# Texas Family Code

2022 Edition
[Supersedes 2020 Edition]

WITH TABLES AND INDEX

THOMSON REUTERS™

Mat #42706687

**ISBN** 978–1–539–22210–1

# PREFACE

Designed for use in the office or courtroom, this pamphlet brings together in the convenient publication the complete Texas Family Code.

## WHAT'S NEW

This product brings up to date statutes through the 2021 Third Called Session of the Texas 87th Legislature.

This pamphlet includes new enactments or important amendments relating to:

- Marriage
- The Parent-Child Relationship
- Protective Orders and Family Violence
- Juvenile Justice Code

## CONTACT US

For additional information or research assistance, contact the Reference Attorneys at 1-800-REF-ATTY (1-800-733-2889) or by Live Chat: Access via Westlaw. Contact our U.S. legal editorial department directly with your questions and suggestions by e-mail at editors.us-legal@tr.com.

Thank you for subscribing to this product. Should you have any questions regarding this product, please contact Customer Service at 1-800-328-4880 or by fax at 1-800-340-9378. If you would like to inquire about related publications, or to place an order, please contact us at 1-888-728-7677 or visit us at legalsolutions.thomsonreuters.com.

THE PUBLISHER

November, 2021

# THOMSON REUTERS PROVIEW™

# EFFECTIVE DATES

The following table shows the date of adjournment and the effective date of ninety day bills enacted at sessions of the legislature beginning with the year 1945:

| Year | Leg. | Session | Adjournment Date | Effective Date |
|---|---|---|---|---|
| 1945 | 49 | Regular | June 5, 1945 | September 4, 1945 |
| 1947 | 50 | Regular | June 6, 1947 | September 5, 1947 |
| 1949 | 51 | Regular | June 6, 1949 | September 5, 1949 |
| 1951 | 52 | Regular | June 8, 1951 | September 7, 1951 |
| 1953 | 53 | Regular | May 27, 1953 | August 26, 1953 |
| 1954 | 53 | 1st C.S. | May 13, 1954 | August 12, 1954 |
| 1955 | 54 | Regular | June 7, 1955 | September 6, 1955 |
| 1957 | 55 | Regular | May 23, 1957 | August 22, 1957 |
| 1957 | 55 | 1st C.S. | November 12, 1957 | February 11, 1958 |
| 1957 | 55 | 2nd C.S. | December 3, 1957 | March 4, 1958 |
| 1959 | 56 | Regular | May 12, 1959 | August 11, 1959 |
| 1959 | 56 | 1st C.S. | June 16, 1959 | September 15, 1959 |
| 1959 | 56 | 2nd C.S. | July 16, 1959 | October 15, 1959 |
| 1959 | 56 | 3rd C.S. | August 6, 1959 | November 5, 1959 |
| 1961 | 57 | Regular | May 29, 1961 | August 28, 1961 |
| 1961 | 57 | 1st C.S. | August 8, 1961 | November 7, 1961 |
| 1961 | 57 | 2nd C.S. | August 14, 1961 | November 13, 1961 |
| 1962 | 57 | 3rd C.S. | February 1, 1962 | May 3, 1962 |
| 1963 | 58 | Regular | May 24, 1963 | August 23, 1963 |
| 1965 | 59 | Regular | May 31, 1965 | August 30, 1965 |
| 1966 | 59 | 1st C.S. | February 23, 1966 | * |
| 1967 | 60 | Regular | May 29, 1967 | August 28, 1967 |
| 1968 | 60 | 1st C.S. | July 3, 1968 | * |
| 1969 | 61 | Regular | June 2, 1969 | September 1, 1969 |
| 1969 | 61 | 1st C.S. | August 26, 1969 | * |
| 1969 | 61 | 2nd C.S. | September 9, 1969 | December 9, 1969 |
| 1971 | 62 | Regular | May 31, 1971 | August 30, 1971 |
| 1971 | 62 | 1st C.S. | June 4, 1971 | September 3, 1971 |
| 1972 | 62 | 2nd C.S. | March 30, 1972 | June 29, 1972 |
| 1972 | 62 | 3rd C.S. | July 7, 1972 | * |
| 1972 | 62 | 4th C.S. | October 17, 1972 | January 16, 1973 |
| 1973 | 63 | Regular | May 28, 1973 | August 27, 1973 |
| 1973 | 63 | 1st C.S. | December 20, 1973 | * |
| 1975 | 64 | Regular | June 2, 1975 | September 1, 1975 |
| 1977 | 65 | Regular | May 30, 1977 | August 29, 1977 |
| 1977 | 65 | 1st C.S. | July 21, 1977 | * |
| 1978 | 65 | 2nd C.S. | August 8, 1978 | November 7, 1978 |
| 1979 | 66 | Regular | May 28, 1979 | August 27, 1979 |
| 1981 | 67 | Regular | June 1, 1981 | August 31, 1981 |

## EFFECTIVE DATES

| Year | Leg. | Session | Adjournment Date | Effective Date |
|---|---|---|---|---|
| 1981 | 67 | 1st C.S. | August 11, 1981 | November 10, 1981 |
| 1982 | 67 | 2nd C.S. | May 28, 1982 | * |
| 1982 | 67 | 3rd C.S. | September 9, 1982 | * |
| 1983 | 68 | Regular | May 30, 1983 | August 29, 1983 |
| 1983 | 68 | 1st C.S. | June 25, 1983 | September 23, 1983 |
| 1984 | 68 | 2nd C.S. | July 3, 1984 | October 2, 1984 |
| 1985 | 69 | Regular | May 27, 1985 | August 26, 1985 |
| 1985 | 69 | 1st C.S. | May 30, 1985 | August 29, 1985 |
| 1986 | 69 | 2nd C.S. | September 4, 1986 | December 4, 1986 |
| 1986 | 69 | 3rd C.S. | September 30, 1986 | December 30, 1986 |
| 1987 | 70 | Regular | June 1, 1987 | August 31, 1987 |
| 1987 | 70 | 1st C.S. | June 3, 1987 | September 2, 1987 |
| 1987 | 70 | 2nd C.S. | July 21, 1987 | October 20, 1987 |
| 1989 | 71 | Regular | May 29, 1989 | August 28, 1989 |
| 1989 | 71 | 1st C.S. | July 19, 1989 | October 18, 1989 |
| 1989 | 71 | 2nd C.S. | December 12, 1989 | * |
| 1990 | 71 | 3rd C.S. | March 28, 1990 | * |
| 1990 | 71 | 4th C.S. | May 1, 1990 | * |
| 1990 | 71 | 5th C.S. | May 30, 1990 | * |
| 1990 | 71 | 6th C.S. | June 7, 1990 | September 6, 1990 |
| 1991 | 72 | Regular | May 27, 1991 | August 26, 1991 |
| 1991 | 72 | 1st C.S. | August 13, 1991 | November 12, 1991 |
| 1991 | 72 | 2nd C.S. | August 25, 1991 | November 24, 1991 |
| 1992 | 72 | 3rd C.S. | January 8, 1992 | April 8, 1992 |
| 1992 | 72 | 4th C.S. | December 3, 1992 | * |
| 1993 | 73 | Regular | May 31, 1993 | August 30, 1993 |
| 1995 | 74 | Regular | May 29, 1995 | August 28, 1995 |
| 1997 | 75 | Regular | June 2, 1997 | September 1, 1997 |
| 1999 | 76 | Regular | May 31, 1999 | August 30, 1999 |
| 2001 | 77 | Regular | May 28, 2001 | September 1, 2001 |
| 2003 | 78 | Regular | June 2, 2003 | September 1, 2003 |
| 2003 | 78 | 1st C.S. | July 28, 2003 | * |
| 2003 | 78 | 2nd C.S. | August 26, 2003 | * |
| 2005 | 79 | 2nd C.S. | August 19, 2005 | November 18, 2005 |
| 2006 | 79 | 3rd C.S. | May 16, 2006 | August 15, 2006 |
| 2007 | 80 | Regular | May 28, 2007 | August 27, 2007 |
| 2009 | 81 | Regular | June 1, 2009 | August 31, 2009 |
| 2009 | 81 | 1st C.S. | July 2, 2009 | * |
| 2011 | 82 | Regular | May 30, 2011 | August 29, 2011 |
| 2011 | 82 | 1st C.S. | June 29, 2011 | September 28, 2011** |
| 2013 | 83 | Regular | May 27, 2013 | August 26, 2013 |
| 2013 | 83 | 1st C.S. | June 25, 2013 | September 24, 2013** |
| 2013 | 83 | 2nd C.S. | July 30, 2013 | October 29, 2013** |
| 2013 | 83 | 3rd C.S. | August 5, 2013 | * |
| 2015 | 84 | Regular | June 1, 2015 | August 31, 2015 |

## EFFECTIVE DATES

| Year | Leg. | Session | Adjournment Date | Effective Date |
|---|---|---|---|---|
| 2017 | 85 | Regular | May 29, 2017 | August 28, 2017 |
| 2017 | 85 | 1st C.S. | August 15, 2017 | November 14, 2017 |
| 2019 | 86 | Regular | May 27, 2019 | August 26, 2019 |
| 2021 | 87 | Regular | May 31, 2021 | August 30, 2021 |
| 2021 | 87 | 1st C.S. | August 6, 2021 | * |
| 2021 | 87 | 2nd C.S. | September 2, 2021 | December 2, 2021 |
| 2021 | 87 | 3rd C.S. | October 19, 2021 | January 18, 2022 |

* No legislation for which the ninety day effective date is applicable.

** Legislation effective on the 91st day after session.

# DISPOSITION TABLE

Showing where provisions of former articles of Vernon's Annotated Civil Statutes and Penal Code of 1925 are covered in the Texas Family Code as originally enacted.

| Vernon's Ann. Civ.St.Article | | V.T.C.A. Family Code Section |
|---|---|---|
| 46a, | § 1 | 11.04(b) |
| | | 11.08 |
| | | 16.01 to 16.03 |
| | § 1a | 11.08 |
| | § 1b | — |
| | § 1c | — |
| | § 1d | 11.09 |
| | § 1e | — |
| | § 2 | 11.12 |
| | § 3 | 16.04 |
| | § 4 | 11.14 |
| | § 5 | 16.07 |
| | § 6(a) | 15.02 |
| | § 6(b) | 16.05(c) |
| | § 6(c) | — |
| | § 6(d) | 16.03(d) |
| | § 6(e) | 16.03(e) |
| | § 6(f) | 15.03 |
| | § 7 | — |
| | § 8 | — |
| | § 9 | 16.09 |
| | § 10 | 11.17 |
| | § 10a | — |
| 46b | | |
| 46b–1, | § 1 | 16.51 |
| | | 16.53 |
| | § 2 | 16.52 |
| | § 3 | 16.54 |
| | § 4 | — |
| | § 5 | 16.55 |
| | § 6 | — |
| 201 to 223 | | — |
| 695c–2, | § 1 | — |
| | § 2 | 34.01 |
| | § 3 | 34.02 |
| | § 4 | 34.03 |
| | § 5 | 34.04 |
| | § 6 | 34.05 |
| | § 7 | 34.06 |
| | § 8 | — |
| 2328b–4, | § 1 | 21.02 |
| | § 2 | 21.03 |
| | § 3 | 21.04 |
| | § 4 | 21.05 |
| | § 5 | 21.11 |
| | § 6 | 21.12 |
| | § 7 | 21.21 |
| | § 8 | 21.22 |
| | § 9 | 21.23 |
| | § 10 | 21.24 |
| | § 11 | 21.25 |
| | § 12 | 21.26 |
| | § 13 | 21.27 |
| | § 14 | 21.28(b) |
| | § 15 | 21.29 |
| | § 16 | 21.30 |
| | § 17 | 21.31(1), (2) |
| | § 18 | 21.32 |
| | § 19 | 21.33 |
| | § 20 | 21.34 |
| | § 21 | 21.35 |
| | § 22 | 21.36 |
| | § 23 | 21.37 |
| | § 24 | 21.38 |
| | § 25 | 21.39 |
| | § 26 | 21.40 |
| | § 27 | 21.41 |
| | § 28 | 21.42 |
| | § 29 | 21.43 |
| | § 30 | 21.44 |
| | § 31 | 21.45(a), (c) |
| | § 32 | 21.61 |
| | § 33 | 21.62 |
| | § 34 | 21.63 |
| | § 35 | 21.64 |
| | § 36 | 21.65 |
| | § 37 | 21.66 |
| | § 38 | — |
| | § 39 | — |
| | § 40 | 21.06 |
| | § 41 | 21.01 |
| 2330 | | 15.02 |
| 2331 | | 11.08 |
| 2332 | | 11.09 |
| 2332a | | 11.17 |
| 2333 | | 11.14 |
| 2334 | | 11.13 |
| 2335 to 2337 | | 15.05 |
| 2338–1, | § 1 | 51.01 |
| | § 2 | — |
| | § 3 | 51.02 |
| | | 51.03(a) |
| | § 4 | 51.04(b), (c), (e), (f) |
| | § 5(a) | 51.04(a) |
| | | 51.05 |
| | § 5(b) | — |
| | § 5(c) | 54.05(a), (b) |
| | § 5(d) | 51.03(c) |
| | § 6(a) | 51.07(b) |
| | § 6(b) | 54.02(a)(1), (2) |

## DISPOSITION TABLE

| Vernon's Ann. Civ.St.Article | V.T.C.A. Family Code Section |
|---|---|
| § 6(c) | 54.02(c) |
| § 6(d) | 54.02(d) |
| § 6(e) | 51.10(h), (i) |
| § 6(f) | 54.02(e) |
| § 6(g) | 54.02(a)(3) |
| § 6(h) | 54.02(f) |
| § 6(i) | 54.02(g) |
| § 6(j) | 54.02(h) |
| § 6(k) | 54.02(i) |
| § 7 | 53.01 |
| | 53.04 |
| § 7–A | 51.06(a) |
| § 7–B(a) | 51.10(d), (e) |
| | 54.07 |
| § 7–B(b) | 51.10(f) |
| § 7–B(c) | 51.10(h) |
| § 7–B(d), (e) | 51.10(i) |
| § 8 | 53.06 |
| § 9 | 53.07 |
| § 10 | 53.06 |
| § 11 | 52.01 |
| | 52.02 |
| § 12 | 51.08 |
| § 13(a) | 54.08 |
| § 13(b) | 54.02(c) |
| § 13(c) | 54.04(d) |
| § 13(d) | 51.13(a) |
| § 13(e) | 51.13(a), (b) |
| § 13(f) | —— |
| § 13–A | 54.06 |
| | 54.07 |
| § 13–B | —— |
| § 14 | 54.05 |
| § 15 | 51.14 |
| § 15–A | 54.08 |
| § 16 | 55.01 |
| | 55.02(a) |
| § 17 | 51.12(a), (b) |
| § 18 | 51.05 |
| § 19 | —— |
| § 20 | 54.07 |
| § 21 | 56.01 |
| § 21–A | 56.02 |
| § 22 to § 24–A | —— |
| 2338–5, § 10 | 11.12 |
| 2338–8, § 20 | 11.12 |
| 2338–11, § 10 | 11.12 |
| 2338–11a, § 10 | 11.12 |
| 2338–11b, § 10 | 11.12 |
| 2338–13, § 20 | 11.12 |
| 2338–14, § 10 | 11.12 |
| 2338–15, § 12 | 11.12 |
| 2338–15a, § 12 | 11.12 |
| 2338–15b, § 12 | 11.12 |
| 2338–15c, § 12 | 11.12 |
| 2338–16, § 13 | 11.12 |
| 2338–17, § 17 | 11.12 |
| 2338–20, § 19 | 11.12 |
| 4445b | 35.03 |
| 4447h, § 1 | —— |
| § 2 | 35.02 |
| § 3 | 35.01 |
| 4602 | 1.83 |
| 4603 | 1.51(a) |
| 4604 | 1.01 |
| | 1.82 |
| 4604c | 1.21 |
| 4604d, § 1 | 1.31 |
| | 1.32 |
| | 1.33 |
| § 2 | 1.26 |
| | 1.27 |
| § 3 | 1.23 |
| § 4 | 1.24 |
| | 1.25 |
| | 1.29 |
| | 1.30 |
| § 5 | 1.34 |
| § 6 | 1.26 |
| | 1.28 |
| § 7 | 1.07(a) |
| § 8 | 1.22 |
| § 9 | 1.35 |
| § 10 | 1.32 |
| § 13 | 1.36 |
| | 1.37 |
| 4605 | 1.02 |
| subsec. (a) | 1.51(b) |
| | 1.52 |
| subsec. (b) | 1.03 |
| | 1.04 |
| | 1.06 |
| subsec. (c) | 1.05 |
| subsec. (d) | 1.03 |
| 4606 | 1.08 |
| | 1.84(a) |
| | 1.85 |
| 4607 | —— |
| 4608 | —— |
| 4609 | —— |
| 4610 | 5.41 |
| 4613 | 5.01(a)(1) |
| | 5.01(a)(2) |
| | 5.01(b) |
| | 5.21 |
| | 5.61(a) |
| 4614 | 4.02 |
| 4615 | 5.01(a)(3) |
| 4617 | 5.25 |
| 4618, § 1 | 5.81 |
| § 2 | 5.82 |
| | 5.83 |
| § 3 | 5.84 |
| | 5.85 |
| 4619 | 5.02 |
| 4620 | 5.61(b) |
| | 5.61(c) |
| | 5.61(d) |
| 4621 | 5.22 |
| | 5.23 |
| 4622 | 5.24(a) |
| | 5.24(b) |
| 4624 | 5.62 |
| 4624a | 5.42 |
| 4625 | 4.03 |
| 4626 | 4.04 |
| 4627 | 4.01 |
| 4628 | 2.43 |

# DISPOSITION TABLE

| Vernon's Ann. Civ.St.Article | V.T.C.A. Family Code Section |
|---|---|
| 4629, subsec. (1) | 3.02 |
| subsec. (2) | 3.05 |
| subsec. (3) | 3.03 |
| subsec. (4) | 3.06 |
| subsec. (5) | 3.04 |
| subsec. (6) | 3.07 |
| 4630 | 3.08 |
| 4631 | 3.21<br>3.22<br>3.23 |
| 4632 | 3.53<br>3.60<br>3.61<br>3.64 |
| 4633 | 3.62 |
| 4634 | 3.57 |
| 4635 | 3.56 |
| 4636 | 3.58 |
| 4637 | 3.59 |
| 4638 | 3.63 |
| 4639 | 11.11<br>14.01 |
| 4639a, § 1 | 11.05<br>11.13<br>14.03<br>14.05(a)<br>14.08(a)<br>14.09 |
| § 1a to § 3 | —— |
| 4639a–1 | 14.05(b) |
| 4640 | 3.66 |
| 4641 | 3.65 |
| 5143 | —— |
| 5143a | —— |
| 5143e, § 1 | 25.01 |
| § 2 | 25.02 |
| § 3 | 25.03 |
| § 4 | 25.04 |
| § 5 | 25.05 |
| § 6 | 25.06 |
| § 7 | 25.07 |
| § 8 | 25.08 |
| § 9 | 25.09 |
| 5921 | 31.01 |
| 5921a | —— |
| 5921b | 31.01<br>31.08 |
| 5922 | 31.02<br>31.03 |
| 5922a | 31.02<br>31.03<br>31.05 |
| 5923 | 31.04<br>31.06<br>31.07 |
| 5923a | 31.04<br>31.06<br>31.07<br>31.08 |
| 5923–1, § 1 | 33.01 |
| § 2 | 33.02<br>33.03 |
| § 3 | —— |
| 5928 | 32.21<br>32.22 |
| 5929 | 32.01<br>32.02<br>32.04 |
| 5930 | 32.05<br>32.23 |
| 5931 | 32.24 |
| 6632 | 5.03<br>5.24(c) |
| 6647 | 5.03<br>5.24(c) |

| Vernon's Ann. P.C. (1925) Article | V.T.C.A. Family Code Section |
|---|---|
| 404 | 1.09 |
| 406 | 1.81(b) |
| 492 | —— |
| 493 | —— |
| 496 | 2.21 |
| 497 | 2.21 |

# DERIVATION TABLE

Showing where provisions of the Texas Family Code as originally enacted were formerly covered in Vernon's Annotated Civil Statutes and Penal Code of 1925.

| V.T.C.A. Family Code Section | Vernon's Ann. Civ.St.Article |
|---|---|
| 1.01 | 4604 |
| 1.02 | 4605 |
| 1.03 | 4605(b), (d) |
| 1.04 | 4605(b) |
| 1.05 | 4605(c) |
| 1.06 | 4605(b) |
| 1.07 | 4604d, § 7 |
| 1.08 | 4606 |
| 1.09 | P.C. 404 |
| 1.21 | 4604c |
| 1.22 | 4604d, § 8 |
| 1.23 | 4604d, § 3 |
| 1.24 | 4604d, § 4 |
| 1.25 | 4604d, § 4 |
| 1.26 | 4604d, §§ 2, 6 |
| 1.27 | 4604d, § 2 |
| 1.28 | 4604d, § 6 |
| 1.29 | 4604d, § 4 |
| 1.30 | 4604d, § 4 |
| 1.31 | 4604d, § 1 |
| 1.32 | 4604d, §§ 1, 10 |
| 1.33 | 4604d, § 1 |
| 1.34 | 4604d, § 5 |
| 1.35 | 4604d, § 9 |
| 1.36 | 4604d, § 13 |
| 1.37 | 4604d, § 13 |
| 1.38 | — |
| 1.51 | 4603<br>4605(a) |
| 1.52 | 4605(a) |
| 1.53 | — |
| 1.81 | P.C. 406 |
| 1.82 | 4604 |
| 1.83 | 4602 |
| 1.84 | 4606 |
| 1.85 | 4606 |
| 1.91 to 1.95 | — |
| 2.01 to 2.03 | — |
| 2.21 | P.C. 496<br>P.C. 497 |
| 2.22 to 2.24 | — |
| 2.41 | — |
| 2.42 | — |
| 2.43 | 4628 |
| 2.44 to | |

| V.T.C.A. Family Code Section | Vernon's Ann. Civ.St.Article |
|---|---|
| 2.47 | — |
| 3.01 | — |
| 3.02 | 4629(1) |
| 3.03 | 4629(3) |
| 3.04 | 4629(5) |
| 3.05 | 4629(2) |
| 3.06 | 4629(4) |
| 3.07 | 4629(6) |
| 3.08 | 4630 |
| 3.21 to 3.23 | 4631 |
| 3.24 | — |
| 3.25 | — |
| 3.51 | — |
| 3.52 | — |
| 3.53 | 4632 |
| 3.54 | — |
| 3.55 | — |
| 3.56 | 4635 |
| 3.57 | 4634 |
| 3.58 | 4636 |
| 3.59 | 4637 |
| 3.60 | 4632 |
| 3.61 | 4632 |
| 3.62 | 4633 |
| 3.63 | 4638 |
| 3.64 | 4632 |
| 3.65 | 4641 |
| 3.66 | 4640 |
| 4.01 | 4627 |
| 4.02 | 4614 |
| 4.03 | 4625 |
| 4.04 | 4626<br>4613 |
| 5.01 | 4615 |
| 5.02 | 4619<br>6632 |
| 5.03 | 6647 |
| 5.21 | 4613 |
| 5.22 | 4621 |
| 5.23 | 4621 |
| 5.24 | 4622<br>6632<br>6647 |
| 5.25 | 4617 |
| 5.26 | — |
| 5.27 | — |
| 5.41 | 4610 |
| 5.42 | 4624a |
| 5.61 | 4613<br>4620 |

| V.T.C.A. Family Code Section | Vernon's Ann. Civ.St.Article |
|---|---|
| 5.62 | 4624 |
| 5.81 | 4618, § 1 |
| 5.82 | 4618, § 2 |
| 5.83 | 4618, § 2 |
| 5.831 | — |
| 5.84 | 4618, § 3 |
| 5.85 | 4618, § 3 |
| 5.86 | — |
| 5.87 | — |
| 11.01 to 11.03 | — |
| 11.04(a) | — |
| 11.04(b) | 46a, § 1 |
| 11.04(c) | — |
| 11.05 | 4639a, § 1 |
| 11.06 | — |
| 11.07 | — |
| 11.08 | 46a, §§ 1, 1a |
| | 2331 |
| 11.09 | 46a, § 1d |
| | 2332 |
| 11.10 | — |
| 11.11 | 4639 |
| 11.12 | 46a, § 2 |
| | 2338—5, § 10 |
| | 2338—8, § 20 |
| | 2338–11, § 10 |
| | 2338–11a, § 10 |
| | 2338–11b, § 10 |
| | 2338–13, § 20 |
| 11.12 | 2338–14, § 10 |
| | 2338–15, § 12 |
| | 2338–15a, § 12 |
| | 2338–15b, § 12 |
| | 2338–15c, § 12 |
| | 2338–16, § 13 |
| | 2338–17, § 17 |
| | 2338—20, § 19 |
| 11.13 | 2334 |
| | 4639a, § 1 |
| 11.14 | 46a, § 4 |
| | 2333 |
| 11.15 | — |
| 11.16 | — |
| 11.17 | 46a, § 10 |
| | 2332a |
| 11.18 | — |
| 11.19 | — |
| 12.01 to 12.04 | — |
| 13.01 to 13.06 | — |
| 14.01 | 4639 |
| 14.02 | — |
| 14.03 | 4639a, § 1 |
| 14.04 | — |
| 14.05(a) | 4639a, § 1 |
| 14.05(b) | 4639a–1 |
| 14.05(c) | — |
| 14.05(d) | — |
| 14.06 | — |
| 14.07 | — |
| 14.08(a) | 4639a, § 1 |
| 14.08(b) to 14.08(d) | — |
| 14.09 | 4639a, § 1 |
| 14.10 | — |
| 15.01 | — |
| 15.02 | 46a, § 6(a) |
| | 2330 |
| 15.03 | 46a, § 6(f) |
| 15.04 | — |
| 15.05 | 2335 to 2337 |
| 15.06 | — |
| 15.07 | — |
| 16.01 | 46a, § 1 |
| 16.02 | 46a, § 1 |
| 16.03(a) | 46a, § 1 |
| 16.03(b) | — |
| 16.03(c) | — |
| 16.03(d) | 46a, § 6(d) |
| 16.03(e) | 46a, § 6(e) |
| 16.04 | 46a, § 3 |
| 16.05(a) | — |
| 16.05(b) | — |
| 16.05(c) | 46a, § 6(b) |
| 16.05(d) | — |
| 16.06 | — |
| 16.07 | 46a, § 5 |
| 16.08 | — |
| 16.09 | 46a, § 9 |
| 16.10 to 16.12 | — |
| 16.51 | 46b–1, § 1 |
| 16.52 | 46b–1, § 2 |
| 16.53 | 46b–1, § 1 |
| 16.54 | 46b–1, § 3 |
| 16.55 | 46b–1, § 5 |
| 17.01 to 17.09 | — |
| 21.01 to 21.66 | 2328b—4 |
| 25.01 to 25.09 | 5143e |
| 31.01 | 5921 |
| | 5921b |
| 31.02 | 5922 |
| | 5922a |
| 31.03 | 5922 |
| | 5922a |
| 31.04 | 5923 |
| | 5923a |
| 31.05 | 5922a |
| 31.06 | 5923 |
| | 5923a |
| 31.07 | 5923 |
| | 5923a |
| 31.08 | 5921b |
| | 5923a |
| 32.01 | 5929 |

# DERIVATION TABLE

| V.T.C.A. Family Code Section | Vernon's Ann. Civ.St.Article |
|---|---|
| 32.02 | 5929 |
| 32.03 | — |
| 32.04 | 5929 |
| 32.05 | 5930 |
| 32.21 | 5928 |
| 32.22 | 5928 |
| 32.23 | 5930 |
| 32.24 | 5931 |
| 33.01 | 5923–1, § 1 |
| 33.02 | 5923–1, § 2 |
| 33.03 | 5923–1, § 2 |
| 34.01 | 695c—2, § 2 |
| 34.02 | 695c—2, § 3 |
| 34.03 | 695c—2, § 4 |
| 34.04 | 695c—2, § 5 |
| 34.05 | 695c—2, § 6 |
| 34.06 | 695c—2, § 7 |
| 35.01 | 4447h, § 3 |
| 35.02 | 4447h, § 2 |
| 35.03 | 4445b |
| 51.01 | 2338–1, § 1 |
| 51.02 | 2338–1, § 3 |
| 51.03(a) | 2338–1, § 3 |
| 51.03(b) | — |
| 51.03(c) | 2338–1, § 5(d) |
| 51.04(a) | 2338–1, § 5(a) |
| 51.04(b) | 2338–1, § 4 |
| 51.04(c) | 2338–1, § 4 |
| 51.04(d) | — |
| 51.04(e) | 2338–1, § 4 |
| 51.04(f) | 2338–1, § 4 |
| 51.05 | 2338–1, §§ 5(a), 18 |
| 51.06(a) | 2338–1, § 7–A |
| 51.06(b) | — |
| 51.07(a) | — |
| 51.07(b) | 2338–1, § 6(a) |
| 51.08 | 2338–1, § 12 |
| 51.09 | — |
| 51.10(a) to 51.10(c) | — |
| 51.10(d) | 2338–1, § 7–B(a) |
| 51.10(e) | 2338–1, § 7–B(a) |
| 51.10(f) | 2338–1, § 7–B(b) |
| 51.10(g) | — |
| 51.10(h) | 2338–1, §§ 6(e), 7–B(c) |
| 51.10(i) | 2338–1, §§ 6(e), 7–B(d), (e) |
| 51.11 | — |
| 51.12(a) | 2338–1, § 17 |
| 51.12(b) | 2338–1, § 17 |
| 51.12(c) | — |
| 51.12(d) | — |
| 51.13(a) | 2338–1, § 13(d), (e) |
| 51.13(b) | 2338–1, § 13(e) |
| 51.13(c) | — |
| 51.14 | 2338–1, § 15 |
| 51.15 to 51.17 | — |
| 52.01 | 2338–1, § 11 |
| 52.02 | 2338–1, § 11 |
| 52.03 | — |
| 52.04 | — |
| 53.01 | 2338–1, § 7 |
| 53.02 | — |
| 53.03 | — |
| 53.04 | 2338–1, § 7 |
| 53.05 | — |
| 53.06 | 2338–1, §§ 8, 10 |
| 53.07 | 2338–1, § 9 |
| 54.01 | — |
| 54.02(a)(1), (2) | 2338–1, § 6(b) |
| 54.02(a)(3) | 2338–1, § 6(g) |
| 54.02(b) | — |
| 54.02(c) | 2338–1, §§ 6(c), 13(b) |
| 54.02(d) | 2338–1, § 6(d) |
| 54.02(e) | 2338–1, § 6(f) |
| 54.02(f) | 2338–1, § 6(h) |
| 54.02(g) | 2338–1, § 6(i) |
| 54.02(h) | 2338–1, § 6(j) |
| 54.02(i) | 2338–1, § 6(k) |
| 54.03 | — |
| 54.04(a) to 54.04(c) | — |
| 54.04(d) | 2338–1, § 13(c) |
| 54.04(e) to 54.04(h) | — |
| 54.05 | 2338–1, §§ 5(c), 14 |
| 54.06 | 2338–1, § 13–A |
| 54.07 | 2338–1, §§ 7–B(a). 13–A, 20 |
| 54.08 | 2338–1, §§ 13(a), 15–A |
| 54.09 | — |
| 55.01 | 2338–1, § 16 |
| 55.02(a) | 2338–1, § 16 |
| 55.02(b) to 55.02(e) | — |
| 55.03 to 55.05 | — |
| 56.01 | 2338–1, § 21 |
| 56.02 | 2338–1, § 21–A |

# FAMILY CODE
# TABLE OF SECTIONS AFFECTED BY THE 87TH LEGISLATURE, THROUGH THIRD CALLED SESSION

| Sec. | Effect | Acts 2021 Ch. | Sec. |
|---|---|---|---|
| 2.0091 | Added | 857 | 1 |
| 6.712 | Added | 934 | 4.01 |
| 6.712 note | – | 934 | 4.06 |
| 8.057(a) | Amended | 64 | 1 |
| 8.057(b) | Amended | 64 | 1 |
| 8.057(c) | Amended | 64 | 1 |
| 8.057(c–1) | Added | 227 | 1 |
| 8.057 note | – | 64 | 6(a) |
| | | | 6(b) |
| | | 227 | 3 |
| 8.059(b) | Amended | 64 | 2 |
| 8.062 | Added | 552 | 1 |
| 8.062 note | – | 552 | 13 |
| 8.351 | Added | 64 | 3 |
| 8.352 | Added | 64 | 3 |
| 8.353 | Added | 64 | 3 |
| 8.354 | Added | 64 | 3 |
| 8.355 | Added | 64 | 3 |
| 8.356 | Added | 64 | 3 |
| 8.357 | Added | 64 | 3 |
| 8.358 | Added | 64 | 3 |
| 8.359 | Added | 64 | 3 |
| 33.006 | Amended | 915 | 7.001 |
| 45.102(c) | Added | 339 | 1 |
| 45.102 note | – | 339 | 3 |
| 45.103(a–1) | Added | 339 | 2 |
| 45.103(c–1) | Added | 339 | 2 |
| 51.02(3–a) | Added | 934 | 4.02 |
| 51.03(b) | Amended | 807 | 38 |
| | | 945 | 5 |
| 51.04(h) | Amended | 934 | 4.03 |
| 51.0414(a) | Amended | 934 | 4.04 |
| 51.11(a) | Amended | 971 | 1 |
| 51.11(a–1) | Added | 971 | 1 |
| 51.11(d) | Added | 971 | 1 |
| 51.11(e) | Added | 971 | 1 |
| 53.03(h–1) | Amended | 948 | 12 |
| 53.03(h–2) | Amended | 948 | 12 |
| 54.01(c) | Amended | 971 | 2 |
| 54.02(e) | Amended | 971 | 3 |
| 54.032(e) | Repealed | 472 | 5.01(b)(1) |
| 54.032(g) | Repealed | 472 | 5.01(b)(1) |
| 54.032(h) | Repealed | 472 | 5.01(b)(1) |
| 54.0325(g) | Repealed | 472 | 5.01(b)(2) |
| 54.0325(h) | Repealed | 472 | 5.01(b)(2) |
| 54.04(b) | Amended | 971 | 4 |
| 54.04012(b) | Amended | 704 | 2 |
| 54.0405(d) | Amended | 663 | 2.02 |
| 54.041(a) | Amended | 472 | 4.03 |
| 54.0411 | Repealed | 472 | 5.01(b)(3) |
| 54.0461 | Repealed | 472 | 5.01(b)(4) |
| 54.0462 | Repealed | 472 | 5.01(b)(4) |
| 54.047(a) | Amended | 948 | 13 |
| 54.047(b) | Amended | 948 | 13 |

## TABLE OF SECTIONS AFFECTED

| Sec. | Effect | Acts 2021 Ch. | Sec. |
|---|---|---|---|
| 54.047(e) | Repealed | 948 | 19(3) |
| 54.047(f) | Amended | 948 | 13 |
| | Repealed | 472 | 5.01(b)(5) |
| 54.05(e) | Amended | 971 | 5 |
| 54.06(a) | Repealed | 472 | 5.01(b)(6) |
| 54.11(d) | Amended | 971 | 6 |
| 55.33 | Amended | 814 | 1 |
| 55.34(a) | Amended | 814 | 2 |
| 55.35(b) | Amended | 814 | 3 |
| 55.43(a) | Amended | 814 | 4 |
| 55.52 | Amended | 814 | 5 |
| 55.53(a) | Amended | 814 | 6 |
| 55.54(b) | Amended | 814 | 7 |
| 58.106(a) | Amended | 423 | 1 |
| 58.256(a–1) | Added | 248 | 1 |
| 58.258(c) | Amended | 248 | 2 |
| 61.002(a) | Amended | 472 | 4.04 |
| 65.003(c) | Amended | 272 | 1 |
| 65.003(d) | Added | 272 | 1 |
| 65.003(e) | Added | 272 | 1 |
| 65.003(f) | Added | 272 | 1 |
| 65.003 note | – | 272 | 2 |
| 85.005(a) | Amended | 787 | 1 |
| 85.005(b) | Amended | 787 | 1 |
| 85.005 note | – | 787 | 13 |
| | | | 18 |
| 85.006(a) | Amended | 787 | 2 |
| 85.006 note | – | 787 | 14 |
| 85.0225 | Added | 245 | 1 |
| 85.0225 note | – | 245 | 3 |
| 85.026(a) | Amended | 787 | 3 |
| 85.026 note | – | 787 | 15 |
| 86.0011(a) | Amended | 787 | 4 |
| 86.0011 note | – | 787 | 15 |
| 101.011 | Amended | 446 | 1 |
| 105.002(c) | Amended | 228 | 1 |
| 105.002 note | – | 228 | 2 |
| 105.008 | Amended | 175 | 1 |
| 105.008 note | – | 175 | 8 |
| 107.003(b) | Amended | 8 | 1 |
| 107.003 note | – | 8 | 15 |
| 107.004(b–1) | Amended | 430 | 1 |
| 107.004(b–2) | Added | 430 | 1 |
| 107.004(b–3) | Added | 430 | 1 |
| 107.004(b–4) | Added | 430 | 1 |
| 107.004(d) | Amended | 8 | 2 |
| | | 934 | 4.05 |
| 107.004(d–2) | Amended | 8 | 2 |
| 107.004(d–3) | Amended | 8 | 2 |
| 107.004(e) | Amended | 8 | 2 |
| | | 934 | 4.05 |
| 107.004 note | – | 430 | 2 |
| 107.011(e) | Added | 971 | 7 |
| 107.016 | Amended | 801 | 1 |
| 107.016 note | – | 801 | 2 |
| 107.103(e) | Added | 1002 | 1 |
| 107.103(f) | Added | 1002 | 1 |
| 107.103(g) | Added | 1002 | 1 |
| 107.103 note | – | 1002 | 2 |
| 108.006(b) | Repealed | 472 | 5.01(b)(7) |
| 108.006(c) | Repealed | 472 | 5.01(b)(7) |

| Sec. | Effect | Acts 2021 Ch. | Sec. |
|---|---|---|---|
| 111.001(b) | Amended | 175 | 2 |
| 153.317(a) | Amended | 896 | 1 |
| | | 967 | 2 |
| 153.317 note | – | 896 | 5 |
| 153.3171 | Added | 896 | 2 |
| | | 967 | 1 |
| 153.3171 note | – | 967 | 5 |
| 154.001(b) | Amended | 238 | 1 |
| 154.001(b–1) | Added | 238 | 1 |
| 154.001 note | – | 238 | 2 |
| 154.003 | Amended | 64 | 4 |
| 154.0655 | Added | 552 | 2 |
| 154.0655 note | – | 552 | 14 |
| 154.066(c) | Added | 552 | 3 |
| 154.125 | Amended | 552 | 4 |
| 154.125 note | – | 552 | 15 |
| 154.129 | Amended | 552 | 5 |
| 154.129 note | – | 552 | 15 |
| 155.207 | Amended | 934 | 7.01 |
| 156.007 | Added | 227 | 2 |
| 156.106 | Added | 672 | 2 |
| 156.106 note | – | 672 | 3 |
| 156.401(c–1) | Added | 552 | 6 |
| 156.401 note | – | 552 | 16 |
| 157.005(b) | Amended | 552 | 7 |
| 157.263(a) | Amended | 552 | 8 |
| 157.263(b) | Amended | 552 | 8 |
| 157.263(b–1) | Amended | 552 | 8 |
| 157.263(b–2) | Added | 552 | 8 |
| 157.263(b–3) | Added | 552 | 8 |
| 157.263 note | – | 552 | 17 |
| 157.3171(c) | Amended | 893 | 2 |
| 157.501 | Added | 64 | 5 |
| 157.502 | Added | 64 | 5 |
| 157.503 | Added | 64 | 5 |
| 157.504 | Added | 64 | 5 |
| 157.505 | Added | 64 | 5 |
| 157.506 | Added | 64 | 5 |
| 157.507 | Added | 64 | 5 |
| 157.508 | Added | 64 | 5 |
| 159.605(b) | Amended | 552 | 9 |
| 159.605 note | – | 552 | 18 |
| 161.001(b) | Amended | 221 | 2.17 |
| 161.001(c) | Amended | 8 | 3 |
| | | 29 | 1 |
| 161.001(d–1) | Added | 831 | 1 |
| 161.001 note | – | 831 | 3 |
| 161.101 | Amended | 8 | 4 |
| 161.101 note | – | 8 | 14 |
| 161.2081 | Added | 710 | 2 |
| 161.301 | Added | 710 | 1 |
| 161.302 | Added | 710 | 1 |
| 161.303 | Added | 710 | 1 |
| 161.304 | Added | 710 | 1 |
| 203.004 | Amended | 53 | 1 |
| 231.0011(c) | Amended | 175 | 3 |
| 231.0011(d) | Amended | 175 | 3 |
| 231.0011 note | – | 175 | 8 |
| 231.104(c) | Added | 175 | 4 |
| 231.1211 | Added | 896 | 3 |
| | | 967 | 3 |

| Sec. | Effect | Acts 2021 Ch. | Acts 2021 Sec. |
|---|---|---|---|
| 231.202 | Amended | 472 | 4.05 |
| 233.018(c) | Added | 175 | 5 |
| 233.018(d) | Added | 175 | 5 |
| 233.018(e) | Added | 175 | 5 |
| 233.021(c) | Amended | 175 | 6 |
| 233.021 note | – | 175 | 9 |
| 233.024(a) | Amended | 175 | 7 |
| 233.024 note | – | 175 | 10 |
| 234.007(a) | Amended | 552 | 10 |
| 234.101 | Amended | 446 | 2 |
| 261.001(1) | Amended | 221 | 2.18 |
| | | 807 | 39 |
| 261.001(4) | Amended | 8 | 5 |
| | | 29 | 2 |
| 261.101(a) | Amended | 902 | 1 |
| 261.101(b) | Amended | 902 | 1 |
| 261.101(b–1) | Amended | 902 | 1 |
| 261.101 note | – | 902 | 2 |
| 261.3017(b) | Amended | 1047 | 1 |
| 261.3017(c) | Amended | 1047 | 1 |
| 261.3017(c–1) | Added | 1047 | 1 |
| 261.3017(c–2) | Added | 1047 | 1 |
| 261.3017(e) | Added | 1047 | 1 |
| 261.3017 note | – | 1047 | 8 |
| 261.30171 | Added | 1047 | 2 |
| 261.30175 | Added | 1047 | 3 |
| 261.3027 | Added | 789 | 1 |
| 261.3091 | Added | 789 | 2 |
| 261.504(a–1) | Added | 1047 | 4 |
| 262.102(b–1) | Added | 1047 | 5 |
| 262.104(c) | Added | 1047 | 6 |
| 262.1095(a) | Amended | 269 | 1 |
| | | 710 | 3 |
| 262.1095(b) | Amended | 269 | 1 |
| 262.1095(d–1) | Added | 269 | 1 |
| 262.1095 note | – | 269 | 5 |
| 262.113 | Repealed | 8 | 13(1) |
| 262.1131 | Repealed | 8 | 13(2) |
| 262.114(d) | Added | 710 | 4 |
| 262.116(a) | Amended | 8 | 6 |
| | | 29 | 3 |
| 262.201(b) | Repealed | 8 | 13(3) |
| 262.201(e) | Amended | 8 | 7 |
| 262.201(g) | Amended | 8 | 7 |
| 262.201(g–1) | Added | 8 | 7 |
| 262.201(h) | Amended | 8 | 7 |
| 262.201(i–1) | Added | 1047 | 7 |
| 262.201(j) | Repealed | 8 | 13(3) |
| 262.201(n) | Amended | 8 | 7 |
| 262.201(q) | Added | 8 | 7 |
| 262.2015(b) | Amended | 221 | 2.19 |
| | | 831 | 2 |
| 262.2015 note | – | 831 | 3 |
| 262.351(1) | Amended | 579 | 1 |
| 262.351(1–a) | Added | 579 | 1 |
| 262.351(1–b) | Added | 579 | 1 |
| 262.353 | Added | 579 | 2 |
| 262.401 | Added | 269 | 2 |
| 262.402 | Added | 269 | 2 |
| 262.403 | Added | 269 | 2 |
| 262.404 | Added | 269 | 2 |

| Sec. | Effect | Acts 2021 Ch. | Sec. |
|---|---|---|---|
| 262.405 | Added | 269 | 2 |
| 262.406 | Added | 269 | 2 |
| 262.407 | Added | 269 | 2 |
| 262.408 | Added | 269 | 2 |
| 262.409 | Added | 269 | 2 |
| 262.410 | Added | 269 | 2 |
| 262.411 | Added | 269 | 2 |
| 262.412 | Added | 269 | 2 |
| 262.413 | Added | 269 | 2 |
| 262.414 | Added | 269 | 2 |
| 262.415 | Added | 269 | 2 |
| 262.416 | Added | 269 | 2 |
| 262.417 | Added | 269 | 2 |
| 263.002(c) | Amended | 8 | 8 |
| 263.002(d) | Added | 8 | 8 |
| 263.00201 | Added | 616 | 1 |
| 263.202(b) | Amended | 269 | 3 |
| 263.401(b–3) | Added | 8 | 9 |
| 263.4011 | Added | 8 | 10 |
| 263.403(a–1) | Amended | 8 | 11 |
| 263.409 | Added | 621 | 1 |
| 263.409 note | – | 621 | 35 |
| 263.503 | Repealed | 683 | 2 |
| 263.5031 | Amended | 683 | 1 |
| 263.5031 note | – | 683 | 3 |
| 264.004(d) | Added | 704 | 3 |
| 264.018(a)(5) | Amended | 616 | 2 |
| 264.107(g) | Amended | 621 | 2 |
| 264.1071 | Added | 621 | 3 |
| 264.1073 | Added | 621 | 3 |
| 264.1077 | Added | 616 | 3 |
| 264.117 | Added | 621 | 4 |
| 264.121(a) | Amended | 793 | 1 |
| 264.121(a–2) | Amended | 793 | 1 |
| 264.121(a–6) | Amended | 793 | 1 |
| 264.121(a–7) | Added | 793 | 1 |
| 264.121(e–1) | Amended | 793 | 1 |
| 264.121(e–4) | Added | 793 | 1 |
| 264.121(g) | Amended | 793 | 1 |
| 264.1214 | Added | 793 | 2 |
| 264.1261(a) | Repealed | 621 | 5(b) |
| 264.1261(b) | Repealed | 621 | 5(b) |
| 264.1261(b–1) | Added | 621 | 5(a) |
| 264.1261(b–2) | Added | 621 | 5(a) |
| 264.1261(b–3) | Added | 621 | 5(a) |
| 264.1261(b–4) | Added | 621 | 5(a) |
| 264.152(4) | Amended | 621 | 6 |
| 264.154(a) | Amended | 621 | 7 |
| 264.154(c) | Added | 621 | 7 |
| 264.155 | Amended | 621 | 8 |
| 264.156(c) | Repealed | 621 | 26(1) |
| 264.157(a) | Amended | 621 | 9 |
| 264.157(b) | Amended | 621 | 9 |
| 264.157(c) | Amended | 621 | 9 |
| 264.158(d) | Added | 621 | 10 |
| 264.159 | Amended | 621 | 11 |
| 264.169 | Repealed | 621 | 26(2) |
| | | 858 | 2(1) |
| 264.1691 | Added | 858 | 1 |
| 264.1691 note | – | 858 | 3 |
| | | | 4 |

| Sec. | Effect | Acts 2021 Ch. | Sec. |
|---|---|---|---|
| 264.171 | Added | 621 | 12 |
| 264.172 | Added | 621 | 12 |
| 264.201(d) | Amended | 515 | 1 |
| 264.203 | Amended | 8 | 12 |
| 264.2031 | Added | 269 | 4 |
| 264.603(a) | Amended | 98 | 1 |
| | | 855 | 17 |
| 265.004(a–1) | Amended | 515 | 2 |
| Ch. 265, Subch. D heading | Amended | 515 | 3 |
| 265.151 heading | Amended | 515 | 4 |
| 265.151(a) | Repealed | 515 | 9 |
| 265.151(b) | Amended | 515 | 5 |
| 265.151(c) | Amended | 515 | 5 |
| 265.151(d) | Added | 515 | 5 |
| 265.152 | Amended | 515 | 6 |
| 265.153 | Amended | 515 | 7 |
| 265.154 | Amended | 515 | 8 |

# TABLE OF CONTENTS

## FAMILY CODE

*Section Analysis, see beginning of each Chapter.*

### TITLE 1. THE MARRIAGE RELATIONSHIP
SUBTITLE A. MARRIAGE



SUBTITLE B. PROPERTY RIGHTS AND LIABILITIES



SUBTITLE C. DISSOLUTION OF MARRIAGE



### TITLE 1-A. COLLABORATIVE FAMILY LAW



### TITLE 2. CHILD IN RELATION TO THE FAMILY
SUBTITLE A. LIMITATIONS OF MINORITY

## TABLE OF CONTENTS

### SUBTITLE D. ADMINISTRATIVE SERVICES



### SUBTITLE E. PROTECTION OF THE CHILD



## PENAL CODE
## TITLE 6. OFFENSES AGAINST THE FAMILY



## CONSTITUTION



## INDEX

# FAMILY CODE

## TITLE 5. THE PARENT–CHILD RELATIONSHIP AND THE SUIT AFFECTING THE PARENT–CHILD RELATIONSHIP

### SUBTITLE A. GENERAL PROVISIONS

Chapter



### SUBTITLE B. SUITS AFFECTING THE PARENT–CHILD RELATIONSHIP



### SUBTITLE C. JUDICIAL RESOURCES AND SERVICES

Chapter



### SUBTITLE D. ADMINISTRATIVE SERVICES



### SUBTITLE E. PROTECTION OF THE CHILD

## TITLE 1. THE MARRIAGE RELATIONSHIP

*Acts 1997, 75th Leg., ch. 7, § 1 reenacted Title 1 effective April 17, 1997. A former Title 1, Husband and Wife, was repealed by Acts 1997, 75th Leg., ch. 7, § 3.*

### DISPOSITION TABLE

Showing where provisions of former Title 1 of the Family Code are covered in Title 1 as reenacted by Acts 1997, 75th Leg., ch. 7.

| Former Section | New Section |
|---|---|
| 1.01 | 2.001 |
| 1.02 | 2.002 |
| (2)(B) | 2.003 |
| 1.03 | 2.004 |
| 1.04 | 2.005 |
| 1.045 | |
| 1.05 (a), (b) | 2.006 |
| (c) | 2.007 |
| 1.06 | 2.008 |
| 1.07 | 2.009 |
| (e) | 2.010 |
| 1.08 | 2.011 |
| 1.09 | 2.012 |
| 1.51 | 2.101 |
| 1.52 | 2.102 |
| 1.53 | 2.103 |
| 1.81 | 2.201 |
| | 2.207 |
| 1.82 | 2.203 |
| | 2.204 |
| 1.83 | 2.202 |
| | 2.205 |
| 1.84 | 2.206 |
| 1.85 | 2.208 |
| 1.86 | 2.209 |
| 1.91 | 2.401 |
| 1.92 | 2.402 |
| 1.93 | 2.403 |
| 1.94 | 2.404 |
| 1.95 | 2.405 |
| 2.01 | 1.101 |
| | 1.102 |
| 2.02 | 2.301 |
| 2.03 | 2.302 |
| 2.21 | 6.201 |
| 2.22 | 6.202 |
| 2.23 | 6.203 |
| 2.24 | 6.307 |
| 2.41 (a) | 6.101 |
| (b) | 6.102 |
| (a), (b) | 6.103 |
| (c) | 6.104 |
| 2.42 | 6.105 |
| 2.43 | 6.106 |
| 2.44 | 6.107 |
| 2.45 | 6.108 |
| 2.46 | 6.109 |

| Former Section | New Section |
|---|---|
| 2.47 | 6.111 |
| 2.48 | 6.110 |
| 3.01 | 6.001 |
| 3.02 | 6.002 |
| 3.03 | 6.003 |
| 3.04 | 6.004 |
| 3.05 | 6.005 |
| 3.06 | 6.006 |
| 3.07 | 6.007 |
| 3.08 | 6.008 |
| 3.21 | 6.301 |
| 3.22 | 6.303 |
| 3.23 | 6.304 |
| 3.24 | 6.302 |
| 3.25 | 6.306 |
| (b) | 6.307 |
| 3.26 | 6.305 |
| 3.51 | 6.401 |
| 3.52 | 6.402 |
| 3.521 | 6.409 |
| 3.522 | 6.404 |
| 3.523 | 6.405 |
| 3.53 | 6.403 |
| | 6.701 |
| 3.54 (a) to (c) | 6.505 |
| (d) | 6.705 |
| (e) | 6.708 |
| 3.55 (a), (b) | 6.406 |
| (c), (d) | 6.407 |
| 3.57 | 6.707 |
| 3.58 (a), (b) | 6.501 |
| (c) | 6.502 |
| (d), (e) | 6.503 |
| (f) | 6.506 |
| (g) | 6.507 |
| (h), (i) | 6.709 |
| 3.581 | 6.504 |
| 3.59 | 6.502 |
| 3.60 | 6.702 |
| 3.61 | 6.703 |
| 3.62 | 6.704 |
| 3.63 (a) | 7.001 |
| (b) | 7.002 |
| 3.631 | 7.006 |
| 3.632 (a) | 7.004 |
| (b), (c) | 9.301 |
| (d), (e) | 7.005 |
| 3.633 (a) | 7.003 |
| (b) to (e) | 9.302 |
| 3.64 | 6.706 |
| 3.65 | 6.708 |
| 3.66 (a), (b) | 6.801 |
| (c) | 6.802 |
| 3.70 (a), (b) | 9.001 |
| (c) | 9.002 |
| | 9.003 |
| (d) | 9.004 |
| (e) | 9.005 |
| 3.71 | 9.007 |
| (a) | 9.006 |
| 3.711 | 9.101 to 9.105 |

| Former Section | New Section |
|---|---|
| 3.72 | 9.008 |
| 3.73 | 9,009 |
| 3.74 | 9.010 |
| 3.75 | 9.011 |
| 3.76 | 9.012 |
| 3.77 | 9.013 |
| | 9.014 |
| 3.90 (a), (b) | 9,201 |
| (c) | 9.202 |
| 3.91 | 9.203 |
| 3.92 | 9.204 |
| 3.93 | 9.205 |
| 3.9601 | 8.001 |
| 3.9602 | 8.002 |
| 3.9603 | 8.003 |
| 3.9604 | 8.004 |
| 3.9605 | 8.005 |
| 3.9606 | 8.006 |
| 3.9607 | 8.007 |
| 3.9608 | 8.008 |
| 3.9609 | 8.009 |
| 3.9610 | 8.010 |
| 3.9611 | 8.011 |
| 4.01 | 1.103 |
| 4.02 | 2.501 |
| 4.03 | 1.104 |
| 4.031 | 3.201 |
| 4.04 | 1.105 |
| 4.05 | 1.106 |
| 4.06 | 1.107 |
| 5.01 (a) | 3.001 |
| (b) | 3.002 |
| 5.02 | 3.003 |
| 5.03 | 3.004 |
| 5.04 | 3.005 |
| 5.21 | 3.101 |
| 5.22 | 3.102 |
| 5.23 | 3.103 |
| 5:24 | 3.104 |
| 5.25 (a), (b) | 3.301 |
| (c) | 3.303 |
| (d) | 3.304 |
| (e) | 3.305 |
| (f) | 3.306 |
| (h) | 3.308 |
| 5.26 | 3.302 |
| (c) | 3.303 |
| (d) | 3.304 |
| (e) | 3.306 |
| (f) | 3.307 |
| (g) | 3.308 |
| 5.27 | 3.309 |
| 5.41 | 4.001 |
| 5.42 | 4.002 |
| 5.43 | 4.003 |
| 5.44 | 4.004 |
| 5.45 | 4.005 |
| 5.46 | 4.006 |
| 5.47 | 4.007 |
| 5.48 | 4.008 |
| 5.49 | 4.009 |
| 5.50 | 4.010 |

| Former Section | New Section |
|---|---|
| 5.51 | 4.101 |
| 5.52 | 4.102 |
| 5.53 | 4.103 |
| 5.54 | 4.104 |
| 5.55 | 4.105 |
| 5.56 | 4.106 |
| 5.61 | 3.202 |
| 5.62 | 3.203 |
| 5.81 | 5.001 |
| 5.82 | 5.002 |
| 5.83 | 5.101 |
| 5.831 | 5.107 |
| 5.84 | 5.107 |
| 5.85 (a) | 5.102, 5.103 |
| (b) | 5.103 to 5.105 |
| (c) | 5.106 |
| 5.86 | 5.108 |
| 5.87 (a) | 5.102 |
| (b) | 5.103 to 5.105 |
| (c) | 5.106 |

# SUBTITLE A. MARRIAGE

## CHAPTER 1. GENERAL PROVISIONS

### SUBCHAPTER A. DEFINITIONS

**Section**



### SUBCHAPTER B. PUBLIC POLICY



*Acts 1997, 75th Leg., ch. 7, § 1, reenacted and revised Title 1 of the Family Code. For the subject matter of former Chapter 1, Entering the Marriage Relationship, see the disposition table in the preliminary material of Title 1.*

### SUBCHAPTER A. DEFINITIONS

#### § 1.001. Applicability of Definitions

(a) The definitions in this subchapter apply to this title.

(b) Except as provided by this subchapter, the definitions in Chapter 101 apply to terms used in this title.

(c) If, in another part of this title, a term defined by this subchapter has a meaning different from the meaning provided by this subchapter, the meaning of that other provision prevails.

Added by Acts 1997, 75th Leg., ch. 7, § 1, eff. April 17, 1997.

**§ 1.002. Court**

"Court" means the district court, juvenile court having the jurisdiction of a district court, or other court expressly given jurisdiction of a suit under this title.

Added by Acts 1997, 75th Leg., ch. 7, § 1, eff. April 17, 1997.

**§ 1.003. Suit for Dissolution of Marriage**

"Suit for dissolution of a marriage" includes a suit for divorce or annulment or to declare a marriage void.

Added by Acts 1997, 75th Leg., ch. 7, § 1, eff. April 17, 1997.

**§§ 1.01 to 1.09. Repealed by Acts 1997, 75th Leg., ch. 7, § 3, eff. April 17, 1997**

## SUBCHAPTER B. PUBLIC POLICY

**§ 1.101. Every Marriage Presumed Valid**

In order to promote the public health and welfare and to provide the necessary records, this code specifies detailed rules to be followed in establishing the marriage relationship. However, in order to provide stability for those entering into the marriage relationship in good faith and to provide for an orderly determination of parentage and security for the children of the relationship, it is the policy of this state to preserve and uphold each marriage against claims of invalidity unless a strong reason exists for holding the marriage void or voidable. Therefore, every marriage entered into in this state is presumed to be valid unless expressly made void by Chapter 6 or unless expressly made voidable by Chapter 6 and annulled as provided by that chapter.

Added by Acts 1997, 75th Leg., ch. 7, § 1, eff. April 17, 1997.

**§ 1.102. Most Recent Marriage Presumed Valid**

When two or more marriages of a person to different spouses are alleged, the most recent marriage is presumed to be valid as against each marriage that precedes the most recent marriage until one who asserts the validity of a prior marriage proves the validity of the prior marriage.

Added by Acts 1997, 75th Leg., ch. 7, § 1, eff. April 17, 1997.

**§ 1.103. Persons Married Elsewhere**

The law of this state applies to persons married elsewhere who are domiciled in this state.

Added by Acts 1997, 75th Leg., ch. 7, § 1, eff. April 17, 1997.

**§ 1.104. Capacity of Spouse**

Except as expressly provided by statute or by the constitution, a person, regardless of age, who has been married in accordance with the law of this state has the capacity and power of an adult, including the capacity to contract.

Added by Acts 1997, 75th Leg., ch. 7, § 1, eff. April 17, 1997.

**§ 1.105. Joinder in Civil Suits**

(a) A spouse may sue and be sued without the joinder of the other spouse.

(b) When claims or liabilities are joint and several, the spouses may be joined under the rules relating to joinder of parties generally.

Added by Acts 1997, 75th Leg., ch. 7, § 1, eff. April 17, 1997.

**§ 1.106. Criminal Conversation Not Authorized**

A right of action by one spouse against a third party for criminal conversation is not authorized in this state.

Added by Acts 1997, 75th Leg., ch. 7, § 1, eff. April 17, 1997.

**§ 1.107. Alienation of Affection Not Authorized**

A right of action by one spouse against a third party for alienation of affection is not authorized in this state.

Added by Acts 1997, 75th Leg., ch. 7, § 1, eff. April 17, 1997.

**§ 1.108. Promise or Agreement Must Be in Writing**

A promise or agreement made on consideration of marriage or nonmarital conjugal cohabitation is not enforceable unless the promise or agreement or a memorandum of the promise or agreement is in writing and signed by the person obligated by the promise or agreement.

Added by Acts 1997, 75th Leg., ch. 7, § 1, eff. April 17, 1997.

**§ 1.109. Use of Digitized Signature**

(a) A digitized signature on an original petition under this title or any other pleading or order in a proceeding under this title satisfies the requirements for and imposes the duties of signatories to pleadings, motions, and other papers identified under Rule 13, Texas Rules of Civil Procedure.

(b) A digitized signature under this section may be applied only by, and must remain under the sole control of, the person whose signature is represented.

Added by Acts 2015, 84th Leg., ch. 1165 (S.B. 813), § 1, eff. Sept. 1, 2015.

### §§ 1.21 to 1.38. Repealed by Acts 1983, 68th Leg., p. 2899, ch. 493, § 2, eff. Aug. 29, 1983

### §§ 1.51 to 1.95. Repealed by Acts 1997, 75th Leg., ch. 7, § 3, eff. April 17, 1997

## CHAPTER 2. THE MARRIAGE RELATIONSHIP



*Acts 1997, 75th Leg., ch. 7, § 1, reenacted and revised Title 1 of the Family Code. For the subject matter of former Chapter 2, Validity of Marriage, see the disposition table in the preliminary material of Title 1.*

### SUBCHAPTER A. APPLICATION FOR MARRIAGE LICENSE

#### § 2.001. Marriage License

(a) A man and a woman desiring to enter into a ceremonial marriage must obtain a marriage license from the county clerk of any county of this state.

(b) A license may not be issued for the marriage of persons of the same sex.

Added by Acts 1997, 75th Leg., ch. 7, § 1, eff. April 17, 1997.

**Validity**

*For validity of this section, see Obergefell v. Hodges, 576 U.S. 644, 576 U.S. 644, 135 S.Ct. 2584, 192 L.Ed.2d 609 (2015).*

#### § 2.002. Application for License

Except as provided by Section 2.006, each person applying for a license must:

(1) appear before the county clerk;

(2) submit the person's proof of identity and age as provided by Section 2.005(b);

(3) provide the information applicable to that person for which spaces are provided in the application for a marriage license;

(4) mark the appropriate boxes provided in the application; and

(5) take the oath printed on the application and sign the application before the county clerk.

Added by Acts 1997, 75th Leg., ch. 7, § 1, eff. April 17, 1997. Amended by Acts 2009, 81st Leg., ch. 978, § 1, eff. Sept. 1, 2009.

### § 2.003. Application for License by Minor

(a) A person under 18 years of age may not marry unless the person has been granted by this state or another state a court order removing the disabilities of minority of the person for general purposes.

(b) In addition to the other requirements provided by this chapter, a person under 18 years of age applying for a license must provide to the county clerk:

(1) a court order granted by this state under Chapter 31 removing the disabilities of minority of the person for general purposes; or

(2) if the person is a nonresident minor, a certified copy of an order removing the disabilities of minority of the person for general purposes filed with this state under Section 31.007.

Added by Acts 1997, 75th Leg., ch. 7, § 1, eff. April 17, 1997. Amended by Acts 2017, 85th Leg., ch. 934 (S.B. 1705), § 1, eff. Sept. 1, 2017.

### § 2.004. Application Form

(a) The county clerk shall furnish the application form as prescribed by the bureau of vital statistics.

(b) The application form must contain:

(1) a heading entitled "Application for Marriage License, ____________ County, Texas";

(2) spaces for each applicant's full name, including the woman's maiden surname, address, social security number, if any, date of birth, and place of birth, including city, county, and state;

(3) a space for indicating the document tendered by each applicant as proof of identity and age;

(4) spaces for indicating whether each applicant has been divorced within the last 30 days;

(5) printed boxes for each applicant to check "true" or "false" in response to the following statement: "I am not presently married and the other applicant is not presently married.";

(6) printed boxes for each applicant to check "true" or "false" in response to the following statement: "The other applicant is not related to me as:

(A) an ancestor or descendant, by blood or adoption;

(B) a brother or sister, of the whole or half blood or by adoption;

(C) a parent's brother or sister, of the whole or half blood or by adoption;

(D) a son or daughter of a brother or sister, of the whole or half blood or by adoption;

(E) a current or former stepchild or stepparent; or

(F) a son or daughter of a parent's brother or sister, of the whole or half blood or by adoption.";

(7) printed boxes for each applicant to check "true" or "false" in response to the following statement: "I am not presently delinquent in the payment of court-ordered child support.";

(8) a printed oath reading: "I SOLEMNLY SWEAR (OR AFFIRM) THAT THE INFORMATION I HAVE GIVEN IN THIS APPLICATION IS CORRECT.";

(9) spaces immediately below the printed oath for the applicants' signatures;

(10) a certificate of the county clerk that:

(A) each applicant made the oath and the date and place that it was made; or

(B) an applicant did not appear personally but the prerequisites for the license have been fulfilled as provided by this chapter;

(11) spaces for indicating the date of the marriage and the county in which the marriage is performed;

(12) a space for the address to which the applicants desire the completed license to be mailed; and

(13) a printed box for each applicant to check indicating that the applicant wishes to make a voluntary contribution of $5 to promote healthy early childhood by supporting the Texas Home Visiting Program administered by the Office of Early Childhood Coordination of the Health and Human Services Commission.

(c) An applicant commits an offense if the applicant knowingly provides false information under Subsection (b)(1), (2), (3), or (4). An offense under this subsection is a Class C misdemeanor.

(d) An applicant commits an offense if the applicant knowingly provides false information under Subsection (b)(5) or (6). An offense under this subsection is a Class A misdemeanor.

Added by Acts 1997, 75th Leg., ch. 7, § 1, eff. April 17, 1997. Amended by Acts 1997, 75th Leg., ch. 776, § 1, eff. Sept. 1, 1997; Acts 2005, 79th Leg., ch. 268, § 4.05, eff. Sept. 1, 2005; Acts 2013, 83rd Leg., ch. 820 (S.B. 1836), § 1, eff. June 14, 2013.

### § 2.005. Proof of Identity and Age

(a) The county clerk shall require proof of the identity and age of each applicant.

(b) The proof must be established by:

(1) a driver's license or identification card issued by this state, another state, or a Canadian province that is current or has expired not more than two years preceding the date the identification is submitted to the county clerk in connection with an application for a license;

(2) a United States passport;

(3) a current passport issued by a foreign country or a consular document issued by a state or national government;

(4) an unexpired Certificate of United States Citizenship, Certificate of Naturalization, United States Citizen Identification Card, Permanent Resident Card, Temporary Resident Card, Employment Authorization Card, or other document issued by the federal Department of Homeland Security or the United States Department of State including an identification photograph;

(5) an unexpired military identification card for active duty, reserve, or retired personnel with an identification photograph;

(6) an original or certified copy of a birth certificate issued by a bureau of vital statistics for a state or a foreign government;

(7) an original or certified copy of a Consular Report of Birth Abroad or Certificate of Birth Abroad issued by the United States Department of State;

(8) an original or certified copy of a court order relating to the applicant's name change or sex change;

(9) school records from a secondary school or institution of higher education;

(10) an insurance policy continuously valid for the two years preceding the date of the application for a license;

(11) a motor vehicle certificate of title;

(12) military records, including documentation of release or discharge from active duty or a draft record;

(13) an unexpired military dependent identification card;

(14) an original or certified copy of the applicant's marriage license or divorce decree;

(15) a voter registration certificate;

(16) a pilot's license issued by the Federal Aviation Administration or another authorized agency of the United States;

(17) a license to carry a handgun under Subchapter H, Chapter 411, Government Code;

(18) a temporary driving permit or a temporary identification card issued by the Department of Public Safety; or

(19) an offender identification card issued by the Texas Department of Criminal Justice.

(c) A person commits an offense if the person knowingly provides false, fraudulent, or otherwise inaccurate proof of an applicant's identity or age under this section. An offense under this subsection is a Class A misdemeanor.

Added by Acts 1997, 75th Leg., ch. 7, § 1, eff. April 17, 1997. Amended by Acts 2005, 79th Leg., ch. 268, § 4.06, eff. Sept. 1, 2005; Acts 2009, 81st Leg., ch. 978, § 2, eff. Sept. 1, 2009; Acts 2015, 84th Leg., ch. 437 (H.B. 910), § 10, eff. Jan. 1, 2016.

### § 2.006. Absent Applicant

(a) If an applicant who is 18 years of age or older is unable to appear personally before the county clerk to apply for a marriage license, any adult person or the other applicant may apply on behalf of the absent applicant.

(b) The person applying on behalf of an absent applicant shall provide to the clerk:

(1) notwithstanding Section 132.001, Civil Practice and Remedies Code, the notarized affidavit of the absent applicant as provided by this subchapter; and

(2) proof of the identity and age of the absent applicant under Section 2.005(b).

(c) Notwithstanding Subsection (a), the clerk may not issue a marriage license for which both applicants are absent unless the person applying on behalf of each absent applicant provides to the clerk an affidavit of the applicant declaring that the applicant is a member of the armed forces of the United States stationed in another country in support of combat or another military operation.

Added by Acts 1997, 75th Leg., ch. 7, § 1, eff. April 17, 1997. Amended by Acts 2005, 79th Leg., ch. 947, § 1, eff. Sept. 1, 2005; Acts 2009, 81st Leg., ch. 978, § 3, eff. Sept. 1, 2009; Acts 2013, 83rd Leg., ch. 650 (H.B. 869), § 1, eff. Sept. 1, 2013; Acts 2017, 85th Leg., ch. 934 (S.B. 1705), § 2, eff. Sept. 1, 2017.

### § 2.007. Affidavit of Absent Applicant

The affidavit of an absent applicant must include:

(1) the absent applicant's full name, including the maiden surname of a female applicant, address, date of birth, place of birth, including city, county, and state, citizenship, and social security number, if any;

(2) a declaration that the absent applicant has not been divorced within the last 30 days;

(3) a declaration that the absent applicant is:

(A) not presently married; or

(B) married to the other applicant and they wish to marry again;

(4) a declaration that the other applicant is not presently married and is not related to the absent applicant as:

(A) an ancestor or descendant, by blood or adoption;

(B) a brother or sister, of the whole or half blood or by adoption;

(C) a parent's brother or sister, of the whole or half blood or by adoption;

(D) a son or daughter of a brother or sister, of the whole or half blood or by adoption;

(E) a current or former stepchild or stepparent; or

(F) a son or daughter of a parent's brother or sister, of the whole or half blood or by adoption;

(5) a declaration that the absent applicant desires to marry and the name, age, and address of the person to whom the absent applicant desires to be married;

(6) the approximate date on which the marriage is to occur;

(7) the reason the absent applicant is unable to appear personally before the county clerk for the issuance of the license; and

(8) the appointment of any adult, other than the other applicant, to act as proxy for the purpose of participating in the ceremony, if the absent applicant is:

(A) a member of the armed forces of the United States stationed in another country in support of combat or another military operation; and

(B) unable to attend the ceremony.

Added by Acts 1997, 75th Leg., ch. 7, § 1, eff. April 17, 1997. Amended by Acts 2005, 79th Leg., ch. 268, § 4.07, eff. Sept. 1, 2005; Acts 2013, 83rd Leg., ch. 650 (H.B. 869), § 2, eff. Sept. 1, 2013.

### § 2.0071. Maintenance of Records by Clerk Relating to License for Absent Applicant

A county clerk who issues a marriage license for an absent applicant shall maintain the affidavit of the absent applicant and the application for the marriage license in the same manner that the clerk maintains an application for a marriage license submitted by two applicants in person.

Added by Acts 2013, 83rd Leg., ch. 650 (H.B. 869), § 3, eff. Sept. 1, 2013.

### § 2.008. Execution of Application by Clerk

(a) The county clerk shall:

(1) determine that all necessary information, other than the date of the marriage ceremony, the county in which the ceremony is conducted, and the name of the person who performs the ceremony, is recorded on the application and that all necessary documents are submitted;

(2) administer the oath to each applicant appearing before the clerk;

(3) have each applicant appearing before the clerk sign the application in the clerk's presence; and

(4) execute the clerk's certificate on the application.

(b) A person appearing before the clerk on behalf of an absent applicant is not required to take the oath on behalf of the absent applicant.

Added by Acts 1997, 75th Leg., ch. 7, § 1, eff. April 17, 1997.

### § 2.009. Issuance of License

(a) Except as provided by Subsections (b) and (d), the county clerk may not issue a license if either applicant:

(1) fails to provide the information required by this subchapter;

(2) fails to submit proof of age and identity;

(3) is under 18 years of age and has not presented:

(A) a court order granted by this state under Chapter 31 removing the disabilities of minority of the applicant for general purposes; or

(B) if the applicant is a nonresident minor, a certified copy of an order removing the disabilities of minority of the applicant for general purposes filed with this state under Section 31.007;

(4) checks "false" in response to a statement in the application, except as provided by Subsection (b) or (d), or fails to make a required declaration in an affidavit required of an absent applicant; or

(5) indicates that the applicant has been divorced within the last 30 days, unless:

(A) the applicants were divorced from each other; or

(B) the prohibition against remarriage is waived as provided by Section 6.802.

(b) If an applicant checks "false" in response to the statement "I am not presently married and the other applicant is not presently married," the county clerk shall inquire as to whether the applicant is presently married to the other applicant. If the applicant states that the applicant is currently married to the other applicant, the county clerk shall record that statement on the license before the administration of the oath. The county clerk may not refuse to issue a license on the ground that the applicants are already married to each other.

(c) On the proper execution of the application, the clerk shall:

(1) prepare the license;

(2) enter on the license the names of the licensees, the date that the license is issued, and, if applicable, the name of the person appointed to act as proxy for an absent applicant, if any;

(3) record the time at which the license was issued;

(4) distribute to each applicant written notice of the online location of the information prepared under Section 2.010 regarding acquired immune deficiency syndrome (AIDS) and human immunodeficiency virus (HIV) and note on the license that the distribution was made; and

(5) inform each applicant:

(A) that a premarital education handbook developed by the child support division of the office of the attorney general under Section 2.014 is available on the child support division's Internet website; or

(B) if the applicant does not have Internet access, how the applicant may obtain a paper copy of the handbook described by Paragraph (A).

(d) The county clerk may not refuse to issue a license to an applicant on the ground that the applicant checked "false" in response to the statement "I am not presently delinquent in the payment of court-ordered child support."

(e) A license issued by a county clerk under this section:

(1) must identify the county in which the license is issued; and

(2) may include the name of the county clerk.

Added by Acts 1997, 75th Leg., ch. 7, § 1, eff. April 17, 1997. Amended by Acts 1997, 75th Leg., ch. 776, § 2, eff. Sept. 1, 1997; Acts 1999, 76th Leg., ch. 62, § 6.01(a), eff. Sept. 1, 1999; Acts 1999, 76th Leg., ch. 185, § 1, eff. Sept. 1, 1999; Acts 2005, 79th Leg., ch. 268, § 4.08, eff. Sept. 1, 2005; Acts 2009, 81st Leg., ch. 978, § 4, eff. Sept. 1, 2009; Acts 2013, 83rd Leg., ch. 742 (S.B. 355), § 1, eff. Sept. 1, 2013; Acts 2013, 83rd Leg., ch. 890 (H.B. 984), § 1, eff. Sept. 1, 2013; Acts 2017, 85th Leg., ch. 695 (H.B. 555), § 1, eff. June 12, 2017; Acts 2017, 85th Leg., ch. 934 (S.B. 1705), § 3, eff. Sept. 1, 2017.

### § 2.0091. Application for and Issuance of License Through Remote Technology

(a) This section applies only in a county in which the county clerk has been certified by the Texas Judicial Council under Section 71.039, Government Code, to issue a marriage license through the use of remote technology.

(b) In a county to which this section applies:

(1) a person who applies for a marriage license through the use of remote technology is considered to have appeared before the court for purposes of this subchapter; and

(2) the county clerk may issue a marriage license through the use of remote technology only in accordance with the procedures adopted by the Texas Judicial Council under Section 71.039, Government Code.

Added by Acts 2021, 87th Leg., ch. 857 (S.B. 907), § 1, eff. Sept. 1, 2021.

### § 2.01. Repealed by Acts 1997, 75th Leg., ch. 7, § 3, eff. April 17, 1997

### § 2.010. AIDS Information; Posting on Internet

The Department of State Health Services shall prepare and make available to the public on its Internet website information about acquired immune deficiency syndrome (AIDS) and human immunodeficiency virus (HIV). The information must be designed to inform an applicant for a marriage license about:

(1) the incidence and mode of transmission of AIDS and HIV;

(2) the local availability of medical procedures, including voluntary testing, designed to show or help show whether a person has AIDS or HIV infection, antibodies to HIV, or infection with any other probable causative agent of AIDS; and

(3) available and appropriate counseling services regarding AIDS and HIV infection.

Added by Acts 1997, 75th Leg., ch. 7, § 1, eff. April 17, 1997. Amended by Acts 2013, 83rd Leg., ch. 890 (H.B. 984), § 2, eff. Sept. 1, 2013.

### § 2.011. Repealed by Acts 2009, 81st Leg., ch. 978, § 10, eff. Sept. 1, 2009

### § 2.012. Violation by County Clerk; Penalty

A county clerk or deputy county clerk who violates or fails to comply with this subchapter commits an offense. An offense under this section is a misdemeanor punishable by a fine of not less than $200 and not more than $500.

Added by Acts 1997, 75th Leg., ch. 7, § 1, eff. April 17, 1997.

### § 2.013. Premarital Education Courses

(a) Each person applying for a marriage license is encouraged to attend a premarital education course of at least eight hours during the year preceding the date of the application for the license.

(b) A premarital education course must include instruction in:

(1) conflict management;

(2) communication skills; and

(3) the key components of a successful marriage.

(c) A course under this section should be offered by instructors trained in a skills-based and research-based marriage preparation curricula. The following individuals and organizations may provide courses:

(1) marriage educators;

(2) clergy or their designees;

(3) licensed mental health professionals;

(4) faith-based organizations; and

(5) community-based organizations.

(d) The curricula of a premarital education course must meet the requirements of this section and provide the skills-based and research-based curricula of:

(1) the United States Department of Health and Human Services healthy marriage initiative;

(2) the National Healthy Marriage Resource Center;

(3) criteria developed by the Health and Human Services Commission; or

(4) other similar resources.

(e) The Health and Human Services Commission shall maintain an Internet website on which individuals and organizations described by Subsection (c) may electronically register with the commission to indicate the skills-based and research-based curriculum in which the registrant is trained.

(f) A person who provides a premarital education course shall provide a signed and dated completion certificate to each individual who completes the course. The certificate must include the name of the course, the name of the course provider, and the completion date.

Added by Acts 1999, 76th Leg., ch. 185, § 2, eff. Sept. 1, 1999. Amended by Acts 2007, 80th Leg., ch. 327, § 1, eff. Sept. 1, 2008.

### § 2.014. Family Trust Fund

(a) The family trust fund is created as a trust fund with the state comptroller and shall be administered by the attorney general for the beneficiaries of the fund.

(b) Money in the trust fund is derived from depositing $3 of each marriage license fee as authorized under Section 118.018(c), Local Government Code, and may be used only for:

(1) the development of a premarital education handbook;

(2) grants to institutions of higher education having academic departments that are capable of research on marriage and divorce that will assist in determining programs, courses, and policies to help strengthen families and assist children whose parents are divorcing;

(3) support for counties to create or administer free or low-cost premarital education courses;

(4) programs intended to reduce the amount of delinquent child support; and

(5) other programs the attorney general determines will assist families in this state.

(c) The premarital education handbook under Subsection (b)(1) must:

(1) as provided by Section 2.009(c)(5), be made available to each applicant for a marriage license in an electronic form on the Internet website of the child support division of the office of the attorney general or, for an applicant who does not have Internet access, in paper copy form; and

(2) contain information on:

(A) conflict management;

(B) communication skills;

(C) children and parenting responsibilities; and

(D) financial responsibilities.

(d) Repealed by Acts 2017, 85th Leg., ch. 553 (S.B. 526), § 6(b); Acts 2017, 85th Leg., ch. 755 (S.B. 1731), § 15(b).

Added by Acts 1999, 76th Leg., ch. 185, § 2, eff. Sept. 1, 1999. Amended by Acts 2013, 83rd Leg., ch. 742 (S.B. 355), § 2, eff. Sept. 1, 2013; Acts 2013, 83rd Leg., ch. 890 (H.B. 984), § 3, eff. Sept. 1, 2013; Acts 2017, 85th Leg., ch. 553 (S.B. 526), § 6(b), eff. Sept. 1, 2017; Acts 2017, 85th Leg., ch. 755 (S.B. 1731), § 15(b), eff. Sept. 1, 2017.

### §§ 2.02, 2.03. Repealed by Acts 1997, 75th Leg., ch. 7, § 3, eff. April 17, 1997

## SUBCHAPTER B. UNDERAGE APPLICANTS

### § 2.101. General Age Requirement

A county clerk may not issue a marriage license if either applicant is under 18 years of age, unless each underage applicant shows that the applicant has been granted by this state or another state a court order removing the disabilities of minority of the applicant for general purposes.

Added by Acts 1997, 75th Leg., ch. 7, § 1, eff. April 17, 1997. Amended by Acts 2017, 85th Leg., ch. 934 (S.B. 1705), § 4, eff. Sept. 1, 2017.

### § 2.102. Repealed by Acts 2017, 85th Leg., ch. 934 (S.B. 1705), § 6, eff. Sept. 1, 2017

### § 2.103. Repealed by Acts 2017, 85th Leg., ch. 934 (S.B. 1705), § 6, eff. Sept. 1, 2017

## SUBCHAPTER C. CEREMONY AND RETURN OF LICENSE

### § 2.201. Expiration of License

If a marriage ceremony has not been conducted before the 90th day after the date the license is issued, the marriage license expires.

Added by Acts 1997, 75th Leg., ch. 7, § 1, eff. April 17, 1997. Amended by Acts 2013, 83rd Leg., ch. 1350 (S.B. 1317), § 1, eff. Sept. 1, 2013.

### § 2.202. Persons Authorized to Conduct Ceremony

(a) The following persons are authorized to conduct a marriage ceremony:

(1) a licensed or ordained Christian minister or priest;

(2) a Jewish rabbi;

(3) a person who is an officer of a religious organization and who is authorized by the organization to conduct a marriage ceremony;

(4) a justice of the supreme court, judge of the court of criminal appeals, justice of the courts of appeals, judge of the district, county, and probate courts, judge of the county courts at law, judge of the courts of domestic relations, judge of the juvenile courts, retired justice or judge of those courts, justice of the peace, retired justice of the peace, judge of a municipal court, retired judge of a municipal court, associate judge of a statutory probate court, retired associate judge of a statutory probate court, associate judge of a county court at law, retired associate judge of a county court at law, or judge or magistrate of a federal court of this state; and

(5) a retired judge or magistrate of a federal court of this state.

(b) For the purposes of Subsection (a)(4), a retired judge or justice is a former judge or justice who is vested in the Judicial Retirement System of Texas Plan One or the Judicial Retirement System of Texas Plan Two or who has an aggregate of at least 12 years of service as judge or justice of any type listed in Subsection (a)(4).

(b–1) For the purposes of Subsection (a)(5), a retired judge or magistrate is a former judge or magistrate of a federal court of this state who is fully vested in the Federal Employees Retirement System under 28 U.S.C. Section 371 or 377.

(c) Except as provided by Subsection (d), a person commits an offense if the person knowingly conducts a marriage ceremony without authorization under this section. An offense under this subsection is a Class A misdemeanor.

(d) A person commits an offense if the person knowingly conducts a marriage ceremony of a minor whose marriage is prohibited by law or of a person who by marrying commits an offense under Section

25.01, Penal Code. An offense under this subsection is a felony of the third degree.

Added by Acts 1997, 75th Leg., ch. 7, § 1, eff. April 17, 1997. Amended by Acts 2005, 79th Leg., ch. 268, § 4.10, eff. Sept. 1, 2005; Acts 2009, 81st Leg., ch. 134, § 1, eff. Sept. 1, 2009; Acts 2013, 83rd Leg., ch. 1350 (S.B. 1317), § 2, eff. Sept. 1, 2013; Acts 2015, 84th Leg., ch. 1069 (H.B. 2278), § 1, eff. Sept. 1, 2015.

### § 2.203. Ceremony

(a) On receiving an unexpired marriage license, an authorized person may conduct the marriage ceremony as provided by this subchapter.

(b) A person may assent to marriage by the appearance of a proxy appointed in the affidavit authorized by Subchapter A if the person is:

(1) a member of the armed forces of the United States stationed in another country in support of combat or another military operation; and

(2) unable to attend the ceremony.

Added by Acts 1997, 75th Leg., ch. 7, § 1, eff. April 17, 1997. Amended by Acts 2013, 83rd Leg., ch. 650 (H.B. 869), § 4, eff. Sept. 1, 2013.

### § 2.204. 72-Hour Waiting Period; Exceptions

(a) Except as provided by this section, a marriage ceremony may not take place during the 72-hour period immediately following the issuance of the marriage license.

(b) The 72–hour waiting period after issuance of a marriage license does not apply to an applicant who:

(1) is a member of the armed forces of the United States and on active duty;

(2) is not a member of the armed forces of the United States but performs work for the United States Department of Defense as a department employee or under a contract with the department;

(3) obtains a written waiver under Subsection (c); or

(4) completes a premarital education course described by Section 2.013, and who provides to the county clerk a premarital education course completion certificate indicating completion of the premarital education course not more than one year before the date the marriage license application is filed with the clerk.

(c) An applicant may request a judge of a court with jurisdiction in family law cases, a justice of the supreme court, a judge of the court of criminal appeals, a county judge, or a judge of a court of appeals for a written waiver permitting the marriage ceremony to take place during the 72-hour period immediately following the issuance of the marriage license. If the judge finds that there is good cause for the marriage to take place during the period, the judge shall sign the waiver. Notwithstanding any other provision of law, a judge under this section has the authority to sign a waiver under this section.

Added by Acts 1997, 75th Leg., ch. 7, § 1, eff. April 17, 1997. Amended by Acts 1999, 76th Leg., ch. 1052, § 1, eff. Sept. 1, 1999; Acts 2005, 79th Leg., ch. 1196, § 1, eff. June 18, 2005; Acts 2007, 80th Leg., ch. 327, § 2, eff. Sept. 1, 2008.

### § 2.205. Discrimination in Conducting Marriage Prohibited

(a) A person authorized to conduct a marriage ceremony by this subchapter is prohibited from discriminating on the basis of race, religion, or national origin against an applicant who is otherwise competent to be married.

(b) On a finding by the State Commission on Judicial Conduct that a person has intentionally violated Subsection (a), the commission may recommend to the supreme court that the person be removed from office.

Added by Acts 1997, 75th Leg., ch. 7, § 1, eff. April 17, 1997.

### § 2.206. Return of License; Penalty

(a) The person who conducts a marriage ceremony shall record on the license the date on which and the county in which the ceremony is performed and the person's name, subscribe the license, and return the license to the county clerk who issued it not later than the 30th day after the date the ceremony is conducted.

(b) A person who fails to comply with this section commits an offense. An offense under this section is a misdemeanor punishable by a fine of not less than $200 and not more than $500.

Added by Acts 1997, 75th Leg., ch. 7, § 1, eff. April 17, 1997.

### § 2.207. Marriage Conducted After License Expired; Penalty

(a) A person who is to conduct a marriage ceremony shall determine whether the license has expired from the county clerk's endorsement on the license.

(b) A person who conducts a marriage ceremony after the marriage license has expired commits an offense. An offense under this section is a misdemeanor punishable by a fine of not less than $200 and not more than $500.

Added by Acts 1997, 75th Leg., ch. 7, § 1, eff. April 17, 1997.

### § 2.208. Recording and Delivery of License

(a) The county clerk shall record a returned marriage license and mail the license to the address indicated on the application. On request by the applicants, the county clerk may e-mail the marriage license to an e-mail address provided to the county clerk by the applicants in addition to mailing the license.

(b) On the application form the county clerk shall record:

(1) the date of the marriage ceremony;

(2) the county in which the ceremony was conducted; and

(3) the name of the person who conducted the ceremony.

Added by Acts 1997, 75th Leg., ch. 7, § 1, eff. April 17, 1997. Amended by Acts 2019, 86th Leg., ch. 538 (H.B. 2767), § 1, eff. Sept. 1, 2019.

### § 2.209. Duplicate License

(a) On request, the county clerk shall issue a certified copy of a recorded marriage license.

(b) If a marriage license issued by a county clerk is lost, destroyed, or rendered useless, the clerk shall issue a duplicate license.

(c) If one or both parties to a marriage license discover an error on the recorded marriage license, both parties to the marriage shall execute a notarized affidavit stating the error. The county clerk shall file and record the affidavit as an amendment to the marriage license, and the affidavit is considered part of the marriage license. The clerk shall include a copy of the affidavit with any future certified copy of the marriage license issued by the clerk.

(d) The executive commissioner of the Health and Human Services Commission by rule shall prescribe the form of the affidavit under Subsection (c).

Added by Acts 1997, 75th Leg., ch. 7, § 1, eff. April 17, 1997. Amended by Acts 2009, 81st Leg., ch. 978, § 6, eff. Sept. 1, 2009.

### § 2.21. Repealed by Acts 1997, 75th Leg., ch. 7, § 3, eff. April 17, 1997

### §§ 2.22 to 2.24. Repealed by Acts 1997, 75th Leg., ch. 7, § 3, eff. April 17, 1997

## SUBCHAPTER D. VALIDITY OF MARRIAGE

### § 2.301. Fraud, Mistake, or Illegality in Obtaining License

Except as otherwise provided by this chapter, the validity of a marriage is not affected by any fraud, mistake, or illegality that occurred in obtaining the marriage license.

Added by Acts 1997, 75th Leg., ch. 7, § 1, eff. April 17, 1997.

### § 2.302. Ceremony Conducted by Unauthorized Person

The validity of a marriage is not affected by the lack of authority of the person conducting the marriage ceremony if:

(1) there was a reasonable appearance of authority by that person;

(2) at least one party to the marriage participated in the ceremony in good faith and that party treats the marriage as valid; and

(3) neither party to the marriage:

(A) is a minor whose marriage is prohibited by law; or

(B) by marrying commits an offense under Section 25.01, Penal Code.

Added by Acts 1997, 75th Leg., ch. 7, § 1, eff. April 17, 1997. Amended by Acts 2005, 79th Leg., ch. 268, § 4.11, eff. Sept. 1, 2005.

## SUBCHAPTER E. MARRIAGE WITHOUT FORMALITIES

### § 2.401. Proof of Informal Marriage

(a) In a judicial, administrative, or other proceeding, the marriage of a man and woman may be proved by evidence that:

(1) a declaration of their marriage has been signed as provided by this subchapter; or

(2) the man and woman agreed to be married and after the agreement they lived together in this state as husband and wife and there represented to others that they were married.

(b) If a proceeding in which a marriage is to be proved as provided by Subsection (a)(2) is not commenced before the second anniversary of the date on which the parties separated and ceased living together, it is rebuttably presumed that the parties did not enter into an agreement to be married.

(c) A person under 18 years of age may not:

(1) be a party to an informal marriage; or

(2) execute a declaration of informal marriage under Section 2.402.

(d) A person may not be a party to an informal marriage or execute a declaration of an informal marriage if the person is presently married to a person who is not the other party to the informal marriage or declaration of an informal marriage, as applicable.

Added by Acts 1997, 75th Leg., ch. 7, § 1, eff. April 17, 1997. Amended by Acts 1997, 75th Leg., ch. 1362, § 1, eff. Sept. 1, 1997; Acts 2005, 79th Leg., ch. 268, § 4.12, eff. Sept. 1, 2005.

### § 2.402. Declaration and Registration of Informal Marriage

(a) A declaration of informal marriage must be signed on a form prescribed by the bureau of vital statistics and provided by the county clerk. Each party to the declaration shall provide the information required in the form.

(b) The declaration form must contain:

(1) a heading entitled "Declaration and Registration of Informal Marriage, ________ County, Texas";

(2) spaces for each party's full name, including the woman's maiden surname, address, date of birth, place of birth, including city, county, and state, and social security number, if any;

(3) a space for indicating the type of document tendered by each party as proof of age and identity;

(4) printed boxes for each party to check "true" or "false" in response to the following statement: "The other party is not related to me as:

(A) an ancestor or descendant, by blood or adoption;

(B) a brother or sister, of the whole or half blood or by adoption;

(C) a parent's brother or sister, of the whole or half blood or by adoption;

(D) a son or daughter of a brother or sister, of the whole or half blood or by adoption;

(E) a current or former stepchild or stepparent; or

(F) a son or daughter of a parent's brother or sister, of the whole or half blood or by adoption.";

(5) a printed declaration and oath reading: "I SOLEMNLY SWEAR (OR AFFIRM) THAT WE, THE UNDERSIGNED, ARE MARRIED TO EACH OTHER BY VIRTUE OF THE FOLLOWING FACTS: ON OR ABOUT (DATE) WE AGREED TO BE MARRIED, AND AFTER THAT DATE WE LIVED TOGETHER AS HUSBAND AND WIFE AND IN THIS STATE WE REPRESENTED TO OTHERS THAT WE WERE MARRIED. SINCE THE DATE OF MARRIAGE TO THE OTHER PARTY I HAVE NOT BEEN MARRIED TO ANY OTHER PERSON. THIS DECLARATION IS TRUE AND THE INFORMATION IN IT WHICH I HAVE GIVEN IS CORRECT.";

(6) spaces immediately below the printed declaration and oath for the parties' signatures; and

(7) a certificate of the county clerk that the parties made the declaration and oath and the place and date it was made.

(c) Repealed by Acts 1997, 75th Leg., ch. 1362, § 4, eff. Sept. 1, 1997.

Added by Acts 1997, 75th Leg., ch. 7, § 1, eff. April 17, 1997. Amended by Acts 1997, 75th Leg., ch. 1362, § 4, eff. Sept. 1, 1997; Acts 2005, 79th Leg., ch. 268, § 4.13, eff. Sept. 1, 2005.

### § 2.403. Proof of Identity and Age; Offense

(a) The county clerk shall require proof of the identity and age of each party to the declaration of informal marriage to be established by a document listed in Section 2.005(b).

(b) A person commits an offense if the person knowingly provides false, fraudulent, or otherwise inaccurate proof of the person's identity or age under this section. An offense under this subsection is a Class A misdemeanor.

Added by Acts 1997, 75th Leg., ch. 7, § 1, eff. April 17, 1997. Amended by Acts 2005, 79th Leg., ch. 268, § 4.14, eff. Sept. 1, 2005; Acts 2009, 81st Leg., ch. 978, § 7, eff. Sept. 1, 2009.

### § 2.404. Recording of Certificate or Declaration of Informal Marriage

(a) The county clerk shall:

(1) determine that all necessary information is recorded on the declaration of informal marriage form and that all necessary documents are submitted to the clerk;

(2) administer the oath to each party to the declaration;

(3) have each party sign the declaration in the clerk's presence; and

(4) execute the clerk's certificate to the declaration.

(a–1) On the proper execution of the declaration, the clerk may:

(1) prepare a certificate of informal marriage;

(2) enter on the certificate the names of the persons declaring their informal marriage and the date the certificate or declaration is issued; and

(3) record the time at which the certificate or declaration is issued.

(b) The county clerk may not certify the declaration or issue or record the certificate of informal marriage or declaration if:

(1) either party fails to supply any information or provide any document required by this subchapter;

(2) either party is under 18 years of age; or

(3) either party checks "false" in response to the statement of relationship to the other party.

(c) On execution of the declaration, the county clerk shall record the declaration or certificate of informal marriage, deliver the original of the declaration to the parties, deliver the original of the certificate of informal marriage to the parties, if a certificate was prepared, and send a copy of the declaration of informal marriage to the bureau of vital statistics.

(d) An executed declaration or a certificate of informal marriage recorded as provided in this section is prima facie evidence of the marriage of the parties.

(e) At the time the parties sign the declaration, the clerk shall distribute to each party printed materials about acquired immune deficiency syndrome (AIDS) and human immunodeficiency virus (HIV). The clerk shall note on the declaration that the distribution was made. The materials shall be prepared and provided to the clerk by the Texas Department of Health and shall be designed to inform the parties about:

(1) the incidence and mode of transmission of AIDS and HIV;

(2) the local availability of medical procedures, including voluntary testing, designed to show or help show whether a person has AIDS or HIV infection, antibodies to HIV, or infection with any other probable causative agent of AIDS; and

(3) available and appropriate counseling services regarding AIDS and HIV infection.

Added by Acts 1997, 75th Leg., ch. 7, § 1, eff. April 17, 1997. Amended by Acts 1997, 75th Leg., ch. 1362, § 2, eff. Sept. 1, 1997; Acts 2009, 81st Leg., ch. 978, §§ 8, 9, eff. Sept. 1, 2009.

### § 2.405. Violation by County Clerk; Penalty

A county clerk or deputy county clerk who violates this subchapter commits an offense. An offense under this section is a misdemeanor punishable by a fine of not less than $200 and not more than $500.

Added by Acts 1997, 75th Leg., ch. 7, § 1, eff. April 17, 1997.

### §§ 2.41 to 2.48. Repealed by Acts 1997, 75th Leg., ch. 7, § 3, eff. April 17, 1997

## SUBCHAPTER F. RIGHTS AND DUTIES OF SPOUSES

### § 2.501. Duty to Support

(a) Each spouse has the duty to support the other spouse.

(b) A spouse who fails to discharge the duty of support is liable to any person who provides necessaries to the spouse to whom support is owed.

Added by Acts 1997, 75th Leg., ch. 7, § 1, eff. April 17, 1997.

## SUBCHAPTER G. FREEDOM OF RELIGION WITH RESPECT TO RECOGNIZING OR PERFORMING CERTAIN MARRIAGES

### § 2.601. Rights of Certain Religious Organizations

A religious organization, an organization supervised or controlled by or in connection with a religious organization, an individual employed by a religious organization while acting in the scope of that employment, or a clergy or minister may not be required to solemnize any marriage or provide services, accommodations, facilities, goods, or privileges for a purpose related to the solemnization, formation, or celebration of any marriage if the action would cause the organization or individual to violate a sincerely held religious belief.

Added by Acts 2015, 84th Leg., ch. 434 (S.B. 2065), § 1, eff. June 11, 2015.

### § 2.602. Discrimination Against Religious Organization Prohibited

A refusal to provide services, accommodations, facilities, goods, or privileges under Section 2.601 is not the basis for a civil or criminal cause of action or any other action by this state or a political subdivision of this state to penalize or withhold benefits or privileges, including tax exemptions or governmental contracts, grants, or licenses, from any protected organization or individual.

Added by Acts 2015, 84th Leg., ch. 434 (S.B. 2065), § 1, eff. June 11, 2015.

# SUBTITLE B. PROPERTY RIGHTS AND LIABILITIES

## CHAPTER 3. MARITAL PROPERTY RIGHTS AND LIABILITIES



*Acts 1997, 75th Leg., ch. 7, § 1, reenacted and revised Title 1 of the Family Code. For the subject matter of former Chapter 3, Dissolution of Marriage, see the disposition table in the preliminary material of Title 1.*

### SUBCHAPTER A. GENERAL RULES FOR SEPARATE AND COMMUNITY PROPERTY

#### § 3.001. Separate Property

A spouse's separate property consists of:

(1) the property owned or claimed by the spouse before marriage;

(2) the property acquired by the spouse during marriage by gift, devise, or descent; and

(3) the recovery for personal injuries sustained by the spouse during marriage, except any recovery for loss of earning capacity during marriage.

Added by Acts 1997, 75th Leg., ch. 7, § 1, eff. April 17, 1997.

#### § 3.002. Community Property

Community property consists of the property, other than separate property, acquired by either spouse during marriage.

Added by Acts 1997, 75th Leg., ch. 7, § 1, eff. April 17, 1997.

#### § 3.003. Presumption of Community Property

(a) Property possessed by either spouse during or on dissolution of marriage is presumed to be community property.

(b) The degree of proof necessary to establish that property is separate property is clear and convincing evidence.

Added by Acts 1997, 75th Leg., ch. 7, § 1, eff. April 17, 1997.

#### § 3.004. Recordation of Separate Property

(a) A subscribed and acknowledged schedule of a spouse's separate property may be recorded in the deed records of the county in which the parties, or one of them, reside and in the county or counties in which the real property is located.

(b) A schedule of a spouse's separate real property is not constructive notice to a good faith purchaser for value or a creditor without actual notice unless the instrument is acknowledged and recorded in the deed records of the county in which the real property is located.

Added by Acts 1997, 75th Leg., ch. 7, § 1, eff. April 17, 1997.

### § 3.005. Gifts Between Spouses

If one spouse makes a gift of property to the other spouse, the gift is presumed to include all the income and property that may arise from that property.

Added by Acts 1997, 75th Leg., ch. 7, § 1, eff. April 17, 1997.

### § 3.006. Proportional Ownership of Property by Marital Estates

If the community estate of the spouses and the separate estate of a spouse have an ownership interest in property, the respective ownership interests of the marital estates are determined by the rule of inception of title.

Added by Acts 1999, 76th Leg., ch. 692, § 1, eff. Sept. 1, 1999. Amended by Acts 2001, 77th Leg., ch. 838, § 3, eff. Sept. 1, 2001.

### § 3.007. Property Interest in Certain Employee Benefits

(a), (b) Repealed by Acts 2009, 81st Leg., ch. 768, § 11(1).

(c) The separate property interest of a spouse in a defined contribution retirement plan may be traced using the tracing and characterization principles that apply to a nonretirement asset.

(d) A spouse who is a participant in an employer-provided stock option plan or an employer-provided restricted stock plan has a separate property interest in the options or restricted stock granted to the spouse under the plan as follows:

(1) if the option or stock was granted to the spouse before marriage but required continued employment during marriage before the grant could be exercised or the restriction removed, the spouse's separate property interest is equal to the fraction of the option or restricted stock in which:

(A) the numerator is the sum of:

(i) the period from the date the option or stock was granted until the date of marriage; and

(ii) if the option or stock also required continued employment following the date of dissolution of the marriage before the grant could be exercised or the restriction removed, the period from the date of dissolution of the marriage until the date the grant could be exercised or the restriction removed; and

(B) the denominator is the period from the date the option or stock was granted until the date the grant could be exercised or the restriction removed; and

(2) if the option or stock was granted to the spouse during the marriage but required continued employment following the date of dissolution of the marriage before the grant could be exercised or the restriction removed, the spouse's separate property interest is equal to the fraction of the option or restricted stock in which:

(A) the numerator is the period from the date of dissolution of the marriage until the date the grant could be exercised or the restriction removed; and

(B) the denominator is the period from the date the option or stock was granted until the date the grant could be exercised or the restriction removed.

(e) The computation described by Subsection (d) applies to each component of the benefit requiring varying periods of employment before the grant could be exercised or the restriction removed.

(f) Repealed by Acts 2009, 81st Leg., ch. 768, § 11(1).

Added by Acts 2005, 79th Leg., ch. 490, § 1, eff. Sept. 1, 2005. Amended by Acts 2009, 81st Leg., ch. 768, §§ 1, 11(1), eff. Sept. 1, 2009.

### § 3.008. Property Interest in Certain Insurance Proceeds

(a) Insurance proceeds paid or payable that arise from a casualty loss to property during marriage are characterized in the same manner as the property to which the claim is attributable.

(b) If a person becomes disabled or is injured, any disability insurance payment or workers' compensation payment is community property to the extent it is intended to replace earnings lost while the disabled or injured person is married. To the extent that any insurance payment or workers' compensation payment is intended to replace earnings while the disabled or injured person is not married, the recovery is the separate property of the disabled or injured spouse.

Added by Acts 2005, 79th Leg., ch. 490, § 1, eff. Sept. 1, 2005.

### §§ 3.01 to 3.08. Repealed by Acts 1997, 75th Leg., ch. 7, § 3, eff. April 17, 1997

## SUBCHAPTER B. MANAGEMENT, CONTROL, AND DISPOSITION OF MARITAL PROPERTY

### § 3.101. Managing Separate Property

Each spouse has the sole management, control, and disposition of that spouse's separate property.

Added by Acts 1997, 75th Leg., ch. 7, § 1, eff. April 17, 1997.

### § 3.102. Managing Community Property

(a) During marriage, each spouse has the sole management, control, and disposition of the community property that the spouse would have owned if single, including:

(1) personal earnings;

(2) revenue from separate property;

(3) recoveries for personal injuries; and

(4) the increase and mutations of, and the revenue from, all property subject to the spouse's sole management, control, and disposition.

(b) If community property subject to the sole management, control, and disposition of one spouse is mixed or combined with community property subject to the sole management, control, and disposition of the other spouse, then the mixed or combined community property is subject to the joint management, control, and disposition of the spouses, unless the spouses provide otherwise by power of attorney in writing or other agreement.

(c) Except as provided by Subsection (a), community property is subject to the joint management, control, and disposition of the spouses unless the spouses provide otherwise by power of attorney in writing or other agreement.

Added by Acts 1997, 75th Leg., ch. 7, § 1, eff. April 17, 1997.

### § 3.103. Managing Earnings of Minor

Except as provided by Section 264.0111, during the marriage of the parents of an unemancipated minor for whom a managing conservator has not been appointed, the earnings of the minor are subject to the joint management, control, and disposition of the parents of the minor, unless otherwise provided by agreement of the parents or by judicial order.

Added by Acts 1997, 75th Leg., ch. 7, § 1, eff. April 17, 1997. Amended by Acts 2001, 77th Leg., ch. 964, § 1, eff. Sept. 1, 2001.

### § 3.104. Protection of Third Persons

(a) During marriage, property is presumed to be subject to the sole management, control, and disposition of a spouse if it is held in that spouse's name, as shown by muniment, contract, deposit of funds, or other evidence of ownership, or if it is in that spouse's possession and is not subject to such evidence of ownership.

(b) A third person dealing with a spouse is entitled to rely, as against the other spouse or anyone claiming from that spouse, on that spouse's authority to deal with the property if:

(1) the property is presumed to be subject to the sole management, control, and disposition of the spouse; and

(2) the person dealing with the spouse:

(A) is not a party to a fraud on the other spouse or another person; and

(B) does not have actual or constructive notice of the spouse's lack of authority.

Added by Acts 1997, 75th Leg., ch. 7, § 1, eff. April 17, 1997.

## SUBCHAPTER C. MARITAL PROPERTY LIABILITIES

### § 3.201. Spousal Liability

(a) A person is personally liable for the acts of the person's spouse only if:

(1) the spouse acts as an agent for the person; or

(2) the spouse incurs a debt for necessaries as provided by Subchapter F,[1] Chapter 2.

(b) Except as provided by this subchapter, community property is not subject to a liability that arises from an act of a spouse.

(c) A spouse does not act as an agent for the other spouse solely because of the marriage relationship.

Added by Acts 1997, 75th Leg., ch. 7, § 1, eff. April 17, 1997.

[1] V.T.C.A., Family Code § 2.501.

### § 3.202. Rules of Marital Property Liability

(a) A spouse's separate property is not subject to liabilities of the other spouse unless both spouses are liable by other rules of law.

(b) Unless both spouses are personally liable as provided by this subchapter, the community property subject to a spouse's sole management, control, and disposition is not subject to:

(1) any liabilities that the other spouse incurred before marriage; or

(2) any nontortious liabilities that the other spouse incurs during marriage.

(c) The community property subject to a spouse's sole or joint management, control, and disposition is subject to the liabilities incurred by the spouse before or during marriage.

(d) All community property is subject to tortious liability of either spouse incurred during marriage.

(e) For purposes of this section, all retirement allowances, annuities, accumulated contributions, optional benefits, and money in the various public retirement system accounts of this state that are community property subject to the participating spouse's sole management, control, and disposition are not subject to any claim for payment of a criminal restitution judgment entered against the nonparticipant spouse except to the extent of the nonparticipant spouse's interest as determined in a qualified domestic relations order under Chapter 804, Government Code.

Added by Acts 1997, 75th Leg., ch. 7, § 1, eff. April 17, 1997. Amended by Acts 2009, 81st Leg., ch. 1244, § 1, eff. Sept. 1, 2009.

### § 3.203. Order in Which Property is Subject to Execution

(a) A judge may determine, as deemed just and equitable, the order in which particular separate or community property is subject to execution and sale to satisfy a judgment, if the property subject to liability for a judgment includes any combination of:

(1) a spouse's separate property;

(2) community property subject to a spouse's sole management, control, and disposition;

(3) community property subject to the other spouse's sole management, control, and disposition; and

(4) community property subject to the spouses' joint management, control, and disposition.

(b) In determining the order in which particular property is subject to execution and sale, the judge shall consider the facts surrounding the transaction or occurrence on which the suit is based.

Added by Acts 1997, 75th Leg., ch. 7, § 1, eff. April 17, 1997.

### §§ 3.21 to 3.26. Repealed by Acts 1997, 75th Leg., ch. 7, § 3, eff. April 17, 1997

## SUBCHAPTER D. MANAGEMENT, CONTROL, AND DISPOSITION OF MARITAL PROPERTY UNDER UNUSUAL CIRCUMSTANCES

### § 3.301. Missing, Abandoned, or Separated Spouse

(a) A spouse may file a sworn petition stating the facts that make it desirable for the petitioning spouse to manage, control, and dispose of community property described or defined in the petition that would otherwise be subject to the sole or joint management, control, and disposition of the other spouse if:

(1) the other spouse has disappeared and that spouse's location remains unknown to the petitioning spouse, unless the spouse is reported to be a prisoner of war or missing on public service;

(2) the other spouse has permanently abandoned the petitioning spouse; or

(3) the spouses are permanently separated.

(b) The petition may be filed in a court in the county in which the petitioner resided at the time the separation began, or the abandonment or disappearance occurred, not earlier than the 60th day after the date of the occurrence of the event. If both spouses are nonresidents of this state at the time the petition is filed, the petition may be filed in a court in a county in which any part of the described or defined community property is located.

Added by Acts 1997, 75th Leg., ch. 7, § 1, eff. April 17, 1997. Amended by Acts 2001, 77th Leg., ch. 217, § 23, eff. Sept. 1, 2001.

### § 3.302. Spouse Missing on Public Service

(a) If a spouse is reported by an executive department of the United States to be a prisoner of war or missing on the public service of the United States, the spouse of the prisoner of war or missing person may file a sworn petition stating the facts that make it desirable for the petitioner to manage, control, and dispose of the community property described or defined in the petition that would otherwise be subject to the sole or joint management, control, and disposition of the imprisoned or missing spouse.

(b) The petition may be filed in a court in the county in which the petitioner resided at the time the report was made not earlier than six months after the date of the notice that a spouse is reported to be a prisoner of war or missing on public service. If both spouses were nonresidents of this state at the time the report was made, the petition shall be filed in a court in a county in which any part of the described or defined property is located.

Added by Acts 1997, 75th Leg., ch. 7, § 1, eff. April 17, 1997.

### § 3.303. Appointment of Attorney

(a) Except as provided by Subsection (b), the court may appoint an attorney in a suit filed under this subchapter for the respondent.

(b) The court shall appoint an attorney in a suit filed under this subchapter for a respondent reported to be a prisoner of war or missing on public service.

(c) The court shall allow a reasonable fee for an appointed attorney's services as a part of the costs of the suit.

Added by Acts 1997, 75th Leg., ch. 7, § 1, eff. April 17, 1997.

### § 3.304. Notice of Hearing; Citation

(a) Notice of the hearing, accompanied by a copy of the petition, shall be issued and served on the attorney representing the respondent, if an attorney has been appointed.

(b) If an attorney has not been appointed for the respondent, citation shall be issued and served on the respondent as in other civil cases.

Added by Acts 1997, 75th Leg., ch. 7, § 1, eff. April 17, 1997.

### § 3.305. Citation by Publication

(a) Except as provided by Section 17.032, Civil Practice and Remedies Code, if the residence of the respondent, other than a respondent reported to be a prisoner of war or missing on public service, is unknown, citation shall be published on the public information Internet website maintained as required by Section 72.034, Government Code, and in a newspaper of general circulation published in the county in which the petition was filed.

(b) The notice shall be published on the public information Internet website for at least two consecutive weeks before the hearing and in a newspaper once a week for two consecutive weeks before the hearing. Neither notice may be initially published after the 20th day before the date set for the hearing.

Added by Acts 1997, 75th Leg., ch. 7, § 1, eff. April 17, 1997. Amended by Acts 2019, 86th Leg., ch. 606 (S.B. 891), § 10.09, eff. June 1, 2020.

Section 15.05 of Acts 2019, 86th Leg., ch. 606 (S.B. 891) provides:

"The Office of Court Administration of the Texas Judicial System is required to implement a provision of this Act only if the legislature appropriates money specifically for that purpose. If the legislature does not appropriate money specifically for that purpose, the office may, but is not required to, implement a provision of this Act using other appropriations available for that purpose."

### § 3.306. Court Order for Management, Control, and Disposition of Community Property

(a) After hearing the evidence in a suit under this subchapter, the court, on terms the court considers just and equitable, shall render an order describing or defining the community property at issue that will be subject to the management, control, and disposition of each spouse during marriage.

(b) The court may:

(1) impose any condition and restriction the court deems necessary to protect the rights of the respondent;

(2) require a bond conditioned on the faithful administration of the property; and

(3) require payment to the registry of the court of all or a portion of the proceeds of the sale of the property, to be disbursed in accordance with the court's further directions.

Added by Acts 1997, 75th Leg., ch. 7, § 1, eff. April 17, 1997.

### § 3.307. Continuing Jurisdiction of Court; Vacating Original Order

(a) The court has continuing jurisdiction over the court's order rendered under this subchapter.

(b) On the motion of either spouse, the court shall amend or vacate the original order after notice and hearing if:

(1) the spouse who disappeared reappears;

(2) the abandonment or permanent separation ends; or

(3) the spouse who was reported to be a prisoner of war or missing on public service returns.

Added by Acts 1997, 75th Leg., ch. 7, § 1, eff. April 17, 1997. Amended by Acts 2001, 77th Leg., ch. 217, § 24, eff. Sept. 1, 2001.

### § 3.308. Recording Order to Affect Real Property

An order authorized by this subchapter affecting real property is not constructive notice to a good faith purchaser for value or to a creditor without actual notice unless the order is recorded in the deed records of the county in which the real property is located.

Added by Acts 1997, 75th Leg., ch. 7, § 1, eff. April 17, 1997.

### § 3.309. Remedies Cumulative

The remedies provided in this subchapter are cumulative of other rights, powers, and remedies afforded spouses by law.

Added by Acts 1997, 75th Leg., ch. 7, § 1, eff. April 17, 1997.

## SUBCHAPTER E. CLAIMS FOR REIMBURSEMENT

### § 3.401. Definitions

In this subchapter:

(1) to (3) Repealed by Acts 2009, 81st Leg., ch. 768, § 11(2).

(4) "Marital estate" means one of three estates:

(A) the community property owned by the spouses together and referred to as the community marital estate;

(B) the separate property owned individually by the husband and referred to as a separate marital estate; or

(C) the separate property owned individually by the wife, also referred to as a separate marital estate.

(5) "Spouse" means a husband, who is a man, or a wife, who is a woman. A member of a civil union or similar relationship entered into in another state between persons of the same sex is not a spouse.

Added by Acts 1999, 76th Leg., ch. 692, § 2, eff. Sept. 1, 1999. Amended by Acts 2001, 77th Leg., ch. 838, § 2, eff. Sept. 1, 2001; Acts 2009, 81st Leg., ch. 768, § 11(2), eff. Sept. 1, 2009.

### § 3.402. Claim for Reimbursement; Offsets

(a) For purposes of this subchapter, a claim for reimbursement includes:

(1) payment by one marital estate of the unsecured liabilities of another marital estate;

(2) inadequate compensation for the time, toil, talent, and effort of a spouse by a business entity under the control and direction of that spouse;

(3) the reduction of the principal amount of a debt secured by a lien on property owned before marriage, to the extent the debt existed at the time of marriage;

(4) the reduction of the principal amount of a debt secured by a lien on property received by a spouse by gift, devise, or descent during a marriage, to the extent the debt existed at the time the property was received;

(5) the reduction of the principal amount of that part of a debt, including a home equity loan:

(A) incurred during a marriage;

(B) secured by a lien on property; and

(C) incurred for the acquisition of, or for capital improvements to, property;

(6) the reduction of the principal amount of that part of a debt:

(A) incurred during a marriage;

(B) secured by a lien on property owned by a spouse;

(C) for which the creditor agreed to look for repayment solely to the separate marital estate of the spouse on whose property the lien attached; and

(D) incurred for the acquisition of, or for capital improvements to, property;

(7) the refinancing of the principal amount described by Subdivisions (3)–(6), to the extent the refinancing reduces that principal amount in a manner described by the applicable subdivision;

(8) capital improvements to property other than by incurring debt; and

(9) the reduction by the community property estate of an unsecured debt incurred by the separate estate of one of the spouses.

(b) The court shall resolve a claim for reimbursement by using equitable principles, including the principle that claims for reimbursement may be offset against each other if the court determines it to be appropriate.

(c) Benefits for the use and enjoyment of property may be offset against a claim for reimbursement for expenditures to benefit a marital estate, except that the separate estate of a spouse may not claim an offset for use and enjoyment of a primary or secondary residence owned wholly or partly by the separate estate against contributions made by the community estate to the separate estate.

(d) Reimbursement for funds expended by a marital estate for improvements to another marital estate shall be measured by the enhancement in value to the benefited marital estate.

(e) The party seeking an offset to a claim for reimbursement has the burden of proof with respect to the offset.

Added by Acts 1999, 76th Leg., ch. 692, § 2, eff. Sept. 1, 1999. Amended by Acts 2001, 77th Leg., ch. 838, § 2, eff. Sept. 1, 2001; Acts 2009, 81st Leg., ch. 768, § 3, eff. Sept. 1, 2009.

### § 3.403. Repealed by Acts 2009, 81st Leg., ch. 768, § 11(3), eff. Sept. 1, 2009

### § 3.404. Application of Inception of Title Rule; Ownership Interest Not Created

(a) This subchapter does not affect the rule of inception of title under which the character of property is determined at the time the right to own or claim the property arises.

(b) A claim for reimbursement under this subchapter does not create an ownership interest in property, but does create a claim against the property of the benefited estate by the contributing estate. The claim matures on dissolution of the marriage or the death of either spouse.

Added by Acts 1999, 76th Leg., ch. 692, § 2, eff. Sept. 1, 1999. Amended by Acts 2001, 77th Leg., ch. 838, § 2, eff. Sept. 1, 2001; Acts 2009, 81st Leg., ch. 768, § 4, eff. Sept. 1, 2009.

### § 3.405. Management Rights

This subchapter does not affect the right to manage, control, or dispose of marital property as provided by this chapter.

Added by Acts 1999, 76th Leg., ch. 692, § 2, eff. Sept. 1, 1999. Amended by Acts 2001, 77th Leg., ch. 838, § 2, eff. Sept. 1, 2001.

### § 3.406. Equitable Lien

(a) On dissolution of a marriage, the court may impose an equitable lien on the property of a benefited marital estate to secure a claim for reimbursement against that property by a contributing marital estate.

(b) On the death of a spouse, a court may, on application for a claim for reimbursement brought by the surviving spouse, the personal representative of the estate of the deceased spouse, or any other person interested in the estate, as defined by Chapter 22, Estates Code, impose an equitable lien on the property of a benefited marital estate to secure a claim for reimbursement against that property by a contributing marital estate.

(c) Repealed by Acts 2009, 81st Leg., ch. 768, § 11(4).

Added by Acts 1999, 76th Leg., ch. 692, § 2, eff. Sept. 1, 1999. Amended by Acts 2001, 77th Leg., ch. 838, § 2, eff. Sept. 1, 2001; Acts 2009, 81st Leg., ch. 768, §§ 5, 11(4), eff. Sept. 1, 2009; Acts 2017, 85th Leg., ch. 324 (S.B. 1488), § 22.013, eff. Sept. 1, 2017.

### § 3.407. Repealed by Acts 2009, 81st Leg., ch. 768, § 11(5), eff. Sept. 1, 2009

### § 3.408. Repealed by Acts 2009, 81st Leg., ch. 768, § 11(5), eff. Sept. 1, 2009

### § 3.409. Nonreimbursable Claims

The court may not recognize a marital estate's claim for reimbursement for:

(1) the payment of child support, alimony, or spousal maintenance;

(2) the living expenses of a spouse or child of a spouse;

(3) contributions of property of a nominal value;

(4) the payment of a liability of a nominal amount; or

(5) a student loan owed by a spouse.

Added by Acts 2001, 77th Leg., ch. 838, § 2, eff. Sept. 1, 2001.

### § 3.410. Effect of Marital Property Agreements

A premarital or marital property agreement, whether executed before, on, or after September 1, 2009, that satisfies the requirements of Chapter 4 is effective to waive, release, assign, or partition a claim for economic contribution, reimbursement, or both, under this subchapter to the same extent the agreement would have been effective to waive, release, assign, or partition a claim for economic contribution, reimbursement, or both under the law as it existed immediately before September 1, 2009, unless the agreement provides otherwise.

Added by Acts 2001, 77th Leg., ch. 838, § 2, eff. Sept. 1, 2001. Amended by Acts 2009, 81st Leg., ch. 768, § 6, eff. Sept. 1, 2009.

### §§ 3.51 to 3.55. Repealed by Acts 1997, 75th Leg., ch. 7, § 3, eff. April 17, 1997

### § 3.56. Repealed by Acts 1981, 67th Leg., p. 2655, ch. 711, § 3, eff. Sept. 1, 1981

### §§ 3.57 to 3.9611. Repealed by Acts 1997, 75th Leg., ch. 7, § 3, eff. April 17, 1997

## CHAPTER 4. PREMARITAL AND MARITAL PROPERTY AGREEMENTS

SUBCHAPTER A. UNIFORM PREMARITAL AGREEMENT ACT

**Section**



SUBCHAPTER B. MARITAL PROPERTY AGREEMENT

SUBCHAPTER C. AGREEMENT TO CONVERT SEPARATE PROPERTY TO COMMUNITY PROPERTY



*Acts 1997, 75th Leg., ch. 7, § 1, reenacted and revised Title 1 of the Family Code. For the subject matter of former Chapter 4, Rights, Duties, Powers, and Liabilities of Spouses, see the disposition table in the preliminary material of Title 1.*

## SUBCHAPTER A. UNIFORM PREMARITAL AGREEMENT ACT

### § 4.001. Definitions

In this subchapter:

(1) "Premarital agreement" means an agreement between prospective spouses made in contemplation of marriage and to be effective on marriage.

(2) "Property" means an interest, present or future, legal or equitable, vested or contingent, in real or personal property, including income and earnings.

Added by Acts 1997, 75th Leg., ch. 7, § 1, eff. April 17, 1997.

### § 4.002. Formalities

A premarital agreement must be in writing and signed by both parties. The agreement is enforceable without consideration.

Added by Acts 1997, 75th Leg., ch. 7, § 1, eff. April 17, 1997.

### § 4.003. Content

(a) The parties to a premarital agreement may contract with respect to:

(1) the rights and obligations of each of the parties in any of the property of either or both of them whenever and wherever acquired or located;

(2) the right to buy, sell, use, transfer, exchange, abandon, lease, consume, expend, assign, create a security interest in, mortgage, encumber, dispose of, or otherwise manage and control property;

(3) the disposition of property on separation, marital dissolution, death, or the occurrence or nonoccurrence of any other event;

(4) the modification or elimination of spousal support;

(5) the making of a will, trust, or other arrangement to carry out the provisions of the agreement;

(6) the ownership rights in and disposition of the death benefit from a life insurance policy;

(7) the choice of law governing the construction of the agreement; and

(8) any other matter, including their personal rights and obligations, not in violation of public policy or a statute imposing a criminal penalty.

(b) The right of a child to support may not be adversely affected by a premarital agreement.

Added by Acts 1997, 75th Leg., ch. 7, § 1, eff. April 17, 1997.

### § 4.004. Effect of Marriage

A premarital agreement becomes effective on marriage.

Added by Acts 1997, 75th Leg., ch. 7, § 1, eff. April 17, 1997.

### § 4.005. Amendment or Revocation

After marriage, a premarital agreement may be amended or revoked only by a written agreement signed by the parties. The amended agreement or the revocation is enforceable without consideration.

Added by Acts 1997, 75th Leg., ch. 7, § 1, eff. April 17, 1997.

### § 4.006. Enforcement

(a) A premarital agreement is not enforceable if the party against whom enforcement is requested proves that:

(1) the party did not sign the agreement voluntarily; or

(2) the agreement was unconscionable when it was signed and, before signing the agreement, that party:

(A) was not provided a fair and reasonable disclosure of the property or financial obligations of the other party;

(B) did not voluntarily and expressly waive, in writing, any right to disclosure of the property or financial obligations of the other party beyond the disclosure provided; and

(C) did not have, or reasonably could not have had, adequate knowledge of the property or financial obligations of the other party.

(b) An issue of unconscionability of a premarital agreement shall be decided by the court as a matter of law.

(c) The remedies and defenses in this section are the exclusive remedies or defenses, including common law remedies or defenses.

Added by Acts 1997, 75th Leg., ch. 7, § 1, eff. April 17, 1997.

### § 4.007. Enforcement: Void Marriage

If a marriage is determined to be void, an agreement that would otherwise have been a premarital agreement is enforceable only to the extent necessary to avoid an inequitable result.

Added by Acts 1997, 75th Leg., ch. 7, § 1, eff. April 17, 1997.

### § 4.008. Limitation of Actions

A statute of limitations applicable to an action asserting a claim for relief under a premarital agreement is tolled during the marriage of the parties to the agreement. However, equitable defenses limiting the time for enforcement, including laches and estoppel, are available to either party.

Added by Acts 1997, 75th Leg., ch. 7, § 1, eff. April 17, 1997.

### § 4.009. Application and Construction

This subchapter shall be applied and construed to effect its general purpose to make uniform the law with respect to the subject of this subchapter among states enacting these provisions.

Added by Acts 1997, 75th Leg., ch. 7, § 1, eff. April 17, 1997.

### § 4.01. Repealed by Acts 1997, 75th Leg., ch. 7, § 3, eff. April 17, 1997

### § 4.010. Short Title

This subchapter may be cited as the Uniform Premarital Agreement Act.

Added by Acts 1997, 75th Leg., ch. 7, § 1, eff. April 17, 1997.

### §§ 4.02 to 4.06. Repealed by Acts 1997, 75th Leg., ch. 7, § 3, eff. April 17, 1997

## SUBCHAPTER B. MARITAL PROPERTY AGREEMENT

### § 4.101. Definition

In this subchapter, "property" has the meaning assigned by Section 4.001.

Added by Acts 1997, 75th Leg., ch. 7, § 1, eff. April 17, 1997.

### § 4.102. Partition or Exchange of Community Property

At any time, the spouses may partition or exchange between themselves all or part of their community property, then existing or to be acquired, as the spouses may desire. Property or a property interest transferred to a spouse by a partition or exchange agreement becomes that spouse's separate property. The partition or exchange of property may also provide that future earnings and income arising from the transferred property shall be the separate property of the owning spouse.

Added by Acts 1997, 75th Leg., ch. 7, § 1, eff. April 17, 1997. Amended by Acts 2003, 78th Leg., ch. 230, § 2, eff. Sept. 1, 2003; Acts 2005, 79th Leg., ch. 477, § 1, eff. Sept. 1, 2005.

### § 4.103. Agreement Between Spouses Concerning Income or Property From Separate Property

At any time, the spouses may agree that the income or property arising from the separate property that is then owned by one of them, or that may thereafter be acquired, shall be the separate property of the owner.

Added by Acts 1997, 75th Leg., ch. 7, § 1, eff. April 17, 1997.

### § 4.104. Formalities

A partition or exchange agreement under Section 4.102 or an agreement under Section 4.103 must be in writing and signed by both parties. Either agreement is enforceable without consideration.

Added by Acts 1997, 75th Leg., ch. 7, § 1, eff. April 17, 1997. Amended by Acts 2005, 79th Leg., ch. 477, § 2, eff. Sept. 1, 2005.

### § 4.105. Enforcement

(a) A partition or exchange agreement is not enforceable if the party against whom enforcement is requested proves that:

(1) the party did not sign the agreement voluntarily; or

(2) the agreement was unconscionable when it was signed and, before execution of the agreement, that party:

(A) was not provided a fair and reasonable disclosure of the property or financial obligations of the other party;

(B) did not voluntarily and expressly waive, in writing, any right to disclosure of the property or financial obligations of the other party beyond the disclosure provided; and

(C) did not have, or reasonably could not have had, adequate knowledge of the property or financial obligations of the other party.

(b) An issue of unconscionability of a partition or exchange agreement shall be decided by the court as a matter of law.

(c) The remedies and defenses in this section are the exclusive remedies or defenses, including common law remedies or defenses.

Added by Acts 1997, 75th Leg., ch. 7, § 1, eff. April 17, 1997.

### § 4.106. Rights of Creditors and Recordation Under Partition or Exchange Agreement

(a) A provision of a partition or exchange agreement made under this subchapter is void with respect to the rights of a preexisting creditor whose rights are intended to be defrauded by it.

(b) A partition or exchange agreement made under this subchapter may be recorded in the deed records of the county in which a party resides and in the county in which the real property affected is located. An agreement made under this subchapter is constructive notice to a good faith purchaser for value or a creditor without actual notice only if the instrument is acknowledged and recorded in the county in which the real property is located.

Added by Acts 1997, 75th Leg., ch. 7, § 1, eff. April 17, 1997.

## SUBCHAPTER C. AGREEMENT TO CONVERT SEPARATE PROPERTY TO COMMUNITY PROPERTY

### § 4.201. Definition

In this subchapter, "property" has the meaning assigned by Section 4.001.

Added by Acts 1999, 76th Leg., ch. 692, § 3, eff. Jan. 1, 2000.

### § 4.202. Agreement to Convert to Community Property

At any time, spouses may agree that all or part of the separate property owned by either or both spouses is converted to community property.

Added by Acts 1999, 76th Leg., ch. 692, § 3, eff. Jan. 1, 2000.

### § 4.203. Formalities of Agreement

(a) An agreement to convert separate property to community property:

(1) must be in writing and:

(A) be signed by the spouses;

(B) identify the property being converted; and

(C) specify that the property is being converted to the spouses' community property; and

(2) is enforceable without consideration.

(b) The mere transfer of a spouse's separate property to the name of the other spouse or to the name of both spouses is not sufficient to convert the property to community property under this subchapter.

Added by Acts 1999, 76th Leg., ch. 692, § 3, eff. Jan. 1, 2000.

### § 4.204. Management of Converted Property

Except as specified in the agreement to convert the property and as provided by Subchapter B, Chapter 3, and other law, property converted to community property under this subchapter is subject to:

(1) the sole management, control, and disposition of the spouse in whose name the property is held;

(2) the sole management, control, and disposition of the spouse who transferred the property if the property is not subject to evidence of ownership;

(3) the joint management, control, and disposition of the spouses if the property is held in the name of both spouses; or

(4) the joint management, control, and disposition of the spouses if the property is not subject to evidence of ownership and was owned by both spouses before the property was converted to community property.

Added by Acts 1999, 76th Leg., ch. 692, § 3, eff. Jan. 1, 2000.

### § 4.205. Enforcement

(a) An agreement to convert property to community property under this subchapter is not enforceable if the spouse against whom enforcement is sought proves that the spouse did not:

(1) execute the agreement voluntarily; or

(2) receive a fair and reasonable disclosure of the legal effect of converting the property to community property.

(b) An agreement that contains the following statement, or substantially similar words, prominently displayed in bold-faced type, capital letters, or underlined, is rebuttably presumed to provide a fair and reasonable disclosure of the legal effect of converting property to community property:

"THIS INSTRUMENT CHANGES SEPARATE PROPERTY TO COMMUNITY PROPERTY. THIS MAY HAVE ADVERSE CONSEQUENCES DURING MARRIAGE AND ON TERMINATION

OF THE MARRIAGE BY DEATH OR DIVORCE. FOR EXAMPLE:

"EXPOSURE TO CREDITORS. IF YOU SIGN THIS AGREEMENT, ALL OR PART OF THE SEPARATE PROPERTY BEING CONVERTED TO COMMUNITY PROPERTY MAY BECOME SUBJECT TO THE LIABILITIES OF YOUR SPOUSE. IF YOU DO NOT SIGN THIS AGREEMENT, YOUR SEPARATE PROPERTY IS GENERALLY NOT SUBJECT TO THE LIABILITIES OF YOUR SPOUSE UNLESS YOU ARE PERSONALLY LIABLE UNDER ANOTHER RULE OF LAW.

"LOSS OF MANAGEMENT RIGHTS. IF YOU SIGN THIS AGREEMENT, ALL OR PART OF THE SEPARATE PROPERTY BEING CONVERTED TO COMMUNITY PROPERTY MAY BECOME SUBJECT TO EITHER THE JOINT MANAGEMENT, CONTROL, AND DISPOSITION OF YOU AND YOUR SPOUSE OR THE SOLE MANAGEMENT, CONTROL, AND DISPOSITION OF YOUR SPOUSE ALONE. IN THAT EVENT, YOU WILL LOSE YOUR MANAGEMENT RIGHTS OVER THE PROPERTY. IF YOU DO NOT SIGN THIS AGREEMENT, YOU WILL GENERALLY RETAIN THOSE RIGHTS."

"LOSS OF PROPERTY OWNERSHIP. IF YOU SIGN THIS AGREEMENT AND YOUR MARRIAGE IS SUBSEQUENTLY TERMINATED BY THE DEATH OF EITHER SPOUSE OR BY DIVORCE, ALL OR PART OF THE SEPARATE PROPERTY BEING CONVERTED TO COMMUNITY PROPERTY MAY BECOME THE SOLE PROPERTY OF YOUR SPOUSE OR YOUR SPOUSE'S HEIRS. IF YOU DO NOT SIGN THIS AGREEMENT, YOU GENERALLY CANNOT BE DEPRIVED OF OWNERSHIP OF YOUR SEPARATE PROPERTY ON TERMINATION OF YOUR MARRIAGE, WHETHER BY DEATH OR DIVORCE."

(c) If a proceeding regarding enforcement of an agreement under this subchapter occurs after the death of the spouse against whom enforcement is sought, the proof required by Subsection (a) may be made by an heir of the spouse or the personal representative of the estate of that spouse.

Added by Acts 1999, 76th Leg., ch. 692, § 3, eff. Jan. 1, 2000. Amended by Acts 2003, 78th Leg., ch. 230, § 3, eff. Sept. 1, 2003.

### § 4.206. Rights of Creditors; Recording

(a) A conversion of separate property to community property does not affect the rights of a preexisting creditor of the spouse whose separate property is being converted.

(b) A conversion of separate property to community property may be recorded in the deed records of the county in which a spouse resides and of the county in which any real property is located.

(c) A conversion of real property from separate property to community property is constructive notice to a good faith purchaser for value or a creditor without actual notice only if the agreement to convert the property is acknowledged and recorded in the deed records of the county in which the real property is located.

Added by Acts 1999, 76th Leg., ch. 692, § 3, eff. Jan. 1, 2000.

## CHAPTER 5. HOMESTEAD RIGHTS

SUBCHAPTER A. SALE OF HOMESTEAD; GENERAL RULE

**Section**



SUBCHAPTER B. SALE OF HOMESTEAD UNDER UNUSUAL CIRCUMSTANCES



*Acts 1997, 75th Leg., ch. 7, § 1, reenacted and revised Title 1 of the Family Code. For the subject matter of former Chapter 5, Marital Property, see the disposition table in the preliminary material of Title 1.*

### SUBCHAPTER A. SALE OF HOMESTEAD; GENERAL RULE

### § 5.001. Sale, Conveyance, or Encumbrance of Homestead

Whether the homestead is the separate property of either spouse or community property, neither spouse may sell, convey, or encumber the homestead without the joinder of the other spouse except as provided in this chapter or by other rules of law.

Added by Acts 1997, 75th Leg., ch. 7, § 1, eff. April 17, 1997.

### § 5.002. Sale of Separate Homestead After Spouse Judicially Declared Incapacitated

If the homestead is the separate property of a spouse and the other spouse has been judicially declared incapacitated by a court exercising original jurisdiction over guardianship and other matters under Title 3, Estates Code, the owner may sell, convey, or encumber the homestead without the joinder of the other spouse.

Added by Acts 1997, 75th Leg., ch. 7, § 1, eff. April 17, 1997. Amended by Acts 2001, 77th Leg., ch. 217, § 25, eff. Sept. 1, 2001; Acts 2017, 85th Leg., ch. 324 (S.B. 1488), § 22.014, eff. Sept. 1, 2017.

### § 5.003. Sale of Community Homestead After Spouse Judicially Declared Incapacitated

If the homestead is the community property of the spouses and one spouse has been judicially declared incapacitated by a court exercising original jurisdiction over guardianship and other matters under Title 3, Estates Code, the competent spouse may sell, convey, or encumber the homestead without the joinder of the other spouse.

Added by Acts 1997, 75th Leg., ch. 7, § 1, eff. April 17, 1997. Renumbered from V.T.C.A., Family Code § 5.107 and amended by Acts 2001, 77th Leg., ch. 217, § 29, eff. Sept. 1, 2001. Amended by Acts 2017, 85th Leg., ch. 324 (S.B. 1488), § 22.015, eff. Sept. 1, 2017.

### §§ 5.01 to 5.04. Repealed by Acts 1997, 75th Leg., ch. 7, § 3, eff. April 17, 1997

## SUBCHAPTER B. SALE OF HOMESTEAD UNDER UNUSUAL CIRCUMSTANCES

### § 5.101. Sale of Separate Homestead Under Unusual Circumstances

If the homestead is the separate property of a spouse, that spouse may file a sworn petition that gives a description of the property, states the facts that make it desirable for the spouse to sell, convey, or encumber the homestead without the joinder of the other spouse, and alleges that the other spouse:

(1) has disappeared and that the location of the spouse remains unknown to the petitioning spouse;

(2) has permanently abandoned the homestead and the petitioning spouse;

(3) has permanently abandoned the homestead and the spouses are permanently separated; or

(4) has been reported by an executive department of the United States to be a prisoner of war or missing on public service of the United States.

Added by Acts 1997, 75th Leg., ch. 7, § 1, eff. April 17, 1997. Amended by Acts 2001, 77th Leg., ch. 217, § 26, eff. Sept. 1, 2001.

### § 5.102. Sale of Community Homestead Under Unusual Circumstances

If the homestead is the community property of the spouses, one spouse may file a sworn petition that gives a description of the property, states the facts that make it desirable for the petitioning spouse to sell, convey, or encumber the homestead without the joinder of the other spouse, and alleges that the other spouse:

(1) has disappeared and that the location of the spouse remains unknown to the petitioning spouse;

(2) has permanently abandoned the homestead and the petitioning spouse;

(3) has permanently abandoned the homestead and the spouses are permanently separated; or

(4) has been reported by an executive department of the United States to be a prisoner of war or missing on public service of the United States.

Added by Acts 1997, 75th Leg., ch. 7, § 1, eff. April 17, 1997. Amended by Acts 2001, 77th Leg., ch. 217, § 27, eff. Sept. 1, 2001.

### § 5.103. Time for Filing Petition

The petitioning spouse may file the petition in a court of the county in which any portion of the property is located not earlier than the 60th day after the date of the occurrence of an event described by Sections 5.101(1)–(3) and 5.102(1)–(3) or not less than six months after the date the other spouse has been reported to be a prisoner of war or missing on public service.

Added by Acts 1997, 75th Leg., ch. 7, § 1, eff. April 17, 1997. Amended by Acts 2001, 77th Leg., ch. 217, § 28, eff. Sept. 1, 2001.

### § 5.104. Appointment of Attorney

(a) Except as provided by Subsection (b), the court may appoint an attorney in a suit filed under this subchapter for the respondent.

(b) The court shall appoint an attorney in a suit filed under this subchapter for a respondent reported to be a prisoner of war or missing on public service.

(c) The court shall allow a reasonable fee for the appointed attorney's services as a part of the costs of the suit.

Added by Acts 1997, 75th Leg., ch. 7, § 1, eff. April 17, 1997.

### § 5.105. Citation; Notice of Hearing

Citation and notice of hearing for a suit filed as provided by this subchapter shall be issued and served in the manner provided in Subchapter D,[1] Chapter 3.

Added by Acts 1997, 75th Leg., ch. 7, § 1, eff. April 17, 1997.

[1] V.T.C.A., Family Code § 3.301 et seq.

### § 5.106. Court Order

(a) After notice and hearing, the court shall render an order the court deems just and equitable with respect to the sale, conveyance, or encumbrance of a separate property homestead.

(b) After hearing the evidence, the court, on terms the court deems just and equitable, shall render an order describing or defining the community property at issue that will be subject to the management, control, and disposition of each spouse during marriage.

(c) The court may:

(1) impose any conditions and restrictions the court deems necessary to protect the rights of the respondent;

(2) require a bond conditioned on the faithful administration of the property; and

(3) require payment to the registry of the court of all or a portion of the proceeds of the sale of the property to be disbursed in accordance with the court's further directions.

Added by Acts 1997, 75th Leg., ch. 7, § 1, eff. April 17, 1997.

### § 5.107. Renumbered as V.T.C.A., Family Code § 5.003 by Acts 2001, 77th Leg., ch. 217, § 29, eff. Sept. 1, 2001

### § 5.108. Remedies and Powers Cumulative

The remedies and the powers of a spouse provided by this subchapter are cumulative of the other rights, powers, and remedies afforded the spouses by law.

Added by Acts 1997, 75th Leg., ch. 7, § 1, eff. April 17, 1997.

### §§ 5.21 to 5.87. Repealed by Acts 1997, 75th Leg., ch. 7, § 3, eff. April 17, 1997

# SUBTITLE C. DISSOLUTION OF MARRIAGE

## CHAPTER 6. SUIT FOR DISSOLUTION OF MARRIAGE

### SUBCHAPTER A. GROUNDS FOR DIVORCE AND DEFENSES

**Section**



### SUBCHAPTER B. GROUNDS FOR ANNULMENT



### SUBCHAPTER C. DECLARING A MARRIAGE VOID



### SUBCHAPTER D. JURISDICTION, VENUE, AND RESIDENCE QUALIFICATIONS



### SUBCHAPTER E. FILING SUIT

## SUBCHAPTER A. GROUNDS FOR DIVORCE AND DEFENSES

### § 6.001. Insupportability

On the petition of either party to a marriage, the court may grant a divorce without regard to fault if the marriage has become insupportable because of discord or conflict of personalities that destroys the legitimate ends of the marital relationship and prevents any reasonable expectation of reconciliation.

Added by Acts 1997, 75th Leg., ch. 7, § 1, eff. April 17, 1997.

### § 6.002. Cruelty

The court may grant a divorce in favor of one spouse if the other spouse is guilty of cruel treatment toward the complaining spouse of a nature that renders further living together insupportable.

Added by Acts 1997, 75th Leg., ch. 7, § 1, eff. April 17, 1997.

### § 6.003. Adultery

The court may grant a divorce in favor of one spouse if the other spouse has committed adultery.

Added by Acts 1997, 75th Leg., ch. 7, § 1, eff. April 17, 1997.

### § 6.004. Conviction of Felony

(a) The court may grant a divorce in favor of one spouse if during the marriage the other spouse:

(1) has been convicted of a felony;

(2) has been imprisoned for at least one year in the Texas Department of Criminal Justice, a federal penitentiary, or the penitentiary of another state; and

(3) has not been pardoned.

(b) The court may not grant a divorce under this section against a spouse who was convicted on the testimony of the other spouse.

Added by Acts 1997, 75th Leg., ch. 7, § 1, eff. April 17, 1997. Amended by Acts 2009, 81st Leg., ch. 87, § 25.056, eff. Sept. 1, 2009.

### § 6.005. Abandonment

The court may grant a divorce in favor of one spouse if the other spouse:

(1) left the complaining spouse with the intention of abandonment; and

(2) remained away for at least one year.

Added by Acts 1997, 75th Leg., ch. 7, § 1, eff. April 17, 1997.

### § 6.006. Living Apart

The court may grant a divorce in favor of either spouse if the spouses have lived apart without cohabitation for at least three years.

Added by Acts 1997, 75th Leg., ch. 7, § 1, eff. April 17, 1997.

### § 6.007. Confinement in Mental Hospital

The court may grant a divorce in favor of one spouse if at the time the suit is filed:

(1) the other spouse has been confined in a state mental hospital or private mental hospital, as defined in Section 571.003, Health and Safety Code, in

this state or another state for at least three years; and

(2) it appears that the hospitalized spouse's mental disorder is of such a degree and nature that adjustment is unlikely or that, if adjustment occurs, a relapse is probable.

Added by Acts 1997, 75th Leg., ch. 7, § 1, eff. April 17, 1997.

### § 6.008. Defenses

(a) The defenses to a suit for divorce of recrimination and adultery are abolished.

(b) Condonation is a defense to a suit for divorce only if the court finds that there is a reasonable expectation of reconciliation.

Added by Acts 1997, 75th Leg., ch. 7, § 1, eff. April 17, 1997.

## SUBCHAPTER B. GROUNDS FOR ANNULMENT

### § 6.101. Repealed by Acts 2007, 80th Leg., ch. 52, § 8, eff. Sept. 1, 2007

### § 6.102. Annulment of Marriage of Person Under Age 18.

(a) The court may grant an annulment of a marriage of a person 16 years of age or older but under 18 years of age that occurred without parental consent or without a court order as provided by Subchapters B and E,[1] Chapter 2.

(b) A petition for annulment under this section may be filed by:

(1) a next friend for the benefit of the underage party;

(2) a parent; or

(3) the judicially designated managing conservator or guardian of the person of the underage party, whether an individual, authorized agency, or court.

(c) A suit filed under this subsection by a next friend is barred unless it is filed within 90 days after the date of the marriage.

Added by Acts 1997, 75th Leg., ch. 7, § 1, eff. April 17, 1997. Amended by Acts 2005, 79th Leg., ch. 268, § 4.16, eff. Sept. 1, 2005; Acts 2007, 80th Leg., ch. 52, § 3, eff. Sept. 1, 2007.

[1] Subchapters B & E, V.T.C.A., Family Code §§ 2.101 et seq. and 2.401 et seq.

### § 6.103. Underage Annulment Barred by Adulthood

A suit to annul a marriage may not be filed under Section 6.102 by a parent, managing conservator, or guardian of a person after the 18th birthday of the person.

Added by Acts 1997, 75th Leg., ch. 7, § 1, eff. April 17, 1997. Amended by Acts 2007, 80th Leg., ch. 52, § 4, eff. Sept. 1, 2007.

### § 6.104. Discretionary Annulment of Underage Marriage

(a) An annulment under Section 6.102 of a marriage may be granted at the discretion of the court sitting without a jury.

(b) In exercising its discretion, the court shall consider the pertinent facts concerning the welfare of the parties to the marriage, including whether the female is pregnant.

Added by Acts 1997, 75th Leg., ch. 7, § 1, eff. April 17, 1997. Amended by Acts 2007, 80th Leg., ch. 52, § 5, eff. Sept. 1, 2007.

### § 6.105. Under Influence of Alcohol or Narcotics

The court may grant an annulment of a marriage to a party to the marriage if:

(1) at the time of the marriage the petitioner was under the influence of alcoholic beverages or narcotics and as a result did not have the capacity to consent to the marriage; and

(2) the petitioner has not voluntarily cohabited with the other party to the marriage since the effects of the alcoholic beverages or narcotics ended.

Added by Acts 1997, 75th Leg., ch. 7, § 1, eff. April 17, 1997.

### § 6.106. Impotency

The court may grant an annulment of a marriage to a party to the marriage if:

(1) either party, for physical or mental reasons, was permanently impotent at the time of the marriage;

(2) the petitioner did not know of the impotency at the time of the marriage; and

(3) the petitioner has not voluntarily cohabited with the other party since learning of the impotency.

Added by Acts 1997, 75th Leg., ch. 7, § 1, eff. April 17, 1997.

### § 6.107. Fraud, Duress, or Force

The court may grant an annulment of a marriage to a party to the marriage if:

(1) the other party used fraud, duress, or force to induce the petitioner to enter into the marriage; and

(2) the petitioner has not voluntarily cohabited with the other party since learning of the fraud or since being released from the duress or force.

Added by Acts 1997, 75th Leg., ch. 7, § 1, eff. April 17, 1997.

### § 6.108. Mental Incapacity

(a) The court may grant an annulment of a marriage to a party to the marriage on the suit of the party or the party's guardian or next friend, if the court finds it to be in the party's best interest to be represented by a guardian or next friend, if:

(1) at the time of the marriage the petitioner did not have the mental capacity to consent to marriage or to understand the nature of the marriage ceremony because of a mental disease or defect; and

(2) since the marriage ceremony, the petitioner has not voluntarily cohabited with the other party during a period when the petitioner possessed the mental capacity to recognize the marriage relationship.

(b) The court may grant an annulment of a marriage to a party to the marriage if:

(1) at the time of the marriage the other party did not have the mental capacity to consent to marriage or to understand the nature of the marriage ceremony because of a mental disease or defect;

(2) at the time of the marriage the petitioner neither knew nor reasonably should have known of the mental disease or defect; and

(3) since the date the petitioner discovered or reasonably should have discovered the mental disease or defect, the petitioner has not voluntarily cohabited with the other party.

Added by Acts 1997, 75th Leg., ch. 7, § 1, eff. April 17, 1997.

### § 6.109. Concealed Divorce

(a) The court may grant an annulment of a marriage to a party to the marriage if:

(1) the other party was divorced from a third party within the 30-day period preceding the date of the marriage ceremony;

(2) at the time of the marriage ceremony the petitioner did not know, and a reasonably prudent person would not have known, of the divorce; and

(3) since the petitioner discovered or a reasonably prudent person would have discovered the fact of the divorce, the petitioner has not voluntarily cohabited with the other party.

(b) A suit may not be brought under this section after the first anniversary of the date of the marriage.

Added by Acts 1997, 75th Leg., ch. 7, § 1, eff. April 17, 1997.

### § 6.110. Marriage Less Than 72 Hours After Issuance of License

(a) The court may grant an annulment of a marriage to a party to the marriage if the marriage ceremony took place in violation of Section 2.204 during the 72-hour period immediately following the issuance of the marriage license.

(b) A suit may not be brought under this section after the 30th day after the date of the marriage.

Added by Acts 1997, 75th Leg., ch. 7, § 1, eff. April 17, 1997.

### § 6.111. Death of Party to Voidable Marriage

Except as provided by Subchapter C, Chapter 123, Estates Code,[1] a marriage subject to annulment may not be challenged in a proceeding instituted after the death of either party to the marriage.

Added by Acts 1997, 75th Leg., ch. 7, § 1, eff. April 17, 1997. Amended by Acts 2007, 80th Leg., ch. 1170, § 4.03, eff. Sept. 1, 2007; Acts 2017, 85th Leg., ch. 324 (S.B. 1488), § 22.016, eff. Sept. 1, 2017.

[1] V.T.C.A., Estates Code § 123.101 et seq.

## SUBCHAPTER C. DECLARING A MARRIAGE VOID

### § 6.201. Consanguinity

A marriage is void if one party to the marriage is related to the other as:

(1) an ancestor or descendant, by blood or adoption;

(2) a brother or sister, of the whole or half blood or by adoption;

(3) a parent's brother or sister, of the whole or half blood or by adoption; or

(4) a son or daughter of a brother or sister, of the whole or half blood or by adoption.

Added by Acts 1997, 75th Leg., ch. 7, § 1, eff. April 17, 1997.

### § 6.202. Marriage During Existence of Prior Marriage

(a) A marriage is void if entered into when either party has an existing marriage to another person that has not been dissolved by legal action or terminated by the death of the other spouse.

(b) The later marriage that is void under this section becomes valid when the prior marriage is dissolved if, after the date of the dissolution, the parties have lived together as husband and wife and represented themselves to others as being married.

Added by Acts 1997, 75th Leg., ch. 7, § 1, eff. April 17, 1997.

### § 6.203. Certain Void Marriages Validated

Except for a marriage that would have been void under Section 6.201, a marriage that was entered into before January 1, 1970, in violation of the prohibitions of Article 496, Penal Code of Texas, 1925, is validated from the date the marriage commenced if the parties continued until January 1, 1970, to live together as husband and wife and to represent themselves to others as being married.

Added by Acts 1997, 75th Leg., ch. 7, § 1, eff. April 17, 1997.

### § 6.204. Recognition of Same-Sex Marriage or Civil Union

(a) In this section, "civil union" means any relationship status other than marriage that:

(1) is intended as an alternative to marriage or applies primarily to cohabitating persons; and

(2) grants to the parties of the relationship legal protections, benefits, or responsibilities granted to the spouses of a marriage.

(b) A marriage between persons of the same sex or a civil union is contrary to the public policy of this state and is void in this state.

(c) The state or an agency or political subdivision of the state may not give effect to a:

(1) public act, record, or judicial proceeding that creates, recognizes, or validates a marriage between persons of the same sex or a civil union in this state or in any other jurisdiction; or

(2) right or claim to any legal protection, benefit, or responsibility asserted as a result of a marriage between persons of the same sex or a civil union in this state or in any other jurisdiction.

Added by Acts 2003, 78th Leg., ch. 124, § 1, eff. Sept. 1, 2003.

#### Validity

*For validity of this section, see Obergefell v. Hodges, 135 S.Ct. 2584, 576 U.S. 644, 192 L.Ed.2d 609 (2015).*

### § 6.205. Marriage to Minor

A marriage is void if either party to the marriage is younger than 18 years of age, unless a court order removing the disabilities of minority of the party for general purposes has been obtained in this state or in another state.

Added by Acts 2005, 79th Leg., ch. 268, § 4.17, eff. Sept. 1, 2005. Amended by Acts 2007, 80th Leg., ch. 52, § 6, eff. Sept. 1, 2007; Acts 2017, 85th Leg., ch. 934 (S.B. 1705), § 5, eff. Sept. 1, 2017.

### § 6.206. Marriage to Stepchild or Stepparent

A marriage is void if a party is a current or former stepchild or stepparent of the other party.

Added by Acts 2005, 79th Leg., ch. 268, § 4.17, eff. Sept. 1, 2005.

## SUBCHAPTER D. JURISDICTION, VENUE, AND RESIDENCE QUALIFICATIONS

### § 6.301. General Residency Rule for Divorce Suit

A suit for divorce may not be maintained in this state unless at the time the suit is filed either the petitioner or the respondent has been:

(1) a domiciliary of this state for the preceding six-month period; and

(2) a resident of the county in which the suit is filed for the preceding 90-day period.

Added by Acts 1997, 75th Leg., ch. 7, § 1, eff. April 17, 1997.

### § 6.302. Suit for Divorce by Nonresident Spouse

If one spouse has been a domiciliary of this state for at least the last six months, a spouse domiciled in another state or nation may file a suit for divorce in the county in which the domiciliary spouse resides at the time the petition is filed.

Added by Acts 1997, 75th Leg., ch. 7, § 1, eff. April 17, 1997.

### § 6.303. Absence on Public Service

Time spent by a Texas domiciliary outside this state or outside the county of residence of the domiciliary while in the service of the armed forces or other service of the United States or of this state, or while accompanying the domiciliary's spouse in the spouse's service of the armed forces or other service of the United States or of this state, is considered residence in this state and in that county.

Added by Acts 1997, 75th Leg., ch. 7, § 1, eff. April 17, 1997. Amended by Acts 2011, 82nd Leg., ch. 436 (S.B. 1159), § 1, eff. June 17, 2011.

**§ 6.304. Armed Forces Personnel Not Previously Residents**

A person not previously a resident of this state who is serving in the armed forces of the United States and has been stationed at one or more military installations in this state for at least the last six months and at a military installation in a county of this state for at least the last 90 days, or who is accompanying the person's spouse during the spouse's military service in those locations and for those periods, is considered to be a Texas domiciliary and a resident of that county for those periods for the purpose of filing suit for dissolution of a marriage.

Added by Acts 1997, 75th Leg., ch. 7, § 1, eff. April 17, 1997. Amended by Acts 2011, 82nd Leg., ch. 436 (S.B. 1159), § 1, eff. June 17, 2011.

**§ 6.305. Acquiring Jurisdiction Over Nonresident Respondent**

(a) If the petitioner in a suit for dissolution of a marriage is a resident or a domiciliary of this state at the time the suit for dissolution is filed, the court may exercise personal jurisdiction over the respondent or over the respondent's personal representative although the respondent is not a resident of this state if:

(1) this state is the last marital residence of the petitioner and the respondent and the suit is filed before the second anniversary of the date on which marital residence ended; or

(2) there is any basis consistent with the constitutions of this state and the United States for the exercise of the personal jurisdiction.

(b) A court acquiring jurisdiction under this section also acquires jurisdiction over the respondent in a suit affecting the parent-child relationship.

Added by Acts 1997, 75th Leg., ch. 7, § 1, eff. April 17, 1997.

**§ 6.306. Jurisdiction to Annul Marriage**

(a) A suit for annulment of a marriage may be maintained in this state only if the parties were married in this state or if either party is domiciled in this state.

(b) A suit for annulment is a suit in rem, affecting the status of the parties to the marriage.

Added by Acts 1997, 75th Leg., ch. 7, § 1, eff. April 17, 1997.

**§ 6.307. Jurisdiction to Declare Marriage Void**

(a) Either party to a marriage made void by this chapter may sue to have the marriage declared void, or the court may declare the marriage void in a collateral proceeding.

(b) The court may declare a marriage void only if:

(1) the purported marriage was contracted in this state; or

(2) either party is domiciled in this state.

(c) A suit to have a marriage declared void is a suit in rem, affecting the status of the parties to the purported marriage.

Added by Acts 1997, 75th Leg., ch. 7, § 1, eff. April 17, 1997.

**§ 6.308. Exercising Partial Jurisdiction**

(a) A court in which a suit for dissolution of a marriage is filed may exercise its jurisdiction over those portions of the suit for which it has authority.

(b) The court's authority to resolve the issues in controversy between the parties may be restricted because the court lacks:

(1) the required personal jurisdiction over a nonresident party in a suit for dissolution of the marriage;

(2) the required jurisdiction under Chapter 152; or

(3) the required jurisdiction under Chapter 159.

Added by Acts 1997, 75th Leg., ch. 7, § 1, eff. April 17, 1997.

## SUBCHAPTER E. FILING SUIT

**§ 6.401. Caption**

(a) Pleadings in a suit for divorce or annulment shall be styled "In the Matter of the Marriage of __________ and __________."

(b) Pleadings in a suit to declare a marriage void shall be styled "A Suit To Declare Void the Marriage of __________ and __________."

Added by Acts 1997, 75th Leg., ch. 7, § 1, eff. April 17, 1997.

**§ 6.402. Pleadings**

(a) A petition in a suit for dissolution of a marriage is sufficient without the necessity of specifying the underlying evidentiary facts if the petition alleges the grounds relied on substantially in the language of the statute.

(b) Allegations of grounds for relief, matters of defense, or facts relied on for a temporary order that are stated in short and plain terms are not subject to special exceptions because of form or sufficiency.

(c) The court shall strike an allegation of evidentiary fact from the pleadings on the motion of a party or on the court's own motion.

Added by Acts 1997, 75th Leg., ch. 7, § 1, eff. April 17, 1997.

### § 6.403. Answer

The respondent in a suit for dissolution of a marriage is not required to answer on oath or affirmation.

Added by Acts 1997, 75th Leg., ch. 7, § 1, eff. April 17, 1997.

### § 6.4035. Waiver of Service

(a) A party to a suit for the dissolution of a marriage may waive the issuance or service of process after the suit is filed by filing with the clerk of the court in which the suit is filed the waiver of the party acknowledging receipt of a copy of the filed petition.

(b) The waiver must contain the mailing address of the party who executed the waiver.

(c) Notwithstanding Section 132.001, Civil Practice and Remedies Code, the waiver must be sworn before a notary public who is not an attorney in the suit. This subsection does not apply if the party executing the waiver is incarcerated.

(d) The Texas Rules of Civil Procedure do not apply to a waiver executed under this section.

(e) The party executing the waiver may not sign the waiver using a digitized signature.

(f) For purposes of this section, "digitized signature" has the meaning assigned by Section 101.0096.

Added by Acts 1997, 75th Leg., ch. 614, § 1, eff. Sept. 1, 1997. Amended by Acts 2013, 83rd Leg., ch. 916 (H.B. 1366), § 2, eff. Sept. 1, 2013; Acts 2015, 84th Leg., ch. 198 (S.B. 814), § 1, eff. Sept. 1, 2015.

### § 6.404. Information Regarding Protective Orders

At any time while a suit for dissolution of a marriage is pending, if the court believes, on the basis of any information received by the court, that a party to the suit or a member of the party's family or household may be a victim of family violence, the court shall inform that party of the party's right to apply for a protective order under Title 4[1].

Added by Acts 2005, 79th Leg., ch. 361, § 2, eff. June 17, 2005.

[1] V.T.C.A., Family Code § 71.001

### § 6.405. Protective Order and Related Orders

(a) The petition in a suit for dissolution of a marriage must state whether, in regard to a party to the suit or a child of a party to the suit:

(1) there is in effect:

(A) a protective order under Title 4;

(B) a protective order under Subchapter A, Chapter 7B,[1] Code of Criminal Procedure; or

(C) an order for emergency protection under Article 17.292, Code of Criminal Procedure; or

(2) an application for an order described by Subdivision (1) is pending.

(b) The petitioner shall attach to the petition a copy of each order described by Subsection (a)(1) in which a party to the suit or the child of a party to the suit was the applicant or victim of the conduct alleged in the application or order and the other party was the respondent or defendant of an action regarding the conduct alleged in the application or order without regard to the date of the order. If a copy of the order is not available at the time of filing, the petition must state that a copy of the order will be filed with the court before any hearing.

Added by Acts 1997, 75th Leg., ch. 7, § 1, eff. April 17, 1997. Amended by Acts 1999, 76th Leg., ch. 62, § 6.04, eff. Sept. 1, 1999; Acts 2017, 85th Leg., ch. 885 (H.B. 3052), § 1, eff. Sept. 1, 2017; Acts 2019, 86th Leg., ch. 469 (H.B. 4173), § 2.30, eff. Jan. 1, 2021.

[1] V.T.C.A., Family Code § 7B.001.

Sections 4.01 and 4.02 of Acts 2019, 86th Leg., ch. 469 (H.B. 4173) provide:

"Sec. 4.01. This Act is enacted under Section 43, Article III, Texas Constitution. This Act is intended as a codification only, and no substantive change in the law is intended by this Act.

"Sec. 4.02. (a) Chapter 311, Government Code (Code Construction Act), applies to the construction of each provision in the Code of Criminal Procedure that is enacted under Section 43, Article III, Texas Constitution (authorizing the continuing statutory revision program), in the same manner as to a code enacted under the continuing statutory revision program, except as otherwise expressly provided by the Code of Criminal Procedure.

"(b) A reference in a law to a statute or a part of a statute in the Code of Criminal Procedure enacted under Section 43, Article III, Texas Constitution (authorizing the continuing statutory revision program), is considered to be a reference to the part of that code that revises that statute or part of that statute."

### § 6.406. Mandatory Joinder of Suit Affecting Parent-Child Relationship

(a) The petition in a suit for dissolution of a marriage shall state whether there are children born or adopted of the marriage who are under 18 years of age or who are otherwise entitled to support as provided by Chapter 154.

(a–1) If the parties to a suit for dissolution of a marriage are the intended parents under a gestational agreement that is in effect and that establishes a parent-child relationship between the parties as intended parents and an unborn child on the birth of the child, the petition in the suit for dissolution of a marriage shall state:

(1) that the parties to the marriage have entered into a gestational agreement establishing a parent-child relationship between the parties as intended parents and an unborn child on the birth of the child;

(2) whether the gestational mother under the agreement is pregnant or a child who is the subject of the agreement has been born; and

(3) whether the agreement has been validated under Section 160.756.

(b) If the parties are parents of a child, as defined by Section 101.003, and the child is not under the continuing jurisdiction of another court as provided by Chapter 155, the suit for dissolution of a marriage must include a suit affecting the parent-child relationship under Title 5.[1]

Added by Acts 1997, 75th Leg., ch. 7, § 1, eff. April 17, 1997. Amended by Acts 2019, 86th Leg., ch. 130 (H.B. 1689), § 1, eff. Sept. 1, 2019.

[1] V.T.C.A., Family Code § 101.001 et seq.

Section 3 of Acts 2019, 86th Leg., ch. 130 (H.B. 1689) provides:

"Section 6.406, Family Code, as amended by this Act, applies only to a petition for dissolution of a marriage that is filed on or after the effective date [Sept. 1, 2019] of this Act. A petition for dissolution of a marriage that is filed before the effective date of this Act is governed by the law in effect on the date the petition is filed, and the former law is continued in effect for that purpose."

### § 6.407. Transfer of Suit Affecting Parent-Child Relationship to Divorce Court

(a) If a suit affecting the parent-child relationship is pending at the time the suit for dissolution of a marriage is filed, the suit affecting the parent-child relationship shall be transferred as provided by Section 103.002 to the court in which the suit for dissolution is filed.

(b) If the parties are parents of a child, as defined by Section 101.003, and the child is under the continuing jurisdiction of another court under Chapter 155, either party to the suit for dissolution of a marriage may move that court for transfer of the suit affecting the parent-child relationship to the court having jurisdiction of the suit for dissolution. The court with continuing jurisdiction shall transfer the proceeding as provided by Chapter 155. On the transfer of the proceedings, the court with jurisdiction of the suit for dissolution of a marriage shall consolidate the two causes of action.

(c) After transfer of a suit affecting the parent-child relationship as provided in Chapter 155, the court with jurisdiction of the suit for dissolution of a marriage has jurisdiction to render an order in the suit affecting the parent-child relationship as provided by Title 5.[1]

Added by Acts 1997, 75th Leg., ch. 7, § 1, eff. April 17, 1997.

[1] V.T.C.A., Family Code § 101.001 et seq.

### § 6.408. Service of Citation

Citation on the filing of an original petition in a suit for dissolution of a marriage shall be issued and served as in other civil cases. Citation may also be served on any other person who has or who may assert an interest in the suit for dissolution of the marriage.

Added by Acts 1997, 75th Leg., ch. 7, § 1, eff. April 17, 1997.

### § 6.409. Citation by Publication

(a) Citation in a suit for dissolution of a marriage may be by publication as in other civil cases, except that notice shall be published one time only.

(b) The notice shall be sufficient if given in substantially the following form:

"STATE OF TEXAS

To (name of person to be served with citation), and to all whom it may concern (if the name of any person to be served with citation is unknown), Respondent(s),

"You have been sued. You may employ an attorney. If you or your attorney do not file a written answer with the clerk who issued this citation by 10 a.m. on the Monday next following the expiration of 20 days after you were served this citation and petition, a default judgment may be taken against you. The petition of ________, Petitioner, was filed in the Court of ________ County, Texas, on the ______ day of ________, against ________, Respondent(s), numbered ______, and entitled 'In the Matter of Marriage of ________ and ________. The suit requests ________ (statement of relief sought).'

"The Court has authority in this suit to enter any judgment or decree dissolving the marriage and providing for the division of property that will be binding on you.

"Issued and given under my hand and seal of said Court at ________, Texas, this the ______ day of ________, ______.

"________
Clerk of the ________ Court of
________ County, Texas
By ________, Deputy."

(c) The form authorized in this section and the form authorized by Section 102.010 may be combined in appropriate situations.

(d) If the citation is for a suit in which a parent-child relationship does not exist, service by publication may be completed by posting the citation at the courthouse door for seven days in the county in which the suit is filed.

(e) If the petitioner or the petitioner's attorney of record makes an oath that no child presently under 18 years of age was born or adopted by the spouses and that no appreciable amount of property was accumulated by the spouses during the marriage, the court may dispense with the appointment of an attorney ad litem. In a case in which citation was by publication, a statement of the evidence, approved and signed by the judge, shall be filed with the papers of the suit as a part of the record.

Added by Acts 1997, 75th Leg., ch. 7, § 1, eff. April 17, 1997.

### § 6.410. Report to Accompany Petition

At the time a petition for divorce or annulment of a marriage is filed, the petitioner shall also file a completed report that may be used by the district clerk, at the time the petition is granted, to comply with Section 194.002, Health and Safety Code.

Added by Acts 2003, 78th Leg., ch. 1128, § 4, eff. Sept. 1, 2003.

### § 6.411. Confidentiality of Pleadings

(a) This section applies only in a county with a population of 3.4 million or more.

(b) Except as otherwise provided by law, all pleadings and other documents filed with the court in a suit for dissolution of a marriage are confidential, are excepted from required public disclosure under Chapter 552, Government Code, and may not be released to a person who is not a party to the suit until after the date of service of citation or the 31st day after the date of filing the suit, whichever date is sooner.

Added by Acts 2003, 78th Leg., ch. 1314, § 1, eff. Sept. 1, 2003. Redesignated from V.T.C.A., Family Code § 6.410 by Acts 2005, 79th Leg., ch. 728, § 23.001(24), eff. Sept. 1, 2005.

## SUBCHAPTER F. TEMPORARY ORDERS

### § 6.501. Temporary Restraining Order

(a) After the filing of a suit for dissolution of a marriage, on the motion of a party or on the court's own motion, the court may grant a temporary restraining order without notice to the adverse party for the preservation of the property and for the protection of the parties as necessary, including an order prohibiting one or both parties from:

(1) intentionally communicating in person or in any other manner, including by telephone or another electronic voice transmission, video chat, in writing, or electronic messaging, with the other party by use of vulgar, profane, obscene, or indecent language or in a coarse or offensive manner, with intent to annoy or alarm the other party;

(2) threatening the other party in person or in any other manner, including by telephone or another electronic voice transmission, video chat, in writing, or electronic messaging, to take unlawful action against any person, intending by this action to annoy or alarm the other party;

(3) placing a telephone call, anonymously, at an unreasonable hour, in an offensive and repetitious manner, or without a legitimate purpose of communication with the intent to annoy or alarm the other party;

(4) intentionally, knowingly, or recklessly causing bodily injury to the other party or to a child of either party;

(5) threatening the other party or a child of either party with imminent bodily injury;

(6) intentionally, knowingly, or recklessly destroying, removing, concealing, encumbering, transferring, or otherwise harming or reducing the value of the property of the parties or either party with intent to obstruct the authority of the court to order a division of the estate of the parties in a manner that the court deems just and right, having due regard for the rights of each party and any children of the marriage;

(7) intentionally falsifying a writing or record, including an electronic record, relating to the property of either party;

(8) intentionally misrepresenting or refusing to disclose to the other party or to the court, on proper request, the existence, amount, or location of any tangible or intellectual property of the parties or either party, including electronically stored or recorded information;

(9) intentionally or knowingly damaging or destroying the tangible or intellectual property of the parties or either party, including electronically stored or recorded information;

(10) intentionally or knowingly tampering with the tangible or intellectual property of the parties or either party, including electronically stored or

recorded information, and causing pecuniary loss or substantial inconvenience to the other party;

(11) except as specifically authorized by the court:

(A) selling, transferring, assigning, mortgaging, encumbering, or in any other manner alienating any of the property of the parties or either party, regardless of whether the property is:

(i) personal property, real property, or intellectual property; or

(ii) separate or community property;

(B) incurring any debt, other than legal expenses in connection with the suit for dissolution of marriage;

(C) withdrawing money from any checking or savings account in a financial institution for any purpose;

(D) spending any money in either party's possession or subject to either party's control for any purpose;

(E) withdrawing or borrowing money in any manner for any purpose from a retirement, profit sharing, pension, death, or other employee benefit plan, employee savings plan, individual retirement account, or Keogh account of either party; or

(F) withdrawing or borrowing in any manner all or any part of the cash surrender value of a life insurance policy on the life of either party or a child of the parties;

(12) entering any safe deposit box in the name of or subject to the control of the parties or either party, whether individually or jointly with others;

(13) changing or in any manner altering the beneficiary designation on any life insurance policy on the life of either party or a child of the parties;

(14) canceling, altering, failing to renew or pay premiums on, or in any manner affecting the level of coverage that existed at the time the suit was filed of, any life, casualty, automobile, or health insurance policy insuring the parties' property or persons, including a child of the parties;

(15) opening or diverting mail or e-mail or any other electronic communication addressed to the other party;

(16) signing or endorsing the other party's name on any negotiable instrument, check, or draft, including a tax refund, insurance payment, and dividend, or attempting to negotiate any negotiable instrument payable to the other party without the personal signature of the other party;

(17) taking any action to terminate or limit credit or charge credit cards in the name of the other party;

(18) discontinuing or reducing the withholding for federal income taxes from either party's wages or salary;

(19) destroying, disposing of, or altering any financial records of the parties, including a canceled check, deposit slip, and other records from a financial institution, a record of credit purchases or cash advances, a tax return, and a financial statement;

(20) destroying, disposing of, or altering any e-mail, text message, video message, or chat message or other electronic data or electronically stored information relevant to the subject matter of the suit for dissolution of marriage, regardless of whether the information is stored on a hard drive, in a removable storage device, in cloud storage, or in another electronic storage medium;

(21) modifying, changing, or altering the native format or metadata of any electronic data or electronically stored information relevant to the subject matter of the suit for dissolution of marriage, regardless of whether the information is stored on a hard drive, in a removable storage device, in cloud storage, or in another electronic storage medium;

(22) deleting any data or content from any social network profile used or created by either party or a child of the parties;

(23) using any password or personal identification number to gain access to the other party's e-mail account, bank account, social media account, or any other electronic account;

(24) terminating or in any manner affecting the service of water, electricity, gas, telephone, cable television, or any other contractual service, including security, pest control, landscaping, or yard maintenance at the residence of either party, or in any manner attempting to withdraw any deposit paid in connection with any of those services;

(25) excluding the other party from the use and enjoyment of a specifically identified residence of the other party; or

(26) entering, operating, or exercising control over a motor vehicle in the possession of the other party.

(b) A temporary restraining order under this subchapter may not include a provision:

(1) the subject of which is a requirement, appointment, award, or other order listed in Section 64.104, Civil Practice and Remedies Code; or

(2) that:

(A) excludes a spouse from occupancy of the residence where that spouse is living except as provided in a protective order made in accordance with Title 4;[1]

(B) prohibits a party from spending funds for reasonable and necessary living expenses; or

(C) prohibits a party from engaging in acts reasonable and necessary to conduct that party's usual business and occupation.

Added by Acts 1997, 75th Leg., ch. 7, § 1, eff. April 17, 1997. Amended by Acts 1999, 76th Leg., ch. 1081, § 6, eff. Sept. 1, 1999; Acts 2015, 84th Leg., ch. 43 (S.B. 815), § 1, eff. Sept. 1, 2015.

[1] V.T.C.A., Family Code § 71.001 et seq.

### § 6.502. Temporary Injunction and Other Temporary Orders

(a) While a suit for dissolution of a marriage is pending and on the motion of a party or on the court's own motion after notice and hearing, the court may render an appropriate order, including the granting of a temporary injunction for the preservation of the property and protection of the parties as deemed necessary and equitable and including an order directed to one or both parties:

(1) requiring a sworn inventory and appraisement of the real and personal property owned or claimed by the parties and specifying the form, manner, and substance of the inventory and appraisal and list of debts and liabilities;

(2) requiring payments to be made for the support of either spouse;

(3) requiring the production of books, papers, documents, and tangible things by a party;

(4) ordering payment of reasonable attorney's fees and expenses;

(5) appointing a receiver for the preservation and protection of the property of the parties;

(6) awarding one spouse exclusive occupancy of the residence during the pendency of the case;

(7) prohibiting the parties, or either party, from spending funds beyond an amount the court determines to be for reasonable and necessary living expenses;

(8) awarding one spouse exclusive control of a party's usual business or occupation; or

(9) prohibiting an act described by Section 6.501(a).

(b) Not later than the 30th day after the date a receiver is appointed under Subsection (a)(5), the receiver shall give notice of the appointment to each lienholder of any property under the receiver's control.

(c) Not later than the seventh day after the date a receiver is appointed under Subsection (a)(5), the court shall issue written findings of fact and conclusions of law in support of the receiver's appointment. If the court dispenses with the issuance of a bond between the spouses as provided by Section 6.503(b) in connection with the receiver's appointment, the court shall include in the court's findings an explanation of the reasons the court dispensed with the issuance of a bond.

Added by Acts 1997, 75th Leg., ch. 7, § 1, eff. April 17, 1997. Amended by Acts 2001, 77th Leg., ch. 695, § 1, eff. Sept. 1, 2001; Acts 2017, 85th Leg., ch. 493 (H.B. 2703), § 1, eff. Sept. 1, 2017.

### § 6.503. Affidavit, Verified Pleading, and Bond Not Required

(a) A temporary restraining order or temporary injunction under this subchapter:

(1) may be granted without an affidavit or a verified pleading stating specific facts showing that immediate and irreparable injury, loss, or damage will result before notice can be served and a hearing can be held; and

(2) need not:

(A) define the injury or state why it is irreparable;

(B) state why the order was granted without notice; or

(C) include an order setting the suit for trial on the merits with respect to the ultimate relief sought.

(b) In a suit for dissolution of a marriage, the court may dispense with the issuance of a bond between the spouses in connection with temporary orders for the protection of the parties and their property.

Added by Acts 1997, 75th Leg., ch. 7, § 1, eff. April 17, 1997.

### § 6.504. Protective Orders

On the motion of a party to a suit for dissolution of a marriage, the court may render a protective order as provided by Subtitle B, Title 4.[1]

Added by Acts 1997, 75th Leg., ch. 7, § 1, eff. April 17, 1997. Amended by Acts 1997, 75th Leg., ch. 1193, § 1, eff. Sept. 1, 1997.

[1] V.T.C.A., Family Code § 81.001 et seq.

### § 6.505. Counseling

(a) While a divorce suit is pending, the court may direct the parties to counsel with a person named by the court.

(b) The person named by the court to counsel the parties shall submit a written report to the court and to the parties before the final hearing. In the report, the counselor shall give only an opinion as to whether there exists a reasonable expectation of reconciliation of the parties and, if so, whether further counseling would be beneficial. The sole purpose of the report is to aid the court in determining whether the suit for divorce should be continued pending further counseling.

(c) A copy of the report shall be furnished to each party.

(d) If the court believes that there is a reasonable expectation of the parties' reconciliation, the court may by written order continue the proceedings and direct the parties to a person named by the court for further counseling for a period fixed by the court not to exceed 60 days, subject to any terms, conditions, and limitations the court considers desirable. In ordering counseling, the court shall consider the circumstances of the parties, including the needs of the parties' family and the availability of counseling services. At the expiration of the period specified by the court, the counselor to whom the parties were directed shall report to the court whether the parties have complied with the court's order. Thereafter, the court shall proceed as in a divorce suit generally.

(e) If the court orders counseling under this section and the parties to the marriage are the parents of a child under 18 years of age born or adopted during the marriage, the counseling shall include counseling on issues that confront children who are the subject of a suit affecting the parent-child relationship.

Added by Acts 1997, 75th Leg., ch. 7, § 1, eff. April 17, 1997. Amended by Acts 1997, 75th Leg., ch. 1325, § 1, eff. Sept. 1, 1997.

### § 6.506. Contempt

The violation of a temporary restraining order, temporary injunction, or other temporary order issued under this subchapter is punishable as contempt.

Added by Acts 1997, 75th Leg., ch. 7, § 1, eff. April 17, 1997.

### § 6.507. Interlocutory Appeal

An order under this subchapter, except an order appointing a receiver, is not subject to interlocutory appeal.

Added by Acts 1997, 75th Leg., ch. 7, § 1, eff. April 17, 1997.

## SUBCHAPTER G. ALTERNATIVE DISPUTE RESOLUTION

### § 6.601. Arbitration Procedures

(a) On written agreement of the parties, the court may refer a suit for dissolution of a marriage to arbitration. The agreement must state whether the arbitration is binding or nonbinding.

(b) If the parties agree to binding arbitration, the court shall render an order reflecting the arbitrator's award.

Added by Acts 1997, 75th Leg., ch. 7, § 1, eff. April 17, 1997.

### § 6.6015. Determination of Validity and Enforceability of Contract Containing Agreement to Arbitrate

(a) If a party to a suit for dissolution of a marriage opposes an application to compel arbitration or makes an application to stay arbitration and asserts that the contract containing the agreement to arbitrate is not valid or enforceable, notwithstanding any provision of the contract to the contrary, the court shall try the issue promptly and may order arbitration only if the court determines that the contract containing the agreement to arbitrate is valid and enforceable against the party seeking to avoid arbitration.

(b) A determination under this section that a contract is valid and enforceable does not affect the court's authority to stay arbitration or refuse to compel arbitration on any other ground provided by law.

(c) This section does not apply to:

(1) a court order;

(2) a mediated settlement agreement described by Section 6.602;

(3) a collaborative law agreement described by Section 6.603;

(4) a written settlement agreement reached at an informal settlement conference described by Section 6.604; or

(5) any other agreement between the parties that is approved by a court.

Added by Acts 2011, 82nd Leg., ch. 1088 (S.B. 1216), § 1, eff. June 17, 2011.

### § 6.602. Mediation Procedures

(a) On the written agreement of the parties or on the court's own motion, the court may refer a suit for dissolution of a marriage to mediation.

(b) A mediated settlement agreement is binding on the parties if the agreement:

(1) provides, in a prominently displayed statement that is in boldfaced type or capital letters or underlined, that the agreement is not subject to revocation;

(2) is signed by each party to the agreement; and

(3) is signed by the party's attorney, if any, who is present at the time the agreement is signed.

(c) If a mediated settlement agreement meets the requirements of this section, a party is entitled to judgment on the mediated settlement agreement notwithstanding Rule 11, Texas Rules of Civil Procedure, or another rule of law.

(d) A party may at any time prior to the final mediation order file a written objection to the referral of a suit for dissolution of a marriage to mediation on the basis of family violence having been committed against the objecting party by the other party. After an objection is filed, the suit may not be referred to mediation unless, on the request of the other party, a hearing is held and the court finds that a preponderance of the evidence does not support the objection. If the suit is referred to mediation, the court shall order appropriate measures be taken to ensure the physical and emotional safety of the party who filed the objection. The order shall provide that the parties not be required to have face-to-face contact and that the parties be placed in separate rooms during mediation.

Added by Acts 1997, 75th Leg., ch. 7, § 1, eff. April 17, 1997. Amended by Acts 1999, 76th Leg., ch. 178, § 2, eff. Aug. 30, 1999; Acts 1999, 76th Leg., ch. 1351, § 1, eff. Sept. 1, 1999.

### § 6.603. Repealed by Acts 2011, 82nd Leg., ch. 1048 (H.B. 3833), § 2, eff. Sept. 1, 2011

### § 6.604. Informal Settlement Conference

(a) The parties to a suit for dissolution of a marriage may agree to one or more informal settlement conferences and may agree that the settlement conferences may be conducted with or without the presence of the parties' attorneys, if any.

(b) A written settlement agreement reached at an informal settlement conference is binding on the parties if the agreement:

(1) provides, in a prominently displayed statement that is in boldfaced type or in capital letters or underlined, that the agreement is not subject to revocation;

(2) is signed by each party to the agreement; and

(3) is signed by the party's attorney, if any, who is present at the time the agreement is signed.

(c) If a written settlement agreement meets the requirements of Subsection (b), a party is entitled to judgment on the settlement agreement notwithstanding Rule 11, Texas Rules of Civil Procedure, or another rule of law.

(d) If the court finds that the terms of the written informal settlement agreement are just and right, those terms are binding on the court. If the court approves the agreement, the court may set forth the agreement in full or incorporate the agreement by reference in the final decree.

(e) If the court finds that the terms of the written informal settlement agreement are not just and right, the court may request the parties to submit a revised agreement or set the case for a contested hearing.

Added by Acts 2005, 79th Leg., ch. 477, § 3, eff. Sept. 1, 2005.

## SUBCHAPTER H. TRIAL AND APPEAL

### § 6.701. Failure to Answer

In a suit for divorce, the petition may not be taken as confessed if the respondent does not file an answer.

Added by Acts 1997, 75th Leg., ch. 7, § 1, eff. April 17, 1997.

### § 6.702. Waiting Period

(a) Except as provided by Subsection (c), the court may not grant a divorce before the 60th day after the date the suit was filed. A decree rendered in violation of this subsection is not subject to collateral attack.

(b) A waiting period is not required before a court may grant an annulment or declare a marriage void other than as required in civil cases generally.

(c) A waiting period is not required under Subsection (a) before a court may grant a divorce in a suit in which the court finds that:

(1) the respondent has been finally convicted of or received deferred adjudication for an offense involving family violence as defined by Section 71.004 against the petitioner or a member of the petitioner's household; or

(2) the petitioner has an active protective order under Title 4[1] or an active magistrate's order for emergency protection under Article 17.292, Code of Criminal Procedure, based on a finding of family

violence, against the respondent because of family violence committed during the marriage.

Added by Acts 1997, 75th Leg., ch. 7, § 1, eff. April 17, 1997. Amended by Acts 2009, 81st Leg., ch. 896, § 1, eff. June 19, 2009.

[1] V.T.C.A., Family Code § 71.001 et seq.

### § 6.703. Jury

In a suit for dissolution of a marriage, either party may demand a jury trial unless the action is a suit to annul an underage marriage under Section 6.102.

Added by Acts 1997, 75th Leg., ch. 7, § 1, eff. April 17, 1997. Amended by Acts 2007, 80th Leg., ch. 52, § 7, eff. Sept. 1, 2007.

### § 6.704. Testimony of Husband or Wife

(a) In a suit for dissolution of a marriage, the husband and wife are competent witnesses for and against each other. A spouse may not be compelled to testify as to a matter that will incriminate the spouse.

(b) If the husband or wife testifies, the court or jury trying the case shall determine the credibility of the witness and the weight to be given the witness's testimony.

Added by Acts 1997, 75th Leg., ch. 7, § 1, eff. April 17, 1997.

### § 6.705. Testimony by Marriage Counselor

(a) The report by the person named by the court to counsel the parties to a suit for divorce may not be admitted as evidence in the suit.

(b) The person named by the court to counsel the parties is not competent to testify in any suit involving the parties or their children.

(c) The files, records, and other work products of the counselor are privileged and confidential for all purposes and may not be admitted as evidence in any suit involving the parties or their children.

Added by Acts 1997, 75th Leg., ch. 7, § 1, eff. April 17, 1997.

### § 6.706. Change of Name

(a) In a decree of divorce or annulment, the court shall change the name of a party specifically requesting the change to a name previously used by the party unless the court states in the decree a reason for denying the change of name.

(b) The court may not deny a change of name solely to keep the last name of family members the same.

(c) A change of name does not release a person from liability incurred by the person under a previous name or defeat a right the person held under a previous name.

(d) A person whose name is changed under this section may apply for a change of name certificate from the clerk of the court as provided by Section 45.106.

Added by Acts 1997, 75th Leg., ch. 7, § 1, eff. April 17, 1997.

### § 6.707. Transfers and Debts Pending Decree

(a) A transfer of real or personal community property or a debt incurred by a spouse while a suit for divorce or annulment is pending that subjects the other spouse or the community property to liability is void with respect to the other spouse if the transfer was made or the debt incurred with the intent to injure the rights of the other spouse.

(b) A transfer or debt is not void if the person dealing with the transferor or debtor spouse did not have notice of the intent to injure the rights of the other spouse.

(c) The spouse seeking to void a transfer or debt incurred while a suit for divorce or annulment is pending has the burden of proving that the person dealing with the transferor or debtor spouse had notice of the intent to injure the rights of the spouse seeking to void the transaction.

Added by Acts 1997, 75th Leg., ch. 7, § 1, eff. April 17, 1997.

### § 6.708. Costs; Attorney's Fees and Expenses

(a) In a suit for dissolution of a marriage, the court as it considers reasonable may award costs to a party. Costs may not be adjudged against a party against whom a divorce is granted for confinement in a mental hospital under Section 6.007.

(b) The expenses of counseling may be taxed as costs against either or both parties.

(c) In a suit for dissolution of a marriage, the court may award reasonable attorney's fees and expenses. The court may order the fees and expenses and any postjudgment interest to be paid directly to the attorney, who may enforce the order in the attorney's own name by any means available for the enforcement of a judgment for debt.

Added by Acts 1997, 75th Leg., ch. 7, § 1, eff. April 17, 1997. Amended by Acts 2013, 83rd Leg., ch. 916 (H.B. 1366), §§ 3, 4, eff. Sept. 1, 2013.

### § 6.709. Temporary Orders During Appeal

(a) In a suit for dissolution of a marriage, on the motion of a party or on the court's own motion, after notice and hearing, the trial court may render a temporary order as considered equitable and necessary for the preservation of the property and for the protection of the parties during an appeal, including an order directed toward one or both parties:

(1) requiring the support of either spouse;

(2) requiring the payment of reasonable and necessary attorney's fees and expenses;

(3) appointing a receiver for the preservation and protection of the property of the parties;

(4) awarding one spouse exclusive occupancy of the parties' residence pending the appeal;

(5) enjoining a party from dissipating or transferring the property awarded to the other party in the trial court's property division; or

(6) suspending the operation of all or part of the property division that is being appealed.

(b) A temporary order under this section enjoining a party from dissipating or transferring the property awarded to the other party in the trial court's property division:

(1) may be rendered without:

(A) the issuance of a bond between the spouses; or

(B) an affidavit or a verified pleading stating specific facts showing that immediate and irreparable injury, loss, or damage will result;

(2) is not required to:

(A) define the injury or state why the injury is irreparable; or

(B) include an order setting the suit for trial on the merits with respect to the ultimate relief sought; and

(3) may not prohibit a party's use, transfer, conveyance, or dissipation of the property awarded to the other party in the trial court's property division if the use, transfer, conveyance, or dissipation of the property is for the purpose of suspending the enforcement of the property division that is the subject of the appeal.

(c) A temporary order under this section that suspends the operation of all or part of the property division that is the subject of the appeal may not be rendered unless the trial court takes reasonable steps to ensure that the party awarded property in the trial court's property division is protected from the other party's dissipation or transfer of that property.

(d) In considering a party's request to suspend the enforcement of the property division, the trial court shall consider whether:

(1) any relief granted under Subsection (a) is adequate to protect the party's interest in the property awarded to the party; or

(2) the party who was not awarded the property should also be required to provide security for the appeal in addition to any relief granted under Subsection (a).

(e) If the trial court determines that the party awarded the property can be adequately protected from the other party's dissipation of assets during the appeal only if the other party provides security for the appeal, the trial court shall set the appropriate amount of security, taking into consideration any relief granted under Subsection (a) and the amount of security that the other party would otherwise have to provide by law if relief under Subsection (a) was not granted.

(f) In rendering a temporary order under this section that suspends enforcement of all or part of the property division, the trial court may grant any relief under Subsection (a), in addition to requiring the party who was not awarded the property to post security for that part of the property division to be suspended. The trial court may require that the party who was not awarded the property post all or only part of the security that would otherwise be required by law.

(g) This section does not prevent a party who was not awarded the property from exercising that party's right to suspend the enforcement of the property division as provided by law.

(h) A motion seeking an original temporary order under this section:

(1) may be filed before trial; and

(2) may not be filed by a party after the date by which that party is required to file the party's notice of appeal under the Texas Rules of Appellate Procedure.

(i) The trial court retains jurisdiction to conduct a hearing and sign an original temporary order under this section until the 60th day after the date any eligible party has filed a notice of appeal from final judgment under the Texas Rules of Appellate Procedure.

(j) The trial court retains jurisdiction to modify and enforce a temporary order under this section unless the appellate court, on a proper showing, supersedes the trial court's order.

(k) On the motion of a party or on the court's own motion, after notice and hearing, the trial court may modify a previous temporary order rendered under this section if:

(1) the circumstances of a party have materially and substantially changed since the rendition of the previous order; and

(2) modification is equitable and necessary for the preservation of the property or for the protection of the parties during the appeal.

(*l*) A party may seek review of the trial court's temporary order under this section by:

(1) motion filed in the court of appeals with jurisdiction or potential jurisdiction over the appeal from the judgment in the case;

(2) proper assignment in the party's brief; or

(3) petition for writ of mandamus.

(m) A temporary order rendered under this section is not subject to interlocutory appeal.

(n) The remedies provided in this section are cumulative of all other remedies allowed by law.

Added by Acts 1997, 75th Leg., ch. 7, § 1, eff. April 17, 1997. Amended by Acts 2017, 85th Leg., ch. 421 (S.B. 1237), § 1, eff. Sept. 1, 2017.

### § 6.710. Notice of Final Decree

The clerk of the court shall mail a notice of the signing of the final decree of dissolution of a marriage to the party who waived service of process under Section 6.4035 at the mailing address contained in the waiver or the office of the party's attorney of record. The notice must state that a copy of the decree is available at the office of the clerk of the court and include the physical address of that office.

Added by Acts 1997, 75th Leg., ch. 614, § 2, eff. Sept. 1, 1997. Amended by Acts 2011, 82nd Leg., ch. 529 (H.B. 2422), § 1, eff. June 17, 2011.

### § 6.711. Findings of Fact and Conclusions of Law

(a) In a suit for dissolution of a marriage in which the court has rendered a judgment dividing the estate of the parties, on request by a party, the court shall state in writing its findings of fact and conclusions of law, including the characterization and value of all assets, liabilities, claims, and offsets on which disputed evidence has been presented.

(b) A request for findings of fact and conclusions of law under this section must conform to the Texas Rules of Civil Procedure.

(c) The findings of fact and conclusions of law required by this section are in addition to any other findings or conclusions required or authorized by law.

Added by Acts 2001, 77th Leg., ch. 297, § 1, eff. Sept. 1, 2001. Amended by Acts 2017, 85th Leg., ch. 421 (S.B. 1237), § 2, eff. Sept. 1, 2017.

### § 6.712. Date of Marriage Requirement in Final Decree

(a) In a suit for dissolution of a marriage in which the court grants a divorce, the court shall state the date of the marriage in the decree of divorce.

(b) This section does not apply to a suit for dissolution of a marriage described by Section 2.401(a)(2).

Added by Acts 2021, 87th Leg., ch. 934 (H.B. 3774), § 4.01, eff. Sept. 1, 2021.

Section 4.06 of Acts 2021, 87th Leg., ch. 934 (H.B. 3774) provides:

"The change in law made by Section 6.712, Family Code, as added by this article, applies only to a suit for dissolution of a marriage filed on or after the effective date [Sept. 1, 2021] of this Act. A suit for dissolution of a marriage filed before the effective date of this Act is governed by the law in effect on the date the suit was filed, and the former law is continued in effect for that purpose."

Section 15.02 of Acts 2021, 87th Leg., ch. 934 (H.B. 3774) provides:

"Not later than May 1, 2022, the Supreme Court of Texas shall adopt rules and promulgate forms under Section 22.0042, Government Code, as added by this article.

Section 18.01 of Acts 2021, 87th Leg., ch. 934 (H.B. 3774) provides:

"A state agency subject to this Act is required to implement a provision of this Act only if the legislature appropriates money specifically for that purpose. If the legislature does not appropriate money specifically for that purpose, the state agency may, but is not required to, implement a provision of this Act using other appropriations available for that purpose."

## SUBCHAPTER I. REMARRIAGE

### § 6.801. Remarriage

(a) Except as otherwise provided by this subchapter, neither party to a divorce may marry a third party before the 31st day after the date the divorce is decreed.

(b) The former spouses may marry each other at any time.

Added by Acts 1997, 75th Leg., ch. 7, § 1, eff. April 17, 1997.

### § 6.802. Waiver of Prohibition Against Remarriage

For good cause shown the court may waive the prohibition against remarriage provided by this subchapter as to either or both spouses if a record of the proceedings is made and preserved or if findings of fact and conclusions of law are filed by the court.

Added by Acts 1997, 75th Leg., ch. 7, § 1, eff. April 17, 1997.

## CHAPTER 7. AWARD OF MARITAL PROPERTY

Section



### § 7.001. General Rule of Property Division

In a decree of divorce or annulment, the court shall order a division of the estate of the parties in a manner that the court deems just and right, having due regard for the rights of each party and any children of the marriage.

Added by Acts 1997, 75th Leg., ch. 7, § 1, eff. April 17, 1997.

### § 7.002. Division and Disposition of Certain Property Under Special Circumstances

(a) In addition to the division of the estate of the parties required by Section 7.001, in a decree of divorce or annulment the court shall order a division of the following real and personal property, wherever situated, in a manner that the court deems just and right, having due regard for the rights of each party and any children of the marriage:

(1) property that was acquired by either spouse while domiciled in another state and that would have been community property if the spouse who acquired the property had been domiciled in this state at the time of the acquisition; or

(2) property that was acquired by either spouse in exchange for real or personal property and that would have been community property if the spouse who acquired the property so exchanged had been domiciled in this state at the time of its acquisition.

(b) In a decree of divorce or annulment, the court shall award to a spouse the following real and personal property, wherever situated, as the separate property of the spouse:

(1) property that was acquired by the spouse while domiciled in another state and that would have been the spouse's separate property if the spouse had been domiciled in this state at the time of acquisition; or

(2) property that was acquired by the spouse in exchange for real or personal property and that would have been the spouse's separate property if the spouse had been domiciled in this state at the time of acquisition.

(c) In a decree of divorce or annulment, the court shall confirm the following as the separate property of a spouse if partitioned or exchanged by written agreement of the spouses:

(1) income and earnings from the spouses' property, wages, salaries, and other forms of compensation received on or after January 1 of the year in which the suit for dissolution of marriage was filed; or

(2) income and earnings from the spouses' property, wages, salaries, and other forms of compensation received in another year during which the spouses were married for any part of the year.

Added by Acts 1997, 75th Leg., ch. 7, § 1, eff. April 17, 1997. Amended by Acts 1999, 76th Leg., ch. 692, § 4, eff. Sept. 1, 1999; Acts 2001, 77th Leg., ch. 838, § 4, eff. Sept. 1, 2001; Acts 2003, 78th Leg., ch. 230, § 4, eff. Sept. 1, 2003.

### § 7.003. Disposition of Retirement and Employment Benefits and Other Plans

In a decree of divorce or annulment, the court shall determine the rights of both spouses in a pension, retirement plan, annuity, individual retirement account, employee stock option plan, stock option, or other form of savings, bonus, profit-sharing, or other employer plan or financial plan of an employee or a participant, regardless of whether the person is self-employed, in the nature of compensation or savings.

Added by Acts 1997, 75th Leg., ch. 7, § 1, eff. April 17, 1997.

### § 7.004. Disposition of Rights in Insurance

In a decree of divorce or annulment, the court shall specifically divide or award the rights of each spouse in an insurance policy.

Added by Acts 1997, 75th Leg., ch. 7, § 1, eff. April 17, 1997.

### § 7.005. Insurance Coverage Not Specifically Awarded

(a) If in a decree of divorce or annulment the court does not specifically award all of the rights of the spouses in an insurance policy other than life insurance in effect at the time the decree is rendered, the policy remains in effect until the policy expires according to the policy's own terms.

(b) The proceeds of a valid claim under the policy are payable as follows:

(1) if the interest in the property insured was awarded solely to one former spouse by the decree, to that former spouse;

(2) if an interest in the property insured was awarded to each former spouse, to those former spouses in proportion to the interests awarded; or

(3) if the insurance coverage is directly related to the person of one of the former spouses, to that former spouse.

(c) The failure of either former spouse to change the endorsement on the policy to reflect the distribution of proceeds established by this section does not relieve the insurer of liability to pay the proceeds or any other obligation on the policy.

(d) This section does not affect the right of a former spouse to assert an ownership interest in an undivided life insurance policy, as provided by Subchapter D,[1] Chapter 9.

Added by Acts 1997, 75th Leg., ch. 7, § 1, eff. April 17, 1997.

[1] V.T.C.A., Family Code §§ 9.301, 9.302.

### § 7.006. Agreement Incident to Divorce or Annulment

(a) To promote amicable settlement of disputes in a suit for divorce or annulment, the spouses may enter into a written agreement concerning the division of the property and the liabilities of the spouses and maintenance of either spouse. The agreement may be revised or repudiated before rendition of the divorce or annulment unless the agreement is binding under another rule of law.

(b) If the court finds that the terms of the written agreement in a divorce or an annulment are just and right, those terms are binding on the court. If the court approves the agreement, the court may set forth the agreement in full or incorporate the agreement by reference in the final decree. If the court incorporates the agreement by reference in the final decree, the agreement is not required to be filed with the court or the court clerk.

(c) If the court finds that the terms of the written agreement in a divorce or annulment are not just and right, the court may request the spouses to submit a revised agreement or may set the case for a contested hearing.

Added by Acts 1997, 75th Leg., ch. 7, § 1, eff. April 17, 1997. Amended by Acts 2019, 86th Leg., ch. 161 (H.B. 559), § 1, eff. May 24, 2019.

Section 2 of Acts 2019, 86th Leg., ch. 161 (H.B. 559) provides:

"Section 7.006(b), Family Code, as amended by this Act, applies to an agreement incorporated by reference in a final decree of divorce or annulment regardless of whether the decree is signed before, on, or after the effective date [May 24, 2019] of this Act."

### § 7.007. Disposition of Claim for Reimbursement

In a decree of divorce or annulment, the court shall determine the rights of both spouses in a claim for reimbursement as provided by Subchapter E,[1] Chapter 3, and shall apply equitable principles to:

(1) determine whether to recognize the claim after taking into account all the relative circumstances of the spouses; and

(2) order a division of the claim for reimbursement, if appropriate, in a manner that the court considers just and right, having due regard for the rights of each party and any children of the marriage.

Added by Acts 2001, 77th Leg., ch. 838, § 5, eff. Sept. 1, 2001. Amended by Acts 2009, 81st Leg., ch. 768, § 7, eff. Sept. 1, 2009.

[1] V.T.C.A., Family Code § 3.401.

### § 7.008. Consideration of Taxes

In ordering the division of the estate of the parties to a suit for dissolution of a marriage, the court may consider:

(1) whether a specific asset will be subject to taxation; and

(2) if the asset will be subject to taxation, when the tax will be required to be paid.

Added by Acts 2005, 79th Leg., ch. 168, § 1, eff. Sept. 1, 2005.

### § 7.009. Fraud on the Community; Division and Disposition of Reconstituted Estate

(a) In this section, "reconstituted estate" means the total value of the community estate that would exist if an actual or constructive fraud on the community had not occurred.

(b) If the trier of fact determines that a spouse has committed actual or constructive fraud on the community, the court shall:

(1) calculate the value by which the community estate was depleted as a result of the fraud on the

community and calculate the amount of the reconstituted estate; and

(2) divide the value of the reconstituted estate between the parties in a manner the court deems just and right.

(c) In making a just and right division of the reconstituted estate under Section 7.001, the court may grant any legal or equitable relief necessary to accomplish a just and right division, including:

(1) awarding to the wronged spouse an appropriate share of the community estate remaining after the actual or constructive fraud on the community;

(2) awarding a money judgment in favor of the wronged spouse against the spouse who committed the actual or constructive fraud on the community; or

(3) awarding to the wronged spouse both a money judgment and an appropriate share of the community estate.

Added by Acts 2011, 82nd Leg., ch. 487 (H.B. 908), § 1, eff. Sept. 1, 2011.

## CHAPTER 8. MAINTENANCE

### SUBCHAPTER A. GENERAL PROVISIONS



### SUBCHAPTER B. SPOUSAL MAINTENANCE



### SUBCHAPTER C. INCOME WITHHOLDING



**Section**

### SUBCHAPTER D. PROCEDURE



### SUBCHAPTER E. RIGHTS AND DUTIES OF EMPLOYER



### SUBCHAPTER F. WRIT OF WITHHOLDING ISSUED BY CLERK



### SUBCHAPTER G. MODIFICATION, REDUCTION, OR TERMINATION OF WITHHOLDING

## DISPOSITION TABLE

Showing where the subject matter of provisions contained in former Chapter 8 of the Family Code may be found in Chapter 8, Maintenance, as amended by Acts 2001, 77th Leg., ch. 807, § 1.

| Former Section | Amended Section |
|---|---|
| 8.001 | 8.001 |
| 8.002 | 8.051 |
| 8.003 | 8.052 |
| 8.004 | 8.053 |
| 8.005 | 8.054 |
| 8.006 | 8.055 |
| 8.007 | 8.056 |
| 8.008 | 8.057 |
| 8.009 | 8.059 |
| 8.010 | 8.060 |
| 8.011 | 8.061 |

## SUBCHAPTER A. GENERAL PROVISIONS

### § 8.001. Definitions

In this chapter:

(1) "Maintenance" means an award in a suit for dissolution of a marriage of periodic payments from the future income of one spouse for the support of the other spouse.

(2) "Notice of application for a writ of withholding" means the document delivered to an obligor and filed with the court as required by this chapter for the nonjudicial determination of arrears and initiation of withholding for spousal maintenance.

(3) "Obligee" means a person entitled to receive payments under the terms of an order for spousal maintenance.

(4) "Obligor" means a person required to make periodic payments under the terms of an order for spousal maintenance.

(5) "Writ of withholding" means the document issued by the clerk of a court and delivered to an employer, directing that earnings be withheld for payment of spousal maintenance as provided by this chapter.

Added by Acts 1997, 75th Leg., ch. 7, § 1, eff. April 17, 1997. Amended by Acts 2001, 77th Leg., ch. 807, § 1, eff. Sept. 1, 2001.

### §§ 8.002 to 8.011. Deleted by Acts 2001, 77th Leg., ch. 807, § 2, eff. Sept. 1, 2001

## SUBCHAPTER B. SPOUSAL MAINTENANCE

### § 8.051. Eligibility for Maintenance

In a suit for dissolution of a marriage or in a proceeding for maintenance in a court with personal jurisdiction over both former spouses following the dissolution of their marriage by a court that lacked personal jurisdiction over an absent spouse, the court may order maintenance for either spouse only if the spouse seeking maintenance will lack sufficient property, including the spouse's separate property, on dissolution of the marriage to provide for the spouse's minimum reasonable needs and:

(1) the spouse from whom maintenance is requested was convicted of or received deferred adjudication for a criminal offense that also constitutes an act of family violence, as defined by Section 71.004, committed during the marriage against the other spouse or the other spouse's child and the offense occurred:

(A) within two years before the date on which a suit for dissolution of the marriage is filed; or

(B) while the suit is pending; or

(2) the spouse seeking maintenance:

(A) is unable to earn sufficient income to provide for the spouse's minimum reasonable needs because of an incapacitating physical or mental disability;

(B) has been married to the other spouse for 10 years or longer and lacks the ability to earn sufficient income to provide for the spouse's minimum reasonable needs; or

(C) is the custodian of a child of the marriage of any age who requires substantial care and personal supervision because of a physical or mental disability that prevents the spouse from earning sufficient income to provide for the spouse's minimum reasonable needs.

Added by Acts 1997, 75th Leg., ch. 7, § 1, eff. April 17, 1997. Amended by Acts 1999, 76th Leg., ch. 62, § 6.05, eff. Sept. 1, 1999; Acts 1999, 76th Leg., ch. 304, § 1, eff. Sept. 1, 1999. Redesignated from § 8.002 and amended by Acts 2001, 77th Leg., ch. 807, § 1, eff. Sept. 1, 2001; Acts 2005, 79th Leg., ch. 914, § 1, eff. Sept. 1, 2005. Amended by Acts 2011, 82nd Leg., ch. 486 (H.B. 901), § 1, eff. Sept. 1, 2011; Acts 2013, 83rd Leg., ch. 242 (H.B. 389), § 2, eff. Sept. 1, 2013.

### § 8.052. Factors in Determining Maintenance

A court that determines that a spouse is eligible to receive maintenance under this chapter shall determine the nature, amount, duration, and manner of periodic payments by considering all relevant factors, including:

(1) each spouse's ability to provide for that spouse's minimum reasonable needs independently, considering that spouse's financial resources on dissolution of the marriage;

(2) the education and employment skills of the spouses, the time necessary to acquire sufficient education or training to enable the spouse seeking maintenance to earn sufficient income, and the availability and feasibility of that education or training;

(3) the duration of the marriage;

(4) the age, employment history, earning ability, and physical and emotional condition of the spouse seeking maintenance;

(5) the effect on each spouse's ability to provide for that spouse's minimum reasonable needs while providing periodic child support payments or maintenance, if applicable;

(6) acts by either spouse resulting in excessive or abnormal expenditures or destruction, concealment, or fraudulent disposition of community property, joint tenancy, or other property held in common;

(7) the contribution by one spouse to the education, training, or increased earning power of the other spouse;

(8) the property brought to the marriage by either spouse;

(9) the contribution of a spouse as homemaker;

(10) marital misconduct, including adultery and cruel treatment, by either spouse during the marriage; and

(11) any history or pattern of family violence, as defined by Section 71.004.

Added by Acts 1997, 75th Leg., ch. 7, § 1, eff. April 17, 1997. Redesignated from § 8.003 by Acts 2001, 77th Leg., ch. 807, § 1, eff. Sept. 1, 2001. Amended by Acts 2011, 82nd Leg., ch. 486 (H.B. 901), § 1, eff. Sept. 1, 2011.

### § 8.053. Presumption

(a) It is a rebuttable presumption that maintenance under Section 8.051(2)(B) is not warranted unless the spouse seeking maintenance has exercised diligence in:

(1) earning sufficient income to provide for the spouse's minimum reasonable needs; or

(2) developing the necessary skills to provide for the spouse's minimum reasonable needs during a period of separation and during the time the suit for dissolution of the marriage is pending.

(b) Repealed by Acts 2011, 82nd Leg., ch. 486 (H.B. 901), § 9(1).

Added by Acts 1997, 75th Leg., ch. 7, § 1, eff. April 17, 1997. Redesignated from § 8.004 by Acts 2001, 77th Leg., ch. 807, § 1, eff. Sept. 1, 2001. Amended by Acts 2005, 79th Leg., ch. 914, § 2, eff. Sept. 1, 2005; Acts 2011, 82nd Leg., ch. 486 (H.B. 901), §§ 2, 9(1), eff. Sept. 1, 2011.

### § 8.054. Duration of Maintenance Order

(a) Except as provided by Subsection (b), a court:

(1) may not order maintenance that remains in effect for more than:

(A) five years after the date of the order, if:

(i) the spouses were married to each other for less than 10 years and the eligibility of the spouse for whom maintenance is ordered is established under Section 8.051(1); or

(ii) the spouses were married to each other for at least 10 years but not more than 20 years;

(B) seven years after the date of the order, if the spouses were married to each other for at least 20 years but not more than 30 years; or

(C) 10 years after the date of the order, if the spouses were married to each other for 30 years or more; and

(2) shall limit the duration of a maintenance order to the shortest reasonable period that allows the spouse seeking maintenance to earn sufficient income to provide for the spouse's minimum reasonable needs, unless the ability of the spouse to provide for the spouse's minimum reasonable needs is substantially or totally diminished because of:

(A) physical or mental disability of the spouse seeking maintenance;

(B) duties as the custodian of an infant or young child of the marriage; or

(C) another compelling impediment to earning sufficient income to provide for the spouse's minimum reasonable needs.

(b) The court may order maintenance for a spouse to whom Section 8.051(2)(A) or (C) applies for as long as the spouse continues to satisfy the eligibility criteria prescribed by the applicable provision.

(c) On the request of either party or on the court's own motion, the court may order the periodic review of its order for maintenance under Subsection (b).

(d) The continuation of maintenance ordered under Subsection (b) is subject to a motion to modify as provided by Section 8.057.

Added by Acts 1997, 75th Leg., ch. 7, § 1, eff. April 17, 1997. Redesignated from V.T.C.A., Family Code § 8.005 and amended by Acts 2001, 77th Leg., ch. 807, § 1, eff. Sept. 1, 2001; Acts 2005, 79th Leg., ch. 914, § 3, eff. Sept. 1, 2005. Amended by Acts 2011, 82nd Leg., ch. 486 (H.B. 901), § 3, eff. Sept. 1, 2011.

### § 8.055. Amount of Maintenance

(a) A court may not order maintenance that requires an obligor to pay monthly more than the lesser of:

(1) $5,000; or

(2) 20 percent of the spouse's average monthly gross income.

(a–1) For purposes of this chapter, gross income:

(1) includes:

(A) 100 percent of all wage and salary income and other compensation for personal services (including commissions, overtime pay, tips, and bonuses);

(B) interest, dividends, and royalty income;

(C) self-employment income;

(D) net rental income (defined as rent after deducting operating expenses and mortgage payments, but not including noncash items such as depreciation); and

(E) all other income actually being received, including severance pay, retirement benefits, pensions, trust income, annuities, capital gains, unemployment benefits, interest income from notes regardless of the source, gifts and prizes, maintenance, and alimony; and

(2) does not include:

(A) return of principal or capital;

(B) accounts receivable;

(C) benefits paid in accordance with federal public assistance programs;

(D) benefits paid in accordance with the Temporary Assistance for Needy Families program;

(E) payments for foster care of a child;

(F) Department of Veterans Affairs service-connected disability compensation;

(G) supplemental security income (SSI), social security benefits, and disability benefits; or

(H) workers' compensation benefits.

(b) Repealed by Acts 2011, 82nd Leg., ch. 486 (H.B. 901), § 9(2).

(c) Repealed by Acts 2011, 82nd Leg., ch. 486 (H.B. 901), § 9(2).

(d) Repealed by Acts 2011, 82nd Leg., ch. 486 (H.B. 901), § 9(2).

Added by Acts 1997, 75th Leg., ch. 7, § 1, eff. April 17, 1997. Redesignated from § 8.006 and amended by Acts 2001, 77th Leg., ch. 807, § 1, eff. Sept. 1, 2001; Acts 2003, 78th Leg., ch. 1138, § 1, eff. Sept. 1, 2003. Amended by Acts 2011, 82nd Leg., ch. 486 (H.B. 901), §§ 4, 9(2), eff. Sept. 1, 2011.

### § 8.056. Termination

(a) The obligation to pay future maintenance terminates on the death of either party or on the remarriage of the obligee.

(b) After a hearing, the court shall order the termination of the maintenance obligation if the court finds that the obligee cohabits with another person with whom the obligee has a dating or romantic relationship in a permanent place of abode on a continuing basis.

(c) Termination of the maintenance obligation does not terminate the obligation to pay any maintenance that accrued before the date of termination, whether as a result of death or remarriage under Subsection (a) or a court order under Subsection (b).

Added by Acts 1997, 75th Leg., ch. 7, § 1, eff. April 17, 1997. Redesignated from § 8.007 and amended by Acts 2001, 77th Leg., ch. 807, § 1, eff. Sept. 1, 2001. Amended by Acts 2011, 82nd Leg., ch. 486 (H.B. 901), § 5, eff. Sept. 1, 2011.

### § 8.057. Modification of Maintenance Order

(a) The amount of maintenance specified in a court order or the portion of a decree that provides for the maintenance of a former spouse may be modified by the filing of a motion in the court that originally rendered the order. A party affected by the order or the portion of the decree to be modified may file the motion.

(b) Notice of a motion to modify maintenance or to establish or modify a maintenance qualified domestic relations order under Subchapter H and the response to the motion, if any, are governed by the Texas Rules of Civil Procedure applicable to the filing of an original lawsuit. Notice must be given by service of citation, and a response must be in the form of an answer due on or before 10 a.m. of the first Monday after 20 days after the date of service. A court shall set a hearing on the motion in the manner provided by Rule 245, Texas Rules of Civil Procedure.

(c) After a hearing, the court may modify an original or modified order or portion of a decree providing for maintenance or a maintenance qualified domestic relations order under Subchapter H on a proper showing of a material and substantial change in circumstances that occurred after the date of the order or decree, including circumstances reflected in the factors specified in Section 8.052, relating to either party or to a child of the marriage described by Section 8.051(2)(C). The court:

(1) shall apply the modification only to payment accruing after the filing of the motion to modify; and

(2) may not increase maintenance to an amount or duration that exceeds the amount or remaining duration of the original maintenance order.

(c–1) A party who files a motion to modify maintenance based on a material and substantial change of circumstances may not be considered on that basis alone to have admitted a material and substantial change of circumstances regarding any other matter.

(d) A loss of employment or circumstances that render a former spouse unable to provide for the spouse's minimum reasonable needs by reason of incapacitating physical or mental disability that occur after the divorce or annulment are not grounds for the institution of spousal maintenance for the benefit of the former spouse.

Added by Acts 1997, 75th Leg., ch. 7, § 1, eff. April 17, 1997. Redesignated from § 8.008 by Acts 2001, 77th Leg., ch. 807, § 1, eff. Sept. 1, 2001. Amended by Acts 2011, 82nd Leg., ch. 486 (H.B. 901), § 6, eff. Sept. 1, 2011; Acts 2021, 87th Leg., ch. 64 (H.B. 867), § 1, eff. Sept. 1, 2021; Acts 2021, 87th Leg., ch. 227 (H.B. 851), § 1, eff. Sept. 1, 2021.

Section 6 of Acts 2021, 87th Leg., ch. 64 (H.B. 867) provides:

"(a) The changes in law made by this Act to Chapters 8, 154, and 157, Family Code, apply to an order for maintenance under Chapter 8, Family Code, or for child support under Chapter 154, Family Code, as applicable, regardless of whether the order was rendered before, on, or after the effective date [Sept. 1, 2021] of this Act.

"(b) The enactment of this Act does not constitute a material and substantial change of circumstances sufficient to warrant modification of a court order or portion of a decree that provides for maintenance or child support rendered before the effective date of this Act."

Section 3 of Acts 2021, 87th Leg., ch. 227 (H.B. 851) provides:

"The changes in law made by this Act apply only to a motion to modify that is filed on or after the effective date [Sept. 1, 2021] of this Act. A motion to modify filed before that date is governed by the law in effect on the date the motion was filed, and that law is continued in effect for that purpose."

### § 8.058. Maintenance Arrearages

A spousal maintenance payment not timely made constitutes an arrearage.

Added by Acts 2001, 77th Leg., ch. 807, § 1, eff. Sept. 1, 2001.

### § 8.059. Enforcement of Maintenance Order

(a) The court may enforce by contempt against the obligor:

(1) the court's maintenance order; or

(2) an agreement for periodic payments of spousal maintenance under the terms of this chapter voluntarily entered into between the parties and approved by the court.

(a–1) The court may not enforce by contempt any provision of an agreed order for maintenance that exceeds the amount of periodic support the court could have ordered under this chapter or for any period of maintenance beyond the period of maintenance the court could have ordered under this chapter.

(b) On the suit to enforce by an obligee, the court may render judgment against a defaulting party for the amount of arrearages after notice by service of citation, answer, if any, and a hearing finding that the defaulting party has failed or refused to comply with the terms of the order. The judgment may be enforced by any means available for the enforcement of judgment for debts, including by an order or writ of withholding and a maintenance qualified domestic relations order under Subchapter H.

(c) It is an affirmative defense to an allegation of contempt of court or the violation of a condition of probation requiring payment of court-ordered maintenance that the obligor:

(1) lacked the ability to provide maintenance in the amount ordered;

(2) lacked property that could be sold, mortgaged, or otherwise pledged to raise the funds needed;

(3) attempted unsuccessfully to borrow the needed funds; and

(4) did not know of a source from which the money could have been borrowed or otherwise legally obtained.

(d) The issue of the existence of an affirmative defense does not arise until pleaded. An obligor must prove the affirmative defense by a preponderance of the evidence.

(e) Repealed by Acts 2011, 82nd Leg., ch. 486 (H.B. 901), § 9(3).

Added by Acts 1997, 75th Leg., ch. 7, § 1, eff. April 17, 1997. Redesignated from § 8.009 and amended by Acts 2001, 77th Leg., ch. 807, § 1, eff. Sept. 1, 2001. Amended by Acts 2011, 82nd Leg., ch. 486 (H.B. 901), §§ 7, 9(3), eff. Sept. 1, 2011; Acts 2013, 83rd Leg., ch. 242 (H.B. 389), § 3, eff. Sept. 1, 2013; Acts 2021, 87th Leg., ch. 64 (H.B. 867), § 2, eff. Sept. 1, 2021.

Section 6 of Acts 2021, 87th Leg., ch. 64 (H.B. 867) provides:

"(a) The changes in law made by this Act to Chapters 8, 154, and 157, Family Code, apply to an order for maintenance under Chapter 8, Family Code, or for child support under Chapter 154, Family Code, as applicable, regardless of whether the order was rendered before, on, or after the effective date [Sept. 1, 2021] of this Act.

"(b) The enactment of this Act does not constitute a material and substantial change of circumstances sufficient to warrant modification of a court order or portion of a decree that provides for maintenance or child support rendered before the effective date of this Act."

### § 8.0591. Overpayment

(a) If an obligor is not in arrears on the obligor's maintenance obligation and the obligor's maintenance obligation has terminated, the obligee must return to the obligor any maintenance payment made by the obligor that exceeds the amount of maintenance ordered or approved by the court, regardless of whether the payment was made before, on, or after the date the maintenance obligation terminated.

(b) An obligor may file a suit to recover overpaid maintenance under Subsection (a). If the court finds that the obligee failed to return overpaid maintenance under Subsection (a), the court shall order the obligee to pay the obligor's attorney's fees and all court costs in addition to the amount of the overpaid maintenance. For good cause shown, the court may waive the requirement that the obligee pay attorney's fees and court costs if the court states in its order the reasons supporting that finding.

Added by Acts 2011, 82nd Leg., ch. 486 (H.B. 901), § 8, eff. Sept. 1, 2011.

### § 8.060. Putative Spouse

In a suit to declare a marriage void, a putative spouse who did not have knowledge of an existing impediment to a valid marriage may be awarded maintenance if otherwise qualified to receive maintenance under this chapter.

Added by Acts 1997, 75th Leg., ch. 7, § 1, eff. April 17, 1997. Redesignated from § 8.010 by Acts 2001, 77th Leg., ch. 807, § 1, eff. Sept. 1, 2001.

### § 8.061. Unmarried Cohabitants

An order for maintenance is not authorized between unmarried cohabitants under any circumstances.

Added by Acts 1997, 75th Leg., ch. 7, § 1, eff. April 17, 1997. Redesignated from § 8.011 by Acts 2001, 77th Leg., ch. 807, § 1, eff. Sept. 1, 2001.

### § 8.062. Place of Payment

If an obligor is ordered to pay an obligee maintenance under this chapter and child support under Chapter 154, the court shall order the payment of maintenance to the state disbursement unit as provided by Chapter 234.

Added by Acts 2021, 87th Leg., ch. 552 (S.B. 286), § 1, eff. Sept. 1, 2021.

Section 12 of Acts 2021, 87th Leg., ch. 552 (S.B. 286) provides:

"The enactment of this Act does not constitute a material and substantial change of circumstances sufficient to warrant modification of a court order or portion of a decree that provides for the support of a child rendered before the effective date [Sept. 1, 2021] of this Act."

Section 13 of Acts 2021, 87th Leg., ch. 552 (S.B. 286) provides:

"(a) Section 8.062, Family Code, as added by this Act, applies only to a maintenance order rendered on or after the effective date [Sept. 1, 2021] of this Act. A maintenance order rendered before the effective date of this Act is governed by the law in effect on the date the order was rendered, and the former law is continued in effect for that purpose.

"(b) Notwithstanding Subsection (a) of this section, an obligor subject to a maintenance order rendered before the effective date of this Act may choose to remit maintenance payments to the state disbursement unit as provided by Chapter 234, Family Code, and the state disbursement unit shall accept those payments."

## SUBCHAPTER C. INCOME WITHHOLDING

### § 8.101. Income Withholding; General Rule

(a) In a proceeding in which periodic payments of spousal maintenance are ordered, modified, or enforced, the court may order that income be withheld from the disposable earnings of the obligor as provided by this chapter.

(a–1) The court may order that income be withheld from the disposable earnings of the obligor in a proceeding in which there is an agreement for periodic payments of spousal maintenance under the terms of this chapter voluntarily entered into between the parties and approved by the court.

(a–2) The court may not order that income be withheld from the disposable earnings of the obligor to the extent that any provision of an agreed order for maintenance exceeds the amount of periodic support the court could have ordered under this chapter or for any period of maintenance beyond the period of maintenance the court could have ordered under this chapter.

(b) This subchapter does not apply to contractual alimony or spousal maintenance, regardless of whether the alimony or maintenance is taxable, unless:

(1) the contract specifically permits income withholding; or

(2) the alimony or maintenance payments are not timely made under the terms of the contract.

(c) An order or writ of withholding for spousal maintenance may be combined with an order or writ of withholding for child support only if the obligee has been appointed managing conservator of the child for whom the child support is owed and is the conservator with whom the child primarily resides.

(d) An order or writ of withholding that combines withholding for spousal maintenance and child support must:

(1) require that the withheld amounts be paid to the appropriate place of payment under Section 154.004;

(2) be in the form prescribed by the Title IV-D agency under Section 158.106;

(3) clearly indicate the amounts withheld that are to be applied to current spousal maintenance and to any maintenance arrearages; and

(4) subject to the maximum withholding allowed under Section 8.106, order that withheld income be applied in the following order of priority:

(A) current child support;

(B) current spousal maintenance;

(C) child support arrearages; and

(D) spousal maintenance arrearages.

(e) Garnishment for the purposes of spousal maintenance does not apply to unemployment insurance benefit payments.

Added by Acts 2001, 77th Leg., ch. 807, § 1, eff. Sept. 1, 2001. Amended by Acts 2013, 83rd Leg., ch. 242 (H.B. 389), § 4, eff. Sept. 1, 2013.

### § 8.102. Withholding for Arrearages in Addition to Current Spousal Maintenance

(a) The court may order that, in addition to income withheld for current spousal maintenance, income be withheld from the disposable earnings of the obligor to be applied toward the liquidation of any arrearages.

(b) The additional amount withheld to be applied toward arrearages must be whichever of the following amounts will discharge the arrearages in the least amount of time:

(1) an amount sufficient to discharge the arrearages in not more than two years; or

(2) 20 percent of the amount withheld for current maintenance.

Added by Acts 2001, 77th Leg., ch. 807, § 1, eff. Sept. 1, 2001.

### § 8.103. Withholding for Arrearages When Current Maintenance Is Not Due

A court may order income withholding to be applied toward arrearages in an amount sufficient to discharge those arrearages in not more than two years if current spousal maintenance is no longer owed.

Added by Acts 2001, 77th Leg., ch. 807, § 1, eff. Sept. 1, 2001.

### § 8.104. Withholding to Satisfy Judgment for Arrearages

The court, in rendering a cumulative judgment for arrearages, may order that a reasonable amount of income be withheld from the disposable earnings of the obligor to be applied toward the satisfaction of the judgment.

Added by Acts 2001, 77th Leg., ch. 807, § 1, eff. Sept. 1, 2001.

### § 8.105. Priority of Withholding

An order or writ of withholding under this chapter has priority over any garnishment, attachment, execution, or other order affecting disposable earnings, except for an order or writ of withholding for child support under Chapter 158.

Added by Acts 2001, 77th Leg., ch. 807, § 1, eff. Sept. 1, 2001.

### § 8.106. Maximum Amount Withheld from Earnings

An order or writ of withholding must direct that an obligor's employer withhold from the obligor's disposable earnings the lesser of:

(1) the amount specified in the order or writ; or

(2) an amount that, when added to the amount of income being withheld by the employer for child support, is equal to 50 percent of the obligor's disposable earnings.

Added by Acts 2001, 77th Leg., ch. 807, § 1, eff. Sept. 1, 2001.

### § 8.107. Order or Writ Binding on Employer Doing Business in This State

An order or writ of withholding issued under this chapter and delivered to an employer doing business in this state is binding on the employer without regard to whether the obligor resides or works outside this state.

Added by Acts 2001, 77th Leg., ch. 807, § 1, eff. Sept. 1, 2001.

### § 8.108. Voluntary Writ of Withholding by Obligor

(a) An obligor may file with the clerk of the court a notarized or acknowledged request signed by the obligor and the obligee for the issuance and delivery to the obligor's employer of a writ of withholding. The obligor may file the request under this section regardless of whether a writ or order has been served on any party or whether the obligor owes arrearages.

(b) On receipt of a request under this section, the clerk shall issue and deliver a writ of withholding in the manner provided by this subchapter.

(c) An employer who receives a writ of withholding issued under this section may request a hearing in the same manner and according to the same terms provided by Section 8.205.

(d) An obligor whose employer receives a writ of withholding issued under this section may request a hearing in the manner provided by Section 8.258.

(e) An obligee may contest a writ of income withholding issued under this section by requesting, not later than the 180th day after the date on which the obligee discovers that the writ was issued, a hearing to be conducted in the manner provided by Section 8.258 for a hearing on a motion to stay.

(f) A writ of withholding under this section may not reduce the total amount of spousal maintenance, including arrearages, owed by the obligor.

Added by Acts 2001, 77th Leg., ch. 807, § 1, eff. Sept. 1, 2001.

## SUBCHAPTER D. PROCEDURE

### § 8.151. Time Limit

The court may issue an order or writ for withholding under this chapter at any time before all spousal maintenance and arrearages are paid.

Added by Acts 2001, 77th Leg., ch. 807, § 1, eff. Sept. 1, 2001.

### § 8.152. Contents of Order of Withholding

(a) An order of withholding must state:

(1) the style, cause number, and court having jurisdiction to enforce the order;

(2) the name, address, and, if available, the social security number of the obligor;

(3) the amount and duration of the spousal maintenance payments, including the amount and duration of withholding for arrearages, if any; and

(4) the name, address, and, if available, the social security number of the obligee.

(b) The order for withholding must require the obligor to notify the court promptly of any material change affecting the order, including a change of employer.

(c) On request by an obligee, the court may exclude from an order of withholding the obligee's address and social security number if the obligee or a member of the obligee's family or household is a victim of family violence and is the subject of a protective order to which the obligor is also subject. On granting a request under this subsection, the court shall order the clerk to:

(1) strike the address and social security number required by Subsection (a) from the order or writ of withholding; and

(2) maintain a confidential record of the obligee's address and social security number to be used only by the court.

Added by Acts 2001, 77th Leg., ch. 807, § 1, eff. Sept. 1, 2001.

### § 8.153. Request for Issuance of Order or Writ of Withholding

An obligor or obligee may file with the clerk of the court a request for issuance of an order or writ of withholding.

Added by Acts 2001, 77th Leg., ch. 807, § 1, eff. Sept. 1, 2001.

### § 8.154. Issuance and Delivery of Order or Writ of Withholding

(a) On receipt of a request for issuance of an order or writ of withholding, the clerk of the court shall deliver a certified copy of the order or writ to the obligor's current employer or to any subsequent employer of the obligor. The clerk shall attach a copy of Subchapter E[1] to the order or writ.

(b) Not later than the fourth working day after the date the order is signed or the request is filed, whichever is later, the clerk shall issue and deliver the certified copy of the order or writ by:

(1) certified or registered mail, return receipt requested, to the employer; or

(2) service of citation to:

(A) the person authorized to receive service of process for the employer in civil cases generally; or

(B) a person designated by the employer by written notice to the clerk to receive orders or notices of income withholding.

Added by Acts 2001, 77th Leg., ch. 807, § 1, eff. Sept. 1, 2001.

[1] V.T.C.A., Family Code § 8.201.

## SUBCHAPTER E. RIGHTS AND DUTIES OF EMPLOYER

### § 8.201. Order or Writ Binding on Employer

(a) An employer required to withhold income from earnings under this chapter is not entitled to notice of the proceedings before the order of withholding is rendered or writ of withholding is issued.

(b) An order or writ of withholding is binding on an employer regardless of whether the employer is specifically named in the order or writ.

Added by Acts 2001, 77th Leg., ch. 807, § 1, eff. Sept. 1, 2001.

### § 8.202. Effective Date and Duration of Income Withholding

An employer shall begin to withhold income in accordance with an order or writ of withholding not later than the first pay period after the date the order or writ was delivered to the employer. The employer shall continue to withhold income as required by the order or writ as long as the obligor is employed by the employer.

Added by Acts 2001, 77th Leg., ch. 807, § 1, eff. Sept. 1, 2001.

### § 8.203. Remitting Withheld Payments

(a) The employer shall remit to the person or office named in the order or writ of withholding the amount of income withheld from an obligor on each pay date. The remittance must include the date on which the income withholding occurred.

(b) The employer shall include with each remittance:

(1) the cause number of the suit under which income withholding is required;

(2) the payor's name; and

(3) the payee's name, unless the remittance is made by electronic funds transfer.

Added by Acts 2001, 77th Leg., ch. 807, § 1, eff. Sept. 1, 2001.

### § 8.204. Employer May Deduct Fee from Earnings

An employer may deduct an administrative fee of not more than $5 each month from the obligor's disposable earnings in addition to the amount withheld as spousal maintenance.

Added by Acts 2001, 77th Leg., ch. 807, § 1, eff. Sept. 1, 2001.

### § 8.205. Hearing Requested by Employer

(a) Not later than the 20th day after the date an order or writ of withholding is delivered to an employer, the employer may file with the court a motion for a hearing on the applicability of the order or writ to the employer.

(b) The hearing under this section must be held on or before the 15th day after the date the motion is made.

(c) An order or writ of withholding is binding and the employer shall continue to withhold income and remit the amount withheld pending further order of the court.

Added by Acts 2001, 77th Leg., ch. 807, § 1, eff. Sept. 1, 2001.

### § 8.206. Liability and Obligation of Employer for Payments

(a) An employer who complies with an order or writ of withholding under this chapter is not liable to the obligor for the amount of income withheld and remitted as required by the order or writ.

(b) An employer who receives, but does not comply with, an order or writ of withholding is liable to:

(1) the obligee for any amount of spousal maintenance not paid in compliance with the order or writ;

(2) the obligor for any amount withheld from the obligor's disposable earnings, but not remitted to the obligee; and

(3) the obligee or obligor for reasonable attorney's fees and court costs incurred in recovering an amount described by Subdivision (1) or (2).

(c) An employer shall comply with an order of withholding for spousal maintenance or alimony issued in another state that appears regular on its face in the same manner as an order issued by a tribunal of this state. The employer shall notify the employee of the order and comply with the order in the manner provided by Subchapter F, Chapter 159[1], with respect to an order of withholding for child support issued by another state. The employer may contest the order of withholding in the manner provided by that subchapter with respect to an order of withholding for child support issued by another state.

Added by Acts 2001, 77th Leg., ch. 807, § 1, eff. Sept. 1, 2001.

[1] V.T.C.A., Family Code 159.501.

### § 8.207. Employer Receiving Multiple Orders or Writs

(a) An employer who receives more than one order or writ of withholding to withhold income from the same obligor shall withhold the combined amounts due under each order or writ unless the combined amounts due exceed the maximum total amount of allowed income withholding under Section 8.106.

(b) If the combined amounts to be withheld under multiple orders or writs for the same obligor exceed the maximum total amount of allowed income withholding under Section 8.106, the employer shall pay, until that maximum is reached, in the following order of priority:

(1) an equal amount toward current child support owed by the obligor in each order or writ until the employer has complied fully with each current child support obligation;

(2) an equal amount toward current maintenance owed by the obligor in each order or writ until the employer has complied fully with each current maintenance obligation;

(3) an equal amount toward child support arrearages owed by the obligor in each order or writ until the employer has complied fully with each order or writ for child support arrearages; and

(4) an equal amount toward maintenance arrearages owed by the obligor in each order or writ until the employer has complied fully with each order or writ for spousal maintenance arrearages.

Added by Acts 2001, 77th Leg., ch. 807, § 1, eff. Sept. 1, 2001.

### § 8.208. Employer's Liability for Discriminatory Hiring or Discharge

(a) An employer may not use an order or writ of withholding as grounds in whole or part for the termination of employment of, or for any other disciplinary action against, an employee.

(b) An employer may not refuse to hire an employee because of an order or writ of withholding.

(c) An employer who intentionally discharges an employee in violation of this section is liable to that employee for current wages, other employment benefits, and reasonable attorney's fees and court costs incurred in enforcing the employee's rights.

(d) In addition to liability imposed under Subsection (c), the court shall order with respect to an employee whose employment was suspended or terminated in violation of this section appropriate injunctive relief, including reinstatement of:

(1) the employee's position with the employer; and

(2) fringe benefits or seniority lost as a result of the suspension or termination.

(e) An employee may bring an action to enforce the employee's rights under this section.

Added by Acts 2001, 77th Leg., ch. 807, § 1, eff. Sept. 1, 2001.

### § 8.209. Penalty for Noncompliance

(a) In addition to the civil remedies provided by this subchapter or any other remedy provided by law, an employer who knowingly violates this chapter by failing to withhold income for spousal maintenance or to remit withheld income in accordance with an order or writ of withholding issued under this chapter commits an offense.

(b) An offense under this section is punishable by a fine not to exceed $200 for each violation.

Added by Acts 2001, 77th Leg., ch. 807, § 1, eff. Sept. 1, 2001.

### § 8.210. Notice of Termination of Employment and of New Employment

(a) An obligor who terminates employment with an employer who has been withholding income and the obligor's employer shall each notify the court and the obligee of:

(1) the termination of employment not later than the seventh day after the date of termination;

(2) the obligor's last known address; and

(3) the name and address of the obligor's new employer, if known.

(b) The obligor shall inform a subsequent employer of the order or writ of withholding after obtaining employment.

Added by Acts 2001, 77th Leg., ch. 807, § 1, eff. Sept. 1, 2001.

## SUBCHAPTER F. WRIT OF WITHHOLDING ISSUED BY CLERK

### § 8.251. Notice of Application for Writ of Withholding; Filing

(a) An obligor or obligee may file a notice of application for a writ of withholding if income withholding was not ordered at the time spousal maintenance was ordered.

(b) The obligor or obligee may file the notice of application for a writ of withholding in the court that ordered the spousal maintenance under Subchapter B.[1]

Added by Acts 2001, 77th Leg., ch. 807, § 1, eff. Sept. 1, 2001.

[1] V.T.C.A., Family Code § 8.051.

### § 8.252. Contents of Notice of Application for Writ of Withholding

The notice of application for a writ of withholding must be verified and:

(1) state the amount of monthly maintenance due, including the amount of arrearages or anticipated arrearages, and the amount of disposable earnings to be withheld under a writ of withholding;

(2) state that the withholding applies to each current or subsequent employer or period of employment;

(3) state that the obligor's employer will be notified to begin the withholding if the obligor does not contest the withholding on or before the 10th day after the date the obligor receives the notice;

(4) describe the procedures for contesting the issuance and delivery of a writ of withholding;

(5) state that the obligor will be provided an opportunity for a hearing not later than the 30th day after the date of receipt of the notice of contest if the obligor contests the withholding;

(6) state that the sole ground for successfully contesting the issuance of a writ of withholding is a dispute concerning the identity of the obligor or the existence or amount of the arrearages;

(7) describe the actions that may be taken if the obligor contests the notice of application for a writ of withholding, including the procedures for suspending issuance of a writ of withholding; and

(8) include with the notice a suggested form for the motion to stay issuance and delivery of the writ of withholding that the obligor may file with the clerk of the appropriate court.

Added by Acts 2001, 77th Leg., ch. 807, § 1, eff. Sept. 1, 2001.

### § 8.253. Interstate Request for Withholding

(a) The registration of a foreign order that provides for spousal maintenance or alimony as provided in Chapter 159 is sufficient for filing a notice of application for a writ of withholding.

(b) The notice must be filed with the clerk of the court having venue as provided in Chapter 159.

(c) The notice of application for a writ of withholding may be delivered to the obligor at the same time that an order is filed for registration under Chapter 159.

Added by Acts 2001, 77th Leg., ch. 807, § 1, eff. Sept. 1, 2001.

### § 8.254. Additional Arrearages

If the notice of application for a writ of withholding states that the obligor has failed to pay more than one spousal maintenance payment according to the terms of the spousal maintenance order, the writ of withholding may include withholding for arrearages that accrue between the filing of the notice and the date of the hearing or the issuance of the writ.

Added by Acts 2001, 77th Leg., ch. 807, § 1, eff. Sept. 1, 2001.

### § 8.255. Delivery of Notice of Application for Writ of Withholding; Time of Delivery

(a) The party who files a notice of application for a writ of withholding shall deliver the notice to the obligor by:

(1) first-class or certified mail, return receipt requested, addressed to the obligor's last known address or place of employment; or

(2) service of citation as in civil cases generally.

(b) If the notice is delivered by mail, the party who filed the notice shall file with the court a certificate stating the name, address, and date the party mailed the notice.

(c) The notice is considered to have been received by the obligor:

(1) on the date of receipt, if the notice was mailed by certified mail;

(2) on the 10th day after the date the notice was mailed, if the notice was mailed by first-class mail; or

(3) on the date of service, if the notice was delivered by service of citation.

Added by Acts 2001, 77th Leg., ch. 807, § 1, eff. Sept. 1, 2001.

### § 8.256. Motion to Stay Issuance of Writ of Withholding

(a) The obligor may stay issuance of a writ of withholding by filing a motion to stay with the clerk of the court not later than the 10th day after the date the notice of application for a writ of withholding was received.

(b) The grounds for filing a motion to stay issuance are limited to a dispute concerning the identity of the obligor or the existence or the amount of the arrearages.

(c) The obligor shall verify that the statements of fact in the motion to stay issuance of the writ are correct.

Added by Acts 2001, 77th Leg., ch. 807, § 1, eff. Sept. 1, 2001.

### § 8.257. Effect of Filing Motion to Stay

If the obligor files a motion to stay as provided by Section 8.256, the clerk of the court may not deliver the writ of withholding to the obligor's employer before a hearing is held.

Added by Acts 2001, 77th Leg., ch. 807, § 1, eff. Sept. 1, 2001.

### § 8.258. Hearing on Motion to Stay

(a) If the obligor files a motion to stay as provided by Section 8.256, the court shall set a hearing on the motion and the clerk of the court shall notify the obligor and obligee of the date, time, and place of the hearing.

(b) The court shall hold a hearing on the motion to stay not later than the 30th day after the date the motion was filed unless the obligor and obligee agree and waive the right to have the motion heard within 30 days.

(c) After the hearing, the court shall:

(1) render an order for income withholding that includes a determination of any amount of arrearages; or

(2) grant the motion to stay.

Added by Acts 2001, 77th Leg., ch. 807, § 1, eff. Sept. 1, 2001.

### § 8.259. Special Exceptions

(a) A defect in a notice of application for a writ of withholding is waived unless the respondent specially excepts in writing and cites with particularity the alleged defect, obscurity, or other ambiguity in the notice.

(b) A special exception under this section must be heard by the court before hearing the motion to stay issuance.

(c) If the court sustains an exception, the court shall provide the party filing the notice an opportunity to refile and shall continue the hearing to a specified date without requiring additional service.

Added by Acts 2001, 77th Leg., ch. 807, § 1, eff. Sept. 1, 2001.

### § 8.260. Writ of Withholding After Arrearages Are Paid

(a) The court may not refuse to order withholding solely on the basis that the obligor paid the arrearages after the obligor received the notice of application for a writ of withholding.

(b) The court shall order that a reasonable amount of income be withheld and applied toward the liquidation of arrearages, even though a judgment confirming arrearages was rendered against the obligor.

Added by Acts 2001, 77th Leg., ch. 807, § 1, eff. Sept. 1, 2001.

### § 8.261. Request for Issuance and Delivery of Writ of Withholding

(a) If a notice of application for a writ of withholding is delivered and the obligor does not file a motion to stay within the time provided by Section 8.256, the party who filed the notice shall file with the clerk of the court a request for issuance of the writ of withholding stating the amount of current spousal maintenance, the amount of arrearages, and the amount to be withheld from the obligor's income.

(b) The party who filed the notice may not file a request for issuance before the 11th day after the date the obligor received the notice of application for a writ of withholding.

Added by Acts 2001, 77th Leg., ch. 807, § 1, eff. Sept. 1, 2001.

### § 8.262. Issuance and Delivery of Writ of Withholding

The clerk of the court shall, on the filing of a request for issuance of a writ of withholding, issue and deliver the writ as provided by Subchapter D[1] not later than the second working day after the date the request is filed. The clerk shall charge a fee in the amount of $15 for issuing the writ of withholding.

Added by Acts 2001, 77th Leg., ch. 807, § 1, eff. Sept. 1, 2001.

[1] V.T.C.A., Family Code § 8.151.

### § 8.263. Contents of Writ of Withholding

A writ of withholding must direct that an obligor's employer or a subsequent employer withhold from the obligor's disposable earnings an amount for current spousal maintenance and arrearages consistent with this chapter.

Added by Acts 2001, 77th Leg., ch. 807, § 1, eff. Sept. 1, 2001.

### § 8.264. Extension of Repayment Schedule by Party; Unreasonable Hardship

A party who files a notice of application for a writ of withholding and who determines that the schedule for repaying arrearages would cause unreasonable hardship to the obligor or the obligor's family may extend the payment period in the writ.

Added by Acts 2001, 77th Leg., ch. 807, § 1, eff. Sept. 1, 2001.

### § 8.265. Remittance of Amount to be Withheld

The obligor's employer shall remit the amount withheld to the person or office named in the writ on each pay date and shall include with the remittance the date on which the withholding occurred.

Added by Acts 2001, 77th Leg., ch. 807, § 1, eff. Sept. 1, 2001.

### § 8.266. Failure to Receive Notice of Application for Writ of Withholding

(a) Not later than the 30th day after the date of the first pay period after the date the obligor's employer receives a writ of withholding, the obligor may file an affidavit with the court stating that:

(1) the obligor did not timely file a motion to stay because the obligor did not receive the notice of application for a writ of withholding; and

(2) grounds exist for a motion to stay.

(b) The obligor may:

(1) file with the affidavit a motion to withdraw the writ of withholding; and

(2) request a hearing on the applicability of the writ.

(c) Income withholding may not be interrupted until after the hearing at which the court renders an order denying or modifying withholding.

Added by Acts 2001, 77th Leg., ch. 807, § 1, eff. Sept. 1, 2001.

### § 8.267. Issuance and Delivery of Writ of Withholding to Subsequent Employer

(a) After the clerk of the court issues a writ of withholding, a party authorized to file a notice of application for a writ of withholding under this subchapter may deliver a copy of the writ to a subsequent employer of the obligor by certified mail.

(b) Except as provided by an order under Section 8.152, the writ of withholding must include the name, address, and signature of the party and clearly indicate that the writ is being issued to a subsequent employer.

(c) The party shall file:

(1) a copy of the writ of withholding with the clerk not later than the third working day after the date of delivery of the writ to the subsequent employer; and

(2) the postal return receipt from the delivery to the subsequent employer not later than the third working day after the date the party receives the receipt.

(d) The party shall pay the clerk a fee in the amount of $15 for filing the copy of the writ.

Added by Acts 2001, 77th Leg., ch. 807, § 1, eff. Sept. 1, 2001.

## SUBCHAPTER G. MODIFICATION, REDUCTION, OR TERMINATION OF WITHHOLDING

### § 8.301. Agreement by Parties Regarding Amount or Duration of Withholding

(a) An obligor and obligee may agree to reduce or terminate income withholding for spousal maintenance on the occurrence of any contingency stated in the order.

(b) The obligor and obligee may file a notarized or acknowledged request with the clerk of the court under Section 8.108 for a revised writ of withholding or notice of termination of withholding.

(c) The clerk shall issue and deliver to the obligor's employer a writ of withholding that reflects the agreed revision or a notice of termination of withholding.

(d) An agreement by the parties under this section does not modify the terms of an order for spousal maintenance.

Added by Acts 2001, 77th Leg., ch. 807, § 1, eff. Sept. 1, 2001.

### § 8.302. Modifications to or Termination of Withholding in Voluntary Withholding Cases

(a) If an obligor initiates voluntary withholding under Section 8.108, the obligee may file with the clerk of the court a notarized request signed by the obligor and the obligee for the issuance and delivery to the obligor of:

(1) a modified writ of withholding that reduces the amount of withholding; or

(2) a notice of termination of withholding.

(b) On receipt of a request under this section, the clerk shall issue and deliver a modified writ of withholding or notice of termination in the manner provided by Section 8.301.

(c) The clerk may charge a fee in the amount of $15 for issuing and delivering the modified writ of withholding or notice of termination.

(d) An obligee may contest a modified writ of withholding or notice of termination issued under this section by requesting a hearing in the manner provided by Section 8.258 not later than the 180th day after the date the obligee discovers that the writ or notice was issued.

Added by Acts 2001, 77th Leg., ch. 807, § 1, eff. Sept. 1, 2001.

### § 8.303. Termination of Withholding in Mandatory Withholding Cases

(a) An obligor for whom withholding for maintenance owed or withholding for maintenance and child support owed is mandatory may file a motion to terminate withholding. On a showing by the obligor that the obligor has complied fully with the terms of the maintenance or child support order, as applicable, the court shall render an order for the issuance and delivery to the obligor of a notice of termination of withholding.

(b) The clerk shall issue and deliver the notice of termination ordered under this section to the obligor.

(c) The clerk may charge a fee in the amount of $15 for issuing and delivering the notice.

Added by Acts 2001, 77th Leg., ch. 807, § 1, eff. Sept. 1, 2001.

### § 8.304. Delivery of Order of Reduction or Termination of Withholding

Any person may deliver to the obligor's employer a certified copy of an order that reduces the amount of spousal maintenance to be withheld or terminates the withholding.

Added by Acts 2001, 77th Leg., ch. 807, § 1, eff. Sept. 1, 2001.

### § 8.305. Liability of Employers

The provisions of this chapter regarding the liability of employers for withholding apply to an order that reduces or terminates withholding.

Added by Acts 2001, 77th Leg., ch. 807, § 1, eff. Sept. 1, 2001.

## SUBCHAPTER H. MAINTENANCE QUALIFIED DOMESTIC RELATIONS ORDER

### § 8.351. Jurisdiction for Qualified Domestic Relations Order

(a) The court that rendered an order for the payment of maintenance, or the court that obtains jurisdiction to enforce a maintenance order, has continuing jurisdiction to render enforceable qualified domestic relations orders or similar orders permitting payment of pension, retirement plan, or other employee benefits to an alternate payee or other lawful payee to satisfy amounts due under the maintenance order. A maintenance order includes a temporary or final order for maintenance and arrears and interest with respect to that order.

(b) Unless prohibited by federal law, a suit seeking a qualified domestic relations order or similar order under this subchapter applies to a pension, retirement plan, or other employee benefit, regardless of whether the pension, retirement plan, or other employee benefit:

(1) is private, state, or federal;

(2) is subject to another qualified domestic relations order or similar order;

(3) is property that is the subject of a pending proceeding for dissolution of a marriage;

(4) is property disposed of in a previous decree for dissolution of a marriage; or

(5) is the subject of an agreement under Chapter 4.

(c) A court described by Subsection (a) retains jurisdiction to render a qualified domestic relations order or similar order under this subchapter until all maintenance due under the maintenance order, including arrearages and interest, has been paid.

Added by Acts 2021, 87th Leg., ch. 64 (H.B. 867), § 3, eff. Sept. 1, 2021.

Section 6 of Acts 2021, 87th Leg., ch. 64 (H.B. 867) provides:

"(a) The changes in law made by this Act to Chapters 8, 154, and 157, Family Code, apply to an order for maintenance under Chapter 8, Family Code, or for child support under Chapter 154, Family Code, as applicable, regardless of whether the order was rendered before, on, or after the effective date [Sept. 1, 2021] of this Act.

"(b) The enactment of this Act does not constitute a material and substantial change of circumstances sufficient to warrant modification of a court order or portion of a decree that provides for maintenance or child support rendered before the effective date of this Act."

## § 8.352. Procedure

(a) A party to a maintenance order may petition the court for a qualified domestic relations order or similar order in an original suit or in an action for enforcement of the maintenance order under this chapter.

(b) Each party whose rights may be affected by the petition is entitled to receive notice.

Added by Acts 2021, 87th Leg., ch. 64 (H.B. 867), § 3, eff. Sept. 1, 2021.

Section 6 of Acts 2021, 87th Leg., ch. 64 (H.B. 867) provides:

"(a) The changes in law made by this Act to Chapters 8, 154, and 157, Family Code, apply to an order for maintenance under Chapter 8, Family Code, or for child support under Chapter 154, Family Code, as applicable, regardless of whether the order was rendered before, on, or after the effective date [Sept. 1, 2021] of this Act.

"(b) The enactment of this Act does not constitute a material and substantial change of circumstances sufficient to warrant modification of a court order or portion of a decree that provides for maintenance or child support rendered before the effective date of this Act."

## § 8.353. Temporary Orders

(a) While a suit for a qualified domestic relations order or similar order is pending or during an appeal of an enforcement order, and on the motion of a party or on the court's own motion after notice and hearing, the court may render an appropriate order, including the granting of a temporary restraining order and temporary injunction, for the preservation of the pension, retirement plan, or other employee benefits and protection of the parties as the court considers necessary.

(b) An order under this section is not subject to interlocutory appeal.

Added by Acts 2021, 87th Leg., ch. 64 (H.B. 867), § 3, eff. Sept. 1, 2021.

Section 6 of Acts 2021, 87th Leg., ch. 64 (H.B. 867) provides:

"(a) The changes in law made by this Act to Chapters 8, 154, and 157, Family Code, apply to an order for maintenance under Chapter 8, Family Code, or for child support under Chapter 154, Family Code, as applicable, regardless of whether the order was rendered before, on, or after the effective date [Sept. 1, 2021] of this Act.

"(b) The enactment of this Act does not constitute a material and substantial change of circumstances sufficient to warrant modification of a court order or portion of a decree that provides for maintenance or child support rendered before the effective date of this Act."

## § 8.354. Defective Prior Domestic Relations Order

If a plan administrator or other person acting in an equivalent capacity determines that a domestic relations order does not satisfy the requirements of a qualified domestic relations order or similar order, the court retains continuing jurisdiction over the parties to the extent necessary to render a qualified domestic relations order.

Added by Acts 2021, 87th Leg., ch. 64 (H.B. 867), § 3, eff. Sept. 1, 2021.

Section 6 of Acts 2021, 87th Leg., ch. 64 (H.B. 867) provides:

"(a) The changes in law made by this Act to Chapters 8, 154, and 157, Family Code, apply to an order for maintenance under Chapter 8, Family Code, or for child support under Chapter 154, Family Code, as applicable, regardless of whether the order was rendered before, on, or after the effective date [Sept. 1, 2021] of this Act.

"(b) The enactment of this Act does not constitute a material and substantial change of circumstances sufficient to warrant modification of a court order or portion of a decree that provides for maintenance or child support rendered before the effective date of this Act."

## § 8.355. Amendment of Qualified Domestic Relations Order

(a) A court that renders a qualified domestic relations order or similar order retains continuing jurisdiction:

(1) to amend the order to correct the order, clarify the terms of the order, or add language to the order to provide for the collection of maintenance;

(2) to convert the amount or frequency of payments under the order to a formula that is in compliance with the terms of the pension, retirement plan, or employee benefit plan; or

(3) to vacate or terminate the order.

(b) An amended domestic relations order or similar order under this section must be submitted to the plan administrator or other person acting in an equivalent capacity to determine whether the amended order satisfies the requirements of a qualified domestic relations order or similar order. Section 8.354 applies to an order amended under this section.

Added by Acts 2021, 87th Leg., ch. 64 (H.B. 867), § 3, eff. Sept. 1, 2021.

Section 6 of Acts 2021, 87th Leg., ch. 64 (H.B. 867) provides:

"(a) The changes in law made by this Act to Chapters 8, 154, and 157, Family Code, apply to an order for maintenance under Chapter 8, Family Code, or for child support under Chapter 154, Family Code, as applicable, regardless of whether the order was rendered before, on, or after the effective date [Sept. 1, 2021] of this Act.

"(b) The enactment of this Act does not constitute a material and substantial change of circumstances sufficient to warrant modification of a court order or portion of a decree that provides for maintenance or child support rendered before the effective date of this Act."

## § 8.356. Liberal Construction

The court shall liberally construe this subchapter to effect payment of pension, retirement plan, or other employee benefits for the satisfaction of the obligor's maintenance obligation.

Added by Acts 2021, 87th Leg., ch. 64 (H.B. 867), § 3, eff. Sept. 1, 2021.

Section 6 of Acts 2021, 87th Leg., ch. 64 (H.B. 867) provides:

"(a) The changes in law made by this Act to Chapters 8, 154, and 157, Family Code, apply to an order for maintenance under Chapter 8, Family Code, or for child support under Chapter 154, Family Code, as applicable, regardless of whether the order was rendered before, on, or after the effective date [Sept. 1, 2021] of this Act.

"(b) The enactment of this Act does not constitute a material and substantial change of circumstances sufficient to warrant modification of a court order or portion of a decree that provides for maintenance or child support rendered before the effective date of this Act."

## § 8.357. Attorney's Fees and Costs

(a) In a proceeding under this subchapter, the court may order the obligor to pay reasonable attorney's fees incurred by a party to obtain the order, all court costs, and all fees charged by a plan administrator for the qualified domestic relations order or similar order.

(b) Fees and costs ordered under this section may be enforced by any means available for the enforcement of a judgment for debt.

Added by Acts 2021, 87th Leg., ch. 64 (H.B. 867), § 3, eff. Sept. 1, 2021.

Section 6 of Acts 2021, 87th Leg., ch. 64 (H.B. 867) provides:

"(a) The changes in law made by this Act to Chapters 8, 154, and 157, Family Code, apply to an order for maintenance under Chapter 8, Family Code, or for child support under Chapter 154, Family Code, as applicable, regardless of whether the order was rendered before, on, or after the effective date [Sept. 1, 2021] of this Act.

"(b) The enactment of this Act does not constitute a material and substantial change of circumstances sufficient to warrant modification of a court order or portion of a decree that provides for maintenance or child support rendered before the effective date of this Act."

## § 8.358. Direct Payment

Payments under a qualified domestic relations order under this subchapter may be made by direct payment or other method ordered by the court.

Added by Acts 2021, 87th Leg., ch. 64 (H.B. 867), § 3, eff. Sept. 1, 2021.

Section 6 of Acts 2021, 87th Leg., ch. 64 (H.B. 867) provides:

"(a) The changes in law made by this Act to Chapters 8, 154, and 157, Family Code, apply to an order for maintenance under Chapter 8, Family Code, or for child support under Chapter 154, Family Code, as applicable, regardless of whether the order was rendered before, on, or after the effective date [Sept. 1, 2021] of this Act.

"(b) The enactment of this Act does not constitute a material and substantial change of circumstances sufficient to warrant modification of a court order or portion of a decree that provides for maintenance or child support rendered before the effective date of this Act."

## § 8.359. Conflicts With Other Law

(a) To the extent of a conflict between this subchapter and Chapter 804, Government Code, Chapter 804, Government Code, prevails.

(b) To the extent of a conflict between this subchapter and federal law, the federal law prevails.

Added by Acts 2021, 87th Leg., ch. 64 (H.B. 867), § 3, eff. Sept. 1, 2021.

Section 6 of Acts 2021, 87th Leg., ch. 64 (H.B. 867) provides:

"(a) The changes in law made by this Act to Chapters 8, 154, and 157, Family Code, apply to an order for maintenance under Chapter 8, Family Code, or for child support under Chapter 154, Family Code, as applicable, regardless of whether the order was rendered before, on, or after the effective date [Sept. 1, 2021] of this Act.

"(b) The enactment of this Act does not constitute a material and substantial change of circumstances sufficient to warrant modification of a court order or portion of a decree that provides for maintenance or child support rendered before the effective date of this Act."

# CHAPTER 9. POST-DECREE PROCEEDINGS

## SUBCHAPTER A. SUIT TO ENFORCE DECREE

**Section**

## SUBCHAPTER A. SUIT TO ENFORCE DECREE

### § 9.001. Enforcement of Decree

(a) A party affected by a decree of divorce or annulment providing for a division of property as provided by Chapter 7, including a division of property and any contractual provisions under the terms of an agreement incident to divorce or annulment under Section 7.006 that was approved by the court, may request enforcement of that decree by filing a suit to enforce as provided by this chapter in the court that rendered the decree.

(b) Except as otherwise provided in this chapter, a suit to enforce shall be governed by the Texas Rules of Civil Procedure applicable to the filing of an original lawsuit.

(c) A party whose rights, duties, powers, or liabilities may be affected by the suit to enforce is entitled to receive notice by citation and shall be commanded to appear by filing a written answer. Thereafter, the proceedings shall be as in civil cases generally.

Added by Acts 1997, 75th Leg., ch. 7, § 1, eff. April 17, 1997. Amended by Acts 2013, 83rd Leg., ch. 242 (H.B. 389), § 5, eff. Sept. 1, 2013.

### § 9.002. Continuing Authority to Enforce Decree

The court that rendered the decree of divorce or annulment retains the power to enforce the property division as provided by Chapter 7, including a property division and any contractual provisions under the terms of an agreement incident to divorce or annulment under Section 7.006 that was approved by the court.

Added by Acts 1997, 75th Leg., ch. 7, § 1, eff. April 17, 1997. Amended by Acts 2013, 83rd Leg., ch. 242 (H.B. 389), § 6, eff. Sept. 1, 2013.

### § 9.003. Filing Deadlines

(a) A suit to enforce the division of tangible personal property in existence at the time of the decree of divorce or annulment must be filed before the second anniversary of the date the decree was signed or becomes final after appeal, whichever date is later, or the suit is barred.

(b) A suit to enforce the division of future property not in existence at the time of the original decree must be filed before the second anniversary of the date the right to the property matures or accrues or the decree becomes final, whichever date is later, or the suit is barred.

Added by Acts 1997, 75th Leg., ch. 7, § 1, eff. April 17, 1997.

### § 9.004. Applicability to Undivided Property

The procedures and limitations of this subchapter do not apply to existing property not divided on divorce, which are governed by Subchapter C [1] and by the rules applicable to civil cases generally.

Added by Acts 1997, 75th Leg., ch. 7, § 1, eff. April 17, 1997.

[1] V.T.C.A., Family Code § 9.201 et seq.

### § 9.005. No Jury

A party may not demand a jury trial if the procedures to enforce a decree of divorce or annulment provided by this subchapter are invoked.

Added by Acts 1997, 75th Leg., ch. 7, § 1, eff. April 17, 1997.

### § 9.006. Enforcement of Division of Property

(a) Except as provided by this subchapter and by the Texas Rules of Civil Procedure, the court may render further orders to enforce the division of property made or approved in the decree of divorce or annulment to assist in the implementation of or to clarify the prior order.

(b) The court may specify more precisely the manner of effecting the property division previously made or approved if the substantive division of property is not altered or changed.

(c) An order of enforcement does not alter or affect the finality of the decree of divorce or annulment being enforced.

Added by Acts 1997, 75th Leg., ch. 7, § 1, eff. April 17, 1997. Amended by Acts 2013, 83rd Leg., ch. 242 (H.B. 389), § 7, eff. Sept. 1, 2013.

### § 9.007. Limitation on Power of Court to Enforce

(a) A court may not amend, modify, alter, or change the division of property made or approved in the decree of divorce or annulment. An order to enforce the division is limited to an order to assist in the implementation of or to clarify the prior order and may not alter or change the substantive division of property.

(b) An order under this section that amends, modifies, alters, or changes the actual, substantive division of property made or approved in a final decree of divorce or annulment is beyond the power of the divorce court and is unenforceable.

(c) The trial court may not render an order to assist in the implementation of or to clarify the property division made or approved in the decree before the 30th day after the date the final judgment is signed. If a timely motion for new trial or to vacate, modify, correct, or reform the decree is filed, the trial court may not render an order to assist in the implementation of or to clarify the property division made or approved in the decree before the 30th day after the date the order overruling the motion is signed or the motion is overruled by operation of law.

Added by Acts 1997, 75th Leg., ch. 7, § 1, eff. April 17, 1997. Amended by Acts 2017, 85th Leg., ch. 421 (S.B. 1237), § 3, eff. Sept. 1, 2017.

### § 9.008. Clarification Order

(a) On the request of a party or on the court's own motion, the court may render a clarifying order before a motion for contempt is made or heard, in conjunction with a motion for contempt or on denial of a motion for contempt.

(b) On a finding by the court that the original form of the division of property is not specific enough to be enforceable by contempt, the court may render a clarifying order setting forth specific terms to enforce compliance with the original division of property.

(c) The court may not give retroactive effect to a clarifying order.

(d) The court shall provide a reasonable time for compliance before enforcing a clarifying order by contempt or in another manner.

Added by Acts 1997, 75th Leg., ch. 7, § 1, eff. April 17, 1997.

### § 9.009. Delivery of Property

To enforce the division of property made or approved in a decree of divorce or annulment, the court may make an order to deliver the specific existing property awarded, without regard to whether the property is of especial value, including an award of an existing sum of money or its equivalent.

Added by Acts 1997, 75th Leg., ch. 7, § 1, eff. April 17, 1997. Amended by Acts 2013, 83rd Leg., ch. 242 (H.B. 389), § 8, eff. Sept. 1, 2013.

### § 9.010. Reduction to Money Judgment

(a) If a party fails to comply with a decree of divorce or annulment and delivery of property awarded in the decree is no longer an adequate remedy, the court may render a money judgment for the damages caused by that failure to comply.

(b) If a party did not receive payments of money as awarded in the decree of divorce or annulment, the court may render judgment against a defaulting party for the amount of unpaid payments to which the party is entitled.

(c) The remedy of a reduction to money judgment is in addition to the other remedies provided by law.

(d) A money judgment rendered under this section may be enforced by any means available for the enforcement of judgment for debt.

Added by Acts 1997, 75th Leg., ch. 7, § 1, eff. April 17, 1997.

### § 9.011. Right to Future Property

(a) The court may, by any remedy provided by this chapter, enforce an award of the right to receive installment payments or a lump-sum payment due on the maturation of an existing vested or nonvested right to be paid in the future.

(b) The subsequent actual receipt by the non-owning party of property awarded to the owner in a decree of divorce or annulment creates a fiduciary obligation in favor of the owner and imposes a constructive trust on the property for the benefit of the owner.

Added by Acts 1997, 75th Leg., ch. 7, § 1, eff. April 17, 1997.

### § 9.012. Contempt

(a) The court may enforce by contempt an order requiring delivery of specific property or an award of a right to future property.

(b) The court may not enforce by contempt an award in a decree of divorce or annulment of a sum of money payable in a lump sum or in future installment payments in the nature of debt, except for:

(1) a sum of money in existence at the time the decree was rendered; or

(2) a matured right to future payments as provided by Section 9.011.

(c) This subchapter does not detract from or limit the general power of a court to enforce an order of the court by appropriate means.

Added by Acts 1997, 75th Leg., ch. 7, § 1, eff. April 17, 1997.

### § 9.013. Costs

The court may award costs in a proceeding to enforce a property division under this subchapter as in other civil cases.

Added by Acts 1997, 75th Leg., ch. 7, § 1, eff. April 17, 1997.

### § 9.014. Attorney's Fees

The court may award reasonable attorney's fees in a proceeding under this subchapter. The court may order the attorney's fees to be paid directly to the attorney, who may enforce the order for fees in the attorney's own name by any means available for the enforcement of a judgment for debt.

Added by Acts 1997, 75th Leg., ch. 7, § 1, eff. April 17, 1997. Amended by Acts 2009, 81st Leg., ch. 768, § 8, eff. Sept. 1, 2009.

## SUBCHAPTER B. POST-DECREE QUALIFIED DOMESTIC RELATIONS ORDER

### § 9.101. Jurisdiction for Qualified Domestic Relations Order

(a) Notwithstanding any other provision of this chapter, the court that rendered a final decree of divorce or annulment or another final order dividing property under this title retains continuing, exclusive jurisdiction to render an enforceable qualified domestic relations order or similar order permitting payment of pension, retirement plan, or other employee benefits divisible under the law of this state or of the United States to an alternate payee or other lawful payee.

(b) Unless prohibited by federal law, a suit seeking a qualified domestic relations order or similar order under this section applies to a previously divided pension, retirement plan, or other employee benefit divisible under the law of this state or of the United States, whether the plan or benefit is private, state, or federal.

Added by Acts 1997, 75th Leg., ch. 7, § 1, eff. April 17, 1997.

### § 9.102. Procedure

(a) A party to a decree of divorce or annulment may petition the court for a qualified domestic relations order or similar order.

(b) Except as otherwise provided by this code, a petition under this subchapter is governed by the Texas Rules of Civil Procedure that apply to the filing of an original lawsuit.

(c) Each party whose rights may be affected by the petition is entitled to receive notice by citation and shall be commanded to appear by filing a written answer.

(d) The proceedings shall be conducted in the same manner as civil cases generally.

Added by Acts 1997, 75th Leg., ch. 7, § 1, eff. April 17, 1997.

### § 9.103. Prior Failure to Render Qualified Domestic Relations Order

A party may petition a court to render a qualified domestic relations order or similar order if the court that rendered a final decree of divorce or annulment or another final order dividing property under this chapter did not provide a qualified domestic relations order or similar order permitting payment of benefits to an alternate payee or other lawful payee.

Added by Acts 1997, 75th Leg., ch. 7, § 1, eff. April 17, 1997.

### § 9.104. Defective Prior Domestic Relations Order

If a plan administrator or other person acting in an equivalent capacity determines that a domestic relations order does not satisfy the requirements of a qualified domestic relations order or similar order, the court retains continuing, exclusive jurisdiction over the parties and their property to the extent necessary to render a qualified domestic relations order.

Added by Acts 1997, 75th Leg., ch. 7, § 1, eff. April 17, 1997.

### § 9.1045. Amendment of Qualified Domestic Relations Order

(a) A court that renders a qualified domestic relations order retains continuing, exclusive jurisdiction to amend the order to correct the order or clarify the terms of the order to effectuate the division of property ordered by the court.

(b) An amended domestic relations order under this section must be submitted to the plan administrator or other person acting in an equivalent capacity to determine whether the amended order satisfies the requirements of a qualified domestic relations order. Section 9.104 applies to a domestic relations order amended under this section.

Added by Acts 2005, 79th Leg., ch. 481, § 1, eff. June 17, 2005.

### § 9.105. Liberal Construction

The court shall liberally construe this subchapter to effect payment of retirement benefits that were divided by a previous decree that failed to contain a qualified domestic relations order or similar order or that contained an order that failed to meet the requirements of a qualified domestic relations order or similar order.

Added by Acts 1997, 75th Leg., ch. 7, § 1, eff. April 17, 1997.

### § 9.106. Attorney's Fees

In a proceeding under this subchapter, the court may award reasonable attorney's fees incurred by a party to a divorce or annulment against the other party to the divorce or annulment. The court may order the attorney's fees to be paid directly to the attorney, who may enforce the order for fees in the attorney's own name by any means available for the enforcement of a judgment for debt.

Added by Acts 2009, 81st Leg., ch. 768, § 9, eff. Sept. 1, 2009.

## SUBCHAPTER C. POST-DECREE DIVISION OF PROPERTY

### § 9.201. Procedure for Division of Certain Property Not Divided on Divorce or Annulment

(a) Either former spouse may file a suit as provided by this subchapter to divide property not divided or awarded to a spouse in a final decree of divorce or annulment.

(b) Except as otherwise provided by this subchapter, the suit is governed by the Texas Rules of Civil Procedure applicable to the filing of an original lawsuit.

Added by Acts 1997, 75th Leg., ch. 7, § 1, eff. April 17, 1997.

### § 9.202. Limitations

(a) A suit under this subchapter must be filed before the second anniversary of the date a former spouse unequivocally repudiates the existence of the ownership interest of the other former spouse and communicates that repudiation to the other former spouse.

(b) The two-year limitations period is tolled for the period that a court of this state does not have jurisdiction over the former spouses or over the property.

Added by Acts 1997, 75th Leg., ch. 7, § 1, eff. April 17, 1997.

### § 9.203. Division of Undivided Assets When Prior Court Had Jurisdiction

(a) If a court of this state failed to dispose of property subject to division in a final decree of divorce or annulment even though the court had jurisdiction over the spouses or over the property, the court shall divide the property in a manner that the court deems just and right, having due regard for the rights of each party and any children of the marriage.

(b) If a final decree of divorce or annulment rendered by a court in another state failed to dispose of property subject to division under the law of that state even though the court had jurisdiction to do so, a court of this state shall apply the law of the other state regarding undivided property as required by Section 1, Article IV, United States Constitution (the full faith and credit clause), and enabling federal statutes.

Added by Acts 1997, 75th Leg., ch. 7, § 1, eff. April 17, 1997.

### § 9.204. Division of Undivided Assets When Prior Court Lacked Jurisdiction

(a) If a court of this state failed to dispose of property subject to division in a final decree of divorce or annulment because the court lacked jurisdiction over a spouse or the property, and if that court subsequently acquires the requisite jurisdiction, that court may divide the property in a manner that the court deems just and right, having due regard for the rights of each party and any children of the marriage.

(b) If a final decree of divorce or annulment rendered by a court in another state failed to dispose of property subject to division under the law of that state because the court lacked jurisdiction over a spouse or the property, and if a court of this state subsequently acquires the requisite jurisdiction over the former spouses or over the property, the court in this state may divide the property in a manner that the court deems just and right, having due regard for the rights of each party and any children of the marriage.

Added by Acts 1997, 75th Leg., ch. 7, § 1, eff. April 17, 1997.

### § 9.205. Attorney's Fees

In a proceeding to divide property previously undivided in a decree of divorce or annulment as provided by this subchapter, the court may award reasonable attorney's fees. The court may order the attorney's fees to be paid directly to the attorney, who may enforce the order in the attorney's own name by any means available for the enforcement of a judgment for debt.

Added by Acts 1997, 75th Leg., ch. 7, § 1, eff. April 17, 1997. Amended by Acts 2009, 81st Leg., ch. 768, § 10, eff. Sept. 1, 2009.

## SUBCHAPTER D. DISPOSITION OF UNDIVIDED BENEFICIAL INTEREST

### § 9.301. Pre-Decree Designation of Ex-Spouse as Beneficiary of Life Insurance

(a) If a decree of divorce or annulment is rendered after an insured has designated the insured's spouse as a beneficiary under a life insurance policy in force at the time of rendition, a provision in the policy in favor of the insured's former spouse is not effective unless:

(1) the decree designates the insured's former spouse as the beneficiary;

(2) the insured redesignates the former spouse as the beneficiary after rendition of the decree; or

(3) the former spouse is designated to receive the proceeds in trust for, on behalf of, or for the benefit of a child or a dependent of either former spouse.

(b) If a designation is not effective under Subsection (a), the proceeds of the policy are payable to the named alternative beneficiary or, if there is not a named alternative beneficiary, to the estate of the insured.

(c) An insurer who pays the proceeds of a life insurance policy issued by the insurer to the beneficiary under a designation that is not effective under Subsection (a) is liable for payment of the proceeds to the person or estate provided by Subsection (b) only if:

(1) before payment of the proceeds to the designated beneficiary, the insurer receives written notice at the home office of the insurer from an interested person that the designation is not effective under Subsection (a); and

(2) the insurer has not interpleaded the proceeds into the registry of a court of competent jurisdiction in accordance with the Texas Rules of Civil Procedure.

Added by Acts 1997, 75th Leg., ch. 7, § 1, eff. April 17, 1997.

### § 9.302. Pre-Decree Designation of Ex-Spouse as Beneficiary in Retirement Benefits and Other Financial Plans

(a) If a decree of divorce or annulment is rendered after a spouse, acting in the capacity of a participant, annuitant, or account holder, has designated the other spouse as a beneficiary under an individual retirement account, employee stock option plan, stock option, or other form of savings, bonus, profit-sharing, or other employer plan or financial plan of an employee or a participant in force at the time of rendition, the designating provision in the plan in favor of the other former spouse is not effective unless:

(1) the decree designates the other former spouse as the beneficiary;

(2) the designating former spouse redesignates the other former spouse as the beneficiary after rendition of the decree; or

(3) the other former spouse is designated to receive the proceeds or benefits in trust for, on behalf of, or for the benefit of a child or dependent of either former spouse.

(b) If a designation is not effective under Subsection (a), the benefits or proceeds are payable to the named alternative beneficiary or, if there is not a named alternative beneficiary, to the designating former spouse.

(c) A business entity, employer, pension trust, insurer, financial institution, or other person obligated to pay retirement benefits or proceeds of a financial plan covered by this section who pays the benefits or proceeds to the beneficiary under a designation of the other former spouse that is not effective under Subsection (a) is liable for payment of the benefits or proceeds to the person provided by Subsection (b) only if:

(1) before payment of the benefits or proceeds to the designated beneficiary, the payor receives written notice at the home office or principal office of the payor from an interested person that the designation of the beneficiary or fiduciary is not effective under Subsection (a); and

(2) the payor has not interpleaded the benefits or proceeds into the registry of a court of competent jurisdiction in accordance with the Texas Rules of Civil Procedure.

(d) This section does not affect the right of a former spouse to assert an ownership interest in an undivided pension, retirement, annuity, or other financial plan described by this section as provided by this subchapter.

(e) This section does not apply to the disposition of a beneficial interest in a retirement benefit or other financial plan of a public retirement system as defined by Section 802.001, Government Code.

Added by Acts 1997, 75th Leg., ch. 7, § 1, eff. April 17, 1997.

# TITLE 1-A. COLLABORATIVE FAMILY LAW

## CHAPTER 11. REMOVAL OF DISABILITIES OF MINORITY [REPEALED]

*Chapter 11 was part of a former Title 2, Parent and Child, and was repealed as part of the reenactment of Title 2 by Acts 1995, 74th Leg., ch. 20.*

**§§ 11.01 to 11.75. Repealed by Acts 1995, 74th Leg., ch. 20, § 2, eff. April 20, 1995**

## CHAPTER 12. THE PARENT—CHILD RELATIONSHIP [REPEALED]

*Chapter 12 was part of a former Title 2, Parent and Child, and was repealed as part of the reenactment of Title 2 by Acts 1995, 74th Leg., ch. 20.*

**§§ 12.01 to 12.06. Repealed by Acts 1995, 74th Leg., ch. 20, § 2, eff. April 20, 1995**

## CHAPTER 13. DETERMINATION OF PATERNITY [REPEALED]

*Chapter 13 was part of a former Title 2, Parent and Child, and was repealed as part of the reenactment of Title 2 by Acts 1995, 74th Leg., ch. 20.*

**§§ 13.01 to 13.44. Repealed by Acts 1995, 74th Leg., ch. 20, § 2, eff. April 20, 1995**

## CHAPTER 14. CONSERVATORSHIP, POSSESSION AND SUPPORT OF CHILDREN [REPEALED]

*Chapter 14 was part of a former Title 2, Parent and Child, and was repealed as part of the reenactment of Title 2 by Acts 1995, 74th Leg., ch. 20.*

**§§ 14.01 to 14.983. Repealed by Acts 1995, 74th Leg., ch. 20, § 2, eff. April 20, 1995**

## CHAPTER 15. COLLABORATIVE FAMILY LAW ACT



*A former Chapter 15, Termination of the Parent-Child Relationship and of the Rights of an Alleged or Probable Father, consisting of §§ 15.01 to 15.07, was repealed by Acts 1995, 74th Leg., ch. 20, § 2, effective April 20, 1995, as part of the reenactment of Title 2.*

### SUBCHAPTER A. APPLICATION AND CONSTRUCTION

**§ 15.001. Policy**

It is the policy of this state to encourage the peaceable resolution of disputes, with special consideration given to disputes involving the parent-child relationship, including disputes involving the conservatorship of, possession of or access to, and support of a child, and the early settlement of pending litigation through voluntary settlement procedures.

Added by Acts 2011, 82nd Leg., ch. 1048 (H.B. 3833), § 1, eff. Sept. 1, 2011.

### § 15.002. Conflicts Between Provisions

If a provision of this chapter conflicts with another provision of this code or another statute or rule of this state and the conflict cannot be reconciled, this chapter prevails.

Added by Acts 2011, 82nd Leg., ch. 1048 (H.B. 3833), § 1, eff. Sept. 1, 2011.

### § 15.003. Uniformity of Application and Construction

In applying and construing this chapter, consideration must be given to the need to promote uniformity of the law with respect to its subject matter among states that enact a collaborative law process Act for family law matters.

Added by Acts 2011, 82nd Leg., ch. 1048 (H.B. 3833), § 1, eff. Sept. 1, 2011.

### § 15.004. Relation to Electronic Signatures in Global and National Commerce Act

This chapter modifies, limits, and supersedes the federal Electronic Signatures in Global and National Commerce Act (15 U.S.C. Section 7001 et seq.) but does not modify, limit, or supersede Section 101(c) of that Act (15 U.S.C. Section 7001(c)), or authorize electronic delivery of any of the notices described in Section 103(b) of that Act (15 U.S.C. Section 7003(b)).

Added by Acts 2011, 82nd Leg., ch. 1048 (H.B. 3833), § 1, eff. Sept. 1, 2011.

## SUBCHAPTER B. GENERAL PROVISIONS

### § 15.051. Short Title

This chapter may be cited as the Collaborative Family Law Act.

Added by Acts 2011, 82nd Leg., ch. 1048 (H.B. 3833), § 1, eff. Sept. 1, 2011.

### § 15.052. Definitions

In this chapter:

(1) "Collaborative family law communication" means a statement made by a party or nonparty participant, whether oral or in a record, or verbal or nonverbal, that:

(A) is made to conduct, participate in, continue, or reconvene a collaborative family law process; and

(B) occurs after the parties sign a collaborative family law participation agreement and before the collaborative family law process is concluded.

(2) "Collaborative family law participation agreement" means an agreement by persons to participate in a collaborative family law process.

(3) "Collaborative family law matter" means a dispute, transaction, claim, problem, or issue for resolution that arises under Title 1 or 5[1] and that is described in a collaborative family law participation agreement. The term includes a dispute, claim, or issue in a proceeding.

(4) "Collaborative family law process" means a procedure intended to resolve a collaborative family law matter without intervention by a tribunal in which parties:

(A) sign a collaborative family law participation agreement; and

(B) are represented by collaborative family law lawyers.

(5) "Collaborative lawyer" means a lawyer who represents a party in a collaborative family law process.

(6) "Law firm" means:

(A) lawyers who practice law together in a partnership, professional corporation, sole proprietorship, limited liability company, or association; and

(B) lawyers employed in a legal services organization or in the legal department of a corporation or other organization or of a government or governmental subdivision, agency, or instrumentality.

(7) "Nonparty participant" means a person, including a collaborative lawyer, other than a party, who participates in a collaborative family law process.

(8) "Party" means a person who signs a collaborative family law participation agreement and whose consent is necessary to resolve a collaborative family law matter.

(9) "Proceeding" means a judicial, administrative, arbitral, or other adjudicative process before a tribunal, including related prehearing and posthearing motions, conferences, and discovery.

(10) "Prospective party" means a person who discusses with a prospective collaborative lawyer the possibility of signing a collaborative family law participation agreement.

(11) "Record" means information that is inscribed on a tangible medium or that is stored in an electronic or other medium and is retrievable in perceivable form.

(12) "Related to a collaborative family law matter" means a matter involving the same parties,

transaction or occurrence, nucleus of operative fact, dispute, claim, or issue as the collaborative family law matter.

(13) "Sign" means, with present intent to authenticate or adopt a record, to:

(A) execute or adopt a tangible symbol; or

(B) attach to or logically associate with the record an electronic symbol, sound, or process.

(14) "Tribunal" means a court, arbitrator, administrative agency, or other body acting in an adjudicative capacity that, after presentation of evidence or legal argument, has jurisdiction to render a decision affecting a party's interests in a matter.

Added by Acts 2011, 82nd Leg., ch. 1048 (H.B. 3833), § 1, eff. Sept. 1, 2011.

[1] V.T.C.A., Family Code § 1.001 et seq. or V.T.C.A., Family Code § 101.001 et seq.

### § 15.053. Applicability

This chapter applies only to a matter arising under Title 1 or 5.[1]

Added by Acts 2011, 82nd Leg., ch. 1048 (H.B. 3833), § 1, eff. Sept. 1, 2011.

[1] V.T.C.A., Family Code § 1.001 et seq., or V.T.C.A., Family Code § 101.001 et seq.

## SUBCHAPTER C. COLLABORATIVE FAMILY LAW PROCESS

### § 15.101. Requirements for Collaborative Family Law Participation Agreement

(a) A collaborative family law participation agreement must:

(1) be in a record;

(2) be signed by the parties;

(3) state the parties' intent to resolve a collaborative family law matter through a collaborative family law process under this chapter;

(4) describe the nature and scope of the collaborative family law matter;

(5) identify the collaborative lawyer who represents each party in the collaborative family law process; and

(6) contain a statement by each collaborative lawyer confirming the lawyer's representation of a party in the collaborative family law process.

(b) A collaborative family law participation agreement must include provisions for:

(1) suspending tribunal intervention in the collaborative family law matter while the parties are using the collaborative family law process; and

(2) unless otherwise agreed in writing, jointly engaging any professionals, experts, or advisors serving in a neutral capacity.

(c) Parties may agree to include in a collaborative family law participation agreement additional provisions not inconsistent with this chapter.

Added by Acts 2011, 82nd Leg., ch. 1048 (H.B. 3833), § 1, eff. Sept. 1, 2011.

### § 15.102. Beginning and Concluding Collaborative Family Law Process

(a) A collaborative family law process begins when the parties sign a collaborative family law participation agreement.

(b) A tribunal may not order a party to participate in a collaborative family law process over that party's objection.

(c) A collaborative family law process is concluded by:

(1) resolution of a collaborative family law matter as evidenced by a signed record;

(2) resolution of a part of a collaborative family law matter, evidenced by a signed record, in which the parties agree that the remaining parts of the matter will not be resolved in the process; or

(3) termination of the process under Subsection (d).

(d) A collaborative family law process terminates:

(1) when a party gives notice to other parties in a record that the process is ended;

(2) when a party:

(A) begins a proceeding related to a collaborative family law matter without the agreement of all parties; or

(B) in a pending proceeding related to the matter:

(i) without the agreement of all parties, initiates a pleading, motion, or request for a conference with the tribunal;

(ii) initiates an order to show cause or requests that the proceeding be put on the tribunal's active calendar; or

(iii) takes similar action requiring notice to be sent to the parties; or

(3) except as otherwise provided by Subsection (g), when a party discharges a collaborative lawyer

or a collaborative lawyer withdraws from further representation of a party.

(e) A party's collaborative lawyer shall give prompt notice in a record to all other parties of the collaborative lawyer's discharge or withdrawal.

(f) A party may terminate a collaborative family law process with or without cause.

(g) Notwithstanding the discharge or withdrawal of a collaborative lawyer, a collaborative family law process continues if, not later than the 30th day after the date the notice of the collaborative lawyer's discharge or withdrawal required by Subsection (e) is sent to the parties:

(1) the unrepresented party engages a successor collaborative lawyer; and

(2) in a signed record:

(A) the parties consent to continue the process by reaffirming the collaborative family law participation agreement;

(B) the agreement is amended to identify the successor collaborative lawyer; and

(C) the successor collaborative lawyer confirms the lawyer's representation of a party in the collaborative process.

(h) A collaborative family law process does not conclude if, with the consent of the parties to a signed record resolving all or part of the collaborative matter, a party requests a tribunal to approve a resolution of the collaborative family law matter or any part of that matter as evidenced by a signed record.

(i) A collaborative family law participation agreement may provide additional methods of concluding a collaborative family law process.

Added by Acts 2011, 82nd Leg., ch. 1048 (H.B. 3833), § 1, eff. Sept. 1, 2011.

### § 15.103. Proceedings Pending Before Tribunal; Status Report

(a) The parties to a proceeding pending before a tribunal may sign a collaborative family law participation agreement to seek to resolve a collaborative family law matter related to the proceeding. The parties shall file promptly with the tribunal a notice of the agreement after the agreement is signed. Subject to Subsection (c) and Sections 15.104 and 15.105, the filing operates as a stay of the proceeding.

(b) A tribunal that is notified, not later than the 30th day before the date of a proceeding, that the parties are using the collaborative family law process to attempt to settle a collaborative family law matter may not, until a party notifies the tribunal that the collaborative family law process did not result in a settlement:

(1) set a proceeding or a hearing in the collaborative family law matter;

(2) impose discovery deadlines;

(3) require compliance with scheduling orders; or

(4) dismiss the proceeding.

(c) The parties shall notify the tribunal in a pending proceeding if the collaborative family law process results in a settlement. If the collaborative family law process does not result in a settlement, the parties shall file a status report:

(1) not later than the 180th day after the date the collaborative family law participation agreement was signed or, if the proceeding was filed by agreement after the collaborative family law participation agreement was signed, not later than the 180th day after the date the proceeding was filed; and

(2) on or before the first anniversary of the date the collaborative family law participation agreement was signed or, if the proceeding was filed by agreement after the collaborative family law participation agreement was signed, on or before the first anniversary of the date the proceeding was filed, accompanied by a motion for continuance.

(d) The tribunal shall grant a motion for continuance filed under Subsection (c)(2) if the status report indicates that the parties desire to continue to use the collaborative family law process.

(e) If the collaborative family law process does not result in a settlement on or before the second anniversary of the date the proceeding was filed, the tribunal may:

(1) set the proceeding for trial on the regular docket; or

(2) dismiss the proceeding without prejudice.

(f) Each party shall file promptly with the tribunal notice in a record when a collaborative family law process concludes. The stay of the proceeding under Subsection (a) is lifted when the notice is filed. The notice may not specify any reason for termination of the process.

(g) A tribunal in which a proceeding is stayed under Subsection (a) may require the parties and collaborative lawyers to provide a status report on the collaborative family law process and the proceeding. A status report:

(1) may include only information on whether the process is ongoing or concluded; and

(2) may not include a report, assessment, evaluation, recommendation, finding, or other communication regarding a collaborative family law process or collaborative family law matter.

(h) A tribunal may not consider a communication made in violation of Subsection (g).

(i) A tribunal shall provide parties notice and an opportunity to be heard before dismissing a proceeding based on delay or failure to prosecute in which a notice of collaborative family law process is filed.

Added by Acts 2011, 82nd Leg., ch. 1048 (H.B. 3833), § 1, eff. Sept. 1, 2011.

### § 15.104. Emergency Order

During a collaborative family law process, a tribunal may issue an emergency order to protect the health, safety, welfare, or interest of a party or a family, as defined by Section 71.003. If the emergency order is granted without the agreement of all parties, the granting of the order terminates the collaborative process.

Added by Acts 2011, 82nd Leg., ch. 1048 (H.B. 3833), § 1, eff. Sept. 1, 2011.

### § 15.105. Effect of Written Settlement Agreement

(a) A settlement agreement under this chapter is enforceable in the same manner as a written settlement agreement under Section 154.071, Civil Practice and Remedies Code.

(b) Notwithstanding Rule 11, Texas Rules of Civil Procedure, or another rule or law, a party is entitled to judgment on a collaborative family law settlement agreement if the agreement:

(1) provides, in a prominently displayed statement that is in boldfaced type, capitalized, or underlined, that the agreement is not subject to revocation; and

(2) is signed by each party to the agreement and the collaborative lawyer of each party.

Added by Acts 2011, 82nd Leg., ch. 1048 (H.B. 3833), § 1, eff. Sept. 1, 2011.

### § 15.106. Disqualification of Collaborative Lawyer and Lawyers in Associated Law Firm; Exception

(a) In this section, "family" has the meaning assigned by Section 71.003.

(b) Except as provided by Subsection (d), a collaborative lawyer is disqualified from appearing before a tribunal to represent a party in a proceeding related to the collaborative family law matter regardless of whether the collaborative lawyer is representing the party for a fee.

(c) Except as provided by Subsection (d) and Sections 15.107 and 15.108, a lawyer in a law firm with which the collaborative lawyer is associated is disqualified from appearing before a tribunal to represent a party in a proceeding related to the collaborative family law matter if the collaborative lawyer is disqualified from doing so under Subsection (b).

(d) A collaborative lawyer or a lawyer in a law firm with which the collaborative lawyer is associated may represent a party:

(1) to request a tribunal to approve an agreement resulting from the collaborative family law process; or

(2) to seek or defend an emergency order to protect the health, safety, welfare, or interest of a party or a family if a successor lawyer is not immediately available to represent that party.

(e) The exception prescribed by Subsection (d) does not apply after the party is represented by a successor lawyer or reasonable measures are taken to protect the health, safety, welfare, or interest of that party or family.

Added by Acts 2011, 82nd Leg., ch. 1048 (H.B. 3833), § 1, eff. Sept. 1, 2011.

### § 15.107. Exception From Disqualification for Representation of Low-Income Parties

After a collaborative family law process concludes, another lawyer in a law firm with which a collaborative lawyer disqualified under Section 15.106(b) is associated may represent a party without a fee in the collaborative family law matter or a matter related to the collaborative family law matter if:

(1) the party has an annual income that qualifies the party for free legal representation under the criteria established by the law firm for free legal representation;

(2) the collaborative family law participation agreement authorizes that representation; and

(3) the collaborative lawyer is isolated from any participation in the collaborative family law matter or a matter related to the collaborative family law matter through procedures within the law firm that

are reasonably calculated to isolate the collaborative lawyer from such participation.

Added by Acts 2011, 82nd Leg., ch. 1048 (H.B. 3833), § 1, eff. Sept. 1, 2011.

### § 15.108. Governmental Entity as Party

(a) In this section, "governmental entity" has the meaning assigned by Section 101.014.

(b) The disqualification prescribed by Section 15.106(b) applies to a collaborative lawyer representing a party that is a governmental entity.

(c) After a collaborative family law process concludes, another lawyer in a law firm with which the collaborative lawyer is associated may represent a governmental entity in the collaborative family law matter or a matter related to the collaborative family law matter if:

(1) the collaborative family law participation agreement authorizes that representation; and

(2) the collaborative lawyer is isolated from any participation in the collaborative family law matter or a matter related to the collaborative family law matter through procedures within the law firm that are reasonably calculated to isolate the collaborative lawyer from such participation.

Added by Acts 2011, 82nd Leg., ch. 1048 (H.B. 3833), § 1, eff. Sept. 1, 2011.

### § 15.109. Disclosure of Information

(a) Except as provided by law other than this chapter, during the collaborative family law process, on the request of another party, a party shall make timely, full, candid, and informal disclosure of information related to the collaborative matter without formal discovery. A party shall update promptly any previously disclosed information that has materially changed.

(b) The parties may define the scope of the disclosure under Subsection (a) during the collaborative family law process.

Added by Acts 2011, 82nd Leg., ch. 1048 (H.B. 3833), § 1, eff. Sept. 1, 2011.

### § 15.110. Standards of Professional Responsibility and Mandatory Reporting Not Affected

This chapter does not affect:

(1) the professional responsibility obligations and standards applicable to a lawyer or other licensed professional; or

(2) the obligation of a person under other law to report abuse or neglect, abandonment, or exploitation of a child or adult.

Added by Acts 2011, 82nd Leg., ch. 1048 (H.B. 3833), § 1, eff. Sept. 1, 2011.

### § 15.111. Informed Consent

Before a prospective party signs a collaborative family law participation agreement, a prospective collaborative lawyer must:

(1) assess with the prospective party factors the lawyer reasonably believes relate to whether a collaborative family law process is appropriate for the prospective party's matter;

(2) provide the prospective party with information that the lawyer reasonably believes is sufficient for the prospective party to make an informed decision about the material benefits and risks of a collaborative family law process as compared to the material benefits and risks of other reasonably available alternatives for resolving the proposed collaborative matter, including litigation, mediation, arbitration, or expert evaluation; and

(3) advise the prospective party that:

(A) after signing an agreement, if a party initiates a proceeding or seeks tribunal intervention in a pending proceeding related to the collaborative family law matter, the collaborative family law process terminates;

(B) participation in a collaborative family law process is voluntary and any party has the right to terminate unilaterally a collaborative family law process with or without cause; and

(C) the collaborative lawyer and any lawyer in a law firm with which the collaborative lawyer is associated may not appear before a tribunal to represent a party in a proceeding related to the collaborative family law matter, except as authorized by Section 15.106(d), 15.107, or 15.108(c).

Added by Acts 2011, 82nd Leg., ch. 1048 (H.B. 3833), § 1, eff. Sept. 1, 2011.

### § 15.112. Family Violence

(a) In this section:

(1) "Dating relationship" has the meaning assigned by Section 71.0021(b).

(2) "Family violence" has the meaning assigned by Section 71.004.

(3) "Household" has the meaning assigned by Section 71.005.

(4) "Member of a household" has the meaning assigned by Section 71.006.

(b) Before a prospective party signs a collaborative family law participation agreement in a collaborative family law matter in which another prospective party is a member of the prospective party's family or household or with whom the prospective party has or has had a dating relationship, a prospective collaborative lawyer must make reasonable inquiry regarding whether the prospective party has a history of family violence with the other prospective party.

(c) If a collaborative lawyer reasonably believes that the party the lawyer represents, or the prospective party with whom the collaborative lawyer consults, as applicable, has a history of family violence with another party or prospective party, the lawyer may not begin or continue a collaborative family law process unless:

(1) the party or prospective party requests beginning or continuing a process; and

(2) the collaborative lawyer or prospective collaborative lawyer determines with the party or prospective party what, if any, reasonable steps could be taken to address the concerns regarding family violence.

Added by Acts 2011, 82nd Leg., ch. 1048 (H.B. 3833), § 1, eff. Sept. 1, 2011.

### § 15.113. Confidentiality of Collaborative Family Law Communication

(a) A collaborative family law communication is confidential to the extent agreed to by the parties in a signed record or as provided by law other than this chapter.

(b) If the parties agree in a signed record, the conduct and demeanor of the parties and nonparty participants, including their collaborative lawyers, are confidential.

(c) If the parties agree in a signed record, communications related to the collaborative family law matter occurring before the signing of the collaborative family law participation agreement are confidential.

Added by Acts 2011, 82nd Leg., ch. 1048 (H.B. 3833), § 1, eff. Sept. 1, 2011.

### § 15.114. Privilege Against Disclosure of Collaborative Family Law Communication

(a) Except as provided by Section 15.115, a collaborative family law communication, whether made before or after the institution of a proceeding, is privileged and not subject to disclosure and may not be used as evidence against a party or nonparty participant in a proceeding.

(b) Any record of a collaborative family law communication is privileged, and neither the parties nor the nonparty participants may be required to testify in a proceeding related to or arising out of the collaborative family law matter or be subject to a process requiring disclosure of privileged information or data related to the collaborative matter.

(c) An oral communication or written material used in or made a part of a collaborative family law process is admissible or discoverable if it is admissible or discoverable independent of the collaborative family law process.

(d) If this section conflicts with other legal requirements for disclosure of communications, records, or materials, the issue of privilege may be presented to the tribunal having jurisdiction of the proceeding to determine, in camera, whether the facts, circumstances, and context of the communications or materials sought to be disclosed warrant a protective order of the tribunal or whether the communications or materials are subject to disclosure. The presentation of the issue of privilege under this subsection does not constitute a termination of the collaborative family law process under Section 15.102(d)(2)(B).

(e) A party or nonparty participant may disclose privileged collaborative family law communications to a party's successor counsel, subject to the terms of confidentiality in the collaborative family law participation agreement. Collaborative family law communications disclosed under this subsection remain privileged.

(f) A person who makes a disclosure or representation about a collaborative family law communication that prejudices the rights of a party or nonparty participant in a proceeding may not assert a privilege under this section. The restriction provided by this subsection applies only to the extent necessary for the person prejudiced to respond to the disclosure or representation.

Added by Acts 2011, 82nd Leg., ch. 1048 (H.B. 3833), § 1, eff. Sept. 1, 2011.

### § 15.115. Limits of Privilege

(a) The privilege prescribed by Section 15.114 does not apply to a collaborative family law communication that is:

(1) in an agreement resulting from the collaborative family law process, evidenced in a record signed by all parties to the agreement;

(2) subject to an express waiver of the privilege in a record or orally during a proceeding if the waiver is made by all parties and nonparty participants;

(3) available to the public under Chapter 552, Government Code, or made during a session of a collaborative family law process that is open, or is required by law to be open, to the public;

(4) a threat or statement of a plan to inflict bodily injury or commit a crime of violence;

(5) a disclosure of a plan to commit or attempt to commit a crime, or conceal an ongoing crime or ongoing criminal activity;

(6) a disclosure in a report of:

(A) suspected abuse or neglect of a child to an appropriate agency under Subchapter B, Chapter 261,[1] or in a proceeding regarding the abuse or neglect of a child, except that evidence may be excluded in the case of communications between an attorney and client under Subchapter C, Chapter 261;[2] or

(B) abuse, neglect, or exploitation of an elderly or disabled person to an appropriate agency under Subchapter B, Chapter 48,[3] Human Resources Code; or

(7) sought or offered to prove or disprove:

(A) a claim or complaint of professional misconduct or malpractice arising from or related to a collaborative family law process;

(B) an allegation that the settlement agreement was procured by fraud, duress, coercion, or other dishonest means or that terms of the settlement agreement are illegal;

(C) the necessity and reasonableness of attorney's fees and related expenses incurred during a collaborative family law process or to challenge or defend the enforceability of the collaborative family law settlement agreement; or

(D) a claim against a third person who did not participate in the collaborative family law process.

(b) If a collaborative family law communication is subject to an exception under Subsection (a), only the part of the communication necessary for the application of the exception may be disclosed or admitted.

(c) The disclosure or admission of evidence excepted from the privilege under Subsection (a) does not make the evidence or any other collaborative family law communication discoverable or admissible for any other purpose.

Added by Acts 2011, 82nd Leg., ch. 1048 (H.B. 3833), § 1, eff. Sept. 1, 2011.

[1] V.T.C.A., Family Code § 261.101 et seq.
[2] V.T.C.A., Family Code § 261.201 et seq.
[3] V.T.C.A., Human Resources Code § 48.051 et seq.

### § 15.116. Authority of Tribunal in Case of Noncompliance

(a) Notwithstanding that an agreement fails to meet the requirements of Section 15.101 or that a lawyer has failed to comply with Section 15.111 or 15.112, a tribunal may find that the parties intended to enter into a collaborative family law participation agreement if the parties:

(1) signed a record indicating an intent to enter into a collaborative family law participation agreement; and

(2) reasonably believed the parties were participating in a collaborative family law process.

(b) If a tribunal makes the findings specified in Subsection (a) and determines that the interests of justice require the following action, the tribunal may:

(1) enforce an agreement evidenced by a record resulting from the process in which the parties participated;

(2) apply the disqualification provisions of Sections 15.106, 15.107, and 15.108; and

(3) apply the collaborative family law privilege under Section 15.114.

Added by Acts 2011, 82nd Leg., ch. 1048 (H.B. 3833), § 1, eff. Sept. 1, 2011.

# TITLE 2. CHILD IN RELATION TO THE FAMILY

## SUBTITLE A. LIMITATIONS OF MINORITY

### CHAPTER 16. ADOPTION [REPEALED]

**§§ 16.01 to 16.55. Repealed by Acts 1995, 74th Leg., ch. 20, § 2, eff. April 20, 1995**

### CHAPTER 17. EMERGENCY PROCEDURES IN SUIT BY GOVERNMENT ENTITY [REPEALED]

**§§ 17.001 to 17.06. Repealed by Acts 1995, 74th Leg., ch. 20, § 2, eff. April 20, 1995**

### CHAPTER 18. REVIEW OF PLACEMENT OF CHILDREN UNDER THE CARE OF THE DEPARTMENT OF HUMAN SERVICES [REPEALED]

**§§ 18.01 to 18.16. Repealed by Acts 1995, 74th Leg., ch. 20, § 2, eff. April 20, 1995**

### CHAPTER 21. REVISED UNIFORM RECIPROCAL ENFORCEMENT OF SUPPORT ACT [REPEALED]

**§§ 21.01 to 21.51. Repealed by Acts 1995, 74th Leg., ch. 20, § 2, eff. April 20, 1995**

### CHAPTER 25. UNIFORM INTERSTATE COMPACT ON JUVENILES [REPEALED]

**§§ 25.01 to 25.09. Repealed by Acts 1995, 74th Leg., ch. 20, § 2, eff. April 20, 1995**

### CHAPTER 31. REMOVAL OF DISABILITIES OF MINORITY

**Section**


*A former Chapter 31, Removal of Disabilities of Minorities, consisting of §§ 31.01 to 31.08, was repealed by Acts 1995, 74th Leg., ch. 20, § 2, effective April 20, 1995, as part of the reenactment of Title 2.*

**§ 31.001. Requirements**

(a) A minor may petition to have the disabilities of minority removed for limited or general purposes if the minor is:

(1) a resident of this state;

(2) 17 years of age, or at least 16 years of age and living separate and apart from the minor's parents, managing conservator, or guardian; and

(3) self-supporting and managing the minor's own financial affairs.

(b) A minor may file suit under this chapter in the minor's own name. The minor need not be represented by next friend.

Added by Acts 1995, 74th Leg., ch. 20, § 1, eff. April 20, 1995.

**§ 31.002. Requisites of Petition; Verification**

(a) The petition for removal of disabilities of minority must state:

(1) the name, age, and place of residence of the petitioner;

(2) the name and place of residence of each living parent;

(3) the name and place of residence of the guardian of the person and the guardian of the estate, if any;

(4) the name and place of residence of the managing conservator, if any;

(5) the reasons why removal would be in the best interest of the minor; and

(6) the purposes for which removal is requested.

(b) A parent of the petitioner must verify the petition, except that if a managing conservator or guardian of the person has been appointed, the petition must be verified by that person. If the person who is to verify the petition is unavailable or that person's whereabouts are unknown, the amicus attorney or attorney ad litem shall verify the petition.

Added by Acts 1995, 74th Leg., ch. 20, § 1, eff. April 20, 1995. Amended by Acts 2005, 79th Leg., ch. 172, § 13, eff. Sept. 1, 2005.

### § 31.003. Venue

The petitioner shall file the petition in the county in which the petitioner resides.

Added by Acts 1995, 74th Leg., ch. 20, § 1, eff. April 20, 1995.

### § 31.004. Representation of Petitioner

The court shall appoint an amicus attorney or attorney ad litem to represent the interest of the petitioner at the hearing.

Added by Acts 1995, 74th Leg., ch. 20, § 1, eff. April 20, 1995. Amended by Acts 2005, 79th Leg., ch. 172, § 14, eff. Sept. 1, 2005.

### § 31.005. Order

The court by order, or the Texas Supreme Court by rule or order, may remove the disabilities of minority of a minor, including any restriction imposed by Chapter 32, if the court or the Texas Supreme Court finds the removal to be in the best interest of the petitioner. The order or rule must state the limited or general purposes for which disabilities are removed.

Added by Acts 1995, 74th Leg., ch. 20, § 1, eff. April 20, 1995. Amended by Acts 1999, 76th Leg., ch. 1303, § 1, eff. Sept. 1, 1999.

### § 31.006. Effect of General Removal

Except for specific constitutional and statutory age requirements, a minor whose disabilities are removed for general purposes has the capacity of an adult, including the capacity to contract. Except as provided by federal law, all educational rights accorded to the parent of a student, including the right to make education decisions under Section 151.001(a)(10), transfer to the minor whose disabilities are removed for general purposes.

Added by Acts 1995, 74th Leg., ch. 20, § 1, eff. April 20, 1995. Amended by Acts 2001, 77th Leg., ch. 767, § 9, eff. June 13, 2001; Acts 2015, 84th Leg., ch. 1236 (S.B. 1296), § 7.001, eff. Sept. 1, 2015.

### § 31.007. Registration of Order of Another State or Nation

(a) A nonresident minor who has had the disabilities of minority removed in the state of the minor's residence may file a certified copy of the order removing disabilities in the deed records of any county in this state.

(b) When a certified copy of the order of a court of another state or nation is filed, the minor has the capacity of an adult, except as provided by Section 31.006 and by the terms of the order.

Added by Acts 1995, 74th Leg., ch. 20, § 1, eff. April 20, 1995.

### § 31.008. Waiver of Citation

(a) A party to a suit under this chapter may waive the issuance or service of citation after the suit is filed by filing with the clerk of the court in which the suit is filed the waiver of the party acknowledging receipt of a copy of the filed petition.

(b) The party executing the waiver may not sign the waiver using a digitized signature.

(c) The waiver must contain the mailing address of the party executing the waiver.

(d) The waiver must be sworn before a notary public who is not an attorney in the suit or conform to the requirements for an unsworn declaration under Section 132.001, Civil Practice and Remedies Code. This subsection does not apply if the party executing the waiver is incarcerated.

(e) The Texas Rules of Civil Procedure do not apply to a waiver executed under this section.

(f) For purposes of this section, "digitized signature" has the meaning assigned by Section 101.0096.

Added by Acts 2015, 84th Leg., ch. 198 (S.B. 814), § 2, eff. Sept. 1, 2015. Amended by Acts 2019, 86th Leg., ch. 606 (S.B. 891), § 11.01, eff. Sept. 1, 2019.

Section 15.05 of Acts 2019, 86th Leg., ch. 606 (S.B. 891) provides:

"The Office of Court Administration of the Texas Judicial System is required to implement a provision of this Act only if the legislature appropriates money specifically for that purpose. If the legislature does not appropriate money specifically for that purpose, the office may, but is not required to, implement a provision of this Act using other appropriations available for that purpose."

## CHAPTER 32. CONSENT TO TREATMENT OF CHILD BY NON–PARENT OR CHILD

### SUBCHAPTER A. CONSENT TO MEDICAL, DENTAL, PSYCHOLOGICAL, AND SURGICAL TREATMENT



### SUBCHAPTER B. IMMUNIZATION

*A former Chapter 32, Change of Name, consisting of §§ 32.01 to 32.23, was repealed by Acts 1995, 74th Leg., ch. 20, § 2, effective April 20, 1995, as part of the reenactment of Title 2.*

## SUBCHAPTER A. CONSENT TO MEDICAL, DENTAL, PSYCHOLOGICAL, AND SURGICAL TREATMENT

### § 32.001. Consent by Non-Parent

(a) The following persons may consent to medical, dental, psychological, and surgical treatment of a child when the person having the right to consent as otherwise provided by law cannot be contacted and that person has not given actual notice to the contrary:

(1) a grandparent of the child;

(2) an adult brother or sister of the child;

(3) an adult aunt or uncle of the child;

(4) an educational institution in which the child is enrolled that has received written authorization to consent from a person having the right to consent;

(5) an adult who has actual care, control, and possession of the child and has written authorization to consent from a person having the right to consent;

(6) a court having jurisdiction over a suit affecting the parent-child relationship of which the child is the subject;

(7) an adult responsible for the actual care, control, and possession of a child under the jurisdiction of a juvenile court or committed by a juvenile court to the care of an agency of the state or county; or

(8) a peace officer who has lawfully taken custody of a minor, if the peace officer has reasonable grounds to believe the minor is in need of immediate medical treatment.

(b) Except as otherwise provided by this subsection, the Texas Juvenile Justice Department may consent to the medical, dental, psychological, and surgical treatment of a child committed to the department under Title 3[1] when the person having the right to consent has been contacted and that person has not given actual notice to the contrary. Consent for medical, dental, psychological, and surgical treatment of a child for whom the Department of Family and Protective Services has been appointed managing conservator and who is committed to the Texas Juvenile Justice Department is governed by Sections 266.004, 266.009, and 266.010.

(c) This section does not apply to consent for the immunization of a child.

(d) A person who consents to the medical treatment of a minor under Subsection (a)(7) or (8) is immune from liability for damages resulting from the examination or treatment of the minor, except to the extent of the person's own acts of negligence. A physician or dentist licensed to practice in this state, or a hospital or medical facility at which a minor is treated is immune from liability for damages resulting from the examination or treatment of a minor under this section, except to the extent of the person's own acts of negligence.

Added by Acts 1995, 74th Leg., ch. 20, § 1, eff. April 20, 1995. Amended by Acts 1995, 74th Leg., ch. 751, § 5, eff. Sept. 1, 1995; Acts 2009, 81st Leg., ch. 108, § 1, eff. May 23, 2009; Acts 2015, 84th Leg., ch. 734 (H.B. 1549), § 37, eff. Sept. 1, 2015.

[1] V.T.C.A., Family Code § 51.01 et seq.

### § 32.002. Consent Form

(a) Consent to medical treatment under this subchapter must be in writing, signed by the person giving consent, and given to the doctor, hospital, or other medical facility that administers the treatment.

(b) The consent must include:

(1) the name of the child;

(2) the name of one or both parents, if known, and the name of any managing conservator or guardian of the child;

(3) the name of the person giving consent and the person's relationship to the child;

(4) a statement of the nature of the medical treatment to be given; and

(5) the date the treatment is to begin.

Added by Acts 1995, 74th Leg., ch. 20, § 1, eff. April 20, 1995.

### § 32.003. Consent to Treatment by Child

(a) A child may consent to medical, dental, psychological, and surgical treatment for the child by a licensed physician or dentist if the child:

(1) is on active duty with the armed services of the United States of America;

(2) is:

(A) 16 years of age or older and resides separate and apart from the child's parents, managing conservator, or guardian, with or without the consent of the parents, managing conservator, or guardian and regardless of the duration of the residence; and

(B) managing the child's own financial affairs, regardless of the source of the income;

(3) consents to the diagnosis and treatment of an infectious, contagious, or communicable disease that is required by law or a rule to be reported by the licensed physician or dentist to a local health officer or the Texas Department of Health, including all diseases within the scope of Section 81.041, Health and Safety Code;

(4) is unmarried and pregnant and consents to hospital, medical, or surgical treatment, other than abortion, related to the pregnancy;

(5) consents to examination and treatment for drug or chemical addiction, drug or chemical dependency, or any other condition directly related to drug or chemical use;

(6) is unmarried, is the parent of a child, and has actual custody of his or her child and consents to medical, dental, psychological, or surgical treatment for the child; or

(7) is serving a term of confinement in a facility operated by or under contract with the Texas Department of Criminal Justice, unless the treatment would constitute a prohibited practice under Section 164.052(a)(19), Occupations Code.

(b) Consent by a child to medical, dental, psychological, and surgical treatment under this section is not subject to disaffirmance because of minority.

(c) Consent of the parents, managing conservator, or guardian of a child is not necessary in order to authorize hospital, medical, surgical, or dental care under this section.

(d) A licensed physician, dentist, or psychologist may, with or without the consent of a child who is a patient, advise the parents, managing conservator, or guardian of the child of the treatment given to or needed by the child.

(e) A physician, dentist, psychologist, hospital, or medical facility is not liable for the examination and treatment of a child under this section except for the provider's or the facility's own acts of negligence.

(f) A physician, dentist, psychologist, hospital, or medical facility may rely on the written statement of the child containing the grounds on which the child has capacity to consent to the child's medical treatment.

Added by Acts 1995, 74th Leg., ch. 20, § 1, eff. April 20, 1995. Amended by Acts 1995, 74th Leg., ch. 751, § 6, eff. Sept. 1, 1995; Acts 2001, 77th Leg., ch. 821, § 2.01, eff. June 14, 2001; Acts 2007, 80th Leg., ch. 1227, § 2, eff. June 15, 2007.

### § 32.004. Consent to Counseling

(a) A child may consent to counseling for:

(1) suicide prevention;

(2) chemical addiction or dependency; or

(3) sexual, physical, or emotional abuse.

(b) A licensed or certified physician, psychologist, counselor, or social worker having reasonable grounds to believe that a child has been sexually, physically, or emotionally abused, is contemplating suicide, or is suffering from a chemical or drug addiction or dependency may:

(1) counsel the child without the consent of the child's parents or, if applicable, managing conservator or guardian;

(2) with or without the consent of the child who is a client, advise the child's parents or, if applicable, managing conservator or guardian of the treatment given to or needed by the child; and

(3) rely on the written statement of the child containing the grounds on which the child has capacity to consent to the child's own treatment under this section.

(c) Unless consent is obtained as otherwise allowed by law, a physician, psychologist, counselor, or social worker may not counsel a child if consent is prohibited by a court order.

(d) A physician, psychologist, counselor, or social worker counseling a child under this section is not liable for damages except for damages resulting from the person's negligence or wilful misconduct.

(e) A parent, or, if applicable, managing conservator or guardian, who has not consented to counseling treatment of the child is not obligated to compensate a physician, psychologist, counselor, or social worker for counseling services rendered under this section.

Added by Acts 1995, 74th Leg., ch. 20, § 1, eff. April 20, 1995.

### § 32.005. Examination Without Consent of Abuse or Neglect of Child

(a) Except as provided by Subsection (c), a physician, dentist, or psychologist having reasonable grounds to believe that a child's physical or mental condition has been adversely affected by abuse or neglect may examine the child without the consent of the child, the child's parents, or other person authorized to consent to treatment under this subchapter.

(b) An examination under this section may include X-rays, blood tests, photographs, and penetration of tissue necessary to accomplish those tests.

(c) Unless consent is obtained as otherwise allowed by law, a physician, dentist, or psychologist may not examine a child:

(1) 16 years of age or older who refuses to consent; or

(2) for whom consent is prohibited by a court order.

(d) A physician, dentist, or psychologist examining a child under this section is not liable for damages except for damages resulting from the physician's or dentist's negligence.

Added by Acts 1995, 74th Leg., ch. 20, § 1, eff. April 20, 1995. Amended by Acts 1997, 75th Leg., ch. 575, § 1, eff. Sept. 1, 1997.

## SUBCHAPTER B. IMMUNIZATION

### § 32.101. Who May Consent to Immunization of Child

(a) In addition to persons authorized to consent to immunization under Chapter 151 and Chapter 153, the following persons may consent to the immunization of a child:

(1) a guardian of the child; and

(2) a person authorized under the law of another state or a court order to consent for the child.

(b) If the persons listed in Subsection (a) are not available and the authority to consent is not denied under Subsection (c), consent to the immunization of a child may be given by:

(1) a grandparent of the child;

(2) an adult brother or sister of the child;

(3) an adult aunt or uncle of the child;

(4) a stepparent of the child;

(5) an educational institution in which the child is enrolled that has written authorization to consent for the child from a parent, managing conservator, guardian, or other person who under the law of another state or a court order may consent for the child;

(6) another adult who has actual care, control, and possession of the child and has written authorization to consent for the child from a parent, managing conservator, guardian, or other person who, under the law of another state or a court order, may consent for the child;

(7) a court having jurisdiction of a suit affecting the parent-child relationship of which the minor is the subject;

(8) an adult having actual care, control, and possession of the child under an order of a juvenile court or by commitment by a juvenile court to the care of an agency of the state or county; or

(9) an adult having actual care, control, and possession of the child as the child's primary caregiver.

(c) A person otherwise authorized to consent under Subsection (a) may not consent for the child if the person has actual knowledge that a parent, managing conservator, guardian of the child, or other person who under the law of another state or a court order may consent for the child:

(1) has expressly refused to give consent to the immunization;

(2) has been told not to consent for the child; or

(3) has withdrawn a prior written authorization for the person to consent.

(d) The Texas Juvenile Justice Department may consent to the immunization of a child committed to it if a parent, managing conservator, or guardian of the minor or other person who, under the law of another state or court order, may consent for the minor has been contacted and:

(1) refuses to consent; and

(2) does not expressly deny to the department the authority to consent for the child.

(e) A person who consents under this section shall provide the health care provider with sufficient and accurate health history and other information about the minor for whom the consent is given and, if necessary, sufficient and accurate health history and information about the minor's family to enable the person who may consent to the minor's immunization and the health care provider to determine adequately the risks and benefits inherent in the proposed immunization and to determine whether immunization is advisable.

(f) Consent to immunization must meet the requirements of Section 32.002(a).

Added by Acts 1995, 74th Leg., ch. 20, § 1, eff. April 20, 1995. Amended by Acts 1997, 75th Leg., ch. 165, § 7.09(a), eff. Sept. 1, 1997; Acts 1999, 76th Leg., ch. 62, § 6.02, eff. Sept. 1, 1999; Acts 2015, 84th Leg., ch. 734 (H.B. 1549), § 38, eff. Sept. 1, 2015.

### § 32.1011. Consent to Immunization by Child

(a) Notwithstanding Section 32.003 or 32.101, a child may consent to the child's own immunization for a disease if:

(1) the child:

(A) is pregnant; or

(B) is the parent of a child and has actual custody of that child; and

(2) the Centers for Disease Control and Prevention recommend or authorize the initial dose of an immunization for that disease to be administered before seven years of age.

(b) Consent to immunization under this section must meet the requirements of Section 32.002(a).

(c) Consent by a child to immunization under this section is not subject to disaffirmance because of minority.

(d) A health care provider or facility may rely on the written statement of the child containing the grounds on which the child has capacity to consent to the child's immunization under this section.

(e) To the extent of any conflict between this section and Section 32.003, this section controls.

Added by Acts 2013, 83rd Leg., ch. 1313 (S.B. 63), § 1, eff. June 14, 2013.

### § 32.102. Informed Consent to Immunization

(a) A person authorized to consent to the immunization of a child has the responsibility to ensure that the consent, if given, is an informed consent. The person authorized to consent is not required to be present when the immunization of the child is requested if a consent form that meets the requirements of Section 32.002 has been given to the health care provider.

(b) The responsibility of a health care provider to provide information to a person consenting to immunization is the same as the provider's responsibility to a parent.

(c) As part of the information given in the counseling for informed consent, the health care provider shall provide information to inform the person authorized to consent to immunization of the procedures available under the National Childhood Vaccine Injury Act of 1986 (42 U.S.C. Section 300aa–1 et seq.) to seek possible recovery for unreimbursed expenses for certain injuries arising out of the administration of certain vaccines.

Added by Acts 1995, 74th Leg., ch. 20, § 1, eff. April 20, 1995. Renumbered from V.T.C.A., Family Code § 32.103 and amended by Acts 1997, 75th Leg., ch. 165, § 7.09(b), (d), eff. Sept. 1, 1997.

### § 32.103. Limited Liability for Immunization

(a) In the absence of wilful misconduct or gross negligence, a health care provider who accepts the health history and other information given by a person who is delegated the authority to consent to the immunization of a child during the informed consent counseling is not liable for an adverse reaction to an immunization or for other injuries to the child resulting from factual errors in the health history or information given by the person to the health care provider.

(b) A person consenting to immunization of a child, a physician, nurse, or other health care provider, or a public health clinic, hospital, or other medical facility is not liable for damages arising from an immunization administered to a child authorized under this subchapter except for injuries resulting from the person's or facility's own acts of negligence.

Added by Acts 1995, 74th Leg., ch. 20, § 1, eff. April 20, 1995. Renumbered from V.T.C.A., Family Code § 32.104 by Acts 1997, 75th Leg., ch. 165, § 7.09(e), eff. Sept. 1, 1997.

### § 32.104. Renumbered as V.T.C.A., Family Code § 32.103 by Acts 1997, 75th Leg., ch. 165, § 7.09(e), eff. Sept. 1, 1997

### § 32.105. Repealed by Acts 1997, 75th Leg., ch. 165, § 7.09(c), eff. Sept. 1, 1997

## SUBCHAPTER C. MISCELLANEOUS PROVISIONS

### § 32.201. Emergency Shelter or Care for Minors

(a) An emergency shelter facility may provide shelter and care to a minor and the minor's child or children, if any.

(b) An emergency shelter facility may provide shelter or care only during an emergency constituting an immediate danger to the physical health or safety of the minor or the minor's child or children.

(c) Shelter or care provided under this section may not be provided after the 15th day after the date the shelter or care is commenced unless:

(1) the facility receives consent to continue services from the minor in accordance with Section 32.202; or

(2) the minor has qualified for financial assistance under Chapter 31, Human Resources Code, and is on the waiting list for housing assistance.

Added by Acts 1995, 74th Leg., ch. 20, § 1, eff. April 20, 1995. Amended by Acts 2003, 78th Leg., ch. 192, § 1, eff. June 2, 2003.

### § 32.202. Consent to Emergency Shelter or Care by Minor

(a) A minor may consent to emergency shelter or care to be provided to the minor or the minor's child or children, if any, under Section 32.201(c) if the minor is:

(1) 16 years of age or older and:

(A) resides separate and apart from the minor's parent, managing conservator, or guardian, regardless of whether the parent, managing conservator, or guardian consents to the residence and regardless of the duration of the residence; and

(B) manages the minor's own financial affairs, regardless of the source of income; or

(2) unmarried and is pregnant or is the parent of a child.

(b) Consent by a minor to emergency shelter or care under this section is not subject to disaffirmance because of minority.

(c) An emergency shelter facility may, with or without the consent of the minor's parent, managing conservator, or guardian, provide emergency shelter or care to the minor or the minor's child or children under Section 32.201(c).

(d) An emergency shelter facility is not liable for providing emergency shelter or care to the minor or the minor's child or children if the minor consents as provided by this section, except that the facility is liable for the facility's own acts of negligence.

(e) An emergency shelter facility may rely on the minor's written statement containing the grounds on which the minor has capacity to consent to emergency shelter or care.

(f) To the extent of any conflict between this section and Section 32.003, Section 32.003 prevails.

Added by Acts 2003, 78th Leg., ch. 192, § 2, eff. June 2, 2003.

### § 32.203. Consent by Minor to Housing or Care Provided Through Transitional Living Program

(a) In this section, "transitional living program" means a residential services program for children provided in a residential child-care facility licensed or certified by the Department of Family and Protective Services under Chapter 42, Human Resources Code, that:

(1) is designed to provide basic life skills training and the opportunity to practice those skills, with a goal of basic life skills development toward independent living; and

(2) is not an independent living program.

(b) A minor may consent to housing or care provided to the minor or the minor's child or children, if any, through a transitional living program if the minor is:

(1) 16 years of age or older and:

(A) resides separate and apart from the minor's parent, managing conservator, or guardian, regardless of whether the parent, managing conservator, or guardian consents to the residence and regardless of the duration of the residence; and

(B) manages the minor's own financial affairs, regardless of the source of income; or

(2) unmarried and is pregnant or is the parent of a child.

(c) Consent by a minor to housing or care under this section is not subject to disaffirmance because of minority.

(d) A transitional living program may, with or without the consent of the parent, managing conservator, or guardian, provide housing or care to the minor or the minor's child or children.

(e) A transitional living program must attempt to notify the minor's parent, managing conservator, or guardian regarding the minor's location.

(f) A transitional living program is not liable for providing housing or care to the minor or the minor's child or children if the minor consents as provided by this section, except that the program is liable for the program's own acts of negligence.

(g) A transitional living program may rely on a minor's written statement containing the grounds on which the minor has capacity to consent to housing or care provided through the program.

(h) To the extent of any conflict between this section and Section 32.003, Section 32.003 prevails.

Added by Acts 2013, 83rd Leg., ch. 587 (S.B. 717), § 1, eff. June 14, 2013.

### § 32.241. Repealed by Acts 1997, 75th Leg., ch. 165, § 7.10(c), eff. Sept. 1, 1997

## CHAPTER 33. NOTICE OF AND CONSENT TO ABORTION

**Section**



*A former Chapter 33, Liability of Parents for Conduct of Child, consisting of §§ 33.01 to 33.03, was repealed by Acts 1995, 74th Leg., ch. 20, § 2, effective April 20, 1995, as part of the reenactment of Title 2.*

### § 33.001. Definitions

In this chapter:

(1) "Abortion" has the meaning assigned by Section 245.002, Health and Safety Code. This definition, as applied in this chapter, may not be construed to limit a minor's access to contraceptives.

(2) "Fetus" means an individual human organism from fertilization until birth.

(3) "Guardian" means a court-appointed guardian of the person of the minor.

(3–a) "Medical emergency" has the meaning assigned by Section 171.002, Health and Safety Code.

(4) "Physician" means an individual licensed to practice medicine in this state.

(5) "Unemancipated minor" includes a minor who:

(A) is unmarried; and

(B) has not had the disabilities of minority removed under Chapter 31.

Added by Acts 1999, 76th Leg., ch. 395, § 1, eff. Sept. 1, 1999. Amended by Acts 2015, 84th Leg., ch. 436 (H.B. 3994), § 2, eff. Jan. 1, 2016; Acts 2017, 85th Leg., ch. 441 (S.B. 8), § 1, eff. Sept. 1, 2017.

### § 33.002. Parental Notice

(a) A physician may not perform an abortion on a pregnant unemancipated minor unless:

(1) the physician performing the abortion gives at least 48 hours actual notice, in person or by telephone, of the physician's intent to perform the abortion to:

(A) a parent of the minor, if the minor has no managing conservator or guardian; or

(B) a court-appointed managing conservator or guardian;

(2) the physician who is to perform the abortion receives an order issued by a court under Section 33.003 or 33.004 authorizing the minor to consent to the abortion as provided by Section 33.003 or 33.004; or

(3) the physician who is to perform the abortion:

(A) concludes that a medical emergency exists;

(B) certifies in writing to the Department of State Health Services and in the patient's medical record the medical indications supporting the physician's judgment that a medical emergency exists; and

(C) provides the notice required by Section 33.0022.

(b) If a person to whom notice may be given under Subsection (a)(1) cannot be notified after a reasonable effort, a physician may perform an abortion if the physician gives 48 hours constructive notice, by certified mail, restricted delivery, sent to the last known address, to the person to whom notice may be given under Subsection (a)(1). The period under this subsection begins when the notice is mailed. If the person required to be notified is not notified within the 48-hour period, the abortion may proceed even if the notice by mail is not received.

(c) The requirement that 48 hours actual notice be provided under this section may be waived by an affidavit of:

(1) a parent of the minor, if the minor has no managing conservator or guardian; or

(2) a court-appointed managing conservator or guardian.

(d) A physician may execute for inclusion in the minor's medical record an affidavit stating that, according to the best information and belief of the physician, notice or constructive notice has been provided as required by this section. Execution of an affidavit under this subsection creates a presumption that the requirements of this section have been satisfied.

(e) The Department of State Health Services shall prepare a form to be used for making the certification required by Subsection (a)(3)(B).

(f) A certification required by Subsection (a)(3)(B) is confidential and privileged and is not subject to disclosure under Chapter 552, Government Code, or to discovery, subpoena, or other legal process. Personal or identifying information about the minor, including her name, address, or social security number, may not be included in a certification under Subsection (a)(3)(B). The physician must keep the medical records on the minor in compliance with the rules adopted by the Texas Medical Board under Section 153.003, Occupations Code.

(g) A physician who intentionally performs an abortion on a pregnant unemancipated minor in violation of this section commits an offense. An offense under this subsection is punishable by a fine not to exceed $10,000. In this subsection, "intentionally" has the meaning assigned by Section 6.03(a), Penal Code.

(h) It is a defense to prosecution under this section that the minor falsely represented her age or identity to the physician to be at least 18 years of age by displaying an apparently valid proof of identity and age described by Subsection (k) such that a reasonable person under similar circumstances would have relied on the representation. The defense does not apply if the physician is shown to have had independent knowledge of the minor's actual age or identity or failed to use due diligence in determining the minor's age or identity. In this subsection, "defense" has the meaning and application assigned by Section 2.03, Penal Code.

(i) In relation to the trial of an offense under this section in which the conduct charged involves a conclusion made by the physician under Subsection (a)(3)(A), the defendant may seek a hearing before the Texas Medical Board on whether the physician's conduct was necessary because of a medical emergency. The findings of the Texas Medical Board under this subsection are admissible on that issue in the trial of the defendant. Notwithstanding any other reason for a continuance provided under the Code of Criminal Procedure or other law, on motion of the defendant, the court shall delay the beginning of the trial for not more than 30 days to permit a hearing under this subsection to take place.

(j) A physician shall use due diligence to determine that any woman on which the physician performs an abortion who claims to have reached the age of majority or to have had the disabilities of minority removed has, in fact, reached the age of majority or has had the disabilities of minority removed.

(k) For the purposes of this section, "due diligence" includes requesting proof of identity and age described by Section 2.005(b) or a copy of the court order removing disabilities of minority.

(*l*) If proof of identity and age cannot be provided, the physician shall provide information on how to obtain proof of identity and age. If the woman is subsequently unable to obtain proof of identity and age and the physician chooses to perform the abortion, the physician shall document that proof of identity and age was not obtained and report to the Department of State Health Services that proof of identity and age was not obtained for the woman on whom the abortion was performed. The department shall report annually to the legislature regarding the number of abortions performed without proof of identity and age.

Added by Acts 1999, 76th Leg., ch. 395, § 1, eff. Sept. 1, 1999. Amended by Acts 2001, 77th Leg., ch. 1420, § 14.741, eff. Sept. 1, 2001; Acts 2015, 84th Leg., ch. 436 (H.B. 3994), § 3, eff. Jan. 1, 2016.

### § 33.0021. Consent Required

A physician may not perform an abortion in violation of Section 164.052(a)(19), Occupations Code.

Added by Acts 2015, 84th Leg., ch. 436 (H.B. 3994), § 4, eff. Jan. 1, 2016.

### § 33.0022. Medical Emergency Notification; Affidavit for Medical Record

(a) If the physician who is to perform the abortion concludes under Section 33.002(a)(3)(A) that a medical emergency exists and that there is insufficient time to provide the notice required by Section 33.002 or obtain the consent required by Section 33.0021, the physician shall make a reasonable effort to inform, in person or by telephone, the parent, managing conservator, or guardian of the unemancipated minor within 24 hours after the time a medical emergency abortion is performed on the minor of:

(1) the performance of the abortion; and

(2) the basis for the physician's determination that a medical emergency existed that required the performance of a medical emergency abortion without fulfilling the requirements of Section 33.002 or 33.0021.

(b) A physician who performs an abortion as described by Subsection (a), not later than 48 hours after the abortion is performed, shall send a written notice that a medical emergency occurred and the ability of the parent, managing conservator, or guardian to contact the physician for more information and medical records, to the last known address of the parent, managing conservator, or guardian by certified mail, restricted delivery, return receipt requested. The physician may rely on last known address information if a reasonable and prudent person, under similar circumstances, would rely on the information as sufficient evidence that the parent, managing conservator, or guardian resides at that address. The physician shall keep in the minor's medical record:

(1) the return receipt from the written notice; or

(2) if the notice was returned as undeliverable, the notice.

(c) A physician who performs an abortion on an unemancipated minor during a medical emergency as described by Subsection (a) shall execute for inclusion in the medical record of the minor an affidavit that explains the specific medical emergency that necessitated the immediate abortion.

Added by Acts 2015, 84th Leg., ch. 436 (H.B. 3994), § 4, eff. Jan. 1, 2016.

### § 33.003. Judicial Approval

(a) A pregnant minor may file an application for a court order authorizing the minor to consent to the performance of an abortion without notification to and consent of a parent, managing conservator, or guardian.

(b) The application must be filed in:

(1) a county court at law, court having probate jurisdiction, or district court, including a family district court, in the minor's county of residence;

(2) if the minor's parent, managing conservator, or guardian is a presiding judge of a court described by Subdivision (1):

(A) a county court at law, court having probate jurisdiction, or district court, including a family district court, in a contiguous county; or

(B) a county court at law, court having probate jurisdiction, or district court, including a family district court, in the county where the minor intends to obtain the abortion;

(3) if the minor's county of residence has a population of less than 10,000:

(A) a court described by Subdivision (1);

(B) a county court at law, court having probate jurisdiction, or district court, including a family district court, in a contiguous county; or

(C) a county court at law, court having probate jurisdiction, or district court, including a family district court, in the county in which the facility at which the minor intends to obtain the abortion is located; or

(4) a county court at law, court having probate jurisdiction, or district court, including a family district court, in the county in which the facility at which the minor intends to obtain the abortion is located, if the minor is not a resident of this state.

(c) The application must:

(1) be made under oath;

(2) include:

(A) a statement that the minor is pregnant;

(B) a statement that the minor is unmarried, is under 18 years of age, and has not had her disabilities removed under Chapter 31;

(C) a statement that the minor wishes to have an abortion without the notification to and consent of a parent, managing conservator, or guardian;

(D) a statement as to whether the minor has retained an attorney and, if she has retained an attorney, the name, address, and telephone number of her attorney; and

(E) a statement about the minor's current residence, including the minor's physical address, mailing address, and telephone number; and

(3) be accompanied by the sworn statement of the minor's attorney under Subsection (r), if the minor has retained an attorney to assist the minor with filing the application under this section.

(d) The clerk of the court shall deliver a courtesy copy of the application made under this section to the judge who is to hear the application.

(e) The court shall appoint a guardian ad litem for the minor who shall represent the best interest of the minor. If the minor has not retained an attorney, the court shall appoint an attorney to represent the minor. The guardian ad litem may not also serve as the minor's attorney ad litem.

(f) The court may appoint to serve as guardian ad litem:

(1) a person who may consent to treatment for the minor under Sections 32.001(a)(1)–(3);

(2) a psychiatrist or an individual licensed or certified as a psychologist under Chapter 501, Occupations Code;

(3) an appropriate employee of the Department of Family and Protective Services;

(4) a member of the clergy; or

(5) another appropriate person selected by the court.

(g) The court shall fix a time for a hearing on an application filed under Subsection (a) and shall keep a record of all testimony and other oral proceedings in the action.

(g–1) The pregnant minor must appear before the court in person and may not appear using videoconferencing, telephone conferencing, or other remote electronic means.

(h) The court shall rule on an application submitted under this section and shall issue written findings of fact and conclusions of law not later than 5 p.m. on the fifth business day after the date the application is filed with the court. On request by the minor, the court shall grant an extension of the period specified by this subsection. If a request for an extension is made, the court shall rule on an application and shall issue written findings of fact and conclusions of law not later than 5 p.m. on the fifth business day after the date the minor states she is ready to proceed to hearing. Proceedings under this section shall be given precedence over other pending matters to the extent necessary to assure that the court reaches a decision promptly, regardless of whether the minor is granted an extension under this subsection.

(i) The court shall determine by clear and convincing evidence, as described by Section 101.007, whether:

(1) the minor is mature and sufficiently well informed to make the decision to have an abortion performed without notification to or consent of a parent, managing conservator, or guardian; or

(2) the notification and attempt to obtain consent would not be in the best interest of the minor.

(i–1) In determining whether the minor meets the requirements of Subsection (i)(1), the court shall consider the experience, perspective, and judgment of the minor. The court may:

(1) consider all relevant factors, including:

(A) the minor's age;

(B) the minor's life experiences, such as working, traveling independently, or managing her own financial affairs; and

(C) steps taken by the minor to explore her options and the consequences of those options;

(2) inquire as to the minor's reasons for seeking an abortion;

(3) consider the degree to which the minor is informed about the state-published informational materials described by Chapter 171, Health and Safety Code; and

(4) require the minor to be evaluated by a licensed mental health counselor, who shall return the evaluation to the court for review within three business days.

(i–2) In determining whether the notification and the attempt to obtain consent would not be in the best interest of the minor, the court may inquire as to:

(1) the minor's reasons for not wanting to notify and obtain consent from a parent, managing conservator, or guardian;

(2) whether notification or the attempt to obtain consent may lead to physical or sexual abuse;

(3) whether the pregnancy was the result of sexual abuse by a parent, managing conservator, or guardian; and

(4) any history of physical or sexual abuse from a parent, managing conservator, or guardian.

(i–3) The court shall enter an order authorizing the minor to consent to the performance of the abortion without notification to and consent of a parent, managing conservator, or guardian and shall execute the required forms if the court finds by clear and convincing evidence, as defined by Section 101.007, that:

(1) the minor is mature and sufficiently well informed to make the decision to have an abortion

performed without notification to or consent of a parent, managing conservator, or guardian; or

(2) the notification and attempt to obtain consent would not be in the best interest of the minor.

(j) If the court finds that the minor does not meet the requirements of Subsection (i–3), the court may not authorize the minor to consent to an abortion without the notification authorized under Section 33.002(a)(1) and consent under Section 33.0021.

(k) The court may not notify a parent, managing conservator, or guardian that the minor is pregnant or that the minor wants to have an abortion. The court proceedings shall be conducted in a manner that protects the confidentiality of the identity of the minor. The application and all other court documents pertaining to the proceedings are confidential and privileged and are not subject to disclosure under Chapter 552, Government Code, or to discovery, subpoena, or other legal process. Confidential records pertaining to a minor under this subsection may be disclosed to the minor.

(*l*) An order of the court issued under this section is confidential and privileged and is not subject to disclosure under Chapter 552, Government Code, or discovery, subpoena, or other legal process. The order may not be released to any person but the pregnant minor, the pregnant minor's guardian ad litem, the pregnant minor's attorney, the physician who is to perform the abortion, another person designated to receive the order by the minor, or a governmental agency or attorney in a criminal or administrative action seeking to assert or protect the interest of the minor. The supreme court may adopt rules to permit confidential docketing of an application under this section.

(*l*–1) The clerk of the court, at intervals prescribed by the Office of Court Administration of the Texas Judicial System, shall submit a report to the office that includes, for each case filed under this section:

(1) the case number and style;

(2) the applicant's county of residence;

(3) the court of appeals district in which the proceeding occurred;

(4) the date of filing;

(5) the date of disposition; and

(6) the disposition of the case.

(*l*–2) The Office of Court Administration of the Texas Judicial System shall annually compile and publish a report aggregating the data received under Subsections (*l*–1)(3) and (6). A report submitted under Subsection (*l*–1) is confidential and privileged and is not subject to disclosure under Chapter 552, Government Code, or to discovery, subpoena, or other legal process. A report under this subsection must protect the confidentiality of:

(1) the identity of all minors and judges who are the subject of the report; and

(2) the information described by Subsection (l–1)(1).

(m) The clerk of the supreme court shall prescribe the application form to be used by the minor filing an application under this section.

(n) A filing fee is not required of and court costs may not be assessed against a minor filing an application under this section.

(*o*) A minor who has filed an application under this section may not withdraw or otherwise non-suit her application without the permission of the court.

(p) Except as otherwise provided by Subsection (q), a minor who has filed an application and has obtained a determination by the court as described by Subsection (i) may not initiate a new application proceeding and the prior proceeding is res judicata of the issue relating to the determination of whether the minor may or may not be authorized to consent to the performance of an abortion without notification to and consent of a parent, managing conservator, or guardian.

(q) A minor whose application is denied may subsequently submit an application to the court that denied the application if the minor shows that there has been a material change in circumstances since the time the court denied the application.

(r) An attorney retained by the minor to assist her in filing an application under this section shall fully inform himself or herself of the minor's prior application history, including the representations made by the minor in the application regarding her address, proper venue in the county in which the application is filed, and whether a prior application has been filed and initiated. If an attorney assists the minor in the application process in any way, with or without payment, the attorney representing the minor must attest to the truth of the minor's claims regarding the venue and prior applications in a sworn statement.

Added by Acts 1999, 76th Leg., ch. 395, § 1, eff. Sept. 1, 1999. Amended by Acts 2001, 77th Leg., ch. 1420, § 14.742, eff. Sept. 1, 2001; Acts 2011, 82nd Leg., ch. 110 (H.B. 841), § 1, eff. May 21, 2011; Acts 2015, 84th Leg., ch. 436 (H.B. 3994), § 5, eff. Jan. 1, 2016.

### § 33.004. Appeal

(a) A minor whose application under Section 33.003 is denied may appeal to the court of appeals having jurisdiction over civil matters in the county in which the application was filed. On receipt of a notice of appeal, the clerk of the court that denied the application shall deliver a copy of the notice of appeal and record on appeal to the clerk of the court of appeals. On receipt of the notice and record, the clerk of the court of appeals shall place the appeal on the docket of the court.

(b) The court of appeals shall rule on an appeal under this section not later than 5 p.m. on the fifth business day after the date the notice of appeal is filed with the court that denied the application. On request by the minor, the court shall grant an extension of the period specified by this subsection. If a request for an extension is made, the court shall rule on the appeal not later than 5 p.m. on the fifth business day after the date the minor states she is ready to proceed. Proceedings under this section shall be given precedence over other pending matters to the extent necessary to assure that the court reaches a decision promptly, regardless of whether the minor is granted an extension under this subsection.

(c) A ruling of the court of appeals issued under this section is confidential and privileged and is not subject to disclosure under Chapter 552, Government Code, or discovery, subpoena, or other legal process. The ruling may not be released to any person but the pregnant minor, the pregnant minor's guardian ad litem, the pregnant minor's attorney, another person designated to receive the ruling by the minor, or a governmental agency or attorney in a criminal or administrative action seeking to assert or protect the interest of the minor. The supreme court may adopt rules to permit confidential docketing of an appeal under this section.

(c–1) Notwithstanding Subsection (c), the court of appeals may publish an opinion relating to a ruling under this section if the opinion is written in a way to preserve the confidentiality of the identity of the pregnant minor.

(d) The clerk of the supreme court shall prescribe the notice of appeal form to be used by the minor appealing a judgment under this section.

(e) A filing fee is not required of and court costs may not be assessed against a minor filing an appeal under this section.

(f) An expedited confidential appeal shall be available to any pregnant minor to whom a court of appeals denies an application to authorize the minor to consent to the performance of an abortion without notification to or consent of a parent, managing conservator, or guardian.

Added by Acts 1999, 76th Leg., ch. 395, § 1, eff. Sept. 1, 1999. Amended by Acts 2015, 84th Leg., ch. 436 (H.B. 3994), § 6, eff. Jan. 1, 2016.

### § 33.005. Affidavit of Physician

(a) A physician may execute for inclusion in the minor's medical record an affidavit stating that, after reasonable inquiry, it is the belief of the physician that:

(1) the minor has made an application or filed a notice of an appeal with a court under this chapter;

(2) the deadline for court action imposed by this chapter has passed; and

(3) the physician has been notified that the court has not denied the application or appeal.

(b) A physician who in good faith has executed an affidavit under Subsection (a) may rely on the affidavit and may perform the abortion as if the court had issued an order granting the application or appeal.

Added by Acts 1999, 76th Leg., ch. 395, § 1, eff. Sept. 1, 1999.

### § 33.006. Guardian Ad Litem Immunity

A guardian ad litem appointed under this chapter and acting in the course and scope of the appointment is not liable for damages arising from an act or omission of the guardian ad litem committed in good faith. The immunity granted by this section does not apply if the conduct of the guardian ad litem is committed in a manner described by Sections 107.009(b)(1)–(3).

Added by Acts 1999, 76th Leg., ch. 395, § 1, eff. Sept. 1, 1999. Amended by Acts 2021, 87th Leg., ch. 915 (H.B. 3607), § 7.001, eff. Sept. 1, 2021.

### § 33.0065. Records

The clerk of the court shall retain the records for each case before the court under this chapter in accordance with rules for civil cases and grant access to the records to the minor who is the subject of the proceeding.

Added by Acts 2015, 84th Leg., ch. 436 (H.B. 3994), § 7, eff. Jan. 1, 2016.

## § 33.007. Costs Paid by State

(a) A court acting under Section 33.003 or 33.004 may issue an order requiring the state to pay:

(1) the cost of any attorney ad litem and any guardian ad litem appointed for the minor;

(2) notwithstanding Sections 33.003(n) and 33.004(e), the costs of court associated with the application or appeal; and

(3) any court reporter's fees incurred.

(b) An order issued under Subsection (a) must be directed to the comptroller, who shall pay the amount ordered from funds appropriated to the Texas Department of Health.

Added by Acts 1999, 76th Leg., ch. 395, § 1, eff. Sept. 1, 1999.

## § 33.008. Physician's Duty to Report Abuse of a Minor; Investigation and Assistance

(a) If a minor claims to have been physically or sexually abused or a physician or physician's agent has reason to believe that a minor has been physically or sexually abused, the physician or physician's agent shall immediately report the suspected abuse and the name of the abuser to the Department of Family and Protective Services and to a local law enforcement agency and shall refer the minor to the department for services or intervention that may be in the best interest of the minor. The local law enforcement agency shall respond and shall write a report within 24 hours of being notified of the alleged abuse. A report shall be made regardless of whether the local law enforcement agency knows or suspects that a report about the abuse may have previously been made.

(b) The appropriate local law enforcement agency and the Department of Family and Protective Services shall investigate suspected abuse reported under this section and, if warranted, shall refer the case to the appropriate prosecuting authority.

(c) When the local law enforcement agency responds to the report of physical or sexual abuse as required by Subsection (a), a law enforcement officer or appropriate agent from the Department of Family and Protective Services may take emergency possession of the minor without a court order to protect the health and safety of the minor as described by Chapter 262.

Added by Acts 1999, 76th Leg., ch. 395, § 1, eff. Sept. 1, 1999. Amended by Acts 2011, 82nd Leg., ch. 110 (H.B. 841), § 2, eff. May 21, 2011; Acts 2015, 84th Leg., ch. 436 (H.B. 3994), § 8, eff. Jan. 1, 2016.

## § 33.0085. Duty of Judge or Justice to Report Abuse of Minor

(a) Notwithstanding any other law, a judge or justice who, as a result of court proceedings conducted under Section 33.003 or 33.004, has reason to believe that a minor has been or may be physically or sexually abused shall:

(1) immediately report the suspected abuse and the name of the abuser to the Department of Family and Protective Services and to a local law enforcement agency; and

(2) refer the minor to the department for services or intervention that may be in the best interest of the minor.

(b) The appropriate local law enforcement agency and the Department of Family and Protective Services shall investigate suspected abuse reported under this section and, if warranted, shall refer the case to the appropriate prosecuting authority.

Added by Acts 2015, 84th Leg., ch. 436 (H.B. 3994), § 9, eff. Jan. 1, 2016.

## § 33.009. Other Reports of Sexual Abuse of a Minor

A court or the guardian ad litem or attorney ad litem for the minor shall report conduct reasonably believed to violate Section 21.02, 22.011, 22.021, or 25.02, Penal Code, based on information obtained during a confidential court proceeding held under this chapter to:

(1) any local or state law enforcement agency;

(2) the Department of Family and Protective Services, if the alleged conduct involves a person responsible for the care, custody, or welfare of the child;

(3) the state agency that operates, licenses, certifies, or registers the facility in which the alleged conduct occurred, if the alleged conduct occurred in a facility operated, licensed, certified, or registered by a state agency; or

(4) an appropriate agency designated by the court.

Added by Acts 1999, 76th Leg., ch. 395, § 1, eff. Sept. 1, 1999. Amended by Acts 2007, 80th Leg., ch. 593, § 3.27, eff. Sept. 1, 2007.

## § 33.010. Confidentiality

Notwithstanding any other law, information obtained by the Department of Family and Protective Services or another entity under Section 33.008,

33.0085, or 33.009 is confidential except to the extent necessary to prove a violation of Section 21.02, 22.011, 22.021, or 25.02, Penal Code.

Added by Acts 1999, 76th Leg., ch. 395, § 1, eff. Sept. 1, 1999. Amended by Acts 2007, 80th Leg., ch. 593, § 3.28, eff. Sept. 1, 2007; Acts 2015, 84th Leg., ch. 436 (H.B. 3994), § 10, eff. Jan. 1, 2016.

### § 33.011. Information Relating to Judicial Bypass

The Texas Department of Health shall produce and distribute informational materials that explain the rights of a minor under this chapter. The materials must explain the procedures established by Sections 33.003 and 33.004 and must be made available in English and in Spanish. The material provided by the department shall also provide information relating to alternatives to abortion and health risks associated with abortion.

Added by Acts 1999, 76th Leg., ch. 395, § 1, eff. Sept. 1, 1999.

### § 33.012. Civil Penalty

(a) A person who is found to have intentionally, knowingly, recklessly, or with gross negligence violated this chapter is liable to this state for a civil penalty of not less than $2,500 and not more than $10,000.

(b) Each performance or attempted performance of an abortion in violation of this chapter is a separate violation.

(c) A civil penalty may not be assessed against:

(1) a minor on whom an abortion is performed or attempted; or

(2) a judge or justice hearing a court proceeding conducted under Section 33.003 or 33.004.

(d) It is not a defense to an action brought under this section that the minor gave informed and voluntary consent.

(e) The attorney general shall bring an action to collect a penalty under this section.

Added by Acts 2015, 84th Leg., ch. 436 (H.B. 3994), § 11, eff. Jan. 1, 2016.

### § 33.013. Capacity to Consent

An unemancipated minor does not have the capacity to consent to any action that violates this chapter.

Added by Acts 2015, 84th Leg., ch. 436 (H.B. 3994), § 11, eff. Jan. 1, 2016.

### § 33.014. Attorney General to Enforce

The attorney general shall enforce this chapter.

Added by Acts 2015, 84th Leg., ch. 436 (H.B. 3994), § 11, eff. Jan. 1, 2016.

## CHAPTER 34. AUTHORIZATION AGREEMENT FOR NONPARENT ADULT CAREGIVER

**Section**



*A former Chapter 34, Report of Child Abuse, consisting of §§ 34.01 to 34.612, was repealed by Acts 1995, 74th Leg., ch. 20, § 2, effective April 20, 1995, as part of the reenactment of Title 2.*

### § 34.001. Repealed by Acts 2017, 85th Leg., ch. 244 (H.B. 871), § 13, eff. Sept. 1, 2017

### § 34.0015. Definitions

In this chapter:

(1) "Adult caregiver" means an adult person whom a parent has authorized to provide temporary care for a child under this chapter.

(2) "Parent" has the meaning assigned by Section 101.024.

Added by Acts 2011, 82nd Leg., ch. 897 (S.B. 482), § 1, eff. Sept. 1, 2011. Amended by Acts 2017, 85th Leg., ch. 244 (H.B. 871), § 2, eff. Sept. 1, 2017.

### § 34.002. Authorization Agreement

(a) A parent or both parents of a child may enter into an authorization agreement with an adult caregiver to authorize the adult caregiver to perform the following acts in regard to the child:

(1) to authorize medical, dental, psychological, or surgical treatment and immunization of the child, including executing any consents or authorizations for the release of information as required by law relating to the treatment or immunization;

(2) to obtain and maintain health insurance coverage for the child and automobile insurance coverage for the child, if appropriate;

(3) to enroll the child in a day-care program or preschool or in a public or private elementary or secondary school;

(4) to authorize the child to participate in age-appropriate extracurricular, civic, social, or recreational activities, including athletic activities;

(5) to authorize the child to obtain a learner's permit, driver's license, or state-issued identification card;

(6) to authorize employment of the child;

(7) to apply for and receive public benefits on behalf of the child; and

(8) to obtain:

(A) copies or originals of state-issued personal identification documents for the child, including the child's birth certificate; and

(B) to the extent authorized under federal law, copies or originals of federally issued personal identification documents for the child, including the child's social security card.

(b) To the extent of any conflict or inconsistency between this chapter and any other law relating to the eligibility requirements other than parental consent to obtain a service under Subsection (a), the other law controls.

(c) An authorization agreement under this chapter does not confer on an adult caregiver the right to authorize the performance of an abortion on the child or the administration of emergency contraception to the child.

(d) Only one authorization agreement may be in effect for a child at any time. An authorization agreement is void if it is executed while a prior authorization agreement remains in effect.

Added by Acts 2009, 81st Leg., ch. 815, § 1, eff. June 19, 2009. Amended by Acts 2011, 82nd Leg., ch. 484 (H.B. 848), § 2, eff. Sept. 1, 2011; Acts 2011, 82nd Leg., ch. 897 (S.B. 482), § 2, eff. Sept. 1, 2011; Acts 2015, 84th Leg., ch. 1167 (S.B. 821), § 1, eff. Sept. 1, 2015; Acts 2017, 85th Leg., ch. 244 (H.B. 871), § 3, eff. Sept. 1, 2017; Acts 2017, 85th Leg., ch. 885 (H.B. 3052), § 2, eff. Sept. 1, 2017.

### § 34.0021. Authorization Agreement by Parent in Child Protective Services Case

A parent may enter into an authorization agreement with an adult caregiver with whom a child is placed under a parental child safety placement agreement approved by the Department of Family and Protective Services to allow the person to perform the acts described by Section 34.002(a) with regard to the child:

(1) during an investigation of abuse or neglect; or

(2) while the department is providing services to the parent.

Added by Acts 2011, 82nd Leg., ch. 484 (H.B. 848), § 3, eff. Sept. 1, 2011. Amended by Acts 2017, 85th Leg., ch. 244 (H.B. 871), § 4, eff. Sept. 1, 2017.

### § 34.0022. Inapplicability of Certain Laws

(a) An authorization agreement executed under this chapter between a child's parent and an adult caregiver does not subject the adult caregiver to any law or rule governing the licensing or regulation of a residential child-care facility under Chapter 42, Human Resources Code.

(b) A child who is the subject of an authorization agreement executed under this chapter is not considered to be placed in foster care and the parties to the authorization agreement are not subject to any law or rule governing foster care providers.

Added by Acts 2017, 85th Leg., ch. 244 (H.B. 871), § 5, eff. Sept. 1, 2017.

### § 34.003. Contents of Authorization Agreement

(a) The authorization agreement must contain:

(1) the following information from the adult caregiver:

(A) the name and signature of the adult caregiver;

(B) the adult caregiver's relationship to the child; and

(C) the adult caregiver's current physical address and telephone number or the best way to contact the adult caregiver;

(2) the following information from the parent:

(A) the name and signature of the parent; and

(B) the parent's current address and telephone number or the best way to contact the parent;

(3) the information in Subdivision (2) with respect to the other parent, if applicable;

(4) a statement that the adult caregiver has been given authorization to perform the functions listed in Section 34.002(a) as a result of a voluntary action of the parent and that the adult caregiver has voluntarily assumed the responsibility of performing those functions;

(5) statements that neither the parent nor the adult caregiver has knowledge that a parent, guardian, custodian, licensed child-placing agency, or other authorized agency asserts any claim or authority inconsistent with the authorization agreement under this chapter with regard to actual physical possession or care, custody, or control of the child;

(6) statements that:

(A) to the best of the parent's and adult caregiver's knowledge:

(i) there is no court order or pending suit affecting the parent-child relationship concerning the child;

(ii) there is no pending litigation in any court concerning:

(a) custody, possession, or placement of the child; or

(b) access to or visitation with the child; and

(iii) a court does not have continuing jurisdiction concerning the child; or

(B) the court with continuing jurisdiction concerning the child has given written approval for the execution of the authorization agreement accompanied by the following information:

(i) the county in which the court is located;

(ii) the number of the court; and

(iii) the cause number in which the order was issued or the litigation is pending;

(7) a statement that to the best of the parent's and adult caregiver's knowledge there is no current, valid authorization agreement regarding the child;

(8) a statement that the authorization is made in conformance with this chapter;

(9) a statement that the parent and the adult caregiver understand that each party to the authorization agreement is required by law to immediately provide to each other party information regarding any change in the party's address or contact information;

(10) a statement by the parent that:

(A) indicates the authorization agreement is for a term of:

(i) six months from the date the parties enter into the agreement, which renews automatically for six-month terms unless the agreement is terminated as provided by Section 34.008; or

(ii) the time provided in the agreement with a specific expiration date earlier than six months after the date the parties enter into the agreement; and

(B) identifies the circumstances under which the authorization agreement may be:

(i) terminated as provided by Section 34.008 before the term of the agreement expires; or

(ii) continued beyond the term of the agreement by a court as provided by Section 34.008(b); and

(11) space for the signature and seal of a notary public.

(b) The authorization agreement must contain the following warnings and disclosures:

(1) that the authorization agreement is an important legal document;

(2) that the parent and the adult caregiver must read all of the warnings and disclosures before signing the authorization agreement;

(3) that the persons signing the authorization agreement are not required to consult an attorney but are advised to do so;

(4) that the parent's rights as a parent may be adversely affected by placing or leaving the parent's child with another person;

(5) that the authorization agreement does not confer on the adult caregiver the rights of a managing or possessory conservator or legal guardian;

(6) that a parent who is a party to the authorization agreement may terminate the authorization agreement and resume custody, possession, care, and control of the child on demand and that at any time the parent may request the return of the child;

(7) that failure by the adult caregiver to return the child to the parent immediately on request may have criminal and civil consequences;

(8) that, under other applicable law, the adult caregiver may be liable for certain expenses relating to the child in the adult caregiver's care but that the parent still retains the parental obligation to support the child;

(9) that, in certain circumstances, the authorization agreement may not be entered into without written permission of the court;

(10) that the authorization agreement may be terminated by certain court orders affecting the child;

(11) that the authorization agreement does not supersede, invalidate, or terminate any prior authorization agreement regarding the child;

(12) that the authorization agreement is void if a prior authorization agreement regarding the child is in effect and has not expired or been terminated;

(13) that, except as provided by Section 34.005(a–2), the authorization agreement is void unless not later than the 10th day after the date the authorization agreement is signed,

the parties mail to a parent who was not a party to the authorization agreement at the parent's last known address, if the parent is living and the parent's parental rights have not been terminated:

(A) one copy of the authorization agreement by certified mail, return receipt requested, or international registered mail, return receipt requested, as applicable; and

(B) one copy of the authorization agreement by first class mail or international first class mail, as applicable; and

(14) that the authorization agreement does not confer on an adult caregiver the right to authorize the performance of an abortion on the child or the administration of emergency contraception to the child.

Added by Acts 2009, 81st Leg., ch. 815, § 1, eff. June 19, 2009. Amended by Acts 2011, 82nd Leg., ch. 897 (S.B. 482), § 3, eff. Sept. 1, 2011; Acts 2017, 85th Leg., ch. 244 (H.B. 871), § 6, eff. Sept. 1, 2017; Acts 2017, 85th Leg., ch. 885 (H.B. 3052), § 3, eff. Sept. 1, 2017.

### § 34.004. Execution of Authorization Agreement

(a) The authorization agreement must be signed and sworn to before a notary public by the parent and the adult caregiver.

(b) A parent may not execute an authorization agreement without a written order by the appropriate court if:

(1) there is a court order or pending suit affecting the parent-child relationship concerning the child;

(2) there is pending litigation in any court concerning:

(A) custody, possession, or placement of the child; or

(B) access to or visitation with the child; or

(3) a court has continuing, exclusive jurisdiction over the child.

(c) An authorization agreement obtained in violation of Subsection (b) is void.

Added by Acts 2009, 81st Leg., ch. 815, § 1, eff. June 19, 2009. Amended by Acts 2017, 85th Leg., ch. 244 (H.B. 871), § 7, eff. Sept. 1, 2017; Acts 2017, 85th Leg., ch. 885 (H.B. 3052), § 4, eff. Sept. 1, 2017.

### § 34.005. Duties of Parties to Authorization Agreement

(a) If both parents did not sign the authorization agreement, not later than the 10th day after the date the authorization agreement is executed the parties shall mail to the parent who was not a party to the authorization agreement at the parent's last known address, if that parent is living and that parent's parental rights have not been terminated:

(1) one copy of the executed authorization agreement by certified mail, return receipt requested, or international registered mail, return receipt requested, as applicable; and

(2) one copy of the executed authorization agreement by first class mail or international first class mail, as applicable.

(a–1) Except as otherwise provided by Subsection (a–2), an authorization agreement is void if the parties fail to comply with Subsection (a).

(a–2) Subsection (a) does not apply to an authorization agreement if the parent who was not a party to the authorization agreement:

(1) does not have court-ordered possession of or access to the child who is the subject of the authorization agreement; and

(2) has previously committed an act of family violence, as defined by Section 71.004, or assault against the parent who is a party to the authorization agreement, the child who is the subject of the authorization agreement, or another child of the parent who is a party to the authorization agreement, as documented by one or more of the following:

(A) the issuance of a protective order against the parent who was not a party to the authorization agreement as provided under Chapter 85 or under a similar law of another state; or

(B) the conviction of the parent who was not a party to the authorization agreement of an offense under Title 5, Penal Code, [1] or of another criminal offense in this state or in another state an element of which involves a violent act or prohibited sexual conduct.

(b) A party to the authorization agreement shall immediately inform each other party of any change in the party's address or contact information. If a party fails to comply with this subsection, the authorization agreement is voidable by the other party.

Added by Acts 2009, 81st Leg., ch. 815, § 1, eff. June 19, 2009. Amended by Acts 2011, 82nd Leg., ch. 897 (S.B. 482), § 4, eff. Sept. 1, 2011; Acts 2017, 85th Leg., ch. 885 (H.B. 3052), § 5, eff. Sept. 1, 2017.

[1] V.T.C.A., Penal Code § 19.01 et seq.

## § 34.006. Authorization Voidable

An authorization agreement is voidable by a party if the other party knowingly:

(1) obtained the authorization agreement by fraud, duress, or misrepresentation; or

(2) made a false statement on the authorization agreement.

Added by Acts 2009, 81st Leg., ch. 815, § 1, eff. June 19, 2009.

## § 34.007. Effect of Authorization Agreement

(a) A person who is not a party to the authorization agreement who relies in good faith on an authorization agreement under this chapter, without actual knowledge that the authorization agreement is void, revoked, or invalid, is not subject to civil or criminal liability to any person, and is not subject to professional disciplinary action, for that reliance if the agreement is completed as required by this chapter.

(b) The authorization agreement does not affect the rights of the child's parent or legal guardian regarding the care, custody, and control of the child, and does not mean that the adult caregiver has legal custody of the child.

(c) An authorization agreement executed under this chapter does not confer or affect standing or a right of intervention in any proceeding under Title 5.[1]

Added by Acts 2009, 81st Leg., ch. 815, § 1, eff. June 19, 2009. Amended by Acts 2017, 85th Leg., ch. 244 (H.B. 871), § 8, eff. Sept. 1, 2017.

[1] V.T.C.A., Family Code § 101.001 et seq.

## § 34.0075. Term of Authorization Agreement

An authorization agreement executed under this chapter is for a term of six months from the date the parties enter into the agreement and renews automatically for six-month terms unless:

(1) an earlier expiration date is stated in the authorization agreement;

(2) the authorization agreement is terminated as provided by Section 34.008; or

(3) a court authorizes the continuation of the agreement as provided by Section 34.008(b).

Added by Acts 2017, 85th Leg., ch. 244 (H.B. 871), § 9, eff. Sept. 1, 2017.

## § 34.008. Termination of Authorization Agreement

(a) Except as provided by Subsection (b), an authorization agreement under this chapter terminates if, after the execution of the authorization agreement, a court enters an order:

(1) affecting the parent-child relationship;

(2) concerning custody, possession, or placement of the child;

(3) concerning access to or visitation with the child; or

(4) regarding the appointment of a guardian for the child under Subchapter B, Chapter 1104, Estates Code.

(b) An authorization agreement may continue after a court order described by Subsection (a) is entered if the court entering the order gives written permission.

(c) An authorization agreement under this chapter terminates on written revocation by a party to the authorization agreement if the party:

(1) gives each party written notice of the revocation;

(2) files the written revocation with the clerk of the county in which:

(A) the child resides;

(B) the child resided at the time the authorization agreement was executed; or

(C) the adult caregiver resides; and

(3) files the written revocation with the clerk of each court:

(A) that has continuing, exclusive jurisdiction over the child;

(B) in which there is a court order or pending suit affecting the parent-child relationship concerning the child;

(C) in which there is pending litigation concerning:

(i) custody, possession, or placement of the child; or

(ii) access to or visitation with the child; or

(D) that has entered an order regarding the appointment of a guardian for the child under Subchapter B, Chapter 1104, Estates Code.

(d) Repealed by Acts 2017, 85th Leg., ch. 244 (H.B. 871), § 13.

(e) If both parents have signed the authorization agreement, either parent may revoke the authorization agreement without the other parent's consent.

(f) Execution of a subsequent authorization agreement does not by itself supersede, invalidate, or terminate a prior authorization agreement.

Added by Acts 2009, 81st Leg., ch. 815, § 1, eff. June 19, 2009. Amended by Acts 2011, 82nd Leg., ch. 897 (S.B. 482), § 5, eff. Sept. 1, 2011; Acts 2017, 85th Leg., ch. 244 (H.B. 871), §§ 10, 13, eff. Sept. 1, 2017; Acts 2017, 85th Leg., ch. 324 (S.B. 1488), § 22.017, eff. Sept. 1, 2017.

### § 34.009. Penalty

(a) A person commits an offense if the person knowingly:

(1) presents a document that is not a valid authorization agreement as a valid authorization agreement under this chapter;

(2) makes a false statement on an authorization agreement; or

(3) obtains an authorization agreement by fraud, duress, or misrepresentation.

(b) An offense under this section is a Class B misdemeanor.

Added by Acts 2009, 81st Leg., ch. 815, § 1, eff. June 19, 2009.

## CHAPTER 35. TEMPORARY AUTHORIZATION FOR CARE OF MINOR CHILD



*A former Chapter 35, Consent to Medical Treatment, consisting of §§ 35.01 to 35.05, was repealed by Acts 1995, 74th Leg., ch. 20, § 2, eff. April 20, 1995.*

### § 35.001. Applicability

This chapter applies to a person whose relationship to a child would make the person eligible to consent to treatment under Section 32.001 or eligible to enter an authorization agreement under Section 34.001.

Added by Acts 2017, 85th Leg., ch. 334 (H.B. 1043), § 1, eff. June 1, 2017.

### § 35.002. Temporary Authorization

A person described by Section 35.001 may seek a court order for temporary authorization for care of a child by filing a petition in the district court in the county in which the person resides if:

(1) the child has resided with the person for at least the 30 days preceding the date the petition was filed; and

(2) the person does not have an authorization agreement under Chapter 34 or other signed, written documentation from a parent, conservator, or guardian that enables the person to provide necessary care for the child.

Added by Acts 2017, 85th Leg., ch. 334 (H.B. 1043), § 1, eff. June 1, 2017.

### § 35.003. Petition for Temporary Authorization for Care of Child

(a) A petition for temporary authorization for care of a child must:

(1) be styled "ex parte" and be in the name of the child;

(2) be verified by the petitioner;

(3) state:

(A) the name, date of birth, and current physical address of the child;

(B) the name, date of birth, and current physical address of the petitioner; and

(C) the name and, if known, the current physical and mailing addresses of the child's parents, conservators, or guardians;

(4) describe the status and location of any court proceeding in this or another state with respect to the child;

(5) describe the petitioner's relationship to the child;

(6) provide the dates during the preceding 12 months that the child has resided with the petitioner;

(7) describe any service or action that the petitioner is unable to obtain or undertake on behalf of the child without authorization from the court;

(8) state any reason that the petitioner is unable to obtain signed, written documentation from a parent, conservator, or guardian of the child;

(9) contain a statement of the period for which the petitioner is requesting temporary authorization; and

(10) contain a statement of any reason supporting the request for the temporary authorization.

(b) If the petition identifies a court proceeding with respect to the child under Subsection (a)(4), the petitioner shall submit a copy of any court order that designates a conservator or guardian of the child.

Added by Acts 2017, 85th Leg., ch. 334 (H.B. 1043), § 1, eff. June 1, 2017.

### § 35.004. Notice; Hearing

(a) On receipt of the petition, the court shall set a hearing.

(b) A copy of the petition and notice of the hearing shall be delivered to the parent, conservator, or guardian of the child by personal service or by certified mail, return receipt requested, at the last known address of the parent, conservator, or guardian.

(c) Proof of service under Subsection (b) must be filed with the court at least three days before the date of the hearing.

Added by Acts 2017, 85th Leg., ch. 334 (H.B. 1043), § 1, eff. June 1, 2017.

### § 35.005. Order for Temporary Authorization

(a) At the hearing on the petition, the court may hear evidence relating to the child's need for care by the petitioner, any other matter raised in the petition, and any objection or other testimony of the child's parent, conservator, or guardian.

(b) The court shall award temporary authorization for care of the child to the petitioner if the court finds it is necessary to the child's welfare and no objection is made by the child's parent, conservator, or guardian. If an objection is made, the court shall dismiss the petition without prejudice.

(c) The court shall grant the petition for temporary authorization only if the court finds by a preponderance of the evidence that the child does not have a parent, conservator, guardian, or other legal representative available to give the necessary consent.

(d) The order granting temporary authorization under this chapter expires on the first anniversary of the date of issuance or at an earlier date determined by the court. The order may authorize the petitioner to:

(1) consent to medical, dental, psychological, and surgical treatment and immunization of the child;

(2) execute any consent or authorization for the release of information as required by law relating to the treatment or immunization under Subdivision (1);

(3) obtain and maintain any public benefit for the child;

(4) enroll the child in a day-care program, preschool, or public or private primary or secondary school;

(5) authorize the child to participate in age-appropriate extracurricular, civic, social, or recreational activities, including athletic activities; and

(6) authorize or consent to any other care for the child essential to the child's welfare.

(e) An order granting temporary authorization under this chapter must state:

(1) the name and date of birth of the person with temporary authorization to care for the child;

(2) the specific areas of authorization granted to the person;

(3) that the order does not supersede any rights of a parent, conservator, or guardian as provided by court order; and

(4) the expiration date of the temporary authorization order.

(f) A copy of an order for temporary authorization must:

(1) be filed under the cause number in any court that has rendered a conservatorship or guardian order regarding the child; and

(2) be sent to the last known address of the child's parent, conservator, or guardian.

Added by Acts 2017, 85th Leg., ch. 334 (H.B. 1043), § 1, eff. June 1, 2017.

### § 35.006. Renewal or Termination of Temporary Authorization

(a) A temporary authorization order may be renewed by court order for a period of not more than one year on a showing by the petitioner of a continuing need for the order.

(b) At any time, the petitioner or the child's parent, conservator, or guardian may request the court to terminate the order. The court shall terminate the order on finding that there is no longer a need for the order.

Added by Acts 2017, 85th Leg., ch. 334 (H.B. 1043), § 1, eff. June 1, 2017.

### § 35.007. Effect of Temporary Authorization

(a) A person who relies in good faith on a temporary authorization order under this chapter is not subject to:

(1) civil or criminal liability to any person; or

(2) professional disciplinary action.

(b) A temporary authorization order does not affect the rights of the child's parent, conservator, or guardian regarding the care, custody, and control of the child, and does not establish legal custody of the child.

(c) A temporary authorization order does not confer or affect standing or a right of intervention in any proceeding under Title 5.

(d) An order under this chapter is not a child custody determination and does not create a court of continuing, exclusive jurisdiction under Title 5.

Added by Acts 2017, 85th Leg., ch. 334 (H.B. 1043), § 1, eff. June 1, 2017.

## CHAPTER 35A. TEMPORARY AUTHORIZATION FOR INPATIENT MENTAL HEALTH SERVICES FOR MINOR CHILD



### § 35A.001. Applicability

This chapter applies to a person whose relationship to a child would make the person eligible to consent to treatment under Section 32.001(a)(1), (2), or (3), and who has had actual care, custody, and control of the child for the six months preceding the filing of a petition under this chapter.

Added by Acts 2019, 86th Leg., ch. 988 (S.B. 1238), § 1, eff. Sept. 1, 2019.

### § 35A.002. Temporary Authorization

A person described by Section 35A.001 may seek a court order for temporary authorization to consent to voluntary inpatient mental health services for a child by filing a petition in the district court in the county in which the person resides.

Added by Acts 2019, 86th Leg., ch. 988 (S.B. 1238), § 1, eff. Sept. 1, 2019.

### § 35A.003. Petition for Temporary Authorization

A petition for temporary authorization to consent to voluntary inpatient mental health services for a child must:

(1) be styled "ex parte" and be in the name of the child;

(2) be verified by the petitioner;

(3) state:

(A) the name, date of birth, and current physical address of the child;

(B) the name, date of birth, and current physical address of the petitioner; and

(C) the name and, if known, the current physical and mailing addresses of the child's parents, conservators, or guardians;

(4) describe the status and location of any court proceeding in this or another state with respect to the child;

(5) describe the petitioner's relationship to the child;

(6) provide the dates during the preceding six months that the child has resided with the petitioner;

(7) contain a certificate of medical examination for mental illness prepared by a physician who has examined the child not earlier than the third day before the date the petition is filed and be accompanied by a sworn statement containing the physician's opinion, and the detailed reasons for that opinion, that the child is a person:

(A) with mental illness or who demonstrates symptoms of a serious emotional disorder; and

(B) who presents a risk of serious harm to self or others if not immediately restrained or hospitalized; and

(8) state any reason that the petitioner is unable to obtain signed, written documentation from a parent, conservator, or guardian of the child.

Added by Acts 2019, 86th Leg., ch. 988 (S.B. 1238), § 1, eff. Sept. 1, 2019.

### § 35A.004. Notice; Hearing

(a) On receipt of the petition, the court shall set a hearing.

(b) A copy of the petition and notice of the hearing shall be delivered to the parent, conservator, or guardian of the child by personal service or by certified mail, return receipt requested, at the last known address of the parent, conservator, or guardian.

Added by Acts 2019, 86th Leg., ch. 988 (S.B. 1238), § 1, eff. Sept. 1, 2019.

### § 35A.005. Order for Temporary Authorization

(a) At the hearing on the petition, the court may hear evidence relating to the child's need for inpatient mental health services by the petitioner, any other matter raised in the petition, and any objection or other testimony of the child's parent, conservator, or guardian.

(b) The court shall dismiss the petition for temporary authorization if an objection is made by the child's parent, conservator, or guardian.

(c) The court shall grant the petition for temporary authorization only if the court finds:

(1) by a preponderance of the evidence that the child does not have available a parent, conservator, guardian, or other legal representative to give consent under Section 572.001, Health and Safety Code, for voluntary inpatient mental health services; and

(2) by clear and convincing evidence that the child is a person:

(A) with mental illness or who demonstrates symptoms of a serious emotional disorder; and

(B) who presents a risk of serious harm to self or others if not immediately restrained or hospitalized.

(d) Subject to Subsection (e), the order granting temporary authorization under this chapter expires on the earliest of:

(1) the date the petitioner requests that the child be discharged from the inpatient mental health facility;

(2) the date a physician determines that the criteria listed in Subsection (c)(2) no longer apply to the child; or

(3) subject to Subsection (e), the 10th day after the date the order for temporary authorization is issued under this section.

(e) The order granting temporary authorization continues in effect until the earlier occurrence of an event described by Subsection (d)(1) or (2) if the petitioner obtains an order for temporary managing conservatorship before the order expires as provided by Subsection (d)(3).

(f) A copy of an order granting temporary authorization must:

(1) be filed under the cause number in any court that has rendered a conservatorship or guardian order regarding the child; and

(2) be sent to the last known address of the child's parent, conservator, or guardian.

Added by Acts 2019, 86th Leg., ch. 988 (S.B. 1238), § 1, eff. Sept. 1, 2019.

## CHAPTER 36. CIVIL LIABILITY FOR INTERFERENCE WITH CHILD CUSTODY [REPEALED]

### §§ 36.01 to 36.08. Repealed by Acts 1995, 74th Leg., ch. 20, § 2, eff. April 20, 1995

# SUBTITLE B. PARENTAL LIABILITY

## CHAPTER 41. LIABILITY OF PARENTS FOR CONDUCT OF CHILD



### § 41.001. Liability

A parent or other person who has the duty of control and reasonable discipline of a child is liable for any property damage proximately caused by:

(1) the negligent conduct of the child if the conduct is reasonably attributable to the negligent failure of the parent or other person to exercise that duty; or

(2) the wilful and malicious conduct of a child who is at least 10 years of age but under 18 years of age.

Added by Acts 1995, 74th Leg., ch. 20, § 1, eff. April 20, 1995. Amended by Acts 2001, 77th Leg., ch. 587, § 1, eff. Sept. 1, 2001.

### § 41.002. Limit of Damages

Recovery for damage caused by wilful and malicious conduct is limited to actual damages, not to exceed $25,000 per occurrence, plus court costs and reasonable attorney's fees.

Added by Acts 1995, 74th Leg., ch. 20, § 1, eff. April 20, 1995. Amended by Acts 1997, 75th Leg., ch. 783, § 1, eff. Sept. 1, 1997.

### § 41.0025. Liability for Property Damage to an Inn or Hotel

(a) Notwithstanding Section 41.002, recovery of damages by an inn or hotel for wilful and malicious conduct is limited to actual damages, not to exceed $25,000 per occurrence, plus court costs and reasonable attorney's fees.

(b) In this section "occurrence" means one incident on a single day in one hotel room. The term does not include incidents in separate rooms or incidents that occur on different days.

Added by Acts 1997, 75th Leg., ch. 40, § 1, eff. Sept. 1, 1997.

### § 41.003. Venue

A suit as provided by this chapter may be filed in the county in which the conduct of the child occurred or in the county in which the defendant resides.

Added by Acts 1995, 74th Leg., ch. 20, § 1, eff. April 20, 1995.

## CHAPTER 42. CIVIL LIABILITY FOR INTERFERENCE WITH POSSESSORY INTEREST IN CHILD

Section



### § 42.001. Definitions

In this chapter:

(1) "Order" means a temporary or final order of a court of this state or another state or nation.

(2) "Possessory right" means a court-ordered right of possession of or access to a child, including conservatorship, custody, and visitation.

Added by Acts 1995, 74th Leg., ch. 20, § 1, eff. April 20, 1995.

### § 42.002. Liability for Interference with Possessory Right

(a) A person who takes or retains possession of a child or who conceals the whereabouts of a child in violation of a possessory right of another person may be liable for damages to that person.

(b) A possessory right is violated by the taking, retention, or concealment of a child at a time when another person is entitled to possession of or access to the child.

Added by Acts 1995, 74th Leg., ch. 20, § 1, eff. April 20, 1995.

### § 42.003. Aiding or Assisting Interference with Possessory Right

(a) A person who aids or assists in conduct for which a cause of action is authorized by this chapter is jointly and severally liable for damages.

(b) A person who was not a party to the suit in which an order was rendered providing for a possessory right is not liable unless the person at the time of the violation:

(1) had actual notice of the existence and contents of the order; or

(2) had reasonable cause to believe that the child was the subject of an order and that the person's actions were likely to violate the order.

Added by Acts 1995, 74th Leg., ch. 20, § 1, eff. April 20, 1995.

### § 42.004. Repealed by Acts 1999, 76th Leg., ch. 437, § 2, eff. Sept. 1, 1999

### § 42.005. Venue

A suit may be filed in a county in which:

(1) the plaintiff resides;

(2) the defendant resides;

(3) a suit affecting the parent-child relationship as provided by Chapter 102 may be brought, concerning the child who is the subject of the court order; or

(4) a court has continuing, exclusive jurisdiction as provided by Chapter 155.

Added by Acts 1995, 74th Leg., ch. 20, § 1, eff. April 20, 1995.

### § 42.006. Damages

(a) Damages may include:

(1) the actual costs and expenses incurred, including attorney's fees, in:

(A) locating a child who is the subject of the order;

(B) recovering possession of the child if the petitioner is entitled to possession; and

(C) enforcing the order and prosecuting the suit; and

(2) mental suffering and anguish incurred by the plaintiff because of a violation of the order.

(b) A person liable for damages who acted with malice or with an intent to cause harm to the plaintiff may be liable for exemplary damages.

Added by Acts 1995, 74th Leg., ch. 20, § 1, eff. April 20, 1995. Amended by Acts 1995, 74th Leg., ch. 751, § 7, eff. Sept. 1, 1995.

### § 42.007. Affirmative Defense

The defendant may plead as an affirmative defense that the defendant acted in violation of the order with the express consent of the plaintiff.

Added by Acts 1995, 74th Leg., ch. 20, § 1, eff. April 20, 1995. Amended by Acts 1999, 76th Leg., ch. 437, § 1, eff. Sept. 1, 1999.

### § 42.008. Remedies Not Affected

This chapter does not affect any other civil or criminal remedy available to any person, including the child, for interference with a possessory right, nor does it affect the power of a parent to represent the interest of a child in a suit filed on behalf of the child.

Added by Acts 1995, 74th Leg., ch. 20, § 1, eff. April 20, 1995.

### § 42.009. Frivolous Suit

A person sued for damages as provided by this chapter is entitled to recover attorney's fees and court costs if:

(1) the claim for damages is dismissed or judgment is awarded to the defendant; and

(2) the court or jury finds that the claim for damages is frivolous, unreasonable, or without foundation.

Added by Acts 1995, 74th Leg., ch. 20, § 1, eff. April 20, 1995.

# SUBTITLE C. CHANGE OF NAME

## CHAPTER 45. CHANGE OF NAME

SUBCHAPTER A. CHANGE OF NAME OF CHILD



### SUBCHAPTER A. CHANGE OF NAME OF CHILD

### § 45.001. Who May File; Venue

A parent, managing conservator, or guardian of a child may file a petition requesting a change of name of the child in the county where the child resides.

Added by Acts 1995, 74th Leg., ch. 20, § 1, eff. April 20, 1995.

### § 45.002. Requirements of Petition

(a) A petition to change the name of a child must be verified and include:

(1) the present name and place of residence of the child;

(2) the reason a change of name is requested;

(3) the full name requested for the child;

(4) whether the child is subject to the continuing exclusive jurisdiction of a court under Chapter 155; and

(5) whether the child is subject to the registration requirements of Chapter 62, Code of Criminal Procedure.

(b) If the child is 10 years of age or older, the child's written consent to the change of name must be attached to the petition.

Added by Acts 1995, 74th Leg., ch. 20, § 1, eff. April 20, 1995. Amended by Acts 1999, 76th Leg., ch. 1390, § 1, eff. Sept. 1, 1999; Acts 2003, 78th Leg., ch. 1300, § 5, eff. Sept. 1, 2003.

### § 45.003. Citation

(a) The following persons are entitled to citation in a suit under this subchapter:

(1) a parent of the child whose parental rights have not been terminated;

(2) any managing conservator of the child; and

(3) any guardian of the child.

(b) Citation must be issued and served in the same manner as under Chapter 102.

Added by Acts 1995, 74th Leg., ch. 20, § 1, eff. April 20, 1995.

### § 45.0031. Waiver of Citation

(a) A party to a suit under this subchapter may waive the issuance or service of citation after the suit is filed by filing with the clerk of the court in which the suit is filed the waiver of the party acknowledging receipt of a copy of the filed petition.

(b) The party executing the waiver may not sign the waiver using a digitized signature.

(c) The waiver must contain the mailing address of the party executing the waiver.

(d) Notwithstanding Section 132.001, Civil Practice and Remedies Code, the waiver must be sworn before a notary public who is not an attorney in the suit. This subsection does not apply if the party executing the waiver is incarcerated.

(e) The Texas Rules of Civil Procedure do not apply to a waiver executed under this section.

(f) For purposes of this section, "digitized signature" has the meaning assigned by Section 101.0096.

Added by Acts 2015, 84th Leg., ch. 198 (S.B. 814), § 3, eff. Sept. 1, 2015.

### § 45.004. Order

(a) The court may order the name of a child changed if:

(1) the change is in the best interest of the child; and

(2) for a child subject to the registration requirements of Chapter 62, Code of Criminal Procedure:

(A) the change is in the interest of the public; and

(B) the person petitioning on behalf of the child provides the court with proof that the child has notified the appropriate local law enforcement authority of the proposed name change.

(b) If the child is subject to the continuing jurisdiction of a court under Chapter 155, the court shall send a copy of the order to the central record file as provided in Chapter 108.

(c) In this section, "local law enforcement authority" has the meaning assigned by Article 62.001, Code of Criminal Procedure.

Added by Acts 1995, 74th Leg., ch. 20, § 1, eff. April 20, 1995. Amended by Acts 2003, 78th Leg., ch. 1300, § 6, eff. Sept. 1, 2003; Acts 2005, 79th Leg., ch. 1008, § 2.05, eff. Sept. 1, 2005.

### § 45.005. Liabilities and Rights Unaffected

A change of name does not:

(1) release a child from any liability incurred in the child's previous name; or

(2) defeat any right the child had in the child's previous name.

Added by Acts 1995, 74th Leg., ch. 20, § 1, eff. April 20, 1995.

## SUBCHAPTER B. CHANGE OF NAME OF ADULT

### § 45.101. Who May File; Venue

An adult may file a petition requesting a change of name in the county of the adult's place of residence.

Added by Acts 1995, 74th Leg., ch. 20, § 1, eff. April 20, 1995.

### § 45.102. Requirements of Petition

(a) A petition to change the name of an adult must be verified and include:

(1) the present name and place of residence of the petitioner;

(2) the full name requested for the petitioner;

(3) the reason the change in name is requested;

(4) whether the petitioner has been the subject of a final felony conviction;

(5) whether the petitioner is subject to the registration requirements of Chapter 62, Code of Criminal Procedure; and

(6) a legible and complete set of the petitioner's fingerprints on a fingerprint card format acceptable to the Department of Public Safety and the Federal Bureau of Investigation.

(b) The petition must include each of the following or a reasonable explanation why the required information is not included:

(1) the petitioner's:

(A) full name;

(B) sex;

(C) race;

(D) date of birth;

(E) driver's license number for any driver's license issued in the 10 years preceding the date of the petition;

(F) social security number; and

(G) assigned FBI number, state identification number, if known, or any other reference number in a criminal history record system that identifies the petitioner;

(2) any offense above the grade of Class C misdemeanor for which the petitioner has been charged; and

(3) the case number and the court if a warrant was issued or a charging instrument was filed or presented for an offense listed in Subsection (b)(2).

(c) A petitioner is not required to provide the street address of the petitioner's place of residence or the petitioner's reason for the requested change of name as otherwise required by Subsection (a) if the petitioner provides a copy of an authorization card certifying in accordance with Article 58.059, Code of Criminal Procedure, that the petitioner is a participant in the address confidentiality program administered by the attorney general under Subchapter B, Chapter 58, Code of Criminal Procedure.

Added by Acts 1995, 74th Leg., ch. 20, § 1, eff. April 20, 1995. Amended by Acts 2003, 78th Leg., ch. 1003, § 1, eff. Sept. 1, 2003; Acts 2003, 78th Leg., ch. 1300, § 7, eff. Sept. 1, 2003; Acts 2005, 79th Leg., ch. 728, § 6.001, eff. Sept. 1, 2005; Acts 2021, 87th Leg., ch. 339 (H.B. 2301), § 1, eff. Sept. 1, 2021.

Section 3 of Acts 2021, 87th Leg., ch. 339 (H.B. 2301) provides:

"The change in law made by this Act applies only to a petition for a change of name that is submitted on or after the effective date [Sept. 1, 2021] of this Act."

## § 45.103. Order

(a) The court shall order a change of name under this subchapter for a person other than a person with a final felony conviction or a person subject to the registration requirements of Chapter 62, Code of Criminal Procedure, if the change is in the interest or to the benefit of the petitioner and in the interest of the public.

(a–1) For purposes of Subsection (a), it is presumed that a change of name is in the interest or to the benefit of the petitioner and in the interest of the public if the petitioner provides a copy of an authorization card certifying in accordance with Article 58.059, Code of Criminal Procedure, that the petitioner is a participant in the address confidentiality program administered by the attorney general under Subchapter B, Chapter 58, Code of Criminal Procedure.

(b) A court may order a change of name under this subchapter for a person with a final felony conviction if:

(1) in addition to the requirements of Subsection (a), the person has:

(A) received a certificate of discharge by the Texas Department of Criminal Justice or completed a period of community supervision or juvenile probation ordered by a court and not less than two years have passed from the date of the receipt of discharge or completion of community supervision or juvenile probation; or

(B) been pardoned; or

(2) the person is requesting to change the person's name to the primary name used in the person's criminal history record information.

(c) A court may order a change of name under this subchapter for a person subject to the registration requirements of Chapter 62, Code of Criminal Procedure, if the person:

(1) meets the requirements of Subsection (a) or is requesting to change the person's name to the primary name used in the person's criminal history record information; and

(2) provides the court with proof that the person has notified the appropriate local law enforcement authority of the proposed name change.

(c–1) An order issued under this section to change the name of a petitioner described by Subsection (a–1) is confidential and may not be released by the court to any person, regardless of whether the petitioner continues to participate in the address confidentiality program following the change of name under this subchapter.

(d) In this section:

(1) "Criminal history record information" has the meaning assigned by Section 411.082, Government Code.

(2) "Local law enforcement authority" has the meaning assigned by Article 62.001, Code of Criminal Procedure.

Added by Acts 1995, 74th Leg., ch. 20, § 1, eff. April 20, 1995. Amended by Acts 2003, 78th Leg., ch. 1300, § 8, eff. Sept. 1, 2003; Acts 2005, 79th Leg., ch. 1008, § 2.06, eff. Sept. 1, 2005; Acts 2009, 81st Leg., ch. 87, § 25.057, eff. Sept. 1, 2009; Acts 2019, 86th Leg., ch. 232 (H.B. 2623), § 1, eff. Sept. 1, 2019; Acts 2021, 87th Leg., ch. 339 (H.B. 2301), § 2, eff. Sept. 1, 2021.

Section 2 of Acts 2019, 86th Leg., ch. 232 (H.B. 2623) provides:

"Section 45.103, Family Code, as amended by this Act, applies only to a petition for a change of name that is filed on or after the effective date [Sept. 1, 2019] of this Act. A petition filed before the effective date of this Act is governed by the law in effect on the date the petition was filed, and the former law is continued in effect for that purpose."

Section 3 of Acts 2021, 87th Leg., ch. 339 (H.B. 2301) provides:

"The change in law made by this Act applies only to a petition for a change of name that is submitted on or after the effective date [Sept. 1, 2021] of this Act."

### § 45.104. Liabilities and Rights Unaffected

A change of name under this subchapter does not release a person from liability incurred in that person's previous name or defeat any right the person had in the person's previous name.

Added by Acts 1995, 74th Leg., ch. 20, § 1, eff. April 20, 1995.

### § 45.105. Change of Name in Divorce Suit

(a) On the final disposition of a suit for divorce, for annulment, or to declare a marriage void, the court shall enter a decree changing the name of a party specially praying for the change to a prior used name unless the court states in the decree a reason for denying the change of name. The court may not deny a change of name solely to keep last names of family members the same.

(b) A person whose name is changed under this section may apply for a change of name certificate from the clerk of the court as provided by Section 45.106.

Added by Acts 1997, 75th Leg., ch. 165, § 7.10(a), eff. Sept. 1, 1997.

### § 45.106. Change of Name Certificate

(a) A person whose name is changed under Section 6.706 or 45.105 may apply to the clerk of the court ordering the name change for a change of name certificate.

(b) A certificate under this section is a one-page document that includes:

(1) the name of the person before the change of name was ordered;

(2) the name to which the person's name was changed by the court;

(3) the date on which the name change was made;

(4) the person's social security number and driver's license number, if any;

(5) the name of the court in which the name change was ordered; and

(6) the signature of the clerk of the court that issued the certificate.

(c) An applicant for a certificate under this section shall pay a $10 fee to the clerk of the court for issuance of the certificate.

(d) A certificate under this section constitutes proof of the change of name of the person named in the certificate.

Added by Acts 1997, 75th Leg., ch. 165, § 7.10(a), eff. Sept. 1, 1997. Amended by Acts 1999, 76th Leg., ch. 62, § 6.06, eff. Sept. 1, 1999.

### § 45.107. Waiver of Citation

(a) A party to a suit under this subchapter may waive the issuance or service of citation after the suit is filed by filing with the clerk of the court in which the suit is filed the waiver of the party acknowledging receipt of a copy of the filed petition.

(b) The party executing the waiver may not sign the waiver using a digitized signature.

(c) The waiver must contain the mailing address of the party executing the waiver.

(d) The waiver must be sworn before a notary public who is not an attorney in the suit or conform to the requirements for an unsworn declaration under Section 132.001, Civil Practice and Remedies Code. This subsection does not apply if the party executing the waiver is incarcerated.

(e) The Texas Rules of Civil Procedure do not apply to a waiver executed under this section.

(f) For purposes of this section, "digitized signature" has the meaning assigned by Section 101.0096.

Added by Acts 2015, 84th Leg., ch. 198 (S.B. 814), § 4, eff. Sept. 1, 2015. Amended by Acts 2019, 86th Leg., ch. 606 (S.B. 891), § 11.02, eff. Sept. 1, 2019.

Section 15.05 of Acts 2019, 86th Leg., ch. 606 (S.B. 891) provides:

"The Office of Court Administration of the Texas Judicial System is required to implement a provision of this Act only if the legislature appropriates money specifically for that purpose. If the legislature does not appropriate money specifically for that purpose, the office may, but is not required to, implement a provision of this Act using other appropriations available for that purpose."

# SUBTITLE E. GENERAL PROVISIONS

## CHAPTER 47. GENERAL PROVISIONS



*This Chapter 47, General Provisions, consisting of §§ 47.001 and 47.002, was added by Acts 2015, 84th Leg., ch. 612 (S.B. 822), § 1.*

*Another Chapter 47, General Provisions, consisting of § 47.001, was added by Acts 2015, 84th Leg., ch. 1165 (S.B. 813), § 2.*

*Acts 2017, 85th Leg., ch. 324 (S.B. 1488), § 7.001 reenacted Chapter 47 to combine the two Chapters and redesignated § 47.001, as added by Acts 2015, 84th Leg., ch. 1165 (S.B. 813), § 2, as § 47.003.*

**§ 47.001. Applicability of Definitions**

(a) Except as provided by Subsection (b), the definitions in Chapter 101 apply to terms used in this title.

(b) If a term defined in this title has a meaning different from the meaning provided by Chapter 101, the meaning provided by this title prevails.

Added by Acts 2015, 84th Leg., ch. 612 (S.B. 822), § 1, eff. Sept. 1, 2015.

**§ 47.002. Applicability of Laws Relating to Attorneys Ad Litem, Guardians Ad Litem, and Amicus Attorneys**

Chapter 107 applies to the appointment of an attorney ad litem, guardian ad litem, or amicus attorney under this title.

Added by Acts 2015, 84th Leg., ch. 612 (S.B. 822), § 1, eff. Sept. 1, 2015.

**§ 47.003. Use of Digitized Signature**

(a) A digitized signature on an original petition or application under this title or any other pleading or order in a proceeding under this title satisfies the requirements for and imposes the duties of signatories to pleadings, motions, and other papers identified under Rule 13, Texas Rules of Civil Procedure.

(b) A digitized signature under this section may be applied only by, and must remain under the sole control of, the person whose signature is represented.

(c) Deleted by Acts 2017, 85th Leg., ch. 324 (S.B. 1488), § 7.001.

Added by Acts 2015, 84th Leg., ch. 1165 (S.B. 813), § 2, eff. Sept. 1, 2015. Redesignated from V.T.C.A., Family Code § 47.001 and amended by Acts 2017, 85th Leg., ch. 324 (S.B. 1488), § 7.001, eff. Sept. 1, 2017.

# TITLE 3. JUVENILE JUSTICE CODE

## CHAPTER 51. GENERAL PROVISIONS



### § 51.01. Purpose and Interpretation

This title shall be construed to effectuate the following public purposes:

(1) to provide for the protection of the public and public safety;

(2) consistent with the protection of the public and public safety:

(A) to promote the concept of punishment for criminal acts;

(B) to remove, where appropriate, the taint of criminality from children committing certain unlawful acts; and

(C) to provide treatment, training, and rehabilitation that emphasizes the accountability and responsibility of both the parent and the child for the child's conduct;

(3) to provide for the care, the protection, and the wholesome moral, mental, and physical development of children coming within its provisions;

(4) to protect the welfare of the community and to control the commission of unlawful acts by children;

(5) to achieve the foregoing purposes in a family environment whenever possible, separating the child from the child's parents only when necessary for the child's welfare or in the interest of public safety and when a child is removed from the child's family, to give the child the care that should be provided by parents; and

(6) to provide a simple judicial procedure through which the provisions of this title are executed and enforced and in which the parties are assured a fair hearing and their constitutional and other legal rights recognized and enforced.

Acts 1973, 63rd Leg., p. 1460, ch. 544, § 1, eff. Sept. 1, 1973. Amended by Acts 1995, 74th Leg., ch. 262, § 2, eff. Jan. 1, 1996.

### § 51.02. Definitions

In this title:

(1) "Aggravated controlled substance felony" means an offense under Subchapter D, Chapter 481, Health and Safety Code,[1] that is punishable by:

(A) a minimum term of confinement that is longer than the minimum term of confinement for a felony of the first degree; or

(B) a maximum fine that is greater than the maximum fine for a felony of the first degree.

(2) "Child" means a person who is:

(A) ten years of age or older and under 17 years of age; or

(B) seventeen years of age or older and under 18 years of age who is alleged or found to have engaged in delinquent conduct or conduct indicating a need for supervision as a result of acts committed before becoming 17 years of age.

(3) "Custodian" means the adult with whom the child resides.

(3–a) "Dual status child" means a child who has been referred to the juvenile justice system and is:

(A) in the temporary or permanent managing conservatorship of the Department of Family and Protective Services;

(B) the subject of a case for which family-based safety services have been offered or provided by the department;

(C) an alleged victim of abuse or neglect in an open child protective investigation; or

(D) a victim in a case in which, after an investigation, the department concluded there was reason to believe the child was abused or neglected.

(4) "Guardian" means the person who, under court order, is the guardian of the person of the child or the public or private agency with whom the child has been placed by a court.

(5) "Judge" or "juvenile court judge" means the judge of a juvenile court.

(6) "Juvenile court" means a court designated under Section 51.04 of this code to exercise jurisdiction over proceedings under this title.

(7) "Law-enforcement officer" means a peace officer as defined by Article 2.12, Code of Criminal Procedure.

(8) "Nonoffender" means a child who:

(A) is subject to jurisdiction of a court under abuse, dependency, or neglect statutes under Title 5 [2] for reasons other than legally prohibited conduct of the child; or

(B) has been taken into custody and is being held solely for deportation out of the United States.

(8–a) "Nonsecure correctional facility" means a facility described by Section 51.126.

(9) "Parent" means the mother or the father of a child, but does not include a parent whose parental rights have been terminated.

(10) "Party" means the state, a child who is the subject of proceedings under this subtitle, or the child's parent, spouse, guardian, or guardian ad litem.

(11) "Prosecuting attorney" means the county attorney, district attorney, or other attorney who regularly serves in a prosecutory capacity in a juvenile court.

(12) "Referral to juvenile court" means the referral of a child or a child's case to the office or official, including an intake officer or probation officer, designated by the juvenile board to process children within the juvenile justice system.

(13) "Secure correctional facility" means any public or private residential facility, including an alcohol or other drug treatment facility, that:

(A) includes construction fixtures designed to physically restrict the movements and activities of juveniles or other individuals held in lawful custody in the facility; and

(B) is used for the placement of any juvenile who has been adjudicated as having committed an offense, any nonoffender, or any other individual convicted of a criminal offense.

(14) "Secure detention facility" means any public or private residential facility that:

(A) includes construction fixtures designed to physically restrict the movements and activities of juveniles or other individuals held in lawful custody in the facility; and

(B) is used for the temporary placement of any juvenile who is accused of having committed an offense, any nonoffender, or any other individual accused of having committed a criminal offense.

(15) "Status offender" means a child who is accused, adjudicated, or convicted for conduct that would not, under state law, be a crime if committed by an adult, including:

(A) running away from home under Section 51.03(b)(2);

(B) a fineable only offense under Section 51.03(b)(1) transferred to the juvenile court under Section 51.08(b), but only if the conduct constituting the offense would not have been criminal if engaged in by an adult;

(C) a violation of standards of student conduct as described by Section 51.03(b)(4);

(D) a violation of a juvenile curfew ordinance or order;

(E) a violation of a provision of the Alcoholic Beverage Code applicable to minors only; or

(F) a violation of any other fineable only offense under Section 8.07(a)(4) or (5), Penal Code, but only if the conduct constituting the offense would not have been criminal if engaged in by an adult.

(16) "Traffic offense" means:

(A) a violation of a penal statute cognizable under Chapter 729, Transportation Code, except for conduct for which the person convicted may be sentenced to imprisonment or confinement in jail; or

(B) a violation of a motor vehicle traffic ordinance of an incorporated city or town in this state.

(17) "Valid court order" means a court order entered under Section 54.04 concerning a child adjudicated to have engaged in conduct indicating a need for supervision as a status offender.

Acts 1973, 63rd Leg., p. 1460, ch. 544, § 1, eff. Sept. 1, 1973. Amended by Acts 1975, 64th Leg., p. 2152, ch. 693, § 1, eff. Sept. 1, 1975; Acts 1995, 74th Leg., ch. 262, § 3, eff. Jan. 1, 1996; Acts 1997, 75th Leg., ch. 165, §§ 6.06, 30.182, eff. Sept. 1, 1997; Acts 1997, 75th Leg., ch. 822, § 2, eff. Sept. 1, 1997; Acts 1997, 75th Leg., ch. 1013, § 13, eff. Sept. 1, 1997; Acts 1997, 75th Leg., ch. 1086, §§ 41, 47, eff. Sept. 1, 1997; Acts 2001, 77th Leg., ch. 821, § 2.02, eff. June 14, 2001; Acts 2001, 77th Leg., ch. 1297, § 1, eff. Sept. 1, 2001; Acts 2003, 78th Leg., ch. 283, § 1, eff. Sept. 1, 2003; Acts 2005, 79th Leg., ch. 949, § 1, eff. Sept. 1, 2005; Acts 2009, 81st Leg., ch. 1187, § 4.004, eff. June 19, 2009; Acts 2013, 83rd Leg., ch. 1299 (H.B. 2862), § 5, eff. Sept. 1, 2013; Acts 2015, 84th Leg., ch. 935 (H.B. 2398), § 17, eff. Sept. 1, 2015; Acts 2021, 87th Leg., ch. 934 (H.B. 3774), § 4.02, eff. Sept. 1, 2021.

[1] V.T.C.A., Health & Safety Code § 481.101 et seq.

[2] V.T.C.A., Family Code § 101.001 et seq.

Section 15.02 of Acts 2021, 87th Leg., ch. 934 (H.B. 3774) provides:

"Not later than May 1, 2022, the Supreme Court of Texas shall adopt rules and promulgate forms under Section 22.0042, Government Code, as added by this article.

Section 18.01 of Acts 2021, 87th Leg., ch. 934 (H.B. 3774) provides:

"A state agency subject to this Act is required to implement a provision of this Act only if the legislature appropriates money specifically for that purpose. If the legislature does not appropriate money specifically for that purpose, the state agency may, but is not required to, implement a provision of this Act using other appropriations available for that purpose."

## § 51.03. Delinquent Conduct; Conduct Indicating a Need for Supervision

(a) Delinquent conduct is:

(1) conduct, other than a traffic offense, that violates a penal law of this state or of the United States punishable by imprisonment or by confinement in jail;

(2) conduct that violates a lawful order of a court under circumstances that would constitute contempt of that court in:

(A) a justice or municipal court;

(B) a county court for conduct punishable only by a fine; or

(C) a truancy court;

(3) conduct that violates Section 49.04, 49.05, 49.06, 49.07, or 49.08, Penal Code; or

(4) conduct that violates Section 106.041, Alcoholic Beverage Code, relating to driving under the influence of alcohol by a minor (third or subsequent offense).

(b) Conduct indicating a need for supervision is:

(1) subject to Subsection (f), conduct, other than a traffic offense, that violates:

(A) the penal laws of this state of the grade of misdemeanor that are punishable by fine only; or

(B) the penal ordinances of any political subdivision of this state;

(2) the voluntary absence of a child from the child's home without the consent of the child's parent or guardian for a substantial length of time or without intent to return;

(3) conduct prohibited by city ordinance or by state law involving the inhalation of the fumes or vapors of paint and other protective coatings or glue and other adhesives and the volatile chemicals itemized in Section 485.001, Health and Safety Code;

(4) an act that violates a school district's previously communicated written standards of student conduct for which the child has been expelled under Section 37.007(c), Education Code;

(5) notwithstanding Subsection (a)(1), conduct described by Section 43.02 or 43.021, Penal Code;

(6) notwithstanding Subsection (a)(1), conduct that violates Section 43.261, Penal Code; or

(7) notwithstanding Subsection (a)(1), conduct that violates Section 42.0601, Penal Code, if the child has not previously been adjudicated as having engaged in conduct violating that section.

(c) Nothing in this title prevents criminal proceedings against a child for perjury.

(d) Repealed by Acts 2015, 84th Leg., ch. 935 (H.B. 2398), § 41(3).

(e) For the purposes of Subsection (b)(2), "child" does not include a person who is married, divorced, or widowed.

(e–1) Repealed by Acts 2015, 84th Leg., ch. 935 (H.B. 2398), § 41(3).

(f) Conduct described under Subsection (b)(1) does not constitute conduct indicating a need for supervision unless the child has been referred to the juvenile court under Section 51.08(b).

(g) Repealed by Acts 2015, 84th Leg., ch. 935 (H.B. 2398), § 41(3).

Acts 1973, 63rd Leg., p. 1460, ch. 544, § 1, eff. Sept. 1, 1973. Amended by Acts 1975, 64th Leg., p. 2153, ch. 693, §§ 2 to 4, eff. Sept. 1, 1975; Acts 1977, 65th Leg., p. 906, ch. 340, § 1, eff. June 6, 1977; Acts 1987, 70th Leg., ch. 511, § 1, eff. Sept. 1, 1987; Acts 1987, 70th Leg., ch. 924, § 1, eff. Sept. 1, 1987; Acts 1987, 70th Leg., ch. 955, § 1, eff. June 19, 1987; Acts 1987, 70th Leg., ch. 1040, § 20, eff. Sept. 1, 1987; Acts 1987, 70th Leg., ch. 1099, § 48, eff. Sept. 1, 1987; Acts 1989, 71st Leg., ch. 1100, § 3.02, eff. Aug. 28, 1989; Acts 1989, 71st Leg., ch. 1245, §§ 1, 4, eff. Sept. 1, 1989; Acts 1991, 72nd Leg., ch. 14, § 284(35), eff. Sept. 1, 1991; Acts 1991, 72nd Leg., ch. 16, § 7.02, eff. Aug. 26, 1991; Acts 1991, 72nd Leg., ch. 169, § 1, eff. Sept. 1, 1991; Acts 1993, 73rd Leg., ch. 46, § 1, eff. Sept. 1, 1993; Acts 1995, 74th Leg., ch. 76, § 14.30, eff. Sept. 1, 1995; Acts 1995, 74th Leg., ch. 262, § 4, eff. Jan. 1, 1996; Acts 1997, 75th Leg., ch. 165, § 6.07, eff. Sept. 1, 1997; Acts 1997, 75th Leg., ch. 1013, § 14, eff. Sept. 1, 1997; Acts 1997, 75th Leg., ch. 1015, § 15, eff. June 19, 1997; Acts 1997, 75th Leg., ch. 1086, § 1, eff. Sept. 1, 1997; Acts 2001, 77th Leg., ch. 1297, § 2, eff. Sept. 1, 2001; Acts 2001, 77th Leg., ch. 1514, § 11, eff. Sept. 1, 2001; Acts 2003, 78th Leg., ch. 137, § 11, eff. Sept. 1, 2003; Acts 2005, 79th Leg., ch. 949, § 2, eff. Sept. 1, 2005; Acts 2007, 80th Leg., ch. 908, § 3, eff. Sept. 1, 2007; Acts 2009, 81st Leg., ch. 311, § 3, eff. Sept. 1, 2009; Acts 2011, 82nd Leg., ch. 1098 (S.B. 1489), § 2, eff. Sept. 1, 2011; Acts 2011, 82nd Leg., ch. 1150 (H.B. 2015), § 1, eff. Sept. 1, 2011; Acts 2011, 82nd Leg., ch. 1322 (S.B. 407), § 4, eff. Sept. 1, 2011; Acts 2013, 83rd Leg., ch. 161 (S.B. 1093), § 7.001, eff. Sept. 1, 2013; Acts 2013, 83rd Leg., ch. 1299 (H.B. 2862), § 6, eff. Sept. 1, 2013; Acts 2015, 84th Leg., ch. 935 (H.B. 2398), §§ 18, 41(3), eff. Sept. 1, 2015; Acts 2015, 84th Leg., ch. 944 (S.B. 206), § 4, eff. Sept. 1, 2015; Acts 2015, 84th Leg., ch. 1273 (S.B. 825), § 3, eff. Sept. 1, 2015; Acts 2017, 85th Leg., ch. 324 (S.B. 1488), § 7.002, eff. Sept. 1, 2017; Acts 2017, 85th Leg., ch. 685 (H.B. 29), § 21, eff. Sept. 1, 2017; Acts 2021, 87th Leg., ch. 807 (H.B. 1540), § 38, eff. Sept. 1, 2021; Acts 2021, 87th Leg., ch. 945 (S.B. 1056), § 5, eff. Sept. 1, 2021.

Section 63(d) of Acts 2021, 87th Leg., ch. 807 (H.B. 1540) provides:

"Except as otherwise provided by this section, the changes in law made by this Act apply only to an offense committed on or after the effective date [Sept. 1, 2021] of this Act. An offense committed before the effective date of this Act is governed by the law in effect on the date the offense was committed, and the former law is continued in effect for that purpose. For purposes of this section, an offense was committed before the effective date of this Act if any element of the offense occurred before that date."

### § 51.031. Habitual Felony Conduct

(a) Habitual felony conduct is conduct violating a penal law of the grade of felony, other than a state jail felony, if:

(1) the child who engaged in the conduct has at least two previous final adjudications as having engaged in delinquent conduct violating a penal law of the grade of felony;

(2) the second previous final adjudication is for conduct that occurred after the date the first previous adjudication became final; and

(3) all appeals relating to the previous adjudications considered under Subdivisions (1) and (2) have been exhausted.

(b) For purposes of this section, an adjudication is final if the child is placed on probation or committed to the Texas Juvenile Justice Department.

(c) An adjudication based on conduct that occurred before January 1, 1996, may not be considered in a disposition made under this section.

Added by Acts 1995, 74th Leg., ch. 262, § 5, eff. Jan. 1, 1996. Amended by Acts 1997, 75th Leg., ch. 1086, § 2, eff. Sept. 1, 1997; Acts 2015, 84th Leg., ch. 734 (H.B. 1549), § 39, eff. Sept. 1, 2015.

### § 51.04. Jurisdiction

(a) This title covers the proceedings in all cases involving the delinquent conduct or conduct indicating a need for supervision engaged in by a person who was a child within the meaning of this title at the time the person engaged in the conduct, and, except as provided by Subsection (h) or Section 51.0414, the juvenile court has exclusive original jurisdiction over proceedings under this title.

(b) In each county, the county's juvenile board shall designate one or more district, criminal district, domestic relations, juvenile, or county courts or county courts at law as the juvenile court, subject to Subsections (c), (d), and (i).

(c) If the county court is designated as a juvenile court, at least one other court shall be designated as the juvenile court. A county court does not have jurisdiction of a proceeding involving a petition approved by a grand jury under Section 53.045 of this code.

(d) If the judge of a court designated in Subsection (b) or (c) of this section is not an attorney licensed in this state, there shall also be designated an alternate court, the judge of which is an attorney licensed in this state.

(e) A designation made under Subsection (b), (c), or (i) may be changed from time to time by the authorized boards or judges for the convenience of the people and the welfare of children. However, there must be at all times a juvenile court designated for each county. It is the intent of the legislature that in selecting a court to be the juvenile court of each county, the selection shall be made as far as practicable so that the court designated as the juvenile court will be one which is presided over by a judge who has a sympathetic understanding of the problems of child welfare and that changes in the designation of juvenile courts be made only when the best interest of the public requires it.

(f) If the judge of the juvenile court or any alternate judge named under Subsection (b) or (c) is not in the county or is otherwise unavailable, any magistrate may make a determination under Section 53.02(f) or may conduct the detention hearing provided for in Section 54.01.

(g) The juvenile board may appoint a referee to make determinations under Section 53.02(f) or to conduct hearings under this title. The referee shall be an attorney licensed to practice law in this state and shall comply with Section 54.10. Payment of any referee services shall be provided from county funds.

(h) A judge exercising jurisdiction over a child in a suit instituted under Subtitle E, Title 5, may refer any aspect of a suit involving a dual status child that is instituted under this title to the appropriate associate judge appointed under Subchapter C, Chapter 201, serving in the county and exercising jurisdiction over the child under Subtitle E, Title 5, if the associate judge consents to the referral. The scope of an associate judge's authority over a suit referred under this subsection is subject to any limitations placed by the court judge in the order of referral.

(i) If the court designated as the juvenile court under Subsection (b) does not have jurisdiction over proceedings under Subtitle E, Title 5, the county's juvenile board may designate at least one other court that does have jurisdiction over proceedings under Subtitle E, Title 5, as a juvenile court or alternative juvenile court.

Acts 1973, 63rd Leg., p. 1460, ch. 544, § 1, eff. Sept. 1, 1973. Amended by Acts 1975, 64th Leg., p. 1357, ch. 514, § 1, eff. June 19, 1975; Acts 1975, 64th Leg., p. 2153, ch. 693, §§ 5 to 7, eff. Sept. 1, 1975; Acts 1977, 65th Leg., p. 1112, ch. 411, § 1, eff. June 15, 1977; Acts 1987, 70th Leg., ch. 385, § 1, eff. Sept. 1, 1987; Acts 1993, 73rd Leg., ch. 168, § 4, eff. Aug. 30, 1993; Acts 1999, 76th Leg., ch. 232, § 2, eff. Sept. 1, 1999; Acts 2001, 77th Leg., ch. 1297, § 3, eff. Sept. 1, 2001; Acts 2001, 77th Leg., ch. 1514, § 12, eff. Sept. 1, 2001; Acts 2013, 83rd Leg., ch. 186 (S.B. 92), § 1, eff. Sept. 1, 2013; Acts 2015, 84th Leg., ch. 935 (H.B. 2398), § 41(3), eff. Sept. 1, 2015; Acts 2019, 86th Leg., ch. 660 (S.B. 1887), § 1, eff. Sept. 1, 2019; Acts 2021, 87th Leg., ch. 934 (H.B. 3774), § 4.03, eff. Sept. 1, 2021.

Section 4 of Acts 2019, 86th Leg., ch. 660 (S.B. 1887) provides:

"The changes in law made by this Act apply only to conduct that occurs on or after the effective date [Sept. 1, 2019] of this Act. Conduct that occurs before the effective date of this Act is governed by the law in effect on the date the conduct occurred, and the former law is continued in effect for that purpose. For the purposes of this section, conduct occurred before the effective date of this Act if any element of the conduct occurred before that date."

Section 15.02 of Acts 2021, 87th Leg., ch. 934 (H.B. 3774) provides:

"Not later than May 1, 2022, the Supreme Court of Texas shall adopt rules and promulgate forms under Section 22.0042, Government Code, as added by this article.

Section 18.01 of Acts 2021, 87th Leg., ch. 934 (H.B. 3774) provides:

"A state agency subject to this Act is required to implement a provision of this Act only if the legislature appropriates money specifically for that purpose. If the legislature does not appropriate money specifically for that purpose, the state agency may, but is not required to, implement a provision of this Act using other appropriations available for that purpose."

### § 51.041. Jurisdiction After Appeal

(a) The court retains jurisdiction over a person, without regard to the age of the person, for conduct engaged in by the person before becoming 17 years of age if, as a result of an appeal by the person or the state under Chapter 56 of an order of the court, the order is reversed or modified and the case remanded to the court by the appellate court.

(b) If the respondent is at least 18 years of age when the order of remand from the appellate court is received by the juvenile court, the juvenile court shall proceed as provided by Sections 54.02(*o*)–(r) for the detention of a person at least 18 years of age in discretionary transfer proceedings. Pending retrial of the adjudication or transfer proceeding, the juvenile court may:

(1) order the respondent released from custody;

(2) order the respondent detained in a juvenile detention facility; or

(3) set bond and order the respondent detained in a county adult facility if bond is not made.

Added by Acts 1995, 74th Leg., ch. 262, § 6, eff. Jan. 1, 1996. Amended by Acts 2001, 77th Leg., ch. 1297, § 4, eff. Sept. 1, 2001; Acts 2003, 78th Leg., ch. 283, § 2, eff. Sept. 1, 2003; Acts 2015, 84th Leg., ch. 74 (S.B. 888), § 2, eff. Sept. 1, 2015.

### § 51.0411. Jurisdiction for Transfer or Release Hearing

The court retains jurisdiction over a person, without regard to the age of the person, who is referred to the court under Section 54.11 for transfer to the Texas Department of Criminal Justice or release under supervision.

Added by Acts 1997, 75th Leg., ch. 1086, § 3, eff. June 19, 1997.

### § 51.0412. Jurisdiction Over Incomplete Proceedings

The court retains jurisdiction over a person, without regard to the age of the person, who is a respondent in an adjudication proceeding, a disposition proceeding, a proceeding to modify disposition, a proceeding for waiver of jurisdiction and transfer to criminal court under Section 54.02(a), or a motion for transfer of determinate sentence probation to an appropriate district court if:

(1) the petition or motion was filed while the respondent was younger than 18 or 19 years of age, as applicable;

(2) the proceeding is not complete before the respondent becomes 18 or 19 years of age, as applicable; and

(3) the court enters a finding in the proceeding that the prosecuting attorney exercised due diligence in an attempt to complete the proceeding before the respondent became 18 or 19 years of age, as applicable.

Added by Acts 2001, 77th Leg., ch. 1297, § 5, eff. Sept. 1, 2001. Amended by Acts 2007, 80th Leg., ch. 908, § 4, eff. Sept. 1, 2007; Acts 2011, 82nd Leg., ch. 438 (S.B. 1208), § 1, eff. Sept. 1, 2011; Acts 2013, 83rd Leg., ch. 1299 (H.B. 2862), § 7, eff. Sept. 1, 2013.

### § 51.0413. Jurisdiction Over and Transfer of Combination of Proceedings

(a) A juvenile court designated under Section 51.04(b) or, if that court does not have jurisdiction over proceedings under Subtitle E, Title 5, the juvenile court designated under Section 51.04(i) may simultaneously exercise jurisdiction over proceedings under this title and proceedings under Subtitle E, Title 5, if there is probable cause to believe that the child who is the subject of those proceedings engaged in delinquent conduct or conduct indicating a need for supervision and cause to believe that the child may be the victim of conduct that constitutes an offense under Section 20A.02, Penal Code.

(b) If a proceeding is instituted under this title in a juvenile court designated under Section 51.04(b) that does not have jurisdiction over proceedings under Subtitle E, Title 5, the court shall assess the case and may transfer the proceedings to a court designated as a juvenile court or alternative juvenile court under Section 51.04(i) if the receiving court agrees and if, in the course of the proceedings, evidence is presented that constitutes cause to believe that the child who is the subject of those proceedings is a child described by Subsection (a).

Added by Acts 2013, 83rd Leg., ch. 186 (S.B. 92), § 2, eff. Sept. 1, 2013.

### § 51.0414. Discretionary Transfer to Combine Proceedings

(a) The juvenile court may transfer a dual status child's case, including transcripts of records and documents for the case, to a district or statutory county court located in another county that is exercising jurisdiction over the child in a suit instituted under Subtitle E, Title 5. A case may only be transferred under this section with the consent of the judge of the court to which the case is being transferred.

(b) Notwithstanding Section 51.04, a district or statutory county court to which a case is transferred under this section has jurisdiction over the transferred case regardless of whether the court is a designated juvenile court or alternative juvenile court in the county.

(c) If the court exercising jurisdiction over the child under Subtitle E, Title 5, consents to a transfer under this section, the juvenile court shall file the transfer order with the clerk of the transferring court. On receipt and without a hearing or further order from the juvenile court, the clerk of the transferring court shall transfer the files, including transcripts of records and documents for the case as soon as practicable but not later than the 10th day after the date an order of transfer is filed.

(d) On receipt of the pleadings, documents, and orders from the transferring court, the clerk of the receiving court shall notify the judge of the receiving court, all parties, and the clerk of the transferring court.

Added by Acts 2019, 86th Leg., ch. 660 (S.B. 1887), § 2, eff. Sept. 1, 2019. Amended by Acts 2021, 87th Leg., ch. 934 (H.B. 3774), § 4.04, eff. Sept. 1, 2021.

Section 15.02 of Acts 2021, 87th Leg., ch. 934 (H.B. 3774) provides:

"Not later than May 1, 2022, the Supreme Court of Texas shall adopt rules and promulgate forms under Section 22.0042, Government Code, as added by this article.

Section 18.01 of Acts 2021, 87th Leg., ch. 934 (H.B. 3774) provides:

"A state agency subject to this Act is required to implement a provision of this Act only if the legislature appropriates money specifically for that purpose. If the legislature does not appropriate money specifically for that purpose, the state agency may, but is not required to, implement a provision of this Act using other appropriations available for that purpose."

### § 51.042. Objection to Jurisdiction Because of Age of the Child

(a) A child who objects to the jurisdiction of the court over the child because of the age of the child must raise the objection at the adjudication hearing or discretionary transfer hearing, if any.

(b) A child who does not object as provided by Subsection (a) waives any right to object to the jurisdiction of the court because of the age of the child at a later hearing or on appeal.

Added by Acts 1995, 74th Leg., ch. 262, § 6, eff. Jan. 1, 1996.

### § 51.045. Juries in County Courts at Law

If a provision of this title requires a jury of 12 persons, that provision prevails over any other law that limits the number of members of a jury in a particular county court at law. The state and the defense are entitled to the same number of peremptory challenges allowed in a district court.

Added by Acts 1987, 70th Leg., ch. 385, § 2, eff. Sept. 1, 1987.

### § 51.05. Court Sessions and Facilities

(a) The juvenile court shall be deemed in session at all times. Suitable quarters shall be provided by the commissioners court of each county for the hearing of cases and for the use of the judge, the probation officer, and other employees of the court.

(b) The juvenile court and the juvenile board shall report annually to the commissioners court on the suitability of the quarters and facilities of the juvenile court and may make recommendations for their improvement.

Acts 1973, 63rd Leg., p. 1460, ch. 544, § 1, eff. Sept. 1, 1973. Amended by Acts 1975, 64th Leg., p. 2154, ch. 693, § 8, eff. Sept. 1, 1975.

### § 51.06. Venue

(a) A proceeding under this title shall be commenced in

(1) the county in which the alleged delinquent conduct or conduct indicating a need for supervision occurred; or

(2) the county in which the child resides at the time the petition is filed, but only if:

(A) the child was under probation supervision in that county at the time of the commission of the delinquent conduct or conduct indicating a need for supervision;

(B) it cannot be determined in which county the delinquent conduct or conduct indicating a need for supervision occurred; or

(C) the county in which the child resides agrees to accept the case for prosecution, in writing, prior to the case being sent to the county of residence for prosecution.

(b) An application for a writ of habeas corpus brought by or on behalf of a person who has been committed to an institution under the jurisdiction of the Texas Juvenile Justice Department and which attacks the validity of the judgment of commitment shall be brought in the county in which the court that entered the judgment of commitment is located.

Acts 1973, 63rd Leg., p. 1460, ch. 544, § 1, eff. Sept. 1, 1973. Amended by Acts 1983, 68th Leg., p. 161, ch. 44, art. 1, § 1, eff. April 26, 1983; Acts 1995, 74th Leg., ch. 262, § 7, eff. Jan. 1, 1996; Acts 1999, 76th Leg., ch. 488, § 1, eff. Sept. 1, 1999; Acts 2015, 84th Leg., ch. 734 (H.B. 1549), § 40, eff. Sept. 1, 2015.

### § 51.07. Transfer to Another County for Disposition

(a) When a child has been found to have engaged in delinquent conduct or conduct indicating a need for supervision under Section 54.03, the juvenile court may transfer the case and transcripts of records and documents to the juvenile court of the county where the child resides for disposition of the case under Section 54.04. Consent by the court of the county where the child resides is not required.

(b) For purposes of Subsection (a), while a child is the subject of a suit under Title 5,[1] the child is considered to reside in the county in which the court of continuing exclusive jurisdiction over the child is located.

Acts 1973, 63rd Leg., p. 1460, ch. 544, § 1, eff. Sept. 1, 1973. Amended by Acts 2005, 79th Leg., ch. 949, § 3, eff. Sept. 1, 2005; Acts 2013, 83rd Leg., ch. 1299 (H.B. 2862), § 8, eff. Sept. 1, 2013.

[1] V.T.C.A., Family Code § 101.001 et seq.

### § 51.071. Transfer of Probation Supervision Between Counties: Courtesy Supervision Prohibited

Except as provided by Section 51.075, a juvenile court or juvenile probation department may not engage in the practice of courtesy supervision of a child on probation.

Added by Acts 2005, 79th Leg., ch. 949, § 4, eff. Sept. 1, 2005.

**§ 51.072. Transfer of Probation Supervision Between Counties: Interim Supervision**

(a) In this section:

(1) "Receiving county" means the county to which a child on probation has moved or intends to move.

(2) "Sending county" means the county that:

(A) originally placed the child on probation; or

(B) assumed permanent supervision of the child under an inter-county transfer of probation supervision.

(b) When a child on probation moves or intends to move from one county to another and intends to remain in the receiving county for at least 60 days, the juvenile probation department of the sending county shall request that the juvenile probation department of the receiving county provide interim supervision of the child. If the receiving county and the sending county are member counties within a judicial district served by one juvenile probation department, then a transfer of probation supervision is not required.

(c) The juvenile probation department of the receiving county may refuse the request to provide interim supervision only if:

(1) the residence of the child in the receiving county is in a residential placement facility arranged by the sending county; or

(2) the residence of the child in the receiving county is in a foster care placement arranged by the Department of Family and Protective Services.

(d) The juvenile probation department of the sending county shall initiate the request for interim supervision by electronic communication to the probation officer designated as the inter-county transfer officer for the juvenile probation department of the receiving county or, in the absence of this designation, to the chief juvenile probation officer.

(e) The juvenile probation department of the sending county shall provide the juvenile probation department of the receiving county with the following information in the request for interim supervision initiated under Subsection (d):

(1) the child's name, sex, age, race, and date of birth;

(2) the name, address, date of birth, and social security or driver's license number, and telephone number, if available, of the person with whom the child proposes to reside or is residing in the receiving county;

(3) the offense for which the child is on probation;

(4) the length of the child's probation term;

(5) a brief summary of the child's history of referrals;

(6) a brief statement of any special needs of the child;

(7) the name and telephone number of the child's school in the receiving county, if available; and

(8) the reason for the child moving or intending to move to the receiving county.

(f) Not later than 10 business days after a receiving county has agreed to provide interim supervision of a child, the juvenile probation department of the sending county shall provide the juvenile probation department of the receiving county with a copy of the following documents:

(1) the petition and the adjudication and disposition orders for the child, including the child's thumbprint;

(2) the child's conditions of probation;

(3) the social history report for the child;

(4) any psychological or psychiatric reports concerning the child;

(5) the Department of Public Safety CR 43J form or tracking incident number concerning the child;

(6) any law enforcement incident reports concerning the offense for which the child is on probation;

(7) any sex offender registration information concerning the child;

(8) any juvenile probation department progress reports concerning the child and any other pertinent documentation for the child's probation officer;

(9) case plans concerning the child;

(10) the Texas Juvenile Justice Department standard assessment tool results for the child;

(11) the computerized referral and case history for the child, including case disposition;

(12) the child's birth certificate;

(13) the child's social security number or social security card, if available;

(14) the name, address, and telephone number of the contact person in the sending county's juvenile probation department;

(15) Title IV–E eligibility screening information for the child, if available;

(16) the address in the sending county for forwarding funds collected to which the sending county is entitled;

(17) any of the child's school or immunization records that the juvenile probation department of the sending county possesses;

(18) any victim information concerning the case for which the child is on probation; and

(19) if applicable, documentation that the sending county has required the child to provide a DNA sample to the Department of Public Safety under Section 54.0405 or 54.0409 or under Subchapter G, Chapter 411, Government Code.[1]

(f–1) The inter-county transfer officers in the sending and receiving counties shall agree on the official start date for the period of interim supervision, which must begin no later than three business days after the date the documents required under Subsection (f) have been received and accepted by the receiving county.

(f–2) On initiating a transfer of probation supervision under this section, for a child ordered to submit a DNA sample as a condition of probation, the sending county shall provide to the receiving county documentation of compliance with the requirements of Section 54.0405 or 54.0409 or of Subchapter G, Chapter 411, Government Code, as applicable. If the sending county has not provided the documentation required under this section within the time provided by Subsection (f), the receiving county may refuse to accept interim supervision until the sending county has provided the documentation.

(g) The juvenile probation department of the receiving county shall supervise the child under the probation conditions imposed by the sending county and provide services similar to those provided to a child placed on probation under the same conditions in the receiving county. On request of the juvenile probation department of the receiving county, the juvenile court of the receiving county may modify the original probation conditions and impose new conditions using the procedures in Section 54.05. The juvenile court of the receiving county may not modify a financial probation condition imposed by the juvenile court of the sending county or the length of the child's probation term. The juvenile court of the receiving county shall designate a cause number for identifying the modification proceedings.

(h) The juvenile court of the sending county may revoke probation for a violation of a condition imposed by the juvenile court of the sending county only if the condition has not been specifically modified or replaced by the juvenile court of the receiving county. The juvenile court of the receiving county may revoke probation for a violation of a condition of probation that the juvenile court of the receiving county has modified or imposed.

(i) If a child is reasonably believed to have violated a condition of probation imposed by the juvenile court of the sending county, the juvenile court of the sending or receiving county may issue a directive to apprehend or detain the child in a certified detention facility, as in other cases of probation violation. In order to respond to a probation violation under this subsection, the juvenile court of the receiving county may:

(1) modify the conditions of probation or extend the probation term; or

(2) require that the juvenile probation department of the sending county resume direct supervision for the child.

(j) On receiving a directive from the juvenile court of the receiving county under Subsection (i)(2), the juvenile probation department of the sending county shall arrange for the prompt transportation of the child back to the sending county at the expense of the sending county. The juvenile probation department in the receiving county shall provide the sending county with supporting written documentation of the incidents of violation of probation on which the request to resume direct supervision is based.

(j–1) Notwithstanding Subsection (j), the sending county may request interim supervision from the receiving county that issued a directive under Subsection (i)(2). Following the conclusion of any judicial proceedings in the sending county or on the completion of any residential placement ordered by the juvenile court of the sending county, the sending and receiving counties may mutually agree to return the child to the receiving county. The sending and receiving counties may take into consideration whether:

(1) the person having legal custody of the child resides in the receiving county;

(2) the child has been ordered by the juvenile court of the sending county to reside with a parent, guardian, or other person who resides in the sending county or any other county; and

(3) the case meets the statutory requirements for collaborative supervision.

(j–2) The period of interim supervision under Subsection (j–1) may not exceed the period under Subsection (m).

(k) The juvenile probation department of the receiving county is entitled to any probation supervision fees collected from the child or the child's parent while providing interim supervision for the child. During the period of interim supervision, the receiving county shall collect and distribute to the victim monetary restitution payments in the manner specified by the sending county. At the expiration of the period of interim supervision, the receiving county shall collect and distribute directly to the victim any remaining payments.

(*l*) The sending county is financially responsible for any special treatment program or placement that the juvenile court of the sending county requires as a condition of probation if the child's family is financially unable to pay for the program or placement.

(m) Except as provided by Subsection (n), a period of interim supervision may not exceed 180 days. Permanent supervision automatically transfers to the juvenile probation department of the receiving county after the expiration of the period of interim supervision. The juvenile probation department of the receiving county may request permanent supervision from the juvenile probation department of the sending county at any time before the 180-day interim supervision period expires. After signing and entry of an order of transfer of permanent supervision by the sending county juvenile court, the juvenile probation department shall, in accordance with Section 51.073(b), promptly send the permanent supervision order and related documents to the receiving county.

(m-1) If a child on interim supervision moves to another county of residence or is otherwise no longer in the receiving county before the expiration of 180 days, the receiving county shall direct the sending county to resume supervision of the child.

(n) Notwithstanding Subsection (m), the period of interim supervision of a child who is placed on probation under Section 54.04(q) does not expire until the child has satisfactorily completed the greater of either 180 days or one-third of the term of probation, including one-third of the term of any extension of the probation term ordered under Section 54.05. Permanent supervision automatically transfers to the probation department of the receiving county after the expiration of the period of interim supervision under this subsection. If the state elects to initiate transfer proceedings under Section 54.051, the juvenile court of the sending county may order transfer of the permanent supervision before the expiration of the period of interim supervision under this subsection.

(*o*) At least once every 90 days during the period of interim supervision, the juvenile probation department of the receiving county shall provide the juvenile probation department of the sending county with a progress report of supervision concerning the child.

Added by Acts 2005, 79th Leg., ch. 949, § 4, eff. Sept. 1, 2005. Amended by Acts 2007, 80th Leg., ch. 908, § 5, eff. Sept. 1, 2007; Acts 2013, 83rd Leg., ch. 1299 (H.B. 2862), § 9, eff. Sept. 1, 2013.

[1] V.T.C.A., Government Code § 411.141 et seq.

### § 51.073. Transfer of Probation Supervision Between Counties: Permanent Supervision

(a) In this section:

(1) "Receiving county" means the county to which a child on probation has moved or intends to move.

(2) "Sending county" means the county that:

(A) originally placed the child on probation; or

(B) assumed permanent supervision of the child under an inter-county transfer of probation supervision.

(b) On transfer of permanent supervision of a child under Section 51.072(m) or (n), the juvenile court of the sending county shall order the juvenile probation department of the sending county to provide the juvenile probation department of the receiving county with the order of transfer. On receipt of the order of transfer, the juvenile probation department of the receiving county shall ensure that the order of transfer, the petition, the order of adjudication, the order of disposition, and the conditions of probation are filed with the clerk of the juvenile court of the receiving county.

(c) The juvenile court of the receiving county shall require that the child be brought before the court in order to impose new or different conditions of probation than those originally ordered by the sending county or ordered by the receiving county during the period of interim supervision. The child shall be represented by counsel as provided by Section 51.10.

(d) Once permanent supervision is transferred to the juvenile probation department of the receiving county, the receiving county is fully responsible for selecting and imposing conditions of probation, providing supervision, modifying conditions of probation, and revoking probation. The sending county has no further jurisdiction over the child's case.

(d-1) On the final transfer of a case involving a child who has been adjudicated as having committed an offense for which registration is required under Chapter 62, Code of Criminal Procedure, the receiving county shall have jurisdiction to conduct a hearing under that chapter. This subsection does not prohibit the receiving county juvenile court from considering the written recommendations of the sending county juvenile court.

(e) This section does not affect the sending county's jurisdiction over any new offense committed by the child in the sending county.

Added by Acts 2005, 79th Leg., ch. 949, § 4, eff. Sept. 1, 2005. Amended by Acts 2007, 80th Leg., ch. 908, § 6, eff. Sept. 1, 2007.

## § 51.074. Transfer of Probation Supervision Between Counties: Deferred Prosecution

(a) A juvenile court may transfer interim supervision, but not permanent supervision, to the county where a child on deferred prosecution resides.

(b) On an extension of a previous order of deferred prosecution authorized under Section 53.03(j), the child shall remain on interim supervision for an additional period not to exceed 180 days.

(c) On a violation of the conditions of the original deferred prosecution agreement, the receiving county shall forward the case to the sending county for prosecution or other action in the manner provided by Sections 51.072(i) and (j), except that the original conditions of deferred prosecution may not be modified by the receiving county.

Added by Acts 2005, 79th Leg., ch. 949, § 4, eff. Sept. 1, 2005. Amended by Acts 2007, 80th Leg., ch. 908, § 7, eff. Sept. 1, 2007.

## § 51.075. Collaborative Supervision Between Adjoining Counties

(a) If a child who is on probation in one county spends substantial time in an adjoining county, including residing, attending school, or working in the adjoining county, the juvenile probation departments of the two counties may enter into a collaborative supervision arrangement regarding the child.

(b) Under a collaborative supervision arrangement, the juvenile probation department of the adjoining county may authorize a probation officer for the county to provide supervision and other services for the child as an agent of the juvenile probation department of the county in which the child was placed on probation. The probation officer providing supervision and other services for the child in the adjoining county shall provide the probation officer supervising the child in the county in which the child was placed on probation with periodic oral, electronic, or written reports concerning the child.

(c) The juvenile court of the county in which the child was placed on probation retains sole authority to modify, amend, extend, or revoke the child's probation.

Added by Acts 2005, 79th Leg., ch. 949, § 4, eff. Sept. 1, 2005.

## § 51.08. Transfer from Criminal Court

(a) If the defendant in a criminal proceeding is a child who is charged with an offense other than perjury, a traffic offense, a misdemeanor punishable by fine only, or a violation of a penal ordinance of a political subdivision, unless the child has been transferred to criminal court under Section 54.02, the court exercising criminal jurisdiction shall transfer the case to the juvenile court, together with a copy of the accusatory pleading and other papers, documents, and transcripts of testimony relating to the case, and shall order that the child be taken to the place of detention designated by the juvenile court, or shall release the child to the custody of the child's parent, guardian, or custodian, to be brought before the juvenile court at a time designated by that court.

(b) A court in which there is pending a complaint against a child alleging a violation of a misdemeanor offense punishable by fine only other than a traffic offense or a violation of a penal ordinance of a political subdivision other than a traffic offense:

(1) except as provided by Subsection (d), shall waive its original jurisdiction and refer the child to juvenile court if:

(A) the complaint pending against the child alleges a violation of a misdemeanor offense under Section 43.261, Penal Code, that is punishable by fine only; or

(B) the child has previously been convicted of:

(i) two or more misdemeanors punishable by fine only other than a traffic offense;

(ii) two or more violations of a penal ordinance of a political subdivision other than a traffic offense; or

(iii) one or more of each of the types of misdemeanors described in Subparagraph (i) or (ii); and

(2) may waive its original jurisdiction and refer the child to juvenile court if the child:

(A) has not previously been convicted of a misdemeanor punishable by fine only other than a traffic offense or a violation of a penal ordinance of a political subdivision other than a traffic offense; or

(B) has previously been convicted of fewer than two misdemeanors punishable by fine only other than a traffic offense or two violations of a penal ordinance of a political subdivision other than a traffic offense.

(c) A court in which there is pending a complaint against a child alleging a violation of a misdemeanor offense punishable by fine only other than a traffic offense or a violation of a penal ordinance of a political subdivision other than a traffic offense shall notify the juvenile court of the county in which the court is located of the pending complaint and shall furnish to the juvenile court a copy of the final disposition of any matter for which the court does not waive its original jurisdiction under Subsection (b).

(d) A court that has implemented a juvenile case manager program under Article 45.056, Code of Criminal Procedure, may, but is not required to, waive its original jurisdiction under Subsection (b)(1)(B).

(e) Repealed by Acts 2015, 84th Leg., ch. 935 (H.B. 2398), § 41(3).

(f) A court shall waive original jurisdiction for a complaint against a child alleging a violation of a misdemeanor offense punishable by fine only, other than a traffic offense, and refer the child to juvenile court if the court or another court has previously dismissed a complaint against the child under Section 8.08, Penal Code.

Acts 1973, 63rd Leg., p. 1460, ch. 544, § 1, eff. Sept. 1, 1973. Amended by Acts 1987, 70th Leg., ch. 1040, § 21, eff. Sept. 1, 1987; Acts 1989, 71st Leg., ch. 1245, § 2, eff. Sept. 1, 1989; Acts 1991, 72nd Leg., ch. 169, § 2, eff. Sept. 1, 1991; Acts 2001, 77th Leg., ch. 1297, § 6, eff. Sept. 1, 2001; Acts 2003, 78th Leg., ch. 283, § 3, eff. Sept. 1, 2003; Acts 2005, 79th Leg., ch. 650, § 1, eff. Sept. 1, 2005; Acts 2009, 81st Leg., ch. 311, § 4, eff. Sept. 1, 2009; Acts 2011, 82nd Leg., ch. 1322 (S.B. 407), § 16, eff. Sept. 1, 2011; Acts 2013, 83rd Leg., ch. 1407 (S.B. 393), § 13, eff. Sept. 1, 2013; Acts 2015, 84th Leg., ch. 935 (H.B. 2398), § 41(3), eff. Sept. 1, 2015.

## § 51.09. Waiver of Rights

Unless a contrary intent clearly appears elsewhere in this title, any right granted to a child by this title or by the constitution or laws of this state or the United States may be waived in proceedings under this title if:

(1) the waiver is made by the child and the attorney for the child;

(2) the child and the attorney waiving the right are informed of and understand the right and the possible consequences of waiving it;

(3) the waiver is voluntary; and

(4) the waiver is made in writing or in court proceedings that are recorded.

Acts 1973, 63rd Leg., p. 1460, ch. 544, § 1, eff. Sept. 1, 1973. Amended by Acts 1975, 64th Leg., p. 2154, ch. 693, § 9, eff. Sept. 1, 1975; Acts 1989, 71st Leg., ch. 84, § 1, eff. Sept. 1, 1989; Acts 1991, 72nd Leg., ch. 64, § 1, eff. Sept. 1, 1991; Acts 1991, 72nd Leg., ch. 429, § 1, eff. Sept. 1, 1991; Acts 1991, 72nd Leg., ch. 557, § 1, eff. Sept. 1, 1991; Acts 1991, 72nd Leg., ch. 593, § 1, eff. Aug. 26, 1991; Acts 1995, 74th Leg., ch. 262, §§ 8, 9, eff. Jan. 1, 1996; Acts 1997, 75th Leg., ch. 1086, § 4, eff. Sept. 1, 1997.

## § 51.095. Admissibility of a Statement of a Child

(a) Notwithstanding Section 51.09, the statement of a child is admissible in evidence in any future proceeding concerning the matter about which the statement was given if:

(1) the statement is made in writing under a circumstance described by Subsection (d) and:

(A) the statement shows that the child has at some time before the making of the statement received from a magistrate a warning that:

(i) the child may remain silent and not make any statement at all and that any statement that the child makes may be used in evidence against the child;

(ii) the child has the right to have an attorney present to advise the child either prior to any questioning or during the questioning;

(iii) if the child is unable to employ an attorney, the child has the right to have an attorney appointed to counsel with the child before or during any interviews with peace officers or attorneys representing the state; and

(iv) the child has the right to terminate the interview at any time;

(B) and:

(i) the statement must be signed in the presence of a magistrate by the child with no law enforcement officer or prosecuting attorney present, except that a magistrate may require a bailiff or a law enforcement officer if a bailiff is not available to be present if the magistrate determines that the presence of the bailiff or law enforcement officer is necessary for the personal safety of the magistrate or other court personnel, provided that the bailiff or law enforcement officer may not carry a weapon in the presence of the child; and

(ii) the magistrate must be fully convinced that the child understands the nature and contents of the statement and that the child is signing the same voluntarily, and if a statement is taken, the magistrate must sign a written statement verifying the foregoing requisites have been met;

(C) the child knowingly, intelligently, and voluntarily waives these rights before and during the making of the statement and signs the statement in the presence of a magistrate; and

(D) the magistrate certifies that the magistrate has examined the child independent of any law enforcement officer or prosecuting attorney, except as required to ensure the personal safety of the magistrate or other court personnel, and has determined that the child understands the nature and contents of the statement and has knowingly, intelligently, and voluntarily waived these rights;

(2) the statement is made orally and the child makes a statement of facts or circumstances that are found to be true and tend to establish the child's guilt, such as the finding of secreted or stolen property, or the instrument with which the child states the offense was committed;

(3) the statement was res gestae of the delinquent conduct or the conduct indicating a need for supervision or of the arrest;

(4) the statement is made:

(A) in open court at the child's adjudication hearing;

(B) before a grand jury considering a petition, under Section 53.045, that the child engaged in delinquent conduct; or

(C) at a preliminary hearing concerning the child held in compliance with this code, other than at a detention hearing under Section 54.01; or

(5) subject to Subsection (f), the statement is made orally under a circumstance described by Subsection (d) and the statement is recorded by an electronic recording device, including a device that records images, and:

(A) before making the statement, the child is given the warning described by Subdivision (1)(A) by a magistrate, the warning is a part of the recording, and the child knowingly, intelligently, and voluntarily waives each right stated in the warning;

(B) the recording device is capable of making an accurate recording, the operator of the device is competent to use the device, the recording is accurate, and the recording has not been altered;

(C) each voice on the recording is identified; and

(D) not later than the 20th day before the date of the proceeding, the attorney representing the child is given a complete and accurate copy of each recording of the child made under this subdivision.

(b) This section and Section 51.09 do not preclude the admission of a statement made by the child if:

(1) the statement does not stem from interrogation of the child under a circumstance described by Subsection (d); or

(2) without regard to whether the statement stems from interrogation of the child under a circumstance described by Subsection (d), the statement is:

(A) voluntary and has a bearing on the credibility of the child as a witness; or

(B) recorded by an electronic recording device, including a device that records images, and is obtained:

(i) in another state in compliance with the laws of that state or this state; or

(ii) by a federal law enforcement officer in this state or another state in compliance with the laws of the United States.

(c) An electronic recording of a child's statement made under Subsection (a)(5) or (b)(2)(B) shall be preserved until all juvenile or criminal matters relating to any conduct referred to in the statement are final, including the exhaustion of all appeals, or barred from prosecution.

(d) Subsections (a)(1) and (a)(5) apply to the statement of a child made:

(1) while the child is in a detention facility or other place of confinement;

(2) while the child is in the custody of an officer; or

(3) during or after the interrogation of the child by an officer if the child is in the possession of the Department of Family and Protective Services and is suspected to have engaged in conduct that violates a penal law of this state.

(e) A juvenile law referee or master may perform the duties imposed on a magistrate under this section without the approval of the juvenile court if the juvenile board of the county in which the statement of the child is made has authorized a referee or master to perform the duties of a magistrate under this section.

(f) A magistrate who provides the warnings required by Subsection (a)(5) for a recorded statement may at the time the warnings are provided request by speaking on the recording that the officer return the child and the recording to the magistrate at the conclusion of the process of questioning. The magistrate may then view the recording with the child or have the child view the recording to enable the magistrate to determine whether the child's statements were given voluntarily. The magistrate's determination of voluntariness shall be reduced to writing and signed and dated by the magistrate. If a magistrate uses the procedure described by this subsection, a child's statement is not admissible unless the magistrate determines that the statement was given voluntarily.

Added by Acts 1997, 75th Leg., ch. 1086, § 4, eff. Sept. 1, 1997. Amended by Acts 1999, 76th Leg., ch. 982, § 1, eff. Sept. 1, 1999; Acts 1999, 76th Leg., ch. 1477, § 1, eff. Sept. 1, 1999; Acts 2001, 77th Leg., ch. 1297, § 7, eff. Sept. 1, 2001; Acts 2001, 77th Leg., ch. 1420, § 21.001(29), eff. Sept. 1, 2001; Acts 2005, 79th Leg., ch. 949, § 5, eff. Sept. 1, 2005; Acts 2007, 80th Leg., ch. 908, § 8, eff. Sept. 1, 2007; Acts 2011, 82nd Leg., ch. 110 (H.B. 841), § 3, eff. May 21, 2011; Acts 2011, 82nd Leg., ch. 1158 (H.B. 2337), § 1, eff. Sept. 1, 2011.

### § 51.10. Right to Assistance of Attorney; Compensation

(a) A child may be represented by an attorney at every stage of proceedings under this title, including:

(1) the detention hearing required by Section 54.01 of this code;

(2) the hearing to consider transfer to criminal court required by Section 54.02 of this code;

(3) the adjudication hearing required by Section 54.03 of this code;

(4) the disposition hearing required by Section 54.04 of this code;

(5) the hearing to modify disposition required by Section 54.05 of this code;

(6) hearings required by Chapter 55 of this code;

(7) habeas corpus proceedings challenging the legality of detention resulting from action under this title; and

(8) proceedings in a court of civil appeals or the Texas Supreme Court reviewing proceedings under this title.

(b) The child's right to representation by an attorney shall not be waived in:

(1) a hearing to consider transfer to criminal court as required by Section 54.02;

(2) an adjudication hearing as required by Section 54.03;

(3) a disposition hearing as required by Section 54.04;

(4) a hearing prior to commitment to the Texas Juvenile Justice Department as a modified disposition in accordance with Section 54.05(f); or

(5) hearings required by Chapter 55.

(c) If the child was not represented by an attorney at the detention hearing required by Section 54.01 of this code and a determination was made to detain the child, the child shall immediately be entitled to representation by an attorney. The court shall order the retention of an attorney according to Subsection (d) or appoint an attorney according to Subsection (f).

(d) The court shall order a child's parent or other person responsible for support of the child to employ an attorney to represent the child, if:

(1) the child is not represented by an attorney;

(2) after giving the appropriate parties an opportunity to be heard, the court determines that the parent or other person responsible for support of the child is financially able to employ an attorney to represent the child; and

(3) the child's right to representation by an attorney:

(A) has not been waived under Section 51.09 of this code; or

(B) may not be waived under Subsection (b) of this section.

(e) The court may enforce orders under Subsection (d) by proceedings under Section 54.07 or by appointing counsel and ordering the parent or other person responsible for support of the child to pay a reasonable attorney's fee set by the court. The order may be enforced under Section 54.07.

(f) The court shall appoint an attorney to represent the interest of a child entitled to representation by an attorney, if:

(1) the child is not represented by an attorney;

(2) the court determines that the child's parent or other person responsible for support of the child is financially unable to employ an attorney to represent the child; and

(3) the child's right to representation by an attorney:

(A) has not been waived under Section 51.09 of this code; or

(B) may not be waived under Subsection (b) of this section.

(g) The juvenile court may appoint an attorney in any case in which it deems representation necessary to protect the interests of the child.

(h) Any attorney representing a child in proceedings under this title is entitled to 10 days to prepare for any adjudication or transfer hearing under this title.

(i) Except as provided in Subsection (d) of this section, an attorney appointed under this section to represent the interests of a child shall be paid from the general fund of the county in which the proceedings were instituted according to the schedule in Article 26.05 of the Texas Code of Criminal Procedure, 1965. For this purpose, a bona fide appeal to a court of civil appeals or proceedings on the merits in the Texas Supreme Court are considered the equivalent of a bona fide appeal to the Texas Court of Criminal Appeals.

(j) The juvenile board of a county may make available to the public the list of attorneys eligible for appointment to represent children in proceedings under this title as provided in the plan adopted under Section 51.102. The list of attorneys must indicate the level of case for which each attorney is eligible for appointment under Section 51.102(b)(2).

(k) Subject to Chapter 61, the juvenile court may order the parent or other person responsible for support of the child to reimburse the county for payments the county made to counsel appointed to represent the child under Subsection (f) or (g). The court may:

(1) order payment for each attorney who has represented the child at any hearing, including a detention hearing, discretionary transfer hearing, adjudication hearing, disposition hearing, or modification of disposition hearing;

(2) include amounts paid to or on behalf of the attorney by the county for preparation time and investigative and expert witness costs; and

(3) require full or partial reimbursement to the county.

(*l*) The court may not order payments under Subsection (k) that exceed the financial ability of the parent or other person responsible for support of the child to meet the payment schedule ordered by the court.

Acts 1973, 63rd Leg., p. 1460, ch. 544, § 1, eff. Sept. 1, 1973. Amended by Acts 1983, 68th Leg., p. 161, ch. 44, art. 1, § 2, eff. April 26, 1983; Acts 1995, 74th Leg., ch. 262, § 11, eff. Jan. 1, 1996; Acts 2001, 77th Leg., ch. 1297, § 8, eff. Sept. 1, 2001; Acts 2003, 78th Leg., ch. 283, § 4, eff. Sept. 1, 2003; Acts 2015, 84th Leg., ch. 734 (H.B. 1549), § 41, eff. Sept. 1, 2015.

### § 51.101. Appointment of Attorney and Continuation of Representation

(a) If an attorney is appointed under Section 54.01(b–1) or (d) to represent a child at the initial detention hearing and the child is detained, the attorney shall continue to represent the child until the case is terminated, the family retains an attorney, or a new attorney is appointed by the juvenile court. Release of the child from detention does not terminate the attorney's representation.

(b) If there is an initial detention hearing without an attorney and the child is detained, the attorney appointed under Section 51.10(c) shall continue to represent the child until the case is terminated, the family retains an attorney, or a new attorney is appointed by the juvenile court. Release of the child from detention does not terminate the attorney's representation.

(c) The juvenile court shall determine, on the filing of a petition, whether the child's family is indigent if:

(1) the child is released by intake;

(2) the child is released at the initial detention hearing; or

(3) the case was referred to the court without the child in custody.

(d) A juvenile court that makes a finding of indigence under Subsection (c) shall appoint an attorney to represent the child on or before the fifth working day after the date the petition for adjudication or discretionary transfer hearing was served on the child. An attorney appointed under this subsection shall continue to represent the child until the case is terminated, the family retains an attorney, or a new attorney is appointed by the juvenile court.

(e) The juvenile court shall determine whether the child's family is indigent if a motion or petition is filed under Section 54.05 seeking to modify disposition by committing the child to the Texas Juvenile Justice Department or placing the child in a secure correctional facility. A court that makes a finding of indigence shall appoint an attorney to represent the child on or before the fifth working day after the date the petition or motion has been filed. An attorney appointed under this subsection shall continue to represent the child until the court rules on the motion or petition, the family retains an attorney, or a new attorney is appointed.

Added by Acts 2001, 77th Leg., ch. 1297, § 9, eff. Sept. 1, 2001. Amended by Acts 2013, 83rd Leg., ch. 912 (H.B. 1318), § 3, eff. Sept. 1, 2013; Acts 2015, 84th Leg., ch. 734 (H.B. 1549), § 42, eff. Sept. 1, 2015.

## § 51.102. Appointment of Counsel Plan

(a) The juvenile board in each county shall adopt a plan that:

(1) specifies the qualifications necessary for an attorney to be included on an appointment list from which attorneys are appointed to represent children in proceedings under this title; and

(2) establishes the procedures for:

(A) including attorneys on the appointment list and removing attorneys from the list; and

(B) appointing attorneys from the appointment list to individual cases.

(b) A plan adopted under Subsection (a) must:

(1) to the extent practicable, comply with the requirements of Article 26.04, Code of Criminal Procedure, except that:

(A) the income and assets of the child's parent or other person responsible for the child's support must be used in determining whether the child is indigent; and

(B) any alternative plan for appointing counsel is established by the juvenile board in the county; and

(2) recognize the differences in qualifications and experience necessary for appointments to cases in which:

(A) the allegation is:

(i) conduct indicating a need for supervision or delinquent conduct, and commitment to the Texas Juvenile Justice Department is not an authorized disposition; or

(ii) delinquent conduct, and commitment to the department without a determinate sentence is an authorized disposition; or

(B) determinate sentence proceedings have been initiated or proceedings for discretionary transfer to criminal court have been initiated.

Added by Acts 2001, 77th Leg., ch. 906, § 11, eff. Jan. 1, 2002. Renumbered from V.T.C.A., Family Code § 51.101 by Acts 2003, 78th Leg., ch. 283, § 5, eff. Sept. 1, 2003; Acts 2003, 78th Leg., ch. 1275, § 2(51), eff. Sept. 1, 2003. Amended by Acts 2015, 84th Leg., ch. 734 (H.B. 1549), § 43, eff. Sept. 1, 2015.

## § 51.11. Guardian ad Litem

(a) In this section:

(1) "Dual-system child" means a child who, at any time before the child's 18th birthday, was referred to the juvenile justice system and was involved in the child welfare system by being:

(A) placed in the temporary or permanent managing conservatorship of the Department of Family and Protective Services;

(B) the subject of a family-based safety services case with the Department of Family and Protective Services;

(C) an alleged victim of abuse or neglect in an active case being investigated by the Department of Family and Protective Services child protective investigations division; or

(D) a victim in a case in which the Department of Family and Protective Services investigation concluded that there was a reason to believe that abuse or neglect occurred.

(2) "Dual-status child" means a dual-system child who is involved with both the child welfare and juvenile justice systems at the same time.

(a–1) If a child appears before the juvenile court without a parent or guardian, the court shall appoint a guardian ad litem to protect the interests of the child. The juvenile court need not appoint a guardian ad litem if a parent or guardian appears with the child.

(b) In any case in which it appears to the juvenile court that the child's parent or guardian is incapable or unwilling to make decisions in the best interest of the child with respect to proceedings under this title, the court may appoint a guardian ad litem to protect the interests of the child in the proceedings.

(c) An attorney for a child may also be his guardian ad litem. A law-enforcement officer, probation officer, or other employee of the juvenile court may not be appointed guardian ad litem.

(d) The juvenile court may appoint the guardian ad litem appointed under Chapter 107 for a child in a suit affecting the parent-child relationship filed by the Department of Family and Protective Services to serve as the guardian ad litem for the child in a proceeding held under this title.

(e) A non-attorney guardian ad litem in a case involving a dual-system child may not:

(1) investigate any charges involving a dual-status child that are pending with the juvenile court; or

(2) offer testimony concerning the guilt or innocence of a dual-status child.

Acts 1973, 63rd Leg., p. 1460, ch. 544, § 1, eff. Sept. 1, 1973. Amended by Acts 2021, 87th Leg., ch. 971 (S.B. 2049), § 1, eff. Sept. 1, 2021.

### § 51.115. Attendance at Hearing: Parent or Other Guardian

(a) Each parent of a child, each managing and possessory conservator of a child, each court-appointed custodian of a child, and a guardian of the person of the child shall attend each hearing affecting the child held under:

(1) Section 54.02 (waiver of jurisdiction and discretionary transfer to criminal court);

(2) Section 54.03 (adjudication hearing);

(3) Section 54.04 (disposition hearing);

(4) Section 54.05 (hearing to modify disposition); and

(5) Section 54.11 (release or transfer hearing).

(b) Subsection (a) does not apply to:

(1) a person for whom, for good cause shown, the court waives attendance;

(2) a person who is not a resident of this state; or

(3) a parent of a child for whom a managing conservator has been appointed and the parent is not a conservator of the child.

(c) A person required under this section to attend a hearing is entitled to reasonable written or oral notice that includes a statement of the place, date, and time of the hearing and that the attendance of the person is required. The notice may be included with or attached to any other notice required by this chapter to be given the person. Separate notice is not required for a disposition hearing that convenes on the adjournment of an adjudication hearing. If a person required under this section fails to attend a hearing, the juvenile court may proceed with the hearing.

(d) A person who is required by Subsection (a) to attend a hearing, who receives the notice of the hearing, and who fails to attend the hearing may be punished by the court for contempt by a fine of not less than $100 and not more than $1,000. In addition to or in lieu of contempt, the court may order the person to receive counseling or to attend an educational course on the duties and responsibilities of parents and skills and techniques in raising children.

Added by Acts 1995, 74th Leg., ch. 262, § 10, eff. Jan. 1, 1996.

### § 51.116. Right to Reemployment

(a) An employer may not terminate the employment of a permanent employee because the employee is required under Section 51.115 to attend a hearing.

(b) An employee whose employment is terminated in violation of this section is entitled to return to the same employment that the employee held when notified of the hearing if the employee, as soon as practical after the hearing, gives the employer actual notice that the employee intends to return.

(c) A person who is injured because of a violation of this section is entitled to reinstatement to the person's former position and to damages, but the damages may not exceed an amount equal to six months' compensation at the rate at which the person was compensated when required to attend the hearing.

(d) The injured person is also entitled to reasonable attorney's fees in an amount approved by the court.

(e) It is a defense to an action brought under this section that the employer's circumstances changed while the employee attended the hearing so that reemployment was impossible or unreasonable. To establish a defense under this subsection, an employer must prove that the termination of employment was because of circumstances other than the employee's attendance at the hearing.

Added by Acts 1995, 74th Leg., ch. 262, § 10, eff. Jan. 1, 1996.

### § 51.12. Place and Conditions of Detention

(a) Except as provided by Subsection (h), a child may be detained only in a:

(1) juvenile processing office in compliance with Section 52.025;

(2) place of nonsecure custody in compliance with Article 45.058, Code of Criminal Procedure;

(3) certified juvenile detention facility that complies with the requirements of Subsection (f);

(4) secure detention facility as provided by Subsection (j);

(5) county jail or other facility as provided by Subsection (*l*); or

(6) nonsecure correctional facility as provided by Subsection (j–1).

(b) The proper authorities in each county shall provide a suitable place of detention for children who are parties to proceedings under this title, but the juvenile board shall control the conditions and terms of detention and detention supervision and shall permit visitation with the child at all reasonable times.

(b–1) A pre-adjudication secure detention facility may be operated only by:

(1) a governmental unit in this state as defined by Section 101.001, Civil Practice and Remedies Code; or

(2) a private entity under a contract with a governmental unit in this state.

(c) In each county, each judge of the juvenile court and a majority of the members of the juvenile board shall personally inspect all public or private juvenile pre-adjudication secure detention facilities that are located in the county at least annually and shall certify in writing to the authorities responsible for operating and giving financial support to the facilities and to the Texas Juvenile Justice Department that the facilities are suitable or unsuitable for the detention of children. In determining whether a facility is suitable or unsuitable for the detention of children, the juvenile court judges and juvenile board members shall consider:

(1) current monitoring and inspection reports and any noncompliance citation reports issued by the department, including the report provided under Subsection (c–1), and the status of any required corrective actions;

(2) current governmental inspector certification regarding the facility's compliance with local fire codes;

(3) current building inspector certification regarding the facility's compliance with local building codes;

(4) for the 12–month period preceding the inspection, the total number of allegations of abuse, neglect, or exploitation reported by the facility and a summary of the findings of any investigations of abuse, neglect, or exploitation conducted by the facility, a local law enforcement agency, and the department;

(5) the availability of health and mental health services provided to facility residents;

(6) the availability of educational services provided to facility residents; and

(7) the overall physical appearance of the facility, including the facility's security, maintenance, cleanliness, and environment.

(c–1) The Texas Juvenile Justice Department shall annually inspect each public or private juvenile pre-adjudication secure detention facility. The department shall provide a report to each juvenile court judge presiding in the same county as an inspected facility indicating whether the facility is suitable or unsuitable for the detention of children in accordance with:

(1) the requirements of Subsections (a), (f), and (g); and

(2) minimum professional standards for the detention of children in pre-adjudication secure confinement promulgated by the department or, at the election of the juvenile board of the county in which the facility is located, the current standards promulgated by the American Correctional Association.

(d) Except as provided by Subsections (j) and (*l*), a child may not be placed in a facility that has not been certified under Subsection (c) as suitable for the detention of children and registered under Subsection (i). Except as provided by Subsections (j) and (*l*), a child detained in a facility that has not been certified under Subsection (c) as suitable for the detention of children or that has not been registered under Subsection (i) shall be entitled to immediate release from custody in that facility.

(e) If there is no certified place of detention in the county in which the petition is filed, the designated place of detention may be in another county.

(f) A child detained in a building that contains a jail, lockup, or other place of secure confinement, including an alcohol or other drug treatment facility, shall be separated by sight and sound from adults detained in the same building. Children and adults are separated by sight and sound only if they are unable to see each other and conversation between them is not possible. The separation must extend to all areas of the facility, including sally ports and passageways, and those areas used for admission, counseling, sleeping, toileting, showering, dining, recreational, educational, or vocational activities, and health care. The separation may be accomplished through architectural design. A person who has been transferred for prosecution in criminal court under Section 54.02 and is under 17 years of age is considered a child for the purposes of this subsection.

(g) Except for a child detained in a juvenile processing office, a place of nonsecure custody, a secure detention facility as provided by Subsection (j), or a facility as provided by Subsection (*l*), a child detained in a building that contains a jail or lockup may not have any contact with:

(1) part-time or full-time security staff, including management, who have contact with adults detained in the same building; or

(2) direct-care staff who have contact with adults detained in the same building.

(h) This section does not apply to a person:

(1) who has been transferred to criminal court for prosecution under Section 54.02 and is at least 17 years of age; or

(2) who is at least 17 years of age and who has been taken into custody after having:

(A) escaped from a juvenile facility operated by or under contract with the Texas Juvenile Justice Department; or

(B) violated a condition of release under supervision of the department.

(i) Except for a facility as provided by Subsection (*l*), a governmental unit or private entity that operates or contracts for the operation of a juvenile pre-adjudication secure detention facility under Subsection (b–1) in this state shall:

(1) register the facility annually with the Texas Juvenile Justice Department; and

(2) adhere to all applicable minimum standards for the facility.

(j) After being taken into custody, a child may be detained in a secure detention facility until the child is released under Section 53.01, 53.012, or 53.02 or until a detention hearing is held under Section 54.01(a), regardless of whether the facility has been certified under Subsection (c), if:

(1) a certified juvenile detention facility is not available in the county in which the child is taken into custody;

(2) the detention facility complies with:

(A) the short-term detention standards adopted by the Texas Juvenile Justice Department; and

(B) the requirements of Subsection (f); and

(3) the detention facility has been designated by the county juvenile board for the county in which the facility is located.

(j–1) After being taken into custody, a child may be detained in a nonsecure correctional facility until the child is released under Section 53. 01, 53.012, or 53.02 or until a detention hearing is held under Section 54.01(a), if:

(1) the nonsecure correctional facility has been appropriately registered and certified;

(2) a certified secure detention facility is not available in the county in which the child is taken into custody;

(3) the nonsecure correctional facility complies with the short-term detention standards adopted by the Texas Juvenile Justice Department; and

(4) the nonsecure correctional facility has been designated by the county juvenile board for the county in which the facility is located.

(k) If a child who is detained under Subsection (j) or (*l*) is not released from detention at the conclusion of the detention hearing for a reason stated in Section 54.01(e), the child may be detained after the hearing only in a certified juvenile detention facility.

(*l*) A child who is taken into custody and required to be detained under Section 53.02(f) may be detained in a county jail or other facility until the child is released under Section 53.02(f) or until a detention hearing is held as required by Section 54.01(p), regardless of whether the facility complies with the requirements of this section, if:

(1) a certified juvenile detention facility or a secure detention facility described by Subsection (j) is not available in the county in which the child is taken into custody or in an adjacent county;

(2) the facility has been designated by the county juvenile board for the county in which the facility is located;

(3) the child is separated by sight and sound from adults detained in the same facility through architectural design or time-phasing;

(4) the child does not have any contact with management or direct-care staff that has contact with adults detained in the same facility on the same work shift;

(5) the county in which the child is taken into custody is not located in a metropolitan statistical area as designated by the United States Bureau of the Census; and

(6) each judge of the juvenile court and a majority of the members of the juvenile board of the county in which the child is taken into custody have personally inspected the facility at least annually and have certified in writing to the Texas Juvenile Justice Department that the facility complies with the requirements of Subdivisions (3) and (4).

(m) The Texas Juvenile Justice Department may deny, suspend, or revoke the registration of any facility required to register under Subsection (i) if the facility fails to:

(1) adhere to all applicable minimum standards for the facility; or

(2) timely correct any notice of noncompliance with minimum standards.

Acts 1973, 63rd Leg., p. 1460, ch. 544, § 1, eff. Sept. 1, 1973. Amended by Acts 1975, 64th Leg., p. 2155, ch. 693, §§ 10, 11, eff. Sept. 1, 1975; Acts 1985, 69th Leg., ch. 293, § 1, eff. Aug. 26, 1985; Acts 1987, 70th Leg., ch. 149, § 31, eff. Sept. 1, 1987; Acts 1995, 74th Leg., ch. 262, § 12, eff. Jan. 1, 1996; Acts 1997, 75th Leg., ch. 772, § 1, eff. Sept. 1, 1997; Acts 1997, 75th Leg., ch. 1374, § 1, eff. Sept. 1, 1997; Acts 1999, 76th Leg., ch. 62, § 6.07, eff. Sept. 1, 1999; Acts 1999, 76th Leg., ch. 232, § 3, eff. Sept. 1, 1999; Acts 1999, 76th Leg., ch. 1477, § 2, eff; Sept. 1, 1999; Acts 2001, 77th Leg., ch. 1297, § 10, eff. Sept. 1, 2001; Acts 2001, 77th Leg., ch. 1514, § 13, eff. Sept. 1, 2001; Acts 2007, 80th Leg., ch. 263, § 5, eff. June 8, 2007; Acts 2011, 82nd Leg., ch. 1087 (S.B. 1209), § 1, eff. Sept. 1, 2011; Acts 2013, 83rd Leg., ch. 1299 (H.B. 2862), § 10, eff. Sept. 1, 2013; Acts 2015, 84th Leg., ch. 734 (H.B. 1549), § 44, eff. Sept. 1, 2015.

### § 51.125. Post–Adjudication Correctional Facilities

(a) A post-adjudication secure correctional facility for juvenile offenders may be operated only by:

(1) a governmental unit in this state as defined by Section 101.001, Civil Practice and Remedies Code; or

(2) a private entity under a contract with a governmental unit in this state.

(b) In each county, each judge of the juvenile court and a majority of the members of the juvenile board shall personally inspect all public or private juvenile post-adjudication secure correctional facilities that are not operated by the Texas Juvenile Justice Department and that are located in the county at least annually and shall certify in writing to the authorities responsible for operating and giving financial support to the facilities and to the department that the facility or facilities are suitable or unsuitable for the confinement of children. In determining whether a facility is suitable or unsuitable for the confinement of children, the juvenile court judges and juvenile board members shall consider:

(1) current monitoring and inspection reports and any noncompliance citation reports issued by the department, including the report provided under Subsection (c), and the status of any required corrective actions; and

(2) the other factors described under Sections 51.12(c)(2)–(7).

(c) The Texas Juvenile Justice Department shall annually inspect each public or private juvenile post-adjudication secure correctional facility that is not operated by the department. The department shall provide a report to each juvenile court judge presiding in the same county as an inspected facility indicating whether the facility is suitable or unsuitable for the confinement of children in accordance with minimum professional standards for the confinement of children in post-adjudication secure confinement promulgated by the department or, at the election of the juvenile board of the county in which the facility is located, the current standards promulgated by the American Correctional Association.

(d) A governmental unit or private entity that operates or contracts for the operation of a juvenile post-adjudication secure correctional facility in this state under Subsection (a), except for a facility operated by or under contract with the Texas Juvenile Justice Department, shall:

(1) register the facility annually with the department; and

(2) adhere to all applicable minimum standards for the facility.

(e) The Texas Juvenile Justice Department may deny, suspend, or revoke the registration of any facility required to register under Subsection (d) if the facility fails to:

(1) adhere to all applicable minimum standards for the facility; or

(2) timely correct any notice of noncompliance with minimum standards.

Added by Acts 2007, 80th Leg., ch. 263, § 6, eff. June 8, 2007. Amended by Acts 2015, 84th Leg., ch. 734 (H.B. 1549), § 45, eff. Sept. 1, 2015.

### § 51.126. Nonsecure Correctional Facilities

(a) A nonsecure correctional facility for juvenile offenders may be operated only by:

(1) a governmental unit, as defined by Section 101.001, Civil Practice and Remedies Code; or

(2) a private entity under a contract with a governmental unit in this state.

(b) In each county, each judge of the juvenile court and a majority of the members of the juvenile board shall personally inspect, at least annually, all nonsecure correctional facilities that are located in the county and shall certify in writing to the authorities responsible for operating and giving financial support to the facilities and to the Texas Juvenile Justice Department that the facility or facilities are suitable or unsuitable for the confinement of children. In determining whether a facility is suitable or unsuitable for the confinement of children, the juvenile court judges and juvenile board members shall consider:

(1) current monitoring and inspection reports and any noncompliance citation reports issued by the

Texas Juvenile Justice Department, including the report provided under Subsection (c), and the status of any required corrective actions; and

(2) the other factors described under Sections 51.12(c)(2)–(7).

(c) The Texas Juvenile Justice Department shall annually inspect each nonsecure correctional facility. The Texas Juvenile Justice Department shall provide a report to each juvenile court judge presiding in the same county as an inspected facility indicating whether the facility is suitable or unsuitable for the confinement of children in accordance with minimum professional standards for the confinement of children in nonsecure confinement promulgated by the Texas Juvenile Justice Department or, at the election of the juvenile board of the county in which the facility is located, the current standards promulgated by the American Correctional Association.

(d) A governmental unit or private entity that operates or contracts for the operation of a juvenile nonsecure correctional facility in this state under Subsection (a), except for a facility operated by or under contract with the Texas Juvenile Justice Department, shall:

(1) register the facility annually with the Texas Juvenile Justice Department; and

(2) adhere to all applicable minimum standards for the facility.

(e) The Texas Juvenile Justice Department may deny, suspend, or revoke the registration of any facility required to register under Subsection (d) if the facility fails to:

(1) adhere to all applicable minimum standards for the facility; or

(2) timely correct any notice of noncompliance with minimum standards.

(f) Expired.

Added by Acts 2009, 81st Leg., ch. 1187, § 4.005, eff. June 19, 2009. Amended by Acts 2011, 82nd Leg., ch. 85 (S.B. 653), § 2.001, eff. Sept. 1, 2011.

### § 51.13. Effect of Adjudication or Disposition

(a) Except as provided by Subsections (d) and (e), an order of adjudication or disposition in a proceeding under this title is not a conviction of crime. Except as provided by Chapter 841, Health and Safety Code, an order of adjudication or disposition does not impose any civil disability ordinarily resulting from a conviction or operate to disqualify the child in any civil service application or appointment.

(b) The adjudication or disposition of a child or evidence adduced in a hearing under this title may be used only in subsequent:

(1) proceedings under this title in which the child is a party;

(2) sentencing proceedings in criminal court against the child to the extent permitted by the Texas Code of Criminal Procedure, 1965; or

(3) civil commitment proceedings under Chapter 841, Health and Safety Code.

(c) A child may not be committed or transferred to a penal institution or other facility used primarily for the execution of sentences of persons convicted of crime, except:

(1) for temporary detention in a jail or lockup pending juvenile court hearing or disposition under conditions meeting the requirements of Section 51.12;

(2) after transfer for prosecution in criminal court under Section 54.02, unless the juvenile court orders the detention of the child in a certified juvenile detention facility under Section 54.02(h);

(3) after transfer from the Texas Juvenile Justice Department under Section 245.151(c), Human Resources Code; or

(4) after transfer from a post-adjudication secure correctional facility, as that term is defined by Section 54.04011.

(d) An adjudication under Section 54.03 that a child engaged in conduct that occurred on or after January 1, 1996, and that constitutes a felony offense resulting in commitment to the Texas Juvenile Justice Department under Section 54.04(d)(2), (d)(3), or (m) or 54.05(f) or commitment to a post-adjudication secure correctional facility under Section 54.04011 for conduct that occurred on or after December 1, 2013, is a final felony conviction only for the purposes of Sections 12.42(a), (b), and (c)(1) or Section 12.425, Penal Code.

(e) A finding that a child engaged in conduct indicating a need for supervision as described by Section 51.03(b)(6) is a conviction only for the purposes of Sections 43.261(c) and (d), Penal Code.

Acts 1973, 63rd Leg., p. 1460, ch. 544, § 1, eff. Sept. 1, 1973. Amended by Acts 1987, 70th Leg., ch. 385, § 3, eff. Sept. 1, 1987; Acts 1993, 73rd Leg., ch. 799, § 1, eff. June 18, 1993; Acts 1995, 74th Leg., ch. 262, § 13, eff. Jan. 1, 1996; Acts 1997, 75th Leg., ch. 1086, § 5, eff. Sept. 1, 1997; Acts 1999, 76th Leg., ch. 1188, § 4.02, eff. Sept. 1, 1999; Acts 2003, 78th Leg., ch. 283, § 6, eff. Sept. 1, 2003; Acts 2011, 82nd Leg., ch. 85 (S.B. 653), § 3.004, eff. Sept. 1, 2011; Acts 2011, 82nd Leg., ch. 1087 (S.B. 1209), § 2, eff. Sept. 1, 2011; Acts 2011, 82nd Leg., ch. 1322 (S.B. 407), § 17, eff. Sept. 1, 2011; Acts 2013, 83rd Leg., ch. 1299 (H.B. 2862), § 11, eff. Sept. 1, 2013; Acts 2013, 83rd Leg., ch. 1323 (S.B. 511), § 1, eff. Dec. 1, 2013; Acts 2015, 84th Leg., ch. 854 (S.B. 1149), § 1, eff. Sept. 1, 2015; Acts 2015, 84th Leg., ch. 935 (H.B. 2398), § 19, eff. Sept. 1, 2015; Acts 2017, 85th Leg., ch. 324 (S.B. 1488), § 7.003, eff. Sept. 1, 2017; Acts 2017, 85th Leg., ch. 685 (H.B. 29), § 22, Sept. 1, 2017.

### § 51.14. Repealed by Acts 1995, 74th Leg., ch. 262, § 100(a), eff. Jan. 1, 1996

### § 51.15. Repealed by Acts 1995, 74th Leg., ch. 262, § 100(a), eff. Jan. 1, 1996

### § 51.151. Polygraph Examination

If a child is taken into custody under Section 52.01 of this code, a person may not administer a polygraph examination to the child without the consent of the child's attorney or the juvenile court unless the child is transferred to criminal court for prosecution under Section 54.02 of this code.

Added by Acts 1987, 70th Leg., ch. 708, § 1, eff. Sept. 1, 1987.

### § 51.16. Repealed by Acts 1995, 74th Leg., ch. 262, § 100(a), eff. Jan. 1, 1996; Acts 1997, 75th Leg., ch. 165, § 10.05(b), eff. Sept. 1, 1997

### § 51.17. Procedure and Evidence

(a) Except as provided by Section 56.01(b–1) and except for the burden of proof to be borne by the state in adjudicating a child to be delinquent or in need of supervision under Section 54.03(f) or otherwise when in conflict with a provision of this title, the Texas Rules of Civil Procedure govern proceedings under this title.

(b) Discovery in a proceeding under this title is governed by the Code of Criminal Procedure and by case decisions in criminal cases.

(c) Except as otherwise provided by this title, the Texas Rules of Evidence applicable to criminal cases and Articles 33.03 and 37.07 and Chapter 38, Code of Criminal Procedure, apply in a judicial proceeding under this title.

(d) When on the motion for appointment of an interpreter by a party or on the motion of the juvenile court, in any proceeding under this title, the court determines that the child, the child's parent or guardian, or a witness does not understand and speak English, an interpreter must be sworn to interpret for the person as provided by Article 38.30, Code of Criminal Procedure.

(e) In any proceeding under this title, if a party notifies the court that the child, the child's parent or guardian, or a witness is deaf, the court shall appoint a qualified interpreter to interpret the proceedings in any language, including sign language, that the deaf person can understand, as provided by Article 38.31, Code of Criminal Procedure.

(f) Any requirement under this title that a document contain a person's signature, including the signature of a judge or a clerk of the court, is satisfied if the document contains the signature of the person as captured on an electronic device or as a digital signature. Article 2.26, Code of Criminal Procedure, applies in a proceeding held under this title.

(g) Articles 21.07, 26.07, 26.08, 26.09, and 26.10, Code of Criminal Procedure, relating to the name of an adult defendant in a criminal case, apply to a child in a proceeding held under this title.

(h) Articles 58.001, 58.101, 58.102, 58.103, 58.104, 58.105, and 58.106, Code of Criminal Procedure, relating to the use of a pseudonym by a victim in a criminal case, apply in a proceeding held under this title.

(i) Except as provided by Section 56.03(f), the state is not required to pay any cost or fee otherwise imposed for court proceedings in either the trial or appellate courts.

Acts 1973, 63rd Leg., p. 1460, ch. 544, § 1, eff. Sept. 1, 1973. Amended by Acts 1995, 74th Leg., ch. 262, § 14, eff. Jan. 1, 1996; Acts 1999, 76th Leg., ch. 1477, § 3, eff. Sept. 1, 1999; Acts 2003, 78th Leg., ch. 283, § 7, eff. Sept. 1, 2003; Acts 2005, 79th Leg., ch. 949, § 6, eff. Sept. 1, 2005; Acts 2007, 80th Leg., ch. 908, § 9, eff. Sept. 1, 2007; Acts 2009, 81st Leg., ch. 642, § 1, eff. Sept. 1, 2009; Acts 2013, 83rd Leg., ch. 1299 (H.B. 2862), § 12, eff. Sept. 1, 2013; Acts 2019, 86th Leg., ch. 469 (H.B. 4173), § 2.31, eff. Jan. 1, 2021.

### § 51.18. Election Between Juvenile Court and Alternate Juvenile Court

(a) This section applies only to a child who has a right to a trial before a juvenile court the judge of which is not an attorney licensed in this state.

(b) On any matter that may lead to an order appealable under Section 56.01 of this code, a child may be tried before either the juvenile court or the alternate juvenile court.

(c) The child may elect to be tried before the alternate juvenile court only if the child files a written notice with that court not later than 10 days before the date of the trial. After the notice is filed, the child may be tried only in the alternate juvenile court. If the child does not file a notice as provided by this subsection, the child may be tried only in the juvenile court.

(d) If the child is tried before the juvenile court, the child is not entitled to a trial de novo before the alternate juvenile court.

(e) The child may appeal any order of the juvenile court or alternate juvenile court only as provided by Section 56.01 of this code.

Added by Acts 1977, 65th Leg., p. 1112, ch. 411, § 2, eff. June 15, 1977. Amended by Acts 1993, 73rd Leg., ch. 168, § 3, eff. Aug. 30, 1993.

## § 51.19. Limitation Periods

(a) The limitation periods and the procedures for applying the limitation periods under Chapter 12, Code of Criminal Procedure, and other statutory law apply to proceedings under this title.

(b) For purposes of computing a limitation period, a petition filed in juvenile court for a transfer or an adjudication hearing is equivalent to an indictment or information and is treated as presented when the petition is filed in the proper court.

(c) The limitation period is two years for an offense or conduct that is not given a specific limitation period under Chapter 12, Code of Criminal Procedure, or other statutory law.

Added by Acts 1997, 75th Leg., ch. 1086, § 6, eff. Sept. 1, 1997.

## § 51.20. Physical or Mental Examination

(a) At any stage of the proceedings under this title, including when a child is initially detained in a pre-adjudication secure detention facility or a post-adjudication secure correctional facility, the juvenile court may, at its discretion or at the request of the child's parent or guardian, order a child who is referred to the juvenile court or who is alleged by a petition or found to have engaged in delinquent conduct or conduct indicating a need for supervision to be examined by a disinterested expert, including a physician, psychiatrist, or psychologist, qualified by education and clinical training in mental health or mental retardation and experienced in forensic evaluation, to determine whether the child has a mental illness as defined by Section 571.003, Health and Safety Code, is a person with mental retardation as defined by Section 591.003, Health and Safety Code, or suffers from chemical dependency as defined by Section 464.001, Health and Safety Code. If the examination is to include a determination of the child's fitness to proceed, an expert may be appointed to conduct the examination only if the expert is qualified under Subchapter B, Chapter 46B, Code of Criminal Procedure, to examine a defendant in a criminal case, and the examination and the report resulting from an examination under this subsection must comply with the requirements under Subchapter B, Chapter 46B, Code of Criminal Procedure, for the examination and resulting report of a defendant in a criminal case.

(b) If, after conducting an examination of a child ordered under Subsection (a) and reviewing any other relevant information, there is reason to believe that the child has a mental illness or mental retardation or suffers from chemical dependency, the probation department shall refer the child to the local mental health or mental retardation authority or to another appropriate and legally authorized agency or provider for evaluation and services, unless the prosecuting attorney has filed a petition under Section 53.04.

(c) If, while a child is under deferred prosecution supervision or court-ordered probation, a qualified professional determines that the child has a mental illness or mental retardation or suffers from chemical dependency and the child is not currently receiving treatment services for the mental illness, mental retardation, or chemical dependency, the probation department shall refer the child to the local mental health or mental retardation authority or to another appropriate and legally authorized agency or provider for evaluation and services.

(d) A probation department shall report each referral of a child to a local mental health or mental retardation authority or another agency or provider made under Subsection (b) or (c) to the Texas Juvenile Justice Department in a format specified by the department.

(e) At any stage of the proceedings under this title, the juvenile court may order a child who has been referred to the juvenile court or who is alleged by the petition or found to have engaged in delinquent conduct or conduct indicating a need for supervision to be subjected to a physical examination by a licensed physician.

Added by Acts 1999, 76th Leg., ch. 1477, § 4, eff. Sept. 1, 1999. Amended by Acts 2001, 77th Leg., ch. 828, § 5(a), eff. Sept. 1, 2001; Acts 2003, 78th Leg., ch. 35, § 6, eff. Jan. 1, 2004; Acts 2005, 79th Leg., ch. 949, § 7, eff. Sept. 1, 2005; Acts 2013, 83rd Leg., ch. 225 (H.B. 144), § 1, eff. Sept. 1, 2013.

## § 51.21. Mental Health Screening and Referral

(a) A probation department that administers the mental health screening instrument or clinical assessment required by Section 221.003, Human Resources Code, shall refer the child to the local mental health authority for assessment and evaluation if:

(1) the child's scores on the screening instrument or clinical assessment indicate a need for further mental health assessment and evaluation; and

(2) the department and child do not have access to an internal, contract, or private mental health professional.

(b) A probation department shall report each referral of a child to a local mental health authority made under Subsection (a) to the Texas Juvenile Justice Department in a format specified by the Texas Juvenile Justice Department.

Added by Acts 2005, 79th Leg., ch. 949, § 8, eff. Sept. 1, 2005. Amended by Acts 2011, 82nd Leg., ch. 85 (S.B. 653), § 3.005, eff. Sept. 1, 2011; Acts 2015, 84th Leg., ch. 734 (H.B. 1549), § 46, eff. Sept. 1, 2015.

## CHAPTER 52. PROCEEDINGS BEFORE AND INCLUDING REFERRAL TO COURT

Section



### § 52.01. Taking into Custody; Issuance of Warning Notice

(a) A child may be taken into custody:

(1) pursuant to an order of the juvenile court under the provisions of this subtitle; [1]

(2) pursuant to the laws of arrest;

(3) by a law-enforcement officer, including a school district peace officer commissioned under Section 37.081, Education Code, if there is probable cause to believe that the child has engaged in:

(A) conduct that violates a penal law of this state or a penal ordinance of any political subdivision of this state;

(B) delinquent conduct or conduct indicating a need for supervision; or

(C) conduct that violates a condition of probation imposed by the juvenile court;

(4) by a probation officer if there is probable cause to believe that the child has violated a condition of probation imposed by the juvenile court;

(5) pursuant to a directive to apprehend issued as provided by Section 52.015; or

(6) by a probation officer if there is probable cause to believe that the child has violated a condition of release imposed by the juvenile court or referee under Section 54.01.

(b) The taking of a child into custody is not an arrest except for the purpose of determining the validity of taking him into custody or the validity of a search under the laws and constitution of this state or of the United States.

(c) A law-enforcement officer authorized to take a child into custody under Subdivisions (2) and (3) of Subsection (a) of this section may issue a warning notice to the child in lieu of taking the child into custody if:

(1) guidelines for warning disposition have been issued by the law-enforcement agency in which the officer works;

(2) the guidelines have been approved by the juvenile board of the county in which the disposition is made;

(3) the disposition is authorized by the guidelines;

(4) the warning notice identifies the child and describes the child's alleged conduct;

(5) a copy of the warning notice is sent to the child's parent, guardian, or custodian as soon as practicable after disposition; and

(6) a copy of the warning notice is filed with the law-enforcement agency and the office or official designated by the juvenile board.

(d) A warning notice filed with the office or official designated by the juvenile board may be used as the basis of further action if necessary.

(e) A law-enforcement officer who has probable cause to believe that a child is in violation of the compulsory school attendance law under Section 25.085, Education Code, may take the child into custody for the purpose of returning the child to the school campus of the child to ensure the child's compliance with compulsory school attendance requirements.

Acts 1973, 63rd Leg., p. 1460, ch. 544, § 1, eff. Sept. 1, 1973. Amended by Acts 1993, 73rd Leg., ch. 115, § 2, eff. May 11, 1993; Acts 1995, 74th Leg., ch. 262, § 15, eff. Jan. 1, 1996; Acts 1997, 75th Leg., ch. 165, § 6.08, eff. Sept. 1, 1997; Acts 2001, 77th Leg., ch. 1297, § 11, eff. Sept. 1, 2001; Acts 2003, 78th Leg., ch. 283, § 8, eff. Sept. 1, 2003; Acts 2005, 79th Leg., ch. 949, § 9, eff. Sept. 1, 2005; Acts 2007, 80th Leg., ch. 1058, § 16, eff. Sept. 1, 2007.

[1] So in enrolled bill; probably should read "this title;".

### § 52.011. Duty of Law Enforcement Officer to Notify Probate Court

(a) In this section, "ward" has the meaning assigned by Section 22.033, Estates Code.

(b) As soon as practicable, but not later than the first working day after the date a law enforcement officer takes a child who is a ward into custody under Section 52.01(a)(2) or (3), the law enforcement officer or other person having custody of the child shall notify the court with jurisdiction over the child's guardianship of the child's detention or arrest.

Added by Acts 2017, 85th Leg., ch. 313 (S.B. 1096), § 7, eff. Sept. 1, 2017.

### § 52.015. Directive to Apprehend

(a) On the request of a law-enforcement or probation officer, a juvenile court may issue a directive to apprehend a child if the court finds there is probable cause to take the child into custody under the provisions of this title.

(b) On the issuance of a directive to apprehend, any law-enforcement or probation officer shall take the child into custody.

(c) An order under this section is not subject to appeal.

Added by Acts 1995, 74th Leg., ch. 262, § 16, eff. Jan. 1, 1996.

### § 52.0151. Bench Warrant; Attachment of Witness in Custody

(a) If a witness is in a placement in the custody of the Texas Juvenile Justice Department, a juvenile secure detention facility, or a juvenile secure correctional facility, the court may issue a bench warrant or direct that an attachment issue to require a peace officer or probation officer to secure custody of the person at the placement and produce the person in court. Once the person is no longer needed as a witness or the period prescribed by Subsection (c) has expired without extension, the court shall order the peace officer or probation officer to return the person to the placement from which the person was released.

(b) The court may order that the person who is the witness be detained in a certified juvenile detention facility if the person is younger than 17 years of age. If the person is at least 17 years of age, the court may order that the person be detained without bond in an appropriate county facility for the detention of adults accused of criminal offenses.

(c) A witness held in custody under this section may be placed in a certified juvenile detention facility for a period not to exceed 30 days. The length of placement may be extended in 30–day increments by the court that issued the original bench warrant. If the placement is not extended, the period under this section expires and the witness may be returned as provided by Subsection (a).

Added by Acts 2005, 79th Leg., ch. 949, § 10, eff. Sept. 1, 2005. Amended by Acts 2013, 83rd Leg., ch. 1299 (H.B. 2862), § 13, eff. Sept. 1, 2013.

### § 52.02. Release or Delivery to Court

(a) Except as provided by Subsection (c), a person taking a child into custody, without unnecessary delay and without first taking the child to any place other than a juvenile processing office designated under Section 52.025, shall do one of the following:

(1) release the child to a parent, guardian, custodian of the child, or other responsible adult upon that person's promise to bring the child before the juvenile court as requested by the court;

(2) bring the child before the office or official designated by the juvenile board if there is probable cause to believe that the child engaged in delinquent conduct, conduct indicating a need for supervision, or conduct that violates a condition of probation imposed by the juvenile court;

(3) bring the child to a detention facility designated by the juvenile board;

(4) bring the child to a secure detention facility as provided by Section 51.12(j);

(5) bring the child to a medical facility if the child is believed to suffer from a serious physical condition or illness that requires prompt treatment;

(6) dispose of the case under Section 52.03; or

(7) if school is in session and the child is a student, bring the child to the school campus to which the child is assigned if the principal, the principal's designee, or a peace officer assigned to the campus agrees to assume responsibility for the child for the remainder of the school day.

(b) A person taking a child into custody shall promptly give notice of the person's action and a statement of the reason for taking the child into custody, to:

(1) the child's parent, guardian, or custodian; and

(2) the office or official designated by the juvenile board.

(c) A person who takes a child into custody and who has reasonable grounds to believe that the child has been operating a motor vehicle in a public place while having any detectable amount of alcohol in the child's system may, before complying with Subsection (a):

(1) take the child to a place to obtain a specimen of the child's breath or blood as provided by Chapter 724, Transportation Code; and

(2) perform intoxilyzer processing and videotaping of the child in an adult processing office of a law enforcement agency.

(d) Notwithstanding Section 51.09(a), a child taken into custody as provided by Subsection (c) may submit to the taking of a breath specimen or refuse to submit to the taking of a breath specimen without the concurrence of an attorney, but only if the request made of the child to give the specimen and the child's response to that request is videotaped. A videotape made under this subsection must be maintained until the disposition of any proceeding against the child relating to the arrest is final and be made available to an attorney representing the child during that period.

Acts 1973, 63rd Leg., p. 1460, ch. 544, § 1, eff. Sept. 1, 1973. Amended by Acts 1991, 72nd Leg., ch. 495, § 1, eff. Sept. 1, 1991; Acts 1997, 75th Leg., ch. 1013, § 15, eff. Sept. 1, 1997; Acts 1997, 75th Leg., ch. 1374, § 2, eff. Sept. 1, 1997; Acts 1999, 76th Leg., ch. 62, § 6.08, eff. Sept. 1, 1999; Acts 1999, 76th Leg., ch. 1477, § 5, eff. Sept. 1, 1999; Acts 2001, 77th Leg., ch. 1297, § 12, eff. Sept. 1, 2001; Acts 2003, 78th Leg., ch. 283, § 9, eff. Sept. 1, 2003; Acts 2007, 80th Leg., ch. 286, § 1, eff. Sept. 1, 2007.

### § 52.025. Designation of Juvenile Processing Office

(a) The juvenile board may designate an office or a room, which may be located in a police facility or sheriff's offices, as the juvenile processing office for the temporary detention of a child taken into custody under Section 52.01. The office may not be a cell or holding facility used for detentions other than detentions under this section. The juvenile board by written order may prescribe the conditions of the designation and limit the activities that may occur in the office during the temporary detention.

(b) A child may be detained in a juvenile processing office only for:

(1) the return of the child to the custody of a person under Section 52.02(a)(1);

(2) the completion of essential forms and records required by the juvenile court or this title;

(3) the photographing and fingerprinting of the child if otherwise authorized at the time of temporary detention by this title;

(4) the issuance of warnings to the child as required or permitted by this title; or

(5) the receipt of a statement by the child under Section 51.095(a)(1), (2), (3), or (5).

(c) A child may not be left unattended in a juvenile processing office and is entitled to be accompanied by the child's parent, guardian, or other custodian or by the child's attorney.

(d) A child may not be detained in a juvenile processing office for longer than six hours.

Added by Acts 1991, 72nd Leg., ch. 495, § 2, eff. Sept. 1, 1991. Amended by Acts 1997, 75th Leg., ch. 1086, § 48, eff. Sept. 1, 1997; Acts 2001, 77th Leg., ch. 1297, § 13, eff. Sept. 1, 2001.

### § 52.026. Responsibility for Transporting Juvenile Offenders

(a) It shall be the duty of the law enforcement officer who has taken a child into custody to transport the child to the appropriate detention facility or to the school campus to which the child is assigned as provided by Section 52.02(a)(7) if the child is not released to the parent, guardian, or custodian of the child.

(b) If the juvenile detention facility is located outside the county in which the child is taken into custody, it shall be the duty of the law enforcement officer who has taken the child into custody or, if authorized by the commissioners court of the county, the sheriff of that county to transport the child to the appropriate juvenile detention facility unless the child is:

(1) detained in a secure detention facility under Section 51.12(j); or

(2) released to the parent, guardian, or custodian of the child.

(c) On adoption of an order by the juvenile board and approval of the juvenile board's order by record vote of the commissioners court, it shall be the duty of the sheriff of the county in which the child is taken into custody to transport the child to and from all scheduled juvenile court proceedings and appearances and other activities ordered by the juvenile court.

Added by Acts 1993, 73rd Leg., ch. 411, § 1, eff. Aug. 30, 1993. Amended by Acts 1997, 75th Leg., ch. 1374, § 3, eff. Sept. 1, 1997; Acts 1999, 76th Leg., ch. 62, § 6.09, eff. Sept. 1, 1999; Acts 1999, 76th Leg., ch. 1082, § 1, eff. June 18, 1999; Acts 2007, 80th Leg., ch. 286, § 2, eff. Sept. 1, 2007.

### § 52.027. Repealed by Acts 2003, 78th Leg., ch. 283, § 61(1), eff. Sept. 1, 2003; Acts 2003,

78th Leg., ch. 1276, § 7.001(a), eff. Sept. 1, 2003.

**§ 52.028. Repealed by Acts 2001, 77th Leg., ch. 1514, § 19(b), eff. Sept. 1, 2001**

**§ 52.03. Disposition Without Referral to Court**

(a) A law-enforcement officer authorized by this title to take a child into custody may dispose of the case of a child taken into custody or accused of a Class C misdemeanor, other than a traffic offense, without referral to juvenile court or charging a child in a court of competent criminal jurisdiction, if:

(1) guidelines for such disposition have been adopted by the juvenile board of the county in which the disposition is made as required by Section 52.032;

(2) the disposition is authorized by the guidelines; and

(3) the officer makes a written report of the officer's disposition to the law-enforcement agency, identifying the child and specifying the grounds for believing that the taking into custody or accusation of criminal conduct was authorized.

(b) No disposition authorized by this section may involve:

(1) keeping the child in law-enforcement custody; or

(2) requiring periodic reporting of the child to a law-enforcement officer, law-enforcement agency, or other agency.

(c) A disposition authorized by this section may involve:

(1) referral of the child to an agency other than the juvenile court;

(2) a brief conference with the child and his parent, guardian, or custodian; or

(3) referral of the child and the child's parent, guardian, or custodian for services under Section 264.302.

(d) Statistics indicating the number and kind of dispositions made by a law-enforcement agency under the authority of this section shall be reported at least annually to the office or official designated by the juvenile board, as ordered by the board.

Acts 1973, 63rd Leg., p. 1460, ch. 544, § 1, eff. Sept. 1, 1973. Amended by Acts 1995, 74th Leg., ch. 262, § 18, eff. Jan. 1, 1996; Acts 1999, 76th Leg., ch. 48, § 1, eff. Sept. 1, 1999; Acts 2001, 77th Leg., ch. 1297, § 15, eff. Sept. 1, 2001; Acts 2003, 78th Leg., ch. 283, § 10, eff. Sept. 1, 2003; Acts 2013, 83rd Leg., ch. 1407 (S.B. 393), § 15, eff. Sept. 1, 2013.

**§ 52.031. First Offender Program**

(a) A juvenile board may establish a first offender program under this section for the referral and disposition of children taken into custody, or accused prior to the filing of a criminal charge, of:

(1) conduct indicating a need for supervision;

(2) a Class C misdemeanor, other than a traffic offense; or

(3) delinquent conduct other than conduct that constitutes:

(A) a felony of the first, second, or third degree, an aggravated controlled substance felony, or a capital felony; or

(B) a state jail felony or misdemeanor involving violence to a person or the use or possession of a firearm, location-restricted knife, or club, as those terms are defined by Section 46.01, Penal Code, or a prohibited weapon, as described by Section 46.05, Penal Code.

(a–1) A child accused of a Class C misdemeanor, other than a traffic offense, may be referred to a first offender program established under this section prior to the filing of a complaint with a criminal court.

(b) Each juvenile board in the county in which a first offender program is established shall designate one or more law enforcement officers and agencies, which may be law enforcement agencies, to process a child under the first offender program.

(c) The disposition of a child under the first offender program may not take place until guidelines for the disposition have been adopted by the juvenile board of the county in which the disposition is made as required by Section 52.032.

*Text of subsec. (d), as amended by Acts 2013, 83rd Leg., ch. 1407 (S.B. 393), § 16*

(d) A law enforcement officer taking a child into custody or accusing a child of an offense described in Subsection (a)(2) may refer the child to the law enforcement officer or agency designated under Subsection (b) for disposition under the first offender program and not refer the child to juvenile court or a court of competent criminal jurisdiction only if:

(1) the child has not previously been adjudicated as having engaged in delinquent conduct;

(2) the referral complies with guidelines for disposition under Subsection (c); and

(3) the officer reports in writing the referral to the agency, identifying the child and specifying the grounds for taking the child into custody or accus-

ing a child of an offense described in Subsection (a)(2).

*Text of subsec. (d), as amended by Acts 2013, 83rd Leg., ch. 1409 (S.B. 1114), § 8*

(d) A law enforcement officer taking a child into custody for conduct described by Subsection (a) or before issuing a citation to a child for an offense described by Subsection (a–1) may refer the child to the law enforcement officer or agency designated under Subsection (b) for disposition under the first offender program and not refer the child to juvenile court for the conduct or file a complaint with a criminal court for the offense only if:

(1) the child has not previously been adjudicated as having engaged in delinquent conduct;

(2) the referral complies with guidelines for disposition under Subsection (c); and

(3) the officer reports in writing the referral to the agency, identifying the child and specifying the grounds for taking the child into custody or for accusing the child of an offense.

(e) A child referred for disposition under the first offender program may not be detained in law enforcement custody.

*Text of subsec. (f), as amended by Acts 2013, 83rd Leg., ch. 1407 (S.B. 393), § 16*

(f) The parent, guardian, or other custodian of the child must receive notice that the child has been referred for disposition under the first offender program. The notice must:

(1) state the grounds for taking the child into custody or accusing a child of an offense described in Subsection (a)(2);

(2) identify the law enforcement officer or agency to which the child was referred;

(3) briefly describe the nature of the program; and

(4) state that the child's failure to complete the program will result in the child being referred to the juvenile court or a court of competent criminal jurisdiction.

*Text of subsec. (f), as amended by Acts 2013, 83rd Leg., ch. 1409 (S.B. 1114), § 8*

(f) The parent, guardian, or other custodian of the child must receive notice that the child has been referred for disposition under the first offender program. The notice must:

(1) state the grounds for taking the child into custody for conduct described by Subsection (a), or for accusing the child of an offense described by Subsection (a–1);

(2) identify the law enforcement officer or agency to which the child was referred;

(3) briefly describe the nature of the program; and

(4) state that the child's failure to complete the program will result in the child being referred to the juvenile court for the conduct or a complaint being filed with a criminal court for the offense.

(g) The child and the parent, guardian, or other custodian of the child must consent to participation by the child in the first offender program.

(h) Disposition under a first offender program may include:

(1) voluntary restitution by the child or the parent, guardian, or other custodian of the child to the victim of the conduct of the child;

(2) voluntary community service restitution by the child;

(3) educational, vocational training, counseling, or other rehabilitative services; and

(4) periodic reporting by the child to the law enforcement officer or agency to which the child has been referred.

*Text of subsec. (i), as amended by Acts 2013, 83rd Leg., ch. 1407 (S.B. 393), § 16*

(i) The case of a child who successfully completes the first offender program is closed and may not be referred to juvenile court or a court of competent criminal jurisdiction, unless the child is taken into custody under circumstances described by Subsection (j)(3).

*Text of subsec. (i), as amended by Acts 2013, 83rd Leg., ch. 1409 (S.B. 1114), § 8*

(i) The case of a child who successfully completes the first offender program is closed and may not be referred to juvenile court or filed with a criminal court, unless the child is taken into custody under circumstances described by Subsection (j)(3).

*Text of subsec. (j), as amended by Acts 2013, 83rd Leg., ch. 1407 (S.B. 393), § 16*

(j) The case of a child referred for disposition under the first offender program shall be referred to juvenile court or a court of competent criminal jurisdiction if:

(1) the child fails to complete the program;

(2) the child or the parent, guardian, or other custodian of the child terminates the child's participation in the program before the child completes it; or

(3) the child completes the program but is taken into custody under Section 52.01 before the 90th day after the date the child completes the program for conduct other than the conduct for which the child was referred to the first offender program.

*Text of subsec. (j), as amended by Acts 2013, 83rd Leg., ch. 1409 (S.B. 1114), § 8*

(j) The case of a child referred for disposition under the first offender program shall be referred to juvenile court or, if the child is accused of an offense described by Subsection (a–1), filed with a criminal court if:

(1) the child fails to complete the program;

(2) the child or the parent, guardian, or other custodian of the child terminates the child's participation in the program before the child completes it; or

(3) the child completes the program but is taken into custody under Section 52.01 before the 90th day after the date the child completes the program for conduct other than the conduct for which the child was referred to the first offender program.

(k) A statement made by a child to a person giving advice or supervision or participating in the first offender program may not be used against the child in any proceeding under this title or any criminal proceeding.

(*l*) The law enforcement agency must report to the juvenile board in December of each year the following:

(1) the last known address of the child, including the census tract;

(2) the gender and ethnicity of the child referred to the program; and

(3) the offense committed by the child.

Added by Acts 1995, 74th Leg., ch. 262, § 19, eff. Jan. 1, 1996. Amended by Acts 1999, 76th Leg., ch. 48, § 2, eff. Sept. 1, 1999; Acts 2013, 83rd Leg., ch. 1407 (S.B. 393), § 16, eff. Sept. 1, 2013; Acts 2013, 83rd Leg., ch. 1409 (S.B. 1114), § 8, eff. Sept. 1, 2013; Acts 2017, 85th Leg., ch. 1049 (H.B. 1935), § 1, eff. Sept. 1, 2017.

### § 52.032. Informal Disposition Guidelines

(a) The juvenile board of each county, in cooperation with each law enforcement agency in the county, shall adopt guidelines for the disposition of a child under Section 52.03 or 52.031. The guidelines adopted under this section shall not be considered mandatory.

(b) The guidelines adopted under Subsection (a) may not allow for the case of a child to be disposed of under Section 52.03 or 52.031 if there is probable cause to believe that the child engaged in delinquent conduct or conduct indicating a need for supervision and cause to believe that the child may be the victim of conduct that constitutes an offense under Section 20A.02, Penal Code.

Added by Acts 1999, 76th Leg., ch. 48, § 3, eff. Sept. 1, 1999. Amended by Acts 2013, 83rd Leg., ch. 186 (S.B. 92), § 3, eff. Sept. 1, 2013.

### § 52.04. Referral to Juvenile Court; Notice to Parents

(a) The following shall accompany referral of a child or a child's case to the office or official designated by the juvenile board or be provided as quickly as possible after referral:

(1) all information in the possession of the person or agency making the referral pertaining to the identity of the child and the child's address, the name and address of the child's parent, guardian, or custodian, the names and addresses of any witnesses, and the child's present whereabouts;

(2) a complete statement of the circumstances of the alleged delinquent conduct or conduct indicating a need for supervision;

(3) when applicable, a complete statement of the circumstances of taking the child into custody; and

(4) when referral is by an officer of a law-enforcement agency, a complete statement of all prior contacts with the child by officers of that law-enforcement agency.

(b) The office or official designated by the juvenile board may refer the case to a law-enforcement agency for the purpose of conducting an investigation to obtain necessary information.

(c) If the office of the prosecuting attorney is designated by the juvenile court to conduct the preliminary investigation under Section 53.01, the referring entity shall first transfer the child's case to the juvenile probation department for statistical reporting purposes only. On the creation of a statistical record or file for the case, the probation department shall within three business days forward the case to the prosecuting attorney for review under Section 53.01.

(d) On referral of the case of a child who has not been taken into custody to the office or official designated by the juvenile board, the office or official designated by the juvenile board shall promptly give notice of the referral and a statement of the reason for the referral to the child's parent, guardian, or custodian.

Acts 1973, 63rd Leg., p. 1460, ch. 544, § 1, eff. Sept. 1, 1973. Amended by Acts 1997, 75th Leg., ch. 1091, § 1, eff. June 19, 1997; Acts 2001, 77th Leg., ch. 136, §§ 1, 2, eff. Sept. 1, 2001; Acts 2001, 77th Leg., ch. 1297, § 16, eff. Sept. 1, 2001; Acts 2003, 78th Leg., ch. 283, § 11, eff. Sept. 1, 2003.

### § 52.041. Referral of Child to Juvenile Court After Expulsion

(a) A school district that expels a child shall refer the child to juvenile court in the county in which the child resides.

(b) The board of the school district or a person designated by the board shall deliver a copy of the order expelling the student and any other information required by Section 52.04 on or before the second working day after the date of the expulsion hearing to the authorized officer of the juvenile court.

(c) Within five working days of receipt of an expulsion notice under this section by the office or official designated by the juvenile board, a preliminary investigation and determination shall be conducted as required by Section 53.01.

(d) The office or official designated by the juvenile board shall within two working days notify the school district that expelled the child if:

(1) a determination was made under Section 53.01 that the person referred to juvenile court was not a child within the meaning of this title;

(2) a determination was made that no probable cause existed to believe the child engaged in delinquent conduct or conduct indicating a need for supervision;

(3) no deferred prosecution or formal court proceedings have been or will be initiated involving the child;

(4) the court or jury finds that the child did not engage in delinquent conduct or conduct indicating a need for supervision and the case has been dismissed with prejudice; or

(5) the child was adjudicated but no disposition was or will be ordered by the court.

(e) In any county where a juvenile justice alternative education program is operated, no student shall be expelled without written notification by the board of the school district or its designated agent to the juvenile board's designated representative. The notification shall be made not later than two business days following the board's determination that the student is to be expelled. Failure to timely notify the designated representative of the juvenile board shall result in the child's duty to continue attending the school district's educational program, which shall be provided to that child until such time as the notification to the juvenile board's designated representative is properly made.

Added by Acts 1995, 74th Leg., ch. 262, § 20, eff. Jan. 1, 1996. Amended by Acts 1997, 75th Leg., ch. 1015, § 16, eff. June 19, 1997; Acts 2001, 77th Leg., ch. 1297, § 17, eff. Sept. 1, 2001.

## CHAPTER 53. PROCEEDINGS PRIOR TO JUDICIAL PROCEEDINGS

Section



### § 53.01. Preliminary Investigation and Determinations; Notice to Parents

(a) On referral of a person believed to be a child or on referral of the person's case to the office or official designated by the juvenile board, the intake officer, probation officer, or other person authorized by the board shall conduct a preliminary investigation to determine whether:

(1) the person referred to juvenile court is a child within the meaning of this title; and

(2) there is probable cause to believe the person:

(A) engaged in delinquent conduct or conduct indicating a need for supervision; or

(B) is a nonoffender who has been taken into custody and is being held solely for deportation out of the United States.

(b) If it is determined that the person is not a child or there is no probable cause, the person shall immediately be released.

(b–1) The person who is conducting the preliminary investigation shall, as appropriate, refer the child's case to a community resource coordination group, a local-level interagency staffing group, or other community juvenile service provider for services under Section 53.011, if the person determines that:

(1) the child is younger than 12 years of age;

(2) there is probable cause to believe the child engaged in delinquent conduct or conduct indicating a need for supervision;

(3) the child's case does not require referral to the prosecuting attorney under Subsection (d) or (f);

(4) the child is eligible for deferred prosecution under Section 53.03; and

(5) the child and the child's family are not currently receiving services under Section 53.011 and would benefit from receiving the services.

(c) When custody of a child is given to the office or official designated by the juvenile board, the intake officer, probation officer, or other person authorized by the board shall promptly give notice of the whereabouts of the child and a statement of the reason the child was taken into custody to the child's parent, guardian, or custodian unless the notice given under Section 52.02(b) provided fair notice of the child's present whereabouts.

(d) Unless the juvenile board approves a written procedure proposed by the office of prosecuting attorney and chief juvenile probation officer which provides otherwise, if it is determined that the person is a child and, regardless of a finding of probable cause, or a lack thereof, there is an allegation that the child engaged in delinquent conduct of the grade of felony, or conduct constituting a misdemeanor offense involving violence to a person or the use or possession of a firearm, location-restricted knife, or club, as those terms are defined by Section 46.01, Penal Code, or prohibited weapon, as described by Section 46.05, Penal Code, the case shall be promptly forwarded to the office of the prosecuting attorney, accompanied by:

(1) all documents that accompanied the current referral; and

(2) a summary of all prior referrals of the child to the juvenile court, juvenile probation department, or a detention facility.

(e) If a juvenile board adopts an alternative referral plan under Subsection (d), the board shall register the plan with the Texas Juvenile Justice Department.

(f) A juvenile board may not adopt an alternate referral plan that does not require the forwarding of a child's case to the prosecuting attorney as provided by Subsection (d) if probable cause exists to believe that the child engaged in delinquent conduct that violates Section 19.03, Penal Code (capital murder), or Section 19.02, Penal Code (murder).

Acts 1973, 63rd Leg., p. 1460, ch. 544, § 1, eff. Sept. 1, 1973. Amended by Acts 1995, 74th Leg., ch. 262, § 21, eff. Jan. 1, 1996; Acts 1997, 75th Leg., ch. 1374, § 5, eff. Sept. 1, 1997; Acts 2001, 77th Leg., ch. 1297, § 18, eff. Sept. 1, 2001; Acts 2003, 78th Leg., ch. 283, § 12, eff. Sept. 1, 2003; Acts 2015, 84th Leg., ch. 734 (H.B. 1549), § 47, eff. Sept. 1, 2015; Acts 2017, 85th Leg., ch. 698 (H.B. 1204), § 1, eff. Sept. 1, 2017; Acts 2017, 85th Leg., ch. 1049 (H.B. 1935), § 2, eff. Sept. 1, 2017.

### § 53.011. Services Provided to Certain Children and Families

(a) In this section:

(1) "Community resource coordination group" has the meaning assigned by Section 531.421, Government Code.

(2) "Local-level interagency staffing group" means a group established under the memorandum of understanding described by Section 531.055, Government Code.

(b) On receipt of a referral under Section 53.01(b–1), a community resource coordination group, a local-level interagency staffing group, or another community juvenile services provider shall evaluate the child's case and make recommendations to the juvenile probation department for appropriate services for the child and the child's family.

(c) The probation officer shall create and coordinate a service plan or system of care for the child or the child's family that incorporates the service recommendations for the child or the child's family provided to the juvenile probation department under Subsection (b). The child and the child's parent, guardian, or custodian must consent to the services with knowledge that consent is voluntary.

(d) For a child who receives a service plan or system of care under this section, the probation officer may hold the child's case open for not more than three months to monitor adherence to the service plan or system of care. The probation officer may adjust the service plan or system of care as necessary during the monitoring period. The probation officer may refer the child to the prosecuting attorney if the child fails to successfully participate in required services during that period.

Added by Acts 2017, 85th Leg., ch. 698 (H.B. 1204), § 2, eff. Sept. 1, 2017.

### § 53.012. Review by Prosecutor

(a) The prosecuting attorney shall promptly review the circumstances and allegations of a referral made under Section 53.01 for legal sufficiency and the desirability of prosecution and may file a petition without regard to whether probable cause was found under Section 53.01.

(b) If the prosecuting attorney does not file a petition requesting the adjudication of the child referred to the prosecuting attorney, the prosecuting attorney shall:

(1) terminate all proceedings, if the reason is for lack of probable cause; or

(2) return the referral to the juvenile probation department for further proceedings.

(c) The juvenile probation department shall promptly refer a child who has been returned to the department under Subsection (b)(2) and who fails or refuses to participate in a program of the department to the prosecuting attorney for review of the child's case and determination of whether to file a petition.

Added by Acts 1995, 74th Leg., ch. 262, § 22, eff. Jan. 1, 1996.

### § 53.013. Progressive Sanctions Program

Each juvenile board may adopt a progressive sanctions program using the model for progressive sanctions in Chapter 59.

Added by Acts 1995, 74th Leg., ch. 262, § 22, eff. Jan. 1, 1996. Amended by Acts 1997, 75th Leg., ch. 1086, § 7, eff. Sept. 1, 1997; Acts 2003, 78th Leg., ch. 479, § 1, eff. Sept. 1, 2003.

### § 53.02. Release from Detention

(a) If a child is brought before the court or delivered to a detention facility as authorized by Sections 51.12(a)(3) and (4), the intake or other authorized officer of the court shall immediately make an investigation and shall release the child unless it appears that his detention is warranted under Subsection (b). The release may be conditioned upon requirements reasonably necessary to insure the child's appearance at later proceedings, but the conditions of the release must be in writing and filed with the office or official designated by the court and a copy furnished to the child.

(b) A child taken into custody may be detained prior to hearing on the petition only if:

(1) the child is likely to abscond or be removed from the jurisdiction of the court;

(2) suitable supervision, care, or protection for the child is not being provided by a parent, guardian, custodian, or other person;

(3) the child has no parent, guardian, custodian, or other person able to return the child to the court when required;

(4) the child may be dangerous to himself or herself or the child may threaten the safety of the public if released;

(5) the child has previously been found to be a delinquent child or has previously been convicted of a penal offense punishable by a term in jail or prison and is likely to commit an offense if released; or

(6) the child's detention is required under Subsection (f).

(c) If the child is not released, a request for detention hearing shall be made and promptly presented to the court, and an informal detention hearing as provided in Section 54.01 of this code shall be held promptly, but not later than the time required by Section 54.01 of this code.

(d) A release of a child to an adult under Subsection (a) must be conditioned on the agreement of the adult to be subject to the jurisdiction of the juvenile court and to an order of contempt by the court if the adult, after notification, is unable to produce the child at later proceedings.

(e) Unless otherwise agreed in the memorandum of understanding under Section 37.011, Education Code, in a county with a population greater than 125,000, if a child being released under this section is expelled under Section 37.007, Education Code, the release shall be conditioned on the child's attending a juvenile justice alternative education program pending a deferred prosecution or formal court disposition of the child's case.

(f) A child who is alleged to have engaged in delinquent conduct and to have used, possessed, or exhibited a firearm, as defined by Section 46.01, Penal Code, in the commission of the offense shall be detained until the child is released at the direction of the judge of the juvenile court, a substitute judge authorized by Section 51.04(f), or a referee appointed under Section 51.04(g), including an oral direction by telephone, or until a detention hearing is held as required by Section 54.01.

Acts 1973, 63rd Leg., p. 1460, ch. 544, § 1, eff. Sept. 1, 1973. Amended by Acts 1979, 66th Leg., p. 1102, ch. 518, § 1, eff. June 11, 1979; Acts 1981, 67th Leg., p. 291, ch. 115, § 1, eff. Aug. 31, 1981; Acts 1995, 74th Leg., ch. 262, § 23, eff. Jan. 1, 1996; Acts 1997, 75th Leg., ch. 1015, § 17, eff. June 19, 1997; Acts 1997, 75th Leg., ch. 1374, § 6, eff. Sept. 1, 1997; Acts 1999, 76th Leg., ch. 232, § 1, eff. Sept. 1, 1999.

### § 53.03. Deferred Prosecution

(a) Subject to Subsections (e) and (g), if the preliminary investigation required by Section 53.01 of this code results in a determination that further proceedings in the case are authorized, the probation officer or other designated officer of the court, subject to the direction of the juvenile court, may advise the parties for a reasonable period of time not to exceed six months concerning deferred prosecution and rehabilitation of a child if:

(1) deferred prosecution would be in the interest of the public and the child;

(2) the child and his parent, guardian, or custodian consent with knowledge that consent is not obligatory; and

(3) the child and his parent, guardian, or custodian are informed that they may terminate the deferred prosecution at any point and petition the court for a court hearing in the case.

(b) Except as otherwise permitted by this title, the child may not be detained during or as a result of the deferred prosecution process.

(c) An incriminating statement made by a participant to the person giving advice and in the discussions or conferences incident thereto may not be used against the declarant in any court hearing.

(d) The juvenile board may adopt a fee schedule for deferred prosecution services and rules for the waiver of a fee for financial hardship in accordance with guidelines that the Texas Juvenile Justice Department shall provide. The maximum fee is $15 a month. If the board adopts a schedule and rules for waiver, the probation officer or other designated officer of the court shall collect the fee authorized by the schedule from the parent, guardian, or custodian of a child for whom a deferred prosecution is authorized under this section or waive the fee in accordance with the rules adopted by the board. The officer shall deposit the fees received under this section in the county treasury to the credit of a special fund that may be used only for juvenile probation or community-based juvenile corrections services or facilities in which a juvenile may be required to live while under court supervision. If the board does not adopt a schedule and rules for waiver, a fee for deferred prosecution services may not be imposed.

(e) A prosecuting attorney may defer prosecution for any child. A probation officer or other designated officer of the court:

(1) may not defer prosecution for a child for a case that is required to be forwarded to the prosecuting attorney under Section 53.01(d); and

(2) may defer prosecution for a child who has previously been adjudicated for conduct that constitutes a felony only if the prosecuting attorney consents in writing.

(f) The probation officer or other officer designated by the court supervising a program of deferred prosecution for a child under this section shall report to the juvenile court any violation by the child of the program.

(g) Prosecution may not be deferred for a child alleged to have engaged in conduct that:

(1) is an offense under Section 49.04, 49.05, 49.06, 49.07, or 49.08, Penal Code; or

(2) is a third or subsequent offense under Section 106.04 or 106.041, Alcoholic Beverage Code.

(h) If the child is alleged to have engaged in delinquent conduct or conduct indicating a need for supervision that violates Section 28.08, Penal Code, deferred prosecution under this section may include:

(1) voluntary attendance in a class with instruction in self-responsibility and empathy for a victim of an offense conducted by a local juvenile probation department, if the class is available; and

(2) voluntary restoration of the property damaged by the child by removing or painting over any markings made by the child, if the owner of the property consents to the restoration.

(h-1) If the child is alleged to have engaged in delinquent conduct or conduct indicating a need for supervision that violates Section 481.115, 481.1151, 481.116, 481.1161, 481.117, 481.118, or 481.121, Health and Safety Code, deferred prosecution under this section may include a condition that the child successfully complete a drug education program that is designed to educate persons on the dangers of drug abuse in accordance with Section 521.374(a)(1), Transportation Code, and that is regulated by the Texas Department of Licensing and Regulation under Chapter 171, Government Code.

(h–2) If the child is alleged to have engaged in delinquent conduct or conduct indicating a need for supervision that violates Section 106.02, 106.025, 106.04, 106.041, 106.05, or 106.07, Alcoholic Beverage Code, or Section 49.02, Penal Code, deferred prosecution under this section may include a condition that the child successfully complete an alcohol awareness program described by Section 106.115, Alcoholic Beverage Code, that is regulated by the Texas Department of Licensing and Regulation under Chapter 171, Government Code.

(i) The court may defer prosecution for a child at any time:

(1) for an adjudication that is to be decided by a jury trial, before the jury is sworn;

(2) for an adjudication before the court, before the first witness is sworn; or

(3) for an uncontested adjudication, before the child pleads to the petition or agrees to a stipulation of evidence.

(j) The court may add the period of deferred prosecution under Subsection (i) to a previous order of deferred prosecution, except that the court may not place the child on deferred prosecution for a combined period longer than one year.

(k) In deciding whether to grant deferred prosecution under Subsection (i), the court may consider professional representations by the parties concerning the nature of the case and the background of the respondent. The representations made under this subsection by the child or counsel for the child are not admissible against the child at trial should the court reject the application for deferred prosecution.

Acts 1973, 63rd Leg., p. 1460, ch. 544, § 1, eff. Sept. 1, 1973. Amended by Acts 1983, 68th Leg., p. 3261, ch. 565, § 1, eff. Sept. 1, 1983; Acts 1987, 70th Leg., ch. 1040, § 22, eff. Sept. 1, 1987; Acts 1995, 74th Leg., ch. 262, § 24, eff. Jan. 1, 1996; Acts 1997, 75th Leg., ch. 593, § 6, eff. Sept. 1, 1997; Acts 1997, 75th Leg., ch. 1013, § 16, eff. Sept. 1, 1997; Acts 1999, 76th Leg., ch. 62, § 19.01(17), eff. Sept. 1, 1999; Acts 2003, 78th Leg., ch. 283, § 13, eff. Sept. 1, 2003; Acts 2005, 79th Leg., ch. 949, § 11, eff. Sept. 1, 2005; Acts 2015, 84th Leg., ch. 734 (H.B. 1549), § 48, eff. Sept. 1, 2015; Acts 2015, 84th Leg., ch. 1004 (H.B. 642), § 5, eff. Sept. 1, 2015; Acts 2021, 87th Leg., ch. 948 (S.B. 1480), § 12, eff. Sept. 1, 2021.

Sections 20 and 21(b) of Acts 2021, 87th Leg., ch. 948 (S.B. 1480) provide:

"Sec. 20(a). For purposes of this section, any reference in law to a license to provide or instruct a court-ordered program includes a certification under the law as it existed immediately before the effective date [Sept. 1, 2021] of this Act.

"(b) On the effective date of this Act, a program provider license or an instructor license issued before the effective date of this Act shall continue to be valid until the license expires.

"(c) An application for an initial program provider or instructor license or for renewal of a program provider or instructor license submitted to the Texas Department of Licensing and Regulation on or after the effective date of this Act is governed by Chapter 171, Government Code, as added by this Act. An application submitted before that date is governed by the laws and rules in effect when the application was submitted, and the former laws and rules are continued in effect for that purpose.

"(d) A person who holds an instructor license prior to the effective date of this Act is eligible to renew that license on or after the effective date of this Act, if:

"(1) the license is current or is within the late renewal period; and

"(2) the person's instructor eligibility requirements remain in effect at the time of renewal.

"(e) On or after the effective date of this Act, if a person's instructor license expires beyond the late renewal period or if the license is revoked, the person must apply for a new license and meet the instructor eligibility and other license requirements in effect at the time of the new application."

"[Sec. 21](b) All rules, fees, policies, procedures, decisions, and forms that relate to a program or activity regulated under this Act and that are in effect on the effective date of this Act remain in effect until changed by the Texas Commission of Licensing and Regulation, the Texas Department of Licensing and Regulation, or the executive director of the Texas Department of Licensing and Regulation, as appropriate."

## § 53.035. Grand Jury Referral

(a) The prosecuting attorney may, before filing a petition under Section 53.04, refer an offense to a grand jury in the county in which the offense is alleged to have been committed.

(b) The grand jury has the same jurisdiction and powers to investigate the facts and circumstances concerning an offense referred to the grand jury under this section as it has to investigate other criminal activity.

(c) If the grand jury votes to take no action on an offense referred to the grand jury under this section, the prosecuting attorney may not file a petition under Section 53.04 concerning the offense unless the same or a successor grand jury approves the filing of the petition.

(d) If the grand jury votes for approval of the prosecution of an offense referred to the grand jury under this section, the prosecuting attorney may file a petition under Section 53.04.

(e) The approval of the prosecution of an offense by a grand jury under this section does not constitute approval of a petition by a grand jury for purposes of Section 53.045.

Added by Acts 1999, 76th Leg., ch. 1477, § 6, eff. Sept. 1, 1999.

## § 53.04. Court Petition; Answer

(a) If the preliminary investigation, required by Section 53.01 of this code results in a determination that further proceedings are authorized and warranted, a petition for an adjudication or transfer hearing of a child alleged to have engaged in delinquent conduct or conduct indicating a need for supervision may be made as promptly as practicable by a prosecuting attorney who has knowledge of the facts alleged or is informed and believes that they are true.

(b) The proceedings shall be styled "In the matter of ____________."

(c) The petition may be on information and belief.

(d) The petition must state:

(1) with reasonable particularity the time, place, and manner of the acts alleged and the penal law or standard of conduct allegedly violated by the acts;

(2) the name, age, and residence address, if known, of the child who is the subject of the petition;

(3) the names and residence addresses, if known, of the parent, guardian, or custodian of the child and of the child's spouse, if any;

(4) if the child's parent, guardian, or custodian does not reside or cannot be found in the state, or if their places of residence are unknown, the name and residence address of any known adult relative residing in the county or, if there is none, the name and residence address of the known adult relative residing nearest to the location of the court; and

(5) if the child is alleged to have engaged in habitual felony conduct, the previous adjudications in which the child was found to have engaged in conduct violating penal laws of the grade of felony.

(e) An oral or written answer to the petition may be made at or before the commencement of the hearing. If there is no answer, a general denial of the alleged conduct is assumed.

Acts 1973, 63rd Leg., p. 1460, ch. 544, § 1, eff. Sept. 1, 1973. Amended by Acts 1995, 74th Leg., ch. 262, § 25, eff. Jan. 1, 1996.

### § 53.045. Offenses Eligible for Determinate Sentence

(a) Except as provided by Subsection (e), the prosecuting attorney may refer the petition to the grand jury of the county in which the court in which the petition is filed presides if the petition alleges that the child engaged in delinquent conduct that constitutes habitual felony conduct as described by Section 51.031 or that included the violation of any of the following provisions:

(1) Section 19.02, Penal Code (murder);

(2) Section 19.03, Penal Code (capital murder);

(3) Section 19.04, Penal Code (manslaughter);

(4) Section 20.04, Penal Code (aggravated kidnapping);

(5) Section 22.011, Penal Code (sexual assault) or Section 22.021, Penal Code (aggravated sexual assault);

(6) Section 22.02, Penal Code (aggravated assault);

(7) Section 29.03, Penal Code (aggravated robbery);

(8) Section 22.04, Penal Code (injury to a child, elderly individual, or disabled individual), if the offense is punishable as a felony, other than a state jail felony;

(9) Section 22.05(b), Penal Code (felony deadly conduct involving discharging a firearm);

(10) Subchapter D, Chapter 481,[1] Health and Safety Code, if the conduct constitutes a felony of the first degree or an aggravated controlled substance felony (certain offenses involving controlled substances);

(11) Section 15.03, Penal Code (criminal solicitation);

(12) Section 21.11(a)(1), Penal Code (indecency with a child);

(13) Section 15.031, Penal Code (criminal solicitation of a minor);

(14) Section 15.01, Penal Code (criminal attempt), if the offense attempted was an offense under Section 19.02, Penal Code (murder), or Section 19.03, Penal Code (capital murder), or an offense listed by Article 42A.054(a), Code of Criminal Procedure;

(15) Section 28.02, Penal Code (arson), if bodily injury or death is suffered by any person by reason of the commission of the conduct;

(16) Section 49.08, Penal Code (intoxication manslaughter); or

(17) Section 15.02, Penal Code (criminal conspiracy), if the offense made the subject of the criminal conspiracy includes a violation of any of the provisions referenced in Subdivisions (1) through (16).

(b) A grand jury may approve a petition submitted to it under this section by a vote of nine members of the grand jury in the same manner that the grand jury votes on the presentment of an indictment.

(c) The grand jury has all the powers to investigate the facts and circumstances relating to a petition submitted under this section as it has to investigate other criminal activity but may not issue an indictment unless the child is transferred to a criminal court as provided by Section 54.02 of this code.

(d) If the grand jury approves of the petition, the fact of approval shall be certified to the juvenile court, and the certification shall be entered in the record of the case. For the purpose of the transfer of a child to the Texas Department of Criminal Justice as provided by Section 152.00161(c) or 245.151(c), Human Resources Code, as applicable, a juvenile court petition approved by a grand jury under this section is an indictment presented by the grand jury.

(e) The prosecuting attorney may not refer a petition that alleges the child engaged in conduct that violated Section 22.011(a)(2), Penal Code, or Sections 22.021(a)(1)(B) and (2)(B), Penal Code, unless the child is more than three years older than the victim of the conduct.

Added by Acts 1987, 70th Leg., ch. 385, § 7, eff. Sept. 1, 1987. Amended by Acts 1991, 72nd Leg., ch. 574, § 1, eff. Sept. 1, 1991; Acts 1995, 74th Leg., ch. 262, §§ 26, 27, eff. Jan. 1, 1996; Acts 1997, 75th Leg., ch. 1086, § 8, eff. Sept. 1, 1997; Acts 2001, 77th Leg., ch. 1297, § 19, eff. Sept. 1, 2001; Acts 2007, 80th Leg., ch. 908, § 10, eff. Sept. 1, 2007; Acts 2011, 82nd Leg., ch. 85 (S.B. 653), § 3.006, eff. Sept. 1, 2011; Acts 2013, 83rd Leg., ch. 1299 (H.B. 2862), § 14, eff. Sept. 1, 2013; Acts 2015, 84th Leg., ch. 770 (H.B. 2299), § 2.31, eff. Jan. 1, 2017; Acts 2015, 84th Leg., ch. 854 (S.B. 1149), § 2, eff. Sept. 1, 2015.

[1] V.T.C.A., Health & Safety Code § 481.101 et seq.

### § 53.05. Time Set for Hearing

(a) After the petition has been filed, the juvenile court shall set a time for the hearing.

(b) The time set for the hearing shall not be later than 10 working days after the day the petition was filed if:

(1) the child is in detention; or

(2) the child will be taken into custody under Section 53.06(d) of this code.

Acts 1973, 63rd Leg., p. 1460, ch. 544, § 1, eff. Sept. 1, 1973. Amended by Acts 1995, 74th Leg., ch. 262, § 28, eff. Jan. 1, 1996.

### § 53.06. Summons

(a) The juvenile court shall direct issuance of a summons to:

(1) the child named in the petition;

(2) the child's parent, guardian, or custodian;

(3) the child's guardian ad litem; and

(4) any other person who appears to the court to be a proper or necessary party to the proceeding.

(b) The summons must require the persons served to appear before the court at the time set to answer the allegations of the petition. A copy of the petition must accompany the summons.

(c) The court may endorse on the summons an order directing the person having the physical custody or control of the child to bring the child to the hearing. A person who violates an order entered under this subsection may be proceeded against under Section 53.08 or 54.07 of this code.

(d) If it appears from an affidavit filed or from sworn testimony before the court that immediate detention of the child is warranted under Section 53.02(b) of this code, the court may endorse on the summons an order that a law-enforcement officer shall serve the summons and shall immediately take the child into custody and bring him before the court.

(e) A party, other than the child, may waive service of summons by written stipulation or by voluntary appearance at the hearing.

Acts 1973, 63rd Leg., p. 1460, ch. 544, § 1, eff. Sept. 1, 1973. Amended by Acts 1995, 74th Leg., ch. 262, § 29, eff. Jan. 1, 1996.

### § 53.07. Service of Summons

(a) If a person to be served with a summons is in this state and can be found, the summons shall be served upon him personally at least two days before the day of the adjudication hearing. If he is in this state and cannot be found, but his address is known or can with reasonable diligence be ascertained, the summons may be served on him by mailing a copy by registered or certified mail, return receipt requested, at least five days before the day of the hearing. If he is outside this state but he can be found or his address is known, or his whereabouts or address can with reasonable diligence be ascertained, service of the summons may be made either by delivering a copy to him personally or mailing a copy to him by registered or certified mail, return receipt requested, at least five days before the day of the hearing.

(b) The juvenile court has jurisdiction of the case if after reasonable effort a person other than the child cannot be found nor his post-office address ascertained, whether he is in or outside this state.

(c) Service of the summons may be made by any suitable person under the direction of the court.

(d) The court may authorize payment from the general funds of the county of the costs of service and of necessary travel expenses incurred by persons summoned or otherwise required to appear at the hearing.

(e) Witnesses may be subpoenaed in accordance with the Texas Code of Criminal Procedure, 1965.

Acts 1973, 63rd Leg., p. 1460, ch. 544, § 1, eff. Sept. 1, 1973.

### § 53.08. Writ of Attachment

(a) The juvenile court may issue a writ of attachment for a person who violates an order entered under Section 53.06(c).

(b) A writ of attachment issued under this section is executed in the same manner as in a criminal proceeding as provided by Chapter 24, Code of Criminal Procedure.

Added by Acts 1995, 74th Leg., ch. 262, § 30, eff. Jan. 1, 1996.

## CHAPTER 54. JUDICIAL PROCEEDINGS



### § 54.01. Detention Hearing

(a) Except as provided by Subsection (p), if the child is not released under Section 53.02, a detention hearing without a jury shall be held promptly, but not later than the second working day after the child is taken into custody; provided, however, that when a child is detained on a Friday or Saturday, then such detention hearing shall be held on the first working day after the child is taken into custody.

(b) Reasonable notice of the detention hearing, either oral or written, shall be given, stating the time, place, and purpose of the hearing. Notice shall be given to the child and, if they can be found, to his parents, guardian, or custodian. Prior to the commencement of the hearing, the court shall inform the parties of the child's right to counsel and to appointed counsel if they are indigent and of the child's right to remain silent with respect to any allegations of delinquent conduct, conduct indicating a need for supervision, or conduct that violates an order of probation imposed by a juvenile court.

(b–1) Unless the court finds that the appointment of counsel is not feasible due to exigent circumstances, the court shall appoint counsel within a reasonable time before the first detention hearing is held to represent the child at that hearing.

(c) At the detention hearing, the court may consider written reports from probation officers, professional court employees, guardians ad litem appointed under Section 51.11(d), or professional consultants in addition to the testimony of witnesses. Prior to the detention hearing, the court shall provide the attorney for the child with access to all written matter to be considered by the court in making the detention decision. The court may order counsel not to reveal items to the child or the child's parent, guardian, or guardian ad litem if such disclosure would materially harm the treatment and rehabilitation of the child or would substantially decrease the likelihood of receiving information from the same or similar sources in the future.

(d) A detention hearing may be held without the presence of the child's parents if the court has been unable to locate them. If no parent or guardian is present, the court shall appoint counsel or a guardian ad litem for the child, subject to the requirements of Subsection (b–1).

(e) At the conclusion of the hearing, the court shall order the child released from detention unless it finds that:

(1) he is likely to abscond or be removed from the jurisdiction of the court;

(2) suitable supervision, care, or protection for him is not being provided by a parent, guardian, custodian, or other person;

(3) he has no parent, guardian, custodian, or other person able to return him to the court when required;

(4) he may be dangerous to himself or may threaten the safety of the public if released; or

(5) he has previously been found to be a delinquent child or has previously been convicted of a penal offense punishable by a term in jail or prison and is likely to commit an offense if released.

(f) Unless otherwise agreed in the memorandum of understanding under Section 37.011, Education Code, a release may be conditioned on requirements reasonably necessary to insure the child's appearance at later proceedings, but the conditions of the release must be in writing and a copy furnished to the child. In a county with a population greater than 125,000, if a child being released under this section is expelled under Section 37.007, Education Code, the release shall be conditioned on the child's attending a juvenile justice alternative education program pending a deferred prosecution or formal court disposition of the child's case.

(g) No statement made by the child at the detention hearing shall be admissible against the child at any other hearing.

(h) A detention order extends to the conclusion of the disposition hearing, if there is one, but in no event for more than 10 working days. Further detention orders may be made following subsequent detention hearings. The initial detention hearing may not be waived but subsequent detention hearings may be waived in accordance with the requirements of Section 51.09. Each subsequent detention order shall extend for no more than 10 working days, except that in a county that does not have a certified juvenile detention facility, as described by Section 51.12(a)(3), each subsequent detention order shall extend for no more than 15 working days.

(i) A child in custody may be detained for as long as 10 days without the hearing described in Subsection (a) of this section if:

(1) a written request for shelter in detention facilities pending arrangement of transportation to his place of residence in another state or country or another county of this state is voluntarily executed by the child not later than the next working day after he was taken into custody;

(2) the request for shelter contains:

(A) a statement by the child that he voluntarily agrees to submit himself to custody and detention for a period of not longer than 10 days without a detention hearing;

(B) an allegation by the person detaining the child that the child has left his place of residence in another state or country or another county of this state, that he is in need of shelter, and that an effort is being made to arrange transportation to his place of residence; and

(C) a statement by the person detaining the child that he has advised the child of his right to demand a detention hearing under Subsection (a) of this section; and

(3) the request is signed by the juvenile court judge to evidence his knowledge of the fact that the child is being held in detention.

(j) The request for shelter may be revoked by the child at any time, and on such revocation, if further detention is necessary, a detention hearing shall be held not later than the next working day in accordance with Subsections (a) through (g) of this section.

(k) Notwithstanding anything in this title to the contrary, the child may sign a request for shelter without the concurrence of an adult specified in Section 51.09 of this code.

(*l*) The juvenile board may appoint a referee to conduct the detention hearing. The referee shall be an attorney licensed to practice law in this state. Such payment or additional payment as may be warranted for referee services shall be provided from county funds. Before commencing the detention hearing, the referee shall inform the parties who have appeared that they are entitled to have the hearing before the juvenile court judge or a substitute judge authorized by Section 51.04(f). If a party objects to the referee conducting the detention hearing, an authorized judge shall conduct the hearing within 24 hours. At the conclusion of the hearing, the referee shall transmit written findings and recommendations to the juvenile court judge or substitute judge. The juvenile court judge or substitute judge shall adopt, modify, or reject the referee's recommendations not later than the next working day after the day that the judge receives the recommendations. Failure to act within that time results in release of the child by operation of law. A recommendation that the child be released operates to secure the child's immediate release, subject to the power of the juvenile court judge or substitute judge to reject or modify that recommendation. The effect of an order detaining a child shall be computed from the time of the hearing before the referee.

(m) The detention hearing required in this section may be held in the county of the designated place of detention where the child is being held even though the designated place of detention is outside the county of residence of the child or the county in which the alleged delinquent conduct, conduct indicating a need for supervision, or probation violation occurred.

(n) An attorney appointed by the court under Section 51.10(c) because a determination was made under this section to detain a child who was not represented by an attorney may request on behalf of the child and is entitled to a de novo detention hearing under this section. The attorney must make the request not later than the 10th working day after the date the attorney is appointed. The hearing must take place not later than the second working day after the date the attorney filed a formal request with the court for a hearing.

(*o*) The court or referee shall find whether there is probable cause to believe that a child taken into custody without an arrest warrant or a directive to apprehend has engaged in delinquent conduct, conduct indicating a need for supervision, or conduct that violates an order of probation imposed by a juvenile court. The court or referee must make the finding within 48 hours, including weekends and holidays, of the time the child was taken into custody. The court or referee may make the finding on any reasonably reliable information without regard to admissibility of that information under the Texas Rules of Evidence. A finding of probable cause is required to detain a child after the 48th hour after the time the child was taken into custody. If a court or referee finds probable cause, additional findings of probable cause are not required in the same cause to authorize further detention.

(p) If a child is detained in a county jail or other facility as provided by Section 51.12(*l*) and the child is not released under Section 53.02(f), a detention hearing without a jury shall be held promptly, but not later than the 24th hour, excluding weekends and holidays, after the time the child is taken into custody.

(q) If a child has not been released under Section 53.02 or this section and a petition has not been filed under Section 53.04 or 54.05 concerning the child, the court shall order the child released from detention not later than:

(1) the 30th working day after the date the initial detention hearing is held, if the child is alleged to have engaged in conduct constituting a capital felony, an aggravated controlled substance felony, or a felony of the first degree; or

(2) the 15th working day after the date the initial detention hearing is held, if the child is alleged to have engaged in conduct constituting an offense other than an offense listed in Subdivision (1) or conduct that violates an order of probation imposed by a juvenile court.

(q–1) The juvenile board may impose an earlier deadline than the specified deadlines for filing petitions under Subsection (q) and may specify the consequences of not filing a petition by the deadline the juvenile board has established. The juvenile board may authorize but not require the juvenile court to release a respondent from detention for failure of the prosecutor to file a petition by the juvenile board's deadline.

(r) On the conditional release of a child from detention by judicial order under Subsection (f), the court, referee, or detention magistrate may order that the child's parent, guardian, or custodian present in court at the detention hearing engage in acts or omissions specified by the court, referee, or detention magistrate that will assist the child in complying with the conditions of release. The order must be in writing and a copy furnished to the parent, guardian, or custodian. An order entered under this subsection may be enforced as provided by Chapter 61.

Acts 1973, 63rd Leg., p. 1460, ch. 544, § 1, eff. Sept. 1, 1973. Amended by Acts 1975, 64th Leg., p. 2156, ch. 693, §§ 14, 15, eff. Sept. 1, 1975; Acts 1979, 66th Leg., p. 1102, ch. 518, § 2, eff. June 11, 1979; Acts 1995, 74th Leg., ch. 262, § 31, eff. Jan. 1, 1996; Acts 1997, 75th Leg., ch. 922, § 1, eff. Sept. 1, 1997; Acts 1997, 75th Leg., ch. 1015, § 18, eff. June 19, 1997; Acts 1997, 75th Leg., ch. 1086, § 9, eff. Sept. 1, 1997; Acts 1999, 76th Leg., ch. 232, § 4, eff. Sept. 1, 1999; Acts 1999, 76th Leg., ch. 1477, § 7, eff. Sept. 1, 1999; Acts 2001, 77th Leg., ch. 1297, § 20, eff. Sept. 1, 2001; Acts 2001, 77th Leg., ch. 1420, § 21.001(30), eff. Sept. 1, 2001; Acts 2003, 78th Leg., ch. 283, § 14, eff. Sept. 1, 2003; Acts 2005, 79th Leg., ch. 949, § 12, eff. Sept. 1, 2005; Acts 2013, 83rd Leg., ch. 912 (H.B. 1318), § 4, eff. Sept. 1, 2013; Acts 2021, 87th Leg., ch. 971 (S.B. 2049), § 2, eff. Sept. 1, 2021.

### § 54.011. Detention Hearings for Status Offenders and Nonoffenders; Penalty

(a) The detention hearing for a status offender or nonoffender who has not been released administratively under Section 53.02 shall be held before the 24th hour after the time the child arrived at a detention facility, excluding hours of a weekend or a holiday. Except as otherwise provided by this section, the judge or referee conducting the detention hearing shall release the status offender or nonoffender from secure detention.

(b) The judge or referee may order a child in detention accused of the violation of a valid court order as defined by Section 51.02 detained not longer than 72 hours after the time the detention order was entered, excluding weekends and holidays, if:

(1) the judge or referee finds at the detention hearing that there is probable cause to believe the child violated the valid court order; and

(2) the detention of the child is justified under Section 54.01(e)(1), (2), or (3).

(c) Except as provided by Subsection (d), a detention order entered under Subsection (b) may be extended for one additional 72-hour period, excluding weekends and holidays, only on a finding of good cause by the juvenile court.

(d) A detention order for a child under this section may be extended on the demand of the child's attorney only to allow the time that is necessary to comply with the requirements of Section 51.10(h), entitling the attorney to 10 days to prepare for an adjudication hearing.

(e) A status offender may be detained for a necessary period, not to exceed the period allowed under the Interstate Compact for Juveniles, to enable the child's return to the child's home in another state under Chapter 60.

(f) Except as provided by Subsection (a), a nonoffender, including a person who has been taken into custody and is being held solely for deportation out of the United States, may not be detained for any period of time in a secure detention facility or secure correctional facility, regardless of whether the facility is publicly or privately operated. A nonoffender who is detained in violation of this subsection is entitled to immediate release from the facility and may bring a civil action for compensation for the illegal detention against any person responsible for the detention. A person commits an offense if the person knowingly detains or assists in detaining a nonoffender in a secure detention facility or secure correctional facility in violation of this subsection. An offense under this subsection is a Class B misdemeanor.

Added by Acts 1995, 74th Leg., ch. 262, § 32, eff. Jan. 1, 1996. Amended by Acts 1997, 75th Leg., ch. 1374, § 7, eff. Sept. 1, 1997; Acts 2003, 78th Leg., ch. 283, §§ 15, 16, eff. Sept. 1, 2003; Acts 2013, 83rd Leg., ch. 1299 (H.B. 2862), § 15, eff. Sept. 1, 2013.

### § 54.012. Interactive Video Recording of Detention Hearing

(a) A detention hearing under Section 54.01 may be held using interactive video equipment if:

(1) the child and the child's attorney agree to the video hearing; and

(2) the parties to the proceeding have the opportunity to cross-examine witnesses.

(b) A detention hearing may not be held using video equipment unless the video equipment for the hearing provides for a two-way communication of image and sound among the child, the court, and other parties at the hearing.

(c) A recording of the communications shall be made. The recording shall be preserved until the earlier of:

(1) the 91st day after the date on which the recording is made if the child is alleged to have engaged in conduct constituting a misdemeanor;

(2) the 120th day after the date on which the recording is made if the child is alleged to have engaged in conduct constituting a felony; or

(3) the date on which the adjudication hearing ends.

(d) An attorney for the child may obtain a copy of the recording on payment of the reasonable costs of reproducing the copy.

Added by Acts 1995, 74th Leg., ch. 262, § 33, eff. Jan. 1, 1996. Amended by Acts 2005, 79th Leg., ch. 949, § 13, eff. Sept. 1, 2005.

## § 54.02. Waiver of Jurisdiction and Discretionary Transfer to Criminal Court

(a) The juvenile court may waive its exclusive original jurisdiction and transfer a child to the appropriate district court or criminal district court for criminal proceedings if:

(1) the child is alleged to have violated a penal law of the grade of felony;

(2) the child was:

(A) 14 years of age or older at the time he is alleged to have committed the offense, if the offense is a capital felony, an aggravated controlled substance felony, or a felony of the first degree, and no adjudication hearing has been conducted concerning that offense; or

(B) 15 years of age or older at the time the child is alleged to have committed the offense, if the offense is a felony of the second or third degree or a state jail felony, and no adjudication hearing has been conducted concerning that offense; and

(3) after a full investigation and a hearing, the juvenile court determines that there is probable cause to believe that the child before the court committed the offense alleged and that because of the seriousness of the offense alleged or the background of the child the welfare of the community requires criminal proceedings.

(b) The petition and notice requirements of Sections 53.04, 53.05, 53.06, and 53.07 of this code must be satisfied, and the summons must state that the hearing is for the purpose of considering discretionary transfer to criminal court.

(c) The juvenile court shall conduct a hearing without a jury to consider transfer of the child for criminal proceedings.

(d) Prior to the hearing, the juvenile court shall order and obtain a complete diagnostic study, social evaluation, and full investigation of the child, his circumstances, and the circumstances of the alleged offense.

(e) At the transfer hearing the court may consider written reports from probation officers, professional court employees, guardians ad litem appointed under Section 51.11(d), or professional consultants in addition to the testimony of witnesses. At least five days prior to the transfer hearing, the court shall provide the attorney for the child and the prosecuting attorney with access to all written matter to be considered by the court in making the transfer decision. The court may order counsel not to reveal items to the child or the child's parent, guardian, or guardian ad litem if such disclosure would materially harm the treatment and rehabilitation of the child or would substantially decrease the likelihood of receiving information from the same or similar sources in the future.

(f) In making the determination required by Subsection (a) of this section, the court shall consider, among other matters:

(1) whether the alleged offense was against person or property, with greater weight in favor of transfer given to offenses against the person;

(2) the sophistication and maturity of the child;

(3) the record and previous history of the child; and

(4) the prospects of adequate protection of the public and the likelihood of the rehabilitation of the child by use of procedures, services, and facilities currently available to the juvenile court.

(g) If the petition alleges multiple offenses that constitute more than one criminal transaction, the juvenile court shall either retain or transfer all offenses relating to a single transaction. Except as provided by Subsection (g–1), a child is not subject to criminal prosecution at any time for any offense arising out of a criminal transaction for which the juvenile court retains jurisdiction.

(g–1) A child may be subject to criminal prosecution for an offense committed under Chapter 19 or Section 49.08, Penal Code, if:

(1) the offense arises out of a criminal transaction for which the juvenile court retained jurisdiction over other offenses relating to the criminal transaction; and

(2) on or before the date the juvenile court retained jurisdiction, one or more of the elements of

the offense under Chapter 19 or Section 49.08, Penal Code, had not occurred.

(h) If the juvenile court waives jurisdiction, it shall state specifically in the order its reasons for waiver and certify its action, including the written order and findings of the court, and shall transfer the person to the appropriate court for criminal proceedings and cause the results of the diagnostic study of the person ordered under Subsection (d), including psychological information, to be transferred to the appropriate criminal prosecutor. On transfer of the person for criminal proceedings, the person shall be dealt with as an adult and in accordance with the Code of Criminal Procedure, except that if detention in a certified juvenile detention facility is authorized under Section 152.0015, Human Resources Code, the juvenile court may order the person to be detained in the facility pending trial or until the criminal court enters an order under Article 4.19, Code of Criminal Procedure. A transfer of custody made under this subsection is an arrest.

(h–1) If the juvenile court orders a person detained in a certified juvenile detention facility under Subsection (h), the juvenile court shall set or deny bond for the person as required by the Code of Criminal Procedure and other law applicable to the pretrial detention of adults accused of criminal offenses.

(i) A waiver under this section is a waiver of jurisdiction over the child and the criminal court may not remand the child to the jurisdiction of the juvenile court.

(j) The juvenile court may waive its exclusive original jurisdiction and transfer a person to the appropriate district court or criminal district court for criminal proceedings if:

(1) the person is 18 years of age or older;

(2) the person was:

(A) 10 years of age or older and under 17 years of age at the time the person is alleged to have committed a capital felony or an offense under Section 19.02, Penal Code;

(B) 14 years of age or older and under 17 years of age at the time the person is alleged to have committed an aggravated controlled substance felony or a felony of the first degree other than an offense under Section 19.02, Penal Code; or

(C) 15 years of age or older and under 17 years of age at the time the person is alleged to have committed a felony of the second or third degree or a state jail felony;

(3) no adjudication concerning the alleged offense has been made or no adjudication hearing concerning the offense has been conducted;

(4) the juvenile court finds from a preponderance of the evidence that:

(A) for a reason beyond the control of the state it was not practicable to proceed in juvenile court before the 18th birthday of the person; or

(B) after due diligence of the state it was not practicable to proceed in juvenile court before the 18th birthday of the person because:

(i) the state did not have probable cause to proceed in juvenile court and new evidence has been found since the 18th birthday of the person;

(ii) the person could not be found; or

(iii) a previous transfer order was reversed by an appellate court or set aside by a district court; and

(5) the juvenile court determines that there is probable cause to believe that the child before the court committed the offense alleged.

(k) The petition and notice requirements of Sections 53.04, 53.05, 53.06, and 53.07 of this code must be satisfied, and the summons must state that the hearing is for the purpose of considering waiver of jurisdiction under Subsection (j). The person's parent, custodian, guardian, or guardian ad litem is not considered a party to a proceeding under Subsection (j) and it is not necessary to provide the parent, custodian, guardian, or guardian ad litem with notice.

(*l*) The juvenile court shall conduct a hearing without a jury to consider waiver of jurisdiction under Subsection (j). Except as otherwise provided by this subsection, a waiver of jurisdiction under Subsection (j) may be made without the necessity of conducting the diagnostic study or complying with the requirements of discretionary transfer proceedings under Subsection (d). If requested by the attorney for the person at least 10 days before the transfer hearing, the court shall order that the person be examined pursuant to Section 51.20(a) and that the results of the examination be provided to the attorney for the person and the attorney for the state at least five days before the transfer hearing.

(m) Notwithstanding any other provision of this section, the juvenile court shall waive its exclusive original jurisdiction and transfer a child to the appropriate district court or criminal court for criminal proceedings if:

(1) the child has previously been transferred to a district court or criminal district court for criminal proceedings under this section, unless:

(A) the child was not indicted in the matter transferred by the grand jury;

(B) the child was found not guilty in the matter transferred;

(C) the matter transferred was dismissed with prejudice; or

(D) the child was convicted in the matter transferred, the conviction was reversed on appeal, and the appeal is final; and

(2) the child is alleged to have violated a penal law of the grade of felony.

(n) A mandatory transfer under Subsection (m) may be made without conducting the study required in discretionary transfer proceedings by Subsection (d). The requirements of Subsection (b) that the summons state that the purpose of the hearing is to consider discretionary transfer to criminal court does not apply to a transfer proceeding under Subsection (m). In a proceeding under Subsection (m), it is sufficient that the summons provide fair notice that the purpose of the hearing is to consider mandatory transfer to criminal court.

(*o*) If a respondent is taken into custody for possible discretionary transfer proceedings under Subsection (j), the juvenile court shall hold a detention hearing in the same manner as provided by Section 54.01, except that the court shall order the respondent released unless it finds that the respondent:

(1) is likely to abscond or be removed from the jurisdiction of the court;

(2) may be dangerous to himself or herself or may threaten the safety of the public if released; or

(3) has previously been found to be a delinquent child or has previously been convicted of a penal offense punishable by a term of jail or prison and is likely to commit an offense if released.

(p) If the juvenile court does not order a respondent released under Subsection (*o*), the court shall, pending the conclusion of the discretionary transfer hearing, order that the respondent be detained in:

(1) a certified juvenile detention facility as provided by Subsection (q); or

(2) an appropriate county facility for the detention of adults accused of criminal offenses.

(q) The detention of a respondent in a certified juvenile detention facility must comply with the detention requirements under this title, except that, to the extent practicable, the person shall be kept separate from children detained in the same facility.

(r) If the juvenile court orders a respondent detained in a county facility under Subsection (p), the county sheriff shall take custody of the respondent under the juvenile court's order. The juvenile court shall set or deny bond for the respondent as required by the Code of Criminal Procedure and other law applicable to the pretrial detention of adults accused of criminal offenses.

(s) If a child is transferred to criminal court under this section, only the petition for discretionary transfer, the order of transfer, and the order of commitment, if any, are a part of the district clerk's public record.

Acts 1973, 63rd Leg., p. 1460, ch. 544, § 1, eff. Sept. 1, 1973. Amended by Acts 1975, 64th Leg., p. 2156, ch. 693, § 16, eff. Sept. 1, 1975; Acts 1987, 70th Leg., ch. 140, §§ 1 to 3, eff. Sept. 1, 1987; Acts 1995, 74th Leg., ch. 262, § 34, eff. Jan. 1, 1996; Acts 1999, 76th Leg., ch. 1477, § 8, eff. Sept. 1, 1999; Acts 2009, 81st Leg., ch. 1354, § 1, eff. Sept. 1, 2009; Acts 2011, 82nd Leg., ch. 1087 (S.B. 1209), § 4, eff. Sept. 1, 2011; Acts 2011, 82nd Leg., ch. 1103 (S.B. 1617), § 1, eff. Sept. 1, 2011; Acts 2013, 83rd Leg., ch. 1299 (H.B. 2862), § 16, eff. Sept. 1, 2013; Acts 2021, 87th Leg., ch. 971 (S.B. 2049), § 3, eff. Sept. 1, 2021.

## § 54.021. Repealed by Acts 2015, 84th Leg., ch. 935 (H.B. 2398), § 41(3), eff. Sept. 1, 2015

## § 54.022. Repealed by Acts 2001, 77th Leg., ch. 1514, § 19(b), eff. Sept. 1, 2001.

## § 54.023. Repealed by Acts 2003, 78th Leg., ch. 283, § 61(1), eff. Sept. 1, 2003.

## § 54.03. Adjudication Hearing

(a) A child may be found to have engaged in delinquent conduct or conduct indicating a need for supervision only after an adjudication hearing conducted in accordance with the provisions of this section.

(b) At the beginning of the adjudication hearing, the juvenile court judge shall explain to the child and his parent, guardian, or guardian ad litem:

(1) the allegations made against the child;

(2) the nature and possible consequences of the proceedings, including the law relating to the admissibility of the record of a juvenile court adjudication in a criminal proceeding;

(3) the child's privilege against self-incrimination;

(4) the child's right to trial and to confrontation of witnesses;

(5) the child's right to representation by an attorney if he is not already represented; and

(6) the child's right to trial by jury.

(c) Trial shall be by jury unless jury is waived in accordance with Section 51.09. If the hearing is on a petition that has been approved by the grand jury under Section 53.045, the jury must consist of 12 persons and be selected in accordance with the requirements in criminal cases. If the hearing is on a petition that alleges conduct that violates a penal law of this state of the grade of misdemeanor, the jury must consist of the number of persons required by Article 33.01(b), Code of Criminal Procedure. Jury verdicts under this title must be unanimous.

(d) Except as provided by Section 54.031, only material, relevant, and competent evidence in accordance with the Texas Rules of Evidence applicable to criminal cases and Chapter 38, Code of Criminal Procedure, may be considered in the adjudication hearing. Except in a detention or discretionary transfer hearing, a social history report or social service file shall not be viewed by the court before the adjudication decision and shall not be viewed by the jury at any time.

(e) A child alleged to have engaged in delinquent conduct or conduct indicating a need for supervision need not be a witness against nor otherwise incriminate himself. An extrajudicial statement which was obtained without fulfilling the requirements of this title or of the constitution of this state or the United States, may not be used in an adjudication hearing. A statement made by the child out of court is insufficient to support a finding of delinquent conduct or conduct indicating a need for supervision unless it is corroborated in whole or in part by other evidence. An adjudication of delinquent conduct or conduct indicating a need for supervision cannot be had upon the testimony of an accomplice unless corroborated by other evidence tending to connect the child with the alleged delinquent conduct or conduct indicating a need for supervision; and the corroboration is not sufficient if it merely shows the commission of the alleged conduct. Evidence illegally seized or obtained is inadmissible in an adjudication hearing.

(f) At the conclusion of the adjudication hearing, the court or jury shall find whether or not the child has engaged in delinquent conduct or conduct indicating a need for supervision. The finding must be based on competent evidence admitted at the hearing. The child shall be presumed to be innocent of the charges against the child and no finding that a child has engaged in delinquent conduct or conduct indicating a need for supervision may be returned unless the state has proved such beyond a reasonable doubt. In all jury cases the jury will be instructed that the burden is on the state to prove that a child has engaged in delinquent conduct or is in need of supervision beyond a reasonable doubt. A child may be adjudicated as having engaged in conduct constituting a lesser included offense as provided by Articles 37.08 and 37.09, Code of Criminal Procedure.

(g) If the court or jury finds that the child did not engage in delinquent conduct or conduct indicating a need for supervision, the court shall dismiss the case with prejudice.

(h) If the finding is that the child did engage in delinquent conduct or conduct indicating a need for supervision, the court or jury shall state which of the allegations in the petition were found to be established by the evidence. The court shall also set a date and time for the disposition hearing.

(i) In order to preserve for appellate or collateral review the failure of the court to provide the child the explanation required by Subsection (b), the attorney for the child must comply with Rule 33.1, Texas Rules of Appellate Procedure, before testimony begins or, if the adjudication is uncontested, before the child pleads to the petition or agrees to a stipulation of evidence.

(j) When the state and the child agree to the disposition of the case, in whole or in part, the prosecuting attorney shall inform the court of the agreement between the state and the child. The court shall inform the child that the court is not required to accept the agreement. The court may delay a decision on whether to accept the agreement until after reviewing a report filed under Section 54.04(b). If the court decides not to accept the agreement, the court shall inform the child of the court's decision and give the child an opportunity to withdraw the plea or stipulation of evidence. If the court rejects the agreement, no document, testimony, or other evidence placed before the court that relates to the rejected agreement may be considered by the court in a subsequent hearing in the case. A statement made by the child before the court's rejection of the agreement to a person writing a report to be filed under Section 54.04(b) may not be admitted into evidence in a subsequent hearing in the case. If the court accepts the agreement, the court shall make a disposition in accordance with the terms of the agreement between the state and the child.

Acts 1973, 63rd Leg., p. 1460, ch. 544, § 1, eff. Sept. 1, 1973. Amended by Acts 1975, 64th Leg., p. 2157, ch. 693, § 17, eff. Sept. 1, 1975; Acts 1979, 66th Leg., p. 1098, ch. 514, § 1, eff. Aug. 27, 1979; Acts 1985, 69th Leg., ch. 590, § 2, eff. Sept. 1, 1985; Acts 1987, 70th Leg., ch. 385, § 8, eff. Sept. 1, 1987; Acts 1987, 70th Leg., ch. 386, § 3, eff. Sept. 1, 1987; Acts 1995, 74th Leg., ch. 262, § 37, eff. Jan. 1, 1996; Acts 1997, 75th Leg., ch. 1086, § 10, eff. Sept. 1, 1997; Acts 1999, 76th Leg., ch. 1477, § 9, eff. Sept. 1, 1999; Acts 2001, 77th Leg., ch. 1297, § 22, eff. Sept. 1, 2001; Acts 2003, 78th Leg., ch. 283, § 17, eff. Sept. 1, 2003; Acts 2009, 81st Leg., ch. 28, § 1, eff. Sept. 1, 2009.

### § 54.031. Hearsay Statement of Certain Abuse Victims

(a) This section applies to a hearing under this title in which a child is alleged to be a delinquent child on the basis of a violation of any of the following provisions of the Penal Code, if a child 12 years of age or younger or a person with a disability is the alleged victim of the violation:

(1) Chapter 21 (Sexual Offenses) or 22 (Assaultive Offenses);

(2) Section 25.02 (Prohibited Sexual Conduct);

(3) Section 43.25 (Sexual Performance by a Child);

(4) Section 20A.02(a)(7) or (8) (Trafficking of Persons); or

(5) Section 43.05(a)(2) (Compelling Prostitution).

(b) This section applies only to statements that describe the alleged violation that:

(1) were made by the child or person with a disability who is the alleged victim of the violation; and

(2) were made to the first person, 18 years of age or older, to whom the child or person with a disability made a statement about the violation.

(c) A statement that meets the requirements of Subsection (b) is not inadmissible because of the hearsay rule if:

(1) on or before the 14th day before the date the hearing begins, the party intending to offer the statement:

(A) notifies each other party of its intention to do so;

(B) provides each other party with the name of the witness through whom it intends to offer the statement; and

(C) provides each other party with a written summary of the statement;

(2) the juvenile court finds, in a hearing conducted outside the presence of the jury, that the statement is reliable based on the time, content, and circumstances of the statement; and

(3) the child or person with a disability who is the alleged victim testifies or is available to testify at the hearing in court or in any other manner provided by law.

(d) In this section, "person with a disability" means a person 13 years of age or older who because of age or physical or mental disease, disability, or injury is substantially unable to protect the person's self from harm or to provide food, shelter, or medical care for the person's self.

Added by Acts 1985, 69th Leg., ch. 590, § 3, eff. Sept. 1, 1985. Amended by Acts 1995, 74th Leg., ch. 76, § 14.31, eff. Sept. 1, 1995; Acts 2009, 81st Leg., ch. 284, § 3, eff. June 11, 2009; Acts 2011, 82nd Leg., ch. 1 (S.B. 24), § 4.01, eff. Sept. 1, 2011.

### § 54.032. Deferral of Adjudication and Dismissal of Certain Cases on Completion of Teen Court Program

(a) A juvenile court may defer adjudication proceedings under Section 54.03 for not more than 180 days if the child:

(1) is alleged to have engaged in conduct indicating a need for supervision that violated a penal law of this state of the grade of misdemeanor that is punishable by fine only or a penal ordinance of a political subdivision of this state;

(2) waives, under Section 51.09, the privilege against self-incrimination and testifies under oath that the allegations are true;

(3) presents to the court an oral or written request to attend a teen court program; and

(4) has not successfully completed a teen court program in the two years preceding the date that the alleged conduct occurred.

(b) The teen court program must be approved by the court.

(c) A child for whom adjudication proceedings are deferred under Subsection (a) shall complete the teen court program not later than the 90th day after the date the teen court hearing to determine punishment is held or the last day of the deferral period, whichever date is earlier. The court shall dismiss the case with prejudice at the time the child presents satisfactory evidence that the child has successfully completed the teen court program.

(d) A case dismissed under this section may not be part of the child's records for any purpose.

(e) The court may require a child who requests a teen court program to pay a reimbursement fee not to exceed $10 that is set by the court to cover the costs of administering this section. The court shall deposit the fee in the county treasury of the county in which the court is located. A child who requests a teen court program and does not complete the program is not entitled to a refund of the fee.

(f) A court may transfer a case in which proceedings have been deferred as provided by this section to a court in another county if the court to which the case is transferred consents. A case may not be transferred unless it is within the jurisdiction of the court to which it is transferred.

(g) In addition to the reimbursement fee authorized by Subsection (e), the court may require a child who requests a teen court program to pay a $10 reimbursement fee to cover the cost to the teen court for performing its duties under this section. The court shall pay the fee to the teen court program, and the teen court program must account to the court for the receipt and disbursal of the fee. A child who pays a fee under this subsection is not entitled to a refund of the fee, regardless of whether the child successfully completes the teen court program.

(h) Notwithstanding Subsection (e) or (g), a juvenile court that is located in the Texas–Louisiana border region, as defined by Section 2056.002, Government Code, may charge a reimbursement fee of $20 under those subsections.

Added by Acts 1989, 71st Leg., ch. 1031, § 2, eff. Sept. 1, 1989. Amended by Acts 1995, 74th Leg., ch. 748, § 1, eff. Sept. 1, 1995; Acts 2001, 77th Leg., ch. 216, § 2, eff. Sept. 1, 2001; Acts 2003, 78th Leg., ch. 283, § 18, eff. Sept. 1, 2003; Acts 2007, 80th Leg., ch. 910, § 2, eff. Sept. 1, 2007; Acts 2019, 86th Leg., ch. 1352 (S.B. 346), § 2.42, eff. Jan. 1, 2020.

### Repeal of (e), (g), and (h)

*Acts 2021, 87th Leg., ch. 472 (S.B. 41), § 5.01(b)(1) repeals (e), (g), and (h) effective Jan. 1, 2022.*

Section 5.01 of Acts 2019, 86th Leg., ch. 1352 (S.B. 346) provides:

"Except as otherwise provided by this Act, the changes in law made by this Act apply only to a cost, fee, or fine on conviction for an offense committed on or after the effective date [Jan. 1, 2020] of this Act. An offense committed before the effective date of this Act is governed by the law in effect on the date the offense was committed, and the former law is continued in effect for that purpose. For purposes of this section, an offense was committed before the effective date of this Act if any element of the offense occurred before that date."

## § 54.0325. Deferral of Adjudication and Dismissal of Certain Cases on Completion of Teen Dating Violence Court Program

(a) In this section:

(1) "Dating violence" has the meaning assigned by Section 71.0021.

(2) "Family violence" has the meaning assigned by Section 71.004.

(3) "Teen dating violence court program" means a program that includes:

(A) a 12–week program designed to educate children who engage in dating violence and encourage them to refrain from engaging in that conduct;

(B) a dedicated teen victim advocate who assists teen victims by offering referrals to additional services, providing counseling and safety planning, and explaining the juvenile justice system;

(C) a court-employed resource coordinator to monitor children's compliance with the 12–week program;

(D) one judge who presides over all of the cases in the jurisdiction that qualify for the program; and

(E) an attorney in the district attorney's office or the county attorney's office who is assigned to the program.

(b) On the recommendation of the prosecuting attorney, the juvenile court may defer adjudication proceedings under Section 54.03 for not more than 180 days if the child is a first offender who is alleged to have engaged in conduct:

(1) that violated a penal law of this state of the grade of misdemeanor; and

(2) involving dating violence.

(c) For the purposes of Subsection (b), a first offender is a child who has not previously been referred to juvenile court for allegedly engaging in conduct constituting dating violence, family violence, or an assault.

(d) Before implementation, the teen dating violence court program must be approved by:

(1) the court; and

(2) the commissioners court of the county.

(e) A child for whom adjudication proceedings are deferred under Subsection (b) shall:

(1) complete the teen dating violence court program not later than the last day of the deferral period; and

(2) appear in court once a month for monitoring purposes.

(f) The court shall dismiss the case with prejudice at the time the child presents satisfactory evidence that the child has successfully completed the teen dating violence court program.

(g) The court may require a child who participates in a teen dating violence court program to pay a fee not to exceed $10 that is set by the court to cover the costs of administering this section. The court shall deposit the fee in the county treasury of the county in which the court is located.

(h) In addition to the fee authorized by Subsection (g), the court may require a child who participates in a teen dating violence court program to pay a fee of $10 to cover the cost to the teen dating violence court program for performing its duties under this section. The court shall pay the fee to the teen dating violence court program, and the teen dating violence court program must account to the court for the receipt and disbursal of the fee.

(i) The court shall track the number of children ordered to participate in the teen dating violence court program, the percentage of victims meeting with the teen victim advocate, and the compliance rate of the children ordered to participate in the program.

Added by Acts 2011, 82nd Leg., ch. 1299 (H.B. 2496), § 1, eff. Sept. 1, 2011.

### Repeal of (g) and (h)

*Acts 2021, 87th Leg., ch. 472 (S.B. 41), § 5.01(b)(2) repeals (g) and (h) effective Jan. 1, 2022.*

## § 54.0326. Deferral of Adjudication and Dismissal of Certain Cases on Completion of Trafficked Persons Program

(a) This section applies to a juvenile court or to an alternative juvenile court exercising simultaneous jurisdiction over proceedings under this title and Subtitle E, Title 5, in the manner authorized by Section 51.0413.

(b) A juvenile court may defer adjudication proceedings under Section 54.03 until the child's 18th birthday and require a child to participate in a program established under Section 152.0017, Human Resources Code, if the child:

(1) is alleged to have engaged in delinquent conduct or conduct indicating a need for supervision and may be a victim of conduct that constitutes an offense under Section 20A.02, Penal Code; and

(2) presents to the court an oral or written request to participate in the program.

(c) Following a child's completion of the program, the court shall dismiss the case with prejudice at the time the child presents satisfactory evidence that the child successfully completed the program.

Added by Acts 2013, 83rd Leg., ch. 186 (S.B. 92), § 4, eff. Sept. 1, 2013. Amended by Acts 2015, 84th Leg., ch. 1236 (S.B. 1296), § 21.002(5), eff. Sept. 1, 2015.

## § 54.033. Sexually Transmitted Disease, AIDS, and HIV Testing

(a) A child found at the conclusion of an adjudication hearing under Section 54.03 of this code to have engaged in delinquent conduct that included a violation of Sections 21.11(a)(1), 22.011, or 22.021, Penal Code, shall undergo a medical procedure or test at the direction of the juvenile court designed to show or help show whether the child has a sexually transmitted disease, acquired immune deficiency syndrome (AIDS), human immunodeficiency virus (HIV) infection, antibodies to HIV, or infection with any other probable causative agent of AIDS. The court may direct the child to undergo the procedure or test on the court's own motion or on the request of the victim of the delinquent conduct.

(b) If the child or another person who has the power to consent to medical treatment for the child refuses to submit voluntarily or consent to the procedure or test, the court shall require the child to submit to the procedure or test.

(c) The person performing the procedure or test shall make the test results available to the local health authority. The local health authority shall be required to notify the victim of the delinquent conduct and the person found to have engaged in the delinquent conduct of the test result.

(d) The state may not use the fact that a medical procedure or test was performed on a child under this section or use the results of the procedure or test in any proceeding arising out of the delinquent conduct.

(e) Testing under this section shall be conducted in accordance with written infectious disease control protocols adopted by the Texas Board of Health that clearly establish procedural guidelines that provide criteria for testing and that respect the rights of the child and the victim of the delinquent conduct.

(f) Nothing in this section allows a court to release a test result to anyone other than a person specifically authorized under this section. Section 81.103(d), Health and Safety Code, may not be construed to allow the disclosure of test results under this section except as provided by this section.

Added by Acts 1993, 73rd Leg., ch. 811, § 2, eff. Sept. 1, 1993.

### § 54.034. Limited Right to Appeal: Warning

Before the court may accept a child's plea or stipulation of evidence in a proceeding held under this title, the court shall inform the child that if the court accepts the plea or stipulation and the court makes a disposition in accordance with the agreement between the state and the child regarding the disposition of the case, the child may not appeal an order of the court entered under Section 54.03, 54.04, or 54.05, unless:

(1) the court gives the child permission to appeal; or

(2) the appeal is based on a matter raised by written motion filed before the proceeding in which the child entered the plea or agreed to the stipulation of evidence.

Added by Acts 1999, 76th Leg., ch. 74, § 1, eff. Sept. 1, 1999.

### § 54.04. Disposition Hearing

(a) The disposition hearing shall be separate, distinct, and subsequent to the adjudication hearing. There is no right to a jury at the disposition hearing unless the child is in jeopardy of a determinate sentence under Subsection (d)(3) or (m), in which case, the child is entitled to a jury of 12 persons to determine the sentence, but only if the child so elects in writing before the commencement of the voir dire examination of the jury panel. If a finding of delinquent conduct is returned, the child may, with the consent of the attorney for the state, change the child's election of one who assesses the disposition.

(b) At the disposition hearing, the juvenile court, notwithstanding the Texas Rules of Evidence or Chapter 37, Code of Criminal Procedure, may consider written reports from probation officers, professional court employees, guardians ad litem appointed under Section 51.11(d), or professional consultants in addition to the testimony of witnesses. On or before the second day before the date of the disposition hearing, the court shall provide the attorney for the child and the prosecuting attorney with access to all written matter to be considered by the court in disposition. The court may order counsel not to reveal items to the child or the child's parent, guardian, or guardian ad litem if such disclosure would materially harm the treatment and rehabilitation of the child or would substantially decrease the likelihood of receiving information from the same or similar sources in the future.

(c) No disposition may be made under this section unless the child is in need of rehabilitation or the protection of the public or the child requires that disposition be made. If the court or jury does not so find, the court shall dismiss the child and enter a final judgment without any disposition. No disposition placing the child on probation outside the child's home may be made under this section unless the court or jury finds that the child, in the child's home, cannot be provided the quality of care and level of support and supervision that the child needs to meet the conditions of the probation.

(d) If the court or jury makes the finding specified in Subsection (c) allowing the court to make a disposition in the case:

(1) the court or jury may, in addition to any order required or authorized under Section 54.041 or 54.042, place the child on probation on such reasonable and lawful terms as the court may determine:

(A) in the child's own home or in the custody of a relative or other fit person; or

(B) subject to the finding under Subsection (c) on the placement of the child outside the child's home, in:

(i) a suitable foster home;

(ii) a suitable public or private residential treatment facility licensed by a state governmental entity or exempted from licensure by state law, except a facility operated by the Texas Juvenile Justice Department; or

(iii) a suitable public or private post-adjudication secure correctional facility that meets the requirements of Section 51.125, except a facility operated by the Texas Juvenile Justice Department;

(2) if the court or jury found at the conclusion of the adjudication hearing that the child engaged in delinquent conduct that violates a penal law of this state or the United States of the grade of felony, the court or jury made a special commitment finding under Section 54.04013, and the petition was not approved by the grand jury under Section 53.045, the court may commit the child to the Texas Juvenile Justice Department under Section 54.04013, or a post-adjudication secure correctional facility under Section 54.04011(c)(1), as applicable, without a determinate sentence;

(3) if the court or jury found at the conclusion of the adjudication hearing that the child engaged in delinquent conduct that included a violation of a penal law listed in Section 53.045(a) and if the petition was approved by the grand jury under Section 53.045, the court or jury may sentence the child to commitment in the Texas Juvenile Justice Department or a post-adjudication secure correctional facility under Section 54.04011(c)(2) with a possible transfer to the Texas Department of Criminal Justice for a term of:

(A) not more than 40 years if the conduct constitutes:

(i) a capital felony;

(ii) a felony of the first degree; or

(iii) an aggravated controlled substance felony;

(B) not more than 20 years if the conduct constitutes a felony of the second degree; or

(C) not more than 10 years if the conduct constitutes a felony of the third degree;

(4) the court may assign the child an appropriate sanction level and sanctions as provided by the assignment guidelines in Section 59.003;

(5) the court may place the child in a suitable nonsecure correctional facility that is registered and meets the applicable standards for the facility as provided by Section 51.126; or

(6) if applicable, the court or jury may make a disposition under Subsection (m) or Section 54.04011(c)(2)(A).

(e) The Texas Juvenile Justice Department shall accept a person properly committed to it by a juvenile court even though the person may be 17 years of age or older at the time of commitment.

(f) The court shall state specifically in the order its reasons for the disposition and shall furnish a copy of the order to the child. If the child is placed on probation, the terms of probation shall be written in the order.

(g) If the court orders a disposition under Subsection (d)(3) or (m) and there is an affirmative finding that the defendant used or exhibited a deadly weapon during the commission of the conduct or during immediate flight from commission of the conduct, the court shall enter the finding in the order. If there is an affirmative finding that the deadly weapon was a firearm, the court shall enter that finding in the order.

(h) At the conclusion of the dispositional hearing, the court shall inform the child of:

(1) the child's right to appeal, as required by Section 56.01; and

(2) the procedures for the sealing of the child's records under Subchapter C–1, Chapter 58.

(i) If the court places the child on probation outside the child's home or commits the child to the Texas Juvenile Justice Department, the court:

(1) shall include in its order its determination that:

(A) it is in the child's best interests to be placed outside the child's home;

(B) reasonable efforts were made to prevent or eliminate the need for the child's removal from the home and to make it possible for the child to return to the child's home; and

(C) the child, in the child's home, cannot be provided the quality of care and level of support and supervision that the child needs to meet the conditions of probation; and

(2) may approve an administrative body to conduct permanency hearings pursuant to 42 U.S.C. Section 675 if required during the placement or commitment of the child.

(j) If the court or jury found that the child engaged in delinquent conduct that included a violation of a penal law of the grade of felony or jailable misdemeanor, the court:

(1) shall require that the child's thumbprint be affixed or attached to the order; and

(2) may require that a photograph of the child be attached to the order.

(k) Except as provided by Subsection (m), the period to which a court or jury may sentence a person to commitment to the Texas Juvenile Justice Department with a transfer to the Texas Department of Criminal Justice under Subsection (d)(3) applies without regard to whether the person has previously been adjudicated as having engaged in delinquent conduct.

(*l*) Except as provided by Subsection (q), a court or jury may place a child on probation under Subsection (d)(1) for any period, except that probation may not continue on or after the child's 18th birthday. Except as provided by Subsection (q), the court may, before the period of probation ends, extend the probation for any period, except that the probation may not extend to or after the child's 18th birthday.

(m) The court or jury may sentence a child adjudicated for habitual felony conduct as described by Section 51.031 to a term prescribed by Subsection (d)(3) and applicable to the conduct adjudicated in the pending case if:

(1) a petition was filed and approved by a grand jury under Section 53.045 alleging that the child engaged in habitual felony conduct; and

(2) the court or jury finds beyond a reasonable doubt that the allegation described by Subdivision (1) in the grand jury petition is true.

(n) A court may order a disposition of secure confinement of a status offender adjudicated for violating a valid court order only if:

(1) before the order is issued, the child received the full due process rights guaranteed by the Constitution of the United States or the Texas Constitution; and

(2) the juvenile probation department in a report authorized by Subsection (b):

(A) reviewed the behavior of the child and the circumstances under which the child was brought before the court;

(B) determined the reasons for the behavior that caused the child to be brought before the court; and

(C) determined that all dispositions, including treatment, other than placement in a secure detention facility or secure correctional facility, have been exhausted or are clearly inappropriate.

(*o*) In a disposition under this title:

(1) a status offender may not, under any circumstances, be committed to the Texas Juvenile Justice Department for engaging in conduct that would not, under state or local law, be a crime if committed by an adult;

(2) a status offender may not, under any circumstances other than as provided under Subsection (n), be placed in a post-adjudication secure correctional facility; and

(3) a child adjudicated for contempt of a county, justice, or municipal court order may not, under any circumstances, be placed in a post-adjudication secure correctional facility or committed to the Texas Juvenile Justice Department for that conduct.

(p) Except as provided by Subsection (*l*), a court that places a child on probation under Subsection (d)(1) for conduct described by Section 54.0405(b) and punishable as a felony shall specify a minimum probation period of two years.

(q) If a court or jury sentences a child to commitment in the Texas Juvenile Justice Department or a post-adjudication secure correctional facility under Subsection (d)(3) for a term of not more than 10 years, the court or jury may place the child on probation under Subsection (d)(1) as an alternative to making the disposition under Subsection (d)(3). The court shall prescribe the period of probation ordered under this subsection for a term of not more than 10 years. The court may, before the sentence of probation expires, extend the probationary period under Section 54.05, except that the sentence of probation and any extension may not exceed 10 years. The court may, before the child's 19th birthday, discharge the child from the sentence of probation. If a sentence of probation ordered under this subsection and any extension of probation ordered under Section 54.05 will continue after the child's 19th birthday, the court shall discharge the child from the sentence of probation on the child's 19th birthday unless the court transfers the child to an appropriate district court under Section 54.051.

(r) If the judge orders a disposition under this section and there is an affirmative finding that the victim or intended victim was younger than 17 years of age at the time of the conduct, the judge shall enter the finding in the order.

(s), (t) Repealed by Acts 2007, 80th Leg., ch. 263, § 64(1).

(u) For the purposes of disposition under Subsection (d)(2), delinquent conduct that violates a penal law of this state of the grade of felony does not include conduct that violates a lawful order of a county, municipal, justice, or juvenile court under circumstances that would constitute contempt of that court.

(v) If the judge orders a disposition under this section for delinquent conduct based on a violation of an offense, on the motion of the attorney representing the state the judge shall make an affirmative finding of fact and enter the affirmative finding in the papers in the case if the judge determines that, regardless of whether the conduct at issue is the subject of the prosecution or part of the same criminal episode as the conduct that is the subject of the prosecution, a victim in the trial:

(1) is or has been a victim of a severe form of trafficking in persons, as defined by 22 U.S.C. Section 7102(8); or

(2) has suffered substantial physical or mental abuse as a result of having been a victim of criminal activity described by 8 U.S.C. Section 1101(a)(15)(U)(iii).

(w) That part of the papers in the case containing an affirmative finding under Subsection (v):

(1) must include specific information identifying the victim, as available;

(2) may not include information identifying the victim's location; and

(3) is confidential, unless written consent for the release of the affirmative finding is obtained from the victim or, if the victim is younger than 18 years of age, the victim's parent or guardian.

(x) A child may be detained in an appropriate detention facility following disposition of the child's case under Subsection (d) or (m) pending:

(1) transportation of the child to the ordered placement; and

(2) the provision of medical or other health care services for the child that may be advisable before transportation, including health care services for children in the late term of pregnancy.

(y) A juvenile court conducting a hearing under this section involving a child for whom the Department of Family and Protective Services has been appointed managing conservator may communicate with the court having continuing jurisdiction over the child before the disposition hearing. The juvenile court may allow the parties to the suit affecting the parent-child relationship in which the Department of Family and Protective Services is a party to participate in the communication under this subsection.

(z) Nothing in this section may be construed to prohibit a juvenile court or jury in a county to which Section 54.04011 applies from committing a child to a post-adjudication secure correctional facility in accordance with that section after a disposition hearing held in accordance with this section.

Acts 1973, 63rd Leg., p. 1460, ch. 544, § 1, eff. Sept. 1, 1973. Amended by Acts 1975, 64th Leg., p. 2158, ch. 693, § 23, eff. Sept. 1, 1975; Acts 1981, 67th Leg., p. 1802, ch. 394, § 1, eff. Aug. 31, 1981; Acts 1983, 68th Leg., p. 161, ch. 44, art. 1, § 3, eff. April 26, 1983; Acts 1983, 68th Leg., p. 3261, ch. 565, § 2, eff. Sept. 1, 1983; Acts 1987, 70th Leg., ch. 385, § 9, eff. Sept. 1, 1987; Acts 1987, 70th Leg., ch. 1052, § 6.11, eff. Sept. 1, 1987; Acts 1989, 71st Leg., ch. 2, § 16.01(17), eff. Aug. 28, 1989; Acts 1989, 71st Leg., ch. 80, § 1, eff. Sept. 1, 1989; Acts 1991, 72nd Leg., ch. 557, § 2, eff. Sept. 1, 1991; Acts 1991, 72nd Leg., ch. 574, § 2, eff. Sept. 1, 1991; Acts 1991, 72nd Leg., ch. 784, § 8, eff. Sept. 1, 1991; Acts 1993, 73rd Leg., ch. 1048, § 1, eff. Sept. 1, 1993; Acts 1995, 74th Leg., ch. 262, § 38, eff. Jan. 1, 1996; Acts 1997, 75th Leg., ch. 669, § 2, eff. Sept. 1, 1997; Acts 1997, 75th Leg., ch. 1086, § 11, eff. Sept. 1, 1997; Acts 1999, 76th Leg., ch. 1193, § 9, eff. Sept. 1, 1999; Acts 1999, 76th Leg., ch. 1415, § 19, eff. Sept. 1, 1999; Acts 1999, 76th Leg., ch. 1448, § 1, eff. Sept. 1, 1999; Acts 1999, 76th Leg., ch. 1477, § 10, eff. Sept. 1, 1999; Acts 2001, 77th Leg., ch. 1297, § 23, eff. Sept. 1, 2001; Acts 2001, 77th Leg., ch. 1420, § 5.001, eff. Sept. 1, 2001; Acts 2003, 78th Leg., ch. 137, § 13, eff. Sept. 1, 2003; Acts 2007, 80th Leg., ch. 263, §§ 7, 64(1), eff. June 8, 2007; Acts 2007, 80th Leg., ch. 849, § 3, eff. June 15, 2007; Acts 2007, 80th Leg., ch. 908, § 11, eff. Sept. 1, 2007; Acts 2009, 81st Leg., ch. 87, § 27.001(13), eff. Sept. 1, 2009; Acts 2009, 81st Leg., ch. 108, § 2, eff. May 23, 2009; Acts 2011, 82nd Leg., ch. 438 (S.B. 1208), § 2, eff. Sept. 1, 2011; Acts 2013, 83rd Leg., ch. 1299 (H.B. 2862), § 17, eff. Sept. 1, 2013; Acts 2013, 83rd Leg., ch. 1323 (S.B. 511), § 2, eff. Dec. 1, 2013; Acts 2015, 84th Leg., ch. 734 (H.B. 1549), § 49, eff. Sept. 1, 2015; Acts 2015, 84th Leg., ch. 962 (S.B. 1630), § 1, eff. Sept. 1, 2015; Acts 2017, 85th Leg., ch. 746 (S.B. 1304), § 2, eff. Sept. 1, 2017; Acts 2021, 87th Leg., ch. 971 (S.B. 2049), § 4, eff. Sept. 1, 2021.

## § 54.0401. Community–Based Programs

(a) This section applies only to a county that has a population of at least 335,000.

(b) A juvenile court of a county to which this section applies may require a child who is found to have engaged in delinquent conduct that violates a penal law of the grade of misdemeanor and for whom the requirements of Subsection (c) are met to participate in a community-based program administered by the county's juvenile board.

(c) A juvenile court of a county to which this section applies may make a disposition under Subsection (b) for delinquent conduct that violates a penal law of the grade of misdemeanor:

(1) if:

(A) the child has been adjudicated as having engaged in delinquent conduct violating a penal law of the grade of misdemeanor on at least two previous occasions;

(B) of the previous adjudications, the conduct that was the basis for one of the adjudications occurred after the date of another previous adjudication; and

(C) the conduct that is the basis of the current adjudication occurred after the date of at least two previous adjudications; or

(2) if:

(A) the child has been adjudicated as having engaged in delinquent conduct violating a penal law of the grade of felony on at least one previous occasion; and

(B) the conduct that is the basis of the current adjudication occurred after the date of that previous adjudication.

(d) The Texas Juvenile Justice Department shall establish guidelines for the implementation of community-based programs described by this section. The juvenile board of each county to which this section applies shall implement a community-based program that complies with those guidelines.

(e) The Texas Juvenile Justice Department shall provide grants to selected juvenile boards to assist with the implementation of a system of community-based programs under this section.

(f) Expired.

Added by Acts 2007, 80th Leg., ch. 263, § 8, eff. June 8, 2007. Amended by Acts 2015, 84th Leg., ch. 734 (H.B. 1549), § 50, eff. Sept. 1, 2015.

## § 54.04011. Expired

### § 54.04012. Trafficked Persons Program

(a) This section applies to a juvenile court or to an alternative juvenile court exercising simultaneous jurisdiction over proceedings under this title and Subtitle E, Title 5, in the manner authorized by Section 51.0413.

(b) A juvenile court may require a child adjudicated to have engaged in delinquent conduct or conduct indicating a need for supervision and who is believed to be a victim of an offense of trafficking of persons as defined by Article 56B.003, Code of Criminal Procedure, to participate in a program established under Section 152.0017, Human Resources Code.

(c) The court may require a child participating in the program to periodically appear in court for monitoring and compliance purposes.

(d) Following a child's successful completion of the program, the court may order the sealing of the records of the case in the manner provided by Subchapter C–1, Chapter 58.

Added by Acts 2013, 83rd Leg., ch. 186 (S.B. 92), § 5, eff. Sept. 1, 2013. Redesignated from V.T.C.A., Family Code § 54.04011 and amended by Acts 2015, 84th Leg., ch. 1236 (S.B. 1296), §§ 21.001(17), 21.002(6), eff. Sept. 1, 2015. Amended by Acts 2017, 85th Leg., ch. 746 (S.B. 1304), § 3, eff. Sept. 1, 2017; Acts 2021, 87th Leg., ch. 704 (H.B. 2633), § 2, eff. Sept. 1, 2021.

### § 54.04013. Special Commitment to Texas Juvenile Justice Department

Notwithstanding any other provision of this code, after a disposition hearing held in accordance with Section 54.04, the juvenile court may commit a child who is found to have engaged in delinquent conduct that constitutes a felony offense to the Texas Juvenile Justice Department without a determinate sentence if the court makes a special commitment finding that the child has behavioral health or other special needs that cannot be met with the resources available in the community. The court should consider the findings of a validated risk and needs assessment and the findings of any other appropriate professional assessment available to the court.

Added by Acts 2015, 84th Leg., ch. 962 (S.B. 1630), § 2, eff. Sept. 1, 2015.

### § 54.0402. Repealed by Acts 2015, 84th Leg., ch. 935 (H.B. 2398), § 41(3), eff. Sept. 1, 2015

### § 54.0404. Electronic Transmission of Certain Visual Material Depicting Minor: Educational Programs

(a) If a child is found to have engaged in conduct indicating a need for supervision described by Section 51.03(b)(6), the juvenile court may enter an order requiring the child to attend and successfully complete an educational program described by Section 37.218, Education Code, or another equivalent educational program.

(b) A juvenile court that enters an order under Subsection (a) shall require the child or the child's parent or other person responsible for the child's support to pay the cost of attending an educational program under Subsection (a) if the court determines that the child, parent, or other person is financially able to make payment.

Added by Acts 2011, 82nd Leg., ch. 1322 (S.B. 407), § 18, eff. Sept. 1, 2011. Amended by Acts 2013, 83rd Leg., ch. 1299 (H.B. 2862), § 18, eff. Sept. 1, 2013; Acts 2015, 84th Leg., ch. 935 (H.B. 2398), § 20, eff. Sept. 1, 2015; Acts 2017, 85th Leg., ch. 324 (S.B. 1488), § 7.004, eff. Sept. 1, 2017; Acts 2017, 85th Leg., ch. 685 (H.B. 29), § 23, eff. Sept. 1, 2017.

### § 54.0405. Child Placed on Probation for Conduct Constituting Sexual Offense

(a) If a court or jury makes a disposition under Section 54.04 in which a child described by Subsection (b) is placed on probation, the court:

(1) may require as a condition of probation that the child:

(A) attend psychological counseling sessions for sex offenders as provided by Subsection (e); and

(B) submit to a polygraph examination as provided by Subsection (f) for purposes of evaluating the child's treatment progress; and

(2) shall require as a condition of probation that the child:

(A) register under Chapter 62, Code of Criminal Procedure; and

(B) submit a blood sample or other specimen to the Department of Public Safety under Subchapter G, Chapter 411, Government Code,[1] for the purpose of creating a DNA record of the child, unless the child has already submitted the required specimen under other state law.

(b) This section applies to a child placed on probation for conduct constituting an offense for which the child is required to register as a sex offender under Chapter 62, Code of Criminal Procedure.

(c) Psychological counseling required as a condition of probation under Subsection (a) must be with an individual or organization that:

(1) provides sex offender treatment or counseling;

(2) is specified by the local juvenile probation department supervising the child; and

(3) meets minimum standards of counseling established by the local juvenile probation department.

(d) A polygraph examination required as a condition of probation under Subsection (a) must be administered by an individual who is specified by the local juvenile probation department supervising the child.

(e) A local juvenile probation department that specifies a sex offender treatment provider under Subsection (c) to provide counseling to a child shall:

(1) establish with the cooperation of the treatment provider the date, time, and place of the first counseling session between the child and the treatment provider;

(2) notify the child and the treatment provider, not later than the 21st day after the date the order making the disposition placing the child on probation under Section 54.04 becomes final, of the date, time, and place of the first counseling session between the child and the treatment provider; and

(3) require the treatment provider to notify the department immediately if the child fails to attend any scheduled counseling session.

(f) A local juvenile probation department that specifies a polygraph examiner under Subsection (d) to administer a polygraph examination to a child shall arrange for a polygraph examination to be administered to the child:

(1) not later than the 60th day after the date the child attends the first counseling session established under Subsection (e); and

(2) after the initial polygraph examination, as required by Subdivision (1), on the request of the treatment provider specified under Subsection (c).

(g) A court that requires as a condition of probation that a child attend psychological counseling under Subsection (a) may order the parent or guardian of the child to:

(1) attend four sessions of instruction with an individual or organization specified by the court relating to:

(A) sexual offenses;

(B) family communication skills;

(C) sex offender treatment;

(D) victims' rights;

(E) parental supervision; and

(F) appropriate sexual behavior; and

(2) during the period the child attends psychological counseling, participate in monthly treatment groups conducted by the child's treatment provider relating to the child's psychological counseling.

(h) A court that orders a parent or guardian of a child to attend instructional sessions and participate in treatment groups under Subsection (g) shall require:

(1) the individual or organization specified by the court under Subsection (g) to notify the court immediately if the parent or guardian fails to attend any scheduled instructional session; and

(2) the child's treatment provider specified under Subsection (c) to notify the court immediately if the parent or guardian fails to attend a session in which the parent or guardian is required to participate in a scheduled treatment group.

(i) A court that requires as a condition of probation that a child attend psychological counseling under Subsection (a) may, before the date the probation period ends, extend the probation for any additional period necessary to complete the required counseling as determined by the treatment provider, except that the probation may not be extended to a date after the date of the child's 18th birthday, or 19th birthday if the child is placed on determinate sentence probation under Section 54.04(q).

Added by Acts 1997, 75th Leg., ch. 669, § 1, eff. Sept. 1, 1997. Amended by Acts 2001, 77th Leg., ch. 211, § 13, eff. Sept. 1, 2001; Acts 2001, 77th Leg., ch. 1420, § 14.743, eff. Sept. 1, 2001; Acts 2011, 82nd Leg., ch. 438 (S.B. 1208), § 3, eff. Sept. 1, 2011; Acts 2021, 87th Leg., ch. 663 (H.B. 1560), § 2.02, eff. Sept. 1, 2021.

[1] V.T.C.A., Government Code § 411.141 et seq.

### § 54.0406. Child Placed on Probation for Conduct Involving a Handgun

(a) If a court or jury places a child on probation under Section 54.04(d) for conduct that violates a penal law that includes as an element of the offense the possession, carrying, using, or exhibiting of a handgun, as defined by Section 46.01, Penal Code, and if at the adjudication hearing the court or jury affirmatively finds that the child personally possessed, carried, used, or exhibited the handgun, the court shall require as a condition of probation that the child, not later than the 30th day after the date the court places the child on probation, notify the juvenile probation officer who is supervising the child of the manner in which the child acquired the handgun, including the date and place of and any person involved in the acquisition.

(b) On receipt of information described by Subsection (a), a juvenile probation officer shall promptly notify the appropriate local law enforcement agency of the information.

(c) Information provided by a child to a juvenile probation officer as required by Subsection (a) and any other information derived from that information may not be used as evidence against the child in any juvenile or criminal proceeding.

Added by Acts 1999, 76th Leg., ch. 1446, § 1, eff. Sept. 1, 1999.

### § 54.0407. Cruelty to Animals: Counseling Required

If a child is found to have engaged in delinquent conduct constituting an offense under Section 42.09 or 42.092, Penal Code, the juvenile court shall order the child to participate in psychological counseling for a period to be determined by the court.

Added by Acts 2001, 77th Leg., ch. 450, § 2, eff. Sept. 1, 2001. Amended by Acts 2007, 80th Leg., ch. 886, § 3, eff. Sept. 1, 2007.

### § 54.0408. Referral of Child Exiting Probation to Mental Health or Mental Retardation Authority

A juvenile probation officer shall refer a child who has been determined to have a mental illness or mental retardation to an appropriate local mental health or mental retardation authority at least three months before the child is to complete the child's juvenile probation term unless the child is currently receiving treatment from the local mental health or mental retardation authority of the county in which the child resides.

Added by Acts 2005, 79th Leg., ch. 949, § 14, eff. Sept. 1, 2005.

### § 54.0409. DNA Sample Required on Certain Felony Adjudications

(a) This section applies only to conduct constituting the commission of a felony:

(1) that is listed in Article 42A.054(a), Code of Criminal Procedure; or

(2) for which it is shown that a deadly weapon, as defined by Section 1.07, Penal Code, was used or exhibited during the commission of the conduct or during immediate flight from the commission of the conduct.

(b) If a court or jury makes a disposition under Section 54.04 in which a child is adjudicated as having engaged in conduct constituting the commission of a felony to which this section applies and the child is placed on probation, the court shall require as a condition of probation that the child provide a DNA sample under Subchapter G, Chapter 411, Government Code,[1] for the purpose of creating a DNA record of the child, unless the child has already submitted the required sample under other state law.

Added by Acts 2009, 81st Leg., ch. 1209, § 3, eff. Sept. 1, 2009. Amended by Acts 2015, 84th Leg., ch. 770 (H.B. 2299), § 2.32, eff. Jan. 1, 2017.

[1] V.T.C.A., Government Code § 411.141 et seq.

### § 54.041. Orders Affecting Parents and Others

*Text of (a) effective until January 1, 2022*

(a) When a child has been found to have engaged in delinquent conduct or conduct indicating a need for supervision and the juvenile court has made a finding that the child is in need of rehabilitation or that the protection of the public or the child requires that disposition be made, the juvenile court, on notice by any reasonable method to all persons affected, may:

(1) order any person found by the juvenile court to have, by a wilful act or omission, contributed to, caused, or encouraged the child's delinquent conduct or conduct indicating a need for supervision to do any act that the juvenile court determines to be reasonable and necessary for the welfare of the child or to refrain from doing any act that the juvenile court determines to be injurious to the welfare of the child;

(2) enjoin all contact between the child and a person who is found to be a contributing cause of the child's delinquent conduct or conduct indicating a need for supervision;

(3) after notice and a hearing of all persons affected order any person living in the same household with the child to participate in social or psychological counseling to assist in the rehabilitation of the child and to strengthen the child's family environment; or

(4) after notice and a hearing of all persons affected order the child's parent or other person responsible for the child's support to pay all or part of the reasonable costs of treatment programs in which the child is required to participate during the

period of probation if the court finds the child's parent or person responsible for the child's support is able to pay the costs.

*Text of (a) effective January 1, 2022*

(a) When a child has been found to have engaged in delinquent conduct or conduct indicating a need for supervision and the juvenile court has made a finding that the child is in need of rehabilitation or that the protection of the public or the child requires that disposition be made, the juvenile court, on notice by any reasonable method to all persons affected, may:

(1) order any person found by the juvenile court to have, by a wilful act or omission, contributed to, caused, or encouraged the child's delinquent conduct or conduct indicating a need for supervision to do any act that the juvenile court determines to be reasonable and necessary for the welfare of the child or to refrain from doing any act that the juvenile court determines to be injurious to the welfare of the child;

(2) enjoin all contact between the child and a person who is found to be a contributing cause of the child's delinquent conduct or conduct indicating a need for supervision; or

(3) after notice and a hearing of all persons affected order any person living in the same household with the child to participate in social or psychological counseling to assist in the rehabilitation of the child and to strengthen the child's family environment.

(b) If a child is found to have engaged in delinquent conduct or conduct indicating a need for supervision arising from the commission of an offense in which property damage or loss or personal injury occurred, the juvenile court, on notice to all persons affected and on hearing, may order the child or a parent to make full or partial restitution to the victim of the offense. The program of restitution must promote the rehabilitation of the child, be appropriate to the age and physical, emotional, and mental abilities of the child, and not conflict with the child's schooling. When practicable and subject to court supervision, the court may approve a restitution program based on a settlement between the child and the victim of the offense. An order under this subsection may provide for periodic payments by the child or a parent of the child for the period specified in the order but except as provided by Subsection (h), that period may not extend past the date of the 18th birthday of the child or past the date the child is no longer enrolled in an accredited secondary school in a program leading toward a high school diploma, whichever date is later.

(c) Restitution under this section is cumulative of any other remedy allowed by law and may be used in addition to other remedies; except that a victim of an offense is not entitled to receive more than actual damages under a juvenile court order.

(d) A person subject to an order proposed under Subsection (a) of this section is entitled to a hearing on the order before the order is entered by the court.

(e) An order made under this section may be enforced as provided by Section 54.07 of this code.

(f) Repealed by Acts 2015, 84th Leg., ch. 935 (H.B. 2398), § 41(3).

(g) Repealed by Acts 2015, 84th Leg., ch. 935 (H.B. 2398), § 41(3).

(h) If the juvenile court places the child on probation in a determinate sentence proceeding initiated under Section 53.045 and transfers supervision on the child's 19th birthday to a district court for placement on community supervision, the district court shall require the payment of any unpaid restitution as a condition of the community supervision. The liability of the child's parent for restitution may not be extended by transfer to a district court for supervision.

Added by Acts 1975, 64th Leg., p. 2157, ch. 693, § 18, eff. Sept. 1, 1975. Amended by Acts 1979, 66th Leg., p. 338, ch. 154, § 2, eff. Sept. 1, 1979; Acts 1983, 68th Leg., p. 528, ch. 110, § 1, eff. Aug. 29, 1983; Acts 1983, 68th Leg., p. 3262, ch. 565, § 3, eff. Sept. 1, 1983; Acts 1989, 71st Leg., ch. 1170, § 3, eff. June 16, 1989; Acts 1995, 74th Leg., ch. 262, § 39, eff. Jan. 1, 1996; Acts 1997, 75th Leg., ch. 165, § 6.09, eff. Sept. 1, 1997; Acts 2001, 77th Leg., ch. 1297, § 24, eff. Sept. 1, 2001; Acts 2001, 77th Leg., ch. 1514, § 15, eff. Sept. 1, 2001; Acts 2003, 78th Leg., ch. 283, § 19, eff. Sept. 1, 2003; Acts 2011, 82nd Leg., ch. 438 (S.B. 1208), § 4, eff. Sept. 1, 2011; Acts 2015, 84th Leg., ch. 935 (H.B. 2398), § 41(3), eff. Sept. 1, 2015; Acts 2021, 87th Leg., ch. 472 (S.B. 41), § 4.03, eff. Jan. 1, 2022.

### § 54.0411. Juvenile Probation Diversion Fund

(a) If a disposition hearing is held under Section 54.04 of this code, the juvenile court, after giving the child, parent, or other person responsible for the child's support a reasonable opportunity to be heard, shall order the child, parent, or other person, if financially able to do so, to pay a fee as costs of court of $20.

(b) Orders for the payment of fees under this section may be enforced as provided by Section 54.07 of this code.

(c) An officer collecting costs under this section shall keep separate records of the funds collected as costs under this section and shall deposit the funds in the county treasury.

(d) Each officer collecting court costs under this section shall file the reports required under Article 103.005, Code of Criminal Procedure. If no funds due as costs under this section have been collected in any quarter, the report required for each quarter shall be filed in the regular manner, and the report must state that no funds due under this section were collected.

(e) The custodian of the county treasury may deposit the funds collected under this section in interest-bearing accounts. The custodian shall keep records of the amount of funds on deposit collected under this section and not later than the last day of the month following each calendar quarter shall send to the comptroller of public accounts the funds collected under this section during the preceding quarter. A county may retain 10 percent of the funds as a service fee and may retain the interest accrued on the funds if the custodian of a county treasury keeps records of the amount of funds on deposit collected under this section and remits the funds to the comptroller within the period prescribed under this subsection.

(f) Funds collected are subject to audit by the comptroller and funds expended are subject to audit by the State Auditor.

(g) The comptroller shall deposit the funds in a special fund to be known as the juvenile probation diversion fund.

(h) The legislature shall determine and appropriate the necessary amount from the juvenile probation diversion fund to the Texas Juvenile Justice Department for the purchase of services the department considers necessary for the diversion of any juvenile who is at risk of commitment to the department. The department shall develop guidelines for the use of the fund. The department may not purchase the services if a person responsible for the child's support or a local juvenile probation department is financially able to provide the services.

Added by Acts 1987, 70th Leg., ch. 1040, § 23, eff. Sept. 1, 1987. Amended by Acts 1989, 71st Leg., ch. 347, § 8, eff. Oct. 1, 1989; Acts 2015, 84th Leg., ch. 734 (H.B. 1549), § 51, eff. Sept. 1, 2015.

**Repeal**

*Acts 2021, 87th Leg., ch. 472 (S.B. 41), § 5.01(b)(3) repeals this section effective Jan. 1, 2022.*

## § 54.042. License Suspension

(a) A juvenile court, in a disposition hearing under Section 54.04, shall:

(1) order the Department of Public Safety to suspend a child's driver's license or permit, or if the child does not have a license or permit, to deny the issuance of a license or permit to the child if the court finds that the child has engaged in conduct that:

(A) violates a law of this state enumerated in Section 521.342(a), Transportation Code; or

(B) violates a penal law of this state or the United States, an element or elements of which involve a severe form of trafficking in persons, as defined by 22 U.S.C. Section 7102; or

(2) notify the Department of Public Safety of the adjudication, if the court finds that the child has engaged in conduct that violates a law of this state enumerated in Section 521.372(a), Transportation Code.

(b) A juvenile court, in a disposition hearing under Section 54.04, may order the Department of Public Safety to suspend a child's driver's license or permit or, if the child does not have a license or permit, to deny the issuance of a license or permit to the child, if the court finds that the child has engaged in conduct that violates Section 28.08, Penal Code.

(c) The order under Subsection (a)(1) shall specify a period of suspension or denial of 365 days.

(d) The order under Subsection (b) shall specify a period of suspension or denial:

(1) not to exceed 365 days; or

(2) of 365 days if the court finds the child has been previously adjudicated as having engaged in conduct violating Section 28.08, Penal Code.

(e) A child whose driver's license or permit has been suspended or denied pursuant to this section may, if the child is otherwise eligible for, and fulfills the requirements for issuance of, a provisional driver's license or permit under Chapter 521, Transportation Code, apply for and receive an occupational license in accordance with the provisions of Subchapter L of that chapter.[1]

(f) A juvenile court, in a disposition hearing under Section 54.04, may order the Department of Public Safety to suspend a child's driver's license or permit or, if the child does not have a license or permit, to deny the issuance of a license or permit to the child for a period not to exceed 12 months if the court finds that the child has engaged in conduct in need of supervision or delinquent conduct other than the conduct described by Subsection (a).

(g) A juvenile court that places a child on probation under Section 54.04 may require as a reasonable condition of the probation that if the child violates the probation, the court may order the Department of Public Safety to suspend the child's driver's license or permit or, if the child does not have a license or permit, to deny the issuance of a license or permit to the child for a period not to exceed 12 months. The court may make this order if a child that is on probation under this condition violates the probation. A suspension under this subsection is cumulative of any other suspension under this section.

(h) If a child is adjudicated for conduct that violates Section 49.04, 49.07, or 49.08, Penal Code, and if any conduct on which that adjudication is based is a ground for a driver's license suspension under Chapter 524 or 724, Transportation Code, each of the suspensions shall be imposed. The court imposing a driver's license suspension under this section shall credit a period of suspension imposed under Chapter 524 or 724, Transportation Code, toward the period of suspension required under this section, except that if the child was previously adjudicated for conduct that violates Section 49.04, 49.07, or 49.08, Penal Code, credit may not be given.

Added by Acts 1983, 68th Leg., p. 1605, ch. 303, § 25, eff. Jan. 1, 1984. Amended by Acts 1985, 69th Leg., ch. 629, § 1, eff. Sept. 1, 1985; Acts 1991, 72nd Leg., ch. 14, § 284(42), eff. Sept. 1, 1991; Acts 1991, 72nd Leg., ch. 784, § 7, eff. Sept. 1, 1991; Acts 1993, 73rd Leg., ch. 491, § 3, eff. June 15, 1993; Acts 1995, 74th Leg., ch. 76, § 14.32, eff. Sept. 1, 1995; Acts 1995, 74th Leg., ch. 262, § 40, eff. Jan. 1, 1996; Acts 1997, 75th Leg., ch. 165, § 30.183, eff. Sept. 1, 1997; Acts 1997, 75th Leg., ch. 593, § 3, eff. Sept. 1, 1997; Acts 1997, 75th Leg., ch. 1013, § 17, eff. Sept. 1, 1997; Acts 1999, 76th Leg., ch. 62, § 19.01(18), eff. Sept. 1, 1999; Acts 2003, 78th Leg., ch. 283, § 20, eff. Sept. 1, 2003; Acts 2009, 81st Leg., ch. 1146, § 18.02, eff. Sept. 1, 2009.

[1] V.T.C.A., Transportation Code § 521.241 et seq.

### § 54.043. Monitoring School Attendance

If the court places a child on probation under Section 54.04(d) and requires as a condition of probation that the child attend school, the probation officer charged with supervising the child shall monitor the child's school attendance and report to the court if the child is voluntarily absent from school.

Added by Acts 1993, 73rd Leg., ch. 347, § 6.02, eff. Sept. 1, 1993.

### § 54.044. Community Service

(a) If the court places a child on probation under Section 54.04(d), the court shall require as a condition of probation that the child work a specified number of hours at a community service project approved by the court and designated by the juvenile probation department as provided by Subsection (e), unless the court determines and enters a finding on the order placing the child on probation that:

(1) the child is physically or mentally incapable of participating in the project;

(2) participating in the project will be a hardship on the child or the family of the child; or

(3) the child has shown good cause that community service should not be required.

(b) The court may also order under this section that the child's parent perform community service with the child.

(c) The court shall order that the child and the child's parent perform a total of not more than 500 hours of community service under this section.

(d) A municipality or county that establishes a program to assist children and their parents in rendering community service under this section may purchase insurance policies protecting the municipality or county against claims brought by a person other than the child or the child's parent for a cause of action that arises from an act of the child or parent while rendering community service. The municipality or county is not liable under this section to the extent that damages are recoverable under a contract of insurance or under a plan of self-insurance authorized by statute. The liability of the municipality or county for a cause of action that arises from an action of the child or the child's parent while rendering community service may not exceed $100,000 to a single person and $300,000 for a single occurrence in the case of personal injury or death, and $10,000 for a single occurrence of property damage. Liability may not extend to punitive or exemplary damages. This subsection does not waive a defense, immunity, or jurisdictional bar available to the municipality or county or its officers or employees, nor shall this section be construed to waive, repeal, or modify any provision of Chapter 101, Civil Practice and Remedies Code.

(e) For the purposes of this section, a court may submit to the juvenile probation department a list of organizations or projects approved by the court for community service. The juvenile probation department may:

(1) designate an organization or project for community service only from the list submitted by the court; and

(2) reassign or transfer a child to a different organization or project on the list submitted by the court under this subsection without court approval.

(f) A person subject to an order proposed under Subsection (a) or (b) is entitled to a hearing on the order before the order is entered by the court.

(g) On a finding by the court that a child's parents or guardians have made a reasonable good faith effort to prevent the child from engaging in delinquent conduct or engaging in conduct indicating a need for supervision and that, despite the parents' or guardians' efforts, the child continues to engage in such conduct, the court shall waive any requirement for community service that may be imposed on a parent under this section.

(h) An order made under this section may be enforced as provided by Section 54.07.

(i) In a disposition hearing under Section 54.04 in which the court finds that a child engaged in conduct violating Section 521.453, Transportation Code, the court, in addition to any other order authorized under this title and if the court is located in a municipality or county that has established a community service program, may order the child to perform eight hours of community service as a condition of probation under Section 54.04(d) unless the child is shown to have previously engaged in conduct violating Section 521.453, Transportation Code, in which case the court may order the child to perform 12 hours of community service.

Added by Acts 1995, 74th Leg., ch. 262, § 41, eff. Jan. 1, 1996. Amended by Acts 1997, 75th Leg., ch. 1358, § 2, eff. Sept. 1, 1997; Acts 2001, 77th Leg., ch. 1297, § 25, eff. Sept. 1, 2001.

### § 54.045. Admission of Unadjudicated Conduct

(a) During a disposition hearing under Section 54.04, a child may:

(1) admit having engaged in delinquent conduct or conduct indicating a need for supervision for which the child has not been adjudicated; and

(2) request the court to take the admitted conduct into account in the disposition of the child.

(b) If the prosecuting attorney agrees in writing, the court may take the admitted conduct into account in the disposition of the child.

(c) A court may take into account admitted conduct over which exclusive venue lies in another county only if the court obtains the written permission of the prosecuting attorney for that county.

(d) A child may not be adjudicated by any court for having engaged in conduct taken into account under this section, except that, if the conduct taken into account included conduct over which exclusive venue lies in another county and the written permission of the prosecuting attorney of that county was not obtained, the child may be adjudicated for that conduct, but the child's admission under this section may not be used against the child in the adjudication.

Added by Acts 1995, 74th Leg., ch. 262, § 41, eff. Jan. 1, 1996.

### § 54.046. Conditions of Probation for Damaging Property with Graffiti

(a) If a juvenile court places on probation under Section 54.04(d) a child adjudicated as having engaged in conduct in violation of Section 28.08, Penal Code, in addition to other conditions of probation, the court:

(1) shall order the child to:

(A) reimburse the owner of the property for the cost of restoring the property; or

(B) with consent of the owner of the property, restore the property by removing or painting over any markings made by the child on the property; and

(2) if the child made markings on public property, a street sign, or an official traffic-control device in violation of Section 28.08, Penal Code, shall order the child to:

(A) make to the political subdivision that owns the public property or erected the street sign or official traffic-control device restitution in an amount equal to the lesser of the cost to the political subdivision of replacing or restoring the public property, street sign, or official traffic-control device; or

(B) with the consent of the political subdivision, restore the public property, street sign, or official traffic-control device by removing or painting over any markings made by the child on the property, sign, or device.

(a–1) For purposes of Subsection (a), "official traffic-control device" has the meaning assigned by Section 541.304, Transportation Code.

(b) In addition to a condition imposed under Subsection (a), the court may require the child as a condition of probation to attend a class with instruction in self-responsibility and empathy for a victim of an offense conducted by a local juvenile probation department.

(c) If a juvenile court orders a child to make restitution under Subsection (a) and the child, child's parent, or other person responsible for the child's support is financially unable to make the restitution, the court may order the child to perform a specific number of hours of community service, in addition to the hours required under Subsection (d), to satisfy the restitution.

(d) If a juvenile court places on probation under Section 54.04(d) a child adjudicated as having engaged in conduct in violation of Section 28.08, Penal Code, in addition to other conditions of probation, the court shall order the child to perform:

(1) at least 15 hours of community service if the amount of pecuniary loss resulting from the conduct is $50 or more but less than $500; or

(2) at least 30 hours of community service if the amount of pecuniary loss resulting from the conduct is $500 or more.

(e) The juvenile court shall direct a child ordered to make restitution under this section to deliver the amount or property due as restitution to a juvenile probation department for transfer to the owner. The juvenile probation department shall notify the juvenile court when the child has delivered the full amount of restitution ordered.

Added by Acts 1997, 75th Leg., ch. 593, § 7, eff. Sept. 1, 1997. Amended by Acts 2007, 80th Leg., ch. 1053, § 4, eff. Sept. 1, 2007; Acts 2009, 81st Leg., ch. 639, § 3, eff. Sept. 1, 2009.

### § 54.0461. Payment of Juvenile Delinquency Prevention Fees

(a) If a child is adjudicated as having engaged in delinquent conduct that violates Section 28.08, Penal Code, the juvenile court shall order the child, parent, or other person responsible for the child's support to pay to the court a $50 juvenile delinquency prevention fee as a cost of court.

(b) The court shall deposit fees received under this section to the credit of the county juvenile delinquency prevention fund provided for under Article 102.0171, Code of Criminal Procedure.

(c) If the court finds that a child, parent, or other person responsible for the child's support is unable to pay the juvenile delinquency prevention fee required under Subsection (a), the court shall enter into the child's case records a statement of that finding. The court may waive a fee under this section only if the court makes the finding under this subsection.

Added by Acts 1999, 76th Leg., ch. 174, § 1, eff. Sept. 1, 1999. Amended by Acts 2003, 78th Leg., ch. 601, § 3, eff. Sept. 1, 2003; Acts 2007, 80th Leg., ch. 1053, § 5, eff. Sept. 1, 2007.

#### Repeal

*Acts 2021, 87th Leg., ch. 472 (S.B. 41), § 5.01(b)(4) repeals this section effective Jan. 1, 2022.*

### § 54.0462. Payment of Fees for Offenses Requiring DNA Testing

(a) If a child is adjudicated as having engaged in delinquent conduct that constitutes the commission of a felony and the provision of a DNA sample is required under Section 54.0409 or other law, the juvenile court shall order the child, parent, or other person responsible for the child's support to pay to the court as a cost of court:

(1) a $50 fee if the disposition of the case includes a commitment to a facility operated by or under contract with the Texas Juvenile Justice Department; and

(2) a $34 fee if the disposition of the case does not include a commitment described by Subdivision (1) and the child is required to submit a DNA sample under Section 54.0409 or other law.

(b) The clerk of the court shall transfer to the comptroller any funds received under this section. The comptroller shall credit the funds to the Department of Public Safety to help defray the cost of any analyses performed on DNA samples provided by children with respect to whom a court cost is collected under this section.

(c) If the court finds that a child, parent, or other person responsible for the child's support is unable to pay the fee required under Subsection (a), the court shall enter into the child's case records a statement of that finding. The court may waive a fee under this section only if the court makes the finding under this subsection.

Added by Acts 2009, 81st Leg., ch. 1209, § 4, eff. Sept. 1, 2009. Amended by Acts 2015, 84th Leg., ch. 734 (H.B. 1549), § 52, eff. Sept. 1, 2015.

#### Repeal

*Acts 2021, 87th Leg., ch. 472 (S.B. 41), § 5.01(b)(4) repeals this section effective Jan. 1, 2022.*

### § 54.047. Alcohol or Drug Related Offense

(a) If the court or jury finds at an adjudication hearing for a child that the child engaged in delinquent conduct or conduct indicating a need for supervision that constitutes a violation of Section 481.115, 481.1151, 481.116, 481.1161, 481.117, 481.118, or 481.121, Health and Safety Code, the court may order that the child successfully complete a drug education program that is designed to educate persons on the dangers of drug abuse in accordance with Section 521.374(a)(1), Transportation Code, and that is regulated by the Texas Department of Licensing and Regulation under Chapter 171, Government Code.

(b) If the court or jury finds at an adjudication hearing for a child that the child engaged in delinquent conduct or conduct indicating a need for supervision that violates the alcohol-related offenses in Section 106.02, 106.025, 106.04, 106.041, 106.05, or 106.07, Alcoholic Beverage Code, or Section 49.02, Penal Code, the court may order that the child successfully complete an alcohol awareness program described by Section 106.115, Alcoholic Beverage Code, that is regulated by the Texas Department of Licensing and Regulation under Chapter 171, Government Code.

(c) The court shall, in addition to any order described by Subsection (a) or (b), order that, in the manner provided by Section 106.071(d), Alcoholic Beverage Code:

(1) the child perform community service; and

(2) the child's driver's license or permit be suspended or that the child be denied issuance of a driver's license or permit.

(d) An order under this section:

(1) is subject to a finding under Section 54.04(c); and

(2) may be issued in addition to any other order authorized by this title.

(e) Repealed by Acts 2021, 87th Leg., ch. 948 (S.B. 1480), § 19(3).

(f) If the court orders a child under Subsection (a) or (b) to successfully complete a drug education program or alcohol awareness program, unless the court determines that the parent or guardian of the child is indigent and unable to pay the cost, the court shall require the child's parent or a guardian of the child to pay the cost of the program. The court shall allow the child's parent or guardian to pay the cost of the program in installments.

Added by Acts 1997, 75th Leg., ch. 1013, § 18, eff. Sept. 1, 1997. Renumbered from V.T.C.A., Family Code § 54.046 by Acts 1999, 76th Leg., ch. 62, § 19.01(19), eff. Sept. 1, 1999. Amended by Acts 2015, 84th Leg., ch. 1004 (H.B. 642), § 6, eff. Sept. 1, 2015; Acts 2021, 87th Leg., ch. 472 (S.B. 41), § 5.01(b)(5), eff. Jan. 1, 2022; Acts 2021, 87th Leg., ch. 948 (S.B. 1480), §§ 13, 19(3), eff. Sept. 1, 2021.

**Repeal of (f)**

*Without reference to the amendment of (f) by Acts 2021, 87th Leg., ch. 948 (S.B. 1480), § 13, Acts 2021, 87th Leg., ch. 472 (S.B. 41), § 5.01(b)(5) repeals (f) effective Jan. 1, 2022.*

Sections 20 and 21(b) of Acts 2021, 87th Leg., ch. 948 (S.B. 1480) provide:

"Sec. 20(a). For purposes of this section, any reference in law to a license to provide or instruct a court-ordered program includes a certification under the law as it existed immediately before the effective date [Sept. 1, 2021] of this Act.

"(b) On the effective date of this Act, a program provider license or an instructor license issued before the effective date of this Act shall continue to be valid until the license expires.

"(c) An application for an initial program provider or instructor license or for renewal of a program provider or instructor license submitted to the Texas Department of Licensing and Regulation on or after the effective date of this Act is governed by Chapter 171, Government Code, as added by this Act. An application submitted before that date is governed by the laws and rules in effect when the application was submitted, and the former laws and rules are continued in effect for that purpose.

"(d) A person who holds an instructor license prior to the effective date of this Act is eligible to renew that license on or after the effective date of this Act, if:

"(1) the license is current or is within the late renewal period; and

"(2) the person's instructor eligibility requirements remain in effect at the time of renewal.

"(e) On or after the effective date of this Act, if a person's instructor license expires beyond the late renewal period or if the license is revoked, the person must apply for a new license and meet the instructor eligibility and other license requirements in effect at the time of the new application."

"[Sec. 21](b) All rules, fees, policies, procedures, decisions, and forms that relate to a program or activity regulated under this Act and that are in effect on the effective date of this Act remain in effect until changed by the Texas Commission of Licensing and Regulation, the Texas Department of Licensing and Regulation, or the executive director of the Texas Department of Licensing and Regulation, as appropriate."

### § 54.048. Restitution

(a) A juvenile court, in a disposition hearing under Section 54.04, may order restitution to be made by the child and the child's parents.

(b) This section applies without regard to whether the petition in the case contains a plea for restitution.

Added by Acts 2001, 77th Leg., ch. 1297, § 26, eff. Sept. 1, 2001.

### § 54.0481. Restitution for Damaging Property with Graffiti

(a) A juvenile court, in a disposition hearing under Section 54.04 regarding a child who has been adjudicated to have engaged in delinquent conduct that violates Section 28.08, Penal Code:

(1) may order the child or a parent or other person responsible for the child's support to make restitution by:

(A) reimbursing the owner of the property for the cost of restoring the property; or

(B) with the consent of the owner of the property, personally restoring the property by removing or painting over any markings the child made; and

(2) if the child made markings on public property, a street sign, or an official traffic-control device in violation of Section 28.08, Penal Code, may order the child or a parent or other person responsible for the child's support to:

(A) make to the political subdivision that owns the public property or erected the street sign or official traffic-control device restitution in an amount equal to the lesser of the cost to the political subdivision of replacing or restoring the public property, street sign, or official traffic-control device; or

(B) with the consent of the political subdivision, restore the public property, street sign, or official traffic-control device by removing or painting over any markings made by the child on the property, sign, or device.

(b) If a juvenile court orders a child to make restitution under Subsection (a) and the child, child's parent, or other person responsible for the child's support is financially unable to make the restitution, the court may order the child to perform a specific number of hours of community service to satisfy the restitution.

(c) For purposes of Subsection (a), "official traffic-control device" has the meaning assigned by Section 541.304, Transportation Code.

Added by Acts 2007, 80th Leg., ch. 1053, § 6, eff. Sept. 1, 2007.

### § 54.0482. Treatment of Restitution Payments

(a) A juvenile probation department that receives a payment to a victim as the result of a juvenile court order for restitution shall immediately:

(1) deposit the payment in an interest-bearing account in the county treasury; and

(2) notify the victim that a payment has been received.

(b) The juvenile probation department shall promptly remit the payment to a victim who has been notified under Subsection (a) and makes a claim for payment.

(b-1) If the victim does not make a claim for payment on or before the 30th day after the date of being notified under Subsection (a), the juvenile probation department shall notify the victim by certified mail, sent to the last known address of the victim, that a payment has been received.

(c) On or before the fifth anniversary of the date the juvenile probation department receives a payment for a victim that is not claimed by the victim, the department shall make and document a good faith effort to locate and notify the victim that an unclaimed payment exists, including:

(1) confirming, if possible, the victim's most recent address with the Department of Public Safety; and

(2) making at least one additional certified mailing to the victim.

(d) A juvenile probation department satisfies the good faith requirement under Subsection (c) by sending by certified mail to the victim, during the period the child is required by the juvenile court order to make payments to the victim, a notice that the victim is entitled to an unclaimed payment.

(e) If a victim claims a payment on or before the fifth anniversary of the date on which the juvenile probation department mailed a notice to the victim under Subsection (b-1), the juvenile probation department shall pay the victim the amount of the original payment, less any interest earned while holding the payment.

(f) If a victim does not claim a payment on or before the fifth anniversary of the date on which the juvenile probation department mailed a notice to the victim under Subsection (b-1), the department:

(1) has no liability to the victim or anyone else in relation to the payment; and

(2) shall transfer the payment from the interest-bearing account to a special fund of the county treasury, the unclaimed juvenile restitution fund.

(g) The county may spend money in the unclaimed juvenile restitution fund only for the same purposes for which the county may spend juvenile state aid.

Added by Acts 2007, 80th Leg., ch. 908, § 12, eff. Sept. 1, 2007. Renumbered from V.T.C.A., Family Code § 54.0481 by Acts 2009, 81st Leg., ch. 87, § 27.001(14), eff. Sept. 1, 2009. Amended by Acts 2013, 83rd Leg., ch. 1299 (H.B. 2862), § 19, eff. Sept. 1, 2013.

### § 54.049. Conditions of Probation for Desecrating a Cemetery or Abusing a Corpse

(a) If a juvenile court places on probation under Section 54.04(d) a child adjudicated to have engaged in conduct in violation of Section 28.03(f), Penal Code, involving damage or destruction inflicted on a place of human burial or under Section 42.08, Penal Code, in addition to other conditions of probation, the court shall order the child to make restitution to a cemetery organization operating a cemetery affected by the conduct in an amount equal to the cost to the cemetery of repairing any damage caused by the conduct.

(b) If a juvenile court orders a child to make restitution under Subsection (a) and the child is financially unable to make the restitution, the court may order:

(1) the child to perform a specific number of hours of community service to satisfy the restitution; or

(2) a parent or other person responsible for the child's support to make the restitution in the amount described by Subsection (a).

(c) In this section, "cemetery" and "cemetery organization" have the meanings assigned by Section 711.001, Health and Safety Code.

Added by Acts 2005, 79th Leg., ch. 1025, § 3, eff. June 18, 2005.

### § 54.0491. Gang-Related Conduct

(a) In this section:

(1) "Criminal street gang" has the meaning assigned by Section 71.01, Penal Code.

(2) "Gang-related conduct" means conduct that violates a penal law of the grade of Class B misdemeanor or higher and in which a child engages with the intent to:

(A) further the criminal activities of a criminal street gang of which the child is a member;

(B) gain membership in a criminal street gang; or

(C) avoid detection as a member of a criminal street gang.

(b) A juvenile court, in a disposition hearing under Section 54.04 regarding a child who has been adjudicated to have engaged in delinquent conduct that is also gang-related conduct, shall order the child to participate in a criminal street gang intervention program that is appropriate for the child based on the child's level of involvement in the criminal activities of a criminal street gang. The intervention program:

(1) must include at least 12 hours of instruction; and

(2) may include voluntary tattoo removal.

(c) If a child required to attend a criminal street gang intervention program is committed to the Texas Juvenile Justice Department as a result of the gang-related conduct, the child must complete the intervention program before being discharged from the custody of or released under supervision by the department.

Added by Acts 2009, 81st Leg., ch. 1130, § 19, eff. Sept. 1, 2009. Amended by Acts 2015, 84th Leg., ch. 734 (H.B. 1549), § 53, eff. Sept. 1, 2015.

### § 54.05. Hearing to Modify Disposition

(a) Except as provided by Subsection (a–1), any disposition, except a commitment to the Texas Juvenile Justice Department, may be modified by the juvenile court as provided in this section until:

(1) the child reaches:

(A) the child's 18th birthday; or

(B) the child's 19th birthday, if the child was placed on determinate sentence probation under Section 54.04(q); or

(2) the child is earlier discharged by the court or operation of law.

(a–1) Repealed by Acts 2015, 84th Leg., ch. 935 (H.B. 2398), § 41(3).

(b) Except for a commitment to the Texas Juvenile Justice Department or to a post-adjudication secure correctional facility under Section 54.04011 or a placement on determinate sentence probation under Section 54.04(q), all dispositions automatically terminate when the child reaches the child's 18th birthday.

(c) There is no right to a jury at a hearing to modify disposition.

(d) A hearing to modify disposition shall be held on the petition of the child and his parent, guardian, guardian ad litem, or attorney, or on the petition of the state, a probation officer, or the court itself. Reasonable notice of a hearing to modify disposition shall be given to all parties.

(e) After the hearing on the merits or facts, the court may consider written reports from probation officers, professional court employees, guardians ad litem appointed under Section 51.11(d), or professional consultants in addition to the testimony of other witnesses. On or before the second day before the date of the hearing to modify disposition, the court shall provide the attorney for the child and the prosecuting attorney with access to all written matter to be considered by the court in deciding whether to modify disposition. The court may order counsel not to reveal items to the child or the child's parent, guardian, or guardian ad litem if such disclosure would materially harm the treatment and rehabilitation of the child or would substantially decrease the likelihood of receiving information from the same or similar sources in the future.

(f) Except as provided by Subsection (j), a disposition based on a finding that the child engaged in delinquent conduct that violates a penal law of this state or the United States of the grade of felony may be modified so as to commit the child to the Texas Juvenile Justice Department or, if applicable, a post-adjudication secure correctional facility operated under Section 152.0016, Human Resources Code, if the court after a hearing to modify disposition finds by a preponderance of the evidence that the child violated a reasonable and lawful order of the court. A disposition based on a finding that the child engaged in habitual felony conduct as described by Section 51.031 or in delinquent conduct that included a violation of a penal law listed in Section 53.045(a) may be modified to commit the child to the Texas Juvenile Justice Department or, if applicable, a post-adjudication secure correctional facility operated under Section 152.0016, Human Resources Code, with a possible transfer to the Texas Department of Criminal Justice for a definite term prescribed by, as applicable, Section 54.04(d)(3) or Section 152.0016(g), Human Resources Code, if the original petition was approved by the grand jury under Section 53.045 and if after a hearing to modify the disposition the court finds that the child violated a reasonable and lawful order of the court.

(g) Except as provided by Subsection (j), a disposition based solely on a finding that the child engaged in conduct indicating a need for supervision may not be modified to commit the child to the Texas Juvenile Justice Department. A new finding in compliance with Section 54.03 must be made that the child engaged in delinquent conduct that meets the requirements for commitment under Section 54.04.

(h) A hearing shall be held prior to placement in a post-adjudication secure correctional facility for a period longer than 30 days or commitment to the Texas Juvenile Justice Department as a modified disposition. In other disposition modifications, the child and the child's parent, guardian, guardian ad litem, or attorney may waive hearing in accordance with Section 51.09.

(i) The court shall specifically state in the order its reasons for modifying the disposition and shall furnish a copy of the order to the child.

(j) If, after conducting a hearing to modify disposition without a jury, the court finds by a preponderance of the evidence that a child violated a reasonable and lawful condition of probation ordered under Section 54.04(q), the court may modify the disposition to commit the child to the Texas Juvenile Justice Department under Section 54.04(d)(3) or, if applicable, a post-adjudication secure correctional facility operated under Section 152.0016, Human Resources Code, for a term that does not exceed the original sentence assessed by the court or jury.

(k) Repealed by Acts 2007, 80th Leg., ch. 263, § 64(2).

(*l*) The court may extend a period of probation under this section at any time during the period of probation or, if a motion for revocation or modification of probation is filed before the period of supervision ends, before the first anniversary of the date on which the period of probation expires.

(m) If the court places the child on probation outside the child's home or commits the child to the Texas Juvenile Justice Department or to a post-adjudication secure correctional facility operated under Section 152.0016, Human Resources Code, the court:

(1) shall include in the court's order a determination that:

(A) it is in the child's best interests to be placed outside the child's home;

(B) reasonable efforts were made to prevent or eliminate the need for the child's removal from the child's home and to make it possible for the child to return home; and

(C) the child, in the child's home, cannot be provided the quality of care and level of support and supervision that the child needs to meet the conditions of probation; and

(2) may approve an administrative body to conduct a permanency hearing pursuant to 42 U.S.C. Section 675 if required during the placement or commitment of the child.

Acts 1973, 63rd Leg., p. 1460, ch. 544, § 1, eff. Sept. 1, 1973. Amended by Acts 1979, 66th Leg., p. 1829, ch. 743, § 1, eff. Aug. 27, 1979; Acts 1983, 68th Leg., p. 162, ch. 44, art. 1, § 4, eff. April 26, 1983; Acts 1985, 69th Leg., ch. 45, § 3, eff. Sept. 1, 1985; Acts 1987, 70th Leg., ch. 385, § 10, eff. Sept. 1, 1987; Acts 1991, 72nd Leg., ch. 557, § 3, eff. Sept. 1, 1991; Acts 1995, 74th Leg., ch. 262, § 42, eff. Jan. 1, 1996; Acts 1999, 76th Leg., ch. 1448, § 2, eff. Sept. 1, 1999; Acts 1999, 76th Leg., ch. 1477, § 11, eff. Sept. 1, 1999; Acts 2001, 77th Leg., ch. 1297, § 27, eff. Sept. 1, 2001; Acts 2001, 77th Leg., ch. 1420, § 5.002, eff. Sept. 1, 2001; Acts 2003, 78th Leg., ch. 283, § 21, eff. Sept. 1, 2003; Acts 2005, 79th Leg., ch. 949, § 15, eff. Sept. 1, 2005; Acts 2007, 80th Leg., ch. 263, §§ 9, 64(2), eff. June 8, 2007; Acts 2011, 82nd Leg., ch. 438 (S.B. 1208), § 5, eff. Sept. 1, 2011; Acts 2011, 82nd Leg., ch. 1098 (S.B. 1489), § 5, eff. Sept. 1, 2011; Acts 2013, 83rd Leg., ch. 1299 (H.B. 2862), § 20, eff. Sept. 1, 2013; Acts 2013, 83rd Leg., ch. 1323 (S.B. 511), § 4, eff. Dec. 1, 2013; Acts 2015, 84th Leg., ch. 734 (H.B. 1549), § 54, eff. Sept. 1, 2015; Acts 2015, 84th Leg., ch. 935 (H.B. 2398), §§ 21, 41(3), eff. Sept. 1, 2015; Acts 2021, 87th Leg., ch. 971 (S.B. 2049), § 5, eff. Sept. 1, 2021.

### § 54.051. Transfer of Determinate Sentence Probation to Appropriate District Court

(a) On motion of the state concerning a child who is placed on probation under Section 54.04(q) for a period, including any extension ordered under Section 54.05, that will continue after the child's 19th birthday, the juvenile court shall hold a hearing to determine whether to transfer the child to an appropriate district court or discharge the child from the sentence of probation.

(b) The hearing must be conducted before the person's 19th birthday, or before the person's 18th birthday if the offense for which the person was placed on probation occurred before September 1, 2011, and must be conducted in the same manner as a hearing to modify disposition under Section 54.05.

(c) If, after a hearing, the court determines to discharge the child, the court shall specify a date on or before the child's 19th birthday to discharge the child from the sentence of probation.

(d) If, after a hearing, the court determines to transfer the child, the court shall transfer the child to an appropriate district court on the child's 19th birthday.

(d–1) After a transfer to district court under Subsection (d), only the petition, the grand jury approval, the judgment concerning the conduct for which the person was placed on determinate sentence probation, and the transfer order are a part of the district clerk's public record.

(e) A district court that exercises jurisdiction over a person transferred under Subsection (d) shall place the person on community supervision under Chapter 42A, Code of Criminal Procedure, for the remainder of the person's probationary period and under conditions consistent with those ordered by the juvenile court.

(e–1) The restrictions on a judge placing a defendant on community supervision imposed by Article 42A.054, Code of Criminal Procedure, do not apply to a case transferred from the juvenile court. The minimum period of community supervision imposed by Article 42A.053(d), Code of Criminal Procedure, does not apply to a case transferred from the juvenile court.

(e–2) If a person who is placed on community supervision under this section violates a condition of that supervision or if the person violated a condition of probation ordered under Section 54.04(q) and that probation violation was not discovered by the state before the person's 19th birthday, the district court shall dispose of the violation of community supervision or probation, as appropriate, in the same manner as if the court had originally exercised jurisdiction over the case. If the judge revokes community supervision, the judge may reduce the prison sentence to any length without regard to the minimum term imposed by Article 42A.755(a), Code of Criminal Procedure.

(e–3) The time that a person serves on probation ordered under Section 54.04(q) is the same as time served on community supervision ordered under this section for purposes of determining the person's eligibility for early discharge from community supervision under Article 42A.701, Code of Criminal Procedure.

(f) The juvenile court may transfer a child to an appropriate district court as provided by this section without a showing that the child violated a condition of probation ordered under Section 54.04(q).

(g) If the juvenile court places the child on probation for an offense for which registration as a sex offender is required by Chapter 62, Code of Criminal Procedure, and defers the registration requirement until completion of treatment for the sex offense under Subchapter H, Chapter 62, Code of Criminal Procedure, [1] the authority under that article to reexamine the need for registration on completion of treatment is transferred to the court to which probation is transferred.

(h) If the juvenile court places the child on probation for an offense for which registration as a sex offender is required by Chapter 62, Code of Criminal Procedure, and the child registers, the authority of the court to excuse further compliance with the registration requirement under Subchapter H, Chapter 62, Code of Criminal Procedure, is transferred to the court to which probation is transferred.

(i) If the juvenile court exercises jurisdiction over a person who is 18 or 19 years of age or older, as applicable, under Section 51.041 or 51.0412, the court or jury may, if the person is otherwise eligible, place the person on probation under Section 54.04(q). The juvenile court shall set the conditions of probation and immediately transfer supervision of the person to the appropriate court exercising criminal jurisdiction under Subsection (e).

Added by Acts 1999, 76th Leg., ch. 1477, § 12, eff. Sept. 1, 1999. Amended by Acts 2003, 78th Leg., ch. 283, § 22, eff. Sept. 1, 2003; Acts 2005, 79th Leg., ch. 1008, § 2.07, eff. Sept. 1, 2005; Acts 2011, 82nd Leg., ch. 438 (S.B. 1208), § 6, eff. Sept. 1, 2011; Acts 2013, 83rd Leg., ch. 1299 (H.B. 2862), § 21, eff. Sept. 1, 2013; Acts 2015, 84th Leg., ch. 770 (H.B. 2299), § 2.33, eff. Jan. 1, 2017.

[1] Vernon's Ann.C.C.P. art. 62.351 et seq.

**§ 54.052. Credit for Time Spent in Detention Facility for Child with Determinate Sentence**

(a) This section applies only to a child who is committed to:

(1) the Texas Juvenile Justice Department under a determinate sentence under Section 54.04(d)(3) or (m) or Section 54.05(f); or

(2) a post-adjudication secure correctional facility under a determinate sentence under Section 54.04011(c)(2).

(b) The judge of the court in which a child is adjudicated shall give the child credit on the child's sentence for the time spent by the child, in connection with the conduct for which the child was adjudicated, in a secure detention facility before the child's transfer to a Texas Juvenile Justice Department facility or a post-adjudication secure correctional facility, as applicable.

(c) If a child appeals the child's adjudication and is retained in a secure detention facility pending the appeal, the judge of the court in which the child was adjudicated shall give the child credit on the child's sentence for the time spent by the child in a secure detention facility pending disposition of the child's appeal. The court shall endorse on both the commitment and the mandate from the appellate court all credit given the child under this subsection.

(d) The Texas Juvenile Justice Department or the juvenile board or local juvenile probation department operating or contracting for the operation of the post-adjudication secure correctional facility under Section 152.0016, Human Resources Code, as applicable, shall grant any credit under this section in computing the child's eligibility for parole and discharge.

Added by Acts 2007, 80th Leg., ch. 263, § 10, eff. June 8, 2007. Amended by Acts 2013, 83rd Leg., ch. 1323 (S.B. 511), § 5, eff. Dec. 1, 2013.

**§ 54.06. Judgments for Support**

(a) At any stage of the proceeding, when a child has been placed outside the child's home, the juvenile court, after giving the parent or other person responsible for the child's support a reasonable opportunity to be heard, shall order the parent or other person to pay in a manner directed by the court a reasonable sum for the support in whole or in part of the child or the court shall waive the payment by order. The court shall order that the payment for support be made to the local juvenile probation department to be used only for residential care and other support for the child unless the child has been committed to the Texas Juvenile Justice Department, in which case the court shall order that the payment be made to the Texas Juvenile Justice Department for deposit in a special account in the general revenue fund that may be appropriated only for the care of children committed to the Texas Juvenile Justice Department.

(b) At any stage of the proceeding, when a child has been placed outside the child's home and the parent of the child is obligated to pay support for the child under a court order under Title 5,[1] the juvenile court shall order that the person entitled to receive the support assign the person's right to support for the child placed outside the child's home to the local juvenile probation department to be used for residential care and other support for the child unless the child has been committed to the Texas Juvenile Justice Department, in which event the court shall order that the assignment be made to the Texas Juvenile Justice Department.

(c) A court may enforce an order for support under this section by ordering garnishment of the wages of the person ordered to pay support or by any other means available to enforce a child support order under Title 5.

(d) Repealed by Acts 2003, 78th Leg., ch. 283, § 61(1).

(e) The court shall apply the child support guidelines under Subchapter C, Chapter 154,[2] in an order requiring the payment of child support under this section. The court shall also require in an order to pay child support under this section that health insurance and dental insurance be provided for the child. Subchapter D, Chapter 154,[3] applies to an order requiring health insurance and dental insurance for a child under this section.

(f) An order under this section prevails over any previous child support order issued with regard to the child to the extent of any conflict between the orders.

Acts 1973, 63rd Leg., p. 1460, ch. 544, § 1, eff. Sept. 1, 1973. Amended by Acts 1983, 68th Leg., p. 163, ch. 44, art. 1, § 5, eff. April 26, 1983; Acts 1987, 70th Leg., ch. 1040, § 24, eff. Sept. 1, 1987; Acts 1993, 73rd Leg., ch. 798, § 23, eff. Sept. 1, 1993; Acts 1993, 73rd Leg., ch. 1048, § 2, eff. Sept. 1, 1993; Acts 1995, 74th Leg., ch. 262, § 43, eff. Jan. 1, 1996; Acts 1997, 75th Leg., ch. 165, § 7.11, eff. Sept. 1, 1997; Acts 2003, 78th Leg., ch. 283, § 61(1), eff. Sept. 1, 2003; Acts 2015, 84th Leg., ch. 734 (H.B. 1549), § 55, eff. Sept. 1, 2015; Acts 2015, 84th Leg., ch. 1150 (S.B. 550), § 1, eff. Sept. 1, 2018.

[1] V.T.C.A., Family Code § 101.001 et seq.

[2] V.T.C.A., Family Code § 154.121 et seq.

[3] V.T.C.A., Family Code § 154.181 et seq.

**Repeal of (a)**

*Acts 2021, 87th Leg., ch. 472 (S.B. 41), § 5.01(b)(6) repeals (a) effective Jan. 1, 2022.*

### § 54.061. Payment of Probation Fees

(a) If a child is placed on probation under Section 54.04(d)(1) of this code, the juvenile court, after giving the child, parent, or other person responsible for the child's support a reasonable opportunity to be heard, shall order the child, parent, or other person, if financially able to do so, to pay to the court a fee of not more than $15 a month during the period that the child continues on probation.

(b) Orders for the payment of fees under this section may be enforced as provided by Section 54.07 of this code.

(c) The court shall deposit the fees received under this section in the county treasury to the credit of a special fund that may be used only for juvenile probation or community-based juvenile corrections services or facilities in which a juvenile may be required to live while under court supervision.

(d) If the court finds that a child, parent, or other person responsible for the child's support is financially unable to pay the probation fee required under Subsection (a), the court shall enter into the records of the child's case a statement of that finding. The court may waive a fee under this section only if the court makes the finding under this subsection.

Added by Acts 1979, 66th Leg., p. 338, ch. 154, § 1, eff. Sept. 1, 1979. Amended by Acts 1981, 67th Leg., p. 2425, ch. 617, § 4, eff. Sept. 1, 1981; Acts 1987, 70th Leg., ch. 1040, § 25, eff. Sept. 1, 1987; Acts 1995, 74th Leg., ch. 262, § 44, eff. Jan. 1, 1996.

### § 54.07. Enforcement of Order

(a) Except as provided by Subsection (b) or a juvenile court child support order, any order of the juvenile court may be enforced as provided by Chapter 61.

(b) A violation of any of the following orders of the juvenile court may not be enforced by contempt of court proceedings against the child:

(1) an order setting conditions of probation;

(2) an order setting conditions of deferred prosecution; and

(3) an order setting conditions of release from detention.

(c) This section and Chapter 61 do not preclude a juvenile court from summarily finding a child or other person in direct contempt of the juvenile court for conduct occurring in the presence of the judge of the court. Direct contempt of the juvenile court by a child is punishable by a maximum of 10 days' confinement in a secure juvenile detention facility or by a maximum of 40 hours of community service, or both. The juvenile court may not impose a fine on a child for direct contempt.

(d) This section and Chapter 61 do not preclude a juvenile court in an appropriate case from using a civil or coercive contempt proceeding to enforce an order.

Acts 1973, 63rd Leg., p. 1460, ch. 544, § 1, eff. Sept. 1, 1973. Amended by Acts 1979, 66th Leg., p. 339, ch. 154, § 3, eff. Sept. 1, 1979; Acts 2003, 78th Leg., ch. 283, § 23, eff. Sept. 1, 2003.

### § 54.08. Public Access to Court Hearings

(a) Except as provided by this section, the court shall open hearings under this title to the public unless the court, for good cause shown, determines that the public should be excluded.

(b) The court may not prohibit a person who is a victim of the conduct of a child, or the person's family, from personally attending a hearing under this title relating to the conduct by the child unless the victim or member of the victim's family is to testify in the hearing or any subsequent hearing relating to the conduct and the court determines that the victim's or family member's testimony would be materially affected if the victim or member of the victim's family hears other testimony at trial.

(c) If a child is under the age of 14 at the time of the hearing, the court shall close the hearing to the public unless the court finds that the interests of the child or the interests of the public would be better served by opening the hearing to the public.

(d) In this section, "family" has the meaning assigned by Section 71.003.

Acts 1973, 63rd Leg., p. 1460, ch. 544, § 1, eff. Sept. 1, 1973. Amended by Acts 1987, 70th Leg., ch. 385, § 11, eff. Sept. 1, 1987; Acts 1995, 74th Leg., ch. 262, § 45, eff. Jan. 1, 1996; Acts 1997, 75th Leg., ch. 1086, § 12, eff. Sept. 1, 1997.

### § 54.09. Recording of Proceedings

All judicial proceedings under this chapter except detention hearings shall be recorded by stenographic notes or by electronic, mechanical, or other appropriate means. Upon request of any party, a detention hearing shall be recorded.

Acts 1973, 63rd Leg., p. 1460, ch. 544, § 1, eff. Sept. 1, 1973.

### § 54.10. Hearings Before Referee

(a) Except as provided by Subsection (e), a hearing under Section 54.03, 54.04, or 54.05, including a jury trial, a hearing under Chapter 55, including a jury trial, or a hearing under the Interstate Compact for Juveniles (Chapter 60) may be held by a referee appointed in accordance with Section 51.04(g) or an associate judge appointed under Chapter 54A, Government Code, provided:

(1) the parties have been informed by the referee or associate judge that they are entitled to have the hearing before the juvenile court judge; and

(2) after each party is given an opportunity to object, no party objects to holding the hearing before the referee or associate judge.

(b) The determination under Section 53.02(f) whether to release a child may be made by a referee appointed in accordance with Section 51.04(g) if:

(1) the child has been informed by the referee that the child is entitled to have the determination made by the juvenile court judge or a substitute judge authorized by Section 51.04(f); or

(2) the child and the attorney for the child have in accordance with Section 51.09 waived the right to have the determination made by the juvenile court judge or a substitute judge.

(c) If a child objects to a referee making the determination under Section 53.02(f), the juvenile court judge or a substitute judge authorized by Section 51.04(f) shall make the determination.

(d) At the conclusion of the hearing or immediately after making the determination, the referee shall transmit written findings and recommendations to the juvenile court judge. The juvenile court judge shall adopt, modify, or reject the referee's recommendations not later than the next working day after the day that the judge receives the recommendations. Failure to act within that time results in release of the child by operation of law and a recommendation that the child be released operates to secure the child's immediate release subject to the power of the juvenile court judge to modify or reject that recommendation.

(e) Except as provided by Subsection (f), the hearings provided by Sections 54.03, 54.04, and 54.05 may not be held before a referee if the grand jury has approved of the petition and the child is subject to a determinate sentence.

(f) When the state and a child who is subject to a determinate sentence agree to the disposition of the case, wholly or partly, a referee or associate judge may hold a hearing for the purpose of allowing the child to enter a plea or stipulation of evidence. After the hearing under this subsection, the referee or associate judge shall transmit the referee's or associate judge's written findings and recommendations regarding the plea or stipulation of evidence to the juvenile court judge for consideration. The juvenile court judge may accept or reject the plea or stipulation of evidence in accordance with Section 54.03(j).

Added by Acts 1975, 64th Leg., p. 2157, ch. 693, § 19, eff. Sept. 1, 1975. Amended by Acts 1979, 66th Leg., p. 1830, ch. 743, § 2, eff. Aug. 27, 1979; Acts 1987, 70th Leg., ch. 385, § 12, eff. Sept. 1, 1987; Acts 1991, 72nd Leg., ch. 74, § 1, eff. Sept. 1, 1991; Acts 1997, 75th Leg., ch. 1086, § 13, eff. Sept. 1, 1997; Acts 1999, 76th Leg., ch. 232, § 5, eff. Sept. 1, 1999; Acts 1999, 76th Leg., ch. 1477, § 13, eff. Sept. 1, 1999; Acts 2005, 79th Leg., ch. 1007, § 2.03, eff. Aug. 26, 2008; Acts 2011, 82nd Leg., 1st C.S., ch. 3 (H.B. 79), § 6.08, eff. Jan. 1, 2012; Acts 2017, 85th Leg., ch. 981 (H.B. 678), § 1, eff. Sept. 1, 2017.

### § 54.11. Release or Transfer Hearing

(a) On receipt of a referral under Section 244.014(a), Human Resources Code, for the transfer to the Texas Department of Criminal Justice of a person committed to the Texas Juvenile Justice Department under Section 54.04(d)(3), 54.04(m), or 54.05(f), on receipt of a request by the Texas Juvenile Justice Department under Section 245.051(d), Human Resources Code, for approval of the release under supervision of a person committed to the Texas Juvenile Justice Department under Section 54.04(d)(3), 54.04(m), or 54.05(f), or on receipt of a referral under Section 152.0016(g) or (j), Human Resources Code, the court shall set a time and place for a hearing on the possible transfer or release of the person, as applicable.

(b) The court shall notify the following of the time and place of the hearing:

(1) the person to be transferred or released under supervision;

(2) the parents of the person;

(3) any legal custodian of the person, including the Texas Juvenile Justice Department or a juvenile board or local juvenile probation department if the child is committed to a post-adjudication secure correctional facility;

(4) the office of the prosecuting attorney that represented the state in the juvenile delinquency proceedings;

(5) the victim of the offense that was included in the delinquent conduct that was a ground for the disposition, or a member of the victim's family; and

(6) any other person who has filed a written request with the court to be notified of a release hearing with respect to the person to be transferred or released under supervision.

(c) Except for the person to be transferred or released under supervision and the prosecuting attorney, the failure to notify a person listed in Subsection (b) of this section does not affect the validity of a hearing conducted or determination made under this section if the record in the case reflects that the whereabouts of the persons who did not receive notice were unknown to the court and a reasonable effort was made by the court to locate those persons.

(d) At a hearing under this section the court may consider written reports and supporting documents from probation officers, professional court employees, guardians ad litem appointed under Section 51.11(d), professional consultants, employees of the Texas Juvenile Justice Department, or employees of a post-adjudication secure correctional facility in addition to the testimony of witnesses. On or before the fifth day before the date of the hearing, the court shall provide the attorney for the person to be transferred or released under supervision with access to all written matter to be considered by the court. All written matter is admissible in evidence at the hearing.

(e) At the hearing, the person to be transferred or released under supervision is entitled to an attorney, to examine all witnesses against him, to present evidence and oral argument, and to previous examination of all reports on and evaluations and examinations of or relating to him that may be used in the hearing.

(f) A hearing under this section is open to the public unless the person to be transferred or released under supervision waives a public hearing with the consent of his attorney and the court.

(g) A hearing under this section must be recorded by a court reporter or by audio or video tape recording, and the record of the hearing must be retained by the court for at least two years after the date of the final determination on the transfer or release of the person by the court.

(h) The hearing on a person who is referred for transfer under Section 152.0016(j) or 244.014(a), Human Resources Code, shall be held not later than the 60th day after the date the court receives the referral.

(i) On conclusion of the hearing on a person who is referred for transfer under Section 152.0016(j) or 244.014(a), Human Resources Code, the court may, as applicable, order:

(1) the return of the person to the Texas Juvenile Justice Department or post-adjudication secure correctional facility; or

(2) the transfer of the person to the custody of the Texas Department of Criminal Justice for the completion of the person's sentence.

(j) On conclusion of the hearing on a person who is referred for release under supervision under Section 152.0016(g) or 245.051(c), Human Resources Code, the court may, as applicable, order the return of the person to the Texas Juvenile Justice Department or post-adjudication secure correctional facility:

(1) with approval for the release of the person under supervision; or

(2) without approval for the release of the person under supervision.

(k) In making a determination under this section, the court may consider the experiences and character of the person before and after commitment to the Texas Juvenile Justice Department or post-adjudication secure correctional facility, the nature of the penal offense that the person was found to have committed and the manner in which the offense was committed, the abilities of the person to contribute to society, the protection of the victim of the offense or any member of the victim's family, the recommendations of the Texas Juvenile Justice Department, county juvenile board, local juvenile probation department, and prosecuting attorney, the best interests of the person, and any other factor relevant to the issue to be decided.

(*l*) Pending the conclusion of a transfer hearing, the juvenile court shall order that the person who is referred for transfer be detained in a certified juvenile detention facility as provided by Subsection (m). If the person is at least 17 years of age, the juvenile court may order that the person be detained without bond in an appropriate county facility for the detention of adults accused of criminal offenses.

(m) The detention of a person in a certified juvenile detention facility must comply with the detention requirements under this title, except that, to the extent practicable, the person must be kept separate from children detained in the same facility.

(n) If the juvenile court orders that a person who is referred for transfer be detained in a county facility under Subsection (*l*), the county sheriff shall take custody of the person under the juvenile court's order.

(*o*) In this section, "post-adjudication secure correctional facility" has the meaning assigned by Section 54.04011.

Added by Acts 1987, 70th Leg., ch. 385, § 13, eff. Sept. 1, 1987. Amended by Acts 1991, 72nd Leg., ch. 574, § 3, eff. Sept. 1, 1991; Acts 1995, 74th Leg., ch. 262, § 46, eff. Jan. 1, 1996; Acts 2001, 77th Leg., ch. 1297, § 29, eff. Sept. 1, 2001; Acts 2003, 78th Leg., ch. 283, § 24, eff. Sept. 1, 2003; Acts 2009, 81st Leg., ch. 87, § 25.058, eff. Sept. 1, 2009; Acts 2011, 82nd Leg., ch. 85 (S.B. 653), § 3.007, eff. Sept. 1, 2011; Acts 2013, 83rd Leg., ch. 1299 (H.B. 2862), § 22, eff. Sept. 1, 2013; Acts 2013, 83rd Leg., ch. 1323 (S.B. 511), § 6, eff. Dec. 1, 2013; Acts 2015, 84th Leg., ch. 854 (S.B. 1149), § 3, eff. Sept. 1, 2015; Acts 2021, 87th Leg., ch. 971 (S.B. 2049), § 6, eff. Sept. 1, 2021.

# CHAPTER 55. PROCEEDINGS CONCERNING CHILDREN WITH MENTAL ILLNESS OR INTELLECTUAL DISABILITY

SUBCHAPTER A. GENERAL PROVISIONS

**Section**



SUBCHAPTER B. CHILD WITH MENTAL ILLNESS



SUBCHAPTER C. CHILD UNFIT TO PROCEED AS A RESULT OF MENTAL ILLNESS OR INTELLECTUAL DISABILITY



**Section**



SUBCHAPTER D. LACK OF RESPONSIBILITY FOR CONDUCT AS A RESULT OF MENTAL ILLNESS OR INTELLECTUAL DISABILITY



## SUBCHAPTER A. GENERAL PROVISIONS

### § 55.01. Meaning of "Having a Mental Illness"

For purposes of this chapter, a child who is described as having a mental illness means a child with a mental illness as defined by Section 571.003, Health and Safety Code.

Added by Acts 1999, 76th Leg., ch. 1477, § 14, eff. Sept. 1, 1999. Amended by Acts 2015, 84th Leg., ch. 1 (S.B. 219), § 1.002, eff. April 2, 2015.

### § 55.02. Mental Health and Intellectual Disability Jurisdiction

For the purpose of initiating proceedings to order mental health or intellectual disability services for a child or for commitment of a child as provided by this chapter, the juvenile court has jurisdiction of proceedings under Subtitle C or D, Title 7, Health and Safety Code. [1]

Added by Acts 1999, 76th Leg., ch. 1477, § 14, eff. Sept. 1, 1999. Amended by Acts 2015, 84th Leg., ch. 1 (S.B. 219), § 1.003, eff. April 2, 2015.

[1] V.T.C.A., Health and Safety Code § 571.001 et seq. or V.T.C.A., Health and Safety Code § 591.001 et seq.

### § 55.03. Standards of Care

(a) Except as provided by this chapter, a child for whom inpatient mental health services is ordered by a court under this chapter shall be cared for as provided by Subtitle C, Title 7, Health and Safety Code. [1]

(b) Except as provided by this chapter, a child who is committed by a court to a residential care facility due to an intellectual disability shall be cared for as provided by Subtitle D, Title 7, Health and Safety Code. [2]

Added by Acts 1999, 76th Leg., ch. 1477, § 14, eff. Sept. 1, 1999. Amended by Acts 2015, 84th Leg., ch. 1 (S.B. 219), § 1.004, eff. April 2, 2015.

[1] V.T.C.A., Health and Safety Code § 571.001 et seq.

[2] V.T.C.A., Health and Safety Code § 591.001 et seq.

### § 55.04. Renumbered as V.T.C.A., Family Code §§ 55.31, 55.32 by Acts 1999, 76th Leg., ch. 1477, § 14, eff. Sept. 1, 1999

### § 55.05. Renumbered as V.T.C.A., Family Code § 55.51 by Acts 1999, 76th Leg., ch. 1477, § 14, eff. Sept. 1, 1999

## SUBCHAPTER B. CHILD WITH MENTAL ILLNESS

### § 55.11. Mental Illness Determination; Examination

(a) On a motion by a party, the juvenile court shall determine whether probable cause exists to believe that a child who is alleged by petition or found to have engaged in delinquent conduct or conduct indicating a need for supervision has a mental illness. In making its determination, the court may:

(1) consider the motion, supporting documents, professional statements of counsel, and witness testimony; and

(2) make its own observation of the child.

(b) If the court determines that probable cause exists to believe that the child has a mental illness, the court shall temporarily stay the juvenile court proceedings and immediately order the child to be examined under Section 51.20. The information obtained from the examination must include expert opinion as to whether the child has a mental illness and whether the child meets the commitment criteria under Subtitle C, Title 7, Health and Safety Code.[1] If ordered by the court, the information must also include expert opinion as to whether the child is unfit to proceed with the juvenile court proceedings.

(c) After considering all relevant information, including information obtained from an examination under Section 51.20, the court shall:

(1) if the court determines that evidence exists to support a finding that the child has a mental illness and that the child meets the commitment criteria under Subtitle C, Title 7, Health and Safety Code, proceed under Section 55.12; or

(2) if the court determines that evidence does not exist to support a finding that the child has a mental illness or that the child meets the commitment criteria under Subtitle C, Title 7, Health and Safety Code, dissolve the stay and continue the juvenile court proceedings.

Added by Acts 1999, 76th Leg., ch. 1477, § 14, eff. Sept. 1, 1999.

[1] V.T.C.A., Health and Safety Code § 571.001 et seq.

### § 55.12. Initiation of Commitment Proceedings

If, after considering all relevant information, the juvenile court determines that evidence exists to support a finding that a child has a mental illness and that the child meets the commitment criteria under Subtitle C, Title 7, Health and Safety Code,[1] the court shall:

(1) initiate proceedings as provided by Section 55.13 to order temporary or extended mental health services, as provided in Subchapter C, Chapter 574, Health and Safety Code; [2] or

(2) refer the child's case as provided by Section 55.14 to the appropriate court for the initiation of proceedings in that court for commitment of the child under Subchapter C, Chapter 574, Health and Safety Code.

Acts 1973, 63rd Leg., p. 1460, ch. 544, § 1, eff. Sept. 1, 1973. Amended by Acts 1995, 74th Leg., ch. 262, § 47, eff. May 31, 1995. Redesignated from V.T.C.A., Family Code § 55.02(a) and amended by Acts 1999, 76th Leg., ch. 1477, § 14, eff. Sept. 1, 1999.

[1] V.T.C.A., Health and Safety Code § 571.001 et seq.

[2] V.T.C.A., Health and Safety Code § 574.031 et seq.

### § 55.13. Commitment Proceedings in Juvenile Court

(a) If the juvenile court initiates proceedings for temporary or extended mental health services under Section 55.12(1), the prosecuting attorney or the attorney for the child may file with the juvenile court an application for court-ordered mental health services under Section 574.001, Health and Safety Code. The juvenile court shall:

(1) set a date for a hearing and provide notice as required by Sections 574.005 and 574.006, Health and Safety Code; and

(2) conduct the hearing in accordance with Subchapter C, Chapter 574, Health and Safety Code.[1]

(b) The burden of proof at the hearing is on the party who filed the application.

(c) The juvenile court shall appoint the number of physicians necessary to examine the child and to complete the certificates of medical examination for mental illness required under Section 574.009, Health and Safety Code.

(d) After conducting a hearing on an application under this section, the juvenile court shall:

(1) if the criteria under Section 574.034 or 574.0345, Health and Safety Code, are satisfied, order temporary mental health services for the child; or

(2) if the criteria under Section 574.035 or 574.0355, Health and Safety Code, are satisfied, order extended mental health services for the child.

Added by Acts 1999, 76th Leg., ch. 1477, § 14, eff. Sept. 1, 1999. Amended by Acts 2019, 86th Leg., ch. 582 (S.B. 362), § 3, eff. Sept. 1, 2019.

[1] V.T.C.A., Health and Safety Code § 574.031 et seq.

Section 28 of Acts 2019, 86th Leg., ch. 582 (S.B. 362) provides:

"The Health and Human Services Commission is required to implement a provision of this Act only if the legislature appropriates money specifically for that purpose. If the legislature does not appropriate money specifically for that purpose, the Health and Human Services Commission may, but is not required to, implement a provision of this Act using other appropriations available for that purpose."

### § 55.14. Referral for Commitment Proceedings

(a) If the juvenile court refers the child's case to the appropriate court for the initiation of commitment proceedings under Section 55.12(2), the juvenile court shall:

(1) send all papers relating to the child's mental illness to the clerk of the court to which the case is referred;

(2) send to the office of the appropriate county attorney or, if a county attorney is not available, to the office of the appropriate district attorney, copies of all papers sent to the clerk of the court under Subdivision (1); and

(3) if the child is in detention:

(A) order the child released from detention to the child's home or another appropriate place;

(B) order the child detained in an appropriate place other than a juvenile detention facility; or

(C) if an appropriate place to release or detain the child as described by Paragraph (A) or (B) is not available, order the child to remain in the juvenile detention facility subject to further detention orders of the court.

(b) The papers sent to the clerk of a court under Subsection (a)(1) constitute an application for mental health services under Section 574.001, Health and Safety Code.

Added by Acts 1999, 76th Leg., ch. 1477, § 14, eff. Sept. 1, 1999.

### § 55.15. Standards of Care; Expiration of Court Order for Mental Health Services

If the juvenile court or a court to which the child's case is referred under Section 55.12(2) orders mental health services for the child, the child shall be cared for, treated, and released in conformity to Subtitle C, Title 7, Health and Safety Code,[1] except:

(1) a court order for mental health services for a child automatically expires on the 120th day after the date the child becomes 18 years of age; and

(2) the administrator of a mental health facility shall notify, in writing, by certified mail, return receipt requested, the juvenile court that ordered mental health services or the juvenile court that referred the case to a court that ordered the mental health services of the intent to discharge the child at least 10 days prior to discharge.

Acts 1973, 63rd Leg., p. 1460, ch. 544, § 1, eff. Sept. 1, 1973. Amended by Acts 1975, 64th Leg., p. 2157, ch. 693, §§ 20 and 21, eff. Sept. 1, 1975; Acts 1991, 72nd Leg., ch. 76, § 9, eff. Sept. 1, 1991; Acts 1995, 74th Leg., ch. 262, § 47, eff. May 31, 1995. Redesignated from V.T.C.A., Family Code § 55.02(c) and amended by Acts 1999, 76th Leg., ch. 1477, § 14, eff. Sept. 1, 1999.

[1] V.T.C.A., Health and Safety Code § 571.001 et seq.

### § 55.16. Order for Mental Health Services; Stay of Proceedings

(a) If the court to which the child's case is referred under Section 55.12(2) orders temporary or extended inpatient mental health services for the child, the court shall immediately notify in writing the referring juvenile court of the court's order for mental health services.

(b) If the juvenile court orders temporary or extended inpatient mental health services for the child or if the juvenile court receives notice under Subsection (a) from the court to which the child's case is referred, the proceedings under this title then pending in juvenile court shall be stayed.

Acts 1973, 63rd Leg., p. 1460, ch. 544, § 1, eff. Sept. 1, 1973. Amended by Acts 1995, 74th Leg., ch. 262, § 47, eff. May 31, 1995. Redesignated from V.T.C.A., Family Code § 55.02(d) and amended by Acts 1999, 76th Leg., ch. 1477, § 14, eff. Sept. 1, 1999.

### § 55.17. Mental Health Services Not Ordered; Dissolution of Stay

(a) If the court to which a child's case is referred under Section 55.12(2) does not order temporary or extended inpatient mental health services for the child, the court shall immediately notify in writing the referring juvenile court of the court's decision.

(b) If the juvenile court does not order temporary or extended inpatient mental health services for the child or if the juvenile court receives notice under Subsection (a) from the court to which the child's case is referred, the juvenile court shall dissolve the stay and continue the juvenile court proceedings.

Added by Acts 1999, 76th Leg., ch. 1477, § 14, eff. Sept. 1, 1999.

### § 55.18. Discharge from Mental Health Facility Before Reaching 18 Years of Age

If the child is discharged from the mental health facility before reaching 18 years of age, the juvenile court may:

(1) dismiss the juvenile court proceedings with prejudice; or

(2) continue with proceedings under this title as though no order of mental health services had been made.

Acts 1973, 63rd Leg., p. 1460, ch. 544, § 1, eff. Sept. 1, 1973. Amended by Acts 1995, 74th Leg., ch. 262, § 47, eff. May 31, 1995. Redesignated from V.T.C.A., Family Code § 55.02(e) by Acts 1999, 76th Leg., ch. 1477, § 14, eff. Sept. 1, 1999.

### § 55.19. Transfer to Criminal Court on 18th Birthday

(a) The juvenile court shall transfer all pending proceedings from the juvenile court to a criminal court on the 18th birthday of a child for whom the juvenile court or a court to which the child's case is referred under Section 55.12(2) has ordered inpatient mental health services if:

(1) the child is not discharged or furloughed from the inpatient mental health facility before reaching 18 years of age; and

(2) the child is alleged to have engaged in delinquent conduct that included a violation of a penal law listed in Section 53.045 and no adjudication concerning the alleged conduct has been made.

(b) The juvenile court shall send notification of the transfer of a child under Subsection (a) to the inpatient mental health facility. The criminal court shall, within 90 days of the transfer, institute proceedings under Chapter 46B, Code of Criminal Procedure. If those or any subsequent proceedings result in a determination that the defendant is competent to stand trial, the defendant may not receive a punishment for the delinquent conduct described by Subsection (a)(2) that results in confinement for a period longer than the maximum period of confinement the defendant could have received if the defendant had been adjudicated for the delinquent conduct while still a child and within the jurisdiction of the juvenile court.

Added by Acts 1995, 74th Leg., ch. 262, § 47, eff. May 31, 1995. Redesignated from § 55.02(f) and (g) and amended by Acts 1999, 76th Leg., ch. 1477, § 14, eff. Sept. 1, 1999; Acts 2003, 78th Leg., ch. 35, § 7, eff. Jan. 1, 2004.

## SUBCHAPTER C. CHILD UNFIT TO PROCEED AS A RESULT OF MENTAL ILLNESS OR INTELLECTUAL DISABILITY

### § 55.31. Unfitness to Proceed Determination; Examination

(a) A child alleged by petition or found to have engaged in delinquent conduct or conduct indicating a need for supervision who as a result of mental illness or an intellectual disability lacks capacity to understand the proceedings in juvenile court or to assist in the child's own defense is unfit to proceed and shall not be subjected to discretionary transfer to criminal court, adjudication, disposition, or modification of disposition as long as such incapacity endures.

(b) On a motion by a party, the juvenile court shall determine whether probable cause exists to believe that a child who is alleged by petition or who is found to have engaged in delinquent conduct or conduct indicating a need for supervision is unfit to proceed as a result of mental illness or an intellectual disability. In making its determination, the court may:

(1) consider the motion, supporting documents, professional statements of counsel, and witness testimony; and

(2) make its own observation of the child.

(c) If the court determines that probable cause exists to believe that the child is unfit to proceed, the court shall temporarily stay the juvenile court proceedings and immediately order the child to be examined under Section 51.20. The information obtained from the examination must include expert opinion as to whether the child is unfit to proceed as a result of mental illness or an intellectual disability.

(d) After considering all relevant information, including information obtained from an examination under Section 51.20, the court shall:

(1) if the court determines that evidence exists to support a finding that the child is unfit to proceed, proceed under Section 55.32; or

(2) if the court determines that evidence does not exist to support a finding that the child is unfit to proceed, dissolve the stay and continue the juvenile court proceedings.

Acts 1973, 63rd Leg., p. 1460, ch. 544, § 1, eff. Sept. 1, 1973. Amended by Acts 1995, 74th Leg., ch. 262, § 47, eff. May 31, 1995. Redesignated from V.T.C.A., Family Code § 55.04(a) and (b) and amended by Acts 1999, 76th Leg., ch. 1477, § 14, eff. Sept. 1, 1999. Amended by Acts 2015, 84th Leg., ch. 1 (S.B. 219), § 1.006, eff. April 2, 2015.

### § 55.32. Hearing on Issue of Fitness to Proceed

(a) If the juvenile court determines that evidence exists to support a finding that a child is unfit to proceed as a result of mental illness or an intellectual disability, the court shall set the case for a hearing on that issue.

(b) The issue of whether the child is unfit to proceed as a result of mental illness or an intellectual disability shall be determined at a hearing separate from any other hearing.

(c) The court shall determine the issue of whether the child is unfit to proceed unless the child or the attorney for the child demands a jury before the 10th day before the date of the hearing.

(d) Unfitness to proceed as a result of mental illness or an intellectual disability must be proved by a preponderance of the evidence.

(e) If the court or jury determines that the child is fit to proceed, the juvenile court shall continue with proceedings under this title as though no question of fitness to proceed had been raised.

(f) If the court or jury determines that the child is unfit to proceed as a result of mental illness or an intellectual disability, the court shall:

(1) stay the juvenile court proceedings for as long as that incapacity endures; and

(2) proceed under Section 55.33.

(g) The fact that the child is unfit to proceed as a result of mental illness or an intellectual disability does not preclude any legal objection to the juvenile court proceedings which is susceptible of fair determination prior to the adjudication hearing and without the personal participation of the child.

Acts 1973, 63rd Leg., p. 1460, ch. 544, § 1, eff. Sept. 1, 1973. Amended by Acts 1995, 74th Leg., ch. 262, § 47, eff. May 31, 1995. Redesignated from V.T.C.A., Family Code § 55.04(c) to (f) and (h) and amended by Acts 1999, 76th Leg., ch. 1477, § 14, eff. Sept. 1, 1999. Amended by Acts 2015, 84th Leg., ch. 1 (S.B. 219), § 1.007, eff. April 2, 2015.

### § 55.33. Proceedings Following Finding of Unfitness to Proceed

(a) If the juvenile court or jury determines under Section 55.32 that a child is unfit as a result of mental illness or an intellectual disability to proceed with the juvenile court proceedings for delinquent conduct, the court shall:

(1) provided that the child meets the commitment criteria under Subtitle C or D, Title 7, Health and Safety Code,[1] order the child placed with the Department of State Health Services or the Department of Aging and Disability Services, as appropriate, for a period of not more than 90 days, which order may not specify a shorter period, for placement in a facility designated by the department;

(2) on application by the child's parent, guardian, or guardian ad litem, order the child placed in a private psychiatric inpatient facility for a period of not more than 90 days, which order may not specify a shorter period, but only if:

(A) the unfitness to proceed is a result of mental illness; and

(B) the placement is agreed to in writing by the administrator of the facility; or

(3) subject to Subsection (c), if the court determines that the child may be adequately treated or served in an alternative setting, order the child to receive treatment for mental illness or services for the child's intellectual disability, as appropriate, on an outpatient basis for a period of not more than 90 days, which order may not specify a shorter period.

(b) If the court orders a child placed in a private psychiatric inpatient facility under Subsection (a)(2), the state or a political subdivision of the state may be ordered to pay any costs associated with the child's placement, subject to an express appropriation of funds for the purpose.

(c) Before issuing an order described by Subsection (a)(3), the court shall consult with the probation department and with local treatment or service providers to determine the appropriate treatment or services for the child.

Added by Acts 1999, 76th Leg., ch. 1477, § 14, eff. Sept. 1, 1999. Amended by Acts 2015, 84th Leg., ch. 1 (S.B. 219), § 1.008, eff. April 2, 2015; Acts 2021, 87th Leg., ch. 814 (H.B. 2107), § 1, eff. Sept. 1, 2021.

[1] V.T.C.A., Health and Safety Code § 571.001 et seq. or V.T.C.A., Health and Safety Code § 591.001 et seq.

### § 55.34. Transportation to and from Facility

(a) If the court issues a placement order under Section 55.33(a)(1) or (2), the court shall order the probation department or sheriff's department to transport the child to the designated facility.

(b) On receipt of a report from a facility to which a child has been transported under Subsection (a), the court shall order the probation department or sheriff's department to transport the child from the facility to the court. If the child is not transported to the court before the 11th day after the date of the court's order, an authorized representative of the facility shall transport the child from the facility to the court.

(c) The county in which the juvenile court is located shall reimburse the facility for the costs incurred in transporting the child to the juvenile court as required by Subsection (b).

Added by Acts 1999, 76th Leg., ch. 1477, § 14, eff. Sept. 1, 1999. Amended by Acts 2021, 87th Leg., ch. 814 (H.B. 2107), § 2, eff. Sept. 1, 2021.

### § 55.35. Information Required to Be Sent to Facility; Report to Court

(a) If the juvenile court issues a placement order under Section 55.33(a), the court shall order the probation department to send copies of any information in the possession of the department and relevant to the issue of the child's mental illness or intellectual disability to the public or private facility or outpatient center, as appropriate.

(b) Not later than the 75th day after the date the court issues a placement order under Section 55.33(a), the public or private facility or outpatient center, as appropriate, shall submit to the court a report that:

(1) describes the treatment or services provided to the child by the facility or center; and

(2) states the opinion of the director of the facility or center as to whether the child is fit or unfit to proceed.

(c) The court shall provide a copy of the report submitted under Subsection (b) to the prosecuting attorney and the attorney for the child.

Added by Acts 1999, 76th Leg., ch. 1477, § 14, eff. Sept. 1, 1999. Amended by Acts 2015, 84th Leg., ch. 1 (S.B. 219), § 1.009, eff. April 2, 2015; Acts 2021, 87th Leg., ch. 814 (H.B. 2107), § 3, eff. Sept. 1, 2021.

### § 55.36. Report That Child Is Fit to Proceed; Hearing on Objection

(a) If a report submitted under Section 55.35(b) states that a child is fit to proceed, the juvenile court shall find that the child is fit to proceed unless the child's attorney objects in writing or in open court not later than the second day after the date the attorney receives a copy of the report under Section 55.35(c).

(b) On objection by the child's attorney under Subsection (a), the juvenile court shall promptly hold a hearing to determine whether the child is fit to proceed, except that the hearing may be held after the date that the placement order issued under Section 55.33(a) expires. At the hearing, the court shall determine the issue of the fitness of the child to proceed unless the child or the child's attorney demands in writing a jury before the 10th day before the date of the hearing.

(c) If, after a hearing, the court or jury finds that the child is fit to proceed, the court shall dissolve the stay and continue the juvenile court proceedings as though a question of fitness to proceed had not been raised.

(d) If, after a hearing, the court or jury finds that the child is unfit to proceed, the court shall proceed under Section 55.37.

Added by Acts 1999, 76th Leg., ch. 1477, § 14, eff. Sept. 1, 1999.

### § 55.37. Report That Child Is Unfit to Proceed as a Result of Mental Illness; Initiation of Commitment Proceedings

If a report submitted under Section 55.35(b) states that a child is unfit to proceed as a result of mental illness and that the child meets the commitment criteria for civil commitment under Subtitle C, Title 7,

Health and Safety Code,[1] the director of the public or private facility or outpatient center, as appropriate, shall submit to the court two certificates of medical examination for mental illness. On receipt of the certificates, the court shall:

(1) initiate proceedings as provided by Section 55.38 in the juvenile court for commitment of the child under Subtitle C, Title 7, Health and Safety Code; or

(2) refer the child's case as provided by Section 55.39 to the appropriate court for the initiation of proceedings in that court for commitment of the child under Subtitle C, Title 7, Health and Safety Code.

Added by Acts 1999, 76th Leg., ch. 1477, § 14, eff. Sept. 1, 1999.

[1] V.T.C.A., Health and Safety Code § 571.001 et seq.

### § 55.38. Commitment Proceedings in Juvenile Court for Mental Illness

(a) If the juvenile court initiates commitment proceedings under Section 55.37(1), the prosecuting attorney may file with the juvenile court an application for court-ordered mental health services under Section 574.001, Health and Safety Code. The juvenile court shall:

(1) set a date for a hearing and provide notice as required by Sections 574.005 and 574.006, Health and Safety Code; and

(2) conduct the hearing in accordance with Subchapter C, Chapter 574, Health and Safety Code.[1]

(b) After conducting a hearing under Subsection (a)(2), the juvenile court shall:

(1) if the criteria under Section 574.034 or 574.0345, Health and Safety Code, are satisfied, order temporary mental health services; or

(2) if the criteria under Section 574.035 or 574.0355, Health and Safety Code, are satisfied, order extended mental health services.

Added by Acts 1999, 76th Leg., ch. 1477, § 14, eff. Sept. 1, 1999. Amended by Acts 2019, 86th Leg., ch. 582 (S.B. 362), § 4, eff. Sept. 1, 2019.

[1] V.T.C.A., Health and Safety Code § 574.031 et seq.

Section 28 of Acts 2019, 86th Leg., ch. 582 (S.B. 362) provides:

"The Health and Human Services Commission is required to implement a provision of this Act only if the legislature appropriates money specifically for that purpose. If the legislature does not appropriate money specifically for that purpose, the Health and Human Services Commission may, but is not required to, implement a provision of this Act using other appropriations available for that purpose."

### § 55.39. Referral for Commitment Proceedings for Mental Illness

(a) If the juvenile court refers the child's case to an appropriate court for the initiation of commitment proceedings under Section 55.37(2), the juvenile court shall:

(1) send all papers relating to the child's unfitness to proceed, including the verdict and judgment of the juvenile court finding the child unfit to proceed, to the clerk of the court to which the case is referred;

(2) send to the office of the appropriate county attorney or, if a county attorney is not available, to the office of the appropriate district attorney, copies of all papers sent to the clerk of the court under Subdivision (1); and

(3) if the child is in detention:

(A) order the child released from detention to the child's home or another appropriate place;

(B) order the child detained in an appropriate place other than a juvenile detention facility; or

(C) if an appropriate place to release or detain the child as described by Paragraph (A) or (B) is not available, order the child to remain in the juvenile detention facility subject to further detention orders of the court.

(b) The papers sent to a court under Subsection (a)(1) constitute an application for mental health services under Section 574.001, Health and Safety Code.

Added by Acts 1999, 76th Leg., ch. 1477, § 14, eff. Sept. 1, 1999.

### § 55.40. Report That Child Is Unfit to Proceed as a Result of Intellectual Disability

If a report submitted under Section 55.35(b) states that a child is unfit to proceed as a result of an intellectual disability and that the child meets the commitment criteria for civil commitment under Subtitle D, Title 7, Health and Safety Code, the director of the residential care facility shall submit to the court an affidavit stating the conclusions reached as a result of the diagnosis. On receipt of the affidavit, the court shall:

(1) initiate proceedings as provided by Section 55.41 in the juvenile court for commitment of the child under Subtitle D, Title 7, Health and Safety Code; or

(2) refer the child's case as provided by Section 55.42 to the appropriate court for the initiation of proceedings in that court for commitment of the

child under Subtitle D, Title 7, Health and Safety Code.[1]

Added by Acts 1999, 76th Leg., ch. 1477, § 14, eff. Sept. 1, 1999. Amended by Acts 2015, 84th Leg., ch. 1 (S.B. 219), § 1.010, eff. April 2, 2015.

[1] V.T.C.A., Health and Safety Code § 591.001 et seq.

### § 55.41. Commitment Proceedings in Juvenile Court for Children with Intellectual Disability

(a) If the juvenile court initiates commitment proceedings under Section 55.40(1), the prosecuting attorney may file with the juvenile court an application for placement under Section 593.041, Health and Safety Code. The juvenile court shall:

(1) set a date for a hearing and provide notice as required by Sections 593.047 and 593.048, Health and Safety Code; and

(2) conduct the hearing in accordance with Sections 593.049–593.056, Health and Safety Code.

(b) After conducting a hearing under Subsection (a)(2), the juvenile court may order commitment of the child to a residential care facility if the commitment criteria under Section 593.052, Health and Safety Code, are satisfied.

(c) On receipt of the court's order, the Department of Aging and Disability Services or the appropriate community center shall admit the child to a residential care facility.

Added by Acts 1999, 76th Leg., ch. 1477, § 14, eff. Sept. 1, 1999. Amended by Acts 2001, 77th Leg., ch. 1297, § 30, eff. Sept. 1, 2001; Acts 2015, 84th Leg., ch. 1 (S.B. 219), §§ 1.011, 1.012, eff. April 2, 2015.

### § 55.42. Referral for Commitment Proceedings for Children with Intellectual Disability

(a) If the juvenile court refers the child's case to an appropriate court for the initiation of commitment proceedings under Section 55.40(2), the juvenile court shall:

(1) send all papers relating to the child's intellectual disability to the clerk of the court to which the case is referred;

(2) send to the office of the appropriate county attorney or, if a county attorney is not available, to the office of the appropriate district attorney, copies of all papers sent to the clerk of the court under Subdivision (1); and

(3) if the child is in detention:

(A) order the child released from detention to the child's home or another appropriate place;

(B) order the child detained in an appropriate place other than a juvenile detention facility; or

(C) if an appropriate place to release or detain the child as described by Paragraph (A) or (B) is not available, order the child to remain in the juvenile detention facility subject to further detention orders of the court.

(b) The papers sent to a court under Subsection (a)(1) constitute an application for placement under Section 593.041, Health and Safety Code.

Added by Acts 1999, 76th Leg., ch. 1477, § 14, eff. Sept. 1, 1999. Amended by Acts 2015, 84th Leg., ch. 1 (S.B. 219), §§ 1.013, 1.014, eff. April 2, 2015.

### § 55.43. Restoration Hearing

(a) The prosecuting attorney may file with the juvenile court a motion for a restoration hearing concerning a child if:

(1) the child is found unfit to proceed as a result of mental illness or an intellectual disability; and

(2) the child:

(A) is not:

(i) ordered by a court to receive inpatient mental health or intellectual disability services;

(ii) committed by a court to a residential care facility; or

(iii) ordered by a court to receive treatment or services on an outpatient basis; or

(B) is discharged or currently on furlough from a mental health facility or outpatient center before the child reaches 18 years of age.

(b) At the restoration hearing, the court shall determine the issue of whether the child is fit to proceed.

(c) The restoration hearing shall be conducted without a jury.

(d) The issue of fitness to proceed must be proved by a preponderance of the evidence.

(e) If, after a hearing, the court finds that the child is fit to proceed, the court shall continue the juvenile court proceedings.

(f) If, after a hearing, the court finds that the child is unfit to proceed, the court shall dismiss the motion for restoration.

Added by Acts 1999, 76th Leg., ch. 1477, § 14, eff. Sept. 1, 1999. Amended by Acts 2007, 80th Leg., ch. 908, § 13, eff. Sept. 1, 2007; Acts 2015, 84th Leg., ch. 1 (S.B. 219), § 1.015, eff. April 2, 2015; Acts 2021, 87th Leg., ch. 814 (H.B. 2107), § 4, eff. Sept. 1, 2021.

### § 55.44. Transfer to Criminal Court on 18th Birthday of Child

(a) The juvenile court shall transfer all pending proceedings from the juvenile court to a criminal court on the 18th birthday of a child for whom the juvenile court or a court to which the child's case is referred has ordered inpatient mental health services or residential care for persons with an intellectual disability if:

(1) the child is not discharged or currently on furlough from the facility before reaching 18 years of age; and

(2) the child is alleged to have engaged in delinquent conduct that included a violation of a penal law listed in Section 53.045 and no adjudication concerning the alleged conduct has been made.

(b) The juvenile court shall send notification of the transfer of a child under Subsection (a) to the facility. The criminal court shall, before the 91st day after the date of the transfer, institute proceedings under Chapter 46B, Code of Criminal Procedure. If those or any subsequent proceedings result in a determination that the defendant is competent to stand trial, the defendant may not receive a punishment for the delinquent conduct described by Subsection (a)(2) that results in confinement for a period longer than the maximum period of confinement the defendant could have received if the defendant had been adjudicated for the delinquent conduct while still a child and within the jurisdiction of the juvenile court.

Added by Acts 1999, 76th Leg., ch. 1477, § 14, eff. Sept. 1, 1999. Amended by Acts 2003, 78th Leg., ch. 35, § 8, eff. Jan. 1, 2004; Acts 2007, 80th Leg., ch. 908, § 14, eff. Sept. 1, 2007; Acts 2015, 84th Leg., ch. 1 (S.B. 219), § 1.016, eff. April 2, 2015.

### § 55.45. Standards of Care; Notice of Release or Furlough

(a) If the juvenile court or a court to which the child's case is referred under Section 55.37(2) orders mental health services for the child, the child shall be cared for, treated, and released in accordance with Subtitle C, Title 7, Health and Safety Code,[1] except that the administrator of a mental health facility shall notify, in writing, by certified mail, return receipt requested, the juvenile court that ordered mental health services or that referred the case to a court that ordered mental health services of the intent to discharge the child on or before the 10th day before the date of discharge.

(b) If the juvenile court or a court to which the child's case is referred under Section 55.40(2) orders the commitment of the child to a residential care facility, the child shall be cared for, treated, and released in accordance with Subtitle D, Title 7, Health and Safety Code,[2] except that the administrator of the residential care facility shall notify, in writing, by certified mail, return receipt requested, the juvenile court that ordered commitment of the child or that referred the case to a court that ordered commitment of the child of the intent to discharge or furlough the child on or before the 20th day before the date of discharge or furlough.

(c) If the referred child, as described in Subsection (b), is alleged to have committed an offense listed in Article 42A.054, Code of Criminal Procedure, the administrator of the residential care facility shall apply, in writing, by certified mail, return receipt requested, to the juvenile court that ordered commitment of the child or that referred the case to a court that ordered commitment of the child and show good cause for any release of the child from the facility for more than 48 hours. Notice of this request must be provided to the prosecuting attorney responsible for the case. The prosecuting attorney, the juvenile, or the administrator may apply for a hearing on this application. If no one applies for a hearing, the trial court shall resolve the application on the written submission. The rules of evidence do not apply to this hearing. An appeal of the trial court's ruling on the application is not allowed. The release of a child described in this subsection without the express approval of the trial court is punishable by contempt.

Added by Acts 2001, 77th Leg., ch. 1297, § 31, eff. Sept. 1, 2001. Amended by Acts 2007, 80th Leg., ch. 908, § 15, eff. Sept. 1, 2007; Acts 2015, 84th Leg., ch. 770 (H.B. 2299), § 2.34, eff. Jan. 1, 2017.

[1] V.T.C.A., Health and Safety Code § 571.001 et seq.
[2] V.T.C.A., Health and Safety Code § 591.001 et seq.

## SUBCHAPTER D. LACK OF RESPONSIBILITY FOR CONDUCT AS A RESULT OF MENTAL ILLNESS OR INTELLECTUAL DISABILITY

### § 55.51. Lack of Responsibility for Conduct Determination; Examination

(a) A child alleged by petition to have engaged in delinquent conduct or conduct indicating a need for supervision is not responsible for the conduct if at the time of the conduct, as a result of mental illness or an intellectual disability, the child lacks substantial capacity either to appreciate the wrongfulness of the child's conduct or to conform the child's conduct to the requirements of law.

(b) On a motion by a party in which it is alleged that a child may not be responsible as a result of mental illness or an intellectual disability for the child's conduct, the court shall order the child to be examined under Section 51.20. The information obtained from the examinations must include expert opinion as to whether the child is not responsible for the child's conduct as a result of mental illness or an intellectual disability.

(c) The issue of whether the child is not responsible for the child's conduct as a result of mental illness or an intellectual disability shall be tried to the court or jury in the adjudication hearing.

(d) Lack of responsibility for conduct as a result of mental illness or an intellectual disability must be proved by a preponderance of the evidence.

(e) In its findings or verdict the court or jury must state whether the child is not responsible for the child's conduct as a result of mental illness or an intellectual disability.

(f) If the court or jury finds the child is not responsible for the child's conduct as a result of mental illness or an intellectual disability, the court shall proceed under Section 55.52.

(g) A child found to be not responsible for the child's conduct as a result of mental illness or an intellectual disability shall not be subject to proceedings under this title with respect to such conduct, other than proceedings under Section 55.52.

Acts 1973, 63rd Leg., p. 1460, ch. 544, § 1, eff. Sept. 1, 1973. Amended by Acts 1995, 74th Leg., ch. 262, § 47, eff. May 31, 1995. Redesignated from V.T.C.A., Family Code § 55.05 and amended by Acts 1999, 76th Leg., ch. 1477, § 14, eff. Sept. 1, 1999. Amended by Acts 2015, 84th Leg., ch. 1 (S.B. 219), § 1.018, eff. April 2, 2015.

### § 55.52. Proceedings Following Finding of Lack of Responsibility for Conduct

(a) If the court or jury finds that a child is not responsible for the child's conduct under Section 55.51 as a result of mental illness or an intellectual disability, the court shall:

(1) provided that the child meets the commitment criteria under Subtitle C or D, Title 7, Health and Safety Code, [1] order the child placed with the Department of State Health Services or the Department of Aging and Disability Services, as appropriate, for a period of not more than 90 days, which order may not specify a shorter period, for placement in a facility designated by the department;

(2) on application by the child's parent, guardian, or guardian ad litem, order the child placed in a private psychiatric inpatient facility for a period of not more than 90 days, which order may not specify a shorter period, but only if:

(A) the child's lack of responsibility is a result of mental illness; and

(B) the placement is agreed to in writing by the administrator of the facility; or

(3) subject to Subsection (c), if the court determines that the child may be adequately treated or served in an alternative setting, order the child to receive treatment for mental illness or services for the child's intellectual disability, as appropriate, on an outpatient basis for a period of not more than 90 days, which order may not specify a shorter period.

(b) If the court orders a child placed in a private psychiatric inpatient facility under Subsection (a)(2), the state or a political subdivision of the state may be ordered to pay any costs associated with the child's placement, subject to an express appropriation of funds for the purpose.

(c) Before issuing an order described by Subsection (a)(3), the court shall consult with the probation department and with local treatment or service providers to determine the appropriate treatment or services for the child.

Added by Acts 1999, 76th Leg., ch. 1477, § 14, eff. Sept. 1, 1999. Amended by Acts 2015, 84th Leg., ch. 1 (S.B. 219), § 1.019, eff. April 2, 2015; Acts 2021, 87th Leg., ch. 814 (H.B. 2107), § 5, eff. Sept. 1, 2021.

[1] V.T.C.A., Health and Safety Code § 571.001 et seq. or V.T.C.A., Health and Safety Code § 591.001 et seq.

### § 55.53. Transportation to and from Facility

(a) If the court issues a placement order under Section 55.52(a)(1) or (2), the court shall order the probation department or sheriff's department to transport the child to the designated facility.

(b) On receipt of a report from a facility to which a child has been transported under Subsection (a), the court shall order the probation department or sheriff's department to transport the child from the facility to the court. If the child is not transported to the court before the 11th day after the date of the court's order, an authorized representative of the facility shall transport the child from the facility to the court.

(c) The county in which the juvenile court is located shall reimburse the facility for the costs incurred in transporting the child to the juvenile court as required by Subsection (b).

Added by Acts 1999, 76th Leg., ch. 1477, § 14, eff. Sept. 1, 1999. Amended by Acts 2021, 87th Leg., ch. 814 (H.B. 2107), § 6, eff. Sept. 1, 2021.

### § 55.54. Information Required to Be Sent to Facility; Report to Court

(a) If the juvenile court issues a placement order under Section 55.52(a), the court shall order the probation department to send copies of any information in the possession of the department and relevant to the issue of the child's mental illness or intellectual disability to the public or private facility or outpatient center, as appropriate.

(b) Not later than the 75th day after the date the court issues a placement order under Section 55.52(a), the public or private facility or outpatient center, as appropriate, shall submit to the court a report that:

(1) describes the treatment or services provided to the child by the facility or center; and

(2) states the opinion of the director of the facility or center as to whether the child has a mental illness or an intellectual disability.

(c) The court shall send a copy of the report submitted under Subsection (b) to the prosecuting attorney and the attorney for the child.

Added by Acts 1999, 76th Leg., ch. 1477, § 14, eff. Sept. 1, 1999. Amended by Acts 2015, 84th Leg., ch. 1 (S.B. 219), § 1.020, eff. April 2, 2015; Acts 2021, 87th Leg., ch. 814 (H.B. 2107), § 7, eff. Sept. 1, 2021.

### § 55.55. Report That Child Does Not Have Mental Illness or Intellectual Disability; Hearing on Objection

(a) If a report submitted under Section 55.54(b) states that a child does not have a mental illness or an intellectual disability, the juvenile court shall discharge the child unless:

(1) an adjudication hearing was conducted concerning conduct that included a violation of a penal law listed in Section 53.045(a) and a petition was approved by a grand jury under Section 53.045; and

(2) the prosecuting attorney objects in writing not later than the second day after the date the attorney receives a copy of the report under Section 55.54(c).

(b) On objection by the prosecuting attorney under Subsection (a), the juvenile court shall hold a hearing without a jury to determine whether the child has a mental illness or an intellectual disability and whether the child meets the commitment criteria for civil commitment under Subtitle C or D, Title 7, Health and Safety Code. [1]

(c) At the hearing, the burden is on the state to prove by clear and convincing evidence that the child has a mental illness or an intellectual disability and that the child meets the commitment criteria for civil commitment under Subtitle C or D, Title 7, Health and Safety Code.

(d) If, after a hearing, the court finds that the child does not have a mental illness or an intellectual disability and that the child does not meet the commitment criteria under Subtitle C or D, Title 7, Health and Safety Code, the court shall discharge the child.

(e) If, after a hearing, the court finds that the child has a mental illness or an intellectual disability and that the child meets the commitment criteria under Subtitle C or D, Title 7, Health and Safety Code, the court shall issue an appropriate commitment order.

Added by Acts 1999, 76th Leg., ch. 1477, § 14, eff. Sept. 1, 1999. Amended by Acts 2015, 84th Leg., ch. 1 (S.B. 219), § 1.021, eff. April 2, 2015.

[1] V.T.C.A., Health and Safety Code § 571.001 et seq. or V.T.C.A., Health and Safety Code § 591.001 et seq.

### § 55.56. Report That Child Has Mental Illness; Initiation of Commitment Proceedings

If a report submitted under Section 55.54(b) states that a child has a mental illness and that the child meets the commitment criteria for civil commitment under Subtitle C, Title 7, Health and Safety Code,[1] the director of the public or private facility or outpatient center, as appropriate, shall submit to the court two certificates of medical examination for mental illness. On receipt of the certificates, the court shall:

(1) initiate proceedings as provided by Section 55.57 in the juvenile court for commitment of the child under Subtitle C, Title 7, Health and Safety Code; or

(2) refer the child's case as provided by Section 55.58 to the appropriate court for the initiation of proceedings in that court for commitment of the child under Subtitle C, Title 7, Health and Safety Code.

Added by Acts 1999, 76th Leg., ch. 1477, § 14, eff. Sept. 1, 1999.

[1] V.T.C.A., Health and Safety Code § 571.001 et seq.

## § 55.57. Commitment Proceedings in Juvenile Court for Mental Illness

(a) If the juvenile court initiates commitment proceedings under Section 55.56(1), the prosecuting attorney may file with the juvenile court an application for court-ordered mental health services under Section 574.001, Health and Safety Code. The juvenile court shall:

(1) set a date for a hearing and provide notice as required by Sections 574.005 and 574.006, Health and Safety Code; and

(2) conduct the hearing in accordance with Subchapter C, Chapter 574, Health and Safety Code.[1]

(b) After conducting a hearing under Subsection (a)(2), the juvenile court shall:

(1) if the criteria under Section 574.034 or 574.0345, Health and Safety Code, are satisfied, order temporary mental health services; or

(2) if the criteria under Section 574.035 or 574.0355, Health and Safety Code, are satisfied, order extended mental health services.

Added by Acts 1999, 76th Leg., ch. 1477, § 14, eff. Sept. 1, 1999. Amended by Acts 2019, 86th Leg., ch. 582 (S.B. 362), § 5, eff. Sept. 1, 2019.

[1] V.T.C.A., Health and Safety Code § 574.031 et seq.

Section 28 of Acts 2019, 86th Leg., ch. 582 (S.B. 362) provides:

"The Health and Human Services Commission is required to implement a provision of this Act only if the legislature appropriates money specifically for that purpose. If the legislature does not appropriate money specifically for that purpose, the Health and Human Services Commission may, but is not required to, implement a provision of this Act using other appropriations available for that purpose."

## § 55.58. Referral for Commitment Proceedings for Mental Illness

(a) If the juvenile court refers the child's case to an appropriate court for the initiation of commitment proceedings under Section 55.56(2), the juvenile court shall:

(1) send all papers relating to the child's mental illness, including the verdict and judgment of the juvenile court finding that the child was not responsible for the child's conduct, to the clerk of the court to which the case is referred;

(2) send to the office of the appropriate county attorney or, if a county attorney is not available, to the office of the district attorney, copies of all papers sent to the clerk of the court under Subdivision (1); and

(3) if the child is in detention:

(A) order the child released from detention to the child's home or another appropriate place;

(B) order the child detained in an appropriate place other than a juvenile detention facility; or

(C) if an appropriate place to release or detain the child as described by Paragraph (A) or (B) is not available, order the child to remain in the juvenile detention facility subject to further detention orders of the court.

(b) The papers sent to a court under Subsection (a)(1) constitute an application for mental health services under Section 574.001, Health and Safety Code.

Added by Acts 1999, 76th Leg., ch. 1477, § 14, eff. Sept. 1, 1999.

## § 55.59. Report That Child Has Intellectual Disability; Initiation of Commitment Proceedings

If a report submitted under Section 55.54(b) states that a child has an intellectual disability and that the child meets the commitment criteria for civil commitment under Subtitle D, Title 7, Health and Safety Code,[1] the director of the residential care facility shall submit to the court an affidavit stating the conclusions reached as a result of the diagnosis. On receipt of an affidavit, the juvenile court shall:

(1) initiate proceedings in the juvenile court as provided by Section 55.60 for commitment of the child under Subtitle D, Title 7, Health and Safety Code; or

(2) refer the child's case to the appropriate court as provided by Section 55.61 for the initiation of proceedings in that court for commitment of the child under Subtitle D, Title 7, Health and Safety Code.

Added by Acts 1999, 76th Leg., ch. 1477, § 14, eff. Sept. 1, 1999. Amended by Acts 2015, 84th Leg., ch. 1 (S.B. 219), § 1.022, eff. April 2, 2015.

[1] V.T.C.A., Health and Safety Code § 591.001 et seq.

## § 55.60. Commitment Proceedings in Juvenile Court for Children with Intellectual Disability

(a) If the juvenile court initiates commitment proceedings under Section 55.59(1), the prosecuting attorney may file with the juvenile court an application for placement under Section 593.041, Health and Safety Code. The juvenile court shall:

(1) set a date for a hearing and provide notice as required by Sections 593.047 and 593.048, Health and Safety Code; and

(2) conduct the hearing in accordance with Sections 593.049–593.056, Health and Safety Code.

(b) After conducting a hearing under Subsection (a)(2), the juvenile court may order commitment of the child to a residential care facility only if the commitment criteria under Section 593.052, Health and Safety Code, are satisfied.

(c) On receipt of the court's order, the Department of Aging and Disability Services or the appropriate community center shall admit the child to a residential care facility.

Added by Acts 1999, 76th Leg., ch. 1477, § 14, eff. Sept. 1, 1999. Amended by Acts 2001, 77th Leg., ch. 1297, § 32, eff. Sept. 1, 2001; Acts 2015, 84th Leg., ch. 1 (S.B. 219), §§ 1.023, 1.024, eff. April 2, 2015.

### § 55.61. Referral for Commitment Proceedings for Children with Intellectual Disability

(a) If the juvenile court refers the child's case to an appropriate court for the initiation of commitment proceedings under Section 55.59(2), the juvenile court shall:

(1) send all papers relating to the child's intellectual disability to the clerk of the court to which the case is referred;

(2) send to the office of the appropriate county attorney or, if a county attorney is not available, to the office of the appropriate district attorney, copies of all papers sent to the clerk of the court under Subdivision (1); and

(3) if the child is in detention:

(A) order the child released from detention to the child's home or another appropriate place;

(B) order the child detained in an appropriate place other than a juvenile detention facility; or

(C) if an appropriate place to release or detain the child as described by Paragraph (A) or (B) is not available, order the child to remain in the juvenile detention facility subject to further detention orders of the court.

(b) The papers sent to a court under Subsection (a)(1) constitute an application for placement under Section 593.041, Health and Safety Code.

Added by Acts 1999, 76th Leg., ch. 1477, § 14, eff. Sept. 1, 1999. Amended by Acts 2015, 84th Leg., ch. 1 (S.B. 219), §§ 1.025, 1.026, eff. April 2, 2015.

## CHAPTER 56. APPEAL

Section



### § 56.01. Right to Appeal

(a) Except as provided by Subsection (b–1), an appeal from an order of a juvenile court is to a court of appeals and the case may be carried to the Texas Supreme Court by writ of error or upon certificate, as in civil cases generally.

(b) The requirements governing an appeal are as in civil cases generally. When an appeal is sought by filing a notice of appeal, security for costs of appeal, or an affidavit of inability to pay the costs of appeal, and the filing is made in a timely fashion after the date the disposition order is signed, the appeal must include the juvenile court adjudication and all rulings contributing to that adjudication. An appeal of the adjudication may be sought notwithstanding that the adjudication order was signed more than 30 days before the date the notice of appeal, security for costs of appeal, or affidavit of inability to pay the costs of appeal was filed.

(b–1) A motion for new trial seeking to vacate an adjudication is:

(1) timely if the motion is filed not later than the 30th day after the date on which the disposition order is signed; and

(2) governed by Rule 21, Texas Rules of Appellate Procedure.

(c) An appeal may be taken:

(1) except as provided by Subsection (n), by or on behalf of a child from an order entered under:

(A) Section 54.02 respecting transfer of the child for prosecution as an adult;

(B) Section 54.03 with regard to delinquent conduct or conduct indicating a need for supervision;

(C) Section 54.04 disposing of the case;

(D) Section 54.05 respecting modification of a previous juvenile court disposition; or

(E) Chapter 55 by a juvenile court committing a child to a facility for the mentally ill or intellectually disabled; or

(2) by a person from an order entered under Section 54.11(i)(2) transferring the person to the custody of the Texas Department of Criminal Justice.

(d) A child has the right to:

(1) appeal, as provided by this subchapter;

(2) representation by counsel on appeal; and

(3) appointment of an attorney for the appeal if an attorney cannot be obtained because of indigency.

(e) On entering an order that is appealable under this section, the court shall advise the child and the child's parent, guardian, or guardian ad litem of the child's rights listed under Subsection (d) of this section.

(f) If the child and his parent, guardian, or guardian ad litem express a desire to appeal, the attorney who represented the child before the juvenile court shall file a notice of appeal with the juvenile court and inform the court whether that attorney will handle the appeal. Counsel shall be appointed under the standards provided in Section 51.10 of this code unless the right to appeal is waived in accordance with Section 51.09 of this code.

(g) An appeal does not suspend the order of the juvenile court, nor does it release the child from the custody of that court or of the person, institution, or agency to whose care the child is committed, unless the juvenile court so orders. However, the appellate court may provide for a personal bond.

(g–1) An appeal from an order entered under Section 54.02 respecting transfer of the child for prosecution as an adult does not stay the criminal proceedings pending the disposition of that appeal.

(h) If the order appealed from takes custody of the child from the child's parent, guardian, or custodian or waives jurisdiction under Section 54.02 and transfers the child to criminal court for prosecution, the appeal has precedence over all other cases.

(h–1) The supreme court shall adopt rules accelerating the disposition by the appellate court and the supreme court of an appeal of an order waiving jurisdiction under Section 54.02 and transferring a child to criminal court for prosecution.

(i) The appellate court may affirm, reverse, or modify the judgment or order, including an order of disposition or modified disposition, from which appeal was taken. It may reverse or modify an order of disposition or modified order of disposition while affirming the juvenile court adjudication that the child engaged in delinquent conduct or conduct indicating a need for supervision. It may remand an order that it reverses or modifies for further proceedings by the juvenile court.

(j) Neither the child nor his family shall be identified in an appellate opinion rendered in an appeal or habeas corpus proceedings related to juvenile court proceedings under this title. The appellate opinion shall be styled, "In the matter of ..........," identifying the child by his initials only.

(k) The appellate court shall dismiss an appeal on the state's motion, supported by affidavit showing that the appellant has escaped from custody pending the appeal and, to the affiant's knowledge, has not voluntarily returned to the state's custody on or before the 10th day after the date of the escape. The court may not dismiss an appeal, or if the appeal has been dismissed, shall reinstate the appeal, on the filing of an affidavit of an officer or other credible person showing that the appellant voluntarily returned to custody on or before the 10th day after the date of the escape.

(*l*) The court may order the child, the child's parent, or other person responsible for support of the child to pay the child's costs of appeal, including the costs of representation by an attorney, unless the court determines the person to be ordered to pay the costs is indigent.

(m) For purposes of determining indigency of the child under this section, the court shall consider the assets and income of the child, the child's parent, and any other person responsible for the support of the child.

(n) A child who enters a plea or agrees to a stipulation of evidence in a proceeding held under this title may not appeal an order of the juvenile court entered under Section 54.03, 54.04, or 54.05 if the court makes a disposition in accordance with the agreement between the state and the child regarding the disposition of the case, unless:

(1) the court gives the child permission to appeal; or

(2) the appeal is based on a matter raised by written motion filed before the proceeding in which the child entered the plea or agreed to the stipulation of evidence.

(*o*) This section does not limit a child's right to obtain a writ of habeas corpus.

Acts 1973, 63rd Leg., p. 1460, ch. 544, § 1, eff. Sept. 1, 1973. Amended by Acts 1987, 70th Leg., ch. 385, § 14, eff. Sept. 1, 1987; Acts 1991, 72nd Leg., ch. 680, § 1, eff. Sept. 1, 1991; Acts 1995, 74th Leg., ch. 262, § 48, eff. Jan. 1, 1996; Acts 1997, 75th Leg., ch. 1086, § 15, eff. Sept. 1, 1997; Acts 1999, 76th Leg., ch. 74, § 2, eff. Sept. 1, 1999; Acts 1999, 76th Leg., ch. 1477, § 15, eff. Sept. 1, 1999; Acts 2001, 77th Leg., ch. 1297, § 33, eff. Sept. 1, 2001; Acts 2009, 81st Leg., ch. 87, § 25.059, eff. Sept. 1, 2009; Acts 2009, 81st Leg., ch. 642, § 2, eff. Sept. 1, 2009; Acts 2015, 84th Leg., ch. 74 (S.B. 888), § 3, eff. Sept. 1, 2015.

### § 56.02. Transcript on Appeal

(a) An attorney retained to represent a child on appeal who desires to have included in the record on appeal a transcription of notes of the reporter has the responsibility of obtaining and paying for the transcription and furnishing it to the clerk in duplicate in time for inclusion in the record.

(b) The juvenile court shall order the reporter to furnish a transcription without charge to the attorney if the court finds, after hearing or on an affidavit filed by the child's parent or other person responsible for support of the child that the parent or other responsible person is unable to pay or to give security therefor.

(c) On certificate of the court that a transcription has been provided without charge, payment therefor shall be made from the general funds of the county in which the proceedings appealed from occurred.

(d) The court reporter shall report any portion of the proceedings requested by either party or directed by the court and shall report the proceedings in question and answer form unless a narrative transcript is requested.

Acts 1973, 63rd Leg., p. 1460, ch. 544, § 1, eff. Sept. 1, 1973. Amended by Acts 1991, 72nd Leg., ch. 674, § 1, eff. Sept. 1, 1991.

### § 56.03. Appeal by State in Cases of Offenses Eligible for Determinate Sentence

(a) In this section, "prosecuting attorney" means the county attorney, district attorney, or criminal district attorney who has the primary responsibility of presenting cases in the juvenile court. The term does not include an assistant prosecuting attorney.

(b) The state is entitled to appeal an order of a court in a juvenile case in which the grand jury has approved of the petition under Section 53.045 if the order:

(1) dismisses a petition or any portion of a petition;

(2) arrests or modifies a judgment;

(3) grants a new trial;

(4) sustains a claim of former jeopardy; or

(5) grants a motion to suppress evidence, a confession, or an admission and if:

(A) jeopardy has not attached in the case;

(B) the prosecuting attorney certifies to the trial court that the appeal is not taken for the purpose of delay; and

(C) the evidence, confession, or admission is of substantial importance in the case.

(c) The prosecuting attorney may not bring an appeal under Subsection (b) later than the 15th day after the date on which the order or ruling to be appealed is entered by the court.

(d) The state is entitled to a stay in the proceedings pending the disposition of an appeal under Subsection (b).

(e) The court of appeals shall give preference in its docket to an appeal filed under Subsection (b).

(f) The state shall pay all costs of appeal under Subsection (b), other than the cost of attorney's fees for the respondent.

(g) If the respondent is represented by appointed counsel, the counsel shall continue to represent the respondent as appointed counsel on the appeal. If the respondent is not represented by appointed counsel, the respondent may seek the appointment of counsel to represent the respondent on appeal. The juvenile court shall determine whether the parent or other person responsible for support of the child is financially able to obtain an attorney to represent the respondent on appeal. If the court determines that the parent or other person is financially unable to obtain counsel for the appeal, the court shall appoint counsel to represent the respondent on appeal.

(h) If the state appeals under this section and the respondent is not detained, the court shall permit the respondent to remain at large subject only to the condition that the respondent appear in court for further proceedings when required by the court. If the respondent is detained, on the state's filing of notice of appeal under this section, the respondent is entitled to immediate release from detention on the allegation that is the subject of the appeal. The court shall permit the respondent to remain at large regarding that allegation subject only to the condition that the respondent appear in court for further proceedings when required by the court.

(i) The Texas Rules of Appellate Procedure apply to a petition by the state to the supreme court for review of a decision of a court of appeals in a juvenile case.

Added by Acts 2003, 78th Leg., ch. 283, § 25, eff. Sept. 1, 2003. Amended by Acts 2013, 83rd Leg., ch. 1299 (H.B. 2862), § 23, eff. Sept. 1, 2013.

## CHAPTER 57. RIGHTS OF VICTIMS



### § 57.001. Definitions

In this chapter:

(1) "Close relative of a deceased victim" means a person who was the spouse of a deceased victim at the time of the victim's death or who is a parent or adult brother, sister, or child of the deceased victim.

(2) "Guardian of a victim" means a person who is the legal guardian of the victim, whether or not the legal relationship between the guardian and victim exists because of the age of the victim or the physical or mental incompetency of the victim.

(3) "Victim" means a person who as the result of the delinquent conduct of a child suffers a pecuniary loss or personal injury or harm.

Added by Acts 1989, 71st Leg., ch. 633, § 1, eff. June 14, 1989. Amended by Acts 1995, 74th Leg., ch. 262, § 49, eff. Jan. 1, 1996; Acts 1997, 75th Leg., ch. 368, § 1, eff. Sept. 1, 1997.

### § 57.002. Victim's Rights

(a) A victim, guardian of a victim, or close relative of a deceased victim is entitled to the following rights within the juvenile justice system:

(1) the right to receive from law enforcement agencies adequate protection from harm and threats of harm arising from cooperation with prosecution efforts;

(2) the right to have the court or person appointed by the court take the safety of the victim or the victim's family into consideration as an element in determining whether the child should be detained before the child's conduct is adjudicated;

(3) the right, if requested, to be informed of relevant court proceedings, including appellate proceedings, and to be informed in a timely manner if those court proceedings have been canceled or rescheduled;

(4) the right to be informed, when requested, by the court or a person appointed by the court concerning the procedures in the juvenile justice system, including general procedures relating to:

(A) the preliminary investigation and deferred prosecution of a case; and

(B) the appeal of the case;

(5) the right to provide pertinent information to a juvenile court conducting a disposition hearing concerning the impact of the offense on the victim and the victim's family by testimony, written statement, or any other manner before the court renders its disposition;

(6) the right to receive information regarding compensation to victims as provided by Chapter 56B, Code of Criminal Procedure, including information related to the costs that may be compensated under that chapter and the amount of compensation, eligibility for compensation, and procedures for application for compensation under that chapter, the payment of medical expenses under Subchapter F, Chapter 56A[1], Code of Criminal Procedure, for a victim of a sexual assault, and when requested, to referral to available social service agencies that may offer additional assistance;

(7) the right to be informed, upon request, of procedures for release under supervision or transfer of the person to the custody of the Texas Department of Criminal Justice for parole, to participate in the release or transfer for parole process, to be notified, if requested, of the person's release, escape, or transfer for parole proceedings concerning the person, to provide to the Texas Juvenile Justice Department for inclusion in the person's file information to be considered by the department before the release under supervision or transfer for parole of the person, and to be notified, if requested, of the person's release or transfer for parole;

(8) the right to be provided with a waiting area, separate or secure from other witnesses, including the child alleged to have committed the conduct and relatives of the child, before testifying in any proceeding concerning the child, or, if a separate waiting area is not available, other safeguards should be taken to minimize the victim's contact with the child and the child's relatives and witnesses, before and during court proceedings;

(9) the right to prompt return of any property of the victim that is held by a law enforcement agency or the attorney for the state as evidence when the property is no longer required for that purpose;

(10) the right to have the attorney for the state notify the employer of the victim, if requested, of

the necessity of the victim's cooperation and testimony in a proceeding that may necessitate the absence of the victim from work for good cause;

(11) the right to be present at all public court proceedings related to the conduct of the child as provided by Section 54.08, subject to that section; and

(12) any other right appropriate to the victim that a victim of criminal conduct has under Subchapter B, Chapter 56A, Code of Criminal Procedure.

(b) In notifying a victim of the release or escape of a person, the Texas Juvenile Justice Department shall use the same procedure established for the notification of the release or escape of an adult offender under Subchapter K, Chapter 56A, Code of Criminal Procedure.

Added by Acts 1989, 71st Leg., ch. 633, § 1, eff. June 14, 1989. Amended by Acts 1995, 74th Leg., ch. 76, § 5.95(110), eff. Sept. 1, 1995; Acts 1995, 74th Leg., ch. 262, § 50, eff. Jan. 1, 1996; Acts 2001, 77th Leg., ch. 1034, § 8, eff. Sept. 1, 2001; Acts 2009, 81st Leg., ch. 87, § 25.060, eff. Sept. 1, 2009; Acts 2013, 83rd Leg., ch. 1345 (S.B. 1192), § 8, eff. Sept. 1, 2013; Acts 2015, 84th Leg., ch. 734 (H.B. 1549), § 56, eff. Sept. 1, 2015; Acts 2019, 86th Leg., ch. 469 (H.B. 4173), § 2.32, eff. Jan. 1, 2021.

[1] Vernon's Ann.C.C.P. art. 56A.251 et seq.

Sections 4.01 and 4.02 of Acts 2019, 86th Leg., ch. 469 (H.B. 4173) provide:

"Sec. 4.01. This Act is enacted under Section 43, Article III, Texas Constitution. This Act is intended as a codification only, and no substantive change in the law is intended by this Act.

"Sec. 4.02. (a) Chapter 311, Government Code (Code Construction Act), applies to the construction of each provision in the Code of Criminal Procedure that is enacted under Section 43, Article III, Texas Constitution (authorizing the continuing statutory revision program), in the same manner as to a code enacted under the continuing statutory revision program, except as otherwise expressly provided by the Code of Criminal Procedure.

"(b) A reference in a law to a statute or a part of a statute in the Code of Criminal Procedure enacted under Section 43, Article III, Texas Constitution (authorizing the continuing statutory revision program), is considered to be a reference to the part of that code that revises that statute or part of that statute."

## § 57.003. Duties of Juvenile Board and Victim Assistance Coordinator

(a) The juvenile board shall ensure to the extent practicable that a victim, guardian of a victim, or close relative of a deceased victim is afforded the rights granted by Section 57.002 and, on request, an explanation of those rights.

(b) The juvenile board may designate a person to serve as victim assistance coordinator in the juvenile board's jurisdiction for victims of juvenile offenders.

(c) The victim assistance coordinator shall ensure that a victim, or close relative of a deceased victim, is afforded the rights granted victims, guardians, and relatives by Section 57.002 and, on request, an explanation of those rights. The victim assistance coordinator shall work closely with appropriate law enforcement agencies, prosecuting attorneys, and the Texas Juvenile Justice Department in carrying out that duty.

(d) The victim assistance coordinator shall ensure that at a minimum, a victim, guardian of a victim, or close relative of a deceased victim receives:

(1) a written notice of the rights outlined in Section 57.002;

(2) an application for compensation under the Crime Victims' Compensation Act (Chapter 56B, Code of Criminal Procedure); and

(3) a victim impact statement with information explaining the possible use and consideration of the victim impact statement at detention, adjudication, and release proceedings involving the juvenile.

(e) The victim assistance coordinator shall, on request, offer to assist a person receiving a form under Subsection (d) to complete the form.

(f) The victim assistance coordinator shall send a copy of the victim impact statement to the court conducting a disposition hearing involving the juvenile.

(g) The juvenile board, with the approval of the commissioners court of the county, may approve a program in which the victim assistance coordinator may offer not more than 10 hours of posttrial psychological counseling for a person who serves as a juror or an alternate juror in an adjudication hearing involving graphic evidence or testimony and who requests the posttrial psychological counseling not later than the 180th day after the date on which the jury in the adjudication hearing is dismissed. The victim assistance coordinator may provide the counseling using a provider that assists local juvenile justice agencies in providing similar services to victims.

Added by Acts 1989, 71st Leg., ch. 633, § 1, eff. June 14, 1989. Amended by Acts 1995, 74th Leg., ch. 262, § 51, eff. Jan. 1, 1996; Acts 2009, 81st Leg., ch. 93, §§ 2, 3, eff. Sept. 1, 2009; Acts 2015, 84th Leg., ch. 734 (H.B. 1549), § 57, eff. Sept. 1, 2015; Acts 2019, 86th Leg., ch. 469 (H.B. 4173), § 2.33, eff. Jan. 1, 2021.

Sections 4.01 and 4.02 of Acts 2019, 86th Leg., ch. 469 (H.B. 4173) provide:

"Sec. 4.01. This Act is enacted under Section 43, Article III, Texas Constitution. This Act is intended as a codification only, and no substantive change in the law is intended by this Act.

"Sec. 4.02. (a) Chapter 311, Government Code (Code Construction Act), applies to the construction of each provision in the Code of Criminal Procedure that is enacted under Section 43, Article III,

Texas Constitution (authorizing the continuing statutory revision program), in the same manner as to a code enacted under the continuing statutory revision program, except as otherwise expressly provided by the Code of Criminal Procedure.

"(b) A reference in a law to a statute or a part of a statute in the Code of Criminal Procedure enacted under Section 43, Article III, Texas Constitution (authorizing the continuing statutory revision program), is considered to be a reference to the part of that code that revises that statute or part of that statute."

## § 57.0031. Notification of Rights of Victims of Juveniles

At the initial contact or at the earliest possible time after the initial contact between the victim of a reported crime and the juvenile probation office having the responsibility for the disposition of the juvenile, the office shall provide the victim a written notice:

(1) containing information about the availability of emergency and medical services, if applicable;

(2) stating that the victim has the right to receive information regarding compensation to victims of crime as provided by the Crime Victims' Compensation Act (Chapter 56B, Code of Criminal Procedure), including information about:

(A) the costs that may be compensated and the amount of compensation, eligibility for compensation, and procedures for application for compensation;

(B) the payment for a medical examination for a victim of a sexual assault; and

(C) referral to available social service agencies that may offer additional assistance;

(3) stating the name, address, and phone number of the victim assistance coordinator for victims of juveniles;

(4) containing the following statement: "You may call the crime victim assistance coordinator for the status of the case and information about victims' rights.";

(5) stating the rights of victims of crime under Section 57.002;

(6) summarizing each procedural stage in the processing of a juvenile case, including preliminary investigation, detention, informal adjustment of a case, disposition hearings, release proceedings, restitution, and appeals;

(7) suggesting steps the victim may take if the victim is subjected to threats or intimidation;

(8) stating the case number and assigned court for the case; and

(9) stating that the victim has the right to file a victim impact statement and to have it considered in juvenile proceedings.

Added by Acts 1995, 74th Leg., ch. 262, § 51, eff. Jan. 1, 1996. Amended by Acts 2019, 86th Leg., ch. 469 (H.B. 4173), § 2.34, eff. Jan. 1, 2021.

Sections 4.01 and 4.02 of Acts 2019, 86th Leg., ch. 469 (H.B. 4173) provide:

"Sec. 4.01. This Act is enacted under Section 43, Article III, Texas Constitution. This Act is intended as a codification only, and no substantive change in the law is intended by this Act.

"Sec. 4.02. (a) Chapter 311, Government Code (Code Construction Act), applies to the construction of each provision in the Code of Criminal Procedure that is enacted under Section 43, Article III, Texas Constitution (authorizing the continuing statutory revision program), in the same manner as to a code enacted under the continuing statutory revision program, except as otherwise expressly provided by the Code of Criminal Procedure.

"(b) A reference in a law to a statute or a part of a statute in the Code of Criminal Procedure enacted under Section 43, Article III, Texas Constitution (authorizing the continuing statutory revision program), is considered to be a reference to the part of that code that revises that statute or part of that statute."

## § 57.004. Notification

A court, a person appointed by the court, or the Texas Juvenile Justice Department is responsible for notifying a victim, guardian of a victim, or close relative of a deceased victim of a proceeding under this chapter only if the victim, guardian of a victim, or close relative of a deceased victim requests the notification in writing and provides a current address to which the notification is to be sent.

Added by Acts 1989, 71st Leg., ch. 633, § 1, eff. June 14, 1989. Amended by Acts 2015, 84th Leg., ch. 734 (H.B. 1549), § 58, eff. Sept. 1, 2015.

## § 57.005. Liability

The Texas Juvenile Justice Department, a juvenile board, a court, a person appointed by a court, an attorney for the state, a peace officer, or a law enforcement agency is not liable for a failure or inability to provide a right listed under Section 57.002.

Added by Acts 1989, 71st Leg., ch. 633, § 1, eff. June 14, 1989. Amended by Acts 2015, 84th Leg., ch. 734 (H.B. 1549), § 59, eff. Sept. 1, 2015.

## § 57.006. Appeal

The failure or inability of any person to provide a right or service listed under Section 57.002 of this code may not be used by a child as a ground for appeal or for a post conviction writ of habeas corpus.

Added by Acts 1989, 71st Leg., ch. 633, § 1, eff. June 14, 1989.

### § 57.007. Standing

A victim, guardian of a victim, or close relative of a victim does not have standing to participate as a party in a juvenile proceeding or to contest the disposition of any case.

Added by Acts 1989, 71st Leg., ch. 633, § 1, eff. June 14, 1989.

### § 57.008. Court Order for Protection From Juveniles

(a) A court may issue an order for protection from juveniles directed against a child to protect a victim of the child's conduct who, because of the victim's participation in the juvenile justice system, risks further harm by the child.

(b) In the order, the court may prohibit the child from doing specified acts or require the child to do specified acts necessary or appropriate to prevent or reduce the likelihood of further harm to the victim by the child.

Added by Acts 1995, 74th Leg., ch. 262, § 52, eff. Jan. 1, 1996.

## CHAPTER 58. RECORDS; JUVENILE JUSTICE INFORMATION SYSTEM

### SUBCHAPTER A. CREATION AND CONFIDENTIALITY OF JUVENILE RECORDS



### SUBCHAPTER B. JUVENILE JUSTICE INFORMATION SYSTEM



### SUBCHAPTER C. AUTOMATIC RESTRICTION OF ACCESS TO RECORDS [REPEALED]



### SUBCHAPTER C–1. SEALING AND DESTRUCTION OF JUVENILE RECORDS



### SUBCHAPTER D. LOCAL JUVENILE JUSTICE INFORMATION SYSTEM



### SUBCHAPTER D–1. REPORTS ON COUNTY INTERNET WEBSITES

SUBCHAPTER E. STATEWIDE JUVENILE INFORMATION AND CASE MANAGEMENT SYSTEM



## SUBCHAPTER A. CREATION AND CONFIDENTIALITY OF JUVENILE RECORDS

### § 58.001. Law Enforcement Collection and Transmittal of Records of Children

(a) Law enforcement officers and other juvenile justice personnel shall collect information described by Section 58.104 as a part of the juvenile justice information system created under Subchapter B.[1]

(b) Repealed by Acts 2017, 85th Leg., ch. 746 (S.B. 1304), § 21(1).

(c) A law enforcement agency shall forward information, including fingerprints, relating to a child who has been taken into custody under Section 52.01 by the agency to the Department of Public Safety for inclusion in the juvenile justice information system created under Subchapter B, but only if the child is referred to juvenile court on or before the 10th day after the date the child is taken into custody under Section 52.01. If the child is not referred to juvenile court within that time, the law enforcement agency shall destroy all information, including photographs and fingerprints, relating to the child unless the child is placed in a first offender program under Section 52.031 or on informal disposition under Section 52.03. The law enforcement agency may not forward any information to the Department of Public Safety relating to the child while the child is in a first offender program under Section 52.031, or during the 90 days following successful completion of the program or while the child is on informal disposition under Section 52.03. Except as provided by Subsection (f), after the date the child completes an informal disposition under Section 52.03 or after the 90th day after the date the child successfully completes a first offender program under Section 52.031, the law enforcement agency shall destroy all information, including photographs and fingerprints, relating to the child.

(d) If information relating to a child is contained in a document that also contains information relating to an adult and a law enforcement agency is required to destroy all information relating to the child under this section, the agency shall alter the document so that the information relating to the child is destroyed and the information relating to the adult is preserved.

(e) The deletion of a computer entry constitutes destruction of the information contained in the entry.

(f) A law enforcement agency may maintain information relating to a child after the 90th day after the date the child successfully completes a first offender program under Section 52.031 only to determine the child's eligibility to participate in a first offender program.

Added by Acts 1995, 74th Leg., ch. 262, § 53, eff. Jan. 1, 1996. Amended by Acts 1997, 75th Leg., ch. 1086, § 16, eff. Sept. 1, 1997; Acts 1999, 76th Leg., ch. 1477, § 16, eff. Sept. 1, 1999; Acts 2017, 85th Leg., ch. 746 (S.B. 1304), §§ 5, 21(1), eff. Sept. 1, 2017.

[1] V.T.C.A., Family Code § 58.101 et seq.

### § 58.002. Photographs and Fingerprints of Children

(a) Except as provided by Chapter 63, Code of Criminal Procedure, a child may not be photographed or fingerprinted without the consent of the juvenile court unless the child is:

(1) taken into custody; or

(2) referred to the juvenile court for conduct that constitutes a felony or a misdemeanor punishable by confinement in jail, regardless of whether the child has been taken into custody.

(b) On or before December 31 of each year, the head of each municipal or county law enforcement agency located in a county shall certify to the juvenile board for that county that the photographs and fingerprints required to be destroyed under Section 58.001 have been destroyed. The juvenile board may conduct or cause to be conducted an audit of the records of the law enforcement agency to verify the destruction of the photographs and fingerprints and the law enforcement agency shall make its records available for this purpose. If the audit shows that the certification provided by the head of the law enforcement agency is false, that person is subject to prosecution for perjury under Chapter 37, Penal Code.

(c) This section does not prohibit a law enforcement officer from photographing or fingerprinting a child who is not in custody or who has not been referred to the juvenile court for conduct that constitutes a felony or misdemeanor punishable by confinement in jail if the child's parent or guardian voluntarily consents in writing to the photographing or fingerprinting of the child. Consent of the child's parent or guardian is not required to photograph or fingerprint a child described by Subsection (a)(1) or (2).

(d) This section does not apply to fingerprints that are required or authorized to be submitted or obtained for an application for a driver's license or personal identification card.

(e) This section does not prohibit a law enforcement officer from fingerprinting or photographing a child as provided by Section 58.0021.

Added by Acts 1995, 74th Leg., ch. 262, § 53, eff. Jan. 1, 1996. Amended by Acts 1997, 75th Leg., ch. 1086, § 17, eff. Sept. 1, 1997; Acts 1999, 76th Leg., ch. 1477, § 17, eff. Sept. 1, 1999; Acts 2001, 77th Leg., ch. 1297, § 34, eff. Sept. 1, 2001; Acts 2017, 85th Leg., ch. 746 (S.B. 1304), § 6, eff. Sept. 1, 2017.

### § 58.0021. Fingerprints or Photographs for Comparison in Investigation

(a) A law enforcement officer may take temporary custody of a child to take the child's fingerprints if:

(1) the officer has probable cause to believe that the child has engaged in delinquent conduct;

(2) the officer has investigated that conduct and has found other fingerprints during the investigation; and

(3) the officer has probable cause to believe that the child's fingerprints will match the other fingerprints.

(b) A law enforcement officer may take temporary custody of a child to take the child's photograph, or may obtain a photograph of a child from a juvenile probation department in possession of a photograph of the child, if:

(1) the officer has probable cause to believe that the child has engaged in delinquent conduct; and

(2) the officer has probable cause to believe that the child's photograph will be of material assistance in the investigation of that conduct.

(c) Temporary custody for the purpose described by Subsection (a) or (b):

(1) is not a taking into custody under Section 52.01; and

(2) may not be reported to the juvenile justice information system under Subchapter B.[1]

(d) If a law enforcement officer does not take the child into custody under Section 52.01, the child shall be released from temporary custody authorized under this section as soon as the fingerprints or photographs are obtained.

(e) A law enforcement officer who under this section obtains fingerprints or photographs from a child shall:

(1) immediately destroy them if they do not lead to a positive comparison or identification; and

(2) make a reasonable effort to notify the child's parent, guardian, or custodian of the action taken.

(f) A law enforcement officer may under this section obtain fingerprints or photographs from a child at:

(1) a juvenile processing office; or

(2) a location that affords reasonable privacy to the child.

Added by Acts 2001, 77th Leg., ch. 1297, § 35, eff. Sept. 1, 2001. Amended by Acts 2017, 85th Leg., ch. 746 (S.B. 1304), § 7, eff. Sept. 1, 2017.

[1] V.T.C.A., Family Code § 58.101 et seq.

### § 58.0022. Fingerprints or Photographs to Identify Runaways

A law enforcement officer who takes a child into custody with probable cause to believe that the child has engaged in conduct indicating a need for supervision as described by Section 51.03(b)(2) and who after reasonable effort is unable to determine the identity of the child, may fingerprint or photograph the child to establish the child's identity. On determination of the child's identity or that the child cannot be identified by the fingerprints or photographs, the law enforcement officer shall immediately destroy all copies of the fingerprint records or photographs of the child.

Added by Acts 2001, 77th Leg., ch. 1297, § 36, eff. Sept. 1, 2001. Amended by Acts 2015, 84th Leg., ch. 935 (H.B. 2398), § 22, eff. Sept. 1, 2015.

### § 58.003. Repealed by Acts 2017, 85th Leg., ch. 746 (S.B. 1304), § 21(2), eff. Sept. 1, 2017

Section 13 of Acts 2019, 86th Leg., ch. 131 (H.B. 1760) provides:

"The changes in law made by this Act apply to records created before, on, or after the effective date [Sept. 1, 2019] of this Act."

### § 58.004. Redaction of Victim's Personally Identifiable Information

(a) Notwithstanding any other law, before disclosing any juvenile court record of a child as authorized by this chapter or other law, the custodian of the record must redact any personally identifiable information about a victim of the child's delinquent conduct or conduct indicating a need for supervision who was under 18 years of age on the date the conduct occurred.

(b) This section does not apply to information that is:

(1) necessary for an agency to provide services to the victim;

(2) necessary for law enforcement purposes;

(3) shared within the statewide juvenile information and case management system established under Subchapter E;

(4) shared with an attorney representing the child in a proceeding under this title; or

(5) shared with an attorney representing any other person in a juvenile or criminal court proceeding arising from the same act or conduct for which the child was referred to juvenile court.

Added by Acts 2015, 84th Leg., ch. 588 (H.B. 4003), § 1, eff. Sept. 1, 2015. Amended by Acts 2017, 85th Leg., ch. 746 (S.B. 1304), § 8, eff. Sept. 1, 2017.

## § 58.005. Confidentiality of Facility Records

(a) This section applies only to the inspection, copying, and maintenance of a record concerning a child and to the storage of information from which a record could be generated, including personally identifiable information, information obtained for the purpose of diagnosis, examination, evaluation, or treatment of the child or for making a referral for treatment of the child, and other records or information, created by or in the possession of:

(1) the Texas Juvenile Justice Department;

(2) an entity having custody of the child under a contract with the Texas Juvenile Justice Department; or

(3) another public or private agency or institution having custody of the child under order of the juvenile court, including a facility operated by or under contract with a juvenile board or juvenile probation department.

(a–1) Except as provided by Article 15.27, Code of Criminal Procedure, the records and information to which this section applies may be disclosed only to:

(1) the professional staff or consultants of the agency or institution;

(2) the judge, probation officers, and professional staff or consultants of the juvenile court;

(3) an attorney for the child;

(4) a governmental agency if the disclosure is required or authorized by law;

(5) an individual or entity to whom the child is referred for treatment or services, including assistance in transitioning the child to the community after the child's release or discharge from a juvenile facility;

(6) the Texas Department of Criminal Justice and the Texas Juvenile Justice Department for the purpose of maintaining statistical records of recidivism and for diagnosis and classification;

(7) a prosecuting attorney;

(8) a parent, guardian, or custodian with whom a child will reside after the child's release or discharge from a juvenile facility;

(9) a governmental agency or court if the record is necessary for an administrative or legal proceeding and the personally identifiable information about the child is redacted before the record is disclosed; or

(10) with permission from the juvenile court, any other individual, agency, or institution having a legitimate interest in the proceeding or in the work of the court.

(b) This section does not affect the collection, dissemination, or maintenance of information as provided by Subchapter B or D–1. [1]

(c) An individual or entity that receives confidential information under this section may not disclose the information unless otherwise authorized by law.

Added by Acts 1995, 74th Leg., ch. 262, § 53, eff. Jan. 1, 1996. Amended by Acts 2003, 78th Leg., ch. 283, § 27, eff. Sept. 1, 2003; Acts 2007, 80th Leg., ch. 908, § 26(a), eff. Sept. 1, 2007; Acts 2015, 84th Leg., ch. 734 (H.B. 1549), § 60, eff. Sept. 1, 2015; Acts 2017, 85th Leg., ch. 746 (S.B. 1304), § 9, eff. Sept. 1, 2017; Acts 2019, 86th Leg., ch. 131 (H.B. 1760), § 1, eff. Sept. 1, 2019.

[1] V.T.C.A., Family Code § 58.351 et seq.

Section 13 of Acts 2019, 86th Leg., ch. 131 (H.B. 1760) provides:

"The changes in law made by this Act apply to records created before, on, or after the effective date [Sept. 1, 2019] of this Act."

## § 58.0051. Interagency Sharing of Educational Records

(a) In this section:

(1) "Educational records" means records in the possession of a primary or secondary educational institution that contain information relating to a student, including information relating to the student's:

(A) identity;

(B) special needs;

(C) educational accommodations;

(D) assessment or diagnostic test results;

(E) attendance records;

(F) disciplinary records;

(G) medical records; and

(H) psychological diagnoses.

(2) "Juvenile service provider" means a governmental entity that provides juvenile justice or prevention, medical, educational, or other support services to a juvenile. The term includes:

(A) a state or local juvenile justice agency as defined by Section 58.101;

(B) health and human services agencies, as defined by Section 531.001, Government Code, and the Health and Human Services Commission;

(C) the Department of Family and Protective Services;

(D) the Department of Public Safety;

(E) the Texas Education Agency;

(F) an independent school district;

(G) a juvenile justice alternative education program;

(H) a charter school;

(I) a local mental health or mental retardation authority;

(J) a court with jurisdiction over juveniles;

(K) a district attorney's office;

(L) a county attorney's office; and

(M) a children's advocacy center established under Section 264.402.

(3) "Student" means a person who:

(A) is registered or in attendance at a primary or secondary educational institution; and

(B) is younger than 18 years of age.

(b) At the request of a juvenile service provider, an independent school district or a charter school shall disclose to the juvenile service provider confidential information contained in the student's educational records if the student has been:

(1) taken into custody under Section 52.01; or

(2) referred to a juvenile court for allegedly engaging in delinquent conduct or conduct indicating a need for supervision.

(c) An independent school district or charter school that discloses confidential information to a juvenile service provider under Subsection (b) may not destroy a record of the disclosed information before the seventh anniversary of the date the information is disclosed.

(d) An independent school district or charter school shall comply with a request under Subsection (b) regardless of whether other state law makes that information confidential.

(e) A juvenile service provider that receives confidential information under this section shall:

(1) certify in writing that the juvenile service provider receiving the confidential information has agreed not to disclose it to a third party, other than another juvenile service provider; and

(2) use the confidential information only to:

(A) verify the identity of a student involved in the juvenile justice system; and

(B) provide delinquency prevention or treatment services to the student.

(f) A juvenile service provider may establish an internal protocol for sharing information with other juvenile service providers as necessary to efficiently and promptly disclose and accept the information. The protocol may specify the types of information that may be shared under this section without violating federal law, including any federal funding requirements. A juvenile service provider may enter into a memorandum of understanding with another juvenile service provider to share information according to the juvenile service provider's protocols. A juvenile service provider shall comply with this section regardless of whether the juvenile service provider establishes an internal protocol or enters into a memorandum of understanding under this subsection unless compliance with this section violates federal law.

(g) This section does not affect the confidential status of the information being shared. The information may be released to a third party only as directed by a court order or as otherwise authorized by law. Personally identifiable information disclosed to a juvenile service provider under this section is not subject to disclosure to a third party under Chapter 552, Government Code.

(h) A juvenile service provider that requests information under this section shall pay a fee to the disclosing juvenile service provider in the same amounts charged for the provision of public information under Subchapter F, Chapter 552, Government Code, unless:

(1) a memorandum of understanding between the requesting provider and the disclosing provider:

(A) prohibits the payment of a fee;

(B) provides for the waiver of a fee; or

(C) provides an alternate method of assessing a fee;

(2) the disclosing provider waives the payment of the fee; or

(3) disclosure of the information is required by law other than this subchapter.

Added by Acts 1999, 76th Leg., ch. 217, § 1, eff. May 24, 1999. Amended by Acts 2007, 80th Leg., ch. 908, § 16, eff. Sept. 1, 2007; Acts 2011, 82nd Leg., ch. 653 (S.B. 1106), § 2, eff. June 17, 2011; Acts 2017, 85th Leg., ch. 316 (H.B. 5), § 1, eff. Sept. 1, 2017.

### § 58.0052. Interagency Sharing of Certain Noneducational Records

(a) In this section:

(1) "Juvenile justice agency" has the meaning assigned by Section 58.101.

(2) "Juvenile service provider" has the meaning assigned by Section 58.0051.

(3) "Multi-system youth" means a person who:

(A) is younger than 19 years of age; and

(B) has received services from two or more juvenile service providers.

(4) "Personal health information" means personally identifiable information regarding a multi-system youth's physical or mental health or the provision of or payment for health care services, including case management services, to a multi-system youth. The term does not include clinical psychological notes or substance abuse treatment information.

(b) Subject to Subsection (c), at the request of a juvenile service provider, another juvenile service provider shall disclose to that provider a multi-system youth's personal health information or a history of governmental services provided to the multi-system youth, including:

(1) identity records;

(2) medical and dental records;

(3) assessment or diagnostic test results;

(4) special needs;

(5) program placements;

(6) psychological diagnoses; and

(7) other related records or information.

(b–1) In addition to the information provided under Subsection (b), the Department of Family and Protective Services and the Texas Juvenile Justice Department shall coordinate and develop protocols for sharing with each other, on request, any other information relating to a multi-system youth necessary to:

(1) identify and coordinate the provision of services to the youth and prevent duplication of services;

(2) enhance rehabilitation of the youth; and

(3) improve and maintain community safety.

(b–2) At the request of the Department of Family and Protective Services or a single source continuum contractor who contracts with the department to provide foster care services, a state or local juvenile justice agency shall share with the department or contractor information in the possession of the juvenile justice agency that is necessary to improve and maintain community safety or that assists the department or contractor in the continuation of services for or providing services to a multi-system youth who is or has been in the custody or control of the juvenile justice agency.

(b–3) At the request of a state or local juvenile justice agency, the Department of Family and Protective Services or a single source continuum contractor who contracts with the department to provide foster care services shall, not later than the 14th business day after the date of the request, share with the juvenile justice agency information in the possession of the department or contractor that is necessary to improve and maintain community safety or that assists the agency in the continuation of services for or providing services to a multi-system youth who:

(1) is or has been in the temporary or permanent managing conservatorship of the department;

(2) is or was the subject of a family-based safety services case with the department;

(3) has been reported as an alleged victim of abuse or neglect to the department;

(4) is the perpetrator in a case in which the department investigation concluded that there was a reason to believe that abuse or neglect occurred; or

(5) is a victim in a case in which the department investigation concluded that there was a reason to believe that abuse or neglect occurred.

(c) A juvenile service provider may disclose personally identifiable information under this section only for the purposes of:

(1) identifying a multi-system youth;

(2) coordinating and monitoring care for a multi-system youth; and

(3) improving the quality of juvenile services provided to a multi-system youth.

(d) To the extent that this section conflicts with another law of this state with respect to confidential information held by a governmental agency, this section controls.

(e) A juvenile service provider may establish an internal protocol for sharing information with other juvenile service providers as necessary to efficiently and promptly disclose and accept the information. The protocol may specify the types of information that may be shared under this section without violating federal law, including any federal funding requirements. A juvenile service provider may enter into a memorandum of understanding with another juvenile service provider to share information according to the juvenile service provider's protocols. A juvenile service provider shall comply with this section regardless of whether the juvenile service provider establishes an internal protocol or enters into a memorandum of understanding under this subsection unless compliance with this section violates federal law.

(f) This section does not affect the confidential status of the information being shared. The information may be released to a third party only as directed by a court order or as otherwise authorized by law. Personally identifiable information disclosed to a juvenile service provider under this section is not subject to disclosure to a third party under Chapter 552, Government Code.

(g) This section does not affect the authority of a governmental agency to disclose to a third party for research purposes information that is not personally identifiable as provided by the governmental agency's protocol.

(h) A juvenile service provider that requests information under this section shall pay a fee to the disclosing juvenile service provider in the same amounts charged for the provision of public information under Subchapter F, Chapter 552, Government Code, unless:

(1) a memorandum of understanding between the requesting provider and the disclosing provider:

(A) prohibits the payment of a fee;

(B) provides for the waiver of a fee; or

(C) provides an alternate method of assessing a fee;

(2) the disclosing provider waives the payment of the fee; or

(3) disclosure of the information is required by law other than this subchapter.

Added by Acts 2011, 82nd Leg., ch. 653 (S.B. 1106), § 2, eff. June 17, 2011. Amended by Acts 2015, 84th Leg., ch. 944 (S.B. 206), § 5, eff. Sept. 1, 2015; Acts 2017, 85th Leg., ch. 317 (H.B. 7), § 3, eff. Sept. 1, 2017; Acts 2017, 85th Leg., ch. 746 (S.B. 1304), § 10, eff. Sept. 1, 2017; Acts 2017, 85th Leg., ch. 1021 (H.B. 1521), § 1, eff. June 15, 2017; Acts 2019, 86th Leg., ch. 131 (H.B. 1760), § 2, eff. Sept. 1, 2019.

Section 13 of Acts 2019, 86th Leg., ch. 131 (H.B. 1760) provides:

"The changes in law made by this Act apply to records created before, on, or after the effective date [Sept. 1, 2019] of this Act."

### § 58.0053. Repealed by Acts 2019, 86th Leg., ch. 131 (H.B. 1760), § 12(2), eff. Sept. 1, 2019

Section 13 of Acts 2019, 86th Leg., ch. 131 (H.B. 1760) provides:

"The changes in law made by this Act apply to records created before, on, or after the effective date [Sept. 1, 2019] of this Act."

### § 58.006. Repealed by Acts 2017, 85th Leg., ch. 746 (S.B. 1304), § 21(3), eff. Sept. 1, 2017

### § 58.007. Confidentiality of Probation Department, Prosecutor, and Court Records

(a) This section applies only to the inspection, copying, and maintenance of a record concerning a child and the storage of information, by electronic means or otherwise, concerning the child from which a record could be generated and does not affect the collection, dissemination, or maintenance of information as provided by Subchapter B or D–1.[1] This section does not apply to a record relating to a child that is:

(1) required or authorized to be maintained under the laws regulating the operation of motor vehicles in this state;

(2) maintained by a municipal or justice court; or

(3) subject to disclosure under Chapter 62, Code of Criminal Procedure.

(b) Except as provided by Section 54.051(d–1) and by Article 15.27, Code of Criminal Procedure, the records, whether physical or electronic, of a juvenile court, a clerk of court, a juvenile probation department, or a prosecuting attorney relating to a child who is a party to a proceeding under this title may be inspected or copied only by:

(1) the judge, probation officers, and professional staff or consultants of the juvenile court;

(2) a juvenile justice agency as that term is defined by Section 58.101;

(3) an attorney representing the child's parent in a proceeding under this title;

(4) an attorney representing the child;

(5) a prosecuting attorney;

(6) an individual or entity to whom the child is referred for treatment or services, including assistance in transitioning the child to the community after the child's release or discharge from a juvenile facility;

(7) a public or private agency or institution providing supervision of the child by arrangement of the juvenile court, or having custody of the child under juvenile court order; or

(8) with permission from the juvenile court, any other individual, agency, or institution having a legitimate interest in the proceeding or in the work of the court.

(b–1) A person who is the subject of the records is entitled to access the records for the purpose of preparing and presenting a motion or application to seal the records.

(c) An individual or entity that receives confidential information under this section may not disclose the information unless otherwise authorized by law.

(d) Repealed by Acts 2017, 85th Leg., ch. 746 (S.B. 1304), § 21(4).

(e) Repealed by Acts 2017, 85th Leg., ch. 746 (S.B. 1304), § 21(4).

(f) Repealed by Acts 2017, 85th Leg., ch. 746 (S.B. 1304), § 21(4).

(g) For the purpose of offering a record as evidence in the punishment phase of a criminal proceeding, a prosecuting attorney may obtain the record of a defendant's adjudication that is admissible under Section 3(a), Article 37.07, Code of Criminal Procedure, by submitting a request for the record to the juvenile court that made the adjudication. If a court receives a request from a prosecuting attorney under this subsection, the court shall, if the court possesses the requested record of adjudication, certify and provide the prosecuting attorney with a copy of the record. If a record has been sealed under this chapter, the juvenile court may not provide a copy of the record to a prosecuting attorney under this subsection.

(h) The juvenile court may disseminate to the public the following information relating to a child who is the subject of a directive to apprehend or a warrant of arrest and who cannot be located for the purpose of apprehension:

(1) the child's name, including other names by which the child is known;

(2) the child's physical description, including sex, weight, height, race, ethnicity, eye color, hair color, scars, marks, and tattoos;

(3) a photograph of the child; and

(4) a description of the conduct the child is alleged to have committed, including the level and degree of the alleged offense.

(i) In addition to the authority to release information under Subsection (b)(6), a juvenile probation department may release information contained in its records without leave of the juvenile court pursuant to guidelines adopted by the juvenile board.

(j) Repealed by Acts 2019, 86th Leg., ch. 131 (H.B. 1760), § 12(3).

Added by Acts 1995, 74th Leg., ch. 262, § 53, eff. Jan. 1, 1996. Amended by Acts 1997, 75th Leg., ch. 1086, § 19, eff. Sept. 1, 1997; Acts 1997, 75th Leg., ch. 1086, § 20, eff. Sept. 1, 1997; Acts 1999, 76th Leg., ch. 815, § 1, eff. June 18, 1999; Acts 1999, 76th Leg., ch. 1415, § 20, eff. Sept. 1, 1999; Acts 1999, 76th Leg., ch. 1477, § 18, eff. Sept. 1, 1999; Acts 2001, 77th Leg., ch. 1297, § 37, eff. Sept. 1, 2001; Acts 2007, 80th Leg., ch. 879, § 1, eff. Sept. 1, 2007; Acts 2007, 80th Leg., ch. 908, § 17, eff. Sept. 1, 2007; Acts 2009, 81st Leg., ch. 87, § 25.061, eff. Sept. 1, 2009; Acts 2013, 83rd Leg., ch. 124 (S.B. 670), § 1, eff. May 24, 2013; Acts 2013, 83rd Leg., ch. 1299 (H.B. 2862), § 28, eff. Sept. 1, 2013; Acts 2015, 84th Leg., ch. 734 (H.B. 1549), § 61, eff. Sept. 1, 2015; Acts 2017, 85th Leg., ch. 746 (S.B. 1304), §§ 11, 12, 21(4), eff. Sept. 1, 2017; Acts 2019, 86th Leg., ch. 131 (H.B. 1760), §§ 3, 12(3), eff. Sept. 1, 2019.

[1] V.T.C.A., Family Code § 58.101 et seq.

Section 13 of Acts 2019, 86th Leg., ch. 131 (H.B. 1760) provides:

"The changes in law made by this Act apply to records created before, on, or after the effective date [Sept. 1, 2019] of this Act."

### §§ 58.0071 to 58.00711. Repealed by Acts 2017, 85th Leg., ch. 746 (S.B. 1304), § 21(5), (6), eff. Sept. 1, 2017

### § 58.0072. Redesignated as V.T.C.A., Family Code § 58.009 and amended by Acts 2017, 85th Leg., ch. 746 (S.B. 1304), § 14, eff. Sept. 1, 2017

### § 58.008. Confidentiality of Law Enforcement Records

(a) This section applies only to the inspection, copying, and maintenance of a record concerning a child and to the storage of information, by electronic means or otherwise, concerning the child from which a record could be generated and does not affect the collection, dissemination, or maintenance of information as provided by Subchapter B. This section does not apply to a record relating to a child that is:

(1) required or authorized to be maintained under the laws regulating the operation of motor vehicles in this state;

(2) maintained by a municipal or justice court; or

(3) subject to disclosure under Chapter 62, Code of Criminal Procedure.

(b) Except as provided by Subsection (c), law enforcement records concerning a child and information concerning a child that are stored by electronic means or otherwise and from which a record could be generated may not be disclosed to the public and shall be:

(1) if maintained on paper or microfilm, kept separate from adult records;

(2) if maintained electronically in the same computer system as adult records, accessible only under controls that are separate and distinct from the controls to access electronic data concerning adults; and

(3) maintained on a local basis only and not sent to a central state or federal depository, except as provided by Subsection (c) or Subchapter B, D, or E.

(c) The law enforcement records of a person with a determinate sentence who is transferred to the Texas Department of Criminal Justice may be transferred to a central state or federal depository for adult records after the date of transfer and may be shared in accordance with the laws governing the adult records in the depository.

(d) Law enforcement records concerning a child may be inspected or copied by:

(1) a juvenile justice agency, as defined by Section 58.101;

(2) a criminal justice agency, as defined by Section 411.082, Government Code;

(3) the child;

(4) the child's parent or guardian; or

(5) the chief executive officer or the officer's designee of a primary or secondary school where the child is enrolled only for the purpose of conducting a threat assessment or preparing a safety plan related to the child.

(d–1) For purposes of Subsection (d), "chief executive officer" includes:

(1) the superintendent of a public school;

(2) the director of an open-enrollment charter school; and

(3) the chief executive officer of a private school.

(e) Before a child or a child's parent or guardian may inspect or copy a record concerning the child under Subsection (d), the custodian of the record shall redact:

(1) any personally identifiable information about a juvenile suspect, offender, victim, or witness who is not the child; and

(2) any information that is excepted from required disclosure under Chapter 552, Government Code, or any other law.

(f) If a child has been reported missing by a parent, guardian, or conservator of that child, information about the child may be forwarded to and disseminated by the Texas Crime Information Center and the National Crime Information Center.

Added by Acts 2017, 85th Leg., ch. 746 (S.B. 1304), § 13, eff. Sept. 1, 2017. Amended by Acts 2019, 86th Leg., ch. 131 (H.B. 1760), § 4, eff. Sept. 1, 2019; Acts 2019, 86th Leg., ch. 451 (S.B. 2135), § 3, eff. Sept. 1, 2019.

Section 13 of Acts 2019, 86th Leg., ch. 131 (H.B. 1760) provides:

"The changes in law made by this Act apply to records created before, on, or after the effective date [Sept. 1, 2019] of this Act."

### § 58.009. Dissemination of Juvenile Justice Information by the Texas Juvenile Justice Department

(a) Except as provided by this section, juvenile justice information collected and maintained by the Texas Juvenile Justice Department for statistical and research purposes is confidential information for the use of the department and may not be disseminated by the department.

(b) Juvenile justice information consists of information of the type described by Section 58.104, including statistical data in any form or medium collected, maintained, or submitted to the Texas Juvenile Justice Department under Section 221.007, Human Resources Code.

(c) The Texas Juvenile Justice Department may grant the following entities access to juvenile justice information for research and statistical purposes or for any other purpose approved by the department:

(1) criminal justice agencies as defined by Section 411.082, Government Code;

(2) the Texas Education Agency, as authorized under Section 37.084, Education Code;

(3) any agency under the authority of the Health and Human Services Commission;

(4) the Department of Family and Protective Services; or

(5) a public or private university.

(d) The Texas Juvenile Justice Department may grant the following individuals or entities access to juvenile justice information only for a purpose beneficial to and approved by the department to:

(1) an individual or entity working on a research or statistical project that:

(A) is funded in whole or in part by state or federal funds; and

(B) meets the requirements of and is approved by the department; or

(2) an individual or entity that:

(A) is working on a research or statistical project that meets the requirements of and is approved by the department; and

(B) has a specific agreement with the department that:

(i) specifically authorizes access to information;

(ii) limits the use of information to the purposes for which the information is given;

(iii) ensures the security and confidentiality of the information; and

(iv) provides for sanctions if a requirement imposed under Subparagraph (i), (ii), or (iii) is violated.

(e) The Texas Juvenile Justice Department shall grant access to juvenile justice information for legislative purposes under Section 552.008, Government Code.

(f) The Texas Juvenile Justice Department may not release juvenile justice information in identifiable form, except for information released under Subsection (c)(1), (2), (3), or (4) or under the terms of an agreement entered into under Subsection (d)(2). For purposes of this subsection, identifiable information means information that contains a juvenile offender's name or other personal identifiers or that can, by virtue of sample size or other factors, be reasonably interpreted as referring to a particular juvenile offender.

(g) Except as provided by Subsection (e), the Texas Juvenile Justice Department is permitted but not required to release or disclose juvenile justice information to any person identified under this section.

Added by Acts 2005, 79th Leg., ch. 949, § 17, eff. Sept. 1, 2005. Amended by Acts 2007, 80th Leg., ch. 908, § 18, eff. Sept. 1, 2007; Acts 2011, 82nd Leg., ch. 85 (S.B. 653), § 3.009, eff. Sept. 1, 2011; Acts 2015, 84th Leg., ch. 734 (H.B. 1549), § 62, eff. Sept. 1, 2015; Acts 2017, 85th Leg., ch. 316 (H.B. 5), § 2, eff. Sept. 1, 2017. Redesignated from V.T.C.A., Family Code § 58.0072 and amended by Acts 2017, 85th Leg., ch. 746 (S.B. 1304), § 14, eff. Sept. 1, 2017. Amended by Acts 2019, 86th Leg., ch. 131 (H.B. 1760), § 5, eff. Sept. 1, 2019.

Section 13 of Acts 2019, 86th Leg., ch. 131 (H.B. 1760) provides:

"The changes in law made by this Act apply to records created before, on, or after the effective date [Sept. 1, 2019] of this Act."

## SUBCHAPTER B. JUVENILE JUSTICE INFORMATION SYSTEM

### § 58.101. Definitions

In this subchapter:

(1) "Criminal justice agency" has the meaning assigned by Section 411.082, Government Code.

(2) "Department" means the Department of Public Safety of the State of Texas.

(3) "Disposition" means an action that results in the termination, transfer of jurisdiction, or indeterminate suspension of the prosecution of a juvenile offender.

(4) "Incident number" means a unique number assigned to a child during a specific custodial or detention period or for a specific referral to the office or official designated by the juvenile board, if the juvenile offender was not taken into custody before the referral.

(5) "Juvenile justice agency" means an agency that has custody or control over juvenile offenders.

(6) "Juvenile offender" means a child who has been assigned an incident number.

(7) "State identification number" means a unique number assigned by the department to a child in the juvenile justice information system.

(8) "Uniform incident fingerprint card" means a multiple-part form containing a unique incident number with space for information relating to the conduct for which a child has been taken into custody, detained, or referred, the child's fingerprints, and other relevant information.

Added by Acts 1995, 74th Leg., ch. 262, § 53, eff. Jan. 1, 1996. Amended by Acts 2001, 77th Leg., ch. 1297, § 39, eff. Sept. 1, 2001.

### § 58.102. Juvenile Justice Information System

(a) The department is responsible for recording data and maintaining a database for a computerized juvenile justice information system that serves:

(1) as the record creation point for the juvenile justice information system maintained by the state; and

(2) as the control terminal for entry of records, in accordance with federal law, rule, and policy, into the federal records system maintained by the Federal Bureau of Investigation.

(b) The department shall develop and maintain the system with the cooperation and advice of the:

(1) Texas Juvenile Justice Department; and

(2) juvenile courts and clerks of juvenile courts.

(c) The department may not collect, retain, or share information relating to a juvenile except as provided by this chapter.

(d) The database must contain the information required by this subchapter.

(e) The department shall designate the offense codes and has the sole responsibility for designating the state identification number for each juvenile whose name appears in the juvenile justice system.

Added by Acts 1995, 74th Leg., ch. 262, § 53, eff. Jan. 1, 1996. Amended by Acts 2015, 84th Leg., ch. 734 (H.B. 1549), § 63, eff. Sept. 1, 2015; Acts 2017, 85th Leg., ch. 746 (S.B. 1304), § 15, eff. Sept. 1, 2017.

### § 58.103. Purpose of System

The purpose of the juvenile justice information system is to:

(1) provide agencies and personnel within the juvenile justice system accurate information relating to children who come into contact with the juvenile justice system of this state;

(2) provide, where allowed by law, adult criminal justice agencies accurate and easily accessible information relating to children who come into contact with the juvenile justice system;

(3) provide an efficient conversion, where appropriate, of juvenile records to adult criminal records;

(4) improve the quality of data used to conduct impact analyses of proposed legislative changes in the juvenile justice system; and

(5) improve the ability of interested parties to analyze the functioning of the juvenile justice system.

Added by Acts 1995, 74th Leg., ch. 262, § 53, eff. Jan. 1, 1996.

### § 58.104. Types of Information Collected

(a) Subject to Subsection (f), the juvenile justice information system shall consist of information relating to delinquent conduct committed or alleged to have been committed by a juvenile offender that, if the conduct had been committed by an adult, would constitute a criminal offense other than an offense punishable by a fine only, including information relating to:

(1) the juvenile offender;

(2) the intake or referral of the juvenile offender into the juvenile justice system;

(3) the detention of the juvenile offender;

(4) the prosecution of the juvenile offender;

(5) the disposition of the juvenile offender's case, including the name and description of any program to which the juvenile offender is referred;

(6) the probation or commitment of the juvenile offender; and

(7) the termination of probation supervision or discharge from commitment of the juvenile offender.

(b) To the extent possible and subject to Subsection (a), the department shall include in the juvenile justice information system the following information for each juvenile offender taken into custody, detained, or referred under this title for delinquent conduct:

(1) the juvenile offender's name, including other names by which the juvenile offender is known;

(2) the juvenile offender's date and place of birth;

(3) the juvenile offender's physical description, including sex, weight, height, race, ethnicity, eye color, hair color, scars, marks, and tattoos;

(4) the juvenile offender's state identification number, and other identifying information, as determined by the department;

(5) the juvenile offender's fingerprints;

(6) the juvenile offender's last known residential address, including the census tract number designation for the address;

(7) the name and identifying number of the agency that took into custody or detained the juvenile offender;

(8) the date of detention or custody;

(9) the conduct for which the juvenile offender was taken into custody, detained, or referred, including level and degree of the alleged offense;

(10) the name and identifying number of the juvenile intake agency or juvenile probation office;

(11) each disposition by the juvenile intake agency or juvenile probation office;

(12) the date of disposition by the juvenile intake agency or juvenile probation office;

(13) the name and identifying number of the prosecutor's office;

(14) each disposition by the prosecutor;

(15) the date of disposition by the prosecutor;

(16) the name and identifying number of the court;

(17) each disposition by the court, including information concerning probation or custody of a juvenile offender by a juvenile justice agency;

(18) the date of disposition by the court;

(19) the date any probation supervision, including deferred prosecution supervision, was terminated;

(20) any commitment or release under supervision by the Texas Juvenile Justice Department;

(21) the date of any commitment or release under supervision by the Texas Juvenile Justice Department; and

(22) a description of each appellate proceeding.

(c) The department may designate codes relating to the information described by Subsection (b).

(d) The department shall designate a state identification number for each juvenile offender.

(e) This subchapter does not apply to a disposition that represents an administrative status notice of an agency described by Section 58.102(b).

(f) Records maintained by the department in the depository are subject to being sealed under Subchapter C–1.

Added by Acts 1995, 74th Leg., ch. 262, § 53, eff. Jan. 1, 1996. Amended by Acts 1997, 75th Leg., ch. 1086, § 21, eff. Sept. 1, 1997; Acts 2005, 79th Leg., ch. 949, § 18, eff. Sept. 1, 2005; Acts 2015, 84th Leg., ch. 734 (H.B. 1549), § 64, eff. Sept. 1, 2015; Acts 2017, 85th Leg., ch. 746 (S.B. 1304), § 16, eff. Sept. 1, 2017.

### § 58.105. Duties of Juvenile Board

Each juvenile board shall provide for:

(1) the compilation and maintenance of records and information needed for reporting information to the department under this subchapter;

(2) the transmittal to the department, in the manner provided by the department, of all records and information required by the department under this subchapter; and

(3) access by the department to inspect records and information to determine the completeness and accuracy of information reported.

Added by Acts 1995, 74th Leg., ch. 262, § 53, eff. Jan. 1, 1996.

### § 58.106. Dissemination of Confidential Information in Juvenile Justice Information System

(a) Except as otherwise provided by this section, information contained in the juvenile justice information system is confidential information for the use of the department and may not be disseminated by the department except:

(1) with the permission of the juvenile offender, to military personnel of this state or the United States;

(2) to a criminal justice agency as defined by Section 411.082, Government Code;

(3) to a noncriminal justice agency authorized by federal statute or federal executive order to receive juvenile justice record information;

(4) to a juvenile justice agency;

(5) to the Texas Juvenile Justice Department;

(6) to the office of independent ombudsman of the Texas Juvenile Justice Department;

(7) to a district, county, justice, or municipal court exercising jurisdiction over a juvenile; and

(8) to the Department of Family and Protective Services or the Health and Human Services Commission as provided by Section 411.114, Government Code.

(a–1) Repealed by Acts 2017, 85th Leg., ch. 746 (S.B. 1304), § 21(7).

(a–2) Information disseminated under Subsection (a) remains confidential after dissemination and may be disclosed by the recipient only as provided by this title.

(b) Subsection (a) does not apply to a document maintained by a juvenile justice or law enforcement agency that is the source of information collected by the department.

(c) The department may, if necessary to protect the welfare of the community, disseminate to the public the following information relating to a juvenile who has escaped from the custody of the Texas Juvenile Justice Department or from another secure detention or correctional facility:

(1) the juvenile's name, including other names by which the juvenile is known;

(2) the juvenile's physical description, including sex, weight, height, race, ethnicity, eye color, hair color, scars, marks, and tattoos;

(3) a photograph of the juvenile; and

(4) a description of the conduct for which the juvenile was committed to the Texas Juvenile Justice Department or detained in the secure detention or correctional facility, including the level and degree of the alleged offense.

(d) The department may, if necessary to protect the welfare of the community, disseminate to the public the information listed under Subsection (c) relating to a juvenile offender when notified by a law enforcement agency of this state that the law enforcement agency has been issued a directive to apprehend the offender or an arrest warrant for the offender or that the law enforcement agency is otherwise authorized to arrest the offender and that the offender is suspected of having:

(1) committed a felony offense under the following provisions of the Penal Code:

(A) Title 5;[1]

(B) Section 29.02; or

(C) Section 29.03; and

(2) fled from arrest or apprehension for commission of the offense.

Added by Acts 1995, 74th Leg., ch. 262, § 53, eff. Jan. 1, 1996. Amended by Acts 1997, 75th Leg., ch. 380, § 1, eff. Sept. 1, 1997; Acts 1999, 76th Leg., ch. 407, § 1, eff. Sept. 1, 1999; Acts 1999, 76th Leg., ch. 1477, § 19, eff. Sept. 1, 1999; Acts 2007, 80th Leg., ch. 263, § 11, eff. June 8, 2007; Acts 2011, 82nd Leg., ch. 186 (S.B. 1241), § 1, eff. Sept. 1, 2011; Acts 2011, 82nd Leg., ch. 653 (S.B. 1106), § 3, eff. June 17, 2011; Acts 2011, 82nd Leg., ch. 1098 (S.B. 1489), § 11, eff. Sept. 1, 2011; Acts 2013, 83rd Leg., ch. 161 (S.B. 1093), § 7.004, eff. Sept. 1, 2013; Acts 2015, 84th Leg., ch. 598 (S.B. 409), §§ 1, 2, eff. Sept. 1, 2015; Acts 2015, 84th Leg., ch. 734 (H.B. 1549), § 65, eff. Sept. 1, 2015; Acts 2015, 84th Leg., ch. 935 (H.B. 2398), § 24, eff. Sept. 1, 2015; Acts 2017, 85th Leg., ch. 746 (S.B. 1304), §§ 17, 21(7), eff. Sept. 1, 2017; Acts 2021, 87th Leg., ch. 423 (H.B. 4158), § 1, eff. June 8, 2021.

[1] V.T.C.A., Penal Code § 19.01 et seq.

### § 58.107. Compatibility of Data

Data supplied to the juvenile justice information system must be compatible with the system and must contain both incident numbers and state identification numbers.

Added by Acts 1995, 74th Leg., ch. 262, § 53, eff. Jan. 1, 1996.

### § 58.108. Duties of Agencies and Courts

(a) A juvenile justice agency and a clerk of a juvenile court shall:

(1) compile and maintain records needed for reporting data required by the department;

(2) transmit to the department in the manner provided by the department data required by the department;

(3) give the department or its accredited agents access to the agency or court for the purpose of inspection to determine the completeness and accuracy of data reported; and

(4) cooperate with the department to enable the department to perform its duties under this chapter.

(b) A juvenile justice agency and clerk of a court shall retain documents described by this section.

Added by Acts 1995, 74th Leg., ch. 262, § 53, eff. Jan. 1, 1996.

### § 58.109. Uniform Incident Fingerprint Card

(a) The department may provide for the use of a uniform incident fingerprint card in the maintenance of the juvenile justice information system.

(b) The department shall design, print, and distribute to each law enforcement agency and juvenile intake agency uniform incident fingerprint cards.

(c) The incident cards must:

(1) be serially numbered with an incident number in a manner that allows each incident of referral of a juvenile offender who is the subject of the incident fingerprint card to be readily ascertained; and

(2) be multiple-part forms that can be transmitted with the juvenile offender through the juvenile justice process and that allow each agency to report required data to the department.

(d) Subject to available telecommunications capacity, the department shall develop the capability to receive by electronic means from a law enforcement agency the information on the uniform incident fingerprint card. The information must be in a form that is compatible to the form required of data supplied to the juvenile justice information system.

Added by Acts 1995, 74th Leg., ch. 262, § 53, eff. Jan. 1, 1996.

### § 58.110. Reporting

(a) The department by rule shall develop reporting procedures that ensure that the juvenile offender processing data is reported from the time a juvenile offender is initially taken into custody, detained, or referred until the time a juvenile offender is released from the jurisdiction of the juvenile justice system.

(b) The law enforcement agency or the juvenile intake agency that initiates the entry of the juvenile offender into the juvenile justice information system for a specific incident shall prepare a uniform incident fingerprint card and initiate the reporting process for each incident reportable under this subchapter.

(c) The clerk of the court exercising jurisdiction over a juvenile offender's case shall report the disposition of the case to the department.

(d) In each county, the reporting agencies may make alternative arrangements for reporting the required information, including combined reporting or electronic reporting, if the alternative reporting is approved by the juvenile board and the department.

(e) Except as otherwise required by applicable state laws or regulations, information required by this chapter to be reported to the department shall be reported promptly. The information shall be reported not later than the 30th day after the date the information is received by the agency responsible for reporting the information, except that a juvenile offender's custody or detention without previous custody shall be reported to the department not later than the seventh day after the date of the custody or detention.

(f) Subject to available telecommunications capacity, the department shall develop the capability to receive by electronic means the information required under this section to be reported to the department. The information must be in a form that is compatible to the form required of data to be reported under this section.

Added by Acts 1995, 74th Leg., ch. 262, § 53, eff. Jan. 1, 1996. Amended by Acts 2007, 80th Leg., ch. 908, § 19, eff. Sept. 1, 2007; Acts 2013, 83rd Leg., ch. 1276 (H.B. 1435), § 2, eff. Sept. 1, 2013.

### § 58.111. Local Data Advisory Boards

The commissioners court of each county may create a local data advisory board to perform the same duties relating to the juvenile justice information system as the duties performed by a local data advisory board in relation to the criminal history record system under Article 66.354, Code of Criminal Procedure.

Added by Acts 1995, 74th Leg., ch. 262, § 53, eff. Jan. 1, 1996. Amended by Acts 2017, 85th Leg., ch. 1058 (H.B. 2931), § 4.05, eff. Jan. 1, 2019.

### § 58.112. Redesignated as V.T.C.A., Human Resources Code § 203.019 by Acts 2017, 85th Leg., ch. 746 (S.B. 1304), § 19, eff. Sept. 1, 2017

### § 58.113. Warrants

The department shall maintain in a computerized database that is accessible by the same entities that may access the juvenile justice information system information relating to a warrant of arrest, as that term is defined by Article 15.01, Code of Criminal Procedure, or a directive to apprehend under Section 52.015 for any child, without regard to whether the child has been taken into custody.

Added by Acts 1995, 74th Leg., ch. 262, § 53, eff. Jan. 1, 1996.

## SUBCHAPTER C. AUTOMATIC RESTRICTION OF ACCESS TO RECORDS [REPEALED]

### §§ 58.201 to 58.211. Repealed by Acts 2017, 85th Leg., ch. 746 (S.B. 1304), § 21(8), eff. Sept. 1, 2017

## SUBCHAPTER C–1. SEALING AND DESTRUCTION OF JUVENILE RECORDS

### § 58.251. Definitions

In this subchapter:

(1) "Electronic record" means an entry in a computer file or information on microfilm, microfiche, or any other electronic storage media.

(2) "Juvenile matter" means a referral to a juvenile court or juvenile probation department and all related court proceedings and outcomes, if any.

(3) "Physical record" means a paper copy of a record.

(4) "Record" means any documentation related to a juvenile matter, including information contained in that documentation.

Added by Acts 2017, 85th Leg., ch. 746 (S.B. 1304), § 18, eff. Sept. 1, 2017.

### § 58.252. Exempted Records

The following records are exempt from this subchapter:

(1) records relating to a criminal combination or criminal street gang maintained by the Department of Public Safety or a local law enforcement agency under Chapter 67, Code of Criminal Procedure;

(2) sex offender registration records maintained by the Department of Public Safety or a local law enforcement agency under Chapter 62, Code of Criminal Procedure; and

(3) records collected or maintained by the Texas Juvenile Justice Department for statistical and research purposes, including data submitted under Section 221.007, Human Resources Code, and personally identifiable information.

Added by Acts 2017, 85th Leg., ch. 746 (S.B. 1304), § 18, eff. Sept. 1, 2017. Amended by Acts 2019, 86th Leg., ch. 467 (H.B. 4170), § 7.002, eff. Sept. 1, 2019.

### § 58.253. Sealing Records Without Application: Delinquent Conduct

(a) This section does not apply to the records of a child referred to a juvenile court or juvenile probation department solely for conduct indicating a need for supervision.

(b) A person who was referred to a juvenile probation department for delinquent conduct is entitled to have all records related to the person's juvenile matters, including records relating to any matters involving conduct indicating a need for supervision, sealed without applying to the juvenile court if the person:

(1) is at least 19 years of age;

(2) has not been adjudicated as having engaged in delinquent conduct or, if adjudicated for delinquent conduct, was not adjudicated for delinquent conduct violating a penal law of the grade of felony;

(3) does not have any pending delinquent conduct matters;

(4) has not been transferred by a juvenile court to a criminal court for prosecution under Section 54.02;

(5) has not as an adult been convicted of a felony or a misdemeanor punishable by confinement in jail; and

(6) does not have any pending charges as an adult for a felony or a misdemeanor punishable by confinement in jail.

Added by Acts 2017, 85th Leg., ch. 746 (S.B. 1304), § 18, eff. Sept. 1, 2017.

### § 58.254. Certification of Eligibility for Sealing Records Without Application for Delinquent Conduct

(a) The Department of Public Safety shall certify to a juvenile probation department that has submitted records to the juvenile justice information system that the records relating to a person referred to the juvenile probation department appear to be eligible for sealing under Section 58.253.

(b) The Department of Public Safety may issue the certification described by Subsection (a) by electronic means, including by electronic mail.

(c) Except as provided by Subsection (d), not later than the 60th day after the date the juvenile probation department receives a certification under Subsection (a), the juvenile probation department shall:

(1) give notice of the receipt of the certification to the juvenile court; and

(2) provide the court with a list of all referrals received by the department relating to that person and the outcome of each referral.

(d) If a juvenile probation department has reason to believe the records of the person for whom the department received a certification under Subsection (a) are not eligible to be sealed, the juvenile probation department shall notify the Department of Public Safety not later than the 15th day after the date the juvenile probation department received the certification. If the juvenile probation department later determines that the person's records are eligible to be sealed, the juvenile probation department shall notify the juvenile court and provide the court the information described by Subsection (c) not later than the 30th day after the date of the determination.

(e) If, after receiving a certification under Subsection (a), the juvenile probation department determines that the person's records are not eligible to be sealed, the juvenile probation department and the Department of Public Safety shall update the juvenile justice information system to reflect that determination and no further action related to the records is required.

(f) Not later than the 60th day after the date a juvenile court receives notice from a juvenile probation department under Subsection (c), the juvenile court shall issue an order sealing all records relating to the person named in the certification.

Added by Acts 2017, 85th Leg., ch. 746 (S.B. 1304), § 18, eff. Sept. 1, 2017.

### § 58.255. Sealing Records Without Application: Conduct Indicating Need for Supervision

(a) A person who was referred to a juvenile court for conduct indicating a need for supervision is entitled to have all records related to all conduct indicating a need for supervision matters sealed without applying to the juvenile court if the person:

(1) has records relating to the conduct filed with the court clerk;

(2) is at least 18 years of age;

(3) has not been referred to the juvenile probation department for delinquent conduct;

(4) has not as an adult been convicted of a felony; and

(5) does not have any pending charges as an adult for a felony or a misdemeanor punishable by confinement in jail.

(b) The juvenile probation department shall:

(1) give the juvenile court notice that a person's records are eligible for sealing under Subsection (a); and

(2) provide the juvenile court with a list of all referrals relating to that person received by the department and the outcome of each referral.

(c) Not later than the 60th day after the date the juvenile court receives notice from the juvenile probation department under Subsection (b), the juvenile court shall issue an order sealing all records relating to the person named in the notice.

Added by Acts 2017, 85th Leg., ch. 746 (S.B. 1304), § 18, eff. Sept. 1, 2017. Amended by Acts 2019, 86th Leg., ch. 131 (H.B. 1760), § 6, eff. Sept. 1, 2019.

Section 13 of Acts 2019, 86th Leg., ch. 131 (H.B. 1760) provides:

"The changes in law made by this Act apply to records created before, on, or after the effective date [Sept. 1, 2019] of this Act."

### § 58.2551. Sealing Records Without Application: Finding of Not True

A juvenile court, on the court's own motion and without a hearing, shall immediately order the sealing of all records related to the alleged conduct if the court enters a finding that the allegations are not true.

Added by Acts 2019, 86th Leg., ch. 131 (H.B. 1760), § 7, eff. Sept. 1, 2019.

Section 13 of Acts 2019, 86th Leg., ch. 131 (H.B. 1760) provides:

"The changes in law made by this Act apply to records created before, on, or after the effective date [Sept. 1, 2019] of this Act."

### § 58.256. Application for Sealing Records

(a) Notwithstanding Sections 58.253 and 58.255, a person may file an application for the sealing of records related to the person in the juvenile court served by the juvenile probation department to which the person was referred. The court may not charge a fee for filing the application, regardless of the form of the application.

(a–1) An application filed under this section may be sent to the juvenile court by any reasonable method authorized under Rule 21, Texas Rules of Civil Procedure, including secure electronic means.

(b) An application filed under this section must include either the following information or the reason that one or more of the following is not included in the application:

(1) the person's:

(A) full name;

(B) sex;

(C) race or ethnicity;

(D) date of birth;

(E) driver's license or identification card number; and

(F) social security number;

(2) the conduct for which the person was referred to the juvenile probation department, including the date on which the conduct was alleged or found to have been committed;

(3) the cause number assigned to each petition relating to the person filed in juvenile court, if any, and the court in which the petition was filed; and

(4) a list of all entities the person believes have possession of records related to the person, including the applicable entities listed under Section 58.258(b).

(c) Except as provided by Subsection (d), the juvenile court may order the sealing of records related to all matters for which the person was referred to the juvenile probation department if the person:

(1) is at least 17 years of age, or is younger than 17 years of age and at least one year has elapsed after the date of final discharge in each matter for which the person was referred to the juvenile probation department;

(2) does not have any delinquent conduct matters pending with any juvenile probation department or juvenile court;

(3) was not transferred by a juvenile court to a criminal court for prosecution under Section 54.02;

(4) has not as an adult been convicted of a felony; and

(5) does not have any pending charges as an adult for a felony or a misdemeanor punishable by confinement in jail.

(d) A court may not order the sealing of the records of a person who:

(1) received a determinate sentence for engaging in:

(A) delinquent conduct that violated a penal law listed under Section 53.045; or

(B) habitual felony conduct as described by Section 51.031;

(2) is currently required to register as a sex offender under Chapter 62, Code of Criminal Procedure; or

(3) was committed to the Texas Juvenile Justice Department or to a post-adjudication secure correctional facility under Section 54.04011, unless the person has been discharged from the agency to which the person was committed.

(e) On receipt of an application under this section, the court may:

(1) order the sealing of the person's records immediately, without a hearing; or

(2) hold a hearing under Section 58.257 at the court's discretion to determine whether to order the sealing of the person's records.

Added by Acts 2017, 85th Leg., ch. 746 (S.B. 1304), § 18, eff. Sept. 1, 2017. Amended by Acts 2019, 86th Leg., ch. 131 (H.B. 1760), § 8, eff. Sept. 1, 2019; Acts 2021, 87th Leg., ch. 248 (H.B. 1401), § 1, eff. Sept. 1, 2021.

Section 13 of Acts 2019, 86th Leg., ch. 131 (H.B. 1760) provides:

"The changes in law made by this Act apply to records created before, on, or after the effective date [Sept. 1, 2019] of this Act."

## § 58.257. Hearing Regarding Sealing of Records

(a) A hearing regarding the sealing of a person's records must be held not later than the 60th day after the date the court receives the person's application under Section 58.256.

(b) The court shall give reasonable notice of a hearing under this section to:

(1) the person who is the subject of the records;

(2) the person's attorney who made the application for sealing on behalf of the person, if any;

(3) the prosecuting attorney for the juvenile court;

(4) all entities named in the application that the person believes possess eligible records related to the person; and

(5) any individual or entity whose presence at the hearing is requested by the person or prosecutor.

Added by Acts 2017, 85th Leg., ch. 746 (S.B. 1304), § 18, eff. Sept. 1, 2017.

## § 58.258. Order Sealing Records

(a) An order sealing the records of a person under this subchapter must include either the following information or the reason one or more of the following is not included in the order:

(1) the person's:

(A) full name;

(B) sex;

(C) race or ethnicity;

(D) date of birth;

(E) driver's license or identification card number; and

(F) social security number;

(2) each instance of conduct indicating a need for supervision or delinquent conduct alleged against the person or for which the person was referred to the juvenile justice system;

(3) the date on which and the county in which each instance of conduct was alleged to have occurred;

(4) if any petitions relating to the person were filed in juvenile court, the cause number assigned to each petition and the court and county in which each petition was filed; and

(5) a list of the entities believed to be in possession of the records that have been ordered sealed, including the entities listed under Subsection (b).

(b) Not later than the 60th day after the date of the entry of the order, the court shall provide a copy of the order to:

(1) the Department of Public Safety;

(2) the Texas Juvenile Justice Department, if the person was committed to the department;

(3) the clerk of court;

(4) the juvenile probation department serving the court;

(5) the prosecutor's office;

(6) each law enforcement agency that had contact with the person in relation to the conduct that is the subject of the sealing order;

(7) each public or private agency that had custody of or that provided supervision or services to the person in relation to the conduct that is the subject of the sealing order; and

(8) each official, agency, or other entity that the court has reason to believe has any record containing information that is related to the conduct that is the subject of the sealing order.

(c) On entry of the order, all adjudications relating to the person are vacated and the proceedings are dismissed and treated for all purposes as though the proceedings had never occurred. The clerk of court shall:

(1) seal all court records relating to the proceedings, including any records created in the clerk's case management system; and

(2) send copies of the order to all entities listed in the order by any reasonable method, including certified mail or secure electronic means.

Added by Acts 2017, 85th Leg., ch. 746 (S.B. 1304), § 18, eff. Sept. 1, 2017. Amended by Acts 2019, 86th Leg., ch. 131 (H.B. 1760), § 9, eff. Sept. 1, 2019; Acts 2021, 87th Leg., ch. 248 (H.B. 1401), § 2, eff. Sept. 1, 2021.

Section 13 of Acts 2019, 86th Leg., ch. 131 (H.B. 1760) provides:

"The changes in law made by this Act apply to records created before, on, or after the effective date [Sept. 1, 2019] of this Act."

## § 58.259. Actions Taken on Receipt of Order to Seal Records

(a) An entity receiving an order to seal the records of a person issued under this subchapter shall, not later than the 61st day after the date of receiving the order, take the following actions, as applicable:

(1) the Department of Public Safety shall:

(A) limit access to the records relating to the person in the juvenile justice information system to only the Texas Juvenile Justice Department for the purpose of conducting research and statistical studies;

(B) destroy any other records relating to the person in the department's possession, including DNA records as provided by Section 411.151, Government Code; and

(C) send written verification of the limitation and destruction of the records to the issuing court;

(2) the Texas Juvenile Justice Department shall:

(A) seal all records relating to the person, other than those exempted from sealing under Section 58.252; and

(B) send written verification of the sealing of the records to the issuing court;

(3) a public or private agency or institution that had custody of or provided supervision or services to the person who is the subject of the records, the juvenile probation department, a law enforcement entity, or a prosecuting attorney shall:

(A) seal all records relating to the person; and

(B) send written verification of the sealing of the records to the issuing court; and

(4) any other entity that receives an order to seal a person's records shall:

(A) send any records relating to the person to the issuing court;

(B) delete all index references to the person's records; and

(C) send written verification of the deletion of the index references to the issuing court.

(b) Physical or electronic records are considered sealed if the records are not destroyed but are stored in a manner that allows access to the records only by the custodian of records for the entity possessing the records.

(c) If an entity that received an order to seal records relating to a person later receives an inquiry about a person or the matter contained in the records, the entity must respond that no records relating to the person or the matter exist.

(d) If an entity receiving an order to seal records under this subchapter is unable to comply with the order because the information in the order is incorrect or insufficient to allow the entity to identify the records that are subject to the order, the entity shall notify the issuing court not later than the 30th day after the date of receipt of the order. The court shall take any actions necessary and possible to provide the needed information to the entity, including contacting the person who is the subject of the order or the person's attorney.

(e) If an entity receiving a sealing order under this subchapter has no records related to the person who is the subject of the order, the entity shall provide written verification of that fact to the issuing court not later than the 30th day after the date of receipt of the order.

Added by Acts 2017, 85th Leg., ch. 746 (S.B. 1304), § 18, eff. Sept. 1, 2017.

## § 58.260. Inspection and Release of Sealed Records

(a) A juvenile court may allow, by order, the inspection of records sealed under this subchapter or under Section 58.003, as that law existed before September 1, 2017, only by:

(1) a person named in the order, on the petition of the person who is the subject of the records;

(2) a prosecutor, on the petition of the prosecutor, for the purpose of reviewing the records for possible use:

(A) in a capital prosecution; or

(B) for the enhancement of punishment under Section 12.42, Penal Code; or

(3) a court, the Texas Department of Criminal Justice, or the Texas Juvenile Justice Department

for the purposes of Article 62.007(e), Code of Criminal Procedure.

(b) After a petitioner inspects records under this section, the court may order the release of any or all of the records to the petitioner on the motion of the petitioner.

Added by Acts 2017, 85th Leg., ch. 746 (S.B. 1304), § 18, eff. Sept. 1, 2017.

### § 58.261. Effect of Sealing Records

(a) A person whose records have been sealed under this subchapter or under Section 58.003, as that law existed before September 1, 2017, is not required to state in any proceeding or in any application for employment, licensing, admission, housing, or other public or private benefit that the person has been the subject of a juvenile matter.

(b) If a person's records have been sealed, the information in the records, the fact that the records once existed, or the person's denial of the existence of the records or of the person's involvement in a juvenile matter may not be used against the person in any manner, including in:

(1) a perjury prosecution or other criminal proceeding;

(2) a civil proceeding, including an administrative proceeding involving a governmental entity;

(3) an application process for licensing or certification; or

(4) an admission, employment, or housing decision.

(c) A person who is the subject of the sealed records may not waive the protected status of the records or the consequences of the protected status.

Added by Acts 2017, 85th Leg., ch. 746 (S.B. 1304), § 18, eff. Sept. 1, 2017.

### § 58.262. Information Given to Child Regarding Sealing of Records

(a) When a child is referred to the juvenile probation department, an employee of the juvenile probation department shall give the child and the child's parent, guardian, or custodian a written explanation describing the process of sealing records under this subchapter and a copy of this subchapter.

(b) On the final discharge of a child, or on the last official action in the matter if there is no adjudication, a probation officer or official at the Texas Juvenile Justice Department, as appropriate, shall give the child and the child's parent, guardian, or custodian a written explanation regarding the eligibility of the child's records for sealing under this subchapter and a copy of this subchapter.

(c) The written explanation provided to a child under Subsections (a) and (b) must include the requirements for a record to be eligible for sealing, including an explanation of the records that are exempt from sealing under Section 58.252, and the following information:

(1) that, regardless of whether the child's conduct was adjudicated, the child has a juvenile record with the Department of Public Safety and the Federal Bureau of Investigation;

(2) the child's juvenile record is a permanent record unless the record is sealed under this subchapter;

(3) except as provided by Section 58.260, the child's juvenile record, other than treatment records made confidential by law, may be accessed by a police officer, sheriff, prosecutor, probation officer, correctional officer, or other criminal or juvenile justice official unless the record is sealed as provided by this subchapter;

(4) sealing of the child's records under Section 58.253 or Section 58.255, as applicable, does not require any action by the child or the child's family, including the filing of an application or hiring of a lawyer, but occurs automatically at age 18 or 19 as applicable based on the child's referral and adjudication history;

(5) the child's juvenile record may be eligible for an earlier sealing date under Section 58.256, but an earlier sealing requires the child or an attorney for the child to file an application with the court;

(6) the impact of sealing records on the child; and

(7) the circumstances under which a sealed record may be reopened.

(d) The Texas Juvenile Justice Department shall adopt rules to implement this section and to facilitate the effective explanation of the information required to be communicated by this section.

Added by Acts 2017, 85th Leg., ch. 746 (S.B. 1304), § 18, eff. Sept. 1, 2017.

### § 58.263. Destruction of Records: No Probable Cause

The court shall order the destruction of the records relating to the conduct for which a child is taken into custody or referred to juvenile court without being taken into custody, including records contained in the juvenile justice information system, if:

(1) a determination is made under Section 53.01 that no probable cause exists to believe the child engaged in the conduct and the case is not referred to a prosecutor for review under Section 53.012; or

(2) a determination that no probable cause exists to believe the child engaged in the conduct is made by a prosecutor under Section 53.012.

Added by Acts 2017, 85th Leg., ch. 746 (S.B. 1304), § 18, eff. Sept. 1, 2017. Amended by Acts 2019, 86th Leg., ch. 131 (H.B. 1760), § 10, eff. Sept. 1, 2019.

Section 13 of Acts 2019, 86th Leg., ch. 131 (H.B. 1760) provides:

"The changes in law made by this Act apply to records created before, on, or after the effective date [Sept. 1, 2019] of this Act."

### § 58.264. Permissible Destruction of Records

(a) Subject to Subsections (b) and (c) of this section, Section 202.001, Local Government Code, and any other restrictions imposed by an entity's records retention guidelines, the following persons may authorize the destruction of records in a closed juvenile matter, regardless of the date the records were created:

(1) a juvenile board, in relation to the records in the possession of the juvenile probation department;

(2) the head of a law enforcement agency, in relation to the records in the possession of the agency; and

(3) a prosecuting attorney, in relation to the records in the possession of the prosecuting attorney's office.

(b) The records related to a person referred to a juvenile probation department may be destroyed if the person:

(1) is at least 18 years of age, and:

(A) the most serious conduct for which the person was referred was conduct indicating a need for supervision, whether or not the person was adjudicated; or

(B) the referral or information did not relate to conduct indicating a need for supervision or delinquent conduct and the juvenile probation department, prosecutor, or juvenile court did not take action on the referral or information for that reason;

(2) is at least 21 years of age, and:

(A) the most serious conduct for which the person was adjudicated was delinquent conduct that violated a penal law of the grade of misdemeanor; or

(B) the most serious conduct for which the person was referred was delinquent conduct and the person was not adjudicated as having engaged in the conduct; or

(3) is at least 31 years of age and the most serious conduct for which the person was adjudicated was delinquent conduct that violated a penal law of the grade of felony.

(c) If a record contains information relating to more than one person referred to a juvenile probation department, the record may only be destroyed if:

(1) the destruction of the record is authorized under this section; and

(2) information in the record that may be destroyed under this section can be separated from information that is not authorized to be destroyed.

(d) Electronic records are considered to be destroyed if the electronic records, including the index to the records, are deleted.

(e) Converting physical records to electronic records and subsequently destroying the physical records while maintaining the electronic records is not considered destruction of a record under this subchapter.

(f) This section does not authorize the destruction of the records of the juvenile court or clerk of court.

(g) This section does not authorize the destruction of records maintained for statistical and research purposes by the Texas Juvenile Justice Department in a juvenile information and case management system authorized under Section 58.403.

(h) This section does not affect the destruction of physical records and files authorized by the Texas State Library Records Retention Schedule.

Added by Acts 2017, 85th Leg., ch. 746 (S.B. 1304), § 18, eff. Sept. 1, 2017.

### § 58.265. Juvenile Records Not Subject to Expunction

Records to which this chapter applies are not subject to an order of expunction issued by any court.

Added by Acts 2017, 85th Leg., ch. 746 (S.B. 1304), § 18, eff. Sept. 1, 2017.

## SUBCHAPTER D. LOCAL JUVENILE JUSTICE INFORMATION SYSTEM

### § 58.301. Definitions

In this subchapter:

(1) "County juvenile board" means a juvenile board created under Chapter 152, Human Resources Code.

(2) "Juvenile facility" means a facility that:

(A) serves juveniles under a juvenile court's jurisdiction; and

(B) is operated as a holdover facility, a preadjudication detention facility, a nonsecure facility, or a post-adjudication secure correctional facility.

(2–a) "Governmental juvenile facility" means a juvenile facility operated by a unit of government.

(3) "Governmental service provider" means a juvenile justice service provider operated by a unit of government.

(4) "Local juvenile justice information system" means a county or multicounty computerized database of information concerning children, with data entry and access by the partner agencies that are members of the system.

(5) "Partner agency" means a service provider or juvenile facility that is authorized by this subchapter to be a member of a local juvenile justice information system or that has applied to be a member of a local juvenile justice information system and has been approved by the county juvenile board or regional juvenile board committee as a member of the system.

(6) "Regional juvenile board committee" means a committee that is composed of two members from each county juvenile board in a region that comprises a multicounty local juvenile information system.

Added by Acts 2001, 77th Leg., ch. 1297, § 41, eff. Sept. 1, 2001. Amended by Acts 2005, 79th Leg., ch. 949, § 23, eff. Sept. 1, 2005; Acts 2017, 85th Leg., ch. 1093 (H.B. 3705), § 1, eff. Sept. 1, 2017.

### § 58.302. Purposes of System

The purposes of a local juvenile justice information system are to:

(1) provide accurate information at the county or regional level relating to children who come into contact with the juvenile justice system;

(2) assist in the development and delivery of services to children in the juvenile justice system;

(3) assist in the development and delivery of services to children:

(A) who school officials have reasonable cause to believe have committed an offense for which a report is required under Section 37.015, Education Code; or

(B) who have been expelled, the expulsion of which school officials are required to report under Section 52.041;

(4) provide for an efficient transmission of juvenile records from justice and municipal courts to county juvenile probation departments and the juvenile court and from county juvenile probation departments and juvenile court to the state juvenile justice information system created by Subchapter B;

(5) provide efficient computerized case management resources to juvenile courts, prosecutors, court clerks, county juvenile probation departments, and partner agencies authorized by this subchapter;

(6) provide a directory of services available to children to the partner agencies to facilitate the delivery of services to children;

(7) provide an efficient means for municipal and justice courts to report filing of charges, adjudications, and dispositions of juveniles to the juvenile court as required by Section 51.08; and

(8) provide a method for agencies to fulfill their duties under Section 58.108, including the electronic transmission of information required to be sent to the Department of Public Safety by Section 58.110(f).

Added by Acts 2001, 77th Leg., ch. 1297, § 41, eff. Sept. 1, 2001. Amended by Acts 2007, 80th Leg., ch. 908, § 20, eff. Sept. 1, 2007.

### § 58.303. Local Juvenile Justice Information System

(a) Juvenile justice agencies in a county or region of this state may jointly create and maintain a local juvenile justice information system to aid in processing the cases of children under this code, to facilitate the delivery of services to children in the juvenile justice system, and to aid in the early identification of at-risk and delinquent children.

(b) A local juvenile justice information system may contain the following components:

(1) case management resources for juvenile courts, court clerks, prosecuting attorneys, and county juvenile probation departments;

(2) reporting systems to fulfill statutory requirements for reporting in the juvenile justice system;

(3) service provider directories and indexes of agencies providing services to children;

(4) victim-witness notices required under Chapter 57;

(5) electronic filing of complaints or petitions, court orders, and other documents filed with the court, including documents containing electronic signatures;

(6) electronic offense and intake processing;

(7) case docket management and calendaring;

(8) communications by email or other electronic communications between partner agencies;

(9) reporting of charges filed, adjudications and dispositions of juveniles by municipal and justice courts and the juvenile court, and transfers of cases to the juvenile court as authorized or required by Section 51.08;

(10) reporting to schools under Article 15.27, Code of Criminal Procedure, by law enforcement agencies, prosecuting attorneys, and juvenile courts;

(11) records of adjudications and dispositions, including probation conditions ordered by the juvenile court;

(12) warrant management and confirmation capabilities; and

(13) case management for juveniles in juvenile facilities.

(c) Blank.

(d) Repealed by Acts 2017, 85th Leg., ch. 1093 (H.B. 3705), § 7(1).

Added by Acts 2001, 77th Leg., ch. 1297, § 41, eff. Sept. 1, 2001. Amended by Acts 2005, 79th Leg., ch. 949, § 24, eff. Sept. 1, 2005; Acts 2007, 80th Leg., ch. 908, § 21, eff. Sept. 1, 2007; Acts 2017, 85th Leg., ch. 1093 (H.B. 3705), §§ 2, 7(1), eff. Sept. 1, 2017.

### § 58.304. Types of Information Contained in a Local Juvenile Information System

(a) A local juvenile justice information system must consist of:

(1) information relating to all referrals to the juvenile court of any type, including referrals for conduct indicating a need for supervision and delinquent conduct; and

(2) information relating to:

(A) the juvenile;

(B) the intake or referral of the juvenile into the juvenile justice system for any offense or conduct;

(C) the detention of the juvenile;

(D) the prosecution of the juvenile;

(E) the disposition of the juvenile's case, including the name and description of any program to which the juvenile is referred; and

(F) the probation, placement, or commitment of the juvenile.

(b) To the extent possible and subject to Subsection (a), the local juvenile justice information system may include the following information for each juvenile taken into custody, detained, or referred under this title:

(1) the juvenile's name, including other names by which the juvenile is known;

(2) the juvenile's date and place of birth;

(3) the juvenile's physical description, including sex, weight, height, race, ethnicity, eye color, hair color, scars, marks, and tattoos;

(4) the juvenile's state identification number and other identifying information;

(5) the juvenile's fingerprints and photograph;

(6) the juvenile's last known residential address, including the census tract number designation for the address;

(7) the name, address, and phone number of the juvenile's parent, guardian, or custodian;

(8) the name and identifying number of the agency that took into custody or detained the juvenile;

(9) each date of custody or detention;

(10) a detailed description of the conduct for which the juvenile was taken into custody, detained, or referred, including the level and degree of the alleged offense;

(11) the name and identifying number of the juvenile intake agency or juvenile probation office;

(12) each disposition by the juvenile intake agency or juvenile probation office;

(13) the date of disposition by the juvenile intake agency or juvenile probation office;

(14) the name and identifying number of the prosecutor's office;

(15) each disposition by the prosecutor;

(16) the date of disposition by the prosecutor;

(17) the name and identifying number of the court;

(18) each disposition by the court, including information concerning custody of a juvenile by a juvenile justice agency or county juvenile probation department;

(19) the date of disposition by the court;

(20) any commitment or release under supervision by the Texas Juvenile Justice Department, including the date of the commitment or release;

(21) information concerning each appellate proceeding;

(22) electronic copies of all documents filed with the court; and

(23) information obtained for the purpose of diagnosis, examination, evaluation, treatment, or referral for treatment of a child by a public or private agency or institution providing supervision of a child by arrangement of the juvenile court or having custody of the child under order of the juvenile court.

(c) If the Department of Public Safety assigns a state identification number for the juvenile, the identification number shall be entered in the local juvenile information system.

(d) Repealed by Acts 2017, 85th Leg., ch. 1093 (H.B. 3705), § 7(2).

Added by Acts 2001, 77th Leg., ch. 1297, § 41, eff. Sept. 1, 2001. Amended by Acts 2007, 80th Leg., ch. 908, § 22, eff. Sept. 1, 2007; Acts 2015, 84th Leg., ch. 734 (H.B. 1549), § 67, eff. Sept. 1, 2015; Acts 2017, 85th Leg., ch. 1093 (H.B. 3705), §§ 3, 7(2), eff. Sept. 1, 2017.

### § 58.305. Partner Agencies

(a) A local juvenile justice information system shall to the extent possible include the following partner agencies within that county:

(1) the juvenile court and court clerk;

(2) justice of the peace and municipal courts;

(3) the county juvenile probation department;

(4) the prosecuting attorneys who prosecute juvenile cases in juvenile court, municipal court, or justice court;

(5) law enforcement agencies;

(6) each public school district in the county;

(7) service providers approved by the county juvenile board; and

(8) juvenile facilities approved by the county juvenile board.

(b) A local juvenile justice information system for a multicounty region shall to the extent possible include the partner agencies listed in Subsections (a)(1)–(6) for each county in the region and the following partner agencies from within the multicounty region that have applied for membership in the system and have been approved by the regional juvenile board committee:

(1) service providers; and

(2) juvenile facilities.

Added by Acts 2001, 77th Leg., ch. 1297, § 41, eff. Sept. 1, 2001. Amended by Acts 2005, 79th Leg., ch. 949, § 25, eff. Sept. 1, 2005; Acts 2007, 80th Leg., ch. 908, § 23, eff. Sept. 1, 2007; Acts 2017, 85th Leg., ch. 1093 (H.B. 3705), § 4, eff. Sept. 1, 2017.

### § 58.306. Access to Information; Levels

(a) This section describes the level of access to information to which each partner agency in a local juvenile justice information system is entitled.

(b) Information is at Access Level 1 if the information relates to a child:

(1) who:

(A) a school official has reasonable grounds to believe has committed an offense for which a report is required under Section 37.015, Education Code; or

(B) has been expelled, the expulsion of which is required to be reported under Section 52.041; and

(2) who has not been charged with a fineable only offense, a status offense, or delinquent conduct.

(c) Information is at Access Level 2 if the information relates to a child who:

(1) is alleged in a justice or municipal court to have committed a fineable only offense, municipal ordinance violation, or status offense; and

(2) has not been charged with delinquent conduct or conduct indicating a need for supervision.

(d) Information is at Access Level 3 if the information relates to a child who is alleged to have engaged in delinquent conduct or conduct indicating a need for supervision.

(e) Except as provided by Subsection (i), Level 1 Access is by public school districts in the county or region served by the local juvenile justice information system.

(f) Except as provided by Subsection (i), Level 2 Access is by:

(1) justice of the peace courts that process juvenile cases; and

(2) municipal courts that process juvenile cases.

(g) Except as provided by Subsection (i), Level 3 Access is by:

(1) the juvenile court and court clerk;

(2) the prosecuting attorney;

(3) the county juvenile probation department;

(4) law enforcement agencies;

(5) governmental service providers that are partner agencies;

(6) governmental juvenile facilities that are partner agencies; and

(7) a private juvenile facility that is a partner agency, except the access is limited to information that relates to a child detained or placed in the custody of the facility.

(h) Access for Level 1 agencies is only to information at Level 1. Access for Level 2 agencies is only to information at Levels 1 and 2. Access for Level 3 agencies is to information at Levels 1, 2, and 3.

(i) Information described by Section 58.304(b)(23) may be accessed only by:

(1) the juvenile court and court clerk;

(2) the county juvenile probation department;

(3) a governmental juvenile facility that is a partner agency; and

(4) a private juvenile facility that is a partner agency, except the access is limited to information that relates to a child detained or placed in the custody of the facility.

Added by Acts 2001, 77th Leg., ch. 1297, § 41, eff. Sept. 1, 2001. Amended by Acts 2007, 80th Leg., ch. 908, § 24, eff. Sept. 1, 2007; Acts 2017, 85th Leg., ch. 1093 (H.B. 3705), § 5, eff. Sept. 1, 2017.

### § 58.307. Confidentiality of Information

(a) Information that is part of a local juvenile justice information system is not public information and may not be released to the public, except as authorized by law.

(b) Information that is part of a local juvenile justice information system is for the professional use of the partner agencies that are members of the system and may be used only by authorized employees of those agencies to discharge duties of those agencies.

(c) Information from a local juvenile justice information system may not be disclosed to persons, agencies, or organizations that are not members of the system except to the extent disclosure is authorized or mandated by this title.

(d) Information in a local juvenile justice information system is subject to destruction, sealing, or restricted access as provided by this title.

(e) Information in a local juvenile justice information system, including electronic signature systems, shall be protected from unauthorized access by a system of access security and any access to information in a local juvenile information system performed by browser software shall be at the level of at least 2048-bit encryption. A juvenile board or a regional juvenile board committee shall require all partner agencies to maintain security and restrict access in accordance with the requirements of this title.

Added by Acts 2001, 77th Leg., ch. 1297, § 41, eff. Sept. 1, 2001. Amended by Acts 2007, 80th Leg., ch. 908, § 25, eff. Sept. 1, 2007; Acts 2017, 85th Leg., ch. 1093 (H.B. 3705), § 6, eff. Sept. 1, 2017.

## SUBCHAPTER D–1. REPORTS ON COUNTY INTERNET WEBSITES

### § 58.351. Applicability

This subchapter applies only to a county with a population of 600,000 or more.

Added by Acts 2007, 80th Leg., ch. 908, § 26(b), eff. Sept. 1, 2007.

### § 58.352. Information Posted on County Website

(a) A juvenile court judge in a county to which this subchapter applies shall post a report on the Internet website of the county in which the court is located. The report must include:

(1) the total number of children committed by the judge to:

(A) a correctional facility operated by the Texas Juvenile Justice Department; or

(B) a post-adjudication secure correctional facility as that term is defined by Section 54.04011; and

(2) for each child committed to a facility described by Subdivision (1):

(A) a general description of the offense committed by the child or the conduct of the child that led to the child's commitment to the facility;

(B) the year the child was committed to the facility; and

(C) the age range, race, and gender of the child.

(b) Not later than the 10th day following the first day of each quarter, a juvenile court judge shall update the information posted on a county Internet website under Subsection (a).

Added by Acts 2007, 80th Leg., ch. 908, § 26(b), eff. Sept. 1, 2007. Amended by Acts 2015, 84th Leg., ch. 734 (H.B. 1549), § 68, eff. Sept. 1, 2015; Acts 2015, 84th Leg., ch. 854 (S.B. 1149), § 4, eff. Sept. 1, 2015.

### § 58.353. Confidentiality

A record posted on a county Internet website under this subchapter may not include any information that personally identifies a child.

Added by Acts 2007, 80th Leg., ch. 908, § 26(b), eff. Sept. 1, 2007.

## SUBCHAPTER E. STATEWIDE JUVENILE INFORMATION AND CASE MANAGEMENT SYSTEM

### § 58.401. Definitions

In this subchapter:

(1) "Department" means the Texas Juvenile Justice Department.

(2) "Criminal justice agency" has the meaning assigned by Section 411.082, Government Code.

(3) "Juvenile justice agency" means an agency that has custody or control over juvenile offenders.

(4) "Partner agencies" means those agencies described in Section 58.305 as well as private service providers to the juvenile justice system.

(5) "System" means an automated statewide juvenile information and case management system.

Added by Acts 2007, 80th Leg., ch. 908, § 27, eff. Sept. 1, 2007. Amended by Acts 2015, 84th Leg., ch. 734 (H.B. 1549), § 69, eff. Sept. 1, 2015.

### § 58.402. Purposes of System

The purposes of the system are to:

(1) provide accurate information at the statewide level relating to children who come into contact with the juvenile justice system;

(2) facilitate communication and information sharing between authorized entities in criminal and juvenile justice agencies and partner agencies regarding effective and efficient identification of and service delivery to juvenile offenders; and

(3) provide comprehensive juvenile justice information and case management abilities that will meet the common data collection, reporting, and management needs of juvenile probation departments in this state and provide the flexibility to accommodate individualized requirements.

Added by Acts 2007, 80th Leg., ch. 908, § 27, eff. Sept. 1, 2007.

### § 58.403. Juvenile Information System

(a) Through the adoption of an interlocal contract under Chapter 791, Government Code, with one or more counties, the department may participate in and assist counties in the creation, operation, and maintenance of a system that is intended for statewide use to:

(1) aid in processing the cases of children under this title;

(2) facilitate the delivery of services to children in the juvenile justice system;

(3) aid in the early identification of at-risk and delinquent children; and

(4) facilitate cross-jurisdictional sharing of information related to juvenile offenders between authorized criminal and juvenile justice agencies and partner agencies.

(b) The department may use funds appropriated for the implementation of this section to pay costs incurred under an interlocal contract described by Subsection (a), including license fees, maintenance and operations costs, administrative costs, and any other costs specified in the interlocal contract.

(c) The department may provide training services to counties on the use and operation of a system created, operated, or maintained by one or more counties under Subsection (a).

(d) Subchapter L, Chapter 2054, Government Code, does not apply to the statewide juvenile information and case management system created under this subchapter.

Added by Acts 2007, 80th Leg., ch. 908, § 27, eff. Sept. 1, 2007. Amended by Acts 2009, 81st Leg., ch. 1337, § 1, eff. Sept. 1, 2009; Acts 2011, 82nd Leg., ch. 85 (S.B. 653), § 2.002, eff. Sept. 1, 2011; Acts 2015, 84th Leg., ch. 734 (H.B. 1549), § 70, eff. Sept. 1, 2015.

### § 58.404. Information Collected by Department

The department may collect and maintain all information related to juvenile offenders and all offenses committed by a juvenile offender, including all information collected and maintained under Subchapters B and D.[1]

Added by Acts 2007, 80th Leg., ch. 908, § 27, eff. Sept. 1, 2007. Amended by Acts 2015, 84th Leg., ch. 734 (H.B. 1549), § 71, eff. Sept. 1, 2015.

[1] V.T.C.A., Family Code §§ 58.101 et seq. and 58.301 et seq.

### § 58.405. Authority Cumulative

The authority granted by this subchapter is cumulative of all other authority granted by this chapter to a county, the department, or a juvenile justice agency and nothing in this subchapter limits the authority of a county, the department, or a juvenile justice agency under this chapter to create an information system or to share information related to a juvenile.

Added by Acts 2007, 80th Leg., ch. 908, § 27, eff. Sept. 1, 2007. Amended by Acts 2015, 84th Leg., ch. 734 (H.B. 1549), § 72, eff. Sept. 1, 2015.

## CHAPTER 59. PROGRESSIVE SANCTIONS MODEL



### § 59.001. Purposes

The purposes of the progressive sanctions model are to:

(1) ensure that juvenile offenders face uniform and consistent consequences and punishments that correspond to the seriousness of each offender's current offense, prior delinquent history, special treatment or training needs, and effectiveness of prior interventions;

(2) balance public protection and rehabilitation while holding juvenile offenders accountable;

(3) permit flexibility in the decisions made in relation to the juvenile offender to the extent allowed by law;

(4) consider the juvenile offender's circumstances;

(5) recognize that departure of a disposition from this model is not necessarily undesirable and in some cases is highly desirable; and

(6) improve juvenile justice planning and resource allocation by ensuring uniform and consistent reporting of disposition decisions at all levels.

Added by Acts 1995, 74th Leg., ch. 262, § 53, eff. Jan. 1, 1996. Amended by Acts 2003, 78th Leg., ch. 479, § 3, eff. Sept. 1, 2003.

### § 59.002. Sanction Level Assignment by Probation Department

(a) The probation department may assign a sanction level of one to a child referred to the probation department under Section 53.012.

(b) The probation department may assign a sanction level of two to a child for whom deferred prosecution is authorized under Section 53.03.

Added by Acts 1995, 74th Leg., ch. 262, § 53, eff. Jan. 1, 1996.

### § 59.003. Sanction Level Assignment Model

(a) Subject to Subsection (e), after a child's first commission of delinquent conduct or conduct indicating a need for supervision, the probation department or prosecuting attorney may, or the juvenile court may, in a disposition hearing under Section 54.04 or a modification hearing under Section 54.05, assign a child one of the following sanction levels according to the child's conduct:

(1) for conduct indicating a need for supervision, other than conduct described in Section 51.03(b)(3) or (4) or a Class A or B misdemeanor, the sanction level is one;

(2) for conduct indicating a need for supervision under Section 51.03(b)(3) or (4) or a Class A or B misdemeanor, other than a misdemeanor involving the use or possession of a firearm, or for delinquent conduct under Section 51.03(a)(2), the sanction level is two;

(3) for a misdemeanor involving the use or possession of a firearm or for a state jail felony or a felony of the third degree, the sanction level is three;

(4) for a felony of the second degree, the sanction level is four;

(5) for a felony of the first degree, other than a felony involving the use of a deadly weapon or causing serious bodily injury, the sanction level is five;

(6) for a felony of the first degree involving the use of a deadly weapon or causing serious bodily injury, for an aggravated controlled substance felony, or for a capital felony, the sanction level is six; or

(7) for a felony of the first degree involving the use of a deadly weapon or causing serious bodily injury, for an aggravated controlled substance felony, or for a capital felony, if the petition has been approved by a grand jury under Section 53.045, or if

a petition to transfer the child to criminal court has been filed under Section 54.02, the sanction level is seven.

(b) Subject to Subsection (e), if the child subsequently is found to have engaged in delinquent conduct in an adjudication hearing under Section 54.03 or a hearing to modify a disposition under Section 54.05 on two separate occasions and each involves a violation of a penal law of a classification that is less than the classification of the child's previous conduct, the juvenile court may assign the child a sanction level that is one level higher than the previously assigned sanction level, unless the child's previously assigned sanction level is six.

(c) Subject to Subsection (e), if the child's subsequent commission of delinquent conduct or conduct indicating a need for supervision involves a violation of a penal law of a classification that is the same as or greater than the classification of the child's previous conduct, the juvenile court may assign the child a sanction level authorized by law that is one level higher than the previously assigned sanction level.

(d) Subject to Subsection (e), if the child's previously assigned sanction level is four or five and the child's subsequent commission of delinquent conduct is of the grade of felony, the juvenile court may assign the child a sanction level that is one level higher than the previously assigned sanction level.

(e) The probation department may, in accordance with Section 54.05, request the extension of a period of probation specified under sanction levels one through five if the circumstances of the child warrant the extension.

(f) Before the court assigns the child a sanction level that involves the revocation of the child's probation and the commitment of the child to the Texas Juvenile Justice Department, the court shall hold a hearing to modify the disposition as required by Section 54.05.

Added by Acts 1995, 74th Leg., ch. 262, § 53, eff. Jan. 1, 1996. Amended by Acts 1997, 75th Leg., ch. 1015, § 19, eff. June 19, 1997; Acts 1997, 75th Leg., ch. 1086, § 22, eff. Sept. 1, 1997; Acts 1999, 76th Leg., ch. 1477, § 20, eff. Sept. 1, 1999; Acts 2001, 77th Leg., ch. 1297, § 42, eff. Sept. 1, 2001; Acts 2003, 78th Leg., ch. 479, §§ 4, 5, eff. Sept. 1, 2003; Acts 2007, 80th Leg., ch. 908, § 28, eff. Sept. 1, 2007; Acts 2015, 84th Leg., ch. 734 (H.B. 1549), § 73, eff. Sept. 1, 2015; Acts 2015, 84th Leg., ch. 935 (H.B. 2398), § 25, eff. Sept. 1, 2015.

### § 59.004. Sanction Level One

(a) For a child at sanction level one, the juvenile court or probation department may:

(1) require counseling for the child regarding the child's conduct;

(2) inform the child of the progressive sanctions that may be imposed on the child if the child continues to engage in delinquent conduct or conduct indicating a need for supervision;

(3) inform the child's parents or guardians of the parents' or guardians' responsibility to impose reasonable restrictions on the child to prevent the conduct from recurring;

(4) provide information or other assistance to the child or the child's parents or guardians in securing needed social services;

(5) require the child or the child's parents or guardians to participate in a program for services under Section 264.302, if a program under Section 264.302 is available to the child or the child's parents or guardians;

(6) refer the child to a community-based citizen intervention program approved by the juvenile court;

(7) release the child to the child's parents or guardians; and

(8) require the child to attend and successfully complete an educational program described by Section 37.218, Education Code, or another equivalent educational program.

(b) The probation department shall discharge the child from the custody of the probation department after the provisions of this section are met.

Added by Acts 1995, 74th Leg., ch. 262, § 53, eff. Jan. 1, 1996. Amended by Acts 1997, 75th Leg., ch. 1086, § 23, eff. Sept. 1, 1997; Acts 2011, 82nd Leg., ch. 1322 (S.B. 407), § 20, eff. Sept. 1, 2011.

### § 59.005. Sanction Level Two

(a) For a child at sanction level two, the juvenile court, the prosecuting attorney, or the probation department may, as provided by Section 53.03:

(1) place the child on deferred prosecution for not less than three months or more than six months;

(2) require the child to make restitution to the victim of the child's conduct or perform community service restitution appropriate to the nature and degree of harm caused and according to the child's ability;

(3) require the child's parents or guardians to identify restrictions the parents or guardians will impose on the child's activities and requirements the parents or guardians will set for the child's behavior;

(4) provide the information required under Sections 59.004(a)(2) and (4);

(5) require the child or the child's parents or guardians to participate in a program for services under Section 264.302, if a program under Section 264.302 is available to the child or the child's parents or guardians;

(6) refer the child to a community-based citizen intervention program approved by the juvenile court; and

(7) if appropriate, impose additional conditions of probation.

(b) The juvenile court or the probation department shall discharge the child from the custody of the probation department on the date the provisions of this section are met or on the child's 18th birthday, whichever is earlier.

Added by Acts 1995, 74th Leg., ch. 262, § 53, eff. Jan. 1, 1996. Amended by Acts 1997, 75th Leg., ch. 1086, § 24, eff. Sept. 1, 1997; Acts 1999, 76th Leg., ch. 1477, § 21, eff. Sept. 1, 1999.

### § 59.006. Sanction Level Three

(a) For a child at sanction level three, the juvenile court may:

(1) place the child on probation for not less than six months;

(2) require the child to make restitution to the victim of the child's conduct or perform community service restitution appropriate to the nature and degree of harm caused and according to the child's ability;

(3) impose specific restrictions on the child's activities and requirements for the child's behavior as conditions of probation;

(4) require a probation officer to closely monitor the child's activities and behavior;

(5) require the child or the child's parents or guardians to participate in programs or services designated by the court or probation officer; and

(6) if appropriate, impose additional conditions of probation.

(b) The juvenile court shall discharge the child from the custody of the probation department on the date the provisions of this section are met or on the child's 18th birthday, whichever is earlier.

Added by Acts 1995, 74th Leg., ch. 262, § 53, eff. Jan. 1, 1996. Amended by Acts 1997, 75th Leg., ch. 1086, § 25, eff. Sept. 1, 1997; Acts 2003, 78th Leg., ch. 479, § 6, eff. Sept. 1, 2003.

### § 59.007. Sanction Level Four

(a) For a child at sanction level four, the juvenile court may:

(1) require the child to participate as a condition of probation for not less than three months or more than 12 months in an intensive services probation program that emphasizes frequent contact and reporting with a probation officer, discipline, intensive supervision services, social responsibility, and productive work;

(2) after release from the program described by Subdivision (1), continue the child on probation supervision;

(3) require the child to make restitution to the victim of the child's conduct or perform community service restitution appropriate to the nature and degree of harm caused and according to the child's ability;

(4) impose highly structured restrictions on the child's activities and requirements for behavior of the child as conditions of probation;

(5) require a probation officer to closely monitor the child;

(6) require the child or the child's parents or guardians to participate in programs or services designed to address their particular needs and circumstances; and

(7) if appropriate, impose additional sanctions.

(b) The juvenile court shall discharge the child from the custody of the probation department on the date the provisions of this section are met or on the child's 18th birthday, whichever is earlier.

Added by Acts 1995, 74th Leg., ch. 262, § 53, eff. Jan. 1, 1996. Amended by Acts 1997, 75th Leg., ch. 1086, § 26, eff. Sept. 1, 1997; Acts 2001, 77th Leg., ch. 1297, § 43, eff. Sept. 1, 2001; Acts 2003, 78th Leg., ch. 479, § 7, eff. Sept. 1, 2003.

### § 59.008. Sanction Level Five

(a) For a child at sanction level five, the juvenile court may:

(1) as a condition of probation, place the child for not less than six months or more than 12 months in a post-adjudication secure correctional facility;

(2) after release from the program described by Subdivision (1), continue the child on probation supervision;

(3) require the child to make restitution to the victim of the child's conduct or perform community service restitution appropriate to the nature and

degree of harm caused and according to the child's ability;

(4) impose highly structured restrictions on the child's activities and requirements for behavior of the child as conditions of probation;

(5) require a probation officer to closely monitor the child;

(6) require the child or the child's parents or guardians to participate in programs or services designed to address their particular needs and circumstances; and

(7) if appropriate, impose additional sanctions.

(b) The juvenile court shall discharge the child from the custody of the probation department on the date the provisions of this section are met or on the child's 18th birthday, whichever is earlier.

Added by Acts 1995, 74th Leg., ch. 262, § 53, eff. Jan. 1, 1996. Amended by Acts 1997, 75th Leg., ch. 1086, § 27, eff. Sept. 1, 1997; Acts 2003, 78th Leg., ch. 479, § 8, eff. Sept. 1, 2003.

### § 59.009. Sanction Level Six

(a) For a child at sanction level six, the juvenile court may commit the child to the custody of the Texas Juvenile Justice Department or a post-adjudication secure correctional facility under Section 54.04011(c)(1). The department, juvenile board, or local juvenile probation department, as applicable, may:

(1) require the child to participate in a highly structured residential program that emphasizes discipline, accountability, fitness, training, and productive work for not less than nine months or more than 24 months unless the department, board, or probation department extends the period and the reason for an extension is documented;

(2) require the child to make restitution to the victim of the child's conduct or perform community service restitution appropriate to the nature and degree of the harm caused and according to the child's ability, if there is a victim of the child's conduct;

(3) require the child and the child's parents or guardians to participate in programs and services for their particular needs and circumstances; and

(4) if appropriate, impose additional sanctions.

(b) On release of the child under supervision, the Texas Juvenile Justice Department parole programs or the juvenile board or local juvenile probation department operating parole programs under Section 152.0016(c)(2), Human Resources Code, may:

(1) impose highly structured restrictions on the child's activities and requirements for behavior of the child as conditions of release under supervision;

(2) require a parole officer to closely monitor the child for not less than six months; and

(3) if appropriate, impose any other conditions of supervision.

(c) The Texas Juvenile Justice Department, juvenile board, or local juvenile probation department may discharge the child from the custody of the department, board, or probation department, as applicable, on the date the provisions of this section are met or on the child's 19th birthday, whichever is earlier.

Added by Acts 1995, 74th Leg., ch. 262, § 53, eff. Jan. 1, 1996. Amended by Acts 1997, 75th Leg., ch. 1086, § 28, eff. Sept. 1, 1997; Acts 2013, 83rd Leg., ch. 1323 (S.B. 511), § 7, eff. Dec. 1, 2013.

### § 59.010. Sanction Level Seven

(a) For a child at sanction level seven, the juvenile court may certify and transfer the child under Section 54.02 or sentence the child to commitment to the Texas Juvenile Justice Department under Section 54.04(d)(3), 54.04(m), or 54.05(f) or to a post-adjudication secure correctional facility under Section 54.04011(c)(2). The department, juvenile board, or local juvenile probation department, as applicable, may:

(1) require the child to participate in a highly structured residential program that emphasizes discipline, accountability, fitness, training, and productive work for not less than 12 months or more than 10 years unless the department, board, or probation department extends the period and the reason for the extension is documented;

(2) require the child to make restitution to the victim of the child's conduct or perform community service restitution appropriate to the nature and degree of harm caused and according to the child's ability, if there is a victim of the child's conduct;

(3) require the child and the child's parents or guardians to participate in programs and services for their particular needs and circumstances; and

(4) impose any other appropriate sanction.

(b) On release of the child under supervision, the Texas Juvenile Justice Department parole programs or the juvenile board or local juvenile probation department parole programs under Section 152.0016(c)(2), Human Resources Code, may:

(1) impose highly structured restrictions on the child's activities and requirements for behavior of the child as conditions of release under supervision;

(2) require a parole officer to monitor the child closely for not less than 12 months; and

(3) impose any other appropriate condition of supervision.

Added by Acts 1995, 74th Leg., ch. 262, § 53, eff. Jan. 1, 1996. Amended by Acts 1997, 75th Leg., ch. 1086, § 29, eff. Sept. 1, 1997; Acts 2013, 83rd Leg., ch. 1323 (S.B. 511), § 8, eff. Dec. 1, 2013.

### § 59.011. Duty of Juvenile Board

A juvenile board shall require the juvenile probation department to report progressive sanction data electronically to the Texas Juvenile Justice Department in the format and time frames specified by the Texas Juvenile Justice Department.

Added by Acts 1995, 74th Leg., ch. 262, § 53, eff. Jan. 1, 1996. Amended by Acts 2001, 77th Leg., ch. 1297, § 44, eff. Sept. 1, 2001; Acts 2015, 84th Leg., ch. 734 (H.B. 1549), § 74, eff. Sept. 1, 2015.

### § 59.012. Repealed by Acts 2013, 83rd Leg., ch. 1312 (S.B. 59), § 99(9), eff. Sept. 1, 2013

### § 59.013. Liability

The Texas Juvenile Justice Department, a juvenile board, a court, a person appointed by a court, an attorney for the state, a peace officer, or a law enforcement agency is not liable for a failure or inability to provide a service listed under Sections 59.004–59.010.

Added by Acts 1995, 74th Leg., ch. 262, § 53, eff. Jan. 1, 1996. Amended by Acts 2015, 84th Leg., ch. 734 (H.B. 1549), § 75, eff. Sept. 1, 2015.

### § 59.014. Appeal

A child may not bring an appeal or a postconviction writ of habeas corpus based on:

(1) the failure or inability of any person to provide a service listed under Sections 59.004–59.010;

(2) the failure of a court or of any person to make a sanction level assignment as provided in Section 59.002 or 59.003;

(3) a departure from the sanction level assignment model provided by this chapter; or

(4) the failure of a juvenile court or probation department to report a departure from the model.

Added by Acts 1995, 74th Leg., ch. 262, § 53, eff. Jan. 1, 1996. Amended by Acts 1999, 76th Leg., ch. 1011, § 1, eff. Sept. 1, 1999; Acts 1999, 76th Leg., ch. 1477, § 22, eff. Sept. 1, 1999; Acts 2003, 78th Leg., ch. 479, § 10, eff. Sept. 1, 2003.

### § 59.015. Waiver of Sanctions on Parents or Guardians

On a finding by the juvenile court or probation department that a child's parents or guardians have made a reasonable good faith effort to prevent the child from engaging in delinquent conduct or engaging in conduct indicating a need for supervision and that, despite the parents' or guardians' efforts, the child continues to engage in such conduct, the court or probation department shall waive any sanction that may be imposed on the parents or guardians at any sanction level.

Added by Acts 1995, 74th Leg., ch. 262, § 53, eff. Jan. 1, 1996.

## CHAPTER 60. UNIFORM INTERSTATE COMPACT ON JUVENILES

Section



### § 60.001. Definitions

In this chapter:

(1) "Commission" means the Interstate Commission for Juveniles.

(2) "Compact" means the Interstate Compact for Juveniles.

(3) "Compact administrator" has the meaning assigned by Article II of the compact.

Added by Acts 1995, 74th Leg., ch. 262, § 53, eff. Jan. 1, 1996. Amended by Acts 2005, 79th Leg., ch. 1007, § 2.01, eff. Aug. 26, 2008.

### §§ 60.002 to 60.004. Repealed by Acts 2005, 79th Leg., ch. 1007, § 3.02, eff. Aug. 26, 2008

### § 60.005. Juvenile Compact Administrator

Under the compact, the governor may designate an officer as the compact administrator. The administrator, acting jointly with like officers of other party states, shall adopt regulations to carry out more effectively the terms of the compact. The compact administrator serves at the pleasure of the governor. The compact administrator shall cooperate with all departments, agencies, and officers of and in the government of this state and its subdivisions in facilitating the proper administration of the compact or of a supplementary agreement entered into by this state.

Added by Acts 1995, 74th Leg., ch. 262, § 53, eff. Jan. 1, 1996.

### § 60.006. Supplementary Agreements

A compact administrator may make supplementary agreements with appropriate officials of other states pursuant to the compact. If a supplementary agreement requires or contemplates the use of an institution or facility of this state or requires or contemplates the provision of a service of this state, the supplementary agreement has no force or effect until approved by the head of the department or agency under whose jurisdiction the institution is operated, or whose department or agency is charged with performing the service.

Added by Acts 1995, 74th Leg., ch. 262, § 53, eff. Jan. 1, 1996.

### § 60.007. Financial Arrangements

The compact administrator may make or arrange for the payments necessary to discharge the financial obligations imposed upon this state by the compact or by a supplementary agreement made under the compact, subject to legislative appropriations.

Added by Acts 1995, 74th Leg., ch. 262, § 53, eff. Jan. 1, 1996.

### § 60.008. Enforcement

The courts, departments, agencies, and officers of this state and its subdivisions shall enforce this compact and shall do all things appropriate to effectuate its purposes and intent which are within their respective jurisdictions.

Added by Acts 1995, 74th Leg., ch. 262, § 53, eff. Jan. 1, 1996.

### § 60.009. Additional Procedures Not Precluded

In addition to any procedures developed under the compact for the return of a runaway juvenile, the particular states, the juvenile, or his parents, the courts, or other legal custodian involved may agree upon and adopt any plan or procedure legally authorized under the laws of this state and the other respective party states for the return of the runaway juvenile.

Added by Acts 1995, 74th Leg., ch. 262, § 53, eff. Jan. 1, 1996. Amended by Acts 2005, 79th Leg., ch. 1007, § 2.01, eff. Aug. 26, 2008.

### § 60.010. Interstate Compact for Juveniles

ARTICLE I
PURPOSE

The compacting states to this Interstate Compact recognize that each state is responsible for the proper supervision or return of juveniles, delinquents, and status offenders who are on probation or parole and who have absconded, escaped, or run away from supervision and control and in so doing have endangered their own safety and the safety of others. The compacting states also recognize that each state is responsible for the safe return of juveniles who have run away from home and in doing so have left their state of residence. The compacting states also recognize that congress, by enacting the Crime Control Act, 4 U.S.C. Section 112 (1965), has authorized and encouraged compacts for cooperative efforts and mutual assistance in the prevention of crime.

It is the purpose of this compact, through means of joint and cooperative action among the compacting states to: (A) ensure that the juveniles who are moved under this compact to another state for probation or parole supervision and services are governed in the receiving state by the same standards that apply to juveniles receiving such supervision and services in the receiving state; (B) ensure that the public safety interests of the citizens, including the victims of juvenile offenders, in both the sending and receiving states are adequately protected and balanced with the juvenile's and the juvenile's family's best interests and welfare when an interstate movement is under consideration; (C) return juveniles who have run away, absconded, or escaped from supervision or control or have been accused of an offense to the state requesting their return through a fair and prompt judicial review process that ensures that the requisition is in order and that the transport is properly supervised; (D) make provisions for contracts between member states for the cooperative institutionalization in public facilities in member states for delinquent youth needing special services; (E) provide for the effective tracking of juveniles who move interstate under the compact's provisions; (F) equitably allocate the costs, benefits, and obligations of the compacting states; (G) establish procedures to manage the movement between states of juvenile offenders released to the community under the jurisdiction of courts, juvenile departments, or any other criminal or juvenile justice agency which has jurisdiction over juvenile offenders, ensuring that a receiving state accepts supervision of a juvenile when the juvenile's parent or other person having legal custody resides or is undertaking residence there; (H) ensure immediate notice to jurisdictions where defined offenders are authorized to travel or to relocate across state lines; (I) establish a system of uniform data collection on information pertaining to juveniles who move interstate under this compact that prevents public disclosure of identity and individual treatment information but allows access by authorized juvenile justice and criminal justice officials and regular reporting of compact activities to heads of state executive, judicial, and legislative branches and juvenile and criminal justice administrators; (J) monitor compliance with rules governing interstate movement of juveniles and initiate interventions to address and correct noncompliance; (K) coordinate training and education regarding the regulation of interstate movement of juveniles for officials involved in such activity; and (L) coordinate the implementation and operation of the compact with the Interstate Compact for the Placement of Children, the Interstate Compact for Adult Offender Supervision and other compacts affecting juveniles particularly in those cases where concurrent or overlapping supervision issues arise. It is the policy of the compacting states that the activities conducted by the Interstate Commission created herein are the formation of public policies and therefore are public business. Furthermore, the compacting states shall cooperate and observe their individual and collective duties and responsibilities for the prompt return and acceptance of juveniles subject to the provisions of this compact. The provisions of this compact shall be reasonably and liberally construed to accomplish the purposes and policies of the compact.

ARTICLE II
DEFINITIONS

As used in this compact, unless the context clearly requires a different construction:

A. "Bylaws" means those bylaws established by the Interstate Commission for its governance or for directing or controlling the Interstate Commission's actions or conduct.

B. "Compact administrator" means the individual in each compacting state appointed pursuant to the terms of this compact responsible for the administration and management of the state's supervision and transfer of juveniles subject to the terms of this compact and to the rules adopted by the Interstate Commission under this compact.

C. "Compacting state" means any state which has enacted the enabling legislation for this compact.

D. "Commissioner" means the voting representative of each compacting state appointed pursuant to Article III of this compact.

E. "Court" means any court having jurisdiction over delinquent, neglected, or dependent children.

F. "Deputy compact administrator" means the individual, if any, in each compacting state appointed to act on behalf of a compact administrator pursuant to the terms of this compact, responsible for the administration and management of the state's supervision and transfer of juveniles subject to the terms of this compact and to the rules adopted by the Interstate Commission under this compact.

G. "Interstate Commission" means the Interstate Commission for Juveniles created by Article III of this compact.

H. "Juvenile" means any person defined as a juvenile in any member state or by the rules of the Interstate Commission, including:

(1) Accused Delinquent—a person charged with an offense that, if committed by an adult, would be a criminal offense;

(2) Adjudicated Delinquent—a person found to have committed an offense that, if committed by an adult, would be a criminal offense;

(3) Accused Status Offender—a person charged with an offense that would not be a criminal offense if committed by an adult;

(4) Adjudicated Status Offender—a person found to have committed an offense that would not be a criminal offense if committed by an adult; and

(5) Nonoffender—a person in need of supervision who has not been accused or adjudicated a status offender or delinquent.

I. "Noncompacting state" means any state which has not enacted the enabling legislation for this compact.

J. "Probation or parole" means any kind of supervision or conditional release of juveniles authorized under the laws of the compacting states.

K. "Rule" means a written statement by the Interstate Commission promulgated pursuant to Article VI of this compact that is of general applicability, implements, interprets, or prescribes a policy or provision of the compact, or an organizational, procedural, or practice requirement of the Interstate Commission, and has the force and effect of statutory law in a compacting state, and includes the amendment, repeal, or suspension of an existing rule.

L. "State" means a state of the United States, the District of Columbia (or its designee), the Commonwealth of Puerto Rico, the U.S. Virgin Islands, Guam, American Samoa, and the Northern Marianas Islands.

### ARTICLE III
### INTERSTATE COMMISSION FOR JUVENILES

A. The compacting states hereby create the Interstate Commission for Juveniles. The Interstate Commission shall be a body corporate and joint agency of the compacting states. The commission shall have all the responsibilities, powers, and duties set forth herein, and such additional powers as may be conferred upon it by subsequent action of the respective legislatures of the compacting states in accordance with the terms of this compact.

B. The Interstate Commission shall consist of commissioners appointed by the appropriate appointing authority in each state pursuant to the rules and requirements of each compacting state. The commissioner shall be the compact administrator, deputy compact administrator, or designee from that state who shall serve on the Interstate Commission in such capacity under or pursuant to the applicable law of the compacting state.

C. In addition to the commissioners who are the voting representatives of each state, the Interstate Commission shall include individuals who are not commissioners, but who are members of interested organizations. Such noncommissioner members must include a member of the national organizations of governors, legislators, state chief justices, attorneys general, Interstate Compact for Adult Offender Supervision, Interstate Compact for the Placement of Children, juvenile justice and juvenile corrections officials, and crime victims. All noncommissioner members of the Interstate Commission shall be ex officio (nonvoting) members. The Interstate Commission may provide in its bylaws for such additional ex officio (nonvoting) members, including members of other national organizations, in such numbers as shall be determined by the commission.

D. Each compacting state represented at any meeting of the Interstate Commission is entitled to one vote. A majority of the compacting states shall constitute a quorum for the transaction of business, unless a larger quorum is required by the bylaws of the Interstate Commission.

E. The Interstate Commission shall meet at least once each calendar year. The chairperson may call additional meetings and, upon the request of a simple majority of the compacting states, shall call additional meetings. Public notice shall be given of all meetings and meetings shall be open to the public.

F. The Interstate Commission shall establish an executive committee, which shall include commission officers, members, and others as determined by the bylaws. The executive committee shall have the power to act on behalf of the Interstate Commission during periods when the Interstate Commission is not in session, with the exception of rulemaking or amendment to the compact. The executive committee shall oversee the day-to-day activities of the administration of the compact managed by an executive director and Interstate Commission staff; administers enforcement and compliance with the provisions of the compact, its bylaws and rules, and performs such other duties as directed by the Interstate Commission or set forth in the bylaws.

G. Each member of the Interstate Commission shall have the right and power to cast a vote to which that compacting state is entitled and to participate in the business and affairs of the Interstate Commission. A member shall vote in person and shall not delegate a vote to another compacting state. However, a commissioner shall appoint another authorized representative, in the absence of the commissioner from that state, to cast a vote on behalf of the compacting state at a specified meeting. The bylaws may provide for members' participation in meetings by telephone or other means of telecommunication or electronic communication.

H. The Interstate Commission's bylaws shall establish conditions and procedures under which the Interstate Commission shall make its information and official records available to the public for inspection or copying. The Interstate Commission may exempt from disclosure any information or official records to the extent they would adversely affect personal privacy rights or proprietary interests.

I. Public notice shall be given of all meetings and all meetings shall be open to the public, except as set forth in the rules or as otherwise provided in the compact. The Interstate Commission and any of its committees may close a meeting to the public when it determines by two-thirds vote that an open meeting would be likely to:

1. Relate solely to the Interstate Commission's internal personnel practices and procedures;

2. Disclose matters specifically exempted from disclosure by statute;

3. Disclose trade secrets or commercial or financial information which is privileged or confidential;

4. Involve accusing any person of a crime or formally censuring any person;

5. Disclose information of a personal nature where disclosure would constitute a clearly unwarranted invasion of personal privacy;

6. Disclose investigative records compiled for law enforcement purposes;

7. Disclose information contained in or related to examination, operating or condition reports prepared by, or on behalf of or for the use of, the Interstate Commission with respect to a regulated person or entity for the purpose of regulation or supervision of such person or entity;

8. Disclose information, the premature disclosure of which would significantly endanger the stability of a regulated person or entity; or

9. Specifically relate to the Interstate Commission's issuance of a subpoena, or its participation in a civil action or other legal proceeding.

J. For every meeting closed pursuant to this provision, the Interstate Commission's legal counsel shall publicly certify that, in the legal counsel's opinion, the meeting may be closed to the public, and shall reference each relevant exemptive provision. The Interstate Commission shall keep minutes which shall fully and clearly describe all matters discussed in any meeting and shall provide a full and accurate summary of any actions taken, and the reasons therefore, including a description of each of the views expressed on any item and the record of any roll call vote (reflected in the vote of each member on the question). All documents considered in connection with any action shall be identified in such minutes.

K. The Interstate Commission shall collect standardized data concerning the interstate movement of juveniles as directed through its rules which shall specify the data to be collected, the means of collection and data exchange, and reporting requirements. Such methods of data collection, exchange, and reporting shall insofar as is reasonably possible conform to up-to-date technology and coordinate the Interstate Commission's information functions with the appropriate repository of records.

## ARTICLE IV
## POWERS AND DUTIES OF THE INTERSTATE COMMISSION

The commission shall have the following powers and duties:

1. To provide for dispute resolution among compacting states.

2. To promulgate rules to effect the purposes and obligations as enumerated in this compact, which shall have the force and effect of statutory law and shall be binding in the compacting states to the extent and in the manner provided in this compact.

3. To oversee, supervise, and coordinate the interstate movement of juveniles subject to the terms of this compact and any bylaws adopted and rules promulgated by the Interstate Commission.

4. To enforce compliance with the compact provisions, the rules promulgated by the Interstate Commission, and the bylaws, using all necessary and proper means, including but not limited to the use of judicial process.

5. To establish and maintain offices which shall be located within one or more of the compacting states.

6. To purchase and maintain insurance and bonds.

7. To borrow, accept, hire, or contract for services of personnel.

8. To establish and appoint committees and hire staff which it deems necessary for the carrying out of its functions including, but not limited to, an executive committee as required by Article III of this compact, which shall have the power to act on behalf of the Interstate Commission in carrying out its powers and duties hereunder.

9. To elect or appoint officers, attorneys, employees, agents, or consultants, and to fix their compensation, define their duties, and determine their qualifications, and to establish the Interstate Commission's personnel policies and programs relating to, inter alia, conflicts of interest, rates of compensation, and qualifications of personnel.

10. To accept any and all donations and grants of money, equipment, supplies, materials, and services, and to receive, utilize, and dispose of same.

11. To lease, purchase, accept contributions or donations of, or otherwise to own, hold, improve, or use any property, whether real, personal, or mixed.

12. To sell, convey, mortgage, pledge, lease, exchange, abandon, or otherwise dispose of any property, whether real, personal, or mixed.

13. To establish a budget and make expenditures and levy dues as provided in Article VIII of this compact.

14. To sue and be sued.

15. To adopt a seal and bylaws governing the management and operation of the Interstate Commission.

16. To perform such functions as may be necessary or appropriate to achieve the purposes of this compact.

17. To report annually to the legislatures, governors, and judiciary of the compacting states concerning the activities of the Interstate Commission during the preceding year. Such reports shall also include any recommendations that may have been adopted by the Interstate Commission.

18. To coordinate education, training, and public awareness regarding the interstate movement of juveniles for officials involved in such activity.

19. To establish uniform standards of the reporting, collecting, and exchanging of data.

20. The Interstate Commission shall maintain its corporate books and records in accordance with the bylaws.

ARTICLE V
ORGANIZATION AND OPERATION OF THE INTERSTATE COMMISSION

Sec. A. Bylaws

1. The Interstate Commission shall, by a majority of the members present and voting, within 12 months of the first Interstate Commission meeting, adopt bylaws to govern its conduct as may be necessary or appropriate to carry out the purposes of the compact, including, but not limited to:

a. Establishing the fiscal year of the Interstate Commission;

b. Establishing an executive committee and such other committees as may be necessary;

c. Providing for the establishment of committees governing any general or specific delegation of any authority or function of the Interstate Commission;

d. Providing reasonable procedures for calling and conducting meetings of the Interstate Commission and ensuring reasonable notice of each such meeting;

e. Establishing the titles and responsibilities of the officers of the Interstate Commission;

f. Providing a mechanism for concluding the operations of the Interstate Commission and the return of any surplus funds that may exist upon the termination of the compact after the payment or reserving of all of its debts and obligations;

g. Providing start-up rules for initial administration of the compact; and

h. Establishing standards and procedures for compliance and technical assistance in carrying out the compact.

Sec. B. Officers and Staff

1. The Interstate Commission shall, by a majority of the members, elect annually from among its members a chairperson and a vice chairperson, each of whom shall have such authority and duties as may be specified in the bylaws. The chairperson or, in the chairperson's absence or disability, the vice chairperson shall preside at all meetings of the Interstate Commission. The officers so elected shall serve without compensation or remuneration from the Interstate Commission, provided that, subject to the availability of budgeted funds, the officers shall be reimbursed for any ordinary and necessary costs and expenses incurred by them in the performance of their duties and responsibilities as officers of the Interstate Commission.

2. The Interstate Commission shall, through its executive committee, appoint or retain an executive director for such period, upon such terms and conditions, and for such compensation as the Interstate Commission may deem appropriate. The executive director shall serve as secretary to the Interstate Commission, but shall not be a member and shall hire and supervise such other staff as may be authorized by the Interstate Commission.

Sec. C. Qualified Immunity, Defense, and Indemnification

1. The Interstate Commission's executive director and employees shall be immune from suit and liability, either personally or in their official capacity, for any claim for damage to or loss of property or personal injury or other civil liability caused or arising out of or relating to any actual or alleged act, error, or omission that occurred, or that such person had a reasonable basis for believing occurred, within the scope of Interstate Commission employment, duties, or responsibilities, provided that any such person shall not be protected from suit or liability for any damage, loss, injury, or liability caused by the intentional or wilful and wanton misconduct of any such person.

2. The liability of any commissioner, or the employee or agent of a commissioner, acting within the scope of such person's employment or duties for acts, errors, or omissions occurring within such person's state may not exceed the limits of liability

set forth under the constitution and laws of that state for state officials, employees, and agents. Nothing in this subsection shall be construed to protect any such person from suit or liability for any damage, loss, injury, or liability caused by the intentional or wilful and wanton misconduct of any such person.

3. The Interstate Commission shall defend the executive director or the employees or representatives of the Interstate Commission and, subject to the approval of the attorney general of the state represented by any commissioner of a compacting state, shall defend such commissioner or the commissioner's representatives or employees in any civil action seeking to impose liability arising out of any actual or alleged act, error, or omission that occurred within the scope of Interstate Commission employment, duties, or responsibilities, or that the defendant had a reasonable basis for believing occurred within the scope of Interstate Commission employment, duties, or responsibilities, provided that the actual or alleged act, error, or omission did not result from intentional or wilful and wanton misconduct on the part of such person.

4. The Interstate Commission shall indemnify and hold the commissioner of a compacting state, or the commissioner's representatives or employees, or the Interstate Commission's representatives or employees, harmless in the amount of any settlement or judgment obtained against such persons arising out of any actual or alleged act, error, or omission that occurred within the scope of Interstate Commission employment, duties, or responsibilities, or that such persons had a reasonable basis for believing occurred within the scope of Interstate Commission employment, duties, or responsibilities, provided that the actual or alleged act, error, or omission did not result from intentional or wilful and wanton misconduct on the part of such persons.

## ARTICLE VI

## RULEMAKING FUNCTIONS OF THE INTERSTATE COMMISSION

A. The Interstate Commission shall promulgate and publish rules in order to effectively and efficiently achieve the purposes of the compact.

B. Rulemaking shall occur pursuant to the criteria set forth in this article and the bylaws and rules adopted pursuant thereto. Such rulemaking shall substantially conform to the principles of the "Model State Administrative Procedures Act," 1981 Act, Uniform Laws Annotated, Vol. 15, p.1 (2000), or such other administrative procedures act, as the Interstate Commission deems appropriate consistent with due process requirements under the United States Constitution as now or hereafter interpreted by the United States Supreme Court. All rules and amendments shall become binding as of the date specified, as published with the final version of the rule as approved by the Interstate Commission.

C. When promulgating a rule, the Interstate Commission shall, at a minimum:

1. Publish the proposed rule's entire text stating the reason or reasons for that proposed rule;

2. Allow and invite persons to submit written data, facts, opinions, and arguments, which information shall be added to the record and be made publicly available;

3. Provide an opportunity for an informal hearing, if petitioned by 10 or more persons; and

4. Promulgate a final rule and its effective date, if appropriate, based on input from state or local officials, or interested parties.

D. Allow, not later than 60 days after a rule is promulgated, any interested person to file a petition in the United States District Court for the District of Columbia or in the federal district court where the Interstate Commission's principal office is located for judicial review of the rule. If the court finds that the Interstate Commission's action is not supported by substantial evidence in the rulemaking record, the court shall hold the rule unlawful and set it aside. For purposes of this subsection, evidence is substantial if it would be considered substantial evidence under the Model State Administrative Procedures Act.

E. If a majority of the legislatures of the compacting states rejects a rule, those states may, by enactment of a statute or resolution in the same manner used to adopt the compact, cause that such rule shall have no further force and effect in any compacting state.

F. The existing rules governing the operation of the Interstate Compact on Juveniles superceded by this Act shall be null and void 12 months after the first meeting of the Interstate Commission created under this compact.

G. Upon determination by the Interstate Commission that an emergency exists, the Interstate Commission may promulgate an emergency rule which shall become effective immediately upon adoption, provided that the usual rulemaking procedures provided hereunder shall be retroactively applied to said rule as soon as reasonably possible, but no later than 90 days after the effective date of the emergency rule.

ARTICLE VII
OVERSIGHT, ENFORCEMENT, AND DISPUTE RESOLUTION BY THE INTERSTATE COMMISSION

Sec. A. Oversight

1. The Interstate Commission shall oversee the administration and operations of the interstate movement of juveniles subject to this compact in the compacting states and shall monitor such activities being administered in noncompacting states which may significantly affect compacting states.

2. The courts and executive agencies in each compacting state shall enforce this compact and shall take all actions necessary and appropriate to effectuate the compact's purposes and intent. The provisions of this compact and the rules promulgated hereunder shall be received by all the judges, public officers, commissions, and departments of the state government as evidence of the authorized statute and administrative rules. All courts shall take judicial notice of the compact and the rules. In any judicial or administrative proceeding in a compacting state pertaining to the subject matter of this compact which may affect the powers, responsibilities, or actions of the Interstate Commission, the Interstate Commission shall be entitled to receive all service of process in any such proceeding, and shall have standing to intervene in the proceeding for all purposes.

Sec. B. Dispute Resolution

1. The compacting states shall report to the Interstate Commission on all issues and activities necessary for the administration of the compact as well as issues and activities pertaining to compliance with the provisions of the compact and its bylaws and rules.

2. The Interstate Commission shall attempt, upon the request of a compacting state, to resolve any disputes or other issues which are subject to the compact and which may arise among compacting states and between compacting and noncompacting states. The Interstate Commission shall promulgate a rule providing for both mediation and binding dispute resolution for disputes among the compacting states.

3. The Interstate Commission, in the reasonable exercise of its discretion, shall enforce the provisions and rules of this compact using any or all means set forth in Article X of this compact.

ARTICLE VIII
FINANCE

A. The Interstate Commission shall pay or provide for the payment of the reasonable expenses of its establishment, organization, and ongoing activities.

B. The Interstate Commission shall levy on and collect an annual assessment from each compacting state to cover the cost of the internal operations and activities of the Interstate Commission and its staff which must be in a total amount sufficient to cover the Interstate Commission's annual budget as approved each year. The aggregate annual assessment amount shall be allocated based upon a formula to be determined by the Interstate Commission, taking into consideration the population of each compacting state and the volume of interstate movement of juveniles in each compacting state. The Interstate Commission shall promulgate a rule binding upon all compacting states that governs said assessment.

C. The Interstate Commission shall not incur any obligations of any kind prior to securing the funds adequate to meet the same, nor shall the Interstate Commission pledge the credit of any of the compacting states, except by and with the authority of the compacting state.

D. The Interstate Commission shall keep accurate accounts of all receipts and disbursements. The receipts and disbursements of the Interstate Commission shall be subject to the audit and accounting procedures established under its bylaws. However, all receipts and disbursements of funds handled by the Interstate Commission shall be audited yearly by a certified or licensed public accountant and the report of the audit shall be included in and become part of the annual report of the Interstate Commission.

ARTICLE IX
COMPACTING STATES, EFFECTIVE DATE, AND AMENDMENT

A. Any state, as defined in Article II of this compact, is eligible to become a compacting state.

B. The compact shall become effective and binding upon legislative enactment of the compact into law by no less than 35 of the states. The initial effective date shall be the later of July 1, 2004, or upon enactment into law by the 35th jurisdiction. Thereafter, the compact shall become effective and binding, as to any other compacting state, upon enactment of the compact into law by that state. The governors of noncompacting states or their designees shall be invited to participate in Interstate Commission activities on a nonvoting basis prior to adoption of the compact by all states.

C. The Interstate Commission may propose amendments to the compact for enactment by the compacting states. No amendment shall become effective and binding upon the Interstate Commission and the compacting states unless and until it is enacted into law by unanimous consent of the compacting states.

## ARTICLE X
## WITHDRAWAL, DEFAULT, TERMINATION, AND JUDICIAL ENFORCEMENT

Sec. A. Withdrawal

1. Once effective, the compact shall continue in force and remain binding upon each and every compacting state, provided that a compacting state may withdraw from the compact by specifically repealing the statute which enacted the compact into law.

2. The effective date of withdrawal is the effective date of the repeal.

3. The withdrawing state shall immediately notify the chairperson of the Interstate Commission in writing upon the introduction of legislation repealing this compact in the withdrawing state. The Interstate Commission shall notify the other compacting states of the withdrawing state's intent to withdraw within 60 days of its receipt thereof.

4. The withdrawing state is responsible for all assessments, obligations, and liabilities incurred through the effective date of withdrawal, including any obligations, the performance of which extend beyond the effective date of withdrawal.

5. Reinstatement following withdrawal of any compacting state shall occur upon the withdrawing state reenacting the compact or upon such later date as determined by the Interstate Commission.

Sec. B. Technical Assistance, Fines, Suspension, Termination, and Default

1. If the Interstate Commission determines that any compacting state has at any time defaulted in the performance of any of its obligations or responsibilities under this compact, or the bylaws or duly promulgated rules, the Interstate Commission may impose any or all of the following penalties:

a. Remedial training and technical assistance as directed by the Interstate Commission;

b. Alternative dispute resolution;

c. Fines, fees, and costs in such amounts as are deemed to be reasonable as fixed by the Interstate Commission; and

d. Suspension or termination of membership in the compact, which shall be imposed only after all other reasonable means of securing compliance under the bylaws and rules have been exhausted and the Interstate Commission has determined that the offending state is in default. Immediate notice of suspension shall be given by the Interstate Commission to the governor, the chief justice or the chief judicial officer of the state, and the majority and minority leaders of the defaulting state's legislature. The grounds for default include, but are not limited to, failure of a compacting state to perform such obligations or responsibilities imposed upon it by this compact, the bylaws or duly promulgated rules, and any other grounds designated in commission bylaws and rules. The Interstate Commission shall immediately notify the defaulting state in writing of the penalty imposed by the Interstate Commission and of the default pending a cure of the default. The Interstate Commission shall stipulate the conditions and the time period within which the defaulting state must cure its default. If the defaulting state fails to cure the default within the time period specified by the Interstate Commission, the defaulting state shall be terminated from the compact upon an affirmative vote of a majority of the compacting states and all rights, privileges, and benefits conferred by this compact shall be terminated from the effective date of termination.

2. Within 60 days of the effective date of termination of a defaulting state, the Interstate Commission shall notify the governor, the chief justice or chief judicial officer of the state, and the majority and minority leaders of the defaulting state's legislature of such termination.

3. The defaulting state is responsible for all assessments, obligations, and liabilities incurred through the effective date of termination including any obligations, the performance of which extends beyond the effective date of termination.

4. The Interstate Commission shall not bear any costs relating to the defaulting state unless otherwise mutually agreed upon in writing between the Interstate Commission and the defaulting state.

5. Reinstatement following termination of any compacting state requires both a reenactment of the compact by the defaulting state and the approval of the Interstate Commission pursuant to the rules.

Sec. C. Judicial Enforcement

The Interstate Commission may, by majority vote of the members, initiate legal action in the United States District Court for the District of Columbia or, at the discretion of the Interstate Commission, in the federal district where the Interstate Commission has its offices, to enforce compliance with the provisions of the compact, its duly promulgated rules and bylaws, against any compacting state in default. In the event judicial enforcement is necessary the prevailing party shall be awarded all costs of such litigation including reasonable attorney's fees.

Sec. D. Dissolution of Compact

1. The compact dissolves effective upon the date of the withdrawal or default of the compacting state, which reduces membership in the compact to one compacting state.

2. Upon the dissolution of this compact, the compact becomes null and void and shall be of no further force or effect, and the business and affairs of the Interstate Commission shall be concluded and any surplus funds shall be distributed in accordance with the bylaws.

ARTICLE XI
SEVERABILITY AND CONSTRUCTION

A. The provisions of this compact shall be severable, and if any phrase, clause, sentence, or provision is deemed unenforceable, the remaining provisions of the compact shall be enforceable.

B. The provisions of this compact shall be liberally construed to effectuate its purposes.

ARTICLE XII
BINDING EFFECT OF COMPACT AND OTHER LAWS

Sec. A. Other Laws

1. Nothing herein prevents the enforcement of any other law of a compacting state that is not inconsistent with this compact.

2. All compacting states' laws other than state constitutions and other interstate compacts conflicting with this compact are superseded to the extent of the conflict.

Sec. B. Binding Effect of the Compact

1. All lawful actions of the Interstate Commission, including all rules and bylaws promulgated by the Interstate Commission, are binding upon the compacting states.

2. All agreements between the Interstate Commission and the compacting states are binding in accordance with their terms.

3. Upon the request of a party to a conflict over meaning or interpretation of Interstate Commission actions, and upon a majority vote of the compacting states, the Interstate Commission may issue advisory opinions regarding such meaning or interpretation.

4. In the event any provision of this compact exceeds the constitutional limits imposed on the legislature of any compacting state, the obligations, duties, powers, or jurisdiction sought to be conferred by such provision upon the Interstate Commission shall be ineffective and such obligations, duties, powers, or jurisdiction shall remain in the compacting state and shall be exercised by the agency thereof to which such obligations, duties, powers, or jurisdiction are delegated by law in effect at the time this compact becomes effective.

Added by Acts 2005, 79th Leg., ch. 1007, § 1.01, eff. Sept. 1, 2005.

### § 60.011. Effect of Texas Laws

If the laws of this state conflict with the compact, the compact controls, except that in the event of a conflict between the compact and the Texas Constitution, as determined by the courts of this state, the Texas Constitution controls.

Added by Acts 2005, 79th Leg., ch. 1007, § 2.02, eff. Aug. 26, 2008.

### § 60.012. Liabilities for Certain Commission Agents

The compact administrator and each member, officer, executive director, employee, or agent of the commission acting within the scope of the person's employment or duties is, for the purpose of acts or omissions occurring within this state, entitled to the same protections under Chapter 104, Civil Practice and Remedies Code, as an employee, a member of the governing board, or any other officer of a state agency, institution, or department.

Added by Acts 2005, 79th Leg., ch. 1007, § 2.02, eff. Aug. 26, 2008.

## CHAPTER 61. RIGHTS AND RESPONSIBILITIES OF PARENTS AND OTHER ELIGIBLE PERSONS

SUBCHAPTER A. ENTRY OF ORDERS AGAINST PARENTS AND OTHER ELIGIBLE PERSONS

Section



SUBCHAPTER B. ENFORCEMENT OF ORDER AGAINST PARENT OR OTHER ELIGIBLE PERSON



SUBCHAPTER C. RIGHTS OF PARENTS



### SUBCHAPTER A. ENTRY OF ORDERS AGAINST PARENTS AND OTHER ELIGIBLE PERSONS

#### § 61.001. Definitions

In this chapter:

(1) "Juvenile court order" means an order by a juvenile court in a proceeding to which this chapter applies requiring a parent or other eligible person to act or refrain from acting.

(2) "Other eligible person" means the respondent's guardian, the respondent's custodian, or any other person described in a provision under this title authorizing the court order.

Added by Acts 2003, 78th Leg., ch. 283, § 28, eff. Sept. 1, 2003.

#### § 61.002. Applicability

*Text of (a) effective until January 1, 2022*

(a) Except as provided by Subsection (b), this chapter applies to a proceeding to enter a juvenile court order:

(1) for payment of probation fees under Section 54.061;

(2) for restitution under Sections 54.041(b) and 54.048;

(3) for payment of graffiti eradication fees under Section 54.0461;

(4) for community service under Section 54.044(b);

(5) for payment of costs of court under Section 54.0411 or other provisions of law;

(6) requiring the person to refrain from doing any act injurious to the welfare of the child under Section 54.041(a)(1);

(7) enjoining contact between the person and the child who is the subject of a proceeding under Section 54.041(a)(2);

(8) ordering a person living in the same household with the child to participate in counseling under Section 54.041(a)(3);

(9) requiring a parent or other eligible person to pay reasonable attorney's fees for representing the child under Section 51.10(e);

(10) requiring the parent or other eligible person to reimburse the county for payments the county has made to an attorney appointed to represent the child under Section 51.10(j);

(11) requiring payment of deferred prosecution supervision fees under Section 53.03(d);

(12) requiring a parent or other eligible person to attend a court hearing under Section 51.115;

(13) requiring a parent or other eligible person to act or refrain from acting to aid the child in complying with conditions of release from detention under Section 54.01(r);

(14) requiring a parent or other eligible person to act or refrain from acting under any law imposing an obligation of action or omission on a parent or other eligible person because of the parent's or person's relation to the child who is the subject of a proceeding under this title;

(15) for payment of fees under Section 54.0462; or

(16) for payment of the cost of attending an educational program under Section 54.0404.

*Text of (a) effective January 1, 2022*

(a) Except as provided by Subsection (b), this chapter applies to a proceeding to enter a juvenile court order:

(1) for payment of probation fees under Section 54.061;

(2) for restitution under Sections 54.041(b) and 54.048;

(3) for community service under Section 54.044(b);

(4) requiring the person to refrain from doing any act injurious to the welfare of the child under Section 54.041(a)(1);

(5) enjoining contact between the person and the child who is the subject of a proceeding under Section 54.041(a)(2);

(6) ordering a person living in the same household with the child to participate in counseling under Section 54.041(a)(3);

(7) requiring a parent or other eligible person to pay reasonable attorney's fees for representing the child under Section 51.10(e);

(8) requiring the parent or other eligible person to reimburse the county for payments the county has made to an attorney appointed to represent the child under Section 51.10(j);

(9) requiring payment of deferred prosecution supervision fees under Section 53.03(d);

(10) requiring a parent or other eligible person to attend a court hearing under Section 51.115;

(11) requiring a parent or other eligible person to act or refrain from acting to aid the child in complying with conditions of release from detention under Section 54.01(r);

(12) requiring a parent or other eligible person to act or refrain from acting under any law imposing an obligation of action or omission on a parent or other eligible person because of the parent's or person's relation to the child who is the subject of a proceeding under this title; or

(13) for payment of the cost of attending an educational program under Section 54.0404.

(b) This subchapter does not apply to the entry and enforcement of a child support order under Section 54.06.

Added by Acts 2003, 78th Leg., ch. 283, § 28, eff. Sept. 1, 2003. Amended by Acts 2009, 81st Leg., ch. 1209, § 5, eff. Sept. 1, 2009; Acts 2011, 82nd Leg., ch. 1322 (S.B. 407), § 21, eff. Sept. 1, 2011; Acts 2015, 84th Leg., ch. 935 (H.B. 2398), § 26, eff. Sept. 1, 2015; Acts 2021, 87th Leg., ch. 472 (S.B. 41), § 4.04, eff. Jan. 1, 2022.

### § 61.003. Entry of Juvenile Court Order Against Parent or Other Eligible Person

(a) To comply with the requirements of due process of law, the juvenile court shall:

(1) provide sufficient notice in writing or orally in a recorded court hearing of a proposed juvenile court order; and

(2) provide a sufficient opportunity for the parent or other eligible person to be heard regarding the proposed order.

(b) A juvenile court order must be in writing and a copy promptly furnished to the parent or other eligible person.

(c) The juvenile court may require the parent or other eligible person to provide suitable identification to be included in the court's file. Suitable identification includes fingerprints, a driver's license number, a social security number, or similar indicia of identity.

Added by Acts 2003, 78th Leg., ch. 283, § 28, eff. Sept. 1, 2003.

### § 61.0031. Transfer of Order Affecting Parent or Other Eligible Person to County of Child's Residence

(a) This section applies only when:

(1) a juvenile court has placed a parent or other eligible person under a court order under this chapter;

(2) the child who was the subject of the juvenile court proceedings in which the order was entered:

(A) resides in a county other than the county in which the order was entered;

(B) has moved to a county other than the county in which the order was entered and intends to remain in that county for at least 60 days; or

(C) intends to move to a county other than the county in which the order was entered and to remain in that county for at least 60 days; and

(3) the parent or other eligible person resides or will reside in the same county as the county in which the child now resides or to which the child has moved or intends to move.

(b) A juvenile court that enters an order described by Subsection (a)(1) may transfer the order to the juvenile court of the county in which the parent now resides or to which the parent has moved or intends to move.

(c) The juvenile court shall provide the parent or other eligible person written notice of the transfer.

The notification must identify the court to which the order has been transferred.

(d) The juvenile court to which the order has been transferred shall require the parent or other eligible person to appear before the court to notify the person of the existence and terms of the order, unless the permanent supervision hearing under Section 51.073(c) has been waived. Failure to do so renders the order unenforceable.

(e) If the notice required by Subsection (d) is provided, the juvenile court to which the order has been transferred may modify, extend, or enforce the order as though the court originally entered the order.

Added by Acts 2005, 79th Leg., ch. 949, § 26, eff. Sept. 1, 2005. Amended by Acts 2013, 83rd Leg., ch. 1299 (H.B. 2862), § 33, eff. Sept. 1, 2013.

### § 61.004. Appeal

(a) The parent or other eligible person against whom a final juvenile court order has been entered may appeal as provided by law from judgments entered in civil cases.

(b) The movant may appeal from a judgment denying requested relief regarding a juvenile court order as provided by law from judgments entered in civil cases.

(c) The pendency of an appeal initiated under this section does not abate or otherwise affect the proceedings in juvenile court involving the child.

Added by Acts 2003, 78th Leg., ch. 283, § 28, eff. Sept. 1, 2003.

## SUBCHAPTER B. ENFORCEMENT OF ORDER AGAINST PARENT OR OTHER ELIGIBLE PERSON

### § 61.051. Motion for Enforcement

(a) A party initiates enforcement of a juvenile court order by filing a written motion. In ordinary and concise language, the motion must:

(1) identify the provision of the order allegedly violated and sought to be enforced;

(2) state specifically and factually the manner of the person's alleged noncompliance;

(3) state the relief requested; and

(4) contain the signature of the party filing the motion.

(b) The movant must allege in the same motion for enforcement each violation by the person of the juvenile court orders described by Section 61. 002(a) that the movant had a reasonable basis for believing the person was violating when the motion was filed.

(c) The juvenile court retains jurisdiction to enter a contempt order if the motion for enforcement is filed not later than six months after the child's 18th birthday.

Added by Acts 2003, 78th Leg., ch. 283, § 28, eff. Sept. 1, 2003.

### § 61.052. Notice and Appearance

(a) On the filing of a motion for enforcement, the court shall by written notice set the date, time, and place of the hearing and order the person against whom enforcement is sought to appear and respond to the motion.

(b) The notice must be given by personal service or by certified mail, return receipt requested, on or before the 10th day before the date of the hearing on the motion. The notice must include a copy of the motion for enforcement. Personal service must comply with the Code of Criminal Procedure.

(c) If a person moves to strike or specially excepts to the motion for enforcement, the court shall rule on the exception or motion to strike before the court hears evidence on the motion for enforcement. If an exception is sustained, the court shall give the movant an opportunity to replead and continue the hearing to a designated date and time without the requirement of additional service.

(d) If a person who has been personally served with notice to appear at the hearing does not appear, the juvenile court may not hold the person in contempt, but may issue a capias for the arrest of the person. The court shall set and enforce bond as provided by Subchapter C,[1] Chapter 157. If a person served by certified mail, return receipt requested, with notice to appear at the hearing does not appear, the juvenile court may require immediate personal service of notice.

Added by Acts 2003, 78th Leg., ch. 283, § 28, eff. Sept. 1, 2003.

[1] V.T.C.A., Family Code § 157.101 et seq.

### § 61.053. Attorney for the Person

(a) In a proceeding on a motion for enforcement where incarceration is a possible punishment against a person who is not represented by an attorney, the court shall inform the person of the right to be represented by an attorney and, if the person is indigent, of the right to the appointment of an attorney.

(b) If the person claims indigency and requests the appointment of an attorney, the juvenile court may require the person to file an affidavit of indigency. The court may hear evidence to determine the issue of indigency.

(c) The court shall appoint an attorney to represent the person if the court determines that the person is indigent.

(d) The court shall allow an appointed or retained attorney at least 10 days after the date of the attorney's appointment or retention to respond to the movant's pleadings and to prepare for the hearing. The attorney may waive the preparation time or agree to a shorter period for preparation.

Added by Acts 2003, 78th Leg., ch. 283, § 28, eff. Sept. 1, 2003.

### § 61.054. Compensation of Appointed Attorney

(a) An attorney appointed to represent an indigent person is entitled to a reasonable fee for services to be paid from the general fund of the county according to the schedule for compensation adopted by the county juvenile board. The attorney must meet the qualifications required of attorneys for appointment to Class B misdemeanor cases in juvenile court.

(b) For purposes of compensation, a proceeding in the supreme court is the equivalent of a proceeding in the court of criminal appeals.

(c) The juvenile court may order the parent or other eligible person for whom it has appointed counsel to reimburse the county for the fees the county pays to appointed counsel.

Added by Acts 2003, 78th Leg., ch. 283, § 28, eff. Sept. 1, 2003.

### § 61.055. Conduct of Enforcement Hearing

(a) The juvenile court shall require that the enforcement hearing be recorded as provided by Section 54.09.

(b) The movant must prove beyond a reasonable doubt that the person against whom enforcement is sought engaged in conduct constituting contempt of a reasonable and lawful court order as alleged in the motion for enforcement.

(c) The person against whom enforcement is sought has a privilege not to be called as a witness or otherwise to incriminate himself or herself.

(d) The juvenile court shall conduct the enforcement hearing without a jury.

(e) The juvenile court shall include in its judgment findings as to each violation alleged in the motion for enforcement and the punishment, if any, to be imposed.

(f) If the person against whom enforcement is sought was not represented by counsel during any previous court proceeding involving a motion for enforcement, the person may through counsel raise any defense or affirmative defense to the proceeding that could have been lodged in the previous court proceeding but was not because the person was not represented by counsel.

(g) It is an affirmative defense to enforcement of a juvenile court order that the juvenile court did not provide the parent or other eligible person with due process of law in the proceeding in which the court entered the order.

Added by Acts 2003, 78th Leg., ch. 283, § 28, eff. Sept. 1, 2003.

### § 61.056. Affirmative Defense of Inability to Pay

(a) In an enforcement hearing in which the motion for enforcement alleges that the person against whom enforcement is sought failed to pay restitution, court costs, supervision fees, or any other payment ordered by the court, it is an affirmative defense that the person was financially unable to pay.

(b) The burden of proof to establish the affirmative defense of inability to pay is on the person asserting it.

(c) In order to prevail on the affirmative defense of inability to pay, the person asserting it must show that the person could not have reasonably paid the court-ordered obligation after the person discharged the person's other important financial obligations, including payments for housing, food, utilities, necessary clothing, education, and preexisting debts.

Added by Acts 2003, 78th Leg., ch. 283, § 28, eff. Sept. 1, 2003.

### § 61.057. Punishment for Contempt

(a) On a finding of contempt, the juvenile court may commit the person to the county jail for a term not to exceed six months or may impose a fine in an amount not to exceed $500, or both.

(b) The court may impose only a single jail sentence not to exceed six months or a single fine not to exceed $500, or both, during an enforcement proceeding, without regard to whether the court has entered multiple findings of contempt.

(c) On a finding of contempt in an enforcement proceeding, the juvenile court may, instead of issuing a commitment to jail, enter an order requiring the person's future conduct to comply with the court's previous orders.

(d) Violation of an order entered under Subsection (c) may be the basis of a new enforcement proceeding.

(e) The juvenile court may assign a juvenile probation officer to assist a person in complying with a court order issued under Subsection (c).

(f) A juvenile court may reduce a term of incarceration or reduce payment of all or part of a fine at any time before the sentence is fully served or the fine fully paid.

(g) A juvenile court may reduce the burden of complying with a court order issued under Subsection (c) at any time before the order is fully satisfied, but may not increase the burden except following a new finding of contempt in a new enforcement proceeding.

Added by Acts 2003, 78th Leg., ch. 283, § 28, eff. Sept. 1, 2003.

## SUBCHAPTER C. RIGHTS OF PARENTS

### § 61.101. Definition

In this subchapter, "parent" includes the guardian or custodian of a child.

Added by Acts 2003, 78th Leg., ch. 283, § 28, eff. Sept. 1, 2003.

### § 61.102. Right to be Informed of Proceeding

(a) The parent of a child referred to a juvenile court is entitled as soon as practicable after the referral to be informed by staff designated by the juvenile board, based on the information accompanying the referral to the juvenile court, of:

(1) the date and time of the offense;

(2) the date and time the child was taken into custody;

(3) the name of the offense and its penal category;

(4) the type of weapon, if any, that was used;

(5) the type of property taken or damaged and the extent of damage, if any;

(6) the physical injuries, if any, to the victim of the offense;

(7) whether there is reason to believe that the offense was gang-related;

(8) whether there is reason to believe that the offense was related to consumption of alcohol or use of an illegal controlled substance;

(9) if the child was taken into custody with adults or other juveniles, the names of those persons;

(10) the aspects of the juvenile court process that apply to the child;

(11) if the child is in detention, the visitation policy of the detention facility that applies to the child;

(12) the child's right to be represented by an attorney and the local standards and procedures for determining whether the parent qualifies for appointment of counsel to represent the child; and

(13) the methods by which the parent can assist the child with the legal process.

(b) If the child was released on field release citation, or from the law enforcement station by the police, by intake, or by the judge or associate judge at the initial detention hearing, the information required by Subsection (a) may be communicated to the parent in person, by telephone, or in writing.

(c) If the child is not released before or at the initial detention hearing, the information required by Subsection (a) shall be communicated in person to the parent unless that is not feasible, in which event it may be communicated by telephone or in writing.

(d) Information disclosed to a parent under Subsection (a) is not admissible in a judicial proceeding under this title as substantive evidence or as evidence to impeach the testimony of a witness for the state.

Added by Acts 2003, 78th Leg., ch. 283, § 28, eff. Sept. 1, 2003.

### § 61.103. Right of Access to Child

(a) The parent of a child taken into custody for delinquent conduct, conduct indicating a need for supervision, or conduct that violates a condition of probation imposed by the juvenile court has the right to communicate in person privately with the child for reasonable periods of time while the child is in:

(1) a juvenile processing office;

(2) a secure detention facility;

(3) a secure correctional facility;

(4) a court-ordered placement facility; or

(5) the custody of the Texas Juvenile Justice Department.

(b) The time, place, and conditions of the private, in-person communication may be regulated to prevent disruption of scheduled activities and to maintain the safety and security of the facility.

Added by Acts 2003, 78th Leg., ch. 283, § 28, eff. Sept. 1, 2003. Amended by Acts 2015, 84th Leg., ch. 734 (H.B. 1549), § 76, eff. Sept. 1, 2015.

### § 61.104. Parental Written Statement

(a) When a petition for adjudication, a motion or petition to modify disposition, or a motion or petition for discretionary transfer to criminal court is served on a parent of the child, the parent must be provided with a form prescribed by the Texas Juvenile Justice Department on which the parent can make a written statement about the needs of the child or family or any other matter relevant to disposition of the case.

(b) The parent shall return the statement to the juvenile probation department, which shall transmit the statement to the court along with the discretionary transfer report authorized by Section 54.02(e), the disposition report authorized by Section 54.04(b), or the modification of disposition report authorized by Section 54.05(e), as applicable. The statement shall be disclosed to the parties as appropriate and may be considered by the court at the disposition, modification, or discretionary transfer hearing.

Added by Acts 2003, 78th Leg., ch. 283, § 28, eff. Sept. 1, 2003. Amended by Acts 2015, 84th Leg., ch. 734 (H.B. 1549), § 77, eff. Sept. 1, 2015.

### § 61.105. Parental Oral Statement

(a) After all the evidence has been received but before the arguments of counsel at a hearing for discretionary transfer to criminal court, a disposition hearing without a jury, or a modification of disposition hearing, the court shall give a parent who is present in court a reasonable opportunity to address the court about the needs or strengths of the child or family or any other matter relevant to disposition of the case.

(b) The parent may not be required to make the statement under oath and may not be subject to cross-examination, but the court may seek clarification or expansion of the statement from the person giving the statement.

(c) The court may consider and act on the statement as the court considers appropriate.

Added by Acts 2003, 78th Leg., ch. 283, § 28, eff. Sept. 1, 2003.

### § 61.106. Appeal or Collateral Challenge

The failure or inability of a person to perform an act or to provide a right or service listed under this subchapter may not be used by the child or any party as a ground for:

(1) appeal;

(2) an application for a post-adjudication writ of habeas corpus; or

(3) exclusion of evidence against the child in any proceeding or forum.

Added by Acts 2003, 78th Leg., ch. 283, § 28, eff. Sept. 1, 2003.

### § 61.107. Liability

The Texas Juvenile Justice Department, a juvenile board, a court, a person appointed by the court, an employee of a juvenile probation department, an attorney for the state, a peace officer, or a law enforcement agency is not liable for a failure or inability to provide a right listed in this chapter.

Added by Acts 2003, 78th Leg., ch. 283, § 28, eff. Sept. 1, 2003. Amended by Acts 2015, 84th Leg., ch. 734 (H.B. 1549), § 78, eff. Sept. 1, 2015.

# TITLE 3A. TRUANCY COURT PROCEEDINGS

## CHAPTER 65. TRUANCY COURT PROCEEDINGS



### SUBCHAPTER A. GENERAL PROVISIONS

#### § 65.001. Scope and Purpose

(a) This chapter details the procedures and proceedings in cases involving allegations of truant conduct.

(b) The purpose of this chapter is to encourage school attendance by creating simple civil judicial procedures through which children are held accountable for excessive school absences.

(c) The best interest of the child is the primary consideration in adjudicating truant conduct of the child.

Added by Acts 2015, 84th Leg., ch. 935 (H.B. 2398), § 27, eff. Sept. 1, 2015.

#### § 65.002. Definitions

In this chapter:

(1) "Child" means a person who is 12 years of age or older and younger than 19 years of age.

(2) "Juvenile court" means a court designated under Section 51.04 to exercise jurisdiction over proceedings under Title 3.[1]

(3) "Qualified telephone interpreter" means a telephone service that employs licensed court interpreters, as defined by Section 157.001, Government Code.

(4) "Truancy court" means a court designated under Section 65.004 to exercise jurisdiction over cases involving allegations of truant conduct.

Added by Acts 2015, 84th Leg., ch. 935 (H.B. 2398), § 27, eff. Sept. 1, 2015.

[1] V.T.C.A., Family Code § 51.01 et seq.&;

### § 65.003. Truant Conduct

(a) A child engages in truant conduct if the child is required to attend school under Section 25.085, Education Code, and fails to attend school on 10 or more days or parts of days within a six-month period in the same school year.

(b) Truant conduct may be prosecuted only as a civil case in a truancy court.

(c) It is an affirmative defense to an allegation of truant conduct that one or more of the absences required to be proven:

(1) have been excused by a school official or by the court;

(2) were involuntary; or

(3) were due to the child's voluntary absence from the child's home because of abuse, as defined by Section 261.001.

(d) The affirmative defense provided by Subsection (c) is not available if, after deducting the absences described by that subsection, there remains a sufficient number of absences to constitute truant conduct.

(e) In asserting an affirmative defense described by Subsection (c), the burden is on the child to show by a preponderance of the evidence that the absence:

(1) has been or should be excused;

(2) was involuntary; or

(3) was due to the child's voluntary absence from the child's home because of abuse, as defined by Section 261.001.

(f) A decision by the court to excuse an absence for purposes of an affirmative defense under Subsection (c) does not affect the ability of the school district to determine whether to excuse the absence for another purpose.

Added by Acts 2015, 84th Leg., ch. 935 (H.B. 2398), § 27, eff. Sept. 1, 2015. Amended by Acts 2021, 87th Leg., ch. 272 (H.B. 3165), § 1, eff. June 4, 2021.

Section 2 of Acts 2021, 87th Leg., ch. 272 (H.B. 3165) provides: "This Act applies beginning with the 2021—2022 school year."

### § 65.004. Truancy Courts; Jurisdiction

(a) The following are designated as truancy courts:

(1) in a county with a population of 1.75 million or more, the constitutional county court;

(2) justice courts; and

(3) municipal courts.

(b) A truancy court has exclusive original jurisdiction over cases involving allegations of truant conduct.

(c) A municipality may enter into an agreement with a contiguous municipality or a municipality with boundaries that are within one-half mile of the municipality seeking to enter into the agreement to establish concurrent jurisdiction of the municipal courts in the municipalities and provide original jurisdiction to a municipal court in which a truancy case is brought as if the municipal court were located in the municipality in which the case arose.

(d) A truancy court retains jurisdiction over a person, without regard to the age of the person, who was referred to the court under Section 65.051 for engaging in truant conduct before the person's 19th birthday, until final disposition of the case.

Added by Acts 2015, 84th Leg., ch. 935 (H.B. 2398), § 27, eff. Sept. 1, 2015.

### § 65.005. Court Sessions

A truancy court is considered to be in session at all times.

Added by Acts 2015, 84th Leg., ch. 935 (H.B. 2398), § 27, eff. Sept. 1, 2015.

### § 65.006. Venue

Venue for a proceeding under this chapter is the county in which the school in which the child is enrolled is located or the county in which the child resides.

Added by Acts 2015, 84th Leg., ch. 935 (H.B. 2398), § 27, eff. Sept. 1, 2015.

### § 65.007. Right to Jury Trial

(a) A child alleged to have engaged in truant conduct is entitled to a jury trial.

(b) The number of jurors in a case involving an allegation of truant conduct is six. The state and the child are each entitled to three peremptory challenges.

(c) There is no jury fee for a trial under this chapter.

Added by Acts 2015, 84th Leg., ch. 935 (H.B. 2398), § 27, eff. Sept. 1, 2015.

### § 65.008. Waiver of Rights

A right granted to a child by this chapter or by the constitution or laws of this state or the United States is waived in proceedings under this chapter if:

(1) the right is one that may be waived;

(2) the child and the child's parent or guardian are informed of the right, understand the right, understand the possible consequences of waiving

the right, and understand that waiver of the right is not required;

(3) the child signs the waiver;

(4) the child's parent or guardian signs the waiver; and

(5) the child's attorney signs the waiver, if the child is represented by counsel.

Added by Acts 2015, 84th Leg., ch. 935 (H.B. 2398), § 27, eff. Sept. 1, 2015.

### § 65.009. Effect of Adjudication

(a) An adjudication of a child as having engaged in truant conduct is not a conviction of crime. An order of adjudication does not impose any civil disability ordinarily resulting from a conviction or operate to disqualify the child in any civil service application or appointment.

(b) The adjudication of a child as having engaged in truant conduct may not be used in any subsequent court proceedings, other than for the purposes of determining an appropriate remedial action under this chapter or in an appeal under this chapter.

Added by Acts 2015, 84th Leg., ch. 935 (H.B. 2398), § 27, eff. Sept. 1, 2015.

### § 65.010. Burden of Proof

A court or jury may not return a finding that a child has engaged in truant conduct unless the state has proved the conduct beyond a reasonable doubt.

Added by Acts 2015, 84th Leg., ch. 935 (H.B. 2398), § 27, eff. Sept. 1, 2015.

### § 65.011. Applicable Statutes Regarding Discovery

Discovery in a proceeding under this chapter is governed by Chapter 39, Code of Criminal Procedure, other than Articles 39.14(i) and (j).

Added by Acts 2015, 84th Leg., ch. 935 (H.B. 2398), § 27, eff. Sept. 1, 2015.

### § 65.012. Procedural Rules

The supreme court may promulgate rules of procedure applicable to proceedings under this chapter, including guidelines applicable to the informal disposition of truancy cases.

Added by Acts 2015, 84th Leg., ch. 935 (H.B. 2398), § 27, eff. Sept. 1, 2015.

### § 65.013. Interpreters

(a) When on the motion for appointment of an interpreter by a party or on the motion of the court, in any proceeding under this chapter, the court determines that the child, the child's parent or guardian, or a witness does not understand and speak English, an interpreter must be sworn to interpret for the person. Articles 38.30(a), (b), and (c), Code of Criminal Procedure, apply in a proceeding under this chapter. A qualified telephone interpreter may be sworn to provide interpretation services if an interpreter is not available to appear in person before the court.

(b) In any proceeding under this chapter, if a party notifies the court that the child, the child's parent or guardian, or a witness is deaf, the court shall appoint a qualified interpreter to interpret the proceedings in any language, including sign language, that the deaf person can understand. Articles 38.31(d), (e), (f), and (g), Code of Criminal Procedure, apply in a proceeding under this chapter.

Added by Acts 2015, 84th Leg., ch. 935 (H.B. 2398), § 27, eff. Sept. 1, 2015.

### § 65.014. Signatures

Any requirement under this chapter that a document be signed or that a document contain a person's signature, including the signature of a judge or a clerk of the court, is satisfied if the document contains the signature of the person as captured on an electronic device or as a digital signature.

Added by Acts 2015, 84th Leg., ch. 935 (H.B. 2398), § 27, eff. Sept. 1, 2015.

### § 65.015. Public Access to Court Hearings

(a) Except as provided by Subsection (b), a truancy court shall open a hearing under this chapter to the public unless the court, for good cause shown, determines that the public should be excluded.

(b) The court may prohibit a person from personally attending a hearing if the person is expected to testify at the hearing and the court determines that the person's testimony would be materially affected if the person hears other testimony at the hearing.

Added by Acts 2015, 84th Leg., ch. 935 (H.B. 2398), § 27, eff. Sept. 1, 2015.

### § 65.016. Recording of Proceedings

(a) The proceedings in a truancy court that is not a court of record may not be recorded.

(b) The proceedings in a truancy court that is a court of record must be recorded by stenographic notes or by electronic, mechanical, or other appropriate means.

Added by Acts 2015, 84th Leg., ch. 935 (H.B. 2398), § 27, eff. Sept. 1, 2015.

### § 65.017. Juvenile Case Managers

A truancy court may employ a juvenile case manager in accordance with Article 45.056, Code of Criminal Procedure, to provide services to children who have been referred to the truancy court or who are in jeopardy of being referred to the truancy court.

Added by Acts 2015, 84th Leg., ch. 935 (H.B. 2398), § 27, eff. Sept. 1, 2015.

## SUBCHAPTER B. INITIAL PROCEDURES

### § 65.051. Initial Referral to Truancy Court

When a truancy court receives a referral under Section 25.0915, Education Code, and the court is not required to dismiss the referral under that section, the court shall forward the referral to a truant conduct prosecutor who serves the court.

Added by Acts 2015, 84th Leg., ch. 935 (H.B. 2398), § 27, eff. Sept. 1, 2015.

### § 65.052. Truant Conduct Prosecutor

In a justice or municipal court or a constitutional county court that is designated as a truancy court, the attorney who represents the state in criminal matters in that court shall serve as the truant conduct prosecutor.

Added by Acts 2015, 84th Leg., ch. 935 (H.B. 2398), § 27, eff. Sept. 1, 2015.

### § 65.053. Review by Prosecutor

(a) The truant conduct prosecutor shall promptly review the facts described in a referral received under Section 65.051.

(b) The prosecutor may, in the prosecutor's discretion, determine whether to file a petition with the truancy court requesting an adjudication of the child for truant conduct. If the prosecutor decides not to file a petition requesting an adjudication, the prosecutor shall inform the truancy court and the school district of the decision.

(c) The prosecutor may not file a petition for an adjudication of a child for truant conduct if the referral was not made in compliance with Section 25.0915, Education Code.

Added by Acts 2015, 84th Leg., ch. 935 (H.B. 2398), § 27, eff. Sept. 1, 2015.

### § 65.054. State's Petition

(a) A petition for an adjudication of a child for truant conduct initiates an action of the state against a child who has allegedly engaged in truant conduct.

(b) The proceedings shall be styled "In the matter of ______________, Child," identifying the child by the child's initials only.

(c) The petition may be on information and belief.

(d) The petition must state:

(1) with reasonable particularity the time, place, and manner of the acts alleged to constitute truant conduct;

(2) the name, age, and residence address, if known, of the child who is the subject of the petition;

(3) the names and residence addresses, if known, of at least one parent, guardian, or custodian of the child and of the child's spouse, if any; and

(4) if the child's parent, guardian, or custodian does not reside or cannot be found in the state, or if their places of residence are unknown, the name and residence address of any known adult relative residing in the county or, if there is none, the name and residence address of the known adult relative residing nearest to the location of the court.

(e) Filing fees may not be charged for the filing of the state's petition.

Added by Acts 2015, 84th Leg., ch. 935 (H.B. 2398), § 27, eff. Sept. 1, 2015.

### § 65.055. Limitations Period

A petition may not be filed after the 45th day after the date of the last absence giving rise to the act of truant conduct.

Added by Acts 2015, 84th Leg., ch. 935 (H.B. 2398), § 27, eff. Sept. 1, 2015.

### § 65.056. Hearing Date

(a) After the petition has been filed, the truancy court shall set a date and time for an adjudication hearing.

(b) The hearing may not be held on or before the 10th day after the date the petition is filed.

Added by Acts 2015, 84th Leg., ch. 935 (H.B. 2398), § 27, eff. Sept. 1, 2015.

### § 65.057. Summons

(a) After setting the date and time of an adjudication hearing, the truancy court shall direct the issuance of a summons to:

(1) the child named in the petition;

(2) the child's parent, guardian, or custodian;

(3) the child's guardian ad litem, if any; and

(4) any other person who appears to the court to be a proper or necessary party to the proceeding.

(b) The summons must require the persons served to appear before the court at the place, date, and time of the adjudication hearing to answer the allegations of the petition. A copy of the petition must accompany the summons. If a person, other than the child, required to appear under this section fails to attend a hearing, the truancy court may proceed with the hearing.

(c) The truancy court may endorse on the summons an order directing the person having the physical custody or control of the child to bring the child to the hearing.

(d) A party, other than the child, may waive service of summons by written stipulation or by voluntary appearance at the hearing.

Added by Acts 2015, 84th Leg., ch. 935 (H.B. 2398), § 27, eff. Sept. 1, 2015.

### § 65.058. Service of Summons

(a) If a person to be served with a summons is in this state and can be found, the summons shall be served on the person personally or by registered or certified mail, return receipt requested, at least five days before the date of the adjudication hearing.

(b) Service of the summons may be made by any suitable person under the direction of the court.

Added by Acts 2015, 84th Leg., ch. 935 (H.B. 2398), § 27, eff. Sept. 1, 2015.

### § 65.059. Representation by Attorney

(a) A child may be represented by an attorney in a case under this chapter. Representation by an attorney is not required.

(b) A child is not entitled to have an attorney appointed to represent the child, but the court may appoint an attorney if the court determines it is in the best interest of the child.

(c) The court may order a child's parent or other responsible person to pay for the cost of an attorney appointed under this section if the court determines that the person has sufficient financial resources.

Added by Acts 2015, 84th Leg., ch. 935 (H.B. 2398), § 27, eff. Sept. 1, 2015.

### § 65.060. Child's Answer

After the petition has been filed, the child may answer, orally or in writing, the petition at or before the commencement of the hearing. If the child does not answer, a general denial of the alleged truant conduct is assumed.

Added by Acts 2015, 84th Leg., ch. 935 (H.B. 2398), § 27, eff. Sept. 1, 2015.

### § 65.061. Guardian Ad Litem

(a) If a child appears before the truancy court without a parent or guardian, or it appears to the court that the child's parent or guardian is incapable or unwilling to make decisions in the best interest of the child with respect to proceedings under this chapter, the court may appoint a guardian ad litem to protect the interests of the child in the proceedings.

(b) An attorney for a child may also be the child's guardian ad litem. A law enforcement officer, probation officer, or other employee of the truancy court may not be appointed as a guardian ad litem.

(c) The court may order a child's parent or other person responsible to support the child to reimburse the county or municipality for the cost of the guardian ad litem. The court may issue the order only after determining that the parent or other responsible person has sufficient financial resources to offset the cost of the child's guardian ad litem wholly or partly.

Added by Acts 2015, 84th Leg., ch. 935 (H.B. 2398), § 27, eff. Sept. 1, 2015.

### § 65.062. Attendance at Hearing

(a) The child must be personally present at the adjudication hearing. The truancy court may not proceed with the adjudication hearing in the absence of the child.

(b) A parent or guardian of a child and any court-appointed guardian ad litem of a child is required to attend the adjudication hearing.

(c) Subsection (b) does not apply to:

(1) a person for whom, for good cause shown, the court excuses attendance;

(2) a person who is not a resident of this state; or

(3) a parent of a child for whom a managing conservator has been appointed and the parent is not a conservator of the child.

Added by Acts 2015, 84th Leg., ch. 935 (H.B. 2398), § 27, eff. Sept. 1, 2015.

### § 65.063. Right to Reemployment

(a) An employer may not terminate the employment of a permanent employee because the employee is required under Section 65.062(b) to attend a hearing.

(b) Notwithstanding any other law, an employee whose employment is terminated in violation of this section is entitled to return to the same employment that the employee held when notified of the hearing if the employee, as soon as practical after the hearing, gives the employer actual notice that the employee intends to return.

(c) A person who is injured because of a violation of this section is entitled to:

(1) reinstatement to the person's former position;

(2) damages not to exceed an amount equal to six times the amount of monthly compensation received by the person on the date of the hearing; and

(3) reasonable attorney's fees in an amount approved by the court.

(d) It is a defense to an action brought under this section that the employer's circumstances changed while the employee attended the hearing and caused reemployment to be impossible or unreasonable. To establish a defense under this subsection, an employer must prove that the termination of employment was because of circumstances other than the employee's attendance at the hearing.

Added by Acts 2015, 84th Leg., ch. 935 (H.B. 2398), § 27, eff. Sept. 1, 2015.

### § 65.064. Subpoena of Witness

A witness may be subpoenaed in accordance with the procedures for the subpoena of a witness under the Code of Criminal Procedure.

Added by Acts 2015, 84th Leg., ch. 935 (H.B. 2398), § 27, eff. Sept. 1, 2015.

### § 65.065. Child Alleged to Be Mentally Ill

(a) A party may make a motion requesting that a petition alleging a child to have engaged in truant conduct be dismissed because the child has a mental illness, as defined by Section 571.003, Health and Safety Code. In response to the motion, the truancy court shall temporarily stay the proceedings to determine whether probable cause exists to believe the child has a mental illness. In making a determination, the court may:

(1) consider the motion, supporting documents, professional statements of counsel, and witness testimony; and

(2) observe the child.

(b) If the court determines that probable cause exists to believe that the child has a mental illness, the court shall dismiss the petition. If the court determines that evidence does not exist to support a finding that the child has a mental illness, the court shall dissolve the stay and continue with the truancy court proceedings.

Added by Acts 2015, 84th Leg., ch. 935 (H.B. 2398), § 27, eff. Sept. 1, 2015.

## SUBCHAPTER C. ADJUDICATION HEARING AND REMEDIES

### § 65.101. Adjudication Hearing; Judgment

(a) A child may be found to have engaged in truant conduct only after an adjudication hearing conducted in accordance with the provisions of this chapter.

(b) At the beginning of the adjudication hearing, the judge of the truancy court shall explain to the child and the child's parent, guardian, or guardian ad litem:

(1) the allegations made against the child;

(2) the nature and possible consequences of the proceedings;

(3) the child's privilege against self-incrimination;

(4) the child's right to trial and to confrontation of witnesses;

(5) the child's right to representation by an attorney if the child is not already represented; and

(6) the child's right to a jury trial.

(c) Trial is by jury unless jury is waived in accordance with Section 65.008. Jury verdicts under this chapter must be unanimous.

(d) The Texas Rules of Evidence do not apply in a truancy proceeding under this chapter except:

(1) when the judge hearing the case determines that a particular rule of evidence applicable to criminal cases must be followed to ensure that the proceedings are fair to all parties; or

(2) as otherwise provided by this chapter.

(e) A child alleged to have engaged in truant conduct need not be a witness against nor otherwise incriminate himself or herself. An extrajudicial statement of the child that was obtained in violation of the constitution of this state or the United States may not be used in an adjudication hearing. A statement made by the child out of court is insufficient to support a finding of truant conduct unless it is corroborated wholly or partly by other evidence.

(f) At the conclusion of the adjudication hearing, the court or jury shall find whether the child has engaged in truant conduct. The finding must be based on competent evidence admitted at the hearing. The child shall be presumed to have not engaged in truant conduct and no finding that a child has engaged in truant conduct may be returned unless the state has proved the conduct beyond a reasonable doubt. In all jury cases the jury will be instructed that the burden is on the state to prove that a child has engaged in truant conduct beyond a reasonable doubt.

(g) If the court or jury finds that the child did not engage in truant conduct, the court shall dismiss the case with prejudice.

(h) If the court or jury finds that the child did engage in truant conduct, the court shall proceed to issue a judgment finding the child has engaged in truant conduct and order the remedies the court finds appropriate under Section 65.103. The jury is not involved in ordering remedies for a child who has been adjudicated as having engaged in truant conduct.

Added by Acts 2015, 84th Leg., ch. 935 (H.B. 2398), § 27, eff. Sept. 1, 2015.

### § 65.102. Remedial Actions

(a) The truancy court shall determine and order appropriate remedial actions in regard to a child who has been found to have engaged in truant conduct.

(b) The truancy court shall orally pronounce the court's remedial actions in the child's presence and enter those actions in a written order.

(c) After pronouncing the court's remedial actions, the court shall advise the child and the child's parent, guardian, or guardian ad litem of:

(1) the child's right to appeal, as detailed in Subchapter D; [1] and

(2) the procedures for the sealing of the child's records under Section 65.201.

Added by Acts 2015, 84th Leg., ch. 935 (H.B. 2398), § 27, eff. Sept. 1, 2015.

[1] V.T.C.A., Family Code § 65.151 et seq.

### § 65.103. Remedial Order

(a) A truancy court may enter a remedial order requiring a child who has been found to have engaged in truant conduct to:

(1) attend school without unexcused absences;

(2) attend a preparatory class for the high school equivalency examination administered under Section 7.111, Education Code, if the court determines that the individual is unlikely to do well in a formal classroom environment due to the individual's age;

(3) if the child is at least 16 years of age, take the high school equivalency examination administered under Section 7.111, Education Code, if that is in the best interest of the child;

(4) attend a nonprofit, community-based special program that the court determines to be in the best interest of the child, including:

(A) an alcohol and drug abuse program;

(B) a rehabilitation program;

(C) a counseling program, including a self-improvement program;

(D) a program that provides training in self-esteem and leadership;

(E) a work and job skills training program;

(F) a program that provides training in parenting, including parental responsibility;

(G) a program that provides training in manners;

(H) a program that provides training in violence avoidance;

(I) a program that provides sensitivity training; and

(J) a program that provides training in advocacy and mentoring;

(5) complete not more than 50 hours of community service on a project acceptable to the court; and

(6) participate for a specified number of hours in a tutorial program covering the academic subjects in which the child is enrolled that are provided by the school the child attends.

(b) A truancy court may not order a child who has been found to have engaged in truant conduct to:

(1) attend a juvenile justice alternative education program, a boot camp, or a for-profit truancy class; or

(2) perform more than 16 hours of community service per week under this section.

(c) In addition to any other order authorized by this section, a truancy court may order the Department of Public Safety to suspend the driver's license or permit of a child who has been found to have engaged in truant conduct. If the child does not have a driver's license or permit, the court may order the Department of Public Safety to deny the issuance of a license or permit to the child. The period of the license or permit suspension or the order that the issuance of a license or permit be denied may not extend beyond the maximum time period that a remedial order is effective as provided by Section 65.104.

Added by Acts 2015, 84th Leg., ch. 935 (H.B. 2398), § 27, eff. Sept. 1, 2015.

### § 65.104. Maximum Time Remedial Order Is Effective

A truancy court's remedial order under Section 65.103 is effective until the later of:

(1) the date specified by the court in the order, which may not be later than the 180th day after the date the order is entered; or

(2) the last day of the school year in which the order was entered.

Added by Acts 2015, 84th Leg., ch. 935 (H.B. 2398), § 27, eff. Sept. 1, 2015.

### § 65.105. Orders Affecting Parents and Others

(a) If a child has been found to have engaged in truant conduct, the truancy court may:

(1) order the child and the child's parent to attend a class for students at risk of dropping out of school that is designed for both the child and the child's parent;

(2) order any person found by the court to have, by a wilful act or omission, contributed to, caused, or encouraged the child's truant conduct to do any act that the court determines to be reasonable and necessary for the welfare of the child or to refrain from doing any act that the court determines to be injurious to the child's welfare;

(3) enjoin all contact between the child and a person who is found to be a contributing cause of the child's truant conduct, unless that person is related to the child within the third degree by consanguinity or affinity, in which case the court may contact the Department of Family and Protective Services, if necessary;

(4) after notice to, and a hearing with, all persons affected, order any person living in the same household with the child to participate in social or psychological counseling to assist in the child's rehabilitation;

(5) order the child's parent or other person responsible for the child's support to pay all or part of the reasonable costs of treatment programs in which the child is ordered to participate if the court finds the child's parent or person responsible for the child's support is able to pay the costs;

(6) order the child's parent to attend a program for parents of students with unexcused absences that provides instruction designed to assist those parents in identifying problems that contribute to the child's unexcused absences and in developing strategies for resolving those problems; and

(7) order the child's parent to perform not more than 50 hours of community service with the child.

(b) A person subject to an order proposed under Subsection (a) is entitled to a hearing before the order is entered by the court.

(c) On a finding by the court that a child's parents have made a reasonable good faith effort to prevent the child from engaging in truant conduct and that, despite the parents' efforts, the child continues to engage in truant conduct, the court shall waive any requirement for community service that may be imposed on a parent under this section.

Added by Acts 2015, 84th Leg., ch. 935 (H.B. 2398), § 27, eff. Sept. 1, 2015.

### § 65.106. Liability for Claims Arising from Community Service

(a) A municipality or county that establishes a program to assist children and their parents in rendering community service under this subchapter may purchase an insurance policy protecting the municipality or county against a claim brought by a person other than the child or the child's parent for a cause of action that arises from an act of the child or parent while rendering the community service. The municipality or county is not liable for the claim to the extent that damages are recoverable under a contract of insurance or under a plan of self-insurance authorized by statute.

(b) The liability of the municipality or county for a claim that arises from an action of the child or the child's parent while rendering community service may not exceed $100,000 to a single person and $300,000 for a single occurrence in the case of personal injury or death, and $10,000 for a single occurrence of property damage. Liability may not extend to punitive or exemplary damages.

(c) This section does not waive a defense, immunity, or jurisdictional bar available to the municipality or county or its officers or employees, nor shall this section be construed to waive, repeal, or modify any provision of Chapter 101, Civil Practice and Remedies Code.

Added by Acts 2015, 84th Leg., ch. 935 (H.B. 2398), § 27, eff. Sept. 1, 2015.

### § 65.107. Court Cost

(a) If a child is found to have engaged in truant conduct, the truancy court, after giving the child, parent, or other person responsible for the child's support a reasonable opportunity to be heard, shall order the child, parent, or other person, if financially able to do so, to pay a court cost of $50 to the clerk of the court.

(b) The court's order to pay the $50 court cost is not effective unless the order is reduced to writing and signed by the judge. The written order to pay the court cost may be part of the court's order detailing the remedial actions in the case.

(c) The clerk of the court shall keep a record of the court costs collected under this section and shall forward the funds to the county treasurer, municipal treasurer, or person fulfilling the role of a county treasurer or municipal treasurer, as appropriate.

(d) The court costs collected under this section shall be deposited in a special account that can be used only to offset the cost of the operations of the truancy court.

Added by Acts 2015, 84th Leg., ch. 935 (H.B. 2398), § 27, eff. Sept. 1, 2015.

### § 65.108. Hearing to Modify Remedy

(a) A truancy court may hold a hearing to modify any remedy imposed by the court. A remedy may only be modified during the period the order is effective under Section 65.104.

(b) There is no right to a jury at a hearing under this section.

(c) A hearing to modify a remedy imposed by the court shall be held on the petition of the state, the court, or the child and the child's parent, guardian, guardian ad litem, or attorney. Reasonable notice of a hearing to modify disposition shall be given to all parties.

(d) Notwithstanding any other law, in considering a motion to modify a remedy imposed by the court, the truancy court may consider a written report from a school district official or employee, juvenile case manager, or professional consultant in addition to the testimony of witnesses. The court shall provide the attorney for the child and the prosecuting attorney with access to all written matters to be considered by the court. The court may order counsel not to reveal items to the child or to the child's parent, guardian, or guardian ad litem if the disclosure would materially harm the treatment and rehabilitation of the child or would substantially decrease the likelihood of receiving information from the same or similar sources in the future.

(e) The truancy court shall pronounce in court, in the presence of the child, the court's changes to the remedy, if any. The court shall specifically state the new remedy and the court's reasons for modifying the remedy in a written order. The court shall furnish a copy of the order to the child.

Added by Acts 2015, 84th Leg., ch. 935 (H.B. 2398), § 27, eff. Sept. 1, 2015.

### § 65.109. Motion for New Trial

The order of a truancy court may be challenged by filing a motion for new trial. Rules 505.3(c) and (e), Texas Rules of Civil Procedure, apply to a motion for new trial.

Added by Acts 2015, 84th Leg., ch. 935 (H.B. 2398), § 27, eff. Sept. 1, 2015.

## SUBCHAPTER D. APPEAL

### § 65.151. Right to Appeal

(a) The child, the child's parent or guardian, or the state may appeal any order of a truancy court. A person subject to an order entered under Section 65.105 may appeal that order.

(b) An appeal from a truancy court shall be to a juvenile court. The case must be tried de novo in the juvenile court. This chapter applies to the de novo trial in the juvenile court. On appeal, the judgment of the truancy court is vacated.

(c) A judgment of a juvenile court in a trial conducted under Subsection (b) may be appealed in the same manner as an appeal under Chapter 56.

Added by Acts 2015, 84th Leg., ch. 935 (H.B. 2398), § 27, eff. Sept. 1, 2015.

### § 65.152. Governing Law

Rule 506, Texas Rules of Civil Procedure, applies to the appeal of an order of a truancy court to a juvenile court in the same manner as the rule applies to an appeal of a judgment of a justice court to a county court, except an appeal bond is not required.

Added by Acts 2015, 84th Leg., ch. 935 (H.B. 2398), § 27, eff. Sept. 1, 2015.

### § 65.153. Counsel on Appeal

(a) A child may be represented by counsel on appeal.

(b) If the child and the child's parent, guardian, or guardian ad litem request an appeal, the attorney who represented the child before the truancy court, if any, shall file a notice of appeal with the court that will hear the appeal and inform that court whether that attorney will handle the appeal.

(c) An appeal serves to vacate the order of the truancy court.

Added by Acts 2015, 84th Leg., ch. 935 (H.B. 2398), § 27, eff. Sept. 1, 2015.

## SUBCHAPTER E. RECORDS

### § 65.201. Sealing of Records

(a) A child who has been found to have engaged in truant conduct may apply, on or after the child's 18th birthday, to the truancy court that made the finding to seal the records relating to the allegation and finding of truant conduct held by:

(1) the court;

(2) the truant conduct prosecutor; and

(3) the school district.

(b) The application must include the following information or an explanation of why one or more of the following is not included:

(1) the child's:

(A) full name;

(B) sex;

(C) race or ethnicity;

(D) date of birth;

(E) driver's license or identification card number; and

(F) social security number;

(2) the dates on which the truant conduct was alleged to have occurred; and

(3) if known, the cause number assigned to the petition and the court and county in which the petition was filed.

(c) The truancy court shall order that the records be sealed after determining the child complied with the remedies ordered by the court in the case.

(d) All index references to the records of the truancy court that are ordered sealed shall be deleted not later than the 30th day after the date of the sealing order.

(e) A truancy court, clerk of the court, truant conduct prosecutor, or school district shall reply to a request for information concerning a child's sealed truant conduct case that no record exists with respect to the child.

(f) Inspection of the sealed records may be permitted by an order of the truancy court on the petition of the person who is the subject of the records and only by those persons named in the order.

(g) A person whose records have been sealed under this section is not required in any proceeding or in any application for employment, information, or licensing to state that the person has been the subject of a proceeding under this chapter. Any statement that the person has never been found to have engaged in truant conduct may not be held against the person in any criminal or civil proceeding.

(h) On or after the fifth anniversary of a child's 16th birthday, on the motion of the child or on the truancy court's own motion, the truancy court may order the destruction of the child's records that have been sealed under this section if the child has not been convicted of a felony.

Added by Acts 2015, 84th Leg., ch. 935 (H.B. 2398), § 27, eff. Sept. 1, 2015.

### § 65.202. Confidentiality of Records

Records and files created under this chapter may be disclosed only to:

(1) the judge of the truancy court, the truant conduct prosecutor, and the staff of the judge and prosecutor;

(2) the child or an attorney for the child;

(3) a governmental agency if the disclosure is required or authorized by law;

(4) a person or entity to whom the child is referred for treatment or services if the agency or institution disclosing the information has entered into a written confidentiality agreement with the person or entity regarding the protection of the disclosed information;

(5) the Texas Department of Criminal Justice and the Texas Juvenile Justice Department for the purpose of maintaining statistical records of recidivism and for diagnosis and classification;

(6) the agency; or

(7) with leave of the truancy court, any other person, agency, or institution having a legitimate interest in the proceeding or in the work of the court.

Added by Acts 2015, 84th Leg., ch. 935 (H.B. 2398), § 27, eff. Sept. 1, 2015.

### § 65.203. Destruction of Certain Records

A truancy court shall order the destruction of records relating to allegations of truant conduct that are held by the court or by the prosecutor if a prosecutor decides not to file a petition for an adjudication of truant conduct after a review of the referral under Section 65.053.

Added by Acts 2015, 84th Leg., ch. 935 (H.B. 2398), § 27, eff. Sept. 1, 2015.

## SUBCHAPTER F. ENFORCEMENT OF ORDERS

### § 65.251. Failure to Obey Truancy Court Order; Child in Contempt of Court

(a) If a child fails to obey an order issued by a truancy court under Section 65.103(a) or a child is in direct contempt of court, the truancy court, after providing notice and an opportunity for a hearing, may hold the child in contempt of court and order either or both of the following:

(1) that the child pay a fine not to exceed $100; or

(2) that the Department of Public Safety suspend the child's driver's license or permit or, if the child does not have a license or permit, order that the Department of Public Safety deny the issuance of a license or permit to the child until the child fully complies with the court's orders.

(b) If a child fails to obey an order issued by a truancy court under Section 65.103(a) or a child is in direct contempt of court and the child has failed to obey an order or has been found in direct contempt of court on two or more previous occasions, the truancy court, after providing notice and an opportunity for a hearing, may refer the child to the juvenile probation department as a request for truancy intervention, unless the child failed to obey the truancy court order or was in direct contempt of court while 17 years of age or older.

(c) On referral of the child to the juvenile probation department, the truancy court shall provide to the juvenile probation department:

(1) documentation of all truancy prevention measures taken by the originating school district;

(2) documentation of all truancy orders for each of the child's previous truancy referrals, including:

(A) court remedies and documentation of the child's failure to comply with the truancy court's orders, if applicable, demonstrating all interventions that were exhausted by the truancy court; and

(B) documentation describing the child's direct contempt of court, if applicable;

(3) the name, birth date, and last known address of the child and the school in which the child is enrolled; and

(4) the name and last known address of the child's parent or guardian.

(d) The juvenile probation department may, on review of information provided under Subsection (c):

(1) offer further remedies related to the local plan for truancy intervention strategies adopted under Section 25.0916, Education Code; or

(2) refer the child to a juvenile court for a hearing to be conducted under Section 65.252.

(e) A truancy court may not order the confinement of a child for the child's failure to obey an order of the court issued under Section 65.103(a).

Added by Acts 2015, 84th Leg., ch. 935 (H.B. 2398), § 27, eff. Sept. 1, 2015.

### § 65.252. Proceedings in Juvenile Court

(a) After a referral by the local juvenile probation department, the juvenile court prosecutor shall determine if probable cause exists to believe that the child engaged in direct contempt of court or failed to obey an order of the truancy court under circumstances that would constitute contempt of court. On a finding that probable cause exists, the prosecutor shall determine whether to request an adjudication. Not later than the 20th day after the date the juvenile court receives a request for adjudication from the prosecutor, the juvenile court shall conduct a hearing to determine if the child engaged in conduct that constitutes contempt of the order issued by the truancy court or engaged in direct contempt of court.

(b) If the juvenile court finds that the child engaged in conduct that constitutes contempt of the order issued by the truancy court or direct contempt of court, the juvenile court shall:

(1) enter an order requiring the child to comply with the truancy court's order;

(2) forward a copy of the order to the truancy court within five days; and

(3) admonish the child, orally and in writing, of the consequences of subsequent referrals to the juvenile court, including:

(A) a possible charge of delinquent conduct for contempt of the truancy court's order or direct contempt of court; and

(B) a possible detention hearing.

(c) If the juvenile court prosecutor finds that probable cause does not exist to believe that the child engaged in direct contempt or in conduct that constitutes contempt of the order issued by the truancy court, or if the juvenile probation department finds that extenuating circumstances caused the original truancy referral, the juvenile court shall enter an order requiring the child's continued compliance with the truancy court's order and notify the truancy court not later than the fifth day after the date the order is entered.

(d) This section does not limit the discretion of a juvenile prosecutor or juvenile court to prosecute a child for conduct under Section 51.03.

Added by Acts 2015, 84th Leg., ch. 935 (H.B. 2398), § 27, eff. Sept. 1, 2015.

### § 65.253. Parent or Other Person in Contempt of Court

(a) A truancy court may enforce the following orders by contempt:

(1) an order that a parent of a child, guardian of a child, or any court-appointed guardian ad litem of a child attend an adjudication hearing under Section 65.062(b);

(2) an order requiring a person other than a child to take a particular action under Section 65.105(a);

(3) an order that a child's parent, or other person responsible to support the child, reimburse the municipality or county for the cost of the guardian ad litem appointed for the child under Section 65.061(c); and

(4) an order that a parent, or person other than the child, pay the $50 court cost under Section 65.107.

(b) A truancy court may find a parent or person other than the child in direct contempt of the court.

(c) The penalty for a finding of contempt under Subsection (a) or (b) is a fine in an amount not to exceed $100.

(d) In addition to the assessment of a fine under Subsection (c), direct contempt of the truancy court by a parent or person other than the child is punishable by:

(1) confinement in jail for a maximum of three days;

(2) a maximum of 40 hours of community service; or

(3) both confinement and community service.

Added by Acts 2015, 84th Leg., ch. 935 (H.B. 2398), § 27, eff. Sept. 1, 2015.

### § 65.254. Writ of Attachment

A truancy court may issue a writ of attachment for a person who violates an order entered under Section 65.057(c). The writ of attachment is executed in the same manner as in a criminal proceeding as provided by Chapter 24, Code of Criminal Procedure.

Added by Acts 2015, 84th Leg., ch. 935 (H.B. 2398), § 27, eff. Sept. 1, 2015.

### § 65.255. Entry of Truancy Court Order Against Parent or Other Eligible Person

(a) The truancy court shall:

(1) provide notice to a person who is the subject of a proposed truancy court order under Section 65.253; and

(2) provide a sufficient opportunity for the person to be heard regarding the proposed order.

(b) A truancy court order under Section 65.253 must be in writing and a copy promptly furnished to the parent or other eligible person.

(c) The truancy court may require the parent or other eligible person to provide suitable identification to be included in the court's file. Suitable identification includes fingerprints, a driver's license number, a social security number, or similar indicia of identity.

Added by Acts 2015, 84th Leg., ch. 935 (H.B. 2398), § 27, eff. Sept. 1, 2015.

### § 65.256. Appeal

(a) The parent or other eligible person against whom a final truancy court order has been entered under Section 65.253 may appeal as provided by law from judgments entered by a justice court in civil cases.

(b) Rule 506, Texas Rules of Civil Procedure, applies to an appeal under this section, except an appeal bond is not required.

(c) The pendency of an appeal initiated under this section does not abate or otherwise affect the proceedings in the truancy court involving the child.

Added by Acts 2015, 84th Leg., ch. 935 (H.B. 2398), § 27, eff. Sept. 1, 2015.

### § 65.257. Motion for Enforcement

(a) The state may initiate enforcement of a truancy court order under Section 65.253 against a parent or person other than the child by filing a written motion. In ordinary and concise language, the motion must:

(1) identify the provision of the order allegedly violated and sought to be enforced;

(2) state specifically and factually the manner of the person's alleged noncompliance;

(3) state the relief requested; and

(4) contain the signature of the party filing the motion.

(b) The state must allege the particular violation by the person of the truancy court order that the state had a reasonable basis for believing the person was violating when the motion was filed.

(c) The truancy court may also initiate enforcement of an order under this section on its own motion.

Added by Acts 2015, 84th Leg., ch. 935 (H.B. 2398), § 27, eff. Sept. 1, 2015.

### § 65.258. Notice and Appearance

(a) On the filing of a motion for enforcement, the truancy court shall by written notice set the date, time, and place of the hearing and order the person against whom enforcement is sought to appear and respond to the motion.

(b) The notice must be given by personal service or by certified mail, return receipt requested, on or before the 10th day before the date of the hearing on the motion. The notice must include a copy of the motion for enforcement. Personal service must comply with the Code of Criminal Procedure.

(c) If a person moves to strike or specially excepts to the motion for enforcement, the truancy court shall rule on the exception or motion to strike before the court hears evidence on the motion for enforcement. If an exception is sustained, the court shall give the movant an opportunity to replead and continue the hearing to a designated date and time without the requirement of additional service.

(d) If a person who has been personally served with notice to appear at the hearing does not appear, the truancy court may not hold the person in contempt, but may issue a warrant for the arrest of the person.

Added by Acts 2015, 84th Leg., ch. 935 (H.B. 2398), § 27, eff. Sept. 1, 2015.

### § 65.259. Conduct of Enforcement Hearing

(a) The movant must prove beyond a reasonable doubt that the person against whom enforcement is sought engaged in conduct constituting contempt of a reasonable and lawful court order as alleged in the motion for enforcement.

(b) The person against whom enforcement is sought has a privilege not to be called as a witness or otherwise to incriminate himself or herself.

(c) The truancy court shall conduct the enforcement hearing without a jury.

(d) The truancy court shall include in the court's judgment:

(1) findings for each violation alleged in the motion for enforcement; and

(2) the punishment, if any, to be imposed.

(e) If the person against whom enforcement is sought was not represented by counsel during any previous court proceeding involving a motion for enforcement, the person may, through counsel, raise any defense or affirmative defense to the proceeding that could have been asserted in the previous court proceeding that was not asserted because the person was not represented by counsel.

(f) It is an affirmative defense to enforcement of a truancy court order under Section 65.253 that the court did not provide the parent or other eligible person with due process of law in the proceeding in which the court entered the order.

Added by Acts 2015, 84th Leg., ch. 935 (H.B. 2398), § 27, eff. Sept. 1, 2015.

# TITLE 4. PROTECTIVE ORDERS AND FAMILY VIOLENCE

## SUBTITLE A. GENERAL PROVISIONS

### CHAPTER 71. DEFINITIONS



*A former Chapter 71, Protective Orders, consisting of §§ 71.01 to 71.19, was repealed by Acts 1997, 75th Leg., ch. 34, § 2, effective May 5, 1997, as part of the reenactment of Title 4.*

#### § 71.001. Applicability of Definitions

(a) Definitions in this chapter apply to this title.

(b) If, in another part of this title, a term defined by this chapter has a meaning different from the meaning provided by this chapter, the meaning of that other provision prevails.

(c) Except as provided by this chapter, the definitions in Chapter 101 apply to terms used in this title.

Added by Acts 1997, 75th Leg., ch. 34, § 1, eff. May 5, 1997.

#### § 71.002. Court

"Court" means the district court, court of domestic relations, juvenile court having the jurisdiction of a district court, statutory county court, constitutional county court, or other court expressly given jurisdiction under this title.

Added by Acts 1997, 75th Leg., ch. 34, § 1, eff. May 5, 1997. Amended by Acts 1997, 75th Leg., ch. 1220, § 1, eff. Sept. 1, 1997.

#### § 71.0021. Dating Violence

(a) "Dating violence" means an act, other than a defensive measure to protect oneself, by an actor that:

(1) is committed against a victim or applicant for a protective order:

(A) with whom the actor has or has had a dating relationship; or

(B) because of the victim's or applicant's marriage to or dating relationship with an individual with whom the actor is or has been in a dating relationship or marriage; and

(2) is intended to result in physical harm, bodily injury, assault, or sexual assault or that is a threat that reasonably places the victim or applicant in fear of imminent physical harm, bodily injury, assault, or sexual assault.

(b) For purposes of this title, "dating relationship" means a relationship between individuals who have or have had a continuing relationship of a romantic or intimate nature. The existence of such a relationship shall be determined based on consideration of:

(1) the length of the relationship;

(2) the nature of the relationship; and

(3) the frequency and type of interaction between the persons involved in the relationship.

(c) A casual acquaintanceship or ordinary fraternization in a business or social context does not constitute a "dating relationship" under Subsection (b).

Added by Acts 2001, 77th Leg., ch. 91, § 1, eff. Sept. 1, 2001. Amended by Acts 2011, 82nd Leg., ch. 872 (S.B. 116), § 2, eff. June 17, 2011; Acts 2015, 84th Leg., ch. 117 (S.B. 817), § 1, eff. Sept. 1, 2015.

#### § 71.003. Family

"Family" includes individuals related by consanguinity or affinity, as determined under Sections 573.022 and 573.024, Government Code, individuals who are former spouses of each other, individuals who are the parents of the same child, without regard to marriage, and a foster child and foster parent, without regard to whether those individuals reside together.

Added by Acts 1997, 75th Leg., ch. 34, § 1, eff. May 5, 1997. Amended by Acts 2001, 77th Leg., ch. 821, § 2.03, eff. June 14, 2001.

#### § 71.004. Family Violence

"Family violence" means:

(1) an act by a member of a family or household against another member of the family or household that is intended to result in physical harm, bodily injury, assault, or sexual assault or that is a threat that reasonably places the member in fear of imminent physical harm, bodily injury, assault, or sexual assault, but does not include defensive measures to protect oneself;

(2) abuse, as that term is defined by Sections 261.001(1)(C), (E), (G), (H), (I), (J), (K), and (M), by a member of a family or household toward a child of the family or household; or

(3) dating violence, as that term is defined by Section 71.0021.

Added by Acts 1997, 75th Leg., ch. 34, § 1, eff. May 5, 1997. Amended by Acts 2001, 77th Leg., ch. 91, § 2, eff. Sept. 1, 2001; Acts 2015, 84th Leg., ch. 117 (S.B. 817), § 2, eff. Sept. 1, 2015; Acts 2017, 85th Leg., ch. 319 (S.B. 11), § 1, eff. Sept. 1, 2017; Acts 2017, 85th Leg., ch. 1136 (H.B. 249), § 1, eff. Sept. 1, 2017.

### § 71.005. Household

"Household" means a unit composed of persons living together in the same dwelling, without regard to whether they are related to each other.

Added by Acts 1997, 75th Leg., ch. 34, § 1, eff. May 5, 1997.

### § 71.006. Member of a Household

"Member of a household" includes a person who previously lived in a household.

Added by Acts 1997, 75th Leg., ch. 34, § 1, eff. May 5, 1997.

### § 71.007. Prosecuting Attorney

"Prosecuting attorney" means the attorney, determined as provided in this title, who represents the state in a district or statutory county court in the county in which venue of the application for a protective order is proper.

Added by Acts 1997, 75th Leg., ch. 34, § 1, eff. May 5, 1997.

### § 71.008. Repealed by Acts 2001, 77th Leg., ch. 48, § 3, eff. Sept. 1, 2001

# SUBTITLE B. PROTECTIVE ORDERS

## CHAPTER 81. GENERAL PROVISIONS

**Section**



### § 81.001. Entitlement to Protective Order

A court shall render a protective order as provided by Section 85.001(b) if the court finds that family violence has occurred and is likely to occur in the future.

Added by Acts 1997, 75th Leg., ch. 34, § 1, eff. May 5, 1997.

### § 81.0015. Presumption

For purposes of this subtitle, there is a presumption that family violence has occurred and is likely to occur in the future if:

(1) the respondent has been convicted of or placed on deferred adjudication community supervision for any of the following offenses against the child for whom the petition is filed:

(A) an offense under Title 5, Penal Code, for which the court has made an affirmative finding that the offense involved family violence under Article 42.013, Code of Criminal Procedure; or

(B) an offense under Title 6, Penal Code;

(2) the respondent's parental rights with respect to the child have been terminated; and

(3) the respondent is seeking or attempting to seek contact with the child.

Added by Acts 2015, 84th Leg., ch. 1241 (H.B. 1782), § 1, eff. Sept. 1, 2015.

### § 81.002. No Fee for Applicant

An applicant for a protective order or an attorney representing an applicant may not be assessed a fee, cost, charge, or expense by a district or county clerk of the court or a sheriff, constable, or other public official or employee in connection with the filing, serving, or entering of a protective order or for any other service described by this subsection, including:

(1) a fee to dismiss, modify, or withdraw a protective order;

(2) a fee for certifying copies;

(3) a fee for comparing copies to originals;

(4) a court reporter fee;

(5) a judicial fund fee;

(6) a fee for any other service related to a protective order; or

(7) a fee to transfer a protective order.

Added by Acts 1997, 75th Leg., ch. 34, § 1, eff. May 5, 1997. Amended by Acts 1997, 75th Leg., ch. 1193, § 3, eff. Sept. 1, 1997.

### § 81.003. Fees and Costs Paid by Party Found to Have Committed Family Violence

(a) Except on a showing of good cause or of the indigence of a party found to have committed family violence, the court shall require in a protective order that the party against whom the order is rendered pay the $16 protective order fee, the standard fees charged by the clerk of the court in a general civil proceeding for the cost of serving the order, the costs of court, and all other fees, charges, or expenses incurred in connection with the protective order.

(b) The court may order a party against whom an agreed protective order is rendered under Section 85.005 to pay the fees required in Subsection (a).

Added by Acts 1997, 75th Leg., ch. 34, § 1, eff. May 5, 1997. Amended by Acts 1997, 75th Leg., ch. 1193, § 4, eff. Sept. 1, 1997.

### § 81.004. Contempt for Nonpayment of Fee

(a) A party who is ordered to pay fees and costs and who does not pay before the date specified by the order may be punished for contempt of court as provided by Section 21.002, Government Code.

(b) If a date is not specified by the court under Subsection (a), payment of costs is required before the 60th day after the date the order was rendered.

Added by Acts 1997, 75th Leg., ch. 34, § 1, eff. May 5, 1997. Amended by Acts 1997, 75th Leg., ch. 1193, § 5, eff. Sept. 1, 1997.

### § 81.005. Attorney's Fees

(a) The court may assess reasonable attorney's fees against the party found to have committed family violence or a party against whom an agreed protective order is rendered under Section 85.005 as compensation for the services of a private or prosecuting attorney or an attorney employed by the Department of Family and Protective Services.

(b) In setting the amount of attorney's fees, the court shall consider the income and ability to pay of the person against whom the fee is assessed.

Added by Acts 1997, 75th Leg., ch. 34, § 1, eff. May 5, 1997. Amended by Acts 1997, 75th Leg., ch. 1193, § 6, eff. Sept. 1, 1997; Acts 2011, 82nd Leg., ch. 110 (H.B. 841), § 4, eff. May 21, 2011.

### § 81.006. Payment of Attorney's Fees

The amount of fees collected under this chapter as compensation for the fees:

(1) of a private attorney shall be paid to the private attorney who may enforce the order for fees in the attorney's own name;

(2) of a prosecuting attorney shall be paid to the credit of the county fund from which the salaries of the employees of the prosecuting attorney are paid or supplemented; and

(3) of an attorney employed by the Department of Family and Protective Services shall be deposited in the general revenue fund to the credit of the Department of Family and Protective Services.

Added by Acts 1997, 75th Leg., ch. 34, § 1, eff. May 5, 1997. Amended by Acts 2011, 82nd Leg., ch. 110 (H.B. 841), § 5, eff. May 21, 2011.

### § 81.007. Prosecuting Attorney

(a) The county attorney or the criminal district attorney is the prosecuting attorney responsible for filing applications under this subtitle unless the district attorney assumes the responsibility by giving notice of that assumption to the county attorney.

(b) The prosecuting attorney responsible for filing an application under this subtitle shall provide notice of that responsibility to all law enforcement agencies in the jurisdiction of the prosecuting attorney.

(c) The prosecuting attorney shall comply with Article 5.06, Code of Criminal Procedure, in filing an application under this subtitle.

Added by Acts 1997, 75th Leg., ch. 34, § 1, eff. May 5, 1997.

### § 81.0075. Representation by Prosecuting Attorney in Certain Other Actions

Subject to the Texas Disciplinary Rules of Professional Conduct, a prosecuting attorney is not precluded from representing a party in a proceeding under this subtitle and the Department of Family and Protective Services in another action involving the party, regardless of whether the proceeding under this subtitle occurs before, concurrently with, or after the other action involving the party.

Added by Acts 1997, 75th Leg., ch. 1193, § 7, eff. Sept. 1, 1997. Amended by Acts 2011, 82nd Leg., ch. 110 (H.B. 841), § 6, eff. May 21, 2011; Acts 2013, 83rd Leg., ch. 393 (S.B. 130), § 1, eff. June 14, 2013.

### § 81.008. Relief Cumulative

Except as provided by this subtitle, the relief and remedies provided by this subtitle are cumulative of other relief and remedies provided by law.

Added by Acts 1997, 75th Leg., ch. 34, § 1, eff. May 5, 1997.

### § 81.009. Appeal

(a) Except as provided by Subsections (b) and (c), a protective order rendered under this subtitle may be appealed.

(b) A protective order rendered against a party in a suit for dissolution of a marriage may not be appealed until the time the final decree of dissolution of the marriage becomes a final, appealable order.

(c) A protective order rendered against a party in a suit affecting the parent-child relationship may not be appealed until the time an order providing for support of the child or possession of or access to the child becomes a final, appealable order.

Added by Acts 2005, 79th Leg., ch. 916, § 2, eff. June 18, 2005.

### § 81.010. Court Enforcement

(a) A court of this state with jurisdiction of proceedings arising under this title may enforce a protective order rendered by another court in the same manner that the court that rendered the order could enforce the order, regardless of whether the order is transferred under Subchapter D, Chapter 85.

(b) A court's authority under this section includes the authority to enforce a protective order through contempt.

(c) A motion for enforcement of a protective order rendered under this title may be filed in:

(1) any court in the county in which the order was rendered with jurisdiction of proceedings arising under this title;

(2) a county in which the movant or respondent resides; or

(3) a county in which an alleged violation of the order occurs.

Added by Acts 2011, 82nd Leg., ch. 632 (S.B. 819), § 1, eff. Sept. 1, 2011.

### § 81.011. Use of Digitized Signature

(a) A digitized signature on an application for a protective order under this title or any other pleading or order in a proceeding under this title satisfies the requirements for and imposes the duties of signatories to pleadings, motions, and other papers identified under Rule 13, Texas Rules of Civil Procedure.

(b) A digitized signature under this section may be applied only by, and must remain under the sole control of, the person whose signature is represented.

Added by Acts 2015, 84th Leg., ch. 1165 (S.B. 813), § 3, eff. Sept. 1, 2015.

## CHAPTER 82. APPLYING FOR PROTECTIVE ORDER

SUBCHAPTER A. APPLICATION FOR PROTECTIVE ORDER

**Section**



SUBCHAPTER B. PLEADINGS BY RESPONDENT



SUBCHAPTER C. NOTICE OF APPLICATION FOR PROTECTIVE ORDER



## SUBCHAPTER A. APPLICATION FOR PROTECTIVE ORDER

### § 82.001. Application

A proceeding under this subtitle is begun by filing "An Application for a Protective Order" with the clerk of the court.

Added by Acts 1997, 75th Leg., ch. 34, § 1, eff. May 5, 1997.

### § 82.002. Who May File Application

(a) With regard to family violence under Section 71.004(1) or (2), an adult member of the family or household may file an application for a protective order to protect the applicant or any other member of the applicant's family or household

*Text of subsec. (b), as added by Acts 2011, 82nd Leg., ch. 632 (S.B. 819), § 2*

(b) With regard to family violence under Section 71.004(3), an application for a protective order to protect the applicant may be filed by a member of the dating relationship, regardless of whether the member is an adult or a child.

*Text of subsec. (b), as added by Acts 2011, 82nd Leg., ch. 872 (S.B. 116), § 3*

(b) With regard to family violence under Section 71.004(3), an application for a protective order to protect the applicant may be filed by:

(1) an adult member of the dating relationship; or

(2) an adult member of the marriage, if the victim is or was married as described by Section 71.0021(a)(1)(B).

(c) Any adult may apply for a protective order to protect a child from family violence.

(d) In addition, an application may be filed for the protection of any person alleged to be a victim of family violence by:

(1) a prosecuting attorney; or

(2) the Department of Family and Protective Services.

(e) The person alleged to be the victim of family violence in an application filed under Subsection (c) or (d) is considered to be the applicant for a protective order under this subtitle.

Added by Acts 1997, 75th Leg., ch. 34, § 1, eff. May 5, 1997. Amended by Acts 1997, 75th Leg., ch. 1193, § 8, eff. Sept. 1, 1997; Acts 2001, 77th Leg., ch. 91, § 3, eff. Sept. 1, 2001; Acts 2011, 82nd Leg., ch. 110 (H.B. 841), § 7, eff. May 21, 2011; Acts 2011, 82nd Leg., ch. 632 (S.B. 819), § 2, eff. Sept. 1, 2011; Acts 2011, 82nd Leg., ch. 872 (S.B. 116), § 3, eff. June 17, 2011.

### § 82.003. Venue

An application may be filed in:

(1) the county in which the applicant resides;

(2) the county in which the respondent resides; or

(3) any county in which the family violence is alleged to have occurred.

Added by Acts 1997, 75th Leg., ch. 34, § 1, eff. May 5, 1997. Amended by Acts 2013, 83rd Leg., ch. 392 (S.B. 129), § 1, eff. June 14, 2013.

### § 82.004. Contents of Application

An application must state:

(1) the name and county of residence of each applicant;

(2) the name and county of residence of each individual alleged to have committed family violence;

(3) the relationships between the applicants and the individual alleged to have committed family violence;

(4) a request for one or more protective orders; and

(5) whether an applicant is receiving services from the Title IV–D agency in connection with a child support case and, if known, the agency case number for each open case.

Added by Acts 1997, 75th Leg., ch. 34, § 1, eff. May 5, 1997. Amended by Acts 2001, 77th Leg., ch. 296, § 1, eff. Sept. 1, 2001; Acts 2013, 83rd Leg., ch. 742 (S.B. 355), § 3, eff. Sept. 1, 2013.

### § 82.005. Application Filed During Suit for Dissolution of Marriage or Suit Affecting Parent-Child Relationship

A person who wishes to apply for a protective order with respect to the person's spouse and who is a party to a suit for the dissolution of a marriage or a suit affecting the parent-child relationship that is pending in a court must file the application as required by Subchapter D,[1] Chapter 85.

Added by Acts 1997, 75th Leg., ch. 34, § 1, eff. May 5, 1997. Amended by Acts 1997, 75th Leg., ch. 1193, § 9, eff. Sept. 1, 1997.

[1] V.T.C.A., Family Code § 85.061 et seq.

### § 82.006. Application Filed After Dissolution of Marriage

If an applicant for a protective order is a former spouse of the individual alleged to have committed family violence, the application must include:

(1) a copy of the decree dissolving the marriage; or

(2) a statement that the decree is unavailable to the applicant and that a copy of the decree will be filed with the court before the hearing on the application.

Added by Acts 1997, 75th Leg., ch. 34, § 1, eff. May 5, 1997.

### § 82.007. Application Filed for Child Subject to Continuing Jurisdiction

An application that requests a protective order for a child who is subject to the continuing exclusive jurisdiction of a court under Title 5[1] or alleges that a child who is subject to the continuing exclusive jurisdiction of a court under Title 5 has committed family violence must include:

(1) a copy of each court order affecting the conservatorship, support, and possession of or access to the child; or

(2) a statement that the orders affecting the child are unavailable to the applicant and that a copy of

the orders will be filed with the court before the hearing on the application.

Added by Acts 1997, 75th Leg., ch. 34, § 1, eff. May 5, 1997.

[1] V.T.C.A., Family Code § 101.001 et seq.

### § 82.008. Application Filed After Expiration of Former Protective Order

(a) An application for a protective order that is filed after a previously rendered protective order has expired must include:

(1) a copy of the expired protective order attached to the application or, if a copy of the expired protective order is unavailable, a statement that the order is unavailable to the applicant and that a copy of the order will be filed with the court before the hearing on the application;

(2) a description of either:

(A) the violation of the expired protective order, if the application alleges that the respondent violated the expired protective order by committing an act prohibited by that order before the order expired; or

(B) the threatened harm that reasonably places the applicant in fear of imminent physical harm, bodily injury, assault, or sexual assault; and

(3) if a violation of the expired order is alleged, a statement that the violation of the expired order has not been grounds for any other order protecting the applicant that has been issued or requested under this subtitle.

(b) The procedural requirements for an original application for a protective order apply to a protective order requested under this section.

Added by Acts 1997, 75th Leg., ch. 34, § 1, eff. May 5, 1997. Amended by Acts 1999, 76th Leg., ch. 1160, § 1, eff. Sept. 1, 1999.

### § 82.0085. Application Filed Before Expiration of Previously Rendered Protective Order

(a) If an application for a protective order alleges that an unexpired protective order applicable to the respondent is due to expire not later than the 30th day after the date the application was filed, the application for the subsequent protective order must include:

(1) a copy of the previously rendered protective order attached to the application or, if a copy of the previously rendered protective order is unavailable, a statement that the order is unavailable to the applicant and that a copy of the order will be filed with the court before the hearing on the application; and

(2) a description of the threatened harm that reasonably places the applicant in fear of imminent physical harm, bodily injury, assault, or sexual assault.

(b) The procedural requirements for an original application for a protective order apply to a protective order requested under this section.

Added by Acts 1999, 76th Leg., ch. 1160, § 2, eff. Sept. 1, 1999.

### § 82.009. Application for Temporary ex Parte Order

(a) An application that requests the issuance of a temporary ex parte order under Chapter 83 must:

(1) contain a detailed description of the facts and circumstances concerning the alleged family violence and the need for the immediate protective order; and

(2) be signed by each applicant under an oath that the facts and circumstances contained in the application are true to the best knowledge and belief of each applicant.

(b) For purposes of this section, a statement signed under oath by a child is valid if the statement otherwise complies with this chapter.

Added by Acts 1997, 75th Leg., ch. 34, § 1, eff. May 5, 1997. Amended by Acts 2011, 82nd Leg., ch. 632 (S.B. 819), § 3, eff. Sept. 1, 2011.

### § 82.010. Confidentiality of Application

(a) This section applies only in a county with a population of 3.4 million or more.

(b) Except as otherwise provided by law, an application for a protective order is confidential, is excepted from required public disclosure under Chapter 552, Government Code, and may not be released to a person who is not a respondent to the application until after the date of service of notice of the application or the date of the hearing on the application, whichever date is sooner.

(c) Except as otherwise provided by law, an application requesting the issuance of a temporary ex parte order under Chapter 83 is confidential, is excepted from required public disclosure under Chapter 552, Government Code, and may not be released to a person who is not a respondent to the application until after the date that the court or law enforcement informs the respondent of the court's order.

Added by Acts 2003, 78th Leg., ch. 1314, § 2, eff. Sept. 1, 2003.

### § 82.011. Confidentiality of Certain Information

On request by an applicant, the court may protect the applicant's mailing address by rendering an order:

(1) requiring the applicant to:

(A) disclose the applicant's mailing address to the court;

(B) designate a person to receive on behalf of the applicant any notice or documents filed with the court related to the application; and

(C) disclose the designated person's mailing address to the court;

(2) requiring the court clerk to:

(A) strike the applicant's mailing address from the public records of the court, if applicable; and

(B) maintain a confidential record of the applicant's mailing address for use only by the court; and

(3) prohibiting the release of the information to the respondent.

Added by Acts 2017, 85th Leg., ch. 422 (S.B. 1242), § 1, eff. Sept. 1, 2017.

## SUBCHAPTER B. PLEADINGS BY RESPONDENT

### § 82.021. Answer

A respondent to an application for a protective order who is served with notice of an application for a protective order may file an answer at any time before the hearing. A respondent is not required to file an answer to the application.

Added by Acts 1997, 75th Leg., ch. 34, § 1, eff. May 5, 1997.

### § 82.022. Request by Respondent for Protective Order

To apply for a protective order, a respondent to an application for a protective order must file a separate application.

Added by Acts 1997, 75th Leg., ch. 34, § 1, eff. May 5, 1997.

## SUBCHAPTER C. NOTICE OF APPLICATION FOR PROTECTIVE ORDER

### § 82.041. Contents of Notice of Application

(a) A notice of an application for a protective order must:

(1) be styled "The State of Texas";

(2) be signed by the clerk of the court under the court's seal;

(3) contain the name and location of the court;

(4) show the date the application was filed;

(5) show the date notice of the application for a protective order was issued;

(6) show the date, time, and place of the hearing;

(7) show the file number;

(8) show the name of each applicant and each person alleged to have committed family violence;

(9) be directed to each person alleged to have committed family violence;

(10) show:

(A) the name and address of the attorney for the applicant; or

(B) if the applicant is not represented by an attorney:

(i) the mailing address of the applicant; or

(ii) if applicable, the name and mailing address of the person designated under Section 82.011; and

(11) contain the address of the clerk of the court.

(b) The notice of an application for a protective order must state: "An application for a protective order has been filed in the court stated in this notice alleging that you have committed family violence. You may employ an attorney to defend you against this allegation. You or your attorney may, but are not required to, file a written answer to the application. Any answer must be filed before the hearing on the application. If you receive this notice within 48 hours before the time set for the hearing, you may request the court to reschedule the hearing not later than 14 days after the date set for the hearing. If you do not attend the hearing, a default judgment may be taken and a protective order may be issued against you."

Added by Acts 1997, 75th Leg., ch. 34, § 1, eff. May 5, 1997. Amended by Acts 1997, 75th Leg., ch. 1193, § 10, eff. Sept. 1, 1997; Acts 2017, 85th Leg., ch. 422 (S.B. 1242), § 2, eff. Sept. 1, 2017.

### § 82.042. Issuance of Notice of Application

(a) On the filing of an application, the clerk of the court shall issue a notice of an application for a protective order and deliver the notice as directed by the applicant.

(b) On request by the applicant, the clerk of the court shall issue a separate or additional notice of an application for a protective order.

Added by Acts 1997, 75th Leg., ch. 34, § 1, eff. May 5, 1997.

### § 82.043. Service of Notice of Application

(a) Each respondent to an application for a protective order is entitled to service of notice of an application for a protective order.

(b) An applicant for a protective order shall furnish the clerk with a sufficient number of copies of the application for service on each respondent.

(c) Notice of an application for a protective order must be served in the same manner as citation under the Texas Rules of Civil Procedure, except that service by publication is not authorized.

(d) Service of notice of an application for a protective order is not required before the issuance of a temporary ex parte order under Chapter 83.

(e) The requirements of service of notice under this subchapter do not apply if the application is filed as a motion in a suit for dissolution of a marriage. Notice for the motion is given in the same manner as any other motion in a suit for dissolution of a marriage.

Added by Acts 1997, 75th Leg., ch. 34, § 1, eff. May 5, 1997.

## CHAPTER 83. TEMPORARY EX PARTE ORDERS

Section



### § 83.001. Requirements for Temporary ex Parte Order

(a) If the court finds from the information contained in an application for a protective order that there is a clear and present danger of family violence, the court, without further notice to the individual alleged to have committed family violence and without a hearing, may enter a temporary ex parte order for the protection of the applicant or any other member of the family or household of the applicant.

(b) In a temporary ex parte order, the court may direct a respondent to do or refrain from doing specified acts.

Added by Acts 1997, 75th Leg., ch. 34, § 1, eff. May 5, 1997. Amended by Acts 2001, 77th Leg., ch. 91, § 4, eff. Sept. 1, 2001.

### § 83.002. Duration of Order; Extension

(a) A temporary ex parte order is valid for the period specified in the order, not to exceed 20 days.

(b) On the request of an applicant or on the court's own motion, a temporary ex parte order may be extended for additional 20-day periods.

Added by Acts 1997, 75th Leg., ch. 34, § 1, eff. May 5, 1997.

### § 83.003. Bond Not Required

The court, at the court's discretion, may dispense with the necessity of a bond for a temporary ex parte order.

Added by Acts 1997, 75th Leg., ch. 34, § 1, eff. May 5, 1997.

### § 83.004. Motion to Vacate

Any individual affected by a temporary ex parte order may file a motion at any time to vacate the order. On the filing of the motion to vacate, the court shall set a date for hearing the motion as soon as possible.

Added by Acts 1997, 75th Leg., ch. 34, § 1, eff. May 5, 1997. Amended by Acts 2001, 77th Leg., ch. 91, § 5, eff. Sept. 1, 2001.

### § 83.005. Conflicting Orders

During the time the order is valid, a temporary ex parte order prevails over any other court order made under Title 5[1] to the extent of any conflict between the orders.

Added by Acts 1997, 75th Leg., ch. 34, § 1, eff. May 5, 1997. Amended by Acts 1997, 75th Leg., ch. 1193, § 11, eff. Sept. 1, 1997.

[1] V.T.C.A., Family Code § 101.001 et seq.

### § 83.006. Exclusion of Party from Residence

(a) Subject to the limitations of Section 85.021(2), a person may only be excluded from the occupancy of the person's residence by a temporary ex parte order under this chapter if the applicant:

(1) files a sworn affidavit that provides a detailed description of the facts and circumstances requiring the exclusion of the person from the residence; and

(2) appears in person to testify at a temporary ex parte hearing to justify the issuance of the order without notice.

(b) Before the court may render a temporary ex parte order excluding a person from the person's residence, the court must find from the required affidavit and testimony that:

(1) the applicant requesting the excluding order either resides on the premises or has resided there within 30 days before the date the application was filed;

(2) the person to be excluded has within the 30 days before the date the application was filed committed family violence against a member of the household; and

(3) there is a clear and present danger that the person to be excluded is likely to commit family violence against a member of the household.

(c) The court may recess the hearing on a temporary ex parte order to contact the respondent by telephone and provide the respondent the opportunity to be present when the court resumes the hearing. Without regard to whether the respondent is able to be present at the hearing, the court shall resume the hearing before the end of the working day.

Added by Acts 1997, 75th Leg., ch. 34, § 1, eff. May 5, 1997. Amended by Acts 2011, 82nd Leg., ch. 632 (S.B. 819), § 4, eff. Sept. 1, 2011.

### § 83.007. Repealed by Acts 2011, 82nd Leg., ch. 632 (S.B. 819), § 6(1), eff. Sept. 1, 2011

## CHAPTER 84. HEARING

**Section**



### § 84.001. Time Set for Hearing

(a) On the filing of an application for a protective order, the court shall set a date and time for the hearing unless a later date is requested by the applicant. Except as provided by Section 84.002, the court may not set a date later than the 14th day after the date the application is filed.

(b) The court may not delay a hearing on an application in order to consolidate it with a hearing on a subsequently filed application.

Added by Acts 1997, 75th Leg., ch. 34, § 1, eff. May 5, 1997.

### § 84.002. Extended Time for Hearing in District Court in Certain Counties

(a) On the request of the prosecuting attorney in a county with a population of more than two million or in a county in a judicial district that is composed of more than one county, the district court shall set the hearing on a date and time not later than 20 days after the date the application is filed or 20 days after the date a request is made to reschedule a hearing under Section 84.003.

(b) The district court shall grant the request of the prosecuting attorney for an extended time in which to hold a hearing on a protective order either on a case-by-case basis or for all cases filed under this subtitle.

Added by Acts 1997, 75th Leg., ch. 34, § 1, eff. May 5, 1997. Amended by Acts 1997, 75th Leg., ch. 1193, § 12, eff. Sept. 1, 1997; Acts 2011, 82nd Leg., ch. 1163 (H.B. 2702), § 17, eff. Sept. 1, 2011.

### § 84.003. Hearing Rescheduled for Failure of Service

(a) If a hearing set under this chapter is not held because of the failure of a respondent to receive service of notice of an application for a protective order, the applicant may request the court to reschedule the hearing.

(b) Except as provided by Section 84.002, the date for a rescheduled hearing shall be not later than 14 days after the date the request is made.

Added by Acts 1997, 75th Leg., ch. 34, § 1, eff. May 5, 1997.

### § 84.004. Hearing Rescheduled for Insufficient Notice

(a) If a respondent receives service of notice of an application for a protective order within 48 hours before the time set for the hearing, on request by the respondent, the court shall reschedule the hearing for a date not later than 14 days after the date set for the hearing.

(b) The respondent is not entitled to additional service for a hearing rescheduled under this section.

Added by Acts 1997, 75th Leg., ch. 34, § 1, eff. May 5, 1997.

### § 84.005. Legislative Continuance

If a proceeding for which a legislative continuance is sought under Section 30.003, Civil Practice and Remedies Code, includes an application for a protective order, the continuance is discretionary with the court.

Added by Acts 1999, 76th Leg., ch. 62, § 6.10(a), eff. Sept. 1, 1999.

### § 84.006. Hearsay Statement of Child Victim of Family Violence

In a hearing on an application for a protective order, a statement made by a child 12 years of age or younger that describes alleged family violence against the child is admissible as evidence in the same manner that a child's statement regarding alleged abuse against the child is admissible under Section 104.006 in a suit affecting the parent-child relationship.

Added by Acts 2011, 82nd Leg., ch. 59 (H.B. 905), § 1, eff. Sept. 1, 2011.

## CHAPTER 85. ISSUANCE OF PROTECTIVE ORDER



### SUBCHAPTER A. FINDINGS AND ORDERS

### § 85.001. Required Findings and Orders

(a) At the close of a hearing on an application for a protective order, the court shall find whether:

(1) family violence has occurred; and

(2) family violence is likely to occur in the future.

(b) If the court finds that family violence has occurred and that family violence is likely to occur in the future, the court:

(1) shall render a protective order as provided by Section 85.022 applying only to a person found to have committed family violence; and

(2) may render a protective order as provided by Section 85.021 applying to both parties that is in the best interest of the person protected by the order or member of the family or household of the person protected by the order.

(c) A protective order that requires the first applicant to do or refrain from doing an act under Section 85.022 shall include a finding that the first applicant has committed family violence and is likely to commit family violence in the future.

(d) If the court renders a protective order for a period of more than two years, the court must include in the order a finding described by Section 85.025(a–1).

Added by Acts 1997, 75th Leg., ch. 34, § 1, eff. May 5, 1997. Amended by Acts 2001, 77th Leg., ch. 91, § 6, eff. Sept. 1, 2001; Acts 2011, 82nd Leg., ch. 627 (S.B. 789), § 1, eff. Sept. 1, 2011.

### § 85.002. Exception for Violation of Expired Protective Order

If the court finds that a respondent violated a protective order by committing an act prohibited by the order as provided by Section 85.022, that the order was in effect at the time of the violation, and that the order has expired after the date that the violation occurred, the court, without the necessity of making the findings described by Section 85.001(a), shall render a protective order as provided by Section

85.022 applying only to the respondent and may render a protective order as provided by Section 85.021.

Added by Acts 1997, 75th Leg., ch. 34, § 1, eff. May 5, 1997. Amended by Acts 1997, 75th Leg., ch. 1193, § 13, eff. Sept. 1, 1997.

### § 85.003. Separate Protective Orders Required

(a) A court that renders separate protective orders that apply to both parties and require both parties to do or refrain from doing acts under Section 85.022 shall render two distinct and separate protective orders in two separate documents that reflect the appropriate conditions for each party.

(b) A court that renders protective orders that apply to both parties and require both parties to do or refrain from doing acts under Section 85.022 shall render the protective orders in two separate documents. The court shall provide one of the documents to the applicant and the other document to the respondent.

(c) A court may not render one protective order under Section 85.022 that applies to both parties.

Added by Acts 1997, 75th Leg., ch. 34, § 1, eff. May 5, 1997.

### § 85.004. Protective Order in Suit for Dissolution of Marriage

A protective order in a suit for dissolution of a marriage must be in a separate document entitled "PROTECTIVE ORDER."

Added by Acts 1997, 75th Leg., ch. 34, § 1, eff. May 5, 1997.

### § 85.005. Agreed Order

(a) To facilitate settlement, the parties to a proceeding may agree in writing to a protective order as provided by Sections 85.021 and 85.022. An agreement under this subsection is subject to the approval of the court. The court may not approve an agreement that requires the applicant for the protective order to do or refrain from doing an act under Section 85.022.

(b) An agreed protective order is enforceable civilly or criminally, regardless of whether the court makes the findings required by Section 85.001.

(c) If the court approves an agreement between the parties, the court shall render an agreed protective order that is in the best interest of the applicant, the family or household, or a member of the family or household.

(d) An agreed protective order is not enforceable as a contract.

(e) An agreed protective order expires on the date the court order expires.

Added by Acts 1997, 75th Leg., ch. 34, § 1, eff. May 5, 1997. Amended by Acts 2005, 79th Leg., ch. 541, § 1, eff. June 17, 2005; Acts 2021, 87th Leg., ch. 787 (H.B. 39), § 1, eff. Sept. 1, 2021.

Section 13 of Acts 2021, 87th Leg., ch. 787 (H.B. 39) provides:

"Section 85.005, Family Code, as amended by this Act, applies only to a protective order approved by the court on or after the effective date [Sept. 1, 2021] of this Act."

### § 85.006. Default Order

(a) Notwithstanding Rule 107, Texas Rules of Civil Procedure, a court may render a protective order that is binding on a respondent who does not attend a hearing if:

(1) the respondent received service of the application and notice of the hearing; and

(2) proof of service was filed with the court before the hearing.

(b) If the court reschedules the hearing under Chapter 84, a protective order may be rendered if the respondent does not attend the rescheduled hearing.

Added by Acts 1997, 75th Leg., ch. 34, § 1, eff. May 5, 1997. Amended by Acts 2021, 87th Leg., ch. 787 (H.B. 39), § 2, eff. Sept. 1, 2021.

Sections 14 and 18 of Acts 2021, 87th Leg., ch. 787 (H.B. 39) provide:

"Sec. 14. Section 85.006, Family Code, as amended by this Act, applies only to a protective order for which the respondent receives service on or after the effective date [Sept. 1, 2021] of this Act."

"Sec. 18. To the extent of any conflict, this Act prevails over another Act of the 87th Legislature, Regular Session, 2021, relating to nonsubstantive additions to and corrections in enacted codes."

### § 85.007. Confidentiality of Certain Information

(a) On request by a person protected by an order or member of the family or household of a person protected by an order, the court may exclude from a protective order the address and telephone number of:

(1) a person protected by the order, in which case the order shall state the county in which the person resides;

(2) the place of employment or business of a person protected by the order; or

(3) the child-care facility or school a child protected by the order attends or in which the child resides.

(b) On granting a request for confidentiality under this section, the court shall order the clerk to:

(1) strike the information described by Subsection (a) from the public records of the court; and

(2) maintain a confidential record of the information for use only by:

(A) the court; or

(B) a law enforcement agency for purposes of entering the information required by Section 411.042(b)(6), Government Code, into the statewide law enforcement information system maintained by the Department of Public Safety.

Added by Acts 1997, 75th Leg., ch. 34, § 1, eff. May 5, 1997. Amended by Acts 2001, 77th Leg., ch. 91, § 7, eff. Sept. 1, 2001; Acts 2017, 85th Leg., ch. 422 (S.B. 1242), § 3, eff. Sept. 1, 2017.

### § 85.008. Repealed by Acts 1997, 75th Leg., ch. 1193, § 24, eff. Sept. 1, 1997

### § 85.009. Order Valid Until Superseded

A protective order rendered under this chapter is valid and enforceable pending further action by the court that rendered the order until the order is properly superseded by another court with jurisdiction over the order.

Added by Acts 1997, 75th Leg., ch. 34, § 1, eff. May 5, 1997.

## SUBCHAPTER B. CONTENTS OF PROTECTIVE ORDER

### § 85.021. Requirements of Order Applying to Any Party

In a protective order, the court may:

(1) prohibit a party from:

(A) removing a child who is a member of the family or household from:

(i) the possession of a person named in the order; or

(ii) the jurisdiction of the court;

(B) transferring, encumbering, or otherwise disposing of property, other than in the ordinary course of business, that is mutually owned or leased by the parties; or

(C) removing a pet, companion animal, or assistance animal, as defined by Section 121.002, Human Resources Code, from the possession or actual or constructive care of a person named in the order;

(2) grant exclusive possession of a residence to a party and, if appropriate, direct one or more parties to vacate the residence if the residence:

(A) is jointly owned or leased by the party receiving exclusive possession and a party being denied possession;

(B) is owned or leased by the party retaining possession; or

(C) is owned or leased by the party being denied possession and that party has an obligation to support the party or a child of the party granted possession of the residence;

(3) provide for the possession of and access to a child of a party if the person receiving possession of or access to the child is a parent of the child;

(4) require the payment of support for a party or for a child of a party if the person required to make the payment has an obligation to support the other party or the child; or

(5) award to a party the use and possession of specified property that is community property or jointly owned or leased property.

Added by Acts 1997, 75th Leg., ch. 34, § 1, eff. May 5, 1997. Amended by Acts 2011, 82nd Leg., ch. 136 (S.B. 279), § 1, eff. Sept. 1, 2011; Acts 2013, 83rd Leg., ch. 543 (S.B. 555), § 1, eff. Sept. 1, 2013.

### § 85.022. Requirements of Order Applying to Person Who Committed Family Violence

(a) In a protective order, the court may order the person found to have committed family violence to perform acts specified by the court that the court determines are necessary or appropriate to prevent or reduce the likelihood of family violence and may order that person to:

(1) complete a battering intervention and prevention program accredited under Article 42.141, Code of Criminal Procedure;

(2) beginning on September 1, 2008, if the referral option under Subdivision (1) is not available, complete a program or counsel with a provider that has begun the accreditation process described by Subsection (a–1); or

(3) if the referral option under Subdivision (1) or, beginning on September 1, 2008, the referral option under Subdivision (2) is not available, counsel with a social worker, family service agency, physician, psychologist, licensed therapist, or licensed professional counselor who has completed family violence intervention training that the community justice assistance division of the Texas Department of Criminal Justice has approved, after consultation with the licensing authorities described by Chapters 152, 501, 502, 503, and 505, Occupations Code, and experts in the field of family violence.

(a–1) Beginning on September 1, 2009, a program or provider serving as a referral option for the courts under Subsection (a)(1) or (2) must be accredited under Section 4A, Article 42.141, Code of Criminal Procedure, as conforming to program guidelines under that article.

(b) In a protective order, the court may prohibit the person found to have committed family violence from:

(1) committing family violence;

(2) communicating:

(A) directly with a person protected by an order or a member of the family or household of a person protected by an order, in a threatening or harassing manner;

(B) a threat through any person to a person protected by an order or a member of the family or household of a person protected by an order; and

(C) if the court finds good cause, in any manner with a person protected by an order or a member of the family or household of a person protected by an order, except through the party's attorney or a person appointed by the court;

(3) going to or near the residence or place of employment or business of a person protected by an order or a member of the family or household of a person protected by an order;

(4) going to or near the residence, child-care facility, or school a child protected under the order normally attends or in which the child normally resides;

(5) engaging in conduct directed specifically toward a person who is a person protected by an order or a member of the family or household of a person protected by an order, including following the person, that is reasonably likely to harass, annoy, alarm, abuse, torment, or embarrass the person;

(6) possessing a firearm, unless the person is a peace officer, as defined by Section 1.07, Penal Code, actively engaged in employment as a sworn, full-time paid employee of a state agency or political subdivision; and

(7) harming, threatening, or interfering with the care, custody, or control of a pet, companion animal, or assistance animal, as defined by Section 121.002, Human Resources Code, that is possessed by or is in the actual or constructive care of a person protected by an order or by a member of the family or household of a person protected by an order.

(c) In an order under Subsection (b)(3) or (4), the court shall specifically describe each prohibited location and the minimum distances from the location, if any, that the party must maintain. This subsection does not apply to an order in which Section 85.007 applies.

(d) In a protective order, the court shall suspend a license to carry a handgun issued under Subchapter H,[1] Chapter 411, Government Code, that is held by a person found to have committed family violence.

(e) In this section, "firearm" has the meaning assigned by Section 46.01, Penal Code.

Added by Acts 1997, 75th Leg., ch. 34, § 1, eff. May 5, 1997. Amended by Acts 1997, 75th Leg., ch. 1193, § 14, eff. Sept. 1, 1997; Acts 1999, 76th Leg., ch. 1412, § 3, eff. Sept. 1, 1999; Acts 2001, 77th Leg., ch. 91, § 8, eff. Sept. 1, 2001; Acts 2001, 77th Leg., ch. 23, § 3, eff. Sept. 1, 2001; Acts 2007, 80th Leg., ch. 113, § 4, eff. Sept. 1, 2007; Acts 2009, 81st Leg., ch. 1146, § 11.21, eff. Sept. 1, 2009; Acts 2011, 82nd Leg., ch. 136 (S.B. 279), § 2, eff. Sept. 1, 2011; Acts 2013, 83rd Leg., ch. 543 (S.B. 555), § 2, eff. Sept. 1, 2013; Acts 2015, 84th Leg., ch. 437 (H.B. 910), § 12, eff. Jan. 1, 2016.

[1] V.T.C.A., Government Code § 411.171 et seq.

### § 85.0225. Separation of Wireless Telephone Service Account

(a) A petitioner who is the primary user of a wireless telephone number associated with the respondent's wireless telephone service account may submit to the court that renders a protective order for the petitioner under this chapter a request for the court to order:

(1) the separation of that wireless telephone number from the respondent's wireless telephone service account; and

(2) if applicable, the separation of each wireless telephone number primarily used by a child in the petitioner's care or custody.

(b) The request must include each wireless telephone number for which the petitioner requests separation.

(c) If the petitioner shows by a preponderance of the evidence that for each wireless telephone number listed in the request the petitioner or, if applicable, a child in the petitioner's care or custody is the primary user, the court shall render a separate order directing the wireless telephone service provider to transfer the billing responsibilities and rights to each listed wireless telephone number to the petitioner.

(d) An order rendered under Subsection (c) must include:

(1) the name and billing wireless telephone number of the wireless telephone service account holder;

(2) each wireless telephone number to be transferred; and

(3) a statement requiring the wireless telephone service provider to transfer to the petitioner all financial responsibility for and the right to use each wireless telephone number transferred.

(e) For purposes of Subsection (d)(3), financial responsibility includes the monthly service costs associated with any mobile device associated with the wireless telephone number.

(f) The court shall serve a copy of the order described by Subsection (c) on the registered agent for the wireless telephone service provider designated under Chapter 5, Business Organizations Code.

(g) The court shall ensure that the contact information of the petitioner is not provided to the respondent as the wireless telephone service account holder in a proceeding under this section.

Added by Acts 2021, 87th Leg., ch. 245 (H.B. 1372), § 1, eff. Sept. 1, 2021.

Section 3 of Acts 2021, 87th Leg., ch. 245 (H.B. 1372) provides:

"The change in law made by this Act applies only to a petition for a protective order filed on or after the effective date [Sept. 1, 2021] of this Act."

### § 85.023. Effect on Property Rights

A protective order or an agreement approved by the court under this subtitle does not affect the title to real property.

Added by Acts 1997, 75th Leg., ch. 34, § 1, eff. May 5, 1997.

### § 85.024. Enforcement of Counseling Requirement

(a) A person found to have engaged in family violence who is ordered to attend a program or counseling under Section 85.022(a)(1), (2), or (3) shall file with the court an affidavit before the 60th day after the date the order was rendered stating either that the person has begun the program or counseling or that a program or counseling is not available within a reasonable distance from the person's residence. A person who files an affidavit that the person has begun the program or counseling shall file with the court before the date the protective order expires a statement that the person completed the program or counseling not later than the 30th day before the expiration date of the protective order or the 30th day before the first anniversary of the date the protective order was issued, whichever date is earlier. An affidavit under this subsection must be accompanied by a letter, notice, or certificate from the program or counselor that verifies the person's completion of the program or counseling. A person who fails to comply with this subsection may be punished for contempt of court under Section 21.002, Government Code.

(b) A protective order under Section 85.022 must specifically advise the person subject to the order of the requirement of this section and the possible punishment if the person fails to comply with the requirement.

Added by Acts 1997, 75th Leg., ch. 34, § 1, eff. May 5, 1997. Amended by Acts 1997, 75th Leg., ch. 1193, § 15, eff. Sept. 1, 1997; Acts 2007, 80th Leg., ch. 113, § 5, eff. Sept. 1, 2007; Acts 2007, 80th Leg., ch. 770, § 1, eff. Sept. 1, 2007.

### § 85.025. Duration of Protective Order

(a) Except as otherwise provided by this section, an order under this subtitle is effective:

(1) for the period stated in the order, not to exceed two years; or

(2) if a period is not stated in the order, until the second anniversary of the date the order was issued.

(a–1) The court may render a protective order sufficient to protect the applicant and members of the applicant's family or household that is effective for a period that exceeds two years if the court finds that the person who is the subject of the protective order:

(1) committed an act constituting a felony offense involving family violence against the applicant or a member of the applicant's family or household, regardless of whether the person has been charged with or convicted of the offense;

(2) caused serious bodily injury to the applicant or a member of the applicant's family or household; or

(3) was the subject of two or more previous protective orders rendered:

(A) to protect the person on whose behalf the current protective order is sought; and

(B) after a finding by the court that the subject of the protective order:

(i) has committed family violence; and

(ii) is likely to commit family violence in the future.

(b) A person who is the subject of a protective order may file a motion not earlier than the first anniversary of the date on which the order was rendered requesting that the court review the protective order and determine whether there is a continuing need for the order.

(b–1) Following the filing of a motion under Subsection (b), a person who is the subject of a protective order issued under Subsection (a–1) that is effective for a period that exceeds two years may file not more than one subsequent motion requesting that the court review the protective order and determine whether there is a continuing need for the order. The subsequent motion may not be filed earlier than the first anniversary of the date on which the court rendered an order on the previous motion by the person.

(b–2) After a hearing on a motion under Subsection (b) or (b–1), if the court does not make a finding that there is no continuing need for the protective order, the protective order remains in effect until the date the order expires under this section. Evidence of the movant's compliance with the protective order does not by itself support a finding by the court that there is no continuing need for the protective order. If the court finds there is no continuing need for the protective order, the court shall order that the protective order expires on a date set by the court.

(b–3) Subsection (b) does not apply to a protective order issued under Subchapter A, Chapter 7B, Code of Criminal Procedure.

(c) If a person who is the subject of a protective order is confined or imprisoned on the date the protective order would expire under Subsection (a) or (a–1), or if the protective order would expire not later than the first anniversary of the date the person is released from confinement or imprisonment, the period for which the order is effective is extended, and the order expires on:

(1) the first anniversary of the date the person is released from confinement or imprisonment, if the person was sentenced to confinement or imprisonment for more than five years; or

(2) the second anniversary of the date the person is released from confinement or imprisonment, if the person was sentenced to confinement or imprisonment for five years or less.

Added by Acts 1997, 75th Leg., ch. 34, § 1, eff. May 5, 1997. Amended by Acts 1999, 76th Leg., ch. 1160, § 3, eff. Sept. 1, 1999; Acts 2011, 82nd Leg., ch. 627 (S.B. 789), § 2, eff. Sept. 1, 2011; Acts 2015, 84th Leg., ch. 336 (H.B. 388), § 1, eff. June 9, 2015; Acts 2017, 85th Leg., ch. 64 (S.B. 712), § 1, eff. Sept. 1, 2017; Acts 2017, 85th Leg., ch. 97 (S.B. 257), § 1, eff. Sept. 1, 2017; Acts 2019, 86th Leg., ch. 469 (H.B. 4173), § 2.35, eff. Jan. 1, 2021.

Sections 4.01 and 4.02 of Acts 2019, 86th Leg., ch. 469 (H.B. 4173) provide:

"Sec. 4.01. This Act is enacted under Section 43, Article III, Texas Constitution. This Act is intended as a codification only, and no substantive change in the law is intended by this Act.

"Sec. 4.02. (a) Chapter 311, Government Code (Code Construction Act), applies to the construction of each provision in the Code of Criminal Procedure that is enacted under Section 43, Article III, Texas Constitution (authorizing the continuing statutory revision program), in the same manner as to a code enacted under the continuing statutory revision program, except as otherwise expressly provided by the Code of Criminal Procedure.

"(b) A reference in a law to a statute or a part of a statute in the Code of Criminal Procedure enacted under Section 43, Article III, Texas Constitution (authorizing the continuing statutory revision program), is considered to be a reference to the part of that code that revises that statute or part of that statute."

## § 85.026. Warning on Protective Order

(a) Each protective order issued under this subtitle, including a temporary ex parte order, must contain the following prominently displayed statements in boldfaced type, capital letters, or underlined:

"A PERSON WHO VIOLATES THIS ORDER MAY BE PUNISHED FOR CONTEMPT OF COURT BY A FINE OF AS MUCH AS $500 OR BY CONFINEMENT IN JAIL FOR AS LONG AS SIX MONTHS, OR BOTH."

"NO PERSON, INCLUDING A PERSON WHO IS PROTECTED BY THIS ORDER, MAY GIVE PERMISSION TO ANYONE TO IGNORE OR VIOLATE ANY PROVISION OF THIS ORDER. DURING THE TIME IN WHICH THIS ORDER IS VALID, EVERY PROVISION OF THIS ORDER IS IN FULL FORCE AND EFFECT UNLESS A COURT CHANGES THE ORDER."

"IT IS UNLAWFUL FOR ANY PERSON, OTHER THAN A PEACE OFFICER, AS DEFINED BY SECTION 1.07, PENAL CODE, ACTIVELY ENGAGED IN EMPLOYMENT AS A SWORN, FULL–TIME PAID EMPLOYEE OF A STATE AGENCY OR POLITICAL SUBDIVISION, WHO IS SUBJECT TO A PROTECTIVE ORDER TO POSSESS A FIREARM OR AMMUNITION."

"IF A PERSON SUBJECT TO A PROTECTIVE ORDER IS RELEASED FROM CONFINEMENT OR IMPRISONMENT FOLLOWING THE DATE THE ORDER WOULD HAVE EXPIRED, OR IF THE ORDER WOULD HAVE EXPIRED NOT LATER THAN THE FIRST ANNIVERSARY OF THE DATE THE PERSON IS RELEASED FROM CONFINEMENT OR IMPRISONMENT, THE ORDER IS AUTOMATICALLY EXTENDED TO EXPIRE ON:

"(1) THE FIRST ANNIVERSARY OF THE DATE THE PERSON IS RELEASED, IF THE PERSON WAS SENTENCED TO CONFINEMENT OR IMPRISONMENT FOR A TERM OF MORE THAN FIVE YEARS; OR

"(2) THE SECOND ANNIVERSARY OF THE DATE THE PERSON IS RELEASED, IF THE PERSON WAS SENTENCED TO CONFINEMENT OR IMPRISONMENT FOR A TERM OF FIVE YEARS OR LESS."

"A VIOLATION OF THIS ORDER BY COMMISSION OF AN ACT PROHIBITED BY THE ORDER MAY BE PUNISHABLE BY A FINE OF AS MUCH AS $4,000 OR BY CONFINEMENT IN JAIL FOR AS LONG AS ONE YEAR, OR BOTH. AN ACT THAT RESULTS IN FAMILY VIOLENCE MAY BE PROSECUTED AS A SEPARATE MISDEMEANOR OR FELONY OFFENSE. IF THE ACT IS PROSECUTED AS A SEPARATE FELONY OFFENSE, IT IS PUNISHABLE BY CONFINEMENT IN PRISON FOR AT LEAST TWO YEARS."

(b) Repealed by Acts 2011, 82nd Leg., ch. 632 (S.B. 819), § 6(2).

(c) Each protective order issued under this subtitle, including a temporary ex parte order, must contain the following prominently displayed statement in boldfaced type, capital letters, or underlined:

"NO PERSON, INCLUDING A PERSON WHO IS PROTECTED BY THIS ORDER, MAY GIVE PERMISSION TO ANYONE TO IGNORE OR VIOLATE ANY PROVISION OF THIS ORDER. DURING THE TIME IN WHICH THIS ORDER IS VALID, EVERY PROVISION OF THIS ORDER IS IN FULL FORCE AND EFFECT UNLESS A COURT CHANGES THE ORDER."

Added by Acts 1997, 75th Leg., ch. 34, § 1, eff. May 5, 1997. Amended by Acts 1999, 76th Leg., ch. 178, § 3, eff. Aug. 30, 1999; Acts 1999, 76th Leg., ch. 1160, § 4, eff. Sept. 1, 1999; Acts 2001, 77th Leg., ch. 23, § 5, eff. Sept. 1, 2001; Acts 2011, 82nd Leg., ch. 632 (S.B. 819), §§ 5, 6(2), eff. Sept. 1, 2011; Acts 2021, 87th Leg., ch. 787 (H.B. 39), § 3, eff. Sept. 1, 2021.

*Without reference to the amendment of subsec. (c) by Acts 1999, 76th Leg., ch. 178, § 3, Acts 1999, 76th Leg., ch. 1160, § 4 deleted subsec. (c) effective September 1, 1999.*

Sections 15 and 18 of Acts 2021, 87th Leg., ch. 787 (H.B. 39) provide:

"Sec. 15. Sections 85.026 and 86.0011, Family Code, as amended by this Act, apply only to a protective order issued on or after the effective date [Sept. 1, 2021] of this Act."

"Sec. 18. To the extent of any conflict, this Act prevails over another Act of the 87th Legislature, Regular Session, 2021, relating to nonsubstantive additions to and corrections in enacted codes."

## SUBCHAPTER C. DELIVERY OF PROTECTIVE ORDER

### § 85.041. Delivery to Respondent

(a) A protective order rendered under this subtitle shall be:

(1) delivered to the respondent as provided by Rule 21a, Texas Rules of Civil Procedure;

(2) served in the same manner as a writ of injunction; or

(3) served in open court at the close of the hearing as provided by this section.

(b) The court shall serve an order in open court to a respondent who is present at the hearing by giving to the respondent a copy of the order, reduced to writing and signed by the judge or master. A certified copy of the signed order shall be given to the applicant at the time the order is given to the respondent. If the applicant is not in court at the conclusion of the hearing, the clerk of the court shall mail a certified copy of the order to the applicant not later than the third business day after the date the hearing is concluded.

(c) If the order has not been reduced to writing, the court shall give notice orally to a respondent who is present at the hearing of the part of the order that contains prohibitions under Section 85.022 or any other part of the order that contains provisions necessary to prevent further family violence. The clerk of the court shall mail a copy of the order to the respondent and a certified copy of the order to the applicant not later than the third business day after the date the hearing is concluded.

(d) If the respondent is not present at the hearing and the order has been reduced to writing at the conclusion of the hearing, the clerk of the court shall immediately provide a certified copy of the order to the applicant and mail a copy of the order to the respondent not later than the third business day after the date the hearing is concluded.

Added by Acts 1997, 75th Leg., ch. 34, § 1, eff. May 5, 1997.

### § 85.042. Delivery of Order to Other Persons

(a) Not later than the next business day after the date the court issues an original or modified protective order under this subtitle, the clerk of the court shall send a copy of the order, along with the information provided by the applicant or the applicant's attorney that is required under Section 411.042(b)(6), Government Code, to:

(1) the chief of police of the municipality in which the person protected by the order resides, if the person resides in a municipality;

(2) the appropriate constable and the sheriff of the county in which the person resides, if the person does not reside in a municipality; and

(3) the Title IV–D agency, if the application for the protective order indicates that the applicant is receiving services from the Title IV–D agency.

(a–1) This subsection applies only if the respondent, at the time of issuance of an original or modified protective order under this subtitle, is a member of the state military forces or is serving in the armed forces of the United States in an active-duty status and the applicant or the applicant's attorney provides to the clerk of the court the mailing address of the staff judge advocate or provost marshal, as applicable. In addition to complying with Subsection (a), the clerk of the court shall also provide a copy of the protective order and the information described by that subsection to the staff judge advocate at Joint Force Headquarters or the provost marshal of the military installation to which the respondent is assigned with the intent that the commanding officer will be notified, as applicable.

(b) If a protective order made under this chapter prohibits a respondent from going to or near a child-care facility or school, the clerk of the court shall send a copy of the order to the child-care facility or school.

(c) The clerk of a court that vacates an original or modified protective order under this subtitle shall notify each individual or entity who received a copy of the original or modified order from the clerk under this section that the order is vacated.

(d) The applicant or the applicant's attorney shall provide to the clerk of the court:

(1) the name and address of each law enforcement agency, child-care facility, school, and other individual or entity to which the clerk is required to send a copy of the order under this section; and

(2) any other information required under Section 411.042(b)(6), Government Code.

(e) The clerk of the court issuing an original or modified protective order under Section 85.022 that suspends a license to carry a handgun shall send a copy of the order to the appropriate division of the Department of Public Safety at its Austin headquarters. On receipt of the order suspending the license, the department shall:

(1) record the suspension of the license in the records of the department;

(2) report the suspension to local law enforcement agencies, as appropriate; and

(3) demand surrender of the suspended license from the license holder.

(f) A clerk of the court may transmit the order and any related information electronically or in another manner that can be accessed by the recipient.

(g) A clerk of the court may delay sending a copy of the order under Subsection (a) only if the clerk lacks information necessary to ensure service and enforcement.

(h) In this section, "business day" means a day other than a Saturday, Sunday, or state or national holiday.

Added by Acts 1997, 75th Leg., ch. 34, § 1, eff. May 5, 1997. Amended by Acts 1997, 75th Leg., ch. 614, § 3, eff. Sept. 1, 1997; Acts 1999, 76th Leg., ch. 1412, § 4, eff. Sept. 1, 1999; Acts 2001, 77th Leg., ch. 35, § 1, eff. Sept. 1, 2001; Acts 2001, 77th Leg., ch. 91, § 9, eff. Sept. 1, 2001; Acts 2011, 82nd Leg., ch. 327 (H.B. 2624), § 1, eff. Sept. 1, 2011; Acts 2013, 83rd Leg., ch. 742 (S.B. 355), § 4, eff. Sept. 1, 2013; Acts 2013, 83rd Leg., ch. 1276 (H.B. 1435), § 3, eff. Sept. 1, 2013; Acts 2015, 84th Leg., ch. 243 (S.B. 737), § 3, eff. Sept. 1, 2015; Acts 2015, 84th Leg., ch. 437 (H.B. 910), § 13, eff. Jan. 1, 2016.

## SUBCHAPTER D. RELATIONSHIP BETWEEN PROTECTIVE ORDER AND SUIT FOR DISSOLUTION OF MARRIAGE AND SUIT AFFECTING PARENT-CHILD RELATIONSHIP

### § 85.061. Dismissal of Application Prohibited; Subsequently Filed Suit for Dissolution of Marriage or Suit Affecting Parent-Child Relationship

If an application for a protective order is pending, a court may not dismiss the application or delay a hearing on the application on the grounds that a suit for dissolution of marriage or suit affecting the parent-child relationship is filed after the date the application was filed.

Added by Acts 1997, 75th Leg., ch. 1193, § 16, eff. Sept. 1, 1997.

### § 85.062. Application Filed While Suit for Dissolution of Marriage or Suit Affecting Parent-Child Relationship Pending

(a) If a suit for dissolution of a marriage or suit affecting the parent-child relationship is pending, a party to the suit may apply for a protective order against another party to the suit by filing an application:

(1) in the court in which the suit is pending; or

(2) in a court in the county in which the applicant resides if the applicant resides outside the jurisdiction of the court in which the suit is pending.

(b) An applicant subject to this section shall inform the clerk of the court that renders a protective order that a suit for dissolution of a marriage or a suit affecting the parent-child relationship is pending in which the applicant is party.

(c) If a final protective order is rendered by a court other than the court in which a suit for dissolution of a marriage or a suit affecting the parent-child relationship is pending, the clerk of the court that rendered the protective order shall:

(1) inform the clerk of the court in which the suit is pending that a final protective order has been rendered; and

(2) forward a copy of the final protective order to the court in which the suit is pending.

(d) A protective order rendered by a court in which an application is filed under Subsection (a)(2) is subject to transfer under Section 85.064.

Added by Acts 1997, 75th Leg., ch. 1193, § 16, eff. Sept. 1, 1997.

### § 85.063. Application Filed After Final Order Rendered in Suit for Dissolution of Marriage or Suit Affecting Parent-Child Relationship

(a) If a final order has been rendered in a suit for dissolution of marriage or suit affecting the parent-child relationship, an application for a protective order by a party to the suit against another party to the suit filed after the date the final order was rendered, and that is:

(1) filed in the county in which the final order was rendered, shall be filed in the court that rendered the final order; and

(2) filed in another county, shall be filed in a court having jurisdiction to render a protective order under this subtitle.

(b) A protective order rendered by a court in which an application is filed under Subsection (a)(2) is subject to transfer under Section 85.064.

Added by Acts 1997, 75th Leg., ch. 1193, § 16, eff. Sept. 1, 1997.

### § 85.064. Transfer of Protective Order

(a) If a protective order was rendered before the filing of a suit for dissolution of marriage or suit affecting the parent-child relationship or while the suit is pending as provided by Section 85.062, the court that rendered the order may, on the motion of a party or on the court's own motion, transfer the protective order to the court having jurisdiction of the suit if the court makes the finding prescribed by Subsection (c).

(b) If a protective order that affects a party's right to possession of or access to a child is rendered after the date a final order was rendered in a suit affecting the parent-child relationship, on the motion of a party or on the court's own motion, the court may transfer the protective order to the court of continuing, exclusive jurisdiction if the court makes the finding prescribed by Subsection (c).

(c) A court may transfer a protective order under this section if the court finds that the transfer is:

(1) in the interest of justice; or

(2) for the safety or convenience of a party or a witness.

(d) The transfer of a protective order under this section shall be conducted according to the procedures provided by Section 155.207.

(e) Except as provided by Section 81.002, the fees or costs associated with the transfer of a protective order shall be paid by the movant.

Added by Acts 1997, 75th Leg., ch. 1193, § 16, eff. Sept. 1, 1997.

### § 85.065. Effect of Transfer

(a) Repealed by Acts 2011, 82nd Leg., ch. 632 (S.B. 819), § 6(3).

(b) Repealed by Acts 2011, 82nd Leg., ch. 632 (S.B. 819), § 6(3).

(c) A protective order that is transferred is subject to modification by the court that receives the order to the same extent modification is permitted under Chapter 87 by a court that rendered the order.

Added by Acts 1997, 75th Leg., ch. 1193, § 16, eff. Sept. 1, 1997. Amended by Acts 2011, 82nd Leg., ch. 632 (S.B. 819), § 6(3), eff. Sept. 1, 2011.

## CHAPTER 86. LAW ENFORCEMENT DUTIES RELATING TO PROTECTIVE ORDERS

## § 86.001. Adoption of Procedures by Law Enforcement Agency

(a) To ensure that law enforcement officers responding to calls are aware of the existence and terms of protective orders issued under this subtitle, each law enforcement agency shall establish procedures in the agency to provide adequate information or access to information for law enforcement officers of the names of each person protected by an order issued under this subtitle and of each person against whom protective orders are directed.

(b) A law enforcement agency may enter a protective order in the agency's computer records of outstanding warrants as notice that the order has been issued and is currently in effect. On receipt of notification by a clerk of court that the court has vacated or dismissed an order, the law enforcement agency shall remove the order from the agency's computer record of outstanding warrants.

Added by Acts 1997, 75th Leg., ch. 34, § 1, eff. May 5, 1997.

## § 86.0011. Duty to Enter Information into Statewide Law Enforcement Information System

(a) On receipt of an original or modified protective order from the clerk of the issuing court, or on receipt of information pertaining to the date of confinement or imprisonment or date of release of a person subject to the protective order, a law enforcement agency shall immediately, but not later than the third business day after the date the order or information is received, enter the information required by Section 411.042(b)(6), Government Code, into the statewide law enforcement information system maintained by the Department of Public Safety.

(b) In this section, "business day" means a day other than a Saturday, Sunday, or state or national holiday.

Added by Acts 2001, 77th Leg., ch. 35, § 2, eff. Sept. 1, 2001. Amended by Acts 2015, 84th Leg., ch. 243 (S.B. 737), § 4, eff. Sept. 1, 2015; Acts 2021, 87th Leg., ch. 787 (H.B. 39), § 4, eff. Sept. 1, 2021.

Section 15 of Acts 2021, 87th Leg., ch. 787 (H.B. 39) provides:

"Sections 85.026 and 86.0011, Family Code, as amended by this Act, apply only to a protective order issued on or after the effective date [Sept. 1, 2021] of this Act."

## § 86.002. Duty to Provide Information to Firearms Dealers

(a) On receipt of a request for a law enforcement information system record check of a prospective transferee by a licensed firearms dealer under the Brady Handgun Violence Prevention Act, 18 U.S.C. Section 922, the chief law enforcement officer shall determine whether the Department of Public Safety has in the department's law enforcement information system a record indicating the existence of an active protective order directed to the prospective transferee.

(b) If the department's law enforcement information system indicates the existence of an active protective order directed to the prospective transferee, the chief law enforcement officer shall immediately advise the dealer that the transfer is prohibited.

Added by Acts 1997, 75th Leg., ch. 34, § 1, eff. May 5, 1997.

## § 86.003. Court Order for Law Enforcement Assistance Under Temporary Order

On request by an applicant obtaining a temporary ex parte protective order that excludes the respondent from the respondent's residence, the court granting the temporary order shall render a written order to the sheriff, constable, or chief of police to provide a law enforcement officer from the department of the chief of police, constable, or sheriff to:

(1) accompany the applicant to the residence covered by the order;

(2) inform the respondent that the court has ordered that the respondent be excluded from the residence;

(3) protect the applicant while the applicant takes possession of the residence; and

(4) protect the applicant if the respondent refuses to vacate the residence while the applicant takes possession of the applicant's necessary personal property.

Added by Acts 1997, 75th Leg., ch. 34, § 1, eff. May 5, 1997. Amended by Acts 1997, 75th Leg., ch. 852, § 1, eff. June 18, 1997.

## § 86.004. Court Order for Law Enforcement Assistance Under Final Order

On request by an applicant obtaining a final protective order that excludes the respondent from the respondent's residence, the court granting the final order shall render a written order to the sheriff, constable, or chief of police to provide a law enforcement officer from the department of the chief of police, constable, or sheriff to:

(1) accompany the applicant to the residence covered by the order;

(2) inform the respondent that the court has ordered that the respondent be excluded from the residence;

(3) protect the applicant while the applicant takes possession of the residence and the respondent takes possession of the respondent's necessary personal property; and

(4) if the respondent refuses to vacate the residence:

(A) remove the respondent from the residence; and

(B) arrest the respondent for violating the court order.

Added by Acts 1997, 75th Leg., ch. 34, § 1, eff. May 5, 1997. Amended by Acts 1997, 75th Leg., ch. 852, § 2, eff. June 18, 1997.

### § 86.005. Protective Order from Another Jurisdiction

To ensure that law enforcement officers responding to calls are aware of the existence and terms of a protective order from another jurisdiction, each law enforcement agency shall establish procedures in the agency to provide adequate information or access to information for law enforcement officers regarding the name of each person protected by an order rendered in another jurisdiction and of each person against whom the protective order is directed.

Added by Acts 1997, 75th Leg., ch. 1193, § 17, eff. Sept. 1, 1997. Amended by Acts 2001, 77th Leg., ch. 48, § 1, eff. Sept. 1, 2001.

## CHAPTER 87. MODIFICATION OF PROTECTIVE ORDERS

**Section**



### § 87.001. Modification of Protective Order

On the motion of any party, the court, after notice and hearing, may modify an existing protective order to:

(1) exclude any item included in the order; or

(2) include any item that could have been included in the order.

Added by Acts 1997, 75th Leg., ch. 34, § 1, eff. May 5, 1997.

### § 87.002. Modification May Not Extend Duration of Order

A protective order may not be modified to extend the period of the order's validity beyond the second anniversary of the date the original order was rendered or beyond the date the order expires under Section 85.025(a-1) or (c), whichever date occurs later.

Added by Acts 1997, 75th Leg., ch. 34, § 1, eff. May 5, 1997. Amended by Acts 1999, 76th Leg., ch. 1160, § 5, eff. Sept. 1, 1999; Acts 2011, 82nd Leg., ch. 627 (S.B. 789), § 3, eff. Sept. 1, 2011.

### § 87.003. Notification of Motion to Modify

Notice of a motion to modify a protective order is sufficient if delivery of the motion is attempted on the respondent at the respondent's last known address by registered or certified mail as provided by Rule 21a, Texas Rules of Civil Procedure.

Added by Acts 1997, 75th Leg., ch. 34, § 1, eff. May 5, 1997.

### § 87.004. Change of Address or Telephone Number

(a) If a protective order contains the address or telephone number of a person protected by the order, of the place of employment or business of the person, or of the child-care facility or school of a child protected by the order and that information is not confidential under Section 85.007, the person protected by the order may file a notification of change of address or telephone number with the court that rendered the order to modify the information contained in the order.

(b) The clerk of the court shall attach the notification of change to the protective order and shall deliver a copy of the notification to the respondent by registered or certified mail as provided by Rule 21a, Texas Rules of Civil Procedure.

(c) The filing of a notification of change of address or telephone number and the attachment of the notification to a protective order does not affect the validity of the order.

Added by Acts 1997, 75th Leg., ch. 1193, § 18, eff. Sept. 1, 1997.

## CHAPTER 88. UNIFORM INTERSTATE ENFORCEMENT OF PROTECTIVE ORDERS ACT

**Section**



*Acts 2001, 77th Leg., ch. 48, § 2 amended Chapter 88 effective September 1, 2001. The former Chapter 88, Protective Order From Another State, consisting of §§ 88.001 to 88.004, was amended as Chapter 88, Uniform Interstate Enforcement of Protective Orders Act, consisting of §§ 88.001 to 88.008.*

### § 88.001. Short Title

This chapter may be cited as the Uniform Interstate Enforcement of Domestic Violence Protection Orders Act.

Added by Acts 2001, 77th Leg., ch. 48, § 2, eff. Sept. 1, 2001.

### § 88.002. Definitions

In this chapter:

(1) "Foreign protective order" means a protective order issued by a tribunal of another state.

(2) "Issuing state" means the state in which a tribunal issues a protective order.

(3) "Mutual foreign protective order" means a foreign protective order that includes provisions issued in favor of both the protected individual seeking enforcement of the order and the respondent.

(4) "Protected individual" means an individual protected by a protective order.

(5) "Protective order" means an injunction or other order, issued by a tribunal under the domestic violence or family violence laws or another law of the issuing state, to prevent an individual from engaging in violent or threatening acts against, harassing, contacting or communicating with, or being in physical proximity to another individual.

(6) "Respondent" means the individual against whom enforcement of a protective order is sought.

(7) "State" means a state of the United States, the District of Columbia, the Commonwealth of Puerto Rico, the United States Virgin Islands, or a territory or insular possession subject to the jurisdiction of the United States. The term includes a military tribunal of the United States, an Indian tribe or band, and an Alaskan native village that has jurisdiction to issue protective orders.

(8) "Tribunal" means a court, agency, or other entity authorized by law to issue or modify a protective order.

Added by Acts 2001, 77th Leg., ch. 48, § 2, eff. Sept. 1, 2001.

### § 88.003. Judicial Enforcement of Order

(a) A tribunal of this state shall enforce the terms of a foreign protective order, including a term that provides relief that a tribunal of this state would not have power to provide but for this section. The tribunal shall enforce the order regardless of whether the order was obtained by independent action or in another proceeding, if the order is an order issued in response to a complaint, petition, or motion filed by or on behalf of an individual seeking protection. In a proceeding to enforce a foreign protective order, the tribunal shall follow the procedures of this state for the enforcement of protective orders.

(b) A tribunal of this state shall enforce the provisions of the foreign protective order that govern the possession of and access to a child if the provisions were issued in accordance with the jurisdictional requirements governing the issuance of possession and access orders in the issuing state.

(c) A tribunal of this state may enforce a provision of the foreign protective order relating to child support if the order was issued in accordance with the jurisdictional requirements of Chapter 159 and the federal Full Faith and Credit for Child Support Orders Act, 28 U.S.C. Section 1738B, as amended.

(d) A foreign protective order is valid if the order:

(1) names the protected individual and the respondent;

(2) is currently in effect;

(3) was rendered by a tribunal that had jurisdiction over the parties and the subject matter under the law of the issuing state; and

(4) was rendered after the respondent was given reasonable notice and an opportunity to be heard consistent with the right to due process, either:

(A) before the tribunal issued the order; or

(B) in the case of an ex parte order, within a reasonable time after the order was rendered.

(e) A protected individual seeking enforcement of a foreign protective order establishes a prima facie case for its validity by presenting an order that is valid on its face.

(f) It is an affirmative defense in an action seeking enforcement of a foreign protective order that the order does not meet the requirements for a valid order under Subsection (d).

(g) A tribunal of this state may enforce the provisions of a mutual foreign protective order that favor a respondent only if:

(1) the respondent filed a written pleading seeking a protective order from the tribunal of the issuing state; and

(2) the tribunal of the issuing state made specific findings in favor of the respondent.

Added by Acts 2001, 77th Leg., ch. 48, § 2, eff. Sept. 1, 2001.

### § 88.004. Nonjudicial Enforcement of Order

(a) A law enforcement officer of this state, on determining that there is probable cause to believe that a valid foreign protective order exists and that the order has been violated, shall enforce the foreign protective order as if it were an order of a tribunal of this state. A law enforcement officer has probable cause to believe that a foreign protective order exists if the protected individual presents a foreign protective order that identifies both the protected individual and the respondent and on its face, is currently in effect.

(b) For the purposes of this section, a foreign protective order may be inscribed on a tangible medium or may be stored in an electronic or other medium if it is retrievable in a perceivable form. Presentation of a certified copy of a protective order is not required for enforcement.

(c) If a protected individual does not present a foreign protective order, a law enforcement officer may determine that there is probable cause to believe that a valid foreign protective order exists by relying on any relevant information.

(d) A law enforcement officer of this state who determines that an otherwise valid foreign protective order cannot be enforced because the respondent has not been notified or served with the order shall inform the respondent of the order and make a reasonable effort to serve the order on the respondent. After informing the respondent and attempting to serve the order, the officer shall allow the respondent a reasonable opportunity to comply with the order before enforcing the order.

(e) The registration or filing of an order in this state is not required for the enforcement of a valid foreign protective order under this chapter.

Added by Acts 2001, 77th Leg., ch. 48, § 2, eff. Sept. 1, 2001.

### § 88.005. Registration of Order

(a) An individual may register a foreign protective order in this state. To register a foreign protective order, an individual shall:

(1) present a certified copy of the order to a sheriff, constable, or chief of police responsible for the registration of orders in the local computer records and in the statewide law enforcement system maintained by the Texas Department of Public Safety; or

(2) present a certified copy of the order to the Department of Public Safety and request that the order be registered in the statewide law enforcement system maintained by the Department of Public Safety.

(b) On receipt of a foreign protective order, the agency responsible for the registration of protective orders shall register the order in accordance with this section and furnish to the individual registering the order a certified copy of the registered order.

(c) The agency responsible for the registration of protective orders shall register a foreign protective order on presentation of a copy of a protective order that has been certified by the issuing state. A registered foreign protective order that is inaccurate or not currently in effect shall be corrected or removed from the registry in accordance with the law of this state.

(d) An individual registering a foreign protective order shall file an affidavit made by the protected individual that, to the best of the protected individual's knowledge, the order is in effect.

(e) A foreign protective order registered under this section may be entered in any existing state or federal registry of protective orders, in accordance with state or federal law.

(f) A fee may not be charged for the registration of a foreign protective order.

Added by Acts 2001, 77th Leg., ch. 48, § 2, eff. Sept. 1, 2001.

### § 88.006. Immunity

A state or local governmental agency, law enforcement officer, prosecuting attorney, clerk of court, or any state or local governmental official acting in an official capacity is immune from civil and criminal liability for an act or omission arising from the registration or enforcement of a foreign protective order or the detention or arrest of a person alleged to have violated a foreign protective order if the act or omission was done in good faith in an effort to comply with this chapter.

Added by Acts 2001, 77th Leg., ch. 48, § 2, eff. Sept. 1, 2001.

### § 88.007. Other Remedies

A protected individual who pursues a remedy under this chapter is not precluded from pursuing other legal or equitable remedies against the respondent.

Added by Acts 2001, 77th Leg., ch. 48, § 2, eff. Sept. 1, 2001.

### § 88.008. Uniformity of Application and Construction

In applying and construing this chapter, consideration shall be given to the need to promote uniformity of the law with respect to its subject matter among the states that enact the Uniform Interstate Enforcement of Domestic Violence Protection Orders Act.

Added by Acts 2001, 77th Leg., ch. 48, § 2, eff. Sept. 1, 2001.

# SUBTITLE C. FAMILY VIOLENCE REPORTING AND SERVICES

## CHAPTER 91. REPORTING FAMILY VIOLENCE

Section



### § 91.001. Definitions

In this subtitle:

(1) "Family violence" has the meaning assigned by Section 71.004.

(2) "Medical professional" means a licensed doctor, nurse, physician assistant, or emergency medical technician.

Added by Acts 1997, 75th Leg., ch. 34, § 1, eff. May 5, 1997.

### § 91.002. Reporting by Witnesses Encouraged

A person who witnesses family violence is encouraged to report the family violence to a local law enforcement agency.

Added by Acts 1997, 75th Leg., ch. 34, § 1, eff. May 5, 1997.

### § 91.003. Information Provided by Medical Professionals

A medical professional who treats a person for injuries that the medical professional has reason to believe were caused by family violence shall:

(1) immediately provide the person with information regarding the nearest family violence shelter center;

(2) document in the person's medical file:

(A) the fact that the person has received the information provided under Subdivision (1); and

(B) the reasons for the medical professional's belief that the person's injuries were caused by family violence; and

(3) give the person a written notice in substantially the following form, completed with the required information, in both English and Spanish:

"NOTICE TO ADULT VICTIMS OF FAMILY VIOLENCE

"It is a crime for any person to cause you any physical injury or harm even if that person is a member or former member of your family or household.

---

"You may report family violence to a law enforcement officer by calling the following telephone numbers: ________.

"If you, your child, or any other household resident has been injured or if you feel you are going to be in danger after a law enforcement officer investigating family violence leaves your residence or at a later time, you have the right to:

"Ask the local prosecutor to file a criminal complaint against the person committing family violence; and

"Apply to a court for an order to protect you. You may want to consult with a legal aid office, a prosecuting attorney, or a private attorney. A court can enter an order that:

"(1) prohibits the abuser from committing further acts of violence;

"(2) prohibits the abuser from threatening, harassing, or contacting you at home;

"(3) directs the abuser to leave your household; and

"(4) establishes temporary custody of the children or any property.

"A VIOLATION OF CERTAIN PROVISIONS OF COURT-ORDERED PROTECTION MAY BE A FELONY.

"CALL THE FOLLOWING VIOLENCE SHELTERS OR SOCIAL ORGANIZATIONS IF YOU NEED PROTECTION: ________________."

Added by Acts 1997, 75th Leg., ch. 34, § 1, eff. May 5, 1997.

### § 91.004. Application of Subtitle

This subtitle does not affect a duty to report child abuse under Chapter 261.

Added by Acts 1997, 75th Leg., ch. 34, § 1, eff. May 5, 1997.

## CHAPTER 92. IMMUNITY

Section



### § 92.001. Immunity

(a) Except as provided by Subsection (b), a person who reports family violence under Section 91.002 or provides information under Section 91.003 is immune from civil liability that might otherwise be incurred or imposed.

(b) A person who reports the person's own conduct or who otherwise reports family violence in bad faith is not protected from liability under this section.

Added by Acts 1997, 75th Leg., ch. 34, § 1, eff. May 5, 1997.

## CHAPTER 93. CONFIDENTIAL AND PRIVILEGED COMMUNICATIONS

Section



### § 93.001. Definitions

In this chapter:

(1) "Advocate" means a person who has at least 20 hours of training in assisting victims of family violence and is an employee or volunteer of a family violence center.

(2) "Family violence center" means a public or private nonprofit organization that provides, as its primary purpose, services to victims of family violence, including the services described by Section 51.005(b)(3), Human Resources Code.

(3) "Victim" has the meaning assigned to "victim of family violence" by Section 51.002, Human Resources Code.

Added by Acts 2017, 85th Leg., ch. 1091 (H.B. 3649), § 2, eff. Sept. 1, 2017.

### § 93.002. Confidential Communications

A written or oral communication between an advocate and a victim made in the course of advising, advocating for, counseling, or assisting the victim is confidential and may not be disclosed.

Added by Acts 2017, 85th Leg., ch. 1091 (H.B. 3649), § 2, eff. Sept. 1, 2017.

### § 93.003. Privileged Communications

(a) A victim has a privilege to refuse to disclose and to prevent another from disclosing a confidential communication described by Section 93.002.

(b) The privilege may be claimed by:

(1) a victim or a victim's attorney on a victim's behalf;

(2) a parent, guardian, or conservator of a victim under 18 years of age; or

(3) an advocate or a family violence center on a victim's behalf.

Added by Acts 2017, 85th Leg., ch. 1091 (H.B. 3649), § 2, eff. Sept. 1, 2017.

### § 93.004. Exceptions

(a) A communication that is confidential under this chapter may be disclosed only:

(1) to another individual employed by or volunteering for a family violence center for the purpose of furthering the advocacy process;

(2) for the purpose of seeking evidence that is admissible under Article 38.49, Code of Criminal Procedure, following an in camera review and a determination that the communication is admissible under that article;

(3) to other persons in the context of a support group or group counseling in which a victim is a participant; or

(4) for the purposes of making a report under Chapter 261 of this code or Section 48.051, Human Resources Code.

(b) Notwithstanding Subsection (a), the Texas Rules of Evidence govern the disclosure of a communication that is confidential under this chapter in a criminal or civil proceeding by an expert witness who relies on facts or data from the communication to form the basis of the expert's opinion.

(c) If the family violence center, at the request of the victim, discloses a communication privileged under this chapter for the purpose of a criminal or civil proceeding, the family violence center shall disclose the communication to all parties to that criminal or civil proceeding.

Added by Acts 2017, 85th Leg., ch. 1091 (H.B. 3649), § 2, eff. Sept. 1, 2017.

# TITLE 5. THE PARENT–CHILD RELATIONSHIP AND THE SUIT AFFECTING THE PARENT–CHILD RELATIONSHIP

## SUBTITLE A. GENERAL PROVISIONS

### CHAPTER 101. DEFINITIONS



#### § 101.001. Applicability of Definitions

(a) Definitions in this subchapter apply to this title.

(b) If, in another part of this title, a term defined by this chapter has a meaning different from the meaning provided by this chapter, the meaning of that other provision prevails.

Added by Acts 1995, 74th Leg., ch. 20, § 1, eff. April 20, 1995.

#### § 101.0010. Acknowledged Father

"Acknowledged father" means a man who has established a father-child relationship under Chapter 160.

Added by Acts 2001, 77th Leg., ch. 821, § 2.04, eff. June 14, 2001.

#### § 101.0011. Administrative Writ of Withholding

"Administrative writ of withholding" means the document issued by the Title IV–D agency or domestic relations office and delivered to an employer directing that earnings be withheld for payment of child support as provided by Chapter 158.

Added by Acts 1997, 75th Leg., ch. 911, § 5, eff. Sept. 1, 1997. Amended by Acts 2005, 79th Leg., ch. 199, § 1, eff. Sept. 1, 2005.

#### § 101.0015. Alleged Father

(a) "Alleged father" means a man who alleges himself to be, or is alleged to be, the genetic father or a possible genetic father of a child, but whose paternity has not been determined.

(b) The term does not include:

(1) a presumed father;

(2) a man whose parental rights have been terminated or declared to not exist; or

(3) a male donor.

Added by Acts 2001, 77th Leg., ch. 821, § 2.04, eff. June 14, 2001.

#### § 101.0017. Amicus Attorney

"Amicus attorney" has the meaning assigned by Section 107.001.

Added by Acts 2005, 79th Leg., ch. 172, § 15, eff. Sept. 1, 2005.

**§ 101.0018. Attorney ad Litem**

"Attorney ad litem" has the meaning assigned by Section 107.001.

Added by Acts 2005, 79th Leg., ch. 172, § 15, eff. Sept. 1, 2005.

**§ 101.002. Repealed by Acts 2015, 84th Leg., ch. 1 (S.B. 219), § 1.203(1), eff. April 2, 2015**

**§ 101.0021. Redesignated as V.T.C.A., Family Code §§ 101.036 by Acts 2015, 84th Leg., ch. 1 (S.B. 219), § 1.207, eff. April 2, 2015**

**§ 101.003. Child or Minor; Adult**

(a) "Child" or "minor" means a person under 18 years of age who is not and has not been married or who has not had the disabilities of minority removed for general purposes.

(b) In the context of child support, "child" includes a person over 18 years of age for whom a person may be obligated to pay child support.

(c) "Adult" means a person who is not a child.

Added by Acts 1995, 74th Leg., ch. 20, § 1, eff. April 20, 1995.

**§ 101.004. Child Support Agency**

"Child support agency" means:

(1) the Title IV–D agency;

(2) a county or district attorney or any other county officer or county agency that executes a cooperative agreement with the Title IV–D agency to provide child support services under Part D of Title IV of the federal Social Security Act (42 U.S.C. Section 651 et seq.) and Chapter 231; or

(3) a domestic relations office.

Added by Acts 1995, 74th Leg., ch. 20, § 1, eff. April 20, 1995.

**§ 101.005. Child Support Review Officer**

"Child support review officer" means an individual designated and trained by a child support agency to conduct reviews under this title.

Added by Acts 1995, 74th Leg., ch. 20, § 1, eff. April 20, 1995. Amended by Acts 1995, 74th Leg., ch. 341, § 2.01, eff. Sept. 1, 1995.

**§ 101.006. Child Support Services**

"Child support services" means administrative or court actions to:

(1) establish paternity;

(2) establish, modify, or enforce child support, medical support, or dental support obligations;

(3) locate absent parents; or

(4) cooperate with other states in these actions and any other action authorized or required under Part D of Title IV of the federal Social Security Act (42 U.S.C. Section 651 et seq.) or Chapter 231.

Added by Acts 1995, 74th Leg., ch. 20, § 1, eff. April 20, 1995. Amended by Acts 2015, 84th Leg., ch. 1150 (S.B. 550), § 2, eff. Sept. 1, 2018.

**§ 101.007. Clear and Convincing Evidence**

"Clear and convincing evidence" means the measure or degree of proof that will produce in the mind of the trier of fact a firm belief or conviction as to the truth of the allegations sought to be established.

Added by Acts 1995, 74th Leg., ch. 20, § 1, eff. April 20, 1995.

**§ 101.008. Court**

"Court" means the district court, juvenile court having the same jurisdiction as a district court, or other court expressly given jurisdiction of a suit affecting the parent-child relationship.

Added by Acts 1995, 74th Leg., ch. 20, § 1, eff. April 20, 1995.

**§ 101.009. Danger to Physical Health or Safety of Child**

"Danger to the physical health or safety of a child" includes exposure of the child to loss or injury that jeopardizes the physical health or safety of the child without regard to whether there has been an actual prior injury to the child.

Added by Acts 1995, 74th Leg., ch. 20, § 1, eff. April 20, 1995.

**§ 101.0094. Dental Insurance**

"Dental insurance" means insurance coverage that provides preventive dental care and other dental services, including usual dentist services, office visits, examinations, X-rays, and emergency services, that may be provided through a single service health maintenance organization or other private or public organization.

Added by Acts 2015, 84th Leg., ch. 1150 (S.B. 550), § 3, eff. Sept. 1, 2018.

**§ 101.0095. Dental Support**

"Dental support" means periodic payments or a lump-sum payment made under an order to cover dental expenses, including dental insurance coverage, incurred for the benefit of a child.

Added by Acts 2015, 84th Leg., ch. 1150 (S.B. 550), § 3, eff. Sept. 1, 2018.

### § 101.0096. Digitized Signature

"Digitized signature" means a graphic image of a handwritten signature having the same legal force and effect for all purposes as a handwritten signature.

Added by Acts 2013, 83rd Leg., ch. 790 (S.B. 1422), § 1, eff. Sept. 1, 2013.

### § 101.010. Disposable Earnings

"Disposable earnings" means the part of the earnings of an individual remaining after the deduction from those earnings of any amount required by law to be withheld, union dues, nondiscretionary retirement contributions, and medical, hospitalization, and disability insurance coverage for the obligor and the obligor's children.

Added by Acts 1995, 74th Leg., ch. 20, § 1, eff. April 20, 1995.

### § 101.011. Earnings

"Earnings" means a payment to or due an individual, regardless of source and how denominated. The term includes a periodic or lump-sum payment for:

(1) wages, salary, compensation received as an independent contractor, overtime pay, severance pay, commission, bonus, and interest income;

(2) payments made under a pension, an annuity, workers' compensation, and a disability or retirement program;

(3) unemployment benefits;

(4) compensation from a transportation network company as defined by Section 2402.001, Occupations Code; and

(5) compensation from a person that operates a technology platform used to make deliveries to customers.

Added by Acts 1995, 74th Leg., ch. 20, § 1, eff. April 20, 1995. Amended by Acts 1997, 75th Leg., ch. 911, § 1, eff. Sept. 1, 1997; Acts 2021, 87th Leg., ch. 446 (H.B. 458), § 1, eff. Sept. 1, 2021.

### § 101.012. Employer

"Employer" means a person, corporation, partnership, workers' compensation insurance carrier, governmental entity, the United States, or any other entity that pays or owes earnings to an individual. The term includes, for the purposes of enrolling dependents in a group health or dental insurance plan, a union, trade association, or other similar organization.

Added by Acts 1995, 74th Leg., ch. 20, § 1, eff. April 20, 1995. Amended by Acts 1995, 74th Leg., ch. 341, § 4.02, eff. Sept. 1, 1995; Acts 1997, 75th Leg., ch. 911, § 2, eff. Sept. 1, 1997; Acts 2015, 84th Leg., ch. 1150 (S.B. 550), § 4, eff. Sept. 1, 2018.

### § 101.0125. Family Violence

"Family violence" has the meaning assigned by Section 71.004.

Added by Acts 1999, 76th Leg., ch. 787, § 1, eff. Sept. 1, 1999.

### § 101.013. Filed

"Filed" means officially filed with the clerk of the court.

Added by Acts 1995, 74th Leg., ch. 20, § 1, eff. April 20, 1995.

### § 101.0133. Foster Care

"Foster care" means the placement of a child who is in the conservatorship of the Department of Family and Protective Services and in care outside the child's home in a residential child-care facility, including an agency foster home, specialized child-care home, cottage home operation, general residential operation, or another facility licensed or certified under Chapter 42, Human Resources Code, in which care is provided for 24 hours a day.

Added by Acts 2015, 84th Leg., ch. 944 (S.B. 206), § 7, eff. Sept. 1, 2015. Amended by Acts 2017, 85th Leg., ch. 317 (H.B. 7), § 4, eff. Sept. 1, 2017.

### § 101.0134. Foster Child

"Foster child" means a child who is in the managing conservatorship of the Department of Family and Protective Services.

Added by Acts 2015, 84th Leg., ch. 944 (S.B. 206), § 7, eff. Sept. 1, 2015.

### § 101.014. Governmental Entity

"Governmental entity" means the state, a political subdivision of the state, or an agency of the state.

Added by Acts 1995, 74th Leg., ch. 20, § 1, eff. April 20, 1995.

### § 101.0145. Guardian ad Litem

"Guardian ad litem" has the meaning assigned by Section 107.001.

Added by Acts 2005, 79th Leg., ch. 172, § 15, eff. Sept. 1, 2005.

### § 101.015. Health Insurance

"Health insurance" means insurance coverage that provides basic health care services, including usual physician services, office visits, hospitalization, and laboratory, X-ray, and emergency services, that may be provided through a health maintenance organization or other private or public organization, other than medical assistance under Chapter 32, Human Resources Code.

Added by Acts 1995, 74th Leg., ch. 20, § 1, eff. April 20, 1995. Amended by Acts 2001, 77th Leg., ch. 1023, § 1, eff. Sept. 1, 2001.

### § 101.016. Joint Managing Conservatorship

"Joint managing conservatorship" means the sharing of the rights and duties of a parent by two parties, ordinarily the parents, even if the exclusive right to make certain decisions may be awarded to one party.

Added by Acts 1995, 74th Leg., ch. 20, § 1, eff. April 20, 1995.

### § 101.0161. Judicial Writ of Withholding

"Judicial writ of withholding" means the document issued by the clerk of a court and delivered to an employer directing that earnings be withheld for payment of child support as provided by Chapter 158.

Added by Acts 1997, 75th Leg., ch. 911, § 5, eff. Sept. 1, 1997.

### § 101.017. Licensed Child Placing Agency

"Licensed child placing agency" means a person, including an organization or corporation, licensed or certified under Chapter 42, Human Resources Code, by the Department of Family and Protective Services to place a child in an adoptive home or a residential child-care facility, including a child-care facility, agency foster home, cottage home operation, or general residential operation.

Added by Acts 1995, 74th Leg., ch. 20, § 1, eff. April 20, 1995. Amended by Acts 2011, 82nd Leg., ch. 110 (H.B. 841), § 9, eff. May 21, 2011; Acts 2015, 84th Leg., ch. 1 (S.B. 219), § 1.028, eff. April 2, 2015; Acts 2017, 85th Leg., ch. 317 (H.B. 7), § 5, eff. Sept. 1, 2017.

### § 101.018. Local Registry

"Local registry" means a county agency or public entity operated under the authority of a district clerk, county government, juvenile board, juvenile probation office, domestic relations office, or other county agency or public entity that serves a county or a court that has jurisdiction under this title and that:

(1) receives child support payments;

(2) maintains records of child support payments;

(3) distributes child support payments as required by law; and

(4) maintains custody of official child support payment records.

Added by Acts 1995, 74th Leg., ch. 20, § 1, eff. April 20, 1995. Amended by Acts 2005, 79th Leg., ch. 740, § 1, eff. June 17, 2005.

### § 101.019. Managing Conservatorship

"Managing conservatorship" means the relationship between a child and a managing conservator appointed by court order.

Added by Acts 1995, 74th Leg., ch. 20, § 1, eff. April 20, 1995.

### § 101.020. Medical Support

"Medical support" means periodic payments or a lump-sum payment made under an order to cover medical expenses, including health insurance coverage, incurred for the benefit of a child.

Added by Acts 1995, 74th Leg., ch. 20, § 1, eff. April 20, 1995. Amended by Acts 1997, 75th Leg., ch. 911, § 3, eff. Sept. 1, 1997.

### § 101.0201. Notice of Application for Judicial Writ of Withholding

"Notice of application for judicial writ of withholding" means the document delivered to an obligor and filed with the court as required by Chapter 158 for the nonjudicial determination of arrears and initiation of withholding.

Added by Acts 1997, 75th Leg., ch. 911, § 5, eff. Sept. 1, 1997.

### § 101.021. Obligee

"Obligee" means a person or entity entitled to receive payments of child support, including an agency of this state or of another jurisdiction to which a person has assigned the person's right to support.

Added by Acts 1995, 74th Leg., ch. 20, § 1, eff. April 20, 1995. Amended by Acts 1999, 76th Leg., ch. 556, § 1, eff. Sept. 1, 1999.

### § 101.022. Obligor

"Obligor" means a person required to make payments under the terms of a support order for a child.

Added by Acts 1995, 74th Leg., ch. 20, § 1, eff. April 20, 1995.

### § 101.023. Order

"Order" means a final order unless identified as a temporary order or the context clearly requires a different meaning. The term includes a decree and a judgment.

Added by Acts 1995, 74th Leg., ch. 20, § 1, eff. April 20, 1995.

### § 101.024. Parent

(a) "Parent" means the mother, a man presumed to be the father, a man legally determined to be the father, a man who has been adjudicated to be the father by a court of competent jurisdiction, a man who has acknowledged his paternity under applicable law, or an adoptive mother or father. Except as provided by Subsection (b), the term does not include a parent as to whom the parent-child relationship has been terminated.

(b) For purposes of establishing, determining the terms of, modifying, or enforcing an order, a reference in this title to a parent includes a person ordered to pay child support under Section 154.001(a–1) or to provide medical support or dental support for a child.

Added by Acts 1995, 74th Leg., ch. 20, § 1, eff. April 20, 1995. Amended by Acts 1999, 76th Leg., ch. 556, § 1, eff. Sept. 1, 1999; Acts 2001, 77th Leg., ch. 821, § 2.05, eff. June 14, 2001; Acts 2005, 79th Leg., ch. 268, § 1.03, eff. Sept. 1, 2005; Acts 2015, 84th Leg., ch. 1150 (S.B. 550), § 5, eff. Sept. 1, 2018.

### § 101.025. Parent-Child Relationship

"Parent-child relationship" means the legal relationship between a child and the child's parents as provided by Chapter 160. The term includes the mother and child relationship and the father and child relationship.

Added by Acts 1995, 74th Leg., ch. 20, § 1, eff. April 20, 1995. Amended by Acts 2001, 77th Leg., ch. 821, § 2.06, eff. June 14, 2001.

### § 101.0255. Record

"Record" means information that is:

(1) inscribed on a tangible medium or stored in an electronic or other medium; and

(2) retrievable in a perceivable form.

Added by Acts 2007, 80th Leg., ch. 972, § 1, eff. Sept. 1, 2007.

### § 101.026. Render

"Render" means the pronouncement by a judge of the court's ruling on a matter. The pronouncement may be made orally in the presence of the court reporter or in writing, including on the court's docket sheet or by a separate written instrument.

Added by Acts 1995, 74th Leg., ch. 20, § 1, eff. April 20, 1995.

### § 101.027. Parent Locator Service

"Parent locator service" means the service established under 42 U.S.C. Section 653.

Added by Acts 1995, 74th Leg., ch. 20, § 1, eff. April 20, 1995.

### § 101.028. School

"School" means an elementary or secondary school in which a child is enrolled or, if the child is not enrolled in an elementary or secondary school, the public school district in which the child primarily resides. For purposes of this section, a reference to elementary school includes prekindergarten.

Added by Acts 1995, 74th Leg., ch. 20, § 1, eff. April 20, 1995. Amended by Acts 2015, 84th Leg., ch. 1167 (S.B. 821), § 2, eff. Sept. 1, 2015.

### § 101.029. Standard Possession Order

"Standard possession order" means an order that provides a parent with rights of possession of a child in accordance with the terms and conditions of Subchapter F,[1] Chapter 153.

Added by Acts 1995, 74th Leg., ch. 20, § 1, eff. April 20, 1995.

[1] V.T.C.A., Family Code § 153.3101 et seq.

### § 101.030. State

"State" means a state of the United States, the District of Columbia, the Commonwealth of Puerto Rico, or a territory or insular possession subject to the jurisdiction of the United States. The term includes an Indian tribe and a foreign jurisdiction that has established procedures for rendition and enforcement of an order that are substantially similar to the procedures of this title.

Added by Acts 1995, 74th Leg., ch. 20, § 1, eff. April 20, 1995.

### § 101.0301. State Case Registry

"State case registry" means the registry established and operated by the Title IV-D agency under 42 U.S.C. Section 654a that has responsibility for maintaining records with respect to child support orders in all Title IV-D cases and in all other cases in which a support order is rendered or modified under this title on or after October 1, 1998.

Added by Acts 1997, 75th Leg., ch. 911, § 5, eff. Sept. 1, 1997.

### § 101.0302. State Disbursement Unit

"State disbursement unit" means the unit established and operated by the Title IV–D agency under 42 U.S.C. Section 654b that has responsibility for receiving, distributing, maintaining, and furnishing child support payments and records on or after October 1, 1999.

Added by Acts 1999, 76th Leg., ch. 556, § 1, eff. Sept. 1, 1999.

### § 101.031. Suit

"Suit" means a legal action under this title.

Added by Acts 1995, 74th Leg., ch. 20, § 1, eff. April 20, 1995. Amended by Acts 2015, 84th Leg., ch. 859 (S.B. 1726), § 2, eff. Sept. 1, 2015.

### § 101.032. Suit Affecting the Parent-Child Relationship

(a) "Suit affecting the parent-child relationship" means a suit filed as provided by this title in which the appointment of a managing conservator or a possessory conservator, access to or support of a child, or establishment or termination of the parent-child relationship is requested.

(b) The following are not suits affecting the parent-child relationship:

(1) a habeas corpus proceeding under Chapter 157;

(2) a proceeding filed under Chapter 159 to determine parentage or to establish, enforce, or modify child support, whether this state is acting as the initiating or responding state; and

(3) a proceeding under Title 2.

Added by Acts 1995, 74th Leg., ch. 20, § 1, eff. April 20, 1995.

### § 101.033. Title IV–D Agency

"Title IV–D agency" means the state agency designated under Chapter 231 to provide services under Part D of Title IV of the federal Social Security Act (42 U.S.C. Section 651 et seq.).

Added by Acts 1995, 74th Leg., ch. 20, § 1, eff. April 20, 1995.

### § 101.034. Title IV–D Case

"Title IV–D case" means an action in which services are provided by the Title IV–D agency under Part D, Title IV, of the federal Social Security Act (42 U.S.C. Section 651 et seq.), relating to the location of an absent parent, determination of parentage, or establishment, modification, or enforcement of a child support, medical support, or dental support obligation, including a suit for modification filed by the Title IV–D agency under Section 231.101(d) and any other action relating to the services that the Title IV–D agency is required or authorized to provide under Section 231.101.

Added by Acts 1995, 74th Leg., ch. 20, § 1, eff. April 20, 1995. Amended by Acts 1997, 75th Leg., ch. 911, § 4, eff. Sept. 1, 1997; Acts 2015, 84th Leg., ch. 1150 (S.B. 550), § 6, eff. Sept. 1, 2018; Acts 2017, 85th Leg., ch. 912 (S.B. 1329), § 1.02, eff. Sept. 1, 2018.

### § 101.035. Tribunal

"Tribunal" means a court, administrative agency, or quasi-judicial entity of a state authorized to establish, enforce, or modify support orders or to determine parentage.

Added by Acts 1995, 74th Leg., ch. 20, § 1, eff. April 20, 1995.

### § 101.036. Vital Statistics Unit

"Vital statistics unit" means the vital statistics unit of the Department of State Health Services.

Added by Acts 1999, 76th Leg., ch. 556, § 1, eff. Sept. 1, 1999. Redesignated from V.T.C.A., Family Code § 101.0021 and amended by Acts 2015, 84th Leg., ch. 1 (S.B. 219), § 1.027, eff. April 2, 2015.

## CHAPTER 102. FILING SUIT

Section

## § 102.001. Suit Authorized; Scope of Suit

(a) A suit may be filed as provided in this title.

(b) One or more matters covered by this title may be determined in the suit. The court, on its own motion, may require the parties to replead in order that any issue affecting the parent-child relationship may be determined in the suit.

Added by Acts 1995, 74th Leg., ch. 20, § 1, eff. April 20, 1995.

## § 102.002. Commencement of Suit

An original suit begins by the filing of a petition as provided by this chapter.

Added by Acts 1995, 74th Leg., ch. 20, § 1, eff. April 20, 1995.

## § 102.003. General Standing to File Suit

(a) An original suit may be filed at any time by:

(1) a parent of the child;

(2) the child through a representative authorized by the court;

(3) a custodian or person having the right of visitation with or access to the child appointed by an order of a court of another state or country;

(4) a guardian of the person or of the estate of the child;

(5) a governmental entity;

(6) the Department of Family and Protective Services;

(7) a licensed child placing agency;

(8) a man alleging himself to be the father of a child filing in accordance with Chapter 160, subject to the limitations of that chapter, but not otherwise;

(9) a person, other than a foster parent, who has had actual care, control, and possession of the child for at least six months ending not more than 90 days preceding the date of the filing of the petition;

(10) a person designated as the managing conservator in a revoked or unrevoked affidavit of relinquishment under Chapter 161 or to whom consent to adoption has been given in writing under Chapter 162;

(11) a person with whom the child and the child's guardian, managing conservator, or parent have resided for at least six months ending not more than 90 days preceding the date of the filing of the petition if the child's guardian, managing conservator, or parent is deceased at the time of the filing of the petition;

(12) a person who is the foster parent of a child placed by the Department of Family and Protective Services in the person's home for at least 12 months ending not more than 90 days preceding the date of the filing of the petition;

(13) a person who is a relative of the child within the third degree by consanguinity, as determined by Chapter 573, Government Code, if the child's parents are deceased at the time of the filing of the petition;

(14) a person who has been named as a prospective adoptive parent of a child by a pregnant woman or the parent of the child, in a verified written statement to confer standing executed under Section 102.0035, regardless of whether the child has been born; or

(15) subject to Subsection (d), a person who is an intended parent of a child or unborn child under a gestational agreement that complies with the requirements of Section 160.754.

(b) In computing the time necessary for standing under Subsections (a)(9), (11), and (12), the court may not require that the time be continuous and uninterrupted but shall consider the child's principal residence during the relevant time preceding the date of commencement of the suit.

(c) Notwithstanding the time requirements of Subsection (a)(12), a person who is the foster parent of a child may file a suit to adopt a child for whom the person is providing foster care at any time after the person has been approved to adopt the child. The standing to file suit under this subsection applies only to the adoption of a child who is eligible to be adopted.

(d) A person described by Subsection (a)(15) has standing to file an original suit only if:

(1) the person is filing an original suit jointly with the other intended parent under the gestational agreement; or

(2) the person is filing an original suit against the other intended parent under the gestational agreement.

Added by Acts 1995, 74th Leg., ch. 20, § 1, eff. April 20, 1995. Amended by Acts 1995, 74th Leg., ch. 751, § 8, eff. Sept. 1, 1995; Acts 1997, 75th Leg., ch. 575, § 3, eff. Sept. 1, 1997; Acts 1999, 76th Leg., ch. 1048, § 1, eff. June 18, 1999; Acts 1999, 76th Leg., ch. 1390, § 2, eff. Sept. 1, 1999; Acts 2001, 77th Leg., ch. 821, § 2.07, eff. June 14, 2001; Acts 2003, 78th Leg., ch. 37, § 1, eff. Sept. 1, 2003; Acts 2003, 78th Leg., ch. 573, § 1, eff. Sept. 1, 2003; Acts 2011, 82nd Leg., ch. 110 (H.B. 841), § 10, eff. May 21, 2011; Acts 2015, 84th Leg., ch. 1 (S.B. 219), § 1.029, eff. April 2, 2015; Acts 2019, 86th Leg., ch. 130 (H.B. 1689), § 2, eff. Sept. 1, 2019.

## § 102.0035. Statement to Confer Standing

(a) A pregnant woman or a parent of a child may execute a statement to confer standing to a prospective adoptive parent as provided by this section to assert standing under Section 102.003(a)(14). A statement to confer standing under this section may not be executed in a suit brought by a governmental entity under Chapter 262 or 263.

(b) A statement to confer standing must contain:

(1) the signature, name, age, and address of the person named as a prospective adoptive parent;

(2) the signature, name, age, and address of the pregnant woman or of the parent of the child who is consenting to the filing of a petition for adoption or to terminate the parent-child relationship as described by Subsection (a);

(3) the birth date of the child or the anticipated birth date if the child has not been born; and

(4) the name of the county in which the suit will be filed.

(c) The statement to confer standing must be attached to the petition in a suit affecting the parent-child relationship. The statement may not be used for any purpose other than to confer standing in a proceeding for adoption or to terminate the parent-child relationship.

(d) A statement to confer standing may be signed at any time during the pregnancy of the mother of the unborn child whose parental rights are to be terminated.

(e) A statement to confer standing is not required in a suit brought by a person who has standing to file a suit affecting the parent-child relationship under Sections 102.003(a)(1)–(13) or any other law under which the person has standing to file a suit.

(f) A person who executes a statement to confer standing may revoke the statement at any time before the person executes an affidavit for voluntary relinquishment of parental rights. The revocation of the statement must be in writing and must be sent by certified mail, return receipt requested, to the prospective adoptive parent.

(g) On filing with the court proof of the delivery of the revocation of a statement to confer standing under Subsection (f), the court shall dismiss any suit affecting the parent-child relationship filed by the prospective adoptive parent named in the statement.

Added by Acts 2003, 78th Leg., ch. 37, § 2, eff. Sept. 1, 2003.

## § 102.004. Standing for Grandparent or Other Person

(a) In addition to the general standing to file suit provided by Section 102.003, a grandparent, or another relative of the child related within the third degree by consanguinity, may file an original suit requesting managing conservatorship if there is satisfactory proof to the court that:

(1) the order requested is necessary because the child's present circumstances would significantly impair the child's physical health or emotional development; or

(2) both parents, the surviving parent, or the managing conservator or custodian either filed the petition or consented to the suit.

(b) An original suit requesting possessory conservatorship may not be filed by a grandparent or other person. However, the court may grant a grandparent or other person, subject to the requirements of Subsection (b–1) if applicable, deemed by the court to have had substantial past contact with the child leave to intervene in a pending suit filed by a person authorized to do so under this chapter if there is satisfactory proof to the court that appointment of a parent as a sole managing conservator or both parents as joint managing conservators would significantly impair the child's physical health or emotional development.

(b–1) A foster parent may only be granted leave to intervene under Subsection (b) if the foster parent would have standing to file an original suit as provided by Section 102.003(a)(12).

(c) Possession of or access to a child by a grandparent is governed by the standards established by Chapter 153.

Added by Acts 1995, 74th Leg., ch. 20, § 1, eff. April 20, 1995. Amended by Acts 1999, 76th Leg., ch. 1048, § 2, eff. June 18, 1999; Acts 2005, 79th Leg., ch. 916, § 3, eff. June 18, 2005; Acts 2007, 80th Leg., ch. 1406, § 2, eff. Sept. 1, 2007; Acts 2017, 85th Leg., ch. 341 (H.B. 1410), § 1, eff. Sept. 1, 2017.

## § 102.0045. Standing for Sibling

(a) The sibling of a child may file an original suit requesting access to the child as provided by Section 153.551 if the sibling is at least 18 years of age.

(a–1) The sibling of a child who is separated from the sibling as the result of an action by the Department of Family and Protective Services may file an original suit as provided by Section 153.551 requesting access to the child, regardless of the age of the sibling.

A court shall expedite a suit filed under this subsection.

(b) Access to a child by a sibling of the child is governed by the standards established by Section 153.551.

Added by Acts 2005, 79th Leg., ch. 1191, § 1, eff. Sept. 1, 2005. Amended by Acts 2009, 81st Leg., ch. 1113, § 1, eff. Sept. 1, 2009; Acts 2015, 84th Leg., ch. 744 (H.B. 1781), § 1, eff. Sept. 1, 2015.

### § 102.005. Standing to Request Termination and Adoption

An original suit requesting only an adoption or for termination of the parent-child relationship joined with a petition for adoption may be filed by:

(1) a stepparent of the child;

(2) an adult who, as the result of a placement for adoption, has had actual possession and control of the child at any time during the 30–day period preceding the filing of the petition;

(3) an adult who has had actual possession and control of the child for not less than two months during the three-month period preceding the filing of the petition;

(4) an adult who has adopted, or is the foster parent of and has petitioned to adopt, a sibling of the child; or

(5) another adult whom the court determines to have had substantial past contact with the child sufficient to warrant standing to do so.

Added by Acts 1995, 74th Leg., ch. 20, § 1, eff. April 20, 1995. Amended by Acts 2007, 80th Leg., ch. 1406, § 3(a), eff. Sept. 1, 2007.

### § 102.006. Limitations on Standing

(a) Except as provided by Subsections (b) and (c), if the parent-child relationship between the child and every living parent of the child has been terminated, an original suit may not be filed by:

(1) a former parent whose parent-child relationship with the child has been terminated by court order;

(2) the father of the child; or

(3) a family member or relative by blood, adoption, or marriage of either a former parent whose parent-child relationship has been terminated or of the father of the child.

(b) The limitations on filing suit imposed by this section do not apply to a person who:

(1) has a continuing right to possession of or access to the child under an existing court order; or

(2) has the consent of the child's managing conservator, guardian, or legal custodian to bring the suit.

(c) The limitations on filing suit imposed by this section do not apply to an adult sibling of the child, a grandparent of the child, an aunt who is a sister of a parent of the child, or an uncle who is a brother of a parent of the child if the adult sibling, grandparent, aunt, or uncle files an original suit or a suit for modification requesting managing conservatorship of the child not later than the 90th day after the date the parent-child relationship between the child and the parent is terminated in a suit filed by the Department of Family and Protective Services requesting the termination of the parent-child relationship.

Added by Acts 1995, 74th Leg., ch. 20, § 1, eff. April 20, 1995. Amended by Acts 2001, 77th Leg., ch. 821, § 2.08, eff. June 14, 2001; Acts 2007, 80th Leg., ch. 866, § 1, eff. June 15, 2007.

### § 102.007. Standing of Title IV–D Agency

In providing services authorized by Chapter 231, the Title IV–D agency or a political subdivision contracting with the attorney general to provide Title IV–D services under this title may file a child support action authorized under this title, including a suit for modification or a motion for enforcement.

Added by Acts 1995, 74th Leg., ch. 20, § 1, eff. April 20, 1995. Amended by Acts 1995, 74th Leg., ch. 341, § 2.02, eff. Sept. 1, 1995.

### § 102.008. Contents of Petition

(a) The petition and all other documents in a proceeding filed under this title, except a suit for adoption of an adult, shall be entitled "In the interest of ______, a child." In a suit in which adoption of a child is requested, the style shall be "In the interest of a child."

(b) The petition must include:

(1) a statement that:

(A) the court in which the petition is filed has continuing, exclusive jurisdiction or that no court has continuing jurisdiction of the suit; or

(B) in a suit in which adoption of a child is requested, the court in which the petition is filed has jurisdiction of the suit under Section 103.001(b);

(2) the name and date of birth of the child, except that if adoption of a child is requested, the name of the child may be omitted;

(3) the full name of the petitioner and the petitioner's relationship to the child or the fact that no relationship exists;

(4) the names of the parents, except in a suit in which adoption is requested;

(5) the name of the managing conservator, if any, or the child's custodian, if any, appointed by order of a court of another state or country;

(6) the names of the guardians of the person and estate of the child, if any;

(7) the names of possessory conservators or other persons, if any, having possession of or access to the child under an order of the court;

(8) the name of an alleged father of the child or a statement that the identity of the father of the child is unknown;

(9) a full description and statement of value of all property owned or possessed by the child;

(10) a statement describing what action the court is requested to take concerning the child and the statutory grounds on which the request is made;

(11) a statement as to whether, in regard to a party to the suit or a child of a party to the suit:

(A) there is in effect:

(i) a protective order under Title 4;

(ii) a protective order under Subchapter A, Chapter 7B, Code of Criminal Procedure; or

(iii) an order for emergency protection under Article 17.292, Code of Criminal Procedure; or

(B) an application for an order described by Paragraph (A) is pending; and

(12) any other information required by this title.

(c) The petitioner shall attach a copy of each order described by Subsection (b)(11)(A) in which a party to the suit or a child of a party to the suit was the applicant or victim of the conduct alleged in the application or order and the other party was the respondent or defendant of an action regarding the conduct alleged in the application or order without regard to the date of the order. If a copy of the order is not available at the time of filing, the petition must state that a copy of the order will be filed with the court before any hearing.

(d) Notwithstanding any other provision of this section, if the Title IV-D agency files a petition in a suit affecting the parent-child relationship, the agency is not required to:

(1) include in the petition the statement described by Subsection (b)(11); or

(2) attach copies of the documentation described by Subsection (c).

Added by Acts 1995, 74th Leg., ch. 20, § 1, eff. April 20, 1995. Amended by Acts 2001, 77th Leg., ch. 296, § 2, eff. Sept. 1, 2001; Acts 2017, 85th Leg., ch. 885 (H.B. 3052), § 6, eff. Sept. 1, 2017; Acts 2019, 86th Leg., ch. 469 (H.B. 4173), § 2.36, eff. Jan. 1, 2021; Acts 2019, 86th Leg., ch. 722 (H.B. 369), § 1, eff. Sept. 1, 2019.

Sections 4.01 and 4.02 of Acts 2019, 86th Leg., ch. 469 (H.B. 4173) provide:

"Sec. 4.01. This Act is enacted under Section 43, Article III, Texas Constitution. This Act is intended as a codification only, and no substantive change in the law is intended by this Act.

"Sec. 4.02. (a) Chapter 311, Government Code (Code Construction Act), applies to the construction of each provision in the Code of Criminal Procedure that is enacted under Section 43, Article III, Texas Constitution (authorizing the continuing statutory revision program), in the same manner as to a code enacted under the continuing statutory revision program, except as otherwise expressly provided by the Code of Criminal Procedure.

"(b) A reference in a law to a statute or a part of a statute in the Code of Criminal Procedure enacted under Section 43, Article III, Texas Constitution (authorizing the continuing statutory revision program), is considered to be a reference to the part of that code that revises that statute or part of that statute."

Section 5 of Acts 2019, 86th Leg., ch. 722 (H.B. 369) provides:

"Section 102.008(b), Family Code, as amended by this Act, applies to a petition in a suit affecting the parent-child relationship filed on or after the effective date [Sept. 1, 2019] of this Act. A petition filed before the effective date of this Act is governed by the law in effect on the date the petition was filed, and the former law is continued in effect for that purpose."

### § 102.0085. Repealed by Acts 2003, 78th Leg., ch. 1313, § 1, eff. Sept. 1, 2003

### § 102.0086. Confidentiality of Pleadings

(a) This section applies only in a county with a population of 3.4 million or more.

(b) Except as otherwise provided by law, all pleadings and other documents filed with the court in a suit affecting the parent-child relationship are confidential, are excepted from required public disclosure under Chapter 552, Government Code, and may not be released to a person who is not a party to the suit until after the date of service of citation or the 31st day after the date of filing the suit, whichever date is sooner.

Acts 2003, 78th Leg., ch. 1314, § 3, eff. Sept. 1, 2003.

### § 102.009. Service of Citation

(a) Except as provided by Subsection (b), the following are entitled to service of citation on the filing of a petition in an original suit:

(1) a managing conservator;

(2) a possessory conservator;

(3) a person having possession of or access to the child under an order;

(4) a person required by law or by order to provide for the support of the child;

(5) a guardian of the person of the child;

(6) a guardian of the estate of the child;

(7) each parent as to whom the parent-child relationship has not been terminated or process has not been waived under Chapter 161;

(8) an alleged father, unless there is attached to the petition an affidavit of waiver of interest in a child executed by the alleged father as provided by Chapter 161 or unless the petitioner has complied with the provisions of Section 161.002(b)(2), (3), or (4);

(9) a man who has filed a notice of intent to claim paternity as provided by Chapter 160;

(10) the Department of Family and Protective Services, if the petition requests that the department be appointed as managing conservator of the child;

(11) the Title IV–D agency, if the petition requests the termination of the parent-child relationship and support rights have been assigned to the Title IV–D agency under Chapter 231;

(12) a prospective adoptive parent to whom standing has been conferred under Section 102.0035; and

(13) a person designated as the managing conservator in a revoked or unrevoked affidavit of relinquishment under Chapter 161 or to whom consent to adoption has been given in writing under Chapter 162.

(b) Citation may be served on any other person who has or who may assert an interest in the child.

(c) Citation on the filing of an original petition in a suit shall be issued and served as in other civil cases.

(d) If the petition requests the establishment, termination, modification, or enforcement of a support right assigned to the Title IV–D agency under Chapter 231 or the rescission of a voluntary acknowledgment of paternity under Chapter 160, notice shall be given to the Title IV–D agency in a manner provided by Rule 21a, Texas Rules of Civil Procedure.

(e) In a proceeding under Chapter 233, the requirements imposed by Subsections (a) and (c) do not apply to the extent of any conflict between those requirements and the provisions in Chapter 233.

Added by Acts 1995, 74th Leg., ch. 20, § 1, eff. April 20, 1995. Amended by Acts 1995, 74th Leg., ch. 751, § 10, eff. Sept. 1, 1995; Acts 1997, 75th Leg., ch. 561, § 1, eff. Sept. 1, 1997; Acts 1997, 75th Leg., ch. 599, § 1, eff. Sept. 1, 1997; Acts 1999, 76th Leg., ch. 62, § 6.12, eff. Sept. 1, 1999; Acts 1999, 76th Leg., ch. 556, § 2, eff. Sept. 1, 1999; Acts 2001, 77th Leg., ch. 821, § 2.09, eff. June 14, 2001; Acts 2005, 79th Leg., ch. 916, § 4, eff. June 18, 2005; Acts 2007, 80th Leg., ch. 972, § 2, eff. Sept. 1, 2007; Acts 2007, 80th Leg., ch. 1283, § 1, eff. Sept. 1, 2007; Acts 2009, 81st Leg., ch. 767, § 1, eff. June 19, 2009.

### § 102.0091. Waiver of Citation

(a) A party to a suit under this title may waive the issuance or service of citation after the suit is filed by filing with the clerk of the court in which the suit is filed the waiver of the party acknowledging receipt of a copy of the filed petition.

(b) The party executing the waiver may not sign the waiver using a digitized signature.

(c) The waiver must contain the mailing address of the party executing the waiver.

(d) Notwithstanding Section 132.001, Civil Practice and Remedies Code, the waiver must be sworn before a notary public who is not an attorney in the suit. This subsection does not apply if the party executing the waiver is incarcerated.

(e) The Texas Rules of Civil Procedure do not apply to a waiver executed under this section.

Added by Acts 2015, 84th Leg., ch. 198 (S.B. 814), § 5, eff. Sept. 1, 2015.

### § 102.010. Service of Citation by Publication

(a) Except as provided by Section 17.032, Civil Practice and Remedies Code, citation may be served to persons entitled to service of citation who cannot be notified by personal service or registered or certified mail and to persons whose names are unknown by publication on the public information Internet website maintained as required by Section 72.034, Government Code, and in a newspaper of general circulation published in the county in which the petition was filed.

(b) Citation by publication shall be published not later than the 20th day before the date set for the hearing. One or more causes to be heard on a certain day may be included in one notice and hearings may be continued from time to time without further notice.

(c) Citation by publication shall be sufficient if given in substantially the following form:

To (names of persons to be served with citation) and to all whom it may concern (if the name of any person to be served with citation is unknown), Respondent(s),

"STATE OF TEXAS

"You have been sued. You may employ an attorney. If you or your attorney do (does) not file a written answer with the clerk who issued this citation by 10 a.m. on the Monday next following the expiration of 20 days after you were served this citation and petition, a default judgment may be taken against you. The petition of ____________, Petitioner, was filed in the Court of ____________ County, Texas, on the ___ day of _________, _____, against _________, Respondent(s), numbered _____, and entitled 'In the interest of _________, a child (or children).' The suit requests (statement of relief requested, e.g., 'terminate the parent-child relationship'). The date and place of birth of the child (children) who is (are) the subject of the suit: ___________.

"The court has authority in this suit to render an order in the child's (children's) interest that will be binding on you, including the termination of the parent-child relationship, the determination of paternity, and the appointment of a conservator with authority to consent to the child's (children's) adoption.

"Issued and given under my hand and seal of the Court at ________, Texas, this the ___ day of ______, ____.

"____________
Clerk of the District Court of
__________ County, Texas.
By ______, Deputy."

(d) In any suit in which service of citation is by publication, a statement of the evidence of service, approved and signed by the court, must be filed with the papers of the suit as a part of the record.

(e) In a suit filed under Chapter 161 or 262 in which the last name of the respondent is unknown, the court may order substituted service of citation by publication, including publication by posting the citation at the courthouse door for a specified time, if the court finds and states in its order that the method of substituted service is as likely as citation by publication on the public information Internet website maintained as required by Section 72.034, Government Code, or in a newspaper in the manner described by Subsection (b) to give the respondent actual notice of the suit. If the court orders that citation by publication shall be completed by posting the citation at the courthouse door for a specified time, service must be completed on, and the answer date is computed from, the expiration date of the posting period. If the court orders another method of substituted service of citation by publication, service shall be completed as directed by the court.

Added by Acts 1995, 74th Leg., ch. 20, § 1, eff. April 20, 1995. Amended by Acts 2003, 78th Leg., ch. 1015, § 1, eff. Sept. 1, 2003; Acts 2019, 86th Leg., ch. 606 (S.B. 891), § 10.10, eff. June 1, 2020.

Section 15.05 of Acts 2019, 86th Leg., ch. 606 (S.B. 891) provides:

"The Office of Court Administration of the Texas Judicial System is required to implement a provision of this Act only if the legislature appropriates money specifically for that purpose. If the legislature does not appropriate money specifically for that purpose, the office may, but is not required to, implement a provision of this Act using other appropriations available for that purpose."

Section 15.05 of Acts 2019, 86th Leg., ch. 606 (S.B. 891) provides:

"The Office of Court Administration of the Texas Judicial System is required to implement a provision of this Act only if the legislature appropriates money specifically for that purpose. If the legislature does not appropriate money specifically for that purpose, the office may, but is not required to, implement a provision of this Act using other appropriations available for that purpose."

### § 102.011. Acquiring Jurisdiction over Nonresident

(a) The court may exercise status or subject matter jurisdiction over the suit as provided by Chapter 152.

(b) The court may also exercise personal jurisdiction over a person on whom service of citation is required or over the person's personal representative, although the person is not a resident or domiciliary of this state, if:

(1) the person is personally served with citation in this state;

(2) the person submits to the jurisdiction of this state by consent, by entering a general appearance, or by filing a responsive document having the effect of waiving any contest to personal jurisdiction;

(3) the child resides in this state as a result of the acts or directives of the person;

(4) the person resided with the child in this state;

(5) the person resided in this state and provided prenatal expenses or support for the child;

(6) the person engaged in sexual intercourse in this state and the child may have been conceived by that act of intercourse;

(7) the person, as provided by Chapter 160:

(A) registered with the paternity registry maintained by the vital statistics unit; or

(B) signed an acknowledgment of paternity of a child born in this state; or

(8) there is any basis consistent with the constitutions of this state and the United States for the exercise of the personal jurisdiction.

Added by Acts 1995, 74th Leg., ch. 20, § 1, eff. April 20, 1995. Amended by Acts 1997, 75th Leg., ch. 561, § 2, eff. Sept. 1, 1997; Acts 2009, 81st Leg., ch. 767, § 2, eff. June 19, 2009; Acts 2015, 84th Leg., ch. 1 (S.B. 219), § 1.030, eff. April 2, 2015.

### § 102.012. Exercising Partial Jurisdiction

(a) A court in which a suit is filed may exercise its jurisdiction over those portions of the suit for which it has authority.

(b) The court's authority to resolve all issues in controversy between the parties may be restricted because the court lacks:

(1) the required personal jurisdiction over a nonresident party;

(2) the required jurisdiction under Chapter 152; or

(3) the required jurisdiction under Chapter 159.

(c) If a provision of Chapter 152 or Chapter 159 expressly conflicts with another provision of this title and the conflict cannot be reconciled, the provision of Chapter 152 or Chapter 159 prevails.

(d) In exercising jurisdiction, the court shall seek to harmonize the provisions of this code, the federal Parental Kidnapping Prevention Act (28 U.S.C. Section 1738A), and the federal Full Faith and Credit for Child Support Order Act (28 U.S.C. Section 1738B).

Added by Acts 1995, 74th Leg., ch. 20, § 1, eff. April 20, 1995. Amended by Acts 1999, 76th Leg., ch. 62, § 6.13, eff. Sept. 1, 1999.

### § 102.013. Docketing Requirements

(a) In a suit for modification or a motion for enforcement, the clerk shall file the petition or motion and all related papers under the same docket number as the prior proceeding without additional letters, digits, or special designations.

(b) If a suit requests the adoption of a child, the clerk shall file the suit and all other papers relating to the suit in a new file having a new docket number.

(c) In a suit to determine parentage under this title in which the court has rendered an order relating to an earlier born child of the same parents, the clerk shall file the suit and all other papers relating to the suit under the same docket number as the prior parentage action. For all other purposes, including the assessment of fees and other costs, the suit is a separate suit.

Added by Acts 1995, 74th Leg., ch. 20, § 1, eff. April 20, 1995. Amended by Acts 2001, 77th Leg., ch. 1023, § 2, eff. Sept. 1, 2001.

### § 102.014. Use of Digitized Signature

(a) A digitized signature on an original petition under this chapter or any other pleading or order in a suit satisfies the requirements for and imposes the duties of signatories to pleadings, motions, and other papers identified under Rule 13, Texas Rules of Civil Procedure.

(b) A digitized signature under this section may be applied only by, and must remain under the sole control of, the person whose signature is represented.

Added by Acts 2013, 83rd Leg., ch. 790 (S.B. 1422), § 2, eff. Sept. 1, 2013.

## CHAPTER 103. VENUE AND TRANSFER OF ORIGINAL PROCEEDINGS



### § 103.001. Venue for Original Suit

(a) Except as otherwise provided by this title, an original suit shall be filed in the county where the child resides, unless:

(1) another court has continuing exclusive jurisdiction under Chapter 155; or

(2) venue is fixed in a suit for dissolution of a marriage under Subchapter D,[1] Chapter 6.

(b) A suit in which adoption is requested may be filed in the county where the child resides or in the county where the petitioners reside, regardless of whether another court has continuing exclusive jurisdiction under Chapter 155. Except as provided by Section 155.201, a court that has continuing exclusive jurisdiction is not required to transfer the suit affecting the parent-child relationship to the court in which the adoption suit is filed.

(c) A child resides in the county where the child's parents reside or the child's parent resides, if only one parent is living, except that:

(1) if a guardian of the person has been appointed by order of a county or probate court and a managing conservator has not been appointed, the

child resides in the county where the guardian of the person resides;

(2) if the parents of the child do not reside in the same county and if a managing conservator, custodian, or guardian of the person has not been appointed, the child resides in the county where the parent having actual care, control, and possession of the child resides;

(3) if the child is in the care and control of an adult other than a parent and a managing conservator, custodian, or guardian of the person has not been appointed, the child resides where the adult having actual care, control, and possession of the child resides;

(4) if the child is in the actual care, control, and possession of an adult other than a parent and the whereabouts of the parent and the guardian of the person is unknown, the child resides where the adult having actual possession, care, and control of the child resides;

(5) if the person whose residence would otherwise determine venue has left the child in the care and control of the adult, the child resides where that adult resides;

(6) if a guardian or custodian of the child has been appointed by order of a court of another state or country, the child resides in the county where the guardian or custodian resides if that person resides in this state; or

(7) if it appears that the child is not under the actual care, control, and possession of an adult, the child resides where the child is found.

Added by Acts 1995, 74th Leg., ch. 20, § 1, eff. April 20, 1995. Amended by Acts 1999, 76th Leg., ch. 62, § 6.14, eff. Sept. 1, 1999; Acts 2015, 84th Leg., ch. 944 (S.B. 206), § 8, eff. Sept. 1, 2015; Acts 2019, 86th Leg., ch. 722 (H.B. 369), § 2, eff. Sept. 1, 2019.

[1] V.T.C.A., Family Code § 6.301 et seq.

Section 2 of Acts 2019, 86th Leg., ch. 136 (H.B. 1854) provides:

"(a) The change in law made by this Act applies only to an order of adoption rendered on or after the effective date [Sept. 1, 2019] of this Act.

"(b) Notwithstanding Subsection (a) of this section, an order of adoption rendered in a suit filed as described by Section 103.001(b), Family Code, on or after September 1, 2015, but before the effective date of this Act by a court that had jurisdiction under that section to render the order of adoption regardless of whether another court had continuing, exclusive jurisdiction under Chapter 155, Family Code, is a final order and is not subject to an appeal on the basis that the court rendering the order of adoption did not have continuing, exclusive jurisdiction at the time the adoption order was rendered."

Section 6 of Acts 2019, 86th Leg., ch. 722 (H.B. 369) provides:

"The changes in law made by this Act to Sections 103.001, 155.201, and 155.204, Family Code, apply to a motion to transfer a suit affecting the parent-child relationship filed on or after the effective date [Sept. 1, 2019] of this Act. A motion to transfer a suit affecting the parent-child relationship filed before the effective date of this Act is governed by the law in effect on the date that motion was filed, and the former law is continued in effect for that purpose."

## § 103.002. Transfer of Original Proceedings Within State

(a) If venue of a suit is improper in the court in which an original suit is filed and no other court has continuing, exclusive jurisdiction of the suit, on the timely motion of a party other than the petitioner, the court shall transfer the proceeding to the county where venue is proper.

(b) On a showing that a suit for dissolution of the marriage of the child's parents has been filed in another court, a court in which a suit is pending shall transfer the proceedings to the court where the dissolution of the marriage is pending.

(c) The procedures in Chapter 155 apply to a transfer of:

(1) an original suit under this section; or

(2) a suit for modification or a motion for enforcement under this title.

Added by Acts 1995, 74th Leg., ch. 20, § 1, eff. April 20, 1995.

## § 103.003. Transfer of Original Suit Within State when Party or Child Resides Outside State

(a) A court of this state in which an original suit is filed or in which a suit for child support is filed under Chapter 159 shall transfer the suit to the county of residence of the party who is a resident of this state if all other parties and children affected by the proceedings reside outside this state.

(b) If one or more of the parties affected by the suit reside outside this state and if more than one party or one or more children affected by the proceeding reside in this state in different counties, the court shall transfer the suit according to the following priorities:

(1) to the court of continuing, exclusive jurisdiction, if any;

(2) to the county of residence of the child, if applicable, provided that:

(A) there is no court of continuing, exclusive jurisdiction; or

(B) the court of continuing, exclusive jurisdiction finds that neither a party nor a child affected by the proceeding resides in the county of the court of continuing jurisdiction; or

(3) if Subdivisions (1) and (2) are inapplicable, to the county most appropriate to serve the convenience of the resident parties, the witnesses, and the interest of justice.

(c) If a transfer of an original suit or suit for child support under Chapter 159 is sought under this section, Chapter 155 applies to the procedures for transfer of the suit.

Added by Acts 1995, 74th Leg., ch. 20, § 1, eff. April 20, 1995.

## CHAPTER 104. EVIDENCE

Section



### § 104.001. Rules of Evidence

Except as otherwise provided, the Texas Rules of Evidence apply as in other civil cases.

Added by Acts 1995, 74th Leg., ch. 20, § 1, eff. April 20, 1995. Amended by Acts 2005, 79th Leg., ch. 728, § 6.002, eff. Sept. 1, 2005.

### § 104.002. Prerecorded Statement of Child

If a child 12 years of age or younger is alleged in a suit under this title to have been abused, the recording of an oral statement of the child recorded prior to the proceeding is admissible into evidence if:

(1) no attorney for a party was present when the statement was made;

(2) the recording is both visual and aural and is recorded on film or videotape or by other electronic means;

(3) the recording equipment was capable of making an accurate recording, the operator was competent, and the recording is accurate and has not been altered;

(4) the statement was not made in response to questioning calculated to lead the child to make a particular statement;

(5) each voice on the recording is identified;

(6) the person conducting the interview of the child in the recording is present at the proceeding and available to testify or be cross-examined by either party; and

(7) each party is afforded an opportunity to view the recording before it is offered into evidence.

Added by Acts 1995, 74th Leg., ch. 20, § 1, eff. April 20, 1995.

### § 104.003. Prerecorded Videotaped Testimony of Child

(a) The court may, on the motion of a party to the proceeding, order that the testimony of the child be taken outside the courtroom and be recorded for showing in the courtroom before the court, the finder of fact, and the parties to the proceeding.

(b) Only an attorney for each party, an attorney ad litem for the child or other person whose presence would contribute to the welfare and well-being of the child, and persons necessary to operate the equipment may be present in the room with the child during the child's testimony.

(c) Only the attorneys for the parties may question the child.

(d) The persons operating the equipment shall be placed in a manner that prevents the child from seeing or hearing them.

(e) The court shall ensure that:

(1) the recording is both visual and aural and is recorded on film or videotape or by other electronic means;

(2) the recording equipment was capable of making an accurate recording, the operator was competent, and the recording is accurate and is not altered;

(3) each voice on the recording is identified; and

(4) each party to the proceeding is afforded an opportunity to view the recording before it is shown in the courtroom.

Added by Acts 1995, 74th Leg., ch. 20, § 1, eff. April 20, 1995.

### § 104.004. Remote Televised Broadcast of Testimony of Child

(a) If in a suit a child 12 years of age or younger is alleged to have been abused, the court may, on the motion of a party to the proceeding, order that the testimony of the child be taken in a room other than the courtroom and be televised by closed-circuit equipment in the courtroom to be viewed by the court and the parties.

(b) The procedures that apply to prerecorded videotaped testimony of a child apply to the remote broadcast of testimony of a child.

Added by Acts 1995, 74th Leg., ch. 20, § 1, eff. April 20, 1995.

### § 104.005. Substitution for In-Court Testimony of Child

(a) If the testimony of a child is taken as provided by this chapter, the child may not be compelled to testify in court during the proceeding.

(b) The court may allow the testimony of a child of any age to be taken in any manner provided by this chapter if the child, because of a medical condition, is incapable of testifying in open court.

Added by Acts 1995, 74th Leg., ch. 20, § 1, eff. April 20, 1995. Amended by Acts 1995, 74th Leg., ch. 751, § 11, eff. Sept. 1, 1995.

### § 104.006. Hearsay Statement of Child Abuse Victim

In a suit affecting the parent-child relationship, a statement made by a child 12 years of age or younger that describes alleged abuse against the child, without regard to whether the statement is otherwise inadmissible as hearsay, is admissible as evidence if, in a hearing conducted outside the presence of the jury, the court finds that the time, content, and circumstances of the statement provide sufficient indications of the statement's reliability and:

(1) the child testifies or is available to testify at the proceeding in court or in any other manner provided for by law; or

(2) the court determines that the use of the statement in lieu of the child's testimony is necessary to protect the welfare of the child.

Added by Acts 1997, 75th Leg., ch. 575, § 4, eff. Sept. 1, 1997.

### § 104.007. Video Testimony of Certain Professionals

(a) In this section, "professional" has the meaning assigned by Section 261.101(b).

(b) In a proceeding brought by the Department of Family and Protective Services concerning a child who is alleged in a suit to have been abused or neglected, the court may order that the testimony of a professional be taken outside the courtroom by videoconference:

(1) on the agreement of the department's counsel and respondent's counsel; or

(2) if good cause exists, on the court's own motion.

(c) In ordering testimony to be taken as provided by Subsection (b), the court shall ensure that the videoconference testimony allows:

(1) the parties and attorneys involved in the proceeding to be able to see and hear the professional as the professional testifies; and

(2) the professional to be able to see and hear the parties and attorneys examining the professional while the professional is testifying.

(d) If the court permits the testimony of a professional by videoconference as provided by this section to be admitted during the proceeding, the professional may not be compelled to be physically present in court during the same proceeding to provide the same testimony unless ordered by the court.

Added by Acts 2003, 78th Leg., ch. 266, § 1, eff. Sept. 1, 2003. Amended by Acts 2015, 84th Leg., ch. 944 (S.B. 206), § 9, eff. Sept. 1, 2015.

### § 104.008. Certain Testimony Prohibited

(a) A person may not offer an expert opinion or recommendation relating to the conservatorship of or possession of or access to a child at issue in a suit unless the person has conducted a child custody evaluation relating to the child under Subchapter D, Chapter 107.[1]

(b) In a contested suit, a mental health professional may provide other relevant information and opinions, other than those prohibited by Subsection (a), relating to any party that the mental health professional has personally evaluated.

(c) This section does not apply to a suit in which the Department of Family and Protective Services is a party.

Added by Acts 2015, 84th Leg., ch. 1252 (H.B. 1449), § 2.01, eff. Sept. 1, 2015.

[1] V.T.C.A., § 107.0501 et seq.

## CHAPTER 105. SETTINGS, HEARINGS, AND ORDERS

Section

### § 105.001. Temporary Orders Before Final Order

(a) In a suit, the court may make a temporary order, including the modification of a prior temporary order, for the safety and welfare of the child, including an order:

(1) for the temporary conservatorship of the child;

(2) for the temporary support of the child;

(3) restraining a party from disturbing the peace of the child or another party;

(4) prohibiting a person from removing the child beyond a geographical area identified by the court; or

(5) for payment of reasonable attorney's fees and expenses.

(b) Except as provided by Subsection (c), temporary restraining orders and temporary injunctions under this section shall be granted without the necessity of an affidavit or verified pleading stating specific facts showing that immediate and irreparable injury, loss, or damage will result before notice can be served and a hearing can be held. Except as provided by Subsection (h), an order may not be rendered under Subsection (a)(1), (2), or (5) except after notice and a hearing. A temporary restraining order or temporary injunction granted under this section need not:

(1) define the injury or state why it is irreparable;

(2) state why the order was granted without notice; or

(3) include an order setting the cause for trial on the merits with respect to the ultimate relief requested.

(c) Except on a verified pleading or an affidavit in accordance with the Texas Rules of Civil Procedure, an order may not be rendered:

(1) attaching the body of the child;

(2) taking the child into the possession of the court or of a person designated by the court; or

(3) excluding a parent from possession of or access to a child.

(d) In a suit, the court may dispense with the necessity of a bond in connection with temporary orders on behalf of the child.

(e) Temporary orders rendered under this section are not subject to interlocutory appeal.

(f) The violation of a temporary restraining order, temporary injunction, or other temporary order rendered under this section is punishable by contempt and the order is subject to and enforceable under Chapter 157.

(g) The rebuttable presumptions established in favor of the application of the guidelines for a child support order and for the standard possession order under Chapters 153 and 154 apply to temporary orders. The presumptions do not limit the authority of the court to render other temporary orders.

(h) An order under Subsection (a)(1) may be rendered without notice and an adversary hearing if the order is an emergency order sought by a governmental entity under Chapter 262.

Added by Acts 1995, 74th Leg., ch. 20, § 1, eff. April 20, 1995. Amended by Acts 1997, 75th Leg., ch. 575, § 5, eff. Sept. 1, 1997; Acts 1999, 76th Leg., ch. 1390, § 3, eff. Sept. 1, 1999; Acts 2003, 78th Leg., ch. 1036, § 1, eff. Sept. 1, 2003.

### § 105.0011. Information Regarding Protective Orders

At any time while a suit is pending, if the court believes, on the basis of any information received by the court, that a party to the suit or a member of the party's family or household may be a victim of family violence, the court shall inform that party of the party's right to apply for a protective order under Title 4. [1]

Added by Acts 2005, 79th Leg., ch. 361, § 3, eff. June 17, 2005.

[1] V.T.C.A., Family Code § 71.001 et seq.

### § 105.002. Jury

(a) Except as provided by Subsection (b), a party may demand a jury trial.

(b) A party may not demand a jury trial in:

(1) a suit in which adoption is sought, including a trial on the issue of denial or revocation of consent to the adoption by the managing conservator; or

(2) a suit to adjudicate parentage under Chapter 160.

(c) In a jury trial:

(1) a party is entitled to a verdict by the jury and the court may not contravene a jury verdict on the issues of:

(A) the appointment of a sole managing conservator;

(B) the appointment of joint managing conservators;

(C) the appointment of a possessory conservator;

(D) the determination of which joint managing conservator has the exclusive right to designate the primary residence of the child;

(E) the determination of whether to impose a restriction on the geographic area in which a sole managing conservator or joint managing conservator may designate the child's primary residence; and

(F) if a restriction described by Paragraph (E) is imposed, the determination of the geographic area within which the sole managing conservator or joint managing conservator must designate the child's primary residence; and

(2) the court may not submit to the jury questions on the issues of:

(A) support under Chapter 154 or Chapter 159;

(B) a specific term or condition of possession of or access to the child; or

(C) any right or duty of a conservator, other than a determination under Subdivision (1)(D), (E), or (F).

(d) Expired.

Added by Acts 1995, 74th Leg., ch. 20, § 1, eff. April 20, 1995. Amended by Acts 1995, 74th Leg., ch. 751, § 12, eff. Sept. 1, 1995; Acts 1997, 75th Leg., ch. 180, § 1, eff. Sept. 1, 1997; Acts 1999, 76th Leg., ch. 556, § 3, eff. Sept. 1, 1999; Acts 2001, 77th Leg., ch. 821, § 2.10, eff. June 14, 2001; Acts 2003, 78th Leg., ch. 1036, §§ 2, 22, eff. Sept. 1, 2003; Acts 2017, 85th Leg., ch. 317 (H.B. 7), § 6, eff. Sept. 1, 2017; Acts 2021, 87th Leg., ch. 228 (H.B. 868), § 1, eff. Sept. 1, 2021.

Section 2 of Acts 2021, 87th Leg., ch. 228 (H.B. 868) provides:

"The change in law made by this Act applies only to a suit affecting the parent-child relationship filed on or after the effective date [Sept. 1, 2021] of this Act. A suit affecting the parent-child relationship filed before the effective date of this Act is governed by the law in effect on the date the suit was filed, and the former law is continued in effect for that purpose."

## § 105.003. Procedure for Contested Hearing

(a) Except as otherwise provided by this title, proceedings shall be as in civil cases generally.

(b) On the agreement of all parties to the suit, the court may limit attendance at the hearing to only those persons who have a direct interest in the suit or in the work of the court.

(c) A record shall be made as in civil cases generally unless waived by the parties with the consent of the court.

(d) When information contained in a report, study, or examination is before the court, the person making the report, study, or examination is subject to both direct examination and cross-examination as in civil cases generally.

(e) The hearing may be adjourned from time to time.

Added by Acts 1995, 74th Leg., ch. 20, § 1, eff. April 20, 1995.

## § 105.004. Preferential Setting

After a hearing, the court may:

(1) grant a motion filed by a party or by the amicus attorney or attorney ad litem for the child for a preferential setting for a trial on the merits; and

(2) give precedence to that hearing over other civil cases if the court finds that the delay created by ordinary scheduling practices will unreasonably affect the best interest of the child.

Added by Acts 1995, 74th Leg., ch. 20, § 1, eff. April 20, 1995. Amended by Acts 2005, 79th Leg., ch. 172, § 16, eff. Sept. 1, 2005.

## § 105.005. Findings

Except as otherwise provided by this title, the court's findings shall be based on a preponderance of the evidence.

Added by Acts 1995, 74th Leg., ch. 20, § 1, eff. April 20, 1995.

## § 105.006. Contents of Final Order

(a) A final order, other than in a proceeding under Chapter 161 or 162, must contain:

(1) the social security number and driver's license number of each party to the suit, including the child, except that the child's social security number or driver's license number is not required if the child has not been assigned a social security number or driver's license number; and

(2) each party's current residence address, mailing address, home telephone number, name of employer, address of employment, and work telephone number, except as provided by Subsection (c).

(b) Except as provided by Subsection (c), the court shall order each party to inform each other party, the court that rendered the order, and the state case registry under Chapter 234 of an intended change in any of the information required by this section as long as any person, as a result of the order, is under an obligation to pay child support or is entitled to possession of or access to a child. The court shall order that notice of the intended change be given at the earlier of:

(1) the 60th day before the date the party intends to make the change; or

(2) the fifth day after the date that the party knew of the change, if the party did not know or could not have known of the change in sufficient time to comply with Subdivision (1).

(c) If a court finds after notice and hearing that requiring a party to provide the information required by this section to another party is likely to cause the child or a conservator harassment, abuse, serious harm, or injury, or to subject the child or a conservator to family violence, as defined by Section 71.004, the court may:

(1) order the information not to be disclosed to another party; or

(2) render any other order the court considers necessary.

(d) An order in a suit that orders child support or possession of or access to a child must contain the following prominently displayed statement in boldfaced type, capital letters, or underlined:

"FAILURE TO OBEY A COURT ORDER FOR CHILD SUPPORT OR FOR POSSESSION OF OR ACCESS TO A CHILD MAY RESULT IN FURTHER LITIGATION TO ENFORCE THE ORDER, INCLUDING CONTEMPT OF COURT. A FINDING OF CONTEMPT MAY BE PUNISHED BY CONFINEMENT IN JAIL FOR UP TO SIX MONTHS, A FINE OF UP TO $500 FOR EACH VIOLATION, AND A MONEY JUDGMENT FOR PAYMENT OF ATTORNEY'S FEES AND COURT COSTS."

"FAILURE OF A PARTY TO MAKE A CHILD SUPPORT PAYMENT TO THE PLACE AND IN THE MANNER REQUIRED BY A COURT ORDER MAY RESULT IN THE PARTY NOT RECEIVING CREDIT FOR MAKING THE PAYMENT."

"FAILURE OF A PARTY TO PAY CHILD SUPPORT DOES NOT JUSTIFY DENYING THAT PARTY COURT-ORDERED POSSESSION OF OR ACCESS TO A CHILD. REFUSAL BY A PARTY TO ALLOW POSSESSION OF OR ACCESS TO A CHILD DOES NOT JUSTIFY FAILURE TO PAY COURT-ORDERED CHILD SUPPORT TO THAT PARTY."

(e) Except as provided by Subsection (c), an order in a suit that orders child support or possession of or access to a child must also contain the following prominently displayed statement in boldfaced type, capital letters, or underlined:

"EACH PERSON WHO IS A PARTY TO THIS ORDER IS ORDERED TO NOTIFY EACH OTHER PARTY, THE COURT, AND THE STATE CASE REGISTRY OF ANY CHANGE IN THE PARTY'S CURRENT RESIDENCE ADDRESS, MAILING ADDRESS, HOME TELEPHONE NUMBER, NAME OF EMPLOYER, ADDRESS OF EMPLOYMENT, DRIVER'S LICENSE NUMBER, AND WORK TELEPHONE NUMBER. THE PARTY IS ORDERED TO GIVE NOTICE OF AN INTENDED CHANGE IN ANY OF THE REQUIRED INFORMATION TO EACH OTHER PARTY, THE COURT, AND THE STATE CASE REGISTRY ON OR BEFORE THE 60TH DAY BEFORE THE INTENDED CHANGE. IF THE PARTY DOES NOT KNOW OR COULD NOT HAVE KNOWN OF THE CHANGE IN SUFFICIENT TIME TO PROVIDE 60-DAY NOTICE, THE PARTY IS ORDERED TO GIVE NOTICE OF THE CHANGE ON OR BEFORE THE FIFTH DAY AFTER THE DATE THAT THE PARTY KNOWS OF THE CHANGE."

"THE DUTY TO FURNISH THIS INFORMATION TO EACH OTHER PARTY, THE COURT, AND THE STATE CASE REGISTRY CONTINUES AS LONG AS ANY PERSON, BY VIRTUE OF THIS ORDER, IS UNDER AN OBLIGATION TO PAY CHILD SUPPORT OR ENTITLED TO POSSESSION OF OR ACCESS TO A CHILD."

"FAILURE BY A PARTY TO OBEY THE ORDER OF THIS COURT TO PROVIDE EACH OTHER PARTY, THE COURT, AND THE STATE CASE REGISTRY WITH THE CHANGE IN THE REQUIRED INFORMATION MAY RESULT IN FURTHER LITIGATION TO ENFORCE THE ORDER, INCLUDING CONTEMPT OF COURT. A FINDING OF CONTEMPT MAY BE PUNISHED BY CONFINEMENT IN JAIL FOR UP TO SIX MONTHS, A FINE OF UP TO $500 FOR EACH VIOLATION, AND A MONEY JUDGMENT FOR PAYMENT OF ATTORNEY'S FEES AND COURT COSTS."

(e–1) An order in a suit that provides for the possession of or access to a child must contain the following prominently displayed statement in boldfaced type, in capital letters, or underlined:

"NOTICE TO ANY PEACE OFFICER OF THE STATE OF TEXAS: YOU MAY USE REASONABLE EFFORTS TO ENFORCE THE TERMS OF CHILD CUSTODY SPECIFIED IN THIS ORDER. A PEACE OFFICER WHO RELIES ON THE TERMS OF A COURT ORDER AND THE OFFICER'S AGENCY ARE ENTITLED TO THE APPLICABLE IMMUNITY AGAINST ANY CLAIM, CIVIL OR OTHERWISE, REGARDING THE OFFICER'S GOOD FAITH ACTS PERFORMED IN THE SCOPE OF THE OFFICER'S DUTIES IN ENFORCING THE TERMS OF THE ORDER THAT RELATE TO CHILD CUSTODY. ANY PERSON WHO KNOWINGLY PRESENTS FOR ENFORCEMENT AN ORDER THAT IS INVALID OR NO LONGER IN EFFECT COMMITS AN OFFENSE THAT MAY BE PUNISHABLE BY CONFINEMENT IN JAIL FOR AS LONG AS TWO YEARS AND A FINE OF AS MUCH AS $10,000."

(e–2) An order in a suit that orders child support must contain the following prominently displayed statement in boldfaced type, in capital letters, or underlined:

"THE COURT MAY MODIFY THIS ORDER THAT PROVIDES FOR THE SUPPORT OF A CHILD, IF:

(1) THE CIRCUMSTANCES OF THE CHILD OR A PERSON AFFECTED BY THE ORDER HAVE MATERIALLY AND SUBSTANTIALLY CHANGED; OR

(2) IT HAS BEEN THREE YEARS SINCE THE ORDER WAS RENDERED OR LAST MODIFIED AND THE MONTHLY AMOUNT OF THE CHILD SUPPORT AWARD UNDER THE ORDER DIFFERS BY EITHER 20 PERCENT OR $100 FROM THE AMOUNT THAT WOULD BE AWARDED IN ACCORDANCE WITH THE CHILD SUPPORT GUIDELINES."

(f) Except for an action in which contempt is sought, in any subsequent child support enforcement action, the court may, on a showing that diligent effort has been made to determine the location of a party, consider due process requirements for notice and service of process to be met with respect to that party on delivery of written notice to the most recent residential or employer address filed by that party with the court and the state case registry.

(g) The Title IV–D agency shall promulgate and provide forms for a party to use in reporting to the court and the state case registry under Chapter 234 the information required under this section.

(h) The court may include in a final order in a suit in which a party to the suit makes an allegation of child abuse or neglect a finding on whether the party who made the allegation knew that the allegation was false. This finding shall not constitute collateral estoppel for any criminal proceeding. The court may impose on a party found to have made a false allegation of child abuse or neglect any civil sanction permitted under law, including attorney's fees, costs of experts, and any other costs.

Added by Acts 1995, 74th Leg., ch. 20, § 1, eff. April 20, 1995. Amended by Acts 1995, 74th Leg., ch. 751, §§ 13, 128, eff. Sept. 1, 1995; Acts 1997, 75th Leg., ch. 786, § 1, eff. Sept. 1, 1997; Acts 1997, 75th Leg., ch. 911, § 6, eff. Sept. 1, 1997; Acts 1999, 76th Leg., ch. 62, § 19.01(21), eff. Sept. 1, 1999; Acts 1999, 76th Leg., ch. 178, § 5, eff. Aug. 30, 1999; Acts 2001, 77th Leg., ch. 133, § 1, eff. Sept. 1, 2001; Acts 2003, 78th Leg., ch. 184, § 1, eff. Sept. 1, 2003; Acts 2007, 80th Leg., ch. 972, § 3, eff. Sept. 1, 2007; Acts 2015, 84th Leg., ch. 280 (H.B. 826), § 1, eff. Sept. 1, 2015; Acts 2015, 84th Leg., ch. 859 (S.B. 1726), § 3, eff. Sept. 1, 2015.

### § 105.007. Compliance with Order Requiring Notice of Change of Required Information

(a) A party shall comply with the order by giving written notice to each other party of an intended change in the party's current residence address, mailing address, home telephone number, name of employer, address of employment, and work telephone number.

(b) The party must give written notice by registered or certified mail of an intended change in the required information to each other party on or before the 60th day before the change is made. If the party does not know or could not have known of the change in sufficient time to provide 60-day notice, the party shall provide the written notice of the change on or before the fifth day after the date that the party knew of the change.

(c) The court may waive the notice required by this section on motion by a party if it finds that the giving of notice of a change of the required information would be likely to expose the child or the party to harassment, abuse, serious harm, or injury.

Added by Acts 1995, 74th Leg., ch. 20, § 1, eff. April 20, 1995. Amended by Acts 1995, 74th Leg., ch. 751, § 14, eff. Sept. 1, 1995.

### § 105.008. Record of Support Order for State Case Registry

(a) The clerk of the court shall provide the state case registry with a record of a court order for child support, medical support, and dental support. The record of a support order shall include information provided by the parties on a form developed by the Title IV–D agency. The form shall be completed by the petitioner and submitted to the clerk at the time the order is filed for record.

(b) The form described by Subsection (a) may include an option for a party to apply for child support services provided by the Title IV–D agency. If a party applies for child support services, the party or the party's authorized representative must sign the form.

(c) To the extent federal funds are available, the Title IV–D agency shall reimburse the clerk of the court for the costs incurred in providing the record of support order required under this section.

Added by Acts 1997, 75th Leg., ch. 911, § 7, eff. Sept. 1, 1997. Amended by Acts 2005, 79th Leg., ch. 916, § 5, eff. June 18, 2005; Acts 2021, 87th Leg., ch. 175 (S.B. 285), § 1, eff. Sept. 1, 2021.

Section 8 of Acts 2021, 87th Leg., ch. 175 (S.B. 285) provides:

"The changes in law made by this Act to Sections 105.008 and 231.0011, Family Code, apply to a suit affecting the parent-child relationship pending. in a trial court on or filed on or after the effective date [Sept. 1, 2021] of this Act."

### § 105.009. Parent Education and Family Stabilization Course

(a) In a suit affecting the parent-child relationship, including an action to modify an order in a suit affecting the parent-child relationship providing for possession of or access to a child, the court may order the parties to the suit to attend a parent education and family stabilization course if the court determines that the order is in the best interest of the child.

(b) The parties to the suit may not be required to attend the course together. The court, on its own motion or the motion of either party, may prohibit the parties from taking the course together if there is a history of family violence in the marriage.

(c) A course under this section must be at least four hours, but not more than 12 hours, in length and be designed to educate and assist parents with regard to the consequences of divorce on parents and children. The course must include information on the following issues:

(1) the emotional effects of divorce on parents;

(2) the emotional and behavioral reactions to divorce by young children and adolescents;

(3) parenting issues relating to the concerns and needs of children at different development stages;

(4) stress indicators in young children and adolescents;

(5) conflict management;

(6) family stabilization through development of a coparenting relationship;

(7) the financial responsibilities of parenting;

(8) family violence, spousal abuse, and child abuse and neglect; and

(9) the availability of community services and resources.

(d) A course may not be designed to provide individual mental health therapy or individual legal advice.

(e) A course satisfies the requirements of this section if it is offered by:

(1) a mental health professional who has at least a master's degree with a background in family therapy or parent education; or

(2) a religious practitioner who performs counseling consistent with the laws of this state or another person designated as a program counselor by a church or religious institution if the litigant so chooses.

(f) Information obtained in a course or a statement made by a participant to a suit during a course may not be considered in the adjudication of the suit or in any subsequent legal proceeding. Any report that results from participation in the course may not become a record in the suit unless the parties stipulate to the record in writing.

(g) The court may take appropriate action with regard to a party who fails to attend or complete a course ordered by the court under this section, including holding the party in contempt of court, striking pleadings, or invoking any sanction provided by Rule 215, Texas Rules of Civil Procedure.[1] The failure or refusal by a party to attend or complete a course required by this section may not delay the court from rendering a judgment in a suit affecting the parent-child relationship.

(h) The course required under this section may be completed by:

(1) personal instruction;

(2) videotape instruction;

(3) instruction through an electronic medium; or

(4) a combination of those methods.

(i) On completion of the course, the course provider shall issue a certificate of completion to each participant. The certificate must state:

(1) the name of the participant;

(2) the name of the course provider;

(3) the date the course was completed; and

(4) whether the course was provided by:

(A) personal instruction;

(B) videotape instruction;

(C) instruction through an electronic medium; or

(D) a combination of those methods.

(j) The county clerk in each county may establish a registry of course providers in the county and a list of locations at which courses are provided. The clerk shall include information in the registry identifying courses that are offered on a sliding fee scale or without charge.

(k) The court may not order the parties to a suit to attend a course under this section if the parties cannot afford to take the course. If the parties cannot afford to take a course, the court may direct the parties to a course that is offered on a sliding fee scale or without charge, if a course of that type is available. A party to a suit may not be required to pay more than $100 to attend a course ordered under this section.

(*l*) A person who has attended a course under this section may not be required to attend the course more than twice before the fifth anniversary of the date the person completes the course for the first time.

*Text of subsec. (m) as added by Acts 2005, 79th Leg., ch. 916, § 6*

(m) A course under this section must be available in both English and Spanish.

*Text of subsec. (m) as added by Acts 2005, 79th Leg., ch. 1171, § 3*

(m) A course under this section in a suit filed in a county with a population of more than two million that is adjacent to a county with a population of more than one million must be available in both English and Spanish.

Added by Acts 1999, 76th Leg., ch. 946, § 1, eff. Sept. 1, 1999. Amended by Acts 2005, 79th Leg., ch. 916, § 6, eff. June 18, 2005; Acts 2005, 79th Leg., ch. 1171, § 3, eff. Oct. 1, 2005.

[1] Vernon's Ann. Rules Civ.Proc., rule 215.1 et seq.

## CHAPTER 106. COSTS AND ATTORNEY'S FEES

Section



### § 106.001. Costs

The court may award costs in a suit or motion under this title and in a habeas corpus proceeding.

Added by Acts 1995, 74th Leg., ch. 20, § 1, eff. April 20, 1995. Amended by Acts 1997, 75th Leg., ch. 15, § 1, eff. Sept. 1, 1997.

### § 106.002. Attorney's Fees and Expenses

(a) In a suit under this title, the court may render judgment for reasonable attorney's fees and expenses and order the judgment and postjudgment interest to be paid directly to an attorney.

(b) A judgment for attorney's fees and expenses may be enforced in the attorney's name by any means available for the enforcement of a judgment for debt.

Added by Acts 1995, 74th Leg., ch. 20, § 1, eff. April 20, 1995. Amended by Acts 1997, 75th Leg., ch. 15, § 2, eff. Sept. 1, 1997; Acts 2003, 78th Leg., ch. 478, § 1, eff. Sept. 1, 2003.

## CHAPTER 107. SPECIAL APPOINTMENTS, CHILD CUSTODY EVALUATIONS, AND ADOPTION EVALUATIONS

### SUBCHAPTER A. COURT-ORDERED REPRESENTATION IN SUITS AFFECTING THE PARENT-CHILD RELATIONSHIP

Section



### SUBCHAPTER B. APPOINTMENTS IN CERTAIN SUITS

#### PART 1. APPOINTMENTS IN SUITS BY GOVERNMENTAL ENTITY

*Chapter 107, Special Appointments and Social Studies, which as added by Acts 1995, 74th Leg., ch. 20, consisted of §§ 107.001 to 107.005, was amended by Acts 1995, 74th Leg., ch. 751, § 15, effective September 1, 1995, to consist of §§ 107.001 to 107.056.*

## SUBCHAPTER A. COURT–ORDERED REPRESENTATION IN SUITS AFFECTING THE PARENT–CHILD RELATIONSHIP

### § 107.001. Definitions

In this chapter:

(1) "Amicus attorney" means an attorney appointed by the court in a suit, other than a suit filed by a governmental entity, whose role is to provide legal services necessary to assist the court in protecting a child's best interests rather than to provide legal services to the child.

(2) "Attorney ad litem" means an attorney who provides legal services to a person, including a child, and who owes to the person the duties of undivided loyalty, confidentiality, and competent representation.

(3) "Developmentally appropriate" means structured to account for a child's age, level of education, cultural background, and degree of language acquisition.

(4) "Dual role" means the role of an attorney who is appointed under Section 107.0125 to act as both guardian ad litem and attorney ad litem for a child in a suit filed by a governmental entity.

(5) "Guardian ad litem" means a person appointed to represent the best interests of a child. The term includes:

(A) a volunteer advocate from a charitable organization described by Subchapter C[1] who is appointed by the court as the child's guardian ad litem;

(B) a professional, other than an attorney, who holds a relevant professional license and whose training relates to the determination of a child's best interests;

(C) an adult having the competence, training, and expertise determined by the court to be sufficient to represent the best interests of the child; or

(D) an attorney ad litem appointed to serve in the dual role.

Added by Acts 2003, 78th Leg., ch. 262, § 1, eff. Sept. 1, 2003. Amended by Acts 2015, 84th Leg., ch. 1 (S.B. 219), § 1.031, eff. April 2, 2015.

[1] V.T.C.A., Family Code § 107.031.

### § 107.002. Powers and Duties of Guardian ad Litem for Child

(a) A guardian ad litem appointed for a child under this chapter is not a party to the suit but may:

(1) conduct an investigation to the extent that the guardian ad litem considers necessary to determine the best interests of the child; and

(2) obtain and review copies of the child's relevant medical, psychological, and school records as provided by Section 107.006.

(b) A guardian ad litem appointed for the child under this chapter shall:

(1) within a reasonable time after the appointment, interview:

(A) the child in a developmentally appropriate manner, if the child is four years of age or older;

(B) each person who has significant knowledge of the child's history and condition, including educators, child welfare service providers, and any foster parent of the child; and

(C) the parties to the suit;

(2) seek to elicit in a developmentally appropriate manner the child's expressed objectives;

(3) consider the child's expressed objectives without being bound by those objectives;

(4) encourage settlement and the use of alternative forms of dispute resolution; and

(5) perform any specific task directed by the court.

(b–1) In addition to the duties required by Subsection (b), a guardian ad litem appointed for a child in a proceeding under Chapter 262 or 263 shall:

(1) review the medical care provided to the child;

(2) in a developmentally appropriate manner, seek to elicit the child's opinion on the medical care provided;

(3) for a child at least 16 years of age, ascertain whether the child has received the following documents:

(A) a certified copy of the child's birth certificate;

(B) a social security card or a replacement social security card;

(C) a driver's license or personal identification certificate under Chapter 521, Transportation Code; and

(D) any other personal document the Department of Family and Protective Services determines appropriate; and

(4) seek to elicit in a developmentally appropriate manner the name of any adult, particularly an adult residing in the child's community, who could be a relative or designated caregiver for the child and immediately provide the names of those individuals to the Department of Family and Protective Services.

(c) A guardian ad litem appointed for the child under this chapter is entitled to:

(1) receive a copy of each pleading or other paper filed with the court in the case in which the guardian ad litem is appointed;

(2) receive notice of each hearing in the case;

(3) participate in case staffings by the Department of Family and Protective Services concerning the child;

(4) attend all legal proceedings in the case but may not call or question a witness or otherwise provide legal services unless the guardian ad litem is a licensed attorney who has been appointed in the dual role;

(5) review and sign, or decline to sign, an agreed order affecting the child;

(6) explain the basis for the guardian ad litem's opposition to the agreed order if the guardian ad litem does not agree to the terms of a proposed order;

(7) have access to the child in the child's placement;

(8) be consulted and provide comments on decisions regarding placement, including kinship, foster care, and adoptive placements;

(9) evaluate whether the child welfare services providers are protecting the child's best interests regarding appropriate care, treatment, services, and all other foster children's rights listed in Section 263.008;

(10) receive notification regarding and an invitation to attend meetings related to the child's service plan and a copy of the plan; and

(11) attend court-ordered mediation regarding the child's case.

(d) The court may compel the guardian ad litem to attend a trial or hearing and to testify as necessary for the proper disposition of the suit.

(e) Unless the guardian ad litem is an attorney who has been appointed in the dual role and subject to the Texas Rules of Evidence, the court shall ensure in a hearing or in a trial on the merits that a guardian ad litem has an opportunity to testify regarding, and is permitted to submit a report regarding, the guardian ad litem's recommendations relating to:

(1) the best interests of the child; and

(2) the bases for the guardian ad litem's recommendations.

(f) In a nonjury trial, a party may call the guardian ad litem as a witness for the purpose of cross-examination regarding the guardian's report without the guardian ad litem being listed as a witness by a party. If the guardian ad litem is not called as a witness, the court shall permit the guardian ad litem to testify in the narrative.

(g) In a contested case, the guardian ad litem shall provide copies of the guardian ad litem's report, if any, to the attorneys for the parties as directed by the court, but not later than the earlier of:

(1) the date required by the scheduling order; or

(2) the 10th day before the date of the commencement of the trial.

(h) Disclosure to the jury of the contents of a guardian ad litem's report to the court is subject to the Texas Rules of Evidence.

(i) A guardian ad litem appointed to represent a child in the managing conservatorship of the Department of Family and Protective Services shall, before each scheduled hearing under Chapter 263, determine whether the child's educational needs and goals have been identified and addressed.

Added by Acts 1995, 74th Leg., ch. 20, § 1, eff. Sept. 1, 1995. Amended by Acts 1997, 75th Leg., ch. 1294, § 2, eff. Sept. 1, 1997; Acts 2003, 78th Leg., ch. 262, § 1, eff. Sept. 1, 2003; Acts 2005, 79th Leg., ch. 172, § 1, eff. Sept. 1, 2005; Acts 2013, 83rd Leg., ch. 204 (H.B. 915), § 1, eff. Sept. 1, 2013; Acts 2013, 83rd Leg., ch. 688 (H.B. 2619), § 1, eff. Sept. 1, 2013; Acts 2015, 84th Leg., ch. 1 (S.B. 219), § 1.032, eff. April 2, 2015; Acts 2017, 85th Leg., ch. 317 (H.B. 7), § 7, eff. Sept. 1, 2017; Acts 2017, 85th Leg., ch. 319 (S.B. 11), § 2, eff. Sept. 1, 2017; Acts 2017, 85th Leg., ch. 937 (S.B. 1758), § 1, eff. Sept. 1, 2017; Acts 2019, 86th Leg., ch. 1294 (H.B. 3390), § 1, eff. June 14, 2019.

**§ 107.003. Powers and Duties of Attorney ad Litem for Child and Amicus Attorney**

(a) An attorney ad litem appointed to represent a child or an amicus attorney appointed to assist the court:

(1) shall:

(A) subject to Rules 4.02, 4.03, and 4.04, Texas Disciplinary Rules of Professional Conduct, and within a reasonable time after the appointment, interview:

(i) the child in a developmentally appropriate manner, if the child is four years of age or older;

(ii) each person who has significant knowledge of the child's history and condition, including any foster parent of the child; and

(iii) the parties to the suit;

(B) seek to elicit in a developmentally appropriate manner the child's expressed objectives of representation;

(C) consider the impact on the child in formulating the attorney's presentation of the child's expressed objectives of representation to the court;

(D) investigate the facts of the case to the extent the attorney considers appropriate;

(E) obtain and review copies of relevant records relating to the child as provided by Section 107.006;

(F) participate in the conduct of the litigation to the same extent as an attorney for a party;

(G) take any action consistent with the child's interests that the attorney considers necessary to expedite the proceedings;

(H) encourage settlement and the use of alternative forms of dispute resolution; and

(I) review and sign, or decline to sign, a proposed or agreed order affecting the child;

(2) must be trained in child advocacy or have experience determined by the court to be equivalent to that training; and

(3) is entitled to:

(A) request clarification from the court if the role of the attorney is ambiguous;

(B) request a hearing or trial on the merits;

(C) consent or refuse to consent to an interview of the child by another attorney;

(D) receive a copy of each pleading or other paper filed with the court;

(E) receive notice of each hearing in the suit;

(F) participate in any case staffing concerning the child conducted by the Department of Family and Protective Services; and

(G) attend all legal proceedings in the suit.

(b) In addition to the duties required by Subsection (a), an attorney ad litem appointed for a child in a proceeding under Chapter 262, 263, or 264 shall:

(1) review the medical care provided to the child;

(2) in a developmentally appropriate manner, seek to elicit the child's opinion on the medical care provided;

(3) for a child at least 16 years of age:

(A) advise the child of the child's right to request the court to authorize the child to consent to the child's own medical care under Section 266.010; and

(B) ascertain whether the child has received the following documents:

(i) a certified copy of the child's birth certificate;

(ii) a social security card or a replacement social security card;

(iii) a driver's license or personal identification certificate under Chapter 521, Transportation Code; and

(iv) any other personal document the Department of Family and Protective Services determines appropriate; and

(4) seek to elicit in a developmentally appropriate manner the name of any adult, particularly an adult residing in the child's community, who could be a relative or designated caregiver for the child and immediately provide the names of those individuals to the Department of Family and Protective Services.

Added by Acts 1997, 75th Leg., ch. 1294, § 3, eff. Sept. 1, 1997. Amended by Acts 2003, 78th Leg., ch. 262, § 1, eff. Sept. 1, 2003; Acts 2005, 79th Leg., ch. 172, § 2, eff. Sept. 1, 2005; Acts 2013, 83rd Leg., ch. 204 (H.B. 915), § 2, eff. Sept. 1, 2013; Acts 2015, 84th Leg., ch. 1 (S.B. 219), § 1.033, eff. April 2, 2015; Acts 2017, 85th Leg., ch. 319 (S.B. 11), § 3, eff. Sept. 1, 2017; Acts 2017, 85th Leg., ch. 937 (S.B. 1758), § 2, eff. Sept. 1, 2017; Acts 2019, 86th Leg., ch. 1294 (H.B. 3390), § 2, eff. June 14, 2019; Acts 2021, 87th Leg., ch. 8 (H.B. 567), § 1, eff. Sept. 1, 2021.

Section 15 of Acts 2021, 87th Leg., ch. 8 (H.B. 567) provides:

"The changes in law made by this Act apply only to a suit filed by the Department of Family and Protective Services on or after the effective date [Sept. 1, 2021] of this Act. A suit filed by the department before that date is governed by the law in effect on the date the suit was filed, and the former law is continued in effect for that purpose."

## § 107.004. Additional Duties of Attorney ad Litem for Child

(a) Except as otherwise provided by this chapter, the attorney ad litem appointed for a child shall, in a developmentally appropriate manner:

(1) advise the child;

(2) represent the child's expressed objectives of representation and follow the child's expressed objectives of representation during the course of litigation if the attorney ad litem determines that the child is competent to understand the nature of an attorney-client relationship and has formed that relationship with the attorney ad litem; and

(3) as appropriate, considering the nature of the appointment, become familiar with the American Bar Association's standards of practice for attorneys who represent children in abuse and neglect cases, the suggested amendments to those standards adopted by the National Association of Counsel for Children, and the American Bar Association's standards of practice for attorneys who represent children in custody cases.

(b) An attorney ad litem appointed for a child in a proceeding under Subtitle E[1] shall complete at least three hours of continuing legal education relating to representing children in child protection cases as described by Subsection (c) as soon as practicable after the attorney ad litem is appointed. An attorney ad litem is not required to comply with this subsection if the court finds that the attorney ad litem has experience equivalent to the required education.

(b–1) An attorney who is on the list maintained by the court as being qualified for appointment as an attorney ad litem for a child in a child protection case must:

(1) complete at least three hours of continuing legal education relating to the representation of a child in a proceeding under Subtitle E each year before the anniversary date of the attorney's listing; and

(2) provide proof that the attorney has completed a training program regarding trauma-informed care and the effect of trauma on children in the conservatorship of the Department of Family and Protective Services.

(b–2) The training described by Subsection (b–1)(2) may satisfy the training requirement under Subsection (b–1)(1) in a year in which an attorney completes the training.

(b–3) An attorney described by Subsection (b–1) shall complete the training required by Subsection (b–1)(2) as soon as practicable after the attorney is placed on the list described by Subsection (b–1).

(b–4) The training required by Subsection (b–1)(2) must be designed to educate an attorney regarding the attorney's duty under Subsection (d–3) and include information regarding:

(1) the symptoms of trauma and the impact that trauma has on a child, including how trauma may affect a child's development, emotions, memories, behavior, and decision-making;

(2) attachment and how a lack of attachment may affect a child;

(3) the role that trauma-informed care and services can have in a child's ability to build connections, feel safe, and regulate the child's emotions to help the child build resiliency and overcome the effects of trauma and adverse childhood experiences;

(4) the importance of screening children for trauma and the risk of mislabeling and inappropriate treatment of children without proper screening, including the risks and benefits associated with the use of psychotropic medication;

(5) the potential for re-traumatization of children in the conservatorship of the Department of Family and Protective Services; and

(6) the availability of:

(A) research-supported, trauma-informed, non-pharmacological interventions; and

(B) trauma-informed advocacy to increase a child's access, while the child is in the conservatorship of the Department of Family and Protective Services, to:

(i) trauma-informed care; and

(ii) trauma-informed mental and behavioral health services.

(c) The continuing legal education required by Subsections (b) and (b–1) must:

(1) be low-cost and available to persons throughout this state, including on the Internet provided through the State Bar of Texas; and

(2) focus on the duties of an attorney ad litem in, and the procedures of and best practices for, representing a child in a proceeding under Subtitle E.

(d) Except as provided by Subsection (e), an attorney ad litem appointed for a child in a proceeding under Chapter 262, 263, or 264 shall:

(1) meet before each court hearing with:

(A) the child, if the child is at least four years of age; or

(B) the individual with whom the child ordinarily resides, including the child's parent, conservator, guardian, caretaker, or custodian, if the child is younger than four years of age; and

(2) report to the court whether the attorney ad litem:

(A) complied with Subdivision (1); or

(B) requests that the court find good cause for noncompliance because compliance was not feasible or in the best interest of the child under Subsection (e).

(d–1) A meeting required by Subsection (d) must take place:

(1) a sufficient time before the hearing to allow the attorney ad litem to prepare for the hearing in accordance with the child's expressed objectives of representation; and

(2) in a private setting that allows for confidential communications between the attorney ad litem and the child or individual with whom the child ordinarily resides, as applicable.

(d–2) An attorney ad litem appointed to represent a child in the managing conservatorship of the Department of Family and Protective Services or a child who is the subject of a proceeding under Chapter 264 shall, before each scheduled hearing under Chapter 263 or 264, determine whether the child's educational needs and goals have been identified and addressed.

(d–3) An attorney ad litem appointed to represent a child in the managing conservatorship of the Department of Family and Protective Services or a child who is the subject of a proceeding under Chapter 264 shall periodically continue to review the child's safety and well-being, including any effects of trauma to the child, and take appropriate action, including requesting a review hearing when necessary to address an issue of concern.

(e) An attorney ad litem appointed for a child in a proceeding under Chapter 262, 263, or 264 is not required to comply with Subsection (d) before a hearing if the court finds at that hearing that the attorney ad litem has shown good cause why the attorney ad litem's compliance with that subsection is not feasible or in the best interest of the child. Additionally, a court may, on a showing of good cause, authorize an attorney ad litem to comply with Subsection (d) by conferring with the child or other individual, as appropriate, by telephone or video conference.

Added by Acts 2003, 78th Leg., ch. 262, § 1, eff. Sept. 1, 2003. Amended by Acts 2005, 79th Leg., ch. 172, § 3, eff. Sept. 1, 2005; Acts 2005, 79th Leg., ch. 268, § 1.04(a), eff. Sept. 1, 2005; Acts 2007, 80th Leg., ch. 310, § 1, eff. June 15, 2007; Acts 2011, 82nd Leg., ch. 572 (H.B. 3311), § 1, eff. Sept. 1, 2011; Acts 2011, 82nd Leg., ch. 573 (H.B. 3314), § 1, eff. Sept. 1, 2011; Acts 2013, 83rd Leg., ch. 688 (H.B. 2619), § 2, eff. Sept. 1, 2013; Acts 2013, 83rd Leg., ch. 810 (S.B. 1759), § 1, eff. Sept. 1, 2013; Acts 2017, 85th Leg., ch. 317 (H.B. 7), § 8, eff. Sept. 1, 2017; Acts 2021, 87th Leg., ch. 8 (H.B. 567), § 2, eff. Sept. 1, 2021; Acts 2021, 87th Leg., ch. 430 (S.B. 904), § 1, eff. Sept. 1, 2021; Acts 2021, 87th Leg., ch. 934 (H.B. 3774), § 4.05, eff. Sept. 1, 2021.

[1] V.T.C.A., Family Code § 261.001 et seq.

Section 15 of Acts 2021, 87th Leg., ch. 8 (H.B. 567) provides:

"The changes in law made by this Act apply only to a suit filed by the Department of Family and Protective Services on or after the effective date [Sept. 1, 2021] of this Act. A suit filed by the department before that date is governed by the law in effect on the date the suit was filed, and the former law is continued in effect for that purpose."

Section 2 of Acts 2021, 87th Leg., ch. 430 (S.B. 904) provides:

"An attorney who is on the list maintained by a court as being qualified for appointment as an attorney ad litem for a child in a child protection case on the effective date of this Act [Sept. 1, 2021] shall complete the training required by Section 107.004(b–1)(2), Family Code, as added by this Act, not later than September 1, 2022."

Section 15.02 of Acts 2021, 87th Leg., ch. 934 (H.B. 3774) provides:

"Not later than May 1, 2022, the Supreme Court of Texas shall adopt rules and promulgate forms under Section 22.0042, Government Code, as added by this article."

Section 18.01 of Acts 2021, 87th Leg., ch. 934 (H.B. 3774) provides:

"A state agency subject to this Act is required to implement a provision of this Act only if the legislature appropriates money specifically for that purpose. If the legislature does not appropriate money specifically for that purpose, the state agency may, but is not required to, implement a provision of this Act using other appropriations available for that purpose."

### § 107.0045. Discipline of Attorney ad Litem

An attorney ad litem who fails to perform the duties required by Sections 107.003 and 107.004 is subject to disciplinary action under Subchapter E, Chapter 81, Government Code. [1]

Added by Acts 2005, 79th Leg., ch. 268, § 1.05, eff. Sept. 1, 2005.

[1] V.T.C.A., Government Code § 81.071 et seq.

### § 107.005. Additional Duties of Amicus Attorney

(a) Subject to any specific limitation in the order of appointment, an amicus attorney shall advocate the best interests of the child after reviewing the facts and circumstances of the case. Notwithstanding Subsection (b), in determining the best interests of the child, an amicus attorney is not bound by the child's expressed objectives of representation.

(b) An amicus attorney shall, in a developmentally appropriate manner:

(1) with the consent of the child, ensure that the child's expressed objectives of representation are made known to the court;

(2) explain the role of the amicus attorney to the child;

(3) inform the child that the amicus attorney may use information that the child provides in providing assistance to the court; and

(4) become familiar with the American Bar Association's standards of practice for attorneys who represent children in custody cases.

(c) An amicus attorney may not disclose confidential communications between the amicus attorney and the child unless the amicus attorney determines that disclosure is necessary to assist the court regarding the best interests of the child.

Added by Acts 2003, 78th Leg., ch. 262, § 1, eff. Sept. 1, 2003. Amended by Acts 2005, 79th Leg., ch. 172, § 4, eff. Sept. 1, 2005.

### § 107.006. Access to Child and Information Relating to Child

(a) In conjunction with an appointment under this chapter, other than an appointment of an attorney ad litem for an adult or a parent, the court shall issue an order authorizing the attorney ad litem, guardian ad litem for the child, or amicus attorney to have immediate access to thc child and any information relating to the child.

(b) Without requiring a further order or release, the custodian of any relevant records relating to the child, including records regarding social services, law enforcement records, school records, records of a probate or court proceeding, and records of a trust or account for which the child is a beneficiary, shall provide access to a person authorized to access the records under Subsection (a).

(c) Without requiring a further order or release, the custodian of a medical, mental health, or drug or alcohol treatment record of a child that is privileged or confidential under other law shall release the record to a person authorized to access the record under Subsection (a), except that a child's drug or alcohol treatment record that is confidential under 42 U.S.C. Section 290dd–2 may only be released as provided under applicable federal regulations.

(d) The disclosure of a confidential record under this section does not affect the confidentiality of the record, and the person provided access to the record may not disclose the record further except as provided by court order or other law.

(e) Notwithstanding the provisions of this section, the requirements of Section 159.008, Occupations Code, apply.

(f) Repealed by Acts 2013, 83rd Leg., ch. 904 (H.B. 1185), § 1.

Added by Acts 1995, 74th Leg., ch. 943, § 11, eff. Sept. 1, 1995. Amended by Acts 1997, 75th Leg., ch. 1294, § 4, eff. Sept. 1, 1997; Acts 2003, 78th Leg., ch. 262, § 1, eff. Sept. 1, 2003; Acts 2005, 79th Leg., ch. 172, § 5, eff. Sept. 1, 2005; Acts 2011, 82nd Leg., ch. 206 (H.B. 2488), § 1, eff. May 30, 2011; Acts 2013, 83rd Leg., ch. 904 (H.B. 1185), § 1, eff. Sept. 1, 2013.

### § 107.007. Attorney Work Product and Testimony

(a) An attorney ad litem, an attorney serving in the dual role, or an amicus attorney may not:

(1) be compelled to produce attorney work product developed during the appointment as an attorney;

(2) be required to disclose the source of any information;

(3) submit a report into evidence; or

(4) testify in court except as authorized by Rule 3.08, Texas Disciplinary Rules of Professional Conduct.

(b) Subsection (a) does not apply to the duty of an attorney to report child abuse or neglect under Section 261.101.

Added by Acts 2003, 78th Leg., ch. 262, § 1, eff. Sept. 1, 2003.

### § 107.008. Substituted Judgment of Attorney for Child

(a) An attorney ad litem appointed to represent a child or an attorney appointed in the dual role may determine that the child cannot meaningfully formulate the child's objectives of representation in a case because the child:

(1) lacks sufficient maturity to understand and form an attorney-client relationship with the attorney;

(2) despite appropriate legal counseling, continues to express objectives of representation that would be seriously injurious to the child; or

(3) for any other reason is incapable of making reasonable judgments and engaging in meaningful communication.

(b) An attorney ad litem or an attorney appointed in the dual role who determines that the child cannot meaningfully formulate the child's expressed objectives of representation may present to the court a position that the attorney determines will serve the best interests of the child.

(c) If a guardian ad litem has been appointed for the child in a suit filed by a governmental entity requesting termination of the parent-child relationship or appointment of the entity as conservator of the child, an attorney ad litem who determines that the child cannot meaningfully formulate the child's expressed objectives of representation:

(1) shall consult with the guardian ad litem and, without being bound by the guardian ad litem's opinion or recommendation, ensure that the guardian ad litem's opinion and basis for any recommendation regarding the best interests of the child are presented to the court; and

(2) may present to the court a position that the attorney determines will serve the best interests of the child.

Added by Acts 2003, 78th Leg., ch. 262, § 1, eff. Sept. 1, 2003. Amended by Acts 2005, 79th Leg., ch. 172, § 6, eff. Sept. 1, 2005.

### § 107.009. Immunity

(a) A guardian ad litem, an attorney ad litem, a child custody evaluator, or an amicus attorney appointed under this chapter is not liable for civil damages arising from an action taken, a recommendation made, or an opinion given in the capacity of guardian ad litem, attorney ad litem, child custody evaluator, or amicus attorney.

(b) Subsection (a) does not apply to an action taken, a recommendation made, or an opinion given:

(1) with conscious indifference or reckless disregard to the safety of another;

(2) in bad faith or with malice; or

(3) that is grossly negligent or wilfully wrongful.

Added by Acts 2003, 78th Leg., ch. 262, § 1, eff. Sept. 1, 2003. Amended by Acts 2005, 79th Leg., ch. 172, § 7, eff. Sept. 1, 2005; Acts 2017, 85th Leg., ch. 257 (H.B. 1501), § 1, eff. Sept. 1, 2017.

### § 107.010. Discretionary Appointment of Attorney ad Litem for Incapacitated Person

The court may appoint an attorney to serve as an attorney ad litem for a person entitled to service of citation in a suit if the court finds that the person is incapacitated. The attorney ad litem shall follow the person's expressed objectives of representation and, if appropriate, refer the proceeding to the proper court for guardianship proceedings.

Added by Acts 2003, 78th Leg., ch. 262, § 1, eff. Sept. 1, 2003.

## SUBCHAPTER B. APPOINTMENTS IN CERTAIN SUITS

## PART 1. APPOINTMENTS IN SUITS BY GOVERNMENTAL ENTITY

### § 107.011. Mandatory Appointment of Guardian ad Litem

(a) Except as otherwise provided by this subchapter, in a suit filed by a governmental entity seeking termination of the parent-child relationship or the appointment of a conservator for a child, the court shall appoint a guardian ad litem to represent the best interests of the child immediately after the filing of the petition but before the full adversary hearing.

(b) The guardian ad litem appointed for a child under this section may be:

(1) a charitable organization composed of volunteer advocates or an individual volunteer advocate appointed under Subchapter C;

(2) an adult having the competence, training, and expertise determined by the court to be sufficient to represent the best interests of the child; or

(3) an attorney appointed in the dual role.

(c) The court may not appoint a guardian ad litem in a suit filed by a governmental entity if an attorney is appointed in the dual role unless the court appoints another person to serve as guardian ad litem for the child and restricts the role of the attorney to acting as an attorney ad litem for the child.

(d) The court may appoint an attorney to serve as guardian ad litem for a child without appointing the attorney to serve in the dual role only if the attorney is specifically appointed to serve only in the role of guardian ad litem. An attorney appointed solely as a guardian ad litem:

(1) may take only those actions that may be taken by a nonattorney guardian ad litem; and

(2) may not:

(A) perform legal services in the case; or

(B) take any action that is restricted to a licensed attorney, including engaging in discovery other than as a witness, making opening and closing statements, or examining witnesses.

(e) The court may appoint the person appointed as guardian ad litem for the child under Section 51.11 to also serve as the guardian ad litem for the child under this section if the person is qualified under this chapter to serve as guardian ad litem.

Added by Acts 1995, 74th Leg., ch. 751, § 15, eff. Sept. 1, 1995. Amended by Acts 2003, 78th Leg., ch. 262, § 1, eff. Sept. 1, 2003; Acts 2021, 87th Leg., ch. 971 (S.B. 2049), § 7, eff. Sept. 1, 2021.

## § 107.012. Mandatory Appointment of Attorney ad Litem for Child

In a suit filed by a governmental entity requesting termination of the parent-child relationship or to be named conservator of a child, the court shall appoint an attorney ad litem to represent the interests of the child immediately after the filing, but before the full adversary hearing, to ensure adequate representation of the child.

Added by Acts 1995, 74th Leg., ch. 751, § 15, eff. Sept. 1, 1995. Amended by Acts 2003, 78th Leg., ch. 262, § 1, eff. Sept. 1, 2003.

## § 107.0125. Appointment of Attorney in Dual Role

(a) In order to comply with the mandatory appointment of a guardian ad litem under Section 107.011 and the mandatory appointment of an attorney ad litem under Section 107.012, the court may appoint an attorney to serve in the dual role.

(b) If the court appoints an attorney to serve in the dual role under this section, the court may at any time during the pendency of the suit appoint another person to serve as guardian ad litem for the child and restrict the attorney to acting as an attorney ad litem for the child.

(c) An attorney appointed to serve in the dual role may request the court to appoint another person to serve as guardian ad litem for the child. If the court grants the attorney's request, the attorney shall serve only as the attorney ad litem for the child.

(d) Unless the court appoints another person as guardian ad litem in a suit filed by a governmental entity, an appointment of an attorney to serve as an attorney ad litem in a suit filed by a governmental entity is an appointment to serve in the dual role regardless of the terminology used in the appointing order.

Added by Acts 2003, 78th Leg., ch. 262, § 1, eff. Sept. 1, 2003.

## § 107.013. Mandatory Appointment of Attorney ad Litem for Parent

(a) In a suit filed by a governmental entity under Subtitle E [1] in which termination of the parent-child relationship or the appointment of a conservator for a child is requested, the court shall appoint an attorney ad litem to represent the interests of:

(1) an indigent parent of the child who responds in opposition to the termination or appointment;

(2) a parent served by citation by publication;

(3) an alleged father who failed to register with the registry under Chapter 160 and whose identity or location is unknown; and

(4) an alleged father who registered with the paternity registry under Chapter 160, but the petitioner's attempt to personally serve citation at the address provided to the registry and at any other address for the alleged father known by the petitioner has been unsuccessful.

(a–1) In a suit described by Subsection (a), if a parent is not represented by an attorney at the parent's first appearance in court, the court shall inform the parent of:

(1) the right to be represented by an attorney; and

(2) if the parent is indigent and appears in opposition to the suit, the right to an attorney ad litem appointed by the court.

(b) If both parents of the child are entitled to the appointment of an attorney ad litem under this section and the court finds that the interests of the parents are not in conflict and that there is no history or pattern of past or present family violence by one parent directed against the other parent, a spouse, or a child of the parties, the court may appoint an attorney ad litem to represent the interests of both parents.

(c) Repealed by Acts 2013, 83rd Leg., ch. 810 (S.B. 1759), § 11.

(d) The court shall require a parent who claims indigence under Subsection (a) to file an affidavit of indigence in accordance with Rule 145(b) of the Texas Rules of Civil Procedure before the court may conduct a hearing to determine the parent's indigence under this section. The court may consider additional evidence at that hearing, including evidence relating to the parent's income, source of income, assets, property ownership, benefits paid in accordance with a federal, state, or local public assistance program, outstanding obligations, and necessary expenses and the number and ages of the parent's dependents. If the court determines the parent is indigent, the court shall appoint an attorney ad litem to represent the parent.

(e) A parent who the court has determined is indigent for purposes of this section is presumed to remain indigent for the duration of the suit and any subsequent appeal unless the court, after reconsideration on the motion of the parent, the attorney ad litem for the parent, or the attorney representing the governmental entity, determines that the parent is no longer indigent due to a material and substantial change in the parent's financial circumstances.

Added by Acts 1995, 74th Leg., ch. 751, § 15, eff. Sept. 1, 1995. Amended by Acts 1997, 75th Leg., ch. 561, § 3, eff. Sept. 1, 1997; Acts 2001, 77th Leg., ch. 821, § 2.11, eff. June 14, 2001; Acts 2003, 78th Leg., ch. 262, § 1, eff. Sept. 1, 2003; Acts 2005, 79th Leg., ch. 268, § 1.06, eff. Sept. 1, 2005; Acts 2007, 80th Leg., ch. 526, § 1, eff. June 16, 2007; Acts 2011, 82nd Leg., ch. 75 (H.B. 906), § 1, eff. Sept. 1, 2011; Acts 2013, 83rd Leg., ch. 810 (S.B. 1759), §§ 2, 11, eff. Sept. 1, 2013; Acts 2015, 84th Leg., ch. 128 (S.B. 1931), § 1, eff. Sept. 1, 2015.

[1] V.T.C.A., Family Code § 261.001 et seq.

## § 107.0131. Powers and Duties of Attorney ad Litem for Parent

(a) An attorney ad litem appointed under Section 107.013 to represent the interests of a parent:

(1) shall:

(A) subject to Rules 4.02, 4.03, and 4.04, Texas Disciplinary Rules of Professional Conduct, and within a reasonable time after the appointment, interview:

(i) the parent, unless the parent's location is unknown;

(ii) each person who has significant knowledge of the case; and

(iii) the parties to the suit;

(B) investigate the facts of the case;

(C) to ensure competent representation at hearings, mediations, pretrial matters, and the trial on the merits:

(i) obtain and review copies of all court files in the suit during the attorney ad litem's course of representation; and

(ii) when necessary, conduct formal discovery under the Texas Rules of Civil Procedure or the discovery control plan;

(D) take any action consistent with the parent's interests that the attorney ad litem considers necessary to expedite the proceedings;

(E) encourage settlement and the use of alternative forms of dispute resolution;

(F) review and sign, or decline to sign, a proposed or agreed order affecting the parent;

(G) meet before each court hearing with the parent, unless the court:

(i) finds at that hearing that the attorney ad litem has shown good cause why the attorney ad litem's compliance is not feasible; or

(ii) on a showing of good cause, authorizes the attorney ad litem to comply by conferring with the parent, as appropriate, by telephone or video conference;

(H) abide by the parent's objectives for representation;

(I) become familiar with the American Bar Association's standards of practice for attorneys who represent parents in abuse and neglect cases; and

(J) complete at least three hours of continuing legal education relating to representing parents in child protection cases as described by Subsection (b) as soon as practicable after the attorney ad litem is appointed, unless the court finds that the attorney ad litem has experience equivalent to that education; and

(2) is entitled to:

(A) request clarification from the court if the role of the attorney ad litem is ambiguous;

(B) request a hearing or trial on the merits;

(C) consent or refuse to consent to an interview of the parent by another attorney;

(D) receive a copy of each pleading or other paper filed with the court;

(E) receive notice of each hearing in the suit;

(F) participate in any case staffing conducted by the Department of Family and Protective Services in which the parent is invited to participate, including, as appropriate, a case staffing to develop a family plan of service, a family group conference, a permanency conference, a mediation, a case staffing to plan for the discharge and return of the child to the parent, and any other case staffing that the department determines would be appropriate for the parent to attend, but excluding any internal department staffing or staffing between the department and the department's legal representative; and

(G) attend all legal proceedings in the suit.

(b) The continuing legal education required by Subsection (a)(1)(J) must:

(1) be low-cost and available to persons throughout this state, including on the Internet provided through the State Bar of Texas; and

(2) focus on the duties of an attorney ad litem in, and the procedures of and best practices for, representing a parent in a proceeding under Subtitle E[1].

(c) An attorney who is on the list maintained by the court as being qualified for appointment as an attorney ad litem for a parent in a child protection case must complete at least three hours of continuing legal education relating to the representation of a parent in a proceeding under Subtitle E each year before the anniversary date of the attorney's listing.

Added by Acts 2011, 82nd Leg., ch. 647 (S.B. 1026), § 1, eff. Sept. 1, 2011. Amended by Acts 2013, 83rd Leg., ch. 810 (S.B. 1759), § 3, eff. Sept. 1, 2013.

[1] V.T.C.A., Family Code § 261.001 et seq.

### § 107.0132. Powers and Duties of Attorney ad Litem for Alleged Father

(a) Except as provided by Subsections (b) and (d), an attorney ad litem appointed under Section 107.013 to represent the interests of an alleged father is only required to:

(1) conduct an investigation regarding the petitioner's due diligence in locating the alleged father, including by verifying that the petitioner has obtained a certificate of the results of a search of the paternity registry under Chapter 160;

(2) interview any party or other person who has significant knowledge of the case who may have information relating to the identity or location of the alleged father; and

(3) conduct an independent investigation to identify or locate the alleged father, as applicable.

(b) If the attorney ad litem identifies and locates the alleged father, the attorney ad litem shall:

(1) provide to each party and the court the alleged father's name and address and any other locating information; and

(2) if appropriate, request the court's approval for the attorney ad litem to assist the alleged father in establishing paternity.

(c) If the alleged father is adjudicated to be a parent of the child and is determined by the court to be indigent, the court may appoint the attorney ad litem to continue to represent the father's interests as a parent under Section 107.013(a)(1) or (c).

(d) If the attorney ad litem is unable to identify or locate the alleged father, the attorney ad litem shall submit to the court a written summary of the attorney ad litem's efforts to identify or locate the alleged father with a statement that the attorney ad litem was unable to identify or locate the alleged father. On receipt of the summary required by this subsection, the court shall discharge the attorney from the appointment.

Added by Acts 2011, 82nd Leg., ch. 647 (S.B. 1026), § 1, eff. Sept. 1, 2011. Amended by Acts 2013, 83rd Leg., ch. 810 (S.B. 1759), § 4, eff. Sept. 1, 2013.

### § 107.0133. Discipline of Attorney ad Litem for Parent or Alleged Father

An attorney ad litem appointed for a parent or an alleged father who fails to perform the duties required by Section 107.0131 or 107.0132, as applicable, is subject to disciplinary action under Subchapter E, Chapter 81, Government Code.[1]

Added by Acts 2011, 82nd Leg., ch. 647 (S.B. 1026), § 1, eff. Sept. 1, 2011.

[1] V.T.C.A., Government Code § 81.071 et seq.

### § 107.0135. Deleted by Acts 2003, 78th Leg., ch. 262, § 1, eff. Sept. 1, 2003

### § 107.014. Powers and Duties of Attorney ad Litem for Certain Parents

(a) Except as provided by Subsections (b) and (e), an attorney ad litem appointed under Section 107.013 to represent the interests of a parent whose identity or location is unknown or who has been served by citation by publication is only required to:

(1) conduct an investigation regarding the petitioner's due diligence in locating the parent;

(2) interview any party or other person who has significant knowledge of the case who may have information relating to the identity or location of the parent; and

(3) conduct an independent investigation to identify or locate the parent, as applicable.

(b) If the attorney ad litem identifies and locates the parent, the attorney ad litem shall:

(1) provide to each party and the court the parent's name and address and any other available locating information unless the court finds that:

(A) disclosure of a parent's address is likely to cause that parent harassment, serious harm, or injury; or

(B) the parent has been a victim of family violence; and

(2) if appropriate, assist the parent in making a claim of indigence for the appointment of an attorney.

(c) If the court makes a finding described by Subsection (b)(1)(A) or (B), the court may:

(1) order that the information not be disclosed; or

(2) render any other order the court considers necessary.

(d) If the court determines the parent is indigent, the court may appoint the attorney ad litem to continue to represent the parent under Section 107.013(a)(1).

(e) If the attorney ad litem is unable to identify or locate the parent, the attorney ad litem shall submit to the court a written summary of the attorney ad litem's efforts to identify or locate the parent with a statement that the attorney ad litem was unable to identify or locate the parent. On receipt of the summary required by this subsection, the court shall discharge the attorney from the appointment.

Added by Acts 2013, 83rd Leg., ch. 810 (S.B. 1759), § 5, eff. Sept. 1, 2013.

### § 107.0141. Temporary Appointment of Attorney ad Litem for Certain Parents

(a) The court may appoint an attorney ad litem to represent the interests of a parent for a limited period beginning at the time the court issues a temporary restraining order or attachment of the parent's child under Chapter 262 and ending on the court's determination of whether the parent is indigent before commencement of the full adversary hearing.

(b) An attorney ad litem appointed for a parent under this section:

(1) has the powers and duties of an attorney ad litem appointed under Section 107.0131; and

(2) if applicable, shall:

(A) conduct an investigation regarding the petitioner's due diligence in locating and serving citation on the parent; and

(B) interview any party or other person who may have information relating to the identity or location of the parent.

(c) If the attorney ad litem identifies and locates the parent, the attorney ad litem shall:

(1) inform the parent of the parent's right to be represented by an attorney and of the parent's right to an attorney ad litem appointed by the court, if the parent is indigent and appears in opposition to the suit;

(2) if the parent claims indigence and requests an attorney ad litem beyond the period of the temporary appointment under this section, assist the parent in making a claim of indigence for the appointment of an attorney ad litem; and

(3) assist the parent in preparing for the full adversary hearing under Subchapter C, Chapter 262.[1]

(d) If the court determines the parent is indigent, the court may appoint the attorney ad litem to continue to represent the parent under Section 107.013(a)(1).

(e) If the attorney ad litem is unable to identify or locate the parent, the attorney ad litem shall submit to the court a written summary of the attorney ad litem's efforts to identify or locate the parent with a statement that the attorney ad litem was unable to identify or locate the parent. On receipt of the summary required by this subsection, the court shall discharge the attorney ad litem from the appointment.

(f) If the attorney ad litem identifies or locates the parent, and the court determines that the parent is not indigent, the court shall discharge the attorney ad litem from the appointment.

Added by Acts 2015, 84th Leg., ch. 128 (S.B. 1931), § 2, eff. Sept. 1, 2015.

[1] V.T.C.A., Family Code § 262.201 et seq.

### § 107.015. Attorney Fees

(a) An attorney appointed under this chapter to serve as an attorney ad litem for a child, an attorney in the dual role, or an attorney ad litem for a parent is entitled to reasonable fees and expenses in the amount set by the court to be paid by the parents of the child unless the parents are indigent.

(b) If the court determines that one or more of the parties are able to defray the fees and expenses of an attorney ad litem or guardian ad litem for the child as determined by the reasonable and customary fees for similar services in the county of jurisdiction, the fees and expenses may be ordered paid by one or more of those parties, or the court may order one or more of those parties, prior to final hearing, to pay the sums into the registry of the court or into an account authorized by the court for the use and benefit of the payee on order of the court. The sums may be taxed as costs to be assessed against one or more of the parties.

(c) If indigency of the parents is shown, an attorney ad litem appointed to represent a child or parent in a suit filed by a governmental entity shall be paid from the general funds of the county according to the fee schedule that applies to an attorney appointed to represent a child in a suit under Title 3 as provided by Chapter 51. The court may not award attorney ad litem fees under this chapter against the state, a state agency, or a political subdivision of the state except as provided by this subsection.

(d) A person appointed as a guardian ad litem or attorney ad litem shall complete and submit to the court a voucher or claim for payment that lists the fees charged and hours worked by the guardian ad litem or attorney ad litem. Information submitted under this section is subject to disclosure under Chapter 552, Government Code.

Added by Acts 1995, 74th Leg., ch. 20, § 1, eff. April 20, 1995. Redesignated from V.T.C.A., Family Code § 107.003 by Acts 1995, 74th Leg., ch. 751, § 15, eff. Sept. 1, 1995. Amended by Acts 1999, 76th Leg., ch. 1390, § 6, eff. Sept. 1, 1999; Acts 2003, 78th Leg., ch. 262, § 1, eff. Sept. 1, 2003; Acts 2005, 79th Leg., ch. 268, § 1.07, eff. Sept. 1, 2005.

### § 107.016. Continued Representation; Duration of Appointment

In a suit filed by a governmental entity in which termination of the parent-child relationship or appointment of the entity as conservator of the child is requested:

(1) an order appointing the Department of Family and Protective Services as the child's managing conservator:

(A) shall provide for the continuation of the appointment of the guardian ad litem or the attorney ad litem for the child, or an attorney appointed to serve in the dual role, as long as the child remains in the conservatorship of the department; and

(B) may provide for the continuation of the appointment of both the attorney ad litem and the guardian ad litem for the child if both have been appointed, as long as the child remains in the conservatorship of the department; and

(2) an attorney appointed under this subchapter to serve as an attorney ad litem for a parent or an alleged father continues to serve in that capacity until the earliest of:

(A) the date the suit affecting the parent-child relationship is dismissed;

(B) the date all appeals in relation to any final order terminating parental rights are exhausted or waived; or

(C) the date the attorney is relieved of the attorney's duties or replaced by another attorney after a finding of good cause is rendered by the court on the record.

Added by Acts 1995, 74th Leg., ch. 751, § 15, eff. Sept. 1, 1995. Amended by Acts 1997, 75th Leg., ch. 575, § 6, eff. Sept. 1, 1997; Acts 2003, 78th Leg., ch. 262, § 1, eff. Sept. 1, 2003; Acts 2011, 82nd Leg., ch. 75 (H.B. 906), § 2, eff. Sept. 1, 2011; Acts 2017, 85th Leg., ch. 317 (H.B. 7), § 9, eff. Sept. 1, 2017; Acts 2021, 87th Leg., ch. 801 (H.B. 1315), § 1, eff. Sept. 1, 2021.

Section 2 of Acts 2021, 87th Leg., ch. 878 (H.B. 1315) provides:

"The changes in law made by this Act apply to a suit affecting the parent-child relationship filed before, on, or after the effective date [Sept. 1, 2021] of this Act."

### § 107.0161. Ad Litem Appointments for Child Committed to Texas Juvenile Justice Department

If an order appointing the Department of Family and Protective Services as managing conservator of a child does not continue the appointment of the child's guardian ad litem or attorney ad litem and the child is committed to the Texas Juvenile Justice Department or released under supervision by the Texas Juvenile Justice Department, the court may appoint a guardian ad litem or attorney ad litem for the child.

Added by Acts 2009, 81st Leg., ch. 108, § 3, eff. May 23, 2009. Amended by Acts 2015, 84th Leg., ch. 734 (H.B. 1549), § 79, eff. Sept. 1, 2015.

### § 107.017. Appointment of Amicus Attorney Prohibited

The court may not appoint a person to serve as an amicus attorney in a suit filed by a governmental entity under this chapter.

Added by Acts 2003, 78th Leg., ch. 262, § 1, eff. Sept. 1, 2003.

## PART 2. APPOINTMENTS IN SUITS OTHER THAN SUITS BY GOVERNMENTAL ENTITY

### § 107.021. Discretionary Appointments

(a) In a suit in which the best interests of a child are at issue, other than a suit filed by a governmental entity requesting termination of the parent-child relationship or appointment of the entity as conservator of the child, the court may appoint one of the following:

(1) an amicus attorney;

(2) an attorney ad litem; or

(3) a guardian ad litem.

(a–1) In a suit requesting termination of the parent-child relationship that is not filed by a governmental entity, the court shall, unless the court finds that the interests of the child will be represented adequately by a party to the suit whose interests are not in conflict with the child's interests, appoint one of the following:

(1) an amicus attorney; or

(2) an attorney ad litem.

(b) In determining whether to make an appointment under this section, the court:

(1) shall:

(A) give due consideration to the ability of the parties to pay reasonable fees to the appointee; and

(B) balance the child's interests against the cost to the parties that would result from an appointment by taking into consideration the cost of available alternatives for resolving issues without making an appointment;

(2) may make an appointment only if the court finds that the appointment is necessary to ensure the determination of the best interests of the child, unless the appointment is otherwise required by this code; and

(3) may not require a person appointed under this section to serve without reasonable compensation for the services rendered by the person.

Added by Acts 2003, 78th Leg., ch. 262, § 1, eff. Sept. 1, 2003. Amended by Acts 2005, 79th Leg., ch. 172, § 8, eff. Sept. 1, 2005.

### § 107.022. Certain Prohibited Appointments

In a suit other than a suit filed by a governmental entity requesting termination of the parent-child relationship or appointment of the entity as conservator of the child, the court may not appoint:

(1) an attorney to serve in the dual role; or

(2) a volunteer advocate to serve as guardian ad litem for a child unless the training of the volunteer advocate is designed for participation in suits other than suits filed by a governmental entity requesting termination of the parent-child relationship or appointment of the entity as conservator of the child.

Added by Acts 2003, 78th Leg., ch. 262, § 1, eff. Sept. 1, 2003. Amended by Acts 2005, 79th Leg., ch. 172, § 9, eff. Sept. 1, 2005.

### § 107.023. Fees in Suits Other Than Suits by Governmental Entity

(a) In a suit other than a suit filed by a governmental entity requesting termination of the parent-child relationship or appointment of the entity as conservator of the child, in addition to the attorney's fees that may be awarded under Chapter 106, the following persons are entitled to reasonable fees and expenses in an amount set by the court and ordered to be paid by one or more parties to the suit:

(1) an attorney appointed as an amicus attorney or as an attorney ad litem for the child; and

(2) a professional who holds a relevant professional license and who is appointed as guardian ad litem for the child, other than a volunteer advocate.

(b) The court shall:

(1) determine the fees and expenses of an amicus attorney, an attorney ad litem, or a guardian ad litem by reference to the reasonable and customary fees for similar services in the county of jurisdiction;

(2) order a reasonable cost deposit to be made at the time the court makes the appointment; and

(3) before the final hearing, order an additional amount to be paid to the credit of a trust account for the use and benefit of the amicus attorney, attorney ad litem, or guardian ad litem.

(c) A court may not award costs, fees, or expenses to an amicus attorney, attorney ad litem, or guardian ad litem against the state, a state agency, or a political subdivision of the state under this part.

(d) The court may determine that fees awarded under this subchapter to an amicus attorney, an attorney ad litem for the child, or a guardian ad litem for the child are necessaries for the benefit of the child.

Added by Acts 2003, 78th Leg., ch. 262, § 1, eff. Sept. 1, 2003. Amended by Acts 2005, 79th Leg., ch. 172, § 10, eff. Sept. 1, 2005.

## SUBCHAPTER C. APPOINTMENT OF VOLUNTEER ADVOCATES

### § 107.031. Volunteer Advocates

(a) In a suit filed by a governmental entity requesting termination of the parent-child relationship or appointment of the entity as conservator of the child, the court may appoint a charitable organization composed of volunteer advocates whose charter mandates the provision of services to allegedly abused and neglected children or an individual who has received the court's approved training regarding abused and neglected children and who has been certified by the court to appear at court hearings as a guardian ad litem for the child or as a volunteer advocate for the child.

(b) In a suit other than a suit filed by a governmental entity requesting termination of the parent-child relationship or appointment of the entity as conservator of the child, the court may appoint a charitable organization composed of volunteer advocates whose training provides for the provision of services in private custody disputes or a person who has received the court's approved training regarding the subject matter of the suit and who has been certified by the court to appear at court hearings as a guardian ad litem for the child or as a volunteer advocate for the child. A person appointed under this subsection is not entitled to fees under Section 107.023.

(c) A court-certified volunteer advocate appointed under this section may be assigned to act as a surrogate parent for the child, as provided by 20 U.S.C. Section 1415(b), if:

(1) the child is in the conservatorship of the Department of Family and Protective Services;

(2) the volunteer advocate is serving as guardian ad litem for the child;

(3) a foster parent of the child is not acting as the child's parent under Section 29.015, Education Code; and

(4) the volunteer advocate completes a training program for surrogate parents that complies with minimum standards established by rule by the Texas Education Agency within the time specified by Section 29.015(b), Education Code.

Added by Acts 1995, 74th Leg., ch. 751, § 15, eff. Sept. 1, 1995. Amended by Acts 1997, 75th Leg., ch. 1294, § 6, eff. Sept. 1, 1997; Acts 1999, 76th Leg., ch. 430, § 3, eff. Sept. 1, 1999; Acts 2003, 78th Leg., ch. 262, § 1, eff. Sept. 1, 2003; Acts 2005, 79th Leg., ch. 172, § 11, eff. Sept. 1, 2005; Acts 2017, 85th Leg., ch. 1025 (H.B. 1556), § 3, eff. Sept. 1, 2017.

## SUBCHAPTER D. CHILD CUSTODY EVALUATION

*Acts 2015, 84th Leg., ch. 1252 (H.B. 1449), §§ 1.01 to 1.17 revised Subchapter D, Child Custody Evaluation, to consist of §§ 107.101 to 107.115.*

*Acts 2015, 84th Leg., ch. 571 (H.B. 3003), § 1, added a Subchapter F, Managed Assigned Counsel Program for the Representation of Certain Children and Parents, consisting of §§ 107.101 to 107.108. Acts 2017, 85th Leg., ch. 324 (S.B. 1488), § 24.001(7) redesignated this Subchapter as Subchapter H, consisting of §§ 107.301 to 107.308.*

**§ 107.0501. Redesignated as V.T.C.A., Family Code § 107.101 and amended by Acts 2015, 84th Leg., ch. 1252 (H.B. 1449), § 1.03, eff. Sept. 1, 2015**

**§ 107.051. Redesignated as V.T.C.A., Family Code § 107.103 and amended by Acts 2015, 84th Leg., ch. 1252 (H.B. 1449), § 1.05, eff. Sept. 1, 2015**

**§ 107.0511. Redesignated as V.T.C.A., Family Code § 107.104 and amended by Acts 2015, 84th Leg., ch. 1252 (H.B. 1449), § 1.06, eff. Sept. 1, 2015**

**§ 107.0512. Redesignated as V.T.C.A., Family Code § 107.107 and amended by Acts 2015, 84th Leg., ch. 1252 (H.B. 1449), § 1.08, eff. Sept. 1, 2015**

**§ 107.0513. Redesignated as V.T.C.A., Family Code § 107.108 and amended by Acts 2015, 84th Leg., ch. 1252 (H.B. 1449), § 1.09, eff. Sept. 1, 2015**

**§ 107.0514. Redesignated as V.T.C.A., Family Code § 107.109 and amended by Acts 2015, 84th Leg., ch. 1252 (H.B. 1449), § 1.10, eff. Sept. 1, 2015**

**§ 107.05145. Redesignated as V.T.C.A., Family Code § 107.111 and amended by Acts 2015, 84th Leg., ch. 1252 (H.B. 1449), § 1.13, eff. Sept. 1, 2015**

**§ 107.0515. Repealed by Acts 2015, 84th Leg., ch. 1252 (H.B. 1449), § 4.01, eff. Sept. 1, 2015**

**§ 107.0519. Repealed by Acts 2015, 84th Leg., ch. 1252 (H.B. 1449), § 4.01, eff. Sept. 1, 2015**

**§ 107.052. Repealed by Acts 2015, 84th Leg., ch. 1252 (H.B. 1449) § 4.01, eff. Sept. 1, 2015**

**§ 107.053. Repealed by Acts 2015, 84th Leg., ch. 1252 (H.B. 1449), § 4.01, eff. Sept. 1, 2015**

**§ 107.054. Redesignated as V.T.C.A., Family Code § 107.113 and amended by Acts 2015, 84th Leg., ch. 1252 (H.B. 1449), § 1.15, eff. Sept. 1, 2015**

**§ 107.055. Redesignated as V.T.C.A., Family Code § 107.114 and amended by Acts 2015, 84th Leg., ch. 1252 (H.B. 1449), § 1.16, eff. Sept. 1, 2015**

**§ 107.056. Redesignated as V.T.C.A., Family Code § 107.115 and amended by Acts 2015, 84th Leg., ch. 1252 (H.B. 1449), § 1.17, eff. Sept. 1, 2015**

**§§ 107.061 to 107.072. Redesignated as V.T.C.A., Family Code §§ 107.251 to 107.262 by Acts 2017, 85th Leg., ch. 324 (S.B. 1488), § 24.001(6), eff. Sept. 1, 2017**

**§ 107.101. Definitions**

In this subchapter:

(1) "Child custody evaluation" means an evaluative process ordered by a court in a contested case through which information, opinions, recommendations, and answers to specific questions asked by the court may be:

(A) made regarding:

(i) conservatorship of a child, including the terms and conditions of conservatorship;

(ii) possession of or access to a child, including the terms and conditions of possession or access; or

(iii) any other issue affecting the best interest of a child; and

(B) made to the court, the parties to the suit, the parties' attorneys, and any other person appointed under this chapter by the court in the suit.

(2) "Child custody evaluator" means an individual who conducts a child custody evaluation under this subchapter. The term includes a private child custody evaluator.

(3) "Department" means the Department of Family and Protective Services.

(4) "Person" includes an agency or a domestic relations office.

(5) "Private child custody evaluator" means a person conducting a child custody evaluation who is not conducting the evaluation as an employee of or contractor with a domestic relations office.

(6) "Supervision" means directing, regularly reviewing, and meeting with a person with respect to the completion of work for which the supervisor is responsible for the outcome. The term does not require the constant physical presence of the person providing supervision and may include telephonic or other electronic communication.

Added by Acts 2007, 80th Leg., ch. 832, § 1, eff. Sept. 1, 2007. Redesignated from V.T.C.A., Family Code § 107.0501 and amended by Acts 2015, 84th Leg., ch. 1252 (H.B. 1449), § 1.03, eff. Sept. 1, 2015.

**§ 107.102. Applicability**

(a) For purposes of this subchapter, a child custody evaluation does not include services provided in accordance with the Interstate Compact on the Placement of Children adopted under Subchapter B, Chapter 162, or an evaluation conducted in accordance with Section 262.114 by an employee of or contractor with the department.

(b) The department may not conduct a child custody evaluation.

(c) Except as provided by Subsections (a) and (b), this subchapter does not apply to the department or to a suit to which the department is a party.

Added by Acts 2015, 84th Leg., ch. 1252 (H.B. 1449), § 1.04, eff. Sept. 1, 2015.

**§ 107.1025. Effect of Mental Examination**

A mental examination described by Rule 204.4, Texas Rules of Civil Procedure, does not by itself satisfy the requirements for a child custody evaluation under this subchapter. A mental examination may be included in the report required under this subchapter and relied on by the child custody evaluator to the extent the evaluator considers appropriate under the circumstances.

Added by Acts 2015, 84th Leg., ch. 1252 (H.B. 1449), § 1.04, eff. Sept. 1, 2015.

**§ 107.103. Order for Child Custody Evaluation**

(a) The court, after notice and hearing or on agreement of the parties, may order the preparation of a child custody evaluation regarding:

(1) the circumstances and condition of:

(A) a child who is the subject of a suit;

(B) a party to a suit; and

(C) if appropriate, the residence of any person requesting conservatorship of, possession of, or access to a child who is the subject of the suit; and

(2) any issue or question relating to the suit at the request of the court before or during the evaluation process.

(b) The court may not appoint a child custody evaluator in a suit involving a nonparent seeking conservatorship of a child unless, after notice and hearing or on agreement of the parties, the court makes a specific finding that good cause has been shown for the appointment of a child custody evaluator.

(c) Except for an order appointing a child custody evaluator who is qualified under Section 107.104(b)(3), an order for a child custody evaluation must include:

(1) the name of each person who will conduct the evaluation;

(2) the purpose of the evaluation;

(3) a list of the basic elements of an evaluation required by Section 107.109(c);

(4) a list of any additional elements of an evaluation required by the court to be completed, including any additional elements specified in Section 107.109(d); and

(5) the specific issues or questions to be addressed in the evaluation.

(d) Except as provided by Section 107.106, each individual who conducts a child custody evaluation must be qualified under Section 107.104.

(e) In appointing a child custody evaluator in a suit in which a party subject to the child custody evaluation does not speak English as a primary language, the court shall ensure that the child custody evaluator:

(1) is able to effectively communicate in the primary language of the party; or

(2) will be assisted by a licensed or certified interpreter.

(f) A licensed or certified interpreter assisting a child custody evaluator under Subsection (e)(2) may accompany the evaluator in person or assist through use of audio or video conferencing technology.

(g) The court may require the parties to pay any costs associated with obtaining assistance for a child custody evaluator from a licensed or certified interpreter.

Added by Acts 1995, 74th Leg., ch. 751, § 15, eff. Sept. 1, 1995. Amended by Acts 1999, 76th Leg., ch. 1390, § 7, eff. Sept. 1, 1999; Acts 2001, 77th Leg., ch. 133, § 2, eff. Sept. 1, 2001; Acts 2001, 77th Leg., ch. 488, § 1, eff. June 11, 2001; Acts 2007, 80th Leg., ch. 832, § 2, eff. Sept. 1, 2007. Redesignated from V.T.C.A., Family Code § 107.051 and amended by Acts 2015, 84th Leg., ch. 1252 (H.B. 1449), § 1.05, eff. Sept. 1, 2015. Amended by Acts 2017, 85th Leg., ch. 257 (H.B. 1501), § 2, eff. Sept. 1, 2017; Acts 2021, 87th Leg., ch. 1002 (H.B. 3009), § 1, eff. Sept. 1, 2021.

Section 2 of Acts 2021, 87th Leg., ch. 1002 (H.B. 3009) provides:

"The change in law made by this Act applies only to a child custody evaluation conducted on or after the effective date [Sept. 1, 2021] of this Act, regardless of whether the suit affecting the parent-child relationship was filed before, on, or after that date."

### § 107.104. Child Custody Evaluator: Minimum Qualifications

(a) In this section:

(1) "Full-time experience" means a period during which an individual works at least 30 hours per week.

(2) "Human services field of study" means a field of study designed to prepare an individual in the disciplined application of counseling, family therapy, psychology, or social work values, principles, and methods.

(b) To be qualified to conduct a child custody evaluation, an individual must:

(1) have at least a master's degree from an accredited college or university in a human services field of study and a license to practice in this state as a social worker, professional counselor, marriage and family therapist, or psychologist, or have a license to practice medicine in this state and a board certification in psychiatry and:

(A) after completing any degree required by this subdivision, have two years of full-time experience or equivalent part-time experience under professional supervision during which the individual performed functions involving the evaluation of physical, intellectual, social, and psychological functioning and needs and developed an understanding of the social and physical environment, both present and prospective, to meet those needs; and

(B) after obtaining a license required by this subdivision, have performed at least 10 court-ordered child custody evaluations under the supervision of an individual qualified under this section;

(2) meet the requirements of Subdivision (1)(A) and be practicing under the direct supervision of an

individual qualified under this section in order to complete at least 10 court-ordered child custody evaluations under supervision; or

(3) be employed by or under contract with a domestic relations office, provided that the individual conducts child custody evaluations relating only to families ordered by a court to participate in child custody evaluations conducted by the domestic relations office.

(c) Notwithstanding Subsections (b)(1) and (2), an individual with a doctoral degree and who holds a license in a human services field of study is qualified to conduct a child custody evaluation if the individual has completed a number of hours of professional development coursework and practice experience directly related to the performance of child custody evaluations as described by this chapter, satisfactory to the licensing agency that issues the individual's license.

(d) The licensing agency that issues a license to an individual described by Subsection (c) may determine by rule that internships, practicums, and other professional preparatory activities completed by the individual during the course of achieving the person's doctoral degree satisfy the requirements of Subsection (c) in whole or in part.

(e) In addition to the qualifications prescribed by this section, an individual must complete at least eight hours of family violence dynamics training provided by a family violence service provider to be qualified to conduct a child custody evaluation under this subchapter.

Added by Acts 2001, 77th Leg., ch. 133, § 3, eff. Sept. 1, 2001. Amended by Acts 2007, 80th Leg., ch. 832, § 3, eff. Sept. 1, 2007; Acts 2009, 81st Leg., ch. 1113, § 2, eff. Sept. 1, 2009. Redesignated from V.T.C.A., Family Code § 107.0511 and amended by Acts 2015, 84th Leg., ch. 1252 (H.B. 1449), § 1.06, eff. Sept. 1, 2015.

### § 107.105. Child Custody Evaluation: Specialized Training Required

(a) The court shall determine whether the qualifications of a child custody evaluator satisfy the requirements of this subchapter.

(b) A child custody evaluator must demonstrate, if requested, appropriate knowledge and competence in child custody evaluation services consistent with professional models, standards, and guidelines.

Added by Acts 2015, 84th Leg., ch. 1252 (H.B. 1449), § 1.07, eff. Sept. 1, 2015.

### § 107.106. Exception to Qualifications Required to Conduct Child Custody Evaluation

(a) This section applies only to a county:

(1) with a population of less than 500,000;

(2) that is contiguous to the Gulf of Mexico or a bay or inlet opening into the gulf and that borders the United Mexican States; or

(3) that borders a county described by Subdivision (2).

(a–1) In a county to which this section applies, if a court finds that an individual who meets the requirements of Section 107.104 is not available in the county to conduct a child custody evaluation in a timely manner, the court, after notice and hearing or on agreement of the parties, may appoint an individual the court determines to be otherwise qualified to conduct the evaluation.

(b) An individual appointed under this section shall comply with all provisions of this subchapter, other than Section 107.104.

Added by Acts 2015, 84th Leg., ch. 1252 (H.B. 1449), § 1.07, eff. Sept. 1, 2015. Amended by Acts 2019, 86th Leg., ch. 1236 (H.B. 2514), § 1, eff. Sept. 1, 2019.

### § 107.107. Child Custody Evaluator: Conflicts of Interest and Bias

(a) Before accepting appointment as a child custody evaluator in a suit, a person must disclose to the court, each attorney for a party to the suit, any attorney for a child who is the subject of the suit, and any party to the suit who does not have an attorney:

(1) any conflict of interest that the person believes the person has with any party to the suit or a child who is the subject of the suit;

(2) any previous knowledge that the person has of a party to the suit or a child who is the subject of the suit, other than knowledge obtained in a court-ordered evaluation;

(3) any pecuniary relationship that the person believes the person has with an attorney in the suit;

(4) any relationship of confidence or trust that the person believes the person has with an attorney in the suit; and

(5) any other information relating to the person's relationship with an attorney in the suit that a reasonable, prudent person would believe would affect the ability of the person to act impartially in conducting a child custody evaluation.

(b) The court may not appoint a person as a child custody evaluator in a suit if the person makes any of the disclosures in Subsection (a) unless:

(1) the court finds that:

(A) the person has no conflict of interest with a party to the suit or a child who is the subject of the suit;

(B) the person's previous knowledge of a party to the suit or a child who is the subject of the suit is not relevant;

(C) the person does not have a pecuniary relationship with an attorney in the suit; and

(D) the person does not have a relationship of trust or confidence with an attorney in the suit; or

(2) the parties and any attorney for a child who is the subject of the suit agree in writing to the person's appointment as the child custody evaluator.

(c) After being appointed as a child custody evaluator in a suit, a person shall immediately disclose to the court, each attorney for a party to the suit, any attorney for a child who is the subject of the suit, and any party to the suit who does not have an attorney any discovery of:

(1) a conflict of interest that the person believes the person has with a party to the suit or a child who is the subject of the suit; and

(2) previous knowledge that the person has of a party to the suit or a child who is the subject of the suit, other than knowledge obtained in a court-ordered evaluation.

(d) A person shall resign from the person's appointment as a child custody evaluator in a suit if the person makes any of the disclosures in Subsection (c) unless:

(1) the court finds that:

(A) the person has no conflict of interest with a party to the suit or a child who is the subject of the suit; and

(B) the person's previous knowledge of a party to the suit or a child who is the subject of the suit is not relevant; or

(2) the parties and any attorney for a child who is the subject of the suit agree in writing to the person's continued appointment as the child custody evaluator.

(e) A child custody evaluator who has previously conducted a child custody evaluation for a suit may conduct all subsequent evaluations in the suit unless the court finds that the evaluator is biased.

(f) An individual may not be appointed as a child custody evaluator in a suit if the individual has worked in a professional capacity with a party to the suit, a child who is the subject of the suit, or a member of the party's or child's family who is involved in the suit. This subsection does not apply to an individual who has worked in a professional capacity with a party, a child, or a member of the party's or child's family only as a teacher of parenting skills in a group setting, with no individualized interaction with any party, the child, any party's family, or the child's family, or as a child custody evaluator who performed a previous evaluation. A child custody evaluator who has worked as a teacher of parenting skills in a group setting that included a party, a child, or another person who will be the subject of an evaluation or has worked as a child custody evaluator for a previous evaluation must notify the court and the attorney of each represented party or, if a party is not represented, the evaluator must notify the party. For purposes of this subsection, "family" has the meaning assigned by Section 71.003.

Added by Acts 2007, 80th Leg., ch. 832, § 3, eff. Sept. 1, 2007. Redesignated from V.T.C.A., Family Code § 107.0512 and amended by Acts 2015, 84th Leg., ch. 1252 (H.B. 1449), § 1.08, eff. Sept. 1, 2015.

### § 107.108. General Provisions Applicable to Conduct of Child Custody Evaluation and Preparation of Report

(a) Unless otherwise directed by a court or prescribed by a provision of this title, a child custody evaluator's actions in conducting a child custody evaluation must be in conformance with the professional standard of care applicable to the evaluator's licensure and any administrative rules, ethical standards, or guidelines adopted by the licensing authority that licenses the evaluator.

(b) A court may impose requirements or adopt local rules applicable to a child custody evaluation or a child custody evaluator that do not conflict with this subchapter.

(c) A child custody evaluator shall follow evidence-based practice methods and make use of current best evidence in making assessments and recommendations.

(d) A child custody evaluator shall disclose to each attorney of record any communication regarding a substantive issue between the evaluator and an attorney of record representing a party in a contested suit. This subsection does not apply to a communication between a child custody evaluator and an attorney ad litem or amicus attorney.

(e) To the extent possible, a child custody evaluator shall verify each statement of fact pertinent to a child custody evaluation and shall note the sources of verification and information in the child custody evaluation report prepared under Section 107.113.

(f) A child custody evaluator shall state the basis for the evaluator's conclusions or recommendations, and the extent to which information obtained limits the reliability and validity of the opinion and the conclusions and recommendations of the evaluator, in the child custody evaluation report prepared under Section 107.113. A child custody evaluator who has evaluated only one side of a contested suit shall refrain from making a recommendation regarding conservatorship of a child or possession of or access to a child, but may state whether any information obtained regarding a child's placement with a party indicates concerns for:

(1) the safety of the child;

(2) the party's parenting skills or capability;

(3) the party's relationship with the child; or

(4) the mental health of the party.

(g) A child custody evaluation must be conducted in compliance with this subchapter, regardless of whether the child custody evaluation is conducted:

(1) by a single child custody evaluator or multiple evaluators working separately or together; or

(2) within a county served by the court with continuing jurisdiction or at a geographically distant location.

(h) A child custody evaluation report must include for each child custody evaluator who conducted any portion of the child custody evaluation:

(1) the name and license number of the child custody evaluator; and

(2) a statement that the child custody evaluator:

(A) has read and meets the requirements of Section 107.104; or

(B) was appointed under Section 107.106.

Added by Acts 2007, 80th Leg., ch. 832, § 3, eff. Sept. 1, 2007. Redesignated from V.T.C.A., Family Code § 107.0513 and amended by Acts 2015, 84th Leg., ch. 1252 (H.B. 1449), § 1.09, eff. Sept. 1, 2015.

### § 107.109. Elements of Child Custody Evaluation

(a) A child custody evaluator may not offer an opinion regarding conservatorship of a child who is the subject of a suit or possession of or access to the child unless each basic element of a child custody evaluation as specified in this section and each additional element ordered by the court, if any, has been completed, unless the failure to complete an element is satisfactorily explained as provided by Subsection (b).

(b) A child custody evaluator shall:

(1) identify in the report required by Section 107.113 any basic element or any additional element of a child custody evaluation described by this section that was not completed;

(2) explain the reasons the element was not completed; and

(3) include an explanation of the likely effect of the missing element on the confidence the child custody evaluator has in the evaluator's expert opinion.

(c) The basic elements of a child custody evaluation under this subchapter consist of:

(1) a personal interview of each party to the suit seeking conservatorship of, possession of, or access to the child;

(2) interviews, conducted in a developmentally appropriate manner, of each child who is the subject of the suit who is at least four years of age during a period of possession of each party to the suit but outside the presence of the party;

(3) observation of each child who is the subject of the suit, regardless of the age of the child, in the presence of each party to the suit, including, as appropriate, during supervised visitation, unless contact between a party and a child is prohibited by court order or the person conducting the evaluation has good cause for not conducting the observation and states the good cause in writing provided to the parties to the suit before the completion of the evaluation;

(4) an observation and, if the child is at least four years of age, an interview of any child who is not a subject of the suit who lives on a full-time basis in a residence that is the subject of the evaluation, including with other children or parties who are subjects of the evaluation, where appropriate;

(5) the obtaining of information from relevant collateral sources, including the review of:

(A) relevant school records;

(B) relevant physical and mental health records of each party to the suit and each child who is the subject of the suit;

(C) relevant records of the department obtained under Section 107.111;

(D) criminal history information relating to each child who is the subject of the suit, each party to the suit, and each person who lives with a party to the suit; and

(E) notwithstanding other law, records or information from any other collateral source that may have relevant information;

(6) for each individual residing in a residence subject to the child custody evaluation, consideration of any criminal history information and any contact with the department or a law enforcement agency regarding abuse or neglect; and

(7) assessment of the relationship between each child who is the subject of the suit and each party seeking possession of or access to the child.

(d) The court may order additional elements of a child custody evaluation under this subchapter, including the following:

(1) balanced interviews and observations of each child who is the subject of the suit so that a child who is interviewed or observed while in the care of one party to the suit is also interviewed or observed while in the care of each other party to the suit;

(2) an interview of each individual, including a child who is at least four years of age, residing on a full-time or part-time basis in a residence subject to the child custody evaluation;

(3) evaluation of the residence of each party seeking conservatorship of a child who is the subject of the suit or possession of or access to the child;

(4) observation of a child who is the subject of the suit with each adult who lives in a residence that is the subject of the evaluation;

(5) an interview, if the child is at least four years of age, and observation of a child who is not the subject of the suit but who lives on a full-time or part-time basis in a residence that is the subject of the evaluation;

(6) psychometric testing, if necessary, consistent with Section 107.110; and

(7) the performance of other tasks requested of the evaluator by the court, including:

(A) a joint interview of the parties to the suit; or

(B) the review of any other information that the court determines is relevant.

Added by Acts 2007, 80th Leg., ch. 832, § 3, eff. Sept. 1, 2007. Redesignated from V.T.C.A., Family Code § 107.0514 and amended by Acts 2015, 84th Leg., ch. 1252 (H.B. 1449), § 1.10, eff. Sept. 1, 2015. Amended by Acts 2017, 85th Leg., ch. 257 (H.B. 1501), § 3, eff. Sept. 1, 2017.

### § 107.110. Psychometric Testing

(a) A child custody evaluator may conduct psychometric testing as part of a child custody evaluation if:

(1) ordered by the court or determined necessary by the child custody evaluator; and

(2) the child custody evaluator is:

(A) appropriately licensed and trained to administer and interpret the specific psychometric tests selected; and

(B) trained in the specialized forensic application of psychometric testing.

(b) Selection of a specific psychometric test is at the professional discretion of the child custody evaluator based on the specific issues raised in the suit.

(c) A child custody evaluator may only use psychometric tests if the evaluator is familiar with the reliability, validation, and related standardization or outcome studies of, and proper applications and use of, the tests within a forensic setting.

(d) If a child custody evaluator considers psychometric testing necessary but lacks specialized training or expertise to use the specific tests under this section, the evaluator may designate a licensed psychologist to conduct the testing and may request additional orders from the court.

Added by Acts 2015, 84th Leg., ch. 1252 (H.B. 1449), § 1.11, eff. Sept. 1, 2015. Amended by Acts 2017, 85th Leg., ch. 257 (H.B. 1501), § 4, eff. Sept. 1, 2017.

### § 107.1101. Effect of Potentially Undiagnosed Serious Mental Illness

(a) In this section, "serious mental illness" has the meaning assigned by Section 1355.001, Insurance Code.

(b) If a child custody evaluator identifies the presence of a potentially undiagnosed serious mental illness experienced by an individual who is a subject of the child custody evaluation and the evaluator is not qualified by the evaluator's licensure, experience, and training to assess a serious mental illness, the evaluator shall make one or more appropriate referrals for a mental examination of the individual and may request additional orders from the court.

(c) The child custody evaluation report must include any information that the evaluator considers appropriate under the circumstances regarding the possible effects of an individual's potentially undiagnosed serious mental illness on the evaluation and the evaluator's recommendations.

Added by Acts 2015, 84th Leg., ch. 1252 (H.B. 1449), § 1.12, eff. Sept. 1, 2015. Amended by Acts 2017, 85th Leg., ch. 257 (H.B. 1501), § 5, eff. Sept. 1, 2017.

### § 107.111. Child Custody Evaluator Access to Investigative Records of Department; Offense

(a) A child custody evaluator appointed by a court is entitled to obtain from the department a complete, unredacted copy of any investigative record regarding abuse or neglect that relates to any person residing in the residence subject to the child custody evaluation.

(b) Except as provided by this section, records obtained by a child custody evaluator from the department under this section are confidential and not subject to disclosure under Chapter 552, Government Code, or to disclosure in response to a subpoena or a discovery request.

(c) A child custody evaluator may disclose information obtained under Subsection (a) in the child custody evaluation report prepared under Section 107.113 only to the extent the evaluator determines that the information is relevant to the child custody evaluation or a recommendation made under this subchapter.

(d) A person commits an offense if the person recklessly discloses confidential information obtained from the department in violation of this section. An offense under this subsection is a Class A misdemeanor.

Added by Acts 2013, 83rd Leg., ch. 74 (S.B. 330), § 1, eff. Sept. 1, 2013. Redesignated from V.T.C.A., Family Code § 107.05145 and amended by Acts 2015, 84th Leg., ch. 1252 (H.B. 1449), § 1.13, eff. Sept. 1, 2015.

### § 107.1111. Child Custody Evaluator Access to Other Records

(a) Notwithstanding any other state law regarding confidentiality, a child custody evaluator appointed by a court is entitled to obtain records that relate to any person residing in a residence subject to a child custody evaluation from:

(1) a local law enforcement authority;

(2) a criminal justice agency;

(3) a juvenile justice agency;

(4) a community supervision and corrections department created under Chapter 76, Government Code; or

(5) any other governmental entity.

(b) Except as provided by this section, records obtained by a child custody evaluator under this section are confidential and not subject to disclosure under Chapter 552, Government Code, or to disclosure in response to a subpoena or a discovery request.

(c) A child custody evaluator may disclose information obtained under Subsection (a) in the child custody evaluation report prepared under Section 107.113 only to the extent the evaluator determines that the information is relevant to the child custody evaluation or a recommendation made under this subchapter.

(d) A person commits an offense if the person recklessly discloses confidential information obtained under Subsection (a) in violation of this section. An offense under this subsection is a Class A misdemeanor.

Added by Acts 2017, 85th Leg., ch. 257 (H.B. 1501), § 6, eff. Sept. 1, 2017.

### § 107.112. Communications and Recordkeeping of Child Custody Evaluator

(a) Notwithstanding any rule, standard of care, or privilege applicable to the professional license held by a child custody evaluator, a communication made by a participant in a child custody evaluation is subject to disclosure and may be offered in any judicial or administrative proceeding if otherwise admissible under the rules of evidence.

(b) A child custody evaluator shall:

(1) keep a detailed record of interviews that the evaluator conducts, observations that the evaluator makes, and substantive interactions that the evaluator has as part of a child custody evaluation; and

(2) maintain the evaluator's records consistent with applicable laws, including rules applicable to the evaluator's license.

(c) Except for records obtained from the department in accordance with Section 107.111, a private child custody evaluator shall, after completion of an evaluation and the preparation and filing of a child custody evaluation report under Section 107.113, make available in a reasonable time the evaluator's records relating to the evaluation on the written request of an attorney for a party, a party who does not have an attorney, and any person appointed under this chapter in the suit in which the evaluator conducted the evaluation, unless a court has issued an order restricting disclosure of the records.

(d) Except for records obtained from the department in accordance with Section 107.111, records relating to a child custody evaluation conducted by an employee of or contractor with a domestic relations office shall, after completion of the evaluation and the preparation and filing of a child custody evaluation report under Section 107.113, be made available on written request according to the local rules and policies of the office.

(e) A person maintaining records subject to disclosure under this section may charge a reasonable fee for producing the records before copying the records.

(f) A private child custody evaluator shall retain all records relating to a child custody evaluation conducted by the evaluator until the ending date of the retention period adopted by the licensing authority that issues the professional license held by the evaluator based on the date the evaluator filed the child custody evaluation report prepared under this section with the court.

(g) A domestic relations office shall retain records relating to a child custody evaluation conducted by a child custody evaluator acting as an employee of or contractor with the office for the retention period established by the office.

(h) A person who participates in a child custody evaluation is not a patient as that term is defined by Section 611.001(1), Health and Safety Code.

Added by Acts 2015, 84th Leg., ch. 1252 (H.B. 1449), § 1.14, eff. Sept. 1, 2015.

### § 107.113. Child Custody Evaluation Report Required

(a) A child custody evaluator who conducts a child custody evaluation shall prepare a report containing the evaluator's findings, opinions, recommendations, and answers to specific questions asked by the court relating to the evaluation.

(b) The person conducting a child custody evaluation shall file with the court on a date set by the court notice that the report under this section is complete. On the earlier of the date the notice is filed or the date required under Section 107.114, the person shall provide a copy of the report to:

(1) each party's attorney;

(2) each party who is not represented by an attorney; and

(3) each attorney ad litem, guardian ad litem, and amicus attorney appointed in the suit.

(c) If the suit is settled before completion of the child custody evaluation report, the report under this section is not required.

(d) A report prepared under this section must include the information required by Section 107.108(h) for each child custody evaluator who conducted any portion of the evaluation.

Added by Acts 1995, 74th Leg., ch. 751, § 15, eff. Sept. 1, 1995. Redesignated from V.T.C.A., Family Code § 107.054 and amended by Acts 2015, 84th Leg., ch. 1252 (H.B. 1449), § 1.15, eff. Sept. 1, 2015. Amended by Acts 2017, 85th Leg., ch. 257 (H.B. 1501), § 7, eff. Sept. 1, 2017.

### § 107.114. Introduction and Provision of Child Custody Evaluation Report

(a) Disclosure to the court or the jury of the contents of a child custody evaluation report prepared under Section 107.113 is subject to the rules of evidence.

(b) Unless the court has rendered an order restricting disclosure, a private child custody evaluator shall provide to the attorneys of the parties to a suit, any party who does not have an attorney, and any other person appointed by the court under this chapter in a suit a copy of the child custody evaluation report before the earlier of:

(1) the third day after the date the child custody evaluation report is completed; or

(2) the 30th day before the date of commencement of the trial.

(c) A child custody evaluator who conducts a child custody evaluation as an employee of or under contract with a domestic relations office shall provide to the attorneys of the parties to a suit and any person appointed in the suit under this chapter a copy of the child custody evaluation report before the earlier of:

(1) the seventh day after the date the child custody evaluation report is completed; or

(2) the fifth day before the date the trial commences.

(d) A child custody evaluator who conducts a child custody evaluation as an employee of or under contract with a domestic relations office shall provide a copy of the report to a party to the suit as provided by the local rules and policies of the office or by a court order.

Added by Acts 1995, 74th Leg., ch. 751, § 15, eff. Sept. 1, 1995. Redesignated from V.T.C.A., Family Code § 107.055 and amended by Acts 2015, 84th Leg., ch. 1252 (H.B. 1449), § 1.16, eff. Sept. 1, 2015. Amended by Acts 2017, 85th Leg., ch. 257 (H.B. 1501), § 8, eff. Sept. 1, 2017.

### § 107.115. Child Custody Evaluation Fee

If the court orders a child custody evaluation to be conducted, the court shall award the person appointed as the child custody evaluator a reasonable fee for the preparation of the child custody evaluation that shall be imposed in the form of a money judgment and paid directly to the person. The person may enforce the judgment for the fee by any means available under law for civil judgments.

Added by Acts 1995, 74th Leg., ch. 751, § 15, eff. Sept. 1, 1995. Amended by Acts 2007, 80th Leg., ch. 832, § 5, eff. Sept. 1, 2007. Redesignated from V.T.C.A., Family Code § 107.056 and amended by Acts 2015, 84th Leg., ch. 1252 (H.B. 1449), § 1.17, eff. Sept. 1, 2015.

## SUBCHAPTER E. ADOPTION EVALUATION

*Acts 2015, 84th Leg., ch. 1252 (H.B. 1449), § 1.18, added this Subchapter E, consisting of §§ 107.151 to 107.163.*

*Another Subchapter E, Office of Child Representation and Office of Parent Representation, added by Acts 2015, 84th Leg., ch. 571 (H.B. 3003), § 1, and consisting of §§ 107.061 to 107.072, was redesignated as Subchapter G, consisting of §§ 107.251 to 107.262, by Acts 2017, 85th Leg., ch. 324 (S.B. 1488), § 24.001(6).*

### § 107.151. Definitions

In this subchapter:

(1) "Adoption evaluation" means a pre-placement or post-placement evaluative process through which information and recommendations regarding adoption of a child may be made to the court, the parties, and the parties' attorneys.

(2) "Adoption evaluator" means a person who conducts an adoption evaluation under this subchapter.

(3) "Department" means the Department of Family and Protective Services.

(4) "Supervision" means directing, regularly reviewing, and meeting with a person with respect to the completion of work for which the supervisor is responsible for the outcome. The term does not require the constant physical presence of the person providing supervision and may include telephonic or other electronic communication.

Added by Acts 2015, 84th Leg., ch. 1252 (H.B. 1449), § 1.18, eff. Sept. 1, 2015.

### § 107.152. Applicability

(a) For purposes of this subchapter, an adoption evaluation does not include services provided in accordance with the Interstate Compact on the Placement of Children adopted under Subchapter B, Chapter 162, or an evaluation conducted in accordance with Section 262.114 by an employee of or contractor with the department.

(b) This subchapter does not apply to the pre-placement and post-placement parts of an adoption evaluation conducted by a licensed child-placing agency or the department.

(c) The pre-placement and post-placement parts of an adoption evaluation conducted by a licensed child-placing agency or the department are governed by rules adopted by the commissioner of the department.

(d) In a suit involving a licensed child-placing agency or the department, a licensed child-placing agency or the department shall conduct the pre-placement and post-placement parts of the adoption evaluation and file reports on those parts with the court before the court renders a final order of adoption.

(e) A court may appoint the department to conduct the pre-placement and post-placement parts of an adoption evaluation in a suit only if the department is:

(1) a party to the suit; or

(2) the managing conservator of the child who is the subject of the suit.

Added by Acts 2015, 84th Leg., ch. 1252 (H.B. 1449), § 1.18, eff. Sept. 1, 2015. Amended by Acts 2017, 85th Leg., ch. 316 (H.B. 5), § 3, eff. Sept. 1, 2017.

### § 107.153. Order for Adoption Evaluation

(a) The court shall order the performance of an adoption evaluation to evaluate each party who requests termination of the parent-child relationship or an adoption in a suit for:

(1) termination of the parent-child relationship in which a person other than a parent may be appointed managing conservator of a child; or

(2) an adoption.

(b) The adoption evaluation required under Subsection (a) must include an evaluation of the circumstances and the condition of the home and social environment of any person requesting to adopt a child who is at issue in the suit.

(c) The court may appoint a qualified individual, a qualified private entity, or a domestic relations office to conduct the adoption evaluation.

(d) Except as provided by Section 107.155, a person who conducts an adoption evaluation must meet the requirements of Section 107.154.

(e) The costs of an adoption evaluation under this section shall be paid by the prospective adoptive parent.

Added by Acts 2015, 84th Leg., ch. 1252 (H.B. 1449), § 1.18, eff. Sept. 1, 2015.

### § 107.154. Adoption Evaluator: Minimum Qualifications

(a) In this section:

(1) "Full-time experience" means a period during which a person works at least 30 hours per week.

(2) "Human services field of study" means a field of study designed to prepare a person in the disciplined application of counseling, family therapy, psychology, or social work values, principles, and methods.

(b) To be qualified to conduct an adoption evaluation under this subchapter, a person must:

(1) have a degree from an accredited college or university in a human services field of study and a license to practice in this state as a social worker, professional counselor, marriage and family therapist, or psychologist and:

(A) have one year of full-time experience working at a child-placing agency conducting child-placing activities; or

(B) be practicing under the direct supervision of a person qualified under this section to conduct adoption evaluations;

(2) be employed by or under contract with a domestic relations office, provided that the person conducts adoption evaluations relating only to families ordered to participate in adoption evaluations conducted by the domestic relations office; or

(3) be qualified as a child custody evaluator under Section 107.104.

(c) In addition to the other qualifications prescribed by this section, an individual must complete at least eight hours of family violence dynamics training provided by a family violence service provider to be qualified to conduct an adoption evaluation under this subchapter.

Added by Acts 2015, 84th Leg., ch. 1252 (H.B. 1449), § 1.18, eff. Sept. 1, 2015. Amended by Acts 2017, 85th Leg., ch. 316 (H.B. 5), § 4(a), eff. Sept. 1, 2017.

### § 107.155. Exception to Qualifications Required to Conduct Adoption Evaluation

(a) In a county with a population of less than 500,000, if a court finds that an individual who meets the requirements of Section 107.154 is not available in the county to conduct an adoption evaluation in a timely manner, the court, after notice and hearing or on agreement of the parties, may appoint a person the court determines to be otherwise qualified to conduct the evaluation.

(b) An individual appointed under this section shall comply with all provisions of this subchapter, other than Section 107.154.

Added by Acts 2015, 84th Leg., ch. 1252 (H.B. 1449), § 1.18, eff. Sept. 1, 2015.

### § 107.156. Adoption Evaluator: Conflicts of Interest and Bias

(a) Before accepting appointment as an adoption evaluator in a suit, a person must disclose to the court, each attorney for a party to the suit, any attorney for a child who is the subject of the suit, and any party to the suit who does not have an attorney:

(1) any conflict of interest that the person believes the person has with a party to the suit or a child who is the subject of the suit;

(2) any previous knowledge that the person has of a party to the suit or a child who is the subject of the suit;

(3) any pecuniary relationship that the person believes the person has with an attorney in the suit;

(4) any relationship of confidence or trust that the person believes the person has with an attorney in the suit; and

(5) any other information relating to the person's relationship with an attorney in the suit that a reasonable, prudent person would believe would affect the ability of the person to act impartially in conducting an adoption evaluation.

(b) The court may not appoint a person as an adoption evaluator in a suit if the person makes any of the disclosures in Subsection (a) unless:

(1) the court finds that:

(A) the person has no conflict of interest with a party to the suit or a child who is the subject of the suit;

(B) the person's previous knowledge of a party to the suit or a child who is the subject of the suit is not relevant;

(C) the person does not have a pecuniary relationship with an attorney in the suit; and

(D) the person does not have a relationship of trust or confidence with an attorney in the suit; or

(2) the parties and any attorney for a child who is the subject of the suit agree in writing to the person's appointment as the adoption evaluator.

(c) After being appointed as an adoption evaluator in a suit, a person shall immediately disclose to the court, each attorney for a party to the suit, any attorney for a child who is the subject of the suit, and any party to the suit who does not have an attorney any discovery of:

(1) a conflict of interest that the person believes the person has with a party to the suit or a child who is the subject of the suit; and

(2) previous knowledge that the person has of a party to the suit or a child who is the subject of the suit, other than knowledge obtained in a court-ordered evaluation.

(d) A person shall resign from the person's appointment as an adoption evaluator in a suit if the person makes any of the disclosures in Subsection (c) unless:

(1) the court finds that:

(A) the person has no conflict of interest with a party to the suit or a child who is the subject of the suit; and

(B) the person's previous knowledge of a party to the suit or a child who is the subject of the suit is not relevant; or

(2) the parties and any attorney for a child who is the subject of the suit agree in writing to the person's continued appointment as the adoption evaluator.

(e) An individual may not be appointed as an adoption evaluator in a suit if the individual has worked in a professional capacity with a party to the suit, a child who is the subject of the suit, or a member of the party's or child's family who is involved in the suit. This subsection does not apply to an individual who has worked in a professional capacity with a party, a child, or a member of the party's or child's family only as a teacher of parenting skills in a group setting, with no individualized interaction with any party, the child, any party's family, or the child's family, or as a child custody evaluator or adoption evaluator who performed a previous evaluation. For purposes of this subsection, "family" has the meaning assigned by Section 71.003.

Added by Acts 2015, 84th Leg., ch. 1252 (H.B. 1449), § 1.18, eff. Sept. 1, 2015.

### § 107.157. Reporting Certain Placements for Adoption

An adoption evaluator shall report to the department any adoptive placement that appears to have been made by someone other than a licensed child-placing agency or a child's parent or managing conservator.

Added by Acts 2015, 84th Leg., ch. 1252 (H.B. 1449), § 1.18, eff. Sept. 1, 2015.

### § 107.158. General Provisions Applicable to Conduct of Adoption Evaluator and Preparation of Reports

(a) Unless otherwise directed by a court or prescribed by this subchapter, an adoption evaluator's actions in conducting an adoption evaluation must be in conformance with the professional standard of care applicable to the evaluator's licensure and any administrative rules, ethical standards, or guidelines adopted by the licensing authority that licenses the evaluator.

(b) A court may impose requirements or adopt local rules applicable to an adoption evaluation or an adoption evaluator that do not conflict with this subchapter.

(c) An adoption evaluator shall follow evidence-based practice methods and make use of current best evidence in making assessments and recommendations.

(d) An adoption evaluator shall disclose to each attorney of record any communication regarding a substantive issue between the evaluator and an attorney of record representing a party in a contested suit. This subsection does not apply to a communication between an adoption evaluator and an amicus attorney.

(e) To the extent possible, an adoption evaluator shall verify each statement of fact pertinent to an adoption evaluation and shall note the sources of verification and information in any report prepared on the evaluation.

(f) An adoption evaluator shall state the basis for the evaluator's conclusions or recommendations in any report prepared on the evaluation.

(g) An adoption evaluation report must include for each adoption evaluator who conducted any portion of the adoption evaluation:

(1) the name and license number of the adoption evaluator; and

(2) a statement that the adoption evaluator:

(A) has read and meets the requirements of Section 107.154; or

(B) was appointed under Section 107.155.

Added by Acts 2015, 84th Leg., ch. 1252 (H.B. 1449), § 1.18, eff. Sept. 1, 2015.

## § 107.159. Requirements for Pre–Placement Portion of Adoption Evaluation and Report

(a) Unless otherwise agreed to by the court, the pre-placement part of an adoption evaluation must comply with the minimum requirements for the pre-placement part of an adoption evaluation under rules adopted by the commissioner of the department.

(b) Unless a child who is the subject of the suit begins to reside in a prospective adoptive home before the suit is commenced, an adoption evaluator shall file with the court a report containing the evaluator's findings and conclusions made after completion of the pre-placement portion of the adoption evaluation.

(c) In a suit filed after the date a child who is the subject of the suit begins to reside in a prospective adoptive home, the report required under this section and the post-placement adoption evaluation report required under Section 107.160 may be combined in a single report.

(d) The report required under this section must be filed with the court before the court may sign the final order for termination of the parent-child relationship. The report shall be included in the record of the suit.

(e) A copy of the report prepared under this section must be made available to the prospective adoptive parents before the court renders a final order of adoption.

Added by Acts 2015, 84th Leg., ch. 1252 (H.B. 1449), § 1.18, eff. Sept. 1, 2015. Amended by Acts 2017, 85th Leg., ch. 316 (H.B. 5), § 5, eff. Sept. 1, 2017.

## § 107.160. Requirements for Post–Placement Portion of Adoption Evaluation and Report

(a) Unless otherwise agreed to by the court, the post-placement part of an adoption evaluation must comply with the minimum requirements for the post-placement part of an adoption evaluation under rules adopted by the commissioner of the department.

(b) An adoption evaluator shall file with the court a report containing the evaluator's findings and conclusions made after a child who is the subject of the suit in which the evaluation is ordered begins to reside in a prospective adoptive home.

(c) The report required under this section must be filed with the court before the court renders a final order of adoption. The report shall be included in the record of the suit.

(d) A copy of the report prepared under this section must be made available to the prospective adoptive parents before the court renders a final order of adoption.

Added by Acts 2015, 84th Leg., ch. 1252 (H.B. 1449), § 1.18, eff. Sept. 1, 2015. Amended by Acts 2017, 85th Leg., ch. 316 (H.B. 5), § 6, eff. Sept. 1, 2017.

## § 107.161. Introduction and Provision of Adoption Evaluation Report and Testimony Relating to Adoption Evaluation

(a) Disclosure to the jury of the contents of an adoption evaluation report prepared under Section 107.159 or 107.160 is subject to the rules of evidence.

(b) The court may compel the attendance of witnesses necessary for the proper disposition of a suit, including a representative of an agency that conducts an adoption evaluation, who may be compelled to testify.

Added by Acts 2015, 84th Leg., ch. 1252 (H.B. 1449), § 1.18, eff. Sept. 1, 2015.

## § 107.162. Adoption Evaluation Fee

If the court orders an adoption evaluation to be conducted, the court shall award the adoption evaluator a reasonable fee for the preparation of the evaluation that shall be imposed in the form of a money judgment and paid directly to the evaluator. The evaluator may enforce the judgment for the fee by any means available under law for civil judgments.

Added by Acts 2015, 84th Leg., ch. 1252 (H.B. 1449), § 1.18, eff. Sept. 1, 2015.

## § 107.163. Adoption Evaluator Access to Investigative Records of Department; Offense

(a) An adoption evaluator is entitled to obtain from the department a complete, unredacted copy of any investigative record regarding abuse or neglect that relates to any person residing in the residence subject to the adoption evaluation.

(b) Except as provided by this section, records obtained by an adoption evaluator from the department under this section are confidential and not subject to disclosure under Chapter 552, Government Code, or to disclosure in response to a subpoena or a discovery request.

(c) An adoption evaluator may disclose information obtained under Subsection (a) in the adoption evaluation report prepared under Section 107.159 or 107.160 only to the extent the evaluator determines that the information is relevant to the adoption evaluation or a recommendation made under this subchapter.

(d) A person commits an offense if the person recklessly discloses confidential information obtained from the department in violation of this section. An offense under this subsection is a Class A misdemeanor.

Added by Acts 2015, 84th Leg., ch. 1252 (H.B. 1449), § 1.18, eff. Sept. 1, 2015.

## SUBCHAPTER F. EVALUATIONS IN CONTESTED ADOPTIONS

*Acts 2015, 84th Leg., ch. 1252 (H.B. 1449), § 1.18, added this Subchapter F, consisting of §§ 107.201 and 107.202.*

*Another Subchapter F, Managed Assigned Counsel Program for the Representation of Certain Children and Parents, added by Acts 2015, 84th Leg., ch. 571 (H.B. 3003), § 1, and consisting of §§ 107.101 to 107.108, was redesignated as Subchapter H, consisting of §§ 107.301 to 107.308, by Acts 2017, 85th Leg., ch. 324 (S.B. 1488), § 24.001(7).*

### § 107.201. Applicability

This subchapter does not apply to services provided in accordance with the Interstate Compact on the Placement of Children adopted under Subchapter B, Chapter 162, to an evaluation conducted in accordance with Section 262.114 by an employee of or contractor with the department, or to a suit in which the Department of Family and Protective Services is a party.

Added by Acts 2015, 84th Leg., ch. 1252 (H.B. 1449), § 1.18, eff. Sept. 1, 2015.

### § 107.202. Assignment of Evaluations in Contested Adoptions

(a) In a suit in which the adoption of a child is being contested, the court shall determine the nature of the questions posed before appointing an evaluator to conduct either a child custody evaluation or an adoption evaluation.

(b) If the court is attempting to determine whether termination of parental rights is in the best interest of a child who is the subject of the suit, the court shall order the evaluation as a child custody evaluation under Subchapter D[1] and include termination as one of the specific issues to be addressed in the evaluation.

(c) When appointing an evaluator to assess the issue of termination of parental rights, the court may, through written order, modify the requirements of the child custody evaluation to take into account the circumstances of the family to be assessed. The court may also appoint the evaluator to concurrently address the requirements for an adoption evaluation under Subchapter E[2] if the evaluator recommends that termination of parental rights is in the best interest of the child who is the subject of the suit.

(d) If the court is attempting to determine whether the parties seeking adoption would be suitable to adopt the child who is the subject of the suit if the termination of parental rights is granted, but the court is not attempting to determine whether such termination of parental rights is in the child's best interest, the court may order the evaluation as an adoption evaluation under Subchapter E.

Added by Acts 2015, 84th Leg., ch. 1252 (H.B. 1449), § 1.18, eff. Sept. 1, 2015.

[1] V.T.C.A., Family Code § 107.0501 et seq.

[2] V.T.C.A., Family Code § 107.151 et seq.

## SUBCHAPTER G. OFFICE OF CHILD REPRESENTATION AND OFFICE OF PARENT REPRESENTATION

*Acts 2015, 84th Leg., ch. 571 (H.B. 3003), § 1, added this Subchapter as Subchapter E, consisting of §§ 107.061 to 107.072. Acts 2017, 85th Leg., ch. 324 (S.B. 1488), § 24.001(6) redesignated the Subchapter as Subchapter G, consisting of §§ 107.251 to 107.262.*

### § 107.251. Definition

In this subchapter, "governmental entity" includes a county, a group of counties, a department of a county, an administrative judicial region created by Section 74.042, Government Code, and any entity created under the Interlocal Cooperation Act as permitted by Chapter 791, Government Code.

Added by Acts 2015, 84th Leg., ch. 571 (H.B. 3003), § 1, eff. Sept. 1, 2015. Redesignated from V.T.C.A., Family Code § 107.061 by Acts 2017, 85th Leg., ch. 324 (S.B. 1488), § 24.001(6), eff. Sept. 1, 2017.

### § 107.252. Applicability

This subchapter applies to a suit filed by a governmental entity seeking termination of the parent-child relationship or the appointment of a conservator for a child in which appointment of an attorney is required under Section 107.012 or 107.013.

Added by Acts 2015, 84th Leg., ch. 571 (H.B. 3003), § 1, eff. Sept. 1, 2015. Redesignated from V.T.C.A., Family Code § 107.062 by Acts 2017, 85th Leg., ch. 324 (S.B. 1488), § 24.001(6), eff. Sept. 1, 2017.

### § 107.253. Nonprofit Funding

This subchapter does not limit or prevent a nonprofit corporation from receiving and using money obtained from other entities to provide legal representation and services as authorized by this subchapter.

Added by Acts 2015, 84th Leg., ch. 571 (H.B. 3003), § 1, eff. Sept. 1, 2015. Redesignated from V.T.C.A., Family Code § 107.063 by Acts 2017, 85th Leg., ch. 324 (S.B. 1488), § 24.001(6), eff. Sept. 1, 2017.

### § 107.254. Office of Child Representation

An office of child representation is an entity that uses public money to provide legal representation and services for a child in a suit filed by a governmental entity seeking termination of the parent-child relationship or the appointment of a conservator for the child in which appointment is mandatory for a child under Section 107.012.

Added by Acts 2015, 84th Leg., ch. 571 (H.B. 3003), § 1, eff. Sept. 1, 2015. Redesignated from V.T.C.A., Family Code § 107.064 by Acts 2017, 85th Leg., ch. 324 (S.B. 1488), § 24.001(6), eff. Sept. 1, 2017.

### § 107.255. Office of Parent Representation

An office of parent representation is an entity that uses public money to provide legal representation and services for a parent in a suit filed by a governmental entity seeking termination of the parent-child relationship or the appointment of a conservator for a child in which appointment is mandatory for a parent under Section 107.013.

Added by Acts 2015, 84th Leg., ch. 571 (H.B. 3003), § 1, eff. Sept. 1, 2015. Redesignated from V.T.C.A., Family Code § 107.065 by Acts 2017, 85th Leg., ch. 324 (S.B. 1488), § 24.001(6), eff. Sept. 1, 2017.

### § 107.256. Creation of Office of Child Representation or Office of Parent Representation

(a) An office described by Section 107.254 or 107.255 may be a governmental entity or a nonprofit corporation operating under a written agreement with a governmental entity, other than an individual judge or court.

(b) The commissioners court of any county, on written approval of a judge of a statutory county court or a district court having family law jurisdiction in the county, may create an office of child representation, an office of parent representation, or both offices by establishing a department of the county or designating under a contract a nonprofit corporation to perform the duties of an office.

(c) The commissioners courts of two or more counties may enter into a written agreement to jointly create and jointly fund a regional office of child representation, a regional office of parent representation, or both regional offices.

(d) In creating an office of child representation or office of parent representation under this section, the commissioners court shall specify or the commissioners courts shall jointly specify, as applicable:

(1) the duties of the office;

(2) the types of cases to which the office may be appointed under this chapter and the courts in which an attorney employed by the office may be required to appear;

(3) if the office is a nonprofit corporation, the term during which the contract designating the office is effective and how that contract may be renewed on expiration of the term; and

(4) if an oversight board is established under Section 107.262 for the office, the powers and duties that have been delegated to the oversight board.

Added by Acts 2015, 84th Leg., ch. 571 (H.B. 3003), § 1, eff. Sept. 1, 2015. Redesignated from V.T.C.A., Family Code § 107.066 and amended by Acts 2017, 85th Leg., ch. 324 (S.B. 1488), §§ 24.001(6), 24.002(2), eff. Sept. 1, 2017.

### § 107.257. Nonprofit as Office

(a) Before contracting with a nonprofit corporation to serve as an office of child representation or office of parent representation, the commissioners court or commissioners courts, as applicable, must solicit proposals for the office.

(b) After considering each proposal for an office of child representation or office of parent representation submitted by a nonprofit corporation, the commissioners court or commissioners courts, as applicable, shall select a proposal that reasonably demonstrates that the office will provide adequate quality representation for children for whom appointed counsel is required under Section 107.012 or for parents for whom appointed counsel is required under Section 107.013, as applicable.

(c) The total cost of the proposal may not be the sole consideration in selecting a proposal.

Added by Acts 2015, 84th Leg., ch. 571 (H.B. 3003), § 1, eff. Sept. 1, 2015. Redesignated from V.T.C.A., Family Code § 107.067 by Acts 2017, 85th Leg., ch. 324 (S.B. 1488), § 24.001(6), eff. Sept. 1, 2017.

### § 107.258. Plan of Operation for Office

The applicable commissioners court or commissioners courts shall require a written plan of operation from an entity serving as an office of child representation or office of parent representation. The plan must include:

(1) a budget for the office, including salaries;

(2) a description of each personnel position, including the chief counsel position;

(3) the maximum allowable caseloads for each attorney employed by the office;

(4) provisions for training personnel and attorneys employed by the office;

(5) a description of anticipated overhead costs for the office;

(6) policies regarding the use of licensed investigators and expert witnesses by the office; and

(7) a policy to ensure that the chief of the office and other attorneys employed by the office do not provide representation to a child, a parent, or an alleged father, as applicable, if doing so would create a conflict of interest.

Added by Acts 2015, 84th Leg., ch. 571 (H.B. 3003), § 1, eff. Sept. 1, 2015. Redesignated from V.T.C.A., Family Code § 107.068 by Acts 2017, 85th Leg., ch. 324 (S.B. 1488), § 24.001(6), eff. Sept. 1, 2017.

### § 107.259. Office Personnel

(a) An office of child representation or office of parent representation must be directed by a chief counsel who:

(1) is a member of the State Bar of Texas;

(2) has practiced law for at least three years; and

(3) has substantial experience in the practice of child welfare law.

(b) An office of child representation or office of parent representation may employ attorneys, licensed investigators, licensed social workers, and other personnel necessary to perform the duties of the office as specified by the commissioners court or commissioners courts.

(c) An attorney for the office of child representation or office of parent representation must comply with any applicable continuing education and training requirements of Sections 107.004 and 107.0131 before accepting representation.

(d) Except as authorized by this chapter, the chief counsel and other attorneys employed by an office of child representation or office of parent representation may not:

(1) engage in the private practice of child welfare law; or

(2) accept anything of value not authorized by this chapter for services rendered under this chapter.

(e) A judge may remove from a case a person who violates Subsection (d).

Added by Acts 2015, 84th Leg., ch. 571 (H.B. 3003), § 1, eff. Sept. 1, 2015. Redesignated from V.T.C.A., Family Code § 107.069 by Acts 2017, 85th Leg., ch. 324 (S.B. 1488), § 24.001(6), eff. Sept. 1, 2017.

### § 107.260. Appointments in County in Which Office Created

(a) If there is an office of child representation or office of parent representation serving a county, a court in that county shall appoint for a child or parent, as applicable, an attorney from the office in a suit filed in the county by a governmental entity seeking termination of the parent-child relationship or the appointment of a conservator for the child, unless there is a conflict of interest or other reason to appoint a different attorney from the list maintained by the court of attorneys qualified for appointment under Section 107.012 or 107.013.

(b) An office of child representation or office of parent representation may not accept an appointment if:

(1) a conflict of interest exists;

(2) the office has insufficient resources to provide adequate representation;

(3) the office is incapable of providing representation in accordance with the rules of professional conduct;

(4) the appointment would require one or more attorneys at the office to have a caseload that exceeds the maximum allowable caseload; or

(5) the office shows other good cause for not accepting the appointment.

(c) An office of parent representation may investigate the financial condition of any person the office is appointed to represent under Section 107.013. The office shall report the results of the investigation to the appointing judge. The judge may hold a hearing to determine if the person is indigent and entitled to appointment of representation under Section 107.013.

(d) If it is necessary to appoint an attorney who is not employed by an office of child representation or office of parent representation for one or more parties, the attorney is entitled to the compensation provided by Section 107.015.

Added by Acts 2015, 84th Leg., ch. 571 (H.B. 3003), § 1, eff. Sept. 1, 2015. Redesignated from V.T.C.A., Family Code § 107.070 by Acts 2017, 85th Leg., ch. 324 (S.B. 1488), § 24.001(6), eff. Sept. 1, 2017.

### § 107.261. Funding of Office

An office of child representation or office of parent representation is entitled to receive money for personnel costs and expenses incurred in operating as an office in amounts set by the commissioners court and paid out of the appropriate county fund, or jointly fixed by the commissioners courts and proportionately paid out of each appropriate county fund if the office serves more than one county.

Added by Acts 2015, 84th Leg., ch. 571 (H.B. 3003), § 1, eff. Sept. 1, 2015. Redesignated from V.T.C.A., Family Code § 107.071 by Acts 2017, 85th Leg., ch. 324 (S.B. 1488), § 24.001(6), eff. Sept. 1, 2017.

### § 107.262. Oversight Board

(a) The commissioners court of a county or the commissioners courts of two or more counties may establish an oversight board for an office of child representation or office of parent representation created in accordance with this subchapter.

(b) A commissioners court that establishes an oversight board under this section shall appoint members of the board. Members may include one or more of the following:

(1) an attorney with substantial experience in child welfare law;

(2) the judge of a trial court having family law jurisdiction in the county or counties for which the office was created;

(3) a county commissioner; and

(4) a county judge.

(c) A commissioners court may delegate to the oversight board any power or duty of the commissioners court to provide oversight of an office of child representation or office of parent representation under this subchapter, including:

(1) recommending selection and removal of a chief counsel of the office;

(2) setting policy for the office; and

(3) developing a budget proposal for the office.

(d) An oversight board established under this section may not access privileged or confidential information.

(e) A judge who serves on an oversight board under this section has judicial immunity in a suit arising from the performance of a power or duty described by Subsection (c).

Added by Acts 2015, 84th Leg., ch. 571 (H.B. 3003), § 1, eff. Sept. 1, 2015. Redesignated from V.T.C.A., Family Code § 107.072 by Acts 2017, 85th Leg., ch. 324 (S.B. 1488), § 24.001(6), eff. Sept. 1, 2017.

## SUBCHAPTER H. MANAGED ASSIGNED COUNSEL PROGRAM FOR THE REPRESENTATION OF CERTAIN CHILDREN AND PARENTS

*Acts 2015, 84th Leg., ch. 571 (H.B. 3003), § 1, added this Subchapter as Subchapter F, consisting of §§ 107.101 to 107.108. Acts 2017, 85th Leg., ch. 324 (S.B. 1488), § 24.001(7) redesignated this Subchapter as Subchapter H, consisting of §§ 107.301 to 107.308.*

### § 107.301. Definitions

In this subchapter:

(1) "Governmental entity" includes a county, a group of counties, a department of a county, an administrative judicial region created by Section 74.042, Government Code, and any entity created under the Interlocal Cooperation Act as permitted by Chapter 791, Government Code.

(2) "Program" means a managed assigned counsel program created under this subchapter.

Added by Acts 2015, 84th Leg., ch. 571 (H.B. 3003), § 1, eff. Sept. 1, 2015. Redesignated from V.T.C.A., Family Code § 107.101 by Acts 2017, 85th Leg., ch. 324 (S.B. 1488), § 24.001(7), eff. Sept. 1, 2017.

### § 107.302. Managed Assigned Counsel Program

(a) A managed assigned counsel program may be operated with public money for the purpose of appointing counsel to provide legal representation and services for a child or parent in a suit filed by a governmental entity seeking termination of the parent-child relationship or the appointment of a conservator for the child in which appointment is mandatory for a child under Section 107.012 or for a parent under Section 107.013.

(b) The program may be operated by a governmental entity, nonprofit corporation, or local bar association under a written agreement with a governmental entity, other than an individual judge or court.

Added by Acts 2015, 84th Leg., ch. 571 (H.B. 3003), § 1, eff. Sept. 1, 2015. Redesignated from V.T.C.A., Family Code § 107.102 by Acts 2017, 85th Leg., ch. 324 (S.B. 1488), § 24.001(7), eff. Sept. 1, 2017.

### § 107.303. Creation of Managed Assigned Counsel Program

(a) The commissioners court of a county, on written approval of a judge of a statutory county court or a district court having family law jurisdiction in the county, may appoint a governmental entity, nonprofit corporation, or local bar association to operate a managed assigned counsel program for the legal representation of:

(1) a child in a suit in which appointment is mandatory under Section 107.012; or

(2) a parent in a suit in which appointment is mandatory under Section 107.013.

(b) The commissioners courts of two or more counties may enter into a written agreement to jointly appoint and fund a governmental entity, nonprofit corporation, or bar association to operate a program that provides legal representation for children, parents, or both children and parents.

(c) In appointing an entity to operate a program under this subchapter, the commissioners court shall specify or the commissioners courts shall jointly specify:

(1) the types of cases in which the program may appoint counsel under this section, and the courts in which the counsel appointed by the program may be required to appear; and

(2) the term of any agreement establishing a program and how the agreement may be terminated or renewed.

Added by Acts 2015, 84th Leg., ch. 571 (H.B. 3003), § 1, eff. Sept. 1, 2015. Redesignated from V.T.C.A., Family Code § 107.103 by Acts 2017, 85th Leg., ch. 324 (S.B. 1488), § 24.001(7), eff. Sept. 1, 2017.

### § 107.304. Plan for Program Required

The commissioners court or commissioners courts shall require a written plan of operation from an entity operating a program under this subchapter. The plan of operation must include:

(1) a budget for the program, including salaries;

(2) a description of each personnel position, including the program's director;

(3) the maximum allowable caseload for each attorney appointed under the program;

(4) provisions for training personnel of the program and attorneys appointed under the program;

(5) a description of anticipated overhead costs for the program;

(6) a policy regarding licensed investigators and expert witnesses used by attorneys appointed under the program;

(7) a policy to ensure that appointments are reasonably and impartially allocated among qualified attorneys; and

(8) a policy to ensure that an attorney appointed under the program does not accept appointment in a case that involves a conflict of interest for the attorney.

Added by Acts 2015, 84th Leg., ch. 571 (H.B. 3003), § 1, eff. Sept. 1, 2015. Redesignated from V.T.C.A., Family Code § 107.104 by Acts 2017, 85th Leg., ch. 324 (S.B. 1488), § 24.001(7), eff. Sept. 1, 2017.

### § 107.305. Program Director; Personnel

(a) Unless a program uses a review committee appointed under Section 107.306, a program under this subchapter must be directed by a person who:

(1) is a member of the State Bar of Texas;

(2) has practiced law for at least three years; and

(3) has substantial experience in the practice of child welfare law.

(b) A program may employ personnel necessary to perform the duties of the program and enter into contracts necessary to perform the program's duties as specified by the commissioners court or commissioners courts under this subchapter.

Added by Acts 2015, 84th Leg., ch. 571 (H.B. 3003), § 1, eff. Sept. 1, 2015. Redesignated from V.T.C.A., Family Code § 107.105 and amended by Acts 2017, 85th Leg., ch. 324 (S.B. 1488), §§ 24.001(7), 24.002(3), eff. Sept. 1, 2017.

### § 107.306. Review Committee

(a) The governmental entity, nonprofit corporation, or local bar association operating a program may appoint a review committee of three or more individuals to approve attorneys for inclusion on the program's public appointment list.

(b) Each member of the committee:

(1) must meet the requirements described by Section 107.305(a) for the program director;

(2) may not be employed as a prosecutor; and

(3) may not be included on or apply for inclusion on the public appointment list.

Added by Acts 2015, 84th Leg., ch. 571 (H.B. 3003), § 1, eff. Sept. 1, 2015. Redesignated from V.T.C.A., Family Code § 107.106 and amended by Acts 2017, 85th Leg., ch. 324 (S.B. 1488), §§ 24.001(7), 24.002(4), eff. Sept. 1, 2017.

### § 107.307. Appointment from Program's Public Appointment List

(a) The judge of a county served by a program shall make any appointment required under Section 107.012 or 107.013 in a suit filed in the county by a governmental entity seeking termination of the parent-child relationship or the appointment of a conservator for the child from the program's public appointment list, unless there is a conflict of interest or other reason to appoint a different attorney from the list maintained by the court of attorneys qualified for appointment under Section 107.012 or 107.013.

(b) The program's public appointment list from which an attorney is appointed under this section must contain the names of qualified attorneys, each of whom:

(1) applies to be included on the list;

(2) meets any applicable requirements, including any education and training programs required under Sections 107.004 and 107.0131; and

(3) is approved by the program director or review committee, as applicable.

Added by Acts 2015, 84th Leg., ch. 571 (H.B. 3003), § 1, eff. Sept. 1, 2015. Redesignated from V.T.C.A., Family Code § 107.107 by Acts 2017, 85th Leg., ch. 324 (S.B. 1488), § 24.001(7), eff. Sept. 1, 2017.

### § 107.308. Funding of Program

(a) A program is entitled to receive money for personnel costs and expenses incurred in amounts set by the commissioners court and paid out of the appropriate county fund or jointly fixed by the commissioners courts and proportionately paid out of each appropriate county fund if the program serves more than one county.

(b) An attorney appointed under the program is entitled to reasonable fees as provided by Section 107.015.

Added by Acts 2015, 84th Leg., ch. 571 (H.B. 3003), § 1, eff. Sept. 1, 2015. Redesignated from V.T.C.A., Family Code § 107.108 by Acts 2017, 85th Leg., ch. 324 (S.B. 1488), § 24.001(7), eff. Sept. 1, 2017.

## CHAPTER 108. CENTRAL RECORD FILE; VITAL STATISTICS

Section



### § 108.001. Transmittal of Records of Suit by Clerk

(a) Except as provided by this chapter, the clerk of the court shall transmit to the vital statistics unit a certified record of the order rendered in a suit, together with the name and all prior names, birth date, and place of birth of the child on a form provided by the unit. The form shall be completed by the petitioner and submitted to the clerk at the time the order is filed for record.

(b) The vital statistics unit shall maintain these records in a central file according to the name, birth date, and place of birth of the child, the court that rendered the order, and the docket number of the suit.

(c) Except as otherwise provided by law, the records required under this section to be maintained by the vital statistics unit are confidential.

(d) In a Title IV–D case, the Title IV–D agency may transmit the record and information specified by Subsection (a) directly to the vital statistics unit. The record and information are not required to be certified if transmitted by the Title IV–D agency under this subsection.

Added by Acts 1995, 74th Leg., ch. 20, § 1, eff. April 20, 1995. Amended by Acts 1995, 74th Leg., ch. 751, § 16, eff. Sept. 1, 1995; Acts 1999, 76th Leg., ch. 1390, § 8, eff. Sept. 1, 1999; Acts 2007, 80th Leg., ch. 972, § 4, eff. Sept. 1, 2007; Acts 2015, 84th Leg., ch. 1 (S.B. 219), § 1.034, eff. April 2, 2015; Acts 2015, 84th Leg., ch. 963 (S.B. 1727), § 1, eff. Sept. 1, 2015.

### § 108.002. Dissolution of Marriage Records Maintained by Clerk

A clerk may not transmit to the central record file the pleadings, papers, studies, and records relating to a suit for divorce or annulment or to declare a marriage void.

Added by Acts 1995, 74th Leg., ch. 20, § 1, eff. April 20, 1995.

### § 108.003. Transmittal of Information Regarding Adoption

(a) The clerk of a court that renders a decree of adoption shall, not later than the 10th day of the first month after the month in which the adoption is rendered, transmit to the central registry of the vital statistics unit a certified report of adoption that includes:

(1) the name of the adopted child after adoption as shown in the adoption order;

(2) the birth date of the adopted child;

(3) the docket number of the adoption suit;

(4) the identity of the court rendering the adoption;

(5) the date of the adoption order;

(6) the name and address of each parent, guardian, managing conservator, or other person whose consent to adoption was required or waived under Chapter 162, or whose parental rights were terminated in the adoption suit;

(7) the identity of the licensed child placing agency, if any, through which the adopted child was placed for adoption; and

(8) the identity, address, and telephone number of the registry through which the adopted child may register as an adoptee.

(b) Except as otherwise provided by law, for good cause shown, or on an order of the court that granted the adoption or terminated the proceedings under Section 155.001, the records concerning a child maintained by the district clerk after rendition of a decree of adoption, the records of a child-placing agency that has ceased operations, and the records required under this section to be maintained by the vital statistics unit are confidential, and no person is entitled to access to or information from these records.

(c) If the vital statistics unit determines that a report filed with the unit under this section requires correction, the unit shall mail the report directly to an attorney of record with respect to the adoption. The attorney shall return the corrected report to the unit. If there is no attorney of record, the unit shall mail the report to the clerk of the court for correction.

Added by Acts 1995, 74th Leg., ch. 20, § 1, eff. April 20, 1995. Amended by Acts 1995, 74th Leg., ch. 751, § 17, eff. Sept. 1, 1995; Acts 1999, 76th Leg., ch. 62, § 6.16, eff. Sept. 1, 1999; Acts 1999, 76th Leg., ch. 1390, § 9, eff. Sept. 1, 1999; Acts 2003, 78th Leg., ch. 1128, § 3, eff. Sept. 1, 2003; Acts 2015, 84th Leg., ch. 1 (S.B. 219), § 1.035, eff. April 2, 2015.

### § 108.004. Transmittal of Files on Loss of Jurisdiction

On the loss of jurisdiction of a court under Chapter 155, 159, or 262, the clerk of the court shall transmit to the central registry of the vital statistics unit a certified record, on a form provided by the unit, stating that jurisdiction has been lost, the reason for the loss of jurisdiction, and the name and all previous names, date of birth, and place of birth of the child.

Added by Acts 1995, 74th Leg., ch. 20, § 1, eff. April 20, 1995. Amended by Acts 1995, 74th Leg., ch. 751, § 18, eff. Sept. 1, 1995; Acts 2007, 80th Leg., ch. 972, § 5, eff. Sept. 1, 2007; Acts 2015, 84th Leg., ch. 1 (S.B. 219), § 1.036, eff. April 2, 2015.

### § 108.005. Adoption Records Received by Vital Statistics Unit

(a) When the vital statistics unit receives a record from the district clerk showing that continuing, exclusive jurisdiction of a child has been lost due to the adoption of the child, the unit shall close the records concerning that child.

(b) An inquiry concerning a child who has been adopted shall be handled as though the child had not previously been the subject of a suit affecting the parent-child relationship.

Added by Acts 1995, 74th Leg., ch. 20, § 1, eff. April 20, 1995. Amended by Acts 1995, 74th Leg., ch. 751, § 19, eff. Sept. 1, 1995; Acts 1999, 76th Leg., ch. 1390, § 10, eff. Sept. 1, 1999; Acts 2015, 84th Leg., ch. 1 (S.B. 219), §§ 1.037, 1.038, eff. April 2, 2015.

### § 108.006. Fees

(a) The Department of State Health Services may charge a reasonable fee to cover the cost of determining and sending information concerning the identity of the court with continuing, exclusive jurisdiction.

(b) On the filing of a suit requesting the adoption of a child, the clerk of the court shall collect an additional fee of $15.

(c) The clerk shall send the fees collected under Subsection (b) to the Department of State Health Services for deposit in a special fund in the state treasury from which the legislature may appropriate money only to operate and maintain the central file and central registry of the vital statistics unit.

(d) The receipts from the fees charged under Subsection (a) shall be deposited in a financial institution as determined by the Department of State Health Services and withdrawn as necessary for the sole purpose of operating and maintaining the central record file.

Added by Acts 1995, 74th Leg., ch. 20, § 1, eff. April 20, 1995. Amended by Acts 1995, 74th Leg., ch. 751, § 20, eff. Sept. 1, 1995; Acts 2015, 84th Leg., ch. 1 (S.B. 219), § 1.039, eff. April 2, 2015; Acts 2021, 87th Leg., ch 472 (S.B. 41), § 5.01, eff. Jan. 1, 2022.

**Repeal of (b) and (c)**

*Acts 2021, 87th Leg., ch. 472 (S.B. 41), § 5.01(b)(7) repeals (b) and (c) effective Jan. 1, 2022.*

### § 108.007. Microfilm

(a) The vital statistics unit may use microfilm or other suitable means for maintaining the central record file.

(b) A certified reproduction of a document maintained by the vital statistics unit is admissible in evidence as the original document.

Added by Acts 1995, 74th Leg., ch. 20, § 1, eff. April 20, 1995. Amended by Acts 1995, 74th Leg., ch. 751, § 21, eff. Sept. 1, 1995; Acts 2015, 84th Leg., ch. 1 (S.B. 219), § 1.040, eff. April 2, 2015.

### § 108.008. Filing Information After Determination of Paternity

(a) On a determination of paternity, the petitioner shall provide the clerk of the court in which the order was rendered the information necessary to prepare the report of determination of paternity. The clerk shall:

(1) prepare the report on a form provided by the vital statistics unit; and

(2) complete the report immediately after the order becomes final.

(b) On completion of the report, the clerk of the court shall forward to the state registrar a report for each order that became final in that court.

Added by Acts 1995, 74th Leg., ch. 20, § 1, eff. April 20, 1995. Amended by Acts 1999, 76th Leg., ch. 556, § 4, eff. Sept. 1, 1999; Acts 2015, 84th Leg., ch. 1 (S.B. 219), § 1.041, eff. April 2, 2015.

### § 108.009. Birth Certificate

(a) The state registrar shall substitute a new birth certificate for the original based on the order in accordance with laws or rules that permit the correction or substitution of a birth certificate for an adopted child or a child whose parents marry each other subsequent to the birth of the child.

(b) The new certificate may not show that the father and child relationship was established after the child's birth but may show the child's actual place and date of birth.

Added by Acts 1995, 74th Leg., ch. 20, § 1, eff. April 20, 1995. Amended by Acts 2001, 77th Leg., ch. 821, § 2.12, eff. June 14, 2001.

### § 108.110. Release of Information by Vital Statistics Unit

(a) The vital statistics unit shall provide to the Department of Family and Protective Services:

(1) adoption information as necessary for the department to comply with federal law or regulations regarding the compilation or reporting of adoption information to federal officials; and

(2) other information as necessary for the department to administer its duties.

(b) The unit may release otherwise confidential information from the unit's central record files to another governmental entity that has a specific need for the information and maintains appropriate safeguards to prevent further dissemination of the information.

Added by Acts 1999, 76th Leg., ch. 1390, § 11, eff. Sept. 1, 1999. Amended by Acts 2015, 84th Leg., ch. 1 (S.B. 219), § 1.042, eff. April 2, 2015.

## CHAPTER 109. APPEALS



### § 109.001. Temporary Orders During Pendency of Appeal

(a) In a suit affecting the parent-child relationship, on the motion of any party or on the court's own motion and after notice and hearing, the court may make any order necessary to preserve and protect the safety and welfare of the child during the pendency of an appeal as the court may deem necessary and equitable. In addition to other matters, an order may:

(1) appoint temporary conservators for the child and provide for possession of the child;

(2) require the temporary support of the child by a party;

(3) enjoin a party from molesting or disturbing the peace of the child or another party;

(4) prohibit a person from removing the child beyond a geographical area identified by the court;

(5) require payment of reasonable and necessary attorney's fees and expenses; or

(6) suspend the operation of the order or judgment that is being appealed.

(b) A temporary order under this section enjoining a party from molesting or disturbing the peace of the child or another party:

(1) may be rendered without:

(A) the issuance of a bond between the parties; or

(B) an affidavit or a verified pleading stating specific facts showing that immediate and irreparable injury, loss, or damage will result; and

(2) is not required to:

(A) define the injury or state why the injury is irreparable; or

(B) include an order setting the suit for trial on the merits with respect to the ultimate relief sought.

(b–1) A motion seeking an original temporary order under this section:

(1) may be filed before trial; and

(2) may not be filed by a party after the date by which that party is required to file the party's notice of appeal under the Texas Rules of Appellate Procedure.

(b–2) The trial court retains jurisdiction to conduct a hearing and sign a temporary order under this section until the 60th day after the date any eligible party has filed a notice of appeal from final judgment under the Texas Rules of Appellate Procedure.

(b–3) The trial court retains jurisdiction to modify and enforce a temporary order under this section unless the appellate court, on a proper showing, supersedes the court's order.

(b–4) On the motion of a party or on the court's own motion, after notice and hearing, the trial court may modify a previous temporary order rendered under this section if:

(1) the circumstances of a party have materially and substantially changed since the rendition of the previous order; and

(2) modification is equitable and necessary for the safety and welfare of the child.

(b–5) A party may seek review of the trial court's temporary order under this section by:

(1) petition for writ of mandamus; or

(2) proper assignment in the party's brief.

(c) A temporary order rendered under this section is not subject to interlocutory appeal.

(d) The court may not suspend under Subsection (a)(6) the operation of an order or judgment terminating the parent-child relationship in a suit brought by the state or a political subdivision of the state permitted by law to bring the suit.

(e) The remedies provided in this section are cumulative of all other remedies allowed by law.

Added by Acts 1995, 74th Leg., ch. 20, § 1, eff. April 20, 1995. Amended by Acts 2001, 77th Leg., ch. 539, § 1, eff. Sept. 1, 2001; Acts 2017, 85th Leg., ch. 421 (S.B. 1237), § 4, eff. Sept. 1, 2017; Acts 2019, 86th Leg., ch. 732 (H.B. 554), § 1, eff. Sept. 1, 2019.

Section 2 of Acts 2019, 86th Leg., ch. 732 (H.B. 554) provides:

"(a) The change in law made by this Act applies only to a temporary order rendered on or after the effective date [Sept. 1, 2019] of this Act.

"(b) Notwithstanding Subsection (a) of this section, the change in law made by this Act applies to a temporary order rendered by a court of competent jurisdiction on or after September 1, 2017, but before the effective date of this Act. The legislature ratifies such an order."

## § 109.002. Appellate Review

(a) An appeal from a final order rendered in a suit, when allowed under this section or under other provisions of law, shall be as in civil cases generally under the Texas Rules of Appellate Procedure, except that an appeal from a final order rendered under Subchapter D, Chapter 152, must comply with Section 152.314.

(a–1) An appeal in a suit in which termination of the parent-child relationship is ordered shall be given precedence over other civil cases by the appellate courts, shall be accelerated, and shall follow the procedures for an accelerated appeal under the Texas Rules of Appellate Procedure.

(b) An appeal may be taken by any party to a suit from a final order rendered under this title.

(c) An appeal from a final order, with or without a supersedeas bond, does not suspend the order unless suspension is ordered by the court rendering the order. The appellate court, on a proper showing, may permit the order to be suspended, unless the order provides for the termination of the parent-child relationship in a suit brought by the state or a political subdivision of the state permitted by law to bring the suit.

(d) On the motion of the parties or on the court's own motion, the appellate court in its opinion may identify the parties by fictitious names or by their initials only.

Added by Acts 1995, 74th Leg., ch. 20, § 1, eff. April 20, 1995. Amended by Acts 1999, 76th Leg., ch. 62, § 6.17, eff. Sept. 1, 1999; Acts 2001, 77th Leg., ch. 421, § 1, eff. Sept. 1, 2001; Acts 2001, 77th Leg., ch. 539, § 2, eff. Sept. 1, 2001; Acts 2011, 82nd Leg., ch. 75 (H.B. 906), § 3, eff. Sept. 1, 2011; Acts 2017, 85th Leg., ch. 421 (S.B. 1237), §§ 5, 6, eff. Sept. 1, 2017.

### § 109.003. Payment for Court Reporter's Record

(a) If the party requesting a court reporter's record in an appeal of a suit has filed an affidavit stating the party's inability to pay costs as provided by Rule 20, Texas Rules of Appellate Procedure,[1] and the affidavit is approved by the trial court, the trial court may order the county in which the trial was held to pay the costs of preparing the court reporter's record.

(b) Nothing in this section shall be construed to permit an official court reporter to be paid more than once for the preparation of the court reporter's record.

Added by Acts 1995, 74th Leg., ch. 20, § 1, eff. April 20, 1995. Amended by Acts 1995, 74th Leg., ch. 472, § 1, eff. Sept. 1, 1995; Acts 2001, 77th Leg., ch. 1420, § 5.0025, eff. Sept. 1, 2001; Acts 2017, 85th Leg., ch. 421 (S.B. 1237), § 7, eff. Sept. 1, 2017.

[1] Vernon's Ann.Rules App.Proc., rules 20.1, 20.2.

## CHAPTER 110. COURT FEES



### § 110.001. General Rule

Except as provided by this chapter, fees in a matter covered by this title shall be as in civil cases generally.

Added by Acts 1995, 74th Leg., ch. 20, § 1, eff. April 20, 1995.

### § 110.002. Filing Fees and Deposits

(a) The clerk of the court may collect a filing fee of $15 in a suit for filing:

(1) a suit or motion for modification;

(2) a motion for enforcement;

(3) a notice of application for judicial writ of withholding;

(4) a motion to transfer;

(5) a petition for license suspension;

(6) a motion to revoke a stay of license suspension; or

(7) a motion for contempt.

(b) No other filing fee may be collected or required for an action described in this section.

(c) The clerk may collect a deposit as in other cases, in the amount set by the clerk for payment of expected costs and other expenses arising in the proceeding.

Added by Acts 1995, 74th Leg., ch. 20, § 1, eff. April 20, 1995. Amended by Acts 1997, 75th Leg., ch. 911, § 8, eff. Sept. 1, 1997; Acts 1997, 75th Leg., ch. 976, § 6, eff. Sept. 1, 1997; Acts 2003, 78th Leg., ch. 268, § 1, eff. Sept. 1, 2003.

### § 110.003. No Separate or Additional Filing Fee

The clerk of the court may not require:

(1) a separate filing fee in a suit joined with a suit for dissolution of marriage under Title 1;[1] or

(2) an additional filing fee if more than one form of relief is requested in a suit.

Added by Acts 1995, 74th Leg., ch. 20, § 1, eff. April 20, 1995.

[1] V.T.C.A., Family Code § 1.001 et seq.

### § 110.004. Fee for Issuing and Delivering Withholding Order or Writ

The clerk of the court may charge a reasonable fee, not to exceed $15, for each order or writ of income withholding issued by the clerk and delivered to an employer.

Added by Acts 1995, 74th Leg., ch. 20, § 1, eff. April 20, 1995. Amended by Acts 1997, 75th Leg., ch. 911, § 9, eff. Sept. 1, 1997.

### § 110.005. Transfer Fee

(a) The fee for filing a transferred case is $45 payable to the clerk of the court to which the case is transferred. No portion of this fee may be sent to the state.

(b) A party may not be assessed any other fee, cost, charge, or expense by the clerk of the court or other public official in connection with filing of the transferred case.

(c) The fee limitation in this section does not affect a fee payable to the court transferring the case.

Added by Acts 1995, 74th Leg., ch. 20, § 1, eff. April 20, 1995.

### § 110.006. Domestic Relations Office Operations Fees and Child Support Service Fees

(a) If an administering entity of a domestic relations office adopts an initial operations fee under Section 203.005(a)(1), the clerk of the court shall:

(1) collect the operations fee at the time the original suit, motion for modification, or motion for enforcement, as applicable, is filed; and

(2) send the fee to the domestic relations office.

(b) If an administering entity of a domestic relations office adopts an initial child support service fee under Section 203.005(a)(2), the clerk of the court shall:

(1) collect the child support service fee at the time the original suit is filed; and

(2) send the fee to the domestic relations office.

(c) The fees described by Subsections (a) and (b) are not filing fees for purposes of Section 110.002 or 110.003.

Added by Acts 1997, 75th Leg., ch. 702, § 1, eff. Sept. 1, 1997. Amended by Acts 1999, 76th Leg., ch. 556, § 5, eff. Sept. 1, 1999; Acts 2009, 81st Leg., ch. 767, § 3, eff. June 19, 2009; Acts 2009, 81st Leg., ch. 1035, § 1, eff. June 19, 2009.

## CHAPTER 111. GUIDELINES FOR POSSESSION AND CHILD SUPPORT



### § 111.001. Review of Guidelines

(a) Prior to each regular legislative session, the standing committees of each house of the legislature having jurisdiction over family law issues shall review and, if necessary, recommend revisions to the guidelines for possession of and access to a child under Chapter 153. The committee shall report the results of the review and shall include any recommended revisions in the committee's report to the legislature.

(b) At least once every four years, the Title IV–D agency shall review the child support guidelines under Chapter 154 as required by 42 U.S.C. Section 667(a) and 45 C.F.R. Section 302.56 and report the results of the review and any recommendations for any changes to the guidelines and their manner of application to the standing committees of each house of the legislature having jurisdiction over family law issues.

Added by Acts 1995, 74th Leg., ch. 20, § 1, eff. April 20, 1995. Amended by Acts 1999, 76th Leg., ch. 556, § 6, eff. Sept. 1, 1999; Acts 2011, 82nd Leg., ch. 8 (S.B. 716), § 1, eff. Sept. 1, 2011; Acts 2021, 87th Leg., ch. 175 (S.B. 285), § 2, eff. Sept. 1, 2021.

### § 111.002. Guidelines Supersede Court Rules

(a) The guidelines in this title supersede local court rules and rules of the supreme court that conflict with the guidelines.

(b) Notwithstanding other law, the guidelines may not be repealed or modified by a rule adopted by the supreme court.

Added by Acts 1995, 74th Leg., ch. 20, § 1, eff. April 20, 1995.

### § 111.003. Posting Guidelines

A copy of the guidelines for possession of and access to a child under Chapter 153 and a copy of the guidelines for the support of a child under Chapter 154 shall be prominently displayed at or near the entrance to the courtroom of every court having jurisdiction of a suit.

Added by Acts 1995, 74th Leg., ch. 20, § 1, eff. April 20, 1995.

# SUBTITLE B. SUITS AFFECTING THE PARENT–CHILD RELATIONSHIP

## CHAPTER 151. RIGHTS AND DUTIES IN PARENT-CHILD RELATIONSHIP



*Acts 2001, 77th Leg., ch. 821, § 2.13 amended Chapter 151 effective June 14, 2001. The former Chapter 151, The Parent-Child Relationship, consisting of §§ 151.001 to 151.103, was amended as Chapter 151,*

*Rights and Duties in the Parent-Child Relationship, consisting of §§ 151.001 to 151.003.*

**DISPOSITION TABLE**

Showing where provisions of former Chapter 151 of the Family Code, The Parent-Child Relationship, are covered in new Chapter 151, Rights and Duties in Parent-Child Relationships as enacted by Acts 2001, 77th Leg., ch. 821.

| Former Section | New Section |
|---|---|
| 151.001 | — |
| 151.002 | — |
| 151.003 | 151.001 |
| 151.004 | 151.002 |
| 151.005 | 151.003 |
| 151.101 | — |
| 151.102 | — |
| 151.103 | — |

## § 151.001. Rights and Duties of Parent

(a) A parent of a child has the following rights and duties:

(1) the right to have physical possession, to direct the moral and religious training, and to designate the residence of the child;

(2) the duty of care, control, protection, and reasonable discipline of the child;

(3) the duty to support the child, including providing the child with clothing, food, shelter, medical and dental care, and education;

(4) the duty, except when a guardian of the child's estate has been appointed, to manage the estate of the child, including the right as an agent of the child to act in relation to the child's estate if the child's action is required by a state, the United States, or a foreign government;

(5) except as provided by Section 264.0111, the right to the services and earnings of the child;

(6) the right to consent to the child's marriage, enlistment in the armed forces of the United States, medical and dental care, and psychiatric, psychological, and surgical treatment;

(7) the right to represent the child in legal action and to make other decisions of substantial legal significance concerning the child;

(8) the right to receive and give receipt for payments for the support of the child and to hold or disburse funds for the benefit of the child;

(9) the right to inherit from and through the child;

(10) the right to make decisions concerning the child's education; and

(11) any other right or duty existing between a parent and child by virtue of law.

(b) The duty of a parent to support his or her child exists while the child is an unemancipated minor and continues as long as the child is fully enrolled in a secondary school in a program leading toward a high school diploma and complies with attendance requirements described by Section 154.002(a)(2).

(c) A parent who fails to discharge the duty of support is liable to a person who provides necessaries to those to whom support is owed.

(d) The rights and duties of a parent are subject to:

(1) a court order affecting the rights and duties;

(2) an affidavit of relinquishment of parental rights; and

(3) an affidavit by the parent designating another person or agency to act as managing conservator.

(e) Only the following persons may use corporal punishment for the reasonable discipline of a child:

(1) a parent or grandparent of the child;

(2) a stepparent of the child who has the duty of control and reasonable discipline of the child; and

(3) an individual who is a guardian of the child and who has the duty of control and reasonable discipline of the child.

Added by Acts 1995, 74th Leg., ch. 20, § 1, eff. April 20, 1995. Amended by Acts 1995, 74th Leg., ch. 751, § 23, eff. Sept. 1, 1995. Renumbered from V.T.C.A., Family Code § 151.003 by Acts 2001, 77th Leg., ch. 821, § 2.13, eff. June 14, 2001. Amended by Acts 2001, 77th Leg., ch. 964, § 2, eff. Sept. 1, 2001; Acts 2003, 78th Leg., ch. 1036, § 3, eff. Sept. 1, 2003; Acts 2005, 79th Leg., ch. 924, § 1, eff. Sept. 1, 2005; Acts 2007, 80th Leg., ch. 972, § 6, eff. Sept. 1, 2007.

## § 151.002. Rights of a Living Child After an Abortion or Premature Birth; Civil Penalty; Criminal Offense

(a) A living human child born alive after an abortion or premature birth is entitled to the same rights, powers, and privileges as are granted by the laws of this state to any other child born alive after the normal gestation period.

(b) In this code, "born alive" means the complete expulsion or extraction from its mother of a product of conception, irrespective of the duration of pregnancy, which, after such separation, breathes or shows any other evidence of life such as beating of the heart, pulsation of the umbilical cord, or definite movement of voluntary muscles, whether or not the umbilical cord has been cut or the placenta is attached. Each product of the birth is considered born alive.

(c) For purposes of this section, a physician-patient relationship is established between a child born alive after an abortion and the physician who performed or attempted to perform the abortion. The physician must exercise the same degree of professional skill, care, and diligence to preserve the life and health of the child as a reasonably diligent and conscientious physician would render to any other child born alive at the same gestational age. In this subsection, "professional skill, care, and diligence" includes a requirement that the physician who performed or attempted the abortion ensure that the child born alive be immediately transferred to a hospital.

(d) A woman on whom an abortion, as defined by Section 245.002, Health and Safety Code, is performed or attempted to be performed may not be held liable under this section.

(e) A physician who violates Subsection (c) by failing to provide the appropriate medical treatment to a child born alive after an abortion or an attempted abortion is liable to the state for a civil penalty of not less than $100,000. The attorney general may bring a suit to collect the penalty. In addition to the civil penalty, the attorney general may recover reasonable attorney's fees. The civil penalty described in this subsection is in addition to any other recovery authorized under other law.

(f) A person who has knowledge of a failure to comply with this section shall report to the attorney general. The identity and any personally identifiable information of the person reporting the failure to comply with this section is confidential under Chapter 552, Government Code.

(g) A physician or health care practitioner who violates Subsection (c) by failing to provide the appropriate medical treatment to a child born alive after an abortion or an attempted abortion commits an offense. An offense under this subsection is a felony of the third degree.

Added by Acts 1995, 74th Leg., ch. 20, § 1, eff. April 20, 1995. Renumbered from V.T.C.A., Family Code § 151.004 by Acts 2001, 77th Leg., ch. 821, § 2.13, eff. June 14, 2001. Amended by Acts 2019, 86th Leg., ch. 1272 (H.B. 16), §§ 1, 2, eff. Sept. 1, 2019.

Sections 3 and 4 of Acts 2019, 86th Leg., ch. 1272 (H.B. 16) provide:

"Sec. 3. Section 151.002, Family Code, as amended by this Act, applies only to a child born alive on or after the effective date [Sept. 1, 2019] of this Act.

"Sec. 4. The change in law made by this Act applies only to the prosecution of an offense committed on or after the effective date of this Act. The prosecution of an offense committed before the effective date of this Act is governed by the law in effect on the date the offense was committed, and the former law is continued in effect for that purpose. For purposes of this section, an offense is committed before the effective date of this Act if any element of the offense occurs before the effective date."

### § 151.003. Limitation on State Agency Action

A state agency may not adopt rules or policies or take any other action that violates the fundamental right and duty of a parent to direct the upbringing of the parent's child.

Added by Acts 1999, 76th Leg., ch. 62, § 6.18(a), eff. Sept. 1, 1999. Renumbered from V.T.C.A., Family Code § 151.005 by Acts 2001, 77th Leg., ch. 821, § 2.13, eff. June 14, 2001.

### §§ 151.004, 151.005. Renumbered as V.T.C.A., Family Code §§ 151.002, 151.003 by Acts 2001, 77th Leg., ch. 821, § 2.13, eff. June 14, 2001

### §§ 151.101 to 151.103. Deleted by Acts 2001, 77th Leg., ch. 821, § 2.13, eff. June 14, 2001

## CHAPTER 152. UNIFORM CHILD CUSTODY JURISDICTION AND ENFORCEMENT ACT

SUBCHAPTER A. APPLICATION AND CONSTRUCTION

**Section**



SUBCHAPTER B. GENERAL PROVISIONS



SUBCHAPTER C. JURISDICTION

SUBCHAPTER D. ENFORCEMENT



*Acts 1999, 76th Leg., ch. 34, § 1 amended Chapter 152 effective September 1, 1999. The former Chapter 152, Uniform Child Custody Jurisdiction Act, consisting of §§ 152.001 to 152.025, was amended as Chapter 152, Uniform Child Custody Jurisdiction and Enforcement Act, consisting of §§ 152.001 to 152.317.*

## DISPOSITION TABLE

Showing where the subject matter of provisions contained in former Chapter 152, Uniform Child Custody Jurisdiction Act, may be found in Chapter 152, Uniform Child Custody Jurisdiction and Enforcement Act, as amended by Acts 1999, 76th Leg., ch. 34, § 1.

| Former Section | Amended Section |
|---|---|
| 152.001 | 152.001 |
| 152.002 | 152.102 |
| 152.003 | 152.201 to 152.204 |
| 152.004 | 152.205(a), (b) |
| 152.005 | 152.108 |
| 152.006 | 152.206, 152.307 |
| 152.007 | 152.207 |
| 152.008 | 152.208 |
| 152.009 | 152.209 |
| 152.010 | 152.205(c) |
| 152.011 | 152.210 |
| 152.012 | 152.106 |
| 152.013 | 152.313 |
| 152.014 | 152.305 |
| 152.015 | 152.306 |
| 152.016 | 152.305 |
| 152.017 | — |
| 152.018 | 152.111(a) |
| 152.019 | 152.112(a) |
| 152.020 | 152.112(b) |
| 152.021 | 152.112(d) |
| 152.022 | — |
| 152.023 | 152.105 |
| 152.024 | 152.107 |
| 152.025 | 152.101 |

SUBCHAPTER A. APPLICATION AND CONSTRUCTION

### § 152.001. Application and Construction

This chapter shall be applied and construed to promote the uniformity of the law among the states that enact it.

Added by Acts 1999, 76th Leg., ch. 34, § 1, eff. Sept. 1, 1999.

### § 152.002. Conflicts Between Provisions

If a provision of this chapter conflicts with a provision of this title or another statute or rule of this state and the conflict cannot be reconciled, this chapter prevails.

Added by Acts 1999, 76th Leg., ch. 34, § 1, eff. Sept. 1, 1999.

### §§ 152.003 to 152.025. Deleted by Acts 1999, 76th Leg., ch. 34, § 1, eff. Sept. 1, 1999

SUBCHAPTER B. GENERAL PROVISIONS

### § 152.101. Short Title

This chapter may be cited as the Uniform Child Custody Jurisdiction and Enforcement Act.

Added by Acts 1999, 76th Leg., ch. 34, § 1, eff. Sept. 1, 1999.

### § 152.102. Definitions

In this chapter:

(1) "Abandoned" means left without provision for reasonable and necessary care or supervision.

(2) "Child" means an individual who has not attained 18 years of age.

(3) "Child custody determination" means a judgment, decree, or other order of a court providing for legal custody, physical custody, or visitation with respect to a child. The term includes permanent, temporary, initial, and modification orders. The term does not include an order relating to child support or another monetary obligation of an individual.

(4) "Child custody proceeding" means a proceeding in which legal custody, physical custody, or visitation with respect to a child is an issue. The term includes a proceeding for divorce, separation,

neglect, abuse, dependency, guardianship, paternity, termination of parental rights, and protection from domestic violence in which the issue may appear. The term does not include a proceeding involving juvenile delinquency, contractual emancipation, or enforcement under Subchapter D.[1]

(5) "Commencement" means the filing of the first pleading in a proceeding.

(6) "Court" means an entity authorized under the law of a state to establish, enforce, or modify a child custody determination.

(7) "Home state" means the state in which a child lived with a parent or a person acting as a parent for at least six consecutive months immediately before the commencement of a child custody proceeding. In the case of a child less than six months of age, the term means the state in which the child lived from birth with a parent or a person acting as a parent. A period of temporary absence of a parent or a person acting as a parent is part of the period.

(8) "Initial determination" means the first child custody determination concerning a particular child.

(9) "Issuing court" means the court that makes a child custody determination for which enforcement is sought under this chapter.

(10) "Issuing state" means the state in which a child custody determination is made.

(11) "Legal custody" means the managing conservatorship of a child.

(12) "Modification" means a child custody determination that changes, replaces, supersedes, or is otherwise made after a previous determination concerning the same child, whether or not it is made by the court that made the previous determination.

(13) "Person acting as a parent" means a person, other than a parent, who:

(A) has physical custody of the child or has had physical custody for a period of six consecutive months, including any temporary absence, within one year immediately before the commencement of a child custody proceeding; and

(B) has been awarded legal custody by a court or claims a right to legal custody under the law of this state.

(14) "Physical custody" means the physical care and supervision of a child.

(15) "Tribe" means an Indian tribe or band, or Alaskan Native village, that is recognized by federal law or formally acknowledged by a state.

(16) "Visitation" means the possession of or access to a child.

(17) "Warrant" means an order issued by a court authorizing law enforcement officers to take physical custody of a child.

Added by Acts 1999, 76th Leg., ch. 34, § 1, eff. Sept. 1, 1999.

[1] V.T.C.A., Family Code § 152.301 et seq.

### § 152.103. Proceedings Governed by Other Law

This chapter does not govern an adoption proceeding or a proceeding pertaining to the authorization of emergency medical care for a child.

Added by Acts 1999, 76th Leg., ch. 34, § 1, eff. Sept. 1, 1999.

### § 152.104. Application to Indian Tribes

(a) A child custody proceeding that pertains to an Indian child as defined in the Indian Child Welfare Act of 1978 (25 U.S.C. Section 1901 et seq.) is not subject to this chapter to the extent that it is governed by the Indian Child Welfare Act.

(b) A court of this state shall treat a tribe as if it were a state of the United States for the purpose of applying this subchapter and Subchapter C.

(c) A child custody determination made by a tribe under factual circumstances in substantial conformity with the jurisdictional standards of this chapter must be recognized and enforced under Subchapter D.

Added by Acts 1999, 76th Leg., ch. 34, § 1, eff. Sept. 1, 1999.

### § 152.105. International Application of Chapter

(a) A court of this state shall treat a foreign country as if it were a state of the United States for the purpose of applying this subchapter and Subchapter C.

(b) Except as otherwise provided in Subsection (c), a child custody determination made in a foreign country under factual circumstances in substantial conformity with the jurisdictional standards of this chapter must be recognized and enforced under Subchapter D.

(c) A court of this state need not apply this chapter if the child custody law of a foreign country violates fundamental principles of human rights.

(d) A record of all of the proceedings under this chapter relating to a child custody determination made in a foreign country or to the enforcement of an order for the return of the child made under the Hague Convention on the Civil Aspects of International Child Abduction shall be made by a court reporter or as provided by Section 201.009.

Added by Acts 1999, 76th Leg., ch. 34, § 1, eff. Sept. 1, 1999. Amended by Acts 2011, 82nd Leg., ch. 92 (S.B. 1490), § 1, eff. Sept. 1, 2011.

### § 152.106. Effect of Child Custody Determination

A child custody determination made by a court of this state that had jurisdiction under this chapter binds all persons who have been served in accordance with the laws of this state or notified in accordance with Section 152.108 or who have submitted to the jurisdiction of the court and who have been given an opportunity to be heard. As to those persons, the determination is conclusive as to all decided issues of law and fact except to the extent the determination is modified.

Added by Acts 1999, 76th Leg., ch. 34, § 1, eff. Sept. 1, 1999.

### § 152.107. Priority

If a question of existence or exercise of jurisdiction under this chapter is raised in a child custody proceeding, the question, upon request of a party, must be given priority on the calendar and handled expeditiously.

Added by Acts 1999, 76th Leg., ch. 34, § 1, eff. Sept. 1, 1999.

### § 152.108. Notice to Persons Outside State

(a) Notice required for the exercise of jurisdiction when a person is outside this state may be given in a manner prescribed by the law of this state for service of process or by the law of the state in which the service is made. Notice must be given in a manner reasonably calculated to give actual notice but may be by publication if other means are not effective.

(b) Proof of service may be made in the manner prescribed by the law of this state or by the law of the state in which the service is made.

(c) Notice is not required for the exercise of jurisdiction with respect to a person who submits to the jurisdiction of the court.

Added by Acts 1999, 76th Leg., ch. 34, § 1, eff. Sept. 1, 1999.

### § 152.109. Appearance and Limited Immunity

(a) A party to a child custody proceeding, including a modification proceeding, or a petitioner or respondent in a proceeding to enforce or register a child custody determination, is not subject to personal jurisdiction in this state for another proceeding or purpose solely by reason of having participated, or of having been physically present for the purpose of participating, in the proceeding.

(b) A person who is subject to personal jurisdiction in this state on a basis other than physical presence is not immune from service of process in this state. A party present in this state who is subject to the jurisdiction of another state is not immune from service of process allowed under the laws of that state.

(c) The immunity granted by Subsection (a) does not extend to civil litigation based on acts unrelated to the participation in a proceeding under this chapter committed by an individual while present in this state.

Added by Acts 1999, 76th Leg., ch. 34, § 1, eff. Sept. 1, 1999.

### § 152.110. Communication Between Courts

(a) In this section, "record" means information that is inscribed on a tangible medium or that is stored in an electronic or other medium and is retrievable in perceivable form.

(b) A court of this state may communicate with a court in another state concerning a proceeding arising under this chapter.

(c) The court may allow the parties to participate in the communication. If the parties are not able to participate in the communication, they must be given the opportunity to present facts and legal arguments before a decision on jurisdiction is made.

(d) If proceedings involving the same parties are pending simultaneously in a court of this state and a court of another state, the court of this state shall inform the other court of the simultaneous proceedings. The court of this state shall request that the other court hold the proceeding in that court in abeyance until the court in this state conducts a hearing to determine whether the court has jurisdiction over the proceeding.

(e) Communication between courts on schedules, calendars, court records, and similar matters may occur without informing the parties. A record need not be made of the communication.

(f) Except as otherwise provided in Subsection (e), a record must be made of any communication under this section. The parties must be informed promptly of the communication and granted access to the record.

Added by Acts 1999, 76th Leg., ch. 34, § 1, eff. Sept. 1, 1999. Amended by Acts 2001, 77th Leg., ch. 329, § 1, eff. May 24, 2001.

### § 152.111. Taking Testimony in Another State

(a) In addition to other procedures available to a party, a party to a child custody proceeding may offer testimony of witnesses who are located in another state, including testimony of the parties and the child, by deposition or other means allowed in this state for testimony taken in another state. The court on its own motion may order that the testimony of a person be taken in another state and may prescribe the manner in which and the terms upon which the testimony is taken.

(b) A court of this state may permit an individual residing in another state to be deposed or to testify by telephone, audiovisual means, or other electronic means before a designated court or at another location in that state. A court of this state shall cooperate with courts of other states in designating an appropriate location for the deposition or testimony.

(c) Documentary evidence transmitted from another state to a court of this state by technological means that do not produce an original writing may not be excluded from evidence on an objection based on the means of transmission.

Added by Acts 1999, 76th Leg., ch. 34, § 1, eff. Sept. 1, 1999.

### § 152.112. Cooperation Between Courts; Preservation of Records

(a) A court of this state may request the appropriate court of another state to:

(1) hold an evidentiary hearing;

(2) order a person to produce or give evidence pursuant to procedures of that state;

(3) order that an evaluation be made with respect to the custody of a child involved in a pending proceeding;

(4) forward to the court of this state a certified copy of the transcript of the record of the hearing, the evidence otherwise presented, and any evaluation prepared in compliance with the request; and

(5) order a party to a child custody proceeding or any person having physical custody of the child to appear in the proceeding with or without the child.

(b) Upon request of a court of another state, a court of this state may hold a hearing or enter an order described in Subsection (a).

(c) Travel and other necessary and reasonable expenses incurred under Subsections (a) and (b) may be assessed against the parties according to the law of this state.

(d) A court of this state shall preserve the pleadings, orders, decrees, records of hearings, evaluations, and other pertinent records with respect to a child custody proceeding until the child attains 18 years of age. Upon appropriate request by a court or law enforcement official of another state, the court shall forward a certified copy of those records.

Added by Acts 1999, 76th Leg., ch. 34, § 1, eff. Sept. 1, 1999.

## SUBCHAPTER C. JURISDICTION

### § 152.201. Initial Child Custody Jurisdiction

(a) Except as otherwise provided in Section 152.204, a court of this state has jurisdiction to make an initial child custody determination only if:

(1) this state is the home state of the child on the date of the commencement of the proceeding, or was the home state of the child within six months before the commencement of the proceeding and the child is absent from this state but a parent or person acting as a parent continues to live in this state;

(2) a court of another state does not have jurisdiction under Subdivision (1), or a court of the home state of the child has declined to exercise jurisdiction on the ground that this state is the more appropriate forum under Section 152.207 or 152.208, and:

(A) the child and the child's parents, or the child and at least one parent or a person acting as a parent, have a significant connection with this state other than mere physical presence; and

(B) substantial evidence is available in this state concerning the child's care, protection, training, and personal relationships;

(3) all courts having jurisdiction under Subdivision (1) or (2) have declined to exercise jurisdiction on the ground that a court of this state is the more appropriate forum to determine the custody of the child under Section 152.207 or 152.208; or

(4) no court of any other state would have jurisdiction under the criteria specified in Subdivision (1), (2), or (3).

(b) Subsection (a) is the exclusive jurisdictional basis for making a child custody determination by a court of this state.

(c) Physical presence of, or personal jurisdiction over, a party or a child is not necessary or sufficient to make a child custody determination.

Added by Acts 1999, 76th Leg., ch. 34, § 1, eff. Sept. 1, 1999.

**§ 152.202. Exclusive Continuing Jurisdiction**

(a) Except as otherwise provided in Section 152.204, a court of this state which has made a child custody determination consistent with Section 152.201 or 152.203 has exclusive continuing jurisdiction over the determination until:

(1) a court of this state determines that neither the child, nor the child and one parent, nor the child and a person acting as a parent, have a significant connection with this state and that substantial evidence is no longer available in this state concerning the child's care, protection, training, and personal relationships; or

(2) a court of this state or a court of another state determines that the child, the child's parents, and any person acting as a parent do not presently reside in this state.

(b) A court of this state which has made a child custody determination and does not have exclusive, continuing jurisdiction under this section may modify that determination only if it has jurisdiction to make an initial determination under Section 152.201.

Added by Acts 1999, 76th Leg., ch. 34, § 1, eff. Sept. 1, 1999.

**§ 152.203. Jurisdiction to Modify Determination**

Except as otherwise provided in Section 152.204, a court of this state may not modify a child custody determination made by a court of another state unless a court of this state has jurisdiction to make an initial determination under Section 152.201(a)(1) or (2) and:

(1) the court of the other state determines it no longer has exclusive continuing jurisdiction under Section 152.202 or that a court of this state would be a more convenient forum under Section 152.207; or

(2) a court of this state or a court of the other state determines that the child, the child's parents, and any person acting as a parent do not presently reside in the other state.

Added by Acts 1999, 76th Leg., ch. 34, § 1, eff. Sept. 1, 1999.

**§ 152.204. Temporary Emergency Jurisdiction**

(a) A court of this state has temporary emergency jurisdiction if the child is present in this state and the child has been abandoned or it is necessary in an emergency to protect the child because the child, or a sibling or parent of the child, is subjected to or threatened with mistreatment or abuse.

(b) If there is no previous child custody determination that is entitled to be enforced under this chapter and a child custody proceeding has not been commenced in a court of a state having jurisdiction under Sections 152.201 through 152.203, a child custody determination made under this section remains in effect until an order is obtained from a court of a state having jurisdiction under Sections 152.201 through 152.203. If a child custody proceeding has not been or is not commenced in a court of a state having jurisdiction under Sections 152.201 through 152.203, a child custody determination made under this section becomes a final determination, if it so provides and this state becomes the home state of the child.

(c) If there is a previous child custody determination that is entitled to be enforced under this chapter, or a child custody proceeding has been commenced in a court of a state having jurisdiction under Sections 152.201 through 152.203, any order issued by a court of this state under this section must specify in the order a period that the court considers adequate to allow the person seeking an order to obtain an order from the state having jurisdiction under Sections 152.201 through 152.203. The order issued in this state remains in effect until an order is obtained from the other state within the period specified or the period expires.

(d) A court of this state which has been asked to make a child custody determination under this section, upon being informed that a child custody proceeding has been commenced in or a child custody determination has been made by a court of a state having jurisdiction under Sections 152.201 through 152.203, shall immediately communicate with the other court. A court of this state which is exercising jurisdiction pursuant to Sections 152.201 through 152.203, upon being informed that a child custody proceeding has been commenced in or a child custody determination has been made by a court of another state under a statute similar to this section shall immediately communicate with the court of that state to resolve the emergency, protect the safety of the parties and the child, and determine a period for the duration of the temporary order.

Added by Acts 1999, 76th Leg., ch. 34, § 1, eff. Sept. 1, 1999.

**§ 152.205. Notice; Opportunity to be Heard; Joinder**

(a) Before a child custody determination is made under this chapter, notice and an opportunity to be heard in accordance with the standards of Section 152.108 must be given to all persons entitled to notice under the law of this state as in child custody proceedings between residents of this state, any parent whose parental rights have not been previously terminated, and any person having physical custody of the child.

(b) This chapter does not govern the enforceability of a child custody determination made without notice or an opportunity to be heard.

(c) The obligation to join a party and the right to intervene as a party in a child custody proceeding under this chapter are governed by the law of this state as in child custody proceedings between residents of this state.

Added by Acts 1999, 76th Leg., ch. 34, § 1, eff. Sept. 1, 1999.

### § 152.206. Simultaneous Proceedings

(a) Except as otherwise provided in Section 152.204, a court of this state may not exercise its jurisdiction under this subchapter if, at the time of the commencement of the proceeding, a proceeding concerning the custody of the child has been commenced in a court of another state having jurisdiction substantially in conformity with this chapter, unless the proceeding has been terminated or is stayed by the court of the other state because a court of this state is a more convenient forum under Section 152.207.

(b) Except as otherwise provided in Section 152.204, a court of this state, before hearing a child custody proceeding, shall examine the court documents and other information supplied by the parties pursuant to Section 152.209. If the court determines that a child custody proceeding has been commenced in a court in another state having jurisdiction substantially in accordance with this chapter, the court of this state shall stay its proceeding and communicate with the court of the other state. If the court of the state having jurisdiction substantially in accordance with this chapter does not determine that the court of this state is a more appropriate forum, the court of this state shall dismiss the proceeding.

(c) In a proceeding to modify a child custody determination, a court of this state shall determine whether a proceeding to enforce the determination has been commenced in another state. If a proceeding to enforce a child custody determination has been commenced in another state, the court may:

(1) stay the proceeding for modification pending the entry of an order of a court of the other state enforcing, staying, denying, or dismissing the proceeding for enforcement;

(2) enjoin the parties from continuing with the proceeding for enforcement; or

(3) proceed with the modification under conditions it considers appropriate.

Added by Acts 1999, 76th Leg., ch. 34, § 1, eff. Sept. 1, 1999.

### § 152.207. Inconvenient Forum

(a) A court of this state which has jurisdiction under this chapter to make a child custody determination may decline to exercise its jurisdiction at any time if it determines that it is an inconvenient forum under the circumstances and that a court of another state is a more appropriate forum. The issue of inconvenient forum may be raised upon motion of a party, the court's own motion, or request of another court.

(b) Before determining whether it is an inconvenient forum, a court of this state shall consider whether it is appropriate for a court of another state to exercise jurisdiction. For this purpose, the court shall allow the parties to submit information and shall consider all relevant factors, including:

(1) whether domestic violence has occurred and is likely to continue in the future and which state could best protect the parties and the child;

(2) the length of time the child has resided outside this state;

(3) the distance between the court in this state and the court in the state that would assume jurisdiction;

(4) the relative financial circumstances of the parties;

(5) any agreement of the parties as to which state should assume jurisdiction;

(6) the nature and location of the evidence required to resolve the pending litigation, including testimony of the child;

(7) the ability of the court of each state to decide the issue expeditiously and the procedures necessary to present the evidence; and

(8) the familiarity of the court of each state with the facts and issues in the pending litigation.

(c) If a court of this state determines that it is an inconvenient forum and that a court of another state is a more appropriate forum, the court shall stay the proceedings upon condition that a child custody proceeding be promptly commenced in another designated state and may impose any other condition the court considers just and proper.

(d) A court of this state may decline to exercise its jurisdiction under this chapter if a child custody determination is incidental to an action for divorce or another proceeding while still retaining jurisdiction over the divorce or other proceeding.

Added by Acts 1999, 76th Leg., ch. 34, § 1, eff. Sept. 1, 1999.

### § 152.208. Jurisdiction Declined by Reason of Conduct

(a) Except as otherwise provided in Section 152.204 or other law of this state, if a court of this state has jurisdiction under this chapter because a person seeking to invoke its jurisdiction has engaged in unjustifiable conduct, the court shall decline to exercise its jurisdiction unless:

(1) the parents and all persons acting as parents have acquiesced in the exercise of jurisdiction;

(2) a court of the state otherwise having jurisdiction under Sections 152.201 through 152.203 determines that this state is a more appropriate forum under Section 152.207; or

(3) no court of any other state would have jurisdiction under the criteria specified in Sections 152.201 through 152.203.

(b) If a court of this state declines to exercise its jurisdiction pursuant to Subsection (a), it may fashion an appropriate remedy to ensure the safety of the child and prevent a repetition of the unjustifiable conduct, including staying the proceeding until a child custody proceeding is commenced in a court having jurisdiction under Sections 152.201 through 152.203.

(c) If a court dismisses a petition or stays a proceeding because it declines to exercise its jurisdiction pursuant to Subsection (a), it shall assess against the party seeking to invoke its jurisdiction necessary and reasonable expenses including costs, communication expenses, attorney's fees, investigative fees, expenses for witnesses, travel expenses, and child care during the course of the proceedings, unless the party from whom fees are sought establishes that the assessment would be clearly inappropriate. The court may not assess fees, costs, or expenses against this state unless authorized by law other than this chapter.

Added by Acts 1999, 76th Leg., ch. 34, § 1, eff. Sept. 1, 1999.

### § 152.209. Information to Be Submitted to Court

(a) Except as provided by Subsection (e) or unless each party resides in this state, in a child custody proceeding, each party, in its first pleading or in an attached affidavit, shall give information, if reasonably ascertainable, under oath as to the child's present address or whereabouts, the places where the child has lived during the last five years, and the names and present addresses of the persons with whom the child has lived during that period. The pleading or affidavit must state whether the party:

(1) has participated, as a party or witness or in any other capacity, in any other proceeding concerning the custody of or visitation with the child and, if so, identify the court, the case number, and the date of the child custody determination, if any;

(2) knows of any proceeding that could affect the current proceeding, including proceedings for enforcement and proceedings relating to domestic violence, protective orders, termination of parental rights, and adoptions and, if so, identify the court, the case number, and the nature of the proceeding; and

(3) knows the names and addresses of any person not a party to the proceeding who has physical custody of the child or claims rights of legal custody or physical custody of, or visitation with, the child and, if so, the names and addresses of those persons.

(b) If the information required by Subsection (a) is not furnished, the court, upon motion of a party or its own motion, may stay the proceeding until the information is furnished.

(c) If the declaration as to any of the items described in Subsections (a)(1) through (3) is in the affirmative, the declarant shall give additional information under oath as required by the court. The court may examine the parties under oath as to details of the information furnished and other matters pertinent to the court's jurisdiction and the disposition of the case.

(d) Each party has a continuing duty to inform the court of any proceeding in this or any other state that could affect the current proceeding.

(e) If a party alleges in an affidavit or a pleading under oath that the health, safety, or liberty of a party or child would be jeopardized by disclosure of identifying information, the information must be sealed and may not be disclosed to the other party or the public unless the court orders the disclosure to be made after a hearing in which the court takes into consideration the health, safety, or liberty of the party or child and determines that the disclosure is in the interest of justice.

Added by Acts 1999, 76th Leg., ch. 34, § 1, eff. Sept. 1, 1999. Amended by Acts 2003, 78th Leg., ch. 1036, § 4, eff. Sept. 1, 2003.

### § 152.210. Appearance of Parties and Child

(a) In a child custody proceeding in this state, the court may order a party to the proceeding who is in this state to appear before the court in person with or without the child. The court may order any person who is in this state and who has physical custody or control of the child to appear in person with the child.

(b) If a party to a child custody proceeding whose presence is desired by the court is outside this state, the court may order that a notice given pursuant to Section 152.108 include a statement directing the party to appear in person with or without the child and informing the party that failure to appear may result in a decision adverse to the party.

(c) The court may enter any orders necessary to ensure the safety of the child and of any person ordered to appear under this section.

(d) If a party to a child custody proceeding who is outside this state is directed to appear under Subsection (b) or desires to appear personally before the court with or without the child, the court may require another party to pay reasonable and necessary travel and other expenses of the party so appearing and of the child.

Added by Acts 1999, 76th Leg., ch. 34, § 1, eff. Sept. 1, 1999.

## SUBCHAPTER D. ENFORCEMENT

### § 152.301. Definitions

In this subchapter:

(1) "Petitioner" means a person who seeks enforcement of an order for return of a child under the Hague Convention on the Civil Aspects of International Child Abduction or enforcement of a child custody determination.

(2) "Respondent" means a person against whom a proceeding has been commenced for enforcement of an order for return of a child under the Hague Convention on the Civil Aspects of International Child Abduction or enforcement of a child custody determination.

Added by Acts 1999, 76th Leg., ch. 34, § 1, eff. Sept. 1, 1999.

### § 152.302. Enforcement Under Hague Convention

Under this subchapter a court of this state may enforce an order for the return of the child made under the Hague Convention on the Civil Aspects of International Child Abduction as if it were a child custody determination.

Added by Acts 1999, 76th Leg., ch. 34, § 1, eff. Sept. 1, 1999.

### § 152.303. Duty to Enforce

(a) A court of this state shall recognize and enforce a child custody determination of a court of another state if the latter court exercised jurisdiction in substantial conformity with this chapter or the determination was made under factual circumstances meeting the jurisdictional standards of this chapter and the determination has not been modified in accordance with this chapter.

(b) A court of this state may utilize any remedy available under other law of this state to enforce a child custody determination made by a court of another state. The remedies provided in this subchapter are cumulative and do not affect the availability of other remedies to enforce a child custody determination.

Added by Acts 1999, 76th Leg., ch. 34, § 1, eff. Sept. 1, 1999.

### § 152.304. Temporary Visitation

(a) A court of this state which does not have jurisdiction to modify a child custody determination may issue a temporary order enforcing:

(1) a visitation schedule made by a court of another state; or

(2) the visitation provisions of a child custody determination of another state that does not provide for a specific visitation schedule.

(b) If a court of this state makes an order under Subsection (a)(2), the court shall specify in the order a period that it considers adequate to allow the petitioner to obtain an order from a court having jurisdiction under the criteria specified in Subchapter C.[1] The order remains in effect until an order is obtained from the other court or the period expires.

Added by Acts 1999, 76th Leg., ch. 34, § 1, eff. Sept. 1, 1999.

[1] V.T.C.A., Family Code § 152.201 et seq.

### § 152.305. Registration of Child Custody Determination

(a) A child custody determination issued by a court of another state may be registered in this state, with or without a simultaneous request for enforcement, by sending to the appropriate court in this state:

(1) a letter or other document requesting registration;

(2) two copies, including one certified copy, of the determination sought to be registered and a statement under penalty of perjury that to the best of the knowledge and belief of the person seeking registration the order has not been modified; and

(3) except as otherwise provided in Section 152.209, the name and address of the person seeking registration and any parent or person acting as a parent who has been awarded custody or visitation in the child custody determination sought to be registered.

(b) On receipt of the documents required by Subsection (a), the registering court shall:

(1) cause the determination to be filed as a foreign judgment, together with one copy of any accompanying documents and information, regardless of their form; and

(2) serve notice upon the persons named pursuant to Subsection (a)(3) and provide them with an opportunity to contest the registration in accordance with this section.

(c) The notice required by Subsection (b)(2) must state that:

(1) a registered determination is enforceable as of the date of the registration in the same manner as a determination issued by a court of this state;

(2) a hearing to contest the validity of the registered determination must be requested within 20 days after service of notice; and

(3) failure to contest the registration will result in confirmation of the child custody determination and preclude further contest of that determination with respect to any matter that could have been asserted.

(d) A person seeking to contest the validity of a registered order must request a hearing within 20 days after service of the notice. At that hearing, the court shall confirm the registered order unless the person contesting registration establishes that:

(1) the issuing court did not have jurisdiction under Subchapter C;[1]

(2) the child custody determination sought to be registered has been vacated, stayed, or modified by a court having jurisdiction to do so under Subchapter C; or

(3) the person contesting registration was entitled to notice, but notice was not given in accordance with the standards of Section 152.108, in the proceedings before the court that issued the order for which registration is sought.

(e) If a timely request for a hearing to contest the validity of the registration is not made, the registration is confirmed as a matter of law and the person requesting registration and all persons served must be notified of the confirmation.

(f) Confirmation of a registered order, whether by operation of law or after notice and hearing, precludes further contest of the order with respect to any matter that could have been asserted at the time of registration.

Added by Acts 1999, 76th Leg., ch. 34, § 1, eff. Sept. 1, 1999.

[1] V.T.C.A., Family Code § 152.201 et seq.

## § 152.306. Enforcement of Registered Determination

(a) A court of this state may grant any relief normally available under the law of this state to enforce a registered child custody determination made by a court of another state.

(b) A court of this state shall recognize and enforce, but may not modify, except in accordance with Subchapter C,[1] a registered child custody determination of a court of another state.

Added by Acts 1999, 76th Leg., ch. 34, § 1, eff. Sept. 1, 1999.

[1] V.T.C.A., Family Code § 152.201 et seq.

## § 152.307. Simultaneous Proceedings

If a proceeding for enforcement under this subchapter is commenced in a court of this state and the court determines that a proceeding to modify the determination is pending in a court of another state having jurisdiction to modify the determination under Subchapter C, the enforcing court shall immediately communicate with the modifying court. The proceeding for enforcement continues unless the enforcing court, after consultation with the modifying court, stays or dismisses the proceeding.

Added by Acts 1999, 76th Leg., ch. 34, § 1, eff. Sept. 1, 1999.

## § 152.308. Expedited Enforcement of Child Custody Determination

(a) A petition under this subchapter must be verified. Certified copies of all orders sought to be enforced and of any order confirming registration must be attached to the petition. A copy of a certified copy of an order may be attached instead of the original.

(b) A petition for enforcement of a child custody determination must state:

(1) whether the court that issued the determination identified the jurisdictional basis it relied upon in exercising jurisdiction and, if so, what the basis was;

(2) whether the determination for which enforcement is sought has been vacated, stayed, or modified by a court whose decision must be enforced under this chapter and, if so, identify the court, the case number, and the nature of the proceeding;

(3) whether any proceeding has been commenced that could affect the current proceeding, including proceedings relating to domestic violence, protective orders, termination of parental rights, and adoptions and, if so, identify the court, the case number, and the nature of the proceeding;

(4) the present physical address of the child and the respondent, if known;

(5) whether relief in addition to the immediate physical custody of the child and attorney's fees is sought, including a request for assistance from law enforcement officials and, if so, the relief sought; and

(6) if the child custody determination has been registered and confirmed under Section 152.305, the date and place of registration.

(c) Upon the filing of a petition, the court shall issue an order directing the respondent to appear in person with or without the child at a hearing and may enter any order necessary to ensure the safety of the parties and the child. The hearing must be held on the next judicial day after service of the order unless that date is impossible. In that event, the court shall hold the hearing on the first judicial day possible. The court may extend the date of hearing at the request of the petitioner.

(d) An order issued under Subsection (c) must state the time and place of the hearing and advise the respondent that at the hearing the court will award the petitioner immediate physical custody of the child and order the payment of fees, costs, and expenses under Section 152.312, and may schedule a hearing to determine whether further relief is appropriate, unless the respondent appears and establishes that:

(1) the child custody determination has not been registered and confirmed under Section 152.305 and that:

(A) the issuing court did not have jurisdiction under Subchapter C;

(B) the child custody determination for which enforcement is sought has been vacated, stayed, or modified by a court having jurisdiction to do so under Subchapter C; or

(C) the respondent was entitled to notice, but notice was not given in accordance with the standards of Section 152.108, in the proceedings before the court that issued the order for which enforcement is sought; or

(2) the child custody determination for which enforcement is sought was registered and confirmed under Section 152.305, but has been vacated, stayed, or modified by a court of a state having jurisdiction to do so under Subchapter C.

Added by Acts 1999, 76th Leg., ch. 34, § 1, eff. Sept. 1, 1999.

### § 152.309. Service of Petition and Order

Except as otherwise provided in Section 152.311, the petition and order must be served, by any method authorized by the law of this state, upon the respondent and any person who has physical custody of the child.

Added by Acts 1999, 76th Leg., ch. 34, § 1, eff. Sept. 1, 1999.

### § 152.310. Hearing and Order

(a) Unless the court issues a temporary emergency order pursuant to Section 152.204, upon a finding that a petitioner is entitled to immediate physical custody of the child, the court shall order that the petitioner may take immediate physical custody of the child unless the respondent establishes that:

(1) the child custody determination has not been registered and confirmed under Section 152.305 and that:

(A) the issuing court did not have jurisdiction under Subchapter C;

(B) the child custody determination for which enforcement is sought has been vacated, stayed, or modified by a court of a state having jurisdiction to do so under Subchapter C; or

(C) the respondent was entitled to notice, but notice was not given in accordance with the standards of Section 152.108, in the proceedings before the court that issued the order for which enforcement is sought; or

(2) the child custody determination for which enforcement is sought was registered and confirmed under Section 152.305 but has been vacated, stayed, or modified by a court of a state having jurisdiction to do so under Subchapter C.

(b) The court shall award the fees, costs, and expenses authorized under Section 152.312 and may grant additional relief, including a request for the assistance of law enforcement officials, and set a further hearing to determine whether additional relief is appropriate.

(c) If a party called to testify refuses to answer on the ground that the testimony may be self-incriminating, the court may draw an adverse inference from the refusal.

(d) A privilege against disclosure of communications between spouses and a defense of immunity based on the relationship of husband and wife or parent and child may not be invoked in a proceeding under this subchapter.

Added by Acts 1999, 76th Leg., ch. 34, § 1, eff. Sept. 1, 1999.

### § 152.311. Warrant to Take Physical Custody of Child

(a) Upon the filing of a petition seeking enforcement of a child custody determination, the petitioner may file a verified application for the issuance of a warrant to take physical custody of the child if the child is imminently likely to suffer serious physical harm or be removed from this state.

(b) If the court, upon the testimony of the petitioner or other witness, finds that the child is imminently likely to suffer serious physical harm or be removed from this state, it may issue a warrant to take physical custody of the child. The petition must be heard on the next judicial day after the warrant is executed unless that date is impossible. In that event, the court shall hold the hearing on the first judicial day possible. The application for the warrant must include the statements required by Section 152.308(b).

(c) A warrant to take physical custody of a child must:

(1) recite the facts upon which a conclusion of imminent serious physical harm or removal from the jurisdiction is based;

(2) direct law enforcement officers to take physical custody of the child immediately;

(3) state the date for the hearing on the petition; and

(4) provide for the safe interim placement of the child pending further order of the court and impose conditions on placement of the child to ensure the appearance of the child and the child's custodian.

(c–1) If the petition seeks to enforce a child custody determination made in a foreign country or an order for the return of the child made under the Hague Convention on the Civil Aspects of International Child Abduction, the court may place a child with a parent or family member in accordance with Subsection (c)(4) only if the parent or family member has significant ties to the jurisdiction of the court. If a parent or family member of the child does not have significant ties to the jurisdiction of the court, the court shall provide for the delivery of the child to the Department of Family and Protective Services in the manner provided for the delivery of a missing child by Section 262.007(c).

(d) The respondent must be served with the petition, warrant, and order immediately after the child is taken into physical custody.

(e) A warrant to take physical custody of a child is enforceable throughout this state. If the court finds on the basis of the testimony of the petitioner or other witness that a less intrusive remedy is not effective, it may authorize law enforcement officers to enter private property to take physical custody of the child. If required by exigent circumstances of the case, the court may authorize law enforcement officers to make a forcible entry at any hour.

(f) Repealed by Acts 2011, 82nd Leg., ch. 92 (S.B. 1490), § 4.

Added by Acts 1999, 76th Leg., ch. 34, § 1, eff. Sept. 1, 1999. Amended by Acts 2011, 82nd Leg., ch. 92 (S.B. 1490), §§ 2, 4, eff. Sept. 1, 2011.

### § 152.312. Costs, Fees, and Expenses

(a) The court shall award the prevailing party, including a state, necessary and reasonable expenses incurred by or on behalf of the party, including costs, communication expenses, attorney's fees, investigative fees, expenses for witnesses, travel expenses, and child care during the course of the proceedings, unless the party from whom fees or expenses are sought establishes that the award would be clearly inappropriate.

(b) The court may not assess fees, costs, or expenses against a state unless authorized by law other than this chapter.

Added by Acts 1999, 76th Leg., ch. 34, § 1, eff. Sept. 1, 1999.

### § 152.313. Recognition and Enforcement

A court of this state shall accord full faith and credit to an order issued by another state and consistent with this chapter which enforces a child custody determination by a court of another state unless the order has been vacated, stayed, or modified by a court having jurisdiction to do so under Subchapter C.[1]

Added by Acts 1999, 76th Leg., ch. 34, § 1, eff. Sept. 1, 1999.

[1] V.T.C.A., Family Code § 152.201 et seq.

### § 152.314. Accelerated Appeals

An appeal may be taken from a final order in a proceeding under this subchapter in accordance with accelerated appellate procedures in other civil cases. Unless the court enters a temporary emergency order under Section 152.204, the enforcing court may not stay an order enforcing a child custody determination pending appeal.

Added by Acts 1999, 76th Leg., ch. 34, § 1, eff. Sept. 1, 1999. Amended by Acts 2017, 85th Leg., ch. 421 (S.B. 1237), § 8, eff. Sept. 1, 2017.

### § 152.315. Role of Prosecutor or Public Official

(a) In a case arising under this chapter or involving the Hague Convention on the Civil Aspects of International Child Abduction, the prosecutor or other appropriate public official may take any lawful action, including resorting to a proceeding under this subchapter or any other available civil proceeding to locate a child, obtain the return of a child, or enforce a child custody determination if there is:

(1) an existing child custody determination;

(2) a request to do so from a court in a pending child custody proceeding;

(3) a reasonable belief that a criminal statute has been violated; or

(4) a reasonable belief that the child has been wrongfully removed or retained in violation of the Hague Convention on the Civil Aspects of International Child Abduction.

(b) A prosecutor or appropriate public official acting under this section acts on behalf of the court and may not represent any party.

Added by Acts 1999, 76th Leg., ch. 34, § 1, eff. Sept. 1, 1999.

### § 152.316. Role of Law Enforcement

At the request of a prosecutor or other appropriate public official acting under Section 152.315, a law enforcement officer may take any lawful action reasonably necessary to locate a child or a party and assist a prosecutor or appropriate public official with responsibilities under Section 152.315.

Added by Acts 1999, 76th Leg., ch. 34, § 1, eff. Sept. 1, 1999.

### § 152.317. Costs and Expenses

If the respondent is not the prevailing party, the court may assess against the respondent all direct expenses and costs incurred by the prosecutor or other appropriate public official and law enforcement officers under Section 152.315 or 152.316.

Added by Acts 1999, 76th Leg., ch. 34, § 1, eff. Sept. 1, 1999.

## CHAPTER 153. CONSERVATORSHIP, POSSESSION, AND ACCESS

### SUBCHAPTER A. GENERAL PROVISIONS



### SUBCHAPTER B. PARENT APPOINTED AS CONSERVATOR: IN GENERAL



### SUBCHAPTER C. PARENT APPOINTED AS SOLE OR JOINT MANAGING CONSERVATOR

## SUBCHAPTER A. GENERAL PROVISIONS

### § 153.001. Public Policy

(a) The public policy of this state is to:

(1) assure that children will have frequent and continuing contact with parents who have shown the ability to act in the best interest of the child;

(2) provide a safe, stable, and nonviolent environment for the child; and

(3) encourage parents to share in the rights and duties of raising their child after the parents have separated or dissolved their marriage.

(b) A court may not render an order that conditions the right of a conservator to possession of or access to a child on the payment of child support.

Added by Acts 1995, 74th Leg., ch. 20, § 1, eff. April 20, 1995. Amended by Acts 1995, 74th Leg., ch. 751, § 25, eff. Sept. 1, 1995; Acts 1999, 76th Leg., ch. 787, § 2, eff. Sept. 1, 1999.

### § 153.002. Best Interest of Child

The best interest of the child shall always be the primary consideration of the court in determining the issues of conservatorship and possession of and access to the child.

Added by Acts 1995, 74th Leg., ch. 20, § 1, eff. April 20, 1995.

### § 153.003. No Discrimination Based on Sex or Marital Status

The court shall consider the qualifications of the parties without regard to their marital status or to the sex of the party or the child in determining:

(1) which party to appoint as sole managing conservator;

(2) whether to appoint a party as joint managing conservator; and

(3) the terms and conditions of conservatorship and possession of and access to the child.

Added by Acts 1995, 74th Leg., ch. 20, § 1, eff. April 20, 1995.

### § 153.004. History of Domestic Violence or Sexual Abuse

(a) In determining whether to appoint a party as a sole or joint managing conservator, the court shall consider evidence of the intentional use of abusive physical force, or evidence of sexual abuse, by a party directed against the party's spouse, a parent of the child, or any person younger than 18 years of age committed within a two-year period preceding the filing of the suit or during the pendency of the suit.

(b) The court may not appoint joint managing conservators if credible evidence is presented of a history or pattern of past or present child neglect, or physical or sexual abuse by one parent directed against the other parent, a spouse, or a child, including a sexual assault in violation of Section 22.011 or 22.021, Penal Code, that results in the other parent becoming pregnant with the child. A history of sexual abuse includes a sexual assault that results in the other parent becoming pregnant with the child, regardless of the prior relationship of the parents. It is a rebuttable presumption that the appointment of a parent as the sole managing conservator of a child or as the conservator who has the exclusive right to determine the primary residence of a child is not in the best interest of the child if credible evidence is presented of a history or pattern of past or present child neglect, or physical or sexual abuse by that parent directed against the other parent, a spouse, or a child.

(c) The court shall consider the commission of family violence or sexual abuse in determining whether to deny, restrict, or limit the possession of a child by a parent who is appointed as a possessory conservator.

(d) The court may not allow a parent to have access to a child for whom it is shown by a preponderance of the evidence that:

(1) there is a history or pattern of committing family violence during the two years preceding the date of the filing of the suit or during the pendency of the suit; or

(2) the parent engaged in conduct that constitutes an offense under Section 21.02, 22.011, 22.021, or 25.02, Penal Code, and that as a direct result of the conduct, the victim of the conduct became pregnant with the parent's child.

(d–1) Notwithstanding Subsection (d), the court may allow a parent to have access to a child if the court:

(1) finds that awarding the parent access to the child would not endanger the child's physical health or emotional welfare and would be in the best interest of the child; and

(2) renders a possession order that is designed to protect the safety and well-being of the child and any other person who has been a victim of family violence committed by the parent and that may include a requirement that:

(A) the periods of access be continuously supervised by an entity or person chosen by the court;

(B) the exchange of possession of the child occur in a protective setting;

(C) the parent abstain from the consumption of alcohol or a controlled substance, as defined by Chapter 481, Health and Safety Code, within 12 hours prior to or during the period of access to the child; or

(D) the parent attend and complete a battering intervention and prevention program as provided by Article 42.141, Code of Criminal Procedure, or, if such a program is not available, complete a course of treatment under Section 153.010.

(e) It is a rebuttable presumption that it is not in the best interest of a child for a parent to have unsupervised visitation with the child if credible evidence is presented of a history or pattern of past or present child neglect or abuse or family violence by:

(1) that parent; or

(2) any person who resides in that parent's household or who is permitted by that parent to have unsupervised access to the child during that parent's periods of possession of or access to the child.

(f) In determining under this section whether there is credible evidence of a history or pattern of past or present child neglect or abuse or family violence by a parent or other person, as applicable, the court shall consider whether a protective order was rendered under Chapter 85, Title 4, [1] against the parent or other person during the two-year period preceding the filing of the suit or during the pendency of the suit.

(g) In this section:

(1) "Abuse" and "neglect" have the meanings assigned by Section 261.001.

(2) "Family violence" has the meaning assigned by Section 71.004.

Added by Acts 1995, 74th Leg., ch. 20, § 1, eff. April 20, 1995. Amended by Acts 1999, 76th Leg., ch. 774, § 1, eff. Sept. 1, 1999; Acts 1999, 76th Leg., ch. 787, § 3, eff. Sept. 1, 1999; Acts 2001, 77th Leg., ch. 586, § 1, eff. Sept. 1, 2001; Acts 2003, 78th Leg., ch. 642, § 1, eff. Sept. 1, 2003; Acts 2013, 83rd Leg., ch. 907 (H.B. 1228), §§ 1, 2, eff. Sept. 1, 2013; Acts 2017, 85th Leg., ch. 99 (S.B. 495), § 1, eff. Sept. 1, 2017.

[1] V.T.C.A., Family Code § 85.001 et seq.

### § 153.005. Appointment of Sole or Joint Managing Conservator

(a) In a suit, except as provided by Section 153.004, the court:

(1) may appoint a sole managing conservator or may appoint joint managing conservators; and

(2) if the parents are or will be separated, shall appoint at least one managing conservator.

(b) A managing conservator must be a parent, a competent adult, the Department of Family and Protective Services, or a licensed child-placing agency.

(c) In making an appointment authorized by this section, the court shall consider whether, preceding the filing of the suit or during the pendency of the suit:

(1) a party engaged in a history or pattern of family violence, as defined by Section 71.004;

(2) a party engaged in a history or pattern of child abuse or child neglect; or

(3) a final protective order was rendered against a party.

Added by Acts 1995, 74th Leg., ch. 20, § 1, eff. April 20, 1995. Amended by Acts 2015, 84th Leg., ch. 1 (S.B. 219), § 1.043, eff. April 2, 2015; Acts 2015, 84th Leg., ch. 117 (S.B. 817), § 3, eff. Sept. 1, 2015.

### § 153.006. Appointment of Possessory Conservator

(a) If a managing conservator is appointed, the court may appoint one or more possessory conservators.

(b) The court shall specify the rights and duties of a person appointed possessory conservator.

(c) The court shall specify and expressly state in the order the times and conditions for possession of or access to the child, unless a party shows good cause why specific orders would not be in the best interest of the child.

Added by Acts 1995, 74th Leg., ch. 20, § 1, eff. April 20, 1995.

### § 153.007. Agreed Parenting Plan

(a) To promote the amicable settlement of disputes between the parties to a suit, the parties may enter into a written agreed parenting plan containing provisions for conservatorship and possession of the child and for modification of the parenting plan, including variations from the standard possession order.

(b) If the court finds that the agreed parenting plan is in the child's best interest, the court shall render an order in accordance with the parenting plan.

(c) Terms of the agreed parenting plan contained in the order or incorporated by reference regarding conservatorship or support of or access to a child in an order may be enforced by all remedies available for enforcement of a judgment, including contempt, but are not enforceable as a contract.

(d) If the court finds the agreed parenting plan is not in the child's best interest, the court may request the parties to submit a revised parenting plan. If the parties do not submit a revised parenting plan satisfactory to the court, the court may, after notice and hearing, order a parenting plan that the court finds to be in the best interest of the child.

Added by Acts 1995, 74th Leg., ch. 20, § 1, eff. April 20, 1995. Amended by Acts 1995, 74th Leg., ch. 751, § 26, eff. Sept. 1, 1995; Acts 2005, 79th Leg., ch. 482, § 3, eff. Sept. 1, 2005; Acts 2007, 80th Leg., ch. 1181, § 1, eff. Sept. 1, 2007.

### § 153.0071. Alternate Dispute Resolution Procedures

(a) On written agreement of the parties, the court may refer a suit affecting the parent-child relationship to arbitration. The agreement must state whether the arbitration is binding or non-binding.

(b) If the parties agree to binding arbitration, the court shall render an order reflecting the arbitrator's award unless the court determines at a non-jury hearing that the award is not in the best interest of the child. The burden of proof at a hearing under this subsection is on the party seeking to avoid rendition of an order based on the arbitrator's award.

(c) On the written agreement of the parties or on the court's own motion, the court may refer a suit affecting the parent-child relationship to mediation.

(d) A mediated settlement agreement is binding on the parties if the agreement:

(1) provides, in a prominently displayed statement that is in boldfaced type or capital letters or underlined, that the agreement is not subject to revocation;

(2) is signed by each party to the agreement; and

(3) is signed by the party's attorney, if any, who is present at the time the agreement is signed.

(e) If a mediated settlement agreement meets the requirements of Subsection (d), a party is entitled to judgment on the mediated settlement agreement notwithstanding Rule 11, Texas Rules of Civil Procedure, or another rule of law.

(e–1) Notwithstanding Subsections (d) and (e), a court may decline to enter a judgment on a mediated settlement agreement if the court finds:

(1) that:

(A) a party to the agreement was a victim of family violence, and that circumstance impaired the party's ability to make decisions; or

(B) the agreement would permit a person who is subject to registration under Chapter 62, Code of Criminal Procedure, on the basis of an offense committed by the person when the person was 17 years of age or older or who otherwise has a history or pattern of past or present physical or sexual abuse directed against any person to:

(i) reside in the same household as the child; or

(ii) otherwise have unsupervised access to the child; and

(2) that the agreement is not in the child's best interest.

(f) A party may at any time prior to the final mediation order file a written objection to the referral of a suit affecting the parent-child relationship to mediation on the basis of family violence having been committed by another party against the objecting party or a child who is the subject of the suit. After an objection is filed, the suit may not be referred to mediation unless, on the request of a party, a hearing is held and the court finds that a preponderance of the evidence does not support the objection. If the suit is referred to mediation, the court shall order appropriate measures be taken to ensure the physical and emotional safety of the party who filed the objection. The order shall provide that the parties not be required to have face-to-face contact and that the parties be placed in separate rooms during mediation. This subsection does not apply to suits filed under Chapter 262.

(g) The provisions for confidentiality of alternative dispute resolution procedures under Chapter 154, Civil Practice and Remedies Code, apply equally to the work of a parenting coordinator, as defined by Section

153.601, and to the parties and any other person who participates in the parenting coordination. This subsection does not affect the duty of a person to report abuse or neglect under Section 261.101.

Added by Acts 1995, 74th Leg., ch. 751, § 27, eff. Sept. 1, 1995. Amended by Acts 1997, 75th Leg., ch. 937, § 3, eff. Sept. 1, 1997; Acts 1999, 76th Leg., ch. 178, § 7, eff. Aug. 30, 1999; Acts 1999, 76th Leg., ch. 1351, § 2, eff. Sept. 1, 1999; Acts 2005, 79th Leg., ch. 916, § 7, eff. June 18, 2005; Acts 2007, 80th Leg., ch. 1181, § 2, eff. Sept. 1, 2007; Acts 2017, 85th Leg., ch. 99 (S.B. 495), § 2, eff. Sept. 1, 2017.

**§ 153.00715. Determination of Validity and Enforceability of Contract Containing Agreement to Arbitrate**

(a) If a party to a suit affecting the parent-child relationship opposes an application to compel arbitration or makes an application to stay arbitration and asserts that the contract containing the agreement to arbitrate is not valid or enforceable, notwithstanding any provision of the contract to the contrary, the court shall try the issue promptly and may order arbitration only if the court determines that the contract containing the agreement to arbitrate is valid and enforceable against the party seeking to avoid arbitration.

(b) A determination under this section that a contract is valid and enforceable does not affect the court's authority to stay arbitration or refuse to compel arbitration on any other ground provided by law.

(c) This section does not apply to:

(1) a court order;

(2) an agreed parenting plan described by Section 153.007;

(3) a mediated settlement agreement described by Section 153.0071;

(4) a collaborative law agreement described by Section 153.0072; or

(5) any other agreement between the parties that is approved by a court.

Added by Acts 2011, 82nd Leg., ch. 1088 (S.B. 1216), § 2, eff. June 17, 2011.

**§ 153.0072. Repealed by Acts 2011, 82nd Leg., ch. 1048 (H.B. 3833), § 2, eff. Sept. 1, 2011**

**§ 153.008. Repealed by Acts 2009, 81st Leg., ch. 1113, § 31, eff. Sept. 1, 2009; Acts 2009, 81st Leg., ch. 1118, § 10, eff. Sept. 1, 2009**

**§ 153.009. Interview of Child in Chambers**

(a) In a nonjury trial or at a hearing, on the application of a party, the amicus attorney, or the attorney ad litem for the child, the court shall interview in chambers a child 12 years of age or older and may interview in chambers a child under 12 years of age to determine the child's wishes as to conservatorship or as to the person who shall have the exclusive right to determine the child's primary residence. The court may also interview a child in chambers on the court's own motion for a purpose specified by this subsection.

(b) In a nonjury trial or at a hearing, on the application of a party, the amicus attorney, or the attorney ad litem for the child or on the court's own motion, the court may interview the child in chambers to determine the child's wishes as to possession, access, or any other issue in the suit affecting the parent-child relationship.

(c) Interviewing a child does not diminish the discretion of the court in determining the best interests of the child.

(d) In a jury trial, the court may not interview the child in chambers regarding an issue on which a party is entitled to a jury verdict.

(e) In any trial or hearing, the court may permit the attorney for a party, the amicus attorney, the guardian ad litem for the child, or the attorney ad litem for the child to be present at the interview.

(f) On the motion of a party, the amicus attorney, or the attorney ad litem for the child, or on the court's own motion, the court shall cause a record of the interview to be made when the child is 12 years of age or older. A record of the interview shall be part of the record in the case.

Added by Acts 1995, 74th Leg., ch. 20, § 1, eff. April 20, 1995. Amended by Acts 1997, 75th Leg., ch. 781, § 1, eff. Sept. 1, 1997; Acts 2001, 77th Leg., ch. 1289, § 2, eff. Sept. 1, 2001; Acts 2005, 79th Leg., ch. 916, § 9, eff. June 18, 2005.

**§ 153.010. Order for Family Counseling**

(a) If the court finds at the time of a hearing that the parties have a history of conflict in resolving an issue of conservatorship or possession of or access to the child, the court may order a party to:

(1) participate in counseling with a mental health professional who:

(A) has a background in family therapy;

(B) has a mental health license that requires as a minimum a master's degree; and

(C) has training in domestic violence if the court determines that the training is relevant to the type of counseling needed; and

(2) pay the cost of counseling.

(b) If a person possessing the requirements of Subsection (a)(1) is not available in the county in which the court presides, the court may appoint a person the court believes is qualified to conduct the counseling ordered under Subsection (a).

Added by Acts 1995, 74th Leg., ch. 20, § 1, eff. April 20, 1995. Amended by Acts 1997, 75th Leg., ch. 645, § 1, eff. Sept. 1, 1997.

### § 153.011. Security Bond

If the court finds that a person who has a possessory interest in a child may violate the court order relating to the interest, the court may order the party to execute a bond or deposit security. The court shall set the amount and condition the bond or security on compliance with the order.

Added by Acts 1995, 74th Leg., ch. 20, § 1, eff. April 20, 1995.

### § 153.012. Right to Privacy; Deletion of Personal Information in Records

The court may order the custodian of records to delete all references in the records to the place of residence of either party appointed as a conservator of the child before the release of the records to another party appointed as a conservator.

Added by Acts 1995, 74th Leg., ch. 20, § 1, eff. April 20, 1995.

### § 153.013. False Report of Child Abuse

(a) If a party to a pending suit affecting the parent-child relationship makes a report alleging child abuse by another party to the suit that the reporting party knows lacks a factual foundation, the court shall deem the report to be a knowingly false report.

(b) Evidence of a false report of child abuse is admissible in a suit between the involved parties regarding the terms of conservatorship of a child.

(c) If the court makes a finding under Subsection (a), the court shall impose a civil penalty not to exceed $500.

Added by Acts 1995, 74th Leg., ch. 751, § 28, eff. Sept. 1, 1995. Amended by Acts 1997, 75th Leg., ch. 786, § 2, eff. Sept. 1, 1997.

### § 153.014. Visitation Centers and Visitation Exchange Facilities

A county may establish a visitation center or a visitation exchange facility for the purpose of facilitating the terms of a court order providing for the possession of or access to a child.

Added by Acts 2001, 77th Leg., ch. 577, § 1, eff. June 11, 2001.

### § 153.015. Electronic Communication with Child by Conservator

(a) In this section, "electronic communication" means any communication facilitated by the use of any wired or wireless technology via the Internet or any other electronic media. The term includes communication facilitated by the use of a telephone, electronic mail, instant messaging, videoconferencing, or webcam.

(b) If a conservator of a child requests the court to order periods of electronic communication with the child under this section, the court may award the conservator reasonable periods of electronic communication with the child to supplement the conservator's periods of possession of the child. In determining whether to award electronic communication, the court shall consider:

(1) whether electronic communication is in the best interest of the child;

(2) whether equipment necessary to facilitate the electronic communication is reasonably available to all parties subject to the order; and

(3) any other factor the court considers appropriate.

(c) If a court awards a conservator periods of electronic communication with a child under this section, each conservator subject to the court's order shall:

(1) provide the other conservator with the e-mail address and other electronic communication access information of the child;

(2) notify the other conservator of any change in the e-mail address or other electronic communication access information not later than 24 hours after the date the change takes effect; and

(3) if necessary equipment is reasonably available, accommodate electronic communication with the child, with the same privacy, respect, and dignity accorded all other forms of access, at a reasonable time and for a reasonable duration subject to any limitation provided by the court in the court's order.

(d) The court may not consider the availability of electronic communication as a factor in determining child support. The availability of electronic communication under this section is not intended as a substitute for physical possession of or access to the child where otherwise appropriate.

(e) In a suit in which the court's order contains provisions related to a finding of family violence in the suit, including supervised visitation, the court may award periods of electronic communication under this section only if:

(1) the award and terms of the award are mutually agreed to by the parties; and

(2) the terms of the award:

(A) are printed in the court's order in boldfaced, capitalized type; and

(B) include any specific restrictions relating to family violence or supervised visitation, as applicable, required by other law to be included in a possession or access order.

Added by Acts 2007, 80th Leg., ch. 972, § 7, eff. Sept. 1, 2007; Acts 2007, 80th Leg., ch. 1041, § 1, eff. June 15, 2007.

## SUBCHAPTER B. PARENT APPOINTED AS CONSERVATOR: IN GENERAL

### § 153.071. Court to Specify Rights and Duties of Parent Appointed a Conservator

If both parents are appointed as conservators of the child, the court shall specify the rights and duties of a parent that are to be exercised:

(1) by each parent independently;

(2) by the joint agreement of the parents; and

(3) exclusively by one parent.

Added by Acts 1995, 74th Leg., ch. 20, § 1, eff. April 20, 1995.

### § 153.072. Written Finding Required to Limit Parental Rights and Duties

The court may limit the rights and duties of a parent appointed as a conservator if the court makes a written finding that the limitation is in the best interest of the child.

Added by Acts 1995, 74th Leg., ch. 20, § 1, eff. April 20, 1995.

### § 153.073. Rights of Parent at All Times

(a) Unless limited by court order, a parent appointed as a conservator of a child has at all times the right:

(1) to receive information from any other conservator of the child concerning the health, education, and welfare of the child;

(2) to confer with the other parent to the extent possible before making a decision concerning the health, education, and welfare of the child;

(3) of access to medical, dental, psychological, and educational records of the child;

(4) to consult with a physician, dentist, or psychologist of the child;

(5) to consult with school officials concerning the child's welfare and educational status, including school activities;

(6) to attend school activities, including school lunches, performances, and field trips;

(7) to be designated on the child's records as a person to be notified in case of an emergency;

(8) to consent to medical, dental, and surgical treatment during an emergency involving an immediate danger to the health and safety of the child; and

(9) to manage the estate of the child to the extent the estate has been created by the parent or the parent's family.

(b) The court shall specify in the order the rights that a parent retains at all times.

Added by Acts 1995, 74th Leg., ch. 20, § 1, eff. April 20, 1995. Amended by Acts 1995, 74th Leg., ch. 751, § 29, eff. Sept. 1, 1995; Acts 2003, 78th Leg., ch. 1036, § 6, eff. Sept. 1, 2003; Acts 2019, 86th Leg., ch. 1156 (H.B. 3145), § 1, eff. June 14, 2019.

### § 153.074. Rights and Duties During Period of Possession

Unless limited by court order, a parent appointed as a conservator of a child has the following rights and duties during the period that the parent has possession of the child:

(1) the duty of care, control, protection, and reasonable discipline of the child;

(2) the duty to support the child, including providing the child with clothing, food, shelter, and medical and dental care not involving an invasive procedure;

(3) the right to consent for the child to medical and dental care not involving an invasive procedure; and

(4) the right to direct the moral and religious training of the child.

Added by Acts 1995, 74th Leg., ch. 20, § 1, eff. April 20, 1995. Amended by Acts 1995, 74th Leg., ch. 751, § 30, eff. Sept. 1, 1995; Acts 2003, 78th Leg., ch. 1036, § 7, eff. Sept. 1, 2003.

### § 153.075. Duties of Parent Not Appointed Conservator

The court may order a parent not appointed as a managing or a possessory conservator to perform other parental duties, including paying child support.

Added by Acts 1995, 74th Leg., ch. 20, § 1, eff. April 20, 1995.

### § 153.076. Duty to Provide Information

(a) The court shall order that each conservator of a child has a duty to inform the other conservator of the child in a timely manner of significant information concerning the health, education, and welfare of the child.

(b) The court shall order that each conservator of a child has the duty to inform the other conservator of the child if the conservator resides with for at least 30 days, marries, or intends to marry a person who the conservator knows:

(1) is registered as a sex offender under Chapter 62, Code of Criminal Procedure; or

(2) is currently charged with an offense for which on conviction the person would be required to register under that chapter.

(b–1) The court shall order that each conservator of a child has the duty to inform the other conservator of the child if the conservator:

(1) establishes a residence with a person who the conservator knows is the subject of a final protective order sought by an individual other than the conservator that is in effect on the date the residence with the person is established;

(2) resides with, or allows unsupervised access to a child by, a person who is the subject of a final protective order sought by the conservator after the expiration of the 60–day period following the date the final protective order is issued; or

(3) is the subject of a final protective order issued after the date of the order establishing conservatorship.

(c) The notice required to be made under Subsection (b) must be made as soon as practicable but not later than the 40th day after the date the conservator of the child begins to reside with the person or the 10th day after the date the marriage occurs, as appropriate. The notice must include a description of the offense that is the basis of the person's requirement to register as a sex offender or of the offense with which the person is charged.

(c–1) The notice required to be made under Subsection (b–1) must be made as soon as practicable but not later than:

(1) the 30th day after the date the conservator establishes residence with the person who is the subject of the final protective order, if the notice is required by Subsection (b–1)(1);

(2) the 90th day after the date the final protective order was issued, if the notice is required by Subsection (b–1)(2); or

(3) the 30th day after the date the final protective order was issued, if the notice is required by Subsection (b–1)(3).

(d) A conservator commits an offense if the conservator fails to provide notice in the manner required by Subsections (b) and (c), or Subsections (b–1) and (c–1), as applicable. An offense under this subsection is a Class C misdemeanor.

Added by Acts 1995, 74th Leg., ch. 751, § 31, eff. Sept. 1, 1995. Amended by Acts 1999, 76th Leg., ch. 330, § 1, eff. Sept. 1, 1999; Acts 2003, 78th Leg., ch. 1036, § 8, eff. Sept. 1, 2003; Acts 2015, 84th Leg., ch. 1166 (S.B. 818), § 1, eff. Sept. 1, 2015.

## SUBCHAPTER C. PARENT APPOINTED AS SOLE OR JOINT MANAGING CONSERVATOR

### § 153.131. Presumption That Parent to be Appointed Managing Conservator

(a) Subject to the prohibition in Section 153.004, unless the court finds that appointment of the parent or parents would not be in the best interest of the child because the appointment would significantly impair the child's physical health or emotional development, a parent shall be appointed sole managing conservator or both parents shall be appointed as joint managing conservators of the child.

(b) It is a rebuttable presumption that the appointment of the parents of a child as joint managing conservators is in the best interest of the child. A finding of a history of family violence involving the parents of a child removes the presumption under this subsection.

Added by Acts 1995, 74th Leg., ch. 20, § 1, eff. April 20, 1995. Amended by Acts 1995, 74th Leg., ch. 751, § 32, eff. Sept. 1, 1995; Acts 1997, 75th Leg., ch. 1193, § 20, eff. Sept. 1, 1997.

## § 153.132. Rights and Duties of Parent Appointed Sole Managing Conservator

Unless limited by court order, a parent appointed as sole managing conservator of a child has the rights and duties provided by Subchapter B [1] and the following exclusive rights:

(1) the right to designate the primary residence of the child;

(2) the right to consent to medical, dental, and surgical treatment involving invasive procedures;

(3) the right to consent to psychiatric and psychological treatment;

(4) the right to receive and give receipt for periodic payments for the support of the child and to hold or disburse these funds for the benefit of the child;

(5) the right to represent the child in legal action and to make other decisions of substantial legal significance concerning the child;

(6) the right to consent to marriage and to enlistment in the armed forces of the United States;

(7) the right to make decisions concerning the child's education;

(8) the right to the services and earnings of the child;

(9) except when a guardian of the child's estate or a guardian or attorney ad litem has been appointed for the child, the right to act as an agent of the child in relation to the child's estate if the child's action is required by a state, the United States, or a foreign government; and

(10) the right to:

(A) apply for a passport for the child;

(B) renew the child's passport; and

(C) maintain possession of the child's passport.

Added by Acts 1995, 74th Leg., ch. 20, § 1, eff. April 20, 1995. Amended by Acts 1995, 74th Leg., ch. 751, § 33, eff. Sept. 1, 1995; Acts 2003, 78th Leg., ch. 1036, § 9, eff. Sept. 1, 2003; Acts 2005, 79th Leg., ch. 916, § 10, eff. June 18, 2005; Acts 2019, 86th Leg., ch. 733 (H.B. 555), § 1, eff. Sept. 1, 2019.

[1] V.T.C.A., Family Code § 153.071 et seq.

Section 3 of Acts 2019, 86th Leg., ch. 733 (H.B. 555) provides:

"The changes in law made by this Act apply only to a suit affecting the parent-child relationship that is pending in a trial court on or filed on or after the effective date [Sept. 1, 2019] of this Act."

## § 153.133. Parenting Plan for Joint Managing Conservatorship

(a) If a written agreed parenting plan is filed with the court, the court shall render an order appointing the parents as joint managing conservators only if the parenting plan:

(1) designates the conservator who has the exclusive right to designate the primary residence of the child and:

(A) establishes, until modified by further order, the geographic area within which the conservator shall maintain the child's primary residence; or

(B) specifies that the conservator may designate the child's primary residence without regard to geographic location;

(2) specifies the rights and duties of each parent regarding the child's physical care, support, and education;

(3) includes provisions to minimize disruption of the child's education, daily routine, and association with friends;

(4) allocates between the parents, independently, jointly, or exclusively, all of the remaining rights and duties of a parent provided by Chapter 151;

(5) is voluntarily and knowingly made by each parent and has not been repudiated by either parent at the time the order is rendered; and

(6) is in the best interest of the child.

(b) The agreed parenting plan may contain an alternative dispute resolution procedure that the parties agree to use before requesting enforcement or modification of the terms and conditions of the joint conservatorship through litigation, except in an emergency.

(c) Notwithstanding Subsection (a)(1), the court shall render an order adopting the provisions of a written agreed parenting plan appointing the parents as joint managing conservators if the parenting plan:

(1) meets all the requirements of Subsections (a)(2) through (6); and

(2) provides that the child's primary residence shall be within a specified geographic area.

Added by Acts 1995, 74th Leg., ch. 20, § 1, eff. April 20, 1995. Amended by Acts 1999, 76th Leg., ch. 936, § 1, eff. Sept. 1, 1999; Acts 2003, 78th Leg., ch. 1036, § 10, eff. Sept. 1, 2003; Acts 2005, 79th Leg., ch. 482, § 4, eff. Sept. 1, 2005; Acts 2007, 80th Leg., ch. 1181, § 3, eff. Sept. 1, 2007; Acts 2009, 81st Leg., ch. 1113, § 3, eff. Sept. 1, 2009.

**§ 153.134. Court-Ordered Joint Conservatorship**

(a) If a written agreed parenting plan is not filed with the court, the court may render an order appointing the parents joint managing conservators only if the appointment is in the best interest of the child, considering the following factors:

(1) whether the physical, psychological, or emotional needs and development of the child will benefit from the appointment of joint managing conservators;

(2) the ability of the parents to give first priority to the welfare of the child and reach shared decisions in the child's best interest;

(3) whether each parent can encourage and accept a positive relationship between the child and the other parent;

(4) whether both parents participated in child rearing before the filing of the suit;

(5) the geographical proximity of the parents' residences;

(6) if the child is 12 years of age or older, the child's preference, if any, regarding the person to have the exclusive right to designate the primary residence of the child; and

(7) any other relevant factor.

(b) In rendering an order appointing joint managing conservators, the court shall:

(1) designate the conservator who has the exclusive right to determine the primary residence of the child and:

(A) establish, until modified by further order, a geographic area within which the conservator shall maintain the child's primary residence; or

(B) specify that the conservator may determine the child's primary residence without regard to geographic location;

(2) specify the rights and duties of each parent regarding the child's physical care, support, and education;

(3) include provisions to minimize disruption of the child's education, daily routine, and association with friends;

(4) allocate between the parents, independently, jointly, or exclusively, all of the remaining rights and duties of a parent as provided by Chapter 151; and

(5) if feasible, recommend that the parties use an alternative dispute resolution method before requesting enforcement or modification of the terms and conditions of the joint conservatorship through litigation, except in an emergency.

Added by Acts 1995, 74th Leg., ch. 20, § 1, eff. April 20, 1995. Amended by Acts 1999, 76th Leg., ch. 936, § 2, eff. Sept. 1, 1999; Acts 2003, 78th Leg., ch. 1036, § 11, eff. Sept. 1, 2003; Acts 2005, 79th Leg., ch. 482, § 5, eff. Sept. 1, 2005; Acts 2005, 79th Leg., ch. 916, § 11, eff. June 18, 2005.

**§ 153.135. Equal Possession Not Required**

Joint managing conservatorship does not require the award of equal or nearly equal periods of physical possession of and access to the child to each of the joint conservators.

Added by Acts 1995, 74th Leg., ch. 20, § 1, eff. April 20, 1995.

**§ 153.136. Repealed by Acts 2003, 78th Leg., ch. 1036, § 22, eff. Sept. 1, 2003**

**§ 153.137. Repealed by Acts 2009, 81st Leg., ch. 1113, § 31, eff. Sept. 1, 2009**

**§ 153.138. Child Support Order Affecting Joint Conservators**

The appointment of joint managing conservators does not impair or limit the authority of the court to order a joint managing conservator to pay child support to another joint managing conservator.

Added by Acts 1995, 74th Leg., ch. 20, § 1, eff. April 20, 1995.

**§ 153.139. Repealed by Acts 1997, 75th Leg., ch. 561, § 30, eff. Sept. 1, 1997**

## SUBCHAPTER D. PARENT APPOINTED AS POSSESSORY CONSERVATOR

**§ 153.191. Presumption that Parent to be Appointed Possessory Conservator**

The court shall appoint as a possessory conservator a parent who is not appointed as a sole or joint managing conservator unless it finds that the appointment is not in the best interest of the child and that parental possession or access would endanger the physical or emotional welfare of the child.

Added by Acts 1995, 74th Leg., ch. 20, § 1, eff. April 20, 1995.

**§ 153.192. Rights and Duties of Parent Appointed Possessory Conservator**

(a) Unless limited by court order, a parent appointed as possessory conservator of a child has the rights and duties provided by Subchapter B [1] and any other right or duty expressly granted to the possessory conservator in the order.

(b) In ordering the terms and conditions for possession of a child by a parent appointed possessory conservator, the court shall be guided by the guidelines in Subchapter E.[2]

Added by Acts 1995, 74th Leg., ch. 20, § 1, eff. April 20, 1995.

[1] V.T.C.A., Family Code § 153.071 et seq.

[2] V.T.C.A., Family Code § 153.251 et seq.

### § 153.193. Minimal Restriction on Parent's Possession or Access

The terms of an order that denies possession of a child to a parent or imposes restrictions or limitations on a parent's right to possession of or access to a child may not exceed those that are required to protect the best interest of the child.

Added by Acts 1995, 74th Leg., ch. 20, § 1, eff. April 20, 1995.

## SUBCHAPTER E. GUIDELINES FOR THE POSSESSION OF A CHILD BY A PARENT NAMED AS POSSESSORY CONSERVATOR

### § 153.251. Policy and General Application of Guidelines

(a) The guidelines established in the standard possession order are intended to guide the courts in ordering the terms and conditions for possession of a child by a parent named as a possessory conservator or as the minimum possession for a joint managing conservator.

(b) It is the policy of this state to encourage frequent contact between a child and each parent for periods of possession that optimize the development of a close and continuing relationship between each parent and child.

(c) It is preferable for all children in a family to be together during periods of possession.

(d) The standard possession order is designed to apply to a child three years of age or older.

Added by Acts 1995, 74th Leg., ch. 20, § 1, eff. April 20, 1995.

### § 153.252. Rebuttable Presumption

In a suit, there is a rebuttable presumption that the standard possession order in Subchapter F:[1]

(1) provides reasonable minimum possession of a child for a parent named as a possessory conservator or joint managing conservator; and

(2) is in the best interest of the child.

Added by Acts 1995, 74th Leg., ch. 20, § 1, eff. April 20, 1995.

[1] V.T.C.A., Family Code § 153.3101 et seq.

### § 153.253. Standard Possession Order Inappropriate or Unworkable

The court shall render an order that grants periods of possession of the child as similar as possible to those provided by the standard possession order if the work schedule or other special circumstances of the managing conservator, the possessory conservator, or the child, or the year-round school schedule of the child, make the standard order unworkable or inappropriate.

Added by Acts 1995, 74th Leg., ch. 20, § 1, eff. April 20, 1995.

### § 153.254. Child Less Than Three Years of Age

(a) The court shall render an order appropriate under the circumstances for possession of a child less than three years of age. In rendering the order, the court shall consider evidence of all relevant factors, including:

(1) the caregiving provided to the child before and during the current suit;

(2) the effect on the child that may result from separation from either party;

(3) the availability of the parties as caregivers and the willingness of the parties to personally care for the child;

(4) the physical, medical, behavioral, and developmental needs of the child;

(5) the physical, medical, emotional, economic, and social conditions of the parties;

(6) the impact and influence of individuals, other than the parties, who will be present during periods of possession;

(7) the presence of siblings during periods of possession;

(8) the child's need to develop healthy attachments to both parents;

(9) the child's need for continuity of routine;

(10) the location and proximity of the residences of the parties;

(11) the need for a temporary possession schedule that incrementally shifts to the schedule provid-

ed in the prospective order under Subsection (d) based on:

(A) the age of the child; or

(B) minimal or inconsistent contact with the child by a party;

(12) the ability of the parties to share in the responsibilities, rights, and duties of parenting; and

(13) any other evidence of the best interest of the child.

(b) Repealed by Acts 2017, 85th Leg., ch. 421 (S.B. 1237), § 12(1).

(c) Repealed by Acts 2017, 85th Leg., ch. 421 (S.B. 1237), § 12(1).

(d) The court shall render a prospective order to take effect on the child's third birthday, which presumptively will be the standard possession order.

Added by Acts 1995, 74th Leg., ch. 20, § 1, eff. April 20, 1995. Amended by Acts 2011, 82nd Leg., ch. 86 (S.B. 820), § 1, eff. Sept. 1, 2011; Acts 2017, 85th Leg., ch. 421 (S.B. 1237), § 12(1), eff. Sept. 1, 2017.

### § 153.255. Agreement

The court may render an order for periods of possession of a child that vary from the standard possession order based on the agreement of the parties.

Added by Acts 1995, 74th Leg., ch. 20, § 1, eff. April 20, 1995.

### § 153.256. Factors for Court to Consider

In ordering the terms of possession of a child under an order other than a standard possession order, the court shall be guided by the guidelines established by the standard possession order and may consider:

(1) the age, developmental status, circumstances, needs, and best interest of the child;

(2) the circumstances of the managing conservator and of the parent named as a possessory conservator; and

(3) any other relevant factor.

Added by Acts 1995, 74th Leg., ch. 20, § 1, eff. April 20, 1995. Amended by Acts 1995, 74th Leg., ch. 751, § 35, eff. Sept. 1, 1995.

### § 153.257. Means of Travel

In an order providing for the terms and conditions of possession of a child, the court may restrict the means of travel of the child by a legal mode of transportation only after a showing of good cause contained in the record and a finding by the court that the restriction is in the best interest of the child. The court shall specify the duties of the conservators to provide transportation to and from the transportation facilities.

Added by Acts 1995, 74th Leg., ch. 20, § 1, eff. April 20, 1995.

### § 153.258. Request for Findings When Order Varies from Standard Order

(a) In all cases in which possession of a child by a parent is contested and the possession of the child varies from the standard possession order, including a possession order for a child under three years of age, on request by a party, the court shall state in writing the specific reasons for the variance from the standard order.

(b) A request for findings of fact under this section must conform to the Texas Rules of Civil Procedure.

Added by Acts 1995, 74th Leg., ch. 20, § 1, eff. April 20, 1995. Amended by Acts 2017, 85th Leg., ch. 421 (S.B. 1237), § 9, eff. Sept. 1, 2017.

## SUBCHAPTER F. STANDARD POSSESSION ORDER

### § 153.3101. Reference to "School" in Standard Possession Order

In a standard possession order, "school" means the elementary or secondary school in which the child is enrolled or, if the child is not enrolled in an elementary or secondary school, the public school district in which the child primarily resides.

Added by Acts 2009, 81st Leg., ch. 1113, § 4, eff. Sept. 1, 2009. Amended by Acts 2015, 84th Leg., ch. 1167 (S.B. 821), § 3, eff. Sept. 1, 2015.

### § 153.311. Mutual Agreement or Specified Terms for Possession

The court shall specify in a standard possession order that the parties may have possession of the child at times mutually agreed to in advance by the parties and, in the absence of mutual agreement, shall have possession of the child under the specified terms set out in the standard possession order.

Added by Acts 1995, 74th Leg., ch. 20, § 1, eff. April 20, 1995. Amended by Acts 2009, 81st Leg., ch. 1113, § 5, eff. Sept. 1, 2009.

### § 153.312. Parents Who Reside 100 Miles or Less Apart

(a) If the possessory conservator resides 100 miles or less from the primary residence of the child, the possessory conservator shall have the right to possession of the child as follows:

(1) on weekends throughout the year beginning at 6 p.m. on the first, third, and fifth Friday of each month and ending at 6 p.m. on the following Sunday; and

(2) on Thursdays of each week during the regular school term beginning at 6 p.m. and ending at 8 p.m., unless the court finds that visitation under this subdivision is not in the best interest of the child.

(b) The following provisions govern possession of the child for vacations and certain specific holidays and supersede conflicting weekend or Thursday periods of possession. The possessory conservator and the managing conservator shall have rights of possession of the child as follows:

(1) the possessory conservator shall have possession in even-numbered years, beginning at 6 p.m. on the day the child is dismissed from school for the school's spring vacation and ending at 6 p.m. on the day before school resumes after that vacation, and the managing conservator shall have possession for the same period in odd-numbered years;

(2) if a possessory conservator:

(A) gives the managing conservator written notice by April 1 of each year specifying an extended period or periods of summer possession, the possessory conservator shall have possession of the child for 30 days beginning not earlier than the day after the child's school is dismissed for the summer vacation and ending not later than seven days before school resumes at the end of the summer vacation, to be exercised in not more than two separate periods of at least seven consecutive days each, with each period of possession beginning and ending at 6 p.m. on each applicable day; or

(B) does not give the managing conservator written notice by April 1 of each year specifying an extended period or periods of summer possession, the possessory conservator shall have possession of the child for 30 consecutive days beginning at 6 p.m. on July 1 and ending at 6 p.m. on July 31;

(3) if the managing conservator gives the possessory conservator written notice by April 15 of each year, the managing conservator shall have possession of the child on any one weekend beginning Friday at 6 p.m. and ending at 6 p.m. on the following Sunday during one period of possession by the possessory conservator under Subdivision (2), provided that the managing conservator picks up the child from the possessory conservator and returns the child to that same place; and

(4) if the managing conservator gives the possessory conservator written notice by April 15 of each year or gives the possessory conservator 14 days' written notice on or after April 16 of each year, the managing conservator may designate one weekend beginning not earlier than the day after the child's school is dismissed for the summer vacation and ending not later than seven days before school resumes at the end of the summer vacation, during which an otherwise scheduled weekend period of possession by the possessory conservator will not take place, provided that the weekend designated does not interfere with the possessory conservator's period or periods of extended summer possession or with Father's Day if the possessory conservator is the father of the child.

(c) Notwithstanding Section 153.316, after receiving notice from the managing conservator under Subsection (b)(3) of this section designating the summer weekend during which the managing conservator is to have possession of the child, the possessory conservator, not later than the 15th day before the Friday that begins that designated weekend, must give the managing conservator written notice of the location at which the managing conservator is to pick up and return the child.

Added by Acts 1995, 74th Leg., ch. 20, § 1, eff. April 20, 1995. Amended by Acts 1997, 75th Leg., ch. 802, § 1, eff. Sept. 1, 1997; Acts 1999, 76th Leg., ch. 236, § 1, eff. Sept. 1, 1999; Acts 2003, 78th Leg., ch. 1036, § 13, eff. Sept. 1, 2003; Acts 2005, 79th Leg., ch. 916, § 12, eff. June 18, 2005; Acts 2007, 80th Leg., ch. 1041, § 2, eff. June 15, 2007; Acts 2009, 81st Leg., ch. 1113, § 6, eff. Sept. 1, 2009; Acts 2019, 86th Leg., ch. 358 (H.B. 553), § 1, eff. Sept. 1, 2019.

Section 2 of Acts 2019, 86th Leg., ch. 358 (H.B. 553) provides:

"Section 153.312(c), Family Code, as added by this Act, applies only to a court order providing for possession of or access to a child rendered on or after the effective date [Sept. 1, 2019] of this Act. A court order rendered before the effective date of this Act is governed by the law in effect on the date the order was rendered, and the former law is continued in effect for that purpose."

### § 153.313. Parents Who Reside Over 100 Miles Apart

If the possessory conservator resides more than 100 miles from the residence of the child, the possessory conservator shall have the right to possession of the child as follows:

(1) either regular weekend possession beginning on the first, third, and fifth Friday as provided under the terms applicable to parents who reside 100 miles or less apart or not more than one

weekend per month of the possessory conservator's choice beginning at 6 p.m. on the day school recesses for the weekend and ending at 6 p.m. on the day before school resumes after the weekend, provided that the possessory conservator gives the managing conservator 14 days' written or telephonic notice preceding a designated weekend, and provided that the possessory conservator elects an option for this alternative period of possession by written notice given to the managing conservator within 90 days after the parties begin to reside more than 100 miles apart, as applicable;

(2) each year beginning at 6 p.m. on the day the child is dismissed from school for the school's spring vacation and ending at 6 p.m. on the day before school resumes after that vacation;

(3) if the possessory conservator:

(A) gives the managing conservator written notice by April 1 of each year specifying an extended period or periods of summer possession, the possessory conservator shall have possession of the child for 42 days beginning not earlier than the day after the child's school is dismissed for the summer vacation and ending not later than seven days before school resumes at the end of the summer vacation, to be exercised in not more than two separate periods of at least seven consecutive days each, with each period of possession beginning and ending at 6 p.m. on each applicable day; or

(B) does not give the managing conservator written notice by April 1 of each year specifying an extended period or periods of summer possession, the possessory conservator shall have possession of the child for 42 consecutive days beginning at 6 p.m. on June 15 and ending at 6 p.m. on July 27;

(4) if the managing conservator gives the possessory conservator written notice by April 15 of each year the managing conservator shall have possession of the child on one weekend beginning Friday at 6 p.m. and ending at 6 p.m. on the following Sunday during one period of possession by the possessory conservator under Subdivision (3), provided that if a period of possession by the possessory conservator exceeds 30 days, the managing conservator may have possession of the child under the terms of this subdivision on two nonconsecutive weekends during that time period, and further provided that the managing conservator picks up the child from the possessory conservator and returns the child to that same place; and

(5) if the managing conservator gives the possessory conservator written notice by April 15 of each year, the managing conservator may designate 21 days beginning not earlier than the day after the child's school is dismissed for the summer vacation and ending not later than seven days before school resumes at the end of the summer vacation, to be exercised in not more than two separate periods of at least seven consecutive days each, with each period of possession beginning and ending at 6 p.m. on each applicable day, during which the possessory conservator may not have possession of the child, provided that the period or periods so designated do not interfere with the possessory conservator's period or periods of extended summer possession or with Father's Day if the possessory conservator is the father of the child.

Added by Acts 1995, 74th Leg., ch. 20, § 1, eff. April 20, 1995. Amended by Acts 1995, 74th Leg., ch. 751, § 36, eff. Sept. 1, 1995; Acts 1999, 76th Leg., ch. 236, § 2, eff. Sept. 1, 1999; Acts 2009, 81st Leg., ch. 1113, § 7, eff. Sept. 1, 2009.

### § 153.314. Holiday Possession Unaffected by Distance Parents Reside Apart

The following provisions govern possession of the child for certain specific holidays and supersede conflicting weekend or Thursday periods of possession without regard to the distance the parents reside apart. The possessory conservator and the managing conservator shall have rights of possession of the child as follows:

(1) the possessory conservator shall have possession of the child in even-numbered years beginning at 6 p.m. on the day the child is dismissed from school for the Christmas school vacation and ending at noon on December 28, and the managing conservator shall have possession for the same period in odd-numbered years;

(2) the possessory conservator shall have possession of the child in odd-numbered years beginning at noon on December 28 and ending at 6 p.m. on the day before school resumes after that vacation, and the managing conservator shall have possession for the same period in even-numbered years;

(3) the possessory conservator shall have possession of the child in odd-numbered years, beginning at 6 p.m. on the day the child is dismissed from school before Thanksgiving and ending at 6 p.m. on the following Sunday, and the managing conservator shall have possession for the same period in even-numbered years;

(4) the parent not otherwise entitled under this standard possession order to present possession of a child on the child's birthday shall have possession of the child beginning at 6 p.m. and ending at 8 p.m. on that day, provided that the parent picks up the child from the residence of the conservator entitled to possession and returns the child to that same place;

(5) if a conservator, the father shall have possession of the child beginning at 6 p.m. on the Friday preceding Father's Day and ending on Father's Day at 6 p.m., provided that, if he is not otherwise entitled under this standard possession order to present possession of the child, he picks up the child from the residence of the conservator entitled to possession and returns the child to that same place; and

(6) if a conservator, the mother shall have possession of the child beginning at 6 p.m. on the Friday preceding Mother's Day and ending on Mother's Day at 6 p.m., provided that, if she is not otherwise entitled under this standard possession order to present possession of the child, she picks up the child from the residence of the conservator entitled to possession and returns the child to that same place.

Added by Acts 1995, 74th Leg., ch. 20, § 1, eff. April 20, 1995. Amended by Acts 2003, 78th Leg., ch. 1036, § 14, eff. Sept. 1, 2003; Acts 2007, 80th Leg., ch. 1041, § 3, eff. June 15, 2007; Acts 2009, 81st Leg., ch. 1113, § 8, eff. Sept. 1, 2009.

### § 153.315. Weekend Possession Extended by Holiday

(a) If a weekend period of possession of the possessory conservator coincides with a student holiday or teacher in-service day that falls on a Monday during the regular school term, as determined by the school in which the child is enrolled, or with a federal, state, or local holiday that falls on a Monday during the summer months in which school is not in session, the weekend possession shall end at 6 p.m. on Monday.

(b) If a weekend period of possession of the possessory conservator coincides with a student holiday or teacher in-service day that falls on a Friday during the regular school term, as determined by the school in which the child is enrolled, or with a federal, state, or local holiday that falls on a Friday during the summer months in which school is not in session, the weekend possession shall begin at 6 p.m. on Thursday.

Added by Acts 1995, 74th Leg., ch. 20, § 1, eff. April 20, 1995. Amended by Acts 2009, 81st Leg., ch. 1113, § 9, eff. Sept. 1, 2009.

### § 153.316. General Terms and Conditions

The court shall order the following general terms and conditions of possession of a child to apply without regard to the distance between the residence of a parent and the child:

(1) the managing conservator shall surrender the child to the possessory conservator at the beginning of each period of the possessory conservator's possession at the residence of the managing conservator;

(2) if the possessory conservator elects to begin a period of possession at the time the child's school is regularly dismissed, the managing conservator shall surrender the child to the possessory conservator at the beginning of each period of possession at the school in which the child is enrolled;

(3) the possessory conservator shall be ordered to do one of the following:

(A) the possessory conservator shall surrender the child to the managing conservator at the end of each period of possession at the residence of the possessory conservator; or

(B) the possessory conservator shall return the child to the residence of the managing conservator at the end of each period of possession, except that the order shall provide that the possessory conservator shall surrender the child to the managing conservator at the end of each period of possession at the residence of the possessory conservator if:

(i) at the time the original order or a modification of an order establishing terms and conditions of possession or access the possessory conservator and the managing conservator lived in the same county, the possessory conservator's county of residence remains the same after the rendition of the order, and the managing conservator's county of residence changes, effective on the date of the change of residence by the managing conservator; or

(ii) the possessory conservator and managing conservator lived in the same residence at any time during a six-month period preceding the date on which a suit for dissolution of the marriage was filed and the possessory conservator's county of residence remains the same and the managing conservator's county of residence changes after they no longer live in the same residence, effective on the date the order is rendered;

(4) if the possessory conservator elects to end a period of possession at the time the child's school resumes, the possessory conservator shall surrender the child to the managing conservator at the

end of each period of possession at the school in which the child is enrolled;

(5) each conservator shall return with the child the personal effects that the child brought at the beginning of the period of possession;

(6) either parent may designate a competent adult to pick up and return the child, as applicable; a parent or a designated competent adult shall be present when the child is picked up or returned;

(7) a parent shall give notice to the person in possession of the child on each occasion that the parent will be unable to exercise that parent's right of possession for a specified period;

(8) written notice, including notice provided by electronic mail or facsimile, shall be deemed to have been timely made if received or, if applicable, postmarked before or at the time that notice is due; and

(9) if a conservator's time of possession of a child ends at the time school resumes and for any reason the child is not or will not be returned to school, the conservator in possession of the child shall immediately notify the school and the other conservator that the child will not be or has not been returned to school.

Added by Acts 1995, 74th Leg., ch. 20, § 1, eff. April 20, 1995. Amended by Acts 1995, 74th Leg., ch. 751, § 37, eff. Sept. 1, 1995; Acts 1997, 75th Leg., ch. 9, § 1, eff. Sept. 1, 1997; Acts 2013, 83rd Leg., ch. 277 (H.B. 845), § 1, eff. Sept. 1, 2013.

**§ 153.3161. Repealed by Acts 2009, 81st Leg., ch. 727, § 6; Acts 2009, 81st Leg., ch. 1113, § 31, eff. Sept. 1, 2009**

**§ 153.3162. Repealed by Acts 2013, 83rd Leg., ch. 277 (H.B. 845), § 3, eff. Sept. 1, 2013**

**§ 153.317. Alternative Beginning and Ending Possession Times**

(a) If elected by a conservator, the court shall alter the standard possession order under Sections 153.312, 153.314, and 153.315 to provide for one or more of the following alternative beginning and ending possession times for the described periods of possession, unless the court finds that the election is not in the best interest of the child:

(1) for weekend periods of possession under Section 153.312(a)(1) during the regular school term:

(A) beginning at the time the child's school is regularly dismissed;

(B) ending at the time the child's school resumes after the weekend; or

(C) beginning at the time described by Paragraph (A) and ending at the time described by Paragraph (B);

(2) for Thursday periods of possession under Section 153.312(a)(2):

(A) beginning at the time the child's school is regularly dismissed;

(B) ending at the time the child's school resumes on Friday; or

(C) beginning at the time described by Paragraph (A) and ending at the time described by Paragraph (B);

(3) for spring vacation periods of possession under Section 153.312(b)(1), beginning at the time the child's school is dismissed for those vacations;

(4) for Christmas school vacation periods of possession under Section 153.314(1), beginning at the time the child's school is dismissed for the vacation;

(5) for Thanksgiving holiday periods of possession under Section 153.314(3), beginning at the time the child's school is dismissed for the holiday;

(6) for Father's Day periods of possession under Section 153.314(5), ending at 8 a.m. on the Monday after Father's Day weekend;

(7) for Mother's Day periods of possession under Section 153.314(6):

(A) beginning at the time the child's school is regularly dismissed on the Friday preceding Mother's Day;

(B) ending at the time the child's school resumes after Mother's Day; or

(C) beginning at the time described by Paragraph (A) and ending at the time described by Paragraph (B);

(8) for weekend periods of possession that are extended under Section 153.315(b) by a student holiday or teacher in-service day that falls on a Friday, beginning at the time the child's school is regularly dismissed on Thursday; or

(9) for weekend periods of possession that are extended under Section 153.315(a) by a student holiday or teacher in-service day that falls on a Monday, ending at 8 a.m. Tuesday.

(b) A conservator must make an election under Subsection (a) before or at the time of the rendition of a possession order. The election may be made:

(1) in a written document filed with the court; or

(2) through an oral statement made in open court on the record.

Added by Acts 1995, 74th Leg., ch. 20, § 1, eff. April 20, 1995. Amended by Acts 1997, 75th Leg., ch. 9, § 1, eff. Sept. 1, 1997; Acts 2003, 78th Leg., ch. 1036, § 15, eff. Sept. 1, 2003; Acts 2009, 81st Leg., ch. 1113, § 10, eff. Sept. 1, 2009; Acts 2013, 83rd Leg., ch. 277 (H.B. 845), § 2, eff. Sept. 1, 2013; Acts 2021, 87th Leg., ch. 896 (H.B. 3203), § 1, eff. Sept. 1, 2021; Acts 2021, 87th Leg., ch. 967 (S.B. 1936), § 2, eff. Sept. 1, 2021.

Sections 4 and 5 of Acts 2021, 87th Leg., ch. 896 (H.B. 3203) provide:

"Sec. 4. The enactment of this Act does not constitute a material and substantial change of circumstances sufficient to warrant modification of a court order or portion of a decree that provides for the possession of or access to a child rendered before the effective date [Sept. 1, 2021] of this Act."

"Sec. 5. The change in law made by this Act applies to a suit affecting the parent-child relationship that is pending in a trial court on the effective date of this Act or that is filed on or after the effective date [Sept. 1, 2021] of this Act."

Sections 4 and 5 of Acts 2021, 87th Leg., ch. 967 (S.B. 1936) provide:

"Sec. 4. The enactment of this Act does not constitute a material and substantial change of circumstances sufficient to warrant modification of a court order or portion of a decree that provides for the possession of or access to a child rendered before the effective date [Sept. 1, 2021] of this Act."

"Sec. 5. The change in law made by this Act applies to a suit affecting the parent-child relationship that is pending in a trial court on the effective date [Sept. 1, 2021] of this Act or that is filed on or after the effective date of this Act."

### § 153.3171. Beginning and Ending Possession Times for Parents Who Reside 50 Miles or Less Apart

(a) Except as provided by Subsection (b), if the possessory conservator resides not more than 50 miles from the primary residence of the child, the court shall alter the standard possession order under Sections 153.312, 153.314, and 153.315 to provide that the conservator has the right to possession of the child as if the conservator had made the elections for alternative beginning and ending possession times under Sections 153.317(a)(1)(C), (2)(C), (3), (4), (5), (6), (7)(C), (8), and (9).

(b) Subsection (a) does not apply if:

(1) the possessory conservator declines one or more of the alternative beginning and ending possession times under Subsection (a) in a written document filed with the court or through an oral statement made in open court on the record;

(2) the court is denying, restricting, or limiting the possessory conservator's possession of or access to the child in the best interest of the child under Section 153.004; or

(3) the court finds that one or more of the alternative beginning and ending possession times under Subsection (a) are not in the best interest of the child, including:

(A) because the distances between residences make the possession schedule described by Subsection (a) unworkable or inappropriate considering the circumstances of the parties or the area in which the parties reside;

(B) because before the filing of the suit, the possessory conservator did not frequently and continuously exercise the rights and duties of a parent with respect to the child; or

(C) for any other reason the court considers relevant.

(c) On the request of a party, the court shall make findings of fact and conclusions of law regarding the order under this section.

Added by Acts 2021, 87th Leg., ch. 896 (H.B. 3203), § 2, eff. Sept. 1, 2021; Acts 2021, 87th Leg., ch. 967 (S.B. 1936), § 1, eff. Sept. 1, 2021.

Sections 4 and 5 of Acts 2021, 87th Leg., ch. 896 (H.B. 3203) provide:

"Sec. 4. The enactment of this Act does not constitute a material and substantial change of circumstances sufficient to warrant modification of a court order or portion of a decree that provides for the possession of or access to a child rendered before the effective date [Sept. 1, 2021] of this Act.

"Sec. 5. The change in law made by this Act applies to a suit affecting the parent-child relationship that is pending in a trial court on the effective date of this Act or that is filed on or after the effective date of this Act."

Sections 4 and 5 of Acts 2021, 87th Leg., ch. 967 (S.B. 1936) provide:

"Sec. 4. The enactment of this Act does not constitute a material and substantial change of circumstances sufficient to warrant modification of a court order or portion of a decree that provides for the possession of or access to a child rendered before the effective date [Sept. 1, 2021] of this Act.

"Sec. 5. The change in law made by this Act applies to a suit affecting the parent-child relationship that is pending in a trial court on the effective date of this Act or that is filed on or after the effective date of this Act."

## SUBCHAPTER G. APPOINTMENT OF NONPARENT AS CONSERVATOR

### § 153.371. Rights and Duties of Nonparent Appointed as Sole Managing Conservator

Unless limited by court order or other provisions of this chapter, a nonparent, a licensed child-placing agency, or the Department of Family and Protective Services appointed as a managing conservator of the child has the following rights and duties:

(1) the right to have physical possession and to direct the moral and religious training of the child;

(2) the duty of care, control, protection, and reasonable discipline of the child;

(3) the duty to provide the child with clothing, food, shelter, education, and medical, psychological, and dental care;

(4) the right to consent for the child to medical, psychiatric, psychological, dental, and surgical treatment and to have access to the child's medical records;

(5) the right to receive and give receipt for payments for the support of the child and to hold or disburse funds for the benefit of the child;

(6) the right to the services and earnings of the child;

(7) the right to consent to marriage and to enlistment in the armed forces of the United States;

(8) the right to represent the child in legal action and to make other decisions of substantial legal significance concerning the child;

(9) except when a guardian of the child's estate or a guardian or attorney ad litem has been appointed for the child, the right to act as an agent of the child in relation to the child's estate if the child's action is required by a state, the United States, or a foreign government;

(10) the right to designate the primary residence of the child and to make decisions regarding the child's education;

(11) if the parent-child relationship has been terminated with respect to the parents, or only living parent, or if there is no living parent, the right to consent to the adoption of the child and to make any other decision concerning the child that a parent could make; and

(12) the right to:

(A) apply for a passport for the child;

(B) renew the child's passport; and

(C) maintain possession of the child's passport.

Added by Acts 1995, 74th Leg., ch. 20, § 1, eff. April 20, 1995. Amended by Acts 1995, 74th Leg., ch. 751, § 34, eff. Sept. 1, 1995; Acts 1999, 76th Leg., ch. 949, § 1, eff. Sept. 1, 1999; Acts 2003, 78th Leg., ch. 1036, § 16, eff. Sept. 1, 2003; Acts 2015, 84th Leg., ch. 1 (S.B. 219), § 1.044, eff. April 2, 2015; Acts 2019, 86th Leg., ch. 733 (H.B. 555), § 2, eff. Sept. 1, 2019.

Section 3 of Acts 2019, 86th Leg., ch. 733 (H.B. 555) provides:

"The changes in law made by this Act apply only to a suit affecting the parent-child relationship that is pending in a trial court on or filed on or after the effective date [Sept. 1, 2019] of this Act."

### § 153.372. Nonparent Appointed as Joint Managing Conservator

(a) A nonparent, the Department of Family and Protective Services, or a licensed child-placing agency appointed as a joint managing conservator may serve in that capacity with either another nonparent or with a parent of the child.

(b) The procedural and substantive standards regarding an agreed or court-ordered joint managing conservatorship provided by Subchapter C [1] apply to a nonparent joint managing conservator.

Added by Acts 1995, 74th Leg., ch. 20, § 1, eff. April 20, 1995. Amended by Acts 2015, 84th Leg., ch. 1 (S.B. 219), § 1.045, eff. April 2, 2015.

[1] V.T.C.A., Family Code § 153.131 et seq.

### § 153.3721. Access to Certain Records by Nonparent Joint Managing Conservator

Unless limited by court order or other provisions of this chapter, a nonparent joint managing conservator has the right of access to the medical records of the child, without regard to whether the right is specified in the order.

Added by Acts 1999, 76th Leg., ch. 949, § 2, eff. Sept. 1, 1999.

### § 153.373. Voluntary Surrender of Possession Rebuts Parental Presumption

The presumption that a parent should be appointed or retained as managing conservator of the child is rebutted if the court finds that:

(1) the parent has voluntarily relinquished actual care, control, and possession of the child to a nonparent, a licensed child-placing agency, or the Department of Family and Protective Services for a period of one year or more, a portion of which was within 90 days preceding the date of intervention in or filing of the suit; and

(2) the appointment of the nonparent, agency, or Department of Family and Protective Services as managing conservator is in the best interest of the child.

Added by Acts 1995, 74th Leg., ch. 20, § 1, eff. April 20, 1995. Amended by Acts 2015, 84th Leg., ch. 1 (S.B. 219), § 1.046, eff. April 2, 2015.

### § 153.374. Designation of Managing Conservator in Affidavit of Relinquishment

(a) A parent may designate a competent person, the Department of Family and Protective Services, or a licensed child-placing agency to serve as managing conservator of the child in an unrevoked or irrevocable affidavit of relinquishment of parental rights executed as provided by Chapter 161.

(b) The person, Department of Family and Protective Services, or agency designated to serve as managing conservator shall be appointed managing conservator unless the court finds that the appointment would not be in the best interest of the child.

Added by Acts 1995, 74th Leg., ch. 20, § 1, eff. April 20, 1995. Amended by Acts 1995, 74th Leg., ch. 751, § 38, eff. Sept. 1, 1995; Acts 2015, 84th Leg., ch. 1 (S.B. 219), § 1.047, eff. April 2, 2015.

### § 153.375. Annual Report by Nonparent Managing Conservator

(a) A nonparent appointed as a managing conservator of a child shall each 12 months after the appointment file with the court a report of facts concerning the child's welfare, including the child's whereabouts and physical condition.

(b) The report may not be admitted in evidence in a subsequent suit.

Added by Acts 1995, 74th Leg., ch. 20, § 1, eff. April 20, 1995.

### § 153.376. Rights and Duties of Nonparent Possessory Conservator

(a) Unless limited by court order or other provisions of this chapter, a nonparent, a licensed child-placing agency, or the Department of Family and Protective Services appointed as a possessory conservator has the following rights and duties during the period of possession:

(1) the duty of care, control, protection, and reasonable discipline of the child;

(2) the duty to provide the child with clothing, food, and shelter; and

(3) the right to consent to medical, dental, and surgical treatment during an emergency involving an immediate danger to the health and safety of the child.

(b) A nonparent possessory conservator has any other right or duty specified in the order.

Added by Acts 1995, 74th Leg., ch. 20, § 1, eff. April 20, 1995. Amended by Acts 2015, 84th Leg., ch. 1 (S.B. 219), § 1.048, eff. April 2, 2015.

### § 153.377. Access to Child's Records

A nonparent possessory conservator has the right of access to medical, dental, psychological, and educational records of the child to the same extent as the managing conservator, without regard to whether the right is specified in the order.

Added by Acts 1995, 74th Leg., ch. 20, § 1, eff. April 20, 1995.

## SUBCHAPTER H. RIGHTS OF GRANDPARENT, AUNT, OR UNCLE

### § 153.431. Appointment of Grandparent, Aunt, or Uncle as Managing Conservator

If both of the parents of a child are deceased, the court may consider appointment of a parent, sister, or brother of a deceased parent as a managing conservator of the child, but that consideration does not alter or diminish the discretionary power of the court.

Added by Acts 1995, 74th Leg., ch. 20, § 1, eff. April 20, 1995. Amended by Acts 2005, 79th Leg., ch. 484, § 2, eff. Sept. 1, 2005.

### § 153.432. Suit for Possession or Access by Grandparent

(a) A biological or adoptive grandparent may request possession of or access to a grandchild by filing:

(1) an original suit; or

(2) a suit for modification as provided by Chapter 156.

(b) A grandparent may request possession of or access to a grandchild in a suit filed for the sole purpose of requesting the relief, without regard to whether the appointment of a managing conservator is an issue in the suit.

(c) In a suit described by Subsection (a), the person filing the suit must execute and attach an affidavit on knowledge or belief that contains, along with supporting facts, the allegation that denial of possession of or access to the child by the petitioner would significantly impair the child's physical health or emotional well-being. The court shall deny the relief sought and dismiss the suit unless the court determines that the facts stated in the affidavit, if true, would be sufficient to support the relief authorized under Section 153.433.

Added by Acts 1995, 74th Leg., ch. 20, § 1, eff. April 20, 1995. Amended by Acts 2005, 79th Leg., ch. 484, § 3, eff. Sept. 1, 2005; Acts 2009, 81st Leg., ch. 1113, § 11, eff. Sept. 1, 2009.

### § 153.433. Possession of or Access to Grandchild

(a) The court may order reasonable possession of or access to a grandchild by a grandparent if:

(1) at the time the relief is requested, at least one biological or adoptive parent of the child has not had that parent's parental rights terminated;

(2) the grandparent requesting possession of or access to the child overcomes the presumption that a parent acts in the best interest of the parent's child by proving by a preponderance of the evidence that denial of possession of or access to the child would significantly impair the child's physical health or emotional well-being; and

(3) the grandparent requesting possession of or access to the child is a parent of a parent of the child and that parent of the child:

(A) has been incarcerated in jail or prison during the three-month period preceding the filing of the petition;

(B) has been found by a court to be incompetent;

(C) is dead; or

(D) does not have actual or court-ordered possession of or access to the child.

(b) An order granting possession of or access to a child by a grandparent that is rendered over a parent's objections must state, with specificity that:

(1) at the time the relief was requested, at least one biological or adoptive parent of the child had not had that parent's parental rights terminated;

(2) the grandparent requesting possession of or access to the child has overcome the presumption that a parent acts in the best interest of the parent's child by proving by a preponderance of the evidence that the denial of possession of or access to the child would significantly impair the child's physical health or emotional well-being; and

(3) the grandparent requesting possession of or access to the child is a parent of a parent of the child and that parent of the child:

(A) has been incarcerated in jail or prison during the three-month period preceding the filing of the petition;

(B) has been found by a court to be incompetent;

(C) is dead; or

(D) does not have actual or court-ordered possession of or access to the child.

Added by Acts 1995, 74th Leg., ch. 20, § 1, eff. April 20, 1995. Amended by Acts 1997, 75th Leg., ch. 1397, § 1, eff. Sept. 1, 1997; Acts 2005, 79th Leg., ch. 484, § 4, eff. Sept. 1, 2005; Acts 2009, 81st Leg., ch. 1113, § 12, eff. Sept. 1, 2009.

### § 153.434. Limitation on Right to Request Possession or Access

A biological or adoptive grandparent may not request possession of or access to a grandchild if:

(1) each of the biological parents of the grandchild has:

(A) died;

(B) had the person's parental rights terminated; or

(C) executed an affidavit of waiver of interest in child or an affidavit of relinquishment of parental rights under Chapter 161 and the affidavit designates the Department of Family and Protective Services, a licensed child-placing agency, or a person other than the child's stepparent as the managing conservator of the child; and

(2) the grandchild has been adopted, or is the subject of a pending suit for adoption, by a person other than the child's stepparent.

Added by Acts 1995, 74th Leg., ch. 20, § 1, eff. April 20, 1995. Amended by Acts 1997, 75th Leg., ch. 561, § 4, eff. Sept. 1, 1997; Acts 1999, 76th Leg., ch. 1390, § 13, eff. Sept. 1, 1999; Acts 2005, 79th Leg., ch. 484, § 5, eff. Sept. 1, 2005; Acts 2015, 84th Leg., ch. 1 (S.B. 219), § 1.049, eff. April 2, 2015.

## SUBCHAPTER I. PREVENTION OF INTERNATIONAL PARENTAL CHILD ABDUCTION

### § 153.501. Necessity of Measures to Prevent International Parental Child Abduction

(a) In a suit, if credible evidence is presented to the court indicating a potential risk of the international abduction of a child by a parent of the child, the court, on its own motion or at the request of a party to the suit, shall determine under this section whether it is necessary for the court to take one or more of the measures described by Section 153.503 to protect the child from the risk of abduction by the parent.

(b) In determining whether to take any of the measures described by Section 153.503, the court shall consider:

(1) the public policies of this state described by Section 153.001(a) and the consideration of the best interest of the child under Section 153.002;

(2) the risk of international abduction of the child by a parent of the child based on the court's evaluation of the risk factors described by Section 153.502;

(3) any obstacles to locating, recovering, and returning the child if the child is abducted to a foreign country; and

(4) the potential physical or psychological harm to the child if the child is abducted to a foreign country.

Added by Acts 2003, 78th Leg., ch. 612, § 1, eff. June 20, 2003.

### § 153.502. Abduction Risk Factors

(a) To determine whether there is a risk of the international abduction of a child by a parent of the child, the court shall consider evidence that the parent:

(1) has taken, enticed away, kept, withheld, or concealed a child in violation of another person's right of possession of or access to the child, unless the parent presents evidence that the parent believed in good faith that the parent's conduct was necessary to avoid imminent harm to the child or the parent;

(2) has previously threatened to take, entice away, keep, withhold, or conceal a child in violation of another person's right of possession of or access to the child;

(3) lacks financial reason to stay in the United States, including evidence that the parent is financially independent, is able to work outside of the United States, or is unemployed;

(4) has recently engaged in planning activities that could facilitate the removal of the child from the United States by the parent, including:

(A) quitting a job;

(B) selling a primary residence;

(C) terminating a lease;

(D) closing bank accounts;

(E) liquidating other assets;

(F) hiding or destroying documents;

(G) applying for a passport or visa or obtaining other travel documents for the parent or the child; or

(H) applying to obtain the child's birth certificate or school or medical records;

(5) has a history of domestic violence that the court is required to consider under Section 153.004; or

(6) has a criminal history or a history of violating court orders.

(a–1) In considering evidence of planning activities under Subsection (a)(4), the court also shall consider any evidence that the parent was engaging in those activities as a part of a safety plan to flee from family violence.

(b) If the court finds that there is credible evidence of a risk of abduction of the child by a parent of the child based on the court's consideration of the factors in Subsection (a), the court shall also consider evidence regarding the following factors to evaluate the risk of international abduction of the child by a parent:

(1) whether the parent has strong familial, emotional, or cultural ties to another country, particularly a country that is not a signatory to or compliant with the Hague Convention on the Civil Aspects of International Child Abduction; and

(2) whether the parent lacks strong ties to the United States, regardless of whether the parent is a citizen or permanent resident of the United States.

(c) If the court finds that there is credible evidence of a risk of abduction of the child by a parent of the child based on the court's consideration of the factors in Subsection (a), the court may also consider evidence regarding the following factors to evaluate the risk of international abduction of the child by a parent:

(1) whether the parent is undergoing a change in status with the United States Immigration and Naturalization Service that would adversely affect that parent's ability to legally remain in the United States;

(2) whether the parent's application for United States citizenship has been denied by the United States Immigration and Naturalization Service;

(3) whether the parent has forged or presented misleading or false evidence to obtain a visa, a passport, a social security card, or any other identification card or has made any misrepresentation to the United States government; or

(4) whether the foreign country to which the parent has ties:

(A) presents obstacles to the recovery and return of a child who is abducted to the country from the United States;

(B) has any legal mechanisms for immediately and effectively enforcing an order regarding the possession of or access to the child issued by this state;

(C) has local laws or practices that would:

(i) enable the parent to prevent the child's other parent from contacting the child without due cause;

(ii) restrict the child's other parent from freely traveling to or exiting from the country because of that parent's gender, nationality, or religion; or

(iii) restrict the child's ability to legally leave the country after the child reaches the age of majority because of the child's gender, nationality, or religion;

(D) is included by the United States Department of State on a list of state sponsors of terrorism;

(E) is a country for which the United States Department of State has issued a travel warning to United States citizens regarding travel to the country;

(F) has an embassy of the United States in the country;

(G) is engaged in any active military action or war, including a civil war;

(H) is a party to and compliant with the Hague Convention on the Civil Aspects of International Child Abduction according to the most recent report on compliance issued by the United States Department of State;

(I) provides for the extradition of a parental abductor and the return of the child to the United States; or

(J) poses a risk that the child's physical health or safety would be endangered in the country because of specific circumstances relating to the child or because of human rights violations committed against children, including arranged marriages, lack of freedom of religion, child labor, lack of child abuse laws, female genital mutilation, and any form of slavery.

Added by Acts 2003, 78th Leg., ch. 612, § 1, eff. June 20, 2003. Amended by Acts 2009, 81st Leg., ch. 1113, § 13, eff. Sept. 1, 2009.

### § 153.503. Abduction Prevention Measures

If the court finds that it is necessary under Section 153.501 to take measures to protect a child from international abduction by a parent of the child, the court may take any of the following actions:

(1) appoint a person other than the parent of the child who presents a risk of abducting the child as the sole managing conservator of the child;

(2) require supervised visitation of the parent by a visitation center or independent organization until the court finds under Section 153.501 that supervised visitation is no longer necessary;

(3) enjoin the parent or any person acting on the parent's behalf from:

(A) disrupting or removing the child from the school or child-care facility in which the child is enrolled; or

(B) approaching the child at any location other than a site designated for supervised visitation;

(4) order passport and travel controls, including controls that:

(A) prohibit the parent and any person acting on the parent's behalf from removing the child from this state or the United States;

(B) require the parent to surrender any passport issued in the child's name, including any passport issued in the name of both the parent and the child; and

(C) prohibit the parent from applying on behalf of the child for a new or replacement passport or international travel visa;

(5) require the parent to provide:

(A) to the United States Department of State's Office of Children's Issues and the relevant foreign consulate or embassy:

(i) written notice of the court-ordered passport and travel restrictions for the child; and

(ii) a properly authenticated copy of the court order detailing the restrictions and documentation of the parent's agreement to the restrictions; and

(B) to the court proof of receipt of the written notice required by Paragraph (A)(i) by the United States Department of State's Office of Children's Issues and the relevant foreign consulate or embassy;

(6) order the parent to execute a bond or deposit security in an amount sufficient to offset the cost of recovering the child if the child is abducted by the parent to a foreign country;

(7) authorize the appropriate law enforcement agencies to take measures to prevent the abduction of the child by the parent; or

(8) include in the court's order provisions:

(A) identifying the United States as the country of habitual residence of the child;

(B) defining the basis for the court's exercise of jurisdiction; and

(C) stating that a party's violation of the order may subject the party to a civil penalty or criminal penalty or to both civil and criminal penalties.

Added by Acts 2003, 78th Leg., ch. 612, § 1, eff. June 20, 2003.

## SUBCHAPTER J. RIGHTS OF SIBLINGS

*Another Subchapter J, Parenting Plan and Parenting Coordinator, consisting of §§ 153.601 to 153.611, was relettered as Subchapter K by Acts 2007, 80th Leg., ch. 921, § 17.001(21), eff. Sept. 1, 2007.*

### § 153.551. Suit for Access

(a) The sibling of a child who is separated from the child because of an action taken by the Department of Family and Protective Services may request access to the child by filing:

(1) an original suit; or

(2) a suit for modification as provided by Chapter 156.

(b) A sibling described by Subsection (a) may request access to the child in a suit filed for the sole purpose of requesting the relief, without regard to whether the appointment of a managing conservator is an issue in the suit.

(c) The court shall order reasonable access to the child by the child's sibling described by Subsection (a) if the court finds that access is in the best interest of the child.

Added by Acts 2005, 79th Leg., ch. 1191, § 2, eff. Sept. 1, 2005. Amended by Acts 2009, 81st Leg., ch. 1113, § 14, eff. Sept. 1, 2009.

### § 153.552. Repealed by Acts 2009, 81st Leg., ch. 1113, § 31, eff. Sept. 1, 2009

## SUBCHAPTER K. PARENTING PLAN, PARENTING COORDINATOR, AND PARENTING FACILITATOR

*Acts 2007, 80th Leg., ch. 921, § 17.001(21) relettered a former Subchapter J, Parenting Plan and Parenting Coordinator, consisting of V.T.C.A., Family Code §§ 153.601 et seq., as Subchapter K, consisting of the same sections.*

### § 153.601. Definitions

In this subchapter:

(1) "Dispute resolution process" means:

(A) a process of alternative dispute resolution conducted in accordance with Section 153.0071 of this chapter and Chapter 154, Civil Practice and Remedies Code; or

(B) any other method of voluntary dispute resolution.

(2) "High-conflict case" means a suit affecting the parent-child relationship in which the court finds that the parties have demonstrated an unusual degree of:

(A) repetitiously resorting to the adjudicative process;

(B) anger and distrust; and

(C) difficulty in communicating about and cooperating in the care of their children.

(3) "Parenting coordinator" means an impartial third party:

(A) who, regardless of the title by which the person is designated by the court, performs any function described by Section 153.606 in a suit; and

(B) who:

(i) is appointed under this subchapter by the court on its own motion or on a motion or agreement of the parties to assist parties in resolving parenting issues through confidential procedures; and

(ii) is not appointed under another statute or a rule of civil procedure.

(3–a) "Parenting facilitator" means an impartial third party:

(A) who, regardless of the title by which the person is designated by the court, performs any function described by Section 153.6061 in a suit; and

(B) who:

(i) is appointed under this subchapter by the court on its own motion or on a motion or agreement of the parties to assist parties in resolving parenting issues through procedures that are not confidential; and

(ii) is not appointed under another statute or a rule of civil procedure.

(4) "Parenting plan" means the provisions of a final court order that:

(A) set out rights and duties of a parent or a person acting as a parent in relation to the child;

(B) provide for periods of possession of and access to the child, which may be the terms set out in the standard possession order under Subchapter F and any amendments to the standard possession order agreed to by the parties or found by the court to be in the best interest of the child;

(C) provide for child support; and

(D) optimize the development of a close and continuing relationship between each parent and the child.

Added by Acts 2005, 79th Leg., ch. 482, § 2, eff. Sept. 1, 2005. Amended by Acts 2007, 80th Leg., ch. 1181, § 4, eff. Sept. 1, 2007; Acts 2009, 81st Leg., ch. 1113, § 16, eff. Sept. 1, 2009.

### § 153.602. Parenting Plan Not Required in Temporary Order

A temporary order in a suit affecting the parent-child relationship rendered in accordance with Section 105.001 is not required to include a temporary parenting plan. The court may not require the submission of a temporary parenting plan in any case or by local rule or practice.

Added by Acts 2005, 79th Leg., ch. 482, § 2, eff. Sept. 1, 2005. Amended by Acts 2007, 80th Leg., ch. 1181, § 4, eff. Sept. 1, 2007.

### § 153.603. Requirement of Parenting Plan in Final Order

(a) Except as provided by Subsection (b), a final order in a suit affecting the parent-child relationship must include a parenting plan.

(b) The following orders are not required to include a parenting plan:

(1) an order that only modifies child support;

(2) an order that only terminates parental rights; or

(3) a final order described by Section 155.001(b).

(c) If the parties have not reached agreement on a final parenting plan on or before the 30th day before the date set for trial on the merits, a party may file with the court and serve a proposed parenting plan.

(d) This section does not preclude the parties from requesting the appointment of a parenting coordinator to resolve parental conflicts.

Added by Acts 2005, 79th Leg., ch. 482, § 2, eff. Sept. 1, 2005. Amended by Acts 2007, 80th Leg., ch. 1181, § 4, eff. Sept. 1, 2007.

### § 153.6031. Exception to Dispute Resolution Process Requirement

A requirement in a parenting plan that a party initiate or participate in a dispute resolution process before filing a court action does not apply to an action:

(1) to modify the parenting plan in an emergency;

(2) to modify child support;

(3) alleging that the child's present circumstances will significantly impair the child's physical health or significantly impair the child's emotional development;

(4) to enforce; or

(5) in which the party shows that enforcement of the requirement is precluded or limited by Section 153.0071.

Added by Acts 2007, 80th Leg., ch. 1181, § 4, eff. Sept. 1, 2007.

### § 153.604. Repealed by Acts 2007, 80th Leg., ch. 1181, § 11(1), eff. Sept. 1, 2007

### § 153.605. Appointment of Parenting Coordinator

(a) In a suit affecting the parent-child relationship, the court may, on its own motion or on a motion or agreement of the parties, appoint a parenting coordinator or assign a domestic relations office under Chapter 203 to appoint an employee or other person to serve as parenting coordinator.

(b) The court may not appoint a parenting coordinator unless, after notice and hearing, the court makes a specific finding that:

(1) the case is a high-conflict case or there is good cause shown for the appointment of a parenting coordinator and the appointment is in the best interest of any minor child in the suit; and

(2) the person appointed has the minimum qualifications required by Section 153.610, as documented by the person, unless those requirements have been waived by the court with the agreement of the parties in accordance with Section 153.610(c).

(c) Notwithstanding any other provision of this subchapter, a party may at any time file a written objection to the appointment of a parenting coordinator on the basis of family violence having been committed by another party against the objecting party or a child who is the subject of the suit. After an objection is filed, a parenting coordinator may not be appointed unless, on the request of a party, a hearing is held and the court finds that a preponderance of the evidence does not support the objection. If a parenting coordinator is appointed, the court shall order appropriate measures be taken to ensure the physical and emotional safety of the party who filed the objection. The order may provide that the parties not be required to have face-to-face contact and that the parties be placed in separate rooms during the parenting coordination.

(d) An individual appointed as a parenting coordinator may not serve in any nonconfidential capacity in the same case, including serving as an amicus attorney, guardian ad litem, child custody evaluator, or adoption evaluator under Chapter 107, as a friend of the court under Chapter 202, or as a parenting facilitator under this subchapter.

Added by Acts 2005, 79th Leg., ch. 482, § 2, eff. Sept. 1, 2005. Amended by Acts 2007, 80th Leg., ch. 1181, § 5, eff. Sept. 1, 2007; Acts 2009, 81st Leg., ch. 1113, § 17, eff. Sept. 1, 2009; Acts 2015, 84th Leg., ch. 1252 (H.B. 1449), § 3.01, eff. Sept. 1, 2015.

## § 153.6051. Appointment of Parenting Facilitator

(a) In a suit affecting the parent-child relationship, the court may, on its own motion or on a motion or agreement of the parties, appoint a parenting facilitator or assign a domestic relations office under Chapter 203 to appoint an employee or other person as a parenting facilitator.

(b) The court may not appoint a parenting facilitator unless, after notice and hearing, the court makes a specific finding that:

(1) the case is a high-conflict case or there is good cause shown for the appointment of a parenting facilitator and the appointment is in the best interest of any minor child in the suit; and

(2) the person appointed has the minimum qualifications required by Section 153.6101, as documented by the person.

(c) Notwithstanding any other provision of this subchapter, a party may at any time file a written objection to the appointment of a parenting facilitator on the basis of family violence having been committed by another party against the objecting party or a child who is the subject of the suit. After an objection is filed, a parenting facilitator may not be appointed unless, on the request of a party, a hearing is held and the court finds that a preponderance of the evidence does not support the objection. If a parenting facilitator is appointed, the court shall order appropriate measures be taken to ensure the physical and emotional safety of the party who filed the objection. The order may provide that the parties not be required to have face-to-face contact and that the parties be placed in separate rooms during the parenting facilitation.

Added by Acts 2009, 81st Leg., ch. 1113, § 18, eff. Sept. 1, 2009.

## § 153.606. Duties of Parenting Coordinator

(a) The court shall specify the duties of a parenting coordinator in the order appointing the parenting coordinator. The duties of the parenting coordinator are limited to matters that will aid the parties in:

(1) identifying disputed issues;

(2) reducing misunderstandings;

(3) clarifying priorities;

(4) exploring possibilities for problem solving;

(5) developing methods of collaboration in parenting;

(6) understanding parenting plans and reaching agreements about parenting issues to be included in a parenting plan;

(7) complying with the court's order regarding conservatorship or possession of and access to the child;

(8) implementing parenting plans;

(9) obtaining training regarding problem solving, conflict management, and parenting skills; and

(10) settling disputes regarding parenting issues and reaching a proposed joint resolution or statement of intent regarding those disputes.

(b) The appointment of a parenting coordinator does not divest the court of:

(1) its exclusive jurisdiction to determine issues of conservatorship, support, and possession of and access to the child; and

(2) the authority to exercise management and control of the suit.

(c) The parenting coordinator may not modify any order, judgment, or decree.

(d) Meetings between the parenting coordinator and the parties may be informal and are not required to follow any specific procedures unless otherwise provided by this subchapter.

(e) Repealed by Acts 2007, 80th Leg., ch. 1181, §11(2).

(f) A parenting coordinator appointed under this subchapter shall comply with the Ethical Guidelines for Mediators as adopted by the Supreme Court of Texas (Misc. Docket No. 05–9107, June 13, 2005). On request by the court, the parties, or the parties' attorneys, the parenting coordinator shall sign a statement of agreement to comply with those guidelines and submit the statement to the court on acceptance of the appointment. A failure to comply with the guidelines is grounds for removal of the parenting coordinator.

Added by Acts 2005, 79th Leg., ch. 482, § 2, eff. Sept. 1, 2005. Amended by Acts 2007, 80th Leg., ch. 1181, §§ 6, 7, 11(2), eff. Sept. 1, 2007; Acts 2009, 81st Leg., ch. 1113, § 19, eff. Sept. 1, 2009.

### § 153.6061. Duties of Parenting Facilitator

(a) The court shall specify the duties of a parenting facilitator in the order appointing the parenting facilitator. The duties of the parenting facilitator are limited to those matters described with regard to a parenting coordinator under Section 153.606(a), except that the parenting facilitator may also monitor compliance with court orders.

(b) A parenting facilitator appointed under this subchapter shall comply with the standard of care applicable to the professional license held by the parenting facilitator in performing the parenting facilitator's duties.

(c) The appointment of a parenting facilitator does not divest the court of:

(1) the exclusive jurisdiction to determine issues of conservatorship, support, and possession of and access to the child; and

(2) the authority to exercise management and control of the suit.

(d) The parenting facilitator may not modify any order, judgment, or decree.

(e) Meetings between the parenting facilitator and the parties may be informal and are not required to follow any specific procedures unless otherwise provided by this subchapter or the standards of practice of the professional license held by the parenting facilitator.

Added by Acts 2009, 81st Leg., ch. 1113, § 20, eff. Sept. 1, 2009.

### § 153.607. Presumption of Good Faith; Removal of Parenting Coordinator

(a) It is a rebuttable presumption that a parenting coordinator is acting in good faith if the parenting coordinator's services have been conducted as provided by this subchapter and the Ethical Guidelines for Mediators described by Section 153.606(f).

(a–1) Except as otherwise provided by this section, the court may remove the parenting coordinator in the court's discretion.

(b) The court shall remove the parenting coordinator:

(1) on the request and agreement of all parties;

(2) on the request of the parenting coordinator;

(3) on the motion of a party, if good cause is shown; or

(4) if the parenting coordinator ceases to satisfy the minimum qualifications required by Section 153.610.

Added by Acts 2005, 79th Leg., ch. 482, § 2, eff. Sept. 1, 2005. Amended by Acts 2007, 80th Leg., ch. 1181, § 8, eff. Sept. 1, 2007; Acts 2009, 81st Leg., ch. 1113, § 21, eff. Sept. 1, 2009.

### § 153.6071. Presumption of Good Faith; Removal of Parenting Facilitator

(a) It is a rebuttable presumption that a parenting facilitator is acting in good faith if the parenting facilitator's services have been conducted as provided by this subchapter and the standard of care applicable to the professional license held by the parenting facilitator.

(b) Except as otherwise provided by this section, the court may remove the parenting facilitator in the court's discretion.

(c) The court shall remove the parenting facilitator:

(1) on the request and agreement of all parties;

(2) on the request of the parenting facilitator;

(3) on the motion of a party, if good cause is shown; or

(4) if the parenting facilitator ceases to satisfy the minimum qualifications required by Section 153.6101.

Added by Acts 2009, 81st Leg., ch. 1113, § 22, eff. Sept. 1, 2009.

### § 153.608. Report of Parenting Coordinator

A parenting coordinator shall submit a written report to the court and to the parties as often as ordered by the court. The report must be limited to a statement of whether the parenting coordination should continue.

Added by Acts 2005, 79th Leg., ch. 482, § 2, eff. Sept. 1, 2005. Amended by Acts 2007, 80th Leg., ch. 1181, § 9, eff. Sept. 1, 2007.

### § 153.6081. Report of Parenting Facilitator

A parenting facilitator shall submit a written report to the court and to the parties as ordered by the court. The report may include a recommendation described by Section 153.6082(e) and any other information required by the court, except that the report may not include recommendations regarding the conservatorship of or the possession of or access to the child who is the subject of the suit.

Added by Acts 2009, 81st Leg., ch. 1113, § 22, eff. Sept. 1, 2009.

### § 153.6082. Report of Joint Proposal or Statement of Intent; Agreements and Recommendations

(a) If the parties have been ordered by the court to attempt to settle parenting issues with the assistance of a parenting coordinator or parenting facilitator and to attempt to reach a proposed joint resolution or statement of intent regarding the dispute, the parenting coordinator or parenting facilitator, as applicable, shall submit a written report describing the parties' joint proposal or statement to the parties, any attorneys for the parties, and any attorney for the child who is the subject of the suit.

(b) The proposed joint resolution or statement of intent is not an agreement unless the resolution or statement is:

(1) prepared by the parties' attorneys, if any, in a form that meets the applicable requirements of:

(A) Rule 11, Texas Rules of Civil Procedure;

(B) a mediated settlement agreement described by Section 153.0071;

(C) a collaborative law agreement described by Section 153.0072;

(D) a settlement agreement described by Section 154.071, Civil Practice and Remedies Code; or

(E) a proposed court order; and

(2) incorporated into an order signed by the court.

(c) A parenting coordinator or parenting facilitator may not draft a document listed in Subsection (b)(1).

(d) The actions of a parenting coordinator or parenting facilitator under this section do not constitute the practice of law.

(e) If the parties have been ordered by the court to attempt to settle parenting issues with the assistance of a parenting facilitator and are unable to settle those issues, the parenting facilitator may make recommendations, other than recommendations regarding the conservatorship of or possession of or access to the child, to the parties and attorneys to implement or clarify provisions of an existing court order that are consistent with the substantive intent of the court order and in the best interest of the child who is the subject of the suit. A recommendation authorized by this subsection does not affect the terms of an existing court order.

Added by Acts 2009, 81st Leg., ch. 1113, § 22, eff. Sept. 1, 2009.

### § 153.6083. Communications and Recordkeeping of Parenting Facilitator

(a) Notwithstanding any rule, standard of care, or privilege applicable to the professional license held by a parenting facilitator, a communication made by a participant in parenting facilitation is subject to disclosure and may be offered in any judicial or administrative proceeding, if otherwise admissible under the rules of evidence. The parenting facilitator may be required to testify in any proceeding relating to or arising from the duties of the parenting facilitator, including as to the basis for any recommendation made to the parties that arises from the duties of the parenting facilitator.

(b) A parenting facilitator shall keep a detailed record regarding meetings and contacts with the parties, attorneys, or other persons involved in the suit.

(c) A person who participates in parenting facilitation is not a patient as defined by Section 611.001, Health and Safety Code, and no record created as part of the parenting facilitation that arises from the parenting facilitator's duties is confidential.

(d) On request, records of parenting facilitation shall be made available by the parenting facilitator to an attorney for a party, an attorney for a child who is the subject of the suit, and a party who does not have an attorney.

(e) A parenting facilitator shall keep parenting facilitation records from the suit until the seventh anniversary of the date the facilitator's services are terminated, unless a different retention period is established by a rule adopted by the licensing authority that issues the professional license held by the parenting facilitator.

Added by Acts 2009, 81st Leg., ch. 1113, § 22, eff. Sept. 1, 2009.

### § 153.609. Compensation of Parenting Coordinator

(a) A court may not appoint a parenting coordinator, other than a domestic relations office or a comparable county agency appointed under Subsection (c) or a volunteer appointed under Subsection (d), unless, after notice and hearing, the court finds that the parties have the means to pay the fees of the parenting coordinator.

(b) Any fees of a parenting coordinator appointed under Subsection (a) shall be allocated between the parties as determined by the court.

(c) Public funds may not be used to pay the fees of a parenting coordinator. Notwithstanding this prohibition, a court may appoint the domestic relations office or a comparable county agency to act as a parenting coordinator if personnel are available to serve that function.

(d) If due to hardship the parties are unable to pay the fees of a parenting coordinator, and a domestic relations office or a comparable county agency is not available under Subsection (c), the court, if feasible, may appoint a person who meets the minimum qualifications prescribed by Section 153.610, including an employee of the court, to act as a parenting coordinator on a volunteer basis and without compensation.

Added by Acts 2005, 79th Leg., ch. 482, § 2, eff. Sept. 1, 2005. Amended by Acts 2007, 80th Leg., ch. 1181, § 10, eff. Sept. 1, 2007; Acts 2011, 82nd Leg., ch. 682 (H.B. 149), § 1, eff. June 17, 2011.

### § 153.6091. Compensation of Parenting Facilitator

Section 153.609 applies to a parenting facilitator in the same manner as provided for a parenting coordinator, except that a person appointed in accordance with Section 153.609(d) to act as a parenting facilitator must meet the minimum qualifications prescribed by Section 153.6101.

Added by Acts 2009, 81st Leg., ch. 1113, § 22, eff. Sept. 1, 2009. Amended by Acts 2011, 82nd Leg., ch. 682 (H.B. 149), § 2, eff. June 17, 2011.

### § 153.610. Qualifications of Parenting Coordinator

(a) The court shall determine the required qualifications of a parenting coordinator, provided that a parenting coordinator must have experience working in a field relating to families, have practical experience with high-conflict cases or litigation between parents, and:

(1) hold at least:

(A) a bachelor's degree in counseling, education, family studies, psychology, or social work; or

(B) a graduate degree in a mental health profession, with an emphasis in family and children's issues; or

(2) be licensed in good standing as an attorney in this state.

(b) In addition to the qualifications prescribed by Subsection (a), a parenting coordinator must complete at least:

(1) eight hours of family violence dynamics training provided by a family violence service provider;

(2) 40 classroom hours of training in dispute resolution techniques in a course conducted by an alternative dispute resolution system or other dispute resolution organization approved by the court; and

(3) 24 classroom hours of training in the fields of family dynamics, child development, family law and the law governing parenting coordination, and parenting coordination styles and procedures.

(c) In appropriate circumstances, a court may, with the agreement of the parties, appoint a person as parenting coordinator who does not satisfy the requirements of Subsection (a) or Subsection (b)(2) or (3) if the court finds that the person has sufficient legal or other professional training or experience in dispute resolution processes to serve in that capacity.

(d) The actions of a parenting coordinator who is not an attorney do not constitute the practice of law.

Added by Acts 2005, 79th Leg., ch. 482, § 2, eff. Sept. 1, 2005. Amended by Acts 2009, 81st Leg., ch. 1113, § 23, eff. Sept. 1, 2009.

### § 153.6101. Qualifications of Parenting Facilitator

(a) The court shall determine whether the qualifications of a proposed parenting facilitator satisfy the requirements of this section. On request by a party, an attorney for a party, or any attorney for a child who is the subject of the suit, a person under consideration for appointment as a parenting facilitator in the suit shall provide proof that the person satisfies the minimum qualifications required by this section.

(b) A parenting facilitator must:

(1) hold a license to practice in this state as a social worker, licensed professional counselor, licensed marriage and family therapist, psychologist, or attorney; and

(2) have completed at least:

(A) eight hours of family violence dynamics training provided by a family violence service provider;

(B) 40 classroom hours of training in dispute resolution techniques in a course conducted by an alternative dispute resolution system or other dispute resolution organization approved by the court;

(C) 24 classroom hours of training in the fields of family dynamics, child development, and family law; and

(D) 16 hours of training in the laws governing parenting coordination and parenting facilitation and the multiple styles and procedures used in different models of service.

(c) The actions of a parenting facilitator who is not an attorney do not constitute the practice of law.

Added by Acts 2009, 81st Leg., ch. 1113, § 24, eff. Sept. 1, 2009.

### § 153.6102. Parenting Facilitator; Conflicts of Interest and Bias

(a) A person who has a conflict of interest with, or has previous knowledge of, a party or a child who is the subject of a suit must, before being appointed as parenting facilitator in a suit:

(1) disclose the conflict or previous knowledge to the court, each attorney for a party, any attorney for a child, and any party who does not have an attorney; and

(2) decline appointment in the suit unless, after the disclosure, the parties and the child's attorney, if any, agree in writing to the person's appointment as parenting facilitator.

(b) A parenting facilitator who, after being appointed in a suit, discovers that the parenting facilitator has a conflict of interest with, or has previous knowledge of, a party or a child who is the subject of the suit shall:

(1) immediately disclose the conflict or previous knowledge to the court, each attorney for a party, any attorney for a child, and any party who does not have an attorney; and

(2) withdraw from the suit unless, after the disclosure, the parties and the child's attorney, if any, agree in writing to the person's continuation as parenting facilitator.

(c) A parenting facilitator, before accepting appointment in a suit, must disclose to the court, each attorney for a party, any attorney for a child who is the subject of the suit, and any party who does not have an attorney:

(1) a pecuniary relationship with an attorney, party, or child in the suit;

(2) a relationship of confidence or trust with an attorney, party, or child in the suit; and

(3) other information regarding any relationship with an attorney, party, or child in the suit that might reasonably affect the ability of the person to act impartially during the person's service as parenting facilitator.

(d) A person who makes a disclosure required by Subsection (c) shall decline appointment as parenting facilitator unless, after the disclosure, the parties and the child's attorney, if any, agree in writing to the person's service as parenting facilitator in the suit.

(e) A parenting facilitator may not serve in any other professional capacity at any other time with any person who is a party to, or the subject of, the suit in which the person serves as parenting facilitator, or with any member of the family of a party or subject. A person who, before appointment as a parenting facilitator in a suit, served in any other professional capacity with a person who is a party to, or subject of, the suit, or with any member of the family of a party or subject, may not serve as parenting facilitator in a suit involving any family member who is a party to or subject of the suit. This subsection does not apply to a person whose only other service in a professional capacity with a family or any member of a family that is a party to or the subject of a suit to which this section applies is as a teacher of coparenting skills in a class conducted in a group setting. For purposes of this subsection, "family" has the meaning assigned by Section 71.003.

(f) A parenting facilitator shall promptly and simultaneously disclose to each party's attorney, any attorney for a child who is a subject of the suit, and any party who does not have an attorney the existence and substance of any communication between the parenting facilitator and another person, including a party, a party's attorney, a child who is the subject of the suit, and any attorney for a child who is the subject of the suit, if the communication occurred outside of a parenting facilitator session and involved the substance of parenting facilitation.

Added by Acts 2009, 81st Leg., ch. 1113, § 24, eff. Sept. 1, 2009.

### § 153.611. Exception for Certain Title IV–D Proceedings

Notwithstanding any other provision of this subchapter, this subchapter does not apply to a proceeding in a Title IV–D case relating to the determination of parentage or establishment, modification, or enforcement of a child support, medical support, or dental support obligation.

Added by Acts 2005, 79th Leg., ch. 482, § 2, eff. Sept. 1, 2005. Amended by Acts 2015, 84th Leg., ch. 1150 (S.B. 550), § 7, eff. Sept. 1, 2018.

SUBCHAPTER L. MILITARY DUTY

### § 153.701. Definitions

In this subchapter:

(1) "Designated person" means the person ordered by the court to temporarily exercise a conservator's rights, duties, and periods of possession and access with regard to a child during the conservator's military deployment, military mobilization, or temporary military duty.

(2) "Military deployment" means the temporary transfer of a service member of the armed forces of this state or the United States serving in an active-duty status to another location in support of combat or some other military operation.

(3) "Military mobilization" means the call-up of a National Guard or Reserve service member of the armed forces of this state or the United States to extended active duty status. The term does not include National Guard or Reserve annual training.

(4) "Temporary military duty" means the transfer of a service member of the armed forces of this state or the United States from one military base to a different location, usually another base, for a limited time for training or to assist in the performance of a noncombat mission.

Added by Acts 2009, 81st Leg., ch. 727, § 1, eff. Sept. 1, 2009; Acts 2009, 81st Leg., ch. 1113, § 25, eff. Sept. 1, 2009.

### § 153.702. Temporary Orders

(a) If a conservator is ordered to military deployment, military mobilization, or temporary military duty that involves moving a substantial distance from the conservator's residence so as to materially affect the conservator's ability to exercise the conservator's rights and duties in relation to a child, either conservator may file for an order under this subchapter without the necessity of showing a material and substantial change of circumstances other than the military deployment, military mobilization, or temporary military duty.

(b) The court may render a temporary order in a proceeding under this subchapter regarding:

(1) possession of or access to the child; or

(2) child support.

(c) A temporary order rendered by the court under this subchapter may grant rights to and impose duties on a designated person regarding the child, except that if the designated person is a nonparent, the court may not require the designated person to pay child support.

(d) After a conservator's military deployment, military mobilization, or temporary military duty is concluded, and the conservator returns to the conservator's usual residence, the temporary orders under this section terminate and the rights of all affected parties are governed by the terms of any court order applicable when the conservator is not ordered to military deployment, military mobilization, or temporary military duty.

Added by Acts 2009, 81st Leg., ch. 727, § 1, eff. Sept. 1, 2009; Acts 2009, 81st Leg., ch. 1113, § 25, eff. Sept. 1, 2009. Amended by Acts 2011, 82nd Leg., ch. 112 (H.B. 1404), § 1, eff. Sept. 1, 2011.

### § 153.703. Appointing Designated Person for Conservator with Exclusive Right to Designate Primary Residence of Child

(a) If the conservator with the exclusive right to designate the primary residence of the child is ordered to military deployment, military mobilization, or temporary military duty, the court may render a temporary order to appoint a designated person to exercise the exclusive right to designate the primary residence of the child during the military deployment, military mobilization, or temporary military duty in the following order of preference:

(1) the conservator who does not have the exclusive right to designate the primary residence of the child;

(2) if appointing the conservator described by Subdivision (1) is not in the child's best interest, a designated person chosen by the conservator with the exclusive right to designate the primary residence of the child; or

(3) if appointing the conservator described by Subdivision (1) or the person chosen under Subdivision (2) is not in the child's best interest, another person chosen by the court.

(b) A nonparent appointed as a designated person in a temporary order rendered under this section has the rights and duties of a nonparent appointed as sole managing conservator under Section 153.371.

(c) The court may limit or expand the rights of a nonparent named as a designated person in a temporary order rendered under this section as appropriate to the best interest of the child.

Added by Acts 2009, 81st Leg., ch. 727, § 1, eff. Sept. 1, 2009; Acts 2009, 81st Leg., ch. 1113, § 25, eff. Sept. 1, 2009. Amended by Acts 2011, 82nd Leg., ch. 112 (H.B. 1404), § 2, eff. Sept. 1, 2011.

### § 153.704. Appointing Designated Person to Exercise Visitation for Conservator with Exclusive Right to Designate Primary Residence of Child in Certain Circumstances

(a) If the court appoints the conservator without the exclusive right to designate the primary residence of the child under Section 153.703(a)(1), the court may award visitation with the child to a designated person chosen by the conservator with the exclusive right to designate the primary residence of the child.

(b) The periods of visitation shall be the same as the visitation to which the conservator without the exclusive right to designate the primary residence of the child was entitled under the court order in effect immediately before the date the temporary order is rendered.

(c) The temporary order for visitation must provide that:

(1) the designated person under this section has the right to possession of the child for the periods and in the manner in which the conservator without the exclusive right to designate the primary residence of the child is entitled under the court order in effect immediately before the date the temporary order is rendered;

(2) the child's other conservator and the designated person under this section are subject to the requirements of Section 153.316, with the designated person considered for purposes of that section to be the possessory conservator;

(3) the designated person under this section has the rights and duties of a nonparent possessory conservator under Section 153.376(a) during the period that the person has possession of the child; and

(4) the designated person under this section is subject to any provision in a court order restricting or prohibiting access to the child by any specified individual.

(d) The court may limit or expand the rights of a nonparent designated person named in a temporary order rendered under this section as appropriate to the best interest of the child.

Added by Acts 2009, 81st Leg., ch. 727, § 1, eff. Sept. 1, 2009; Acts 2009, 81st Leg., ch. 1113, § 25, eff. Sept. 1, 2009.

### § 153.705. Appointing Designated Person to Exercise Visitation for Conservator without Exclusive Right to Designate Primary Residence of Child

(a) If the conservator without the exclusive right to designate the primary residence of the child is ordered to military deployment, military mobilization, or temporary military duty, the court may award visitation with the child to a designated person chosen by the conservator, if the visitation is in the best interest of the child.

(b) The temporary order for visitation must provide that:

(1) the designated person under this section has the right to possession of the child for the periods and in the manner in which the conservator described by Subsection (a) would be entitled if not ordered to military deployment, military mobilization, or temporary military duty;

(2) the child's other conservator and the designated person under this section are subject to the requirements of Section 153.316, with the designated person considered for purposes of that section to be the possessory conservator;

(3) the designated person under this section has the rights and duties of a nonparent possessory conservator under Section 153.376(a) during the period that the designated person has possession of the child; and

(4) the designated person under this section is subject to any provision in a court order restricting or prohibiting access to the child by any specified individual.

(c) The court may limit or expand the rights of a nonparent designated person named in a temporary order rendered under this section as appropriate to the best interest of the child.

Added by Acts 2009, 81st Leg., ch. 727, § 1, eff. Sept. 1, 2009; Acts 2009, 81st Leg., ch. 1113, § 25, eff. Sept. 1, 2009.

### § 153.706. Repealed by Acts 2011, 82nd Leg., ch. 112 (H.B. 1404), § 3, eff. Sept. 1, 2011

### § 153.707. Expedited Hearing

(a) On a motion by the conservator who has been ordered to military deployment, military mobilization, or temporary military duty, the court shall, for good cause shown, hold an expedited hearing if the court finds that the conservator's military duties have a material effect on the conservator's ability to appear in person at a regularly scheduled hearing.

(b) A hearing under this section shall, if possible, take precedence over other suits affecting the parent-child relationship not involving a conservator who has been ordered to military deployment, military mobilization, or temporary military duty.

(c) On a motion by any party, the court shall, after reasonable advance notice and for good cause shown, allow a party to present testimony and evidence by electronic means, including by teleconference or through the Internet.

Added by Acts 2009, 81st Leg., ch. 727, § 1, Sept. 1, 2009; Acts 2009, 81st Leg., ch. 1113, § 25, eff. Sept. 1, 2009.

### § 153.708. Enforcement

Temporary orders rendered under this subchapter may be enforced by or against the designated person to the same extent that an order would be enforceable against the conservator who has been ordered to military deployment, military mobilization, or temporary military duty.

Added by Acts 2009, 81st Leg., ch. 727, § 1, eff. Sept. 1, 2009; Acts 2009, 81st Leg., ch. 1113, § 25, eff. Sept. 1, 2009.

### § 153.709. Additional Periods of Possession or Access

(a) Not later than the 90th day after the date a conservator without the exclusive right to designate the primary residence of the child who is a member of the armed services concludes the conservator's military deployment, military mobilization, or temporary military duty, the conservator may petition the court to:

(1) compute the periods of possession of or access to the child to which the conservator would have otherwise been entitled during the conservator's deployment; and

(2) award the conservator additional periods of possession of or access to the child to compensate for the periods described by Subdivision (1).

(b) If the conservator described by Subsection (a) petitions the court under Subsection (a), the court:

(1) shall compute the periods of possession or access to the child described by Subsection (a)(1); and

(2) may award to the conservator additional periods of possession of or access to the child for a length of time and under terms the court considers reasonable, if the court determines that:

(A) the conservator was on military deployment, military mobilization, or temporary military duty in a location where access to the child was not reasonably possible; and

(B) the award of additional periods of possession of or access to the child is in the best interest of the child.

(c) In making the determination under Subsection (b)(2), the court:

(1) shall consider:

(A) the periods of possession of or access to the child to which the conservator would otherwise have been entitled during the conservator's military deployment, military mobilization, or temporary military duty, as computed under Subsection (b)(1);

(B) whether the court named a designated person under Section 153.705 to exercise limited possession of the child during the conservator's deployment; and

(C) any other factor the court considers appropriate; and

(2) is not required to award additional periods of possession of or access to the child that equals the possession or access to which the conservator would have been entitled during the conservator's military deployment, military mobilization, or temporary military duty, as computed under Subsection (b)(1).

(d) After the conservator described by Subsection (a) has exercised all additional periods of possession or access awarded under this section, the rights of all affected parties are governed by the terms of the court order applicable when the conservator is not ordered to military deployment, military mobilization, or temporary military duty.

Added by Acts 2009, 81st Leg., ch. 727, § 1, eff. Sept. 1, 2009; Acts 2009, 81st Leg., ch. 1113, § 25, eff. Sept. 1, 2009.

## CHAPTER 154. CHILD SUPPORT

### SUBCHAPTER A. COURT-ORDERED CHILD SUPPORT

Section

## SUBCHAPTER A. COURT–ORDERED CHILD SUPPORT

### § 154.001. Support of Child

(a) The court may order either or both parents to support a child in the manner specified by the order:

(1) until the child is 18 years of age or until graduation from high school, whichever occurs later;

(2) until the child is emancipated through marriage, through removal of the disabilities of minority by court order, or by other operation of law;

(3) until the death of the child; or

(4) if the child is disabled as defined in this chapter, for an indefinite period.

(a–1) The court may order each person who is financially able and whose parental rights have been terminated with respect to a child in substitute care for whom the department has been appointed managing conservator, a child for a reason described by Section 161.001(b)(1)(T)(iv) or (b)(1)(U), or a child who was conceived as a direct result of conduct that constitutes an offense under Section 21.02, 22.011, 22.021, or 25.02, Penal Code, to support the child in the manner specified by the order:

(1) until the earliest of:

(A) the child's adoption;

(B) the child's 18th birthday or graduation from high school, whichever occurs later;

(C) removal of the child's disabilities of minority by court order, marriage, or other operation of law; or

(D) the child's death; or

(2) if the child is disabled as defined in this chapter, for an indefinite period.

(b) The court may order either or both parents to make periodic payments for the support of a child in a proceeding in which the Department of Family and Protective Services is named temporary managing conservator. In a proceeding in which the Department of Family and Protective Services is named permanent managing conservator of a child whose parents' rights have not been terminated, the court shall order each parent that is financially able to make periodic payments for the support of the child.

(b–1) In a proceeding described by Subsection (b) in which the court renders an order modifying an existing order for the support of the child to require that the payments be made to the Department of Family and Protective Services, the court shall provide notice of the order to the office of the attorney general not later than the 10th day after the date the order is rendered.

(c) In a Title IV–D case, if neither parent has physical possession or conservatorship of the child, the court may render an order providing that a nonparent or agency having physical possession may receive, hold, or disburse child support payments for the benefit of the child.

Added by Acts 1995, 74th Leg., ch. 20, § 1, eff. April 20, 1995. Amended by Acts 1995, 74th Leg., ch. 751, § 39, eff. Sept. 1, 1995; Acts 1999, 76th Leg., ch. 556, § 8, eff. Sept. 1, 1999; Acts 2005, 79th Leg., ch. 268, § 1.08(a), eff. Sept. 1, 2005; Acts 2013, 83rd Leg., ch. 907 (H.B. 1228), § 3, eff. Sept. 1, 2013; Acts 2017, 85th Leg., ch. 40 (S.B. 77), § 1, eff. Sept. 1, 2017; Acts 2021, 87th Leg., ch. 238 (H.B. 1227), § 1, eff. Sept. 1, 2021.

Section 2 of Acts 2021, 87th Leg., ch. 238 (H.B. 1227) provides:

"The change in law made by this Act applies only to a proceeding that is pending in a trial court on or filed on or after the effective date [Sept. 1, 2021] of this Act."

### § 154.002. Child Support Through High School Graduation

(a) The court may render an original support order, or modify an existing order, providing child support past the 18th birthday of the child to be paid only if the child is:

(1) enrolled:

(A) under Chapter 25, Education Code, in an accredited secondary school in a program leading toward a high school diploma;

(B) under Section 130.008, Education Code, in courses for joint high school and junior college credit; or

(C) on a full-time basis in a private secondary school in a program leading toward a high school diploma; and

(2) complying with:

(A) the minimum attendance requirements of Subchapter C, Chapter 25, Education Code; [1] or

(B) the minimum attendance requirements imposed by the school in which the child is enrolled, if the child is enrolled in a private secondary school.

(b) The request for a support order through high school graduation may be filed before or after the child's 18th birthday.

(c) The order for periodic support may provide that payments continue through the end of the month in which the child graduates.

Added by Acts 1995, 74th Leg., ch. 20, § 1, eff. April 20, 1995. Amended by Acts 1999, 76th Leg., ch. 506, § 1, eff. Aug. 30, 1999; Acts 2003, 78th Leg., ch. 38, § 1, eff. Sept. 1, 2003.

[1] V.T.C.A., Education Code § 25.081 et seq.

### § 154.003. Manner of Payment

The court may order that child support be paid by:

(1) periodic payments;

(2) a lump-sum payment;

(3) an annuity purchase;

(4) the setting aside of property to be administered for the support of the child as specified in the order;

(5) pension, retirement, or other employee benefits in accordance with an enforceable qualified domestic relations order or similar order under Subchapter J, Chapter 157; or

(6) any combination of periodic payments, lump-sum payments, annuity purchases, or setting aside of property.

Added by Acts 1995, 74th Leg., ch. 20, § 1, eff. April 20, 1995. Amended by Acts 2021, 87th Leg., ch. 64 (H.B. 867), § 4, eff. Sept. 1, 2021.

Section 6 of Acts 2021, 87th Leg., ch. 64 (H.B. 867) provides:

"(a) The changes in law made by this Act to Chapters 8, 154, and 157, Family Code, apply to an order for maintenance under Chapter 8, Family Code, or for child support under Chapter 154, Family Code, as applicable, regardless of whether the order was rendered before, on, or after the effective date [Sept. 1, 2021] of this Act.

"(b) The enactment of this Act does not constitute a material and substantial change of circumstances sufficient to warrant modification of a court order or portion of a decree that provides for maintenance or child support rendered before the effective date of this Act."

## § 154.004. Place of Payment

(a) The court shall order the payment of child support to the state disbursement unit as provided by Chapter 234.

(b) In a Title IV–D case, the court or the Title IV–D agency shall order that income withheld for child support be paid to the state disbursement unit of this state or, if appropriate, to the state disbursement unit of another state.

(c) This section does not apply to a child support order that:

(1) was initially rendered by a court before January 1, 1994; and

(2) is not being enforced by the Title IV–D agency.

Added by Acts 1995, 74th Leg., ch. 20, § 1, eff. April 20, 1995. Amended by Acts 1999, 76th Leg., ch. 556, § 9, eff. Sept. 1, 1999; Acts 2003, 78th Leg., ch. 1247, § 1, eff. Sept. 1, 2003.

## § 154.005. Payments of Support Obligation by Trust

(a) The court may order the trustees of a spendthrift or other trust to make disbursements for the support of a child to the extent the trustees are required to make payments to a beneficiary who is required to make child support payments as provided by this chapter.

(b) If disbursement of the assets of the trust is discretionary, the court may order child support payments from the income of the trust but not from the principal.

Added by Acts 1995, 74th Leg., ch. 20, § 1, eff. April 20, 1995.

## § 154.006. Termination of Duty of Support

(a) Unless otherwise agreed in writing or expressly provided in the order or as provided by Subsection (b), the child support order terminates on:

(1) the marriage of the child;

(2) the removal of the child's disabilities for general purposes;

(3) the death of the child;

(4) a finding by a court that the child:

(A) is 18 years of age or older; and

(B) has failed to comply with the enrollment or attendance requirements described by Section 154.002(a);

(5) the issuance under Section 161.005(h) of an order terminating the parent-child relationship between the obligor and the child based on the results of genetic testing that exclude the obligor as the child's genetic father; or

(6) if the child enlists in the armed forces of the United States, the date on which the child begins active service as defined by 10 U.S.C. Section 101.

(b) Unless a nonparent or agency has been appointed conservator of the child under Chapter 153, the order for current child support, and any provision relating to conservatorship, possession, or access terminates on the marriage or remarriage of the obligor and obligee to each other.

Added by Acts 1995, 74th Leg., ch. 20, § 1, eff. April 20, 1995. Amended by Acts 1999, 76th Leg., ch. 556, § 9, eff. Sept. 1, 1999; Acts 2003, 78th Leg., ch. 38, § 2, eff. Sept. 1, 2003; Acts 2007, 80th Leg., ch. 972, § 9(a), eff. Sept. 1, 2007; Acts 2007, 80th Leg., ch. 1404, § 1, eff. Sept. 1, 2007; Acts 2011, 82nd Leg., ch. 54 (S.B. 785), § 1, eff. May 12, 2011.

## § 154.007. Order to Withhold Child Support from Income

(a) In a proceeding in which periodic payments of child support are ordered, modified, or enforced, the court or Title IV-D agency shall order that income be withheld from the disposable earnings of the obligor as provided by Chapter 158.

(b) If the court does not order income withholding, an order for support must contain a provision for income withholding to ensure that withholding may be effected if a delinquency occurs.

(c) A child support order must be construed to contain a withholding provision even if the provision has been omitted from the written order.

(d) If the order was rendered or last modified before January 1, 1987, the order is presumed to contain a provision for income withholding procedures to take effect in the event a delinquency occurs without further amendment to the order or future action by the court.

Added by Acts 1995, 74th Leg., ch. 20, § 1, eff. April 20, 1995. Amended by Acts 1997, 75th Leg., ch. 911, § 10, eff. Sept. 1, 1997.

## § 154.008. Provision for Medical Support and Dental Support

The court shall order medical support and dental support for the child as provided by Subchapters B and D. [1]

Added by Acts 1995, 74th Leg., ch. 20, § 1, eff. April 20, 1995. Amended by Acts 2001, 77th Leg., ch. 1023, § 3, eff. Sept. 1, 2001; Acts 2015, 84th Leg., ch. 1150 (S.B. 550), § 8, eff. Sept. 1, 2018.

[1] V.T.C.A., Family Code § 154.061 et seq. and V.T.C.A., Family Code § 154.181 et seq.

### § 154.009. Retroactive Child Support

(a) The court may order a parent to pay retroactive child support if the parent:

(1) has not previously been ordered to pay support for the child; and

(2) was not a party to a suit in which support was ordered.

(b) In ordering retroactive child support, the court shall apply the child support guidelines provided by this chapter.

(c) Unless the Title IV–D agency is a party to an agreement concerning support or purporting to settle past, present, or future support obligations by prepayment or otherwise, an agreement between the parties does not reduce or terminate retroactive support that the agency may request.

(d) Notwithstanding Subsection (a), the court may order a parent subject to a previous child support order to pay retroactive child support if:

(1) the previous child support order terminated as a result of the marriage or remarriage of the child's parents;

(2) the child's parents separated after the marriage or remarriage; and

(3) a new child support order is sought after the date of the separation.

(e) In rendering an order under Subsection (d), the court may order retroactive child support back to the date of the separation of the child's parents.

Added by Acts 1995, 74th Leg., ch. 20, § 1, eff. April 20, 1995. Amended by Acts 2001, 77th Leg., ch. 1023, § 4, eff. Sept. 1, 2001.

### § 154.010. No Discrimination Based on Marital Status of Parents or Sex

The amount of support ordered for the benefit of a child shall be determined without regard to:

(1) the sex of the obligor, obligee, or child; or

(2) the marital status of the parents of the child.

Added by Acts 1995, 74th Leg., ch. 20, § 1, eff. April 20, 1995.

### § 154.011. Support Not Conditioned on Possession or Access

A court may not render an order that conditions the payment of child support on whether a managing conservator allows a possessory conservator to have possession of or access to a child.

Added by Acts 1995, 74th Leg., ch. 751, § 40, eff. Sept. 1, 1995.

### § 154.012. Support Paid in Excess of Support Order

(a) If an obligor is not in arrears and the obligor's child support obligation has terminated, the obligee shall return to the obligor a child support payment made by the obligor that exceeds the amount of support ordered, regardless of whether the payment was made before, on, or after the date the child support obligation terminated.

(b) An obligor may file a suit to recover a child support payment under Subsection (a). If the court finds that the obligee failed to return a child support payment under Subsection (a), the court shall order the obligee to pay to the obligor attorney's fees and all court costs in addition to the amount of support paid after the date the child support order terminated. For good cause shown, the court may waive the requirement that the obligee pay attorney's fees and costs if the court states the reasons supporting that finding.

Added by Acts 1999, 76th Leg., ch. 363, § 1, eff. Sept. 1, 1999. Amended by Acts 2001, 77th Leg., ch. 1023, § 5, eff. Sept. 1, 2001.

### § 154.013. Continuation of Duty to Pay Support After Death of Obligee

(a) A child support obligation does not terminate on the death of the obligee but continues as an obligation to the child named in the support order, as required by this section.

(b) Notwithstanding any provision of the Estates Code, a child support payment held by the Title IV–D agency, a local registry, or the state disbursement unit or any uncashed check or warrant representing a child support payment made before, on, or after the date of death of the obligee shall be paid proportionately for the benefit of each surviving child named in the support order and not to the estate of the obligee. The payment is free of any creditor's claim against the deceased obligee's estate and may be disbursed as provided by Subsection (c).

(c) On the death of the obligee, current child support owed by the obligor for the benefit of the child or any amount described by Subsection (b) shall be paid to:

(1) a person, other than a parent, who is appointed as managing conservator of the child;

(2) a person, including the obligor, who has assumed actual care, control, and possession of the child, if a managing conservator or guardian of the child has not been appointed;

(3) the county clerk, as provided by Chapter 1355, Estates Code, in the name of and for the account of the child for whom the support is owed;

(4) a guardian of the child appointed under Title 3, Estates Code, as provided by that code; or

(5) the surviving child, if the child is an adult or has otherwise had the disabilities of minority removed.

(d) On presentation of the obligee's death certificate, the court shall render an order directing payment of child support paid but not disbursed to be made as provided by Subsection (c). A copy of the order shall be provided to:

(1) the obligor;

(2) as appropriate:

(A) the person having actual care, control, and possession of the child;

(B) the county clerk; or

(C) the managing conservator or guardian of the child, if one has been appointed;

(3) the local registry or state disbursement unit and, if appropriate, the Title IV-D agency; and

(4) the child named in the support order, if the child is an adult or has otherwise had the disabilities of minority removed.

(e) The order under Subsection (d) must contain:

(1) a statement that the obligee is deceased and that child support amounts otherwise payable to the obligee shall be paid for the benefit of a surviving child named in the support order as provided by Subsection (c);

(2) the name and age of each child named in the support order; and

(3) the name and mailing address of, as appropriate:

(A) the person having actual care, control, and possession of the child;

(B) the county clerk; or

(C) the managing conservator or guardian of the child, if one has been appointed.

(f) On receipt of the order required under this section, the local registry, state disbursement unit, or Title IV-D agency shall disburse payments as required by the order.

Added by Acts 2001, 77th Leg., ch. 1023, § 6, eff. Sept. 1, 2001. Amended by Acts 2017, 85th Leg., ch. 324 (S.B. 1488), § 22.018, eff. Sept. 1, 2017.

### § 154.014. Payments in Excess of Court-Ordered Amount

(a) If a child support agency or local child support registry receives from an obligor who is not in arrears a child support payment in an amount that exceeds the court-ordered amount, the agency or registry, to the extent possible, shall give effect to any expressed intent of the obligor for the application of the amount that exceeds the court-ordered amount.

(b) If the obligor does not express an intent for the application of the amount paid in excess of the court-ordered amount, the agency or registry shall:

(1) credit the excess amount to the obligor's future child support obligation; and

(2) promptly disburse the excess amount to the obligee.

(c) This section does not apply to an obligee who is a recipient of public assistance under Chapter 31, Human Resources Code.

Added by Acts 2001, 77th Leg., ch. 1491, § 2, eff. Jan. 1, 2002. Renumbered from V.T.C.A., Family Code § 154.013 by Acts 2003, 78th Leg., ch. 1275, § 2(52), eff. Sept. 1, 2003.

### § 154.015. Acceleration of Unpaid Child Support Obligation

(a) In this section, "estate" has the meaning assigned by Chapter 22, Estates Code.

(b) If the child support obligor dies before the child support obligation terminates, the remaining unpaid balance of the child support obligation becomes payable on the date the obligor dies.

(c) For purposes of this section, the court of continuing jurisdiction shall determine the amount of the unpaid child support obligation for each child of the deceased obligor. In determining the amount of the unpaid child support obligation, the court shall consider all relevant factors, including:

(1) the present value of the total amount of monthly periodic child support payments that would become due between the month in which the obligor dies and the month in which the child turns 18 years of age, based on the amount of the periodic monthly child support payments under the child support order in effect on the date of the obligor's death;

(2) the present value of the total amount of health insurance and dental insurance premiums payable for the benefit of the child from the month in which the obligor dies until the month in which the child turns 18 years of age, based on the cost of health insurance and dental insurance for the child ordered to be paid on the date of the obligor's death;

(3) in the case of a disabled child under 18 years of age or an adult disabled child, an amount to be determined by the court under Section 154.306;

(4) the nature and amount of any benefit to which the child would be entitled as a result of the obligor's death, including life insurance proceeds, annuity payments, trust distributions, social security death benefits, and retirement survivor benefits; and

(5) any other financial resource available for the support of the child.

(d) If, after considering all relevant factors, the court finds that the child support obligation has been satisfied, the court shall render an order terminating the child support obligation. If the court finds that the child support obligation is not satisfied, the court shall render a judgment in favor of the obligee, for the benefit of the child, in the amount of the unpaid child support obligation determined under Subsection (c). The order must designate the obligee as constructive trustee, for the benefit of the child, of any money received in satisfaction of the judgment.

(e) The obligee has a claim, on behalf of the child, against the deceased obligor's estate for the unpaid child support obligation determined under Subsection (c). The obligee may present the claim in the manner provided by the Estates Code.

(f) If money paid to the obligee for the benefit of the child exceeds the amount of the unpaid child support obligation remaining at the time of the obligor's death, the obligee shall hold the excess amount as constructive trustee for the benefit of the deceased obligor's estate until the obligee delivers the excess amount to the legal representative of the deceased obligor's estate.

Added by Acts 2007, 80th Leg., ch. 1404, § 2, eff. Sept. 1, 2007. Amended by Acts 2015, 84th Leg., ch. 1150 (S.B. 550), § 9, eff. Sept. 1, 2018; Acts 2017, 85th Leg., ch. 324 (S.B. 1488), § 22.019, eff. Sept. 1, 2017.

### § 154.016. Provision of Support in Event of Death of Parent

(a) The court may order a child support obligor to obtain and maintain a life insurance policy, including a decreasing term life insurance policy, that will establish an insurance-funded trust or an annuity payable to the obligee for the benefit of the child that will satisfy the support obligation under the child support order in the event of the obligor's death.

(b) In determining the nature and extent of the obligation to provide for the support of the child in the event of the death of the obligor, the court shall consider all relevant factors, including:

(1) the present value of the total amount of monthly periodic child support payments from the date the child support order is rendered until the month in which the child turns 18 years of age, based on the amount of the periodic monthly child support payment under the child support order;

(2) the present value of the total amount of health insurance and dental insurance premiums payable for the benefit of the child from the date the child support order is rendered until the month in which the child turns 18 years of age, based on the cost of health insurance and dental insurance for the child ordered to be paid; and

(3) in the case of a disabled child under 18 years of age or an adult disabled child, an amount to be determined by the court under Section 154.306.

(c) The court may, on its own motion or on a motion of the obligee, require the child support obligor to provide proof satisfactory to the court verifying compliance with the order rendered under this section.

Added by Acts 2007, 80th Leg., ch. 1404, § 2, eff. Sept. 1, 2007. Amended by Acts 2015, 84th Leg., ch. 1150 (S.B. 550), § 10, eff. Sept. 1, 2018.

## SUBCHAPTER B. COMPUTING NET RESOURCES AVAILABLE FOR PAYMENT OF CHILD SUPPORT

### § 154.061. Computing Net Monthly Income

(a) Whenever feasible, gross income should first be computed on an annual basis and then should be recalculated to determine average monthly gross income.

(b) The Title IV–D agency shall annually promulgate tax charts to compute net monthly income, subtracting from gross income social security taxes and federal income tax withholding for a single person claiming one personal exemption and the standard deduction.

Added by Acts 1995, 74th Leg., ch. 20, § 1, eff. April 20, 1995.

## OFFICE OF THE ATTORNEY GENERAL
## 2021 TAX CHARTS
## Effective January 1, 2021

Pursuant to § 154.061(b) of the Texas Family Code, the Office of the Attorney General of Texas, as the Title IV–D agency, has promulgated the following tax charts to assist courts in establishing the amount of a child support order. These tax charts are applicable to employed and self-employed persons in computing net monthly income.

INSTRUCTIONS FOR USE

To use these tables, first compute the obligor's annual gross income. Then recompute to determine the obligor's average monthly gross income. These tables provide a method for calculating "monthly net income" for child support purposes, subtracting from monthly gross income the social security taxes and the federal income tax withholding for a single person claiming one personal exemption and the standard deduction.

Thereafter, in many cases the guidelines call for a number of additional steps to complete the necessary calculations. For example, §§ 154.061–154.070 provide for appropriate additions to "income" as that term is defined for federal income tax purposes, and for certain subtractions from monthly net income, in order to arrive at the net resources of the obligor available for child support purposes. If necessary, one may compute an obligee's net resources using similar steps.

LIMITATIONS ON USE

These charts are intended to assist courts in common situations, and do not account for all deductions and adjustments allowable under the Internal Revenue Code. For instance, these charts do not take into account the qualified business income deduction which might be taken by some owners of sole proprietorships, S corporations, partnerships, or stand-alone rental properties (pass-thru entities). In some situations, section 199A of the Internal Revenue Code allows owners of pass-thru entities to take a deduction against their income resulting in a reduction of the effective tax rate. These charts should not be used to estimate the net income of owners of pass-thru entities. The computation of net income for parties with complex tax situations may require consultation with an income tax professional.

EMPLOYED PERSONS
2021 TAX CHART

| | Federal Insurance Contributions Act Taxes | | | |
|---|---|---|---|---|
| Monthly Gross Wages | Old–Age, Survivors and Disability Insurance Program (Social Security) Tax (6.2%)* | Medicare's Hospital Insurance Program (Medicare) Tax (1.45%)* | Federal Income Tax*** | Net Monthly Income |
| 1,200.00 | 74.40 | 17.40 | 15.42 | 1,092.78 |
| 1,256.67**** | 77.91 | 18.22 | 21.08 | 1,139.46 |
| 1,300.00 | 80.60 | 18.85 | 25.42 | 1,175.13 |
| 1,400.00 | 86.80 | 20.30 | 35.42 | 1,257.48 |
| 1,500.00 | 93.00 | 21.75 | 45.42 | 1,339.83 |
| 1,600.00 | 99.20 | 23.20 | 55.42 | 1,422.18 |
| 1,700.00 | 105.40 | 24.65 | 65.42 | 1,504.53 |
| 1,800.00 | 111.60 | 26.10 | 75.42 | 1,586.88 |
| 1,900.00 | 117.80 | 27.55 | 85.92 | 1,668.73 |
| 2,000.00 | 124.00 | 29.00 | 97.92 | 1,749.08 |
| 2,100.00 | 130.20 | 30.45 | 109.92 | 1,829.43 |
| 2,200.00 | 136.40 | 31.90 | 121.92 | 1,909.78 |
| 2,300.00 | 142.60 | 33.35 | 133.92 | 1,990.13 |
| 2,400.00 | 148.80 | 34.80 | 145.92 | 2,070.48 |
| 2,500.00 | 155.00 | 36.25 | 157.92 | 2,150.83 |
| 2,600.00 | 161.20 | 37.70 | 169.92 | 2,231.18 |
| 2,700.00 | 167.40 | 39.15 | 181.92 | 2,311.53 |
| 2,800.00 | 173.60 | 40.60 | 193.92 | 2,391.88 |
| 2,900.00 | 179.80 | 42.05 | 205.92 | 2,472.23 |
| 3,000.00 | 186.00 | 43.50 | 217.92 | 2,552.58 |
| 3,100.00 | 192.20 | 44.95 | 229.92 | 2,632.93 |
| 3,200.00 | 198.40 | 46.40 | 241.92 | 2,713.28 |
| 3,300.00 | 204.60 | 47.85 | 253.92 | 2,793.63 |
| 3,400.00 | 210.80 | 49.30 | 265.92 | 2,873.98 |

| Monthly Gross Wages | Federal Insurance Contributions Act Taxes: Old–Age, Survivors and Disability Insurance Program (Social Security) Tax (6.2%)* | Medicare's Hospital Insurance Program (Medicare) Tax (1.45%)* | Federal Income Tax*** | Net Monthly Income |
|---|---|---|---|---|
| 3,500.00 | 217.00 | 50.75 | 277.92 | 2,954.33 |
| 3,600.00 | 223.20 | 52.20 | 289.92 | 3,034.68 |
| 3,700.00 | 229.40 | 53.65 | 301.92 | 3,115.03 |
| 3,800.00 | 235.60 | 55.10 | 313.92 | 3,195.38 |
| 3,900.00 | 241.80 | 56.55 | 325.92 | 3,275.73 |
| 4,000.00 | 248.00 | 58.00 | 337.92 | 3,356.08 |
| 4,100.00 | 254.20 | 59.45 | 349.92 | 3,436.43 |
| 4,200.00 | 260.40 | 60.90 | 361.92 | 3,516.78 |
| 4,300.00 | 266.60 | 62.35 | 373.92 | 3,597.13 |
| 4,400.00 | 272.80 | 63.80 | 385.92 | 3,677.48 |
| 4,500.00 | 279.00 | 65.25 | 405.63 | 3,750.12 |
| 4,600.00 | 285.20 | 66.70 | 427.63 | 3,820.47 |
| 4,700.00 | 291.40 | 68.15 | 449.63 | 3,890.82 |
| 4,800.00 | 297.60 | 69.60 | 471.63 | 3,961.17 |
| 4,900.00 | 303.80 | 71.05 | 493.63 | 4,031.52 |
| 5,000.00 | 310.00 | 72.50 | 515.63 | 4,101.87 |
| 5,100.00 | 316.20 | 73.95 | 537.63 | 4,172.22 |
| 5,200.00 | 322.40 | 75.40 | 559.63 | 4,242.57 |
| 5,300.00 | 328.60 | 76.85 | 581.63 | 4,312.92 |
| 5,400.00 | 334.80 | 78.30 | 603.63 | 4,383.27 |
| 5,500.00 | 341.00 | 79.75 | 625.63 | 4,453.62 |
| 5,600.00 | 347.20 | 81.20 | 647.63 | 4,523.97 |
| 5,700.00 | 353.40 | 82.65 | 669.63 | 4,594.32 |
| 5,800.00 | 359.60 | 84.10 | 691.63 | 4,664.67 |
| 5,900.00 | 365.80 | 85.55 | 713.63 | 4,735.02 |
| 6,000.00 | 372.00 | 87.00 | 735.63 | 4,805.37 |
| 6,250.00 | 387.50 | 90.63 | 790.63 | 4,981.24 |
| 6,500.00 | 403.00 | 94.25 | 845.63 | 5,157.12 |
| 6,750.00 | 418.50 | 97.88 | 900.63 | 5,332.99 |
| 7,000.00 | 434.00 | 101.50 | 955.63 | 5,508.87 |
| 7,500.00 | 465.00 | 108.75 | 1,065.63 | 5,860.62 |
| 8,000.00 | 496.00 | 116.00 | 1,175.63 | 6,212.37 |
| 8,500.00 | 527.00 | 123.25 | 1,290.75 | 6,559.00 |
| 9,000.00 | 558.00 | 130.50 | 1,410.75 | 6,900.75 |
| 9,500.00 | 589.00 | 137.75 | 1,530.75 | 7,242.50 |
| 10,000.00 | 620.00 | 145.00 | 1,650.75 | 7,584.25 |
| 10,500.00 | 651.00 | 152.25 | 1,770.75 | 7,926.00 |
| 11,000.00 | 682.00 | 159.50 | 1,890.75 | 8,267.75 |
| 11,500.00 | 713.00 | 166.75 | 2,010.75 | 8,609.50 |
| 11,900.00** | 737.80 | 172.55 | 2,106.75 | 8,882.90 |
| 12,000.00 | 737.80 | 174.00 | 2,130.75 | 8,957.45 |
| 12,325.35***** | 737.80 | 178.72 | 2,208.83 | 9,200.00 |

**Footnotes to Employed Persons 2021 Tax Chart:**

References to "the Code" refer to the Internal Revenue Code of 1986, as amended (26 U.S.C.)

* An employed person not subject to the Social Security Tax and the Medicare Tax will be allowed the reductions reflected in these columns, unless it is shown that such person has no similar contributory plan such as teacher retirement, federal railroad retirement, federal civil service retirement, etc.

** In 2021 the maximum level of Monthly Gross Wages for an employed person subject to the 6.2% Social Security tax is $142,800 per year, or $11,900 per month ($142,800 / 12 = $11,900). The maximum monthly Social Security Tax in 2021 is $737.80 based on the maximum OASDI Contribution and Benefit Base amount of $142,800 for 2021.

| | |
|---|---|
| Monthly Gross Wages | $142,800 for the year, or $11,900 monthly average |
| Social Security tax rate = 6.2% | $142,800 is equal to the 2021 OASDI contribution and benefit base, so $142,800 is taxed at this rate. |

$142,800 x .062 = $8,853.60 for the year, or $737.80 monthly average

*** These amounts represent one-twelfth (1/12) of the annual federal income tax calculated for a single taxpayer claiming one personal exemption (in the case of a taxable year beginning after December 31, 2017, and before January 1, 2026 the exemption amount is zero), and taking the standard deduction ($12,550).

Examples:

| | | |
|---|---|---|
| Monthly Gross Wages | $72,000 for the year, or $6,000 monthly average | $132,000 for the year, or $11,000 monthly average |
| Personal Exemption Section 151(d) of the Code | $0 for tax years 2018 through 2025 | $0 for tax years 2018 through 2025 |
| Standard Deduction Section 63(c) of the Code | $12,550 | $12,550 |
| Income amount to be used in the income tax computation | $72,000 - $0 - $12,550 = $59,450 | $132,000 - $0 - $12,550 = $119,450 |
| Income tax computation for 2021 | *If taxable income is over $40,525 but not over $86,375, the tax is $4,664.00 plus 22% of the excess over $40,525 (Section 1(j) of the Code)* $4,664 + (($59,450 - $40,525) x .22) = $8,827.50 for the year, or $735.63 monthly average | *If taxable income is over $86,375 but not over $164,925, the tax is $14,751 plus 24% of the excess over $86,375 (Section 1(j) of the Code)* $14,751 + (($119,450 - $86,375) x .24) = $22,689 for the year, or $1,890.75 monthly average |

**** This amount represents one-twelfth (1/12) of the gross income of an individual earning the federal minimum wage ($7.25 per hour) for a 40-hour week for a full year.

| | |
|---|---|
| Federal Minimum Wage = $7.25 per hour | $7.25 x 40 hours per week x 52 weeks per year = $15,080 per year |
| Monthly average | $15,080 / 12 = $1,256.67 monthly average |

***** This amount represents the point where the monthly gross wages of an employed individual would result in $9,200.00 of net resources. Texas Family Code section 154.125 provides "The guidelines for the support of a child in this section are specifically designed to apply to situations in which the obligor's monthly net resources are not greater than $7,500 or the adjusted amount determined under Subsection (a-1), whichever is greater." Effective September 1, 2019 the adjusted amount determined under Subsection (a-1) is $9,200.00. Texas Family Code section 154.126(a) provides, "If the obligor's net resources exceed the amount provided by Section 154.125(a), the court shall presumptively apply the percentage guidelines to the portion of the obligor's net resources that does not exceed that amount. Without further reference to the percentage recommendation by these guidelines, the court may order additional amounts of child support as appropriate, depending on the income of the parties and the proven needs of the child." The tax charts promulgated by the Office of the Attorney General include net monthly income amounts up to the amount specified in Texas Family Code section 154.125.

* * * * * * * * * * * * * * * * * * * * *

**Citations Relating to Employed Persons 2021 Tax Chart:**

1. Old–Age, Survivors and Disability Insurance Tax
   (a) Contribution Base
      (1) Social Security Administration's notice appearing in 85 Fed. Reg. 67413 (October 22, 2020)
      (2) Section 3121(a) of the Internal Revenue Code of 1986, as amended (26 U.S.C. § 3121(a))
      (3) Section 230 of the Social Security Act, as amended (42 U.S.C. § 430)
   (b) Tax Rate
      (1) Section 3101(a) of the Internal Revenue Code of 1986, as amended (26 U.S.C. § 3101(a))
2. Hospital (Medicare) Insurance Tax
   (a) Contribution Base
      (1) Section 3121(a) of the Internal Revenue Code of 1986, as amended (26 U.S.C. § 3121(a))
      (2) Omnibus Budget Reconciliation Act of 1993, Pub.L.No. 103–66, § 13207, 107 Stat. 312, 467–69 (1993)
   (b) Tax Rate
      (1) Section 3101(b) of the Internal Revenue Code of 1986, as amended (26 U.S.C. § 3101(b))
3. Federal Income Tax
   (a) Tax Rate Schedule for 2021 for Single Taxpayers

(1) Revenue Procedure 2020-45, Section 3.01, Table 3 which appears in Internal Revenue Bulletin 2020-46, dated November 9, 2020,
(2) Section 1(j) of the Internal Revenue Code of 1986, as amended (26 U.S.C. § 1(j))
(b) Standard Deduction
(1) Revenue Procedure 2020-45, Section 3.16, which appears in Internal Revenue Bulletin 2020-46, dated November 9, 2020
(2) Section 63(c) of the Internal Revenue Code of 1986, as amended (26 U.S.C. § 63(c))
(c) Personal Exemption
(1) An Act to provide for reconciliation pursuant to titles II and V of the concurrent resolution on the budget for fiscal year 2018, Pub. L. No. 115-97, 131 Stat. 2054 (codified as amended in scattered sections of 26 U.S.C.) amended the Internal Revenue Code of 1986, by adding a new paragraph to Section 151(d), which dictates that the personal exemption amount is zero for the taxable years 2018 through 2025.
(2) Section 151(d) of the Internal Revenue Code of 1986, as amended (26 U.S.C. § 151(d))

4. Adjusted amount determined under Subsection (a–1) of Texas Family Code section 154.125
Office of the Attorney General "Announcement of Adjustment Required by Texas Family Code section 154.125" appearing in 44 TexReg 3559 (July 12, 2019)

SELF–EMPLOYED PERSONS
2021 TAX CHART

| Monthly Self-Employment Income TFC 154.065* | Old–Age, Survivors and Disability Insurance Program (Social Security) Tax (12.4%)** | Medicare's Hospital Insurance Program (Medicare) Tax (2.9%)** | Federal Income Tax**** | Net Monthly Income |
|---|---|---|---|---|
| 1,200.00 | 137.42 | 32.14 | 6.94 | 1,023.50 |
| 1,300.00 | 148.87 | 34.82 | 16.23 | 1,100.08 |
| 1,400.00 | 160.32 | 37.49 | 25.53 | 1,176.66 |
| 1,500.00 | 171.77 | 40.17 | 34.82 | 1,253.24 |
| 1,600.00 | 183.22 | 42.85 | 44.11 | 1,329.82 |
| 1,700.00 | 194.67 | 45.53 | 53.41 | 1,406.39 |
| 1,800.00 | 206.13 | 48.21 | 62.70 | 1,482.96 |
| 1,900.00 | 217.58 | 50.88 | 71.99 | 1,559.55 |
| 2,000.00 | 229.03 | 53.56 | 81.29 | 1,636.12 |
| 2,100.00 | 240.48 | 56.24 | 92.11 | 1,711.17 |
| 2,200.00 | 251.93 | 58.92 | 103.27 | 1,785.88 |
| 2,300.00 | 263.38 | 61.60 | 114.42 | 1,860.60 |
| 2,400.00 | 274.83 | 64.28 | 125.57 | 1,935.32 |
| 2,500.00 | 286.29 | 66.95 | 136.72 | 2,010.04 |
| 2,600.00 | 297.74 | 69.63 | 147.87 | 2,084.76 |
| 2,700.00 | 309.19 | 72.31 | 159.03 | 2,159.47 |
| 2,800.00 | 320.64 | 74.99 | 170.18 | 2,234.19 |
| 2,900.00 | 332.09 | 77.67 | 181.33 | 2,308.91 |
| 3,000.00 | 343.54 | 80.34 | 192.48 | 2,383.64 |
| 3,100.00 | 354.99 | 83.02 | 203.64 | 2,458.35 |
| 3,200.00 | 366.44 | 85.70 | 214.79 | 2,533.07 |
| 3,300.00 | 377.90 | 88.38 | 225.94 | 2,607.78 |
| 3,400.00 | 389.35 | 91.06 | 237.09 | 2,682.50 |
| 3,500.00 | 400.80 | 93.74 | 248.24 | 2,757.22 |
| 3,600.00 | 412.25 | 96.41 | 259.40 | 2,831.94 |
| 3,700.00 | 423.70 | 99.09 | 270.55 | 2,906.66 |
| 3,800.00 | 435.15 | 101.77 | 281.70 | 2,981.38 |
| 3,900.00 | 446.60 | 104.45 | 292.85 | 3,056.10 |
| 4,000.00 | 458.06 | 107.13 | 304.01 | 3,130.80 |
| 4,100.00 | 469.51 | 109.80 | 315.16 | 3,205.53 |
| 4,200.00 | 480.96 | 112.48 | 326.31 | 3,280.25 |
| 4,300.00 | 492.41 | 115.16 | 337.46 | 3,354.97 |
| 4,400.00 | 503.86 | 117.84 | 348.61 | 3,429.69 |
| 4,500.00 | 515.31 | 120.52 | 359.77 | 3,504.40 |
| 4,600.00 | 526.76 | 123.19 | 370.92 | 3,579.13 |
| 4,700.00 | 538.22 | 125.87 | 382.07 | 3,653.84 |
| 4,800.00 | 549.67 | 128.55 | 397.02 | 3,724.76 |
| 4,900.00 | 561.12 | 131.23 | 417.47 | 3,790.18 |
| 5,000.00 | 572.57 | 133.91 | 437.91 | 3,855.61 |

| Monthly Self-Employment Income TFC 154.065* | Old–Age, Survivors and Disability Insurance Program (Social Security) Tax (12.4%)** | Medicare's Hospital Insurance Program (Medicare) Tax (2.9%)** | Federal Income Tax**** | Net Monthly Income |
|---|---|---|---|---|
| 5,100.00 | 584.02 | 136.59 | 458.36 | 3,921.03 |
| 5,200.00 | 595.47 | 139.26 | 478.80 | 3,986.47 |
| 5,300.00 | 606.92 | 141.94 | 499.25 | 4,051.89 |
| 5,400.00 | 618.38 | 144.62 | 519.70 | 4,117.30 |
| 5,500.00 | 629.83 | 147.30 | 540.14 | 4,182.73 |
| 5,600.00 | 641.28 | 149.98 | 560.59 | 4,248.15 |
| 5,700.00 | 652.73 | 152.65 | 581.03 | 4,313.59 |
| 5,800.00 | 664.18 | 155.33 | 601.48 | 4,379.01 |
| 5,900.00 | 675.63 | 158.01 | 621.92 | 4,444.44 |
| 6,000.00 | 687.08 | 160.69 | 642.37 | 4,509.86 |
| 6,250.00 | 715.71 | 167.38 | 693.48 | 4,673.43 |
| 6,500.00 | 744.34 | 174.08 | 744.60 | 4,836.98 |
| 6,750.00 | 772.97 | 180.78 | 795.71 | 5,000.54 |
| 7,000.00 | 801.60 | 187.47 | 846.83 | 5,164.10 |
| 7,500.00 | 858.86 | 200.86 | 949.06 | 5,491.22 |
| 8,000.00 | 916.11 | 214.25 | 1,051.28 | 5,818.36 |
| 8,500.00 | 973.37 | 227.64 | 1,153.51 | 6,145.48 |
| 9,000.00 | 1,030.63 | 241.03 | 1,258.15 | 6,470.19 |
| 9,500.00 | 1,087.88 | 254.42 | 1,369.67 | 6,788.03 |
| 10,000.00 | 1,145.14 | 267.81 | 1,481.20 | 7,105.85 |
| 10,500.00 | 1,202.40 | 281.21 | 1,592.72 | 7,423.67 |
| 11,000.00 | 1,259.65 | 294.60 | 1,704.24 | 7,741.51 |
| 11,500.00 | 1,316.91 | 307.99 | 1,815.76 | 8,059.34 |
| 12,000.00 | 1,374.17 | 321.38 | 1,927.28 | 8,377.17 |
| 12,885.76*** | 1,475.60 | 345.10 | 2,124.85 | 8,940.21 |
| 13,000.00 | 1,475.60 | 348.16 | 2,151.90 | 9,024.34 |
| 13,238.53***** | 1,475.60 | 354.55 | 2,208.38 | 9,200.00 |

**Footnotes to Self–Employed Persons 2021 Tax Chart:**

References to "the Code" refer to the Internal Revenue Code of 1986, as amended (26 U.S.C.)

* Texas Family Code Section 154.065 defines what is included in, and what may be excluded from, self-employment income for Texas child support guideline computation purposes. The values displayed in the first column of this chart are the full amount of net earnings from self-employment income (determined before the deduction required by Section 1402(a)(12) of the Code explained in the next footnote, **[2]).

** The tax rates for self-employment taxes are 12.4% for the Social Security tax and 2.9% for the Medicare tax, however, only a portion of the net earnings from self-employment are subject to these taxes. Section 1402(a)(12) of the Code permits a self-employed person a deduction in net earnings from self-employment (as defined in sections 1401 and 1402 of the Code) equal to one-half of the combined rates. The purpose is to adjust net income downward by the amount that would have been paid by an employer, had the individual been classified as an employee. The sum of these rates is 15.3% (12.4% + 2.9% = 15.3%). One-half (1/2) of the combined rate is 7.65% (15.3% x 1/2 = 7.65%). Self-employed taxpayers compute this deduction by multiplying net earnings from self-employment by .9235 (100% - 7.65% = 92.35%) to determine the portion of self-employment income subject to self-employment taxes.

Social Security tax is owed on the portion of self-employment income subject to self-employment taxes that do not exceed the maximum OASDI Contribution and Benefit Base amount of $142,800 (for tax year 2021). Medicare's Hospital Insurance Program (Medicare) tax is owed on the full amount of self-employment income subject to self-employment taxes. Section 1401 of the Code.

Examples:

| | | |
|---|---|---|
| Monthly Self-Employment Income, TFC 154.065 | $72,000 for the year, or $6,000 monthly average | $156,000 for the year, or $13,000 monthly average |
| 92.35% of self-employment income is subject to self-employment taxes | $72,000 x .9235 = $66,492 for the year | $156,000 x .9235 = $144,066 for the year |
| Social Security tax rate = 12.4% | $66,492 does not exceed the OASDI contribution and benefit base, so $66,492 is taxed at this rate. | $144,066 exceeds the OASDI contribution and benefit base, so only the first $142,800 is taxed at this rate. |

| | | |
|---|---|---|
| | $66,492 x .124 = $8,245 for the year, or $687.08 monthly average | $142,800 x .124 = $17,707.20 for the year, or $1,475.60 monthly average |
| Medicare tax rate = 2.9% | $66,492 x .029 = $1,928.27 for the year, or $160.69 monthly average | $144,066 x .029 = $4,177.91 for the year, or $348.16 monthly average |

*** In 2021 the maximum level of Monthly Self-Employment Income subject to the 12.4% Social Security tax is $154,629.13 per year, or $12,885.76 per month ($154,629.13 / 12 = $12,885.76). This is the income amount before the deduction required by Section 1402(a)(12) of the Code. The maximum monthly Social Security Tax in 2021 is $1,475.60 based on the maximum OASDI Contribution and Benefit Base amount of $142,800 for 2021.

| | |
|---|---|
| Monthly Self-Employment Income, TFC 154.065 | $154,629.13 for the year, or $12,885.76 monthly average |
| 92.35% of self-employment income is subject to self-employment taxes | $154,629.13 x .9235 = $142,800 for the year |
| Social Security tax rate = 12.4% | $142,800 is equal to the 2021 OASDI contribution and benefit base, so $142,800 is taxed at this rate.<br><br>142,800 x .124 = $17,707.20 for the year, or $1,475.60 monthly average |

**** These amounts represent one-twelfth (1/12) of the annual federal income tax calculated for a single taxpayer claiming one personal exemption (in the case of a taxable year beginning after December 31, 2017, and before January 1, 2026 the exemption amount is zero), and taking the standard deduction ($12,550).

The calculation of federal income taxes on self-employment income requires the determination of the total self-employment taxes imposed, as described above. The calculation of federal income taxes permits the taxpayer to reduce net income from self-employment by one half of the actual taxes imposed thereby approximating the employment taxes (Social Security and Medicare) that are paid by an employed person. Section 164(f) of the Code.

Examples:

| | | |
|---|---|---|
| Monthly Self-Employment Income, TFC 154.065 | $72,000 for the year, or $6,000 monthly average | $156,000 for the year, or $13,000 monthly average |
| Social security tax | $8,245 for the year, or $687.08 monthly average | $17,707.20 for the year, or $1,475.60 monthly average |
| Medicare tax | $1,928.27 for the year, or $160.69 monthly average | $4,177.91 for the year, or $348.16 monthly average |
| Total self-employment taxes imposed | $8,245 + $1,928.27 = $10,173.27 for the year | $17,707.20 + $4,177.91 = $21,885.11 for the year |
| Tax deductible portion of self-employment taxes. Section 164(f) of the Code | $10,173.27 x 1/2 = $5,086.64 for the year | $21,885.11 x 1/2 = $10,942.56 for the year |
| Personal Exemption Section 151(d) of the Code | $0 for tax years 2018 through 2025 | $0 for tax years 2018 through 2025 |
| Standard Deduction Section 63(c) of the Code | $12,550 | $12,550 |
| Income amount to be used in the income tax computation | $72,000 - $5,086.64 - $0 - $12,550 = $54,363.36 | $156,000 - $10,942.56 - $0 - $12,550 = $132,507.44 |
| Income tax computation for 2021 | *If taxable income is over $40,525 but not over $86,375, the tax is $4,664 plus 22% of the excess over $40,525 (Section 1(j) of the Code)*<br><br>$4,664 + (($54,363.36 - $40,525) x .22) = $7,708.44 for the year, or $642.37 monthly average | *If taxable income is over $86,375 but not over $164,925 the tax is $14,751 plus 24% of the excess over $86,375 (Section 1(j) of the Code)*<br><br>$14,751 + (($132,507.44 - $86,375) x .24) = $25,822.79 for the year, or $2,151.90 monthly average |

Note: For tax years 2018 through 2025, the personal exemption amount is zero. Section 63(c) of the Code. For 2021, the computations do not include the subtraction of any personal exemptions.

***** This amount represents the point where the monthly gross income of a self-employed individual would result in $9,200.00 of net resources. Texas Family Code section 154.125 provides, "The guidelines for the support of a child in this section are specifically designed to apply to situations in which the obligor's monthly net resources are not greater than $7,500 or the adjusted amount determined under Subsection (a-1), whichever is greater." Effective September 1, 2019 the adjusted amount determined under Subsection (a-1) is $9,200.00. Texas Family Code section 154.126(a) provides, "If the obligor's net resources exceed the amount provided by Section 154.125(a), the court shall presumptively apply the percentage guidelines to the portion of the obligor's net resources that does not exceed that amount. Without further reference to the percentage recommendation by these guidelines, the court may order additional amounts of child support as appropriate, depending on the income of the parties and the proven needs of the child." The tax charts promulgated by the Office of the Attorney General include net monthly income amounts up to the amount specified in Texas Family Code section 154.125.

* * * * * * * * * * * * * * * * * * * * * *

**Citations Relating to Self-Employed Persons 2021 Tax Chart:**

1. Old–Age, Survivors and Disability Insurance Tax
   - (a) Contribution Base
     - (1) Social Security Administration's notice appearing in 85 Fed. Reg. 67413 (October 22, 2020)
     - (2) Section 1402(b) of the Internal Revenue Code of 1986, as amended (26 U.S.C. § 1402(b))
     - (3) Section 230 of the Social Security Act, as amended (42 U.S.C. § 430)
   - (b) Tax Rate
     - (1) Section 1401(a) of the Internal Revenue Code of 1986, as amended (26 U.S.C. § 1401(a))
   - (c) Deduction Under Section 1402(a)(12)
     - (1) Section 1402(a)(12) of the Internal Revenue Code of 1986, as amended (26 U.S.C. § 1402(a)(12))
2. Hospital (Medicare) Insurance Tax
   - (a) Contribution Base
     - (1) Section 1402(b) of the Internal Revenue Code of 1986, as amended (26 U.S.C. § 1402(b))
     - (2) Omnibus Budget Reconciliation Act of 1993, Pub. L. No. 103–66, § 13207, 107 Stat. 312, 467–69 (1993)
   - (b) Tax Rate
     - (1) Section 1401(b) of the Internal Revenue Code of 1986, as amended (26 U.S.C. § 1401(b))
   - (c) Deduction Under Section 1402(a)(12)
     - (1) Section 1402(a)(12) of the Internal Revenue Code of 1986, as amended (26 U.S.C. § 1402(a)(12))
3. Federal Income Tax
   - (a) Tax Rate Schedule for 2021 for Single Taxpayers
     - (1) Revenue Procedure 2020-45, Section 3.01, Table 3 which appears in Internal Revenue Bulletin 2020-46, dated November 9, 2020,
     - (2) Section 1(j), of the Internal Revenue Code of 1986, as amended (26 U.S.C. § 1(j))
   - (b) Standard Deduction
     - (1) Revenue Procedure 2020-45, Section 3.16, which appears in Internal Revenue Bulletin 2020-46, dated November 9, 2020
     - (2) Section 63(c) of the Internal Revenue Code of 1986, as amended (26 U.S.C. § 63(c))
   - (c) Personal Exemption
     - (1) An Act to provide for reconciliation pursuant to titles II and V of the concurrent resolution on the budget for fiscal year 2018, Pub. L. No. 115-97, 131 Stat. 2054 (codified as amended in scattered sections of 26 U.S.C.) amended the Internal Revenue Code of 1986, by adding a new paragraph to Section 151(d), which dictates that the personal exemption amount is zero for the taxable years 2018 through 2025.
     - (2) Section 151(d) of the Internal Revenue Code of 1986, as amended (26 U.S.C. § 151(d))
   - (d) Deduction Under Section 164(f)
     - (1) Section 164(f) of the Internal Revenue Code of 1986, as amended (26 U.S.C. § 164(f))
4. Adjusted amount determined under Subsection (a–1) of Texas Family Code section 154.125 Office of the Attorney General "Announcement of Adjustment Required by Texas Family Code section 154.125" appearing in 44 TexReg 3559 (July 12, 2019)

### § 154.062. Net Resources

(a) The court shall calculate net resources for the purpose of determining child support liability as provided by this section.

(b) Resources include:

(1) 100 percent of all wage and salary income and other compensation for personal services (including commissions, overtime pay, tips, and bonuses);

(2) interest, dividends, and royalty income;

(3) self-employment income;

(4) net rental income (defined as rent after deducting operating expenses and mortgage payments, but not including noncash items such as depreciation); and

(5) all other income actually being received, including severance pay, retirement benefits, pensions, trust income, annuities, capital gains, social security benefits other than supplemental security income, United States Department of Veterans Affairs disability benefits other than non-service-connected disability pension benefits, as defined by 38 U.S.C. Section 101(17), unemployment benefits, disability and workers' compensation benefits, interest income from notes regardless of the source, gifts and prizes, spousal maintenance, and alimony.

(c) Resources do not include:

(1) return of principal or capital;

(2) accounts receivable;

(3) benefits paid in accordance with the Temporary Assistance for Needy Families program or another federal public assistance program; or

(4) payments for foster care of a child.

(d) The court shall deduct the following items from resources to determine the net resources available for child support:

(1) social security taxes;

(2) federal income tax based on the tax rate for a single person claiming one personal exemption and the standard deduction;

(3) state income tax;

(4) union dues;

(5) expenses for the cost of health insurance, dental insurance, or cash medical support for the obligor's child ordered by the court under Sections 154.182 and 154.1825; and

(6) if the obligor does not pay social security taxes, nondiscretionary retirement plan contributions.

(e) In calculating the amount of the deduction for health care or dental coverage for a child under Subsection (d)(5), if the obligor has other minor dependents covered under the same health or dental insurance plan, the court shall divide the total cost to the obligor for the insurance by the total number of minor dependents, including the child, covered under the plan.

(f) For purposes of Subsection (d)(6), a nondiscretionary retirement plan is a plan to which an employee is required to contribute as a condition of employment.

Added by Acts 1995, 74th Leg., ch. 20, § 1, eff. April 20, 1995. Amended by Acts 1995, 74th Leg., ch. 751, § 41, eff. Sept. 1, 1995; Acts 2007, 80th Leg., ch. 363, § 1, eff. Sept. 1, 2007; Acts 2007, 80th Leg., ch. 620, § 1, eff. Sept. 1, 2007; Acts 2009, 81st Leg., ch. 87, § 9.001, eff. Sept. 1, 2009; Acts 2009, 81st Leg., ch. 767, § 4, eff. June 19, 2009; Acts 2009, 81st Leg., ch. 834, § 1, eff. Sept. 1, 2009; Acts 2009, 81st Leg., ch. 1118, § 1, eff. Sept. 1, 2009; Acts 2011, 82nd Leg., ch. 91 (S.B. 1303), § 9.001, eff. Sept. 1, 2011; Acts 2011, 82nd Leg., ch. 932 (S.B. 1751), § 1, eff. Sept. 1, 2012; Acts 2013, 83rd Leg., ch. 1046 (H.B. 3017), § 1, eff. Sept. 1, 2013; Acts 2015, 84th Leg., ch. 1150 (S.B. 550), § 11, eff. Sept. 1, 2018.

## § 154.063. Party to Furnish Information

The court shall require a party to:

(1) furnish information sufficient to accurately identify that party's net resources and ability to pay child support; and

(2) produce copies of income tax returns for the past two years, a financial statement, and current pay stubs.

Added by Acts 1995, 74th Leg., ch. 20, § 1, eff. April 20, 1995.

## § 154.064. Medical Support and Dental Support for Child Presumptively Provided by Obligor

The guidelines for support of a child are based on the assumption that the court will order the obligor to provide medical support and dental support for the child in addition to the amount of child support calculated in accordance with those guidelines.

Added by Acts 1995, 74th Leg., ch. 20, § 1, eff. April 20, 1995. Amended by Acts 2001, 77th Leg., ch. 1023, § 7, eff. Sept. 1, 2001; Acts 2015, 84th Leg., ch. 1150 (S.B. 550), § 12, eff. Sept. 1, 2018.

## § 154.065. Self-Employment Income

(a) Income from self-employment, whether positive or negative, includes benefits allocated to an individual from a business or undertaking in the form of a proprietorship, partnership, joint venture, close corporation, agency, or independent contractor, less ordinary and necessary expenses required to produce that income.

(b) In its discretion, the court may exclude from self-employment income amounts allowable under federal income tax law as depreciation, tax credits, or any other business expenses shown by the evidence to be inappropriate in making the determination of income available for the purpose of calculating child support.

Added by Acts 1995, 74th Leg., ch. 20, § 1, eff. April 20, 1995.

## § 154.0655. Imputation of Income

(a) In this section, "resources" has the meaning assigned by Section 154.062(b).

(b) To the extent possible, the court shall rely on evidence of a party's resources when applying the support guidelines.

(c) In the absence of evidence of a party's resources, the court, when applying Section 154.066 or 154.068, shall consider relevant background circumstances regarding the obligor, including:

(1) the obligor's:

(A) assets;

(B) residence;

(C) employment;

(D) earnings history;

(E) job skills;

(F) educational attainment;

(G) literacy;

(H) age;

(I) health;

(J) criminal history;

(K) barriers to employment; and

(L) record of seeking work;

(2) job opportunities in the obligor's community;

(3) the prevailing wage in the obligor's community; and

(4) whether there are employers willing to hire the obligor.

Added by Acts 2021, 87th Leg., ch. 552 (S.B. 286), § 2, eff. Sept. 1, 2021.

Section 12 of Acts 2021, 87th Leg., ch. 552 (S.B. 286) provides:

"The enactment of this Act does not constitute a material and substantial change of circumstances sufficient to warrant modification of a court order or portion of a decree that provides for the support of a child rendered before the effective date [Sept. 1, 2021] of this Act."

Section 14 of Acts 2021, 87th Leg., ch. 552 (S.B. 286) provides:

"Section 154.0655, Family Code, as added by this Act, and Section 154.066, Family Code, as amended by this Act, apply only to a proceeding to establish or modify a child support obligation that is pending in a trial court on or filed on or after the effective date [Sept. 1, 2021] of this Act."

## § 154.066. Intentional Unemployment or Underemployment

(a) If the actual income of the obligor is significantly less than what the obligor could earn because of intentional unemployment or underemployment, the court may apply the support guidelines to the earning potential of the obligor.

(b) In determining whether an obligor is intentionally unemployed or underemployed, the court may consider evidence that the obligor is a veteran, as defined by 38 U.S.C. Section 101(2), who is seeking or has been awarded:

(1) United States Department of Veterans Affairs disability benefits, as defined by 38 U.S.C. Section 101(16); or

(2) non-service-connected disability pension benefits, as defined by 38 U.S.C. Section 101(17).

(c) The court may not consider incarceration as intentional unemployment or underemployment when establishing or modifying a support order.

Added by Acts 1995, 74th Leg., ch. 20, § 1, eff. April 20, 1995. Amended by Acts 2013, 83rd Leg., ch. 1046 (H.B. 3017), § 2, eff. Sept. 1, 2013; Acts 2021, 87th Leg., ch. 552 (S.B. 286), § 3, eff. Sept. 1, 2021.

Section 12 of Acts 2021, 87th Leg., ch. 552 (S.B. 286) provides:

"The enactment of this Act does not constitute a material and substantial change of circumstances sufficient to warrant modification of a court order or portion of a decree that provides for the support of a child rendered before the effective date [Sept. 1, 2021] of this Act."

## § 154.067. Deemed Income

(a) When appropriate, in order to determine the net resources available for child support, the court may assign a reasonable amount of deemed income attributable to assets that do not currently produce income. The court shall also consider whether certain property that is not producing income can be liquidated without an unreasonable financial sacrifice because of cyclical or other market conditions. If there is no effective market for the property, the carrying costs of such an investment, including property taxes and note payments, shall be offset against the income attributed to the property.

(b) The court may assign a reasonable amount of deemed income to income-producing assets that a party has voluntarily transferred or on which earnings have intentionally been reduced.

Added by Acts 1995, 74th Leg., ch. 20, § 1, eff. April 20, 1995.

## § 154.068. Wage and Salary Presumption

(a) In the absence of evidence of a party's resources, as defined by Section 154.062(b), the court shall presume that the party has income equal to the federal minimum wage for a 40-hour week to which the support guidelines may be applied.

(b) The presumption required by Subsection (a) does not apply if the court finds that the party is subject to an order of confinement that exceeds 90 days and is incarcerated in a local, state, or federal jail or prison at the time the court makes the determination regarding the party's income.

Added by Acts 1995, 74th Leg., ch. 20, § 1, eff. April 20, 1995. Amended by Acts 2013, 83rd Leg., ch. 1046 (H.B. 3017), § 3, eff. Sept. 1, 2013; Acts 2015, 84th Leg., ch. 1249 (H.B. 943), § 1, eff. Sept. 1, 2015.

### § 154.069. Net Resources of Spouse

(a) The court may not add any portion of the net resources of a spouse to the net resources of an obligor or obligee in order to calculate the amount of child support to be ordered.

(b) The court may not subtract the needs of a spouse, or of a dependent of a spouse, from the net resources of the obligor or obligee.

Added by Acts 1995, 74th Leg., ch. 20, § 1, eff. April 20, 1995.

### § 154.070. Child Support Received by Obligor

In a situation involving multiple households due child support, child support received by an obligor shall be added to the obligor's net resources to compute the net resources before determining the child support credit or applying the percentages in the multiple household table in this chapter.

Added by Acts 1995, 74th Leg., ch. 20, § 1, eff. April 20, 1995.

## SUBCHAPTER C. CHILD SUPPORT GUIDELINES

### § 154.121. Guidelines for the Support of a Child

The child support guidelines in this subchapter are intended to guide the court in determining an equitable amount of child support.

Added by Acts 1995, 74th Leg., ch. 20, § 1, eff. April 20, 1995.

### § 154.122. Application of Guidelines Rebuttably Presumed in Best Interest of Child

(a) The amount of a periodic child support payment established by the child support guidelines in effect in this state at the time of the hearing is presumed to be reasonable, and an order of support conforming to the guidelines is presumed to be in the best interest of the child.

(b) A court may determine that the application of the guidelines would be unjust or inappropriate under the circumstances.

Added by Acts 1995, 74th Leg., ch. 20, § 1, eff. April 20, 1995.

### § 154.123. Additional Factors for Court to Consider

(a) The court may order periodic child support payments in an amount other than that established by the guidelines if the evidence rebuts the presumption that application of the guidelines is in the best interest of the child and justifies a variance from the guidelines.

(b) In determining whether application of the guidelines would be unjust or inappropriate under the circumstances, the court shall consider evidence of all relevant factors, including:

(1) the age and needs of the child;

(2) the ability of the parents to contribute to the support of the child;

(3) any financial resources available for the support of the child;

(4) the amount of time of possession of and access to a child;

(5) the amount of the obligee's net resources, including the earning potential of the obligee if the actual income of the obligee is significantly less than what the obligee could earn because the obligee is intentionally unemployed or underemployed and including an increase or decrease in the income of the obligee or income that may be attributed to the property and assets of the obligee;

(6) child care expenses incurred by either party in order to maintain gainful employment;

(7) whether either party has the managing conservatorship or actual physical custody of another child;

(8) the amount of alimony or spousal maintenance actually and currently being paid or received by a party;

(9) the expenses for a son or daughter for education beyond secondary school;

(10) whether the obligor or obligee has an automobile, housing, or other benefits furnished by his or her employer, another person, or a business entity;

(11) the amount of other deductions from the wage or salary income and from other compensation for personal services of the parties;

(12) provision for health care insurance and payment of uninsured medical expenses;

(13) special or extraordinary educational, health care, or other expenses of the parties or of the child;

(14) the cost of travel in order to exercise possession of and access to a child;

(15) positive or negative cash flow from any real and personal property and assets, including a business and investments;

(16) debts or debt service assumed by either party; and

(17) any other reason consistent with the best interest of the child, taking into consideration the circumstances of the parents.

Added by Acts 1995, 74th Leg., ch. 20, § 1, eff. April 20, 1995.

### § 154.124. Agreement Concerning Support

(a) To promote the amicable settlement of disputes between the parties to a suit, the parties may enter into a written agreement containing provisions for support of the child and for modification of the agreement, including variations from the child support guidelines provided by Subchapter C.[1]

(b) If the court finds that the agreement is in the child's best interest, the court shall render an order in accordance with the agreement.

(c) Terms of the agreement pertaining to child support in the order may be enforced by all remedies available for enforcement of a judgment, including contempt, but are not enforceable as a contract.

(d) If the court finds the agreement is not in the child's best interest, the court may request the parties to submit a revised agreement or the court may render an order for the support of the child.

Added by Acts 1995, 74th Leg., ch. 20, § 1, eff. April 20, 1995. Amended by Acts 2003, 78th Leg., ch. 480, § 1, eff. Sept. 1, 2003.

[1] V.T.C.A., Family Code § 154.121 et seq.

### § 154.125. Application of Guidelines to Net Resources

(a) The guidelines for the support of a child in this section are specifically designed to apply to situations in which the obligor's monthly net resources are not greater than the maximum amount of net resources to which the statutory guidelines are applicable, as most recently published by the Title IV–D agency in the Texas Register.

(a–1) The amount prescribed by Subsection (a) is adjusted every six years as necessary to reflect inflation. The Title IV–D agency shall compute the adjusted amount, to take effect beginning September 1 of the year of the adjustment, based on the percentage change in the consumer price index during the 72–month period preceding March 1 of the year of the adjustment, as rounded to the nearest $50 increment. The Title IV–D agency shall publish the adjusted amount in the Texas Register before September 1 of the year in which the adjustment takes effect. For purposes of this subsection, "consumer price index" has the meaning assigned by Section 341.201, Finance Code.

(b) If the obligor's monthly net resources are not greater than the amount described by Subsection (a) and the obligor's monthly net resources are equal to or greater than the amount described by Subsection (c), the court shall presumptively apply the following schedule in rendering the child support order:

CHILD SUPPORT GUIDELINES
BASED ON THE MONTHLY NET RESOURCES OF THE OBLIGOR

| | |
|---|---|
| 1 child | 20% of Obligor's Net Resources |
| 2 children | 25% of Obligor's Net Resources |
| 3 children | 30% of Obligor's Net Resources |
| 4 children | 35% of Obligor's Net Resources |
| 5 children | 40% of Obligor's Net Resources |
| 6+ children | Not less than the amount for 5 children |

(c) If the obligor's monthly net resources are less than $1,000, the court shall presumptively apply the following schedule in rendering the child support order:

LOW-INCOME CHILD SUPPORT GUIDELINES
BASED ON THE MONTHLY NET RESOURCES OF THE OBLIGOR

| | |
|---|---|
| 1 child | 15% of Obligor's Net Resources |
| 2 children | 20% of Obligor's Net Resources |
| 3 children | 25% of Obligor's Net Resources |
| 4 children | 30% of Obligor's Net Resources |
| 5 children | 35% of Obligor's Net Resources |
| 6+ children | Not less than the amount for 5 children |

Added by Acts 1995, 74th Leg., ch. 20, § 1, eff. April 20, 1995. Amended by Acts 2007, 80th Leg., ch. 620, § 2, eff. Sept. 1, 2007; Acts 2009, 81st Leg., ch. 767, § 5, eff. June 19, 2009; Acts 2021, 87th Leg., ch. 552 (S.B. 286), § 4, eff. Sept. 1, 2021.

Sections 12 and 15 of Acts 2021, 87th Leg., ch. 552 (S.B. 286) provide:

"Sec. 12. The enactment of this Act does not constitute a material and substantial change of circumstances sufficient to warrant modification of a court order or portion of a decree that provides for the support of a child rendered before the effective date [Sept. 1, 2021] of this Act."

"Sec. 15. The changes in law made by this Act to Sections 154.125 and 154.129, Family Code, apply to a suit affecting the parent-child relationship that is filed on or after the effective date of this Act. A suit filed before the effective date of this Act is governed by the law in effect on the date the suit is filed, and the former law is continued in effect for that purpose."

### § 154.126. Application of Guidelines to Additional Net Resources

(a) If the obligor's net resources exceed the amount provided by Section 154.125(a), the court shall presumptively apply the percentage guidelines to the portion of the obligor's net resources that does not exceed that amount. Without further reference to the percentage recommended by these guidelines, the court may order additional amounts of child support as appropriate, depending on the income of the parties and the proven needs of the child.

(b) The proper calculation of a child support order that exceeds the presumptive amount established for the portion of the obligor's net resources provided by Section 154.125(a) requires that the entire amount of the presumptive award be subtracted from the proven total needs of the child. After the presumptive award is subtracted, the court shall allocate between the parties the responsibility to meet the additional needs of the child according to the circumstances of the parties. However, in no event may the obligor be required to pay more child support than the greater of the presumptive amount or the amount equal to 100 percent of the proven needs of the child.

Added by Acts 1995, 74th Leg., ch. 20, § 1, eff. April 20, 1995. Amended by Acts 2007, 80th Leg., ch. 620, § 3, eff. Sept. 1, 2007.

### § 154.127. Partial Termination of Support Obligation

(a) A child support order for more than one child shall provide that, on the termination of support for a child, the level of support for the remaining child or children is in accordance with the child support guidelines.

(b) A child support order is in compliance with the requirement imposed by Subsection (a) if the order contains a provision that specifies:

(1) the events, including a child reaching the age of 18 years or otherwise having the disabilities of minority removed, that have the effect of terminating the obligor's obligation to pay child support for that child; and

(2) the reduced total amount that the obligor is required to pay each month after the occurrence of an event described by Subdivision (1).

Added by Acts 1995, 74th Leg., ch. 20, § 1, eff. April 20, 1995. Amended by Acts 2007, 80th Leg., ch. 972, § 10, eff. Sept. 1, 2007.

### § 154.128. Computing Support for Children in More Than One Household

(a) In applying the child support guidelines for an obligor who has children in more than one household, the court shall apply the percentage guidelines in this subchapter by making the following computation:

(1) determine the amount of child support that would be ordered if all children whom the obligor has the legal duty to support lived in one household by applying the schedule in this subchapter;

(2) compute a child support credit for the obligor's children who are not before the court by dividing the amount determined under Subdivision (1) by the total number of children whom the obligor is obligated to support and multiplying that number by the number of the obligor's children who are not before the court;

(3) determine the adjusted net resources of the obligor by subtracting the child support credit computed under Subdivision (2) from the net resources of the obligor; and

(4) determine the child support amount for the children before the court by applying the percentage guidelines for one household for the number of children of the obligor before the court to the obligor's adjusted net resources.

(b) For the purpose of determining a child support credit, the total number of an obligor's children includes the children before the court for the establishment or modification of a support order and any other children, including children residing with the obligor, whom the obligor has the legal duty of support.

(c) The child support credit with respect to children for whom the obligor is obligated by an order to pay support is computed, regardless of whether the obligor is delinquent in child support payments, without regard to the amount of the order.

Added by Acts 1995, 74th Leg., ch. 20, § 1, eff. April 20, 1995.

### § 154.129. Alternative Method of Computing Support for Children in More than One Household

(a) If the obligor's monthly net resources are not greater than the amount described by Section 154.125(a) and if the obligor's monthly net resources are equal to or greater than the amount described by Section 154.125(c), in lieu of performing the computation under the preceding section, the court may determine the child support amount for the children before the court by applying the percentages in the table below to the obligor's net resources:

MULTIPLE FAMILY ADJUSTED GUIDELINES
(% OF NET RESOURCES)

| Number of other children for whom the obligor has a duty of support | Number of children before the court: 1 | 2 | 3 | 4 | 5 | 6 | 7 |
|---|---|---|---|---|---|---|---|
| 0 | 20.00 | 25.00 | 30.00 | 35.00 | 40.00 | 40.00 | 40.00 |
| 1 | 17.50 | 22.50 | 27.38 | 32.20 | 37.33 | 37.71 | 38.00 |
| 2 | 16.00 | 20.63 | 25.20 | 30.33 | 35.43 | 36.00 | 36.44 |
| 3 | 14.75 | 19.00 | 24.00 | 29.00 | 34.00 | 34.67 | 35.20 |
| 4 | 13.60 | 18.33 | 23.14 | 28.00 | 32.89 | 33.60 | 34.18 |
| 5 | 13.33 | 17.86 | 22.50 | 27.22 | 32.00 | 32.73 | 33.33 |
| 6 | 13.14 | 17.50 | 22.00 | 26.60 | 31.27 | 32.00 | 32.62 |
| 7 | 13.00 | 17.22 | 21.60 | 26.09 | 30.67 | 31.38 | 32.00 |

(b) If the obligor's monthly net resources are less than the amount described by Section 154.125(c), in lieu of performing the computation under the preceding section, the court may determine the child support amount for the children before the court by applying the percentages in the table below to the obligor's net resources:

LOW-INCOME MULTIPLE FAMILY ADJUSTED GUIDELINES
(% OF NET RESOURCES)

| Number of other children for whom the obligor has a duty of support | Number of children before the court: 1 | 2 | 3 | 4 | 5 | 6 | 7 |
|---|---|---|---|---|---|---|---|
| 0 | 15.00 | 20.00 | 25.00 | 30.00 | 35.00 | 35.00 | 35.00 |
| 1 | 13.50 | 18.33 | 23.13 | 27.90 | 32.96 | 33.25 | 33.47 |
| 2 | 12.50 | 17.00 | 21.50 | 26.50 | 31.50 | 31.94 | 32.28 |
| 3 | 11.63 | 15.80 | 20.63 | 25.50 | 30.41 | 30.92 | 31.33 |
| 4 | 10.80 | 15.33 | 20.00 | 24.75 | 29.56 | 30.10 | 30.55 |
| 5 | 10.63 | 15.00 | 19.53 | 24.17 | 28.88 | 29.43 | 29.90 |
| 6 | 10.50 | 14.75 | 19.17 | 23.70 | 28.32 | 28.88 | 29.35 |
| 7 | 10.41 | 14.56 | 18.88 | 23.32 | 27.85 | 28.40 | 28.88 |

Added by Acts 1995, 74th Leg., ch. 20, § 1, eff. April 20, 1995. Amended by Acts 2021, 87th Leg., ch. 552 (S.B. 286), § 5, eff. Sept. 1, 2021.

Sections 12 and 15 of Acts 2021, 87th Leg., ch. 552 (S.B. 286) provide:

"Sec. 12. The enactment of this Act does not constitute a material and substantial change of circumstances sufficient to warrant modification of a court order or portion of a decree that provides for the support of a child rendered before the effective date [Sept. 1, 2021] of this Act."

"Sec. 15. The changes in law made by this Act to Sections 154.125 and 154.129, Family Code, apply to a suit affecting the parent-child relationship that is filed on or after the effective date of this Act. A suit filed before the effective date of this Act is governed by the law in effect on the date the suit is filed, and the former law is continued in effect for that purpose."

## § 154.130. Findings in Child Support Order

(a) Without regard to Rules 296 through 299, Texas Rules of Civil Procedure, in rendering an order of child support, the court shall make the findings required by Subsection (b) if:

(1) a party files a written request with the court before the final order is signed, but not later than 20 days after the date of rendition of the order;

(2) a party makes an oral request in open court during the hearing; or

(3) the amount of child support ordered by the court varies from the amount computed by applying the percentage guidelines under Section 154.125 or 154.129, as applicable.

(a–1) Repealed by Acts 2017, 85th Leg., ch. 421 (S.B. 1237), § 12(2).

(b) If findings are required by this section, the court shall state whether the application of the guidelines would be unjust or inappropriate and shall state the following in the child support order:

"(1) the net resources of the obligor per month are $______;

"(2) the net resources of the obligee per month are $______;

"(3) the percentage applied to the obligor's net resources for child support is ______%; and

"(4) if applicable, the specific reasons that the amount of child support per month ordered by the court varies from the amount computed by applying the percentage guidelines under Section 154.125 or 154.129, as applicable."

(c) Findings under Subsection (b)(2) are required only if evidence of the monthly net resources of the obligee has been offered.

Added by Acts 1995, 74th Leg., ch. 20, § 1, eff. April 20, 1995. Amended by Acts 2001, 77th Leg., ch. 1023, § 8, eff. Sept. 1, 2001; Acts 2007, 80th Leg., ch. 620, § 4, eff. Sept. 1, 2007; Acts 2009, 81st Leg., ch. 767, § 6, 37, eff. June 19, 2009; Acts 2017, 85th Leg., ch. 421 (S.B. 1237), §§ 10, 12(2), eff. Sept. 1, 2017.

## § 154.131. Retroactive Child Support

(a) The child support guidelines are intended to guide the court in determining the amount of retroactive child support, if any, to be ordered.

(b) In ordering retroactive child support, the court shall consider the net resources of the obligor during the relevant time period and whether:

(1) the mother of the child had made any previous attempts to notify the obligor of his paternity or probable paternity;

(2) the obligor had knowledge of his paternity or probable paternity;

(3) the order of retroactive child support will impose an undue financial hardship on the obligor or the obligor's family; and

(4) the obligor has provided actual support or other necessaries before the filing of the action.

(c) It is presumed that a court order limiting the amount of retroactive child support to an amount that does not exceed the total amount of support that would have been due for the four years preceding the date the petition seeking support was filed is reasonable and in the best interest of the child.

(d) The presumption created under this section may be rebutted by evidence that the obligor:

(1) knew or should have known that the obligor was the father of the child for whom support is sought; and

(2) sought to avoid the establishment of a support obligation to the child.

(e) An order under this section limiting the amount of retroactive support does not constitute a variance from the guidelines requiring the court to make specific findings under Section 154.130.

(f) Notwithstanding any other provision of this subtitle, the court retains jurisdiction to render an order for retroactive child support in a suit if a petition requesting retroactive child support is filed not later than the fourth anniversary of the date of the child's 18th birthday.

Added by Acts 1995, 74th Leg., ch. 20, § 1, eff. April 20, 1995. Amended by Acts 2001, 77th Leg., ch. 392, § 1, eff. Sept. 1, 2001; Acts 2001, 77th Leg., ch. 821, § 2.14, eff. June 14, 2001; Acts 2001, 77th Leg., ch. 1023, § 9, eff. Sept. 1, 2001; Acts 2007, 80th Leg., ch. 972, § 11(a), eff. Sept. 1, 2007.

### § 154.132. Application of Guidelines to Children of Certain Disabled Obligors

In applying the child support guidelines for an obligor who has a disability and who is required to pay support for a child who receives benefits as a result of the obligor's disability, the court shall apply the guidelines by determining the amount of child support that would be ordered under the child support guidelines and subtracting from that total the amount of benefits or the value of the benefits paid to or for the child as a result of the obligor's disability.

Added by Acts 1999, 76th Leg., ch. 891, § 1, eff. Sept. 1, 1999.

### § 154.133. Application of Guidelines to Children of Obligors Receiving Social Security

In applying the child support guidelines for an obligor who is receiving social security old age benefits and who is required to pay support for a child who receives benefits as a result of the obligor's receipt of social security old age benefits, the court shall apply the guidelines by determining the amount of child support that would be ordered under the child support guidelines and subtracting from that total the amount of benefits or the value of the benefits paid to or for the child as a result of the obligor's receipt of social security old age benefits.

Added by Acts 2001, 77th Leg., ch. 544, § 1, eff. Sept. 1, 2001.

## SUBCHAPTER D. MEDICAL AND DENTAL SUPPORT FOR CHILD

### § 154.181. Medical Support Order

(a) The court shall render an order for the medical support of the child as provided by this section and Section 154.182 in:

(1) a proceeding in which periodic payments of child support are ordered under this chapter or modified under Chapter 156;

(2) any other suit affecting the parent-child relationship in which the court determines that medical support of the child must be established, modified, or clarified; or

(3) a proceeding under Chapter 159.

(b) Before a hearing on temporary orders or a final order, if no hearing on temporary orders is held, the court shall require the parties to the proceedings to disclose in a pleading or other statement:

(1) if private health insurance is in effect for the child, the identity of the insurance company providing the coverage, the policy number, which parent is responsible for payment of any insurance premium for the coverage, whether the coverage is provided through a parent's employment, and the cost of the premium; or

(2) if private health insurance is not in effect for the child, whether:

(A) the child is receiving medical assistance under Chapter 32, Human Resources Code;

(B) the child is receiving health benefits coverage under the state child health plan under Chapter 62, Health and Safety Code, and the cost of any premium; and

(C) either parent has access to private health insurance at reasonable cost to the obligor.

(c) In rendering temporary orders, the court shall, except for good cause shown, order that any health insurance coverage in effect for the child continue in effect pending the rendition of a final order, except that the court may not require the continuation of any health insurance that is not available to the parent at reasonable cost to the obligor. If there is no health insurance coverage in effect for the child or if the insurance in effect is not available at a reasonable cost to the obligor, the court shall, except for good cause shown, order health care coverage for the child as provided under Section 154.182.

(d) On rendering a final order the court shall:

(1) make specific findings with respect to the manner in which health care coverage is to be provided for the child, in accordance with the priorities identified under Section 154.182; and

(2) except for good cause shown or on agreement of the parties, require the parent ordered to provide health care coverage for the child as provided under Section 154.182 to produce evidence to the court's satisfaction that the parent has applied for or secured health insurance or has otherwise taken necessary action to provide for health care coverage for the child, as ordered by the court.

(e) In this section, "reasonable cost" means the cost of health insurance coverage for a child that does not exceed nine percent of the obligor's annual resources, as described by Section 154.062(b), if the obligor is responsible under a medical support order for the cost of health insurance coverage for only one child. If the obligor is responsible under a medical support order for the cost of health insurance coverage for more than one child, "reasonable cost" means the total cost of health insurance coverage for all children for which the obligor is responsible under a medical support order that does not exceed nine percent of the obligor's annual resources, as described by Section 154.062(b).

Added by Acts 1995, 74th Leg., ch. 20, § 1, eff. April 20, 1995. Amended by Acts 2001, 77th Leg., ch. 449, § 1, eff. June 5, 2001; Acts 2003, 78th Leg., ch. 610, § 1, eff. Sept. 1, 2003; Acts 2007, 80th Leg., ch. 363, § 2, eff. Sept. 1, 2007; Acts 2009, 81st Leg., ch. 767, § 7, eff. June 19, 2009.

### § 154.1815. Dental Support Order

(a) In this section, "reasonable cost" means the cost of a dental insurance premium that does not exceed 1.5 percent of the obligor's annual resources, as described by Section 154.062(b), if the obligor is responsible under a dental support order for the cost of dental insurance coverage for only one child. If the obligor is responsible under a dental support order for the cost of dental insurance coverage for more than one child, "reasonable cost" means the total cost of dental insurance coverage for all children for which the obligor is responsible under a dental support order that does not exceed 1.5 percent of the obligor's annual resources, as described by Section 154.062(b).

(b) In a suit affecting the parent-child relationship or in a proceeding under Chapter 159, the court shall render an order for the dental support of the child as provided by this section and Section 154.1825.

(c) Before a hearing on temporary orders, or a final order if no hearing on temporary orders is held, the court shall require the parties to the proceedings to disclose in a pleading or other document whether the child is covered by dental insurance and, if the child is covered, the identity of the insurer providing the coverage, the policy number, which parent is responsible for payment of any insurance premium for the coverage, whether the coverage is provided through a parent's employment, and the cost of the premium. If dental insurance is not in effect for the child, the parties must disclose to the court whether either parent has access to dental insurance at a reasonable cost to the obligor.

(d) In rendering temporary orders, the court shall, except for good cause shown, order that any dental insurance coverage in effect for the child continue in effect pending the rendition of a final order, except that the court may not require the continuation of any dental insurance that is not available to the parent at a reasonable cost to the obligor. If dental insurance coverage is not in effect for the child or if the insurance in effect is not available at a reasonable cost to the obligor, the court shall, except for good cause shown, order dental insurance coverage for the child as provided by Section 154.1825.

(e) On rendering a final order the court shall:

(1) make specific findings with respect to the manner in which dental insurance coverage is to be provided for the child, in accordance with the priorities identified under Section 154.1825; and

(2) except for good cause shown or on agreement of the parties, require the parent ordered to provide dental insurance coverage for the child as provided by Section 154.1825 to produce evidence to the court's satisfaction that the parent has applied for or secured dental insurance or has otherwise taken necessary action to provide for dental insurance coverage for the child, as ordered by the court.

Added by Acts 2015, 84th Leg., ch. 1150 (S.B. 550), § 14, eff. Sept. 1, 2018.

### § 154.182. Health Care Coverage for Child

(a) The court shall consider the cost, accessibility, and quality of health insurance coverage available to the parties and shall give priority to health insurance coverage available through the employment of one of the parties if the coverage is available at a reasonable cost to the obligor.

(b) In determining the manner in which health care coverage for the child is to be ordered, the court shall render its order in accordance with the following priorities, unless a party shows good cause why a particular order would not be in the best interest of the child:

(1) if health insurance is available for the child through a parent's employment or membership in a union, trade association, or other organization at reasonable cost, the court shall order that parent to include the child in the parent's health insurance;

(2) if health insurance is not available for the child under Subdivision (1) but is available to a parent at reasonable cost from another source, including the program under Section 154.1826 to provide health insurance in Title IV-D cases, the court may order that parent to provide health insurance for the child; or

(3) if health insurance coverage is not available for the child under Subdivision (1) or (2), the court shall order the obligor to pay the obligee, in addition to any amount ordered under the guidelines for child support, an amount, not to exceed nine percent of the obligor's annual resources, as described by Section 154.062(b), as cash medical support for the child.

(b–1) If the parent ordered to provide health insurance under Subsection (b)(1) or (2) is the obligee, the court shall order the obligor to pay the obligee, as additional child support, an amount equal to the actual cost of health insurance for the child, but not to exceed a reasonable cost to the obligor. In calculating the actual cost of health insurance for the child, if the obligee has other minor dependents covered under the same health insurance plan, the court shall divide the total cost to the obligee for the insurance by the total number of minor dependents, including the child covered under the plan.

(b–2) If the court finds that neither parent has access to private health insurance at a reasonable cost to the obligor, the court shall order the parent awarded the exclusive right to designate the child's primary residence or, to the extent permitted by law, the other parent to apply immediately on behalf of the child for participation in a government medical assistance program or health plan. If the child participates in a government medical assistance program or health plan, the court shall order cash medical support under Subsection (b)(3).

(b–3) An order requiring the payment of cash medical support under Subsection (b)(3) must allow the obligor to discontinue payment of the cash medical support if:

(1) health insurance for the child becomes available to the obligor at a reasonable cost; and

(2) the obligor:

(A) enrolls the child in the insurance plan; and

(B) provides the obligee and, in a Title IV–D case, the Title IV–D agency, the information required under Section 154.185.

(c) In this section:

(1) "Accessibility" means the extent to which health insurance coverage for a child provides for the availability of medical care within a reasonable traveling distance and time from the child's primary residence, as determined by the court.

(2) "Reasonable cost" has the meaning assigned by Section 154.181(e).

(d) Repealed by Acts 2009, 81st Leg., ch. 767, § 37.

Added by Acts 1995, 74th Leg., ch. 20, § 1, eff. April 20, 1995. Amended by Acts 1997, 75th Leg., ch. 550, § 2, eff. June 2, 1997; Acts 2001, 77th Leg., ch. 449, § 2, eff. June 5, 2001; Acts 2003, 78th Leg., ch. 610, § 2, eff. Sept. 1, 2003; Acts 2007, 80th Leg., ch. 363, §§ 3, 4, eff. Sept. 1, 2007; Acts 2007, 80th Leg., ch. 620, § 5, eff. Sept. 1, 2007; Acts 2009, 81st Leg., ch. 767, §§ 8, 37, eff. June 19, 2009.

### § 154.1825. Dental Care Coverage for Child

(a) In this section:

(1) "Accessibility" means the extent to which dental insurance coverage for a child provides for the availability of dental care within a reasonable traveling distance and time from the child's primary residence, as determined by the court.

(2) "Reasonable cost" has the meaning assigned by Section 154.1815(a).

(b) The court shall consider the cost, accessibility, and quality of dental insurance coverage available to the parties and shall give priority to dental insurance coverage available through the employment of one of the parties if the coverage is available at a reasonable cost to the obligor.

(c) In determining the manner in which dental care coverage for the child is to be ordered, the court shall render its order in accordance with the following priorities, unless a party shows good cause why a particular order is not in the best interest of the child:

(1) if dental insurance is available for the child through a parent's employment or membership in a

union, trade association, or other organization at reasonable cost, the court shall order that parent to include the child in the parent's dental insurance; or

(2) if dental insurance is not available for the child under Subdivision (1) but is available to a parent from another source and at a reasonable cost, the court may order that parent to provide dental insurance for the child.

(d) If the parent ordered to provide dental insurance under Subsection (c)(1) or (2) is the obligee, the court shall order the obligor to pay the obligee, as additional child support, an amount equal to the actual cost of dental insurance for the child, but not to exceed a reasonable cost to the obligor. In calculating the actual cost of dental insurance for the child, if the obligee has other minor dependents covered under the same dental insurance plan, the court shall divide the total cost to the obligee for the insurance by the total number of minor dependents, including the child covered under the plan.

Added by Acts 2015, 84th Leg., ch. 1150 (S.B. 550), § 15, eff. Sept. 1, 2018.

### § 154.1826. Health Care Program for Certain Children in Title IV–D Cases

(a) In this section:

(1) "Health benefit plan issuer" means an insurer, health maintenance organization, or other entity authorized to provide health benefits coverage under the laws of this state.

(2) "Health care provider" means a physician or other person who is licensed, certified, or otherwise authorized to provide a health care service in this state.

(3) "Program" means the child health care program developed under this section.

(4) "Reasonable cost" has the meaning assigned by Section 154.181(e).

(5) "Third-party administrator" means a person who is not a health benefit plan issuer or agent of a health benefit plan issuer and who provides administrative services for the program, including processing enrollment of eligible children in the program and processing premium payments on behalf of the program.

(b) In consultation with the Texas Department of Insurance, the Health and Human Services Commission, and representatives of the insurance industry in this state, the Title IV–D agency shall develop and implement a statewide program to address the health care needs of children in Title IV–D cases for whom health insurance is not available to either parent at reasonable cost under Section 154.182(b)(1) or under Section 154.182(b)(2) from a source other than the program.

(c) The director of the Title IV–D agency may establish an advisory committee to consult with the director regarding the implementation and operation of the program. If the director establishes an advisory committee, the director may appoint any of the following persons to the advisory committee:

(1) representatives of appropriate public and private entities, including state agencies concerned with health care management;

(2) members of the judiciary;

(3) members of the legislature; and

(4) representatives of the insurance industry.

(d) The principal objective of the program is to provide basic health care services, including office visits with health care providers, hospitalization, and diagnostic and emergency services, to eligible children in Title IV–D cases at reasonable cost to the parents obligated by court order to provide medical support for the children.

(e) The Title IV–D agency may use available private resources, including gifts and grants, in administering the program.

(f) The Title IV–D agency shall adopt rules as necessary to implement the program. The Title IV–D agency shall consult with the Texas Department of Insurance and the Health and Human Services Commission in establishing policies and procedures for the administration of the program and in determining appropriate benefits to be provided under the program.

(g) A health benefit plan issuer that participates in the program may not deny health care coverage under the program to eligible children because of preexisting conditions or chronic illnesses. A child who is determined to be eligible for coverage under the program continues to be eligible until the termination of the parent's duty to pay child support as specified by Section 154.006. Enrollment of a child in the program does not preclude the subsequent enrollment of the child in another health care plan that becomes available to the child's parent at reasonable cost, including a health care plan available through the parent's employment or the state child health plan under Chapter 62, Health and Safety Code.

(h) The Title IV–D agency shall contract with an independent third-party administrator to provide necessary administrative services for operation of the program.

(i) A person acting as a third-party administrator under Subsection (h) is not considered an administrator for purposes of Chapter 4151, Insurance Code.

(j) The Title IV–D agency shall solicit applications for participation in the program from health benefit plan issuers that meet requirements specified by the agency. Each health benefit plan issuer that participates in the program must hold a certificate of authority issued by the Texas Department of Insurance.

(k) The Title IV–D agency shall promptly notify the courts of this state when the program has been implemented and is available to provide for the health care needs of children described by Subsection (b). The notification must specify a date beginning on which children may be enrolled in the program.

(*l*) On or after the date specified in the notification required by Subsection (k), a court that orders health care coverage for a child in a Title IV–D case shall order that the child be enrolled in the program authorized by this section unless other health insurance is available for the child at reasonable cost, including the state child health plan under Chapter 62, Health and Safety Code.

(m) Payment of premium costs for the enrollment of a child in the program may be enforced by the Title IV–D agency against the obligor by any means available for the enforcement of a child support obligation, including income withholding under Chapter 158.

(n) The program is not subject to any provision of the Insurance Code or other law that requires coverage or the offer of coverage of a health care service or benefit.

(*o*) Any health information obtained by the program, or by a third-party administrator providing program services, that is subject to the Health Insurance Portability and Accountability Act of 1996 (42 U.S.C. Section 1320d et seq.) or Chapter 181, Health and Safety Code, is confidential and not open to public inspection. Any personally identifiable financial information or supporting documentation of a parent whose child is enrolled in the program that is obtained by the program, or by a third-party administrator providing program services, is confidential and not open to public inspection.

Added by Acts 2009, 81st Leg., ch. 767, § 9, eff. June 19, 2009.

### § 154.1827. Administrative Adjustment of Medical Support Order

(a) In each Title IV–D case in which a medical support order requires that a child be enrolled in a health care program under Section 154.1826, the Title IV–D agency may administratively adjust the order as necessary on an annual basis to reflect changes in the amount of premium costs associated with the child's enrollment.

(b) The Title IV–D agency shall provide notice of the administrative adjustment to the obligor and the clerk of the court that rendered the order.

Added by Acts 2009, 81st Leg., ch. 767, § 9, eff. June 19, 2009.

### § 154.183. Medical and Dental Support Additional Support Duty of Obligor

(a) An amount that an obligor is ordered to pay as medical support or dental support for the child under this chapter, including the costs of health insurance coverage or cash medical support under Section 154.182 and the costs of dental insurance under Section 154.1825:

(1) is in addition to the amount that the obligor is required to pay for child support under the guidelines for child support;

(2) is a child support obligation; and

(3) may be enforced by any means available for the enforcement of child support, including withholding from earnings under Chapter 158.

(b) If the court finds and states in the child support order that the obligee will maintain health insurance coverage, dental insurance coverage, or both, for the child at the obligee's expense, the court shall increase the amount of child support to be paid by the obligor in an amount not exceeding the actual cost to the obligee for maintaining the coverage, as provided under Sections 154.182(b–1) and 154.1825(d).

(c) As additional child support, the court shall allocate between the parties, according to their circumstances:

(1) the reasonable and necessary health care expenses, including vision and dental expenses, of the child that are not reimbursed by health or dental insurance or are not otherwise covered by the amount of cash medical support ordered under Section 154.182; and

(2) amounts paid by either party as deductibles or copayments in obtaining health care or dental

care services for the child covered under a health insurance or dental insurance policy.

Added by Acts 1995, 74th Leg., ch. 20, § 1, eff. April 20, 1995. Amended by Acts 2007, 80th Leg., ch. 363, § 5, eff. Sept. 1, 2007; Acts 2007, 80th Leg., ch. 620, § 6, eff. Sept. 1, 2007; Acts 2009, 81st Leg., ch. 87, § 9.002, eff. Sept. 1, 2009; Acts 2009, 81st Leg., ch. 767, § 10, eff. June 19, 2009; Acts 2015, 84th Leg., ch. 1150 (S.B. 550), § 16, eff. Sept. 1, 2018.

### § 154.184. Effect of Order

(a) Receipt of a medical support order requiring that health insurance be provided for a child or a dental support order requiring that dental insurance be provided for a child shall be considered a change in the family circumstances of the employee or member, for health insurance purposes and dental insurance purposes, equivalent to the birth or adoption of a child.

(b) If the employee or member is eligible for dependent health coverage or dependent dental coverage, the employer shall automatically enroll the child for the first 31 days after the receipt of the order or notice of the medical support order or the dental support order under Section 154.186 on the same terms and conditions as apply to any other dependent child.

(c) The employer shall notify the insurer of the automatic enrollment.

(d) During the 31–day period, the employer and insurer shall complete all necessary forms and procedures to make the enrollment permanent or shall report in accordance with this subchapter the reasons the coverage cannot be made permanent.

Added by Acts 1995, 74th Leg., ch. 20, § 1, eff. April 20, 1995. Amended by Acts 1995, 74th Leg., ch. 341, § 4.03, eff. Sept. 1, 1995; Acts 1997, 75th Leg., ch. 911, § 11, eff. Sept. 1, 1997; Acts 2015, 84th Leg., ch. 1150 (S.B. 550), § 17, eff. Sept. 1, 2018.

### § 154.185. Parent to Furnish Information

(a) The court shall order a parent providing health insurance or dental insurance to furnish to either the obligee, obligor, or child support agency the following information not later than the 30th day after the date the notice of rendition of the order is received:

(1) the social security number of the parent;

(2) the name and address of the parent's employer;

(3) with regard to health insurance:

(A) whether the employer is self-insured or has health insurance available;

(B) proof that health insurance has been provided for the child;

(C) if the employer has health insurance available, the name of the health insurance carrier, the number of the policy, a copy of the policy and schedule of benefits, a health insurance membership card, claim forms, and any other information necessary to submit a claim; and

(D) if the employer is self-insured, a copy of the schedule of benefits, a membership card, claim forms, and any other information necessary to submit a claim; and

(4) with regard to dental insurance:

(A) whether the employer is self-insured or has dental insurance available;

(B) proof that dental insurance has been provided for the child;

(C) if the employer has dental insurance available, the name of the dental insurance carrier, the number of the policy, a copy of the policy and schedule of benefits, a dental insurance membership card, claim forms, and any other information necessary to submit a claim; and

(D) if the employer is self-insured, a copy of the schedule of benefits, a membership card, claim forms, and any other information necessary to submit a claim.

(b) The court shall also order a parent providing health insurance or dental insurance to furnish the obligor, obligee, or child support agency with additional information regarding the health insurance coverage or dental insurance coverage not later than the 15th day after the date the information is received by the parent.

Added by Acts 1995, 74th Leg., ch. 20, § 1, eff. April 20, 1995. Amended by Acts 2001, 77th Leg., ch. 1023, § 10, eff. Sept. 1, 2001; Acts 2015, 84th Leg., ch. 1150 (S.B. 550), § 18, eff. Sept. 1, 2018.

### § 154.186. Notice to Employer Concerning Medical Support or Dental Support

(a) The obligee, obligor, or a child support agency of this state or another state may send to the employer a copy of the order requiring an employee to provide health insurance coverage or dental insurance coverage for a child or may include notice of the medical support order or dental support order in an order or writ of withholding sent to the employer in accordance with Chapter 158.

(b) In an appropriate Title IV–D case, the Title IV–D agency of this state or another state shall send to the employer the national medical support notice required under Part D, Title IV of the federal Social Security Act (42 U.S.C. Section 651 et seq.), as amended. The notice may be used in any other suit in which an obligor is ordered to provide health insurance coverage for a child.

(c) The Title IV–D agency by rule shall establish procedures consistent with federal law for use of the national medical support notice and may prescribe forms for the efficient use of the notice. The agency shall provide the notice and forms, on request, to obligees, obligors, domestic relations offices, friends of the court, and attorneys.

Added by Acts 1995, 74th Leg., ch. 20, § 1, eff. April 20, 1995. Amended by Acts 1995, 74th Leg., ch. 341, § 4.04, eff. Sept. 1, 1995; Acts 1997, 75th Leg., ch. 911, § 12, eff. Sept. 1, 1997; Acts 2003, 78th Leg., ch. 120, § 1, eff. July 1, 2003; Acts 2007, 80th Leg., ch. 972, § 12, eff. Sept. 1, 2007; Acts 2015, 84th Leg., ch. 1150 (S.B. 550), §§ 19, 20, eff. Sept. 1, 2018.

## § 154.187. Duties of Employer

(a) An order or notice under this subchapter to an employer directing that health insurance coverage or dental insurance coverage be provided to a child of an employee or member is binding on a current or subsequent employer on receipt without regard to the date the order was rendered. If the employee or member is eligible for dependent health coverage or dental coverage for the child, the employer shall immediately enroll the child in a health insurance plan or dental insurance plan regardless of whether the employee is enrolled in the plan. If dependent coverage is not available to the employee or member through the employer's health insurance plan or dental insurance plan or enrollment cannot be made permanent or if the employer is not responsible or otherwise liable for providing such coverage, the employer shall provide notice to the sender in accordance with Subsection (c).

(b) If additional premiums are incurred as a result of adding the child to the health insurance plan or the dental insurance plan, the employer shall deduct the health insurance premium or the dental insurance premium from the earnings of the employee in accordance with Chapter 158 and apply the amount withheld to payment of the insurance premium.

(c) An employer who has received an order or notice under this subchapter shall provide to the sender, not later than the 40th day after the date the employer receives the order or notice, a statement that the child:

(1) has been enrolled in the employer's health insurance plan or dental insurance plan, or is already enrolled in another health insurance plan or dental insurance plan in accordance with a previous child support, medical support, or dental support order to which the employee is subject; or

(2) cannot be enrolled or cannot be enrolled permanently in the employer's health insurance plan or dental insurance plan and provide the reason why coverage or permanent coverage cannot be provided.

(d) If the employee ceases employment or if the health insurance coverage or dental insurance coverage lapses, the employer shall provide to the sender, not later than the 15th day after the date of the termination of employment or the lapse of the coverage, notice of the termination or lapse and of the availability of any conversion privileges.

(e) On request, the employer shall release to the sender information concerning the available health insurance coverage or dental insurance coverage, including the name of the health insurance carrier or dental insurance carrier, the policy number, a copy of the policy and schedule of benefits, a health insurance or dental insurance membership card, and claim forms.

(f) In this section, "sender" means the person sending the order or notice under Section 154.186.

(g) An employer who fails to enroll a child, fails to withhold or remit premiums or cash medical support, or discriminates in hiring or employment on the basis of a medical support order or notice or a dental support order or notice under this subchapter shall be subject to the penalties and fines in Subchapter C, Chapter 158. [1]

(h) An employer who receives a national medical support notice under Section 154.186 shall comply with the requirements of the notice.

(i) The notices required by Subsections (c) and (d) must be provided to the sender by first class mail, unless the sender is the Title IV–D agency. Notices to the Title IV–D agency may be provided electronically or via first class mail.

Added by Acts 1995, 74th Leg., ch. 20, § 1, eff. April 20, 1995. Amended by Acts 1995, 74th Leg., ch. 341, § 4.05, eff. Sept. 1, 1995; Acts 1997, 75th Leg., ch. 911, § 13, eff. Sept. 1, 1997; Acts 2003, 78th Leg., ch. 120, § 2, eff. July 1, 2003; Acts 2009, 81st Leg., ch. 767, § 11, eff. June 19, 2009; Acts 2011, 82nd Leg., ch. 508 (H.B. 1674), § 1, eff. Sept. 1, 2011; Acts 2015, 84th Leg., ch. 859 (S.B. 1726), § 4, eff. Sept. 1, 2015; Acts 2015, 84th Leg., ch. 1150 (S.B. 550), § 21, eff. Sept. 1, 2018.

[1] V.T.C.A., Family Code § 158.201 et seq.

### § 154.188. Failure to Provide or Pay for Required Health Insurance or Dental Insurance

A parent ordered to provide health insurance or dental insurance or to pay the other parent additional child support for the cost of health insurance or dental insurance who fails to do so is liable for:

(1) necessary medical expenses or dental expenses of the child, without regard to whether the expenses would have been paid if health insurance or dental insurance had been provided; and

(2) the cost of health insurance premiums, dental insurance premiums, or contributions, if any, paid on behalf of the child.

Added by Acts 1995, 74th Leg., ch. 20, § 1, eff. April 20, 1995. Amended by Acts 2001, 77th Leg., ch. 295, § 1, eff. Sept. 1, 2001; Acts 2003, 78th Leg., ch. 610, § 3, eff. Sept. 1, 2003; Acts 2015, 84th Leg., ch. 1150 (S.B. 550), § 22, eff. Sept. 1, 2018.

### § 154.189. Notice of Termination or Lapse of Insurance Coverage

(a) An obligor ordered to provide health insurance coverage or dental insurance coverage for a child must notify the obligee and any child support agency enforcing a support obligation against the obligor of the:

(1) termination or lapse of health insurance coverage or dental insurance coverage for the child not later than the 15th day after the date of a termination or lapse; and

(2) availability of additional health insurance or dental insurance to the obligor for the child after a termination or lapse of coverage not later than the 15th day after the date the insurance becomes available.

(b) If termination of coverage results from a change of employers, the obligor, the obligee, or the child support agency may send the new employer a copy of the order requiring the employee to provide health insurance or dental insurance for a child or notice of the medical support order or the dental support order as provided by this subchapter.

Added by Acts 1995, 74th Leg., ch. 20, § 1, eff. April 20, 1995. Amended by Acts 1997, 75th Leg., ch. 911, § 14, eff. Sept. 1, 1997; Acts 2015, 84th Leg., ch. 1150 (S.B. 550), § 23, eff. Sept. 1, 2018.

### § 154.190. Reenrolling Child for Insurance Coverage

After health insurance or dental insurance has been terminated or has lapsed, an obligor ordered to provide health insurance coverage or dental insurance coverage for the child must enroll the child in a health insurance plan or a dental insurance plan at the next available enrollment period.

Added by Acts 1995, 74th Leg., ch. 20, § 1, eff. April 20, 1995. Amended by Acts 2015, 84th Leg., ch. 1150 (S.B. 550), § 24, eff. Sept. 1, 2018.

### § 154.191. Remedy Not Exclusive

(a) This subchapter does not limit the rights of the obligor, obligee, local domestic relations office, or Title IV–D agency to enforce, modify, or clarify the medical support order or dental support order.

(b) This subchapter does not limit the authority of the court to render or modify a medical support order or dental support order to provide for payment of uninsured health expenses, health care costs, health insurance premiums, uninsured dental expenses, dental costs, or dental insurance premiums in a manner consistent with this subchapter.

Added by Acts 1995, 74th Leg., ch. 20, § 1, eff. April 20, 1995. Amended by Acts 2009, 81st Leg., ch. 767, § 12, eff. June 19, 2009; Acts 2015, 84th Leg., ch. 1150 (S.B. 550), § 25, eff. Sept. 1, 2018.

### § 154.192. Cancellation or Elimination of Insurance Coverage for Child

Unless the employee or member ceases to be eligible for dependent coverage, or the employer has eliminated dependent health coverage or dental coverage for all of the employer's employees or members, the employer may not cancel or eliminate coverage of a child enrolled under this subchapter until the employer is provided satisfactory written evidence that:

(1) the court order or administrative order requiring the coverage is no longer in effect; or

(2) the child is enrolled in comparable insurance coverage or will be enrolled in comparable coverage that will take effect not later than the effective date of the cancellation or elimination of the employer's coverage.

Added by Acts 1995, 74th Leg., ch. 20, § 1, eff. April 20, 1995. Amended by Acts 1995, 74th Leg., ch. 341, § 4.06, eff. Sept. 1, 1995; Acts 2015, 84th Leg., ch. 1150 (S.B. 550), § 26, eff. Sept. 1, 2018.

### § 154.193. Medical Support Order or Dental Support Order Not Qualified

(a) If a plan administrator or other person acting in an equivalent position determines that a medical support order or dental support order issued under this subchapter does not qualify for enforcement under federal law, the tribunal may, on its own motion or the motion of a party, render an order that qualifies for enforcement under federal law.

(b) The procedure for filing a motion for enforcement of a final order applies to a motion under this section. Service of citation is not required, and a person is not entitled to a jury in a proceeding under this section.

(c) The employer or plan administrator is not a necessary party to a proceeding under this section.

Added by Acts 1997, 75th Leg., ch. 911, § 15, eff. Sept. 1, 1997. Amended by Acts 2015, 84th Leg., ch. 1150 (S.B. 550), §§ 27, 28, eff. Sept. 1, 2018.

## SUBCHAPTER E. LOCAL CHILD SUPPORT REGISTRY

### § 154.241. Local Registry

(a) A local registry shall receive a court-ordered child support payment or a payment otherwise authorized by law and shall forward the payment, as appropriate, to the Title IV–D agency, local domestic relations office, or obligee within two working days after the date the local registry receives the payment.

(b) A local registry may not require an obligor, obligee, or other party or entity to furnish a certified copy of a court order as a condition of processing child support payments and shall accept as sufficient authority to process the payments a photocopy, facsimile copy, or conformed copy of the court's order.

(c) A local registry shall include with each payment it forwards to the Title IV–D agency the date it received the payment and the withholding date furnished by the employer.

(d) A local registry shall accept child support payments made by personal check, money order, or cashier's check. A local registry may refuse payment by personal check if a pattern of abuse regarding the use of personal checks has been established. Abuse includes checks drawn on insufficient funds, abusive or offensive language written on the check, intentional mutilation of the instrument, or other actions that delay or disrupt the registry's operation.

(e) Subject to Section 154.004, at the request of an obligee, a local registry shall redirect and forward a child support payment to an address and in care of a person or entity designated by the obligee. A local registry may require that the obligee's request be in writing or be made on a form provided by the local registry for that purpose, but may not charge a fee for receiving the request or redirecting the payments as requested.

(f) A local registry may accept child support payments made by credit card, debit card, or automatic teller machine card.

(g) Notwithstanding any other law, a private entity may perform the duties and functions of a local registry under this section either under a contract with a county commissioners court or domestic relations office executed under Section 204.002 or under an appointment by a court.

Added by Acts 1995, 74th Leg., ch. 20, § 1, eff. April 20, 1995. Amended by Acts 1995, 74th Leg., ch. 751, § 42, eff. Sept. 1, 1995; Acts 2003, 78th Leg., ch. 645, § 1, eff. Sept. 1, 2003; Acts 2005, 79th Leg., ch. 740, § 2, eff. June 17, 2005.

### § 154.242. Payment or Transfer of Child Support Payments by Electronic Funds Transfer

(a) A child support payment may be made by electronic funds transfer to:

(1) the Title IV–D agency;

(2) a local registry if the registry agrees to accept electronic payment; or

(3) the state disbursement unit.

(b) A local registry may transmit child support payments to the Title IV–D agency by electronic funds transfer. Unless support payments are required to be made to the state disbursement unit, an obligor may make payments, with the approval of the court entering the order, directly to the bank account of the obligee by electronic transfer and provide verification of the deposit to the local registry. A local registry in a county that makes deposits into personal bank accounts by electronic funds transfer as of April 1, 1995, may transmit a child support payment to an obligee by electronic funds transfer if the obligee maintains a bank account and provides the local registry with the necessary bank account information to complete electronic payment.

Added by Acts 1995, 74th Leg., ch. 20, § 1, eff. April 20, 1995. Amended by Acts 1995, 74th Leg., ch. 597, § 1, eff. Jan. 1, 1996; Acts 1997, 75th Leg., ch. 702, § 2, eff. Jan. 1, 1998; Acts 1997, 75th Leg., ch. 1053, § 2, eff. Sept. 1, 1997; Acts 1999, 76th Leg., ch. 556, § 10, eff. Sept. 1, 1999.

### § 154.243. Production of Child Support Payment Record

The Title IV–D agency, a local registry, or the state disbursement unit may comply with a subpoena or other order directing the production of a child support payment record by sending a certified copy of the record or an affidavit regarding the payment record to the court that directed production of the record.

Added by Acts 1995, 74th Leg., ch. 20, § 1, eff. April 20, 1995. Amended by Acts 1999, 76th Leg., ch. 556, § 10, eff. Sept. 1, 1999.

## SUBCHAPTER F. SUPPORT FOR A MINOR OR ADULT DISABLED CHILD

### § 154.301. Definitions

In this subchapter:

(1) "Adult child" means a child 18 years of age or older.

(2) "Child" means a son or daughter of any age.

Added by Acts 1995, 74th Leg., ch. 20, § 1, eff. April 20, 1995.

### § 154.302. Court-Ordered Support for Disabled Child

(a) The court may order either or both parents to provide for the support of a child for an indefinite period and may determine the rights and duties of the parents if the court finds that:

(1) the child, whether institutionalized or not, requires substantial care and personal supervision because of a mental or physical disability and will not be capable of self-support; and

(2) the disability exists, or the cause of the disability is known to exist, on or before the 18th birthday of the child.

(b) A court that orders support under this section shall designate a parent of the child or another person having physical custody or guardianship of the child under a court order to receive the support for the child. The court may designate a child who is 18 years of age or older to receive the support directly.

(c) Notwithstanding Subsection (b), a court that orders support under this section for an adult child with a disability may designate a special needs trust and provide that the support may be paid directly to the trust for the benefit of the adult child. The court shall order that support payable to a special needs trust under this subsection be paid directly to the trust and may not order the support be paid to the state disbursement unit. This subsection does not apply in a Title IV–D case.

Added by Acts 1995, 74th Leg., ch. 20, § 1, eff. April 20, 1995. Amended by Acts 1997, 75th Leg., ch. 1173, § 1, eff. Sept. 1, 1997; Acts 2019, 86th Leg., ch. 359 (H.B. 558), § 1, eff. Sept. 1, 2019.

Section 2 of Acts 2019, 86th Leg., ch. 359 (H.B. 558) provides:

"The change in law made by this Act constitutes a material and substantial change of circumstances under Section 156.401, Family Code, sufficient to warrant modification of a court order or a portion of a decree that provides for the support of a child rendered before the effective date [Sept. 1, 2019] of this Act."

### § 154.303. Standing to Sue

(a) A suit provided by this subchapter may be filed only by:

(1) a parent of the child or another person having physical custody or guardianship of the child under a court order; or

(2) the child if the child:

(A) is 18 years of age or older;

(B) does not have a mental disability; and

(C) is determined by the court to be capable of managing the child's financial affairs.

(b) The parent, the child, if the child is 18 years of age or older, or other person may not transfer or assign the cause of action to any person, including a governmental or private entity or agency, except for an assignment made to the Title IV–D agency under Section 231.104 or in the provision of child support enforcement services under Section 159.307.

Added by Acts 1995, 74th Leg., ch. 20, § 1, eff. April 20, 1995. Amended by Acts 1997, 75th Leg., ch. 1173, § 2, eff. Sept. 1, 1997; Acts 2011, 82nd Leg., ch. 508 (H.B. 1674), § 2, eff. Sept. 1, 2011.

### § 154.304. General Procedure

Except as otherwise provided by this subchapter, the substantive and procedural rights and remedies in a suit affecting the parent-child relationship relating to the establishment, modification, or enforcement of a child support order apply to a suit filed and an order rendered under this subchapter.

Added by Acts 1995, 74th Leg., ch. 20, § 1, eff. April 20, 1995.

### § 154.305. Specific Procedures

(a) A suit under this subchapter may be filed:

(1) regardless of the age of the child; and

(2) as an independent cause of action or joined with any other claim or remedy provided by this code.

(b) If no court has continuing, exclusive jurisdiction of the child, an action under this subchapter may be filed as an original suit affecting the parent-child relationship.

(c) If there is a court of continuing, exclusive jurisdiction, an action under this subchapter may be filed as a suit for modification as provided by Chapter 156.

Added by Acts 1995, 74th Leg., ch. 20, § 1, eff. April 20, 1995.

### § 154.306. Amount of Support After Age 18

In determining the amount of support to be paid after a child's 18th birthday, the specific terms and conditions of that support, and the rights and duties of both parents with respect to the support of the child, the court shall determine and give special consideration to:

(1) any existing or future needs of the adult child directly related to the adult child's mental or physical disability and the substantial care and personal supervision directly required by or related to that disability;

(2) whether the parent pays for or will pay for the care or supervision of the adult child or provides or will provide substantial care or personal supervision of the adult child;

(3) the financial resources available to both parents for the support, care, and supervision of the adult child; and

(4) any other financial resources or other resources or programs available for the support, care, and supervision of the adult child.

Added by Acts 1995, 74th Leg., ch. 20, § 1, eff. April 20, 1995.

### § 154.307. Modification and Enforcement

An order provided by this subchapter may contain provisions governing the rights and duties of both parents with respect to the support of the child and may be modified or enforced in the same manner as any other order provided by this title.

Added by Acts 1995, 74th Leg., ch. 20, § 1, eff. April 20, 1995.

### § 154.308. Remedy Not Exclusive

(a) This subchapter does not affect a parent's:

(1) cause of action for the support of a disabled child under any other law; or

(2) ability to contract for the support of a disabled child.

(b) This subchapter does not affect the substantive or procedural rights or remedies of a person other than a parent, including a governmental or private entity or agency, with respect to the support of a disabled child under any other law.

Added by Acts 1995, 74th Leg., ch. 20, § 1, eff. April 20, 1995.

### § 154.309. Possession of or Access to Adult Disabled Child

(a) A court may render an order for the possession of or access to an adult disabled child that is appropriate under the circumstances.

(b) Possession of or access to an adult disabled child is enforceable in the manner provided by Chapter 157. An adult disabled child may refuse possession or access if the adult disabled child is mentally competent.

(c) A court that obtains continuing, exclusive jurisdiction of a suit affecting the parent-child relationship involving a disabled person who is a child retains continuing, exclusive jurisdiction of subsequent proceedings involving the person, including proceedings after the person is an adult. Notwithstanding this subsection and any other law, a probate court may exercise jurisdiction in a guardianship proceeding for the person after the person is an adult.

Added by Acts 1995, 74th Leg., ch. 751, § 43, eff. Sept. 1, 1995. Amended by Acts 2007, 80th Leg., ch. 453, § 1, eff. June 16, 2007.

## CHAPTER 155. CONTINUING, EXCLUSIVE JURISDICTION; TRANSFER

SUBCHAPTER A. CONTINUING, EXCLUSIVE JURISDICTION

**Section**



SUBCHAPTER B. IDENTIFICATION OF COURT OF CONTINUING, EXCLUSIVE JURISDICTION



SUBCHAPTER C. TRANSFER OF CONTINUING, EXCLUSIVE JURISDICTION

## SUBCHAPTER A. CONTINUING, EXCLUSIVE JURISDICTION

### § 155.001. Acquiring Continuing, Exclusive Jurisdiction

(a) Except as otherwise provided by this section, a court acquires continuing, exclusive jurisdiction over the matters provided for by this title in connection with a child on the rendition of a final order.

(b) The following final orders do not create continuing, exclusive jurisdiction in a court:

(1) a voluntary or involuntary dismissal of a suit affecting the parent-child relationship;

(2) in a suit to determine parentage, a final order finding that an alleged or presumed father is not the father of the child, except that the jurisdiction of the court is not affected if the child was subject to the jurisdiction of the court or some other court in a suit affecting the parent-child relationship before the commencement of the suit to adjudicate parentage; and

(3) a final order of adoption, after which a subsequent suit affecting the child must be commenced as though the child had not been the subject of a suit for adoption or any other suit affecting the parent-child relationship before the adoption.

(c) If a court of this state has acquired continuing, exclusive jurisdiction, no other court of this state has jurisdiction of a suit with regard to that child except as provided by this chapter, Section 103.001(b), or Chapter 262.

(d) Unless a final order has been rendered by a court of continuing, exclusive jurisdiction, a subsequent suit shall be commenced as an original proceeding.

Added by Acts 1995, 74th Leg., ch. 20, § 1, eff. April 20, 1995. Amended by Acts 1999, 76th Leg., ch. 62, § 6.19, eff. Sept. 1, 1999; Acts 2001, 77th Leg., ch. 821, § 2.15, eff. June 14, 2001; Acts 2015, 84th Leg., ch. 944 (S.B. 206), § 10, eff. Sept. 1, 2015.

### § 155.002. Retaining Continuing, Exclusive Jurisdiction

Except as otherwise provided by this subchapter, a court with continuing, exclusive jurisdiction retains jurisdiction of the parties and matters provided by this title.

Added by Acts 1995, 74th Leg., ch. 20, § 1, eff. April 20, 1995. Amended by Acts 1999, 76th Leg., ch. 62, § 6.20, eff. Sept. 1, 1999.

### § 155.003. Exercise of Continuing, Exclusive Jurisdiction

(a) Except as otherwise provided by this section, a court with continuing, exclusive jurisdiction may exercise its jurisdiction to modify its order regarding managing conservatorship, possessory conservatorship, possession of and access to the child, and support of the child.

(b) A court of this state may not exercise its continuing, exclusive jurisdiction to modify managing conservatorship if:

(1) the child's home state is other than this state; or

(2) modification is precluded by Chapter 152.

(c) A court of this state may not exercise its continuing, exclusive jurisdiction to modify possessory conservatorship or possession of or access to a child if:

(1) the child's home state is other than this state and all parties have established and continue to maintain their principal residence outside this state; or

(2) each individual party has filed written consent with the tribunal of this state for a tribunal of another state to modify the order and assume continuing, exclusive jurisdiction of the suit.

(d) A court of this state may not exercise its continuing, exclusive jurisdiction to modify its child support order if modification is precluded by Chapter 159.

Added by Acts 1995, 74th Leg., ch. 20, § 1, eff. April 20, 1995.

### § 155.004. Loss of Continuing, Exclusive Jurisdiction

(a) A court of this state loses its continuing, exclusive jurisdiction to modify its order if:

(1) an order of adoption is rendered by another court in an original suit filed as described by Section 103.001(b);

(2) the parents of the child have remarried each other after the dissolution of a previous marriage

between them and file a suit for the dissolution of their subsequent marriage combined with a suit affecting the parent-child relationship as if there had not been a prior court with continuing, exclusive jurisdiction over the child; or

(3) another court assumed jurisdiction over a suit and rendered a final order based on incorrect information received from the vital statistics unit that there was no court of continuing, exclusive jurisdiction.

(b) This section does not affect the power of the court to enforce its order for a violation that occurred before the time continuing, exclusive jurisdiction was lost under this section.

Added by Acts 1995, 74th Leg., ch. 20, § 1, eff. April 20, 1995. Amended by Acts 1997, 75th Leg., ch. 575, § 8, eff. Sept. 1, 1997; Acts 2015, 84th Leg., ch. 1 (S.B. 219), § 1.050, eff. April 2, 2015; Acts 2019, 86th Leg., ch. 136 (H.B. 1854), § 1, eff. Sept. 1, 2019.

Section 2 of Acts 2019, 86th Leg., ch. 136 (H.B. 1854) provides:

"(a) The change in law made by this Act applies only to an order of adoption rendered on or after the effective date [Sept. 1, 2019] of this Act.

"(b) Notwithstanding Subsection (a) of this section, an order of adoption rendered in a suit filed as described by Section 103.001(b), Family Code, on or after September 1, 2015, but before the effective date of this Act by a court that had jurisdiction under that section to render the order of adoption regardless of whether another court had continuing, exclusive jurisdiction under Chapter 155, Family Code, is a final order and is not subject to an appeal on the basis that the court rendering the order of adoption did not have continuing, exclusive jurisdiction at the time the adoption order was rendered."

### § 155.005. Jurisdiction Pending Transfer

(a) During the transfer of a suit from a court with continuing, exclusive jurisdiction, the transferring court retains jurisdiction to render temporary orders.

(b) The jurisdiction of the transferring court terminates on the docketing of the case in the transferee court.

Added by Acts 1995, 74th Leg., ch. 20, § 1, eff. April 20, 1995.

## SUBCHAPTER B. IDENTIFICATION OF COURT OF CONTINUING, EXCLUSIVE JURISDICTION

### § 155.101. Request for Identification of Court of Continuing, Exclusive Jurisdiction

(a) The petitioner or the court shall request from the vital statistics unit identification of the court that last had continuing, exclusive jurisdiction of the child in a suit unless:

(1) the petition alleges that no court has continuing, exclusive jurisdiction of the child and the issue is not disputed by the pleadings; or

(2) the petition alleges that the court in which the suit or petition to modify has been filed has acquired and retains continuing, exclusive jurisdiction of the child as the result of a prior proceeding and the issue is not disputed by the pleadings.

(b) The vital statistics unit shall, on the written request of the court, an attorney, or a party:

(1) identify the court that last had continuing, exclusive jurisdiction of the child in a suit and give the docket number of the suit; or

(2) state that the child has not been the subject of a suit.

(c) The child shall be identified in the request by name, birthdate, and place of birth.

(d) The vital statistics unit shall transmit the information not later than the 10th day after the date on which the request is received.

Added by Acts 1995, 74th Leg., ch. 20, § 1, eff. April 20, 1995. Amended by Acts 1995, 74th Leg., ch. 751, § 44, eff. Sept. 1, 1995; Acts 1999, 76th Leg., ch. 178, § 8, eff. Aug. 30, 1999; Acts 2015, 84th Leg., ch. 1 (S.B. 219), § 1.051, eff. April 2, 2015.

### § 155.102. Dismissal

If a court in which a suit is filed determines that another court has continuing, exclusive jurisdiction of the child, the court in which the suit is filed shall dismiss the suit without prejudice.

Added by Acts 1995, 74th Leg., ch. 20, § 1, eff. April 20, 1995.

### § 155.103. Reliance on Vital Statistics Unit Information

(a) A court shall have jurisdiction over a suit if it has been, correctly or incorrectly, informed by the vital statistics unit that the child has not been the subject of a suit and the petition states that no other court has continuing, exclusive jurisdiction over the child.

(b) If the vital statistics unit notifies the court that the unit has furnished incorrect information regarding the existence of another court with continuing, exclusive jurisdiction before the rendition of a final order, the provisions of this chapter apply.

Added by Acts 1995, 74th Leg., ch. 20, § 1, eff. April 20, 1995. Amended by Acts 1995, 74th Leg., ch. 751, § 45, eff. Sept. 1, 1995; Acts 2015, 84th Leg., ch. 1 (S.B. 219), § 1.052, eff. April 2, 2015.

### § 155.104. Voidable Order

(a) If a request for information from the vital statistics unit relating to the identity of the court having continuing, exclusive jurisdiction of the child has been made under this subchapter, a final order, except an order of dismissal, may not be rendered until the information is filed with the court.

(b) If a final order is rendered in the absence of the filing of the information from the vital statistics unit, the order is voidable on a showing that a court other than the court that rendered the order had continuing, exclusive jurisdiction.

Added by Acts 1995, 74th Leg., ch. 20, § 1, eff. April 20, 1995. Amended by Acts 1995, 74th Leg., ch. 751, § 46, eff. Sept. 1, 1995; Acts 2015, 84th Leg., ch. 1 (S.B. 219), § 1.053, eff. April 2, 2015.

## SUBCHAPTER C. TRANSFER OF CONTINUING, EXCLUSIVE JURISDICTION

### § 155.201. Mandatory Transfer

(a) On the filing of a motion showing that a suit for dissolution of the marriage of the child's parents has been filed in another court and requesting a transfer to that court, the court having continuing, exclusive jurisdiction of a suit affecting the parent-child relationship shall, within the time required by Section 155.204, transfer the proceedings to the court in which the dissolution of the marriage is pending.

(a–1) On the filing of a motion showing that a suit in which adoption of a child is requested has been filed in another court located in the county in which the child resides as provided by Section 103.001 and requesting a transfer to that court, the court having continuing, exclusive jurisdiction of a suit affecting the parent-child relationship with regard to that child shall, within the time required by Section 155.204, transfer the proceedings to the court in which the suit for adoption is pending.

(a–2) A motion described by Subsection (a) or (a–1) must comply with the requirements of Section 155.204(a).

(b) If a suit to modify or a motion to enforce an order is filed in the court having continuing, exclusive jurisdiction of a suit, on the timely motion of a party the court shall, within the time required by Section 155. 204, transfer the proceeding to another county in this state if the child has resided in the other county for six months or longer.

(c) If a suit to modify or a motion to enforce an order is pending at the time a subsequent suit to modify or motion to enforce is filed, the court may transfer the proceeding as provided by Subsection (b) only if the court could have transferred the proceeding at the time the first motion or suit was filed.

(d) On receiving notice that a court exercising jurisdiction under Chapter 262 has ordered the transfer of a suit under Section 262.203(a)(2), the court of continuing, exclusive jurisdiction shall, in accordance with the requirements of Section 155.204(i), transfer the proceedings to the court in which the suit under Chapter 262 is pending within the time required by Section 155.207(a).

Added by Acts 1995, 74th Leg., ch. 20, § 1, eff. April 20, 1995. Amended by Acts 1999, 76th Leg., ch. 1135, § 1, eff. Sept. 1, 1999; Acts 2005, 79th Leg., ch. 916, § 14, eff. June 18, 2005; Acts 2017, 85th Leg., ch. 317 (H.B. 7), § 10, eff. Sept. 1, 2017; Acts 2017, 85th Leg., ch. 572 (S.B. 738), § 1; Acts 2017, 85th Leg., ch. 910 (S.B. 999), § 1, eff. Sept. 1, 2017; Acts 2019, 86th Leg., ch. 467 (H.B. 4170), § 7.003, eff. Sept. 1, 2019; Acts 2019, 86th Leg., ch. 722 (H.B. 369), § 3, eff. Sept. 1, 2019.

Section 6 of Acts 2019, 86th Leg., ch. 722 (H.B. 369) provides:

"The changes in law made by this Act to Sections 103.001, 155.201, and 155.204, Family Code, apply to a motion to transfer a suit affecting the parent-child relationship filed on or after the effective date [Sept. 1, 2019] of this Act. A motion to transfer a suit affecting the parent-child relationship filed before the effective date of this Act is governed by the law in effect on the date that motion was filed, and the former law is continued in effect for that purpose."

### § 155.202. Discretionary Transfer

(a) If the basis of a motion to transfer a proceeding under this subchapter is that the child resides in another county, the court may deny the motion if it is shown that the child has resided in that county for less than six months at the time the proceeding is commenced.

(b) For the convenience of the parties and witnesses and in the interest of justice, the court, on the timely motion of a party, may transfer the proceeding to a proper court in another county in the state.

Added by Acts 1995, 74th Leg., ch. 20, § 1, eff. April 20, 1995.

### § 155.203. Determining County of Child's Residence

In computing the time during which the child has resided in a county, the court may not require that the period of residence be continuous and uninterrupted but shall look to the child's principal residence during the six-month period preceding the commencement of the suit.

Added by Acts 1995, 74th Leg., ch. 20, § 1, eff. April 20, 1995.

### § 155.204. Procedure for Transfer

(a) A motion to transfer under Section 155.201(a) or (a–1) may be filed at any time. The motion must contain a certification that all other parties, including the attorney general, if applicable, have been informed of the filing of the motion.

(b) Except as provided by Subsection (a) or Section 262.203, a motion to transfer by a petitioner or movant is timely if it is made at the time the initial pleadings are filed. A motion to transfer by another party is timely if it is made on or before the first Monday after the 20th day after the date of service of citation or notice of the suit or before the commencement of the hearing, whichever is sooner.

(c) If a timely motion to transfer has been filed and no controverting affidavit is filed within the period allowed for its filing, the proceeding shall, not later than the 21st day after the final date of the period allowed for the filing of a controverting affidavit, be transferred without a hearing to the proper court.

(d) On or before the first Monday after the 20th day after the date of notice of a motion to transfer is served, a party desiring to contest the motion must file a controverting affidavit denying that grounds for the transfer exist.

(e) If a controverting affidavit contesting the motion to transfer is filed, each party is entitled to notice not less than 10 days before the date of the hearing on the motion to transfer.

(f) Only evidence pertaining to the transfer may be taken at the hearing.

(g) If the court finds after the hearing on the motion to transfer that grounds for the transfer exist, the proceeding shall be transferred to the proper court not later than the 21st day after the date the hearing is concluded.

(h) An order transferring or refusing to transfer the proceeding is not subject to interlocutory appeal.

(i) If a transfer order has been signed by a court exercising jurisdiction under Chapter 262, the Department of Family and Protective Services shall file the transfer order with the clerk of the court of continuing, exclusive jurisdiction. On receipt and without a hearing or further order from the court of continuing, exclusive jurisdiction, the clerk of the court of continuing, exclusive jurisdiction shall transfer the files as provided by this subchapter within the time required by Section 155.207(a).

Added by Acts 1995, 74th Leg., ch. 20, § 1, eff. April 20, 1995. Amended by Acts 1999, 76th Leg., ch. 1150, § 1, eff. Sept. 1, 1999; Acts 1999, 76th Leg., ch. 1390, § 14, eff. Sept. 1, 1999; Acts 2005, 79th Leg., ch. 916, § 15, eff. June 18, 2005; Acts 2017, 85th Leg., ch. 317 (H.B. 7), § 11, eff. Sept. 1, 2017; Acts 2017, 85th Leg., ch. 572 (S.B. 738), § 2; Acts 2017, 85th Leg., ch. 910 (S.B. 999), § 2, eff. Sept. 1, 2017; Acts 2019, 86th Leg., ch. 722 (H.B. 369), § 4, eff. Sept. 1, 2019.

Section 6 of Acts 2019, 86th Leg., ch. 722 (H.B. 369) provides:

"The changes in law made by this Act to Sections 103.001, 155.201, and 155.204, Family Code, apply to a motion to transfer a suit affecting the parent-child relationship filed on or after the effective date [Sept. 1, 2019] of this Act. A motion to transfer a suit affecting the parent-child relationship filed before the effective date of this Act is governed by the law in effect on the date that motion was filed, and the former law is continued in effect for that purpose."

### § 155.205. Transfer of Child Support Registry

(a) On rendition of an order transferring continuing, exclusive jurisdiction to another court, the transferring court shall also order that all future payments of child support be made to the local registry of the transferee court or, if payments have previously been directed to the state disbursement unit, to the state disbursement unit.

(b) The transferring court's local registry or the state disbursement unit shall continue to receive, record, and forward child support payments to the payee until it receives notice that the transferred case has been docketed by the transferee court.

(c) After receiving notice of docketing from the transferee court, the transferring court's local registry shall send a certified copy of the child support payment record to the clerk of the transferee court and shall forward any payments received to the transferee court's local registry or to the state disbursement unit, as appropriate.

Added by Acts 1995, 74th Leg., ch. 20, § 1, eff. April 20, 1995. Amended by Acts 1999, 76th Leg., ch. 556, § 11, eff. Sept. 1, 1999; Acts 2001, 77th Leg., ch. 1023, § 11, eff. Sept. 1, 2001.

### § 155.206. Effect of Transfer

(a) A court to which a transfer is made becomes the court of continuing, exclusive jurisdiction and all proceedings in the suit are continued as if it were brought there originally.

(b) A judgment or order transferred has the same effect and shall be enforced as if originally rendered in the transferee court.

(c) The transferee court shall enforce a judgment or order of the transferring court by contempt or by any other means by which the transferring court could have enforced its judgment or order. The transferee court shall have the power to punish disobedience of the transferring court's order, whether occurring before or after the transfer, by contempt.

(d) After the transfer, the transferring court does not retain jurisdiction of the child who is the subject of the suit, nor does it have jurisdiction to enforce its order for a violation occurring before or after the transfer of jurisdiction.

Added by Acts 1995, 74th Leg., ch. 20, § 1, eff. April 20, 1995.

### § 155.207. Transfer of Court Files

(a) Not later than the 10th working day after the date an order of transfer is signed, the clerk of the court transferring a proceeding shall send, using the electronic filing system established under Section 72.031, Government Code, to the proper court in the county to which transfer is being made:

(1) a transfer certificate and index of transferred documents;

(2) a copy of each final order;

(3) a copy of the order of transfer signed by the transferring court;

(4) a copy of the original papers filed in the transferring court;

(5) a copy of the transfer certificate and index of transferred documents from each previous transfer; and

(6) a bill of any costs that have accrued in the transferring court.

(a-1) The clerk of the transferring court shall use the standardized transfer certificate and index of transferred documents form created by the Office of Court Administration of the Texas Judicial System under Section 72.037, Government Code, when transferring a proceeding under this section.

(b) The clerk of the transferring court shall keep a copy of transferred pleadings.

(c) The clerk of the transferee court shall:

(1) accept documents transferred under Subsection (a);

(2) docket the suit; and

(3) notify, using the electronic filing system established under Section 72.031, Government Code, all parties, the clerk of the transferring court, and, if appropriate, the transferring court's local registry that the suit has been docketed.

(c-1) The clerk of the transferee court shall physically or electronically mark or stamp the transfer certificate and index of transferred documents to evidence the date and time of acceptance under Subsection (c), but may not physically or electronically mark or stamp any other document transferred under Subsection (a).

(d) The clerk of the transferring court shall send a certified copy of the order directing payments to the transferee court:

(1) to any party affected by the order, and, if appropriate, to the local registry of the transferee court using the electronic filing system established under Section 72.031, Government Code; and

(2) to an employer affected by the order electronically or by first class mail.

(e) The clerks of both the transferee and transferring courts may each produce under Chapter 51, Government Code, certified or uncertified copies of documents filed in a case transferred under this section, but shall also include a copy of the transfer certificate and index of transferred documents with each document produced.

(f) Sections 80.001 and 80.002, Government Code, do not apply to the transfer of documents under this section.

Added by Acts 1995, 74th Leg., ch. 20, § 1, eff. April 20, 1995. Amended by Acts 2001, 77th Leg., ch. 1023, § 12, eff. Sept. 1, 2001; Acts 2005, 79th Leg., ch. 916, § 16, eff. June 18, 2005; Acts 2015, 84th Leg., ch. 211 (S.B. 1929), § 1, eff. Sept. 1, 2015; Acts 2021, 87th Leg., ch. 934 (H.B. 3774), § 7.01, eff. Sept. 1, 2021.

Section 15.02 of Acts 2021, 87th Leg., ch. 934 (H.B. 3774) provides:

"Not later than May 1, 2022, the Supreme Court of Texas shall adopt rules and promulgate forms under Section 22.0042, Government Code, as added by this article.

Section 18.01 of Acts 2021, 87th Leg., ch. 934 (H.B. 3774) provides:

"A state agency subject to this Act is required to implement a provision of this Act only if the legislature appropriates money specifically for that purpose. If the legislature does not appropriate money specifically for that purpose, the state agency may, but is not required to, implement a provision of this Act using other appropriations available for that purpose."

## SUBCHAPTER D. TRANSFER OF PROCEEDINGS WITHIN THE STATE WHEN PARTY OR CHILD RESIDES OUTSIDE THE STATE

### § 155.301. Authority to Transfer

(a) A court of this state with continuing, exclusive jurisdiction over a child custody proceeding under Chapter 152 or a child support proceeding under

Chapter 159 shall transfer the proceeding to the county of residence of the resident party if one party is a resident of this state and all other parties including the child or all of the children affected by the proceeding reside outside this state.

(b) If one or more of the parties affected by the proceedings reside outside the state and if more than one party or one or more children affected by the proceeding reside in this state in different counties, the court shall transfer the proceeding according to the following priorities:

(1) to the court of continuing, exclusive jurisdiction, if any;

(2) to the county of residence of the child, if applicable, provided that:

(A) Subdivision (1) is inapplicable; or

(B) the court of continuing, exclusive jurisdiction finds that neither a party nor a child affected by the proceeding resides in the county of the court of continuing, exclusive jurisdiction; or

(3) if Subdivisions (1) and (2) are inapplicable, to the county most appropriate to serve the convenience of the resident parties, the witnesses, and the interest of justice.

(c) Except as otherwise provided by this subsection, if a transfer of continuing, exclusive jurisdiction is sought under this section, the procedures for determining and effecting a transfer of proceedings provided by this chapter apply. If the parties submit to the court an agreed order for transfer, the court shall sign the order without the need for other pleadings.

Added by Acts 1995, 74th Leg., ch. 20, § 1, eff. April 20, 1995. Amended by Acts 2003, 78th Leg., ch. 1036, § 17, eff. Sept. 1, 2003; Acts 2007, 80th Leg., ch. 972, § 13, eff. Sept. 1, 2007.

## CHAPTER 156. MODIFICATION

SUBCHAPTER A. GENERAL PROVISIONS



SUBCHAPTER B. MODIFICATION OF CONSERVATORSHIP, POSSESSION AND ACCESS, OR DETERMINATION OF RESIDENCE



SUBCHAPTER C. MODIFICATION OF JOINT MANAGING CONSERVATORSHIP [REPEALED]



SUBCHAPTER D. MODIFICATION OF POSSESSION OF OR ACCESS TO CHILD [REPEALED]



SUBCHAPTER E. MODIFICATION OF CHILD SUPPORT



### SUBCHAPTER A. GENERAL PROVISIONS

#### § 156.001. Orders Subject to Modification

A court with continuing, exclusive jurisdiction may modify an order that provides for the conservatorship, support, or possession of and access to a child.

Added by Acts 1995, 74th Leg., ch. 20, § 1, eff. April 20, 1995.

#### § 156.002. Who Can File

(a) A party affected by an order may file a suit for modification in the court with continuing, exclusive jurisdiction.

(b) A person or entity who, at the time of filing, has standing to sue under Chapter 102 may file a suit for modification in the court with continuing, exclusive jurisdiction.

(c) The sibling of a child who is separated from the child because of the actions of the Department of

Family and Protective Services may file a suit for modification requesting access to the child in the court with continuing, exclusive jurisdiction.

Added by Acts 1995, 74th Leg., ch. 20, § 1, eff. April 20, 1995. Amended by Acts 2009, 81st Leg., ch. 1113, § 26, eff. Sept. 1, 2009.

### § 156.003. Notice

A party whose rights and duties may be affected by a suit for modification is entitled to receive notice by service of citation.

Added by Acts 1995, 74th Leg., ch. 20, § 1, eff. April 20, 1995. Amended by Acts 1999, 76th Leg., ch. 178, § 9, eff. Aug. 30, 1999.

### § 156.004. Procedure

The Texas Rules of Civil Procedure applicable to the filing of an original lawsuit apply to a suit for modification under this chapter.

Added by Acts 1995, 74th Leg., ch. 20, § 1, eff. April 20, 1995.

### § 156.005. Frivolous Filing of Suit for Modification

Notwithstanding Rules 296 through 299, Texas Rules of Civil Procedure, if the court finds that a suit for modification is filed frivolously or is designed to harass a party, the court shall state that finding in the order and assess attorney's fees as costs against the offending party.

Added by Acts 1995, 74th Leg., ch. 20, § 1, eff. April 20, 1995. Amended by Acts 2017, 85th Leg., ch. 421 (S.B. 1237), § 11, eff. Sept. 1, 2017.

### § 156.006. Temporary Orders

(a) Except as provided by Subsection (b), the court may render a temporary order in a suit for modification.

(b) While a suit for modification is pending, the court may not render a temporary order that has the effect of creating a designation, or changing the designation, of the person who has the exclusive right to designate the primary residence of the child, or the effect of creating a geographic area, or changing or eliminating the geographic area, within which a conservator must maintain the child's primary residence, under the final order unless the temporary order is in the best interest of the child and:

(1) the order is necessary because the child's present circumstances would significantly impair the child's physical health or emotional development;

(2) the person designated in the final order has voluntarily relinquished the primary care and possession of the child for more than six months; or

(3) the child is 12 years of age or older and has expressed to the court in chambers as provided by Section 153.009 the name of the person who is the child's preference to have the exclusive right to designate the primary residence of the child.

(b–1) A person who files a motion for a temporary order authorized by Subsection (b)(1) shall execute and attach to the motion an affidavit on the person's personal knowledge or the person's belief based on representations made to the person by a person with personal knowledge that contains facts that support the allegation that the child's present circumstances would significantly impair the child's physical health or emotional development. The court shall deny the relief sought and decline to schedule a hearing on the motion unless the court determines, on the basis of the affidavit, that facts adequate to support the allegation are stated in the affidavit. If the court determines that the facts stated are adequate to support the allegation, the court shall set a time and place for the hearing.

(c) Subsection (b)(2) does not apply to a conservator who has the exclusive right to designate the primary residence of the child and who has temporarily relinquished the primary care and possession of the child to another person during the conservator's military deployment, military mobilization, or temporary military duty, as those terms are defined by Section 153.701.

Added by Acts 1995, 74th Leg., ch. 20, § 1, eff. April 20, 1995. Amended by Acts 1999, 76th Leg., ch. 1390, § 15, eff. Sept. 1, 1999; Acts 2001, 77th Leg., ch. 1289, § 3, eff. Sept. 1, 2001; Acts 2003, 78th Leg., ch. 1036, § 18, eff. Sept. 1, 2003; Acts 2005, 79th Leg., ch. 916, § 17, eff. June 18, 2005; Acts 2009, 81st Leg., ch. 727, § 2, eff. Sept. 1, 2009; Acts 2009, 81st Leg., ch. 1113, § 27, eff. Sept. 1, 2009; Acts 2009, 81st Leg., ch. 1118, § 2, eff. Sept. 1, 2009; Acts 2015, 84th Leg., ch. 397 (H.B. 1500), § 1, eff. Sept. 1, 2015; Acts 2017, 85th Leg., ch. 91 (H.B. 1495), § 1, eff. Sept. 1, 2017.

### § 156.007. Certain Filings Not Admissions

A party who files a motion to modify an order that provides for the appointment of a conservator of a child, provides the terms and conditions of conservatorship, provides for the possession of or access to a child, or provides for the support of a child based on a material and substantial change of circumstances may not be considered on that basis alone to have admitted a material and substantial change of circumstances regarding any other matter.

Added by Acts 2021, 87th Leg., ch. 227 (H.B. 851), § 2, eff. Sept. 1, 2021.

Section 3 of Acts 2021, 87th Leg., ch. 227 (H.B. 851) provides:

"The changes in law made by this Act apply only to a motion to modify that is filed on or after the effective date [Sept. 1, 2021] of this Act. A motion to modify filed before that date is governed by the law in effect on the date the motion was filed, and that law is continued in effect for that purpose."

## SUBCHAPTER B. MODIFICATION OF CONSERVATORSHIP, POSSESSION AND ACCESS, OR DETERMINATION OF RESIDENCE

### § 156.101. Grounds for Modification of Order Establishing Conservatorship or Possession and Access

(a) The court may modify an order that provides for the appointment of a conservator of a child, that provides the terms and conditions of conservatorship, or that provides for the possession of or access to a child if modification would be in the best interest of the child and:

(1) the circumstances of the child, a conservator, or other party affected by the order have materially and substantially changed since the earlier of:

(A) the date of the rendition of the order; or

(B) the date of the signing of a mediated or collaborative law settlement agreement on which the order is based;

(2) the child is at least 12 years of age and has expressed to the court in chambers as provided by Section 153.009 the name of the person who is the child's preference to have the exclusive right to designate the primary residence of the child; or

(3) the conservator who has the exclusive right to designate the primary residence of the child has voluntarily relinquished the primary care and possession of the child to another person for at least six months.

(b) Subsection (a)(3) does not apply to a conservator who has the exclusive right to designate the primary residence of the child and who has temporarily relinquished the primary care and possession of the child to another person during the conservator's military deployment, military mobilization, or temporary military duty, as those terms are defined by Section 153.701.

Added by Acts 1995, 74th Leg., ch. 20, § 1, eff. April 20, 1995. Amended by Acts 1995, 74th Leg., ch. 751, § 47, eff. Sept. 1, 1995; Acts 1999, 76th Leg., ch. 1390, § 16, eff. Sept. 1, 1999; Acts 2001, 77th Leg., ch. 1289, § 5, eff. Sept. 1, 2001; Acts 2003, 78th Leg., ch. 1036, § 19, eff. Sept. 1, 2003; Acts 2009, 81st Leg., ch. 727, § 3, eff. Sept. 1, 2009; Acts 2009, 81st Leg., ch. 1113, § 28, eff. Sept. 1, 2009; Acts 2009, 81st Leg., ch. 1118, § 3, eff. Sept. 1, 2009.

### § 156.102. Modification of Exclusive Right to Determine Primary Residence of Child Within One Year of Order

(a) If a suit seeking to modify the designation of the person having the exclusive right to designate the primary residence of a child is filed not later than one year after the earlier of the date of the rendition of the order or the date of the signing of a mediated or collaborative law settlement agreement on which the order is based, the person filing the suit shall execute and attach an affidavit as provided by Subsection (b).

(b) The affidavit must contain, along with supporting facts, at least one of the following allegations:

(1) that the child's present environment may endanger the child's physical health or significantly impair the child's emotional development;

(2) that the person who has the exclusive right to designate the primary residence of the child is the person seeking or consenting to the modification and the modification is in the best interest of the child; or

(3) that the person who has the exclusive right to designate the primary residence of the child has voluntarily relinquished the primary care and possession of the child for at least six months and the modification is in the best interest of the child.

(c) The court shall deny the relief sought and refuse to schedule a hearing for modification under this section unless the court determines, on the basis of the affidavit, that facts adequate to support an allegation listed in Subsection (b) are stated in the affidavit. If the court determines that the facts stated are adequate to support an allegation, the court shall set a time and place for the hearing.

(d) Subsection (b)(3) does not apply to a person who has the exclusive right to designate the primary residence of the child and who has temporarily relinquished the primary care and possession of the child to another person during the conservator's military deployment, military mobilization, or temporary military duty, as those terms are defined by Section 153.701.

Added by Acts 1995, 74th Leg., ch. 20, § 1, eff. April 20, 1995. Amended by Acts 2001, 77th Leg., ch. 1289, § 6, eff. Sept. 1, 2001; Acts 2003, 78th Leg., ch. 1036, § 20, eff. Sept. 1, 2003; Acts 2009, 81st Leg., ch. 727, § 4, eff. Sept. 1, 2009; Acts 2009, 81st Leg., ch. 1113, § 29, eff. Sept. 1, 2009.

### § 156.103. Increased Expenses Because of Change of Residence

(a) If a change of residence results in increased expenses for a party having possession of or access to a child, the court may render appropriate orders to allocate those increased expenses on a fair and equitable basis, taking into account the cause of the increased expenses and the best interest of the child.

(b) The payment of increased expenses by the party whose residence is changed is rebuttably presumed to be in the best interest of the child.

(c) The court may render an order without regard to whether another change in the terms and conditions for the possession of or access to the child is made.

Added by Acts 1995, 74th Leg., ch. 20, § 1, eff. April 20, 1995. Amended by Acts 2001, 77th Leg., ch. 1289, § 7, eff. Sept. 1, 2001.

### § 156.104. Modification of Order on Conviction for Child Abuse; Penalty

(a) Except as provided by Section 156.1045, the conviction of a conservator for an offense under Section 21.02, Penal Code, or the conviction of a conservator or an order deferring adjudication with regard to the conservator, for an offense involving the abuse of a child under Section 21.11, 22.011, or 22.021, Penal Code, is a material and substantial change of circumstances sufficient to justify a temporary order and modification of an existing court order or portion of a decree that provides for the appointment of a conservator or that sets the terms and conditions of conservatorship or for the possession of or access to a child.

(b) A person commits an offense if the person files a suit to modify an order or portion of a decree based on the grounds permitted under Subsection (a) and the person knows that the person against whom the motion is filed has not been convicted of an offense, or received deferred adjudication for an offense, under Section 21.02, 21.11, 22.011, or 22.021, Penal Code. An offense under this subsection is a Class B misdemeanor.

Added by Acts 1995, 74th Leg., ch. 20, § 1, eff. April 20, 1995. Amended by Acts 2001, 77th Leg., ch. 1289, § 8, eff. Sept. 1, 2001; Acts 2007, 80th Leg., ch. 593, § 3.29, eff. Sept. 1, 2007.

### § 156.1045. Modification of Order on Conviction for Family Violence

(a) The conviction or an order deferring adjudication of a person who is a possessory conservator or a sole or joint managing conservator for an offense involving family violence is a material and substantial change of circumstances sufficient to justify a temporary order and modification of an existing court order or portion of a decree that provides for the appointment of a conservator or that sets the terms and conditions of conservatorship or for the possession of or access to a child to conform the order to the requirements of Section 153.004(d).

(b) A person commits an offense if the person files a suit to modify an order or portion of a decree based on the grounds permitted under Subsection (a) and the person knows that the person against whom the motion is filed has not been convicted of an offense, or received deferred adjudication for an offense, involving family violence. An offense under this subsection is a Class B misdemeanor.

Added by Acts 2001, 77th Leg., ch. 1289, § 9, eff. Sept. 1, 2001.

### § 156.105. Modification of Order Based on Military Duty

The military duty of a conservator who is ordered to military deployment, military mobilization, or temporary military duty, as those terms are defined by Section 153.701, does not by itself constitute a material and substantial change of circumstances sufficient to justify a modification of an existing court order or portion of a decree that sets the terms and conditions for the possession of or access to a child except that the court may render a temporary order under Subchapter L,[1] Chapter 153.

Added by Acts 2005, 79th Leg., ch. 916, § 18, eff. June 18, 2005. Amended by Acts 2007, 80th Leg., ch. 972, § 14, eff. Sept. 1, 2007; Acts 2007, 80th Leg., ch. 1041, § 5, eff. June 15, 2007; Acts 2009, 81st Leg., ch. 727, § 5, eff. Sept. 1, 2009; Acts 2009, 81st Leg., ch. 1113, § 30, eff. Sept. 1, 2009.

[1] V.T.C.A., Family Code § 153.701 et seq.

### § 156.106. Modification of Order Based on Death of Conservator

(a) The death of a person who is a conservator of a child is a material and substantial change of circumstances sufficient to justify a temporary order and modification of an existing court order or portion of a decree that provides for the appointment of a conservator or that sets the terms and conditions of conservatorship or for the possession of or access to the child.

(b) Before modifying an order under Section 156.101 based on a material and substantial change of circumstances described by Subsection (a), the court must consider any term or condition of the order or portion of a decree that denies possession of the child to a parent or imposes restrictions or limitations on the parent's right to possession of or access to the child. The court may include those restrictions or limitations in a modification of the order if the court finds that the restrictions or limitations continue to be in the best interest of the child.

Added by Acts 2021, 87th Leg., ch. 672 (H.B. 1849), § 2, eff. Sept. 1, 2021.

Sections 1 and 3 of Acts 2021, 87th Leg., ch. 672 (H.B. 1849) provide:

"Sec. 1. This Act may be cited as Chelsea Maddux's Law."

"Sec. 3. The change in law made by this Act applies to a suit for modification that is pending in a trial court on the effective date [Sept. 1, 2021] of this Act or that is filed on or after that date."

## SUBCHAPTER C. MODIFICATION OF JOINT MANAGING CONSERVATORSHIP [REPEALED]

### §§ 156.201 to 156.203. Repealed by Acts 2001, 77th Leg., ch. 1289, § 12(2), eff. Sept. 1, 2001

## SUBCHAPTER D. MODIFICATION OF POSSESSION OF OR ACCESS TO CHILD [REPEALED]

### §§ 156.301 to 156.304. Repealed by Acts 2001, 77th Leg., ch. 1289, § 12(2), eff. Sept. 1, 2001

## SUBCHAPTER E. MODIFICATION OF CHILD SUPPORT

### § 156.401. Grounds for Modification of Child Support

(a) Except as provided by Subsection (a–1), (a–2), or (b), the court may modify an order that provides for the support of a child, including an order for health care coverage under Section 154.182 or an order for dental care coverage under Section 154.1825, if:

(1) the circumstances of the child or a person affected by the order have materially and substantially changed since the earlier of:

(A) the date of the order's rendition; or

(B) the date of the signing of a mediated or collaborative law settlement agreement on which the order is based; or

(2) it has been three years since the order was rendered or last modified and the monthly amount of the child support award under the order differs by either 20 percent or $100 from the amount that would be awarded in accordance with the child support guidelines.

(a–1) If the parties agree to an order under which the amount of child support differs from the amount that would be awarded in accordance with the child support guidelines, the court may modify the order only if the circumstances of the child or a person affected by the order have materially and substantially changed since the date of the order's rendition.

(a–2) A court or administrative order for child support in a Title IV–D case may be modified at any time, and without a showing of material and substantial change in the circumstances of the child or a person affected by the order, to provide for medical support or dental support of the child if the order does not provide health care coverage as required under Section 154.182 or dental care coverage as required under Section 154.1825.

(b) A support order may be modified with regard to the amount of support ordered only as to obligations accruing after the earlier of:

(1) the date of service of citation; or

(2) an appearance in the suit to modify.

(c) An order of joint conservatorship, in and of itself, does not constitute grounds for modifying a support order.

(c–1) Incarceration of a child support obligor in a local, state, or federal jail or prison for a period exceeding 180 days is a material and substantial change of circumstances for the purposes of this section.

(d) Release of a child support obligor from incarceration is a material and substantial change in circumstances for purposes of this section if the obligor's child support obligation was abated, reduced, or suspended during the period of the obligor's incarceration.

Added by Acts 1995, 74th Leg., ch. 20, § 1, eff. April 20, 1995. Amended by Acts 1997, 75th Leg., ch. 911, § 16, eff. Sept. 1, 1997; Acts 1999, 76th Leg., ch. 43, § 1, eff. Sept. 1, 1999; Acts 2003, 78th Leg., ch. 1036, § 21, eff. Sept. 1, 2003; Acts 2005, 79th Leg., ch. 916, § 19, eff. June 18, 2005; Acts 2007, 80th Leg., ch. 363, § 6, eff. Sept. 1, 2007; Acts 2007, 80th Leg., ch. 972, § 15, eff. Sept. 1, 2007; Acts 2011, 82nd Leg., ch. 508 (H.B. 1674), § 3, eff. Sept. 1, 2011; Acts 2013, 83rd Leg., ch. 742 (S.B. 355), § 5, eff. Sept. 1, 2013; Acts 2015, 84th Leg., ch. 1150 (S.B. 550), § 29, eff. Sept. 1, 2018; Acts 2021, 87th Leg., ch. 552 (S.B. 286), § 6, eff. Sept. 1, 2021.

Section 2 of Acts 2019, 86th Leg., ch. 359 (H.B. 558) provides:

"The change in law made by this Act [Acts 2019, 86th Leg., ch. 359 (H.B. 558) in V.T.C.A., Family Code 154.302 added (c)] constitutes a material and substantial change of circumstances under Section 156.401, Family Code, sufficient to warrant modification of a court order or a portion of a decree that provides for the support of a child rendered before the effective date [Sept. 1, 2019] of this Act."

Sections 12 and 16 of Acts 2021, 87th Leg., ch. 552 (S.B. 286) provide:

"Sec. 12. The enactment of this Act does not constitute a material and substantial change of circumstances sufficient to warrant modification of a court order or portion of a decree that provides for the support of a child rendered before the effective date [Sept. 1, 2021] of this Act."

"Sec. 16. Section 156.401, Family Code, as amended by this Act, applies only to a suit for modification of a child support order that is filed on or after the effective date of this Act. A suit for modification that is filed before the effective date of this Act is governed by the law in effect on the date the suit was filed, and the former law is continued in effect for that purpose."

### § 156.402. Effect of Guidelines

(a) The court may consider the child support guidelines for single and multiple families under Chapter 154 to determine whether there has been a material or substantial change of circumstances under this chapter that warrants a modification of an existing child support order if the modification is in the best interest of the child.

(b) If the amount of support contained in the order does not substantially conform with the guidelines for single and multiple families under Chapter 154, the court may modify the order to substantially conform with the guidelines if the modification is in the best interest of the child. A court may consider other relevant evidence in addition to the factors listed in the guidelines.

Added by Acts 1995, 74th Leg., ch. 20, § 1, eff. April 20, 1995. Amended by Acts 1999, 76th Leg., ch. 62, § 6.22, eff. Sept. 1, 1999; Acts 1999, 76th Leg., ch. 556, § 12, eff. Sept. 1, 1999.

### § 156.403. Voluntary Additional Support

A history of support voluntarily provided in excess of the court order does not constitute cause to increase the amount of an existing child support order.

Added by Acts 1995, 74th Leg., ch. 20, § 1, eff. April 20, 1995.

### § 156.404. Net Resources of New Spouse

(a) The court may not add any portion of the net resources of a new spouse to the net resources of an obligor or obligee in order to calculate the amount of child support to be ordered in a suit for modification.

(b) The court may not subtract the needs of a new spouse, or of a dependent of a new spouse, from the net resources of the obligor or obligee in a suit for modification.

Added by Acts 1995, 74th Leg., ch. 20, § 1, eff. April 20, 1995.

### § 156.405. Change in Lifestyle

An increase in the needs, standard of living, or lifestyle of the obligee since the rendition of the existing order does not warrant an increase in the obligor's child support obligation.

Added by Acts 1995, 74th Leg., ch. 20, § 1, eff. April 20, 1995.

### § 156.406. Use of Guidelines for Children in More Than One Household

In applying the child support guidelines in a suit under this subchapter, if the obligor has the duty to support children in more than one household, the court shall apply the percentage guidelines for multiple families under Chapter 154.

Added by Acts 1995, 74th Leg., ch. 20, § 1, eff. April 20, 1995. Amended by Acts 1999, 76th Leg., ch. 62, § 6.23, eff. Sept. 1, 1999; Acts 1999, 76th Leg., ch. 556, § 13, eff. Sept. 1, 1999.

### § 156.407. Assignment of Child Support Right

A notice of assignment filed under Chapter 231 does not constitute a modification of an order to pay child support.

Added by Acts 1995, 74th Leg., ch. 20, § 1, eff. April 20, 1995.

### § 156.408. Modification of Support Order Rendered by Another State

(a) Unless both parties and the child reside in this state, a court of this state may modify an order of child support rendered by an appropriate tribunal of another state only as provided by Chapter 159.

(b) If both parties and the child reside in this state, a court of this state may modify an order of child support rendered by an appropriate tribunal of another state after registration of the order as provided by Chapter 159.

Added by Acts 1995, 74th Leg., ch. 20, § 1, eff. April 20, 1995. Amended by Acts 2001, 77th Leg., ch. 1023, § 13, eff. Sept. 1, 2001.

### § 156.409. Change in Physical Possession

(a) The court shall, on the motion of a party or a person having physical possession of the child, modify an order providing for the support of the child to provide that the person having physical possession of the child for at least six months shall have the right to receive and give receipt for payments of support for the child and to hold or disburse money for the benefit of the child if the sole managing conservator of the child or the joint managing conservator who has the exclusive right to determine the primary residence of the child has:

(1) voluntarily relinquished the primary care and possession of the child;

(2) been incarcerated or sentenced to be incarcerated for at least 90 days; or

(3) relinquished the primary care and possession of the child in a proceeding under Title 3[1] or Chapter 262.

(a–1) If the court modifies a support order under this section, the court shall order the obligor to pay the person or entity having physical possession of the child any unpaid child support that is not subject to offset or reimbursement under Section 157.008 and that accrues after the date the sole or joint managing conservator:

(1) relinquishes possession and control of the child, whether voluntarily or in a proceeding under Title 3 or Chapter 262; or

(2) is incarcerated.

(a–2) This section does not affect the ability of the court to render a temporary order for the payment of child support that is in the best interest of the child.

(a–3) An order under this section that modifies a support order because of the incarceration of the sole or joint managing conservator of a child must provide that on the conservator's release from incarceration the conservator may file an affidavit with the court stating that the conservator has been released from incarceration, that there has not been a modification of the conservatorship of the child during the incarceration, and that the conservator has resumed physical possession of the child. A copy of the affidavit shall be delivered to the obligor and any other party, including the Title IV–D agency if appropriate. On receipt of the affidavit, the court on its own motion shall order the obligor to make support payments to the conservator.

(b) Notice of a motion for modification under this section may be served in the manner for serving a notice under Section 157.065.

Added by Acts 1999, 76th Leg., ch. 556, § 14, eff. Sept. 1, 1999. Amended by Acts 2001, 77th Leg., ch. 1023, § 14, eff. Sept. 1, 2001; Acts 2001, 77th Leg., ch. 1289, § 10, eff. Sept. 1, 2001; Acts 2005, 79th Leg., ch. 261, § 1, eff. May 30, 2005; Acts 2007, 80th Leg., ch. 972, § 16, eff. Sept. 1, 2007.

[1] V.T.C.A., Family Code §§ 51.01 et seq. or 262.001 et seq.

### § 156.410. Repealed by Acts 2009, 81st Leg., ch. 727, § 6, eff. Sept. 1, 2009; Acts 2009, 81st Leg., ch. 1113, § 31, eff. Sept. 1, 2009

## CHAPTER 157. ENFORCEMENT

SUBCHAPTER A. PLEADINGS AND DEFENSES



SUBCHAPTER B. PROCEDURE



SUBCHAPTER C. FAILURE TO APPEAR; BOND OR SECURITY

## SUBCHAPTER A. PLEADINGS AND DEFENSES

### § 157.001. Motion for Enforcement

(a) A motion for enforcement as provided in this chapter may be filed to enforce any provision of a temporary or final order rendered in a suit.

(b) The court may enforce by contempt any provision of a temporary or final order.

(c) The court may enforce a temporary or final order for child support as provided in this chapter or Chapter 158.

(d) A motion for enforcement shall be filed in the court of continuing, exclusive jurisdiction.

(e) For purposes of this section, "temporary order" includes a temporary restraining order, standing order, injunction, and any other temporary order rendered by a court.

Added by Acts 1995, 74th Leg., ch. 20, § 1, eff. April 20, 1995. Amended by Acts 2015, 84th Leg., ch. 1105 (H.B. 3121), § 1, eff. Sept. 1, 2015.

### § 157.002. Contents of Motion

(a) A motion for enforcement must, in ordinary and concise language:

(1) identify the provision of the order allegedly violated and sought to be enforced;

(2) state the manner of the respondent's alleged noncompliance;

(3) state the relief requested by the movant; and

(4) contain the signature of the movant or the movant's attorney.

(b) A motion for enforcement of child support:

(1) must include the amount owed as provided in the order, the amount paid, and the amount of arrearages;

(2) if contempt is requested, must include the portion of the order allegedly violated and, for each date of alleged contempt, the amount due and the amount paid, if any;

(3) may include as an attachment a copy of a record of child support payments maintained by the Title IV-D registry or a local registry; and

(4) if the obligor owes arrearages for a child receiving assistance under Part A of Title IV of the federal Social Security Act (42 U.S.C. Section 601 et seq.), may include a request that:

(A) the obligor pay the arrearages in accordance with a plan approved by the court; or

(B) if the obligor is already subject to a plan and is not incapacitated, the obligor participate in work activities, as defined under 42 U.S.C. Section 607(d), that the court determines appropriate.

(c) A motion for enforcement of the terms and conditions of conservatorship or possession of or access to a child must include the date, place, and, if applicable, the time of each occasion of the respondent's failure to comply with the order.

(d) The movant is not required to plead that the underlying order is enforceable by contempt to obtain other appropriate enforcement remedies.

(e) The movant may allege repeated past violations of the order and that future violations of a similar nature may occur before the date of the hearing.

Added by Acts 1995, 74th Leg., ch. 20, § 1, eff. April 20, 1995. Amended by Acts 1997, 75th Leg., ch. 911, § 17, eff. Sept. 1, 1997.

### § 157.003. Joinder of Claims and Remedies; No Election of Remedies

(a) A party requesting enforcement may join in the same proceeding any claim and remedy provided for in this chapter, other provisions of this title, or other rules of law.

(b) A motion for enforcement does not constitute an election of remedies that limits or precludes:

(1) the use of any other civil or criminal proceeding to enforce a final order; or

(2) a suit for damages under Chapter 42.

Added by Acts 1995, 74th Leg., ch. 20, § 1, eff. April 20, 1995. Amended by Acts 1999, 76th Leg., ch. 62, § 6.24, eff. Sept. 1, 1999.

### § 157.004. Time Limitations; Enforcement of Possession

The court retains jurisdiction to render a contempt order for failure to comply with the order of possession and access if the motion for enforcement is filed not later than the sixth month after the date:

(1) the child becomes an adult; or

(2) on which the right of possession and access terminates under the order or by operation of law.

Added by Acts 1995, 74th Leg., ch. 20, § 1, eff. April 20, 1995.

### § 157.005. Time Limitations; Enforcement of Child Support

(a) The court retains jurisdiction to render a contempt order for failure to comply with the child support order if the motion for enforcement is filed not later than the second anniversary of the date:

(1) the child becomes an adult; or

(2) on which the child support obligation terminates under the order or by operation of law.

(b) The court retains jurisdiction to confirm the total amount of child support, medical support, and dental support arrearages and render cumulative money judgments for past-due child support, medical support, and dental support, as provided by Section 157.263, if a motion for enforcement requesting a money judgment is filed not later than the 10th anniversary after the date:

(1) the child becomes an adult; or

(2) on which the child support obligation terminates under the child support order or by operation of law.

Added by Acts 1995, 74th Leg., ch. 20, § 1, eff. April 20, 1995. Amended by Acts 1999, 76th Leg., ch. 556, § 15, eff. Sept. 1, 1999; Acts 2005, 79th Leg., ch. 916, § 21, eff. June 18, 2005; Acts 2007, 80th Leg., ch. 972, § 17, eff. Sept. 1, 2007; Acts 2009, 81st Leg., ch. 767, § 13, eff. June 19, 2009; Acts 2021, 87th Leg., ch. 552 (S.B. 286), § 7, eff. Sept. 1, 2021.

Section 12 of Acts 2021, 87th Leg., ch. 552 (S.B. 286) provides:

"The enactment of this Act does not constitute a material and substantial change of circumstances sufficient to warrant modification of a court order or portion of a decree that provides for the support of a child rendered before the effective date [Sept. 1, 2021] of this Act."

### § 157.006. Affirmative Defense to Motion for Enforcement

(a) The issue of the existence of an affirmative defense to a motion for enforcement does not arise unless evidence is admitted supporting the defense.

(b) The respondent must prove the affirmative defense by a preponderance of the evidence.

Added by Acts 1995, 74th Leg., ch. 20, § 1, eff. April 20, 1995.

### § 157.007. Affirmative Defense to Motion for Enforcement of Possession or Access

(a) The respondent may plead as an affirmative defense to contempt for failure to comply with an order for possession or access to a child that the movant voluntarily relinquished actual possession and control of the child.

(b) The voluntary relinquishment must have been for the time encompassed by the court-ordered periods during which the respondent is alleged to have interfered.

Added by Acts 1995, 74th Leg., ch. 20, § 1, eff. April 20, 1995.

### § 157.008. Affirmative Defense to Motion for Enforcement of Child Support

(a) An obligor may plead as an affirmative defense in whole or in part to a motion for enforcement of child support that the obligee voluntarily relinquished to the obligor actual possession and control of a child.

(b) The voluntary relinquishment must have been for a time period in excess of any court-ordered periods of possession of and access to the child and actual support must have been supplied by the obligor.

(c) An obligor may plead as an affirmative defense to an allegation of contempt or of the violation of a condition of community service requiring payment of child support that the obligor:

(1) lacked the ability to provide support in the amount ordered;

(2) lacked property that could be sold, mortgaged, or otherwise pledged to raise the funds needed;

(3) attempted unsuccessfully to borrow the funds needed; and

(4) knew of no source from which the money could have been borrowed or legally obtained.

(d) An obligor who has provided actual support to the child during a time subject to an affirmative defense under this section may request reimbursement for that support as a counterclaim or offset against the claim of the obligee.

(e) An action against the obligee for support supplied to a child is limited to the amount of periodic payments previously ordered by the court.

Added by Acts 1995, 74th Leg., ch. 20, § 1, eff. April 20, 1995.

### § 157.009. Credit for Payment of Disability Benefits

In addition to any other credit or offset available to an obligor under this title, if a child for whom the obligor owes child support receives a lump-sum payment as a result of the obligor's disability and that payment is made to the obligee as the representative payee of the child, the obligor is entitled to a credit. The credit under this section is equal to the amount of the lump-sum payment and shall be applied to any child support arrearage and interest owed by the obligor on behalf of that child at the time the payment is made.

Added by Acts 2009, 81st Leg., ch. 538, § 1, eff. June 19, 2009; Acts 2009, 81st Leg., ch. 767, § 14, eff. June 19, 2009.

## SUBCHAPTER B. PROCEDURE

### § 157.061. Setting Hearing

(a) On filing a motion for enforcement requesting contempt, the court shall set the date, time, and place of the hearing and order the respondent to personally appear and respond to the motion.

(b) If the motion for enforcement does not request contempt, the court shall set the motion for hearing on the request of a party.

(c) The court shall give preference to a motion for enforcement of child support in setting a hearing date and may not delay the hearing because a suit for modification of the order requested to be enforced has been or may be filed.

Added by Acts 1995, 74th Leg., ch. 20, § 1, eff. April 20, 1995.

### § 157.062. Notice of Hearing

(a) The notice of hearing must include the date, time, and place of the hearing.

(b) The notice of hearing need not repeat the allegations contained in the motion for enforcement.

(c) Notice of hearing on a motion for enforcement of a final order providing for child support or possession of or access to a child, any provision of a final order rendered against a party who has already appeared in a suit under this title, or any provision of a temporary order shall be given to the respondent by personal service of a copy of the motion and notice not later than the 10th day before the date of the hearing. For purposes of this subsection, "temporary order" includes a temporary restraining order, standing order, injunction, and any other temporary order rendered by a court.

(d) If a motion for enforcement of a final order, other than a final order rendered against a party who has already appeared in a suit under this title, is joined with another claim:

(1) the hearing may not be held before 10 a.m. on the first Monday after the 20th day after the date of service; and

(2) the provisions of the Texas Rules of Civil Procedure applicable to the filing of an original lawsuit apply.

Added by Acts 1995, 74th Leg., ch. 20, § 1, eff. April 20, 1995. Amended by Acts 1995, 74th Leg., ch. 751, § 49, eff. Sept. 1, 1995; Acts 2015, 84th Leg., ch. 1105 (H.B. 3121), § 2, eff. Sept. 1, 2015.

### § 157.063. Appearance

A party makes a general appearance for all purposes in an enforcement proceeding if:

(1) the party appears at the hearing or is present when the case is called; and

(2) the party does not object to the court's jurisdiction or the form or manner of the notice of hearing.

Added by Acts 1995, 74th Leg., ch. 20, § 1, eff. April 20, 1995.

### § 157.064. Special Exception

(a) If a respondent specially excepts to the motion for enforcement or moves to strike, the court shall rule on the exception or the motion to strike before it hears the motion for enforcement.

(b) If an exception is sustained, the court shall give the movant an opportunity to replead and continue the hearing to a designated date and time without the requirement of additional service.

Added by Acts 1995, 74th Leg., ch. 20, § 1, eff. April 20, 1995.

### § 157.065. Notice of Hearing, First Class Mail

(a) If a party has been ordered under Chapter 105 to provide the court and the state case registry with the party's current mailing address, notice of a hearing on a motion for enforcement of a final order or on a request for a court order implementing a post-judgment remedy for the collection of child support may be served by mailing a copy of the notice to the respondent, together with a copy of the motion or request, by first class mail to the last mailing address of the respondent on file with the court and the registry.

(b) The notice may be sent by the clerk of the court, the attorney for the movant or party requesting a court order, or any person entitled to the address information as provided in Chapter 105.

(c) A person who sends the notice shall file of record a certificate of service showing the date of mailing and the name of the person who sent the notice.

(d) Repealed by Acts 1997, 75th Leg., ch. 911, § 97(a), eff. Sept. 1, 1997.

Added by Acts 1995, 74th Leg., ch. 20, § 1, eff. April 20, 1995. Amended by Acts 1997, 75th Leg., ch. 911, §§ 18, 97(a), eff. Sept. 1, 1997; Acts 2007, 80th Leg., ch. 972, § 18, eff. Sept. 1, 2007; Acts 2015, 84th Leg., ch. 859 (S.B. 1726), § 5, eff. Sept. 1, 2015; Acts 2015, 84th Leg., ch. 1105 (H.B. 3121), § 3, eff. Sept. 1, 2015.

### § 157.066. Failure to Appear

If a respondent who has been personally served with notice to appear at a hearing does not appear at the designated time, place, and date to respond to a motion for enforcement of an existing court order, regardless of whether the motion is joined with other claims or remedies, the court may not hold the respondent in contempt but may, on proper proof, grant a default judgment for the relief sought and issue a capias for the arrest of the respondent.

Added by Acts 1995, 74th Leg., ch. 20, § 1, eff. April 20, 1995. Amended by Acts 1995, 74th Leg., ch. 751, § 50, eff. Sept. 1, 1995.

## SUBCHAPTER C. FAILURE TO APPEAR; BOND OR SECURITY

### § 157.101. Bond or Security for Release of Respondent

(a) When the court orders the issuance of a capias as provided in this chapter, the court shall also set an appearance bond or security, payable to the obligee or to a person designated by the court, in a reasonable amount.

(b) An appearance bond or security in the amount of $1,000 or a cash bond in the amount of $250 is presumed to be reasonable. Evidence that the respondent has attempted to evade service of process, has previously been found guilty of contempt, or has accrued arrearages over $1,000 is sufficient to rebut the presumption. If the presumption is rebutted, the court shall set a reasonable bond.

Added by Acts 1995, 74th Leg., ch. 20, § 1, eff. April 20, 1995.

### § 157.102. Capias or Warrant; Duty of Law Enforcement Officials

Law enforcement officials shall treat a capias or arrest warrant ordered under this chapter in the same manner as an arrest warrant for a criminal offense and shall enter the capias or warrant in the computer records for outstanding warrants maintained by the local police, sheriff, and Department of Public Safety. The capias or warrant shall be forwarded to and disseminated by the Texas Crime Information Center and the National Crime Information Center.

Added by Acts 1995, 74th Leg., ch. 20, § 1, eff. April 20, 1995. Amended by Acts 1997, 75th Leg., ch. 702, § 3, eff. Sept. 1, 1997; Acts 1999, 76th Leg., ch. 556, § 16, eff. Sept. 1, 1999; Acts 2007, 80th Leg., ch. 972, § 19, eff. Sept. 1, 2007.

### § 157.103. Capias Fees

(a) The fee for issuing a capias as provided in this chapter is the same as the fee for issuance of a writ of attachment.

(b) The fee for serving a capias is the same as the fee for service of a writ in civil cases generally.

Added by Acts 1995, 74th Leg., ch. 20, § 1, eff. April 20, 1995.

### § 157.104. Conditional Release

If the respondent is taken into custody and released on bond, the court shall condition the bond on the respondent's promise to appear in court for a hearing as required by the court without the necessity of further personal service of notice on the respondent.

Added by Acts 1995, 74th Leg., ch. 20, § 1, eff. April 20, 1995.

### § 157.105. Release Hearing

(a) If the respondent is taken into custody and not released on bond, the respondent shall be brought before the court that issued the capias on or before the third working day after the arrest. The court shall determine whether the respondent's appearance in court at a designated time and place can be assured by a method other than by posting the bond or security previously established.

(a–1) The court may conduct the release hearing under Subsection (a) through the use of teleconferencing, videoconferencing, or other remote electronic means if the court determines that the method of appearance will facilitate the hearing.

(b) If the respondent is released without posting bond or security, the court shall set a hearing on the alleged contempt at a designated date, time, and place and give the respondent notice of hearing in open court. No other notice to the respondent is required.

(c) If the court is not satisfied that the respondent's appearance in court can be assured and the respondent remains in custody, a hearing on the alleged contempt shall be held as soon as practicable, but not later than the seventh day after the date that the respondent was taken into custody, unless the respondent and the respondent's attorney waive the accelerated hearing.

Added by Acts 1995, 74th Leg., ch. 20, § 1, eff. April 20, 1995. Amended by Acts 2007, 80th Leg., ch. 972, § 21, eff. Sept. 1, 2007; Acts 2017, 85th Leg., ch. 961 (S.B. 1965), § 1, eff. Sept. 1, 2017.

### § 157.106. Cash Bond as Support

(a) If the respondent has posted a cash bond and is found to be in arrears in the payment of court-ordered child support, the court shall order that the proceeds of the cash bond be paid to the child support obligee or to a person designated by the court, not to exceed the amount of child support arrearages determined to exist.

(b) This section applies without regard to whether the respondent appears at the hearing.

Added by Acts 1995, 74th Leg., ch. 20, § 1, eff. April 20, 1995.

### § 157.107. Appearance Bond or Security Other Than Cash Bond as Support

(a) If the respondent fails to appear at the hearing as directed, the court shall order that the appearance bond or security be forfeited and that the proceeds of any judgment on the bond or security, not to exceed the amount of child support arrearages determined to exist, be paid to the obligee or to a person designated by the court.

(b) The obligee may file suit on the bond.

Added by Acts 1995, 74th Leg., ch. 20, § 1, eff. April 20, 1995.

### § 157.108. Cash Bond as Property of Respondent

A court shall treat a cash bond posted for the benefit of the respondent as the property of the respondent. A person who posts the cash bond does not have recourse in relation to an order regarding the bond other than against the respondent.

Added by Acts 1995, 74th Leg., ch. 20, § 1, eff. April 20, 1995.

### § 157.109. Security for Compliance with Order

(a) The court may order the respondent to execute a bond or post security if the court finds that the respondent:

(1) has on two or more occasions denied possession of or access to a child who is the subject of the order; or

(2) is employed by an employer not subject to the jurisdiction of the court or for whom income withholding is unworkable or inappropriate.

(b) The court shall set the amount of the bond or security and condition the bond or security on compliance with the court order permitting possession or access or the payment of past-due or future child support.

(c) The court shall order the bond or security payable through the registry of the court:

(1) to the obligee or other person or entity entitled to receive child support payments designated by the court if enforcement of child support is requested; or

(2) to the person who is entitled to possession or access if enforcement of possession or access is requested.

Added by Acts 1995, 74th Leg., ch. 20, § 1, eff. April 20, 1995.

### § 157.110. Forfeiture of Security for Failure to Comply with Order

(a) On the motion of a person or entity for whose benefit a bond has been executed or security deposited, the court may forfeit all or part of the bond or security deposit on a finding that the person who furnished the bond or security:

(1) has violated the court order for possession of and access to a child; or

(2) failed to make child support payments.

(b) The court shall order the registry to pay the funds from a forfeited bond or security deposit to the obligee or person or entity entitled to receive child support payments in an amount that does not exceed the child support arrearages or, in the case of possession of or access to a child, to the person entitled to possession or access.

(c) The court may order that all or part of the forfeited amount be applied to pay attorney's fees and costs incurred by the person or entity bringing the motion for contempt or motion for forfeiture.

Added by Acts 1995, 74th Leg., ch. 20, § 1, eff. April 20, 1995.

### § 157.111. Forfeiture Not Defense to Contempt

The forfeiture of bond or security is not a defense in a contempt proceeding.

Added by Acts 1995, 74th Leg., ch. 20, § 1, eff. April 20, 1995.

### § 157.112. Joinder of Forfeiture and Contempt Proceedings

A motion for enforcement requesting contempt may be joined with a forfeiture proceeding.

Added by Acts 1995, 74th Leg., ch. 20, § 1, eff. April 20, 1995.

### § 157.113. Application of Bond Pending Writ

If the obligor requests to execute a bond or to post security pending a hearing by an appellate court on a writ, the bond or security on forfeiture shall be payable to the obligee.

Added by Acts 1995, 74th Leg., ch. 20, § 1, eff. April 20, 1995.

### § 157.114. Failure to Appear

The court may order a capias to be issued for the arrest of the respondent if:

(1) the motion for enforcement requests contempt;

(2) the respondent was personally served; and

(3) the respondent fails to appear.

Added by Acts 1995, 74th Leg., ch. 20, § 1, eff. April 20, 1995.

### § 157.115. Default Judgment

(a) The court may render a default order for the relief requested if the respondent:

(1) has been personally served, has filed an answer, or has entered an appearance; and

(2) does not appear at the designated time, place, and date to respond to the motion.

(b) If the respondent fails to appear, the court may not hold the respondent in contempt but may order a capias to be issued.

Added by Acts 1995, 74th Leg., ch. 20, § 1, eff. April 20, 1995. Amended by Acts 1995, 74th Leg., ch. 751, § 51, eff. Sept. 1, 1995.

## SUBCHAPTER D. HEARING AND ENFORCEMENT ORDER

### § 157.161. Record

(a) Except as provided by Subsection (b), a record of the hearing in a motion for enforcement shall be made by a court reporter or as provided by Chapter 201.

(b) A record is not required if:

(1) the parties agree to an order; or

(2) the motion does not request incarceration and the parties waive the requirement of a record at the time of hearing, either in writing or in open court, and the court approves waiver.

Added by Acts 1995, 74th Leg., ch. 20, § 1, eff. April 20, 1995.

### § 157.162. Proof

(a) The movant is not required to prove that the underlying order is enforceable by contempt to obtain other appropriate enforcement remedies.

(b) A finding that the respondent is not in contempt does not preclude the court from awarding the petitioner court costs and reasonable attorney's fees or ordering any other enforcement remedy, including rendering a money judgment, posting a bond or other security, or withholding income.

(c) The movant may attach to the motion a copy of a payment record. The movant may subsequently update that payment record at the hearing. If a payment record was attached to the motion as authorized by this subsection, the payment record, as updated if applicable, is admissible to prove:

(1) the dates and in what amounts payments were made;

(2) the amount of any accrued interest;

(3) the cumulative arrearage over time; and

(4) the cumulative arrearage as of the final date of the record.

(c–1) A respondent may offer evidence controverting the contents of a payment record under Subsection (c).

(d) Repealed by Acts 2013, 83rd Leg., ch. 649 (H.B. 847), § 2.

(e) Repealed by Acts 2013, 83rd Leg., ch. 649 (H.B. 847), § 2.

Added by Acts 1995, 74th Leg., ch. 20, § 1, eff. April 20, 1995. Amended by Acts 2007, 80th Leg., ch. 1189, § 1, eff. June 15, 2007; Acts 2009, 81st Leg., ch. 767, § 15, eff. June 19, 2009; Acts 2011, 82nd Leg., ch. 508 (H.B. 1674), § 4, eff. Sept. 1, 2011; Acts 2013, 83rd Leg., ch. 649 (H.B. 847), §§ 1, 2, eff. June 14, 2013.

### § 157.163. Appointment of Attorney

(a) In a motion for enforcement or motion to revoke community service, the court must first determine whether incarceration of the respondent is a possible result of the proceedings.

(b) If the court determines that incarceration is a possible result of the proceedings, the court shall inform a respondent not represented by an attorney of the right to be represented by an attorney and, if the respondent is indigent, of the right to the appointment of an attorney.

(c) If the court determines that the respondent will not be incarcerated as a result of the proceedings, the court may require a respondent who is indigent to proceed without an attorney.

(d) If the respondent claims indigency and requests the appointment of an attorney, the court shall require the respondent to file an affidavit of indigency. The court may hear evidence to determine the issue of indigency.

(d–1) The court may conduct a hearing on the issue of indigency through the use of teleconferencing, videoconferencing, or other remote electronic means if the court determines that conducting the hearing in that manner will facilitate the hearing.

(e) Except as provided by Subsection (c), the court shall appoint an attorney to represent the respondent if the court determines that the respondent is indigent.

(f) If the respondent is not in custody, an appointed attorney is entitled to not less than 10 days from the date of the attorney's appointment to respond to the movant's pleadings and prepare for the hearing.

(g) If the respondent is in custody, an appointed attorney is entitled to not less than five days from the date the respondent was taken into custody to respond to the movant's pleadings and prepare for the hearing.

(h) The court may shorten or extend the time for preparation if the respondent and the respondent's attorney sign a waiver of the time limit.

(i) The scope of the court appointment of an attorney to represent the respondent is limited to the allegation of contempt or of violation of community supervision contained in the motion for enforcement or motion to revoke community supervision.

Added by Acts 1995, 74th Leg., ch. 20, § 1, eff. April 20, 1995. Amended by Acts 2017, 85th Leg., ch. 961 (S.B. 1965), § 2, eff. Sept. 1, 2017.

## § 157.164. Payment of Appointed Attorney

(a) An attorney appointed to represent an indigent respondent is entitled to a reasonable fee for services within the scope of the appointment in the amount set by the court.

(b) The fee shall be paid from the general funds of the county according to the schedule for the compensation of counsel appointed to defend criminal defendants as provided in the Code of Criminal Procedure.

(c) For purposes of this section, a proceeding in a court of appeals or the Supreme Court of Texas is considered the equivalent of a bona fide appeal to the Texas Court of Criminal Appeals.

Added by Acts 1995, 74th Leg., ch. 20, § 1, eff. April 20, 1995.

## § 157.165. Probation of Contempt Order

The court may place the respondent on community supervision and suspend commitment if the court finds that the respondent is in contempt of court for failure or refusal to obey an order rendered as provided in this title.

Added by Acts 1995, 74th Leg., ch. 20, § 1, eff. April 20, 1995. Amended by Acts 1999, 76th Leg., ch. 62, § 6.25, eff. Sept. 1, 1999.

## § 157.166. Contents of Enforcement Order

(a) An enforcement order must include:

(1) in ordinary and concise language the provisions of the order for which enforcement was requested;

(2) the acts or omissions that are the subject of the order;

(3) the manner of the respondent's noncompliance; and

(4) the relief granted by the court.

(b) If the order imposes incarceration or a fine for criminal contempt, an enforcement order must contain findings identifying, setting out, or incorporating by reference the provisions of the order for which enforcement was requested and the date of each occasion when the respondent's failure to comply with the order was found to constitute criminal contempt.

(c) If the enforcement order imposes incarceration for civil contempt, the order must state the specific conditions on which the respondent may be released from confinement.

Added by Acts 1995, 74th Leg., ch. 20, § 1, eff. April 20, 1995. Amended by Acts 1999, 76th Leg., ch. 556, § 17, eff. Sept. 1, 1999.

## § 157.167. Respondent to Pay Attorney's Fees and Costs

(a) If the court finds that the respondent has failed to make child support payments, the court shall order the respondent to pay the movant's reasonable attorney's fees and all court costs in addition to the arrearages. Fees and costs ordered under this subsection may be enforced by any means available for the enforcement of child support, including contempt.

(b) If the court finds that the respondent has failed to comply with the terms of an order providing for the possession of or access to a child, the court shall order the respondent to pay the movant's reasonable attorney's fees and all court costs in addition to any other remedy. If the court finds that the enforcement of the order with which the respondent failed to comply was necessary to ensure the child's physical or emotional health or welfare, the fees and costs ordered under this subsection may be enforced by any means available for the enforcement of child support, including contempt, but not including income withholding.

(c) Except as provided by Subsection (d), for good cause shown, the court may waive the requirement that the respondent pay attorney's fees and costs if the court states the reasons supporting that finding.

(d) If the court finds that the respondent is in contempt of court for failure or refusal to pay child support and that the respondent owes $20,000 or more in child support arrearages, the court may not waive the requirement that the respondent pay attorney's fees and costs unless the court also finds that the respondent:

(1) is involuntarily unemployed or is disabled; and

(2) lacks the financial resources to pay the attorney's fees and costs.

Added by Acts 1995, 74th Leg., ch. 20, § 1, eff. April 20, 1995. Amended by Acts 1999, 76th Leg., ch. 556, § 18, eff. Sept. 1, 1999; Acts 2003, 78th Leg., ch. 477, § 1, eff. Sept. 1, 2003; Acts 2003, 78th Leg., ch. 1262, § 1, eff. Sept. 1, 2003; Acts 2005, 79th Leg., ch. 253, § 1, eff. Sept. 1, 2005.

### § 157.168. Additional Periods of Possession or Access

(a) A court may order additional periods of possession of or access to a child to compensate for the denial of court-ordered possession or access. The additional periods of possession or access:

(1) must be of the same type and duration of the possession or access that was denied;

(2) may include weekend, holiday, and summer possession or access; and

(3) must occur on or before the second anniversary of the date the court finds that court-ordered possession or access has been denied.

(b) The person denied possession or access is entitled to decide the time of the additional possession or access, subject to the provisions of Subsection (a)(1).

Added by Acts 1995, 74th Leg., ch. 751, § 52, eff. Sept. 1, 1995. Amended by Acts 1997, 75th Leg., ch. 974, § 1, eff. Sept. 1, 1997; Acts 1999, 76th Leg., ch. 1034, § 1, eff. Sept. 1, 1999.

## SUBCHAPTER E. COMMUNITY SUPERVISION

### § 157.211. Conditions of Community Supervision

If the court places the respondent on community supervision and suspends commitment, the terms and conditions of community supervision may include the requirement that the respondent:

(1) report to the community supervision officer as directed;

(2) permit the community supervision officer to visit the respondent at the respondent's home or elsewhere;

(3) obtain counseling on financial planning, budget management, conflict resolution, parenting skills, alcohol or drug abuse, or other matters causing the respondent to fail to obey the order;

(4) pay required child support and any child support arrearages;

(5) pay court costs and attorney's fees ordered by the court;

(6) seek employment assistance services offered by the Texas Workforce Commission under Section 302.0035, Labor Code, if appropriate; and

(7) participate in mediation or other services to alleviate conditions that prevent the respondent from obeying the court's order.

Added by Acts 1995, 74th Leg., ch. 20, § 1, eff. April 20, 1995. Amended by Acts 1997, 75th Leg., ch. 702, § 4, eff. Sept. 1, 1997; Acts 1999, 76th Leg., ch. 946, § 2, eff. Sept. 1, 1999; Acts 2001, 77th Leg., ch. 311, § 1, eff. Sept. 1, 2001.

### § 157.212. Term of Community Supervision

The initial period of community supervision may not exceed 10 years. The court may continue the community supervision beyond 10 years until the earlier of:

(1) the second anniversary of the date on which the community supervision first exceeded 10 years; or

(2) the date on which all child support, including arrearages and interest, has been paid.

Added by Acts 1995, 74th Leg., ch. 20, § 1, eff. April 20, 1995. Amended by Acts 1999, 76th Leg., ch. 1313, § 1, eff. Sept. 1, 1999; Acts 2007, 80th Leg., ch. 972, § 22, eff. Sept. 1, 2007.

### § 157.213. Community Supervision Fees

(a) The court may require the respondent to pay a fee to the court in an amount equal to that required of a criminal defendant subject to community supervision.

(b) The court may make payment of the fee a condition of granting or continuing community supervision.

(c) The court shall deposit the fees received under this subchapter as follows:

(1) if the community supervision officer is employed by a community supervision and corrections department, in the special fund of the county treasury provided by the Code of Criminal Procedure to be used for community supervision; or

(2) if the community supervision officer is employed by a domestic relations office, in one of the following funds, as determined by the office's administering entity:

(A) the general fund for the county in which the domestic relations office is located; or

(B) the office fund established by the administering entity for the domestic relations office.

Added by Acts 1995, 74th Leg., ch. 20, § 1, eff. April 20, 1995. Amended by Acts 2001, 77th Leg., ch. 311, § 2, eff. Sept. 1, 2001.

### § 157.214. Motion to Revoke Community Supervision

A prosecuting attorney, the Title IV-D agency, a domestic relations office, or a party affected by the order may file a verified motion alleging specifically that certain conduct of the respondent constitutes a violation of the terms and conditions of community supervision.

Added by Acts 1995, 74th Leg., ch. 20, § 1, eff. April 20, 1995. Amended by Acts 2001, 77th Leg., ch. 311, § 3, eff. Sept. 1, 2001.

### § 157.215. Arrest for Alleged Violation of Community Supervision

(a) If the motion to revoke community supervision alleges a prima facie case that the respondent has violated a term or condition of community supervision, the court may order the respondent's arrest by warrant.

(b) The respondent shall be brought promptly before the court ordering the arrest.

Added by Acts 1995, 74th Leg., ch. 20, § 1, eff. April 20, 1995.

### § 157.216. Hearing on Motion to Revoke Community Supervision

(a) The court shall hold a hearing without a jury not later than the third working day after the date the respondent is arrested under Section 157.215. If the court is unavailable for a hearing on that date, the hearing shall be held not later than the third working day after the date the court becomes available.

(b) The hearing under this section may not be held later than the seventh working day after the date the respondent is arrested.

(c) After the hearing, the court may continue, modify, or revoke the community supervision.

Added by Acts 1995, 74th Leg., ch. 20, § 1, eff. April 20, 1995. Amended by Acts 2007, 80th Leg., ch. 972, § 23, eff. Sept. 1, 2007.

### § 157.217. Discharge From Community Supervision

(a) When a community supervision period has been satisfactorily completed, the court on its own motion shall discharge the respondent from community supervision.

(b) The court may discharge the respondent from community supervision on the motion of the respondent if the court finds that the respondent:

(1) has satisfactorily completed one year of community supervision; and

(2) has fully complied with the community supervision order.

Added by Acts 1995, 74th Leg., ch. 20, § 1, eff. April 20, 1995.

## SUBCHAPTER F. JUDGMENT AND INTEREST

### § 157.261. Unpaid Child Support as Judgment

(a) A child support payment not timely made constitutes a final judgment for the amount due and owing, including interest as provided in this chapter.

(b) For the purposes of this subchapter, interest begins to accrue on the date the judge signs the order for the judgment unless the order contains a statement that the order is rendered on another specific date.

Added by Acts 1995, 74th Leg., ch. 20, § 1, eff. April 20, 1995. Amended by Acts 1997, 75th Leg., ch. 702, § 5, eff. Sept. 1, 1997.

### § 157.262. Repealed by Acts 2011, 82nd Leg., ch. 508 (H.B. 1674), § 24, eff. Sept. 1, 2011

### § 157.263. Confirmation of Arrearages

(a) If a motion for enforcement of child support requests a money judgment for arrearages, the court shall confirm the amount of arrearages and render cumulative money judgments as follows:

(1) a cumulative money judgment for the amount of child support owed under Subsection (b);

(2) a cumulative money judgment for the amount of medical support owed under Subsection (b–1); and

(3) a cumulative money judgment for the amount of dental support owed under Subsection (b–2).

(b) A cumulative money judgment for the amount of child support owed includes:

(1) unpaid child support not previously confirmed;

(2) the balance owed on previously confirmed child support arrearages or lump sum or retroactive child support judgments;

(3) interest on the child support arrearages; and

(4) a statement that it is a cumulative judgment for the amount of child support owed.

(b–1) A cumulative money judgment for the amount of medical support owed includes:

(1) unpaid medical support not previously confirmed;

(2) the balance owed on previously confirmed medical support arrearages or lump sum or retroactive medical support judgments;

(3) interest on the medical support arrearages; and

(4) a statement that it is a cumulative judgment for the amount of medical support owed.

(b–2) A cumulative money judgment for the amount of dental support owed includes:

(1) unpaid dental support not previously confirmed;

(2) the balance owed on previously confirmed dental support arrearages or lump sum or retroactive dental support judgments;

(3) interest on the dental support arrearages; and

(4) a statement that it is a cumulative judgment for the amount of dental support owed.

(b–3) In rendering a money judgment under this section, the court may not reduce or modify the amount of child support, medical support, or dental support arrearages but, in confirming the amount of arrearages, may allow a counterclaim or offset as provided by this title.

(c) If the amount of arrearages confirmed by the court reflects a credit to the obligor for support arrearages collected from a federal tax refund under 42 U.S.C. Section 664, and, subsequently, the amount of that credit is reduced because the refund was adjusted because of an injured spouse claim by a jointly filing spouse, the tax return was amended, the return was audited by the Internal Revenue Service, or for another reason permitted by law, the court shall render a new cumulative judgment to include as arrearages an amount equal to the amount by which the credit was reduced.

Added by Acts 1995, 74th Leg., ch. 20, § 1, eff. April 20, 1995. Amended by Acts 2003, 78th Leg., ch. 610, § 4, eff. Sept. 1, 2003; Acts 2007, 80th Leg., ch. 972, § 24, eff. Sept. 1, 2007; Acts 2011, 82nd Leg., ch. 508 (H.B. 1674), § 5, eff. Sept. 1, 2011; Acts 2021, 87th Leg., ch. 552 (S.B. 286), § 8, eff. Sept. 1, 2021.

Section 12 of Acts 2021, 87th Leg., ch. 552 (S.B. 286) provides:

"The enactment of this Act does not constitute a material and substantial change of circumstances sufficient to warrant modification of a court order or portion of a decree that provides for the support of a child rendered before the effective date [Sept. 1, 2021] of this Act."

Section 17 of Acts 2021, 87th Leg., ch. 552 (S.B. 286) provides:

"Section 157.263, Family Code, as amended by this Act, applies only to a cumulative money judgment rendered on or after the effective date [Sept. 1, 2021] of this Act. A judgment rendered before the effective date of this Act is governed by the law in effect at the time the judgment was rendered, and the former law is continued in effect for that purpose."

### § 157.264. Enforcement of Judgment

(a) A money judgment rendered as provided in this subchapter or a judgment for retroactive child support rendered under Chapter 154 may be enforced by any means available for the enforcement of a judgment for debts or the collection of child support.

(b) The court shall render an order requiring that the obligor make periodic payments on the judgment, including by income withholding under Chapter 158 if the obligor is subject to income withholding.

(c) An order rendered under Subsection (b) does not preclude or limit the use of any other means for enforcement of the judgment.

Added by Acts 1995, 74th Leg., ch. 20, § 1, eff. April 20, 1995. Amended by Acts 2001, 77th Leg., ch. 1023, § 16, eff. Sept. 1, 2001; Acts 2007, 80th Leg., ch. 972, § 25, eff. Sept. 1, 2007; Acts 2009, 81st Leg., ch. 767, § 17, eff. June 19, 2009; Acts 2015, 84th Leg., ch. 859 (S.B. 1726), § 6, eff. Sept. 1, 2015.

### § 157.265. Accrual of Interest on Child Support

(a) Interest accrues on the portion of delinquent child support that is greater than the amount of the monthly periodic support obligation at the rate of six percent simple interest per year from the date the support is delinquent until the date the support is paid or the arrearages are confirmed and reduced to money judgment.

(b) Interest accrues on child support arrearages that have been confirmed and reduced to money judgment as provided in this subchapter at the rate of six percent simple interest per year from the date the order is rendered until the date the judgment is paid.

(c) Interest accrues on a money judgment for retroactive or lump-sum child support at the annual rate of six percent simple interest from the date the order is rendered until the judgment is paid.

(d) Subsection (a) applies to a child support payment that becomes due on or after January 1, 2002.

(e) Child support arrearages in existence on January 1, 2002, that were not confirmed and reduced to a money judgment on or before that date accrue interest as follows:

(1) before January 1, 2002, the arrearages are subject to the interest rate that applied to the arrearages before that date; and

(2) on and after January 1, 2002, the cumulative total of arrearages and interest accumulated on those arrearages described by Subdivision (1) is subject to Subsection (a).

(f) Subsections (b) and (c) apply to a money judgment for child support rendered on or after January 1, 2002. A money judgment for child support rendered before that date is governed by the law in effect on the date the judgment was rendered, and the former law is continued in effect for that purpose.

Added by Acts 1995, 74th Leg., ch. 20, § 1, eff. April 20, 1995. Amended by Acts 1995, 74th Leg., ch. 751, § 53, eff. Sept. 1, 1995; Acts 1999, 76th Leg., ch. 943, § 1, eff. Jan. 1, 2000; Acts 2001, 77th Leg., ch. 1491, § 1, eff. Jan. 1, 2002; Acts 2005, 79th Leg., ch. 185, § 1, eff. May 27, 2005.

### § 157.266. Date of Delinquency

(a) A child support payment is delinquent for the purpose of accrual of interest if the payment is not received before the 31st day after the payment date stated in the order by:

(1) the local registry, Title IV-D registry, or state disbursement unit; or

(2) the obligee or entity specified in the order, if payments are not made through a registry.

(b) If a payment date is not stated in the order, a child support payment is delinquent if payment is not received by the registry or the obligee or entity specified in the order on the date that an amount equal to the support payable for one month becomes past due.

Added by Acts 1995, 74th Leg., ch. 20, § 1, eff. April 20, 1995. Amended by Acts 1999, 76th Leg., ch. 943, § 2, eff. Jan. 1, 2000.

### § 157.267. Interest Enforced as Child Support

Accrued interest is part of the child support obligation and may be enforced by any means provided for the collection of child support.

Added by Acts 1995, 74th Leg., ch. 20, § 1, eff. April 20, 1995.

### § 157.268. Application of Child Support Payment

Child support collected shall be applied in the following order of priority:

(1) current child support;

(2) non-delinquent child support owed;

(3) the principal amount of child support that has not been confirmed and reduced to money judgment;

(4) the principal amount of child support that has been confirmed and reduced to money judgment;

(5) interest on the principal amounts specified in Subdivisions (3) and (4); and

(6) the amount of any ordered attorney's fees or costs, or Title IV–D service fees authorized under Section 231.103 for which the obligor is responsible.

Added by Acts 1995, 74th Leg., ch. 20, § 1, eff. April 20, 1995. Amended by Acts 2001, 77th Leg., ch. 1023, § 17, eff. Sept. 1, 2001; Acts 2007, 80th Leg., ch. 972, § 20, eff. Sept. 1, 2007; Acts 2009, 81st Leg., ch. 767, § 18, eff. Jan. 1, 2010.

### § 157.269. Retention of Jurisdiction

A court that renders an order providing for the payment of child support retains continuing jurisdiction to enforce the order, including by adjusting the amount of the periodic payments to be made by the obligor or the amount to be withheld from the obligor's disposable earnings, until all current support, medical support, dental support, and child support arrearages, including interest and any applicable fees and costs, have been paid.

Added by Acts 1995, 74th Leg., ch. 751, § 54, eff. Sept. 1, 1995. Amended by Acts 1999, 76th Leg., ch. 556, § 19, eff. Sept. 1, 1999; Acts 2007, 80th Leg., ch. 972, § 26, eff. Sept. 1, 2007; Acts 2015, 84th Leg., ch. 1150 (S.B. 550), § 30, eff. Sept. 1, 2018.

## SUBCHAPTER G. CHILD SUPPORT LIEN

### § 157.311. Definitions

In this subchapter:

(1) "Account" means:

(A) any type of a demand deposit account, checking or negotiable withdrawal order account, savings account, time deposit account, mutual fund account, certificate of deposit, or any other instrument of deposit in which an individual has a beneficial ownership either in its entirety or on a shared or multiple party basis, including any accrued interest and dividends; and

(B) an insurance policy, including a life insurance policy or annuity contract, in which an individual has a beneficial ownership or against which an individual may file a claim or counterclaim.

(2) "Claimant" means:

(A) the obligee or a private attorney representing the obligee;

(B) the Title IV-D agency providing child support services;

(C) a domestic relations office or local registry; or

(D) an attorney appointed as a friend of the court.

(3) "Court having continuing jurisdiction" is the court of continuing, exclusive jurisdiction in this state or a tribunal of another state having jurisdiction under the Uniform Interstate Family Support Act or a substantially similar act.

(4) "Financial institution" has the meaning assigned by 42 U.S.C. Section 669a(d)(1) and includes a depository institution, depository institution holding company as defined by 12 U.S.C. Section 1813(w), credit union, benefit association, insurance company, mutual fund, and any similar entity authorized to do business in this state.

(5) "Lien" means a child support lien issued in this or another state.

Added by Acts 1995, 74th Leg., ch. 20, § 1, eff. April 20, 1995. Amended by Acts 1997, 75th Leg., ch. 420, § 1, eff. Sept. 1, 1997; Acts 1997, 75th Leg., ch. 911, § 19, eff. Sept. 1, 1997; Acts 2001, 77th Leg., ch. 1023, § 18, eff. Sept. 1, 2001; Acts 2003, 78th Leg., ch. 610, § 5, eff. Sept. 1, 2003; Acts 2011, 82nd Leg., ch. 508 (H.B. 1674), § 6, eff. Sept. 1, 2011.

### § 157.312. General Provisions

(a) A claimant may enforce child support by a lien as provided in this subchapter.

(b) The remedies provided by this subchapter do not affect the availability of other remedies provided by law.

(c) The lien is in addition to any other lien provided by law.

(d) A child support lien arises by operation of law against real and personal property of an obligor for all amounts of child support due and owing, including any accrued interest, regardless of whether the amounts have been adjudicated or otherwise determined, subject to the requirements of this subchapter for perfection of the lien.

(e) A child support lien arising in another state may be enforced in the same manner and to the same extent as a lien arising in this state.

(f) A foreclosure action under this subchapter is not required as a prerequisite to levy and execution on a judicial or administrative determination of arrearages as provided by Section 157.327.

(g) A child support lien under this subchapter may not be directed to an employer to attach to the disposable earnings of an obligor paid by the employer.

Added by Acts 1995, 74th Leg., ch. 20, § 1, eff. April 20, 1995. Amended by Acts 1997, 75th Leg., ch. 420, § 2, eff. Sept. 1, 1997; Acts 1997, 75th Leg., ch. 911, § 20, eff. Sept. 1, 1997; Acts 2001, 77th Leg., ch. 1023, § 19, eff. Sept. 1, 2001; Acts 2003, 78th Leg., ch. 610, § 6, eff. Sept. 1, 2003.

### § 157.313. Contents of Child Support Lien Notice

(a) Except as provided by Subsection (e), a child support lien notice must contain:

(1) the name and address of the person to whom the notice is being sent;

(2) the style, docket or cause number, and identity of the tribunal of this or another state having continuing jurisdiction of the child support action and, if the case is a Title IV–D case, the case number;

(3) the full name, address, and, if known, the birth date, driver's license number, social security number, and any aliases of the obligor;

(4) the full name and, if known, social security number of the obligee;

(5) the amount of the current or prospective child support obligation, the frequency with which current or prospective child support is ordered to be paid, and the amount of child support arrearages owed by the obligor and the date of the signing of the court order, administrative order, or writ that

determined the arrearages or the date and manner in which the arrearages were determined;

(6) the rate of interest specified in the court order, administrative order, or writ or, in the absence of a specified interest rate, the rate provided for by law;

(7) the name and address of the person or agency asserting the lien;

(8) the motor vehicle identification number as shown on the obligor's title if the property is a motor vehicle;

(9) a statement that the lien attaches to all nonexempt real and personal property of the obligor that is located or recorded in the state, including any property specifically identified in the notice and any property acquired after the date of filing or delivery of the notice;

(10) a statement that any ordered child support not timely paid in the future constitutes a final judgment for the amount due and owing, including interest, and accrues up to an amount that may not exceed the lien amount; and

(11) a statement that the obligor is being provided a copy of the lien notice and that the obligor may dispute the arrearage amount by filing suit under Section 157.323.

(b) A claimant may include any other information that the claimant considers necessary.

(c) Except as provided by Subsection (e), the lien notice must be verified.

(d) A claimant must file a notice for each after-acquired motor vehicle.

(e) A notice of a lien for child support under this section may be in the form authorized by federal law or regulation. The federal form of lien notice does not require verification when used by the Title IV–D agency.

(f) The requirement under Subsections (a)(3) and (4) to provide a social security number, if known, does not apply to a lien notice for a lien on real property.

Added by Acts 1995, 74th Leg., ch. 20, § 1, eff. April 20, 1995. Amended by Acts 1997, 75th Leg., ch. 420, § 3, eff. Sept. 1, 1997; Acts 1997, 75th Leg., ch. 911, § 21, eff. Sept. 1, 1997; Acts 2001, 77th Leg., ch. 1023, § 20, eff. Sept. 1, 2001; Acts 2007, 80th Leg., ch. 972, § 27, eff. Sept. 1, 2007.

### § 157.314. Filing Lien Notice or Abstract of Judgment; Notice to Obligor

(a) A child support lien notice or an abstract of judgment for past due child support may be filed by the claimant with the county clerk of:

(1) any county in which the obligor is believed to own nonexempt real or personal property;

(2) the county in which the obligor resides; or

(3) the county in which the court having continuing jurisdiction has venue of the suit affecting the parent-child relationship.

(b) A child support lien notice may be filed with or delivered to the following, as appropriate:

(1) the clerk of the court in which a claim, counterclaim, or suit by, or on behalf of, the obligor, including a claim or potential right to proceeds from an estate as an heir, beneficiary, or creditor, is pending, provided that a copy of the lien is mailed to the attorney of record for the obligor, if any;

(2) an attorney who represents the obligor in a claim or counterclaim that has not been filed with a court;

(3) any other individual or organization believed to be in possession of real or personal property of the obligor; or

(4) any governmental unit or agency that issues or records certificates, titles, or other indicia of property ownership.

(c) Not later than the 21st day after the date of filing or delivering the child support lien notice, the claimant shall provide a copy of the notice to the obligor by first class or certified mail, return receipt requested, addressed to the obligor at the obligor's last known address. If another person is known to have an ownership interest in the property subject to the lien, the claimant shall provide a copy of the lien notice to that person at the time notice is provided to the obligor.

(d) If a child support lien notice is delivered to a financial institution with respect to an account of the obligor, the institution shall immediately:

(1) provide the claimant with the last known address of the obligor; and

(2) notify any other person having an ownership interest in the account that the account has been frozen in an amount not to exceed the amount of the child support arrearage identified in the notice.

Added by Acts 1995, 74th Leg., ch. 20, § 1, eff. April 20, 1995. Amended by Acts 1997, 75th Leg., ch. 420, § 4, eff. Sept. 1, 1997; Acts 1997, 75th Leg., ch. 911, § 22, eff. Sept. 1, 1997; Acts 2001, 77th Leg., ch. 1023, § 21, eff. Sept. 1, 2001.

### § 157.3145. Service on Financial Institution

(a) Service of a child support lien notice on a financial institution relating to property held by the institution in the name of, or in behalf of, an obligor is governed by Section 59.008, Finance Code, if the institution is subject to that law, or may be delivered to the registered agent, the institution's main business office in this state, or another address provided by the institution under Section 231.307.

(b) A financial institution doing business in this state shall comply with the notice of lien and levy under this section regardless of whether the institution's corporate headquarters is located in this state.

Added by Acts 2001, 77th Leg., ch. 1023, § 22, eff. Sept. 1, 2001. Amended by Acts 2003, 78th Leg., ch. 610, § 7, eff. Sept. 1, 2003.

### § 157.315. Recording and Indexing Lien

(a) On receipt of a child support lien notice, the county clerk shall immediately record the notice in the county judgment records as provided in Chapter 52, Property Code.

(b) The county clerk may not charge the Title IV-D agency, a domestic relations office, a friend of the court, or any other party a fee for recording the notice of a lien. To qualify for this exemption, the lien notice must be styled "Notice of Child Support Lien" or be in the form authorized by federal law or regulation.

(c) The county clerk may not charge the Title IV-D agency, a domestic relations office, or a friend of the court a fee for recording the release of a child support lien. The lien release must be styled "Release of Child Support Lien."

Added by Acts 1995, 74th Leg., ch. 20, § 1, eff. April 20, 1995. Amended by Acts 1999, 76th Leg., ch. 595, § 1, eff. Sept. 1, 1999; Acts 1999, 76th Leg., ch. 769, § 1, eff. Sept. 1, 1999; Acts 2001, 77th Leg., ch. 1023, § 23, eff. Sept. 1, 2001.

### § 157.316. Perfection of Child Support Lien

(a) Except as provided by Subsection (b), a child support lien is perfected when an abstract of judgment for past due child support or a child support lien notice is filed or delivered as provided by Section 157.314.

(b) If a lien established under this subchapter attaches to a motor vehicle, the lien must be perfected in the manner provided by Chapter 501, Transportation Code, and the court or Title IV–D agency that rendered the order of child support shall include in the order a requirement that the obligor surrender to the court or Title IV–D agency evidence of the legal ownership of the motor vehicle against which the lien may attach. A lien against a motor vehicle under this subchapter is not perfected until the obligor's title to the vehicle has been surrendered to the court or Title IV–D agency and the Texas Department of Motor Vehicles has issued a subsequent title that discloses on its face the fact that the vehicle is subject to a child support lien under this subchapter.

Added by Acts 1995, 74th Leg., ch. 20, § 1, eff. April 20, 1995. Amended by Acts 1997, 75th Leg., ch. 420, § 5, eff. Sept. 1, 1997; Acts 1997, 75th Leg., ch. 911, § 23, eff. Sept. 1, 1997; Acts 2001, 77th Leg., ch. 1023, § 24, eff. Sept. 1, 2001; Acts 2009, 81st Leg., ch. 933, § 3C.01, eff. Sept. 1, 2009.

### § 157.317. Property to Which Lien Attaches

(a) A child support lien attaches to all real and personal property not exempt under the Texas Constitution or other law, including:

(1) an account in a financial institution;

(2) a retirement plan, including an individual retirement account;

(3) the proceeds of an insurance policy, including the proceeds from a life insurance policy or annuity contract and the proceeds from the sale or assignment of life insurance or annuity benefits, a claim for compensation, or a settlement or award for the claim for compensation, due to or owned by the obligor;

(4) property seized and subject to forfeiture under Chapter 59, Code of Criminal Procedure; and

(5) the proceeds derived from the sale of oil or gas production from an oil or gas well located in this state.

(a–1) A lien attaches to all property owned or acquired on or after the date the lien notice or abstract of judgment is filed with the county clerk of the county in which the property is located, with the court clerk as to property or claims in litigation, or, as to property of the obligor in the possession or control of a third party, from the date the lien notice is delivered to that party.

(b) A lien attaches to all nonhomestead real property of the obligor but does not attach to a homestead exempt under the Texas Constitution or the Property Code.

Added by Acts 1995, 74th Leg., ch. 20, § 1, eff. April 20, 1995. Amended by Acts 1997, 75th Leg., ch. 420, § 6, eff. Sept. 1, 1997; Acts 1997, 75th Leg., ch. 911, § 24, eff. Sept. 1, 1997; Acts 1999, 76th Leg., ch. 344, § 7.007, eff. Sept. 1, 1999; Acts 1999, 76th Leg., ch. 556, § 20, eff. Sept. 1, 1999; Acts 2001, 77th Leg., ch. 1023, § 25, eff. Sept. 1, 2001; Acts 2003, 78th Leg., ch. 610, § 8, eff. Sept. 1, 2003; Acts 2007, 80th Leg., ch. 972, § 28, eff. Sept. 1, 2007; Acts 2011, 82nd Leg., ch. 508 (H.B. 1674), § 7, eff. Sept. 1, 2011; Acts 2017, 85th Leg., ch. 961 (S.B. 1965), § 3, eff. Sept. 1, 2017.

## § 157.3171. Release of Lien on Homestead Property

(a) An obligor who believes that a child support lien has attached to real property of the obligor that is the obligor's homestead, as defined by Section 41.002, Property Code, may file an affidavit to release the lien against the homestead in the same manner that a judgment debtor may file an affidavit under Section 52.0012, Property Code, to release a judgment lien against a homestead.

(b) Except as provided by Subsection (c), the obligor must comply with all requirements imposed by Section 52.0012, Property Code. For purposes of complying with that section, the obligor is considered to be a judgment debtor under that section and the claimant under the child support lien is considered to be a judgment creditor under that section.

(c) For purposes of Section 52.0012(d), Property Code, and the requirements of the certificate of mailing prescribed by Section 52.0012(g), Property Code, the obligor is required only to send the letter and affidavit described in Section 52.0012(g) to the claimant under the child support lien at the claimant's last known address.

(d) The claimant under the child support lien may dispute the obligor's affidavit by filing a contradicting affidavit in the manner provided by Section 52.0012(e), Property Code.

(e) Subject to Subsection (f), an affidavit filed by an obligor under this section has the same effect with respect to a child support lien as an affidavit filed under Section 52.0012, Property Code, has with respect to a judgment lien.

(f) If the claimant files a contradicting affidavit as described by Subsection (d), the issue of whether the real property is subject to the lien must be resolved in an action brought for that purpose in the district court of the county in which the real property is located and the lien was filed.

Added by Acts 2009, 81st Leg., ch. 164, § 1, eff. May 26, 2009. Amended by Acts 2021, 87th Leg., ch. 893 (H.B. 3115), § 2, eff. Sept. 1, 2021.

Section 3 of Acts 2021, 87th Leg., ch. 893 (H.B. 3115) provides:

"The change in law made by this Act applies only to an affidavit filed under Section 52.0012(b), Property Code, as amended by this Act, on or after the effective date [Sept. 1, 2021] of this Act. An affidavit filed under Section 52.0012(b), Property Code, as amended by this Act, before the effective date of this Act is governed by the law in effect immediately before that date, and that law is continued in effect for that purpose."

## § 157.318. Duration and Effect of Child Support Lien

(a) Subject to Subsection (d), a lien is effective until all current support and child support arrearages, including interest, any costs and reasonable attorney's fees, and any Title IV–D service fees authorized under Section 231.103 for which the obligor is responsible, have been paid or the lien is otherwise released as provided by this subchapter.

(b) The lien secures payment of all child support arrearages owed by the obligor under the underlying child support order, including arrearages that accrue after the lien notice was filed or delivered as provided by Section 157.314.

(c) The filing of a lien notice or abstract of judgment with the county clerk is a record of the notice and has the same effect as any other lien notice with respect to real property records.

(d) A lien is effective with respect to real property until the 10th anniversary of the date on which the lien notice was filed with the county clerk. A lien subject to the limitation prescribed by this subsection may be renewed for subsequent 10–year periods by filing a renewed lien notice in the same manner as the original lien notice. For purposes of establishing priority, a renewed lien notice filed before the applicable 10th anniversary relates back to the date the original lien notice was filed. A renewed lien notice filed on or after the applicable 10th anniversary has priority over any other lien recorded with respect to the real property only on the basis of the date the renewed lien notice is filed.

Added by Acts 1995, 74th Leg., ch. 20, § 1, eff. April 20, 1995. Amended by Acts 1997, 75th Leg., ch. 420, § 7, eff. Sept. 1, 1997; Acts 1997, 75th Leg., ch. 911, § 25, eff. Sept. 1, 1997; Acts 2001, 77th Leg., ch. 1023, § 26, eff. Sept. 1, 2001; Acts 2007, 80th Leg., ch. 972, § 29, eff. Sept. 1, 2007; Acts 2009, 81st Leg., ch. 164, § 2, eff. May 26, 2009.

## § 157.319. Effect of Lien Notice

(a) If a person having actual notice of the lien possesses nonexempt personal property of the obligor that may be subject to the lien, the property may not be paid over, released, sold, transferred, encumbered, or conveyed unless:

(1) a release of lien signed by the claimant is delivered to the person in possession; or

(2) a court, after notice to the claimant and hearing, has ordered the release of the lien because arrearages do not exist.

(b) A person having notice of a child support lien who violates this section may be joined as a party to a foreclosure action under this chapter and is subject to the penalties[1] provided by this subchapter.

(c) This section does not affect the validity or priority of a lien of a health care provider, a lien for attorney's fees, or a lien of a holder of a security interest. This section does not affect the assignment of rights or subrogation of a claim under Title XIX of the federal Social Security Act (42 U.S.C. Section 1396 et seq.), as amended.

Added by Acts 1995, 74th Leg., ch. 20, § 1, eff. April 20, 1995. Amended by Acts 1997, 75th Leg., ch. 420, § 8, eff. Sept. 1, 1997; Acts 1997, 75th Leg., ch. 911, § 26, eff. Sept. 1, 1997; Acts 2001, 77th Leg., ch. 1023, § 27, eff. Sept. 1, 2001.

[1] Acts 1997, 75th Leg., ch. 420, § 8 here read "remedies" in lieu of "penalties".

## § 157.320. Priority of Lien as to Real Property

(a) A lien created under this subchapter does not have priority over a lien or conveyance of an interest in the nonexempt real property recorded before the child support lien notice is recorded in the county where the real property is located.

(b) A lien created under this subchapter has priority over any lien or conveyance of an interest in the nonexempt real property recorded after the child support lien notice is recorded in the county clerk's office in the county where the property of the obligor is located.

(c) A conveyance of real property by the obligor after a lien notice has been recorded in the county where the real property is located is subject to the lien and may not impair the enforceability of the lien against the real property.

(d) A lien created under this subchapter is subordinate to a vendor's lien retained in a conveyance to the obligor.

Added by Acts 1995, 74th Leg., ch. 20, § 1, eff. April 20, 1995. Amended by Acts 1997, 75th Leg., ch. 911, § 27, eff. Sept. 1, 1997.

## § 157.321. Discretionary Release of Lien

A child support lien claimant may at any time release a lien on all or part of the property of the obligor or return seized property, without liability, if assurance of payment is considered adequate by the claimant or if the release or return will facilitate the collection of the arrearages. The release or return may not operate to prevent future action to collect from the same or other property owned by the obligor.

Added by Acts 1995, 74th Leg., ch. 20, § 1, eff. April 20, 1995. Amended by Acts 1997, 75th Leg., ch. 420, § 9, eff. Sept. 1, 1997; Acts 1997, 75th Leg., ch. 911, § 28, eff. Sept. 1, 1997; Acts 2001, 77th Leg., ch. 1023, § 28, eff. Sept. 1, 2001.

## § 157.322. Mandatory Release of Lien

(a) On payment in full of the amount of child support due, together with any costs and reasonable attorney's fees, the child support lien claimant shall execute and deliver to the obligor or the obligor's attorney a release of the child support lien.

(b) The release of the child support lien is effective when:

(1) filed with the county clerk with whom the lien notice or abstract of judgment was filed; or

(2) delivered to any other individual or organization that may have been served with a lien notice under this subchapter.

Added by Acts 1995, 74th Leg., ch. 20, § 1, eff. April 20, 1995. Amended by Acts 1997, 75th Leg., ch. 420, § 10, eff. Sept. 1, 1997; Acts 1997, 75th Leg., ch. 911, §§ 29, 97(a), eff. Sept. 1, 1997; Acts 2001, 77th Leg., ch. 1023, § 29, eff. Sept. 1, 2001.

## § 157.323. Foreclosure or Suit to Determine Arrearages

(a) In addition to any other remedy provided by law, an action to foreclose a child support lien, to dispute the amount of arrearages stated in the lien, or to resolve issues of ownership interest with respect to property subject to a child support lien may be brought in:

(1) the court in which the lien notice was filed under Section 157. 314(b)(1);

(2) the district court of the county in which the property is or was located and the lien was filed; or

(3) the court of continuing jurisdiction.

(b) The procedures provided by Subchapter B[1] apply to a foreclosure action under this section, except that a person or organization in possession of the property of the obligor or known to have an ownership interest in property that is subject to the lien may be joined as an additional respondent.

(c) If arrearages are owed by the obligor, the court shall:

(1) render judgment against the obligor for the amount due, plus costs and reasonable attorney's fees;

(2) order any official authorized to levy execution to satisfy the lien, costs, and attorney's fees by selling any property on which a lien is established under this subchapter; or

(3) order an individual or organization in possession of nonexempt personal property or cash owned by the obligor to dispose of the property as the court may direct.

(d) For execution and sale under this section, publication of notice is necessary only for three consecutive weeks in a newspaper published in the county where the property is located or, if there is no newspaper in that county, in the most convenient newspaper in circulation in the county.

Added by Acts 1995, 74th Leg., ch. 20, § 1, eff. April 20, 1995. Amended by Acts 1997, 75th Leg., ch. 420, § 11, eff. Sept. 1, 1997; Acts 1997, 75th Leg., ch. 911, § 30, eff. Sept. 1, 1997; Acts 2001, 77th Leg., ch. 1023, § 30, eff. Sept. 1, 2001.

[1] V.T.C.A., Family Code § 157.061 et seq.

### § 157.324. Liability for Failure to Comply with Order or Lien

A person who knowingly disposes of property subject to a child support lien or who, after a foreclosure hearing, fails to surrender on demand nonexempt personal property as directed by a court under this subchapter is liable to the claimant in an amount equal to the value of the property disposed of or not surrendered, not to exceed the amount of the child support arrearages for which the lien or foreclosure judgment was issued.

Added by Acts 1995, 74th Leg., ch. 20, § 1, eff. April 20, 1995. Amended by Acts 1997, 75th Leg., ch. 420, § 12, eff. Sept. 1, 1997; Acts 1997, 75th Leg., ch. 911, § 31, eff. Sept. 1, 1997; Acts 2001, 77th Leg., ch. 1023, § 31, eff. Sept. 1, 2001; Acts 2007, 80th Leg., ch. 972, § 30, eff. Sept. 1, 2007.

### § 157.325. Release of Excess Funds to Debtor or Obligor

(a) If a person has in the person's possession earnings, deposits, accounts, balances, or other funds or assets of the obligor, including the proceeds of a judgment or other settlement of a claim or counterclaim due to the obligor that are in excess of the amount of arrearages specified in the child support lien, the holder of the nonexempt personal property or the obligor may request that the claimant release any excess amount from the lien. The claimant shall grant the request and discharge any lien on the excess amount unless the security for the arrearages would be impaired.

(b) If the claimant refuses the request, the holder of the personal property or the obligor may file suit under this subchapter for an order determining the amount of arrearages and discharging excess personal property or money from the lien.

Added by Acts 1995, 74th Leg., ch. 20, § 1, eff. April 20, 1995. Amended by Acts 1997, 75th Leg., ch. 420, § 13, eff. Sept. 1, 1997; Acts 1997, 75th Leg., ch. 911, § 32, eff. Sept. 1, 1997; Acts 2001, 77th Leg., ch. 1023, § 32, eff. Sept. 1, 2001.

### § 157.326. Interest of Obligor's Spouse or Another Person Having Ownership Interest

(a) A spouse of an obligor or another person having an ownership interest in property that is subject to a child support lien may file suit under Section 157.323 to determine the extent, if any, of the spouse's or other person's interest in real or personal property that is subject to:

(1) a lien perfected under this subchapter; or

(2) an action to foreclose under this subchapter.

(b) After notice to the obligor, the obligor's spouse, any other person alleging an ownership interest, the claimant, and the obligee, the court shall conduct a hearing and determine the extent, if any, of the ownership interest in the property held by the obligor's spouse or other person. If the court finds that:

(1) the property is the separate property of the obligor's spouse or the other person, the court shall order that the lien against the property be released and that any action to foreclose on the property be dismissed;

(2) the property is jointly owned by the obligor and the obligor's spouse, the court shall determine whether the sale of the obligor's interest in the property would result in an unreasonable hardship on the obligor's spouse or family and:

(A) if so, the court shall render an order that the obligor's interest in the property not be sold and that the lien against the property should be released; or

(B) if not, the court shall render an order partitioning the property and directing that the property be sold and the proceeds applied to the child support arrearages; or

(3) the property is owned in part by another person, other than the obligor's spouse, the court shall render an order partitioning the property and directing that the obligor's share of the property be applied to the child support arrearages.

(c) In a proceeding under this section, the spouse or other person claiming an ownership interest in the property has the burden to prove the extent of that ownership interest.

Added by Acts 1995, 74th Leg., ch. 20, § 1, eff. April 20, 1995. Amended by Acts 1997, 75th Leg., ch. 420, § 14, eff. Sept. 1, 1997; Acts 1997, 75th Leg., ch. 911, § 33, eff. Sept. 1, 1997; Acts 2001, 77th Leg., ch. 1023, § 33, eff. Sept. 1, 2001.

### § 157.327. Execution and Levy on Financial Assets of Obligor

(a) Notwithstanding any other provision of law, if a judgment or administrative determination of arrearages has been rendered, a claimant may deliver a notice of levy to any financial institution possessing or controlling assets or funds owned by, or owed to, an obligor and subject to a child support lien, including a lien for child support arising in another state.

(b) The notice under this section must:

(1) identify the amount of child support arrearages owing at the time the amount of arrearages was determined or, if the amount is less, the amount of arrearages owing at the time the notice is prepared and delivered to the financial institution; and

(2) direct the financial institution to pay to the claimant, not earlier than the 15th day or later than the 21st day after the date of delivery of the notice, an amount from the assets of the obligor or from funds due to the obligor that are held or controlled by the institution, not to exceed the amount of the child support arrearages identified in the notice, unless:

(A) the institution is notified by the claimant that the obligor has paid the arrearages or made arrangements satisfactory to the claimant for the payment of the arrearages;

(B) the obligor or another person files a suit under Section 157.323 requesting a hearing by the court; or

(C) if the claimant is the Title IV–D agency, the obligor has requested an agency review under Section 157.328.

(c) A financial institution that receives a notice of levy under this section may not close an account in which the obligor has an ownership interest, permit a withdrawal from any account the obligor owns, in whole or in part, or pay funds to the obligor so that any amount remaining in the account is less than the amount of the arrearages identified in the notice, plus any fees due to the institution and any costs of the levy identified by the claimant.

(d) A financial institution that receives a notice of levy under this section shall notify any other person having an ownership interest in an account in which the obligor has an ownership interest that the account has been levied on in an amount not to exceed the amount of the child support arrearages identified in the notice of levy.

(e) The notice of levy may be delivered to a financial institution as provided by Section 59.008, Finance Code, if the institution is subject to that law or may be delivered to the registered agent, the institution's main business office in this state, or another address provided by the institution under Section 231.307.

(f) A financial institution may deduct the fees and costs identified in Subsection (c) from the obligor's assets before paying the appropriate amount to the claimant.

Added by Acts 2001, 77th Leg., ch. 1023, § 34, eff. Sept. 1, 2001. Amended by Acts 2007, 80th Leg., ch. 972, § 31, eff. Sept. 1, 2007.

### § 157.3271. Levy on Financial Institution Account of Deceased Obligor

(a) Subject to Subsection (b), the Title IV–D agency may, not earlier than the 90th day after the date of death of an obligor in a Title IV–D case, deliver a notice of levy to a financial institution in which the obligor was the sole owner of an account, regardless of whether the Title IV–D agency has issued a child support lien notice regarding the account.

(b) The Title IV–D agency may not deliver a notice of levy under this section if probate proceedings relating to the obligor's estate have commenced.

(c) The notice of levy must:

(1) identify the amount of child support arrearages determined by the Title IV–D agency to be owing and unpaid by the obligor on the date of the obligor's death; and

(2) direct the financial institution to pay to the Title IV–D agency, not earlier than the 45th day or later than the 60th day after the date of delivery of the notice, an amount from the assets of the obligor or from funds due to the obligor that are held or controlled by the institution, not to exceed the amount of the child support arrearages identified in the notice.

(d) Not later than the 35th day after the date of delivery of the notice, the financial institution must notify any other person asserting a claim against the account that:

(1) the account has been levied on for child support arrearages in the amount shown on the notice of levy; and

(2) the person may contest the levy by filing suit and requesting a court hearing in the same manner that a person may challenge a child support lien under Section 157.323.

(e) A person who contests a levy under this section, as authorized by Subsection (d)(2), may bring the suit in:

(1) the district court of the county in which the property is located or in which the obligor resided; or

(2) the court of continuing jurisdiction.

(f) The notice of levy may be delivered to a financial institution as provided by Section 59.008, Finance Code, if the institution is subject to that law or may be delivered to the registered agent, the institution's main business office in this state, or another address provided by the institution under Section 231.307.

(g) A financial institution may deduct its fees and costs, including any costs for complying with this section, from the deceased obligor's assets before paying the appropriate amount to the Title IV–D agency.

Added by Acts 2011, 82nd Leg., ch. 508 (H.B. 1674), § 8, eff. Sept. 1, 2011.

### § 157.328. Notice of Levy Sent to Obligor

(a) At the time the notice of levy under Section 157.327 is delivered to a financial institution, the claimant shall serve the obligor with a copy of the notice.

(b) The notice of levy delivered to the obligor must inform the obligor that:

(1) the claimant will not proceed with levy if, not later than the 10th day after the date of receipt of the notice, the obligor pays in full the amount of arrearages identified in the notice or otherwise makes arrangements acceptable to the claimant for the payment of the arrearage amounts; and

(2) the obligor may contest the levy by filing suit under Section 157.323 not later than the 10th day after the date of receipt of the notice.

(c) If the claimant is the Title IV-D agency, the obligor receiving a notice of levy may request review by the agency not later than the 10th day after the date of receipt of the notice to resolve any issue in dispute regarding the existence or amount of the arrearages. The agency shall provide an opportunity for a review, by telephone conference or in person, as appropriate to the circumstances, not later than the fifth business day after the date an oral or written request from the obligor for the review is received. If the review fails to resolve any issue in dispute, the obligor may file suit under Section 157.323 for a hearing by the court not later than the fifth day after the date of the conclusion of the agency review. If the obligor fails to timely file suit, the Title IV-D agency may request the financial institution to release and remit the funds subject to levy.

(d) The notice under this section may be delivered to the last known address of the obligor by first class mail, certified mail, or registered mail.

Added by Acts 2001, 77th Leg., ch. 1023, § 34, eff. Sept. 1, 2001.

### § 157.329. No Liability for Compliance with Notice of Levy

A financial institution that possesses or has a right to an obligor's assets for which a notice of levy has been delivered and that surrenders the assets or right to assets to a child support lien claimant is not liable to the obligor or any other person for the property or rights surrendered.

Added by Acts 2001, 77th Leg., ch. 1023, § 34, eff. Sept. 1, 2001.

### § 157.330. Failure to Comply with Notice of Levy

(a) A person who possesses or has a right to property that is the subject of a notice of levy delivered to the person and who refuses to surrender the property or right to property to the claimant on demand is liable to the claimant in an amount equal to the value of the property or right to property not surrendered but that does not exceed the amount of the child support arrearages for which the notice of levy has been filed.

(b) A claimant may recover costs and reasonable attorney's fees incurred in an action under this section.

Added by Acts 2001, 77th Leg., ch. 1023, § 34, eff. Sept. 1, 2001. Amended by Acts 2007, 80th Leg., ch. 972, § 32, eff. Sept. 1, 2007.

### § 157.331. Additional Levy to Satisfy Arrearages

If the property or right to property on which a notice of levy has been filed does not produce money sufficient to satisfy the amount of child support arrearages identified in the notice of levy, the claimant may proceed to levy on other property of the obligor until the total amount of child support due is paid.

Added by Acts 2001, 77th Leg., ch. 1023, § 34, eff. Sept. 1, 2001.

## SUBCHAPTER H. HABEAS CORPUS

### § 157.371. Jurisdiction

(a) The relator may file a petition for a writ of habeas corpus in either the court of continuing, exclusive jurisdiction or in a court with jurisdiction to issue a writ of habeas corpus in the county in which the child is found.

(b) Although a habeas corpus proceeding is not a suit affecting the parent-child relationship, the court may refer to the provisions of this title for definitions and procedures as appropriate.

Added by Acts 1995, 74th Leg., ch. 20, § 1, eff. April 20, 1995.

### § 157.372. Return of Child

(a) Subject to Chapter 152 and the Parental Kidnapping Prevention Act (28 U.S.C. Section 1738A), if the right to possession of a child is governed by a court order, the court in a habeas corpus proceeding involving the right to possession of the child shall compel return of the child to the relator only if the court finds that the relator is entitled to possession under the order.

(b) If the court finds that the previous order was granted by a court that did not give the contestants reasonable notice of the proceeding and an opportunity to be heard, the court may not render an order in the habeas corpus proceeding compelling return of the child on the basis of that order.

Added by Acts 1995, 74th Leg., ch. 20, § 1, eff. April 20, 1995.

### § 157.373. Relator Relinquished Possession; Temporary Orders

(a) If the relator has by consent or acquiescence relinquished actual possession and control of the child for not less than 6 months preceding the date of the filing of the petition for the writ, the court may either compel or refuse to order return of the child.

(b) The court may disregard brief periods of possession and control by the relator during the 6-month period.

(c) In a suit in which the court does not compel return of the child, the court may issue temporary orders under Chapter 105 if a suit affecting the parent-child relationship is pending and the parties have received notice of a hearing on temporary orders set for the same time as the habeas corpus proceeding.

Added by Acts 1995, 74th Leg., ch. 20, § 1, eff. April 20, 1995.

### § 157.374. Welfare of Child

Notwithstanding any other provision of this subchapter, the court may render an appropriate temporary order if there is a serious immediate question concerning the welfare of the child.

Added by Acts 1995, 74th Leg., ch. 20, § 1, eff. April 20, 1995.

### § 157.375. Immunity to Civil Process

(a) While in this state for the sole purpose of compelling the return of a child through a habeas corpus proceeding, the relator is not amenable to civil process and is not subject to the jurisdiction of any civil court except the court in which the writ is pending. The relator is subject to process and jurisdiction in that court only for the purpose of prosecuting the writ.

(b) A request by the relator for costs, attorney's fees, and necessary travel and other expenses under Chapter 106 or 152 is not a waiver of immunity to civil process.

Added by Acts 1995, 74th Leg., ch. 20, § 1, eff. April 20, 1995.

### § 157.376. No Existing Order

(a) If the right to possession of a child is not governed by an order, the court in a habeas corpus proceeding involving the right of possession of the child:

(1) shall compel return of the child to the parent if the right of possession is between a parent and a nonparent and a suit affecting the parent-child relationship has not been filed; or

(2) may either compel return of the child or issue temporary orders under Chapter 105 if a suit affecting the parent-child relationship is pending and the parties have received notice of a hearing on temporary orders set for the same time as the habeas corpus proceeding.

(b) The court may not use a habeas corpus proceeding to adjudicate the right of possession of a child between two parents or between two or more nonparents.

Added by Acts 1995, 74th Leg., ch. 20, § 1, eff. April 20, 1995.

## SUBCHAPTER I. CLARIFICATION OF ORDERS

### § 157.421. Clarifying Nonspecific Order

(a) A court may clarify an order rendered by the court in a proceeding under this title if the court finds, on the motion of a party or on the court's own motion, that the order is not specific enough to be enforced by contempt.

(b) The court shall clarify the order by rendering an order that is specific enough to be enforced by contempt.

(c) A clarified order does not affect the finality of the order that it clarifies.

Added by Acts 1995, 74th Leg., ch. 20, § 1, eff. April 20, 1995.

### § 157.422. Procedure

(a) The procedure for filing a motion for enforcement of a final order applies to a motion for clarification.

(b) A person is not entitled to a jury in a proceeding under this subchapter.

Added by Acts 1995, 74th Leg., ch. 20, § 1, eff. April 20, 1995.

### § 157.423. Substantive Change Not Enforceable

(a) A court may not change the substantive provisions of an order to be clarified under this subchapter.

(b) A substantive change made by a clarification order is not enforceable.

Added by Acts 1995, 74th Leg., ch. 20, § 1, eff. April 20, 1995.

### § 157.424. Relation to Motion for Contempt

The court may render a clarification order before a motion for contempt is made or heard, in conjunction with a motion for contempt, or after the denial of a motion for contempt.

Added by Acts 1995, 74th Leg., ch. 20, § 1, eff. April 20, 1995.

### § 157.425. Order Not Retroactive

The court may not provide that a clarification order is retroactive for the purpose of enforcement by contempt.

Added by Acts 1995, 74th Leg., ch. 20, § 1, eff. April 20, 1995.

### § 157.426. Time Allowed to Comply

(a) In a clarification order, the court shall provide a reasonable time for compliance.

(b) The clarification order may be enforced by contempt after the time for compliance has expired.

Added by Acts 1995, 74th Leg., ch. 20, § 1, eff. April 20, 1995.

## SUBCHAPTER J. CHILD SUPPORT QUALIFIED DOMESTIC RELATIONS ORDER

### § 157.501. Jurisdiction for Qualified Domestic Relations Order

(a) The court that rendered an order for the payment of child support, or the court that obtains jurisdiction to enforce a child support order under Chapter 159, has continuing jurisdiction to render enforceable qualified domestic relations orders or similar orders permitting payment of pension, retirement plan, or other employee benefits to an alternate payee or other lawful payee to satisfy support amounts due under the child support order. A child support order includes a temporary or final order for child support, medical support, or dental support and arrears and interest with respect to that order.

(b) Unless prohibited by federal law, a suit seeking a qualified domestic relations order or similar order under this subchapter applies to a pension, retirement plan, or other employee benefit, regardless of whether the pension, retirement plan, or other employee benefit:

(1) is private, state, or federal;

(2) is subject to another qualified domestic relations order or similar order;

(3) is property that is the subject of a pending proceeding for dissolution of a marriage;

(4) is property disposed of in a previous decree for dissolution of a marriage; or

(5) is the subject of an agreement under Chapter 4.

(c) A court described by Subsection (a) retains jurisdiction to render a qualified domestic relations order or similar order under this subchapter until all support due under the child support order, including arrearages and interest, has been paid.

Added by Acts 2021, 87th Leg., ch. 64 (H.B. 867), § 5, eff. Sept. 1, 2021.

Section 6 of Acts 2021, 87th Leg., ch. 64 (H.B. 867) provides:

"(a) The changes in law made by this Act to Chapters 8, 154, and 157, Family Code, apply to an order for maintenance under Chapter 8, Family Code, or for child support under Chapter 154, Family Code, as applicable, regardless of whether the order was rendered before, on, or after the effective date [Sept. 1, 2021] of this Act.

"(b) The enactment of this Act does not constitute a material and substantial change of circumstances sufficient to warrant modification of a court order or portion of a decree that provides for maintenance or child support rendered before the effective date of this Act."

## § 157.502. Procedure

(a) A party to a child support order, or the Title IV–D agency in a Title IV–D case, may petition the court for a qualified domestic relations order or similar order in an original suit or in an action for child support enforcement under this chapter.

(b) Each party whose rights may be affected by the petition is entitled to receive notice under Subchapter B.

Added by Acts 2021, 87th Leg., ch. 64 (H.B. 867), § 5, eff. Sept. 1, 2021.

Section 6 of Acts 2021, 87th Leg., ch. 64 (H.B. 867) provides:

"(a) The changes in law made by this Act to Chapters 8, 154, and 157, Family Code, apply to an order for maintenance under Chapter 8, Family Code, or for child support under Chapter 154, Family Code, as applicable, regardless of whether the order was rendered before, on, or after the effective date [Sept. 1, 2021] of this Act.

"(b) The enactment of this Act does not constitute a material and substantial change of circumstances sufficient to warrant modification of a court order or portion of a decree that provides for maintenance or child support rendered before the effective date of this Act."

## § 157.503. Temporary Orders

(a) While a suit for a qualified domestic relations order or similar order is pending or during an appeal of an enforcement order, and on the motion of a party or on the court's own motion after notice and hearing, the court may render an appropriate order, including the granting of a temporary restraining order and temporary injunction, for the preservation of the pension, retirement plan, or other employee benefits and protection of the parties as the court considers necessary.

(b) An order under this section is not subject to interlocutory appeal.

Added by Acts 2021, 87th Leg., ch. 64 (H.B. 867), § 5, eff. Sept. 1, 2021.

Section 6 of Acts 2021, 87th Leg., ch. 64 (H.B. 867) provides:

"(a) The changes in law made by this Act to Chapters 8, 154, and 157, Family Code, apply to an order for maintenance under Chapter 8, Family Code, or for child support under Chapter 154, Family Code, as applicable, regardless of whether the order was rendered before, on, or after the effective date [Sept. 1, 2021] of this Act.

"(b) The enactment of this Act does not constitute a material and substantial change of circumstances sufficient to warrant modification of a court order or portion of a decree that provides for maintenance or child support rendered before the effective date of this Act."

## § 157.504. Defective Prior Domestic Relations Order

If a plan administrator or other person acting in an equivalent capacity determines that a domestic relations order does not satisfy the requirements of a qualified domestic relations order or similar order, the court retains continuing jurisdiction over the parties to the extent necessary to render a qualified domestic relations order.

Added by Acts 2021, 87th Leg., ch. 64 (H.B. 867), § 5, eff. Sept. 1, 2021.

Section 6 of Acts 2021, 87th Leg., ch. 64 (H.B. 867) provides:

"(a) The changes in law made by this Act to Chapters 8, 154, and 157, Family Code, apply to an order for maintenance under Chapter 8, Family Code, or for child support under Chapter 154, Family Code, as applicable, regardless of whether the order was rendered before, on, or after the effective date [Sept. 1, 2021] of this Act.

"(b) The enactment of this Act does not constitute a material and substantial change of circumstances sufficient to warrant modification of a court order or portion of a decree that provides for maintenance or child support rendered before the effective date of this Act."

## § 157.505. Amendment of Qualified Domestic Relations Order

(a) A court that renders a qualified domestic relations order or similar order retains continuing jurisdiction:

(1) to amend the order to correct the order, clarify the terms of the order, or add language to the order to provide for the collection of child support;

(2) to convert the amount or frequency of payments under the order to a formula that is in compliance with the terms of the pension, retirement plan, or employee benefit plan; or

(3) to vacate or terminate the order.

(b) An amended domestic relations order or similar order under this section must be submitted to the plan administrator or other person acting in an equivalent capacity to determine whether the amended order satisfies the requirements of a qualified domestic relations order or similar order. Section 157.504 applies to an order amended under this section.

Added by Acts 2021, 87th Leg., ch. 64 (H.B. 867), § 5, eff. Sept. 1, 2021.

Section 6 of Acts 2021, 87th Leg., ch. 64 (H.B. 867) provides:

"(a) The changes in law made by this Act to Chapters 8, 154, and 157, Family Code, apply to an order for maintenance under Chapter 8, Family Code, or for child support under Chapter 154, Family Code, as applicable, regardless of whether the order was rendered before, on, or after the effective date [Sept. 1, 2021] of this Act.

"(b) The enactment of this Act does not constitute a material and substantial change of circumstances sufficient to warrant modification of a court order or portion of a decree that provides for maintenance or child support rendered before the effective date of this Act."

## § 157.506. Liberal Construction

The court shall liberally construe this subchapter to effect payment of pension, retirement plan, or other employee benefits for the satisfaction of the obligor's child support obligation.

Added by Acts 2021, 87th Leg., ch. 64 (H.B. 867), § 5, eff. Sept. 1, 2021.

Section 6 of Acts 2021, 87th Leg., ch. 64 (H.B. 867) provides:

"(a) The changes in law made by this Act to Chapters 8, 154, and 157, Family Code, apply to an order for maintenance under Chapter 8, Family Code, or for child support under Chapter 154, Family Code, as applicable, regardless of whether the order was rendered before, on, or after the effective date [Sept. 1, 2021] of this Act.

"(b) The enactment of this Act does not constitute a material and substantial change of circumstances sufficient to warrant modification of a court order or portion of a decree that provides for maintenance or child support rendered before the effective date of this Act."

## § 157.507. Attorney's Fees and Costs

(a) In a proceeding under this subchapter, the court may order the obligor to pay reasonable attorney's fees incurred by a party to obtain the order, all court costs, and all fees charged by a plan administrator for the qualified domestic relations order or similar order.

(b) Fees and costs ordered under this section may be enforced by any means available for the enforcement of child support, including contempt.

Added by Acts 2021, 87th Leg., ch. 64 (H.B. 867), § 5, eff. Sept. 1, 2021.

Section 6 of Acts 2021, 87th Leg., ch. 64 (H.B. 867) provides:

"(a) The changes in law made by this Act to Chapters 8, 154, and 157, Family Code, apply to an order for maintenance under Chapter 8, Family Code, or for child support under Chapter 154, Family Code, as applicable, regardless of whether the order was rendered before, on, or after the effective date [Sept. 1, 2021] of this Act.

"(b) The enactment of this Act does not constitute a material and substantial change of circumstances sufficient to warrant modification of a court order or portion of a decree that provides for maintenance or child support rendered before the effective date of this Act."

## § 157.508. Conflicts With Other Law

(a) To the extent of a conflict between this subchapter and Chapter 804, Government Code, Chapter 804, Government Code, prevails.

(b) To the extent of a conflict between this subchapter and federal law, the federal law prevails.

Added by Acts 2021, 87th Leg., ch. 64 (H.B. 867), § 5, eff. Sept. 1, 2021.

Section 6 of Acts 2021, 87th Leg., ch. 64 (H.B. 867) provides:

"(a) The changes in law made by this Act to Chapters 8, 154, and 157, Family Code, apply to an order for maintenance under Chapter 8, Family Code, or for child support under Chapter 154, Family Code, as applicable, regardless of whether the order was rendered before, on, or after the effective date [Sept. 1, 2021] of this Act.

"(b) The enactment of this Act does not constitute a material and substantial change of circumstances sufficient to warrant modification of a court order or portion of a decree that provides for maintenance or child support rendered before the effective date of this Act."

# CHAPTER 158. WITHHOLDING FROM EARNINGS FOR CHILD SUPPORT

### SUBCHAPTER A. INCOME WITHHOLDING REQUIRED; GENERAL PROVISIONS

**Section**



### SUBCHAPTER B. PROCEDURE



### SUBCHAPTER C. RIGHTS AND DUTIES OF EMPLOYER

SUBCHAPTER D. JUDICIAL WRIT OF WITHHOLDING ISSUED BY CLERK



SUBCHAPTER E. MODIFICATION, REDUCTION, OR TERMINATION OF WITHHOLDING



SUBCHAPTER F. ADMINISTRATIVE WRIT OF WITHHOLDING



## SUBCHAPTER A. INCOME WITHHOLDING REQUIRED; GENERAL PROVISIONS

### § 158.001. Income Withholding; General Rule

In a proceeding in which periodic payments of child support are ordered, modified, or enforced, the court or the Title IV-D agency shall order that income be withheld from the disposable earnings of the obligor as provided by this chapter.

Added by Acts 1995, 74th Leg., ch. 20, § 1, eff. April 20, 1995. Amended by Acts 1997, 75th Leg., ch. 911, § 34, eff. Sept. 1, 1997.

### § 158.002. Suspension of Income Withholding

Except in a Title IV-D case, the court may provide, for good cause shown or on agreement of the parties, that the order withholding income need not be issued or delivered to an employer until:

(1) the obligor has been in arrears for an amount due for more than 30 days;

(2) the amount of the arrearages is an amount equal to or greater than the amount due for a one-month period; or

(3) any other violation of the child support order has occurred.

Added by Acts 1995, 74th Leg., ch. 20, § 1, eff. April 20, 1995. Amended by Acts 1997, 75th Leg., ch. 911, § 35, eff. Sept. 1, 1997.

### § 158.003. Withholding for Arrearages in Addition to Current Support

(a) In addition to income withheld for the current support of a child, income shall be withheld from the disposable earnings of the obligor to be applied toward the liquidation of any child support arrearages, including accrued interest as provided in Chapter 157.

(b) The additional amount to be withheld for arrearages shall be an amount sufficient to discharge those arrearages in not more than two years or an additional 20 percent added to the amount of the current monthly support order, whichever amount will result in the arrearages being discharged in the least amount of time.

Added by Acts 1995, 74th Leg., ch. 20, § 1, eff. April 20, 1995. Amended by Acts 1999, 76th Leg., ch. 556, § 21, eff. Sept. 1, 1999.

### § 158.004. Withholding for Arrearages When No Current Support Is Due

If current support is no longer owed, the court or the Title IV–D agency shall order that income be withheld for arrearages, including accrued interest as provided in Chapter 157, in an amount sufficient to discharge those arrearages in not more than two years.

Added by Acts 1995, 74th Leg., ch. 20, § 1, eff. April 20, 1995. Amended by Acts 1999, 76th Leg., ch. 556, § 22, eff. Sept. 1, 1999.

## § 158.005. Withholding to Satisfy Judgment for Arrearages

In rendering a cumulative judgment for arrearages, the court shall order that a reasonable amount of income be withheld from the disposable earnings of the obligor to be applied toward the satisfaction of the judgment.

Added by Acts 1995, 74th Leg., ch. 20, § 1, eff. April 20, 1995.

## § 158.0051. Order for Withholding for Costs and Fees

(a) In addition to an order for income to be withheld for child support, including child support and child support arrearages, the court may render an order that income be withheld from the disposable earnings of the obligor to be applied towards the satisfaction of any ordered attorney's fees and costs resulting from an action to enforce child support under this title.

(b) An order rendered under this section is subordinate to an order or writ of withholding for child support under this chapter and is subject to the maximum amount allowed to be withheld under Section 158.009.

(c) The court shall order that amounts withheld for fees and costs under this section be remitted directly to the person entitled to the ordered attorney's fees or costs or be paid through a local registry for disbursement to that person.

Added by Acts 2001, 77th Leg., ch. 1023, § 35, eff. Sept. 1, 2001.

## § 158.006. Income Withholding in Title IV-D Suits

In a Title IV-D case, the court or the Title IV-D agency shall order that income be withheld from the disposable earnings of the obligor and may not suspend, stay, or delay issuance of the order or of a judicial or administrative writ of withholding.

Added by Acts 1995, 74th Leg., ch. 20, § 1, eff. April 20, 1995. Amended by Acts 1997, 75th Leg., ch. 911, § 36, eff. Sept. 1, 1997.

## § 158.007. Extension of Repayment Schedule by Court or Title IV–D Agency; Unreasonable Hardship

If the court or the Title IV–D agency finds that the schedule for discharging arrearages would cause the obligor, the obligor's family, or children for whom support is due from the obligor to suffer unreasonable hardship, the court or agency may extend the payment period for a reasonable length of time.

Added by Acts 1995, 74th Leg., ch. 20, § 1, eff. April 20, 1995. Amended by Acts 1999, 76th Leg., ch. 556, § 22, eff. Sept. 1, 1999.

## § 158.008. Priority of Withholding

An order or writ of withholding has priority over any garnishment, attachment, execution, or other assignment or order affecting disposable earnings.

Added by Acts 1995, 74th Leg., ch. 20, § 1, eff. April 20, 1995.

## § 158.009. Maximum Amount Withheld From Earnings

An order or writ of withholding shall direct that any employer of the obligor withhold from the obligor's disposable earnings the amount specified up to a maximum amount of 50 percent of the obligor's disposable earnings.

Added by Acts 1995, 74th Leg., ch. 20, § 1, eff. April 20, 1995. Amended by Acts 1997, 75th Leg., ch. 911, § 37, eff. Sept. 1, 1997.

## § 158.010. Order or Writ Binding on Employer Doing Business in State

An order or writ of withholding issued under this chapter and delivered to an employer doing business in this state is binding on the employer without regard to whether the obligor resides or works outside this state.

Added by Acts 1995, 74th Leg., ch. 20, § 1, eff. April 20, 1995. Amended by Acts 1997, 75th Leg., ch. 911, § 38, eff. Sept. 1, 1997.

## § 158.011. Voluntary Withholding by Obligor

(a) An obligor may file with the clerk of the court a notarized or acknowledged request signed by the obligor and the obligee for the issuance and delivery to the obligor's employer of a writ of withholding. A notarized or acknowledged request may be filed under this section regardless of whether a writ or order has been served on any party or of the existence or amount of an arrearage.

(b) On receipt of a request under this section, the clerk shall issue and deliver a writ of withholding in the manner provided by this chapter.

(c) An employer that receives a writ of withholding issued under this section may request a hearing in the same manner and according to the same terms provided by Section 158.205.

(d) An obligor whose employer receives a writ of withholding issued under this section may request a hearing in the manner provided by Section 158.309.

(e) An obligee may contest a writ of withholding issued under this section by requesting, not later than the 180th day after the date on which the obligee discovers that the writ has been issued, a hearing in the manner provided by Section 158.309.

(f) A writ of withholding under this section may not reduce the total amount of child support, including arrearages, owed by the obligor.

Added by Acts 1995, 74th Leg., ch. 751, § 55, eff. Sept. 1, 1995. Amended by Acts 1997, 75th Leg., ch. 911, § 39, eff. Sept. 1, 1997.

## SUBCHAPTER B. PROCEDURE

### § 158.101. Applicability of Procedure

Except as otherwise provided in this chapter, the procedure for a motion for enforcement of child support as provided in Chapter 157 applies to an action for income withholding.

Added by Acts 1995, 74th Leg., ch. 20, § 1, eff. April 20, 1995.

### § 158.102. Time Limitations

An order or writ for income withholding under this chapter may be issued until all current support and child support arrearages, interest, and any applicable fees and costs, including ordered attorney's fees and court costs, have been paid.

Added by Acts 1995, 74th Leg., ch. 20, § 1, eff. April 20, 1995. Amended by Acts 1997, 75th Leg., ch. 911, § 40, eff. Sept. 1, 1997; Acts 1999, 76th Leg., ch. 556, § 23, eff. Sept. 1, 1999.

### § 158.103. Contents of Order or Writ of Withholding

An order of withholding or writ of withholding issued under this chapter must contain the information required by the forms prescribed by the Title IV-D agency under Section 158.106.

Added by Acts 1995, 74th Leg., ch. 20, § 1, eff. April 20, 1995. Amended by Acts 1997, 75th Leg., ch. 911, § 41, eff. Sept. 1, 1997; Acts 1999, 76th Leg., ch. 556, § 23, eff. Sept. 1, 1999; Acts 2001, 77th Leg., ch. 1023, § 36, eff. Sept. 1, 2001.

### § 158.104. Request for Issuance of Order or Judicial Writ of Withholding

A request for issuance of an order or judicial writ of withholding may be filed with the clerk of the court by the prosecuting attorney, the Title IV–D agency, the friend of the court, a domestic relations office, the obligor, the obligee, or an attorney representing the obligee or obligor.

Added by Acts 1995, 74th Leg., ch. 20, § 1, eff. April 20, 1995. Amended by Acts 1997, 75th Leg., ch. 702, § 6, eff. Sept. 1, 1997; Acts 1999, 76th Leg., ch. 556, § 23, eff. Sept. 1, 1999.

### § 158.105. Issuance and Delivery of Order or Judicial Writ of Withholding

(a) On filing a request for issuance of an order or judicial writ of withholding, the clerk of the court shall cause a certified copy of the order or writ to be delivered to the obligor's current employer or to any subsequent employer of the obligor.

(b) The clerk shall issue and deliver the certified copy of the order or judicial writ not later than the fourth working day after the date the order is signed or the request is filed, whichever is later.

(c) An order or judicial writ of withholding shall be delivered to the employer by first class mail or, if requested, by certified or registered mail, return receipt requested, by electronic transmission, including electronic mail or facsimile transmission, or by service of citation to:

(1) the person authorized to receive service of process for the employer in civil cases generally; or

(2) a person designated by the employer, by written notice to the clerk, to receive orders or writs of withholding.

(d) The clerk may deliver an order or judicial writ of withholding under Subsection (c) by electronic mail if the employer has an electronic mail address or by facsimile transmission if the employer is capable of receiving documents transmitted in that manner. If delivery is accomplished by electronic mail, the clerk must request acknowledgment of receipt from the employer or use an electronic mail system with a read receipt capability. If delivery is accomplished by facsimile transmission, the clerk's facsimile machine must create a delivery confirmation report.

Added by Acts 1995, 74th Leg., ch. 20, § 1, eff. April 20, 1995. Amended by Acts 1997, 75th Leg., ch. 702, § 7, eff. Sept. 1, 1997; Acts 1999, 76th Leg., ch. 556, § 24, eff. Sept. 1, 1999; Acts 2001, 77th Leg., ch. 1023, § 37, eff. Sept. 1, 2001; Acts 2005, 79th Leg., ch. 1113, § 1, eff. Sept. 1, 2005.

### § 158.106. Required Forms for Income Withholding

(a) The Title IV–D agency shall prescribe forms as required by federal law in a standard format entitled order or notice to withhold income for child support under this chapter.

(b) The Title IV–D agency shall make the required forms available to obligors, obligees, domestic relations offices, friends of the court, clerks of the court, and private attorneys.

(c) The Title IV–D agency may prescribe additional forms for the efficient collection of child support from earnings and to promote the administration of justice for all parties.

(d) The forms prescribed by the Title IV–D agency under this section shall be used:

(1) for an order or judicial writ of income withholding under this chapter; and

(2) to request voluntary withholding under Section 158.011.

Added by Acts 1995, 74th Leg., ch. 20, § 1, eff. April 20, 1995. Amended by Acts 1997, 75th Leg., ch. 911, § 42, eff. Sept. 1, 1997; Acts 1999, 76th Leg., ch. 556, § 25, eff. Sept. 1, 1999; Acts 2001, 77th Leg., ch. 1023, § 38, eff. Sept. 1, 2001; Acts 2013, 83rd Leg., ch. 742 (S.B. 355), § 6, eff. Sept. 1, 2013.

### § 158.107. Repealed by Acts 1997, 75th Leg., ch. 911, § 97(a), eff. Sept. 1, 1997

## SUBCHAPTER C. RIGHTS AND DUTIES OF EMPLOYER

### § 158.201. Order or Writ Binding on Employer

(a) An employer required to withhold income from earnings is not entitled to notice of the proceedings before the order is rendered or writ of withholding is issued.

(b) An order or writ of withholding is binding on an employer regardless of whether the employer is specifically named in the order or writ.

Added by Acts 1995, 74th Leg., ch. 20, § 1, eff. April 20, 1995. Amended by Acts 1997, 75th Leg., ch. 911, § 43, eff. Sept. 1, 1997.

### § 158.202. Effective Date of and Duration of Withholding

An employer shall begin to withhold income in accordance with an order or writ of withholding not later than the first pay period following the date on which the order or writ was delivered to the employer and shall continue to withhold income as required by the order or writ as long as the obligor is employed by the employer.

Added by Acts 1995, 74th Leg., ch. 20, § 1, eff. April 20, 1995. Amended by Acts 1997, 75th Leg., ch. 911, § 44, eff. Sept. 1, 1997.

### § 158.203. Remitting Withheld Payments

(a) The employer shall remit the amount to be withheld to the person or office named in the order or writ on each pay date. The payment must include the date on which the withholding occurred.

(b) An employer with 50 or more employees shall remit a payment required under this section by electronic funds transfer or electronic data interchange not later than the second business day after the pay date.

(b–1) An employer with fewer than 50 employees may remit a payment required under this section by electronic funds transfer or electronic data interchange. A payment remitted by the employer electronically must be remitted not later than the date specified by Subsection (b).

(c) The employer shall include with each payment transmitted:

(1) the number assigned by the Title IV–D agency, if available, and the county identification number, if available;

(2) the name of the county or the county's federal information processing standard code;

(3) the cause number of the suit under which withholding is required;

(4) the payor's name and social security number; and

(5) the payee's name and, if available, social security number, unless the payment is transmitted by electronic funds transfer.

(d) In a case in which an obligor's income is subject to withholding, the employer shall remit the payment of child support directly to the state disbursement unit.

(e) The state disbursement unit may impose on an employer described by Subsection (b) a payment processing surcharge in an amount of not more than $25 for each remittance made on behalf of an employee that is not made by electronic funds transfer or electronic data exchange. The payment processing surcharge under this subsection may not be charged against the employee or taken from amounts withheld from the employee's wages.

(f) The state disbursement unit shall:

(1) notify an employer described by Subsection (b) who fails to remit withheld income by electronic funds transfer or electronic data exchange that the employer is subject to a payment processing surcharge under Subsection (e); and

(2) inform the employer of the amount of the surcharge owed and the manner in which the surcharge is required to be paid to the unit.

Added by Acts 1995, 74th Leg., ch. 20, § 1, eff. April 20, 1995. Amended by Acts 1997, 75th Leg., ch. 702, § 8, eff. Jan. 1, 1998; Acts 1999, 76th Leg., ch. 556, § 26, eff. Sept. 1, 1999; Acts 2009, 81st Leg., ch. 767, § 19, eff. Sept. 1, 2009; Acts 2011, 82nd Leg., ch. 508 (H.B. 1674), § 9, eff. Sept. 1, 2011; Acts 2013, 83rd Leg., ch. 742 (S.B. 355), § 7, eff. Sept. 1, 2013.

### § 158.204. Employer May Deduct Fee From Earnings

An employer may deduct an administrative fee of not more than $10 each month from the obligor's disposable earnings in addition to the amount to be withheld as child support.

Added by Acts 1995, 74th Leg., ch. 20, § 1, eff. April 20, 1995. Amended by Acts 1999, 76th Leg., ch. 859, § 1, eff. Sept. 1, 1999.

### § 158.205. Hearing Requested by Employer

(a) Not later than the 20th day after the date an order or writ of withholding is delivered, the employer may, as appropriate, file a motion with the court or file a request with the Title IV-D agency for a hearing on the applicability of the order or writ to the employer. The Title IV-D agency by rule shall establish procedures for an agency hearing under this section.

(b) The hearing under this section shall be held not later than the 15th day after the date the motion or request was made.

(c) An order or writ of withholding remains binding and payments shall continue to be made pending further order of the court or, in the case of an administrative writ, action of the Title IV-D agency.

Added by Acts 1995, 74th Leg., ch. 20, § 1, eff. April 20, 1995. Amended by Acts 1997, 75th Leg., ch. 911, § 45, eff. Sept. 1, 1997.

### § 158.206. Liability and Obligation of Employer; Workers' Compensation Claims

(a) An employer receiving an order or a writ of withholding under this chapter, including an order or writ directing that health insurance or dental insurance be provided to a child, who complies with the order or writ is not liable to the obligor for the amount of income withheld and paid as required by the order or writ.

(b) An employer receiving an order or writ of withholding who does not comply with the order or writ is liable:

(1) to the obligee for the amount not paid in compliance with the order or writ, including the amount the obligor is required to pay for health insurance or dental insurance under Chapter 154;

(2) to the obligor for:

(A) the amount withheld and not paid as required by the order or writ; and

(B) an amount equal to the interest that accrues under Section 157.265 on the amount withheld and not paid; and

(3) for reasonable attorney's fees and court costs.

(c) If an obligor has filed a claim for workers' compensation, the obligor's employer shall send a copy of the income withholding order or writ to the insurance carrier with whom the claim has been filed in order to continue the ordered withholding of income.

Added by Acts 1995, 74th Leg., ch. 20, § 1, eff. April 20, 1995. Amended by Acts 1995, 74th Leg., ch. 341, § 4.07, eff. Sept. 1, 1995; Acts 1997, 75th Leg., ch. 911, § 46, eff. Sept. 1, 1997; Acts 1999, 76th Leg., ch. 859, § 2, eff. Sept. 1, 1999; Acts 1999, 76th Leg., ch. 1580, § 1, eff. Sept. 1, 1999; Acts 2001, 77th Leg., ch. 1023, § 39, eff. Sept. 1, 2001; Acts 2015, 84th Leg., ch. 1150 (S.B. 550), § 31, eff. Sept. 1, 2018.

### § 158.207. Employer Receiving More Than One Order or Writ

(a) An employer receiving two or more orders or writs for one obligor shall comply with each order or writ to the extent possible.

(b) If the total amount due under the orders or writs exceeds the maximum amount allowed to be withheld under Section 158.009, the employer shall pay an equal amount towards the current support in each order or writ until the employer has complied fully with each current support obligation and, thereafter, equal amounts on the arrearages until the employer has complied with each order or writ, or until the maximum total amount of allowed withholding is reached, whichever occurs first.

(c) An employer who receives more than one order or writ of withholding that combines withholding for child support and spousal maintenance as provided by Section 8.101 shall withhold income and pay the amount withheld in accordance with Section 8.207.

Added by Acts 1995, 74th Leg., ch. 20, § 1, eff. April 20, 1995. Amended by Acts 1997, 75th Leg., ch. 911, § 47, eff. Sept. 1, 1997; Acts 2001, 77th Leg., ch. 807, § 2, eff. Sept. 1, 2001.

### § 158.208. Employer May Combine Amounts Withheld

An employer required to withhold from more than one obligor may combine the amounts withheld and make a single payment to each agency designated if the employer separately identifies the amount of the payment that is attributable to each obligor.

Added by Acts 1995, 74th Leg., ch. 20, § 1, eff. April 20, 1995.

### § 158.209. Employer's Penalty for Discriminatory Hiring or Discharge

(a) An employer may not use an order or writ of withholding as grounds in whole or part for the termination of employment or for any other disciplinary action against an employee.

(b) An employer may not refuse to hire an employee because of an order or writ of withholding.

(c) If an employer intentionally discharges an employee in violation of this section, the employer continues to be liable to the employee for current wages and other benefits and for reasonable attorney's fees and court costs incurred in enforcing the employee's rights as provided in this section.

(d) An action under this section may be brought by the employee, a friend of the court, the domestic relations office, or the Title IV-D agency.

Added by Acts 1995, 74th Leg., ch. 20, § 1, eff. April 20, 1995. Amended by Acts 1997, 75th Leg., ch. 911, § 48, eff. Sept. 1, 1997.

### § 158.210. Fine for Noncompliance

(a) In addition to the civil remedies provided by this subchapter or any other remedy provided by law, an employer who knowingly violates the provisions of this chapter may be subject to a fine not to exceed $200 for each occurrence in which the employer fails to:

(1) withhold income for child support as instructed in an order or writ issued under this chapter; or

(2) remit withheld income within the time required by Section 158.203 to the payee identified in the order or writ or to the state disbursement unit.

(b) A fine recovered under this section shall be paid to the county in which the obligee resides and shall be used by the county to improve child support services.

Added by Acts 1995, 74th Leg., ch. 20, § 1, eff. April 20, 1995. Amended by Acts 1997, 75th Leg., ch. 420, § 15, eff. Sept. 1, 1997; Acts 1999, 76th Leg., ch. 556, § 27, eff. Sept. 1, 1999.

### § 158.211. Notice of Termination of Employment and of New Employment

(a) If an obligor terminates employment with an employer who has been withholding income, both the obligor and the employer shall notify the court or the Title IV–D agency and the obligee of that fact not later than the seventh day after the date employment terminated and shall provide the obligor's last known address and the name and address of the obligor's new employer, if known.

(b) The obligor has a continuing duty to inform any subsequent employer of the order or writ of withholding after obtaining employment.

Added by Acts 1995, 74th Leg., ch. 20, § 1, eff. April 20, 1995. Amended by Acts 1999, 76th Leg., ch. 556, § 28, eff. Sept. 1, 1999.

### § 158.212. Improper Payment

An employer who remits a payment to an incorrect office or person shall remit the payment to the agency or person identified in the order of withholding not later than the second business day after the date the employer receives the returned payment.

Added by Acts 1999, 76th Leg., ch. 556, § 29, eff. Sept. 1, 1999.

### § 158.213. Withholding From Workers' Compensation Benefits

(a) An insurance carrier that receives an order or writ of withholding under Section 158.206 for workers' compensation benefits payable to an obligor shall withhold an amount not to exceed the maximum amount allowed to be withheld from income under Section 158.009 regardless of whether the benefits payable to the obligor for lost income are paid as lump sum amounts or as periodic payments.

(b) An insurance carrier subject to this section shall send the amount withheld for child support to the place of payment designated in the order or writ of withholding.

Added by Acts 2003, 78th Leg., ch. 610, § 9, eff. Sept. 1, 2003.

### § 158.214. Withholding From Severance Pay

(a) In this section, "severance pay" means income paid on termination of employment in addition to the employee's usual earnings from the employer at the time of termination.

(b) An employer receiving an order or writ of withholding under this chapter shall withhold from any severance pay owed an obligor an amount equal to the amount the employer would have withheld under the order or writ if the severance pay had been paid as the obligor's usual earnings as a current employee.

(c) The total amount that may be withheld under this section is subject to the maximum amount allowed to be withheld under Section 158.009.

Added by Acts 2007, 80th Leg., ch. 972, § 33, eff. Sept. 1, 2007.

### § 158.215. Withholding From Lump–Sum Payments

(a) In this section, "lump-sum payment" means income in the form of a bonus or an amount paid in lieu of vacation or other leave time. The term does not include an employee's usual earnings or an amount paid as severance pay on termination of employment.

(b) This section applies only to an employer who receives an administrative writ of withholding in a Title IV–D case.

(c) An employer to whom this section applies may not make a lump-sum payment to the obligor in the amount of $500 or more without first notifying the Title IV–D agency to determine whether all or a portion of the payment should be applied to child support arrearages owed by the obligor.

(d) After notifying the Title IV–D agency in compliance with Subsection (c), the employer may not make the lump-sum payment before the earlier of:

(1) the 10th day after the date on which the employer notified the Title IV–D agency; or

(2) the date on which the employer receives authorization from the Title IV–D agency to make the payment.

(e) If the employer receives a timely authorization from the Title IV–D agency under Subsection (d)(2), the employer may make the payment only in accordance with the terms of that authorization.

Added by Acts 2007, 80th Leg., ch. 972, § 34, eff. Sept. 1, 2007. Amended by Acts 2009, 81st Leg., ch. 767, § 20, eff. June 19, 2009.

## SUBCHAPTER D. JUDICIAL WRIT OF WITHHOLDING ISSUED BY CLERK

### § 158.301. Notice of Application for Judicial Writ of Withholding; Filing

(a) A notice of application for judicial writ of withholding may be filed if:

(1) a delinquency occurs in child support payments in an amount equal to or greater than the total support due for one month; or

(2) income withholding was not ordered at the time child support was ordered.

(b) The notice of application for judicial writ of withholding may be filed in the court of continuing jurisdiction by:

(1) the Title IV-D agency;

(2) the attorney representing the local domestic relations office;

(3) the attorney appointed a friend of the court as provided in Chapter 202;

(4) the obligor or obligee; or

(5) a private attorney representing the obligor or obligee.

(c) The Title IV-D agency may in a Title IV-D case file a notice of application for judicial writ of withholding on request of the obligor or obligee.

Added by Acts 1995, 74th Leg., ch. 20, § 1, eff. April 20, 1995. Amended by Acts 1995, 74th Leg., ch. 751, § 57, eff. Sept. 1, 1995; Acts 1997, 75th Leg., ch. 911, § 50, eff. Sept. 1, 1997.

### § 158.302. Contents of Notice of Application for Judicial Writ of Withholding

The notice of application for judicial writ of withholding shall be verified and:

(1) state the amount of monthly support due, including medical support and dental support, the amount of arrearages or anticipated arrearages, including accrued interest, and the amount of wages that will be withheld in accordance with a judicial writ of withholding;

(2) state that the withholding applies to each current or subsequent employer or period of employment;

(3) state that if the obligor does not contest the withholding within 10 days after the date of receipt of the notice, the obligor's employer will be notified to begin the withholding;

(4) describe the procedures for contesting the issuance and delivery of a writ of withholding;

(5) state that if the obligor contests the withholding, the obligor will be afforded an opportunity for a hearing by the court not later than the 30th day after the date of receipt of the notice of contest;

(6) state that the sole ground for successfully contesting the issuance of a writ of withholding is a dispute concerning the identity of the obligor or the existence or amount of the arrearages, including accrued interest;

(7) describe the actions that may be taken if the obligor contests the notice of application for judicial writ of withholding, including the procedures for suspending issuance of a writ of withholding; and

(8) include with the notice a suggested form for the motion to stay issuance and delivery of the judicial writ of withholding that the obligor may file with the clerk of the appropriate court.

Added by Acts 1995, 74th Leg., ch. 20, § 1, eff. April 20, 1995. Amended by Acts 1997, 75th Leg., ch. 911, § 51, eff. Sept. 1, 1997; Acts 2015, 84th Leg., ch. 1150 (S.B. 550), § 32, eff. Sept. 1, 2018.

### § 158.303. Interstate Request for Income Withholding

(a) The registration of a foreign support order as provided in Chapter 159 is sufficient for the filing of a notice of application for judicial writ of withholding.

(b) The notice shall be filed with the clerk of the court having venue as provided in Chapter 159.

(c) Notice of application for judicial writ of withholding may be delivered to the obligor at the same time that an order is filed for registration under Chapter 159.

Added by Acts 1995, 74th Leg., ch. 20, § 1, eff. April 20, 1995. Amended by Acts 1995, 74th Leg., ch. 751, § 58, eff. Sept. 1, 1995; Acts 1997, 75th Leg., ch. 911, § 52, eff. Sept. 1, 1997.

### § 158.304. Additional Arrearages

If the notice of application for judicial writ of withholding states that the obligor has repeatedly failed to pay support in accordance with the underlying support order, the judicial writ may include arrearages that accrue between the filing of the notice and the date of the hearing or the issuance of a judicial writ of withholding.

Added by Acts 1995, 74th Leg., ch. 20, § 1, eff. April 20, 1995. Amended by Acts 1997, 75th Leg., ch. 911, § 53, eff. Sept. 1, 1997.

### § 158.305. Repealed by Acts 1997, 75th Leg., ch. 911, § 97(a), eff. Sept. 1, 1997

### § 158.306. Delivery of Notice of Application for Judicial Writ of Withholding; Time of Delivery

(a) A notice of application for judicial writ of withholding may be delivered to the obligor by:

(1) hand delivery by a person designated by the Title IV-D agency or local domestic relations office;

(2) first-class or certified mail, return receipt requested, addressed to the obligor's last known address or place of employment; or

(3) by service of citation as in civil cases generally.

(b) If the notice is delivered by mailing or hand delivery, the party who filed the notice shall file with the court a certificate stating the name, address, and date on which the mailing or hand delivery was made.

(c) Notice is considered to have been received by the obligor:

(1) if hand delivered, on the date of delivery;

(2) if mailed by certified mail, on the date of receipt;

(3) if mailed by first-class mail, on the 10th day after the date the notice was mailed; or

(4) if delivered by service of citation, on the date of service.

Added by Acts 1995, 74th Leg., ch. 20, § 1, eff. April 20, 1995. Amended by Acts 1997, 75th Leg., ch. 911, § 54, eff. Sept. 1, 1997.

### § 158.307. Motion to Stay Issuance of Writ of Withholding

(a) The obligor may stay issuance of a judicial writ of withholding by filing a motion to stay with the clerk of court not later than the 10th day after the date the notice of application for judicial writ of withholding was received.

(b) The grounds for filing a motion to stay issuance are limited to a dispute concerning the identity of the obligor or the existence or the amount of the arrearages.

(c) The obligor shall verify that statements of fact in the motion to stay issuance of the writ are true and correct.

Added by Acts 1995, 74th Leg., ch. 20, § 1, eff. April 20, 1995. Amended by Acts 1997, 75th Leg., ch. 911, § 55, eff. Sept. 1, 1997.

### § 158.308. Effect of Filing Motion to Stay

The filing of a motion to stay by an obligor in the manner provided by Section 158.307 prohibits the clerk of court from delivering the judicial writ of withholding to any employer of the obligor before a hearing is held.

Added by Acts 1995, 74th Leg., ch. 20, § 1, eff. April 20, 1995. Amended by Acts 1997, 75th Leg., ch. 911, § 56, eff. Sept. 1, 1997.

### § 158.309. Hearing on Motion to Stay

(a) If a motion to stay is filed in the manner provided by Section 158.307, the court shall set a hearing on the motion and the clerk of court shall notify the obligor, obligee, or their authorized representatives, and the party who filed the application for judicial writ of withholding of the date, time, and place of the hearing.

(b) The court shall hold a hearing on the motion to stay not later than the 30th day after the date the motion was filed, except that a hearing may be held later than the 30th day after filing if both the obligor and obligee agree and waive the right to have the motion heard within 30 days.

(c) Upon hearing, the court shall:

(1) render an order for income withholding that includes a determination of the amount of child support arrearages, including medical support, dental support, and interest; or

(2) grant the motion to stay.

Added by Acts 1995, 74th Leg., ch. 20, § 1, eff. April 20, 1995. Amended by Acts 1995, 74th Leg., ch. 751, § 59, eff. Sept. 1, 1995; Acts 1997, 75th Leg., ch. 911, § 57, eff. Sept. 1, 1997; Acts 2015, 84th Leg., ch. 1150 (S.B. 550), § 33, eff. Sept. 1, 2018.

### § 158.310. Special Exceptions

(a) A defect in a notice of application for judicial writ of withholding is waived unless the respondent specially excepts in writing and cites with particularity the alleged defect, obscurity, or other ambiguity in the notice.

(b) A special exception under this section must be heard by the court before hearing the motion to stay issuance.

(c) If the court sustains an exception, the court shall provide the party filing the notice an opportunity to refile and the court shall continue the hearing to a date certain without the requirement of additional service.

Added by Acts 1995, 74th Leg., ch. 20, § 1, eff. April 20, 1995. Amended by Acts 1997, 75th Leg., ch. 911, § 58, eff. Sept. 1, 1997.

### § 158.311. Arrearages

(a) Payment of arrearages after receipt of notice of application for judicial writ of withholding may not be the sole basis for the court to refuse to order withholding.

(b) The court shall order that a reasonable amount of income be withheld to be applied toward the liquidation of arrearages, even though a judgment confirming arrearages has been rendered against the obligor.

Added by Acts 1995, 74th Leg., ch. 20, § 1, eff. April 20, 1995. Amended by Acts 1997, 75th Leg., ch. 911, § 59, eff. Sept. 1, 1997.

### § 158.312. Request for Issuance and Delivery of Writ of Withholding

(a) If a notice of application for judicial writ of withholding is delivered and a motion to stay is not filed within the time limits provided by Section 158.307, the party who filed the notice shall file with the clerk of the court a request for issuance of the writ of withholding stating the amount of current support, including medical support and dental support, the amount of arrearages, and the amount to be withheld from the obligor's income.

(b) The request for issuance may not be filed before the 11th day after the date of receipt of the notice of application for judicial writ of withholding by the obligor.

Added by Acts 1995, 74th Leg., ch. 20, § 1, eff. April 20, 1995. Amended by Acts 1997, 75th Leg., ch. 911, § 60, eff. Sept. 1, 1997; Acts 1999, 76th Leg., ch. 556, § 30, eff. Sept. 1, 1999; Acts 2015, 84th Leg., ch. 1150 (S.B. 550), § 34, eff. Sept. 1, 2018.

### § 158.313. Issuance and Delivery of Writ of Withholding

(a) On the filing of a request for issuance of a writ of withholding, the clerk of the court shall issue the writ.

(b) The writ shall be delivered as provided by Subchapter B.[1]

(c) The clerk shall issue and mail the writ not later than the second working day after the date the request is filed.

Added by Acts 1995, 74th Leg., ch. 20, § 1, eff. April 20, 1995.

[1] V.T.C.A., Family Code § 158.101 et seq.

### § 158.314. Contents of Writ of Withholding

The judicial writ of income withholding issued by the clerk must direct that the employer or a subsequent employer withhold from the obligor's disposable income for current child support, including medical support and dental support, and child support arrearages an amount that is consistent with the provisions of this chapter regarding orders of withholding.

Added by Acts 1995, 74th Leg., ch. 20, § 1, eff. April 20, 1995. Amended by Acts 1997, 75th Leg., ch. 911, § 61, eff. Sept. 1, 1997; Acts 2015, 84th Leg., ch. 1150 (S.B. 550), § 35, eff. Sept. 1, 2018.

### § 158.315. Extension of Repayment Schedule by Party; Unreasonable Hardship

If the party who filed the notice of application for judicial writ of withholding finds that the schedule for repaying arrearages would cause the obligor, the obligor's family, or the children for whom the support is due from the obligor to suffer unreasonable hardship, the party may extend the payment period in the writ.

Added by Acts 1995, 74th Leg., ch. 20, § 1, eff. April 20, 1995. Amended by Acts 1997, 75th Leg., ch. 911, § 62, eff. Sept. 1, 1997.

### § 158.316. Payment of Amount to Be Withheld

The amount to be withheld shall be paid to the person or office named in the writ on each pay date and shall include with the payment the date on which the withholding occurred.

Added by Acts 1995, 74th Leg., ch. 20, § 1, eff. April 20, 1995.

### § 158.317. Failure to Receive Notice of Application for Judicial Writ of Withholding

(a) Not later than the 30th day after the date of the first pay period following the date of delivery of the writ of withholding to the obligor's employer, the obligor may file an affidavit with the court that a motion to stay was not timely filed because the notice of application for judicial writ of withholding was not received by the obligor and that grounds exist for a motion to stay.

(b) Concurrently with the filing of the affidavit, the obligor may file a motion to withdraw the writ of withholding and request a hearing on the applicability of the writ.

(c) Income withholding may not be interrupted until after the hearing at which the court renders an order denying or modifying withholding.

Added by Acts 1995, 74th Leg., ch. 20, § 1, eff. April 20, 1995. Amended by Acts 1997, 75th Leg., ch. 911, § 63, eff. Sept. 1, 1997.

### § 158.318. [Blank]

### § 158.319. Issuance and Delivery of Judicial Writ of Withholding to Subsequent Employer

(a) After the issuance of a judicial writ of withholding by the clerk, a party authorized to file a notice of application for judicial writ of withholding under this subchapter may issue the judicial writ of withholding to a subsequent employer of the obligor by delivering to the employer by certified mail a copy of the writ.

(b) The judicial writ of withholding must include the name, address, and signature of the party and clearly indicate that the writ is being issued to a subsequent employer.

(c) The party shall file a copy of the judicial writ of withholding with the clerk not later than the third working day following delivery of the writ to the subsequent employer. The party shall pay the clerk a fee of $15 at the time the copy of the writ is filed.

(d) The party shall file the postal return receipt from the delivery to the subsequent employer not later than the third working day after the party receives the receipt.

Added by Acts 1995, 74th Leg., ch. 751, § 60, eff. Sept. 1, 1995. Amended by Acts 1997, 75th Leg., ch. 911, § 64, eff. Sept. 1, 1997.

## SUBCHAPTER E. MODIFICATION, REDUCTION, OR TERMINATION OF WITHHOLDING

### § 158.401. Modifications to or Termination of Withholding by Title IV–D Agency

(a) The Title IV–D agency shall establish procedures for the reduction in the amount of or termination of withholding from income on the liquidation of an arrearages or the termination of the obligation of support in Title IV–D cases. The procedures shall provide that the payment of overdue support may not be used as the sole basis for terminating withholding.

(b) At the request of the Title IV-D agency, the clerk of the court shall issue a judicial writ of withholding to the obligor's employer reflecting any modification or changes in the amount to be withheld or the termination of withholding.

Added by Acts 1995, 74th Leg., ch. 20, § 1, eff. April 20, 1995. Amended by Acts 1997, 75th Leg., ch. 911, § 65, eff. Sept. 1, 1997.

### § 158.402. Agreement by Parties Regarding Amount or Duration of Withholding

(a) An obligor and obligee may agree on a reduction in or termination of income withholding for child support on the occurrence of one of the following contingencies stated in the order:

(1) the child becomes 18 years of age or is graduated from high school, whichever is later;

(2) the child's disabilities of minority are removed by marriage, court order, or other operation of law; or

(3) the child dies.

(b) The obligor and obligee may file a notarized or acknowledged request with the clerk of the court under Section 158.011 for a revised judicial writ of withholding, including the termination of withholding.

(c) The clerk shall issue and deliver to an employer of the obligor a judicial writ of withholding that reflects the agreed revision or termination of withholding.

(d) An agreement by the parties under this section does not modify the terms of a support order.

Added by Acts 1995, 74th Leg., ch. 751, § 61, eff. Sept. 1, 1995. Amended by Acts 1997, 75th Leg., ch. 911, § 66, eff. Sept. 1, 1997.

### § 158.403. Modifications to or Termination of Withholding in Voluntary Withholding Cases

(a) If an obligor initiates voluntary withholding under Section 158.011, the obligee or an agency providing child support services may file with the clerk of the court a notarized request signed by the obligor and the obligee or agency, as appropriate, for the issuance and delivery to the obligor of a:

(1) modified writ of withholding that reduces the amount of withholding; or

(2) notice of termination of withholding.

(b) On receipt of a request under this section, the clerk shall issue and deliver a modified writ of withholding or notice of termination in the manner provided by Section 158.402.

(c) The clerk may charge a reasonable fee not to exceed $15 for filing the request.

(d) An obligee may contest a modified writ of withholding or notice of termination issued under this section by requesting a hearing in the manner provided by Section 158.309 not later than the 180th day after the date the obligee discovers that the writ or notice has been issued.

Added by Acts 1995, 74th Leg., ch. 751, § 61, eff. Sept. 1, 1995.

### § 158.404. Delivery of Order of Reduction or Termination of Withholding

If a court has rendered an order that reduces the amount of child support to be withheld or terminates withholding for child support, any person or governmental entity may deliver to the employer a certified copy of the order without the requirement that the clerk of the court deliver the order.

Added by Acts 1995, 74th Leg., ch. 20, § 1, eff. April 20, 1995. Renumbered from V.T.C.A., Family Code § 158.402 by Acts 1995, 74th Leg., ch. 751, § 61, eff. Sept. 1, 1995.

### § 158.405. Liability of Employers

The provisions of this chapter regarding the liability of employers for withholding apply to an order that reduces or terminates withholding.

Added by Acts 1995, 74th Leg., ch. 20, § 1, eff. April 20, 1995. Renumbered from V.T.C.A., Family Code § 158.403 by Acts 1995, 74th Leg., ch. 751, § 61, eff. Sept. 1, 1995.

## SUBCHAPTER F. ADMINISTRATIVE WRIT OF WITHHOLDING

### § 158.501. Issuance of Administrative Writ of Withholding

(a) The Title IV–D agency may initiate income withholding by issuing an administrative writ of withholding for the enforcement of an existing order as authorized by this subchapter.

(b) Except as provided by Subsection (d), the Title IV–D agency is the only entity that may issue an administrative writ under this subchapter.

(c) The Title IV-D agency may use the procedures authorized by this subchapter to enforce a support order rendered by a tribunal of another state regardless of whether the order has been registered under Chapter 159.

(d) A domestic relations office may issue an administrative writ of withholding under this chapter in a proceeding in which the office is providing child support enforcement services. A reference in this code to the Title IV–D agency that relates to an administrative writ includes a domestic relations office, except that the writ must be in the form prescribed by the Title IV–D agency under Section 158.504.

Added by Acts 1997, 75th Leg., ch. 911, § 67, eff. Sept. 1, 1997. Amended by Acts 1999, 76th Leg., ch. 556, § 31, eff. Sept. 1, 1999; Acts 2001, 77th Leg., ch. 1023, § 40, eff. Sept. 1, 2001; Acts 2005, 79th Leg., ch. 199, §§ 3, 4, eff. Sept. 1, 2005.

### § 158.502. When Administrative Writ of Withholding May Be Issued

(a) An administrative writ of withholding under this subchapter may be issued by the Title IV–D agency at any time until all current support, including medical support and dental support, child support arrearages, and Title IV–D service fees authorized under Section 231.103 for which the obligor is responsible have been paid. The writ issued under this subsection may be based on an obligation in more than one support order.

(b) The Title IV–D agency may issue an administrative writ of withholding that directs that an amount be withheld for an arrearage or adjusts the amount to be withheld for an arrearage. An administrative writ issued under this subsection may be contested as provided by Section 158.506.

(c) The Title IV-D agency may issue an administrative writ of withholding as a reissuance of an existing withholding order on file with the court of continuing jurisdiction or a tribunal of another state. The administrative writ under this subsection is not subject to the contest provisions of Sections 158.505(a)(2) and 158.506.

(d) The Title IV–D agency may issue an administrative writ of withholding to direct child support payments to the state disbursement unit of another state.

Added by Acts 1997, 75th Leg., ch. 911, § 67, eff. Sept. 1, 1997. Amended by Acts 1999, 76th Leg., ch. 556, § 31, eff. Sept. 1, 1999; Acts 2001, 77th Leg., ch. 1023, § 41, eff. Sept. 1, 2001; Acts 2003, 78th Leg., ch. 1247, § 2, eff. Sept. 1, 2003; Acts 2007, 80th Leg., ch. 972, § 35, eff. Sept. 1, 2007; Acts 2015, 84th Leg., ch. 1150 (S.B. 550), § 36, eff. Sept. 1, 2018.

### § 158.503. Delivery of Administrative Writ to Employer; Filing with Court or Maintaining Record

(a) An administrative writ of withholding issued under this subchapter may be delivered to an employer by mail or by electronic transmission.

(b) The Title IV–D agency shall:

(1) not later than the third business day after the date of delivery of the administrative writ of withholding to an employer, file a copy of the writ, together with a signed certificate of service, in the court of continuing jurisdiction; or

(2) maintain a record of the writ until all support obligations of the obligor have been satisfied or income withholding has been terminated as provided by this chapter.

(b–1) The certificate of service required under Subsection (b)(1) may be signed electronically.

(c) The copy of the administrative writ of withholding filed with the clerk of court must include:

(1) the name, address, and signature of the authorized attorney or individual that issued the writ;

(2) the name and address of the employer served with the writ; and

(3) a true copy of the information provided to the employer.

(d) The clerk of the court may charge a reasonable fee not to exceed $15 for filing an administrative writ under this section.

Added by Acts 1997, 75th Leg., ch. 911, § 67, eff. Sept. 1, 1997. Amended by Acts 1999, 76th Leg., ch. 556, § 32, eff. Sept. 1, 1999; Acts 2001, 77th Leg., ch. 116, § 1, eff. Sept. 1, 2001; Acts 2001, 77th Leg., ch. 1023, § 42, eff. Sept. 1, 2001; Acts 2011, 82nd Leg., ch. 508 (H.B. 1674), §§ 10, 11, eff. Sept. 1, 2011.

### § 158.504. Contents of Administrative Writ of Withholding

(a) The administrative writ of withholding must be in the form prescribed by the Title IV-D agency as required by this chapter and in a standard format authorized by the United States Department of Health and Human Services.

(b) An administrative writ of withholding issued under this subchapter may contain only the information that is necessary for the employer to withhold income for child support, medical support, and dental support and shall specify the place where the withheld income is to be paid.

Added by Acts 1997, 75th Leg., ch. 911, § 67, eff. Sept. 1, 1997. Amended by Acts 1999, 76th Leg., ch. 556, § 33, eff. Sept. 1, 1999; Acts 2001, 77th Leg., ch. 1023, § 43, eff. Sept. 1, 2001; Acts 2015, 84th Leg., ch. 1150 (S.B. 550), § 37, eff. Sept. 1, 2018.

### § 158.505. Notice to Obligor

(a) On issuance of an administrative writ of withholding, the Title IV-D agency shall send the obligor:

(1) notice that the withholding has commenced, including, if the writ is issued as provided by Section 158.502(b), the amount of the arrearages, including accrued interest;

(2) except as provided by Section 158.502(c), notice of the procedures to follow if the obligor desires to contest withholding on the grounds that the identity of the obligor or the existence or amount of arrearages is incorrect; and

(3) a copy of the administrative writ, including the information concerning income withholding provided to the employer.

(b) The notice required under this section may be sent to the obligor by:

(1) personal delivery by a person designated by the Title IV-D agency;

(2) first-class mail or certified mail, return receipt requested, addressed to the obligor's last known address; or

(3) service of citation as in civil cases generally.

(c) Repealed by Acts 1999, 76th Leg., ch. 556, § 81, eff. Sept. 1, 1999.

Added by Acts 1997, 75th Leg., ch. 911, § 67, eff. Sept. 1, 1997. Amended by Acts 1999, 76th Leg., ch. 556, §§ 34, 81, eff. Sept. 1, 1999; Acts 2001, 77th Leg., ch. 1023, § 44, eff. Sept. 1, 2001.

### § 158.506. Contest by Obligor to Administrative Writ of Withholding

(a) Except as provided by Section 158.502(c), an obligor receiving the notice under Section 158.505 may request a review by the Title IV–D agency to resolve any issue in dispute regarding the identity of the obligor or the existence or amount of arrearages. The Title IV–D agency shall provide an opportunity for a review, by telephonic conference or in person, as may be appropriate under the circumstances.

(b) After a review under this section, the Title IV-D agency may issue a new administrative writ of withholding to the employer, including a writ modifying the amount to be withheld or terminating withholding.

(c) If a review under this section fails to resolve any issue in dispute, the obligor may file a motion with the court to withdraw the administrative writ of withholding and request a hearing with the court not later than the 30th day after receiving notice of the agency's determination. Income withholding may not be interrupted pending a hearing by the court.

(d) If an administrative writ of withholding issued under this subchapter is based on an order of a tribunal of another state that has not been registered under Chapter 159, the obligor may file a motion with an appropriate court in accordance with Subsection (c).

Added by Acts 1997, 75th Leg., ch. 911, § 67, eff. Sept. 1, 1997. Amended by Acts 1999, 76th Leg., ch. 556, § 35, eff. Sept. 1, 1999; Acts 2007, 80th Leg., ch. 972, § 36, eff. Sept. 1, 2007.

### § 158.507. Administrative Writ Terminating Withholding

An administrative writ to terminate withholding may be issued and delivered to an employer by the Title IV–D agency when all current support, including medical support and dental support, child support arrearages, and Title IV–D service fees authorized under Section 231.103 for which the obligor is responsible have been paid.

Added by Acts 1997, 75th Leg., ch. 911, § 67, eff. Sept. 1, 1997. Amended by Acts 2007, 80th Leg., ch. 972, § 37, eff. Sept. 1, 2007; Acts 2015, 84th Leg., ch. 1150 (S.B. 550), § 38, eff. Sept. 1, 2018.

### § 158.508. Repealed by Acts 2001, 77th Leg., ch. 1023, § 76, eff. Sept. 1, 2001

## CHAPTER 159. UNIFORM INTERSTATE FAMILY SUPPORT ACT

### SUBCHAPTER A. CONFLICTS BETWEEN PROVISIONS



### SUBCHAPTER B. GENERAL PROVISIONS



### SUBCHAPTER C. JURISDICTION

## SUBCHAPTER A. CONFLICTS BETWEEN PROVISIONS

### § 159.001. Conflicts Between Provisions

If a provision of this chapter conflicts with a provision of this title or another statute or rule of this state and the conflict cannot be reconciled, this chapter prevails.

Added by Acts 1995, 74th Leg., ch. 20, § 1, eff. April 20, 1995.

## SUBCHAPTER B. GENERAL PROVISIONS

### § 159.101. Short Title

This chapter may be cited as the Uniform Interstate Family Support Act.

Added by Acts 2003, 78th Leg., ch. 1247, § 3, eff. Sept. 1, 2003.

### § 159.102. Definitions

In this chapter:

(1) "Child" means an individual, whether over or under the age of majority, who:

(A) is or is alleged to be owed a duty of support by the individual's parent; or

(B) is or is alleged to be the beneficiary of a support order directed to the parent.

(2) "Child support order" means a support order for a child, including a child who has attained the age of majority under the law of the issuing state or foreign country.

(3) "Convention" means the Convention on the International Recovery of Child Support and Other Forms of Family Maintenance, concluded at The Hague on November 23, 2007.

(4) "Duty of support" means an obligation imposed or imposable by law to provide support for a child, spouse, or former spouse, including an unsatisfied obligation to provide support.

(5) "Foreign country" means a country, including a political subdivision thereof, other than the United States, that authorizes the issuance of support orders and:

(A) which has been declared under the law of the United States to be a foreign reciprocating country;

(B) which has established a reciprocal arrangement for child support with this state as provided in Section 159.308;

(C) which has enacted a law or established procedures for the issuance and enforcement of support orders which are substantially similar to the procedures under this chapter; or

(D) in which the Convention is in force with respect to the United States.

(6) "Foreign support order" means a support order of a foreign tribunal.

(7) "Foreign tribunal" means a court, administrative agency, or quasi-judicial entity of a foreign country which is authorized to establish, enforce, or modify support orders or to determine parentage of a child. The term includes a competent authority under the Convention.

(8) "Home state" means the state or foreign country in which a child lived with a parent or a person acting as parent for at least six consecutive months immediately preceding the time of filing of a petition or a comparable pleading for support and, if a child is less than six months old, the state or foreign country in which the child lived from birth with any of them. A period of temporary absence of any of them is counted as part of the six-month or other period.

(9) "Income" includes earnings or other periodic entitlements to money from any source and any other property subject to withholding for support under the law of this state.

(10) "Income-withholding order" means an order or other legal process directed to an obligor's employer, as provided in Chapter 158, to withhold support from the income of the obligor.

(11) "Initiating tribunal" means the tribunal of a state or foreign country from which a petition or comparable pleading is forwarded or a petition or comparable pleading is filed for forwarding to another state or foreign country.

(12) "Issuing foreign country" means the foreign country in which a tribunal issues a support order or a judgment determining parentage of a child.

(13) "Issuing state" means the state in which a tribunal issues a support order or a judgment determining parentage of a child.

(14) "Issuing tribunal" means the tribunal of a state or foreign country that issues a support order or a judgment determining parentage of a child.

(15) "Law" includes decisional and statutory law and rules and regulations having the force of law.

(16) "Obligee" means:

(A) an individual to whom a duty of support is or is alleged to be owed or in whose favor a support order or a judgment determining parentage of a child has been issued;

(B) a foreign country, state, or political subdivision of a state to which the rights under a duty of support or support order have been assigned or that has independent claims based on financial assistance provided to an individual obligee in place of child support;

(C) an individual seeking a judgment determining parentage of the individual's child; or

(D) a person that is a creditor in a proceeding under Subchapter H.

(17) "Obligor" means an individual, or the estate of a decedent, that:

(A) owes or is alleged to owe a duty of support;

(B) is alleged but has not been adjudicated to be a parent of a child;

(C) is liable under a support order; or

(D) is a debtor in a proceeding under Subchapter H.

(18) "Outside this state" means a location in another state or a country other than the United States, whether or not the country is a foreign country.

(19) "Person" means an individual, corporation, business trust, estate, trust, partnership, limited liability company, association, joint venture, public corporation, government or governmental subdivision, agency, or instrumentality, or any other legal or commercial entity.

(20) "Record" means information that is:

(A) inscribed on a tangible medium or that is stored in an electronic or other medium; and

(B) retrievable in a perceivable form.

(21) "Register" means to file in a tribunal of this state a support order or judgment determining parentage of a child issued in another state or a foreign country.

(22) "Registering tribunal" means a tribunal in which a support order or judgment determining parentage of a child is registered.

(23) "Responding state" means a state in which a petition or comparable pleading for support or to determine parentage of a child is filed or to which a petition or comparable pleading is forwarded for filing from another state or a foreign country.

(24) "Responding tribunal" means the authorized tribunal in a responding state or foreign country.

(25) "Spousal support order" means a support order for a spouse or former spouse of the obligor.

(26) "State" means a state of the United States, the District of Columbia, Puerto Rico, the United States Virgin Islands, or any territory or insular possession subject to the jurisdiction of the United States. The term includes an Indian nation or tribe.

(27) "Support enforcement agency" means a public official, governmental entity, or private agency authorized to:

(A) seek enforcement of support orders or laws relating to the duty of support;

(B) seek establishment or modification of child support;

(C) request determination of parentage of a child;

(D) attempt to locate obligors or their assets; or

(E) request determination of the controlling child support order.

"Support enforcement agency" does not include a domestic relations office unless that office has entered into a cooperative agreement with the Title IV–D agency to perform duties under this chapter.

(28) "Support order" means a judgment, decree, order, decision, or directive, whether temporary, final, or subject to modification, issued in a state or foreign country for the benefit of a child, a spouse, or a former spouse that provides for monetary support, health care, arrearages, retroactive support, or reimbursement for financial assistance provided to an individual obligee in place of child support. The term may include related costs and fees, interest, income withholding, automatic adjustment, reasonable attorney's fees, and other relief.

(29) "Tribunal" means a court, administrative agency, or quasi-judicial entity authorized to establish, enforce, or modify support orders or to determine parentage of a child.

Added by Acts 1995, 74th Leg., ch. 20, § 1, eff. April 20, 1995. Amended by Acts 1997, 75th Leg., ch. 607, § 1, eff. Sept. 1, 1997. Renumbered from V.T.C.A., Family Code § 159.101 and amended by Acts 2003, 78th Leg., ch. 1247, § 3, eff. Sept. 1, 2003; Acts 2007, 80th Leg., ch. 972, § 38, eff. Sept. 1, 2007. Amended by Acts 2015, 84th Leg., ch. 368 (H.B. 3538), § 1, eff. July 1, 2015.

## § 159.103. State Tribunal and Support Enforcement Agency

(a) The court is the tribunal of this state.

(b) The office of the attorney general is the support enforcement agency of this state.

Added by Acts 1995, 74th Leg., ch. 20, § 1, eff. April 20, 1995. Amended by Acts 1997, 75th Leg., ch. 607, § 2, eff. Sept. 1, 1997. Renumbered from V.T.C.A., Family Code § 159.102 by Acts 2003, 78th Leg., ch. 1247, § 3, eff. Sept. 1, 2003. Amended by Acts 2015, 84th Leg., ch. 368 (H.B. 3538), § 2, eff. July 1, 2015.

### § 159.104. Remedies Cumulative

(a) Remedies provided by this chapter are cumulative and do not affect the availability of remedies under other law or the recognition of a foreign support order on the basis of comity.

(b) This chapter does not:

(1) provide the exclusive method of establishing or enforcing a support order under the law of this state; or

(2) grant a tribunal of this state jurisdiction to render judgment or issue an order relating to child custody or visitation in a proceeding under this chapter.

Added by Acts 1995, 74th Leg., ch. 20, § 1, eff. April 20, 1995. Renumbered from V.T.C.A., Family Code § 159.103 and amended by Acts 2003, 78th Leg., ch. 1247, § 3, eff. Sept. 1, 2003. Amended by Acts 2015, 84th Leg., ch. 368 (H.B. 3538), § 3, eff. July 1, 2015.

### § 159.105. Application of Chapter to Resident of Foreign Country and Foreign Support Proceeding

(a) A tribunal of this state shall apply Subchapters B through G and, as applicable, Subchapter H to a support proceeding involving:

(1) a foreign support order;

(2) a foreign tribunal; or

(3) an obligee, obligor, or child residing in a foreign country.

(b) A tribunal of this state that is requested to recognize and enforce a support order on the basis of comity may apply the procedural and substantive provisions of Subchapters B through G.

(c) Subchapter H applies only to a support proceeding under the Convention. In such a proceeding, if a provision of Subchapter H is inconsistent with Subchapters B through G, Subchapter H controls.

Added by Acts 2015, 84th Leg., ch. 368 (H.B. 3538), § 4, eff. July 1, 2015.

## SUBCHAPTER C. JURISDICTION

### § 159.201. Bases for Jurisdiction over Nonresident

(a) In a proceeding to establish or enforce a support order or to determine parentage of a child, a tribunal of this state may exercise personal jurisdiction over a nonresident individual or the individual's guardian or conservator if:

(1) the individual is personally served with citation in this state;

(2) the individual submits to the jurisdiction of this state by consent in a record, by entering a general appearance, or by filing a responsive document having the effect of waiving any contest to personal jurisdiction;

(3) the individual resided with the child in this state;

(4) the individual resided in this state and provided prenatal expenses or support for the child;

(5) the child resides in this state as a result of the acts or directives of the individual;

(6) the individual engaged in sexual intercourse in this state and the child may have been conceived by that act of intercourse;

(7) the individual asserted parentage of a child in the paternity registry maintained in this state by the vital statistics unit; or

(8) there is any other basis consistent with the constitutions of this state and the United States for the exercise of personal jurisdiction.

(b) The bases of personal jurisdiction listed in Subsection (a) or in any other law of this state may not be used to acquire personal jurisdiction for a tribunal of this state to modify a child support order of another state unless the requirements of Section 159.611 are met, or, in the case of a foreign support order, unless the requirements of Section 159.615 are met.

Added by Acts 1995, 74th Leg., ch. 20, § 1, eff. April 20, 1995. Amended by Acts 1997, 75th Leg., ch. 561, § 5, eff. Sept. 1, 1997; Acts 2003, 78th Leg., ch. 1247, § 4, eff. Sept. 1, 2003; Acts 2015, 84th Leg., ch. 1 (S.B. 219), § 1.054, eff. April 2, 2015; Acts 2015, 84th Leg., ch. 368 (H.B. 3538), § 5, eff. July 1, 2015.

### § 159.202. Duration of Personal Jurisdiction

Personal jurisdiction acquired by a tribunal of this state in a proceeding under this chapter or other law of this state relating to a support order continues as long as the tribunal of this state has continuing, exclusive jurisdiction to modify its order or continuing jurisdiction to enforce its order as provided by Sections 159.205, 159.206, and 159.211.

Added by Acts 1995, 74th Leg., ch. 20, § 1, eff. April 20, 1995. Amended by Acts 2003, 78th Leg., ch. 1247, § 5, eff. Sept. 1, 2003; Acts 2015, 84th Leg., ch. 368 (H.B. 3538), § 6, eff. July 1, 2015.

### § 159.203. Initiating and Responding Tribunal of State

Under this chapter, a tribunal of this state may serve as an initiating tribunal to forward proceedings to a tribunal of another state and as a responding tribunal for proceedings initiated in another state or a foreign country.

Added by Acts 1995, 74th Leg., ch. 20, § 1, eff. April 20, 1995. Amended by Acts 1997, 75th Leg., ch. 607, § 3, eff. Sept. 1, 1997; Acts 2015, 84th Leg., ch. 368 (H.B. 3538), § 7, eff. July 1, 2015.

### § 159.204. Simultaneous Proceedings

(a) A tribunal of this state may exercise jurisdiction to establish a support order if the petition or comparable pleading is filed after a pleading is filed in another state or a foreign country only if:

(1) the petition or comparable pleading in this state is filed before the expiration of the time allowed in the other state or the foreign country for filing a responsive pleading challenging the exercise of jurisdiction by the other state or the foreign country;

(2) the contesting party timely challenges the exercise of jurisdiction in the other state or the foreign country; and

(3) if relevant, this state is the home state of the child.

(b) A tribunal of this state may not exercise jurisdiction to establish a support order if the petition or comparable pleading is filed before a petition or comparable pleading is filed in another state or a foreign country if:

(1) the petition or comparable pleading in the other state or foreign country is filed before the expiration of the time allowed in this state for filing a responsive pleading challenging the exercise of jurisdiction by this state;

(2) the contesting party timely challenges the exercise of jurisdiction in this state; and

(3) if relevant, the other state or foreign country is the home state of the child.

Added by Acts 1995, 74th Leg., ch. 20, § 1, eff. April 20, 1995. Amended by Acts 2003, 78th Leg., ch. 1247, § 6, eff. Sept. 1, 2003; Acts 2015, 84th Leg., ch. 368 (H.B. 3538), § 8, eff. July 1, 2015.

### § 159.205. Continuing, Exclusive Jurisdiction to Modify Child Support Order

(a) A tribunal of this state that has issued a child support order consistent with the law of this state has and shall exercise continuing, exclusive jurisdiction to modify its child support order if the order is the controlling order and:

(1) at the time of the filing of a request for modification this state is the residence of the obligor, the individual obligee, or the child for whose benefit the support order is issued; or

(2) even if this state is not the residence of the obligor, the individual obligee, or the child for whose benefit the support order is issued, the parties consent in a record or in open court that the tribunal of this state may continue to exercise jurisdiction to modify its order.

(b) A tribunal of this state that has issued a child support order consistent with the law of this state may not exercise continuing, exclusive jurisdiction to modify the order if:

(1) all of the parties who are individuals file consent in a record with the tribunal of this state that a tribunal of another state that has jurisdiction over at least one of the parties who is an individual or that is located in the state of residence of the child may modify the order and assume continuing, exclusive jurisdiction; or

(2) the tribunal's order is not the controlling order.

(c) If a tribunal of another state has issued a child support order pursuant to the Uniform Interstate Family Support Act or a law substantially similar to that Act that modifies a child support order of a tribunal of this state, tribunals of this state shall recognize the continuing, exclusive jurisdiction of the tribunal of the other state.

(d) A tribunal of this state that lacks continuing, exclusive jurisdiction to modify a child support order may serve as an initiating tribunal to request a tribunal of another state to modify a support order issued in that state.

(e) A temporary support order issued ex parte or pending resolution of a jurisdictional conflict does not create continuing, exclusive jurisdiction in the issuing tribunal.

(f) Repealed by Acts 2003, 78th Leg., ch. 1247, § 46.

Added by Acts 1995, 74th Leg., ch. 20, § 1, eff. April 20, 1995. Amended by Acts 1997, 75th Leg., ch. 607, § 4, eff. Sept. 1, 1997; Acts 2003, 78th Leg., ch. 1247, §§ 7, 8, 46, eff. Sept. 1, 2003; Acts 2015, 84th Leg., ch. 368 (H.B. 3538), § 9, eff. July 1, 2015.

### § 159.206. Continuing Jurisdiction to Enforce Child Support Order

(a) A tribunal of this state that has issued a child support order consistent with the law of this state may serve as an initiating tribunal to request a tribunal of another state to enforce:

(1) the order, if the order:

(A) is the controlling order; and

(B) has not been modified by a tribunal of another state that assumed jurisdiction under the Uniform Interstate Family Support Act; or

(2) a money judgment for arrears of support and interest on the order accrued before a determination that an order of a tribunal of another state is the controlling order.

(b) A tribunal of this state having continuing jurisdiction over a support order may act as a responding tribunal to enforce the order.

Added by Acts 1995, 74th Leg., ch. 20, § 1, eff. April 20, 1995. Amended by Acts 2003, 78th Leg., ch. 1247, § 9, eff. Sept. 1, 2003; Acts 2015, 84th Leg., ch. 368 (H.B. 3538), § 10, eff. July 1, 2015.

### § 159.207. Determination of Controlling Child Support Order

(a) If a proceeding is brought under this chapter and only one tribunal has issued a child support order, the order of that tribunal controls and must be recognized.

(b) If a proceeding is brought under this chapter and two or more child support orders have been issued by tribunals of this state, another state, or a foreign country with regard to the same obligor and same child, a tribunal of this state having personal jurisdiction over both the obligor and individual obligee shall apply the following rules and by order shall determine which order controls and must be recognized:

(1) if only one of the tribunals would have continuing, exclusive jurisdiction under this chapter, the order of that tribunal controls;

(2) if more than one of the tribunals would have continuing, exclusive jurisdiction under this chapter:

(A) an order issued by a tribunal in the current home state of the child controls; or

(B) if an order has not been issued in the current home state of the child, the order most recently issued controls; and

(3) if none of the tribunals would have continuing, exclusive jurisdiction under this chapter, the tribunal of this state shall issue a child support order that controls.

(c) If two or more child support orders have been issued for the same obligor and same child, on request of a party who is an individual or that is a support enforcement agency, a tribunal of this state having personal jurisdiction over both the obligor and the obligee who is an individual shall determine which order controls under Subsection (b). The request may be filed with a registration for enforcement or registration for modification under Subchapter G[1] or may be filed as a separate proceeding.

(d) A request to determine which is the controlling order must be accompanied by a copy of every child support order in effect and the applicable record of payments. The requesting party shall give notice of the request to each party whose rights may be affected by the determination.

(e) The tribunal that issued the controlling order under Subsection (a), (b), or (c) has continuing jurisdiction to the extent provided by Section 159.205 or 159.206.

(f) A tribunal of this state that determines by order which is the controlling order under Subsection (b)(1) or (2) or Subsection (c), or that issues a new controlling order under Subsection (b)(3), shall state in that order:

(1) the basis upon which the tribunal made its determination;

(2) the amount of prospective support, if any; and

(3) the total amount of consolidated arrears and accrued interest, if any, under all of the orders after all payments made are credited as provided by Section 159.209.

(g) Within 30 days after issuance of an order determining which order is the controlling order, the party obtaining the order shall file a certified copy of the controlling order in each tribunal that issued or registered an earlier order of child support. A party or support enforcement agency obtaining the order that fails to file a certified copy is subject to appropriate sanctions by a tribunal in which the issue of failure to file arises. The failure to file does not affect the validity or enforceability of the controlling order.

(h) An order that has been determined to be the controlling order, or a judgment for consolidated arrears of support and interest, if any, made under this section, must be recognized in proceedings under this chapter.

Added by Acts 1995, 74th Leg., ch. 20, § 1, eff. April 20, 1995. Amended by Acts 1997, 75th Leg., ch. 607, § 5, eff. Sept. 1, 1997; Acts 2003, 78th Leg., ch. 1247, §§ 10, 11, eff. Sept. 1, 2003; Acts 2015, 84th Leg., ch. 368 (H.B. 3538), § 11, eff. July 1, 2015.

[1] V.T.C.A., Family Code § 159.601 et seq.

### § 159.208. Child Support Orders for Two or More Obligees

In responding to registrations or petitions for enforcement of two or more child support orders in effect at the same time with regard to the same obligor and different individual obligees, at least one of which was issued by a tribunal of another state or a foreign country, a tribunal of this state shall enforce those orders in the same manner as if the orders had been issued by a tribunal of this state.

Added by Acts 1995, 74th Leg., ch. 20, § 1, eff. April 20, 1995. Amended by Acts 2003, 78th Leg., ch. 1247, § 12, eff. Sept. 1, 2003; Acts 2015, 84th Leg., ch. 368 (H.B. 3538), § 12, eff. July 1, 2015.

### § 159.209. Credit for Payments

A tribunal of this state shall credit amounts collected for a particular period under any child support order against the amounts owed for the same period under any other child support order for support of the same child issued by a tribunal of this state, another state, or a foreign country.

Added by Acts 1995, 74th Leg., ch. 20, § 1, eff. April 20, 1995. Amended by Acts 2003, 78th Leg., ch. 1247, § 12, eff. Sept. 1, 2003; Acts 2015, 84th Leg., ch. 368 (H.B. 3538), § 13, eff. July 1, 2015.

### § 159.210. Application of Chapter to Nonresident Subject to Personal Jurisdiction

A tribunal of this state exercising personal jurisdiction over a nonresident in a proceeding under this chapter or under other law of this state relating to a support order or recognizing a foreign support order may receive evidence from outside this state as provided by Section 159.316, communicate with a tribunal outside this state as provided by Section 159.317, and obtain discovery through a tribunal outside this state as provided by Section 159.318. In all other respects, Subchapters D, E, F, and G do not apply and the tribunal shall apply the procedural and substantive law of this state.

Added by Acts 2003, 78th Leg., ch. 1247, § 12, eff. Sept. 1, 2003. Amended by Acts 2015, 84th Leg., ch. 368 (H.B. 3538), § 14, eff. July 1, 2015.

### § 159.211. Continuing, Exclusive Jurisdiction to Modify Spousal Support Order

(a) A tribunal of this state issuing a spousal support order consistent with the law of this state has continuing, exclusive jurisdiction to modify the spousal support order throughout the existence of the support obligation.

(b) A tribunal of this state may not modify a spousal support order issued by a tribunal of another state or a foreign country having continuing, exclusive jurisdiction over that order under the law of that state or foreign country.

(c) A tribunal of this state that has continuing, exclusive jurisdiction over a spousal support order may serve as:

(1) an initiating tribunal to request a tribunal of another state to enforce the spousal support order issued in this state; or

(2) a responding tribunal to enforce or modify its own spousal support order.

Added by Acts 2003, 78th Leg., ch. 1247, § 12, eff. Sept. 1, 2003. Amended by Acts 2015, 84th Leg., ch. 368 (H.B. 3538), § 15, eff. July 1, 2015.

## SUBCHAPTER D. CIVIL PROVISIONS OF GENERAL APPLICATION

### § 159.301. Proceedings Under Chapter

(a) Except as otherwise provided in this chapter, this subchapter applies to all proceedings under this chapter.

(b) Repealed by Acts 2003, 78th Leg., ch. 1247, § 46.

(c) An individual petitioner or a support enforcement agency may initiate a proceeding authorized under this chapter by filing a petition in an initiating tribunal for forwarding to a responding tribunal or by filing a petition or a comparable pleading directly in a tribunal of another state or foreign country that has or can obtain personal jurisdiction over the respondent.

Added by Acts 1995, 74th Leg., ch. 20, § 1, eff. April 20, 1995. Amended by Acts 1997, 75th Leg., ch. 607, § 6, eff. Sept. 1, 1997; Acts 2003, 78th Leg., ch. 1247, §§ 13, 46, eff. Sept. 1, 2003; Acts 2015, 84th Leg., ch. 368 (H.B. 3538), § 16, eff. July 1, 2015.

### § 159.302. Proceeding by Minor Parent

A minor parent or a guardian or other legal representative of a minor parent may maintain a proceeding on behalf of or for the benefit of the minor's child.

Added by Acts 1995, 74th Leg., ch. 20, § 1, eff. April 20, 1995. Amended by Acts 2003, 78th Leg., ch. 1247, § 14, eff. Sept. 1, 2003.

### § 159.303. Application of Law of State

Except as otherwise provided in this chapter, a responding tribunal of this state shall:

(1) apply the procedural and substantive law generally applicable to similar proceedings originating in this state and may exercise all powers and provide all remedies available in those proceedings; and

(2) determine the duty of support and the amount payable in accordance with the law and support guidelines of this state.

Added by Acts 1995, 74th Leg., ch. 20, § 1, eff. April 20, 1995. Amended by Acts 1997; 75th Leg., ch. 607, § 7, eff. Sept. 1, 1997; Acts 2003, 78th Leg., ch. 1247, § 15, eff. Sept. 1, 2003.

### § 159.304. Duties of Initiating Tribunal

(a) On the filing of a petition authorized by this chapter, an initiating tribunal of this state shall forward the petition and its accompanying documents:

(1) to the responding tribunal or appropriate support enforcement agency in the responding state; or

(2) if the identity of the responding tribunal is unknown, to the state information agency of the responding state with a request that they be forwarded to the appropriate tribunal and that receipt be acknowledged.

(b) If requested by the responding tribunal, a tribunal of this state shall issue a certificate or other document and make findings required by the law of the responding state. If the responding tribunal is in a foreign country, on request the tribunal of this state shall specify the amount of support sought, convert that amount into the equivalent amount in the foreign currency under the applicable official or market exchange rate as publicly reported, and provide any other documents necessary to satisfy the requirements of the responding foreign tribunal.

Added by Acts 1995, 74th Leg., ch. 20, § 1, eff. April 20, 1995. Amended by Acts 1997, 75th Leg., ch. 607, § 8, eff. Sept. 1, 1997; Acts 2003, 78th Leg., ch. 1247, § 15, eff. Sept. 1, 2003; Acts 2015, 84th Leg., ch. 368 (H.B. 3538), § 17, eff. July 1, 2015.

### § 159.305. Duties and Powers of Responding Tribunal

(a) When a responding tribunal of this state receives a petition or comparable pleading from an initiating tribunal or directly under Section 159.301(c), the responding tribunal shall cause the petition or pleading to be filed and notify the petitioner where and when it was filed.

(b) A responding tribunal of this state, to the extent not prohibited by other law, may do one or more of the following:

(1) establish or enforce a support order, modify a child support order, determine the controlling child support order, or determine parentage of a child;

(2) order an obligor to comply with a support order, specifying the amount and the manner of compliance;

(3) order income withholding;

(4) determine the amount of any arrearages and specify a method of payment;

(5) enforce orders by civil or criminal contempt, or both;

(6) set aside property for satisfaction of the support order;

(7) place liens and order execution on the obligor's property;

(8) order an obligor to keep the tribunal informed of the obligor's current residential address, electronic mail address, telephone number, employer, address of employment, and telephone number at the place of employment;

(9) issue a bench warrant or capias for an obligor who has failed after proper notice to appear at a hearing ordered by the tribunal and enter the bench warrant or capias in any local and state computer systems for criminal warrants;

(10) order the obligor to seek appropriate employment by specified methods;

(11) award reasonable attorney's fees and other fees and costs; and

(12) grant any other available remedy.

(c) A responding tribunal of this state shall include in a support order issued under this chapter, or in the documents accompanying the order, the calculations on which the support order is based.

(d) A responding tribunal of this state may not condition the payment of a support order issued under this chapter on compliance by a party with provisions for visitation.

(e) If a responding tribunal of this state issues an order under this chapter, the tribunal shall send a copy of the order to the petitioner and the respondent and to the initiating tribunal, if any.

(f) If requested to enforce a support order, arrears, or judgment or modify a support order stated in a foreign currency, a responding tribunal of this state shall convert the amount stated in the foreign currency to the equivalent amount in dollars under the applicable official or market exchange rate as publicly reported.

Added by Acts 1995, 74th Leg., ch. 20, § 1, eff. April 20, 1995. Amended by Acts 1997, 75th Leg., ch. 607, § 9, eff. Sept. 1, 1997; Acts 2003, 78th Leg., ch. 1247, § 16, eff. Sept. 1, 2003; Acts 2015, 84th Leg., ch. 368 (H.B. 3538), § 18, eff. July 1, 2015.

### § 159.306. Inappropriate Tribunal

If a petition or comparable pleading is received by an inappropriate tribunal of this state, that tribunal shall forward the pleading and accompanying documents to an appropriate tribunal in this state or another state and notify the petitioner where and when the pleading was sent.

Added by Acts 1995, 74th Leg., ch. 20, § 1, eff. April 20, 1995. Amended by Acts 1997, 75th Leg., ch. 607, § 10, eff. Sept. 1, 1997.

### § 159.307. Duties of Support Enforcement Agency

(a) A support enforcement agency of this state, on request, shall provide services to a petitioner in a proceeding under this chapter.

(b) A support enforcement agency of this state that is providing services to the petitioner shall:

(1) take all steps necessary to enable an appropriate tribunal of this state, another state, or a foreign country to obtain jurisdiction over the respondent;

(2) request an appropriate tribunal to set a date, time, and place for a hearing;

(3) make a reasonable effort to obtain all relevant information, including information as to income and property of the parties;

(4) within two days, exclusive of Saturdays, Sundays, and legal holidays, after receipt of notice in a record from an initiating, responding, or registering tribunal, send a copy of the notice to the petitioner;

(5) within two days, exclusive of Saturdays, Sundays, and legal holidays, after receipt of communication in a record from the respondent or the respondent's attorney, send a copy of the communication to the petitioner; and

(6) notify the petitioner if jurisdiction over the respondent cannot be obtained.

(c) A support enforcement agency of this state that requests registration of a child support order in this state for enforcement or for modification shall make reasonable efforts:

(1) to ensure that the order to be registered is the controlling order; or

(2) if two or more child support orders exist and the identity of the controlling order has not been determined, to ensure that a request for such a determination is made in a tribunal having jurisdiction to do so.

(d) A support enforcement agency of this state that requests registration and enforcement of a support order, arrears, or a judgment stated in a foreign currency shall convert the amount stated in the foreign currency into the equivalent amount in dollars under the applicable official or market exchange rate as publicly reported.

(e) A support enforcement agency of this state shall issue, or request a tribunal of this state to issue, a child support order and an income-withholding order that redirects payment of current support, arrears, and interest if requested to do so by a support enforcement agency of another state under Section 159.319.

(f) This chapter does not create or negate a relationship of attorney and client or other fiduciary relationship between a support enforcement agency or the attorney for the agency and the individual being assisted by the agency.

Added by Acts 1995, 74th Leg., ch. 20, § 1, eff. April 20, 1995. Amended by Acts 1997, 75th Leg., ch. 607, § 11, eff. Sept. 1, 1997; Acts 2003, 78th Leg., ch. 1247, § 17, eff. Sept. 1, 2003; Acts 2015, 84th Leg., ch. 368 (H.B. 3538), § 19, eff. July 1, 2015.

### § 159.308. Duty of Attorney General and Governor

(a) If the attorney general determines that the support enforcement agency is neglecting or refusing to provide services to an individual, the attorney general may order the agency to perform its duties under this chapter or may provide those services directly to the individual.

(b) The governor may determine that a foreign country has established a reciprocal arrangement for child support with this state and take appropriate action for notification of the determination.

Added by Acts 1995, 74th Leg., ch. 20, § 1, eff. April 20, 1995. Amended by Acts 2003, 78th Leg., ch. 1247, § 18, eff. Sept. 1, 2003; Acts 2015, 84th Leg., ch. 368 (H.B. 3538), §§ 20, 21, eff. July 1, 2015.

### § 159.309. Private Counsel

An individual may employ private counsel to represent the individual in proceedings authorized by this chapter.

Added by Acts 1995, 74th Leg., ch. 20, § 1, eff. April 20, 1995.

### § 159.310. Duties of State Information Agency

(a) The Title IV–D agency is the state information agency under this chapter.

(b) The state information agency shall:

(1) compile and maintain a current list, including addresses, of the tribunals in this state that have jurisdiction under this chapter and any support enforcement agencies in this state and transmit a copy to the state information agency of every other state;

(2) maintain a register of names and addresses of tribunals and support enforcement agencies received from other states;

(3) forward to the appropriate tribunal in the county in this state in which the obligee who is an individual or the obligor resides, or in which the obligor's property is believed to be located, all documents concerning a proceeding under this chapter received from another state or a foreign country; and

(4) obtain information concerning the location of the obligor and the obligor's property in this state not exempt from execution, by such means as postal verification and federal or state locator services, examination of telephone directories, requests for the obligor's address from employers, and examination of governmental records, including, to the extent not prohibited by other law, those relating to real property, vital statistics, law enforcement, taxation, motor vehicles, driver's licenses, and social security.

Added by Acts 1995, 74th Leg., ch. 20, § 1, eff. April 20, 1995. Amended by Acts 2003, 78th Leg., ch. 1247, § 19, eff. Sept. 1, 2003; Acts 2015, 84th Leg., ch. 368 (H.B. 3538), § 22, eff. July 1, 2015.

### § 159.311. Pleadings and Accompanying Documents

(a) In a proceeding under this chapter, a petitioner seeking to establish a support order, to determine parentage of a child, or to register and modify a support order of a tribunal of another state or foreign country must file a petition. Unless otherwise ordered under Section 159.312, the petition or accompanying documents must provide, so far as known, the name, residential address, and social security numbers of the obligor and the obligee or the parent and alleged parent, and the name, sex, residential address, social security number, and date of birth of each child for whose benefit support is sought or whose parentage is to be determined. Unless filed at the time of registration, the petition must be accompanied by a copy of any support order known to have been issued by another tribunal. The petition may include any other information that may assist in locating or identifying the respondent.

(b) The petition must specify the relief sought. The petition and accompanying documents must conform substantially with the requirements imposed by the forms mandated by federal law for use in cases filed by a support enforcement agency.

Added by Acts 1995, 74th Leg., ch. 20, § 1, eff. April 20, 1995. Amended by Acts 2003, 78th Leg., ch. 1247, § 20, eff. Sept. 1, 2003; Acts 2015, 84th Leg., ch. 368 (H.B. 3538), § 23, eff. July 1, 2015.

### § 159.312. Nondisclosure of Information in Exceptional Circumstances

If a party alleges in an affidavit or pleading under oath that the health, safety, or liberty of a party or child would be jeopardized by disclosure of specific identifying information, that information must be sealed and may not be disclosed to the other party or the public. After a hearing in which a tribunal takes into consideration the health, safety, or liberty of the party or child, the tribunal may order disclosure of information that the tribunal determines to be in the interest of justice.

Added by Acts 1995, 74th Leg., ch. 20, § 1, eff. April 20, 1995. Amended by Acts 2003, 78th Leg., ch. 1247, § 21, eff. Sept. 1, 2003; Acts 2015, 84th Leg., ch. 368 (H.B. 3538), § 24, eff. July 1, 2015.

### § 159.313. Costs and Fees

(a) The petitioner may not be required to pay a filing fee or other costs.

(b) If an obligee prevails, a responding tribunal of this state may assess against an obligor filing fees, reasonable attorney's fees, other costs, and necessary travel and other reasonable expenses incurred by the obligee and the obligee's witnesses. The tribunal may not assess fees, costs, or expenses against the obligee or the support enforcement agency of either the initiating or responding state or foreign country, except as provided by other law. Attorney's fees may be taxed as costs, and may be ordered paid directly to the attorney, who may enforce the order in the attorney's own name. Payment of support owed to the obligee has priority over fees, costs, and expenses.

(c) The tribunal shall order the payment of costs and reasonable attorney's fees if it determines that a hearing was requested primarily for delay. In a proceeding under Subchapter G, a hearing is presumed to have been requested primarily for delay if a registered support order is confirmed or enforced without change.

Added by Acts 1995, 74th Leg., ch. 20, § 1, eff. April 20, 1995. Amended by Acts 1997, 75th Leg., ch. 607, § 12, eff. Sept. 1, 1997; Acts 2015, 84th Leg., ch. 368 (H.B. 3538), § 25, eff. July 1, 2015.

### § 159.314. Limited Immunity of Petitioner

(a) Participation by a petitioner in a proceeding under this chapter before a responding tribunal, whether in person, by private attorney, or through services provided by the support enforcement agency, does not confer personal jurisdiction over the petitioner in another proceeding.

(b) A petitioner is not amenable to service of civil process while physically present in this state to participate in a proceeding under this chapter.

(c) The immunity granted by this section does not extend to civil litigation based on acts unrelated to a proceeding under this chapter committed by a party while physically present in this state to participate in the proceeding.

Added by Acts 1995, 74th Leg., ch. 20, § 1, eff. April 20, 1995. Amended by Acts 2003, 78th Leg., ch. 1247, § 22, eff. Sept. 1, 2003; Acts 2015, 84th Leg., ch. 368 (H.B. 3538), § 26, eff. July 1, 2015.

### § 159.315. Nonparentage as Defense

A party whose parentage of a child has been previously determined by or under law may not plead nonparentage as a defense to a proceeding under this chapter.

Added by Acts 1995, 74th Leg., ch. 20, § 1, eff. April 20, 1995.

### § 159.316. Special Rules of Evidence and Procedure

(a) The physical presence of a nonresident party who is an individual in a tribunal of this state is not required for the establishment, enforcement, or modification of a support order or the rendition of a judgment determining parentage of a child.

(b) An affidavit, a document substantially complying with federally mandated forms, or a document incorporated by reference in an affidavit or document, that would not be excluded under the hearsay rule if given in person, is admissible in evidence if given under penalty of perjury by a party or witness residing outside this state.

(c) A copy of the record of child support payments certified as a true copy of the original by the custodian of the record may be forwarded to a responding tribunal. The copy is evidence of facts asserted in it and is admissible to show whether payments were made.

(d) Copies of bills for testing for parentage of a child, and for prenatal and postnatal health care of the mother and child furnished to the adverse party at least 10 days before trial are admissible in evidence to prove the amount of the charges billed and that the charges were reasonable, necessary, and customary.

(e) Documentary evidence transmitted from outside this state to a tribunal of this state by telephone, telecopier, or other electronic means that does not provide an original record may not be excluded from evidence on an objection based on the means of transmission.

(f) In a proceeding under this chapter, a tribunal of this state shall permit a party or witness residing outside this state to be deposed or to testify under penalty of perjury by telephone, audiovisual means, or other electronic means at a designated tribunal or other location. A tribunal of this state shall cooperate with other tribunals in designating an appropriate location for the deposition or testimony.

(g) If a party called to testify at a civil hearing refuses to answer on the ground that the testimony may be self-incriminating, the trier of fact may draw an adverse inference from the refusal.

(h) A privilege against disclosure of communications between spouses does not apply in a proceeding under this chapter.

(i) The defense of immunity based on the relationship of husband and wife or parent and child does not apply in a proceeding under this chapter.

(j) A voluntary acknowledgment of paternity, certified as a true copy, is admissible to establish parentage of the child.

Added by Acts 1995, 74th Leg., ch. 20, § 1, eff. April 20, 1995. Amended by Acts 2003, 78th Leg., ch. 1247, § 23, eff. Sept. 1, 2003; Acts 2005, 79th Leg., ch. 344, § 1, eff. June 17, 2005; Acts 2015, 84th Leg., ch. 368 (H.B. 3538), § 27, eff. July 1, 2015.

### § 159.317. Communications Between Tribunals

A tribunal of this state may communicate with a tribunal outside this state in a record or by telephone, electronic mail, or by other means, to obtain information concerning the laws, the legal effect of a judgment, decree, or order of that tribunal, and the status of a proceeding. A tribunal of this state may furnish similar information by similar means to a tribunal outside this state.

Added by Acts 1995, 74th Leg., ch. 20, § 1, eff. April 20, 1995. Amended by Acts 2003, 78th Leg., ch. 1247, § 24, eff. Sept. 1, 2003; Acts 2015, 84th Leg., ch. 368 (H.B. 3538), § 28, eff. July 1, 2015.

### § 159.318. Assistance With Discovery

A tribunal of this state may:

(1) request a tribunal outside this state to assist in obtaining discovery; and

(2) on request, compel a person over whom the tribunal has jurisdiction to respond to a discovery order issued by a tribunal outside this state.

Added by Acts 1995, 74th Leg., ch. 20, § 1, eff. April 20, 1995. Amended by Acts 2015, 84th Leg., ch. 368 (H.B. 3538), § 29, eff. July 1, 2015.

### § 159.319. Receipt and Disbursement of Payments

(a) A support enforcement agency or tribunal of this state shall disburse promptly any amounts received under a support order, as directed by the order. The agency or tribunal shall furnish to a requesting party or tribunal of another state or a foreign country a certified statement by the custodian of the record of the amounts and dates of all payments received.

(b) If the obligor, the obligee who is an individual, and the child do not reside in this state, on request from the support enforcement agency of this state or another state, the support enforcement agency of this state or a tribunal of this state shall:

(1) direct that the support payment be made to the support enforcement agency in the state in which the obligee is receiving services; and

(2) issue and send to the obligor's employer a conforming income-withholding order or an administrative notice of change of payee reflecting the redirected payments.

(c) The support enforcement agency of this state on receiving redirected payments from another state under a law similar to Subsection (b) shall provide to a requesting party or a tribunal of the other state a certified statement by the custodian of the record of the amount and dates of all payments received.

Added by Acts 1995, 74th Leg., ch. 20, § 1, eff. April 20, 1995. Amended by Acts 2003, 78th Leg., ch. 1247, § 25, eff. Sept. 1, 2003; Acts 2015, 84th Leg., ch. 368 (H.B. 3538), § 30, eff. July 1, 2015.

## SUBCHAPTER E. ESTABLISHMENT OF SUPPORT ORDER OR DETERMINATION OF PARENTAGE

### § 159.401. Establishment of Support Order

(a) If a support order entitled to recognition under this chapter has not been issued, a responding tribunal of this state with personal jurisdiction over the parties may issue a support order if:

(1) the individual seeking the order resides outside this state; or

(2) the support enforcement agency seeking the order is located outside this state.

(b) The tribunal may issue a temporary child support order if the tribunal determines that such an order is appropriate and the individual ordered to pay is:

(1) a presumed father of the child;

(2) petitioning to have his paternity adjudicated;

(3) identified as the father of the child through genetic testing;

(4) an alleged father who has declined to submit to genetic testing;

(5) shown by clear and convincing evidence to be the father of the child;

(6) an acknowledged father as provided by applicable state law;

(7) the mother of the child; or

(8) an individual who has been ordered to pay child support in a previous proceeding and the order has not been reversed or vacated.

(c) On finding, after notice and an opportunity to be heard, that an obligor owes a duty of support, the tribunal shall issue a support order directed to the obligor and may issue other orders under Section 159.305.

Added by Acts 1995, 74th Leg., ch. 20, § 1, eff. April 20, 1995. Amended by Acts 2003, 78th Leg., ch. 1247, § 26, eff. Sept. 1, 2003; Acts 2015, 84th Leg., ch. 368 (H.B. 3538), § 32, eff. July 1, 2015.

### § 159.402. Proceeding to Determine Parentage

A tribunal of this state authorized to determine parentage of a child may serve as a responding tribunal in a proceeding to determine parentage of a child brought under this chapter or a law or procedure substantially similar to this chapter.

Added by Acts 2015, 84th Leg., ch. 368 (H.B. 3538), § 33, eff. July 1, 2015.

## SUBCHAPTER F. ENFORCEMENT OF SUPPORT ORDER WITHOUT REGISTRATION

### § 159.501. Employer's Receipt of Income–Withholding Order of Another State

An income-withholding order issued in another state may be sent by or on behalf of the obligee or by the support enforcement agency to the person defined as the obligor's employer under Chapter 158 without first filing a petition or comparable pleading or registering the order with a tribunal of this state.

Added by Acts 1995, 74th Leg., ch. 20, § 1, eff. April 20, 1995. Renumbered from V.T.C.A., Family Code § 159.501(a) and amended by Acts 1997, 75th Leg., ch. 607, § 13, eff. Sept. 1, 1997; Acts 2003, 78th Leg., ch. 1247, § 27, eff. Sept. 1, 2003.

### § 159.502. Employer's Compliance with Income-Withholding Order of Another State

(a) On receipt of an income-withholding order, the obligor's employer shall immediately provide a copy of the order to the obligor.

(b) The employer shall treat an income-withholding order issued in another state that appears regular on its face as if the order had been issued by a tribunal of this state.

(c) Except as otherwise provided in Subsection (d) and Section 159.503, the employer shall withhold and distribute the funds as directed in the withholding order by complying with terms of the order that specify:

(1) the duration and amount of periodic payments of current child support, stated as a sum certain;

(2) the person designated to receive payments and the address to which the payments are to be forwarded;

(3) medical support and dental support, whether in the form of periodic cash payments, stated as a sum certain, or ordering the obligor to provide health insurance coverage or dental insurance coverage for the child under a policy available through the obligor's employment;

(4) the amount of periodic payments of fees and costs for a support enforcement agency, the issuing tribunal, and the obligee's attorney, stated as sums certain; and

(5) the amount of periodic payments of arrearages and interest on arrearages, stated as sums certain.

(d) An employer shall comply with the law of the state of the obligor's principal place of employment for withholding from income with respect to:

(1) the employer's fee for processing an income-withholding order;

(2) the maximum amount permitted to be withheld from the obligor's income; and

(3) the times within which the employer must implement the withholding order and forward the child support payment.

Added by Acts 1995, 74th Leg., ch. 20, § 1, eff. April 20, 1995. Renumbered from V.T.C.A., Family Code § 159.501(a) and amended by Acts 1997, 75th Leg., ch. 607, § 13, eff. Sept. 1, 1997; Acts 2003, 78th Leg., ch. 1247, § 28, eff. Sept. 1, 2003. Amended by Acts 2015, 84th Leg., ch. 1150 (S.B. 550), § 39, eff. Sept. 1, 2018.

### § 159.503. Employer's Compliance with Two or More Income–Withholding Orders

If an obligor's employer receives two or more income-withholding orders with respect to the earnings of the same obligor, the employer satisfies the terms of the orders if the employer complies with the law of the state of the obligor's principal place of employment to establish the priorities for withholding and allocating income withheld for two or more child support obligees.

Added by Acts 1997, 75th Leg., ch. 607, § 13, eff. Sept. 1, 1997. Amended by Acts 2003, 78th Leg., ch. 1247, § 29, eff. Sept. 1, 2003.

### § 159.504. Immunity From Civil Liability

An employer who complies with an income-withholding order issued in another state in accordance with this subchapter is not subject to civil liability to an individual or agency with regard to the employer's withholding of child support from the obligor's income.

Added by Acts 1997, 75th Leg., ch. 607, § 13, eff. Sept. 1, 1997.

### § 159.505. Penalties for Noncompliance

An employer who wilfully fails to comply with an income-withholding order issued by another state and received for enforcement is subject to the same penalties that may be imposed for noncompliance with an order issued by a tribunal of this state.

Added by Acts 1997, 75th Leg., ch. 607, § 13, eff. Sept. 1, 1997.

### § 159.506. Contest by Obligor

(a) An obligor may contest the validity or enforcement of an income-withholding order issued in another state and received directly by an employer in this state by registering the order in a tribunal of this state and filing a contest to that order as provided in Subchapter G[1] or otherwise contesting the order in the same manner as if the order had been issued by a tribunal of this state.

(b) The obligor shall give notice of the contest to:

(1) a support enforcement agency providing services to the obligee;

(2) each employer that has directly received an income-withholding order relating to the obligor; and

(3) the person designated to receive payments in the income-withholding order or, if no person is designated, to the obligee.

Added by Acts 1995, 74th Leg., ch. 20, § 1, eff. April 20, 1995. Renumbered from V.T.C.A., Family Code, § 159.501(b) and amended by Acts 1997, 75th Leg., ch. 607, § 13, eff. Sept. 1, 1997. Amended by Acts 2003, 78th Leg., ch. 1247, § 30, eff. Sept. 1, 2003; Acts 2015, 84th Leg., ch. 368 (H.B. 3538), § 35, eff. July 1, 2015.

[1] V.T.C.A., Family Code § 159.601 et seq.

### § 159.507. Administrative Enforcement of Orders

(a) A party or support enforcement agency seeking to enforce a support order or an income-withholding order, or both, issued in another state or a foreign support order may send the documents required for registering the order to a support enforcement agency of this state.

(b) On receipt of the documents, the support enforcement agency, without initially seeking to register the order, shall consider and, if appropriate, use any administrative procedure authorized by the law of this state to enforce a support order or an income-withholding order, or both. If the obligor does not contest administrative enforcement, the order need not be registered. If the obligor contests the validity or administrative enforcement of the order, the support enforcement agency shall register the order under this chapter.

Added by Acts 1995, 74th Leg., ch. 20, § 1, eff. April 20, 1995. Renumbered from V.T.C.A., Family Code § 159.502 and amended by Acts 1997, 75th Leg., ch. 607, § 13, eff. Sept. 1, 1997. Amended by Acts 2003, 78th Leg., ch. 1247, § 31, eff. Sept. 1, 2003; Acts 2015, 84th Leg., ch. 368 (H.B. 3538), § 36, eff. July 1, 2015.

## SUBCHAPTER G. REGISTRATION, ENFORCEMENT, AND MODIFICATION OF SUPPORT ORDER

## PART 1. REGISTRATION FOR ENFORCEMENT OF SUPPORT ORDER

### § 159.601. Registration of Order for Enforcement

A support order or income-withholding order issued in another state or a foreign support order may be registered in this state for enforcement.

Added by Acts 1995, 74th Leg., ch. 20, § 1, eff. April 20, 1995. Amended by Acts 2015, 84th Leg., ch. 368 (H.B. 3538), § 38, eff. July 1, 2015.

### § 159.602. Procedure to Register Order for Enforcement

(a) Except as otherwise provided by Section 159.706, a support order or income-withholding order of another state or a foreign support order may be registered in this state by sending the following records to the appropriate tribunal in this state:

(1) a letter of transmittal to the tribunal requesting registration and enforcement;

(2) two copies, including one certified copy, of the order to be registered, including any modification of the order;

(3) a sworn statement by the person requesting registration or a certified statement by the custodian of the records showing the amount of any arrearage;

(4) the name of the obligor and, if known:

(A) the obligor's address and social security number;

(B) the name and address of the obligor's employer and any other source of income of the obligor; and

(C) a description of and the location of property of the obligor in this state not exempt from execution; and

(5) except as otherwise provided by Section 159.312, the name and address of the obligee and, if applicable, the person to whom support payments are to be remitted.

(b) On receipt of a request for registration, the registering tribunal shall cause the order to be filed as an order of a tribunal of another state or a foreign support order, together with one copy of the documents and information, regardless of their form.

(c) A petition or comparable pleading seeking a remedy that must be affirmatively sought under other law of this state may be filed at the same time as the request for registration or later. The pleading must specify the grounds for the remedy sought.

(d) If two or more orders are in effect, the person requesting registration shall:

(1) furnish to the tribunal a copy of each support order asserted to be in effect in addition to the documents specified in this section;

(2) specify the order alleged to be the controlling order, if any; and

(3) specify the amount of consolidated arrears, if any.

(e) A request for a determination of which order is the controlling order may be filed separately from or with a request for registration and enforcement or for registration and modification. The person requesting registration shall give notice of the request to each party whose rights may be affected by the determination.

Added by Acts 1995, 74th Leg., ch. 20, § 1, eff. April 20, 1995. Amended by Acts 2001, 77th Leg., ch. 296, § 3, eff. Sept. 1, 2001; Acts 2003, 78th Leg., ch. 1247, § 33, eff. Sept. 1, 2003; Acts 2015, 84th Leg., ch. 368 (H.B. 3538), § 39, eff. July 1, 2015.

### § 159.603. Effect of Registration for Enforcement

(a) A support order or income-withholding order issued in another state or a foreign support order is registered when the order is filed in the registering tribunal of this state.

(b) A registered support order issued in another state or a foreign country is enforceable in the same manner and is subject to the same procedures as an order issued by a tribunal of this state.

(c) Except as otherwise provided in this subchapter, a tribunal of this state shall recognize and enforce, but may not modify, a registered support order if the issuing tribunal had jurisdiction.

Added by Acts 1995, 74th Leg., ch. 20, § 1, eff. April 20, 1995. Amended by Acts 2015, 84th Leg., ch. 368 (H.B. 3538), § 40, eff. July 1, 2015.

### § 159.604. Choice of Law

(a) Except as otherwise provided by Subsection (d), the law of the issuing state or foreign country governs:

(1) the nature, extent, amount, and duration of current payments under a registered support order;

(2) the computation and payment of arrearages and accrual of interest on the arrearages under the support order; and

(3) the existence and satisfaction of other obligations under the support order.

(b) In a proceeding for arrears under a registered support order, the statute of limitation of this state, or of the issuing state or foreign country, whichever is longer, applies.

(c) A responding tribunal of this state shall apply the procedures and remedies of this state to enforce current support and collect arrears and interest due on a support order of another state or a foreign country registered in this state.

(d) After a tribunal of this state or another state determines which is the controlling order and issues an order consolidating arrears, if any, the tribunal of this state shall prospectively apply the law of the state or foreign country issuing the controlling order, including that state's or country's law on interest on arrears, on current and future support, and on consolidated arrears.

Added by Acts 1995, 74th Leg., ch. 20, § 1, eff. April 20, 1995. Amended by Acts 1997, 75th Leg., ch. 607, § 14, eff. Sept. 1, 1997; Acts 2003, 78th Leg., ch. 1247, § 34, eff. Sept. 1, 2003; Acts 2015, 84th Leg., ch. 368 (H.B. 3538), § 41, eff. July 1, 2015.

## PART 2. CONTEST OF VALIDITY OR ENFORCEMENT

### § 159.605. Notice of Registration of Order

(a) When a support order or income-withholding order issued in another state or a foreign support order is registered, the registering tribunal of this state shall notify the nonregistering party. The notice must be accompanied by a copy of the registered order and the documents and relevant information accompanying the order.

(b) A notice must inform the nonregistering party:

(1) that a registered order is enforceable as of the date of registration in the same manner as an order issued by a tribunal of this state;

(2) that a hearing to contest the validity or enforcement of the registered order must be requested within 30 days after notice unless the registered order is under Section 159.707;

(3) that failure to contest the validity or enforcement of the registered order in a timely manner will result in confirmation of the order and enforcement of the order and the alleged arrearages; and

(4) of the amount of any alleged arrearages.

(c) If the registering party asserts that two or more orders are in effect, the notice must also:

(1) identify the two or more orders and the order alleged by the registering party to be the controlling order and the consolidated arrears, if any;

(2) notify the nonregistering party of the right to a determination of which is the controlling order;

(3) state that the procedures provided in Subsection (b) apply to the determination of which is the controlling order; and

(4) state that failure to contest the validity or enforcement of the order alleged to be the controlling order in a timely manner may result in confirmation that the order is the controlling order.

(d) On registration of an income-withholding order for enforcement, the support enforcement agency or the registering tribunal shall notify the obligor's employer under Chapter 158.

Added by Acts 1995, 74th Leg., ch. 20, § 1, eff. April 20, 1995. Amended by Acts 1997, 75th Leg., ch. 607, § 15, eff. Sept. 1, 1997; Acts 2003, 78th Leg., ch. 1247, § 35, eff. Sept. 1, 2003; Acts 2015, 84th Leg., ch. 368 (H.B. 3538), § 43, eff. July 1, 2015; Acts 2021, 87th Leg., ch. 552 (S.B. 286), § 9, eff. Sept. 1, 2021.

Section 12 of Acts 2021, 87th Leg., ch. 552 (S.B. 286) provides:

"The enactment of this Act does not constitute a material and substantial change of circumstances sufficient to warrant modification of a court order or portion of a decree that provides for the support of a child rendered before the effective date [Sept. 1, 2021] of this Act."

Section 18 of Acts 2021, 87th Leg., ch. 552 (S.B. 286) provides:

"Section 159.605, Family Code, as amended by this Act, applies only to a support order or income-withholding order issued by a court of another state that is registered in this state on or after the effective date [Sept. 1, 2021] of this Act. A support order or income-withholding order that is registered in this state before the effective date of this Act is governed by the law in effect on the date the order was registered, and the former law is continued in effect for that purpose."

### § 159.606. Procedure to Contest Validity or Enforcement of Registered Support Order

(a) A nonregistering party seeking to contest the validity or enforcement of a registered support order in this state shall request a hearing within the time required by Section 159.605. The nonregistering party may seek to vacate the registration, to assert any defense to an allegation of noncompliance with the registered order, or to contest the remedies being sought or the amount of any alleged arrearages under Section 159.607.

(b) If the nonregistering party fails to contest the validity or enforcement of the registered support order in a timely manner, the order is confirmed by operation of law.

(c) If a nonregistering party requests a hearing to contest the validity or enforcement of the registered support order, the registering tribunal shall schedule the matter for hearing and give notice to the parties of the date, time, and place of the hearing.

Added by Acts 1995, 74th Leg., ch. 20, § 1, eff. April 20, 1995. Amended by Acts 1997, 75th Leg., ch. 607, § 16, eff. Sept. 1, 1997; Acts 2015, 84th Leg., ch. 368 (H.B. 3538), § 44, eff. July 1, 2015.

### § 159.607. Contest of Registration or Enforcement

(a) A party contesting the validity or enforcement of a registered support order or seeking to vacate the registration has the burden of proving one or more of the following defenses:

(1) the issuing tribunal lacked personal jurisdiction over the contesting party;

(2) the order was obtained by fraud;

(3) the order has been vacated, suspended, or modified by a later order;

(4) the issuing tribunal has stayed the order pending appeal;

(5) there is a defense under the law of this state to the remedy sought;

(6) full or partial payment has been made;

(7) the statute of limitation under Section 159.604 precludes enforcement of some or all of the alleged arrearages; or

(8) the alleged controlling order is not the controlling order.

(b) If a party presents evidence establishing a full or partial defense under Subsection (a), a tribunal may stay enforcement of the registered support order, continue the proceeding to permit production of additional relevant evidence, and issue other appropriate orders. An uncontested portion of the registered support order may be enforced by all remedies available under the law of this state.

(c) If the contesting party does not establish a defense under Subsection (a) to the validity or enforcement of the registered support order, the registering tribunal shall issue an order confirming the order.

Added by Acts 1995, 74th Leg., ch. 20, § 1, eff. April 20, 1995. Amended by Acts 2003, 78th Leg., ch. 1247, § 36, eff. Sept. 1, 2003; Acts 2015, 84th Leg., ch. 368 (H.B. 3538), § 45, eff. July 1, 2015.

### § 159.608. Confirmed Order

Confirmation of a registered support order, whether by operation of law or after notice and hearing, precludes further contest of the order with respect to any matter that could have been asserted at the time of registration.

Added by Acts 1995, 74th Leg., ch. 20, § 1, eff. April 20, 1995. Amended by Acts 2015, 84th Leg., ch. 368 (H.B. 3538), § 46, eff. July 1, 2015.

## PART 3. REGISTRATION AND MODIFICATION OF CHILD SUPPORT ORDER OF ANOTHER STATE

### § 159.609. Procedure to Register Child Support Order of Another State for Modification

A party or support enforcement agency seeking to modify, or to modify and enforce, a child support order issued in another state shall register that order in this state in the same manner provided in Sections 159.601 through 159.608 if the order has not been registered. A petition for modification may be filed at the same time as a request for registration, or later. The pleading must specify the grounds for modification.

Added by Acts 1995, 74th Leg., ch. 20, § 1, eff. April 20, 1995. Amended by Acts 2015, 84th Leg., ch. 368 (H.B. 3538), § 48, eff. July 1, 2015.

### § 159.610. Effect of Registration for Modification

A tribunal of this state may enforce a child support order of another state registered for purposes of modification in the same manner as if the order had been issued by a tribunal of this state, but the registered support order may be modified only if the requirements of Section 159.611 or 159.613 have been met.

Added by Acts 1995, 74th Leg., ch. 20, § 1, eff. April 20, 1995. Amended by Acts 2003, 78th Leg., ch. 1247, § 37, eff. Sept. 1, 2003; Acts 2015, 84th Leg., ch. 368 (H.B. 3538), § 49, eff. July 1, 2015.

### § 159.611. Modification of Child Support Order of Another State

(a) If Section 159.613 does not apply, on petition a tribunal of this state may modify a child support order issued in another state that is registered in this state if, after notice and hearing, the tribunal finds that:

(1) the following requirements are met:

(A) the child, the obligee who is an individual, and the obligor do not reside in the issuing state;

(B) a petitioner who is a nonresident of this state seeks modification; and

(C) the respondent is subject to the personal jurisdiction of the tribunal of this state; or

(2) this state is the residence of the child, or a party who is an individual is subject to the personal jurisdiction of the tribunal of this state, and all of the parties who are individuals have filed consents in a record in the issuing tribunal for a tribunal of this state to modify the support order and assume continuing, exclusive jurisdiction.

(b) Modification of a registered child support order is subject to the same requirements, procedures, and defenses that apply to the modification of an order issued by a tribunal of this state, and the order may be enforced and satisfied in the same manner.

(c) A tribunal of this state may not modify any aspect of a child support order that may not be modified under the law of the issuing state, including the duration of the obligation of support. If two or more tribunals have issued child support orders for the same obligor and same child, the order that controls and must be so recognized under Section 159.207 establishes the aspects of the support order that are nonmodifiable.

(d) In a proceeding to modify a child support order, the law of the state that is determined to have issued the initial controlling order governs the duration of the obligation of support. The obligor's fulfillment of the duty of support established by that order precludes imposition of a further obligation of support by a tribunal of this state.

(e) On issuance of an order by a tribunal of this state modifying a child support order issued in another state, the tribunal of this state becomes the tribunal of continuing, exclusive jurisdiction.

(f) Notwithstanding Subsections (a) through (e) of this section and Section 159.201(b), a tribunal of this state retains jurisdiction to modify an order issued by a tribunal of this state if:

(1) one party resides in another state; and

(2) the other party resides outside the United States.

Added by Acts 1995, 74th Leg., ch. 20, § 1, eff. April 20, 1995. Amended by Acts 1997, 75th Leg., ch. 607, § 17, eff. Sept. 1, 1997; Acts 2001, 77th Leg., ch. 1420, § 5.0026, eff. Sept. 1, 2001; Acts 2003, 78th Leg., ch. 1247, § 38, eff. Sept. 1, 2003; Acts 2009, 81st Leg., ch. 767, § 21, eff. June 19, 2009; Acts 2015, 84th Leg., ch. 368 (H.B. 3538), § 50, eff. July 1, 2015.

### § 159.612. Recognition of Order Modified in Another State

If a child support order issued by a tribunal of this state is modified by a tribunal of another state that assumed jurisdiction under the Uniform Interstate Family Support Act, a tribunal of this state:

(1) may enforce the order that was modified only as to arrears and interest accruing before the modification;

(2) may provide appropriate relief for violations of the order that occurred before the effective date of the modification; and

(3) shall recognize the modifying order of the other state, on registration, for the purpose of enforcement.

Added by Acts 1995, 74th Leg., ch. 20, § 1, eff. April 20, 1995. Amended by Acts 2003, 78th Leg., ch. 1247, § 39, eff. Sept. 1, 2003; Acts 2015, 84th Leg., ch. 368 (H.B. 3538), § 51, eff. July 1, 2015.

### § 159.613. Jurisdiction to Modify Child Support Order of Another State When Individual Parties Reside in This State

(a) If all of the parties who are individuals reside in this state and the child does not reside in the issuing state, a tribunal of this state has jurisdiction to enforce and to modify the issuing state's child support order in a proceeding to register that order.

(b) A tribunal of this state exercising jurisdiction under this section shall apply the provisions of Subchapters B and C, this subchapter, and the procedural and substantive law of this state to the proceeding for enforcement or modification. Subchapters D, E, F, H, and I do not apply.

Added by Acts 1997, 75th Leg., ch. 607, § 18, eff. Sept. 1, 1997. Amended by Acts 2015, 84th Leg., ch. 368 (H.B. 3538), § 52, eff. July 1, 2015.

### § 159.614. Notice to Issuing Tribunal of Modification

Within 30 days after issuance of a modified child support order, the party obtaining the modification shall file a certified copy of the order with the issuing tribunal that had continuing, exclusive jurisdiction over the earlier order and in each tribunal in which the party knows the earlier order has been registered. A party who obtains the order and fails to file a certified copy is subject to appropriate sanctions by a tribunal in which the issue of failure to file arises. The failure to file does not affect the validity or enforceability of the modified order of the new tribunal having continuing, exclusive jurisdiction.

Added by Acts 1997, 75th Leg., ch. 607, § 18, eff. Sept. 1, 1997.

## PART 4. REGISTRATION AND MODIFICATION OF FOREIGN CHILD SUPPORT ORDER

### § 159.615. Jurisdiction to Modify Child Support Order of Foreign Country

(a) Except as otherwise provided by Section 159.711, if a foreign country lacks or refuses to exercise jurisdiction to modify its child support order pursuant to its laws, a tribunal of this state may assume jurisdiction to modify the child support order and bind all individuals subject to the personal jurisdiction of the tribunal regardless of whether the consent to modification of a child support order otherwise required of the individual under Section 159.611 has been given or whether the individual seeking modification is a resident of this state or of the foreign country.

(b) An order issued by a tribunal of this state modifying a foreign child support order under this section is the controlling order.

Added by Acts 2003, 78th Leg., ch. 1247, § 40, eff. Sept. 1, 2003. Amended by Acts 2015, 84th Leg., ch. 368 (H.B. 3538), § 54, eff. July 1, 2015.

### § 159.616. Procedure to Register Child Support Order of Foreign Country for Modification

A party or support enforcement agency seeking to modify, or to modify and enforce, a foreign child support order not under the Convention may register that order in this state under Sections 159.601 through 159.608 if the order has not been registered. A petition for modification may be filed at the same time as a request for registration or at another time. The petition must specify the grounds for modification.

Added by Acts 2015, 84th Leg., ch. 368 (H.B. 3538), § 55, eff. July 1, 2015.

## SUBCHAPTER H. SUPPORT PROCEEDING UNDER CONVENTION

### § 159.701. Definitions

In this subchapter:

(1) "Application" means a request under the Convention by an obligee or obligor, or on behalf of a

child, made through a central authority for assistance from another central authority.

(2) "Central authority" means the entity designated by the United States or a foreign country described in Section 159.102(5)(D) to perform the functions specified in the Convention.

(3) "Convention support order" means a support order of a tribunal of a foreign country described in Section 159.102(5)(D).

(4) "Direct request" means a petition filed by an individual in a tribunal of this state in a proceeding involving an obligee, obligor, or child residing outside the United States.

(5) "Foreign central authority" means the entity designated by a foreign country described in Section 159.102(5)(D) to perform the functions specified in the Convention.

(6) "Foreign support agreement":

(A) means an agreement for support in a record that:

(i) is enforceable as a support order in the country of origin;

(ii) has been:

(a) formally drawn up or registered as an authentic instrument by a foreign tribunal; or

(b) authenticated by, or concluded, registered, or filed with a foreign tribunal; and

(iii) may be reviewed and modified by a foreign tribunal; and

(B) includes a maintenance arrangement or authentic instrument under the Convention.

(7) "United States central authority" means the secretary of the United States Department of Health and Human Services.

Added by Acts 1995, 74th Leg., ch. 20, § 1, eff. April 20, 1995. Amended by Acts 2003, 78th Leg., ch. 1247, § 41, eff. Sept. 1, 2003; Acts 2015, 84th Leg., ch. 368 (H.B. 3538), § 57, eff. July 1, 2015.

### § 159.702. Applicability

This subchapter applies only to a support proceeding under the Convention. In such a proceeding, if a provision of this subchapter is inconsistent with Subchapters B through G, this subchapter controls.

Added by Acts 2015, 84th Leg., ch. 368 (H.B. 3538), § 58, eff. July 1, 2015.

### § 159.703. Relationship of Office of Attorney General to United States Central Authority

The office of the attorney general of this state is recognized as the agency designated by the United States central authority to perform specific functions under the Convention.

Added by Acts 2015, 84th Leg., ch. 368 (H.B. 3538), § 58, eff. July 1, 2015.

### § 159.704. Initiation by Office of Attorney General of Support Proceeding Under Convention

(a) In a support proceeding under this subchapter, the office of the attorney general of this state shall:

(1) transmit and receive applications; and

(2) initiate or facilitate the institution of a proceeding regarding an application in a tribunal of this state.

(b) The following support proceedings are available to an obligee under the Convention:

(1) recognition or recognition and enforcement of a foreign support order;

(2) enforcement of a support order issued or recognized in this state;

(3) establishment of a support order if there is no existing order, including, if necessary, determination of parentage of a child;

(4) establishment of a support order if recognition of a foreign support order is refused under Section 159.708(b)(2), (4), or (9);

(5) modification of a support order of a tribunal of this state; and

(6) modification of a support order of a tribunal of another state or a foreign country.

(c) The following support proceedings are available under the Convention to an obligor against which there is an existing support order:

(1) recognition of an order suspending or limiting enforcement of an existing support order of a tribunal of this state;

(2) modification of a support order of a tribunal of this state; and

(3) modification of a support order of a tribunal of another state or a foreign country.

(d) A tribunal of this state may not require security, bond, or deposit, however described, to guarantee the payment of costs and expenses in proceedings under the Convention.

Added by Acts 2015, 84th Leg., ch. 368 (H.B. 3538), § 58, eff. July 1, 2015.

### § 159.705. Direct Request

(a) A petitioner may file a direct request seeking establishment or modification of a support order or determination of parentage of a child. In the proceeding, the law of this state applies.

(b) A petitioner may file a direct request seeking recognition and enforcement of a support order or support agreement. In the proceeding, Sections 159.706 through 159.713 apply.

(c) In a direct request for recognition and enforcement of a Convention support order or foreign support agreement:

(1) a security, bond, or deposit is not required to guarantee the payment of costs and expenses; and

(2) an obligee or obligor that in the issuing country has benefited from free legal assistance is entitled to benefit, at least to the same extent, from any free legal assistance provided for by the law of this state under the same circumstances.

(d) A petitioner filing a direct request is not entitled to assistance from the office of the attorney general.

(e) This subchapter does not prevent the application of laws of this state that provide simplified, more expeditious rules regarding a direct request for recognition and enforcement of a foreign support order or foreign support agreement.

Added by Acts 2015, 84th Leg., ch. 368 (H.B. 3538), § 58, eff. July 1, 2015.

### § 159.706. Registration of Convention Support Order

(a) Except as otherwise provided in this subchapter, a party who is an individual or a support enforcement agency seeking recognition of a Convention support order shall register the order in this state as provided in Subchapter G.

(b) Notwithstanding Sections 159.311 and 159.602(a), a request for registration of a Convention support order must be accompanied by:

(1) the complete text of the support order or an abstract or extract of the support order drawn up by the issuing foreign tribunal, which may be in the form recommended by the Hague Conference on Private International Law;

(2) a record stating that the support order is enforceable in the issuing country;

(3) if the respondent did not appear and was not represented in the proceedings in the issuing country, a record attesting, as appropriate, either that the respondent had proper notice of the proceedings and an opportunity to be heard or that the respondent had proper notice of the support order and an opportunity to be heard in a challenge or appeal on fact or law before a tribunal;

(4) a record showing the amount of arrears, if any, and the date the amount was calculated;

(5) a record showing a requirement for automatic adjustment of the amount of support, if any, and the information necessary to make the appropriate calculations; and

(6) if necessary, a record showing the extent to which the applicant received free legal assistance in the issuing country.

(c) A request for registration of a Convention support order may seek recognition and partial enforcement of the order.

(d) A tribunal of this state may vacate the registration of a Convention support order without the filing of a contest under Section 159.707 only if, acting on its own motion, the tribunal finds that recognition and enforcement of the order would be manifestly incompatible with public policy.

(e) The tribunal shall promptly notify the parties of the registration or the order vacating the registration of a Convention support order.

Added by Acts 2015, 84th Leg., ch. 368 (H.B. 3538), § 58, eff. July 1, 2015.

### § 159.707. Contest of Registered Convention Support Order

(a) Except as otherwise provided in this subchapter, Sections 159.605 through 159.608 apply to a contest of a registered Convention support order.

(b) A party contesting a registered Convention support order shall file a contest not later than 30 days after notice of the registration. If the contesting party does not reside in the United States, the contest must be filed not later than 60 days after notice of the registration.

(c) If the nonregistering party fails to contest the registered Convention support order by the time specified in Subsection (b), the order is enforceable.

(d) A contest of a registered Convention support order may be based only on grounds set forth in

Section 159.708. The contesting party bears the burden of proof.

(e) In a contest of a registered Convention support order, a tribunal of this state:

(1) is bound by the findings of fact on which the foreign tribunal based its jurisdiction; and

(2) may not review the merits of the order.

(f) A tribunal of this state deciding a contest of a registered Convention support order shall promptly notify the parties of its decision.

(g) A challenge or appeal, if any, does not stay the enforcement of a Convention support order unless there are exceptional circumstances.

Added by Acts 2015, 84th Leg., ch. 368 (H.B. 3538), § 58, eff. July 1, 2015.

### § 159.708. Recognition and Enforcement of Registered Convention Support Order

(a) Except as otherwise provided in Subsection (b), a tribunal of this state shall recognize and enforce a registered Convention support order.

(b) The following grounds are the only grounds on which a tribunal of this state may refuse recognition and enforcement of a registered Convention support order:

(1) recognition and enforcement of the order is manifestly incompatible with public policy, including the failure of the issuing tribunal to observe minimum standards of due process, which include notice and an opportunity to be heard;

(2) the issuing tribunal lacked personal jurisdiction consistent with Section 159.201;

(3) the order is not enforceable in the issuing country;

(4) the order was obtained by fraud in connection with a matter of procedure;

(5) a record transmitted in accordance with Section 159.706 lacks authenticity or integrity;

(6) a proceeding between the same parties and having the same purpose is pending before a tribunal of this state and that proceeding was the first to be filed;

(7) the order is incompatible with a more recent support order involving the same parties and having the same purpose if the more recent support order is entitled to recognition and enforcement under this chapter in this state;

(8) payment, to the extent alleged arrears have been paid in whole or in part;

(9) in a case in which the respondent neither appeared nor was represented in the proceeding in the issuing foreign country:

(A) if the law of that country provides for prior notice of proceedings, the respondent did not have proper notice of the proceedings and an opportunity to be heard; or

(B) if the law of that country does not provide for prior notice of the proceedings, the respondent did not have proper notice of the order and an opportunity to be heard in a challenge or appeal on fact or law before a tribunal; or

(10) the order was made in violation of Section 159.711.

(c) If a tribunal of this state does not recognize a Convention support order under Subsection (b)(2), (4), or (9):

(1) the tribunal may not dismiss the proceeding without allowing a reasonable time for a party to request the establishment of a new Convention support order; and

(2) the office of the attorney general shall take all appropriate measures to request a child support order for the obligee if the application for recognition and enforcement was received under Section 159.704.

Added by Acts 2015, 84th Leg., ch. 368 (H.B. 3538), § 58, eff. July 1, 2015.

### § 159.709. Partial Enforcement

If a tribunal of this state does not recognize and enforce a Convention support order in its entirety, it shall enforce any severable part of the order. An application or direct request may seek recognition and partial enforcement of a Convention support order.

Added by Acts 2015, 84th Leg., ch. 368 (H.B. 3538), § 58, eff. July 1, 2015.

### § 159.710. Foreign Support Agreement

(a) Except as otherwise provided by Subsections (c) and (d), a tribunal of this state shall recognize and enforce a foreign support agreement registered in this state.

(b) An application or direct request for recognition and enforcement of a foreign support agreement must be accompanied by:

(1) the complete text of the foreign support agreement; and

(2) a record stating that the foreign support agreement is enforceable as an order of support in the issuing country.

(c) A tribunal of this state may vacate the registration of a foreign support agreement only if, acting on its own motion, the tribunal finds that recognition and enforcement would be manifestly incompatible with public policy.

(d) In a contest of a foreign support agreement, a tribunal of this state may refuse recognition and enforcement of the agreement if it finds:

(1) recognition and enforcement of the agreement is manifestly incompatible with public policy;

(2) the agreement was obtained by fraud or falsification;

(3) the agreement is incompatible with a support order involving the same parties and having the same purpose in this state, another state, or a foreign country if the support order is entitled to recognition and enforcement under this chapter in this state; or

(4) the record submitted under Subsection (b) lacks authenticity or integrity.

(e) A proceeding for recognition and enforcement of a foreign support agreement must be suspended during the pendency of a challenge to or appeal of the agreement before a tribunal of another state or a foreign country.

Added by Acts 2015, 84th Leg., ch. 368 (H.B. 3538), § 58, eff. July 1, 2015.

### § 159.711. Modification of Convention Child Support Order

(a) A tribunal of this state may not modify a Convention child support order if the obligee remains a resident of the foreign country where the support order was issued unless:

(1) the obligee submits to the jurisdiction of a tribunal of this state, either expressly or by defending on the merits of the case without objecting to the jurisdiction at the first available opportunity; or

(2) the foreign tribunal lacks or refuses to exercise jurisdiction to modify its support order or issue a new support order.

(b) If a tribunal of this state does not modify a Convention child support order because the order is not recognized in this state, Section 159.708(c) applies.

Added by Acts 2015, 84th Leg., ch. 368 (H.B. 3538), § 58, eff. July 1, 2015.

### § 159.712. Personal Information; Limit on Use

Personal information gathered or transmitted under this subchapter may be used only for the purposes for which it was gathered or transmitted.

Added by Acts 2015, 84th Leg., ch. 368 (H.B. 3538), § 58, eff. July 1, 2015.

### § 159.713. Record in Original Language; English Translation

A record filed with a tribunal of this state under this subchapter must be in the original language and, if not in English, must be accompanied by an English translation.

Added by Acts 2015, 84th Leg., ch. 368 (H.B. 3538), § 58, eff. July 1, 2015.

## SUBCHAPTER I. INTERSTATE RENDITION

### § 159.801. Grounds for Rendition

(a) For purposes of this subchapter, "governor" includes an individual performing the functions of governor or the executive authority of a state covered by this chapter.

(b) The governor of this state may:

(1) demand that the governor of another state surrender an individual found in the other state who is charged criminally in this state with having failed to provide for the support of an obligee; or

(2) on the demand of the governor of another state, surrender an individual found in this state who is charged criminally in the other state with having failed to provide for the support of an obligee.

(c) A provision for extradition of individuals not inconsistent with this chapter applies to the demand even if the individual whose surrender is demanded was not in the demanding state when the crime was allegedly committed and has not fled from that state.

Added by Acts 1995, 74th Leg., ch. 20, § 1, eff. April 20, 1995. Amended by Acts 2003, 78th Leg., ch. 1247, § 42, eff. Sept. 1, 2003; Acts 2015, 84th Leg., ch. 368 (H.B. 3538), § 59, eff. July 1, 2015.

### § 159.802. Conditions of Rendition

(a) Before making a demand that the governor of another state surrender an individual charged criminally in this state with having failed to provide for the support of an obligee, the governor of this state may require a prosecutor of this state to demonstrate that, not less than 60 days previously, the obligee had initiated proceedings for support under this chapter or that the proceeding would be of no avail.

(b) If, under this chapter or a law substantially similar to this chapter, the governor of another state makes a demand that the governor of this state surrender an individual charged criminally in that state with having failed to provide for the support of a child or other individual to whom a duty of support is owed, the governor may require a prosecutor to investigate the demand and report whether a proceeding for support has been initiated or would be effective. If it appears that a proceeding would be effective but has not been initiated, the governor may delay honoring the demand for a reasonable time to permit the initiation of a proceeding.

(c) If a proceeding for support has been initiated and the individual whose rendition is demanded prevails, the governor may decline to honor the demand. If the petitioner prevails and the individual whose rendition is demanded is subject to a support order, the governor may decline to honor the demand if the individual is complying with the support order.

Added by Acts 1995, 74th Leg., ch. 20, § 1, eff. April 20, 1995. Amended by Acts 2003, 78th Leg., ch. 1247, § 43, eff. Sept. 1, 2003; Acts 2015, 84th Leg., ch. 368 (H.B. 3538), § 60, eff. July 1, 2015.

## SUBCHAPTER J. MISCELLANEOUS PROVISIONS

### § 159.901. Uniformity of Application and Construction

In applying and construing this uniform act, consideration must be given to the need to promote uniformity of the law with respect to its subject matter among states that enact it.

Added by Acts 1995, 74th Leg., ch. 20, § 1, eff. April 20, 1995. Amended by Acts 2003, 78th Leg., ch. 1247, § 44, eff. Sept. 1, 2003; Acts 2015, 84th Leg., ch. 368 (H.B. 3538), § 61, eff. July 1, 2015.

### § 159.902. Repealed by Acts 2003, 78th Leg., ch. 1247, § 46, eff. Sept. 1, 2003

# CHAPTER 160. UNIFORM PARENTAGE ACT

SUBCHAPTER A. APPLICATION AND CONSTRUCTION



SUBCHAPTER B. GENERAL PROVISIONS



SUBCHAPTER C. PARENT-CHILD RELATIONSHIP



SUBCHAPTER D. VOLUNTARY ACKNOWLEDGMENT OF PATERNITY



SUBCHAPTER E. REGISTRY OF PATERNITY



SUBCHAPTER F. GENETIC TESTING

*Acts 2001, 77th Leg., ch. 821, § 1.01 amended Chapter 160 effective June 14, 2001. The former Chapter 160, Determination of Parentage, consisting of §§ 160.001 to 160.263, was amended as Chapter 160, Uniform Parentage Act, consisting of §§ 160.001 to 160.707.*

## DISPOSITION TABLE

Showing where provisions of former Chapter 160 of the Family Code, Determination of Parentage, are covered in new Chapter 160, Uniform Parentage Act as enacted by Acts 2001, 77th Leg., ch. 821.

| Former Section | New Section |
|---|---|
| 160.001 | 160.001 |
| 160.002 | 160.606, 160.607 |
| 160.003 | 160.603, 160.612 |
| 160.004 | 160.624 |
| 160.005 | 160.636 |
| 160.006 | 160.636 |
| 160.007 | — |
| 160.101 | — |
| 160.102 | 160.502 |
| 160.103 | 160.503 |
| 160.104 | — |
| 160.105 | — |
| 160.106 | 160.505 |
| 160.107 | 160.622 |
| 160.108 | — |
| 160.109 | 160.621 |
| 160.110 | 160.204 |
| 160.201 | 160.301 |
| 160.202 | 160.302 |
| 160.203 | 160.306 |
| 160.204 | 160.303, 160.304 |
| 160.205 | 160.305 |
| 160.206 | 160.307 |
| 160.207 | 160.308, 160.316 |
| 160.208 | 160.309 |
| 160.209 | 160.310 |
| 160.210 | 160.311 |
| 160.211 | — |
| 160.212 | 160.312 |
| 160.213 | 160.312 |
| 160.214 | 160.313 |

| Former Section | New Section |
|---|---|
| 160.215 | 160.314 |
| 160.216 | 160.315 |
| 160.251 | 160.401, 160.402 |
| 160.252 | — |
| 160.253 | — |
| 160.254 | — |
| 160.2545 | — |
| 160.255 | 160.412, 160.413 |
| 160.256 | — |
| 160.257 | — |
| 160.258 | — |
| 160.259 | 160.402 |
| 160.260 | 160.421, 160.422 |
| 160.261 | — |
| 160.262 | 160.416 |
| 160.263 | 160.423 |

## SUBCHAPTER A. APPLICATION AND CONSTRUCTION

### § 160.001. Application and Construction

This chapter shall be applied and construed to promote the uniformity of the law among the states that enact the Uniform Parentage Act.

Added by Acts 2001, 77th Leg., ch. 821, § 1.01, eff. June 14, 2001.

### § 160.002. Conflicts Between Provisions

If a provision of this chapter conflicts with another provision of this title or another state statute or rule and the conflict cannot be reconciled, this chapter prevails.

Added by Acts 2001, 77th Leg., ch. 821, § 1.01, eff. June 14, 2001.

### §§ 160.003 to 160.007. Deleted by Acts 2001, 77th Leg., ch. 821, § 1.01, eff. June 14, 2001

## SUBCHAPTER B. GENERAL PROVISIONS

### § 160.101. Short Title

This chapter may be cited as the Uniform Parentage Act.

Added by Acts 2001, 77th Leg., ch. 821, § 1.01, eff. June 14, 2001.

### § 160.102. Definitions

In this chapter:

(1) "Adjudicated father" means a man who has been adjudicated by a court to be the father of a child.

(2) "Assisted reproduction" means a method of causing pregnancy other than sexual intercourse. The term includes:

(A) intrauterine insemination;

(B) donation of eggs;

(C) donation of embryos;

(D) in vitro fertilization and transfer of embryos; and

(E) intracytoplasmic sperm injection.

(3) "Child" means an individual of any age whose parentage may be determined under this chapter.

(4) "Commence" means to file the initial pleading seeking an adjudication of parentage in a court of this state.

(5) "Determination of parentage" means the establishment of the parent-child relationship by the signing of a valid acknowledgment of paternity under Subchapter D[1] or by an adjudication by a court.

(6) "Donor" means an individual who provides eggs or sperm to a licensed physician to be used for assisted reproduction, regardless of whether the eggs or sperm are provided for consideration. The term does not include:

(A) a husband who provides sperm or a wife who provides eggs to be used for assisted reproduction by the wife;

(B) a woman who gives birth to a child by means of assisted reproduction; or

(C) an unmarried man who, with the intent to be the father of the resulting child, provides sperm to be used for assisted reproduction by an unmarried woman, as provided by Section 160.7031.

(7) "Ethnic or racial group" means, for purposes of genetic testing, a recognized group that an individual identifies as all or part of the individual's ancestry or that is identified by other information.

(8) "Genetic testing" means an analysis of an individual's genetic markers to exclude or identify a man as the father of a child or a woman as the mother of a child. The term includes an analysis of one or more of the following:

(A) deoxyribonucleic acid; and

(B) blood-group antigens, red-cell antigens, human-leukocyte antigens, serum enzymes, serum proteins, or red-cell enzymes.

(9) "Intended parents" means individuals who enter into an agreement providing that the individuals will be the parents of a child born to a gestational mother by means of assisted reproduction, regard-

less of whether either individual has a genetic relationship with the child.

(10) "Man" means a male individual of any age.

(11) "Parent" means an individual who has established a parent-child relationship under Section 160.201.

(12) "Paternity index" means the likelihood of paternity determined by calculating the ratio between:

(A) the likelihood that the tested man is the father of the child, based on the genetic markers of the tested man, the mother of the child, and the child, conditioned on the hypothesis that the tested man is the father of the child; and

(B) the likelihood that the tested man is not the father of the child, based on the genetic markers of the tested man, the mother of the child, and the child, conditioned on the hypothesis that the tested man is not the father of the child and that the father of the child is of the same ethnic or racial group as the tested man.

(13) "Presumed father" means a man who, by operation of law under Section 160.204, is recognized as the father of a child until that status is rebutted or confirmed in a judicial proceeding.

(14) "Probability of paternity" means the probability, with respect to the ethnic or racial group to which the alleged father belongs, that the alleged father is the father of the child, compared to a random, unrelated man of the same ethnic or racial group, expressed as a percentage incorporating the paternity index and a prior probability.

(15) "Record" means information that is inscribed on a tangible medium or that is stored in an electronic or other medium and is retrievable in a perceivable form.

(16) "Signatory" means an individual who authenticates a record and is bound by its terms.

(17) "Support enforcement agency" means a public official or public agency authorized to seek:

(A) the enforcement of child support orders or laws relating to the duty of support;

(B) the establishment or modification of child support;

(C) the determination of parentage;

(D) the location of child-support obligors and their income and assets; or

(E) the conservatorship of a child or the termination of parental rights.

Added by Acts 2001, 77th Leg., ch. 821, § 1.01, eff. June 14, 2001. Amended by Acts 2007, 80th Leg., ch. 972, § 39, eff. Sept. 1, 2007.

[1] V.T.C.A., Family Code § 160.301 et seq.

## § 160.103. Scope of Chapter; Choice of Law

(a) Except as provided by Chapter 233, this chapter governs every determination of parentage in this state.

(b) The court shall apply the law of this state to adjudicate the parent-child relationship. The applicable law does not depend on:

(1) the place of birth of the child; or

(2) the past or present residence of the child.

(c) This chapter does not create, enlarge, or diminish parental rights or duties under another law of this state.

(d) Repealed by Acts 2003, 78th Leg., ch. 457, § 3.

Added by Acts 2001, 77th Leg., ch. 821, § 1.01, eff. June 14, 2001. Amended by Acts 2003, 78th Leg., ch. 457, § 3, eff. Sept. 1, 2003; Acts 2009, 81st Leg., ch. 767, § 22, eff. June 19, 2009.

## § 160.104. Authorized Courts

The following courts are authorized to adjudicate parentage under this chapter:

(1) a court with jurisdiction to hear a suit affecting the parent-child relationship under this title; or

(2) a court with jurisdiction to adjudicate parentage under another law of this state.

Added by Acts 2001, 77th Leg., ch. 821, § 1.01, eff. June 14, 2001.

## § 160.105. Protection of Participants

A proceeding under this chapter is subject to the other laws of this state governing the health, safety, privacy, and liberty of a child or any other individual who may be jeopardized by the disclosure of identifying information, including the person's address, telephone number, place of employment, and social security number and the name of the child's day-care facility and school.

Added by Acts 2001, 77th Leg., ch. 821, § 1.01, eff. June 14, 2001.

### § 160.106. Determination of Maternity

The provisions of this chapter relating to the determination of paternity apply to a determination of maternity.

Added by Acts 2001, 77th Leg., ch. 821, § 1.01, eff. June 14, 2001.

### §§ 160.107 to 160.110. Deleted by Acts 2001, 77th Leg., ch. 821, § 1.01, eff. June 14, 2001

## SUBCHAPTER C. PARENT-CHILD RELATIONSHIP

### § 160.201. Establishment of Parent-Child Relationship

(a) The mother-child relationship is established between a woman and a child by:

(1) the woman giving birth to the child;

(2) an adjudication of the woman's maternity; or

(3) the adoption of the child by the woman.

(b) The father-child relationship is established between a man and a child by:

(1) an unrebutted presumption of the man's paternity of the child under Section 160.204;

(2) an effective acknowledgment of paternity by the man under Subchapter D,[1] unless the acknowledgment has been rescinded or successfully challenged;

(3) an adjudication of the man's paternity;

(4) the adoption of the child by the man; or

(5) the man's consenting to assisted reproduction by his wife under Subchapter H,[2] which resulted in the birth of the child.

Added by Acts 2001, 77th Leg., ch. 821, § 1.01, eff. June 14, 2001.

[1] V.T.C.A., Family Code § 160.301 et seq.

[2] V.T.C.A., Family Code § 160.701 et seq.

### § 160.202. No Discrimination Based on Marital Status

A child born to parents who are not married to each other has the same rights under the law as a child born to parents who are married to each other.

Added by Acts 2001, 77th Leg., ch. 821, § 1.01, eff. June 14, 2001.

### § 160.203. Consequences of Establishment of Parentage

Unless parental rights are terminated, a parent-child relationship established under this chapter applies for all purposes, except as otherwise provided by another law of this state.

Added by Acts 2001, 77th Leg., ch. 821, § 1.01, eff. June 14, 2001.

### § 160.204. Presumption of Paternity

(a) A man is presumed to be the father of a child if:

(1) he is married to the mother of the child and the child is born during the marriage;

(2) he is married to the mother of the child and the child is born before the 301st day after the date the marriage is terminated by death, annulment, declaration of invalidity, or divorce;

(3) he married the mother of the child before the birth of the child in apparent compliance with law, even if the attempted marriage is or could be declared invalid, and the child is born during the invalid marriage or before the 301st day after the date the marriage is terminated by death, annulment, declaration of invalidity, or divorce;

(4) he married the mother of the child after the birth of the child in apparent compliance with law, regardless of whether the marriage is or could be declared invalid, he voluntarily asserted his paternity of the child, and:

(A) the assertion is in a record filed with the vital statistics unit;

(B) he is voluntarily named as the child's father on the child's birth certificate; or

(C) he promised in a record to support the child as his own; or

(5) during the first two years of the child's life, he continuously resided in the household in which the child resided and he represented to others that the child was his own.

(b) A presumption of paternity established under this section may be rebutted only by:

(1) an adjudication under Subchapter G[1]; or

(2) the filing of a valid denial of paternity by a presumed father in conjunction with the filing by another person of a valid acknowledgment of paternity as provided by Section 160.305.

Added by Acts 2001, 77th Leg., ch. 821, § 1.01, eff. June 14, 2001. Amended by Acts 2003, 78th Leg., ch. 610, § 10, eff. Sept. 1, 2003; Acts 2003, 78th Leg., ch. 1248, § 1, eff. Sept. 1, 2003; Acts 2015, 84th Leg., ch. 1 (S.B. 219), § 1.055, eff. April 2, 2015.

[1] V.T.C.A., Family Code § 160.601 et seq.

### §§ 160.205 to 160.263. Deleted by Acts 2001, 77th Leg., ch. 821, § 1.01, eff. June 14, 2001

## SUBCHAPTER D. VOLUNTARY ACKNOWLEDGMENT OF PATERNITY

### § 160.301. Acknowledgment of Paternity

The mother of a child and a man claiming to be the biological father of the child may sign an acknowledgment of paternity with the intent to establish the man's paternity.

Added by Acts 2001, 77th Leg., ch. 821, § 1.01, eff. June 14, 2001. Amended by Acts 2003, 78th Leg., ch. 1248, § 2, eff. Sept. 1, 2003.

### § 160.302. Execution of Acknowledgment of Paternity

(a) An acknowledgment of paternity must:

(1) be in a record;

(2) be signed, or otherwise authenticated, under penalty of perjury by the mother and the man seeking to establish paternity;

(3) state that the child whose paternity is being acknowledged:

(A) does not have a presumed father or has a presumed father whose full name is stated; and

(B) does not have another acknowledged or adjudicated father;

(4) state whether there has been genetic testing and, if so, that the acknowledging man's claim of paternity is consistent with the results of the testing; and

(5) state that the signatories understand that the acknowledgment is the equivalent of a judicial adjudication of the paternity of the child and that a challenge to the acknowledgment is permitted only under limited circumstances.

(b) An acknowledgment of paternity is void if it:

(1) states that another man is a presumed father of the child, unless a denial of paternity signed or otherwise authenticated by the presumed father is filed with the vital statistics unit;

(2) states that another man is an acknowledged or adjudicated father of the child; or

(3) falsely denies the existence of a presumed, acknowledged, or adjudicated father of the child.

(c) A presumed father may sign or otherwise authenticate an acknowledgment of paternity.

(d) An acknowledgment of paternity constitutes an affidavit under Section 666(a)(5)(C)[1], Social Security Act (42 U.S.C. Section 666(a)(5)(C)).

Added by Acts 2001, 77th Leg., ch. 821, § 1.01, eff. June 14, 2001. Amended by Acts 2011, 82nd Leg., ch. 1221 (S.B. 502), § 1, eff. Sept. 1, 2011; Acts 2015, 84th Leg., ch. 1 (S.B. 219), § 1.056, eff. April 2, 2015; Acts 2015, 84th Leg., ch. 859 (S.B. 1726), § 7, eff. Sept. 1, 2015.

[1] So in original. Probably should read "Section 466(a)(5)(C)", because section 466 of the Social Security Act enacted 42 U.S.C.A. § 666.

### § 160.303. Denial of Paternity

A presumed father of a child may sign a denial of his paternity. The denial is valid only if:

(1) an acknowledgment of paternity signed or otherwise authenticated by another man is filed under Section 160.305;

(2) the denial is in a record and is signed or otherwise authenticated under penalty of perjury; and

(3) the presumed father has not previously:

(A) acknowledged paternity of the child, unless the previous acknowledgment has been rescinded under Section 160.307 or successfully challenged under Section 160.308; or

(B) been adjudicated to be the father of the child.

Added by Acts 2001, 77th Leg., ch. 821, § 1.01, eff. June 14, 2001.

### § 160.304. Rules for Acknowledgment and Denial of Paternity

(a) An acknowledgment of paternity and a denial of paternity may be contained in a single document or in different documents and may be filed separately or simultaneously. If the acknowledgment and denial are both necessary, neither document is valid until both documents are filed.

(b) An acknowledgment of paternity or a denial of paternity may be signed before the birth of the child.

(c) Subject to Subsection (a), an acknowledgment of paternity or denial of paternity takes effect on the date of the birth of the child or the filing of the document with the vital statistics unit, whichever occurs later.

(d) An acknowledgment of paternity or denial of paternity signed by a minor is valid if it otherwise complies with this chapter.

Added by Acts 2001, 77th Leg., ch. 821, § 1.01, eff. June 14, 2001. Amended by Acts 2015, 84th Leg., ch. 1 (S.B. 219), § 1.057, eff. April 2, 2015.

## § 160.305. Effect of Acknowledgment or Denial of Paternity

(a) Except as provided by Sections 160.307 and 160.308, a valid acknowledgment of paternity filed with the vital statistics unit is the equivalent of an adjudication of the paternity of a child and confers on the acknowledged father all rights and duties of a parent.

(b) Except as provided by Sections 160.307 and 160.308, a valid denial of paternity filed with the vital statistics unit in conjunction with a valid acknowledgment of paternity is the equivalent of an adjudication of the nonpaternity of the presumed father and discharges the presumed father from all rights and duties of a parent.

Added by Acts 2001, 77th Leg., ch. 821, § 1.01, eff. June 14, 2001. Amended by Acts 2015, 84th Leg., ch. 1 (S.B. 219), § 1.058, eff. April 2, 2015.

## § 160.306. Filing Fee Not Required

The Department of State Health Services may not charge a fee for filing:

(1) an acknowledgment of paternity;

(2) a denial of paternity; or

(3) a rescission of an acknowledgment of paternity or denial of paternity.

Added by Acts 2001, 77th Leg., ch. 821, § 1.01, eff. June 14, 2001. Amended by Acts 2011, 82nd Leg., ch. 1221 (S.B. 502), § 2, eff. Sept. 1, 2011; Acts 2015, 84th Leg., ch. 1 (S.B. 219), § 1.059, eff. April 2, 2015.

## § 160.307. Procedures for Rescission

(a) A signatory may rescind an acknowledgment of paternity or denial of paternity as provided by this section before the earlier of:

(1) the 60th day after the effective date of the acknowledgment or denial, as provided by Section 160.304; or

(2) the date a proceeding to which the signatory is a party is initiated before a court to adjudicate an issue relating to the child, including a proceeding that establishes child support.

(b) A signatory seeking to rescind an acknowledgment of paternity or denial of paternity must file with the vital statistics unit a completed rescission, on the form prescribed under Section 160.312, in which the signatory declares under penalty of perjury that:

(1) as of the date the rescission is filed, a proceeding has not been held affecting the child identified in the acknowledgment of paternity or denial of paternity, including a proceeding to establish child support;

(2) a copy of the completed rescission was sent by certified or registered mail, return receipt requested, to:

(A) if the rescission is of an acknowledgment of paternity, the other signatory of the acknowledgment of paternity and the signatory of any related denial of paternity; or

(B) if the rescission is of a denial of paternity, the signatories of the related acknowledgment of paternity; and

(3) if a signatory to the acknowledgment of paternity or denial of paternity is receiving services from the Title IV–D agency, a copy of the completed rescission was sent by certified or registered mail to the Title IV–D agency.

(c) On receipt of a completed rescission, the vital statistics unit shall void the acknowledgment of paternity or denial of paternity affected by the rescission and amend the birth record of the child, if appropriate.

(d) Any party affected by the rescission, including the Title IV–D agency, may contest the rescission by bringing a proceeding under Subchapter G[1] to adjudicate the parentage of the child.

Added by Acts 2001, 77th Leg., ch. 821, § 1.01, eff. June 14, 2001. Amended by Acts 2011, 82nd Leg., ch. 1221 (S.B. 502), § 3, eff. Sept. 1, 2011; Acts 2015, 84th Leg., ch. 1 (S.B. 219), § 1.060, eff. April 2, 2015.

[1] V.T.C.A., Family Code § 160.601 et seq.

## § 160.308. Challenge After Expiration of Period for Rescission

(a) After the period for rescission under Section 160.307 has expired, a signatory of an acknowledgment of paternity or denial of paternity may commence a proceeding to challenge the acknowledgment or denial only on the basis of fraud, duress, or material mistake of fact. The proceeding may be commenced at any time before the issuance of an order affecting the child identified in the acknowledgment or denial, including an order relating to support of the child.

(b) A party challenging an acknowledgment of paternity or denial of paternity has the burden of proof.

(c) Notwithstanding any other provision of this chapter, a collateral attack on an acknowledgment of paternity signed under this chapter may not be maintained after the issuance of an order affecting the child identified in the acknowledgment, including an order relating to support of the child.

(d) For purposes of Subsection (a), evidence that, based on genetic testing, the man who is the signatory of an acknowledgement of paternity is not rebuttably identified as the father of a child in accordance with Section 160.505 constitutes a material mistake of fact.

Added by Acts 2001, 77th Leg., ch. 821, § 1.01, eff. June 14, 2001. Amended by Acts 2005, 79th Leg., ch. 478, § 1, eff. Sept. 1, 2005; Acts 2011, 82nd Leg., ch. 1221 (S.B. 502), § 4, eff. Sept. 1, 2011.

### § 160.309. Procedure for Challenge

(a) Each signatory to an acknowledgment of paternity and any related denial of paternity must be made a party to a proceeding to challenge the acknowledgment or denial of paternity.

(b) For purposes of a challenge to an acknowledgment of paternity or denial of paternity, a signatory submits to the personal jurisdiction of this state by signing the acknowledgment or denial. The jurisdiction is effective on the filing of the document with the vital statistics unit.

(c) Except for good cause shown, while a proceeding is pending to challenge an acknowledgment of paternity or a denial of paternity, the court may not suspend the legal responsibilities of a signatory arising from the acknowledgment, including the duty to pay child support.

(d) A proceeding to challenge an acknowledgment of paternity or a denial of paternity shall be conducted in the same manner as a proceeding to adjudicate parentage under Subchapter G.[1]

(e) At the conclusion of a proceeding to challenge an acknowledgment of paternity or a denial of paternity, the court shall order the vital statistics unit to amend the birth record of the child, if appropriate.

Added by Acts 2001, 77th Leg., ch. 821, § 1.01, eff. June 14, 2001. Amended by Acts 2011, 82nd Leg., ch. 1221 (S.B. 502), § 5, eff. Sept. 1, 2011; Acts 2015, 84th Leg., ch. 1 (S.B. 219), § 1.061, eff. April 2, 2015.

[1] V.T.C.A., Family Code § 160.601 et seq.

### § 160.310. Ratification Barred

A court or administrative agency conducting a judicial or administrative proceeding may not ratify an unchallenged acknowledgment of paternity.

Added by Acts 2001, 77th Leg., ch. 821, § 1.01, eff. June 14, 2001.

### § 160.311. Full Faith and Credit

A court of this state shall give full faith and credit to an acknowledgment of paternity or a denial of paternity that is effective in another state if the acknowledgment or denial has been signed and is otherwise in compliance with the law of the other state.

Added by Acts 2001, 77th Leg., ch. 821, § 1.01, eff. June 14, 2001.

### § 160.312. Forms

(a) To facilitate compliance with this subchapter, the vital statistics unit shall prescribe forms for the:

(1) acknowledgment of paternity;

(2) denial of paternity; and

(3) rescission of an acknowledgment or denial of paternity.

(b) A valid acknowledgment of paternity, denial of paternity, or rescission of an acknowledgment or denial of paternity is not affected by a later modification of the prescribed form.

Added by Acts 2001, 77th Leg., ch. 821, § 1.01, eff. June 14, 2001. Amended by Acts 2011, 82nd Leg., ch. 1221 (S.B. 502), § 6, eff. Sept. 1, 2011; Acts 2015, 84th Leg., ch. 1 (S.B. 219), § 1.062, eff. April 2, 2015.

### § 160.313. Release of Information

The vital statistics unit may release information relating to the acknowledgment of paternity or denial of paternity to a signatory of the acknowledgment or denial and to the courts and Title IV–D agency of this or another state.

Added by Acts 2001, 77th Leg., ch. 821, § 1.01, eff. June 14, 2001. Amended by Acts 2015, 84th Leg., ch. 1 (S.B. 219), § 1.063, eff. April 2, 2015.

### § 160.314. Adoption of Rules

The Title IV–D agency and the executive commissioner of the Health and Human Services Commission may adopt rules to implement this subchapter.

Added by Acts 2001, 77th Leg., ch. 821, § 1.01, eff. June 14, 2001. Amended by Acts 2015, 84th Leg., ch. 1 (S.B. 219), § 1.064, eff. April 2, 2015.

### § 160.315. Memorandum of Understanding

(a) The Title IV–D agency and the vital statistics unit shall adopt a memorandum of understanding governing the collection and transfer of information for the voluntary acknowledgment of paternity.

(b) The Title IV–D agency and the vital statistics unit shall review the memorandum semiannually and renew or modify the memorandum as necessary.

Added by Acts 2001, 77th Leg., ch. 821, § 1.01, eff. June 14, 2001. Amended by Acts 2015, 84th Leg., ch. 1 (S.B. 219), § 1.065, eff. April 2, 2015.

### § 160.316. Expired

## SUBCHAPTER E. REGISTRY OF PATERNITY

### § 160.401. Establishment of Registry

A registry of paternity is established in the vital statistics unit.

Added by Acts 2001, 77th Leg., ch. 821, § 1.01, eff. June 14, 2001. Amended by Acts 2015, 84th Leg., ch. 1 (S.B. 219), § 1.066, eff. April 2, 2015.

### § 160.402. Registration for Notification

(a) Except as otherwise provided by Subsection (b), a man who desires to be notified of a proceeding for the adoption of or the termination of parental rights regarding a child that he may have fathered may register with the registry of paternity:

(1) before the birth of the child; or

(2) not later than the 31st day after the date of the birth of the child.

(b) A man is entitled to notice of a proceeding described by Subsection (a) regardless of whether he registers with the registry of paternity if:

(1) a father-child relationship between the man and the child has been established under this chapter or another law; or

(2) the man commences a proceeding to adjudicate his paternity before the court has terminated his parental rights.

(c) A registrant shall promptly notify the registry in a record of any change in the information provided by the registrant. The vital statistics unit shall incorporate all new information received into its records but is not required to affirmatively seek to obtain current information for incorporation in the registry.

Added by Acts 2001, 77th Leg., ch. 821, § 1.01, eff. June 14, 2001. Amended by Acts 2015, 84th Leg., ch. 1 (S.B. 219), § 1.067, eff. April 2, 2015.

### § 160.403. Notice of Proceeding

Except as provided by Sections 161.002(b)(2), (3), and (4) and (f), notice of a proceeding to adopt or to terminate parental rights regarding a child must be given to a registrant who has timely registered with regard to that child. Notice must be given in a manner prescribed for service of process in a civil action.

Added by Acts 2001, 77th Leg., ch. 821, § 1.01, eff. June 14, 2001. Amended by Acts 2007, 80th Leg., ch. 1283, § 2, eff. Sept. 1, 2007.

### § 160.404. Termination of Parental Rights: Failure to Register

The parental rights of a man alleged to be the father of a child may be terminated without notice as provided by Section 161.002 if the man:

(1) did not timely register with the vital statistics unit; and

(2) is not entitled to notice under Section 160.402 or 161.002.

Added by Acts 2001, 77th Leg., ch. 821, § 1.01, eff. June 14, 2001. Amended by Acts 2015, 84th Leg., ch. 1 (S.B. 219), § 1.068, eff. April 2, 2015.

### §§ 160.405 to 160.410. [Blank]

### § 160.411. Required Form

The vital statistics unit shall adopt a form for registering with the registry. The form must require the signature of the registrant. The form must state that:

(1) the form is signed under penalty of perjury;

(2) a timely registration entitles the registrant to notice of a proceeding for adoption of the child or for termination of the registrant's parental rights;

(3) a timely registration does not commence a proceeding to establish paternity;

(4) the information disclosed on the form may be used against the registrant to establish paternity;

(5) services to assist in establishing paternity are available to the registrant through the support enforcement agency;

(6) the registrant should also register in another state if the conception or birth of the child occurred in the other state;

(7) information on registries in other states is available from the vital statistics unit; and

(8) procedures exist to rescind the registration of a claim of paternity.

Added by Acts 2001, 77th Leg., ch. 821, § 1.01, eff. June 14, 2001. Amended by Acts 2015, 84th Leg., ch. 1 (S.B. 219), § 1.069, eff. April 2, 2015.

### § 160.412. Furnishing of Information; Confidentiality

(a) The vital statistics unit is not required to attempt to locate the mother of a child who is the subject of a registration. The vital statistics unit shall send a copy of the notice of the registration to a mother who has provided an address.

(b) Information contained in the registry is confidential and may be released on request only to:

(1) a court or a person designated by the court;

(2) the mother of the child who is the subject of the registration;

(3) an agency authorized by another law to receive the information;

(4) a licensed child-placing agency;

(5) a support enforcement agency;

(6) a party, or the party's attorney of record, to a proceeding under this chapter or a proceeding to adopt or to terminate parental rights regarding a child who is the subject of the registration; and

(7) the registry of paternity in another state.

Added by Acts 2001, 77th Leg., ch. 821, § 1.01, eff. June 14, 2001. Amended by Acts 2015, 84th Leg., ch. 1 (S.B. 219), § 1.070, eff. April 2, 2015.

### § 160.413. Offense: Unauthorized Release of Information

(a) A person commits an offense if the person intentionally releases information from the registry of paternity to another person, including an agency, that is not authorized to receive the information under Section 160.412.

(b) An offense under this section is a Class A misdemeanor.

Added by Acts 2001, 77th Leg., ch. 821, § 1.01, eff. June 14, 2001.

### § 160.414. Rescission of Registration

A registrant may rescind his registration at any time by sending to the registry a rescission in a record or another manner authenticated by him and witnessed or notarized.

Added by Acts 2001, 77th Leg., ch. 821, § 1.01, eff. June 14, 2001.

### § 160.415. Untimely Registration

If a man registers later than the 31st day after the date of the birth of the child, the vital statistics unit shall notify the registrant that the registration was not timely filed.

Added by Acts 2001, 77th Leg., ch. 821, § 1.01, eff. June 14, 2001. Amended by Acts 2007, 80th Leg., ch. 627, § 1, eff. June 15, 2007; Acts 2015, 84th Leg., ch. 1 (S.B. 219), § 1.071, eff. April 2, 2015.

### § 160.416. Fees for Registry

(a) A fee may not be charged for filing a registration or to rescind a registration.

(b) Except as otherwise provided by Subsection (c), the vital statistics unit may charge a reasonable fee for making a search of the registry and for furnishing a certificate.

(c) A support enforcement agency is not required to pay a fee authorized by Subsection (b).

Added by Acts 2001, 77th Leg., ch. 821, § 1.01, eff. June 14, 2001. Amended by Acts 2015, 84th Leg., ch. 1 (S.B. 219), § 1.072, eff. April 2, 2015.

### §§ 160.417 to 160.420. [Blank]

### § 160.421. Search of Appropriate Registry

(a) If a father-child relationship has not been established under this chapter, a petitioner for the adoption of or the termination of parental rights regarding the child must obtain a certificate of the results of a search of the registry. The petitioner may request a search of the registry on or after the 32nd day after the date of the birth of the child, and the executive commissioner of the Health and Human Services Commission may not by rule impose a waiting period that must elapse before the vital statistics unit will conduct the requested search.

(b) If the petitioner for the adoption of or the termination of parental rights regarding a child has reason to believe that the conception or birth of the child may have occurred in another state, the petitioner must obtain a certificate of the results of a search of the paternity registry, if any, in the other state.

Added by Acts 2001, 77th Leg., ch. 821, § 1.01, eff. June 14, 2001. Amended by Acts 2007, 80th Leg., ch. 627, § 2, eff. June 15, 2007; Acts 2015, 84th Leg., ch. 1 (S.B. 219), § 1.073, eff. April 2, 2015.

### § 160.422. Certificate of Search of Registry

(a) The vital statistics unit shall furnish a certificate of the results of a search of the registry on request by an individual, a court, or an agency listed in Section 160.412(b).

(b) The certificate of the results of a search must be signed on behalf of the unit and state that:

(1) a search has been made of the registry; and

(2) a registration containing the information required to identify the registrant:

(A) has been found and is attached to the certificate; or

(B) has not been found.

(c) A petitioner must file the certificate of the results of a search of the registry with the court before a proceeding for the adoption of or termination of parental rights regarding a child may be concluded.

(d) A search of the registry is not required if a parent-child relationship exists between a man and the child, as provided by Section 160.201(b), and that man:

(1) has been served with citation of the proceeding for termination of the parent-child relationship; or

(2) has signed a relinquishment of parental rights with regard to the child.

Added by Acts 2001, 77th Leg., ch. 821, § 1.01, eff. June 14, 2001. Amended by Acts 2007, 80th Leg., ch. 1283, § 3, eff. Sept. 1, 2007; Acts 2015, 84th Leg., ch. 1 (S.B. 219), § 1.074, eff. April 2, 2015.

### § 160.423. Admissibility of Certificate

A certificate of the results of a search of the registry in this state or of a paternity registry in another state is admissible in a proceeding for the adoption of or the termination of parental rights regarding a child and, if relevant, in other legal proceedings.

Added by Acts 2001, 77th Leg., ch. 821, § 1.01, eff. June 14, 2001.

## SUBCHAPTER F. GENETIC TESTING

### § 160.501. Application of Subchapter

This subchapter governs genetic testing of an individual to determine parentage, regardless of whether the individual:

(1) voluntarily submits to testing; or

(2) is tested under an order of a court or a support enforcement agency.

Added by Acts 2001, 77th Leg., ch. 821, § 1.01, eff. June 14, 2001.

### § 160.502. Order for Testing

(a) Except as otherwise provided by this subchapter and by Subchapter G, a court shall order a child and other designated individuals to submit to genetic testing if the request is made by a party to a proceeding to determine parentage.

(b) If a request for genetic testing of a child is made before the birth of the child, the court or support enforcement agency may not order in utero testing.

(c) If two or more men are subject to court-ordered genetic testing, the testing may be ordered concurrently or sequentially.

Added by Acts 2001, 77th Leg., ch. 821, § 1.01, eff. June 14, 2001.

### § 160.503. Requirements for Genetic Testing

(a) Genetic testing must be of a type reasonably relied on by experts in the field of genetic testing. The testing must be performed in a testing laboratory accredited by:

(1) the American Association of Blood Banks, or a successor to its functions;

(2) the American Society for Histocompatibility and Immunogenetics, or a successor to its functions; or

(3) an accrediting body designated by the federal secretary of health and human services.

(b) A specimen used in genetic testing may consist of one or more samples, or a combination of samples, of blood, buccal cells, bone, hair, or other body tissue or fluid. The specimen used in the testing is not required to be of the same kind for each individual undergoing genetic testing.

(c) Based on the ethnic or racial group of an individual, the testing laboratory shall determine the databases from which to select frequencies for use in the calculation of the probability of paternity of the individual. If there is disagreement as to the testing laboratory's choice:

(1) the objecting individual may require the testing laboratory, not later than the 30th day after the date of receipt of the report of the test, to recalculate the probability of paternity using an ethnic or racial group different from that used by the laboratory;

(2) the individual objecting to the testing laboratory's initial choice shall:

(A) if the frequencies are not available to the testing laboratory for the ethnic or racial group requested, provide the requested frequencies compiled in a manner recognized by accrediting bodies; or

(B) engage another testing laboratory to perform the calculations; and

(3) the testing laboratory may use its own statistical estimate if there is a question regarding which ethnic or racial group is appropriate and, if available, shall calculate the frequencies using statistics for any other ethnic or racial group requested.

(d) If, after recalculation using a different ethnic or racial group, genetic testing does not rebuttably identify a man as the father of a child under Section 160.505, an individual who has been tested may be required to submit to additional genetic testing.

Added by Acts 2001, 77th Leg., ch. 821, § 1.01, eff. June 14, 2001.

### § 160.504. Report of Genetic Testing

(a) A report of the results of genetic testing must be in a record and signed under penalty of perjury by a designee of the testing laboratory. A report made under the requirements of this subchapter is self-authenticating.

(b) Documentation from the testing laboratory is sufficient to establish a reliable chain of custody that allows the results of genetic testing to be admissible without testimony if the documentation includes:

(1) the name and photograph of each individual whose specimens have been taken;

(2) the name of each individual who collected the specimens;

(3) the places in which the specimens were collected and the date of each collection;

(4) the name of each individual who received the specimens in the testing laboratory; and

(5) the dates the specimens were received.

Added by Acts 2001, 77th Leg., ch. 821, § 1.01, eff. June 14, 2001.

### § 160.505. Genetic Testing Results; Rebuttal

(a) A man is rebuttably identified as the father of a child under this chapter if the genetic testing complies with this subchapter and the results disclose:

(1) that the man has at least a 99 percent probability of paternity, using a prior probability of 0.5, as calculated by using the combined paternity index obtained in the testing; and

(2) a combined paternity index of at least 100 to 1.

(b) A man identified as the father of a child under Subsection (a) may rebut the genetic testing results only by producing other genetic testing satisfying the requirements of this subchapter that:

(1) excludes the man as a genetic father of the child; or

(2) identifies another man as the possible father of the child.

(c) Except as otherwise provided by Section 160.510, if more than one man is identified by genetic testing as the possible father of the child, the court shall order each man to submit to further genetic testing to identify the genetic father.

Added by Acts 2001, 77th Leg., ch. 821, § 1.01, eff. June 14, 2001.

### § 160.506. Costs of Genetic Testing

(a) Subject to the assessment of costs under Subchapter G,[1] the cost of initial genetic testing must be advanced:

(1) by a support enforcement agency, if the agency is providing services in the proceeding;

(2) by the individual who made the request;

(3) as agreed by the parties; or

(4) as ordered by the court.

(b) In cases in which the cost of genetic testing is advanced by the support enforcement agency, the agency may seek reimbursement from a man who is rebuttably identified as the father.

Added by Acts 2001, 77th Leg., ch. 821, § 1.01, eff. June 14, 2001.

[1] V.T.C.A., Family Code § 160.601 et seq.

### § 160.507. Additional Genetic Testing

The court or the support enforcement agency shall order additional genetic testing on the request of a party who contests the result of the original testing. If the previous genetic testing identified a man as the father of the child under Section 160.505, the court or agency may not order additional testing unless the party provides advance payment for the testing.

Added by Acts 2001, 77th Leg., ch. 821, § 1.01, eff. June 14, 2001.

### § 160.508. Genetic Testing When All Individuals Not Available

(a) Subject to Subsection (b), if a genetic testing specimen for good cause and under circumstances the court considers to be just is not available from a man who may be the father of a child, a court may order the following individuals to submit specimens for genetic testing:

(1) the parents of the man;

(2) any brothers or sisters of the man;

(3) any other children of the man and their mothers; and

(4) other relatives of the man necessary to complete genetic testing.

(b) A court may not render an order under this section unless the court finds that the need for genetic testing outweighs the legitimate interests of the individual sought to be tested.

Added by Acts 2001, 77th Leg., ch. 821, § 1.01, eff. June 14, 2001.

### § 160.509. Deceased Individual

For good cause shown, the court may order genetic testing of a deceased individual.

Added by Acts 2001, 77th Leg., ch. 821, § 1.01, eff. June 14, 2001.

### § 160.510. Identical Brothers

(a) The court may order genetic testing of a brother of a man identified as the father of a child if the man is commonly believed to have an identical brother and evidence suggests that the brother may be the genetic father of the child.

(b) If each brother satisfies the requirements of Section 160.505 for being the identified father of the child and there is not another identical brother being identified as the father of the child, the court may rely on nongenetic evidence to adjudicate which brother is the father of the child.

Added by Acts 2001, 77th Leg., ch. 821, § 1.01, eff. June 14, 2001.

### § 160.511. Offense: Unauthorized Release of Specimen

(a) A person commits an offense if the person intentionally releases an identifiable specimen of another person for any purpose not relevant to the parentage proceeding and without a court order or the written permission of the person who furnished the specimen.

(b) An offense under this section is a Class A misdemeanor.

Added by Acts 2001, 77th Leg., ch. 821, § 1.01, eff. June 14, 2001.

### § 160.512. Offense: Falsification of Specimen

(a) A person commits an offense if the person alters, destroys, conceals, fabricates, or falsifies genetic evidence in a proceeding to adjudicate parentage, including inducing another person to provide a specimen with the intent to affect the outcome of the proceeding.

(b) An offense under this section is a felony of the third degree.

(c) An order excluding a man as the biological father of a child based on genetic evidence shown to be altered, fabricated, or falsified is void and unenforceable.

Added by Acts 2011, 82nd Leg., ch. 1221 (S.B. 502), § 7, eff. Sept. 1, 2011.

## SUBCHAPTER G. PROCEEDING TO ADJUDICATE PARENTAGE

### § 160.601. Proceeding Authorized; Rules of Procedure

(a) A civil proceeding may be maintained to adjudicate the parentage of a child.

(b) The proceeding is governed by the Texas Rules of Civil Procedure, except as provided by Chapter 233.

Added by Acts 2001, 77th Leg., ch. 821, § 1.01, eff. June 14, 2001. Amended by Acts 2009, 81st Leg., ch. 767, § 23, eff. June 19, 2009.

### § 160.602. Standing to Maintain Proceeding

(a) Subject to Subchapter D [1] and Sections 160.607 and 160.609 and except as provided by Subsection (b), a proceeding to adjudicate parentage may be maintained by:

(1) the child;

(2) the mother of the child;

(3) a man whose paternity of the child is to be adjudicated;

(4) the support enforcement agency or another government agency authorized by other law;

(5) an authorized adoption agency or licensed child-placing agency;

(6) a representative authorized by law to act for an individual who would otherwise be entitled to maintain a proceeding but who is deceased, is incapacitated, or is a minor;

(7) a person related within the second degree by consanguinity to the mother of the child, if the mother is deceased; or

(8) a person who is an intended parent.

(b) After the date a child having no presumed, acknowledged, or adjudicated father becomes an adult, a proceeding to adjudicate the parentage of the adult child may only be maintained by the adult child.

Added by Acts 2001, 77th Leg., ch. 821, § 1.01, eff. June 14, 2001. Amended by Acts 2003, 78th Leg., ch. 457, § 1, eff. Sept. 1, 2003; Acts 2003, 78th Leg., ch. 1248, § 3, eff. Sept. 1, 2003.

[1] V.T.C.A., Family Code § 160.301 et seq.

## § 160.603. Necessary Parties to Proceeding

The following individuals must be joined as parties in a proceeding to adjudicate parentage:

(1) the mother of the child; and

(2) a man whose paternity of the child is to be adjudicated.

Added by Acts 2001, 77th Leg., ch. 821, § 1.01, eff. June 14, 2001.

## § 160.6035. Contents of Petition; Statement Relating to Certain Protective Orders Required

(a) The petition in a proceeding to adjudicate parentage must include a statement as to whether, in regard to a party to the proceeding or a child of a party to the proceeding:

(1) there is in effect:

(A) a protective order under Title 4;

(B) a protective order under Subchapter A, Chapter 7B, Code of Criminal Procedure; or

(C) an order for emergency protection under Article 17.292, Code of Criminal Procedure; or

(2) an application for an order described by Subdivision (1) is pending.

(b) The petitioner shall attach a copy of each order described by Subsection (a)(1) in which a party to the proceeding or a child of a party to the proceeding was the applicant or victim of the conduct alleged in the application or order and the other party was the respondent or defendant of an action regarding the conduct alleged in the application or order without regard to the date of the order. If a copy of the order is not available at the time of filing, the petition must state that a copy of the order will be filed with the court before any hearing.

(c) Notwithstanding any other provision of this section, if the Title IV–D agency files a petition in a proceeding to adjudicate parentage, the agency is not required to:

(1) include in the petition the statement described by Subsection (a); or

(2) attach copies of the documentation described by Subsection (b).

Added by Acts 2017, 85th Leg., ch. 885 (H.B. 3052), § 7, eff. Sept. 1, 2017. Amended by Acts 2019, 86th Leg., ch. 469 (H.B. 4173), § 2.37, eff. Jan. 1, 2021.

Sections 4.01 and 4.02 of Acts 2019, 86th Leg., ch. 469 (H.B. 4173) provide:

"Sec. 4.01. This Act is enacted under Section 43, Article III, Texas Constitution. This Act is intended as a codification only, and no substantive change in the law is intended by this Act.

"Sec. 4.02. (a) Chapter 311, Government Code (Code Construction Act), applies to the construction of each provision in the Code of Criminal Procedure that is enacted under Section 43, Article III, Texas Constitution (authorizing the continuing statutory revision program), in the same manner as to a code enacted under the continuing statutory revision program, except as otherwise expressly provided by the Code of Criminal Procedure.

"(b) A reference in a law to a statute or a part of a statute in the Code of Criminal Procedure enacted under Section 43, Article III, Texas Constitution (authorizing the continuing statutory revision program), is considered to be a reference to the part of that code that revises that statute or part of that statute."

## § 160.604. Personal Jurisdiction

(a) An individual may not be adjudicated to be a parent unless the court has personal jurisdiction over the individual.

(b) A court of this state having jurisdiction to adjudicate parentage may exercise personal jurisdiction over a nonresident individual or the guardian or conservator of the individual if the conditions in Section 159.201 are satisfied.

(c) Lack of jurisdiction over one individual does not preclude the court from making an adjudication of parentage binding on another individual over whom the court has personal jurisdiction.

Added by Acts 2001, 77th Leg., ch. 821, § 1.01, eff. June 14, 2001.

## § 160.605. Venue

Venue for a proceeding to adjudicate parentage is in the county of this state in which:

(1) the child resides or is found;

(2) the respondent resides or is found if the child does not reside in this state; or

(3) a proceeding for probate or administration of the presumed or alleged father's estate has been commenced.

Added by Acts 2001, 77th Leg., ch. 821, § 1.01, eff. June 14, 2001.

**§ 160.606. No Time Limitation: Child Having No Presumed, Acknowledged, or Adjudicated Father**

A proceeding to adjudicate the parentage of a child having no presumed, acknowledged, or adjudicated father may be commenced at any time, including after the date:

(1) the child becomes an adult; or

(2) an earlier proceeding to adjudicate paternity has been dismissed based on the application of a statute of limitation then in effect.

Added by Acts 2001, 77th Leg., ch. 821, § 1.01, eff. June 14, 2001.

**§ 160.607. Time Limitation: Child Having Presumed Father**

(a) Except as otherwise provided by Subsection (b), a proceeding brought by a presumed father, the mother, or another individual to adjudicate the parentage of a child having a presumed father shall be commenced not later than the fourth anniversary of the date of the birth of the child.

(b) A proceeding seeking to adjudicate the parentage of a child having a presumed father may be maintained at any time if the court determines that:

(1) the presumed father and the mother of the child did not live together or engage in sexual intercourse with each other during the probable time of conception; or

(2) the presumed father was precluded from commencing a proceeding to adjudicate the parentage of the child before the expiration of the time prescribed by Subsection (a) because of the mistaken belief that he was the child's biological father based on misrepresentations that led him to that conclusion.

Added by Acts 2001, 77th Leg., ch. 821, § 1.01, eff. June 14, 2001. Amended by Acts 2003, 78th Leg., ch. 1248, § 4, eff. Sept. 1, 2003; Acts 2011, 82nd Leg., ch. 1221 (S.B. 502), § 8, eff. Sept. 1, 2011.

**§ 160.608. Authority to Deny Motion for Genetic Testing**

(a) In a proceeding to adjudicate parentage, a court may deny a motion for an order for the genetic testing of the mother, the child, and the presumed father if the court determines that:

(1) the conduct of the mother or the presumed father estops that party from denying parentage; and

(2) it would be inequitable to disprove the father-child relationship between the child and the presumed father.

(b) In determining whether to deny a motion for an order for genetic testing under this section, the court shall consider the best interest of the child, including the following factors:

(1) the length of time between the date of the proceeding to adjudicate parentage and the date the presumed father was placed on notice that he might not be the genetic father;

(2) the length of time during which the presumed father has assumed the role of father of the child;

(3) the facts surrounding the presumed father's discovery of his possible nonpaternity;

(4) the nature of the relationship between the child and the presumed father;

(5) the age of the child;

(6) any harm that may result to the child if presumed paternity is successfully disproved;

(7) the nature of the relationship between the child and the alleged father;

(8) the extent to which the passage of time reduces the chances of establishing the paternity of another man and a child support obligation in favor of the child; and

(9) other factors that may affect the equities arising from the disruption of the father-child relationship between the child and the presumed father or the chance of other harm to the child.

(c) In a proceeding involving the application of this section, a child who is a minor or is incapacitated must be represented by an amicus attorney or attorney ad litem.

(d) A denial of a motion for an order for genetic testing must be based on clear and convincing evidence.

(e) If the court denies a motion for an order for genetic testing, the court shall issue an order adjudicating the presumed father to be the father of the child.

(f) This section applies to a proceeding to challenge an acknowledgment of paternity or a denial of paternity as provided by Section 160.309(d).

Added by Acts 2001, 77th Leg., ch. 821, § 1.01, eff. June 14, 2001. Amended by Acts 2003, 78th Leg., ch. 1248, § 5, eff. Sept. 1, 2003; Acts 2005, 79th Leg., ch. 172, § 17, eff. Sept. 1, 2005; Acts 2011, 82nd Leg., ch. 1221 (S.B. 502), § 9, eff. Sept. 1, 2011.

### § 160.609. Time Limitation: Child Having Acknowledged or Adjudicated Father

(a) If a child has an acknowledged father, a signatory to the acknowledgment or denial of paternity may commence a proceeding under this chapter to challenge the paternity of the child only within the time allowed under Section 160.308.

(b) If a child has an acknowledged father or an adjudicated father, an individual, other than the child, who is not a signatory to the acknowledgment or a party to the adjudication and who seeks an adjudication of paternity of the child must commence a proceeding not later than the fourth anniversary of the effective date of the acknowledgment or adjudication.

Added by Acts 2001, 77th Leg., ch. 821, § 1.01, eff. June 14, 2001. Amended by Acts 2011, 82nd Leg., ch. 1221 (S.B. 502), § 10, eff. Sept. 1, 2011.

### § 160.610. Joinder of Proceedings

(a) Except as provided by Subsection (b), a proceeding to adjudicate parentage may be joined with a proceeding for adoption, termination of parental rights, possession of or access to a child, child support, divorce, annulment, or probate or administration of an estate or another appropriate proceeding.

(b) A respondent may not join a proceeding described by Subsection (a) with a proceeding to adjudicate parentage brought under Chapter 159.

Added by Acts 2001, 77th Leg., ch. 821, § 1.01, eff. June 14, 2001.

### § 160.611. Proceedings Before Birth

(a) A proceeding to determine parentage commenced before the birth of the child may not be concluded until after the birth of the child.

(b) In a proceeding described by Subsection (a), the following actions may be taken before the birth of the child:

(1) service of process;

(2) discovery; and

(3) except as prohibited by Section 160.502, collection of specimens for genetic testing.

Added by Acts 2001, 77th Leg., ch. 821, § 1.01, eff. June 14, 2001.

### § 160.612. Child as Party; Representation

(a) A minor child is a permissible party, but is not a necessary party to a proceeding under this subchapter.

(b) The court shall appoint an amicus attorney or attorney ad litem to represent a child who is a minor or is incapacitated if the child is a party or the court finds that the interests of the child are not adequately represented.

Added by Acts 2001, 77th Leg., ch. 821, § 1.01, eff. June 14, 2001. Amended by Acts 2005, 79th Leg., ch. 172, § 18, eff. Sept. 1, 2005.

### §§ 160.613 to 160.620. [Blank]

### § 160.621. Admissibility of Results of Genetic Testing; Expenses

(a) Except as otherwise provided by Subsection (c), a report of a genetic testing expert is admissible as evidence of the truth of the facts asserted in the report. The admissibility of the report is not affected by whether the testing was performed:

(1) voluntarily or under an order of the court or a support enforcement agency; or

(2) before or after the date of commencement of the proceeding.

(b) A party objecting to the results of genetic testing may call one or more genetic testing experts to testify in person or by telephone, videoconference, deposition, or another method approved by the court. Unless otherwise ordered by the court, the party offering the testimony bears the expense for the expert testifying.

(c) If a child has a presumed, acknowledged, or adjudicated father, the results of genetic testing are inadmissible to adjudicate parentage unless performed:

(1) with the consent of both the mother and the presumed, acknowledged, or adjudicated father; or

(2) under an order of the court under Section 160.502.

(d) Copies of bills for genetic testing and for prenatal and postnatal health care for the mother and child that are furnished to the adverse party on or before the 10th day before the date of a hearing are admissible to establish:

(1) the amount of the charges billed; and

(2) that the charges were reasonable, necessary, and customary.

Added by Acts 2001, 77th Leg., ch. 821, § 1.01, eff. June 14, 2001.

## § 160.622. Consequences of Declining Genetic Testing

(a) An order for genetic testing is enforceable by contempt.

(b) A court may adjudicate parentage contrary to the position of an individual whose paternity is being determined on the grounds that the individual declines to submit to genetic testing as ordered by the court.

(c) Genetic testing of the mother of a child is not a prerequisite to testing the child and a man whose paternity is being determined. If the mother is unavailable or declines to submit to genetic testing, the court may order the testing of the child and each man whose paternity is being adjudicated.

Added by Acts 2001, 77th Leg., ch. 821, § 1.01, eff. June 14, 2001.

## § 160.623. Admission of Paternity Authorized

(a) A respondent in a proceeding to adjudicate parentage may admit to the paternity of a child by filing a pleading to that effect or by admitting paternity under penalty of perjury when making an appearance or during a hearing.

(b) If the court finds that the admission of paternity satisfies the requirements of this section and that there is no reason to question the admission, the court shall render an order adjudicating the child to be the child of the man admitting paternity.

Added by Acts 2001, 77th Leg., ch. 821, § 1.01, eff. June 14, 2001.

## § 160.624. Temporary Order

(a) In a proceeding under this subchapter, the court shall render a temporary order for child support for a child if the order is appropriate and the individual ordered to pay child support:

(1) is a presumed father of the child;

(2) is petitioning to have his paternity adjudicated;

(3) is identified as the father through genetic testing under Section 160.505;

(4) is an alleged father who has declined to submit to genetic testing;

(5) is shown by clear and convincing evidence to be the father of the child; or

(6) is the mother of the child.

(b) A temporary order may include provisions for the possession of or access to the child as provided by other laws of this state.

Added by Acts 2001, 77th Leg., ch. 821, § 1.01, eff. June 14, 2001.

## §§ 160.625 to 160.630. [Blank]

## § 160.631. Rules for Adjudication of Paternity

(a) The court shall apply the rules stated in this section to adjudicate the paternity of a child.

(b) The paternity of a child having a presumed, acknowledged, or adjudicated father may be disproved only by admissible results of genetic testing excluding that man as the father of the child or identifying another man as the father of the child.

(c) Unless the results of genetic testing are admitted to rebut other results of genetic testing, the man identified as the father of a child under Section 160.505 shall be adjudicated as being the father of the child.

(d) Unless the results of genetic testing are admitted to rebut other results of genetic testing, a man excluded as the father of a child by genetic testing shall be adjudicated as not being the father of the child.

(e) If the court finds that genetic testing under Section 160.505 does not identify or exclude a man as the father of a child, the court may not dismiss the proceeding. In that event, the results of genetic testing and other evidence are admissible to adjudicate the issue of paternity.

Added by Acts 2001, 77th Leg., ch. 821, § 1.01, eff. June 14, 2001.

## § 160.632. Jury Prohibited

The court shall adjudicate paternity of a child without a jury.

Added by Acts 2001, 77th Leg., ch. 821, § 1.01, eff. June 14, 2001.

## § 160.633. Hearings; Inspection of Records

(a) A proceeding under this subchapter is open to the public as in other civil cases.

(b) Papers and records in a proceeding under this subchapter are available for public inspection.

Added by Acts 2001, 77th Leg., ch. 821, § 1.01, eff. June 14, 2001. Amended by Acts 2003, 78th Leg., ch. 610, § 11, eff. Sept. 1, 2003.

### § 160.634. Order on Default

The court shall issue an order adjudicating the paternity of a man who:

(1) after service of process, is in default; and

(2) is found by the court to be the father of a child.

Added by Acts 2001, 77th Leg., ch. 821, § 1.01, eff. June 14, 2001.

### § 160.635. Dismissal for Want of Prosecution

The court may issue an order dismissing a proceeding commenced under this chapter for want of prosecution only without prejudice. An order of dismissal for want of prosecution purportedly with prejudice is void and has only the effect of a dismissal without prejudice.

Added by Acts 2001, 77th Leg., ch. 821, § 1.01, eff. June 14, 2001.

### § 160.636. Order Adjudicating Parentage; Costs

(a) The court shall render an order adjudicating whether a man alleged or claiming to be the father is the parent of the child.

(b) An order adjudicating parentage must identify the child by name and date of birth.

(c) Except as otherwise provided by Subsection (d), the court may assess filing fees, reasonable attorney's fees, fees for genetic testing, other costs, and necessary travel and other reasonable expenses incurred in a proceeding under this subchapter. Attorney's fees awarded by the court may be paid directly to the attorney. An attorney who is awarded attorney's fees may enforce the order in the attorney's own name.

(d) The court may not assess fees, costs, or expenses against the support enforcement agency of this state or another state, except as provided by other law.

(e) On request of a party and for good cause shown, the court may order that the name of the child be changed.

(f) If the order of the court is at variance with the child's birth certificate, the court shall order the vital statistics unit to issue an amended birth record.

(g) On a finding of parentage, the court may order retroactive child support as provided by Chapter 154 and, on a proper showing, order a party to pay an equitable portion of all of the prenatal and postnatal health care expenses of the mother and the child.

(h) In rendering an order for retroactive child support under this section, the court shall use the child support guidelines provided by Chapter 154, together with any relevant factors.

Added by Acts 2001, 77th Leg., ch. 821, § 1.01, eff. June 14, 2001. Amended by Acts 2015, 84th Leg., ch. 1 (S.B. 219), § 1.075, eff. April 2, 2015.

### § 160.637. Binding Effect of Determination of Parentage

(a) Except as otherwise provided by Subsection (b) or Section 160.316, a determination of parentage is binding on:

(1) all signatories to an acknowledgment or denial of paternity as provided by Subchapter D;[1] and

(2) all parties to an adjudication by a court acting under circumstances that satisfy the jurisdictional requirements of Section 159.201.

(b) A child is not bound by a determination of parentage under this chapter unless:

(1) the determination was based on an unrescinded acknowledgment of paternity and the acknowledgment is consistent with the results of genetic testing;

(2) the adjudication of parentage was based on a finding consistent with the results of genetic testing and the consistency is declared in the determination or is otherwise shown; or

(3) the child was a party or was represented in the proceeding determining parentage by an attorney ad litem.

(c) In a proceeding to dissolve a marriage, the court is considered to have made an adjudication of the parentage of a child if the court acts under circumstances that satisfy the jurisdictional requirements of Section 159.201, and the final order:

(1) expressly identifies the child as "a child of the marriage" or "issue of the marriage" or uses similar words indicating that the husband is the father of the child; or

(2) provides for the payment of child support for the child by the husband unless paternity is specifically disclaimed in the order.

(d) Except as otherwise provided by Subsection (b), a determination of parentage may be a defense in a subsequent proceeding seeking to adjudicate parentage by an individual who was not a party to the earlier proceeding.

(e) A party to an adjudication of paternity may challenge the adjudication only under the laws of this state relating to appeal, the vacating of judgments, or other judicial review.

Added by Acts 2001, 77th Leg., ch. 821, § 1.01, eff. June 14, 2001.

[1] V.T.C.A., Family Code § 160.301 et seq.

## SUBCHAPTER H. CHILD OF ASSISTED REPRODUCTION

### § 160.701. Scope of Subchapter

This subchapter applies only to a child conceived by means of assisted reproduction.

Added by Acts 2001, 77th Leg., ch. 821, § 1.01, eff. June 14, 2001.

### § 160.702. Parental Status of Donor

A donor is not a parent of a child conceived by means of assisted reproduction.

Added by Acts 2001, 77th Leg., ch. 821, § 1.01, eff. June 14, 2001.

### § 160.703. Husband's Paternity of Child of Assisted Reproduction

If a husband provides sperm for or consents to assisted reproduction by his wife as provided by Section 160.704, he is the father of a resulting child.

Added by Acts 2001, 77th Leg., ch. 821, § 1.01, eff. June 14, 2001.

### § 160.7031. Unmarried Man's Paternity of Child of Assisted Reproduction

(a) If an unmarried man, with the intent to be the father of a resulting child, provides sperm to a licensed physician and consents to the use of that sperm for assisted reproduction by an unmarried woman, he is the father of a resulting child.

(b) Consent by an unmarried man who intends to be the father of a resulting child in accordance with this section must be in a record signed by the man and the unmarried woman and kept by a licensed physician.

Added by Acts 2007, 80th Leg., ch. 972, § 40, eff. Sept. 1, 2007.

### § 160.704. Consent to Assisted Reproduction

(a) Consent by a married woman to assisted reproduction must be in a record signed by the woman and her husband and kept by a licensed physician. This requirement does not apply to the donation of eggs by a married woman for assisted reproduction by another woman.

(b) Failure by the husband to sign a consent required by Subsection (a) before or after the birth of the child does not preclude a finding that the husband is the father of a child born to his wife if the wife and husband openly treated the child as their own.

Added by Acts 2001, 77th Leg., ch. 821, § 1.01, eff. June 14, 2001. Amended by Acts 2007, 80th Leg., ch. 972, § 41, eff. Sept. 1, 2007.

### § 160.705. Limitation on Husband's Dispute of Paternity

(a) Except as otherwise provided by Subsection (b), the husband of a wife who gives birth to a child by means of assisted reproduction may not challenge his paternity of the child unless:

(1) before the fourth anniversary of the date of learning of the birth of the child he commences a proceeding to adjudicate his paternity; and

(2) the court finds that he did not consent to the assisted reproduction before or after the birth of the child.

(b) A proceeding to adjudicate paternity may be maintained at any time if the court determines that:

(1) the husband did not provide sperm for or, before or after the birth of the child, consent to assisted reproduction by his wife;

(2) the husband and the mother of the child have not cohabited since the probable time of assisted reproduction; and

(3) the husband never openly treated the child as his own.

(c) The limitations provided by this section apply to a marriage declared invalid after assisted reproduction.

Added by Acts 2001, 77th Leg., ch. 821, § 1.01, eff. June 14, 2001.

### § 160.706. Effect of Dissolution of Marriage

(a) If a marriage is dissolved before the placement of eggs, sperm, or embryos, the former spouse is not a parent of the resulting child unless the former spouse consented in a record kept by a licensed physician that if assisted reproduction were to occur after a divorce the former spouse would be a parent of the child.

(b) The consent of a former spouse to assisted reproduction may be withdrawn by that individual in a record kept by a licensed physician at any time before the placement of eggs, sperm, or embryos.

Added by Acts 2001, 77th Leg., ch. 821, § 1.01, eff. June 14, 2001. Amended by Acts 2007, 80th Leg., ch. 972, § 42, eff. Sept. 1, 2007.

### § 160.707. Parental Status of Deceased Spouse

If a spouse dies before the placement of eggs, sperm, or embryos, the deceased spouse is not a parent of the resulting child unless the deceased spouse consented in a record kept by a licensed physician that if assisted reproduction were to occur after death the deceased spouse would be a parent of the child.

Added by Acts 2001, 77th Leg., ch. 821, § 1.01, eff. June 14, 2001. Amended by Acts 2007, 80th Leg., ch. 972, § 43, eff. Sept. 1, 2007.

## SUBCHAPTER I. GESTATIONAL AGREEMENTS

### § 160.751. Definition

In this subchapter, "gestational mother" means a woman who gives birth to a child conceived under a gestational agreement.

Added by Acts 2003, 78th Leg., ch. 457, § 2, eff. Sept. 1, 2003.

### § 160.752. Scope of Subchapter; Choice of Law

(a) Notwithstanding any other provision of this chapter or another law, this subchapter authorizes an agreement between a woman and the intended parents of a child in which the woman relinquishes all rights as a parent of a child conceived by means of assisted reproduction and that provides that the intended parents become the parents of the child.

(b) This subchapter controls over any other law with respect to a child conceived under a gestational agreement under this subchapter.

Added by Acts 2003, 78th Leg., ch. 457, § 2, eff. Sept. 1, 2003.

### § 160.753. Establishment of Parent–Child Relationship

(a) Notwithstanding any other provision of this chapter or another law, the mother-child relationship exists between a woman and a child by an adjudication confirming the woman as a parent of the child born to a gestational mother under a gestational agreement if the gestational agreement is validated under this subchapter or enforceable under other law, regardless of the fact that the gestational mother gave birth to the child.

(b) The father-child relationship exists between a child and a man by an adjudication confirming the man as a parent of the child born to a gestational mother under a gestational agreement if the gestational agreement is validated under this subchapter or enforceable under other law.

Added by Acts 2003, 78th Leg., ch. 457, § 2, eff. Sept. 1, 2003.

### § 160.754. Gestational Agreement Authorized

(a) A prospective gestational mother, her husband if she is married, each donor, and each intended parent may enter into a written agreement providing that:

(1) the prospective gestational mother agrees to pregnancy by means of assisted reproduction;

(2) the prospective gestational mother, her husband if she is married, and each donor other than the intended parents, if applicable, relinquish all parental rights and duties with respect to a child conceived through assisted reproduction;

(3) the intended parents will be the parents of the child; and

(4) the gestational mother and each intended parent agree to exchange throughout the period covered by the agreement all relevant information regarding the health of the gestational mother and each intended parent.

(b) The intended parents must be married to each other. Each intended parent must be a party to the gestational agreement.

(c) The gestational agreement must require that the eggs used in the assisted reproduction procedure be retrieved from an intended parent or a donor. The gestational mother's eggs may not be used in the assisted reproduction procedure.

(d) The gestational agreement must state that the physician who will perform the assisted reproduction procedure as provided by the agreement has informed the parties to the agreement of:

(1) the rate of successful conceptions and births attributable to the procedure, including the most recent published outcome statistics of the procedure at the facility at which it will be performed;

(2) the potential for and risks associated with the implantation of multiple embryos and consequent multiple births resulting from the procedure;

(3) the nature of and expenses related to the procedure;

(4) the health risks associated with, as applicable, fertility drugs used in the procedure, egg retrieval procedures, and egg or embryo transfer procedures; and

(5) reasonably foreseeable psychological effects resulting from the procedure.

(e) The parties to a gestational agreement must enter into the agreement before the 14th day preceding the date the transfer of eggs, sperm, or embryos to the gestational mother occurs for the purpose of conception or implantation.

(f) A gestational agreement does not apply to the birth of a child conceived by means of sexual intercourse.

(g) A gestational agreement may not limit the right of the gestational mother to make decisions to safeguard her health or the health of an embryo.

Added by Acts 2003, 78th Leg., ch. 457, § 2, eff. Sept. 1, 2003.

### § 160.755. Petition to Validate Gestational Agreement

(a) The intended parents and the prospective gestational mother under a gestational agreement may commence a proceeding to validate the agreement.

(b) A person may maintain a proceeding to validate a gestational agreement only if:

(1) the prospective gestational mother or the intended parents have resided in this state for the 90 days preceding the date the proceeding is commenced;

(2) the prospective gestational mother's husband, if she is married, is joined as a party to the proceeding; and

(3) a copy of the gestational agreement is attached to the petition.

Added by Acts 2003, 78th Leg., ch. 457, § 2, eff. Sept. 1, 2003.

### § 160.756. Hearing to Validate Gestational Agreement

(a) A gestational agreement must be validated as provided by this section.

(b) The court may validate a gestational agreement as provided by Subsection (c) only if the court finds that:

(1) the parties have submitted to the jurisdiction of the court under the jurisdictional standards of this chapter;

(2) the medical evidence provided shows that the intended mother is unable to carry a pregnancy to term and give birth to the child or is unable to carry the pregnancy to term and give birth to the child without unreasonable risk to her physical or mental health or to the health of the unborn child;

(3) unless waived by the court, an agency or other person has conducted a home study of the intended parents and has determined that the intended parents meet the standards of fitness applicable to adoptive parents;

(4) each party to the agreement has voluntarily entered into and understands the terms of the agreement;

(5) the prospective gestational mother has had at least one previous pregnancy and delivery and carrying another pregnancy to term and giving birth to another child would not pose an unreasonable risk to the child's health or the physical or mental health of the prospective gestational mother; and

(6) the parties have adequately provided for which party is responsible for all reasonable health care expenses associated with the pregnancy, including providing for who is responsible for those expenses if the agreement is terminated.

(c) If the court finds that the requirements of Subsection (b) are satisfied, the court may render an order validating the gestational agreement and declaring that the intended parents will be the parents of a child born under the agreement.

(d) The court may validate the gestational agreement at the court's discretion. The court's determination of whether to validate the agreement is subject to review only for abuse of discretion.

Added by Acts 2003, 78th Leg., ch. 457, § 2, eff. Sept. 1, 2003.

### § 160.757. Inspection of Records

The proceedings, records, and identities of the parties to a gestational agreement under this subchapter are subject to inspection under the same standards of confidentiality that apply to an adoption under the laws of this state.

Added by Acts 2003, 78th Leg., ch. 457, § 2, eff. Sept. 1, 2003.

## § 160.758. Continuing, Exclusive Jurisdiction

Subject to Section 152.201, a court that conducts a proceeding under this subchapter has continuing, exclusive jurisdiction of all matters arising out of the gestational agreement until the date a child born to the gestational mother during the period covered by the agreement reaches 180 days of age.

Added by Acts 2003, 78th Leg., ch. 457, § 2, eff. Sept. 1, 2003.

## § 160.759. Termination of Gestational Agreement

(a) Before a prospective gestational mother becomes pregnant by means of assisted reproduction, the prospective gestational mother, her husband if she is married, or either intended parent may terminate a gestational agreement validated under Section 160.756 by giving written notice of the termination to each other party to the agreement.

(b) A person who terminates a gestational agreement under Subsection (a) shall file notice of the termination with the court. A person having the duty to notify the court who does not notify the court of the termination of the agreement is subject to appropriate sanctions.

(c) On receipt of the notice of termination, the court shall vacate the order rendered under Section 160.756 validating the gestational agreement.

(d) A prospective gestational mother and her husband, if she is married, may not be liable to an intended parent for terminating a gestational agreement if the termination is in accordance with this section.

Added by Acts 2003, 78th Leg., ch. 457, § 2, eff. Sept. 1, 2003.

## § 160.760. Parentage Under Validated Gestational Agreement

(a) On the birth of a child to a gestational mother under a validated gestational agreement, the intended parents shall file a notice of the birth with the court not later than the 300th day after the date assisted reproduction occurred.

(b) After receiving notice of the birth, the court shall render an order that:

(1) confirms that the intended parents are the child's parents;

(2) requires the gestational mother to surrender the child to the intended parents, if necessary; and

(3) requires the vital statistics unit to issue a birth certificate naming the intended parents as the child's parents.

(c) If a person alleges that a child born to a gestational mother did not result from assisted reproduction, the court shall order that scientifically accepted parentage testing be conducted to determine the child's parentage.

(d) If the intended parents fail to file the notice required by Subsection (a), the gestational mother or an appropriate state agency may file the notice required by that subsection. On a showing that an order validating the gestational agreement was rendered in accordance with Section 160.756, the court shall order that the intended parents are the child's parents and are financially responsible for the child.

Added by Acts 2003, 78th Leg., ch. 457, § 2, eff. Sept. 1, 2003. Amended by Acts 2005, 79th Leg., ch. 916, § 22, eff. June 18, 2005; Acts 2015, 84th Leg., ch. 1 (S.B. 219), § 1.076, eff. April 2, 2015.

## § 160.761. Effect of Gestational Mother's Marriage After Validation of Agreement

If a gestational mother is married after the court renders an order validating a gestational agreement under this subchapter:

(1) the validity of the gestational agreement is not affected;

(2) the gestational mother's husband is not required to consent to the agreement; and

(3) the gestational mother's husband is not a presumed father of the child born under the terms of the agreement.

Added by Acts 2003, 78th Leg., ch. 457, § 2, eff. Sept. 1, 2003.

## § 160.762. Effect of Gestational Agreement That is Not Validated

(a) A gestational agreement that is not validated as provided by this subchapter is unenforceable, regardless of whether the agreement is in a record.

(b) The parent-child relationship of a child born under a gestational agreement that is not validated as provided by this subchapter is determined as otherwise provided by this chapter.

(c) A party to a gestational agreement that is not validated as provided by this subchapter who is an intended parent under the agreement may be held liable for the support of a child born under the agreement, even if the agreement is otherwise unenforceable.

(d) The court may assess filing fees, reasonable attorney's fees, fees for genetic testing, other costs, and necessary travel and other reasonable expenses incurred in a proceeding under this section. Attorney's fees awarded by the court may be paid directly to the attorney. An attorney who is awarded attorney's fees may enforce the order in the attorney's own name.

Added by Acts 2003, 78th Leg., ch. 457, § 2, eff. Sept. 1, 2003.

## § 160.763. Health Care Facility Reporting Requirement

(a) The executive commissioner of the Health and Human Services Commission by rule shall develop and implement a confidential reporting system that requires each health care facility in this state at which assisted reproduction procedures are performed under gestational agreements to report statistics related to those procedures.

(b) In developing the reporting system, the executive commissioner shall require each health care facility described by Subsection (a) to annually report:

(1) the number of assisted reproduction procedures under a gestational agreement performed at the facility during the preceding year; and

(2) the number and current status of embryos created through assisted reproduction procedures described by Subdivision (1) that were not transferred for implantation.

Added by Acts 2003, 78th Leg., ch. 457, § 2, eff. Sept. 1, 2003. Amended by Acts 2015, 84th Leg., ch. 1 (S.B. 219), § 1.077, eff. April 2, 2015.

# CHAPTER 161. TERMINATION OF THE PARENT–CHILD RELATIONSHIP

SUBCHAPTER A. GROUNDS



## SUBCHAPTER A. GROUNDS

## § 161.001. Involuntary Termination of Parent–Child Relationship

(a) In this section, "born addicted to alcohol or a controlled substance" means a child:

(1) who is born to a mother who during the pregnancy used a controlled substance, as defined by Chapter 481, Health and Safety Code, other than a controlled substance legally obtained by prescription, or alcohol; and

(2) who, after birth as a result of the mother's use of the controlled substance or alcohol:

(A) experiences observable withdrawal from the alcohol or controlled substance;

(B) exhibits observable or harmful effects in the child's physical appearance or functioning; or

(C) exhibits the demonstrable presence of alcohol or a controlled substance in the child's bodily fluids.

(b) The court may order termination of the parent-child relationship if the court finds by clear and convincing evidence:

(1) that the parent has:

(A) voluntarily left the child alone or in the possession of another not the parent and expressed an intent not to return;

(B) voluntarily left the child alone or in the possession of another not the parent without expressing an intent to return, without providing for the adequate support of the child, and remained away for a period of at least three months;

(C) voluntarily left the child alone or in the possession of another without providing adequate support of the child and remained away for a period of at least six months;

(D) knowingly placed or knowingly allowed the child to remain in conditions or surroundings which endanger the physical or emotional well-being of the child;

(E) engaged in conduct or knowingly placed the child with persons who engaged in conduct which endangers the physical or emotional well-being of the child;

(F) failed to support the child in accordance with the parent's ability during a period of one year ending within six months of the date of the filing of the petition;

(G) abandoned the child without identifying the child or furnishing means of identification, and the child's identity cannot be ascertained by the exercise of reasonable diligence;

(H) voluntarily, and with knowledge of the pregnancy, abandoned the mother of the child beginning at a time during her pregnancy with the child and continuing through the birth, failed to provide adequate support or medical care for the mother during the period of abandonment before the birth of the child, and remained apart from the child or failed to support the child since the birth;

(I) contumaciously refused to submit to a reasonable and lawful order of a court under Subchapter D, Chapter 261;[1]

(J) been the major cause of:

(i) the failure of the child to be enrolled in school as required by the Education Code; or

(ii) the child's absence from the child's home without the consent of the parents or guardian for a substantial length of time or without the intent to return;

(K) executed before or after the suit is filed an unrevoked or irrevocable affidavit of relinquishment of parental rights as provided by this chapter;

(L) been convicted or has been placed on community supervision, including deferred adjudication community supervision, for being criminally responsible for the death or serious injury of a child under the following sections of the Penal Code, or under a law of another jurisdiction that contains elements that are substantially similar to the elements of an offense under one of the following Penal Code sections, or adjudicated under Title 3 for conduct that caused the death or serious injury of a child and that would constitute a violation of one of the following Penal Code sections:

(i) Section 19.02 (murder);

(ii) Section 19.03 (capital murder);

(iii) Section 19.04 (manslaughter);

(iv) Section 21.11 (indecency with a child);

(v) Section 22.01 (assault);

(vi) Section 22.011 (sexual assault);

(vii) Section 22.02 (aggravated assault);

(viii) Section 22.021 (aggravated sexual assault);

(ix) Section 22.04 (injury to a child, elderly individual, or disabled individual);

(x) Section 22.041 (abandoning or endangering child);

(xi) Section 25.02 (prohibited sexual conduct);

(xii) Section 43.25 (sexual performance by a child);

(xiii) Section 43.26 (possession or promotion of child pornography);

(xiv) Section 21.02 (continuous sexual abuse of young child or disabled individual );

(xv) Section 20A.02(a)(7) or (8) (trafficking of persons); and

(xvi) Section 43.05(a)(2) (compelling prostitution);

(M) had his or her parent-child relationship terminated with respect to another child based on a finding that the parent's conduct was in violation of Paragraph (D) or (E) or substantially equivalent provisions of the law of another state;

(N) constructively abandoned the child who has been in the permanent or temporary managing conservatorship of the Department of Family and

Protective Services for not less than six months, and:

(i) the department has made reasonable efforts to return the child to the parent;

(ii) the parent has not regularly visited or maintained significant contact with the child; and

(iii) the parent has demonstrated an inability to provide the child with a safe environment;

(O) failed to comply with the provisions of a court order that specifically established the actions necessary for the parent to obtain the return of the child who has been in the permanent or temporary managing conservatorship of the Department of Family and Protective Services for not less than nine months as a result of the child's removal from the parent under Chapter 262 for the abuse or neglect of the child;

(P) used a controlled substance, as defined by Chapter 481, Health and Safety Code, in a manner that endangered the health or safety of the child, and:

(i) failed to complete a court-ordered substance abuse treatment program; or

(ii) after completion of a court-ordered substance abuse treatment program, continued to abuse a controlled substance;

(Q) knowingly engaged in criminal conduct that has resulted in the parent's:

(i) conviction of an offense; and

(ii) confinement or imprisonment and inability to care for the child for not less than two years from the date of filing the petition;

(R) been the cause of the child being born addicted to alcohol or a controlled substance, other than a controlled substance legally obtained by prescription;

(S) voluntarily delivered the child to a designated emergency infant care provider under Section 262.302 without expressing an intent to return for the child;

(T) been convicted of:

(i) the murder of the other parent of the child under Section 19.02 or 19.03, Penal Code, or under a law of another state, federal law, the law of a foreign country, or the Uniform Code of Military Justice that contains elements that are substantially similar to the elements of an offense under Section 19.02 or 19.03, Penal Code;

(ii) criminal attempt under Section 15.01, Penal Code, or under a law of another state, federal law, the law of a foreign country, or the Uniform Code of Military Justice that contains elements that are substantially similar to the elements of an offense under Section 15.01, Penal Code, to commit the offense described by Subparagraph (i);

(iii) criminal solicitation under Section 15.03, Penal Code, or under a law of another state, federal law, the law of a foreign country, or the Uniform Code of Military Justice that contains elements that are substantially similar to the elements of an offense under Section 15.03, Penal Code, of the offense described by Subparagraph (i); or

(iv) the sexual assault of the other parent of the child under Section 22.011 or 22.021, Penal Code, or under a law of another state, federal law, or the Uniform Code of Military Justice that contains elements that are substantially similar to the elements of an offense under Section 22.011 or 22.021, Penal Code; or

(U) been placed on community supervision, including deferred adjudication community supervision, or another functionally equivalent form of community supervision or probation, for being criminally responsible for the sexual assault of the other parent of the child under Section 22.011 or 22.021, Penal Code, or under a law of another state, federal law, or the Uniform Code of Military Justice that contains elements that are substantially similar to the elements of an offense under Section 22.011 or 22.021, Penal Code; and

(2) that termination is in the best interest of the child.

(c) Evidence of one or more of the following does not constitute clear and convincing evidence sufficient for a court to make a finding under Subsection (b) and order termination of the parent-child relationship:

(1) the parent homeschooled the child;

(2) the parent is economically disadvantaged;

(3) the parent has been charged with a nonviolent misdemeanor offense other than:

(A) an offense under Title 5, Penal Code;

(B) an offense under Title 6, Penal Code; or

(C) an offense that involves family violence, as defined by Section 71.004 of this code;

(4) the parent provided or administered low-THC cannabis to a child for whom the low-THC cannabis was prescribed under Chapter 169, Occupations Code;

(5) the parent declined immunization for the child for reasons of conscience, including a religious belief; or

*Text of (c)(6), as added by Acts 2021, 87th Leg., ch. 8 (H.B. 567), § 3*

(6) the parent allowed the child to engage in independent activities that are appropriate and typi-

cal for the child's level of maturity, physical condition, developmental abilities, or culture.

*Text of (c)(6), as added by Acts 2021, 87th Leg., ch. 29 (H.B. 2536), § 1*

(6) sought an opinion from more than one medical provider relating to the child's medical care, transferred the child's medical care to a new medical provider, or transferred the child to another health care facility.

(d) A court may not order termination under Subsection (b)(1)(O) based on the failure by the parent to comply with a specific provision of a court order if a parent proves by a preponderance of evidence that:

(1) the parent was unable to comply with specific provisions of the court order; and

(2) the parent made a good faith effort to comply with the order and the failure to comply with the order is not attributable to any fault of the parent.

(d–1) The court may not order termination under Subsection (b)(1)(M) unless the petition for the termination of the parent-child relationship is filed not later than the first anniversary of the date the department or an equivalent agency in another state was granted managing conservatorship of a child in the case that resulted in the termination of the parent-child relationship with respect to that child based on a finding that the parent's conduct violated Subsection (b)(1)(D) or (E) or substantially equivalent provisions of the law of another state.

(e) This section does not prohibit the Department of Family and Protective Services from offering evidence described by Subsection (c) as part of an action to terminate the parent-child relationship under this subchapter.

Added by Acts 1995, 74th Leg., ch. 20, § 1, eff. April 20, 1995. Amended by Acts 1995, 74th Leg., ch. 709, § 1, eff. Sept. 1, 1995; Acts 1995, 74th Leg., ch. 751, § 65, eff. Sept. 1, 1995; Acts 1997, 75th Leg., ch. 575, § 9, eff. Sept. 1, 1997; Acts 1997, 75th Leg., ch. 1022, § 60, eff. Sept. 1, 1997; Acts 1999, 76th Leg., ch. 1087, § 1, eff. Sept. 1, 1999; Acts 1999, 76th Leg., ch. 1390, § 18, eff. Sept. 1, 1999; Acts 2001, 77th Leg., ch. 809, § 1, eff. Sept. 1, 2001; Acts 2005, 79th Leg., ch. 508, § 2, eff. Sept. 1, 2005; Acts 2007, 80th Leg., ch. 593, § 3.30, eff. Sept. 1, 2007; Acts 2009, 81st Leg., ch. 86, § 1, eff. Sept. 1, 2009; Acts 2011, 82nd Leg., ch. 1 (S.B. 24), § 4.02, eff. Sept. 1, 2011; Acts 2015, 84th Leg., ch. 1 (S.B. 219), § 1.078, eff. April 2, 2015; Acts 2015, 84th Leg., ch. 944 (S.B. 206), § 11, eff. Sept. 1, 2015; Acts 2017, 85th Leg., ch. 40 (S.B. 77), § 2, eff. Sept. 1, 2017; Acts 2017, 85th Leg., ch. 317 (H.B. 7), § 12, eff. Sept. 1, 2017; Acts 2021, 87th Leg., ch. 8 (H.B. 567), § 3, eff. Sept. 1, 2021; Acts 2021, 87th Leg., ch. 29 (H.B. 2536), § 1, eff. May 15, 2021; Acts 2021, 87th Leg., ch. 221 (H.B. 375), § 2.17, eff. Sept. 1, 2021; Acts 2021, 87th Leg., ch. 831 (H.B. 2924), § 1, eff. Sept. 1, 2021.

[1] V.T.C.A., Family Code § 261.301 et seq.

Section 15 of Acts 2021, 87th Leg., ch. 8 (H.B. 567) provides:

"The changes in law made by this Act apply only to a suit filed by the Department of Family and Protective Services on or after the effective date [Sept. 1, 2021] of this Act. A suit filed by the department before that date is governed by the law in effect on the date the suit was filed, and the former law is continued in effect for that purpose."

Section 3.01 of Acts 2021, 87th Leg., ch. 221 (H.B. 375) provides:

"The change in law made by this Act applies only to an offense committed on or after the effective date [Sept. 1, 2021] of this Act. An offense committed before the effective date of this Act is governed by the law in effect on the date the offense was committed, and the former law is continued in effect for that purpose. For purposes of this section, an offense was committed before the effective date of this Act if any element of the offense occurred before that date."

Section 3 of Acts 2021, 87th Leg., ch. 831 (H.B. 2924) provides:

"The change in law made by this Act applies only to a court order for the involuntary termination of the parent-child relationship rendered on or after the effective date of this Act [Sept. 1, 2021]. A court order rendered before the effective date of this Act is governed by the law in effect on the date the order was rendered, and the former law is continued in effect for that purpose."

## § 161.002. Termination of the Rights of an Alleged Biological Father

(a) Except as otherwise provided by this section, the procedural and substantive standards for termination of parental rights apply to the termination of the rights of an alleged father.

(b) The rights of an alleged father may be terminated if:

(1) after being served with citation, he does not respond by timely filing an admission of paternity or a counterclaim for paternity under Chapter 160;

(2) the child is over one year of age at the time the petition for termination of the parent-child relationship or for adoption is filed, he has not registered with the paternity registry under Chapter 160, and after the exercise of due diligence by the petitioner:

(A) his identity and location are unknown; or

(B) his identity is known but he cannot be located;

(3) the child is under one year of age at the time the petition for termination of the parent-child relationship or for adoption is filed and he has not registered with the paternity registry under Chapter 160; or

(4) he has registered with the paternity registry under Chapter 160, but the petitioner's attempt to personally serve citation at the address provided to the registry and at any other address for the alleged father known by the petitioner has been unsuccessful, despite the due diligence of the petitioner.

(c) Repealed by Acts 2015, 84th Leg., ch. 1 (S.B. 219), § 1.203(2).

(c–1) The termination of the rights of an alleged father under Subsection (b)(2) or (3) rendered on or after January 1, 2008, does not require personal service of citation or citation by publication on the alleged father, and there is no requirement to identify or locate an alleged father who has not registered with the paternity registry under Chapter 160.

(d) The termination of rights of an alleged father under Subsection (b)(4) does not require service of citation by publication on the alleged father.

(e) The court shall not render an order terminating parental rights under Subsection (b)(2) or (3) unless the court receives evidence of a certificate of the results of a search of the paternity registry under Chapter 160 from the vital statistics unit indicating that no man has registered the intent to claim paternity.

(f) The court shall not render an order terminating parental rights under Subsection (b)(4) unless the court, after reviewing the petitioner's sworn affidavit describing the petitioner's effort to obtain personal service of citation on the alleged father and considering any evidence submitted by the attorney ad litem for the alleged father, has found that the petitioner exercised due diligence in attempting to obtain service on the alleged father. The order shall contain specific findings regarding the exercise of due diligence of the petitioner.

Added by Acts 1995, 74th Leg., ch. 20, § 1, eff. April 20, 1995. Amended by Acts 1995, 74th Leg., ch. 751, § 66, eff. Sept. 1, 1995; Acts 1997, 75th Leg., ch. 561, § 7, eff. Sept. 1, 1997; Acts 2001, 77th Leg., ch. 821, § 2.16, eff. June 14, 2001; Acts 2001, 77th Leg., ch. 1090, § 1, eff. Sept. 1, 2001; Acts 2007, 80th Leg., ch. 1283, § 4, eff. Sept. 1, 2007; Acts 2015, 84th Leg., ch. 1 (S.B. 219), §§ 1.079, 1.203(2), eff. April 2, 2015.

### § 161.003. Involuntary Termination: Inability to Care for Child

(a) The court may order termination of the parent-child relationship in a suit filed by the Department of Family and Protective Services if the court finds that:

(1) the parent has a mental or emotional illness or a mental deficiency that renders the parent unable to provide for the physical, emotional, and mental needs of the child;

(2) the illness or deficiency, in all reasonable probability, proved by clear and convincing evidence, will continue to render the parent unable to provide for the child's needs until the 18th birthday of the child;

(3) the department has been the temporary or sole managing conservator of the child of the parent for at least six months preceding the date of the hearing on the termination held in accordance with Subsection (c);

(4) the department has made reasonable efforts to return the child to the parent; and

(5) the termination is in the best interest of the child.

(b) Immediately after the filing of a suit under this section, the court shall appoint an attorney ad litem to represent the interests of the parent against whom the suit is brought.

(c) A hearing on the termination may not be held earlier than 180 days after the date on which the suit was filed.

(d) An attorney appointed under Subsection (b) shall represent the parent for the duration of the suit unless the parent, with the permission of the court, retains another attorney.

Added by Acts 1995, 74th Leg., ch. 20, § 1, eff. April 20, 1995. Amended by Acts 1995, 74th Leg., ch. 751, § 67, eff. Sept. 1, 1995; Acts 2001, 77th Leg., ch. 496, § 1, eff. Sept. 1, 2001; Acts 2001, 77th Leg., ch. 1090, § 2, eff. Sept. 1, 2001; Acts 2015, 84th Leg., ch. 1 (S.B. 219), § 1.080, eff. April 2, 2015.

### § 161.004. Termination of Parental Rights After Denial of Prior Petition to Terminate

(a) The court may terminate the parent-child relationship after rendition of an order that previously denied termination of the parent-child relationship if:

(1) the petition under this section is filed after the date the order denying termination was rendered;

(2) the circumstances of the child, parent, sole managing conservator, possessory conservator, or other party affected by the order denying termination have materially and substantially changed since the date that the order was rendered;

(3) the parent committed an act listed under Section 161.001 before the date the order denying termination was rendered; and

(4) termination is in the best interest of the child.

(b) At a hearing under this section, the court may consider evidence presented at a previous hearing in a suit for termination of the parent-child relationship of the parent with respect to the same child.

Added by Acts 1995, 74th Leg., ch. 20, § 1, eff. April 20, 1995.

### § 161.005. Termination When Parent Is Petitioner

(a) A parent may file a suit for termination of the petitioner's parent-child relationship. Except as provided by Subsection (h), the court may order termination if termination is in the best interest of the child.

(b) If the petition designates the Department of Family and Protective Services as managing conservator, the department shall be given service of citation. The court shall notify the department if the court appoints the department as the managing conservator of the child.

(c) Subject to Subsection (d), a man may file a suit for termination of the parent-child relationship between the man and a child if, without obtaining genetic testing, the man signed an acknowledgment of paternity of the child in accordance with Subchapter D, Chapter 160, or was adjudicated to be the father of the child in a previous proceeding under this title in which genetic testing did not occur. The petition must be verified and must allege facts showing that the petitioner:

(1) is not the child's genetic father; and

(2) signed the acknowledgment of paternity or failed to contest parentage in the previous proceeding because of the mistaken belief, at the time the acknowledgment was signed or on the date the court order in the previous proceeding was rendered, that he was the child's genetic father based on misrepresentations that led him to that conclusion.

(d) A man may not file a petition under Subsection (c) if:

(1) the man is the child's adoptive father;

(2) the child was conceived by assisted reproduction and the man consented to assisted reproduction by his wife under Subchapter H, Chapter 160; or

(3) the man is the intended father of the child under a gestational agreement validated by a court under Subchapter I, Chapter 160.

(e) A petition under Subsection (c) must be filed not later than the second anniversary of the date on which the petitioner becomes aware of the facts alleged in the petition indicating that the petitioner is not the child's genetic father.

(e–1) Expired.

(f) In a proceeding initiated under Subsection (c), the court shall hold a pretrial hearing to determine whether the petitioner has established a meritorious prima facie case for termination of the parent-child relationship. If a meritorious prima facie claim is established, the court shall order the petitioner and the child to submit to genetic testing under Subchapter F, Chapter 160.

(g) If the results of genetic testing ordered under Subsection (f) identify the petitioner as the child's genetic father under the standards prescribed by Section 160.505 and the results of any further testing requested by the petitioner and ordered by the court under Subchapter F, Chapter 160, do not exclude the petitioner as the child's genetic father, the court shall deny the petitioner's request for termination of the parent-child relationship.

(h) If the results of genetic testing ordered under Subsection (f) exclude the petitioner as the child's genetic father, the court shall render an order terminating the parent-child relationship.

(i) An order under Subsection (h) terminating the parent-child relationship ends the petitioner's obligation for future support of the child as of the date the order is rendered, as well as the obligation to pay interest that accrues after that date on the basis of a child support arrearage or money judgment for a child support arrearage existing on that date. The order does not affect the petitioner's obligations for support of the child incurred before that date. Those obligations are enforceable until satisfied by any means available for the enforcement of child support other than contempt.

(j) An order under Subsection (h) terminating the parent-child relationship does not preclude:

(1) the initiation of a proceeding under Chapter 160 to adjudicate whether another man is the child's parent; or

(2) if the other man subject to a proceeding under Subdivision (1) is adjudicated as the child's parent, the rendition of an order requiring that man to pay child support for the child under Chapter 154, subject to Subsection (k).

(k) Notwithstanding Section 154.131, an order described by Subsection (j)(2) may not require the other man to pay retroactive child support for any period preceding the date on which the order under Subsection (h) terminated the parent-child relationship between the child and the man seeking termination under this section.

(*l*) At any time before the court renders an order terminating the parent-child relationship under Subsection (h), the petitioner may request that the court also order periods of possession of or access to the child by the petitioner following termination of the parent-child relationship. If requested, the court may order periods of possession of or access to the child only if the court determines that denial of periods of possession of or access to the child would significantly impair the child's physical health or emotional well-being.

(m) The court may include provisions in an order under Subsection (*l*) that require:

(1) the child or any party to the proceeding to participate in counseling with a mental health professional who:

(A) has a background in family therapy; and

(B) holds a professional license that requires the person to possess at least a master's degree; and

(2) any party to pay the costs of the counseling described by Subdivision (1).

(n) Notwithstanding Subsection (m)(1), if a person who possesses the qualifications described by that subdivision is not available in the county in which the court is located, the court may require that the counseling be conducted by another person the court considers qualified for that purpose.

(*o*) During any period of possession of or access to the child ordered under Subsection (*l*) the petitioner has the rights and duties specified by Section 153.074, subject to any limitation specified by the court in its order.

Added by Acts 1995, 74th Leg., ch. 20, § 1, eff. April 20, 1995. Amended by Acts 1995, 74th Leg., ch. 751, § 68, eff. Sept. 1, 1995; Acts 2011, 82nd Leg., ch. 54 (S.B. 785), § 2, eff. May 12, 2011; Acts 2013, 83rd Leg., ch. 227 (H.B. 154), § 1, eff. June 14, 2013; Acts 2015, 84th Leg., ch. 1 (S.B. 219), § 1.081, eff. April 2, 2015.

### § 161.006. Termination After Abortion

(a) A petition requesting termination of the parent-child relationship with respect to a parent who is not the petitioner may be granted if the child was born alive as the result of an abortion.

(b) In this code, "abortion" has the meaning assigned by Section 245.002, Health and Safety Code.

(c) The court or the jury may not terminate the parent-child relationship under this section with respect to a parent who:

(1) had no knowledge of the abortion; or

(2) participated in or consented to the abortion for the sole purpose of preventing the death of the mother.

Added by Acts 1995, 74th Leg., ch. 20, § 1, eff. April 20, 1995. Amended by Acts 2017, 85th Leg., ch. 441 (S.B. 8), § 2, eff. Sept. 1, 2017.

### § 161.007. Termination When Pregnancy Results from Criminal Act

(a) Except as provided by Subsection (b), the court shall order the termination of the parent-child relationship of a parent and a child if the court finds by clear and convincing evidence that:

(1) the parent has engaged in conduct that constitutes an offense under Section 21.02, 22.011, 22.021, or 25.02, Penal Code;

(2) as a direct result of the conduct described by Subdivision (1), the victim of the conduct became pregnant with the parent's child; and

(3) termination is in the best interest of the child.

(b) If, for the two years after the birth of the child, the parent was married to or cohabiting with the other parent of the child, the court may order the termination of the parent-child relationship of the parent and the child if the court finds that:

(1) the parent has been convicted of an offense committed under Section 21.02, 22.011, 22.021, or 25.02, Penal Code;

(2) as a direct result of the commission of the offense by the parent, the other parent became pregnant with the child; and

(3) termination is in the best interest of the child.

Added by Acts 1997, 75th Leg., ch. 561, § 8, eff. Sept. 1, 1997. Amended by Acts 2007, 80th Leg., ch. 593, § 3.31, eff. Sept. 1, 2007; Acts 2013, 83rd Leg., ch. 907 (H.B. 1228), § 4, eff. Sept. 1, 2013.

## SUBCHAPTER B. PROCEDURES

### § 161.101. Petition Allegations; Petition and Motion Requirements

(a) A petition for the termination of the parent-child relationship is sufficient without the necessity of specifying the underlying facts if the petition alleges in the statutory language the ground for the termination and that termination is in the best interest of the child.

(b) A petition or motion filed by the Department of Family and Protective Services in a suit for termination of the parent-child relationship is subject to Chapter 10, Civil Practice and Remedies Code, and Rule 13, Texas Rules of Civil Procedure.

Added by Acts 1995, 74th Leg., ch. 20, § 1, eff. April 20, 1995. Amended by Acts 2021, 87th Leg., ch. 8 (H.B. 567), § 4, eff. Sept. 1, 2021.

Sections 14 and 15 of Acts 2021, 87th Leg., ch. 8 (H.B. 567) provide:

"Sec. 14. Section 161.101, Family Code, as amended by this Act, applies only to a petition or motion filed by the Department of Family and Protective Services on or after the effective date [Sept. 1, 2021] of this Act. A petition or motion filed by the department before that date is governed by the law in effect on the date the petition or motion was filed, and the former law is continued in effect for that purpose.

"Sec. 15. The changes in law made by this Act apply only to a suit filed by the Department of Family and Protective Services on or after the effective date of this Act. A suit filed by the department before that date is governed by the law in effect on the date the suit was filed, and the former law is continued in effect for that purpose."

## § 161.102. Filing Suit for Termination Before Birth

(a) A suit for termination may be filed before the birth of the child.

(b) If the suit is filed before the birth of the child, the petition shall be styled "In the Interest of an Unborn Child." After the birth, the clerk shall change the style of the case to conform to the requirements of Section 102.008.

Added by Acts 1995, 74th Leg., ch. 20, § 1, eff. April 20, 1995.

## § 161.103. Affidavit of Voluntary Relinquishment of Parental Rights

(a) An affidavit for voluntary relinquishment of parental rights must be:

(1) signed after the birth of the child, but not before 48 hours after the birth of the child, by the parent, whether or not a minor, whose parental rights are to be relinquished;

(2) witnessed by two credible persons; and

(3) verified before a person authorized to take oaths.

(b) The affidavit must contain:

(1) the name, county of residence, and age of the parent whose parental rights are being relinquished;

(2) the name, age, and birth date of the child;

(3) the names and addresses of the guardians of the person and estate of the child, if any;

(4) a statement that the affiant is or is not presently obligated by court order to make payments for the support of the child;

(5) a full description and statement of value of all property owned or possessed by the child;

(6) an allegation that termination of the parent-child relationship is in the best interest of the child;

(7) one of the following, as applicable:

(A) the name and county of residence of the other parent;

(B) a statement that the parental rights of the other parent have been terminated by death or court order; or

(C) a statement that the child has no presumed father;

(8) a statement that the parent has been informed of parental rights and duties;

(9) a statement that the relinquishment is revocable, that the relinquishment is irrevocable, or that the relinquishment is irrevocable for a stated period of time;

(10) if the relinquishment is revocable, a statement in boldfaced type concerning the right of the parent signing the affidavit to revoke the relinquishment only if the revocation is made before the 11th day after the date the affidavit is executed;

(11) if the relinquishment is revocable, the name and address of a person to whom the revocation is to be delivered; and

(12) the designation of a prospective adoptive parent, the Department of Family and Protective Services, if the department has consented in writing to the designation, or a licensed child-placing agency to serve as managing conservator of the child and the address of the person or agency.

(c) The affidavit may contain:

(1) a waiver of process in a suit to terminate the parent-child relationship filed under this chapter or in a suit to terminate joined with a petition for adoption; and

(2) a consent to the placement of the child for adoption by the Department of Family and Protective Services or by a licensed child-placing agency.

(d) A copy of the affidavit shall be provided to the parent at the time the parent signs the affidavit.

(e) The relinquishment in an affidavit that designates the Department of Family and Protective Services or a licensed child-placing agency to serve as the managing conservator is irrevocable. A relinquishment in any other affidavit of relinquishment is revocable unless it expressly provides that it is irrevocable for a stated period of time not to exceed 60 days after the date of its execution.

(f) A relinquishment in an affidavit of relinquishment of parental rights that fails to state that the relinquishment is irrevocable for a stated time is revocable as provided by Section 161.1035.

(g) To revoke a relinquishment under Subsection (e) the parent must sign a statement witnessed by two credible persons and verified before a person authorized to take oaths. A copy of the revocation shall be delivered to the person designated in the affidavit. If a parent attempting to revoke a relinquishment under this subsection has knowledge that a suit for termination of the parent-child relationship has been filed based on the parent's affidavit of relinquishment of parental rights, the parent shall file a copy of the revocation with the clerk of the court.

(h) The affidavit may not contain terms for limited post-termination contact between the child and the parent whose parental rights are to be relinquished as a condition of the relinquishment of parental rights.

Added by Acts 1995, 74th Leg., ch. 20, § 1, eff. April 20, 1995. Amended by Acts 1995, 74th Leg., ch. 751, § 69, eff. Sept. 1, 1995; Acts 1997, 75th Leg., ch. 561, § 9, eff. Sept. 1, 1997; Acts 2003, 78th Leg., ch. 561, § 3, eff. Sept. 1, 2003; Acts 2007, 80th Leg., ch. 1283, § 5, eff. Sept. 1, 2007; Acts 2007, 80th Leg., ch. 1412, § 1, eff. Sept. 1, 2007; Acts 2015, 84th Leg., ch. 1 (S.B. 219), § 1.082, eff. April 2, 2015.

### § 161.1031. Medical History Report

(a) A parent who signs an affidavit of voluntary relinquishment of parental rights under Section 161.103 regarding a biological child must also prepare a medical history report that addresses the medical history of the parent and the parent's ancestors.

(b) The Department of Family and Protective Services, in cooperation with the Department of State Health Services, shall adopt a form that a parent may use to comply with this section. The form must be designed to permit a parent to identify any medical condition of the parent or the parent's ancestors that could indicate a predisposition for the child to develop the condition.

(c) The medical history report shall be used in preparing the health, social, educational, and genetic history report required by Section 162.005 and shall be made available to persons granted access under Section 162.006 in the manner provided by that section.

Added by Acts 2005, 79th Leg., ch. 1258, § 1, eff. Sept. 1, 2005.

### § 161.1035. Revocability of Certain Affidavits

An affidavit of relinquishment of parental rights that fails to state that the relinquishment or waiver is irrevocable for a stated time is:

(1) revocable only if the revocation is made before the 11th day after the date the affidavit is executed; and

(2) irrevocable on or after the 11th day after the date the affidavit is executed.

Added by Acts 1997, 75th Leg., ch. 561, § 10, eff. Sept. 1, 1997. Amended by Acts 2007, 80th Leg., ch. 1283, § 6, eff. Sept. 1, 2007.

### § 161.104. Rights of Designated Managing Conservator Pending Court Appointment

A person, licensed child-placing agency, or the Department of Family and Protective Services designated managing conservator of a child in an irrevocable or unrevoked affidavit of relinquishment has a right to possession of the child superior to the right of the person executing the affidavit, the right to consent to medical, surgical, dental, and psychological treatment of the child, and the rights and duties given by Chapter 153 to a possessory conservator until such time as these rights and duties are modified or terminated by court order.

Added by Acts 1995, 74th Leg., ch. 20, § 1, eff. April 20, 1995. Amended by Acts 1995, 74th Leg., ch. 751, § 70, eff. Sept. 1, 1995; Acts 2015, 84th Leg., ch. 1 (S.B. 219), § 1.083, eff. April 2, 2015.

### § 161.105. Repealed by Acts 2007, 80th Leg., ch. 1283, § 13, eff. Sept. 1, 2007

### § 161.106. Affidavit of Waiver of Interest in Child

(a) A man may sign an affidavit disclaiming any interest in a child and waiving notice or the service of citation in any suit filed or to be filed affecting the parent-child relationship with respect to the child.

(b) The affidavit may be signed before the birth of the child.

(c) The affidavit shall be:

(1) signed by the man, whether or not a minor;

(2) witnessed by two credible persons; and

(3) verified before a person authorized to take oaths.

(d) The affidavit may contain a statement that the affiant does not admit being the father of the child or having had a sexual relationship with the mother of the child.

(e) An affidavit of waiver of interest in a child may be used in a suit in which the affiant attempts to establish an interest in the child. The affidavit may not be used in a suit brought by another person, licensed child-placing agency, or the Department of Family and Protective Services to establish the affiant's paternity of the child.

(f) A waiver in an affidavit under this section is irrevocable.

(g), (h) Repealed by Acts 2007, 80th Leg., ch. 1283, § 13.

(i) A copy of the affidavit shall be provided to the person who executed the affidavit at the time the person signs the affidavit.

(j) Repealed by Acts 2007, 80th Leg., ch. 1283, § 13.

Added by Acts 1995, 74th Leg., ch. 20, § 1, eff. April 20, 1995. Amended by Acts 1997, 75th Leg., ch. 561, § 11, eff. Sept. 1, 1997; Acts 2007, 80th Leg., ch. 1283, §§ 7, 13, eff. Sept. 1, 2007; Acts 2015, 84th Leg., ch. 1 (S.B. 219), § 1.084, eff. April 2, 2015.

### § 161.107. Missing Parent or Relative

(a) In this section:

(1) "Parent" means a parent, as defined by Section 160.102, whose parent-child relationship with a child has not been terminated. The term does not include a man who does not have a parent-child relationship established under Chapter 160.

(2) "Relative" means a parent, grandparent, or adult sibling or child.

(b) If a parent of the child has not been personally served in a suit in which the Department of Family and Protective Services seeks termination, the department must make a diligent effort to locate that parent.

(c) If a parent has not been personally served and cannot be located, the department shall make a diligent effort to locate a relative of the missing parent to give the relative an opportunity to request appointment as the child's managing conservator.

(d) If the department is not able to locate a missing parent or a relative of that parent and sufficient information is available concerning the physical whereabouts of the parent or relative, the department shall request the state agency designated to administer a statewide plan for child support to use the parental locator service established under 42 U.S.C. Section 653 to determine the location of the missing parent or relative.

(e) The department shall be required to provide evidence to the court to show what actions were taken by the department in making a diligent effort to locate the missing parent and relative of the missing parent.

Added by Acts 1995, 74th Leg., ch. 20, § 1, eff. April 20, 1995. Amended by Acts 1995, 74th Leg., ch. 751, § 71, eff. Sept. 1, 1995; Acts 2007, 80th Leg., ch. 1283, §§ 8, 9, eff. Sept. 1, 2007.

### § 161.108. Release of Child From Hospital or Birthing Center

(a) Before or at the time an affidavit of relinquishment of parental rights under Section 161.103 is executed, the mother of a newborn child may authorize the release of the child from the hospital or birthing center to a licensed child-placing agency, the Department of Family and Protective Services, or another designated person.

(b) A release under this section must be:

(1) executed in writing;

(2) witnessed by two credible adults; and

(3) verified before a person authorized to take oaths.

(c) A hospital or birthing center shall comply with the terms of a release executed under this section without requiring a court order.

Added by Acts 1997, 75th Leg., ch. 561, § 12, eff. Sept. 1, 1997. Amended by Acts 2015, 84th Leg., ch. 1 (S.B. 219), § 1.085, eff. April 2, 2015.

### § 161.109. Requirement of Paternity Registry Certificate

(a) If a parent-child relationship does not exist between the child and any man, a certificate from the vital statistics unit signed by the registrar that a diligent search has been made of the paternity registry maintained by the unit and that a registration has not been found pertaining to the father of the child in question must be filed with the court before a trial on the merits in the suit for termination may be held.

(b) In a proceeding to terminate parental rights in which the alleged or probable father has not been personally served with citation or signed an affidavit of relinquishment or an affidavit of waiver of interest, the court may not terminate the parental rights of the alleged or probable father, whether known or unknown, unless a certificate from the vital statistics unit signed by the registrar states that a diligent search has been made of the paternity registry maintained by the unit and that a filing or registration has not been found pertaining to the father of the child in question.

Added by Acts 1997, 75th Leg., ch. 561, § 12, eff. Sept. 1, 1997. Amended by Acts 2007, 80th Leg., ch. 1283, § 10, eff. Sept. 1, 2007; Acts 2015, 84th Leg., ch. 1 (S.B. 219), § 1.086, eff. April 2, 2015.

## SUBCHAPTER C. HEARING AND ORDER

### § 161.201. Repealed by Acts 2001, 77th Leg., ch. 130, § 1, eff. Sept. 1, 2001

### § 161.2011. Continuance; Access to Child

(a) A parent whose rights are subject to termination in a suit affecting the parent-child relationship and against whom criminal charges are filed that directly relate to the grounds for which termination is sought may file a motion requesting a continuance of the final trial in the suit until the criminal charges are resolved. The court may grant the motion only if the court finds that a continuance is in the best interest of the child. Notwithstanding any continuance granted, the court shall conduct status and permanency hearings with respect to the child as required by Chapter 263 and shall comply with the dismissal date under Section 263.401.

(b) Nothing in this section precludes the court from issuing appropriate temporary orders as authorized in this code.

(c) The court in which a suit to terminate the parent-child relationship is pending may render an order denying a parent access to a child if the parent is indicted for criminal activity that constitutes a ground for terminating the parent-child relationship under Section 161.001. The denial of access under this section shall continue until the date the criminal charges for which the parent was indicted are resolved and the court renders an order providing for access to the child by the parent.

Added by Acts 1997, 75th Leg., ch. 1022, § 61, eff. Sept. 1, 1997. Amended by Acts 2001, 77th Leg., ch. 1090, § 3, eff. Sept. 1, 2001.

### § 161.202. Preferential Setting

In a termination suit, after a hearing, the court shall grant a motion for a preferential setting for a final hearing on the merits filed by a party to the suit or by the amicus attorney or attorney ad litem for the child and shall give precedence to that hearing over other civil cases if:

(1) termination would make the child eligible for adoption; and

(2) discovery has been completed or sufficient time has elapsed since the filing of the suit for the completion of all necessary and reasonable discovery if diligently pursued.

Added by Acts 1995, 74th Leg., ch. 20, § 1, eff. April 20, 1995. Amended by Acts 2001, 77th Leg., ch. 133, § 5, eff. Sept. 1, 2001; Acts 2005, 79th Leg., ch. 172, § 19, eff. Sept. 1, 2005.

### § 161.2021. Medical History Report

(a) In a termination suit, the court shall order each parent before the court to provide information regarding the medical history of the parent and the parent's ancestors.

(b) A parent may comply with the court's order under this section by completing the medical history report form adopted by the Department of Family and Protective Services under Section 161.1031.

(c) If the Department of Family and Protective Services is a party to the termination suit, the information provided under this section must be maintained in the department records relating to the child and made available to persons with whom the child is placed.

Added by Acts 2005, 79th Leg., ch. 1258, § 2, eff. Sept. 1, 2005.

### § 161.203. Dismissal of Petition

A suit to terminate may not be dismissed nor may a nonsuit be taken unless the dismissal or nonsuit is approved by the court. The dismissal or nonsuit approved by the court is without prejudice.

Added by Acts 1995, 74th Leg., ch. 20, § 1, eff. April 20, 1995. Amended by Acts 2001, 77th Leg., ch. 1090, § 4, eff. Sept. 1, 2001.

### § 161.204. Termination Based on Affidavit of Waiver of Interest

In a suit for termination, the court may render an order terminating the parent-child relationship between a child and a man who has signed an affidavit of waiver of interest in the child, if the termination is in the best interest of the child.

Added by Acts 1995, 74th Leg., ch. 20, § 1, eff. April 20, 1995. Amended by Acts 2001, 77th Leg., ch. 1090, § 5, eff. Sept. 1, 2001.

### § 161.205. Order Denying Termination

If the court does not order termination of the parent-child relationship, the court shall:

(1) deny the petition; or

(2) render any order in the best interest of the child.

Added by Acts 1995, 74th Leg., ch. 20, § 1, eff. April 20, 1995. Amended by Acts 2001, 77th Leg., ch. 1090, § 6, eff. Sept. 1, 2001.

### § 161.206. Order Terminating Parental Rights

(a) If the court finds by clear and convincing evidence grounds for termination of the parent-child relationship,[1] it shall render an order terminating the parent-child relationship.

(a–1) In a suit filed by the Department of Family and Protective Services seeking termination of the parent-child relationship for more than one parent of the child, the court may order termination of the parent-child relationship for the parent only if the court finds by clear and convincing evidence grounds for the termination of the parent-child relationship for that parent.

(b) Except as provided by Section 161.2061, an order terminating the parent-child relationship divests the parent and the child of all legal rights and duties with respect to each other, except that the child retains the right to inherit from and through the parent unless the court otherwise provides.

(c) Nothing in this chapter precludes or affects the rights of a biological or adoptive maternal or paternal grandparent to reasonable access under Chapter 153.

(d) An order rendered under this section must include a finding that:

(1) a request for identification of a court of continuing, exclusive jurisdiction has been made as required by Section 155.101; and

(2) all parties entitled to notice, including the Title IV–D agency, have been notified.

Added by Acts 1995, 74th Leg., ch. 20, § 1, eff. April 20, 1995. Amended by Acts 1995, 74th Leg., ch. 709, § 2, eff. Sept. 1, 1995; Acts 1995, 74th Leg., ch. 751, § 72, eff. Sept. 1, 1995; Acts 2003, 78th Leg., ch. 561, § 1, eff. Sept. 1, 2003; Acts 2007, 80th Leg., ch. 972, § 44, eff. Sept. 1, 2007; Acts 2017, 85th Leg., ch. 317 (H.B. 7), § 13, eff. Sept. 1, 2017.

[1] Acts 1995, 74th Leg., ch. 751 inserted "by clear and convincing evidence" following "relationship".

### § 161.2061. Terms Regarding Limited Post–Termination Contact

(a) If the court finds it to be in the best interest of the child, the court may provide in an order terminating the parent-child relationship that the biological parent who filed an affidavit of voluntary relinquishment of parental rights under Section 161.103 shall have limited post-termination contact with the child as provided by Subsection (b) on the agreement of the biological parent and the Department of Family and Protective Services.

(b) The order of termination may include terms that allow the biological parent to:

(1) receive specified information regarding the child;

(2) provide written communications to the child; and

(3) have limited access to the child.

(c) The terms of an order of termination regarding limited post-termination contact may be enforced only if the party seeking enforcement pleads and proves that, before filing the motion for enforcement, the party attempted in good faith to resolve the disputed matters through mediation.

(d) The terms of an order of termination under this section are not enforceable by contempt.

(e) The terms of an order of termination regarding limited post-termination contact may not be modified.

(f) An order under this section does not:

(1) affect the finality of a termination order; or

(2) grant standing to a parent whose parental rights have been terminated to file any action under this title other than a motion to enforce the terms regarding limited post-termination contact until the court renders a subsequent adoption order with respect to the child.

Added by Acts 2003, 78th Leg., ch. 561, § 2, eff. Sept. 1, 2003. Amended by Acts 2015, 84th Leg., ch. 1 (S.B. 219), § 1.087, eff. April 2, 2015.

### § 161.2062. Provision for Limited Contact Between Biological Parent and Child

(a) An order terminating the parent-child relationship may not require that a subsequent adoption order include terms regarding limited post-termination contact between the child and a biological parent.

(b) The inclusion of a requirement for post-termination contact described by Subsection (a) in a termination order does not:

(1) affect the finality of a termination or subsequent adoption order; or

(2) grant standing to a parent whose parental rights have been terminated to file any action under

this title after the court renders a subsequent adoption order with respect to the child.

Added by Acts 2003, 78th Leg., ch. 561, § 2, eff. Sept. 1, 2003.

### § 161.207. Appointment of Managing Conservator on Termination

(a) If the court terminates the parent-child relationship with respect to both parents or to the only living parent, the court shall appoint a suitable, competent adult, the Department of Family and Protective Services, or a licensed child-placing agency as managing conservator of the child. An agency designated managing conservator in an unrevoked or irrevocable affidavit of relinquishment shall be appointed managing conservator.

(b) The order of appointment may refer to the docket number of the suit and need not refer to the parties nor be accompanied by any other papers in the record.

Added by Acts 1995, 74th Leg., ch. 20, § 1, eff. April 20, 1995. Amended by Acts 2015, 84th Leg., ch. 1 (S.B. 219), § 1.088, eff. April 2, 2015.

### § 161.208. Appointment of Department of Family and Protective Services as Managing Conservator

If a parent of the child has not been personally served in a suit in which the Department of Family and Protective Services seeks termination, the court that terminates a parent-child relationship may not appoint the Department of Family and Protective Services as permanent managing conservator of the child unless the court determines that:

(1) the department has made a diligent effort to locate a missing parent who has not been personally served and a relative of that parent; and

(2) a relative located by the department has had a reasonable opportunity to request appointment as managing conservator of the child or the department has not been able to locate the missing parent or a relative of the missing parent.

Added by Acts 1995, 74th Leg., ch. 20, § 1, eff. April 20, 1995. Amended by Acts 2015, 84th Leg., ch. 1 (S.B. 219), § 1.089, eff. April 2, 2015.

### § 161.2081. Notice of Termination for Certain Relatives

Immediately after a court renders an order terminating the parent-child relationship in a suit filed by the Department of Family and Protective Services, the department shall notify each individual described by Section 102.006(c) who has been identified under Section 262.1095 that:

(1) the parent-child relationship has been terminated; and

(2) the individual has 90 days after the date the order is rendered to file an original suit or a suit for modification requesting managing conservatorship of the child in accordance with Section 102.006(c).

Added by Acts 2021, 87th Leg., ch. 710 (H.B. 2926), § 2, eff. Sept. 1, 2021.

### § 161.209. Copy of Order of Termination

A copy of an order of termination rendered under Section 161.206 is not required to be mailed to parties as provided by Rules 119a and 239a, Texas Rules of Civil Procedure.

Added by Acts 1995, 74th Leg., ch. 20, § 1, eff. April 20, 1995.

### § 161.210. Sealing of File

The court, on the motion of a party or on the court's own motion, may order the sealing of the file, the minutes of the court, or both, in a suit for termination.

Added by Acts 1995, 74th Leg., ch. 20, § 1, eff. April 20, 1995.

### § 161.211. Direct or Collateral Attack on Termination Order

(a) Notwithstanding Rule 329, Texas Rules of Civil Procedure, the validity of an order terminating the parental rights of a person who has been personally served or who has executed an affidavit of relinquishment of parental rights or an affidavit of waiver of interest in a child or whose rights have been terminated under Section 161.002(b) is not subject to collateral or direct attack after the sixth month after the date the order was signed.

(b) Notwithstanding Rule 329, Texas Rules of Civil Procedure, the validity of an order terminating the parental rights of a person who is served by citation by publication is not subject to collateral or direct attack after the sixth month after the date the order was signed.

(c) A direct or collateral attack on an order terminating parental rights based on an unrevoked affidavit of relinquishment of parental rights or affidavit of waiver of interest in a child is limited to issues relating to fraud, duress, or coercion in the execution of the affidavit.

Added by Acts 1997, 75th Leg., ch. 600, § 1, eff. Sept. 1, 1997; Acts 1997, 75th Leg., ch. 601, § 2, eff. Sept. 1, 1997. Amended by Acts 1999, 76th Leg., ch. 1390, § 19, eff. Sept. 1, 1999.

## SUBCHAPTER D. REINSTATEMENT OF PARENTAL RIGHTS AFTER INVOLUNTARY TERMINATION

### § 161.301. Definitions

In this subchapter:

(1) "Commissioner" means the commissioner of the Department of Family and Protective Services.

(2) "Department" means the Department of Family and Protective Services.

Added by Acts 2021, 87th Leg., ch. 710 (H.B. 2926), § 1, eff. Sept. 1, 2021.

### § 161.302. Petition

(a) The following persons may file a petition under this subchapter requesting the court to reinstate the parental rights of a former parent whose parental rights were involuntarily terminated under Section 161.001 or 161.003:

(1) the department;

(2) the single source continuum contractor under Subchapter B–1, Chapter 264, with responsibility for the child who is the subject of the petition;

(3) the attorney ad litem for the child who is the subject of the petition; or

(4) the former parent whose parental rights were involuntarily terminated.

(b) A petition for the reinstatement of parental rights may be filed under this subchapter only if:

(1) the termination of parental rights resulted from a suit filed by the department;

(2) at least two years have passed since the issuance of the order terminating the former parent's parental rights and an appeal of the order is not pending;

(3) the child has not been adopted;

(4) the child is not the subject of an adoption placement agreement; and

(5) the petitioner has provided the notice required by Subsection (d), if the petitioner is the former parent whose parental rights are sought to be reinstated.

(c) The contents of the petition for reinstatement of parental rights must be sworn by the petitioner and must include:

(1) the name of the petitioner;

(2) the name and current residence address of the former parent whose parental rights are sought to be reinstated, if that former parent is not the petitioner;

(3) the child's name, current residence address, and date and place of birth, if known;

(4) the name, current residence address, and contact information, if known, of any party that:

(A) participated in the original termination hearing; and

(B) has information relevant to the determination of conservatorship of or possession of or access to the child;

(5) a summary of the grounds on which the court rendered the order terminating the former parent's parental rights;

(6) a summary statement of the facts and evidence that the petitioner believes demonstrate that the former parent whose parental rights are sought to be reinstated has the capacity and willingness to perform parental duties under Section 151.001, including steps the former parent has taken toward personal rehabilitation since the rendition of the order terminating parental rights, including mental health and substance abuse treatment, employment, or other personal history that demonstrates rehabilitation;

(7) a statement of the former parent whose parental rights are sought to be reinstated requesting the reinstatement of parental rights;

(8) a statement of the intent or willingness of the child to consent to the reinstatement of parental rights, if the child is 12 years of age or older; and

(9) a summary of all prior requests or motions for reinstatement by the former parent whose parental rights are sought to be reinstated and by the petitioner, if the former parent is not the petitioner, with respect to that child.

(d) Before a former parent whose parental rights have been involuntarily terminated may file a petition for reinstatement under this subchapter, the former parent, at least 45 days before the petition is filed, must notify the department of the former parent's intent to file the petition. The commissioner shall create a form to be used by a former parent for that notice that includes the information listed in Subsection (c). A copy of the notice must be filed with the petition.

(e) The petition for the reinstatement of parental rights and notice of hearing on the petition must be served on:

(1) the child or the child's representative;

(2) the county attorney;

(3) the child's attorney ad litem;

(4) the department or single source continuum contractor, if applicable;

(5) the former parent whose parental rights are sought to be reinstated, if that former parent is not the petitioner; and

(6) if the child is subject to the Indian Child Welfare Act of 1978 (25 U.S.C. Section 1901 et seq.), the designated tribal service agent of the child's tribe and any other person required by federal law.

Added by Acts 2021, 87th Leg., ch. 710 (H.B. 2926), § 1, eff. Sept. 1, 2021.

### § 161.303. Hearing

(a) A reinstatement hearing under this subchapter must be held not later than the 60th day after the date the petition is filed.

(b) The petitioner has the burden of proof in the hearing, and each party may call witnesses.

(c) The court may grant the petition and order the reinstatement of the former parent's parental rights only if the court finds by a preponderance of the evidence that:

(1) reinstatement of parental rights is in the child's best interests;

(2) at least two years have passed since issuance of the order terminating parental rights and an appeal of the order is not pending;

(3) the child has not been adopted and is not the subject of an adoption placement agreement;

(4) if the child is 12 years of age or older, the child consents to the reinstatement and desires to reside with the parent;

(5) the former parent has remedied the conditions that were grounds for rendering the order terminating parental rights; and

(6) the former parent is willing and has the capability to perform parental duties as provided in Section 151.001, including maintaining the health, safety, and welfare of the child.

(d) In determining whether to grant a petition for reinstatement of parental rights under this subchapter in regard to a child who is 11 years of age or younger on the date the petition is filed, the court shall consider the child's age, maturity, and ability to express a preference and may consider the child's preference regarding the reinstatement as one factor, considered along with all other relevant factors, in making the determination.

Added by Acts 2021, 87th Leg., ch. 710 (H.B. 2926), § 1, eff. Sept. 1, 2021.

### § 161.304. Orders

(a) Following a hearing under this subchapter, the court may render an order:

(1) granting the petition;

(2) denying the petition; or

(3) deferring the decision on the petition and rendering a temporary order expiring after a period of six months during which the department remains the managing conservator of the child and the former parent is the possessory conservator.

(b) If the court defers granting the petition under Subsection (a)(3):

(1) the department shall monitor the possessory conservatorship of the former parent during the period of the temporary order; and

(2) when the temporary order expires, the court shall hold a hearing to determine whether to grant or deny the petition for reinstatement.

(c) If, following a hearing under this subchapter, the court renders an order for reinstatement of parental rights, the court shall enter the court's findings in a written order stating that all legal rights, powers, privileges, immunities, duties, and obligations of the former parent regarding the child, including with respect to custody, care, control, and support, are reinstated.

(d) If, following a hearing under this subchapter, the court denies a petition for reinstatement of parental rights, the court shall render a written order that includes:

(1) the court's findings and detailing reasons for denial of the petition; and

(2) a statement prohibiting the filing of a subsequent petition in regard to the former parent's parental rights before the first anniversary of the date the order of denial was issued.

Added by Acts 2021, 87th Leg., ch. 710 (H.B. 2926), § 1, eff. Sept. 1, 2021.

## CHAPTER 162. ADOPTION

### SUBCHAPTER A. ADOPTION OF A CHILD



### SUBCHAPTER B. INTERSTATE COMPACT ON THE PLACEMENT OF CHILDREN



### SUBCHAPTER C. INTERSTATE COMPACT ON ADOPTION AND MEDICAL ASSISTANCE



### SUBCHAPTER D. ADOPTION SERVICES BY THE DEPARTMENT OF FAMILY AND PROTECTIVE SERVICES



### SUBCHAPTER E. VOLUNTARY ADOPTION REGISTRIES



### SUBCHAPTER F. ADOPTION OF AN ADULT



### SUBCHAPTER G. MISCELLANEOUS PROVISIONS

SUBCHAPTER H. EMBRYO DONATION INFORMATION



## SUBCHAPTER A. ADOPTION OF A CHILD

### § 162.001. Who May Adopt and Be Adopted

(a) Subject to the requirements for standing to sue in Chapter 102, an adult may petition to adopt a child who may be adopted.

(b) A child residing in this state may be adopted if:

(1) the parent-child relationship as to each living parent of the child has been terminated or a suit for termination is joined with the suit for adoption;

(2) the parent whose rights have not been terminated is presently the spouse of the petitioner and the proceeding is for a stepparent adoption;

(3) the child is at least two years old, the parent-child relationship has been terminated with respect to one parent, the person seeking the adoption has been a managing conservator or has had actual care, possession, and control of the child for a period of six months preceding the adoption or is the child's former stepparent, and the nonterminated parent consents to the adoption; or

(4) the child is at least two years old, the parent-child relationship has been terminated with respect to one parent, and the person seeking the adoption is the child's former stepparent and has been a managing conservator or has had actual care, possession, and control of the child for a period of one year preceding the adoption.

(c) If an affidavit of relinquishment of parental rights contains a consent for the Department of Family and Protective Services or a licensed child-placing agency to place the child for adoption and appoints the department or agency managing conservator of the child, further consent by the parent is not required and the adoption order shall terminate all rights of the parent without further termination proceedings.

Added by Acts 1995, 74th Leg., ch. 20, § 1, eff. April 20, 1995. Amended by Acts 1997, 75th Leg., ch. 561, § 14, eff. Sept. 1, 1997; Acts 2003, 78th Leg., ch. 493, § 1, eff. Sept. 1, 2003; Acts 2015, 84th Leg., ch. 1 (S.B. 219), § 1.090, eff. April 2, 2015.

### § 162.002. Prerequisites to Petition

(a) If a petitioner is married, both spouses must join in the petition for adoption.

(b) A petition in a suit for adoption or a suit for appointment of a nonparent managing conservator with authority to consent to adoption of a child must include:

(1) a verified allegation that there has been compliance with Subchapter B[1]; or

(2) if there has not been compliance with Subchapter B, a verified statement of the particular reasons for noncompliance.

Added by Acts 1995, 74th Leg., ch. 20, § 1, eff. April 20, 1995.

[1] V.T.C.A., Family Code § 162.101 et seq.

### § 162.0025. Adoption Sought by Military Service Member

In a suit for adoption, the fact that a petitioner is a member of the armed forces of the United States, a member of the Texas National Guard or the National Guard of another state, or a member of a reserve component of the armed forces of the United States may not be considered by the court, or any person performing an adoption evaluation or home screening, as a negative factor in determining whether the adoption is in the best interest of the child or whether the petitioner would be a suitable parent.

Added by Acts 2007, 80th Leg., ch. 768, § 1, eff. June 15, 2007. Amended by Acts 2015, 84th Leg., ch. 1252 (H.B. 1449), § 3.02, eff. Sept. 1, 2015.

### § 162.003. Adoption Evaluation

In a suit for adoption, an adoption evaluation must be conducted as provided in Chapter 107.

Added by Acts 1995, 74th Leg., ch. 20, § 1, eff. April 20, 1995. Amended by Acts 1995, 74th Leg., ch. 751, § 73, eff. Sept. 1, 1995; Acts 1995, 74th Leg., ch. 800, § 1, eff. Sept. 1, 1995; Acts 2001, 77th Leg., ch. 133, § 6, eff. Sept. 1, 2001; Acts 2007, 80th Leg., ch. 832, § 6, eff. Sept. 1, 2007; Acts 2015, 84th Leg., ch. 1252 (H.B. 1449), § 3.03, eff. Sept. 1, 2015.

### § 162.004. Repealed by Acts 2001, 77th Leg., ch. 133, § 7, eff. Sept. 1, 2001

### § 162.0045. Preferential Setting

The court shall grant a motion for a preferential setting for a final hearing on an adoption and shall give precedence to that hearing over all other civil cases not given preference by other law if the adoption evaluation has been filed and the criminal history for the person seeking to adopt the child has been obtained.

Added by Acts 1997, 75th Leg., ch. 561, § 15, eff. Sept. 1, 1997. Amended by Acts 2015, 84th Leg., ch. 1252 (H.B. 1449), § 3.04, eff. Sept. 1, 2015.

### § 162.005. Preparation of Health, Social, Educational, and Genetic History Report

(a) This section does not apply to an adoption by the child's:

(1) grandparent;

(2) aunt or uncle by birth, marriage, or prior adoption; or

(3) stepparent.

(b) Before placing a child for adoption, the Department of Family and Protective Services, a licensed child-placing agency, or the child's parent or guardian shall compile a report on the available health, social, educational, and genetic history of the child to be adopted.

(c) The department shall ensure that each licensed child-placing agency, single source continuum contractor, or other person placing a child for adoption receives a copy of any portion of the report prepared by the department.

(d) If the child has been placed for adoption by a person or entity other than the department, a licensed child-placing agency, or the child's parent or guardian, it is the duty of the person or entity who places the child for adoption to prepare the report.

(e) The person or entity who places the child for adoption shall provide the prospective adoptive parents a copy of the report as early as practicable before the first meeting of the adoptive parents with the child. The copy of the report shall be edited to protect the identity of birth parents and their families.

(f) The department, licensed child-placing agency, parent, guardian, person, or entity who prepares and files the original report is required to furnish supplemental medical, psychological, and psychiatric information to the adoptive parents if that information becomes available and to file the supplemental information where the original report is filed. The supplemental information shall be retained for as long as the original report is required to be retained.

Added by Acts 1995, 74th Leg., ch. 20, § 1, eff. April 20, 1995. Amended by Acts 2015, 84th Leg., ch. 1 (S.B. 219), § 1.091, eff. April 2, 2015; Acts 2015, 84th Leg., ch. 944 (S.B. 206), § 12, eff. Sept. 1, 2015; Acts 2017, 85th Leg., ch. 319 (S.B. 11), § 4, eff. Sept. 1, 2017.

### § 162.006. Access to Health, Social, Educational, and Genetic History Report; Retention

(a) Redesignated as V.T.C.A., Family Code § 162.0062(a) and amended by Acts 2015, 84th Leg., ch. 944 (S.B. 206), § 15(a).

(a–1) Redesignated as V.T.C.A., Family Code § 162.0062(b) and amended by Acts 2015, 84th Leg., ch. 944 (S.B. 206), § 15(a).

(b) The department, licensed child-placing agency, or court retaining a copy of the report shall provide a copy of the report that has been edited to protect the identity of the birth parents and any other person whose identity is confidential to the following persons on request:

(1) an adoptive parent of the adopted child;

(2) the managing conservator, guardian of the person, or legal custodian of the adopted child;

(3) the adopted child, after the child is an adult;

(4) the surviving spouse of the adopted child if the adopted child is dead and the spouse is the parent or guardian of a child of the deceased adopted child; or

(5) a progeny of the adopted child if the adopted child is dead and the progeny is an adult.

(c) A copy of the report may not be furnished to a person who cannot furnish satisfactory proof of identity and legal entitlement to receive a copy.

(d) A person requesting a copy of the report shall pay the actual and reasonable costs of providing a copy and verifying entitlement to the copy.

(e) The report shall be retained for 99 years from the date of the adoption by the department or licensed child-placing agency placing the child for adoption. If the agency ceases to function as a child-placing agency, the agency shall transfer all the reports to the department or, after giving notice to the department, to a transferee agency that is assuming responsibility for the preservation of the agency's adoption records. If the child has not been placed for adoption by the department or a licensed child-placing agency and if the child is being adopted by a person other than the child's stepparent, grandparent, aunt, or uncle by birth, marriage, or prior adoption, the person or entity who places the child for adoption shall file the report with the department, which shall retain the copies for 99 years from the date of the adoption.

Added by Acts 1995, 74th Leg., ch. 20, § 1, eff. April 20, 1995. Amended by Acts 2013, 83rd Leg., ch. 1069 (H.B. 3259), § 1, eff. Sept. 1, 2013; Acts 2015, 84th Leg., ch. 1 (S.B. 219), § 1.092, eff. April 2, 2015; Acts 2015, 84th Leg., ch. 944 (S.B. 206), §§ 13, 15(a), eff. Sept. 1, 2015.

### § 162.0062. Access to Information

(a) Except as provided by Subsection (c), the prospective adoptive parents of a child are entitled to examine the records and other information relating to the history of the child. The Department of Family and Protective Services, licensed child-placing agency, or other person placing a child for adoption shall inform the prospective adoptive parents of their right to examine the records and other information relating to the history of the child. The department, licensed child-placing agency, or other person placing the child for adoption shall edit the records and information to protect the identity of the biological parents and any other person whose identity is confidential.

(a–1) If a child is placed with a prospective adoptive parent prior to adoption, the prospective adoptive parent is entitled to examine any record or other information relating to the child's health history, including the portion of the report prepared under Section 162.005 for the child that relates to the child's health. The department, licensed child-placing agency, single source continuum contractor, or other person placing a child for adoption shall inform the prospective adoptive parent of the prospective adoptive parent's right to examine the records and other information relating to the child's health history. The department, licensed child-placing agency, single source continuum contractor, or other person placing the child for adoption shall edit the records and information to protect the identity of the biological parents and any other person whose identity is confidential.

(b) The records described by Subsection (a) must include any records relating to an investigation of abuse in which the child was an alleged or confirmed victim of sexual abuse while residing in a foster home or other residential child-care facility. If the licensed child-placing agency or other person placing the child for adoption does not have the information required by this subsection, the department, at the request of the licensed child-placing agency or other person placing the child for adoption, shall provide the information to the prospective adoptive parents of the child.

(c) If the prospective adoptive parents of a child have reviewed the health, social, educational, and genetic history report for the child and indicated that they want to proceed with the adoption, the department may, but is not required to, allow the prospective adoptive parents of the child to examine the records and other information relating to the history of the child, unless the prospective adoptive parents request the child's case record. The department shall provide the child's case record to the prospective adoptive parents on the request of the prospective adoptive parents.

(c–1) If the prospective adoptive parents of a child indicate they want to proceed with the adoption under Subsection (c), the department, licensed child-placing agency, or single source continuum contractor shall provide the prospective adoptive parents with access to research regarding underlying health issues and other conditions of trauma that could impact child development and permanency.

(d) The adoptive parents and the adopted child, after the child is an adult, are entitled to receive copies of the records that have been edited to protect the identity of the biological parents and any other person whose identity is confidential and other information relating to the history of the child maintained by the department, licensed child-placing agency, person, or entity placing the child for adoption.

(e) It is the duty of the person or entity placing the child for adoption to edit the records and information to protect the identity of the biological parents and any other person whose identity is confidential.

(f) At the time an adoption order is rendered, the court shall provide to the parents of an adopted child information provided by the vital statistics unit that describes the functions of the voluntary adoption registry under Subchapter E.[1] The licensed child-placing agency shall provide to each of the child's biological parents known to the agency, the information when the parent signs an affidavit of relinquishment of parental rights or affidavit of waiver of interest in a child. The information shall include the right of the child or biological parent to refuse to participate in the registry. If the adopted child is 14 years old or older the court shall provide the information to the child.

Added by Acts 1995, 74th Leg., ch. 20, § 1, eff. April 20, 1995. Amended by Acts 1997, 75th Leg., ch. 561, § 17, eff. Sept. 1, 1997; Acts 2007, 80th Leg., ch. 1283, § 11, eff. Sept. 1, 2007; Acts 2013, 83rd Leg., ch. 1069 (H.B. 3259), § 1, eff. Sept. 1, 2013; Acts 2015, 84th Leg., ch. 1 (S.B. 219), §§ 1.092, 1.096, eff. April 2, 2015. Redesignated from V.T.C.A., Family Code §§ 162.006(a), (a–1), 162.018(b) to (d) and amended by Acts 2015, 84th Leg., ch. 944 (S.B. 206), § 15(a), (b), eff. Sept. 1, 2015. Amended by Acts 2017, 85th Leg., ch. 319 (S.B. 11), § 5, eff. Sept. 1, 2017.

[1] V.T.C.A., Family Code § 162.401.

### § 162.0065. Editing Adoption Records in Department Placement

Notwithstanding any other provision of this chapter, in an adoption in which a child is placed for adoption by the Department of Family and Protective Services, the department is not required to edit records to protect the identity of birth parents and other persons whose identity is confidential if the department determines that information is already known to the adoptive parents or is readily available through other sources, including the court records of a suit to terminate the parent-child relationship under Chapter 161.

Added by Acts 2003, 78th Leg., ch. 68, § 1, eff. Sept. 1, 2003. Amended by Acts 2015, 84th Leg., ch. 1 (S.B. 219), § 1.093, eff. April 2, 2015.

### § 162.007. Contents of Health, Social, Educational, and Genetic History Report

(a) The health history of the child must include information about:

(1) the child's health status at the time of placement;

(2) the child's birth, neonatal, and other medical, psychological, psychiatric, and dental history information, including to the extent known by the Department of Family and Protective Services based on the information collected under Section 264.019:

(A) whether the child's birth mother consumed alcohol during pregnancy; and

(B) whether the child has been diagnosed with fetal alcohol spectrum disorder;

(3) a record of immunizations for the child; and

(4) the available results of medical, psychological, psychiatric, and dental examinations of the child.

(b) The social history of the child must include information, to the extent known, about past and existing relationships between the child and the child's siblings, parents by birth, extended family, and other persons who have had physical possession of or legal access to the child.

(c) The educational history of the child must include, to the extent known, information about:

(1) the enrollment and performance of the child in educational institutions;

(2) results of educational testing and standardized tests for the child; and

(3) special educational needs, if any, of the child.

(d) The genetic history of the child must include a description of the child's parents by birth and their parents, any other child born to either of the child's parents, and extended family members and must include, to the extent the information is available, information about:

(1) their health and medical history, including any genetic diseases and disorders;

(2) their health status at the time of placement;

(3) the cause of and their age at death;

(4) their height, weight, and eye and hair color;

(5) their nationality and ethnic background;

(6) their general levels of educational and professional achievements, if any;

(7) their religious backgrounds, if any;

(8) any psychological, psychiatric, or social evaluations, including the date of the evaluation, any diagnosis, and a summary of any findings;

(9) any criminal conviction records relating to a misdemeanor or felony classified as an offense against the person or family or public indecency or a felony violation of a statute intended to control the possession or distribution of a substance included in Chapter 481, Health and Safety Code; and

(10) any information necessary to determine whether the child is entitled to or otherwise eligible for state or federal financial, medical, or other assistance.

(e) The report shall include a history of physical, sexual, or emotional abuse suffered by the child, if any.

(f) Notwithstanding the other provisions of this section, the Department of Family and Protective Services may, in accordance with department rule, modify the form and contents of the health, social, educational, and genetic history report for a child as the department determines appropriate based on:

(1) the relationship between the prospective adoptive parents and the child or the child's birth family;

(2) the provision of the child's case record to the prospective adoptive parents; or

(3) any other factor specified by department rule.

(g) In this section, "fetal alcohol spectrum disorder" means any of a group of conditions that can occur in a person whose mother consumed alcohol during pregnancy.

Added by Acts 1995, 74th Leg., ch. 20, § 1, eff. April 20, 1995. Amended by Acts 2015, 84th Leg., ch. 944 (S.B. 206), §§ 12, 14, eff. Sept. 1, 2015; Acts 2017, 85th Leg., ch. 319 (S.B. 11), § 6, eff. Sept. 1, 2017; Acts 2019, 86th Leg., ch. 417 (S.B. 195), § 1, eff. Jan. 1, 2020.

### § 162.008. Filing of Health, Social, Educational, and Genetic History Report

(a) This section does not apply to an adoption by the child's:

(1) grandparent;

(2) aunt or uncle by birth, marriage, or prior adoption; or

(3) stepparent.

(b) A petition for adoption may not be granted until the following documents have been filed:

(1) a copy of the health, social, educational, and genetic history report signed by the child's adoptive parents; and

(2) if the report is required to be submitted to the Department of Family and Protective Services under Section 162.006(e), a certificate from the department acknowledging receipt of the report.

(c) A court having jurisdiction of a suit affecting the parent-child relationship may by order waive the making and filing of a report under this section if the child's biological parents cannot be located and their absence results in insufficient information being available to compile the report.

Added by Acts 1995, 74th Leg., ch. 20, § 1, eff. April 20, 1995. Amended by Acts 1999, 76th Leg., ch. 1390, § 20, eff. Sept. 1, 1999; Acts 2015, 84th Leg., ch. 1 (S.B. 219), § 1.094, eff. April 2, 2015.

### § 162.0085. Criminal History Report Required

(a) In a suit affecting the parent-child relationship in which an adoption is sought, the court shall order each person seeking to adopt the child to obtain that person's own criminal history record information. The court shall accept under this section a person's criminal history record information that is provided by the Department of Family and Protective Services or by a licensed child-placing agency that received the information from the department if the information was obtained not more than one year before the date the court ordered the history to be obtained.

(b) A person required to obtain information under Subsection (a) shall obtain the information in the manner provided by Section 411.128, Government Code.

Added by Acts 1995, 74th Leg., ch. 751, § 75, eff. Sept. 1, 1995; Acts 1995, 74th Leg., ch. 908, § 2, eff. Sept. 1, 1995. Amended by Acts 1997, 75th Leg., ch. 561, § 16, eff. Sept. 1, 1997; Acts 2015, 84th Leg., ch. 1 (S.B. 219), § 1.095, eff. April 2, 2015.

### § 162.0086. Information Regarding Sibling Access

(a) The Department of Family and Protective Services shall provide information to each person seeking to adopt a child placed for adoption by the department regarding the right of a child's sibling to file a suit for access to the child under Sections 102.0045 and 153.551.

(b) The department may provide the information required under Subsection (a) on any form or application provided to prospective adoptive parents.

Added by Acts 2017, 85th Leg., ch. 316 (H.B. 5), § 7, eff. Sept. 1, 2017; Acts 2017, 85th Leg., ch. 413 (S.B. 948), § 1, eff. Sept. 1, 2017.

### § 162.009. Residence with Petitioner

(a) The court may not grant an adoption until the child has resided with the petitioner for not less than six months.

(b) On request of the petitioner, the court may waive the residence requirement if the waiver is in the best interest of the child.

Added by Acts 1995, 74th Leg., ch. 20, § 1, eff. April 20, 1995.

### § 162.010. Consent Required

(a) Unless the managing conservator is the petitioner, the written consent of a managing conservator to the adoption must be filed. The court may waive the requirement of consent by the managing conservator if the court finds that the consent is being refused or has been revoked without good cause. A hearing on the issue of consent shall be conducted by the court without a jury.

(b) If a parent of the child is presently the spouse of the petitioner, that parent must join in the petition for adoption and further consent of that parent is not required.

(c) A child 12 years of age or older must consent to the adoption in writing or in court. The court may waive this requirement if it would serve the child's best interest.

Added by Acts 1995, 74th Leg., ch. 20, § 1, eff. April 20, 1995. Amended by Acts 1995, 74th Leg., ch. 751, § 76, eff. Sept. 1, 1995.

### § 162.011. Revocation of Consent

At any time before an order granting the adoption of the child is rendered, a consent required by Section 162.010 may be revoked by filing a signed revocation.

Added by Acts 1995, 74th Leg., ch. 20, § 1, eff. April 20, 1995.

### § 162.012. Direct or Collateral Attack

(a) Notwithstanding Rule 329, Texas Rules of Civil Procedure, the validity of an adoption order is not subject to attack after six months after the date the order was signed.

(b) The validity of a final adoption order is not subject to attack because a health, social, educational, and genetic history was not filed.

Added by Acts 1995, 74th Leg., ch. 20, § 1, eff. April 20, 1995. Amended by Acts 1997, 75th Leg., ch. 601, § 1, eff. Sept. 1, 1997; Acts 1997, 75th Leg., ch. 600, § 2, eff. Jan. 1, 1998.

### § 162.013. Abatement or Dismissal

(a) If the sole petitioner dies or the joint petitioners die, the court shall dismiss the suit for adoption.

(b) If one of the joint petitioners dies, the proceeding shall continue uninterrupted.

(c) If the joint petitioners divorce, the court shall abate the suit for adoption. The court shall dismiss the petition unless the petition is amended to request adoption by one of the original petitioners.

Added by Acts 1995, 74th Leg., ch. 20, § 1, eff. April 20, 1995.

### § 162.014. Attendance at Hearing Required

(a) If the joint petitioners are husband and wife and it would be unduly difficult for one of the petitioners to appear at the hearing, the court may waive the attendance of that petitioner if the other spouse is present.

(b) A child to be adopted who is 12 years of age or older shall attend the hearing. The court may waive this requirement in the best interest of the child.

Added by Acts 1995, 74th Leg., ch. 20, § 1, eff. April 20, 1995.

### § 162.015. Race or Ethnicity

(a) In determining the best interest of the child, the court may not deny or delay the adoption or otherwise discriminate on the basis of race or ethnicity of the child or the prospective adoptive parents.

(b) This section does not apply to a person, entity, tribe, organization, or child custody proceeding subject to the Indian Child Welfare Act of 1978 (25 U.S.C. Section 1901 et seq.). In this subsection "child custody proceeding" has the meaning provided by 25 U.S.C. Section 1903.

Added by Acts 1995, 74th Leg., ch. 20, § 1, eff. April 20, 1995. Amended by Acts 1995, 74th Leg., ch. 751, § 77, eff. Sept. 1, 1995.

### § 162.016. Adoption Order

(a) If a petition requesting termination has been joined with a petition requesting adoption, the court shall also terminate the parent-child relationship at the same time the adoption order is rendered. The court must make separate findings that the termination is in the best interest of the child and that the adoption is in the best interest of the child.

(b) If the court finds that the requirements for adoption have been met and the adoption is in the best interest of the child, the court shall grant the adoption.

(c) The name of the child may be changed in the order if requested.

Added by Acts 1995, 74th Leg., ch. 20, § 1, eff. April 20, 1995.

### § 162.017. Effect of Adoption

(a) An order of adoption creates the parent-child relationship between the adoptive parent and the child for all purposes.

(b) An adopted child is entitled to inherit from and through the child's adoptive parents as though the child were the biological child of the parents.

(c) The terms "child," "descendant," "issue," and other terms indicating the relationship of parent and child include an adopted child unless the context or express language clearly indicates otherwise.

(d) Nothing in this chapter precludes or affects the rights of a biological or adoptive maternal or paternal grandparent to reasonable possession of or access to a grandchild, as provided in Chapter 153.

Added by Acts 1995, 74th Leg., ch. 20, § 1, eff. April 20, 1995. Amended by Acts 2005, 79th Leg., ch. 916, § 23, eff. June 18, 2005.

### § 162.018. Deleted in part and redesignated in part as V.T.C.A., Family Code § 162.0062(d) to (f) by Acts 2015, 84th Leg., ch. 944 (S.B. 206), § 15(b), eff. Sept. 1, 2015

### § 162.019. Copy of Order

A copy of the adoption order is not required to be mailed to the parties as provided in Rules 119a and 239a, Texas Rules of Civil Procedure.

Added by Acts 1995, 74th Leg., ch. 20, § 1, eff. April 20, 1995.

### § 162.020. Withdrawal or Denial of Petition

If a petition requesting adoption is withdrawn or denied, the court may order the removal of the child from the proposed adoptive home if removal is in the child's best interest and may enter any order necessary for the welfare of the child.

Added by Acts 1995, 74th Leg., ch. 20, § 1, eff. April 20, 1995.

### § 162.021. Sealing File

(a) The court, on the motion of a party or on the court's own motion, may order the sealing of the file and the minutes of the court, or both, in a suit requesting an adoption.

(b) Rendition of the order does not relieve the clerk from the duty to send information regarding adoption to the vital statistics unit as required by this subchapter and Chapter 108.

Added by Acts 1995, 74th Leg., ch. 20, § 1, eff. April 20, 1995. Amended by Acts 1995, 74th Leg., ch. 751, § 78, eff. Sept. 1, 1995; Acts 2015, 84th Leg., ch. 1 (S.B. 219), § 1.097, eff. April 2, 2015.

### § 162.022. Confidentiality Maintained by Clerk

The records concerning a child maintained by the district clerk after entry of an order of adoption are confidential. No person is entitled to access to the records or may obtain information from the records except for good cause under an order of the court that issued the order.

Added by Acts 1995, 74th Leg., ch. 20, § 1, eff. April 20, 1995.

### § 162.023. Adoption Order from Foreign Country

(a) Except as otherwise provided by law, an adoption order rendered to a resident of this state that is made by a foreign country shall be accorded full faith and credit by the courts of this state and enforced as if the order were rendered by a court in this state unless the adoption law or process of the foreign country violates the fundamental principles of human rights or the laws or public policy of this state.

(b) A person who adopts a child in a foreign country may register the order in this state. A petition for registration of a foreign adoption order may be combined with a petition for a name change. If the court finds that the foreign adoption order meets the requirements of Subsection (a), the court shall order the state registrar to:

(1) register the order under Chapter 192, Health and Safety Code; and

(2) file a certificate of birth for the child under Section 192.006, Health and Safety Code.

Added by Acts 2003, 78th Leg., ch. 19, § 1, eff. Sept. 1, 2003.

### § 162.024. Repealed by Acts 1995, 74th Leg., ch. 751, § 128, eff. Sept. 1, 1995

### § 162.025. Placement by Unauthorized Person; Offense

(a) A person who is not the natural or adoptive parent of the child, the legal guardian of the child, or a child-placing agency licensed under Chapter 42, Human Resources Code, commits an offense if the person:

(1) serves as an intermediary between a prospective adoptive parent and an expectant parent or parent of a minor child to identify the parties to each other; or

(2) places a child for adoption.

(b) It is not an offense under this section if a professional provides legal or medical services to:

(1) a parent who identifies the prospective adoptive parent and places the child for adoption without the assistance of the professional; or

(2) a prospective adoptive parent who identifies a parent and receives placement of a child for adoption without the assistance of the professional.

(c) An offense under this section is a Class B misdemeanor.

Added by Acts 1995, 74th Leg., ch. 411, § 1, eff. Sept. 1, 1995. Amended by Acts 1997, 75th Leg., ch. 561, § 18, eff. Sept. 1, 1997.

### § 162.026. Regulated Custody Transfer of Adopted Child

A parent, managing conservator, or guardian of an adopted child may not transfer permanent physical custody of the child to any person who is not a relative or stepparent of the child or an adult who has a significant and long-standing relationship with the child unless:

(1) the parent, managing conservator, or guardian files a petition with a court of competent jurisdiction requesting a transfer of custody; and

(2) the court approves the petition.

Added by Acts 2017, 85th Leg., ch. 985 (H.B. 834), § 1, eff. Sept. 1, 2017.

## SUBCHAPTER B. INTERSTATE COMPACT ON THE PLACEMENT OF CHILDREN

### § 162.101. Definitions

In this subchapter:

(1) "Appropriate public authorities," with reference to this state, means the commissioner of the Department of Family and Protective Services.

(2) "Appropriate authority in the receiving state," with reference to this state, means the commissioner of the Department of Family and Protective Services.

(3) "Compact" means the Interstate Compact on the Placement of Children.

(4) "Executive head," with reference to this state, means the governor.

Added by Acts 1995, 74th Leg., ch. 20, § 1, eff. April 20, 1995. Amended by Acts 1995, 74th Leg., ch. 846, § 2, eff. June 16, 1995; Acts 2015, 84th Leg., ch. 1 (S.B. 219), § 1.098, eff. April 2, 2015.

### § 162.102. Adoption of Compact; Text

The Interstate Compact on the Placement of Children is adopted by this state and entered into with all other jurisdictions in form substantially as provided by this subchapter.

#### INTERSTATE COMPACT ON THE PLACEMENT OF CHILDREN

#### ARTICLE I. PURPOSE AND POLICY

It is the purpose and policy of the party states to cooperate with each other in the interstate placement of children to the end that:

(a) Each child requiring placement shall receive the maximum opportunity to be placed in a suitable environment and with persons or institutions having appropriate qualifications and facilities to provide a necessary and desirable degree and type of care.

(b) The appropriate authorities in a state where a child is to be placed may have full opportunity to ascertain the circumstances of the proposed placement, thereby promoting full compliance with applicable requirements for the protection of the child.

(c) The proper authorities of the state from which the placement is made may obtain the most complete information on the basis on which to evaluate a projected placement before it is made.

(d) Appropriate jurisdictional arrangements for the care of children will be promoted.

#### ARTICLE II. DEFINITIONS

As used in this compact:

(a) "Child" means a person who, by reason of minority, is legally subject to parental, guardianship, or similar control.

(b) "Sending agency" means a party state, officer, or employee thereof; a subdivision of a party state, or officer or employee thereof; a court of a party state; a person, corporation, association, charitable agency, or other entity which sends, brings, or causes to be sent or brought any child to another party state.

(c) "Receiving state" means the state to which a child is sent, brought, or caused to be sent or brought, whether by public authorities or private persons or agencies, and whether for placement with state or local public authorities or for placement with private agencies or persons.

(d) "Placement" means the arrangement for the care of a child in a family free or boarding home or in a child-caring agency or institution but does not include any institution caring for the mentally ill, mentally defective, or epileptic or any institution primarily educational in character, and any hospital or other medical facility.

#### ARTICLE III. CONDITIONS FOR PLACEMENT

(a) No sending agency shall send, bring, or cause to be sent or brought into any other party state any child for placement in foster care or as a preliminary to a possible adoption unless the sending agency shall comply with each and every requirement set forth in this article and with the applicable laws of the receiving state governing the placement of children therein.

(b) Prior to sending, bringing, or causing any child to be sent or brought into a receiving state for placement in foster care or as a preliminary to a possible adoption, the sending agency shall furnish the appropriate public authorities in the receiving state written notice of the intention to send, bring, or place the child in the receiving state. The notice shall contain:

(1) the name, date, and place of birth of the child;

(2) the identity and address or addresses of the parents or legal guardian;

(3) the name and address of the person, agency, or institution to or with which the sending agency proposes to send, bring, or place the child;

(4) a full statement of the reasons for such proposed action and evidence of the authority pursuant to which the placement is proposed to be made.

(c) Any public officer or agency in a receiving state which is in receipt of a notice pursuant to Paragraph (b) of this article may request of the sending agency, or any other appropriate officer or agency of or in the sending agency's state, and shall be entitled to receive therefrom, such supporting or additional information as it may deem necessary under the circumstances to carry out the purpose and policy of this compact.

(d) The child shall not be sent, brought, or caused to be sent or brought into the receiving state until the appropriate public authorities in the receiving state shall notify the sending agency, in writing, to the effect that the proposed placement does not appear to be contrary to the interests of the child.

## ARTICLE IV. PENALTY FOR ILLEGAL PLACEMENT

The sending, bringing, or causing to be sent or brought into any receiving state of a child in violation of the terms of this compact shall constitute a violation of the laws respecting the placement of children of both the state in which the sending agency is located or from which it sends or brings the child and of the receiving state. Such violation may be punished or subjected to penalty in either jurisdiction in accordance with its laws. In addition to liability for any such punishment or penalty, any such violation shall constitute full and sufficient grounds for the suspension or revocation of any license, permit, or other legal authorization held by the sending agency which empowers or allows it to place or care for children.

## ARTICLE V. RETENTION OF JURISDICTION

(a) The sending agency shall retain jurisdiction over the child sufficient to determine all matters in relation to the custody, supervision, care, treatment, and disposition of the child which it would have had if the child had remained in the sending agency's state, until the child is adopted, reaches majority, becomes self-supporting, or is discharged with the concurrence of the appropriate authority in the receiving state. Such jurisdiction shall also include the power to effect or cause the return of the child or its transfer to another location and custody pursuant to law. The sending agency shall continue to have financial responsibility for support and maintenance of the child during the period of the placement. Nothing contained herein shall defeat a claim of jurisdiction by a receiving state sufficient to deal with an act of delinquency or crime committed therein.

(b) When the sending agency is a public agency, it may enter into an agreement with an authorized public or private agency in the receiving state providing for the performance of one or more services in respect of such case by the latter as agent for the sending agency.

(c) Nothing in this compact shall be construed to prevent a private charitable agency authorized to place children in the receiving state from performing services or acting as agent in that state for a private charitable agency of the sending state; nor to prevent the agency in the receiving state from discharging financial responsibility for the support and maintenance of a child who has been placed on behalf of the sending agency without relieving the responsibility set forth in Paragraph (a) hereof.

## ARTICLE VI. INSTITUTIONAL CARE OF DELINQUENT CHILDREN

A child adjudicated delinquent may be placed in an institution in another party jurisdiction pursuant to this compact but no such placement shall be made unless the child is given a court hearing on notice to the parent or guardian with opportunity to be heard, prior to his being sent to such other party jurisdiction for institutional care and the court finds that:

(1) equivalent facilities for the child are not available in the sending agency's jurisdiction; and

(2) institutional care in the other jurisdiction is in the best interest of the child and will not produce undue hardship.

## ARTICLE VII. COMPACT ADMINISTRATOR

The executive head of each jurisdiction party to this compact shall designate an officer who shall be general coordinator of activities under this compact in his jurisdiction and who, acting jointly with like officers of other party jurisdictions, shall have power to promulgate rules and regulations to carry out more effectively the terms and provisions of this compact.

## ARTICLE VIII. LIMITATIONS

This compact shall not apply to:

(a) the sending or bringing of a child into a receiving state by his parent, stepparent, grandparent, adult brother or sister, adult uncle or aunt, or his guardian and leaving the child with any such relative or nonagency guardian in the receiving state; or

(b) any placement, sending, or bringing of a child into a receiving state pursuant to any other interstate compact to which both the state from which the child is sent or brought and the receiving state are party, or to any other agreement between said states which has the force of law.

### ARTICLE IX. ENACTMENT AND WITHDRAWAL

This compact shall be open to joinder by any state, territory, or possession of the United States, the District of Columbia, the Commonwealth of Puerto Rico, and, with the consent of congress, the government of Canada or any province thereof. It shall become effective with respect to any such jurisdiction when such jurisdiction has enacted the same into law. Withdrawal from this compact shall be by the enactment of a statute repealing the same, but shall not take effect until two years after the effective date of such statute and until written notice of the withdrawal has been given by the withdrawing state to the governor of each other party jurisdiction. Withdrawal of a party state shall not affect the rights, duties, and obligations under this compact of any sending agency therein with respect to a placement made prior to the effective date of withdrawal.

### ARTICLE X. CONSTRUCTION AND SEVERABILITY

The provisions of this compact shall be liberally construed to effectuate the purposes thereof. The provisions of this compact shall be severable and if any phrase, clause, sentence, or provision of this compact is declared to be contrary to the constitution of any party state or of the United States or the applicability thereof to any government, agency, person, or circumstance is held invalid, the validity of the remainder of this compact and the applicability thereof to any government, agency, person, or circumstance shall not be affected thereby. If this compact shall be held contrary to the constitution of any state party thereto, the compact shall remain in full force and effect as to the remaining states and in full force and effect as to the state affected as to all severable matters.

Added by Acts 1995, 74th Leg., ch. 20, § 1, eff. April 20, 1995. Redesignated from V.T.C.A., Family Code § 162.108 and amended by Acts 1995, 74th Leg., ch. 846, § 3, eff. June 16, 1995.

## § 162.103. Financial Responsibility for Child

(a) Financial responsibility for a child placed as provided in the compact is determined, in the first instance, as provided in Article V of the compact. After partial or complete default of performance under the provisions of Article V assigning financial responsibility, the commissioner of the Department of Family and Protective Services may bring suit under Chapter 154 and may file a complaint with the appropriate prosecuting attorney, claiming a violation of Section 25.05, Penal Code.

(b) After default, if the commissioner of the Department of Family and Protective Services determines that financial responsibility is unlikely to be assumed by the sending agency or the child's parents, the commissioner may cause the child to be returned to the sending agency.

(c) After default, the Department of Family and Protective Services shall assume financial responsibility for the child until it is assumed by the child's parents or until the child is safely returned to the sending agency.

Added by Acts 1995, 74th Leg., ch. 20, § 1, eff. April 20, 1995. Redesignated from V.T.C.A., Family Code § 162.109 and amended by Acts 1995, 74th Leg., ch. 846, § 4, eff. June 16, 1995. Amended by Acts 2015, 84th Leg., ch. 1 (S.B. 219), § 1.099, eff. April 2, 2015.

## § 162.104. Approval of Placement

The commissioner of the Department of Family and Protective Services may not approve the placement of a child in this state without the concurrence of the individuals with whom the child is proposed to be placed or the head of an institution with which the child is proposed to be placed.

Added by Acts 1995, 74th Leg., ch. 20, § 1, eff. April 20, 1995. Redesignated from V.T.C.A., Family Code § 162.110 and amended by Acts 1995, 74th Leg., ch. 846, § 5, eff. June 16, 1995. Amended by Acts 2015, 84th Leg., ch. 1 (S.B. 219), § 1.100, eff. April 2, 2015.

## § 162.105. Placement in Another State

A juvenile court may place a delinquent child in an institution in another state as provided by Article VI of the compact. After placement in another state, the court retains jurisdiction of the child as provided by Article V of the compact.

Added by Acts 1995, 74th Leg., ch. 20, § 1, eff. April 20, 1995. Redesignated from V.T.C.A., Family Code § 162.111 by Acts 1995, 74th Leg., ch. 846, § 6, eff. June 16, 1995.

### § 162.106. Compact Authority

(a) The governor shall appoint the commissioner of the Department of Family and Protective Services as compact administrator.

(b) The commissioner of the Department of Family and Protective Services shall designate a deputy compact administrator and staff necessary to execute the terms of the compact in this state.

Added by Acts 1995, 74th Leg., ch. 20, § 1, eff. April 20, 1995. Redesignated from V.T.C.A., Family Code § 162.112 and amended by Acts 1995, 74th Leg., ch. 846, § 7, eff. June 16, 1995. Amended by Acts 2015, 84th Leg., ch. 1 (S.B. 219), § 1.101, eff. April 2, 2015.

### § 162.107. Offenses; Penalties

(a) An individual, agency, corporation, or child-care facility that violates a provision of the compact commits an offense. An offense under this subsection is a Class B misdemeanor.

(b) An individual, agency, corporation, child-care facility, or general residential operation in this state that violates Article IV of the compact commits an offense. An offense under this subsection is a Class B misdemeanor. On conviction, the court shall revoke any license to operate as a child-care facility or general residential operation issued by the Department of Family and Protective Services to the entity convicted and shall revoke any license or certification of the individual, agency, or corporation necessary to practice in the state.

Added by Acts 1995, 74th Leg., ch. 20, § 1, eff. April 20, 1995. Redesignated from V.T.C.A., Family Code § 162.113 and amended by Acts 1995, 74th Leg., ch. 846, § 8, eff. June 16, 1995. Amended by Acts 2015, 84th Leg., ch. 1 (S.B. 219), § 1.102, eff. April 2, 2015.

### §§ 162.108 to 162.113. Redesignated as V.T.C.A., Family Code §§ 162.102 to 162.107 by Acts 1995, 74th Leg., ch. 846, §§ 3 to 8, eff. June 16, 1995

### § 162.114. Repealed by Acts 1995, 74th Leg., ch. 846, § 10, eff. June 16, 1995

## SUBCHAPTER C. INTERSTATE COMPACT ON ADOPTION AND MEDICAL ASSISTANCE

### § 162.201. Adoption of Compact; Text

The Interstate Compact on Adoption and Medical Assistance is adopted by this state and entered into with all other jurisdictions joining in the compact in form substantially as provided under this subchapter.

#### INTERSTATE COMPACT ON ADOPTION AND MEDICAL ASSISTANCE

#### ARTICLE I. FINDINGS

The legislature finds that:

(a) Finding adoptive families for children for whom state assistance is desirable, under Subchapter D,[1] Chapter 162, and assuring the protection of the interest of the children affected during the entire assistance period require special measures when the adoptive parents move to other states or are residents of another state.

(b) The provision of medical and other necessary services for children, with state assistance, encounters special difficulties when the provision of services takes place in other states.

#### ARTICLE II. PURPOSES

The purposes of the compact are to:

(a) authorize the Department of Family and Protective Services, with the concurrence of the Health and Human Services Commission, to enter into interstate agreements with agencies of other states for the protection of children on behalf of whom adoption assistance is being provided by the Department of Family and Protective Services; and

(b) provide procedures for interstate children's adoption assistance payments, including medical payments.

#### ARTICLE III. DEFINITIONS

In this compact:

(a) "Adoption assistance state" means the state that signs an adoption assistance agreement in a particular case.

(b) "Residence state" means the state in which the child resides by virtue of the residence of the adoptive parents.

(c) "State" means a state of the United States, the District of Columbia, the Commonwealth of Puerto Rico, the Virgin Islands, Guam, the Commonwealth of the Northern Mariana Islands, or a territory or possession of or a territory or possession administered by the United States.

ARTICLE IV. COMPACTS AUTHORIZED

The Department of Family and Protective Services, through its commissioner, is authorized to develop, participate in the development of, negotiate, and enter into one or more interstate compacts on behalf of this state with other states to implement one or more of the purposes of this compact. An interstate compact authorized by this article has the force and effect of law.

ARTICLE V. CONTENTS OF COMPACTS

A compact entered into under the authority conferred by this compact shall contain:

(1) a provision making the compact available for joinder by all states;

(2) a provision for withdrawal from the compact on written notice to the parties, with a period of one year between the date of the notice and the effective date of the withdrawal;

(3) a requirement that protections under the compact continue for the duration of the adoption assistance and apply to all children and their adoptive parents who on the effective date of the withdrawal are receiving adoption assistance from a party state other than the one in which they reside and have their principal place of abode;

(4) a requirement that each case of adoption assistance to which the compact applies be covered by a written adoption assistance agreement between the adoptive parents and the state child welfare agency of the state that provides the adoption assistance and that the agreement be expressly for the benefit of the adopted child and enforceable by the adoptive parents and the state agency providing the adoption assistance; and

(5) other provisions that are appropriate for the proper administration of the compact.

ARTICLE VI. OPTIONAL CONTENTS OF COMPACTS

A compact entered into under the authority conferred by this compact may contain the following provisions, in addition to those required under Article V of this compact:

(1) provisions establishing procedures and entitlement to medical, developmental, child-care, or other social services for the child in accordance with applicable laws, even if the child and the adoptive parents are in a state other than the one responsible for or providing the services or the funds to defray part or all of the costs thereof; and

(2) other provisions that are appropriate or incidental to the proper administration of the compact.

ARTICLE VII. MEDICAL ASSISTANCE

(a) A child with special needs who resides in this state and who is the subject of an adoption assistance agreement with another state is entitled to receive a medical assistance identification from this state on the filing in the state medical assistance agency of a certified copy of the adoption assistance agreement obtained from the adoption assistance state. In accordance with rules of the state medical assistance agency, the adoptive parents, at least annually, shall show that the agreement is still in effect or has been renewed.

(b) The state medical assistance agency shall consider the holder of a medical assistance identification under this article as any other holder of a medical assistance identification under the laws of this state and shall process and make payment on claims on the holder's account in the same manner and under the same conditions and procedures as for other recipients of medical assistance.

(c) The state medical assistance agency shall provide coverage and benefits for a child who is in another state and who is covered by an adoption assistance agreement made by the Department of Family and Protective Services for the coverage or benefits, if any, not provided by the residence state. The adoptive parents acting for the child may submit evidence of payment for services or benefit amounts not payable in the residence state and shall be reimbursed for those amounts. Services or benefit amounts covered under any insurance or other third-party medical contract or arrangement held by the child or the adoptive parents may not be reimbursed. The state medical assistance agency shall adopt rules implementing this subsection. The additional coverage and benefit amounts provided under this subsection are for services for which there is no federal contribution or services that, if federally aided, are not provided by the residence state. The rules shall include procedures for obtaining prior approval for services in cases in which prior approval is required for the assistance.

(d) The submission of a false, misleading, or fraudulent claim for payment or reimbursement for services or benefits under this article or the making of a false, misleading, or fraudulent statement in connection with the claim is an offense under this subsection if the person submitting the claim or making the statement knows or should know that the claim or statement is false, misleading, or fraudulent. A person who commits an offense under this subsection may be liable for a fine not to exceed $10,000 or imprisonment for not more than two years, or both the fine and the imprisonment. An offense under this subsection that also constitutes an offense under other law may be punished under either this subsection or the other applicable law.

(e) This article applies only to medical assistance for children under adoption assistance agreements with states that have entered into a compact with this state under which the other state provides medical assistance to children with special needs under adoption assistance agreements made by this state. All other children entitled to medical assistance under adoption assistance agreements entered into by this state are eligible to receive the medical assistance in accordance with the laws and procedures that apply to the agreement.

ARTICLE VIII. FEDERAL PARTICIPATION

Consistent with federal law, the Department of Family and Protective Services and the Health and Human Services Commission, in connection with the administration of this compact or a compact authorized by this compact, shall include the provision of adoption assistance and medical assistance for which the federal government pays some or all of the cost in any state plan made under the Adoption Assistance and Child Welfare Act of 1980 (Pub. L. No. 96–272), Titles IV–E and XIX of the Social Security Act, and other applicable federal laws. The Department of Family and Protective Services and the Health and Human Services Commission shall apply for and administer all relevant federal aid in accordance with law.

Added by Acts 1995, 74th Leg., ch. 846, § 9, eff. June 16, 1995. Amended by Acts 2015, 84th Leg., ch. 1 (S.B. 219), § 1.103, eff. April 2, 2015.

[1] V.T.C.A., Family Code § 162.301 et seq.

### § 162.202. Authority of Department of Family and Protective Services

The Department of Family and Protective Services, with the concurrence of the Health and Human Services Commission, may develop, participate in the development of, negotiate, and enter into one or more interstate compacts on behalf of this state with other states to implement one or more of the purposes of this subchapter. An interstate compact authorized by this subchapter has the force and effect of law.

Added by Acts 1995, 74th Leg., ch. 846, § 9, eff. June 16, 1995. Amended by Acts 2015, 84th Leg., ch. 1 (S.B. 219), § 1.104, eff. April 2, 2015.

### § 162.203. Compact Administration

The commissioner of the Department of Family and Protective Services shall serve as the compact administrator. The administrator shall cooperate with all departments, agencies, and officers of this state and its subdivisions in facilitating the proper administration of the compact and any supplemental agreements entered into by this state. The commissioner of the Department of Family and Protective Services and the executive commissioner of the Health and Human Services Commission shall designate deputy compact administrators to represent adoption assistance services and medical assistance services provided under Title XIX of the Social Security Act.

Added by Acts 1995, 74th Leg., ch. 846, § 9, eff. June 16, 1995. Amended by Acts 2015, 84th Leg., ch. 1 (S.B. 219), § 1.105, eff. April 2, 2015.

### § 162.204. Supplementary Agreements

The compact administrator may enter into supplementary agreements with appropriate officials of other states under the compact. If a supplementary agreement requires or authorizes the use of any institution or facility of this state or requires or authorizes the provision of a service by this state, the supplementary agreement does not take effect until approved by the head of the department or agency under whose jurisdiction the institution or facility is operated or whose department or agency will be charged with rendering the service.

Added by Acts 1995, 74th Leg., ch. 846, § 9, eff. June 16, 1995.

### § 162.205. Payments by State

The compact administrator, subject to the approval of the chief state fiscal officer, may make or arrange for payments necessary to discharge financial obligations imposed on this state by the compact or by a supplementary agreement entered into under the compact.

Added by Acts 1995, 74th Leg., ch. 846, § 9, eff. June 16, 1995.

### § 162.206. Penalties

A person who, under a compact entered into under this subchapter, knowingly obtains or attempts to obtain or aids or abets any person in obtaining, by means of a wilfully false statement or representation or by impersonation or other fraudulent device, any assistance on behalf of a child or other person to which the child or other person is not entitled, or assistance in an amount greater than that to which the child or other person is entitled, commits an offense. An offense under this section is a Class B misdemeanor. An offense under this section that also constitutes an offense under other law may be punished under either this section or the other applicable law.

Added by Acts 1995, 74th Leg., ch. 846, § 9, eff. June 16, 1995.

## SUBCHAPTER D. ADOPTION SERVICES BY THE DEPARTMENT OF FAMILY AND PROTECTIVE SERVICES

### § 162.301. Definitions

In this subchapter:

(1) "Adoption assistance agreement" means a written agreement, binding on the parties to the agreement, between the Department of Family and Protective Services and the prospective adoptive parents that specifies the nature and amount of any payment, services, or assistance to be provided under the agreement and stipulates that the agreement will remain in effect without regard to the state in which the prospective adoptive parents reside at any particular time.

(2) "Child" means a child who cannot be placed for adoption with appropriate adoptive parents without the provision of adoption assistance because of factors including ethnic background, age, membership in a minority or sibling group, the presence of a medical condition, or a physical, mental, or emotional disability.

(3) "Department" means the Department of Family and Protective Services.

Added by Acts 1995, 74th Leg., ch. 20, § 1, eff. April 20, 1995. Amended by Acts 1995, 74th Leg., ch. 412, § 1, eff. Aug. 28, 1995; Acts 2015, 84th Leg., ch. 1 (S.B. 219), § 1.107, eff. April 2, 2015.

### § 162.302. Repealed by Acts 2015, 84th Leg., ch. 944 (S.B. 206), § 86(1), eff. Sept. 1, 2015

### § 162.303. Repealed by Acts 2015, 84th Leg., ch. 944 (S.B. 206), § 86(2), eff. Sept. 1, 2015

### § 162.304. Financial and Medical Assistance

(a) The department shall administer a program to provide adoption assistance for eligible children and enter into adoption assistance agreements with the adoptive parents of a child as authorized by Part E of Title IV of the federal Social Security Act, as amended (42 U.S.C. Section 673).

(b) The adoption of a child may be subsidized by the department. The need for and amount of the subsidy shall be determined by the department under its rules.

(b–1) Subject to the availability of funds, the department shall pay a $150 subsidy each month for the premiums for health benefits coverage for a child with respect to whom a court has entered a final order of adoption if the child:

(1) was in the conservatorship of the department at the time of the child's adoptive placement;

(2) after the adoption, is not receiving medical assistance under Chapter 32, Human Resources Code; and

(3) is younger than 18 years of age.

(b–2) The commissioner of the department shall adopt rules necessary to implement Subsection (b–1), including rules that:

(1) limit eligibility for the subsidy under that subsection to a child whose adoptive family income is less than 300 percent of the federal poverty level;

(2) provide for the manner in which the department shall pay the subsidy under that subsection; and

(3) specify any documentation required to be provided by an adoptive parent as proof that the subsidy is used to obtain and maintain health benefits coverage for the adopted child.

(c) Repealed by Acts 2015, 84th Leg., ch. 944 (S.B. 206), § 86(3).

(d) Repealed by Acts 2015, 84th Leg., ch. 944 (S.B. 206), § 86(3).

(e) Repealed by Acts 2015, 84th Leg., ch. 944 (S.B. 206), § 86(3).

(f) Repealed by Acts 2019, 86th Leg., ch. 1022 (H.B. 72), § 3.

(g) The commissioner of the department by rule shall provide that the maximum amount of the subsidy under Subsection (b) that may be paid to an adoptive parent of a child under an adoption assistance agreement is an amount that is equal to the amount that would have been paid to the foster parent of the child, based on the child's foster care service level on the date the department and the adoptive parent enter into the adoption assistance agreement. This subsection applies only to a child who, based on factors specified in rules of the department, the department determines would otherwise have been expected to remain in foster care until the child's 18th birthday and for whom this state would have made foster care payments for that care. Factors the department may consider in determining whether a child is eligible for the amount of the subsidy authorized by this subsection include the following:

(1) the child's mental or physical disability, age, and membership in a sibling group; and

(2) the number of prior placement disruptions the child has experienced.

(h) In determining the amount that would have been paid to a foster parent for purposes of Subsection (g), the department:

(1) shall use the minimum amount required to be paid to a foster parent for a child assigned the same service level as the child who is the subject of the adoption assistance agreement; and

(2) may not include any amount that a child-placing agency is entitled to retain under the foster care rate structure in effect on the date the department and the adoptive parent enter into the agreement.

(i) A child for whom a subsidy is provided under Subsection (b–1) for premiums for health benefits coverage and who does not receive any other subsidy under this section is not considered to be the subject of an adoption assistance agreement for any other purpose, including for determining eligibility for the exemption from payment of tuition and fees for higher education under Section 54.367, Education Code.

(j) The department shall keep records necessary to evaluate the adoption assistance program's effectiveness in encouraging and promoting the adoption of children.

Added by Acts 1995, 74th Leg., ch. 20, § 1, eff. April 20, 1995. Amended by Acts 1995, 74th Leg., ch. 412, § 4, eff. Aug. 28, 1995; Acts 2005, 79th Leg., ch. 268, § 1.09, eff. Sept. 1, 2005; Acts 2007, 80th Leg., ch. 267, § 2(a), eff. Sept. 1, 2007; Acts 2007, 80th Leg., ch. 1406, § 4(a), eff. Sept. 1, 2007; Acts 2009, 81st Leg., ch. 87, § 27.001(15), eff. Sept. 1, 2009; Acts 2011, 82nd Leg., ch. 359 (S.B. 32), § 11, eff. Jan. 1, 2012; Acts 2015, 84th Leg., ch. 944 (S.B. 206), §§ 16, 86(3), eff. Sept. 1, 2015; Acts 2017, 85th Leg., ch. 316 (H.B. 5), § 8, eff. Sept. 1, 2017; Acts 2019, 86th Leg., ch. 1022 (H.B. 72), §§ 1, 3, eff. Sept. 1, 2019.

### § 162.3041. Continuation of Assistance after Child's 18th Birthday

(a) The department shall, in accordance with department rules, offer adoption assistance after a child's 18th birthday to the child's adoptive parents under an existing adoption assistance agreement entered into under Section 162.304 until:

(1) the first day of the month of the child's 21st birthday if the department determines, as provided by department rules, that:

(A) the child has a mental or physical disability that warrants the continuation of that assistance;

(B) the child, or the child's adoptive parent on behalf of the child, has applied for federal benefits under the supplemental security income program (42 U.S.C. Section 1381 et seq.), as amended; and

(C) the child's adoptive parents are providing the child's financial support; or

(2) if the child does not meet the requirements of Subdivision (1), the earlier of:

(A) the date the child ceases to regularly attend high school or a vocational or technical program;

(B) the date the child obtains a high school diploma or high school equivalency certificate;

(C) the date the child's adoptive parents stop providing financial support to the child; or

(D) the first day of the month of the child's 19th birthday.

(a–1) Notwithstanding Subsection (a), if the department first entered into an adoption assistance agreement with a child's adoptive parents after the child's 16th birthday, the department shall, in accordance with rules adopted by the commissioner of the department, offer adoption assistance after the child's 18th birthday to the child's adoptive parents under an existing adoption agreement until the last day of the month of the child's 21st birthday, provided the child is:

(1) regularly attending high school or enrolled in a program leading toward a high school diploma or high school equivalency certificate;

(2) regularly attending an institution of higher education or a postsecondary vocational or technical program;

(3) participating in a program or activity that promotes, or removes barriers to, employment;

(4) employed for at least 80 hours a month; or

(5) incapable of doing any of the activities described by Subdivisions (1)–(4) due to a documented medical condition.

(b) In determining whether a child meets the requirements of Subdivision (a)(1), the department may conduct an assessment of the child's mental or physical disability or may contract for the assessment to be conducted.

(c) The department and any person with whom the department contracts to conduct an assessment under Subsection (b) shall:

(1) inform the adoptive parents of the child for whom the assessment is conducted of the application requirement under Subsection (a)(1)(B) for federal benefits for the child under the supplemental security income program (42 U.S.C. Section 1381 et seq.), as amended;

(2) provide assistance to the adoptive parents and the child in preparing an application for benefits under that program; and

(3) provide ongoing consultation and guidance to the adoptive parents and the child throughout the eligibility determination process for benefits under that program.

(d) The department is not required to provide adoption assistance benefits under Subsection (a) or (a–1) unless funds are appropriated to the department specifically for purposes of those subsections. If the legislature does not appropriate sufficient money to provide adoption assistance to the adoptive parents of all children described by Subsection (a), the department shall provide adoption assistance only to the adoptive parents of children described by Subsection (a)(1).

Added by Acts 2001, 77th Leg., ch. 1449, § 1, eff. Sept. 1, 2001. Amended by Acts 2009, 81st Leg., ch. 1118, § 4, eff. Sept. 1, 2009; Acts 2009, 81st Leg., ch. 1238, § 6(a), eff. Oct. 1, 2010; Acts 2015, 84th Leg., ch. 944 (S.B. 206), § 17, eff. Sept. 1, 2015; Acts 2017, 85th Leg., ch. 316 (H.B. 5), § 9, eff. Sept. 1, 2017.

### § 162.305. Repealed by Acts 2015, 84th Leg., ch. 1 (S.B. 219) § 1.203(3), eff. April 2, 2015

### § 162.306. Postadoption Services

(a) The department may provide services after adoption to adoptees and adoptive families for whom the department provided services before the adoption.

(b) The department may provide services under this section directly or through contract.

(c) The services may include financial assistance, respite care, placement services, parenting programs, support groups, counseling services, crisis intervention, and medical aid.

Added by Acts 1995, 74th Leg., ch. 20, § 1, eff. April 20, 1995. Amended by Acts 1995, 74th Leg., ch. 412, § 6, eff. Aug. 28, 1995.

### § 162.307. Repealed by Acts 1995, 74th Leg., ch. 412, § 7, eff. Aug. 28, 1995

### § 162.308. Repealed by Acts 2015, 84th Leg., ch. 944 (S.B. 206), § 86(4), eff. Sept. 1, 2015

### § 162.3085. Adoptive Placement in Compliance with Federal Law Required

The department or a licensed child-placing agency making an adoptive placement shall comply with the Multiethnic Placement Act of 1994 (42 U.S.C. Section 1996b).

Added by Acts 2015, 84th Leg., ch. 944 (S.B. 206), § 18, eff. Sept. 1, 2015.

### § 162.309. Repealed by Acts 2015, 84th Leg., ch. 944 (S.B. 206), § 86(5), eff. Sept. 1, 2015; Acts 2015, 84th Leg., ch. 946 (S.B. 277), § 2.37(a), eff. Jan. 1, 2016

## SUBCHAPTER E. VOLUNTARY ADOPTION REGISTRIES

### § 162.401. Purpose

The purpose of this subchapter is to provide for the establishment of mutual consent voluntary adoption registries through which adoptees, birth parents, and biological siblings may voluntarily locate each other. It is not the purpose of this subchapter to inhibit or prohibit persons from locating each other through other legal means or to inhibit or affect in any way the provision of postadoptive services and education, by adoption agencies or others, that go further than the procedures set out for registries established under this subchapter.

Added by Acts 1995, 74th Leg., ch. 20, § 1, eff. April 20, 1995.

### § 162.402. Definitions

In this subchapter:

(1) "Administrator" means the administrator of a mutual consent voluntary adoption registry established under this subchapter.

(2) "Adoptee" means a person 18 years of age or older who has been legally adopted in this state or another state or country.

(3) "Adoption" means the act of creating the legal relationship of parent and child between a person and a child who is not the biological child of that person. The term does not include the act of establishing the legal relationship of parent and child between a man and a child through proof of paternity or voluntary legitimation proceedings.

(4) "Adoption agency" means a person, other than a natural parent or guardian of a child, who plans for the placement of or places a child in the home of a prospective adoptive parent.

(5) "Adoptive parent" means an adult who is a parent of an adoptee through a legal process of adoption.

(6) "Alleged father" means a man who is not deemed by law to be or who has not been adjudicated to be the biological father of an adoptee and who claims or is alleged to be the adoptee's biological father.

(7) "Authorized agency" means a public agency authorized to care for or to place children for adoption or a private entity approved for that purpose by the department through a license, certification, or other means. The term includes a licensed child-placing agency or a previously licensed child-placing agency that has ceased operations and has transferred its adoption records to the vital statistics unit or an agency authorized by the department to place children for adoption and a licensed child-placing agency that has been acquired by, merged with, or otherwise succeeded by an agency authorized by the department to place children for adoption.

(8) "Biological parent" means a man or woman who is the father or mother of genetic origin of a child.

(9) "Biological siblings" means persons who share a common birth parent.

(10) "Birth parent" means:

(A) the biological mother of an adoptee;

(B) the man adjudicated or presumed under Chapter 151 to be the biological father of an adoptee; and

(C) a man who has signed a consent to adoption, affidavit of relinquishment, affidavit of waiver of interest in child, or other written instrument releasing the adoptee for adoption, unless the consent, affidavit, or other instrument includes a sworn refusal to admit or a denial of paternity. The term includes a birth mother and birth father but does not include a person adjudicated by a court of competent jurisdiction as not being the biological parent of an adoptee.

(11) "Central registry" means the mutual consent voluntary adoption registry established and maintained by the vital statistics unit under this subchapter.

(12) "Department" means the Department of Family and Protective Services.

(13) "Registry" means a mutual consent voluntary adoption registry established under this subchapter.

(14) "Vital statistics unit" means the vital statistics unit of the Department of State Health Services.

Added by Acts 1995, 74th Leg., ch. 20, § 1, eff. April 20, 1995. Amended by Acts 1995, 74th Leg., ch. 968, §§ 1, 11, eff. Sept. 1, 1995; Acts 1997, 75th Leg., ch. 561, § 19, eff. Sept. 1, 1997; Acts 2015, 84th Leg., ch. 1 (S.B. 219), § 1.110, eff. April 2, 2015.

### § 162.403. Establishment of Voluntary Adoption Registries

(a) The vital statistics unit shall establish and maintain a mutual consent voluntary adoption registry.

(b) Except as provided by Subsection (c), an agency authorized by the department to place children for adoption and an association comprised exclusively of those agencies may establish a mutual consent voluntary adoption registry. An agency may contract with any other agency authorized by the department to place children for adoption or with an association comprised exclusively of those agencies to perform registry services on its behalf.

(c) An authorized agency that did not directly or by contract provide registry services as required by this subchapter on January 1, 1984, may not provide its own registry service. The vital statistics unit shall operate through the central registry those services for agencies not permitted to provide a registry under this section.

Added by Acts 1995, 74th Leg., ch. 20, § 1, eff. April 20, 1995. Amended by Acts 1997, 75th Leg., ch. 561, § 20, eff. Sept. 1, 1997; Acts 2015, 84th Leg., ch. 1 (S.B. 219), § 1.111, eff. April 2, 2015.

### § 162.404. Requirement to Send Information to Central Registry

An authorized agency that is permitted to provide a registry under this subchapter or that participates in a mutual consent voluntary adoption registry with an association of authorized agencies shall send to the central registry a duplicate of all information the registry maintains in the agency's registry or sends to the registry in which the agency participates.

Added by Acts 1997, 75th Leg., ch. 561, § 21, eff. Sept. 1, 1997.

### § 162.405. Determination of Appropriate Registry

(a) The administrator of the central registry shall determine the appropriate registry to which an applicant is entitled to apply.

(b) On receiving an inquiry by an adoptee, birth parent, or sibling who has provided satisfactory proof of age and identity and paid all required inquiry fees, the administrator of the central registry shall review the information on file in the central index and consult with the administrators of other registries in the state to determine the identity of any appropriate registry through which the adoptee, birth parent, or sibling may register.

(c) Each administrator shall, not later than the 30th day after the date of receiving an inquiry from the administrator of the central registry, respond in writing to the inquiry that the registrant was not placed for adoption by an agency served by that registry or that the registrant was placed for adoption by an agency served by that registry. If the registrant was placed for adoption by an agency served by the registry, the administrator shall file a report with the administrator of the central registry including:

(1) the name of the adopted child as shown in the final adoption decree;

(2) the birth date of the adopted child;

(3) the docket number of the adoption suit;

(4) the identity of the court that granted the adoption;

(5) the date of the final adoption decree;

(6) the identity of the agency, if any, through which the adopted child was placed; and

(7) the identity, address, and telephone number of the registry through which the adopted child may register as an adoptee.

(d) After completing the investigation, the administrator of the central registry shall issue an official certificate stating:

(1) the identity of the registry through which the adoptee, birth parent, or biological sibling may apply for registration, if known; or

(2) if the administrator cannot make a conclusive determination, that the adoptee, birth parent, or biological sibling is entitled to apply for registration through the central registry.

Added by Acts 1995, 74th Leg., ch. 20, § 1, eff. April 20, 1995. Amended by Acts 1995, 74th Leg., ch. 751, § 79, eff. Sept. 1, 1995; Acts 1995, 74th Leg., ch. 968, § 2, eff. Sept. 1, 1995.

### § 162.406. Registration Eligibility

(a) An adoptee who is 18 years of age or older may apply to a registry for information about the adoptee's birth parents and biological siblings.

(b) A birth parent who is 18 years of age or older may apply to a registry for information about an adoptee who is a child by birth of the birth parent.

(c) An alleged father who is 18 years of age or older and who acknowledges paternity but is not, at the time of application, a birth father may register as a birth father but may not otherwise be recognized as a birth father for the purposes of this subchapter unless:

(1) the adoptee's birth mother in her application identifies him as the adoptee's biological father; and

(2) additional information concerning the adoptee obtained from other sources is not inconsistent with his claim of paternity.

(d) A biological sibling who is 18 years of age or older may apply to a registry for information about the person's adopted biological siblings.

(e) Only birth parents, adoptees, and biological siblings may apply for information through a registry.

(f) A person, including an authorized agency, may not apply for information through a registry as an agent, attorney, or representative of an adoptee, birth parent, or biological sibling.

Added by Acts 1995, 74th Leg., ch. 20, § 1, eff. April 20, 1995. Amended by Acts 1995, 74th Leg., ch. 968, § 3, eff. Sept. 1, 1995.

### § 162.407. Registration

(a) The administrator shall require each registration applicant to sign a written application.

(b) An adoptee adopted or placed through an authorized agency may register through the registry maintained by that agency or the registry to which the agency has delegated registry services or through the central registry maintained by the vital statistics unit.

(c) Birth parents and biological siblings shall register through:

(1) the registry of the authorized agency through which the adoptee was adopted or placed; or

(2) the central registry.

(d) The administrator may not accept an application for registration unless the applicant:

(1) provides proof of identity as provided by Section 162.408;

(2) establishes the applicant's eligibility to register; and

(3) pays all required registration fees.

(e) A registration remains in effect until the 99th anniversary of the date the registration is accepted unless a shorter period is specified by the applicant or the registration is withdrawn before that time.

(f) A registrant may withdraw the registrant's registration in writing without charge at any time.

(g) After a registration is withdrawn or expires, the registrant shall be treated as if the person has not previously registered.

(h) A completed registry application must be accepted or rejected before the 46th day after the date the application is received. If an application is rejected, the administrator shall provide the applicant with a written statement of the reason for the rejection.

Added by Acts 1995, 74th Leg., ch. 20, § 1, eff. April 20, 1995. Amended by Acts 1995, 74th Leg., ch. 968, § 4, eff. Sept. 1, 1995; Acts 1997, 75th Leg., ch. 561, § 22, eff. Sept. 1, 1997; Acts 2015, 84th Leg., ch. 1 (S.B. 219), § 1.112, eff. April 2, 2015.

### § 162.408. Proof of Identity

The rules and minimum standards of the Department of State Health Services for the vital statistics unit must provide for proof of identity in order to facilitate the purposes of this subchapter and to protect the privacy rights of adoptees, adoptive parents, birth parents, biological siblings, and their families.

Added by Acts 1995, 74th Leg., ch. 20, § 1, eff. April 20, 1995. Amended by Acts 1997, 75th Leg., ch. 561, § 23, eff. Sept. 1, 1997; Acts 2015, 84th Leg., ch. 1 (S.B. 219), § 1.113, eff. April 2, 2015.

### § 162.409. Application

(a) An application must contain:

(1) the name, address, and telephone number of the applicant;

(2) any other name or alias by which the applicant has been known;

(3) the age, date of birth, and place of birth of the applicant;

(4) the original name of the adoptee, if known;

(5) the adoptive name of the adoptee, if known;

(6) a statement that the applicant is willing to allow the applicant's identity to be disclosed to a registrant who is eligible to learn the applicant's identity;

(7) the name, address, and telephone number of the agency or other entity, organization, or person placing the adoptee for adoption, if known, or, if not known, a statement that the applicant does not know that information;

(8) an authorization to the administrator and the administrator's designees to inspect all vital statistics records, court records, and agency records, including confidential records, relating to the birth, adoption, marriage, and divorce of the applicant or to the birth and death of any child or sibling by birth or adoption of the applicant;

(9) the specific address to which the applicant wishes notice of a successful match to be mailed;

(10) a statement that the applicant either does or does not consent to disclosure of identifying information about the applicant after the applicant's death;

(11) a statement that the registration is to be effective for 99 years or for a stated shorter period selected by the applicant; and

(12) a statement that the adoptee applicant either does or does not desire to be informed that registry records indicate that the applicant has a biological sibling who has registered under this subchapter.

(b) The application may contain the applicant's social security number if the applicant, after being advised of the right not to supply the number, voluntarily furnishes it.

(c) The application of a birth parent must include:

(1) the original name and date of birth or approximate date of birth of each adoptee with respect to whom the parent is registering;

(2) the names of all other birth children, including maiden names, aliases, dates and places of birth, and names of the birth parents;

(3) each name known or thought by the applicant to have been used by the adoptee's other birth parent;

(4) the last known address of the adoptee's other birth parent; and

(5) other available information through which the other birth parent may be identified.

(d) The application of a biological sibling must include:

(1) a statement explaining the applicant's basis for believing that the applicant has one or more biological siblings;

(2) the names, including maiden and married names, and aliases of all the applicant's siblings by birth and adoption and their dates and places of birth, if known;

(3) the names of the applicant's legal parents;

(4) the names of the applicant's birth parents, if known; and

(5) any other information known to the applicant through which the existence and identity of the applicant's biological siblings can be confirmed.

(e) An application may also contain additional information through which the applicant's identity and eligibility to register may be ascertained.

(f) The administrator shall assist the applicant in filling out the application if the applicant is unable to complete the application without assistance, but the administrator may not furnish the applicant with any substantive information necessary to complete the application.

Added by Acts 1995, 74th Leg., ch. 20, § 1, eff. April 20, 1995. Amended by Acts 1995, 74th Leg., ch. 968, § 5, eff. Sept. 1, 1995.

### § 162.410. Repealed by Acts 1995, 74th Leg., ch. 968, § 11, eff. Sept. 1, 1995

### § 162.411. Fees

(a) The costs of establishing, operating, and maintaining a registry may be recovered in whole or in part through users' fees charged to applicants and registrants.

(b) Each registry shall establish a schedule of fees for services provided by the registry. The fees shall be reasonably related to the direct and indirect costs of establishing, operating, and maintaining the registry.

(c) A fee may not be charged for withdrawing a registration.

(d) The fees collected by the vital statistics unit shall be deposited in a special fund in the general revenue fund. Funds in the special fund may be appropriated only for the administration of the central registry.

(e) The administrator may waive users' fees in whole or in part if the applicant provides satisfactory proof of financial inability to pay the fees.

Added by Acts 1995, 74th Leg., ch. 20, § 1, eff. April 20, 1995. Amended by Acts 1995, 74th Leg., ch. 968, § 6, eff. Sept. 1, 1995; Acts 1997, 75th Leg., ch. 561, § 24, eff. Sept. 1, 1997; Acts 2015, 84th Leg., ch. 1 (S.B. 219), § 1.114, eff. April 2, 2015.

### § 162.412. Supplemental Information

(a) A registrant may amend the registrant's registration and submit additional information to the administrator. A registrant shall notify the administrator of any change in the registrant's name or address that occurs after acceptance of the application.

(b) The administrator does not have a duty to search for a registrant who fails to register a change of name or address.

Added by Acts 1995, 74th Leg., ch. 20, § 1, eff. April 20, 1995.

### § 162.413. Counseling

The applicant must participate in counseling for not less than one hour with a social worker or mental health professional with expertise in postadoption counseling after the administrator has accepted the application for registration and before the release of confidential information.

Added by Acts 1995, 74th Leg., ch. 20, § 1, eff. April 20, 1995. Amended by Acts 1995, 74th Leg., ch. 968, § 7, eff. Sept. 1, 1995.

### § 162.414. Matching Procedures

(a) The administrator shall process each registration in an attempt to match the adoptee and the adoptee's birth parents or the adoptee and the adoptee's biological siblings.

(b) The administrator shall determine that there is a match if the adult adoptee and the birth mother or the birth father have registered or if a biological sibling has registered.

(c) To establish or corroborate a match, the administrator shall request confirmation of a possible match from the vital statistics unit. If the agency operating the registry has in its own records sufficient information through which the match may be confirmed, the administrator may, but is not required to, request confirmation from the vital statistics unit. The vital statistics unit may confirm or deny the match without breaching the duty of confidentiality to the adoptee, adoptive parents, birth parents, or biological siblings and without a court order.

(d) To establish a match, the administrator may also request confirmation of a possible match from the agency, if any, that has possession of records concerning the adoption of an adoptee or from the court that granted the adoption, the hospital where the adoptee or any biological sibling was born, the physician who delivered the adoptee or biological sibling, or any other person who has knowledge of the relevant facts. The agency, court, hospital, physician, or person with knowledge may confirm or deny the match without breaching any duty of confidentiality to the adoptee, adoptive parents, birth parents, or biological siblings.

(e) If a match is denied by a source contacted under Subsection (d), the administrator shall make a full and complete investigation into the reliability of the denial. If the match is corroborated by other reliable sources and the administrator is satisfied that the denial is erroneous, the administrator may make disclosures but shall report to the adoptee, birth parents, and biological siblings involved that the match was not confirmed by all information sources.

Added by Acts 1995, 74th Leg., ch. 20, § 1, eff. April 20, 1995. Amended by Acts 1995, 74th Leg., ch. 968, § 8, eff. Sept. 1, 1995; Acts 1997, 75th Leg., ch. 561, § 25, eff. Sept. 1, 1997; Acts 2015, 84th Leg., ch. 1 (S.B. 219), § 1.115, eff. April 2, 2015.

### § 162.415. Repealed by Acts 1995, 74th Leg., ch. 968, § 11, eff. Sept. 1, 1995

### § 162.416. Disclosure of Identifying Information

(a) When a match has been made and confirmed to the administrator's satisfaction, the administrator shall mail to each registrant, at the registrant's last known address, by fax or registered or certified mail, return receipt requested, delivery restricted to addressee only, a written notice:

(1) informing the registrant that a match has been made and confirmed;

(2) reminding the registrant that the registrant may withdraw the registration before disclosures are made, if desired; and

(3) notifying the registrant that before any identifying disclosures are made, the registrant must:

(A) sign a written consent to disclosure that allows the disclosure of identifying information about the other registrants to the registrant and allows the disclosure of identifying information about the registrant to other registrants;

(B) participate in counseling for not less than one hour with a social worker or mental health professional who has expertise in postadoption counseling; and

(C) provide the administrator with written certification that the counseling required under Subdivision (B) has been completed.

(b) Identifying information about a registrant shall be released without the registrant's having consented after the match to disclosure if the registrant is dead, the registrant's registration was valid at the time of death, and the registrant had in writing specifically authorized the postdeath disclosure in the registrant's application or in a supplemental statement filed with the administrator.

(c) Identifying information about a deceased birth parent may not be released until each surviving child of the deceased birth parent is an adult or until each child's surviving parent, guardian, managing conservator, or legal custodian consents in writing to the disclosure.

(d) The administrator shall prepare and release written disclosure statements identifying information about each of the registrants if the registrants complied with Subsection (a) and, before the 60th day after the date notification of match was mailed, the registrant or registrants have not withdrawn their registrations.

(e) If the administrator establishes that a match cannot be made because of the death of an adoptee, birth parent, or biological sibling, the administrator shall promptly notify the affected registrant. The administrator shall disclose the reason why a match cannot be made and may disclose nonidentifying information concerning the circumstances of the person's death.

Added by Acts 1995, 74th Leg., ch. 20, § 1, eff. April 20, 1995. Amended by Acts 1995, 74th Leg., ch. 968, § 9, eff. Sept. 1, 1995.

### §§ 162.417, 162.418. Repealed by Acts 1995, 74th Leg., ch. 968, § 11, eff. Sept. 1, 1995

### § 162.419. Registry Records Confidential

(a) All applications, registrations, records, and other information submitted to, obtained by, or otherwise acquired by a registry are confidential and may not be disclosed to any person or entity except in the manner authorized by this subchapter.

(b) Information acquired by a registry may not be disclosed under freedom of information or sunshine legislation, rules, or practice.

(c) A person may not file or prosecute a class action litigation to force a registry to disclose identifying information.

Added by Acts 1995, 74th Leg., ch. 20, § 1, eff. April 20, 1995.

### § 162.420. Rulemaking

(a) The executive commissioner of the Health and Human Services Commission shall make rules and adopt minimum standards for the Department of State Health Services to:

(1) administer the provisions of this subchapter; and

(2) ensure that each registry respects the right to privacy and confidentiality of an adoptee, birth parent, and biological sibling who does not desire to disclose the person's identity.

(b) The Department of State Health Services shall conduct a comprehensive review of all rules and standards adopted under this subchapter not less than every six years.

(c) In order to provide the administrators an opportunity to review proposed rules and standards and send written suggestions to the executive commissioner of the Health and Human Services Commission, the executive commissioner shall, before adopting rules and minimum standards, send a copy of the proposed rules and standards not less than 60 days before the date they take effect to:

(1) the administrator of each registry established under this subchapter; and

(2) the administrator of each agency authorized by the department to place children for adoption.

Added by Acts 1995, 74th Leg., ch. 20, § 1, eff. April 20, 1995. Amended by Acts 1997, 75th Leg., ch. 561, § 26, eff. Sept. 1, 1997; Acts 2015, 84th Leg., ch. 1 (S.B. 219), § 1.116, eff. April 2, 2015.

### § 162.421. Prohibited Acts; Criminal Penalties

(a) This subchapter does not prevent the Department of State Health Services from making known to the public, by appropriate means, the existence of voluntary adoption registries.

(b) Information received by or in connection with the operation of a registry may not be stored in a data bank used for any purpose other than operation of the registry.

(c) A person commits an offense if the person knowingly or recklessly discloses information from a registry application, registration, record, or other information submitted to, obtained by, or otherwise acquired by a registry in violation of this subchapter. This subsection may not be construed to penalize the disclosure of information from adoption agency records. An offense under this subsection is a felony of the second degree.

(d) A person commits an offense if the person with criminal negligence causes or permits the disclosure of information from a registry application, registration, record, or other information submitted to, obtained by, or otherwise acquired by a registry in violation of this subchapter. This subsection may not be construed to penalize the disclosure of information from adoption agency records. An offense under this subsection is a Class A misdemeanor.

(e) A person commits an offense if the person impersonates an adoptee, birth parent, or biological sibling with the intent to secure confidential information from a registry established under this subchapter. An offense under this subsection is a felony of the second degree.

(f) A person commits an offense if the person impersonates an administrator, agent, or employee of a registry with the intent to secure confidential information from a registry established under this subchapter. An offense under this subsection is a felony of the second degree.

(g) A person commits an offense if the person, with intent to deceive and with knowledge of the statement's meaning, makes a false statement under oath in connection with the operation of a registry. An offense under this subsection is a felony of the third degree.

Added by Acts 1995, 74th Leg., ch. 20, § 1, eff. April 20, 1995. Amended by Acts 1995, 74th Leg., ch. 968, § 10, eff. Sept. 1, 1995; Acts 1997, 75th Leg., ch. 561, § 27, eff. Sept. 1, 1997; Acts 2015, 84th Leg., ch. 1 (S.B. 219), § 1.117, eff. April 2, 2015.

### § 162.422. Immunity from Liability

(a) The Department of State Health Services or authorized agency establishing or operating a registry is not liable to any person for obtaining or disclosing identifying information about a birth parent, adoptee, or biological sibling within the scope of this subchapter and under its provisions.

(b) An employee or agent of the Department of State Health Services or of an authorized agency establishing or operating a registry under this subchapter is not liable to any person for obtaining or disclosing identifying information about a birth parent, adoptee, or biological sibling within the scope of this subchapter and under its provisions.

(c) A person or entity furnishing information to the administrator or an employee or agent of a registry is not liable to any person for disclosing information about a birth parent, adoptee, or biological sibling within the scope of this subchapter and under its provisions.

(d) A person or entity is not immune from liability for performing an act prohibited by Section 162.421.

Added by Acts 1995, 74th Leg., ch. 20, § 1, eff. April 20, 1995. Amended by Acts 1997, 75th Leg., ch. 561, § 28, eff. Sept. 1, 1997; Acts 2015, 84th Leg., ch. 1 (S.B. 219), § 1.118, eff. April 2, 2015.

## SUBCHAPTER F. ADOPTION OF AN ADULT

### § 162.501. Adoption of Adult

The court may grant the petition of an adult residing in this state to adopt another adult according to this subchapter.

Added by Acts 1995, 74th Leg., ch. 20, § 1, eff. April 20, 1995.

### § 162.502. Jurisdiction

The petitioner shall file a suit to adopt an adult in the district court or a statutory county court granted jurisdiction in family law cases and proceedings by Chapter 25, Government Code, in the county of the petitioner's residence.

Added by Acts 1995, 74th Leg., ch. 20, § 1, eff. April 20, 1995.

### § 162.503. Requirements of Petition

(a) A petition to adopt an adult shall be entitled "In the Interest of ________, An Adult."

(b) If the petitioner is married, both spouses must join in the petition for adoption.

Added by Acts 1995, 74th Leg., ch. 20, § 1, eff. April 20, 1995.

### § 162.504. Consent

A court may not grant an adoption unless the adult consents in writing to be adopted by the petitioner.

Added by Acts 1995, 74th Leg., ch. 20, § 1, eff. April 20, 1995.

### § 162.505. Attendance Required

The petitioner and the adult to be adopted must attend the hearing. For good cause shown, the court may waive this requirement, by written order, if the petitioner or adult to be adopted is unable to attend.

Added by Acts 1995, 74th Leg., ch. 20, § 1, eff. April 20, 1995.

### § 162.506. Adoption Order

(a) The court shall grant the adoption if the court finds that the requirements for adoption of an adult are met.

(b) Notwithstanding that both spouses have joined in a petition for the adoption of an adult as required by Section 162.503(b), the court may grant the adoption of the adult to both spouses or, on request of the spouses, to only one spouse.

Added by Acts 1995, 74th Leg., ch. 20, § 1, eff. April 20, 1995. Amended by Acts 2003, 78th Leg., ch. 555, § 1, eff. June 20, 2003.

### § 162.507. Effect of Adoption

(a) The adopted adult is the son or daughter of the adoptive parents for all purposes.

(b) The adopted adult is entitled to inherit from and through the adopted adult's adoptive parents as though the adopted adult were the biological child of the adoptive parents.

(c) The adopted adult may not inherit from or through the adult's biological parent. A biological parent may not inherit from or through an adopted adult.

Added by Acts 1995, 74th Leg., ch. 20, § 1, eff. April 20, 1995. Amended by Acts 2005, 79th Leg., ch. 169, § 1, eff. Sept. 1, 2005.

## SUBCHAPTER G. MISCELLANEOUS PROVISIONS

### § 162.601. Incentives for Licensed Child-Placing Agencies

(a) Subject to the availability of funds, the Department of Family and Protective Services shall pay, in addition to any other amounts due, a monetary incentive to a licensed child-placing agency for the completion of an adoption:

(1) of a child, as defined by Section 162.301, receiving or entitled to receive foster care at department expense; and

(2) arranged with the assistance of the agency.

(b) The incentive may not exceed 25 percent of the amount the department would have spent to provide one year of foster care for the child, determined according to the child's level of care at the time the adoption is completed.

(c) For purposes of this section, an adoption is completed on the date on which the court issues the adoption order.

Added by Acts 1997, 75th Leg., ch. 1309, § 1, eff. Sept. 1, 1997. Amended by Acts 2015, 84th Leg., ch. 1 (S.B. 219), § 1.119, eff. April 2, 2015.

### § 162.602. Documentation to Accompany Petition for Adoption or Annulment or Revocation of Adoption

At the time a petition for adoption or annulment or revocation of adoption is filed, the petitioner shall also file completed documentation that may be used by the clerk of the court, at the time the petition is granted, to comply with Section 192.009, Health and Safety Code, and Section 108.003.

Added by Acts 2003, 78th Leg., ch. 1128, § 5, eff. Sept. 1, 2003.

### § 162.603. Post-Adoption Support Information Provided by Licensed Child-Placing Agencies

A licensed child-placing agency shall provide prospective adoptive parents with information regarding:

(1) the community services and other resources available to support a parent who adopts a child; and

(2) the options available to the adoptive parent if the parent is unable to care for the adopted child.

Added by Acts 2017, 85th Leg., ch. 985 (H.B. 834), § 2, eff. Sept. 1, 2017.

## SUBCHAPTER H. EMBRYO DONATION INFORMATION

### § 162.701. Definitions

In this subchapter:

(1) "Department" means the Department of Family and Protective Services.

(2) "Embryo donation" has the meaning assigned by Section 159.011, Occupations Code.

Added by Acts 2017, 85th Leg., ch. 331 (H.B. 785), § 2, eff. Sept. 1, 2017.

### § 162.702. Information Regarding Embryo Donation

The department shall post information regarding embryo donation on the department's Internet website. The information must include contact information for nonprofit organizations that facilitate embryo donation.

Added by Acts 2017, 85th Leg., ch. 331 (H.B. 785), § 2, eff. Sept. 1, 2017.

# SUBTITLE C. JUDICIAL RESOURCES AND SERVICES

## CHAPTER 201. ASSOCIATE JUDGE

### SUBCHAPTER A. ASSOCIATE JUDGE

Section



### SUBCHAPTER B. ASSOCIATE JUDGE FOR TITLE IV-D CASES

SUBCHAPTER C. ASSOCIATE JUDGE FOR CHILD PROTECTION CASES



SUBCHAPTER D. ASSOCIATE JUDGE FOR JUVENILE MATTERS



## SUBCHAPTER A. ASSOCIATE JUDGE

### § 201.001. Appointment

(a) A judge of a court having jurisdiction of a suit under this title, Title 1, Chapter 45, or Title 4 may appoint a full-time or part-time associate judge to perform the duties authorized by this chapter if the commissioners court of a county in which the court has jurisdiction authorizes the employment of an associate judge.

(b) If a court has jurisdiction in more than one county, an associate judge appointed by that court may serve only in a county in which the commissioners court has authorized the associate judge's appointment.

(c) If more than one court in a county has jurisdiction of a suit under this title, Title 1, Chapter 45, or Title 4 the commissioners court may authorize the appointment of an associate judge for each court or may authorize one or more associate judges to share service with two or more courts.

(d) If an associate judge serves more than one court, the associate judge's appointment must be made with the unanimous approval of all the judges under whom the associate judge serves.

(e) This section does not apply to an associate judge appointed under Subchapter B[1] or C[2].

Added by Acts 1995, 74th Leg., ch. 20, § 1, eff. April 20, 1995. Amended by Acts 1999, 76th Leg., ch. 1302, § 1, eff. Sept. 1, 1999; Acts 2003, 78th Leg., ch. 1258, § 2, eff. Sept. 1, 2003; Acts 2015, 84th Leg., ch. 197 (S.B. 812), § 1, eff. Sept. 1, 2015.

1 V.T.C.A., Family Code § 201.101 et seq.
2 V.T.C.A., Family Code § 201.201 et seq.

### § 201.002. Qualifications

(a) Except as provided by Subsection (b), to be eligible for appointment as an associate judge, a person must meet the requirements and qualifications to serve as a judge of the court or courts for which the associate judge is appointed.

(b) To be eligible for appointment as an associate judge under Subchapter B or C, [1] a person must meet the requirements and qualifications established under those subchapters.

Added by Acts 1995, 74th Leg., ch. 20, § 1, eff. April 20, 1995. Amended by Acts 2007, 80th Leg., ch. 44, § 1, eff. Sept. 1, 2007.

1 V.T.C.A., Family Code § 210.101 et seq. or V.T.C.A., Family Code § 201.201 et seq.

### § 201.003. Compensation

(a) An associate judge shall be paid a salary determined by the commissioners court of the county in which the associate judge serves.

(b) If an associate judge serves in more than one county, the associate judge shall be paid a salary as determined by agreement of the commissioners courts of the counties in which the associate judge serves.

(c) The associate judge's salary is paid from the county fund available for payment of officers' salaries.

(d) This section does not apply to an associate judge appointed under Subchapter B[1] or C[2].

Added by Acts 1995, 74th Leg., ch. 20, § 1, eff. April 20, 1995. Amended by Acts 1999, 76th Leg., ch. 1302, § 2, eff. Sept. 1, 1999; Acts 2003, 78th Leg., ch. 1258, § 3, eff. Sept. 1, 2003.

[1] V.T.C.A., Family Code § 201.101 et seq.
[2] V.T.C.A., Family Code § 201.201 et seq.

### § 201.004. Termination of Associate Judge

(a) An associate judge who serves a single court serves at the will of the judge of that court.

(b) The employment of an associate judge who serves more than two courts may only be terminated by a majority vote of all the judges of the courts which the associate judge serves.

(c) The employment of an associate judge who serves two courts may be terminated by either of the judges of the courts which the associate judge serves.

(d) This section does not apply to an associate judge appointed under Subchapter B[1] or C[2].

Added by Acts 1995, 74th Leg., ch. 20, § 1, eff. April 20, 1995. Amended by Acts 1999, 76th Leg., ch. 1302, § 3, eff. Sept. 1, 1999; Acts 2003, 78th Leg., ch. 1258, § 4, eff. Sept. 1, 2003.

[1] V.T.C.A., Family Code § 201.101 et seq.
[2] V.T.C.A., Family Code § 201.201 et seq.

### § 201.005. Cases That May Be Referred

(a) Except as provided by this section, a judge of a court may refer to an associate judge any aspect of a suit over which the court has jurisdiction under this title, Title 1, Chapter 45, or Title 4, including any matter ancillary to the suit.

(b) Unless a party files a written objection to the associate judge hearing a trial on the merits, the judge may refer the trial to the associate judge. A trial on the merits is any final adjudication from which an appeal may be taken to a court of appeals.

(c) A party must file an objection to an associate judge hearing a trial on the merits or presiding at a jury trial not later than the 10th day after the date the party receives notice that the associate judge will hear the trial. If an objection is filed, the referring court shall hear the trial on the merits or preside at a jury trial.

(d) The requirements of Subsections (b) and (c) shall apply whenever a judge has authority to refer the trial of a suit under this title, Title 1, Chapter 45, or Title 4 to an associate judge, master, or other assistant judge regardless of whether the assistant judge is appointed under this subchapter.

Added by Acts 1995, 74th Leg., ch. 20, § 1, eff. April 20, 1995. Amended by Acts 1999, 76th Leg., ch. 1302, § 4, eff. Sept. 1, 1999; Acts 2015, 84th Leg., ch. 197 (S.B. 812), § 2, eff. Sept. 1, 2015.

### § 201.006. Order of Referral

(a) In referring a case to an associate judge, the judge of the referring court shall render:

(1) an individual order of referral; or

(2) a general order of referral specifying the class and type of cases to be heard by the associate judge.

(b) The order of referral may limit the power or duties of an associate judge.

Added by Acts 1995, 74th Leg., ch. 20, § 1, eff. April 20, 1995.

### § 201.007. Powers of Associate Judge

(a) Except as limited by an order of referral, an associate judge may:

(1) conduct a hearing;

(2) hear evidence;

(3) compel production of relevant evidence;

(4) rule on the admissibility of evidence;

(5) issue a summons for:

(A) the appearance of witnesses; and

(B) the appearance of a parent who has failed to appear before an agency authorized to conduct an investigation of an allegation of abuse or neglect of a child after receiving proper notice;

(6) examine a witness;

(7) swear a witness for a hearing;

(8) make findings of fact on evidence;

(9) formulate conclusions of law;

(10) recommend an order to be rendered in a case;

(11) regulate all proceedings in a hearing before the associate judge;

(12) order the attachment of a witness or party who fails to obey a subpoena;

(13) order the detention of a witness or party found guilty of contempt, pending approval by the referring court as provided by Section 201.013;

(14) without prejudice to the right to a de novo hearing before the referring court under Section 201.015 and subject to Subsection (c), render and sign:

(A) a final order agreed to in writing as to both form and substance by all parties;

(B) a final default order;

(C) a temporary order; or

(D) a final order in a case in which a party files an unrevoked waiver made in accordance with Rule 119, Texas Rules of Civil Procedure, that waives notice to the party of the final hearing or waives the party's appearance at the final hearing;

(15) take action as necessary and proper for the efficient performance of the associate judge's duties; and

(16) render and sign a final order if the parties waive the right to a de novo hearing before the referring court under Section 201.015 in writing before the start of a hearing conducted by the associate judge.

(b) An associate judge may, in the interest of justice, refer a case back to the referring court regardless of whether a timely objection to the associate judge hearing the trial on the merits or presiding at a jury trial has been made by any party.

(c) A final order described by Subsection (a)(14) becomes final after the expiration of the period described by Section 201.015(a) if a party does not request a de novo hearing in accordance with that section. An order described by Subsection (a)(14) or (16) that is rendered and signed by an associate judge constitutes an order of the referring court.

(d) An answer filed by or on behalf of a party who previously filed a waiver described in Subsection (a)(14)(D) shall revoke that waiver.

(e) An order signed before May 1, 2017, by an associate judge under Subsection (a)(16) is a final order rendered as of the date the order was signed.

Added by Acts 1995, 74th Leg., ch. 20, § 1, eff. April 20, 1995. Amended by Acts 1999, 76th Leg., ch. 1302, § 5, eff. Sept. 1, 1999; Acts 2003, 78th Leg., ch. 476, § 1, eff. Sept. 1, 2003; Acts 2005, 79th Leg., ch. 550, § 1, eff. Sept. 1, 2005; Acts 2007, 80th Leg., ch. 839, § 1, eff. June 15, 2007; Acts 2007, 80th Leg., ch. 1406, § 5, eff. Sept. 1, 2007; Acts 2017, 85th Leg., ch. 279 (H.B. 2927), § 1, eff. May 29, 2017; Acts 2017, 85th Leg., ch. 912 (S.B. 1329), § 1.03(a), eff. Sept. 1, 2017.

### § 201.008. Attendance of Bailiff

A bailiff may attend a hearing by an associate judge if directed by the referring court.

Added by Acts 1995, 74th Leg., ch. 20, § 1, eff. April 20, 1995.

### § 201.009. Court Reporter; Record

(a) A court reporter may be provided during a hearing held by an associate judge appointed under this chapter. A court reporter is required to be provided when the associate judge presides over a jury trial or a contested final termination hearing.

(b) A party, the associate judge, or the referring court may provide for a reporter during the hearing, if one is not otherwise provided.

(c) Except as provided by Subsection (a), in the absence of a court reporter or on agreement of the parties, the record may be preserved by any means approved by the associate judge.

(d) The referring court or associate judge may tax the expense of preserving the record under Subsection (c) as costs.

(e) On a request for a de novo hearing, the referring court may consider testimony or other evidence in the record in addition to witnesses or other matters presented under Section 201.015.

Added by Acts 1995, 74th Leg., ch. 20, § 1, eff. April 20, 1995. Amended by Acts 1999, 76th Leg., ch. 1302, § 6, eff. Sept. 1, 1999; Acts 2007, 80th Leg., ch. 839, §§ 2, 3, eff. June 15, 2007; Acts 2007, 80th Leg., ch. 1235, § 1, eff. Sept. 1, 2007; Acts 2009, 81st Leg., ch. 767, § 24, eff. June 19, 2009.

### § 201.010. Witness

(a) A witness appearing before an associate judge is subject to the penalties for perjury provided by law.

(b) A referring court may fine or imprison a witness who:

(1) failed to appear before an associate judge after being summoned; or

(2) improperly refused to answer questions if the refusal has been certified to the court by the associate judge.

Added by Acts 1995, 74th Leg., ch. 20, § 1, eff. April 20, 1995.

### § 201.011. Report

(a) The associate judge's report may contain the associate judge's findings, conclusions, or recommendations and may be in the form of a proposed order. The associate judge's report must be in writing in the form directed by the referring court.

(b) After a hearing, the associate judge shall provide the parties participating in the hearing notice of the substance of the associate judge's report, including any proposed order.

(c) Notice may be given to the parties:

(1) in open court, by an oral statement or a copy of the associate judge's written report, including any proposed order;

(2) by certified mail, return receipt requested; or

(3) by facsimile transmission.

(d) There is a rebuttable presumption that notice is received on the date stated on:

(1) the signed return receipt, if notice was provided by certified mail; or

(2) the confirmation page produced by the facsimile machine, if notice was provided by facsimile transmission.

(e) After a hearing conducted by an associate judge, the associate judge shall send the associate judge's signed and dated report, including any proposed order, and all other papers relating to the case to the referring court.

Added by Acts 1995, 74th Leg., ch. 20, § 1, eff. April 20, 1995. Amended by Acts 1999, 76th Leg., ch. 1302, § 7, eff. Sept. 1, 1999; Acts 2003, 78th Leg., ch. 464, § 1, eff. Sept. 1, 2003; Acts 2007, 80th Leg., ch. 1235, § 2, eff. Sept. 1, 2007.

### § 201.012. Notice of Right to De Novo Hearing Before Referring Court

(a) Notice of the right to a de novo hearing before the referring court shall be given to all parties.

(b) The notice may be given:

(1) by oral statement in open court;

(2) by posting inside or outside the courtroom of the referring court; or

(3) as otherwise directed by the referring court.

Added by Acts 1995, 74th Leg., ch. 20, § 1, eff. April 20, 1995. Amended by Acts 2007, 80th Leg., ch. 1235, §§ 3, 4, eff. Sept. 1, 2007.

### § 201.013. Order of Court

(a) Pending a de novo hearing before the referring court, a proposed order or judgment of the associate judge is in full force and effect and is enforceable as an order or judgment of the referring court, except for an order providing for the appointment of a receiver.

(b) Except as provided by Section 201.007(c), if a request for a de novo hearing before the referring court is not timely filed, the proposed order or judgment of the associate judge becomes the order or judgment of the referring court only on the referring court's signing the proposed order or judgment.

(c) An order by an associate judge for the temporary detention or incarceration of a witness or party shall be presented to the referring court on the day the witness or party is detained or incarcerated. The referring court, without prejudice to the right to a de novo hearing provided by Section 201.015, may approve the temporary detention or incarceration or may order the release of the party or witness, with or without bond, pending a de novo hearing. If the referring court is not immediately available, the associate judge may order the release of the party or witness, with or without bond, pending a de novo hearing or may continue the person's detention or incarceration for not more than 72 hours.

Added by Acts 1995, 74th Leg., ch. 20, § 1, eff. April 20, 1995. Amended by Acts 1999, 76th Leg., ch. 1302, § 8, eff. Sept. 1, 1999; Acts 2003, 78th Leg., ch. 476, § 2, eff. Sept. 1, 2003; Acts 2007, 80th Leg., ch. 1235, § 5, eff. Sept. 1, 2007; Acts 2017, 85th Leg., ch. 279 (H.B. 2927), § 2, eff. May 29, 2017; Acts 2017, 85th Leg., ch. 912 (S.B. 1329), § 1.03(b), eff. Sept. 1, 2017.

### § 201.014. Judicial Action on Associate Judge's Proposed Order or Judgment

(a) Except as otherwise provided in this subchapter, unless a party files a written request for a de novo hearing before the referring court, the referring court may:

(1) adopt, modify, or reject the associate judge's proposed order or judgment;

(2) hear further evidence; or

(3) recommit the matter to the associate judge for further proceedings.

(b) Regardless of whether a party files a written request for a de novo hearing before the referring court, a proposed order or judgment rendered by an associate judge in a suit filed by the Department of Family and Protective Services that meets the requirements of Section 263.401(d) is considered a final order for purposes of Section 263.401.

Added by Acts 1995, 74th Leg., ch. 20, § 1, eff. April 20, 1995. Amended by Acts 1999, 76th Leg., ch. 1302, § 9, eff. Sept. 1, 1999; Acts 2007, 80th Leg., ch. 1235, § 6, eff. Sept. 1, 2007; Acts 2017, 85th Leg., ch. 279 (H.B. 2927), § 3, eff. May 29, 2017; Acts 2017, 85th Leg., ch. 912 (S.B. 1329), § 1.03(c), eff. Sept. 1, 2017.

### § 201.015. De Novo Hearing Before Referring Court

(a) A party may request a de novo hearing before the referring court by filing with the clerk of the referring court a written request not later than the third working day after the date the party receives notice of:

(1) the substance of the associate judge's report as provided by Section 201.011; or

(2) the rendering of the temporary order, if the request concerns a temporary order rendered by an associate judge under Section 201.007(a)(14)(C).

(b) A request for a de novo hearing under this section must specify the issues that will be presented to the referring court.

(c) In the de novo hearing before the referring court, the parties may present witnesses on the issues specified in the request for hearing. The referring court may also consider the record from the hearing before the associate judge, including the charge to and verdict returned by a jury.

(d) Notice of a request for a de novo hearing before the referring court shall be given to the opposing attorney under Rule 21a, Texas Rules of Civil Procedure.

(e) If a request for a de novo hearing before the referring court is filed by a party, any other party may file a request for a de novo hearing before the referring court not later than the third working day after the date the initial request was filed.

(f) The referring court, after notice to the parties, shall hold a de novo hearing not later than the 30th day after the date on which the initial request for a de novo hearing was filed with the clerk of the referring court.

(g) Before the start of a hearing by an associate judge, the parties may waive the right of a de novo hearing before the referring court in writing or on the record.

(h) The denial of relief to a party after a de novo hearing under this section or a party's waiver of the right to a de novo hearing before the referring court does not affect the right of a party to file a motion for new trial, motion for judgment notwithstanding the verdict, or other post-trial motion.

(i) A party may not demand a second jury in a de novo hearing before the referring court if the associate judge's proposed order or judgment resulted from a jury trial.

Added by Acts 1995, 74th Leg., ch. 20, § 1, eff. April 20, 1995. Amended by Acts 1999, 76th Leg., ch. 1302, § 10, eff. Sept. 1, 1999; Acts 2007, 80th Leg., ch. 1043, § 1, eff. Sept. 1, 2007; Acts 2007, 80th Leg., ch. 1235, § 7, eff. Sept. 1, 2007; Acts 2009, 81st Leg., ch. 767, § 25, eff. June 19, 2009; Acts 2013, 83rd Leg., ch. 916 (H.B. 1366), § 5, eff. Sept. 1, 2013; Acts 2015, 84th Leg., ch. 589 (H.B. 4086), § 1, eff. June 16, 2015.

### § 201.016. Appellate Review

(a) A party's failure to request a de novo hearing before the referring court or a party's waiver of the right to request a de novo hearing before the referring court does not deprive the party of the right to appeal to or request other relief from a court of appeals or the supreme court.

(b) Except as provided by Subsection (c), the date an order or judgment by the referring court is signed is the controlling date for the purposes of appeal to or request for other relief from a court of appeals or the supreme court.

(c) The date an agreed order, a default order, or a final order described by Section 201.007(a)(16) is signed by an associate judge is the controlling date for the purpose of an appeal to, or a request for other relief relating to the order from, a court of appeals or the supreme court.

Added by Acts 1995, 74th Leg., ch. 20, § 1, eff. April 20, 1995. Amended by Acts 2003, 78th Leg., ch. 476, § 3, eff. Sept. 1, 2003; Acts 2007, 80th Leg., ch. 1235, § 8, eff. Sept. 1, 2007; Acts 2017, 85th Leg., ch. 279 (H.B. 2927), § 4, eff. May 29, 2017; Acts 2017, 85th Leg., ch. 912 (S.B. 1329), § 1.03(d), eff. Sept. 1, 2017.

### § 201.017. Immunity

An associate judge appointed under this subchapter has the judicial immunity of a district judge. All existing immunity granted an associate judge by law, express or implied, continues in full force and effect.

Added by Acts 1995, 74th Leg., ch. 20, § 1, eff. April 20, 1995.

### § 201.018. Visiting Associate Judge

(a) If an associate judge appointed under this subchapter is temporarily unable to perform the judge's official duties because of absence or illness, injury, or other disability, a judge of a court having jurisdiction of a suit under this title, Title 1, Chapter 45, or Title 4 may appoint a visiting associate judge to perform the duties of the associate judge during the period of the associate judge's absence or disability if the commissioners court of a county in which the court has jurisdiction authorizes the employment of a visiting associate judge.

(b) To be eligible for appointment under this section, a person must have served as an associate judge for at least two years.

(c) Sections 201.001 through 201.017 apply to a visiting associate judge appointed under this section.

(d) This section does not apply to an associate judge appointed under Subchapter B[1].

Added by Acts 1999, 76th Leg., ch. 1355, § 1, eff. Aug. 30, 1999. Amended by Acts 2001, 77th Leg., ch. 308, § 1, eff. Sept. 1, 2001; Acts 2003, 78th Leg., ch. 1258, § 5, eff. Sept. 1, 2003. Amended by Acts 2015, 84th Leg., ch. 197 (S.B. 812), § 3, eff. Sept. 1, 2015.

[1] V.T.C.A., Family Code § 201.101 et seq.

## SUBCHAPTER B. ASSOCIATE JUDGE FOR TITLE IV–D CASES

### § 201.101. Authority of Presiding Judge

(a) The presiding judge of each administrative judicial region, after conferring with the judges of courts in the region having jurisdiction of Title IV–D cases, shall determine which courts require the appointment of a full-time or part-time associate judge to complete each Title IV–D case within the time specified in this subchapter.

(b) If the presiding judge of an administrative judicial region determines under Subsection (a) that the courts in the region require the appointment of an associate judge, the presiding judge shall appoint an associate judge from a list of the qualified applicants who have submitted an application to the office of court administration. Before making the appointment, the presiding judge must provide the list to the judges of the courts from which cases will be referred to the associate judge. Each judge may recommend to the presiding judge the names of one or more applicants for appointment. An associate judge appointed under this subsection serves for a term of four years from the date the associate judge is appointed and qualifies for office. The appointment of an associate judge for a term does not affect the at-will employment status of the associate judge. The presiding judge may terminate an appointment at any time.

(b–1) Before reappointing an associate judge appointed under Subsection (b), the presiding judge must notify each judge of the courts from which cases will be referred to the associate judge of the presiding judge's intent to reappoint the associate judge to another term. Each judge may submit to the presiding judge a recommendation on whether the associate judge should be reappointed.

(c) An associate judge appointed under this subchapter may be appointed to serve more than one court. Two or more judges of administrative judicial regions may jointly appoint one or more associate judges to serve the regions.

(d) Except as provided under Subsection (e), if an associate judge is appointed for a court under this subchapter, all Title IV–D cases shall be referred to the associate judge by a general order for each county issued by the judge of the court for which the associate judge is appointed, or, in the absence of that order, by a general order issued by the presiding judge who appointed the associate judge. Referral of Title IV–D cases may not be made for individual cases or case by case.

(e) If a county has entered into a contract with the Title IV–D agency under Section 231.0011, enforcement services may be directly provided in cases identified under the contract by county personnel as provided under Section 231.0011(d), including judges and associate judges of the courts of the county.

Added by Acts 1995, 74th Leg., ch. 20, § 1, eff. April 20, 1995. Amended by Acts 2003, 78th Leg., ch. 1258, § 7, eff. Sept. 1, 2003; Acts 2013, 83rd Leg., ch. 742 (S.B. 355), § 8, eff. Sept. 1, 2013; Acts 2015, 84th Leg., ch. 1182 (S.B. 1139), § 1.01, eff. Sept. 1, 2015.

### § 201.102. Application of Law Governing Associate Judges

Subchapter A applies to an associate judge appointed under this subchapter, except that, to the extent of any conflict between this subchapter and Subchapter A, this subchapter prevails.

Added by Acts 1995, 74th Leg., ch. 20, § 1, eff. April 20, 1995. Amended by Acts 1999, 76th Leg., ch. 556, § 41, eff. Sept. 1, 1999; Acts 1999, 76th Leg., ch. 1302, § 11, eff. Sept. 1, 1999; Acts 2003, 78th Leg., ch. 1258, § 8, eff. Sept. 1, 2003; Acts 2007, 80th Leg., ch. 44, § 2, eff. Sept. 1, 2007.

### § 201.1021. Qualifications

(a) To be eligible for appointment under this subchapter, a person must be a citizen of the United States, have resided in this state for the two years preceding the date of appointment, and be:

(1) eligible for assignment under Section 74.054, Government Code, because the person is named on the list of retired and former judges maintained by the presiding judge of the administrative region under Section 74.055, Government Code; or

(2) licensed to practice law in this state and have been a practicing lawyer in this state, or a judge of a court in this state who is not otherwise eligible under Subdivision (1), for the four years preceding the date of appointment.

(b) An associate judge appointed under this subchapter shall during the term of appointment reside in the administrative judicial region, or a county adjacent to the region, in which the court to which the associate judge is appointed is located. An associate judge appointed to serve in two or more administrative judicial regions may reside anywhere in the regions.

Added by Acts 2007, 80th Leg., ch. 44, § 3, eff. Sept. 1, 2007. Amended by Acts 2009, 81st Leg., ch. 760, § 1, eff. June 19, 2009.

### § 201.103. Designation of Host County

(a) The presiding judges of the administrative judicial regions by majority vote shall determine the host county of an associate judge appointed under this subchapter.

(b) The host county shall provide an adequate courtroom and quarters, including furniture, necessary utilities, and telephone equipment and service, for the associate judge and other personnel assisting the associate judge.

(c) An associate judge is not required to reside in the host county.

Added by Acts 1995, 74th Leg., ch. 20, § 1, eff. April 20, 1995. Amended by Acts 2003, 78th Leg., ch. 1258, § 8, eff. Sept. 1, 2003.

### § 201.104. Powers of Associate Judge

(a) On the motion of a party or the associate judge, an associate judge may refer a complex case back to the judge for final disposition after the associate judge has recommended temporary support.

(b) An associate judge may render and sign any order that is not a final order on the merits of the case.

(c) An associate judge may recommend to the referring court any order after a trial on the merits.

(d) Only the referring court may hear and render an order on a motion for postjudgment relief, including a motion for a new trial or to vacate, correct, or reform a judgment.

(e) Notwithstanding Subsection (d) and subject to Section 201.1042(g), an associate judge may hear and render an order on any matter necessary to be decided in connection with a Title IV–D service, including:

(1) a suit to modify or clarify an existing child support order;

(2) a motion to enforce a child support order or revoke a respondent's community supervision and suspension of commitment;

(3) a respondent's compliance with the conditions provided in the associate judge's report for suspension of the respondent's commitment;

(4) a motion for postjudgment relief, including a motion for a new trial or to vacate, correct, or reform a judgment, if neither party has requested a de novo hearing before the referring court;

(5) a suit affecting the parent-child relationship; and

(6) a suit for modification under Chapter 156.

Added by Acts 1995, 74th Leg., ch. 20, § 1, eff. April 20, 1995. Amended by Acts 1999, 76th Leg., ch. 556, § 42, eff. Sept. 1, 1999; Acts 2001, 77th Leg., ch. 1023, § 46, eff. Sept. 1, 2001; Acts 2003, 78th Leg., ch. 1258, § 8, eff. Sept. 1, 2003; Acts 2009, 81st Leg., ch. 806, § 1, eff. Sept. 1, 2009; Acts 2017, 85th Leg., ch. 699 (H.B. 2048), § 1, eff. Sept. 1, 2017.

### § 201.1041. Judicial Action on Associate Judge's Proposed Order or Judgment

(a) If a request for a de novo hearing before the referring court is not timely filed or the right to a de novo hearing before the referring court is waived, the proposed order or judgment of the associate judge, other than a proposed order or judgment providing for enforcement by contempt or the immediate incarceration of a party, shall become the order or judgment of the referring court by operation of law without ratification by the referring court.

(b) An associate judge's proposed order or judgment providing for enforcement by contempt or the immediate incarceration of a party becomes an order of the referring court only if:

(1) the referring court signs an order adopting the associate judge's proposed order or judgment; and

(2) the order or judgment meets the requirements of Section 157.166.

(c) Except as provided by Subsection (b), a proposed order or judgment of the associate judge is in full force and effect and is enforceable as an order or judgment of the referring court pending a de novo hearing before the referring court.

Added by Acts 1999, 76th Leg., ch. 556, § 43, eff. Sept. 1, 1999. Amended by Acts 2001, 77th Leg., ch. 1023, § 47, eff. Sept. 1, 2001; Acts 2003, 78th Leg., ch. 1258, § 8, eff. Sept. 1, 2003; Acts 2007, 80th Leg., ch. 1235, § 9, eff. Sept. 1, 2007.

### § 201.1042. De Novo Hearing Before Referring Court

(a) Except as provided by this section, Section 201.015 applies to a request for a de novo hearing before the referring court.

(b) The party requesting a de novo hearing before the referring court shall file notice with the clerk of the referring court not later than the third working day after the date the associate judge signs the proposed order or judgment.

(c) A respondent who timely files a request for a de novo hearing on an associate judge's proposed order or judgment providing for incarceration shall be brought before the referring court not later than the first working day after the date on which the respondent files the request for a de novo hearing. The referring court shall determine whether the respondent should be released on bond or whether the respondent's appearance in court at a designated time and place can be otherwise assured.

(d) If the respondent under Subsection (c) is released on bond or other security, the referring court shall condition the bond or other security on the respondent's promise to appear in court for a de novo hearing at a designated date, time, and place, and the referring court shall give the respondent notice of the hearing in open court. No other notice to the respondent is required.

(e) If the respondent under Subsection (c) is released without posting bond or security, the court shall set a de novo hearing at a designated date, time, and place and give the respondent notice of the hearing in open court. No other notice to the respondent is required.

(f) If the referring court is not satisfied that the respondent's appearance in court can be assured and the respondent remains incarcerated, a de novo hearing shall be held as soon as practicable, but not later than the fifth day after the date the respondent's request for a de novo hearing before the referring court was filed, unless the respondent or, if represented, the respondent's attorney waives the accelerated hearing.

(g) Until a de novo hearing is held under this section and the referring court has signed an order or judgment or has ruled on a timely filed motion for new trial or a motion to vacate, correct, or reform a judgment, an associate judge may not hold a hearing on the respondent's compliance with conditions in the associate judge's proposed order or judgment for suspension of commitment or on a motion to revoke the respondent's community supervision and suspension of commitment.

Added by Acts 1999, 76th Leg., ch. 556, § 43, eff. Sept. 1, 1999. Amended by Acts 2001, 77th Leg., ch. 1023, § 48, eff. Sept. 1, 2001; Acts 2003, 78th Leg., ch. 1258, § 9, eff. Sept. 1, 2003; Acts 2007, 80th Leg., ch. 1235, § 10, eff. Sept. 1, 2007; Acts 2013, 83rd Leg., ch. 916 (H.B. 1366), § 6, eff. Sept. 1, 2013.

### § 201.105. Compensation of Associate Judge

(a) An associate judge appointed under this subchapter is entitled to a salary in the amount equal to 90 percent of the state base salary paid to a district judge as set by the General Appropriations Act in accordance with Section 659.012(a), Government Code.

(b) The associate judge's salary shall be paid from county funds available for payment of officers' salaries or from funds available from the state and federal government as provided by this subchapter.

Added by Acts 1995, 74th Leg., ch. 20, § 1, eff. April 20, 1995. Amended by Acts 2003, 78th Leg., ch. 1258, § 10, eff. Sept. 1, 2003; Acts 2019, 86th Leg., ch. 1121 (H.B. 2384), § 1, eff. Sept. 1, 2019.

Section 37 of Acts 2019, 86th Leg., ch. 1121 (H.B. 2384) provides:

"The comptroller of public accounts is required to implement a provision of this Act only if the legislature appropriates money specifically for that purpose. If the legislature does not appropriate money specifically for that purpose, the comptroller may, but is not required to, implement a provision of this Act using other appropriations available for that purpose."

### § 201.106. Child Support Court Monitor and Other Personnel

(a) The presiding judge of an administrative judicial region or the presiding judges of the administrative judicial regions, by majority vote, may appoint other personnel, including a child support court monitor for each associate judge appointed under this subchapter, as needed to implement and administer the provisions of this subchapter.

(b) The salaries of the personnel and court monitors shall be paid from county funds available for payment of officers' salaries or from funds available from the state and federal government as provided by this subchapter.

Added by Acts 1995, 74th Leg., ch. 20, § 1, eff. April 20, 1995. Amended by Acts 1999, 76th Leg., ch. 1072, § 2, eff. Sept. 1, 1999; Acts 2003, 78th Leg., ch. 1258, § 10, eff. Sept. 1, 2003.

### § 201.1065. Duties of Child Support Court Monitor

(a) A child support court monitor appointed under this subchapter shall monitor child support cases in which the obligor is placed on probation for failure to comply with the requirements of a child support order.

(b) In monitoring a child support case, a court monitor shall:

(1) conduct an intake assessment of the needs of an obligor that, if addressed, would enable the obligor to comply with a child support order;

(2) refer an obligor to employment services offered by the employment assistance program under Section 302.0035, Labor Code, if appropriate;

(3) provide mediation services or referrals to services, if appropriate;

(4) schedule periodic contacts with an obligor to assess compliance with the child support order and whether additional support services are required;

(5) monitor the amount and timeliness of child support payments owed and paid by an obligor; and

(6) if appropriate, recommend that the court:

(A) discharge an obligor from or modify the terms of the obligor's community supervision; or

(B) revoke an obligor's community supervision.

Added by Acts 1999, 76th Leg., ch. 1072, § 3, eff. Sept. 1, 1999. Amended by Acts 2003, 78th Leg., ch. 1258, § 10, eff. Sept. 1, 2003.

### § 201.1066. Supervision of Associate Judges

(a) The office of court administration shall assist the presiding judges in:

(1) monitoring the associate judges' compliance with job performance standards and federal and state laws and policies;

(2) addressing the training needs and resource requirements of the associate judges;

(3) conducting annual performance evaluations for the associate judges and other personnel appointed under this subchapter based on written personnel performance standards adopted by the presiding judges and performance information solicited from the referring courts and other relevant persons; and

(4) receiving, investigating, and resolving complaints about particular associate judges or the associate judge program under this subchapter based on a uniform process adopted by the presiding judges.

(b) The office of court administration shall develop procedures and a written evaluation form to be used by the presiding judges in conducting the annual performance evaluations under Subsection (a)(3).

(c) Each judge of a court that refers cases to an associate judge under this subchapter may submit to the presiding judge or the office of court administration information on the associate judge's performance during the preceding year based on a uniform process adopted by the presiding judges.

Added by Acts 1999, 76th Leg., ch. 556, § 44, eff. Sept. 1, 1999. Redesignated from V.T.C.A., Family Code § 201.1065 by Acts 2001, 77th Leg., ch. 1420, § 21.001(31), eff. Sept. 1, 2001. Amended by Acts 2003, 78th Leg., ch. 1258, § 10, eff. Sept. 1, 2003; Acts 2015, 84th Leg., ch. 1182 (S.B. 1139), § 1.02, eff. Sept. 1, 2015.

### § 201.107. State and Federal Funds

(a) The office of court administration may contract with the Title IV–D agency for available state and federal funds under Title IV–D and may employ personnel needed to implement and administer this subchapter. An associate judge, a court monitor for each associate judge, and other personnel appointed under this subchapter are state employees for all purposes, including accrual of leave time, insurance benefits, retirement benefits, and travel regulations.

(b) The presiding judges of the administrative judicial regions, state agencies, and counties may contract with the Title IV–D agency for available federal funds under Title IV–D to reimburse costs and salaries associated with associate judges, court monitors, and personnel appointed under this subchapter and may also use available state funds and public or private grants.

(c) The presiding judges and the Title IV–D agency shall act and are authorized to take any action necessary to maximize the amount of federal funds available under the Title IV–D program.

Added by Acts 1995, 74th Leg., ch. 20, § 1, eff. April 20, 1995. Amended by Acts 1999, 76th Leg., ch. 556, § 45, eff. Sept. 1, 1999; Acts 1999, 76th Leg., ch. 1072, § 4, eff. Sept. 1, 1999; Acts 2003, 78th Leg., ch. 1258, § 11, eff. Sept. 1, 2003.

### § 201.108. Repealed by Acts 2003, 78th Leg., ch. 1258, § 27, eff. Sept. 1, 2003.

### § 201.1085. Repealed by Acts 1999, 76th Leg., ch. 62, § 6.26, eff. Sept. 1, 1999; Acts 1999, 76th Leg., ch. 1302, § 14, eff. Sept. 1, 1999

### § 201.109. Repealed by Acts 2003, 78th Leg., ch. 1258, § 27, eff. Sept. 1, 2003.

### § 201.110. Time for Disposition of Title IV–D Cases

(a) Title IV–D cases must be completed from the time of successful service to the time of disposition within the following time:

(1) 75 percent within six months; and

(2) 90 percent within one year.

(b) Title IV–D cases shall be given priority over other cases.

(c) A clerk or judge may not restrict the number of Title IV–D cases that are filed or heard in the courts.

Added by Acts 1995, 74th Leg., ch. 20, § 1, eff. April 20, 1995. Amended by Acts 2003, 78th Leg., ch. 1258, § 12, eff. Sept. 1, 2003.

### § 201.111. Time to Act on Associate Judge's Proposed Order or Judgment That Includes Recommended Finding of Contempt

(a) Not later than the 10th day after the date an associate judge's proposed order or judgment recommending a finding of contempt is signed, the referring court shall:

(1) adopt, modify, or reject the proposed order or judgment;

(2) hear further evidence; or

(3) recommit the matter for further proceedings.

(b) The time limit in Subsection (a) does not apply if a party has filed a written request for a de novo hearing before the referring court.

Added by Acts 1995, 74th Leg., ch. 751, § 80, eff. Sept. 1, 1995. Amended by Acts 1999, 76th Leg., ch. 556, § 46, eff. Sept. 1, 1999; Acts 2003, 78th Leg., ch. 1258, §§ 13, 14, eff. Sept. 1, 2003; Acts 2007, 80th Leg., ch. 1235, § 11, eff. Sept. 1, 2007.

### § 201.112. Limitation on Law Practice by Certain Associate Judges

A full-time associate judge appointed under this subchapter may not engage in the private practice of law.

Added by Acts 1999, 76th Leg., ch. 556, § 47, eff. Sept. 1, 1999. Amended by Acts 2003, 78th Leg., ch. 1258, § 15, eff. Sept. 1, 2003.

### § 201.113. Visiting Associate Judge

(a) If an associate judge appointed under this subchapter is temporarily unable to perform the associate judge's official duties because of absence resulting from family circumstances, illness, injury, disability, or military service, or if there is a vacancy in the position of associate judge, the presiding judge of the administrative judicial region in which the associate judge serves or the vacancy occurs may appoint a visiting associate judge for Title IV–D cases to perform the duties of the associate judge during the period the associate judge is unable to perform the associate judge's duties or until another associate judge is appointed to fill the vacancy.

(b) A person is not eligible for appointment under this section unless the person has served as a master or associate judge under this chapter, a district judge, or a statutory county court judge for at least two years before the date of appointment.

(c) A visiting associate judge appointed under this section is subject to each provision of this chapter that applies to an associate judge serving under a regular appointment under this subchapter. A visiting associate judge appointed under this section is entitled to compensation to be determined by a majority vote of the presiding judges of the administrative judicial regions through use of funds under this subchapter. A visiting associate judge is not considered to be a state employee for any purpose.

(d) Section 2252.901, Government Code, does not apply to the appointment of a visiting associate judge under this section.

Added by Acts 2001, 77th Leg., ch. 1023, § 49, eff. Sept. 1, 2001. Amended by Acts 2003, 78th Leg., ch. 1258, § 15, eff. Sept. 1, 2003; Acts 2005, 79th Leg., ch. 343, § 1, eff. June 17, 2005; Acts 2009, 81st Leg., ch. 760, § 2, eff. June 19, 2009.

## SUBCHAPTER C. ASSOCIATE JUDGE FOR CHILD PROTECTION CASES

### § 201.201. Authority of Presiding Judge

(a) The presiding judge of each administrative judicial region, after conferring with the judges of courts in the region having family law jurisdiction and a child protection caseload, shall determine which courts require the appointment of a full-time or part-time associate judge to complete cases under Subtitle E within the times specified under that subtitle.

(b) If the presiding judge of an administrative judicial region determines under Subsection (a) that the courts in the region require the appointment of an associate judge, the presiding judge shall appoint an associate judge from a list of the qualified applicants who have submitted an application to the office of court administration. Before making the appointment, the presiding judge must provide the list to the judges of the courts from which cases will be referred to the associate judge. Each judge may recommend to the presiding judge the names of one or more applicants for appointment. An associate judge appointed under this subsection serves for a term of four years from the date the associate judge is appointed and qualifies for office. The appointment of an associate judge for a term does not affect the at-will employment status of the associate judge. The presiding judge may terminate an appointment at any time.

(b–1) Before reappointing an associate judge appointed under Subsection (b), the presiding judge must notify each judge of the courts from which cases will be referred to the associate judge of the presiding judge's intent to reappoint the associate judge to another term. Each judge may submit to the presiding judge a recommendation on whether the associate judge should be reappointed.

(c) An associate judge appointed under this subchapter may be appointed to serve more than one court. Two or more judges of administrative judicial regions may jointly appoint one or more associate judges to serve the regions.

(d) If an associate judge is appointed for a court, all child protection cases shall be referred to the associate judge by a general order for each county issued by the judge of the court for which the associate judge is appointed or, in the absence of that order, by a general order issued by the presiding judge who appointed the associate judge.

(e) This section does not limit the jurisdiction of a court to issue orders under Subtitle E.

Added by Acts 1999, 76th Leg., ch. 1302, § 12, eff. Sept. 1, 1999. Amended by Acts 2003, 78th Leg., ch. 1258, § 17, eff. Sept. 1, 2003; Acts 2011, 82nd Leg., ch. 377 (S.B. 283), § 1, eff. June 17, 2011; Acts 2015, 84th Leg., ch. 1182 (S.B. 1139), § 1.03, eff. Sept. 1, 2015.

### § 201.202. Application of Law Governing Associate Judges

Except as provided by this subchapter, Subchapter A applies to an associate judge appointed under this subchapter.

Added by Acts 1999, 76th Leg., ch. 1302, § 12, eff. Sept. 1, 1999. Amended by Acts 2007, 80th Leg., ch. 44, § 4, eff. Sept. 1, 2007.

### § 201.2021. Qualifications

(a) To be eligible for appointment under this subchapter, a person must be a citizen of the United States, have resided in this state for the two years preceding the date of appointment, and be:

(1) eligible for assignment under Section 74.054, Government Code, because the person is named on the list of retired and former judges maintained by the presiding judge of the administrative region under Section 74.055, Government Code; or

(2) licensed to practice law in this state and have been a practicing lawyer in this state, or a judge of a court in this state who is not otherwise eligible under Subdivision (1), for the four years preceding the date of appointment.

(b) An associate judge appointed under this subchapter shall during the term of appointment reside in the administrative judicial region, or a county adjacent to the region, in which the court to which the associate judge is appointed is located. An associate judge appointed to serve in two or more administrative judicial regions may reside anywhere in the regions.

Added by Acts 2007, 80th Leg., ch. 44, § 5, eff. Sept. 1, 2007. Amended by Acts 2009, 81st Leg., ch. 760, § 3, eff. June 19, 2009.

### § 201.203. Designation of Host County

(a) Subject to the approval of the commissioners court of the proposed host county, the presiding judges of the administrative judicial regions by majority vote shall determine the host county of an associate judge appointed under this subchapter.

(b) The host county shall provide an adequate courtroom and quarters, including furniture, necessary utilities, and telephone equipment and service, for the associate judge and other personnel assisting the associate judge.

(c) An associate judge is not required to reside in the host county.

Added by Acts 1999, 76th Leg., ch. 1302, § 12, eff. Sept. 1, 1999.

### § 201.204. General Powers of Associate Judge

(a) On the motion of a party or the associate judge, an associate judge may refer a complex case back to the referring court for final disposition after recommending temporary orders for the protection of a child.

(b) An associate judge may render and sign any pretrial order.

(c) An associate judge may recommend to the referring court any order after a trial on the merits.

(d) An associate judge may hear and render an order in a suit for the adoption of a child for whom the Texas Department of Family and Protective Services has been named managing conservator.

(e) An associate judge may hear and render an order in a suit referred to the associate judge by a juvenile court under Section 51.04, subject to the limitations placed on the associate judge's authority in the order of referral.

Added by Acts 1999, 76th Leg., ch. 1302, § 12, eff. Sept. 1, 1999. Amended by Acts 2003, 78th Leg., ch. 1258, § 18, eff. Sept. 1, 2003; Acts 2017, 85th Leg., ch. 912 (S.B. 1329), § 1.04, eff. Sept. 1, 2017; Acts 2019, 86th Leg., ch. 660 (S.B. 1887), § 3, eff. Sept. 1, 2019.

### § 201.2041. Judicial Action on Associate Judge's Proposed Order or Judgment

(a) If a request for a de novo hearing before the referring court is not timely filed or the right to a de novo hearing before the referring court is waived, the proposed order or judgment of the associate judge becomes the order or judgment of the referring court by operation of law without ratification by the referring court.

(b) Regardless of whether a de novo hearing is requested before the referring court, a proposed order or judgment rendered by an associate judge that meets the requirements of Section 263.401(d) is considered a final order for purposes of Section 263.401.

Added by Acts 2003, 78th Leg., ch. 1258, § 19, eff. Sept. 1, 2003. Amended by Acts 2007, 80th Leg., ch. 1235, § 12, eff. Sept. 1, 2007.

### § 201.2042. De Novo Hearing Before Referring Court

(a) Except as provided by this section, Section 201.015 applies to a request for a de novo hearing before the referring court.

(b) The party requesting a de novo hearing before the referring court shall file notice with the referring court and the clerk of the referring court.

Added by Acts 2003, 78th Leg., ch. 1258, § 19, eff. Sept. 1, 2003. Amended by Acts 2007, 80th Leg., ch. 1235, § 13, eff. Sept. 1, 2007.

### § 201.205. Compensation of Associate Judge

(a) An associate judge appointed under this subchapter is entitled to a salary in the amount equal to 90 percent of the state base salary paid to a district judge as set by the General Appropriations Act in accordance with Section 659.012(a), Government Code.

(b) The associate judge's salary shall be paid from county funds available for payment of officers' salaries subject to the approval of the commissioners court or from funds available from the state and federal governments as provided by this subchapter.

Added by Acts 1999, 76th Leg., ch. 1302, § 12, eff. Sept. 1, 1999. Amended by Acts 2003, 78th Leg., ch. 1258, § 20, eff. Sept. 1, 2003; Acts 2019, 86th Leg., ch. 1121 (H.B. 2384), § 2, eff. Sept. 1, 2019.

Section 37 of Acts 2019, 86th Leg., ch. 1121 (H.B. 2384) provides:

"The comptroller of public accounts is required to implement a provision of this Act only if the legislature appropriates money specifically for that purpose. If the legislature does not appropriate money specifically for that purpose, the comptroller may, but is not required to, implement a provision of this Act using other appropriations available for that purpose."

### § 201.206. Personnel

(a) The presiding judge of an administrative judicial region or the presiding judges of the administrative judicial regions, by majority vote, may appoint personnel as needed to implement and administer the provisions of this subchapter.

(b) The salaries of the personnel shall be paid from county funds available for payment of officers' salaries subject to the approval of the commissioners court or from funds available from the state and federal governments as provided by this subchapter.

Added by Acts 1999, 76th Leg., ch. 1302, § 12, eff. Sept. 1, 1999. Amended by Acts 2003, 78th Leg., ch. 1258, § 21, eff. Sept. 1, 2003.

### § 201.2061. Supervision of Associate Judges

(a) The office of court administration shall assist the presiding judges in:

(1) monitoring the associate judges' compliance with any applicable job performance standards, uniform practices adopted by the presiding judges, and federal and state laws and policies;

(2) addressing the training needs and resource requirements of the associate judges;

(3) conducting annual performance evaluations for the associate judges and other personnel appointed under this subchapter based on written personnel performance standards adopted by the presiding judges and performance information solicited from the referring courts and other relevant persons; and

(4) receiving, investigating, and resolving complaints about particular associate judges or the associate judge program under this subchapter based on a uniform process adopted by the presiding judges.

(b) The office of court administration shall develop procedures and a written evaluation form to be used by the presiding judges in conducting the annual performance evaluations under Subsection (a)(3).

(c) Each judge of a court that refers cases to an associate judge under this subchapter may submit to the presiding judge or the office of court administration information on the associate judge's performance during the preceding year based on a uniform process adopted by the presiding judges.

Added by Acts 2003, 78th Leg., ch. 1258, § 22, eff. Sept. 1, 2003. Amended by Acts 2015, 84th Leg., ch. 1182 (S.B. 1139), § 1.04, eff. Sept. 1, 2015.

### § 201.207. State and Federal Funds; Personnel

(a) The office of court administration may contract for available state and federal funds from any source and may employ personnel needed to implement and administer this subchapter. An associate judge and other personnel appointed under this subsection are state employees for all purposes, including accrual of leave time, insurance benefits, retirement benefits, and travel regulations.

(b) The presiding judges of the administrative judicial regions, state agencies, and counties may contract for available federal funds from any source to reimburse costs and salaries associated with associate judges and personnel appointed under this section and may also use available state funds and public or private grants.

(c) The presiding judges and the office of court administration in cooperation with other agencies shall take action necessary to maximize the amount of federal money available to fund the use of associate judges under this subchapter.

Added by Acts 1999, 76th Leg., ch. 1302, § 12, eff. Sept. 1, 1999.

### § 201.208. Assignment of Judges and Appointment of Visiting Associate Judges

(a) This chapter does not limit the authority of a presiding judge to assign a judge eligible for assignment under Chapter 74, Government Code, to assist in processing cases in a reasonable time.

(b) If an associate judge appointed under this subchapter is temporarily unable to perform the associate judge's official duties because of absence resulting from family circumstances, illness, injury, disability, or military service, or if there is a vacancy in the position of associate judge, the presiding judge of the administrative judicial region in which the associate judge serves or the vacancy occurs may appoint a visiting associate judge to perform the duties of the associate judge during the period the associate judge is unable to perform the associate judge's duties or until another associate judge is appointed to fill the vacancy.

(c) A person is not eligible for appointment under this section unless the person has served as a master or associate judge under this chapter, a district judge, or a statutory county court judge for at least two years before the date of appointment.

(d) A visiting associate judge appointed under this section is subject to each provision of this chapter that applies to an associate judge serving under a regular appointment under this subchapter. A visiting associate judge appointed under this section is entitled to compensation, to be determined by a majority vote of the presiding judges of the administrative judicial regions, through use of funds under this subchapter. A visiting associate judge is not considered to be a state employee for any purpose.

(e) Section 2252.901, Government Code, does not apply to the appointment of a visiting associate judge under this section.

Added by Acts 1999, 76th Leg., ch. 1302, § 12, eff. Sept. 1, 1999. Amended by Acts 2003, 78th Leg., ch. 1258, § 23, eff. Sept. 1, 2003; Acts 2005, 79th Leg., ch. 343, § 2, eff. June 17, 2005; Acts 2009, 81st Leg., ch. 760, § 4, eff. June 19, 2009.

### § 201.209. Limitation on Law Practice by Associate Judge

An associate judge appointed under this subchapter may not engage in the private practice of law.

Added by Acts 2003, 78th Leg., ch. 1258, § 24, eff. Sept. 1, 2003.

## SUBCHAPTER D. ASSOCIATE JUDGE FOR JUVENILE MATTERS

### § 201.301. Applicability

This subchapter applies only to an associate judge appointed under this subchapter and does not apply to a juvenile court master appointed under Subchapter K, Chapter 54, Government Code.

Added by Acts 2011, 82nd Leg., 1st C.S., ch. 3 (H.B. 79), § 6.03, eff. Jan. 1, 2012.

### § 201.302. Appointment

(a) A judge of a court that is designated as a juvenile court may appoint a full-time or part-time associate judge to perform the duties authorized by this chapter if the commissioners court of a county in which the court has jurisdiction has authorized creation of an associate judge position.

(b) If a court has jurisdiction in more than one county, an associate judge appointed by that court may serve only in a county in which the commissioners court has authorized the appointment.

(c) If more than one court in a county has been designated as a juvenile court, the commissioners court may authorize the appointment of an associate judge for each court or may authorize one or more associate judges to share service with two or more courts.

(d) If an associate judge serves more than one court, the associate judge's appointment must be made as established by local rule, but in no event by less than a vote of two-thirds of the judges under whom the associate judge serves.

Added by Acts 2011, 82nd Leg., 1st C.S., ch. 3 (H.B. 79), § 6.03, eff. Jan. 1, 2012.

### § 201.303. Qualifications

To qualify for appointment as an associate judge under this subchapter, a person must:

(1) be a resident of this state and one of the counties the person will serve;

(2) have been licensed to practice law in this state for at least four years;

(3) not have been removed from office by impeachment, by the supreme court, by the governor on address to the legislature, by a tribunal reviewing a recommendation of the State Commission on Judicial Conduct, or by the legislature's abolition of the judge's court; and

(4) not have resigned from office after having received notice that formal proceedings by the State Commission on Judicial Conduct had been instituted as provided in Section 33.022, Government Code, and before final disposition of the proceedings.

Added by Acts 2011, 82nd Leg., 1st C.S., ch. 3 (H.B. 79), § 6.03, eff. Jan. 1, 2012.

### § 201.304. Compensation

(a) An associate judge shall be paid a salary determined by the commissioners court of the county in which the associate judge serves.

(b) If an associate judge serves in more than one county, the associate judge shall be paid a salary as determined by agreement of the commissioners courts of the counties in which the associate judge serves.

(c) The associate judge's salary is paid from the county fund available for payment of officers' salaries.

Added by Acts 2011, 82nd Leg., 1st C.S., ch. 3 (H.B. 79), § 6.03, eff. Jan. 1, 2012.

### § 201.305. Termination

(a) An associate judge who serves a single court serves at the will of the judge of that court.

(b) The employment of an associate judge who serves more than two courts may only be terminated by a majority vote of all the judges of the courts which the associate judge serves.

(c) The employment of an associate judge who serves two courts may be terminated by either of the judges of the courts which the associate judge serves.

(d) To terminate an associate judge's employment, the appropriate judges must sign a written order of termination. The order must state:

(1) the associate judge's name and state bar identification number;

(2) each court ordering termination; and

(3) the date the associate judge's employment ends.

Added by Acts 2011, 82nd Leg., 1st C.S., ch. 3 (H.B. 79), § 6.03, eff. Jan. 1, 2012.

### § 201.306. Cases That May Be Referred

(a) Except as provided by this section, a judge of a juvenile court may refer to an associate judge any aspect of a juvenile matter brought:

(1) under this title or Title 3; or

(2) in connection with Rule 308a, Texas Rules of Civil Procedure.

(b) Unless a party files a written objection to the associate judge hearing a trial on the merits, the judge may refer the trial to the associate judge. A trial on the merits is any final adjudication from which an appeal may be taken to a court of appeals.

(c) A party must file an objection to an associate judge hearing a trial on the merits or presiding at a jury trial not later than the 10th day after the date the party receives notice that the associate judge will hear the trial. If an objection is filed, the referring court shall hear the trial on the merits or preside at a jury trial.

(d) The requirements of Subsections (b) and (c) apply when a judge has authority to refer the trial of a suit under this title, Title 1, or Title 4 to an associate judge, master, or other assistant judge regardless of whether the assistant judge is appointed under this subchapter.

Added by Acts 2011, 82nd Leg., 1st C.S., ch. 3 (H.B. 79), § 6.03, eff. Jan. 1, 2012.

### § 201.307. Methods of Referral

(a) A case may be referred to an associate judge by an order of referral in a specific case or by an omnibus order.

(b) The order of referral may limit the power or duties of an associate judge.

Added by Acts 2011, 82nd Leg., 1st C.S., ch. 3 (H.B. 79), § 6.03, eff. Jan. 1, 2012.

### § 201.308. Powers of Associate Judge

(a) Except as limited by an order of referral, an associate judge may:

(1) conduct a hearing;

(2) hear evidence;

(3) compel production of relevant evidence;

(4) rule on the admissibility of evidence;

(5) issue a summons for:

(A) the appearance of witnesses; and

(B) the appearance of a parent who has failed to appear before an agency authorized to conduct an investigation of an allegation of abuse or neglect of a child after receiving proper notice;

(6) examine a witness;

(7) swear a witness for a hearing;

(8) make findings of fact on evidence;

(9) formulate conclusions of law;

(10) recommend an order to be rendered in a case;

(11) regulate proceedings in a hearing;

(12) order the attachment of a witness or party who fails to obey a subpoena;

(13) order the detention of a witness or party found guilty of contempt, pending approval by the referring court; and

(14) take action as necessary and proper for the efficient performance of the associate judge's duties.

(b) An associate judge may, in the interest of justice, refer a case back to the referring court regardless of whether a timely objection to the associate judge hearing the trial on the merits or presiding at a jury trial has been made by any party.

Added by Acts 2011, 82nd Leg., 1st C.S., ch. 3 (H.B. 79), § 6.03, eff. Jan. 1, 2012.

### § 201.309. Referees

(a) An associate judge appointed under this subchapter may serve as a referee as provided by Sections 51.04(g) and 54.10.

(b) A referee appointed under Section 51.04(g) may be appointed to serve as an associate judge under this subchapter.

Added by Acts 2011, 82nd Leg., 1st C.S., ch. 3 (H.B. 79), § 6.03, eff. Jan. 1, 2012.

### § 201.310. Attendance of Bailiff

A bailiff may attend a hearing by an associate judge if directed by the referring court.

Added by Acts 2011, 82nd Leg., 1st C.S., ch. 3 (H.B. 79), § 6.03, eff. Jan. 1, 2012.

### § 201.311. Witness

(a) A witness appearing before an associate judge is subject to the penalties for perjury provided by law.

(b) A referring court may fine or imprison a witness who:

(1) failed to appear before an associate judge after being summoned; or

(2) improperly refused to answer questions if the refusal has been certified to the court by the associate judge.

Added by Acts 2011, 82nd Leg., 1st C.S., ch. 3 (H.B. 79), § 6.03, eff. Jan. 1, 2012.

### § 201.312. Court Reporter; Record

(a) A court reporter may be provided during a hearing held by an associate judge appointed under this subchapter. A court reporter is required to be provided when the associate judge presides over a jury trial or a contested final termination hearing.

(b) A party, the associate judge, or the referring court may provide for a reporter during the hearing if one is not otherwise provided.

(c) Except as provided by Subsection (a), in the absence of a court reporter or on agreement of the parties, the record may be preserved by any means approved by the associate judge.

(d) The referring court or associate judge may assess the expense of preserving the record as costs.

(e) On a request for a de novo hearing, the referring court may consider testimony or other evidence in the record, if the record is taken by a court reporter, in addition to witnesses or other matters presented under Section 201.317.

Added by Acts 2011, 82nd Leg., 1st C.S., ch. 3 (H.B. 79), § 6.03, eff. Jan. 1, 2012.

### § 201.313. Report

(a) The associate judge's report may contain the associate judge's findings, conclusions, or recommendations and may be in the form of a proposed order. The associate judge's report must be in writing and in the form directed by the referring court.

(b) After a hearing, the associate judge shall provide the parties participating in the hearing notice of the substance of the associate judge's report, including any proposed order.

(c) Notice may be given to the parties:

(1) in open court, by an oral statement or by providing a copy of the associate judge's written report, including any proposed order;

(2) by certified mail, return receipt requested; or

(3) by facsimile.

(d) A rebuttable presumption exists that notice is received on the date stated on:

(1) the signed return receipt, if notice was provided by certified mail; or

(2) the confirmation page produced by the facsimile machine, if notice was provided by facsimile.

(e) After a hearing conducted by an associate judge, the associate judge shall send the associate judge's signed and dated report, including any proposed order, and all other papers relating to the case to the referring court.

Added by Acts 2011, 82nd Leg., 1st C.S., ch. 3 (H.B. 79), § 6.03, eff. Jan. 1, 2012.

### § 201.314. Notice of Right to De Novo Hearing; Waiver

(a) An associate judge shall give all parties notice of the right to a de novo hearing to the judge of the referring court.

(b) The notice may be given:

(1) by oral statement in open court;

(2) by posting inside or outside the courtroom of the referring court; or

(3) as otherwise directed by the referring court.

(c) Before the start of a hearing by an associate judge, a party may waive the right of a de novo hearing before the referring court in writing or on the record.

Added by Acts 2011, 82nd Leg., 1st C.S., ch. 3 (H.B. 79), § 6.03, eff. Jan. 1, 2012.

### § 201.315. Order of Court

(a) Pending a de novo hearing before the referring court, a proposed order or judgment of the associate judge is in full force and effect and is enforceable as an order or judgment of the referring court, except for an order providing for the appointment of a receiver.

(b) If a request for a de novo hearing before the referring court is not timely filed or the right to a de novo hearing before the referring court is waived, the proposed order or judgment of the associate judge becomes the order or judgment of the referring court only on the referring court's signing the proposed order or judgment.

(c) An order by an associate judge for the temporary detention or incarceration of a witness or party shall be presented to the referring court on the day the witness or party is detained or incarcerated. The referring court, without prejudice to the right to a de novo hearing provided by Section 201.317, may approve the temporary detention or incarceration or may order the release of the party or witness, with or without bond, pending a de novo hearing. If the referring court is not immediately available, the associate judge may order the release of the party or witness, with or without bond, pending a de novo hearing or may continue the person's detention or incarceration for not more than 72 hours.

Added by Acts 2011, 82nd Leg., 1st C.S., ch. 3 (H.B. 79), § 6.03, eff. Jan. 1, 2012.

### § 201.316. Judicial Action on Associate Judge's Proposed Order or Judgment

Unless a party files a written request for a de novo hearing before the referring court, the referring court may:

(1) adopt, modify, or reject the associate judge's proposed order or judgment;

(2) hear additional evidence; or

(3) recommit the matter to the associate judge for further proceedings.

Added by Acts 2011, 82nd Leg., 1st C.S., ch. 3 (H.B. 79), § 6.03, eff. Jan. 1, 2012.

### § 201.317. De Novo Hearing

(a) A party may request a de novo hearing before the referring court by filing with the clerk of the referring court a written request not later than the third working day after the date the party receives notice of the substance of the associate judge's report as provided by Section 201.313.

(b) A request for a de novo hearing under this section must specify the issues that will be presented to the referring court. The de novo hearing is limited to the specified issues.

(c) Notice of a request for a de novo hearing before the referring court shall be given to the opposing attorney in the manner provided by Rule 21a, Texas Rules of Civil Procedure.

(d) If a request for a de novo hearing before the referring court is filed by a party, any other party may file a request for a de novo hearing before the referring court not later than the third working day after the date the initial request was filed.

(e) The referring court, after notice to the parties, shall hold a de novo hearing not later than the 30th day after the date the initial request for a de novo hearing was filed with the clerk of the referring court.

(f) In the de novo hearing before the referring court, the parties may present witnesses on the issues specified in the request for hearing. The referring court may also consider the record from the hearing before the associate judge, including the charge to and verdict returned by a jury, if the record was taken by a court reporter.

(g) The denial of relief to a party after a de novo hearing under this section or a party's waiver of the right to a de novo hearing before the referring court does not affect the right of a party to file a motion for new trial, a motion for judgment notwithstanding the verdict, or other posttrial motions.

(h) A party may not demand a second jury in a de novo hearing before the referring court if the associate judge's proposed order or judgment resulted from a jury trial.

Added by Acts 2011, 82nd Leg., 1st C.S., ch. 3 (H.B. 79), § 6.03, eff. Jan. 1, 2012. Amended by Acts 2013, 83rd Leg., ch. 916 (H.B. 1366), § 7, eff. Sept. 1, 2013.

### § 201.318. Appellate Review

(a) A party's failure to request a de novo hearing before the referring court or a party's waiver of the right to request a de novo hearing before the referring court does not deprive the party of the right to appeal to or request other relief from a court of appeals or the supreme court.

(b) Except as provided by Subsection (c), the date an order or judgment by the referring court is signed is the controlling date for the purposes of appeal to or request for other relief from a court of appeals or the supreme court.

(c) The date an agreed order or a default order is signed by an associate judge is the controlling date for the purpose of an appeal to, or a request for other relief relating to the order from, a court of appeals or the supreme court.

Added by Acts 2011, 82nd Leg., 1st C.S., ch. 3 (H.B. 79), § 6.03, eff. Jan. 1, 2012.

### § 201.319. Judicial Immunity

An associate judge appointed under this subchapter has the judicial immunity of a district judge.

Added by Acts 2011, 82nd Leg., 1st C.S., ch. 3 (H.B. 79), § 6.03, eff. Jan. 1, 2012.

### § 201.320. Visiting Associate Judge

(a) If an associate judge appointed under this subchapter is temporarily unable to perform the judge's official duties because of absence or illness, injury, or other disability, a judge of a court having jurisdiction of a suit under this title or Title 1 or 4 may appoint a visiting associate judge to perform the duties of the associate judge during the period of the associate judge's absence or disability if the commissioners court of a county in which the court has jurisdiction authorizes the employment of a visiting associate judge.

(b) To be eligible for appointment under this section, a person must have served as an associate judge for at least two years.

(c) Sections 201.001 through 201.017 apply to a visiting associate judge appointed under this section.

Added by Acts 2011, 82nd Leg., 1st C.S., ch. 3 (H.B. 79), § 6.03, eff. Jan. 1, 2012.

## CHAPTER 202. FRIEND OF THE COURT

**Section**



### § 202.001. Appointment

(a) After an order for child support or possession of or access to a child has been rendered, a court may appoint a friend of the court on:

(1) the request of a person alleging that the order has been violated; or

(2) its own motion.

(b) A court may appoint a friend of the court in a proceeding under Part D of Title IV of the federal Social Security Act (42 U.S.C. Section 651 et seq.) only if the Title IV–D agency agrees in writing to the appointment.

(c) The duration of the appointment of a friend of the court is as determined by the court.

(d) In the appointment of a friend of the court, the court shall give preference to:

(1) a local domestic relations office;

(2) a local child support collection office;

(3) the local court official designated to enforce actions as provided in Chapter 159; or

(4) an attorney in good standing with the State Bar of Texas.

(e) In the execution of a friend of the court's duties under this subchapter, a friend of the court shall represent the court to ensure compliance with the court's order.

Added by Acts 1995, 74th Leg., ch. 20, § 1, eff. April 20, 1995.

### § 202.002. Authority and Duties

(a) A friend of the court may coordinate nonjudicial efforts to improve compliance with a court order relating to child support or possession of or access to a child by use of:

(1) telephone communication;

(2) written communication;

(3) one or more volunteer advocates under Chapter 107;

(4) informal pretrial consultation;

(5) one or more of the alternate dispute resolution methods under Chapter 154, Civil Practice and Remedies Code;

(6) a licensed social worker;

(7) a family mediator; and

(8) employment agencies, retraining programs, and any similar resources to ensure that both parents can meet their financial obligations to the child.

(b) A friend of the court, not later than the 15th day of the month following the reporting month:

(1) shall report to the court or monitor reports made to the court on:

(A) the amount of child support collected as a percentage of the amount ordered; and

(B) efforts to ensure compliance with orders relating to possession of or access to a child; and

(2) may file an action to enforce, clarify, or modify a court order relating to child support or possession of or access to a child.

(c) A friend of the court may file a notice of delinquency and a request for a writ of income withholding under Chapter 158 in order to enforce a child support order.

Added by Acts 1995, 74th Leg., ch. 20, § 1, eff. April 20, 1995. Amended by Acts 1995, 74th Leg., ch. 751, § 81, eff. Sept. 1, 1995; Acts 1997, 75th Leg., ch. 702, § 9, eff. Sept. 1, 1997; Acts 2003, 78th Leg., ch. 892, § 21, eff. Sept. 1, 2003.

### § 202.003. Duty of Local Offices and Officials to Report

A local domestic relations office, a local registry, or a court official designated to receive child support under a court order shall, if ordered by the court, report to the court or a friend of the court on a monthly basis:

(1) any delinquency and arrearage in child support payments; and

(2) any violation of an order relating to possession of or access to a child.

Added by Acts 1995, 74th Leg., ch. 20, § 1, eff. April 20, 1995.

### § 202.004. Access to Information

A friend of the court may arrange access to child support payment records by electronic means if the records are computerized.

Added by Acts 1995, 74th Leg., ch. 20, § 1, eff. April 20, 1995.

### § 202.005. Compensation

(a) A friend of the court is entitled to compensation for services rendered and for expenses incurred in rendering the services.

(b) The court may assess the amount that the friend of the court receives in compensation against a party to the suit in the same manner as the court awards costs under Chapter 106.

(c) Repealed by Acts 2019, 86th Leg., ch. 1352 (S.B. 346), § 4.40(4).

(d) Repealed by Acts 2019, 86th Leg., ch. 1352 (S.B. 346), § 4.40(4).

Added by Acts 1995, 74th Leg., ch. 20, § 1, eff. April 20, 1995. Amended by Acts 2019, 86th Leg., ch. 1352 (S.B. 346), § 4.40(4), eff. Jan. 1, 2020.

Section 5.01 of Acts 2019, 86th Leg., ch. 1352 (S.B. 346) provides:

"Except as otherwise provided by this Act, the changes in law made by this Act apply only to a cost, fee, or fine on conviction for an offense committed on or after the effective date [Jan. 1, 2020] of this Act. An offense committed before the effective date of this Act is governed by the law in effect on the date the offense was committed, and the former law is continued in effect for that purpose. For purposes of this section, an offense was committed before the effective date of this Act if any element of the offense occurred before that date."

## CHAPTER 203. DOMESTIC RELATIONS OFFICES

**Section**



### § 203.001. Definitions

In this chapter:

(1) "Administering entity" means a commissioners court, juvenile board, or other entity responsible for administering a domestic relations office under this chapter.

(2) "Domestic relations office" means a county office that serves families, county departments, and courts to ensure effective implementation of this title.

Added by Acts 1995, 74th Leg., ch. 20, § 1, eff. April 20, 1995. Amended by Acts 1995, 74th Leg., ch. 475, § 1, eff. Sept. 1, 1995.

### § 203.002. Establishment of Domestic Relations Office

A commissioners court may establish a domestic relations office.

Added by Acts 1995, 74th Leg., ch. 20, § 1, eff. April 20, 1995. Redesignated from V.T.C.A., Family Code § 203.003 and amended by Acts 1995, 74th Leg., ch. 475, § 1, eff. Sept. 1, 1995.

### § 203.003. Administration

(a) A domestic relations office shall be administered:

(1) as provided by the commissioners court; or

(2) if the commissioners court does not otherwise provide for the administration of the office, by the juvenile board that serves the county in which the domestic relations office is located.

(b) The administering entity shall appoint and assign the duties of a director who shall be responsible for the day-to-day administration of the office. A director serves at the pleasure of the administering entity.

(c) The administering entity shall determine the amount of money needed to operate the office.

(d) A commissioners court that establishes a domestic relations office under this chapter may execute a bond for the office. A bond under this subsection must be:

(1) executed with a solvent surety company authorized to do business in the state; and

(2) conditioned on the faithful performance of the duties of the office.

(e) The administering entity shall establish procedures for the acceptance and use of a grant or donation to the office.

Added by Acts 1995, 74th Leg., ch. 20, § 1, eff. April 20, 1995. Redesignated from V.T.C.A., Family Code § 203.004 and amended by Acts 1995, 74th Leg., ch. 475, § 1, eff. Sept. 1, 1995.

### § 203.004. Powers and Duties

(a) A domestic relations office may:

(1) collect and disburse child support payments that are ordered by a court to be paid through a domestic relations registry;

(2) maintain records of payments and disbursements made under Subdivision (1);

(3) file a suit under this title, including a suit to:

(A) establish paternity; and

(B) enforce, clarify or modify a court order for child support or for possession of and access to a child;

(4) provide an informal forum in which alternative dispute resolution is used to resolve disputes under this code;

(5) prepare a court-ordered child custody evaluation or adoption evaluation under Chapter 107;

(6) represent a child as an amicus attorney, an attorney ad litem, or a guardian ad litem in a suit in which:

(A) termination of the parent-child relationship is sought; or

(B) conservatorship of or access to a child is contested;

(7) serve as a friend of the court;

(8) provide predivorce counseling ordered by a court;

(9) provide community supervision services under Chapter 157;

(10) provide information to assist a party in understanding, complying with, or enforcing the party's duties and obligations under this code;

(11) provide, directly or through a contract, visitation services, including supervision of court-ordered visitation, visitation exchange, or other similar services;

(12) issue an administrative writ of withholding under Subchapter F, Chapter 158; and

(13) provide parenting coordinator services under Chapter 153.

(b) A court having jurisdiction in a proceeding under this title, Title 3, or Section 25.05, Penal Code, may order that child support payments be made through a domestic relations office.

(c) A domestic relations office may:

(1) hire or contract for the services of attorneys to assist the office in providing services under this chapter; and

(2) employ community supervision officers or court monitors.

Added by Acts 1995, 74th Leg., ch. 20, § 1, eff. April 20, 1995. Redesignated from V.T.C.A., Family Code § 203.005 and amended by Acts 1995, 74th Leg., ch. 475, § 1, eff. Sept. 1, 1995. Amended by Acts 1997, 75th Leg., ch. 702, § 10, eff. Sept. 1, 1997; Acts 1999, 76th Leg., ch. 859, § 3, eff. Sept. 1, 1999; Acts 1999, 76th Leg., ch. 1191, § 1, eff. June 18, 1999; Acts 2001, 77th Leg., ch. 1023, § 50, eff. Sept. 1, 2001; Acts 2005, 79th Leg., ch. 172, § 20, eff. Sept. 1, 2005; Acts 2005, 79th Leg., ch. 199, § 5, eff. Sept. 1, 2005; Acts 2007, 80th Leg., ch. 832, § 7, eff. Sept. 1, 2007; Acts 2015, 84th Leg., ch. 1252 (H.B. 1449), § 3.05, eff. Sept. 1, 2015; Acts 2021, 87th Leg., ch. 53 (S.B. 567), § 1, eff. Sept. 1, 2021.

### § 203.005. Fees and Charges

(a) The administering entity may authorize a domestic relations office to assess and collect:

(1) an initial operations fee not to exceed $15 to be paid to the domestic relations office on each filing of an original suit, motion for modification, or motion for enforcement;

(2) in a county that has a child support enforcement cooperative agreement with the Title IV–D agency, an initial child support service fee not to exceed $36 to be paid to the domestic relations office on the filing of an original suit;

(3) a reasonable application fee to be paid by an applicant requesting services from the office;

(4) a reasonable attorney's fee and court costs incurred or ordered by the court;

(5) a monthly service fee not to exceed $3 to be paid annually in advance by a managing conservator and possessory conservator for whom the domestic relations office provides child support services;

(6) community supervision fees as provided by Chapter 157 if community supervision officers are employed by the domestic relations office;

(7) a reasonable fee for preparation of a court-ordered child custody evaluation or adoption evaluation;

(8) in a county that provides visitation services under Sections 153.014 and 203.004 a reasonable fee to be paid to the domestic relations office at the time the visitation services are provided;

(9) a fee to reimburse the domestic relations office for a fee required to be paid under Section 158.503(d) for filing an administrative writ of withholding;

(10) a reasonable fee for parenting coordinator services; and

(11) a reasonable fee for alternative dispute resolution services.

(b) The first payment of a fee under Subsection (a)(5) is due on the date that the person required to pay support is ordered to begin child support, alimony, or separate maintenance payments. Subsequent payments of the fee are due annually and in advance.

(c) The director of a domestic relations office shall attempt to collect all fees in an efficient manner.

(d) The administering entity may provide for an exemption from the payment of a fee authorized under this section if payment of the fee is not practical or in the interest of justice. Fees that may be exempted under this subsection include fees related to:

(1) spousal and child support payments made under an interstate pact;

(2) a suit brought by the Texas Department of Human Services;

(3) activities performed by the Department of Protective and Regulatory Services or another governmental agency, a private adoption agency, or a charitable organization; and

(4) services for a person who has applied for or who receives public assistance under the laws of this state.

(e) A fee authorized by this section for providing child support services is part of the child support obligation and may be enforced against both an obligor and obligee by any method available for the enforcement of child support, including contempt.

Added by Acts 1995, 74th Leg., ch. 20, § 1, eff. April 20, 1995. Redesignated from V.T.C.A., Family Code § 203.009 and amended by Acts 1995, 74th Leg., ch. 475, § 1, eff. Sept. 1, 1995. Amended by Acts 1999, 76th Leg., ch. 556, § 48, eff. Sept. 1, 1999; Acts 2001, 77th Leg., ch. 1023, § 51, eff. Sept. 1, 2001; Acts 2003, 78th Leg., ch. 707, § 1, eff. Sept. 1, 2003; Acts 2003, 78th Leg., ch. 1076, § 1, eff. Sept. 1, 2003; Acts 2005, 79th Leg., ch. 199, § 6, eff. Sept. 1, 2005; Acts 2007, 80th Leg., ch. 832, § 8, eff. Sept. 1, 2007; Acts 2009, 81st Leg., ch. 767, § 26, eff. June 19, 2009; Acts 2009, 81st Leg., ch. 1035, § 2, eff. June 19, 2009; Acts 2011, 82nd Leg., ch. 1341 (S.B. 1233), § 10, eff. June 17, 2011; Acts 2015, 84th Leg., ch. 1252 (H.B. 1449), § 3.06, eff. Sept. 1, 2015.

## § 203.006. Fund

(a) As determined by the administering entity, fees collected or received by a domestic relations office shall be deposited in:

(1) the general fund for the county in which the domestic relations office is located; or

(2) the office fund established for the domestic relations office.

(b) The administering entity shall use the domestic relations office fund to provide money for services authorized by this chapter.

(c) A domestic relations office fund may be supplemented as necessary from the county's general fund or from other money available from the county.

Added by Acts 1995, 74th Leg., ch. 20, § 1, eff. April 20, 1995. Redesignated from V.T.C.A., Family Code § 203.010 and amended by Acts 1995, 74th Leg., ch. 475, § 1, eff. Sept. 1, 1995. Amended by Acts 1997, 75th Leg., ch. 702, § 11, eff. Sept. 1, 1997.

## § 203.007. Access to Records; Offense

(a) A domestic relations office may obtain the records described by Subsections (b), (c), (d), and (e) that relate to a person who has:

(1) been ordered to pay child support;

(2) been designated as a conservator of a child;

(3) been designated to be the father of a child;

(4) executed an acknowledgment of paternity;

(5) court-ordered possession of a child; or

(6) filed suit to adopt a child.

(b) A domestic relations office is entitled to obtain from the Department of Public Safety records that relate to:

(1) a person's date of birth;

(2) a person's most recent address;

(3) a person's current driver's license status;

(4) motor vehicle accidents involving a person;

(5) reported traffic-law violations of which a person has been convicted; and

(6) a person's criminal history record information.

(c) A domestic relations office is entitled to obtain from the Texas Workforce Commission records that relate to:

(1) a person's address;

(2) a person's employment status and earnings;

(3) the name and address of a person's current or former employer; and

(4) unemployment compensation benefits received by a person.

(d) To the extent permitted by federal law, a domestic relations office is entitled to obtain from the national directory of new hires established under 42 U.S.C. Section 653(i), as amended, records that relate to a person described by Subsection (a), including records that relate to:

(1) the name, telephone number, and address of the person's employer;

(2) information provided by the person on a W-4 form; and

(3) information provided by the person's employer on a Title IV-D form.

(e) To the extent permitted by federal law, a domestic relations office is entitled to obtain from the state case registry records that relate to a person described by Subsection (a), including records that relate to:

(1) the street and mailing address and the social security number of the person;

(2) the name, telephone number, and address of the person's employer;

(3) the location and value of real and personal property owned by the person; and

(4) the name and address of each financial institution in which the person maintains an account and the account number for each account.

(f) An agency required to provide records under this section may charge a domestic relations office a fee for providing the records in an amount that does not exceed the amount paid for those records by the agency responsible for Title IV-D cases.

(g) The Department of Public Safety, the Texas Workforce Commission, or the office of the secretary of state may charge a domestic relations office a fee not to exceed the charge paid by the Title IV-D agency for furnishing records under this section.

(h) Information obtained by a domestic relations office under this section that is confidential under a constitution, statute, judicial decision, or rule is privileged and may be used only by that office.

(i) A person commits an offense if the person releases or discloses confidential information obtained under this section without the consent of the person to whom the information relates. An offense under this subsection is a Class C misdemeanor.

(j) A domestic relations office is entitled to obtain from the office of the secretary of state the following information about a registered voter to the extent that the information is available:

(1) complete name;

(2) current and former street and mailing address;

(3) sex;

(4) date of birth;

(5) social security number; and

(6) telephone number.

Added by Acts 1995, 74th Leg., ch. 20, § 1, eff. April 20, 1995. Redesignated from V.T.C.A., Family Code § 203.012 and amended by Acts 1995, 74th Leg., ch. 475, § 1, eff. Sept. 1, 1995. Amended by Acts 1995, 74th Leg., ch. 803, § 1, eff. Sept. 1, 1995; Acts 1997, 75th Leg., ch. 165, § 7.18, eff. Sept. 1, 1997; Acts 1999, 76th Leg., ch. 556, § 49, eff. Sept. 1, 1999; Acts 1999, 76th Leg., ch. 859, § 4, eff. Sept. 1, 1999; Acts 1999, 76th Leg., ch. 1191, § 2, eff. June 18, 1999; Acts 2007, 80th Leg., ch. 832, § 9, eff. Sept. 1, 2007.

### § 203.008. Deleted by Acts 1995, 74th Leg., ch. 475, § 1, eff. Sept. 1, 1995

### § 203.009. Redesignated as V.T.C.A., Family Code § 203.005 by Acts 1995, 74th Leg., ch. 475, § 1, eff. Sept. 1, 1995

### § 203.010. Redesignated as V.T.C.A., Family Code § 203.006 by Acts 1995, 74th Leg., ch. 475, § 1, eff. Sept. 1, 1995

### § 203.011. Deleted by Acts 1995, 74th Leg., ch. 475, § 1, eff. Sept. 1, 1995

### § 203.012. Redesignated as V.T.C.A., Family Code § 203.007 by Acts 1995, 74th Leg., ch. 475, § 1, eff. Sept. 1, 1995

## CHAPTER 204. CHILD SUPPORT COLLECTION BY PRIVATE ENTITY

**Section**



*Acts 1999, 76th Leg., ch. 118, § 1, redesignated Chapter 153 Human Resources Code to Title 5, Family Code, as Chapter 204.*

### § 204.001. Applicability

This chapter applies only to a commissioners court or domestic relations office of a county that did not have the authority to contract with a private entity to receive, disburse, and record payments or restitution of child support on January 1, 1997.

Added by Acts 1997, 75th Leg., ch. 1053, § 1, eff. Sept. 1, 1997. Redesignated from V.T.C.A., Human Resources Code § 153.001 and amended by Acts 1999, 76th Leg., ch. 118, § 1, eff. Sept. 1, 1999; Acts 2005, 79th Leg., ch. 740, § 3, eff. June 17, 2005.

### § 204.002. Authority to Contract

A county, acting through its commissioners court or domestic relations office, may contract with a private entity to:

(1) enforce, collect, receive, and disburse:

(A) child support payments;

(B) other amounts due under a court order containing an order to pay child support; and

(C) fees, including fees provided by this chapter;

(2) maintain appropriate records, including records of child support and other amounts and fees that are due, past due, paid, or delinquent;

(3) locate absent parents;

(4) furnish statements to parents accounting for payments that are due, past due, paid, or delinquent;

(5) send billings and other appropriate notices to parents;

(6) perform any duty or function that a local registry is authorized to perform;

(7) perform any duty or function in connection with the state case registry; or

(8) provide another child support or visitation enforcement service authorized by the commission-

ers court, including mediation of disputes related to child support or visitation.

Added by Acts 1997, 75th Leg., ch. 1053, § 1, eff. Sept. 1, 1997. Redesignated from V.T.C.A., Human Resources Code § 153.002 and amended by Acts 1999, 76th Leg., ch. 118, § 1, eff. Sept. 1, 1999.

### § 204.003. Terms and Conditions of Contract

The commissioners court or domestic relations office shall include all appropriate terms and conditions in the contract that it determines are reasonable to secure the services of a private entity as provided by this chapter, including:

(1) provisions specifying the services to be provided by the entity;

(2) the method, conditions, and amount of compensation for the entity;

(3) provisions for the security of funds collected as child support, fees, or other amounts under the contract or that otherwise provide reasonable assurance to the county of the entity's full and faithful performance of the contract;

(4) provisions specifying the records to be kept by the entity, including any records necessary to fully account for all funds received and disbursed as child support, fees, or other amounts;

(5) requirements governing the inspection, verification, audit, or explanation of the entity's accounting or other records;

(6) the county's right to terminate the contract on 30 days' notice to the private entity if the private entity engages in an ongoing pattern of child support enforcement that constitutes wilful and gross misconduct subjecting delinquent obligors to unconscionable duress, abuse, or harassment;

(7) provisions permitting an obligor and obligee to jointly waive the monitoring procedure, if not required by law, by written request approved by order of the court having jurisdiction of the suit in which the child support order was issued; and

(8) provisions for the disclosure or nondisclosure of information or records maintained or known to the entity as a result of contract performance, including a requirement for the private entity to:

(A) disclose to any child support obligor that the private entity is attempting to enforce the obligor's child support obligation; and

(B) make no disclosure of the information or records other than in furtherance of the effort to enforce the child support order.

Added by Acts 1997, 75th Leg., ch. 1053, § 1, eff. Sept. 1, 1997. Redesignated from V.T.C.A., Human Resources Code § 153.003 and amended by Acts 1999, 76th Leg., ch. 118, § 1, eff. Sept. 1, 1999.

### § 204.004. Funding

(a) To provide or recover the costs of providing services authorized by this chapter, a commissioners court, on its behalf or on behalf of the domestic relations office, may:

(1) provide by order for the assessment and collection of a reasonable fee at the time a party files a suit affecting the parent-child relationship;

(2) provide by order for the assessment and collection of a fee of $3 per month at a time specified for payment of child support;

(3) provide by order for the assessment and collection of a late payment fee of $4 per month to be imposed if an obligor does not make a payment of child support in full when due;

(4) accept or receive funds from public grants or private sources available for providing services authorized by this chapter; or

(5) use any combination of funding sources specified by this subsection.

(b) The commissioners court, on its behalf or on behalf of the domestic relations office, may:

(1) provide by order for reasonable exemptions from the collection of fees authorized by Subsection (a); and

(2) require payment of a fee authorized by Subsection (a)(2) annually and in advance.

(c) The commissioners court may not charge a fee under Subsection (a)(2) if the amount of child support ordered to be paid is less than the equivalent of $100 per month.

(d) The fees established under Subsection (a) may be collected by any means provided for the collection of child support. The commissioners court may provide by order, on its behalf or on behalf of the domestic relations office, for the manner of collection of fees and the apportionment of payments received to meet fee obligations.

Added by Acts 1997, 75th Leg., ch. 1053, § 1, eff. Sept. 1, 1997. Redesignated from V.T.C.A., Human Resources Code § 153.004 and amended by Acts 1999, 76th Leg., ch. 118, § 1, eff. Sept. 1, 1999.

### § 204.005. Cumulative Effect of Chapter

A power or duty conferred on a county, county official, or county instrumentality by this chapter is cumulative of the powers and duties created or conferred by other law.

Added by Acts 1997, 75th Leg., ch. 1053, § 1, eff. Sept. 1, 1997. Redesignated from V.T.C.A., Human Resources Code § 153.005 and amended by Acts 1999, 76th Leg., ch. 118, § 1, eff. Sept. 1, 1999.

## SUBTITLE D. ADMINISTRATIVE SERVICES

## CHAPTER 231. TITLE IV–D SERVICES

### SUBCHAPTER A. ADMINISTRATION OF TITLE IV–D PROGRAM

Section



### SUBCHAPTER B. SERVICES PROVIDED BY TITLE IV–D PROGRAM



Section



### SUBCHAPTER C. PAYMENT OF FEES AND COSTS



### SUBCHAPTER D. LOCATION OF PARENTS AND RESOURCES



### SUBCHAPTER E. CHILD SUPPORT REVIEW PROCESS TO ESTABLISH OR ENFORCE SUPPORT OBLIGATIONS [REDESIGNATED]

## SUBCHAPTER A. ADMINISTRATION OF TITLE IV–D PROGRAM

### § 231.001. Designation of Title IV–D Agency

The office of the attorney general is designated as the state's Title IV–D agency.

Added by Acts 1995, 74th Leg., ch. 20, § 1, eff. April 20, 1995.

### § 231.0011. Development of Statewide Integrated System for Child Support, Medical Support, and Dental Support Enforcement

(a) The Title IV–D agency shall have final approval authority on any contract or proposal for delivery of Title IV–D services under this section and in coordination with the Texas Judicial Council, the Office of Court Administration of the Texas Judicial System, the federal Office of Child Support Enforcement, and state, county, and local officials, shall develop and implement a statewide integrated system for child support, medical support, and dental support enforcement, employing federal, state, local, and private resources to:

(1) unify child support registry functions;

(2) record and track all child support orders entered in the state;

(3) establish an automated enforcement process which will use delinquency monitoring, billing, and other enforcement techniques to ensure the payment of current support;

(4) incorporate existing enforcement resources into the system to obtain maximum benefit from state and federal funding; and

(5) ensure accountability for all participants in the process, including state, county, and local officials, private contractors, and the judiciary.

(b) Counties and other providers of child support services shall be required, as a condition of participation in the unified system, to enter into a contract with the Title IV–D agency, to comply with all federal requirements for the Title IV–D program, and to maintain at least the current level of funding for activities which are proposed to be included in the integrated child support system.

(c) The Title IV–D agency may contract with any county meeting technical system requirements necessary to comply with federal law for provision of Title IV–D services in that county. The clerk of the court of a county participating in the unified enforcement system shall use a record of support order form described by Section 105.008(b) that includes an option for the obligee or obligor to apply for child support services provided by the Title IV–D agency.

(d) Counties participating in the unified enforcement system shall monitor all assigned Title IV–D child support cases and on delinquency may, subject to the approval of the Title IV–D agency, provide enforcement services through:

(1) direct provision of services by county personnel;

(2) subcontracting all or portions of the services to private entities or attorneys; or

(3) such other methods as may be approved by the Title IV–D agency.

(e) The Title IV–D agency may phase in the integrated child support registry and enforcement system, and the requirement to implement the system shall be contingent on the receipt of locally generated funds and federal reimbursement. Locally generated funds include but are not limited to funds contributed by counties and cities.

(f) The Title IV–D agency shall adopt rules to implement this section.

(g) Participation in the statewide integrated system for child support, medical support, and dental support enforcement by a county is voluntary, and nothing in this section shall be construed to mandate participation.

(h) This section does not limit the ability of the Title IV–D agency to enter into an agreement with a county for the provision of services as authorized under Section 231.002.

Added by Acts 1995, 74th Leg., ch. 341, § 1.01, eff. Sept. 1, 1995. Amended by Acts 1997, 75th Leg., ch. 702, § 12, eff. Sept. 1, 1997; Acts 1999, 76th Leg., ch. 556, § 50, eff. Sept. 1, 1999; Acts 2015, 84th Leg., ch. 1150 (S.B. 550), §§ 40, 41, eff. Sept. 1, 2018; Acts 2021, 87th Leg., ch. 175 (S.B. 285), § 3, eff. Sept. 1, 2021.

Section 8 of Acts 2021, 87th Leg., ch. 175 (S.B. 285) provides:

"The changes in law made by this Act to Sections 105.008 and 231.0011, Family Code, apply to a suit affecting the parent-child relationship pending in a trial court on or filed on or after the effective date [Sept. 1, 2021] of this Act."

### § 231.0012. Child Support Enforcement Management

The person appointed by the attorney general as the person responsible for managing the Title IV-D agency's child support enforcement duties shall report directly to the attorney general.

Added by Acts 1997, 75th Leg., ch. 420, § 16, eff. Sept. 1, 1997.

### § 231.0013. Dedication of Funds

Appropriations made to the Title IV–D agency for child support enforcement may be expended only for the purposes for which the money was appropriated.

Added by Acts 1997, 75th Leg., ch. 420, § 16, eff. Sept. 1, 1997.

### § 231.002. Powers and Duties

(a) The Title IV–D agency may:

(1) accept, transfer, and expend funds, subject to the General Appropriations Act, made available by the federal or state government or by another public or private source for the purpose of carrying out this chapter;

(2) adopt rules for the provision of child support services;

(3) initiate legal actions needed to implement this chapter; and

(4) enter into contracts or agreements necessary to administer this chapter.

(b) The Title IV–D agency may perform the duties and functions necessary for locating children under agreements with the federal government as provided by 42 U.S.C. Section 663.

(c) The Title IV–D agency may enter into agreements or contracts with federal, state, or other public or private agencies or individuals for the purpose of carrying out the agency's responsibilities under federal or state law. The agreements or contracts between the agency and other state agencies or political subdivisions of this or another state, including a consortia of multiple states, and agreements or contracts with vendors for the delivery of program services are not subject to Chapter 771 or 783, Government Code.

(d) Consistent with federal law and any international treaty or convention to which the United States is a party and that has been ratified by the United States Congress, the Title IV–D agency may:

(1) on approval by and in cooperation with the governor, pursue negotiations and enter into reciprocal arrangements with the federal government, another state, or a foreign country or a political subdivision of the federal government, state, or foreign country to:

(A) establish and enforce child support obligations; and

(B) establish mechanisms to enforce an order providing for possession of or access to a child rendered under Chapter 153;

(2) spend money appropriated to the agency for child support enforcement to engage in international child support enforcement; and

(3) spend other money appropriated to the agency necessary for the agency to conduct the agency's activities under Subdivision (1).

(e) The Title IV–D agency may take the following administrative actions with respect to the location of a parent, the determination of parentage, and the establishment, modification, and enforcement of child support, medical support, and dental support orders required by 42 U.S.C. Section 666(c), without obtaining an order from any other judicial or administrative tribunal:

(1) issue an administrative subpoena, as provided by Section 231.303, to obtain financial or other information;

(2) order genetic testing for parentage determination, as provided by Chapter 233;

(3) order income withholding, as provided by Chapter 233, and issue an administrative writ of withholding, as provided by Chapter 158; and

(4) take any action with respect to execution, collection, and release of a judgment or lien for child support necessary to satisfy the judgment or lien, as provided by Chapter 157.

(f) The Title IV–D agency shall recognize and enforce the authority of the Title IV–D agency of another state to take actions similar to the actions listed in this section.

(g) The Title IV–D agency shall develop and use procedures for the administrative enforcement of interstate cases meeting the requirements of 42 U.S.C. Section 666(a)(14) under which the agency:

(1) shall promptly respond to a request made by another state for assistance in a Title IV–D case; and

(2) may, by electronic or other means, transmit to another state a request for assistance in a Title IV–D case.

(h) Repealed by Acts 2009, 81st Leg., ch. 164, § 3.

(i) The Title IV–D agency may provide a release or satisfaction of a judgment for all or part of the amount of the arrearages assigned to the Title IV–D agency under Section 231.104(a).

(j) In the enforcement or modification of a child support order, the Title IV–D agency is not:

(1) subject to a mediation or arbitration clause or requirement in the order to which the Title IV–D agency was not a party; or

(2) liable for any costs associated with mediation or arbitration arising from provisions in the order or another agreement of the parties.

Added by Acts 1995, 74th Leg., ch. 20, § 1, eff. April 20, 1995. Amended by Acts 1997, 75th Leg., ch. 874, § 1, eff. Sept. 1, 1997; Acts 1997, 75th Leg., ch. 911, § 68, eff. Sept. 1, 1997; Acts 1999, 76th Leg., ch. 62, § 6.27, eff. Sept. 1, 1999; Acts 1999, 76th Leg., ch. 556, § 51, eff. Sept. 1, 1999; Acts 2003, 78th Leg., ch. 310, § 1, eff. Sept. 1, 2003; Acts 2003, 78th Leg., ch. 610, § 12, eff. Sept. 1, 2003; Acts 2009, 81st Leg., ch. 164, § 3, eff. May 26, 2009; Acts 2013, 83rd Leg., ch. 742 (S.B. 355), § 9, eff. Sept. 1, 2013; Acts 2015, 84th Leg., ch. 1150 (S.B. 550), § 42, eff. Sept. 1, 2018.

### § 231.003. Forms and Procedures

The Title IV–D agency shall by rule promulgate any forms and procedures necessary to comply fully with the intent of this chapter.

Added by Acts 1995, 74th Leg., ch. 20, § 1, eff. April 20, 1995.

### § 231.004. Repealed by Acts 1997, 75th Leg., ch. 911, § 97(a), eff. Sept. 1, 1997

### § 231.005. Biennial Report Required

(a) The Title IV–D agency shall report to the legislature each biennium on:

(1) the effectiveness of the agency's child support enforcement activity in reducing the state's public assistance obligations; and

(2) the use and effectiveness of all enforcement tools authorized by state or federal law or otherwise available to the agency.

(b) The agency shall develop a method for estimating the costs and benefits of the child support enforcement program and the effect of the program on appropriations for public assistance.

Added by Acts 1995, 74th Leg., ch. 20, § 1, eff. April 20, 1995. Amended by Acts 1999, 76th Leg., ch. 556, § 51, eff. Sept. 1, 1999; Acts 2011, 82nd Leg., ch. 990 (H.B. 1781), § 2, eff. June 17, 2011.

### § 231.006. Ineligibility to Receive State Grants or Loans or Receive Payment on State Contracts

(a) A child support obligor who is more than 30 days delinquent in paying child support and a business entity in which the obligor is a sole proprietor, partner, shareholder, or owner with an ownership interest of at least 25 percent is not eligible to:

(1) receive payments from state funds under a contract to provide property, materials, or services; or

(2) receive a state-funded grant or loan.

(a–1) Repealed by Acts 2007, 80th Leg., ch. 972, § 65(1).

(b) A child support obligor or business entity ineligible to receive payments under Subsection (a) remains ineligible until:

(1) all arrearages have been paid;

(2) the obligor is in compliance with a written repayment agreement or court order as to any existing delinquency; or

(3) the court of continuing jurisdiction over the child support order has granted the obligor an exemption from Subsection (a) as part of a court-supervised effort to improve earnings and child support payments.

(c) A bid or an application for a contract, grant, or loan paid from state funds must include the name and social security number of the individual or sole proprietor and each partner, shareholder, or owner with an ownership interest of at least 25 percent of the business entity submitting the bid or application.

(d) A contract, bid, or application subject to the requirements of this section must include the following statement:

"Under Section 231.006, Family Code, the vendor or applicant certifies that the individual or business entity named in this contract, bid, or application is not ineligible to receive the specified grant, loan, or payment and acknowledges that this contract may be terminated and payment may be withheld if this certification is inaccurate."

(e) If a state agency determines that an individual or business entity holding a state contract is ineligible to receive payment under Subsection (a), the contract may be terminated.

(f) If the certificate required under Subsection (d) is shown to be false, the vendor is liable to the state for attorney's fees, the costs necessary to complete the contract, including the cost of advertising and awarding a second contract, and any other damages provided by law or contract.

(g) This section does not create a cause of action to contest a bid or award of a state grant, loan, or contract. This section does not impose a duty on the Title IV-D agency to collect information to send to the comptroller to withhold a payment to a business entity. The Title IV-D agency and other affected agencies are encouraged to develop a system by which the Title IV-D agency may identify a business entity that is ineligible to receive a state payment under Subsection (a) and to ensure that a state payment to the entity is not made. This system should be implemented using existing funds and only if the Title IV-D agency, comptroller, and other affected agencies determine that it will be cost-effective.

(h) This section does not apply to a contract between governmental entities.

(i) The Title IV-D agency may adopt rules or prescribe forms to implement any provision of this section.

(j) A state agency may accept a bid that does not include the information required under Subsection (c) if the state agency collects the information before the contract, grant, or loan is executed.

Added by Acts 1995, 74th Leg., ch. 20, § 1, eff. April 20, 1995. Amended by Acts 1995, 74th Leg., ch. 751, § 82, eff. Sept. 1, 1995; Acts 1999, 76th Leg., ch. 28, § 1, eff. Sept. 1, 1999; Acts 2003, 78th Leg., ch. 437, § 1, eff. Sept. 1, 2003; Acts 2003, 78th Leg., ch. 1015, § 2, eff. Sept. 1, 2003; Acts 2007, 80th Leg., ch. 972, §§ 45, 65(1), eff. Sept. 1, 2007.

### § 231.007. Debts to State

(a) A person obligated to pay child support in a case in which the Title IV-D agency is providing services under this chapter who does not pay the required support is indebted to the state for the purposes of Section 403.055, Government Code, if the Title IV-D agency has reported the person to the comptroller under that section properly.

(b) The amount of a person's indebtedness to the state under Subsection (a) is equal to the sum of:

(1) the amount of the required child support that has not been paid; and

(2) any interest, fees, court costs, or other amounts owed by the person because the person has not paid the support.

(c) The Title IV-D agency is the sole assignee of all payments, including payments of compensation, by the state to a person indebted to the state under Subsection (a).

(d) On request of the Title IV-D agency:

(1) the comptroller shall make payable and deliver to the agency any payments for which the agency is the assignee under Subsection (c), if the comptroller is responsible for issuing warrants or initiating electronic funds transfers to make those payments; and

(2) a state agency shall make payable and deliver to the Title IV-D agency any payments for which the Title IV-D agency is the assignee under Subsection (c) if the comptroller is not responsible for issuing warrants or initiating electronic funds transfers to make those payments.

(e) A person indebted to the state under Subsection (a) may eliminate the debt by:

(1) paying the entire amount of the debt; or

(2) resolving the debt in a manner acceptable to the Title IV-D agency.

(f) The comptroller or a state agency may rely on a representation by the Title IV-D agency that:

(1) a person is indebted to the state under Subsection (a); or

(2) a person who was indebted to the state under Subsection (a) has eliminated the debt.

(g) Except as provided by Subsection (h), the payment of workers' compensation benefits to a person indebted to the state under Subsection (a) is the same for the purposes of this section as any other payment made to the person by the state. Notwithstanding Section 408.203, Labor Code, an order or writ to withhold income from workers' compensation benefits is not required before the benefits are withheld or assigned under this section.

(h) The amount of weekly workers' compensation benefits that may be withheld or assigned under this section may not exceed 50 percent of the person's weekly compensation benefits. The comptroller or a state agency may rely on a representation by the Title IV–D agency that a withholding or assignment under this section would not violate this subsection.

(i) Section 403.055(d), Government Code, does not authorize the comptroller to issue a warrant or initiate an electronic funds transfer to pay the compensation or remuneration of an individual who is indebted to the state under Subsection (a).

(j) Section 2107.008(h), Government Code, does not authorize a state agency to pay the compensation or remuneration of an individual who is indebted to the state under Subsection (a).

(k) In this section, "compensation," "state agency," and "state officer or employee" have the meanings assigned by Section 403.055, Government Code.

Added by Acts 1995, 74th Leg., ch. 20, § 1, eff. April 20, 1995. Amended by Acts 1995, 74th Leg., ch. 751, § 83, eff. Sept. 1, 1995; Acts 1997, 75th Leg., ch. 165, § 7.19, eff. Sept. 1, 1997; Acts 1999, 76th Leg., ch. 1467, § 1.07, eff. Jan. 1, 2000; Acts 2001, 77th Leg., ch. 1158, § 6, eff. June 15, 2001; Acts 2003, 78th Leg., ch. 610, § 13, eff. Sept. 1, 2003.

### § 231.008. Disposition of Funds

(a) The Title IV–D agency shall deposit money received under assignments or as fees in a special fund in the state treasury. The agency may spend money in the fund for the administration of this chapter, subject to the General Appropriations Act.

(b) All other money received under this chapter shall be deposited in a special fund in the state treasury.

(c) Sections 403.094[1] and 403.095, Government Code, do not apply to a fund described by this section.

Added by Acts 1995, 74th Leg., ch. 20, § 1, eff. April 20, 1995.

[1] Repealed.

### § 231.009. Payment of Penalties

From funds appropriated for the Title IV–D agency, the agency shall reimburse the Texas Department of Human Services for any penalty assessed under Title IV–A of the federal Social Security Act (42 U.S.C. Section 651 et seq.) that is assessed because of the agency's administration of this chapter.

Added by Acts 1995, 74th Leg., ch. 20, § 1, eff. April 20, 1995.

### § 231.010. Cooperation with Department of Protective and Regulatory Services

(a) In this section, "department" means the Department of Protective and Regulatory Services.

(b) To the extent possible, the Title IV-D agency shall:

(1) provide to the department access to all of the Title IV-D agency's available child support locating resources;

(2) allow the department to use the Title IV-D agency's child support enforcement system to track child support payments and to have access to the agency's management reports that show payments made;

(3) make reports on Title IV-E, Social Security Act (42 U.S.C. Section 670 et seq.), foster care collections available to the department in a timely manner; and

(4) work with the department to obtain child support payments for protective services cases in which the department is responsible for providing care for children under temporary and final orders.

Added by Acts 1999, 76th Leg., ch. 228, § 1, eff. Sept. 1, 1999. Redesignated from V.T.C.A., Family Code § 231.011 by Acts 2003, 78th Leg., ch. 1275, § 2(53), eff. Sept. 1, 2003.

### § 231.011 Repealed by Acts 2007, 80th Leg., ch. 972, § 65(2), eff. Sept. 1, 2007.

### § 231.012. Child Support Work Group

(a) The director of the Title IV–D agency may convene a work group representing public and private entities with an interest in child support enforcement in this state to work with the director in developing strategies to improve child support enforcement in this state.

(b) The director of the Title IV–D agency shall appoint the members of the work group after consulting with appropriate public and private entities.

(c) The work group shall meet as convened by the director of the Title IV–D agency and consult with the director on matters relating to child support enforcement in this state, including the delivery of Title IV–D services.

(d) A work group member or the member's designee may not receive compensation but is entitled to reimbursement for actual and necessary expenses incurred in performing the member's duties under this section.

(e) The work group is not an advisory committee as defined by Section 2110.001, Government Code. Chapter 2110, Government Code, does not apply to the work group.

Added by Acts 1999, 76th Leg., ch. 556, § 51, eff. Sept. 1, 1999. Amended by Acts 2003, 78th Leg., ch. 1258, § 25, eff. Sept. 1, 2003; Acts 2007, 80th Leg., ch. 972, §§ 46, 47, eff. Sept. 1, 2007.

### § 231.013. Repealed by Acts 2017, 85th Leg., ch. 553 (S.B. 526), § 5(b), eff. Sept. 1, 2017

### § 231.014. Personnel

The director of the Title IV–D agency shall provide to the employees of the Title IV–D agency, as often as necessary, information regarding the requirements for employment under this title, including information regarding a person's responsibilities under applicable laws relating to standards of conduct for state employees.

Added by Acts 1999, 76th Leg., ch. 556, § 51, eff. Sept. 1, 1999.

### § 231.015. Insurance Reporting Program

(a) In consultation with the Texas Department of Insurance and representatives of the insurance industry in this state, including insurance trade associations, the Title IV–D agency by rule shall operate a program under which insurers shall cooperate with the Title IV–D agency in identifying obligors who owe child support arrearages and are subject to liens for child support arrearages to intercept certain insurance settlements or awards for claims in satisfaction of the arrearage amounts.

(b) An insurer that provides information or responds to a notice of child support lien or levy under Subchapter G,[1] Chapter 157, or acts in good faith to comply with procedures established by the Title IV–D agency under this section is not liable for those acts under any law to any person.

(c) An insurer may not be required to report or identify the following types of claims:

(1) a first-party property damage claim under:

(A) a personal automobile insurance policy for actual repair, replacement, or loss of use of an insured vehicle; or

(B) a residential or tenant property insurance policy for actual repair, replacement, or loss of use of an insured dwelling and contents, including additional living expenses actually incurred;

(2) a third-party property damage claim:

(A) that will be paid to a vendor or repair facility for the actual repair, replacement, or loss of use of:

(i) a dwelling, condominium, or other improvements on real property;

(ii) a vehicle, including a motor vehicle, motorcycle, or recreational vehicle; or

(iii) other tangible personal property that has sustained actual damage or loss; or

(B) for the reimbursement to a claimant for payments made by the claimant to a vendor or repair facility for the actual repair, replacement, or loss of use of:

(i) a dwelling, condominium, or other improvements on real property;

(ii) a vehicle, including a motor vehicle, motorcycle, or recreational vehicle; or

(iii) other tangible personal property that has sustained actual damage or loss;

(3) a claim for benefits, or a portion of a claim for benefits, assigned to be paid to a funeral service provider or facility for actual funeral expenses owed by the insured that are not otherwise paid or reimbursed;

(4) a claim for benefits assigned to be paid to a health care provider or facility for actual medical expenses owed by the insured that are not otherwise paid or reimbursed; or

(5) a claim for benefits to be paid under a limited benefit insurance policy that provides:

(A) coverage for one or more specified diseases or illnesses;

(B) dental or vision benefits; or

(C) hospital indemnity or other fixed indemnity coverage.

Added by Acts 2001, 77th Leg., ch. 1023, § 52, eff. Sept. 1, 2001. Amended by Acts 2009, 81st Leg., ch. 767, § 27, eff. June 19, 2009; Acts 2011, 82nd Leg., ch. 508 (H.B. 1674), § 12, eff. Sept. 1, 2011; Acts 2015, 84th Leg., ch. 1185 (S.B. 1174), § 1, eff. June 19, 2015; Acts 2017, 85th Leg., ch. 902 (H.B. 3845), § 1, eff. June 15, 2017.

[1] V.T.C.A., Family Code § 157.311 et seq.

## SUBCHAPTER B. SERVICES PROVIDED BY TITLE IV–D PROGRAM

### § 231.101. Title IV–D Child Support Services

(a) The Title IV–D agency may provide all services required or authorized to be provided by Part D of Title IV of the federal Social Security Act (42 U.S.C. Section 651 et seq.), including:

(1) parent locator services;

(2) paternity determination;

(3) child support, medical support, and dental support establishment;

(4) review and adjustment of child support orders;

(5) enforcement of child support, medical support, and dental support orders; and

(6) collection and distribution of child support payments.

(b) At the request of either the obligee or obligor, the Title IV-D agency shall review a child support order once every three years and, if appropriate, adjust the support amount to meet the requirements of the child support guidelines under Chapter 154.

(c) Except as notice is included in the child support order, a party subject to a support order shall be provided notice not less than once every three years of the party's right to request that the Title IV-D agency review and, if appropriate, adjust the amount of ordered support.

(d) The Title IV–D agency may review a support order at any time on a showing of a material and substantial change in circumstances, taking into consideration the best interests of the child. If the Title IV–D agency determines that the primary care and possession of the child has changed, the Title IV–D agency may file a petition for modification under Chapter 156.

(e) The Title IV-D agency shall distribute a child support payment received by the agency from an employer within two working days after the date the agency receives the payment.

Added by Acts 1995, 74th Leg., ch. 20, § 1, eff. April 20, 1995. Amended by Acts 1997, 75th Leg., ch. 702, § 13, eff. Sept. 1, 1997; Acts 1997, 75th Leg., ch. 911, § 69, eff. Sept. 1, 1997; Acts 1999, 76th Leg., ch. 62, § 19.01(22), eff. Sept. 1, 1999; Acts 2015, 84th Leg., ch. 963 (S.B. 1727), § 2, eff. Sept. 1, 2015; Acts 2015, 84th Leg., ch. 1150 (S.B. 550), § 43, eff. Sept. 1, 2018.

### § 231.102. Eligibility for Child Support Services

The Title IV–D agency on application or as otherwise authorized by law may provide services for the benefit of a child without regard to whether the child has received public assistance.

Added by Acts 1995, 74th Leg., ch. 20, § 1, eff. April 20, 1995.

### § 231.103. Application and Service Fees

(a) The Title IV–D agency may:

(1) charge a reasonable application fee;

(2) charge a $35 annual service fee; and

(3) to the extent permitted by federal law, recover costs for the services provided in a Title IV–D case.

(b) An application fee may not be charged in a case in which the Title IV–D agency provides services because the family receives public assistance.

(c) An application fee may not exceed a maximum amount established by federal law.

(d) Repealed by Acts 2007, 80th Leg., ch. 972, § 65(3).

(e) The Title IV–D agency may impose and collect a fee as authorized by federal law for each request for parent locator services under Section 231.101(a).

(f) The state disbursement unit established and operated by the Title IV–D agency under Chapter 234 may collect a monthly service fee of $3 in each case in which support payments are processed through the unit.

(g) The Title IV–D agency by rule shall establish procedures for the imposition of fees and recovery of costs authorized under this section.

(g–1) A fee authorized under this section for providing child support enforcement services is part of the child support obligation if the obligor is responsible for the fee, and may be enforced against the obligor through any method available for the enforcement of child support, including contempt.

(h) The attorney general child support application and service fee account is an account in the general revenue fund in the state treasury. The account consists of all fees and costs collected under this section. The Title IV–D agency may only use the money in the account for agency program expenditures.

Added by Acts 1995, 74th Leg., ch. 20, § 1, eff. April 20, 1995. Amended by Acts 2003, 78th Leg., ch. 1262, §§ 2, 3, eff. Sept. 1, 2003; Acts 2007, 80th Leg., ch. 972, §§ 48, 65(3), eff. Sept. 1, 2007; Acts 2019, 86th Leg., ch. 606 (S.B. 891), § 13.01, eff. Sept. 1, 2019.

Section 15.05 of Acts 2019, 86th Leg., ch. 606 (S.B. 891) provides:

"The Office of Court Administration of the Texas Judicial System is required to implement a provision of this Act only if the legislature appropriates money specifically for that purpose. If the legislature does not appropriate money specifically for that purpose, the office may, but is not required to, implement a provision of this Act using other appropriations available for that purpose."

### § 231.104. Assignment of Right to Support

(a) To the extent authorized by federal law, the approval of an application for or the receipt of financial assistance as provided by Chapter 31, Human Resources Code, constitutes an assignment to the Title IV-D agency of any rights to support from any other person that the applicant or recipient may have personally or for a child for whom the applicant or recipient is claiming assistance.

(b) An application for child support services is an assignment of support rights to enable the Title IV–D agency to establish and enforce child support, medical support, and dental support obligations, but an assignment is not a condition of eligibility for services.

(c) Filing a notice of assignment of support rights, a notice of change of payee under Section 231.105, or a pleading by the Title IV–D agency in a suit under this title is evidence of the assignment of support rights to the Title IV–D agency in that cause and is admissible as evidence of the truth of the assignment of support rights and does not require further authentication or verification.

Added by Acts 1995, 74th Leg., ch. 20, § 1, eff. April 20, 1995. Amended by Acts 1997, 75th Leg., ch. 911, § 70, eff. Sept. 1, 1997; Acts 2001, 77th Leg., ch. 1023, § 53, eff. Sept. 1, 2001; Acts 2003, 78th Leg., ch. 610, § 14, eff. Sept. 1, 2003; Acts 2015, 84th Leg., ch. 1150 (S.B. 550), § 44, eff. Sept. 1, 2018; Acts 2021, 87th Leg., ch. 175 (S.B. 285), § 4, eff. Sept. 1, 2021.

### § 231.105. Notice of Change of Payee

(a) Child support payments for the benefit of a child whose support rights have been assigned to the Title IV-D agency under Section 231.104 shall be made payable to the Title IV-D agency and transmitted to the state disbursement unit as provided by Chapter 234.

(b) If a court has ordered support payments to be made to an applicant for or recipient of financial assistance or to an applicant for or recipient of Title IV-D services, the Title IV-D agency shall, on providing notice to the obligee and the obligor, direct the obligor or other payor to make support payments payable to the Title IV-D agency and to transmit the payments to the state disbursement unit. The Title IV-D agency shall file a copy of the notice with the court ordering the payments and with the child support registry. The notice must include:

(1) a statement that the child is an applicant for or recipient of financial assistance, or a child other than a recipient child for whom Title IV-D services are provided;

(2) the name of the child and the caretaker for whom support has been ordered by the court;

(3) the style and cause number of the case in which support was ordered; and

(4) instructions for the payment of ordered support to the agency.

(c) On receipt of a copy of the notice under Subsection (b), the clerk of the court shall file the notice in the appropriate case file.

Added by Acts 1995, 74th Leg., ch. 20, § 1, eff. April 20, 1995. Amended by Acts 1997, 75th Leg., ch. 911, § 71, eff. Sept. 1, 1997; Acts 2001, 77th Leg., ch. 1023, § 54, eff. Sept. 1, 2001.

### § 231.106. Notice of Termination of Assignment

(a) On termination of support rights to the Title IV-D agency, the Title IV-D agency shall, after providing notice to the obligee and the obligor, send a notice of termination of assignment to the obligor or other payor, which may direct that all or a portion of the payments be made payable to the agency and to other persons who are entitled to receive the payments.

(b) The Title IV–D agency shall send a copy of the notice of termination of assignment to the court ordering the support and to the child support registry, and on receipt of the notice the clerk of the court shall file the notice in the appropriate case file. The clerk may not require an order of the court to terminate the assignment and direct support payments to the person entitled to receive the payment.

Added by Acts 1995, 74th Leg., ch. 20, § 1, eff. April 20, 1995. Amended by Acts 1997, 75th Leg., ch. 911, § 72, eff. Sept. 1, 1997; Acts 1999, 76th Leg., ch. 556, § 52, eff. Sept. 1, 1999.

### § 231.107. Certificate of Assignment or of Termination of Assignment

If an abstract of judgment or a child support lien on support amounts assigned to the Title IV-D agency under this chapter has previously been filed of record, the agency shall file for recordation, with the county clerk of each county in which such abstract or lien has been filed, a certificate that a notice of change of payee or a notice of termination of assignment has been issued by the agency.

Added by Acts 1995, 74th Leg., ch. 20, § 1, eff. April 20, 1995. Amended by Acts 1997, 75th Leg., ch. 911, § 73, eff. Sept. 1, 1997.

### § 231.108. Confidentiality of Records and Privileged Communications

(a) Except as provided by Subsection (c), all files and records of services provided by the Title IV–D agency under this title, including information concerning a custodial parent, a noncustodial parent, a child, or an alleged or presumed father, are confidential.

(b) Except as provided by Subsection (c), all communications made by a recipient of financial assistance under Chapter 31, Human Resources Code, or an applicant for or recipient of services under this chapter are privileged.

(c) The Title IV–D agency may use or release information from the files and records, including information that results from a communication made by a recipient of financial assistance under Chapter 31,

Human Resources Code, or by an applicant for or recipient of services under this chapter, for purposes directly connected with the administration of the child support, paternity determination, parent locator, or aid to families with dependent children programs. The Title IV–D agency may release information from the files and records to a consumer reporting agency in accordance with Section 231.114.

(d) The Title IV–D agency by rule may provide for the release of information to public officials.

(e) The Title IV-D agency may not release information on the physical location of a person if:

(1) a protective order has been entered with respect to the person; or

(2) there is reason to believe that the release of information may result in physical or emotional harm to the person.

(f) The Title IV–D agency, by rule, may provide for the release of information to persons for purposes not prohibited by federal law.

(g) The final order in a suit adjudicating parentage is available for public inspection as provided by Section 160.633.

Added by Acts 1995, 74th Leg., ch. 20, § 1, eff. April 20, 1995. Amended by Acts 1995, 74th Leg., ch. 341, § 1.08, eff. Sept. 1, 1995; Acts 1997, 75th Leg., ch. 911, § 74, eff. Sept. 1, 1997; Acts 1999, 76th Leg., ch. 556, § 53, eff. Sept. 1, 1999; Acts 2003, 78th Leg., ch. 610, § 15, eff. Sept. 1, 2003; Acts 2015, 84th Leg., ch. 963 (S.B. 1727), § 3, eff. Sept. 1, 2015.

### § 231.109. Attorneys Representing State

(a) Attorneys employed by the Title IV–D agency may represent this state or another state in an action brought under the authority of federal law or this chapter.

(b) The Title IV–D agency may contract with private attorneys, other private entities, or political subdivisions of the state to provide services in Title IV–D cases.

(c) The Title IV–D agency shall provide copies of all contracts entered into under this section to the Legislative Budget Board and the Governor's Office of Budget and Planning, along with a written justification of the need for each contract, within 60 days after the execution of the contract.

(d) An attorney employed to provide Title IV-D services represents the interest of the state and not the interest of any other party. The provision of services by an attorney under this chapter does not create an attorney-client relationship between the attorney and any other party. The agency shall, at the time an application for child support services is made, inform the applicant that neither the Title IV–D agency nor any attorney who provides services under this chapter is the applicant's attorney and that the attorney providing services under this chapter does not provide legal representation to the applicant.

(e) An attorney employed by the Title IV–D agency or as otherwise provided by this chapter may not be appointed or act as an amicus attorney or attorney ad litem for a child or another party.

Added by Acts 1995, 74th Leg., ch. 20, § 1, eff. April 20, 1995. Amended by Acts 1995, 74th Leg., ch. 341, § 1.02, eff. Sept. 1, 1995; Acts 2005, 79th Leg., ch. 172, § 21, eff. Sept. 1, 2005.

### § 231.110. Authorization of Service

The provision of services by the Title IV–D agency under this chapter or Part D of Title IV of the federal Social Security Act (42 U.S.C. Section 651 et seq.) does not authorize service on the agency of any legal notice that is required to be served on any party other than the agency.

Added by Acts 1995, 74th Leg., ch. 20, § 1, eff. April 20, 1995.

### § 231.111. Disqualification of Agency

A court shall not disqualify the Title IV–D agency in a legal action filed under this chapter or Part D of Title IV of the federal Social Security Act (42 U.S.C. Section 651 et seq.) on the basis that the agency has previously provided services to a party whose interests may now be adverse to the relief requested.

Added by Acts 1995, 74th Leg., ch. 20, § 1, eff. April 20, 1995.

### § 231.112. Information on Paternity Establishment

On notification by the state registrar under Section 192.005(d), Health and Safety Code, that the items relating to the child's father are not completed on a birth certificate filed with the state registrar, the Title IV–D agency may provide to:

(1) the child's mother and, if possible, the man claiming to be the child's biological father written information necessary for the man to complete an acknowledgment of paternity as provided by Chapter 160; and

(2) the child's mother written information:

(A) explaining the benefits of having the child's paternity established; and

(B) regarding the availability of paternity establishment and child support enforcement services.

Added by Acts 1995, 74th Leg., ch. 20, § 1, eff. April 20, 1995. Amended by Acts 1999, 76th Leg., ch. 556, § 54, eff. Sept. 1, 1999.

### § 231.113. Enforcement of Support Obligations in Public Assistance Cases

To the extent possible, the Title IV–D agency shall enforce a child support obligation in a case involving a child who receives financial assistance under Chapter 31, Human Resources Code, not later than the first anniversary of the date the agency receives from the Texas Department of Human Services the information the department is required to provide to assist in the enforcement of that obligation.

Added by Acts 1995, 74th Leg., ch. 341, § 1.03, eff. Sept. 1, 1995.

### § 231.114. Reports of Child Support Payments to Consumer Reporting Agencies

(a) The Title IV–D agency shall make information available in accordance with this section to a consumer reporting agency regarding the amount of child support owed and the amount paid by an obligor in a Title IV–D case.

(b) Before disclosing the information to consumer reporting agencies, the Title IV–D agency shall send the obligor a notice by mail to the obligor's last known address. The notice must include:

(1) the information to be released, including the amount of the obligor's child support obligation and delinquency, if any, that will be reported;

(2) the procedure available for the obligor to contest the accuracy of the information; and

(3) a statement that the information will be released if the obligor fails to contest the disclosure before the 30th day after the date of mailing of the notice.

(c) If the obligor does not contest the disclosure within the period specified by Subsection (b), the Title IV–D agency shall make the information available to the consumer reporting agency.

(d) The Title IV–D agency shall regularly update the information released to a consumer reporting agency under this section to ensure the accuracy of the released information.

(e) The Title IV–D agency may charge a consumer reporting agency a reasonable fee for making information available under this section, including all applicable mailing costs.

(f) In this section:

(1) "Consumer reporting agency" means any person that regularly engages in whole or in part in the practice of assembling or evaluating consumer credit information or other information on consumers for monetary fees, for dues, or on a cooperative nonprofit basis, to furnish consumer reports to third parties.

(2) "Obligor" means any person required to make payments under the terms of a support order for a child.

(3) "Title IV–D case" means a case in which services are being provided by the Title IV–D agency under Part D of Title IV of the federal Social Security Act (42 U.S.C. Section 651 et seq.) seeking to locate an absent parent, determine parentage, or establish, modify, enforce, or monitor a child support obligation.

Added by Acts 1995, 74th Leg., ch. 341, § 1.03, eff. Sept. 1, 1995.

### § 231.115. Noncooperation by Recipient of Public Assistance

(a) The failure by a person who is a recipient of public assistance under Chapter 31, Human Resources Code, to provide accurate information as required by Section 31.0315, Human Resources Code, shall serve as the basis for a determination by the Title IV–D agency that the person did not cooperate with the Title IV–D agency.

(b) The Title IV–D agency shall:

(1) identify the actions or failures to act by a recipient of public assistance that constitute noncooperation with the Title IV–D agency;

(2) adopt rules governing noncompliance; and

(3) send noncompliance determinations to the Texas Department of Human Services for immediate imposition of sanctions.

(c) In adopting rules under this section that establish the basis for determining that a person has failed to cooperate with the Title IV–D agency, the Title IV–D agency shall consider whether:

(1) good cause exists for the failure to cooperate;

(2) the person has failed to disclose the name and location of an alleged or probable parent of the child, if known by the person, at the time of apply-

ing for public assistance or at a subsequent time; and

(3) the person named a man as the alleged father and the man was subsequently excluded by parentage testing as being the father if the person has previously named another man as the child's father.

Added by Acts 1997, 75th Leg., ch. 911, § 75, eff. Sept. 1, 1997. Amended by Acts 1999, 76th Leg., ch. 556, § 54, eff. Sept. 1, 1999.

### § 231.116. Information on Internet

The Title IV-D agency shall place on the Internet for public access child support information to assist the public in child support matters, including application forms, child support collection in other states, and profiles of certain obligors who are in arrears in paying child support.

Added by Acts 1997, 75th Leg., ch. 420, § 18, eff. Sept. 1, 1997.

### § 231.1165. Information on Service of Citation

The Title IV-D agency shall update the agency's child support automated system to inform the parties in a suit of the service of citation in the suit not later than the first business day after the date the agency receives notice that citation has been served. The information required by this section must be available by telephone and on the Internet.

Added by Acts 2001, 77th Leg., ch. 141, § 1, eff. Sept. 1, 2001.

### § 231.117. Unemployed and Underemployed Obligors

(a) The Title IV-D agency shall refer to appropriate state and local entities that provide employment services any unemployed or underemployed obligor who is in arrears in court-ordered child support payments.

(b) A referral under Subsection (a) may include:

(1) skills training and job placement through:

(A) the Texas Workforce Commission; or

(B) the agency responsible for the food stamp employment and training program (7 U.S.C. Section 2015(d));

(2) referrals to education and literacy classes; and

(3) counseling regarding:

(A) substance abuse;

(B) parenting skills;

(C) life skills; and

(D) mediation techniques.

(c) The Title IV-D agency may require an unemployed or underemployed obligor to complete the training, classes, or counseling to which the obligor is referred under this section. The agency shall suspend under Chapter 232 the license of an obligor who fails to comply with the requirements of this subsection.

(d) A court or the Title IV–D agency may issue an order that requires the parent to either work, have a plan to pay overdue child support, or participate in work activities appropriate to pay the overdue support.

Added by Acts 1997, 75th Leg., ch. 165, § 7.20(a), eff. Sept. 1, 1997. Amended by Acts 1999, 76th Leg., ch. 1072, § 5, eff. Sept. 1, 1999. Redesignated from V.T.C.A., Family Code § 231.115 and amended by Acts 1999, 76th Leg., ch. 62, § 19.01(23), eff. Sept. 1, 1999; Acts 1999, 76th Leg., ch. 556, § 54, eff. Sept. 1, 1999.

### § 231.118. Service of Citation

(a) The Title IV–D agency may contract with private process servers to serve a citation, a subpoena, an order, or any other document required or appropriate under law to be served a party.

(b) For the purposes of Rule 103 of the Texas Rules of Civil Procedure, a person who serves a citation or any other document under this section is authorized to serve the document without a written court order authorizing the service.

(c) Issuance and return of the process shall be made in accordance with law and shall be verified by the person serving the document.

(d) Notwithstanding Subsection (c), a return of the process made under this section in a suit may not include the address served if:

(1) a pleading filed in the suit requests a finding under Section 105.006(c); or

(2) the court has previously made a finding and ordered nondisclosure under Section 105.006(c) relating to the parties and the order has not been superseded.

Added by Acts 1999, 76th Leg., ch. 556, § 54, eff. Sept. 1, 1999. Amended by Acts 2017, 85th Leg., ch. 699 (H.B. 2048), § 2, eff. Sept. 1, 2017.

### § 231.119. Ombudsman Program

(a) The Title IV–D agency shall establish an ombudsman program to process and track complaints against the Title IV–D agency. The director of the Title IV–D agency shall:

(1) designate an employee to serve as chief ombudsman to manage the ombudsman program; and

(2) designate an employee in each field office to act as the ombudsman for the office.

(b) The Title IV–D agency shall develop and implement a uniform process for receiving and resolving complaints against the Title IV–D agency throughout the state. The process shall include statewide procedures to inform the public and recipients of Title IV–D services of the right to file a complaint against the Title IV–D agency, including the mailing addresses and telephone numbers of appropriate Title IV–D agency personnel responsible for receiving complaints and providing related assistance.

(c) The ombudsman in each field office shall ensure that an employee in the field office responds to and attempts to resolve each complaint that is filed with the field office. If a complaint cannot be resolved at the field office level, the ombudsman in the field office shall refer the complaint to the chief ombudsman.

(d) The Title IV–D agency shall maintain a file on each written complaint filed with the Title IV–D agency. The file must include:

(1) the name of the person who filed the complaint;

(2) the date the complaint is received by the Title IV–D agency;

(3) the subject matter of the complaint;

(4) the name of each person contacted in relation to the complaint;

(5) a summary of the results of the review or investigation of the complaint; and

(6) an explanation of the reason the file was closed, if the agency closed the file without taking action other than to investigate the complaint.

(e) The Title IV–D agency, at least quarterly until final disposition of the complaint, shall notify the person filing the complaint and each person who is a subject of the complaint of the status of the investigation of the complaint unless the notice would jeopardize an undercover investigation.

(f) The Title IV–D agency shall provide to the person filing the complaint and to each person who is a subject of the complaint a copy of the Title IV–D agency's policies and procedures relating to complaint investigation and resolution.

Added by Acts 1999, 76th Leg., ch. 556, § 54, eff. Sept. 1, 1999.

### § 231.120. Toll-free Telephone Number for Employers

The Title IV–D agency shall maintain a toll-free telephone number at which personnel are available during normal business hours to answer questions from employers responsible for withholding child support. The Title IV–D agency shall inform employers about the toll-free telephone number.

Added by Acts 1999, 76th Leg., ch. 556, § 54, eff. Sept. 1, 1999.

### § 231.121. Availability of Brochures

The Title IV-D agency shall ensure that all Title IV-D brochures published by the agency are available to the public at courthouses where family law cases are heard in the state.

Added by Acts 2001, 77th Leg., ch. 141, § 2, eff. Sept. 1, 2001.

### § 231.1211. Informational Materials on Standard Possession Order

(a) The Title IV–D agency shall create informational materials that describe the possession schedule under the standard possession order under Subchapter F, Chapter 153, including any alternate schedules or elections available to conservators.

(b) The Title IV–D agency shall make the informational materials described by Subsection (a) available on the agency's Internet website and distribute printed copies of those materials on request.

Added by Acts 2021, 87th Leg., ch. 896 (H.B. 3203), § 3, eff. Sept. 1, 2021; Acts 2021, 87th Leg., ch. 967 (S.B. 1936), § 3, eff. Sept. 1, 2021.

Sections 4 and 5 of Acts 2021, 87th Leg., ch. 896 (H.B. 3203) provide:

"Sec. 4. The enactment of this Act does not constitute a material and substantial change of circumstances sufficient to warrant modification of a court order or portion of a decree that provides for the possession of or access to a child rendered before the effective date [Sept. 1, 2021] of this Act.

"Sec. 5. The change in law made by this Act applies to a suit affecting the parent-child relationship that is pending in a trial court on the effective date of this Act or that is filed on or after the effective date of this Act."

Sections 4 and 5 of Acts 2021, 87th Leg., ch. 967 (S.B. 1936) provide:

"Sec. 4. The enactment of this Act does not constitute a material and substantial change of circumstances sufficient to warrant modification of a court order or portion of a decree that provides for the possession of or access to a child rendered before the effective date [Sept. 1, 2021] of this Act."

""Sec. 5. The change in law made by this Act applies to a suit affecting the parent-child relationship that is pending in a trial court on the effective date of this Act or that is filed on or after the effective date of this Act."

### § 231.122. Monitoring Child Support Cases; Enforcement

The Title IV–D agency shall monitor each Title IV–D case from the date the agency begins providing services on the case. If a child support obligor in a Title IV–D case becomes more than 60 days delinquent in paying child support, the Title IV–D agency shall expedite the commencement of an action to enforce the child support order.

Added by Acts 2005, 79th Leg., ch. 268, § 1.10, eff. Sept. 1, 2005.

### § 231.123. Cooperation with Volunteer Income Tax Assistance Programs

(a) In order to maximize the amount of any tax refund to which an obligor may be entitled and which may be applied to child support, medical support, and dental support obligations, the Title IV–D agency shall cooperate with volunteer income tax assistance programs in the state in informing obligors of the availability of the programs.

(b) The Title IV–D agency shall publicize the services of the volunteer income tax assistance programs by distributing printed materials regarding the programs and by placing information regarding the programs on the agency's Internet website.

(c) The Title IV–D agency is not responsible for producing or paying the costs of producing the printed materials distributed in accordance with Subsection (b).

Added by Acts 2005, 79th Leg., ch. 925, § 1, eff. Sept. 1, 2005. Redesignated from V.T.C.A., Family Code § 231.122 by Acts 2007, 80th Leg., ch. 921, § 17.001(22), eff. Sept. 1, 2007. Amended by Acts 2015, 84th Leg., ch. 1150 (S.B. 550), § 45, eff. Sept. 1, 2018.

### § 231.124. Child Support Arrearages Payment Incentive Program

(a) The Title IV–D agency may establish and administer a payment incentive program to promote payment by obligors who are delinquent in satisfying child support arrearages assigned to the Title IV–D agency under Section 231.104(a).

(b) A program established under this section must provide to a participating obligor a credit for every dollar amount paid by the obligor on interest and arrearages balances during each month of the obligor's voluntary enrollment in the program. In establishing a program under this section, the Title IV–D agency by rule must prescribe:

(1) criteria for a child support obligor's initial eligibility to participate in the program;

(2) the conditions for a child support obligor's continued participation in the program;

(3) procedures for enrollment in the program; and

(4) the terms of the financial incentives to be offered under the program.

(c) The Title IV–D agency shall provide eligible obligors with notice of the program and enrollment instructions.

Added by Acts 2011, 82nd Leg., ch. 508 (H.B. 1674), § 13, eff. Sept. 1, 2011.

## SUBCHAPTER C. PAYMENT OF FEES AND COSTS

### § 231.201. Definitions

In this subchapter:

(1) "Federal share" means the portion of allowable expenses for fees and other costs that will be reimbursed by the federal government under federal law and regulations regarding the administration of the Title IV–D program.

(2) "State share" means the portion of allowable expenses for fees and other costs that remain after receipt of the federal share of reimbursement and that is to be reimbursed by the state or may be contributed by certified public expenditure by a county.

Added by Acts 1995, 74th Leg., ch. 20, § 1, eff. April 20, 1995.

### § 231.202. Authorized Costs and Fees in Title IV–D Cases

*Text of § 231.202 effective until Jan. 1, 2022. See, also, § 231.202 effective Jan. 1, 2022.*

In a Title IV–D case filed under this title, including a case filed under Chapter 159, the Title IV–D agency shall pay only the following costs and fees:

(1) filing fees and fees for issuance and service of process as provided by Chapter 110 of this code and by Sections 51.317(b)(1), (2), and (3) and (b–1), 51.318(b)(2), and 51.319(2), Government Code;

(2) fees for transfer as provided by Chapter 110;

(3) fees for the issuance and delivery of orders and writs of income withholding in the amounts provided by Chapter 110;

(4) the fee for services provided by sheriffs and constables, including:

(A) a fee authorized under Section 118.131, Local Government Code, for serving each item of process to each individual on whom service is required, including service by certified or registered mail; and

(B) a fee authorized under Section 157.103(b) for serving a capias;

(5) the fee for filing an administrative writ of withholding under Section 158.503(d);

(6) the fee for issuance of a subpoena as provided by Section 51.318(b)(1), Government Code; and

(7) a fee authorized by Section 72.031, Government Code, for the electronic filing of documents with a clerk.

Added by Acts 1995, 74th Leg., ch. 20, § 1, eff. April 20, 1995. Amended by Acts 1995, 74th Leg., ch. 341, § 1.04, eff. Sept. 1, 1995; Acts 1997, 75th Leg., ch. 165, § 7.21(a), eff. Sept. 1, 1997; Acts 2001, 77th Leg., ch. 116, § 2, eff. Sept. 1, 2001; Acts 2003, 78th Leg., ch. 1217, § 1, eff. Sept. 1, 2003; Acts 2007, 80th Leg., ch. 972, § 49, eff. Sept. 1, 2007; Acts 2009, 81st Leg., ch. 767, § 28, eff. Sept. 1, 2009; Acts 2013, 83rd Leg., ch. 1290 (H.B. 2302), § 15, eff. Sept. 1, 2013.

### § 231.202. Authorized Costs and Fees in Title IV–D Cases

*Text of § 231.202 effective Jan. 1, 2022. See, also, § 231.202 effective until Jan. 1, 2022.*

In a Title IV–D case filed under this title, including a case filed under Chapter 159, the Title IV–D agency shall pay only the following costs and fees:

(1) filing fees and fees for issuance and service of process as provided by Chapter 110 of this code and by Sections 51.318(b)(2) and 51.319(2), Government Code;

(2) fees for transfer as provided by Chapter 110;

(3) fees for the issuance and delivery of orders and writs of income withholding in the amounts provided by Chapter 110;

(4) the fee for services provided by sheriffs and constables, including:

(A) a fee authorized under Section 118.131, Local Government Code, for serving each item of process to each individual on whom service is required, including service by certified or registered mail; and

(B) a fee authorized under Section 157.103(b) for serving a capias;

(5) the fee for filing an administrative writ of withholding under Section 158.503(d); and

(6) the fee for issuance of a subpoena as provided by Section 51.318(b)(1), Government Code.

Added by Acts 1995, 74th Leg., ch. 20, § 1, eff. April 20, 1995. Amended by Acts 1995, 74th Leg., ch. 341, § 1.04, eff. Sept. 1, 1995; Acts 1997, 75th Leg., ch. 165, § 7.21(a), eff. Sept. 1, 1997; Acts 2001, 77th Leg., ch. 116, § 2, eff. Sept. 1, 2001; Acts 2003, 78th Leg., ch. 1217, § 1, eff. Sept. 1, 2003; Acts 2007, 80th Leg., ch. 972, § 49, eff. Sept. 1, 2007; Acts 2009, 81st Leg., ch. 767, § 28, eff. Sept. 1, 2009; Acts 2013, 83rd Leg., ch. 1290 (H.B. 2302), § 15, eff. Sept. 1, 2013; Acts 2021, 87th Leg., ch. 472 (S.B. 41), § 4.05, eff. Jan. 1, 2022.

### § 231.2025. Contingency Fees

The Title IV-D agency may pay a contingency fee in a contract or agreement between the agency and a private agency or individual authorized under Section 231.002(c).

Added by Acts 1997, 75th Leg., ch. 420, § 19, eff. Sept. 1, 1997.

### § 231.203. State Exemption from Bond Not Affected

This subchapter does not affect, nor is this subchapter affected by, the exemption from bond provided by Section 6.001, Civil Practice and Remedies Code.

Added by Acts 1995, 74th Leg., ch. 20, § 1, eff. April 20, 1995.

### § 231.204. Prohibited Fees in Title IV–D Cases

Except as provided by this subchapter, an appellate court, a clerk of an appellate court, a district or county clerk, sheriff, constable, or other government officer or employee may not charge the Title IV–D agency or a private attorney or political subdivision that has entered into a contract to provide Title IV–D services any fees or other amounts otherwise imposed by law for services rendered in, or in connection with, a Title IV–D case, including:

(1) a fee payable to a district clerk for:

(A) performing services related to the estates of deceased persons or minors;

(B) certifying copies; or

(C) comparing copies to originals;

(2) a court reporter fee, except as provided by Section 231.209;

(3) a judicial fund fee;

(4) a fee for a child support registry, enforcement office, or domestic relations office;

(5) a fee for alternative dispute resolution services;

(6) a filing fee or other costs payable to a clerk of an appellate court; and

(7) a statewide electronic filing system fund fee.

Added by Acts 1995, 74th Leg., ch. 20, § 1, eff. April 20, 1995. Amended by Acts 1999, 76th Leg., ch. 556, § 55, eff. Sept. 1, 1999; Acts 2001, 77th Leg., ch. 1023, § 55, eff. Sept. 1, 2001; Acts 2013, 83rd Leg., ch. 742 (S.B. 355), § 10, eff. Sept. 1, 2013; Acts 2013, 83rd Leg., ch. 1290 (H.B. 2302), § 16, eff. Sept. 1, 2013.

### § 231.205. Limitations on Liability of Attorney General for Authorized Fees and Costs

(a) The Title IV–D agency is liable for a fee or cost under this subchapter only to the extent that an express, specific appropriation is made to the agency exclusively for that purpose. To the extent that state funds are not available, the amount of costs and fees that are not reimbursed by the federal government and that represent the state share shall be paid by certified public expenditure by the county through the clerk of the court, sheriff, or constable. This section does not prohibit the agency from spending other funds appropriated for child support enforcement to provide the initial expenditures necessary to qualify for the federal share.

(b) The Title IV–D agency is liable for the payment of the federal share of reimbursement for fees and costs under this subchapter only to the extent that the federal share is received, and if an amount is paid by the agency and that amount is disallowed by the federal government or the federal share is not otherwise received, the clerk of the court, sheriff, or constable to whom the payment was made shall return the amount to the agency not later than the 30th day after the date on which notice is given by the agency.

Added by Acts 1995, 74th Leg., ch. 20, § 1, eff. April 20, 1995.

### § 231.206. Restriction on Fees for Child Support or Registry Services in Title IV–D Cases

A district clerk, a county child support registry or enforcement office, or a domestic relations office may not assess or collect fees for processing child support payments or for child support services from the Title IV–D agency, a managing conservator, or a possessory conservator in a Title IV–D case, except as provided by this subchapter.

Added by Acts 1995, 74th Leg., ch. 20, § 1, eff. April 20, 1995.

### § 231.207. Method of Billing for Allowable Fees

(a) To be entitled to reimbursement under this subchapter, the clerk of the court, sheriff, or constable must submit one monthly billing to the Title IV–D agency.

(b) The monthly billing must be in the form and manner prescribed by the Title IV–D agency and be approved by the clerk, sheriff, or constable.

Added by Acts 1995, 74th Leg., ch. 20, § 1, eff. April 20, 1995.

### § 231.208. Agreements for Reimbursement in Lieu of Fees

(a) The Title IV–D agency and a qualified county may enter into a written agreement under which reimbursement for salaries and certain other actual costs incurred by the clerk, sheriff, or constable in Title IV–D cases is provided to the county.

(b) A county may not enter into an agreement for reimbursement under this section unless the clerk, sheriff, or constable providing service has at least two full-time employees each devoted exclusively to providing services in Title IV–D cases.

(c) Reimbursement made under this section is in lieu of all costs and fees provided by this subchapter.

Added by Acts 1995, 74th Leg., ch. 20, § 1, eff. April 20, 1995.

### § 231.209. Payment for Services Not Affected by This Subchapter

Without regard to this subchapter and specifically Section 231.205, the Title IV–D agency may pay the costs for:

(1) the services of an official court reporter for the preparation of statements of facts;

(2) the costs for the publication of citation served by publication; and

(3) mileage or other reasonable travel costs incurred by a sheriff or constable when traveling out of the county to execute an outstanding warrant or capias, to be reimbursed at a rate not to exceed the rate provided for mileage or other costs incurred by state employees in the General Appropriations Act.

Added by Acts 1995, 74th Leg., ch. 20, § 1, eff. April 20, 1995. Amended by Acts 1995, 74th Leg., ch. 341, § 1.05, eff. Sept. 1, 1995.

### § 231.210. Authority to Pay Litigation Expenses

(a) The Title IV–D agency may pay all fees, expenses, costs, and bills necessary to secure evidence and to take the testimony of a witness, including advance payments or purchases for transportation, lodging, meals, and incidental expenses of custodians of evidence or witnesses whose transportation is necessary and proper for the production of evidence or the taking of testimony in a Title IV–D case.

(b) In making payments under this section, the Title IV–D agency shall present vouchers to the comptroller that have been sworn to by the custodian or witness and approved by the agency. The voucher shall be sufficient to authorize payment without the necessity of a written contract.

(c) The Title IV–D agency may directly pay a commercial transportation company or commercial lodging establishment for the expense of transportation or lodging of a custodian or witness.

Added by Acts 1995, 74th Leg., ch. 20, § 1, eff. April 20, 1995.

### § 231.211. Award of Cost Against Nonprevailing Party in Title IV–D Case

(a) At the conclusion of a Title IV–D case, the court may assess attorney's fees and all court costs as authorized by law against the nonprevailing party, except that the court may not assess those amounts against the Title IV–D agency or a private attorney or political subdivision that has entered into a contract under this chapter or any party to whom the agency has provided services under this chapter. Such fees and costs may not exceed reasonable and necessary costs as determined by the court.

(b) The clerk of the court may take any action necessary to collect any fees or costs assessed under this section.

Added by Acts 1995, 74th Leg., ch. 20, § 1, eff. April 20, 1995.

## SUBCHAPTER D. LOCATION OF PARENTS AND RESOURCES

### § 231.301. Title IV–D Parent Locator Services

(a) The parent locator service conducted by the Title IV–D agency shall be used to obtain information for:

(1) child support establishment and enforcement purposes regarding the identity, social security number, location, employer and employment benefits, income, and assets or debts of any individual under an obligation to pay child support, medical support, or dental support or to whom a support obligation is owed; or

(2) the establishment of paternity.

(b) As authorized by federal law, the following persons may receive information under this section:

(1) a person or entity that contracts with the Title IV–D agency to provide services authorized under Title IV–D or an employee of the Title IV–D agency;

(2) an attorney who has the duty or authority, by law, to enforce an order for possession of or access to a child;

(3) a court, or an agent of the court, having jurisdiction to render or enforce an order for possession of or access to a child;

(4) the resident parent, legal guardian, attorney, or agent of a child who is not receiving public assistance; and

(5) a state agency that administers a program operated under a state plan as provided by 42 U.S.C. Section 653(c).

Added by Acts 1995, 74th Leg., ch. 20, § 1, eff. April 20, 1995. Amended by Acts 1997, 75th Leg., ch. 911, § 76, eff. Sept. 1, 1997; Acts 1999, 76th Leg., ch. 556, § 56, eff. Sept. 1, 1999; Acts 2015, 84th Leg., ch. 1150 (S.B. 550), § 46, eff. Sept. 1, 2018.

### § 231.302. Information to Assist in Location of Persons or Property

(a) The Title IV-D agency of this or another state may request and obtain information relating to the identity, location, employment, compensation, benefits, income, and property holdings or other assets of any person from a state or local government agency, private company, institution, or other entity as necessary to establish, modify, or enforce a support order.

(b) A government agency, private company, institution, or other entity shall provide the information requested under Subsection (a) directly to the Title IV–D agency not later than the seventh day after the request to obtain information is received, without the requirement of payment of a fee for the information, and shall, subject to safeguards on privacy and information security, provide the information in the most efficient and expeditious manner available, including electronic or automated transfer and interface. Any individual or entity disclosing information under this section in response to a request from a Title IV–D agency may not be held liable in any civil action or proceeding to any person for the disclosure of information under this subsection.

(c) Except as provided by Subsection (c–1) or (c–2), to assist in the administration of laws relating to child support enforcement under Parts A and D of Title IV of the federal Social Security Act (42 U.S.C. Section 601 et seq. and 42 U.S.C. Section 651 et seq.):

(1) each licensing authority shall request and each applicant for a license shall provide the applicant's social security number;

(2) each agency administering a contract that provides for a payment of state funds shall request and each individual or entity bidding on a state contract shall provide the individual's or entity's social security number as required by Section 231.006; and

(3) each agency administering a state-funded grant or loan program shall request and each applicant for a grant or loan shall provide the applicant's social security number as required by Section 231.006.

(c–1) For purposes of issuing a license to carry a concealed handgun under Subchapter H, Chapter 411, Government Code,[1] the Department of Public Safety is not required to request, and an applicant is not required to provide, the applicant's social security number.

(c–2) For purposes of issuing a fishing or hunting license, the Texas Parks and Wildlife Department is not required to request, and an applicant is not required to provide, the applicant's social security number if the applicant is 13 years of age or younger.

(d) This section does not limit the right of an agency or licensing authority to collect and use a social security number under another provision of law.

(e) Except as provided by Subsection (d), a social security number provided under this section is confidential and may be disclosed only for the purposes of responding to a request for information from an agency operating under the provisions of Part A or D of Title IV of the federal Social Security Act (42 U.S.C. Sections 601 et seq. and 651 et seq).

(f) Information collected by the Title IV-D agency under this section may be used only for child support purposes.

(g) In this section, "licensing authority" has the meaning assigned by Section 232.001.

Added by Acts 1995, 74th Leg., ch. 20, § 1, eff. April 20, 1995. Amended by Acts 1995, 74th Leg., ch. 751, § 84, eff. Sept. 1, 1995; Acts 1997, 75th Leg., ch. 420, § 20, eff. Sept. 1, 1997; Acts 1997, 75th Leg., ch. 911, § 77, eff. Sept. 1, 1997; Acts 1999, 76th Leg., ch. 62, § 6.28, eff. Sept. 1, 1999; Acts 2001, 77th Leg., ch. 1023, § 56, eff. Sept. 1, 2001; Acts 2013, 83rd Leg., ch. 665 (H.B. 1349), § 1, eff. Jan. 1, 2014; Acts 2015, 84th Leg., ch. 153 (H.B. 821), § 1, eff. Sept. 1, 2015; Acts 2015, 84th Leg., ch. 963 (S.B. 1727), § 4, eff. Sept. 1, 2015.

[1] V.T.C.A., Government Code § 411.171 et seq.

### § 231.303. Title IV-D Administrative Subpoena

(a) The Title IV-D agency of this state or another state may issue an administrative subpoena to any individual or private or public entity in this state to furnish information necessary to carry out the purposes of child support enforcement under 42 U.S.C. Section 651 et seq. or this chapter.

(b) An individual or entity receiving an administrative subpoena under this section shall comply with the subpoena. The Title IV-D agency may impose a fine in an amount not to exceed $500 on an individual or entity that fails without good cause to comply with an administrative subpoena. An alleged or presumed father or a parent who fails to comply with a subpoena without good cause may also be subject to license suspension under Chapter 232.

(c) A court may compel compliance with an administrative subpoena and with any administrative fine for failure to comply with the subpoena and may award attorney's fees and costs to the Title IV-D agency in enforcing an administrative subpoena on proof that an individual or organization failed without good cause to comply with the subpoena.

(d) An individual or organization may not be liable in a civil action or proceeding for disclosing financial or other information to a Title IV-D agency under this section. The Title IV-D agency may disclose information in a financial record obtained from a financial institution only to the extent necessary:

(1) to establish, modify, or enforce a child support obligation; or

(2) to comply with Section 233.001, as added by Chapter 420, Acts of the 75th Legislature, Regular Session, 1997.

Added by Acts 1995, 74th Leg., ch. 20, § 1, eff. April 20, 1995. Amended by Acts 1997, 75th Leg., ch. 911, § 78, eff. Sept. 1, 1997; Acts 1999, 76th Leg., ch. 859, § 5, eff. Sept. 1, 1999.

### § 231.304. Repealed by Acts 1997, 75th Leg., ch. 911, § 97(b), eff. October 1, 1998

### § 231.305. Memorandum of Understanding on Child Support for Children Receiving Public Assistance

(a) The Title IV–D agency and the Texas Department of Human Services by rule shall adopt a memorandum of understanding governing the establishment and enforcement of court-ordered child support in cases involving children who receive financial assistance under Chapter 31, Human Resources Code.

The memorandum shall require the agency and the department to:

(1) develop procedures to ensure that the information the department is required to collect to establish and enforce child support:

(A) is collected from the person applying to receive the financial assistance at the time the application is filed;

(B) is accurate and complete when the department forwards the information to the agency;

(C) is not information previously reported to the agency; and

(D) is forwarded to the agency in an expeditious manner;

(2) develop procedures to ensure that the agency does not duplicate the efforts of the department in gathering necessary information;

(3) clarify each agency's responsibilities in the establishment and enforcement of child support;

(4) develop guidelines for use by eligibility workers and child support enforcement officers in obtaining from an applicant the information required to establish and enforce child support for that child;

(5) develop training programs for appropriate department personnel to enhance the collection of information for child support enforcement;

(6) develop a standard time, not to exceed 30 days, for the department to initiate a sanction on request from the agency;

(7) develop procedures for agency participation in department appeal hearings relating to noncompliance sanctions;

(8) develop performance measures regarding the timeliness and the number of sanctions resulting from agency requests for noncompliance sanctions; and

(9) prescribe:

(A) the time in which the department is required to forward information under Subdivision (1)(D); and

(B) what constitutes complete information under Subdivision (1)(B).

(b) The Title IV–D agency and the Texas Department of Human Services shall review and renew or modify the memorandum not later than January 1 of each even-numbered year.

Added by Acts 1995, 74th Leg., ch. 341, § 1.07, eff. Sept. 1, 1995. Amended by Acts 1999, 76th Leg., ch. 556, § 57, eff. Sept. 1, 1999.

### § 231.306. Maximizing Medical Support and Dental Support Establishment and Collection by the Title IV–D Agency

(a) On the installation of an automated child support enforcement system, the Title IV–D agency is strongly encouraged to:

(1) maximize the collection of medical support and dental support; and

(2) establish cash medical support orders for children eligible for medical assistance under the state Medicaid program for whom private insurance coverage is not available.

(b) In this section:

(1) "Medical support" has the meaning assigned by Section 101.020.

(2) "Dental support" has the meaning assigned by Section 101.0095.

Added by Acts 1995, 74th Leg., ch. 341, § 2.03, eff. Sept. 1, 1995. Amended by Acts 2015, 84th Leg., ch. 1150 (S.B. 550), § 47, eff. Sept. 1, 2018.

### § 231.307. Financial Institution Data Matches

(a) The Title IV-D agency shall develop a system meeting the requirements of federal law (42 U.S.C. Sections 666(a)(4) and (17)) for the exchange of data with financial institutions doing business in the state to identify an account of an obligor owing past-due child support and to enforce support obligations against the obligor, including the imposition of a lien and a levy and execution on an obligor's assets held in financial institutions as required by federal law (42 U.S.C. Section 666(c)(1)(G)).

(b) The Title IV-D agency by rule shall establish procedures for data matches authorized under this section.

(c) The Title IV–D agency may enter into an agreement with one or more states to create a consortium for data matches authorized under this section. The Title IV–D agency may contract with a vendor selected by the consortium to perform data matches with financial institutions.

(d) A financial institution providing information or responding to a notice of child support lien or levy provided under Subchapter G,[1] Chapter 157, or otherwise acting in good faith to comply with the Title IV–D agency's procedures under this section may not be liable under any federal or state law for any damages that arise from those acts.

(e) In this section:

(1) "Financial institution" has the meaning assigned by Section 157.311; and

(2) "Account" has the meaning assigned by Section 157.311.

(f) A financial institution participating in data matches authorized by this section may provide the Title IV-D agency an address for the purpose of service of notices or process required in actions under this section or Subchapter G, Chapter 157.

(g) This section does not apply to an insurer subject to the reporting requirements under Section 231.015.

Added by Acts 1997, 75th Leg., ch. 911, § 79, eff. Sept. 1, 1997. Amended by Acts 1999, 76th Leg., ch. 556, § 58, eff. Sept. 1, 1999; Acts 2001, 77th Leg., ch. 1023, § 57, eff. Sept. 1, 2001; Acts 2011, 82nd Leg., ch. 508 (H.B. 1674), § 14, eff. Sept. 1, 2011.

[1] V.T.C.A., Family Code § 157.311 et seq.

### § 231.308. Public Identification of Certain Obligors

(a) The Title IV-D agency shall develop a program to identify publicly certain child support obligors who are delinquent in the payment of child support. The program shall include the displaying of photographs and profiles of obligors in public and private locations. The Title IV-D agency shall use posters, the news media, and other cost-effective methods to display photographs and profiles of certain obligors who are in arrears in paying child support. The Title IV-D agency shall divide the state into at least six regions for local identification of certain child support obligors who are delinquent in the payment of child support.

(b) The Title IV-D agency may not disclose information under this section that is by law required to remain confidential.

Added by Acts 1997, 75th Leg., ch. 420, § 21, eff. Sept. 1, 1997.

### § 231.309. Rewards for Information

(a) The Title IV-D agency may offer a reward to an individual who provides information to the agency that leads to the collection of child support owed by an obligor who is delinquent in paying support.

(b) The Title IV-D agency shall adopt rules providing for the amounts of rewards offered under this section and the circumstances under which an individual providing information described in Subsection (a) is entitled to receive a reward.

(c) A reward paid under this section shall be paid from the child support retained collections account.

Added by Acts 1997, 75th Leg., ch. 420, § 21, eff. Sept. 1, 1997.

### § 231.310. Repealed by Acts 2007, 80th Leg., ch. 972, § 65(4), eff. Sept. 1, 2007.

## SUBCHAPTER E. CHILD SUPPORT REVIEW PROCESS TO ESTABLISH OR ENFORCE SUPPORT OBLIGATIONS [REDESIGNATED]

*Acts 1997, 75th Leg., ch. 911, § 80 redesignated and amended V.T.C.A., Family Code Chapter 231, Subchapter E, consisting of §§ 231.401 to 231.429, to be V.T.C.A., Family Code Chapter 233.*

### §§ 231.401 to 231.429. Redesignated as V.T.C.A., Family Code §§ 233.001 to 233.029 by Acts 1997, 75th Leg., ch. 911, § 80, eff. Sept. 1, 1997

### §§ 231.430, 231.431. Repealed by Acts 1997, 75th Leg., ch. 911, § 97(a), eff. Sept. 1, 1997

## CHAPTER 232. SUSPENSION OF LICENSE

**Section**



### § 232.001. Definitions

In this chapter:

(1) "License" means a license, certificate, registration, permit, or other authorization that:

(A) is issued by a licensing authority;

(B) is subject before expiration to renewal, suspension, revocation, forfeiture, or termination by a licensing authority; and

(C) a person must obtain[1] to:

(i) practice or engage in a particular business, occupation, or profession;

(ii) operate a motor vehicle on a public highway in this state; or

(iii) engage in any other regulated activity, including hunting, fishing, or other recreational activity for which a license or permit is required.

(2) "Licensing authority" means a department, commission, board, office, or other agency of the state or a political subdivision of the state that issues or renews a license or that otherwise has authority to suspend or refuse to renew a license.

(3) "Order suspending license" means an order issued by the Title IV–D agency or a court directing a licensing authority to suspend or refuse to renew a license.

(3–a) "Renewal" means any instance when a licensing authority:

(A) renews, extends, recertifies, or reissues a license; or

(B) periodically certifies a licensee to be in good standing with the licensing authority based on the required payment of fees or dues or the performance of some other mandated action or activity.

(4) "Subpoena" means a judicial or administrative subpoena issued in a parentage determination or child support proceeding under this title.

Added by Acts 1995, 74th Leg., ch. 655, § 5.03, eff. Sept. 1, 1995; Acts 1995, 74th Leg., ch. 751, § 85, eff. Sept. 1, 1995. Amended by Acts 1997, 75th Leg., ch. 911, § 82, eff. Sept. 1, 1997; Acts 2001, 77th Leg., ch. 1023, § 58, eff. Sept. 1, 2001; Acts 2007, 80th Leg., ch. 972, § 50, eff. Sept. 1, 2007; Acts 2015, 84th Leg., ch. 859 (S.B. 1726), § 8, eff. Sept. 1, 2015.

[1] Acts 1995, 74th Leg., ch. 655, § 5.03 here read "is necessary for a person" in lieu of "a person must obtain".

### § 232.002. Licensing Authorities Subject to Chapter

Unless otherwise restricted or exempted, all licensing authorities are subject to this chapter.

Added by Acts 1995, 74th Leg., ch. 655, § 5.03, eff. Sept. 1, 1995; Acts 1995, 74th Leg., ch. 751, § 85, eff. Sept. 1, 1995. Amended by Acts 1997, 75th Leg., ch. 165, § 7.22, eff. Sept. 1, 1997; Acts 1997, 75th Leg., ch. 1280, § 1.02, eff. Sept. 1, 1997; Acts 1997, 75th Leg., ch. 1288, § 2, eff. Sept. 1, 1997; Acts 1999, 76th Leg., ch. 1254, § 4, eff. Sept. 1, 1999; Acts 1999, 76th Leg., ch. 1477, § 23, eff. Sept. 1, 1999; Acts 2001, 77th Leg., ch. 394, § 2, eff. Sept. 1, 2001; Acts 2003, 78th Leg., ch. 553, § 2.003, eff. Feb. 1, 2004; Acts 2005, 79th Leg., ch. 798, § 4.01, eff. Sept. 1, 2005; Acts 2007, 80th Leg., ch. 889, § 53, eff. Sept. 1, 2007; Acts 2007, 80th Leg., ch. 890, § 2.02, eff. Sept. 1, 2007; Acts 2007, 80th Leg., ch. 921, § 6.001, eff. Sept. 1, 2007; Acts 2007, 80th Leg., ch. 972, § 51, eff. Sept. 1, 2007.

### § 232.0021. Application of Chapter to Texas Lottery Commission

With respect to the Texas Lottery Commission, this chapter applies only to a lottery ticket sales agent license issued under Chapter 466, Government Code.

Added by Acts 2001, 77th Leg., ch. 394, § 3, eff. Sept. 1, 2001.

### § 232.0022. Suspension or Nonrenewal of Motor Vehicle Registration

(a) The Texas Department of Motor Vehicles is the appropriate licensing authority for suspension or nonrenewal of a motor vehicle registration under this chapter.

(b) The suspension or nonrenewal of a motor vehicle registration under this chapter does not:

(1) encumber the title to the motor vehicle or otherwise affect the transfer of the title to the vehicle; or

(2) affect the sale, purchase, or registration of the motor vehicle by a person who holds a general distinguishing number issued under Chapter 503, Transportation Code.

Added by Acts 2007, 80th Leg., ch. 972, § 52, eff. Sept. 1, 2007. Amended by Acts 2009, 81st Leg., ch. 933, § 3C.02, eff. Sept. 1, 2009.

### § 232.003. Suspension of License

(a) A court or the Title IV-D agency may issue an order suspending a license as provided by this chapter if an individual who is an obligor:

(1) owes overdue child support in an amount equal to or greater than the total support due for three months under a support order;

(2) has been provided an opportunity to make payments toward the overdue child support under a court-ordered or agreed repayment schedule; and

(3) has failed to comply with the repayment schedule.

(b) A court or the Title IV-D agency may issue an order suspending a license as provided by this chapter if a parent or alleged parent has failed, after receiving appropriate notice, to comply with a subpoena.

(c) A court may issue an order suspending license as provided by this chapter for an individual for whom a court has rendered an enforcement order under Chapter 157 finding that the individual has failed to comply with the terms of a court order providing for the possession of or access to a child.

Added by Acts 1995, 74th Leg., ch. 655, § 5.03, eff. Sept. 1, 1995; Acts 1995, 74th Leg., ch. 751, § 85, eff. Sept. 1, 1995; Amended by Acts 1997, 75th Leg., ch. 420, §§ 22, 23, eff. Sept. 1, 1997; Acts 1997, 75th Leg., ch. 911, § 83, eff. Sept. 1, 1997; Acts 1999, 76th Leg., ch. 556, § 59, eff. Sept. 1, 1999; Acts 2001, 77th Leg., ch. 724, § 2, eff. Sept. 1, 2001; Acts 2001, 77th Leg., ch. 1023, § 59, eff. Sept. 1, 2001.

### § 232.004. Petition for Suspension of License

(a) A child support agency or obligee may file a petition to suspend, as provided by this chapter, a license of an obligor who has an arrearage equal to or greater than the total support due for three months under a support order.

(b) In a Title IV–D case, the petition shall be filed with the Title IV–D agency, the court of continuing jurisdiction, or the tribunal in which a child support order has been registered under Chapter 159. The tribunal in which the petition is filed obtains jurisdiction over the matter.

(c) In a case other than a Title IV-D case, the petition shall be filed in the court of continuing jurisdiction or the court in which a child support order has been registered under Chapter 159.

(d) A proceeding in a case filed with the Title IV-D agency under this chapter is governed by the contested case provisions of Chapter 2001, Government Code, except that Section 2001.054 does not apply to the proceeding. The director of the Title IV-D agency or the director's designee may render a final decision in a contested case proceeding under this chapter.

Added by Acts 1995, 74th Leg., ch. 655, § 5.03, eff. Sept. 1, 1995; Acts 1995, 74th Leg., ch. 751, § 85, eff. Sept. 1, 1995. Amended by Acts 1997, 75th Leg., ch. 420, § 24, eff. Sept. 1, 1997; Acts 1997, 75th Leg., ch. 911, § 84, eff. Sept. 1, 1997; Acts 1999, 76th Leg., ch. 556, § 60, eff. Sept. 1, 1999; Acts 2007, 80th Leg., ch. 972, § 53, eff. Sept. 1, 2007.

### § 232.005. Contents of Petition

(a) A petition under this chapter must state that license suspension is required under Section 232.003 and allege:

(1) the name and, if known, social security number of the individual;

(2) the name of the licensing authority that issued a license the individual is believed to hold; and

(3) the amount of arrearages owed under the child support order or the facts associated with the individual's failure to comply with:

(A) a subpoena; or

(B) the terms of a court order providing for the possession of or access to a child.

(b) A petition under this chapter may include as an attachment a copy of:

(1) the record of child support payments maintained by the Title IV-D registry or local registry;

(2) the subpoena with which the individual has failed to comply, together with proof of service of the subpoena; or

(3) with respect to a petition for suspension under Section 232.003(c):

(A) the enforcement order rendered under Chapter 157 describing the manner in which the individual was found to have not complied with the terms of a court order providing for the possession of or access to a child; and

(B) the court order containing the provisions that the individual was found to have violated.

Added by Acts 1995, 74th Leg., ch. 655, § 5.03, eff. Sept. 1, 1995; Acts 1995, 74th Leg., ch. 751, § 85, eff. Sept. 1, 1995. Amended by Acts 1997, 75th Leg., ch. 911, § 85, eff. Sept. 1, 1997; Acts 2001, 77th Leg., ch. 724, § 3, eff. Sept. 1, 2001; Acts 2001, 77th Leg., ch. 1023, § 60, eff. Sept. 1, 2001; Acts 2009, 81st Leg., ch. 767, § 29, eff. June 19, 2009.

### § 232.006. Notice

(a) On the filing of a petition under Section 232.004, the clerk of the court or the Title IV-D agency shall deliver to the individual:

(1) notice of the individual's right to a hearing before the court or agency;

(2) notice of the deadline for requesting a hearing; and

(3) a hearing request form if the proceeding is in a Title IV-D case.

(b) Notice under this section may be served:

(1) if the party has been ordered under Chapter 105 to provide the court and registry with the party's current mailing address, by mailing a copy of the notice to the respondent, together with a copy of the petition, by first class mail to the last mailing address of the respondent on file with the court and the state case registry; or

(2) as in civil cases generally.

(c) The notice must contain the following prominently displayed statement in boldfaced type, capital letters, or underlined:

"AN ACTION TO SUSPEND ONE OR MORE LICENSES ISSUED TO YOU HAS BEEN FILED AS PROVIDED BY CHAPTER 232, TEXAS FAMI-

LY CODE. YOU MAY EMPLOY AN ATTORNEY TO REPRESENT YOU IN THIS ACTION. IF YOU OR YOUR ATTORNEY DO NOT REQUEST A HEARING BEFORE THE 21ST DAY AFTER THE DATE OF SERVICE OF THIS NOTICE, AN ORDER SUSPENDING YOUR LICENSE MAY BE RENDERED."

Added by Acts 1995, 74th Leg., ch. 655, § 5.03, eff. Sept. 1, 1995; Acts 1995, 74th Leg., ch. 751, § 85, eff. Sept. 1, 1995. Amended by Acts 1997, 75th Leg., ch. 911, § 86, eff. Sept. 1, 1997; Acts 1997, 75th Leg., ch. 976, § 7, eff. Sept. 1, 1997; Acts 1999, 76th Leg., ch. 178, § 11, eff. Aug. 30, 1999; Acts 2007, 80th Leg., ch. 972, § 54, eff. Sept. 1, 2007.

### § 232.007. Hearing on Petition to Suspend License

(a) A request for a hearing and motion to stay suspension must be filed with the court or Title IV-D agency by the individual not later than the 20th day after the date of service of the notice under Section 232.006.

(b) If a request for a hearing is filed, the court or Title IV-D agency shall:

(1) promptly schedule a hearing;

(2) notify each party of the date, time, and location of the hearing; and

(3) stay suspension pending the hearing.

(c) In a case involving support arrearages, a record of child support payments made by the Title IV-D agency or a local registry is evidence of whether the payments were made. A copy of the record appearing regular on its face shall be admitted as evidence at a hearing under this chapter, including a hearing on a motion to revoke a stay. Either party may offer controverting evidence.

(d) In a case in which an individual has failed to comply with a subpoena, proof of service is evidence of delivery of the subpoena.

Added by Acts 1995, 74th Leg., ch. 655, § 5.03, eff. Sept. 1, 1995; Acts 1995, 74th Leg., ch. 751, § 85, eff. Sept. 1, 1995. Amended by Acts 1997, 75th Leg., ch. 911, § 87, eff. Sept. 1, 1997.

### § 232.008. Order Suspending License for Failure to Pay Child Support

(a) On making the findings required by Section 232.003, the court or Title IV-D agency shall render an order suspending the license unless the individual:

(1) proves that all arrearages and the current month's support have been paid;

(2) shows good cause for failure to comply with the subpoena or the terms of the court order providing for the possession of or access to a child; or

(3) establishes an affirmative defense as provided by Section 157.008(c).

(b) Subject to Subsection (b–1), the court or Title IV–D agency may stay an order suspending a license conditioned on the individual's compliance with:

(1) a reasonable repayment schedule that is incorporated in the order;

(2) the requirements of a reissued and delivered subpoena; or

(3) the requirements of any court order pertaining to the possession of or access to a child.

(b–1) The court or Title IV–D agency may not stay an order under Subsection (b)(1) unless the individual makes an immediate partial payment in an amount specified by the court or Title IV–D agency. The amount specified may not be less than $200.

(c) An order suspending a license with a stay of the suspension may not be served on the licensing authority unless the stay is revoked as provided by this chapter.

(d) A final order suspending license rendered by a court or the Title IV-D agency shall be forwarded to the appropriate licensing authority by the clerk of the court or Title IV-D agency. The clerk shall collect from an obligor a fee of $5 for each order mailed.

(e) If the court or Title IV-D agency renders an order suspending license, the individual may also be ordered not to engage in the licensed activity.

(f) If the court or Title IV-D agency finds that the petition for suspension should be denied, the petition shall be dismissed without prejudice, and an order suspending license may not be rendered.

Added by Acts 1995, 74th Leg., ch. 655, § 5.03, eff. Sept. 1, 1995; Acts 1995, 74th Leg., ch. 751, § 85, eff. Sept. 1, 1995. Amended by Acts 1997, 75th Leg., ch. 911, § 88, eff. Sept. 1, 1997; Acts 1997, 75th Leg., ch. 976, § 8, eff. Sept. 1, 1997; Acts 1999, 76th Leg., ch. 556, § 61, eff. Sept. 1, 1999; Acts 2001, 77th Leg., ch. 724, § 4, eff. Sept. 1, 2001; Acts 2013, 83rd Leg., ch. 674 (H.B. 1846), § 1, eff. Sept. 1, 2013.

### § 232.009. Default Order

The court or Title IV-D agency shall consider the allegations of the petition for suspension to be admitted and shall render an order suspending the license of an obligor without the requirement of a hearing if the court or Title IV-D agency determines that the individual failed to respond to a notice issued under Section 232.006 by:

(1) requesting a hearing; or

(2) appearing at a scheduled hearing.

Added by Acts 1995, 74th Leg., ch. 655, § 5.03, eff. Sept. 1, 1995; Acts 1995, 74th Leg., ch. 751, § 85, eff. Sept. 1, 1995. Amended by Acts 1997, 75th Leg., ch. 420, § 25, eff. Sept. 1, 1997; Acts 1997, 75th Leg., ch. 911, § 89, eff. Sept. 1, 1997; Acts 2001, 77th Leg., ch. 1023, § 61, eff. Sept. 1, 2001.

### § 232.010. Review of Final Administrative Order

An order issued by a Title IV-D agency under this chapter is a final agency decision and is subject to review under the substantial evidence rule as provided by Chapter 2001, Government Code.

Added by Acts 1995, 74th Leg., ch. 655, § 5.03, eff. Sept. 1, 1995; Acts 1995, 74th Leg., ch. 751, § 85, eff. Sept. 1, 1995.

### § 232.011. Action by Licensing Authority

(a) On receipt of a final order suspending license, the licensing authority shall immediately determine if the authority has issued a license to the individual named on the order and, if a license has been issued:

(1) record the suspension of the license in the licensing authority's records;

(2) report the suspension as appropriate; and

(3) demand surrender of the suspended license if required by law for other cases in which a license is suspended.

(b) A licensing authority shall implement the terms of a final order suspending license without additional review or hearing. The authority may provide notice as appropriate to the license holder or to others concerned with the license.

(c) A licensing authority may not modify, remand, reverse, vacate, or stay an order suspending license issued under this chapter and may not review, vacate, or reconsider the terms of a final order suspending license.

(d) An individual who is the subject of a final order suspending license is not entitled to a refund for any fee or deposit paid to the licensing authority.

(e) An individual who continues to engage in the business, occupation, profession, or other licensed activity after the implementation of the order suspending license by the licensing authority is liable for the same civil and criminal penalties provided for engaging in the licensed activity without a license or while a license is suspended that apply to any other license holder of that licensing authority.

(f) A licensing authority is exempt from liability to a license holder for any act authorized under this chapter performed by the authority.

(g) Except as provided by this chapter, an order suspending license or dismissing a petition for the suspension of a license does not affect the power of a licensing authority to grant, deny, suspend, revoke, terminate, or renew a license.

(h) The denial or suspension of a driver's license under this chapter is governed by this chapter and not by the general licensing provisions of Chapter 521, Transportation Code.

(i) An order issued under this chapter to suspend a license applies to each license issued by the licensing authority subject to the order for which the obligor is eligible. The licensing authority may not issue or renew any other license for the obligor until the court or the Title IV-D agency renders an order vacating or staying an order suspending license.

Added by Acts 1995, 74th Leg., ch. 655, § 5.03, eff. Sept. 1, 1995; Acts 1995, 74th Leg., ch. 751, § 85, eff. Sept. 1, 1995. Amended by Acts 1997, 75th Leg., ch. 165, § 30.184, eff. Sept. 1, 1997; Acts 1997, 75th Leg., ch. 911, § 90, eff. Sept. 1, 1997; Acts 2001, 77th Leg., ch. 1023, § 62, eff. Sept. 1, 2001.

### § 232.012. Motion to Revoke Stay

(a) The obligee, support enforcement agency, court, or Title IV-D agency may file a motion to revoke the stay of an order suspending license if the individual who is subject of an order suspending license does not comply with:

(1) the terms of a reasonable repayment plan entered into by the individual;

(2) the requirements of a reissued subpoena; or

(3) the terms of any court order pertaining to the possession of or access to a child.

(b) Notice to the individual of a motion to revoke stay under this section may be given by personal service or by mail to the address provided by the individual, if any, in the order suspending license. The notice must include a notice of hearing. The notice must be provided to the individual not less than 10 days before the date of the hearing.

(c) A motion to revoke stay must allege the manner in which the individual failed to comply with the repayment plan, the reissued subpoena, or the court order pertaining to possession of or access to a child.

(d) If the court or Title IV-D agency finds that the individual is not in compliance with the terms of the repayment plan, reissued subpoena, or court order pertaining to possession of or access to a child, the court or agency shall revoke the stay of the order suspending license and render a final order suspending license.

Added by Acts 1995, 74th Leg., ch. 655, § 5.03, eff. Sept. 1, 1995; Acts 1995, 74th Leg., ch. 751, § 85, eff. Sept. 1, 1995. Amended by Acts 1997, 75th Leg., ch. 911, § 91, eff. Sept. 1, 1997; Acts 2001, 77th Leg., ch. 724, § 5, eff. Sept. 1, 2001.

### § 232.013. Vacating or Staying Order Suspending License

(a) The court or Title IV–D agency may render an order vacating or staying an order suspending an individual's license if:

(1) the individual has:

(A) paid all delinquent child support or has established a satisfactory payment record;

(B) complied with the requirements of a reissued subpoena; or

(C) complied with the terms of any court order providing for the possession of or access to a child; or

(2) the court or Title IV–D agency determines that good cause exists for vacating or staying the order.

(b) The clerk of the court or Title IV-D agency shall promptly deliver an order vacating or staying an order suspending license to the appropriate licensing authority. The clerk shall collect from an obligor a fee of $5 for each order mailed.

(c) On receipt of an order vacating or staying an order suspending license, the licensing authority shall promptly issue the affected license to the individual if the individual is otherwise qualified for the license.

(d) An order rendered under this section does not affect the right of the child support agency or obligee to any other remedy provided by law, including the right to seek relief under this chapter. An order rendered under this section does not affect the power of a licensing authority to grant, deny, suspend, revoke, terminate, or renew a license as otherwise provided by law.

Added by Acts 1995, 74th Leg., ch. 655, § 5.03, eff. Sept. 1, 1995; Acts 1995, 74th Leg., ch. 751, § 85, eff. Sept. 1, 1995. Amended by Acts 1997, 75th Leg., ch. 911, § 92, eff. Sept. 1, 1997; Acts 1997, 75th Leg., ch. 976, § 9, eff. Sept. 1, 1997; Acts 2001, 77th Leg., ch. 724, § 6, eff. Sept. 1, 2001; Acts 2003, 78th Leg., ch. 610, § 16, eff. Sept. 1, 2003.

### § 232.0135. Denial of License Issuance or Renewal

(a) A child support agency, as defined by Section 101.004, may provide notice to a licensing authority concerning an obligor who has failed to pay child support under a support order for six months or more that requests the authority to refuse to approve an application for issuance of a license to the obligor or renewal of an existing license of the obligor.

(b) A licensing authority that receives the information described by Subsection (a) shall refuse to approve an application for issuance of a license to the obligor or renewal of an existing license of the obligor until the authority is notified by the child support agency that the obligor has:

(1) paid all child support arrearages;

(2) made an immediate payment of not less than $200 toward child support arrearages owed and established with the agency a satisfactory repayment schedule for the remainder or is in compliance with a court order for payment of the arrearages;

(3) been granted an exemption from this subsection as part of a court-supervised plan to improve the obligor's earnings and child support payments; or

(4) successfully contested the denial of issuance or renewal of license under Subsection (d).

(c) On providing a licensing authority with the notice described by Subsection (a), the child support agency shall send a copy to the obligor by first class mail and inform the obligor of the steps the obligor must take to permit the authority to approve the obligor's application for license issuance or renewal.

(d) An obligor receiving notice under Subsection (c) may request a review by the child support agency to resolve any issue in dispute regarding the identity of the obligor or the existence or amount of child support arrearages. The agency shall promptly provide an opportunity for a review, either by telephone or in person, as appropriate to the circumstances. After the review, if appropriate, the agency may notify the licensing authority that it may approve the obligor's application for issuance or renewal of license. If the agency and the obligor fail to resolve any issue in dispute, the obligor, not later than the 30th day after the date of receiving notice of the agency's determination from the review, may file a motion with the court to direct the agency to withdraw the notice under Subsection (a) and request a hearing on the motion. The obligor's application for license issuance or renewal may not be approved by the licensing authority until the court rules on the motion. If, after a review by the agency or a hearing by the court, the agency withdraws the notice under Subsection (a), the agency shall reimburse the obligor the amount of any fee charged the obligor under Section 232.014.

(e) If an obligor enters into a repayment agreement with the child support agency under this section, the agency may incorporate the agreement in an order to be filed with and confirmed by the court in the manner provided for agreed orders under Chapter 233.

(f) In this section, "licensing authority" does not include the State Securities Board.

Added by Acts 2007, 80th Leg., ch. 972, § 55, eff. Sept. 1, 2007. Amended by Acts 2011, 82nd Leg., ch. 508 (H.B. 1674), §§ 15, 16, eff. Sept. 1, 2011; Acts 2013, 83rd Leg., ch. 674 (H.B. 1846), § 2, eff. Sept. 1, 2013; Acts 2013, 83rd Leg., ch. 742 (S.B. 355), § 11, eff. Sept. 1, 2013; Acts 2015, 84th Leg., ch. 859 (S.B. 1726), § 9, eff. Sept. 1, 2015.

### § 232.014. Fee by Licensing Authority

(a) A licensing authority may charge a fee to an individual who is the subject of an order suspending license or of an action of a child support agency under Section 232.0135 to deny issuance or renewal of license in an amount sufficient to recover the administrative costs incurred by the authority under this chapter.

(b) A fee collected by the Texas Department of Motor Vehicles shall be deposited to the credit of the Texas Department of Motor Vehicles fund. A fee collected by the Department of Public Safety shall be deposited to the credit of the state highway fund.

Added by Acts 1995, 74th Leg., ch. 655, § 5.03, eff. Sept. 1, 1995; Acts 1995, 74th Leg., ch. 751, § 85, eff. Sept. 1, 1995. Amended by Acts 1997, 75th Leg., ch. 911, § 93, eff. Sept. 1, 1997; Acts 2007, 80th Leg., ch. 972, § 56, eff. Sept. 1, 2007; Acts 2009, 81st Leg., ch. 933, § 3C.03, eff. Sept. 1, 2009; Acts 2011, 82nd Leg., ch. 508 (H.B. 1674), § 17, eff. Sept. 1, 2011; Acts 2013, 83rd Leg., ch. 1287 (H.B. 2202), § 1, eff. Sept. 1, 2013.

### § 232.015. Cooperation Between Licensing Authorities and Title IV–D Agency

(a) The Title IV-D agency may request from each licensing authority the name, address, social security number, license renewal date, and other identifying information for each individual who holds, applies for, or renews a license issued by the authority.

(b) A licensing authority shall provide the requested information in the form and manner identified by the Title IV-D agency.

(c) The Title IV-D agency may enter into a cooperative agreement with a licensing authority to administer this chapter in a cost-effective manner.

(d) The Title IV-D agency may adopt a reasonable implementation schedule for the requirements of this section.

(e) The Title IV-D agency, the comptroller, and the Texas Alcoholic Beverage Commission shall by rule specify additional prerequisites for the suspension of licenses relating to state taxes collected under Title 2, Tax Code.[1] The joint rules must be adopted not later than March 1, 1996.

Added by Acts 1995, 74th Leg., ch. 751, § 85, eff. Sept. 1, 1995. Amended by Acts 2001, 77th Leg., ch. 1023, § 63, eff. Sept. 1, 2001.

[1] V.T.C.A., Tax Code § 101.001 et seq.

### § 232.016. Rules, Forms, and Procedures

The Title IV-D agency by rule shall prescribe forms and procedures for the implementation of this chapter.

Added by Acts 1995, 74th Leg., ch. 655, § 5.03, eff. Sept. 1, 1995; Acts 1995, 74th Leg., ch. 751, § 85, eff. Sept. 1, 1995.

## CHAPTER 233. CHILD SUPPORT REVIEW PROCESS TO ESTABLISH OR ENFORCE SUPPORT OBLIGATIONS

**Section**

*Chapter 233, Child Support Review Process to Establish or Enforce Support Obligations, consisting of §§ 233.001 to 233.029, was redesignated from V.T.C.A., Family Code Chapter 231, Subchapter E and amended by Acts 1997, 75th Leg., ch. 911, § 80.*

*Another Chapter 233, Sharing Information in State Case Registry, consisting of §§ 233.001 to 233.004, added by Acts 1997, 75th Leg., ch. 420, § 26, was redesignated as Chapter 235, consisting of §§ 235.001 to 235.004, by Acts 1999, 76th Leg., ch. 62, § 19.01(24).*

### § 233.001. Purpose

(a) The purpose of the procedures specified in the child support review process authorized by this chapter is to enable the Title IV–D agency to take expedited administrative actions to establish, modify, and enforce child support, medical support, and dental support obligations, to determine parentage, or to take any other action authorized or required under Part D, Title IV, of the federal Social Security Act (42 U.S.C. Section 651 et seq.), and Chapter 231.

(b) A child support review order issued under this chapter and confirmed by a court constitutes an order of the court and is enforceable by any means available for the enforcement of child support obligations under this code, including withholding income, filing a child support lien, and suspending a license under Chapter 232.

Added by Acts 1995, 74th Leg., ch. 20, § 1, eff. April 20, 1995. Amended by Acts 1995, 74th Leg., ch. 341, § 2.04, eff. Sept. 1, 1995. Redesignated from V.T.C.A., Family Code § 231.401 and amended by Acts 1997, 75th Leg., ch. 911, § 80, eff. Sept. 1, 1997. Amended by Acts 2015, 84th Leg., ch. 1150 (S.B. 550), § 48, eff. Sept. 1, 2018.

### § 233.002. Agreements Encouraged

To the extent permitted by this chapter, the Title IV-D agency shall encourage agreement of the parties.

Added by Acts 1995, 74th Leg., ch. 20, § 1, eff. April 20, 1995. Amended by Acts 1995, 74th Leg., ch. 341, § 2.04, eff. Sept. 1, 1995. Redesignated from V.T.C.A., Family Code § 231.402 and amended by Acts 1997, 75th Leg., ch. 911, § 80, eff. Sept. 1, 1997.

### § 233.003. Bilingual Forms Required

A notice or other form used to implement administrative procedures under this chapter shall be printed in both Spanish and English.

Added by Acts 1995, 74th Leg., ch. 20, § 1, eff. April 20, 1995. Amended by Acts 1995, 74th Leg., ch. 341, § 2.04, eff. Sept. 1, 1995. Redesignated from V.T.C.A., Family Code § 231.403 and amended by Acts 1997 75th Leg., ch. 911, § 80, eff. Sept. 1, 1997.

### § 233.004. Interpreter Required

If a party participating in an administrative proceeding under this chapter does not speak English or is hearing impaired, the Title IV-D agency shall provide for interpreter services at no charge to the party.

Added by Acts 1995, 74th Leg., ch. 20, § 1, eff. April 20, 1995. Amended by Acts 1995, 74th Leg., ch. 341, § 2.04, eff. Sept. 1, 1995. Redesignated from V.T.C.A., Family Code § 231.404 and amended by Acts 1997 75th Leg., ch. 911, § 80, eff. Sept. 1, 1997.

### § 233.005. Initiating Administrative Actions

An administrative action under this chapter may be initiated by issuing a notice of child support review under Section 233.006 or a notice of proposed child support review order under Section 233.009 or 233.0095 to each party entitled to notice.

Added by Acts 1995, 74th Leg., ch. 20, § 1, eff. April 20, 1995. Amended by Acts 1995, 74th Leg., ch. 341, § 2.04, eff. Sept. 1, 1995. Redesignated from V.T.C.A., Family Code § 231.405 and amended by Acts 1997 75th Leg., ch. 911, § 80, eff. Sept. 1, 1997. Amended by Acts 1999, 76th Leg., ch. 556, § 63, eff. Sept. 1, 1999.

### § 233.006. Contents of Notice of Child Support Review

(a) The notice of child support review issued by the Title IV-D agency must:

(1) describe the procedure for a child support review, including the procedures for requesting a negotiation conference;

(2) inform the recipient that the recipient may be represented by legal counsel during the review process or at a court hearing; and

(3) inform the recipient that the recipient may refuse to participate or cease participation in the child support review process, but that the refusal by the recipient to participate will not prevent the completion of the process or the filing of a child support review order.

(b) In addition to the information required by Subsection (a), the notice of child support review may inform the recipient that:

(1) an affidavit of financial resources included with the notice must be executed by the recipient and returned to the Title IV-D agency not later than the 15th day after the date the notice is received or delivered; and

(2) if the requested affidavit of financial resources is not returned as required, the agency may:

(A) proceed with the review using the information that is available to the agency; and

(B) file a legal action without further notice to the recipient, except as otherwise required by law.

Added by Acts 1995, 74th Leg., ch. 20, § 1, eff. April 20, 1995. Amended by Acts 1995, 74th Leg., ch. 341, § 2.04, eff. Sept. 1, 1995. Redesignated from V.T.C.A., Family Code § 231.406 and amended by Acts 1997 75th Leg., ch. 911, § 80, eff. Sept. 1, 1997. Amended by Acts 2001, 77th Leg., ch. 1023, § 64, eff. Sept. 1, 2001.

### § 233.007. Service of Notice

(a) A notice required in an administrative action under this chapter may be delivered by personal service or first class mail on each party entitled to citation or notice as provided by Chapter 102.

(b) This section does not apply to notice required on filing of a child support review order or to later judicial actions.

Added by Acts 1995, 74th Leg., ch. 20, § 1, eff. April 20, 1995. Amended by Acts 1995, 74th Leg., ch. 341, § 2.04, eff. Sept. 1, 1995. Redesignated from V.T.C.A., Family Code § 231.407 and amended by Acts 1997 75th Leg., ch. 911, § 80, eff. Sept. 1, 1997.

### § 233.008. Administrative Subpoena in Child Support Review

In a child support review under this chapter, the Title IV-D agency may issue an administrative subpoena authorized under Chapter 231 to any individual or organization believed to have financial or other information needed to establish, modify, or enforce a support order.

Added by Acts 1995, 74th Leg., ch. 20, § 1, eff. April 20, 1995. Amended by Acts 1995, 74th Leg., ch. 341, § 2.04, eff. Sept. 1, 1995. Redesignated from V.T.C.A., Family Code § 231.408 and amended by Acts 1997 75th Leg., ch. 911, § 80, eff. Sept. 1, 1997.

### § 233.009. Notice of Proposed Child Support Review Order; Negotiation Conference

(a) After an investigation and assessment of financial resources, the Title IV-D agency may serve on the parties a notice of proposed child support review order in enforcing or modifying an existing order.

(b) The notice of proposed child support review order shall state:

(1) the amount of periodic payment of child support due, the amount of any overdue support that is owed as an arrearage as of the date of the notice, and the amounts that are to be paid by the obligor for current support due and in payment on the arrearage owed;

(2) that the person identified in the notice as the party responsible for payment of the support amounts may contest the notice order on the grounds that:

(A) the respondent is not the responsible party;

(B) the dependent child is no longer entitled to child support; or

(C) the amount of monthly support or arrearage is incorrectly stated; and

(3) that, if the person identified in the notice as the party responsible for payment of the support amounts does not contest the notice in writing or request a negotiation conference to discuss the notice not later than the 15th day after the date the notice was delivered, the Title IV–D agency may file a child support review order for child support, medical support, and dental support for the child as provided by Chapter 154 according to the information available to the agency.

(c) The Title IV-D agency may schedule a negotiation conference without a request from a party.

(d) The Title IV-D agency shall schedule a negotiation conference on the timely request of a party.

(e) The agency may conduct a negotiation conference, or any part of a negotiation conference, by telephone conference call, by video conference, as well as in person and may adjourn the conference for a reasonable time to permit mediation of issues that cannot be resolved by the parties and the agency.

(f) Notwithstanding any other provision of this chapter, if the parties have agreed to the terms of a proposed child support review order and each party has signed the order, including a waiver of the right to service of process as provided by Section 233.018, the Title IV-D agency may immediately present the order and waiver to the court for confirmation without conducting a negotiation conference or requiring the production of financial information.

Added by Acts 1995, 74th Leg., ch. 20, § 1, eff. April 20, 1995. Amended by Acts 1995, 74th Leg., ch. 341, § 2.04, eff. Sept. 1, 1995. Redesignated from V.T.C.A., Family Code § 231.409 and amended by Acts 1997 75th Leg., ch. 911, § 80, eff. Sept. 1, 1997; Acts 2001, 77th Leg., ch. 1023, § 65, eff. Sept. 1, 2001. Amended by Acts 2015, 84th Leg., ch. 1150 (S.B. 550), § 49, eff. Sept. 1, 2018.

### § 233.0095. Notice of Proposed Child Support Review Order in Cases of Acknowledged Paternity

(a) If an individual has signed the acknowledgment of paternity as the father of the child or executed a statement of paternity, the Title IV–D agency may serve on the parties a notice of proposed child support review order.

(b) The notice of proposed child support review order shall state:

(1) the amount of periodic payment of child support due;

(2) that the person identified in the notice as the party responsible for payment of the support amounts may only contest the amount of monthly support; and

(3) that, if the person identified in the notice as the party responsible for payment of the support amounts does not contest the notice in writing or request a negotiation conference to discuss the notice not later than the 15th day after the date the notice was delivered, the Title IV–D agency may file the child support order for child support, medical support, and dental support for the child as provided by Chapter 154 according to the information available to the agency.

(c) The Title IV–D agency may schedule a negotiation conference without a request from a party.

(d) The Title IV–D agency shall schedule a negotiation conference on the timely request of a party.

(e) The Title IV–D agency may conduct a negotiation conference, or any part of a negotiation conference, by telephone conference call, by video conference, or in person and may adjourn the conference for a reasonable time to permit mediation of issues that cannot be resolved by the parties and the agency.

(f) Notwithstanding any other provision of this chapter, if paternity has been acknowledged, the parties have agreed to the terms of a proposed child support review order, and each party has signed the order, including a waiver of the right to service of process as provided by Section 233.018, the Title IV-D agency may immediately present the order and waiver to the court for confirmation without conducting a negotiation conference or requiring the production of financial information.

Added by Acts 1999, 76th Leg., ch. 556, § 64, eff. Sept. 1, 1999. Amended by Acts 2001, 77th Leg., ch. 1023, § 66, eff. Sept. 1, 2001; Acts 2015, 84th Leg., ch. 1150 (S.B. 550), § 50, eff. Sept. 1, 2018.

### § 233.010. Notice of Negotiation Conference; Failure to Attend Conference

(a) The Title IV-D agency shall notify all parties entitled to notice of the negotiation conference of the date, time, and place of the conference not later than the 10th day before the date of the conference.

(b) If a party fails to attend the scheduled conference, the agency may proceed with the review and file a child support review order according to the information available to the agency.

Added by Acts 1995, 74th Leg., ch. 20, § 1, eff. April 20, 1995. Amended by Acts 1995, 74th Leg., ch. 341, § 2.04, eff. Sept. 1, 1995. Redesignated from V.T.C.A., Family Code § 231.410 and amended by Acts 1997 75th Leg., ch. 911, § 80, eff. Sept. 1, 1997.

### § 233.011. Rescheduling Negotiation Conference; Notice Required

(a) The Title IV-D agency may reschedule or adjourn a negotiation conference on the request of any party.

(b) The Title IV-D agency shall give all parties notice of a rescheduled conference not later than the third day before the date of the rescheduled conference.

Added by Acts 1995, 74th Leg., ch. 20, § 1, eff. April 20, 1995. Amended by Acts 1995, 74th Leg., ch. 341, § 2.04, eff. Sept. 1, 1995. Redesignated from V.T.C.A., Family Code § 231.411 and amended by Acts 1997 75th Leg., ch. 911, § 80, eff. Sept. 1, 1997.

### § 233.012. Information Required to be Provided at Negotiation Conference

At the beginning of the negotiation conference, the child support review officer shall review with the parties participating in the conference information provided in the notice of child support review and inform the parties that:

(1) the purpose of the negotiation conference is to provide an opportunity to reach an agreement on a child support order;

(2) if the parties reach an agreement, the review officer will prepare an agreed review order to be effective immediately on being confirmed by the court, as provided by Section 233.024;

(3) a party does not have to sign a review order prepared by the child support review officer but that the Title IV–D agency may file a review order without the agreement of the parties;

(4) the parties may sign a waiver of the right to service of process;

(5) a party may file a request for a court hearing on a nonagreed order not later than the 20th day after the date a copy of the petition for confirmation of the order is delivered to the party; and

(6) a party may file a motion for a new trial not later than the 30th day after an order is confirmed by the court.

Added by Acts 1995, 74th Leg., ch. 20, § 1, eff. April 20, 1995. Amended by Acts 1995, 74th Leg., ch. 341, § 2.04, eff. Sept. 1, 1995. Redesignated from V.T.C.A., Family Code § 231.412 and amended by Acts 1997 75th Leg., ch. 911, § 80, eff. Sept. 1, 1997. Amended by Acts 2011, 82nd Leg., ch. 508 (H.B. 1674), § 18, eff. Sept. 1, 2011.

### § 233.013. Determining Support Amount; Modification

(a) The Title IV–D agency may use any information obtained by the agency from the parties or any other source and shall apply the child support guidelines provided by this code to determine the appropriate amount of child support. In determining the appropriate amount of child support, the agency may consider evidence of the factors a court is required to consider under Section 154.123(b), and, if the agency deviates from the guidelines in determining the amount of monthly child support, with or without the agreement of the parties, the child support review order must include the findings required to be made by a court under Section 154.130(b).

(b) If grounds exist for modification of a child support order under Subchapter E, Chapter 156[1], the Title IV–D agency may file an appropriate child support review order, including an order that has the effect of modifying an existing court or administrative order for child support without the necessity of filing a motion to modify.

(c) Notwithstanding Subsection (b), the Title IV–D agency may, at any time and without a showing of material and substantial change in the circumstances of the parties, file a child support review order that has the effect of modifying an existing order for child support to provide medical support or dental support for a child if the existing order does not provide health care coverage for the child as required under Section 154.182 or dental care coverage for the child as required under Section 154.1825.

Added by Acts 1995, 74th Leg., ch. 20, § 1, eff. April 20, 1995. Amended by Acts 1995, 74th Leg., ch. 341, § 2.04, eff. Sept. 1, 1995. Redesignated from V.T.C.A., Family Code § 231.413 and amended by Acts 1997 75th Leg., ch. 911, § 80, eff. Sept. 1, 1997. Amended by Acts 2011, 82nd Leg., ch. 508 (H.B. 1674), § 19, eff. Sept. 1, 2011; Acts 2013, 83rd Leg., ch. 742 (S.B. 355), § 12, eff. Sept. 1, 2013; Acts 2015, 84th Leg., ch. 963 (S.B. 1727), § 5, eff. Sept. 1, 2015; Acts 2015, 84th Leg., ch. 1150 (S.B. 550), § 51, eff. Sept. 1, 2018.

[1] V.T.C.A., Family Code § 156.401 et seq.

### § 233.014. Record of Proceedings

(a) For the purposes of this chapter, documentary evidence relied on by the child support review officer, including an affidavit of a party, together with the child support review order is a sufficient record of the proceedings.

(b) The Title IV-D agency is not required to make any other record or transcript of the negotiation conference.

Added by Acts 1995, 74th Leg., ch. 20, § 1, eff. April 20, 1995. Amended by Acts 1995, 74th Leg., ch. 341, § 2.04, eff. Sept. 1, 1995. Redesignated from V.T.C.A., Family Code § 231.414 and amended by Acts 1997 75th Leg., ch. 911, § 80, eff. Sept. 1, 1997.

### § 233.015. Issuance of Child Support Review Order or Finding That No Order Should be Issued; Effect

(a) If a negotiation conference does not result in agreement by all parties to the child support review order, the Title IV-D agency shall render a final decision in the form of a child support review order or a determination that the agency should not issue a child support review order not later than the fifth day after the date of the negotiation conference.

(b) If the Title IV-D agency determines that the agency should not issue a child support order, the agency shall immediately provide each party with notice of the determination by personal delivery or by first class mail.

(c) A determination that a child support order should not be issued must include a statement of the reasons that an order is not being issued and a statement that the agency's determination does not affect the right of the Title IV-D agency or a party to request any other remedy provided by law.

Added by Acts 1995, 74th Leg., ch. 20, § 1, eff. April 20, 1995. Amended by Acts 1995, 74th Leg., ch. 341, § 2.04, eff. Sept. 1, 1995. Redesignated from V.T.C.A., Family Code § 231.415 and amended by Acts 1997 75th Leg., ch. 911, § 80, eff. Sept. 1, 1997.

### § 233.016. Vacating Child Support Review Order

(a) The Title IV-D agency may vacate a child support review order at any time before the order is filed with the court.

(b) A new negotiation conference, with notice to all parties, may be scheduled or the Title IV-D agency may make a determination that a child support review order should not be issued and give notice of that determination as provided by this chapter.

Added by Acts 1995, 74th Leg., ch. 20, § 1, eff. April 20, 1995. Amended by Acts 1995, 74th Leg., ch. 341, § 2.04, eff. Sept. 1, 1995. Redesignated from V.T.C.A., Family Code § 231.416 and amended by Acts 1997 75th Leg., ch. 911, § 80, eff. Sept. 1, 1997.

### § 233.017. Contents of Child Support Review Order

(a) An order issued under this chapter must be reviewed and signed by an attorney of the Title IV–D agency and must contain all provisions that are appropriate for an order under this title, including current child support, medical support, dental support, a determination of any arrearages or retroactive support, and, if not otherwise ordered, income withholding.

(b) A child support review order providing for the enforcement of an order may not contain a provision that imposes incarceration or a fine or contains a finding of contempt.

(c) Repealed by Acts 2011, 82nd Leg., ch. 508 (H.B. 1674), § 25.

(d) A child support review order that is not agreed to by all the parties may specify and reserve for the court at the confirmation hearing unresolved issues relating to conservatorship or possession of a child.

Added by Acts 1995, 74th Leg., ch. 20, § 1, eff. April 20, 1995. Amended by Acts 1995, 74th Leg., ch. 341, § 2.04, eff. Sept. 1, 1995. Redesignated from V.T.C.A., Family Code § 231.417 and amended by Acts 1997 75th Leg., ch. 911, § 80, eff. Sept. 1, 1997. Amended by Acts 2011, 82nd Leg., ch. 508 (H.B. 1674), § 25, eff. Sept. 1, 2011; Acts 2015, 84th Leg., ch. 1150 (S.B. 550), § 52, eff. Sept. 1, 2018.

### § 233.018. Additional Contents of Agreed Child Support Review Order

(a) If a negotiation conference results in an agreement of the parties, each party must sign the child support review order and the order must contain as to each party:

(1) a waiver by the party of the right to service of process and a court hearing;

(2) the mailing address of the party; and

(3) the following statement printed on the order in boldfaced type, in capital letters, or underlined:

"I ACKNOWLEDGE THAT I HAVE READ AND UNDERSTAND THIS CHILD SUPPORT REVIEW ORDER. I UNDERSTAND THAT IF I SIGN THIS ORDER, IT WILL BE CONFIRMED BY THE COURT WITHOUT FURTHER NOTICE TO ME. I KNOW THAT I HAVE A RIGHT TO REQUEST THAT A COURT RECONSIDER THE ORDER BY FILING A MOTION FOR A NEW TRIAL AT ANY TIME BEFORE THE 30TH DAY AFTER THE DATE OF THE CONFIRMATION OF THE ORDER BY THE COURT. I KNOW TIIAT IF I DO NOT OBEY THE TERMS OF THIS ORDER I MAY BE HELD IN CONTEMPT OF COURT."

(b) If a negotiation conference results in an agreement on some but not all issues in the case, the parties may sign a waiver of service along with an agreement to appear in court at a specified date and time for a determination by the court of all unresolved issues. Notice of the hearing is not required.

(c) A party may sign a waiver under this section using a digitized signature.

(d) A waiver under this section must be:

(1) sworn before a notary public; or

(2) executed using an unsworn declaration under Section 132.001, Civil Practice and Remedies Code.

(e) Notwithstanding Subsection (a)(2), the mailing address of a party shall be omitted if:

(1) the court has previously made a finding and ordered nondisclosure under Section 105.006(c) re-

lating to the parties and the order has not been superseded; or

(2) the child support review order contains an agreed finding and order under Section 105.006(c).

Added by Acts 1995, 74th Leg., ch. 20, § 1, eff. April 20, 1995. Amended by Acts 1995, 74th Leg., ch. 341, § 2.04, eff. Sept. 1, 1995. Redesignated from V.T.C.A., Family Code § 231.418 and amended by Acts 1997 75th Leg., ch. 911, § 80, eff. Sept. 1, 1997. Amended by Acts 1999, 76th Leg., ch. 556, § 65, eff. Sept. 1, 1999; Acts 2001, 77th Leg., ch. 1023, § 67, eff. Sept. 1, 2001; Acts 2003, 78th Leg., ch. 610, § 17, eff. Sept. 1, 2003; Acts 2021, 87th Leg., ch. 175 (S.B. 285), § 5, eff. Sept. 1, 2021.

### § 233.019. Filing of Agreed Review Order

(a) The Title IV-D agency shall file an agreed child support review order and a waiver of service signed by the parties with the clerk of the court having continuing jurisdiction of the child who is the subject of the order.

(b) If there is not a court of continuing jurisdiction, the Title IV-D agency shall file the agreed review order with the clerk of a court having jurisdiction under this title.

(c) If applicable, an acknowledgment of paternity or a written report of a parentage testing expert and any documentary evidence relied upon by the agency shall be filed with the agreed review order as an exhibit to the order.

(d) A child support order issued by a tribunal of another state and filed with an agreed review order as an exhibit to the agreed review order shall be treated as a confirmed order without the necessity of registration under Subchapter G, Chapter 159.

(e) If a party timely files a motion for a new trial for reconsideration of an agreed review order and the court grants the motion, the agreed review order filed with the clerk constitutes a sufficient pleading by the Title IV–D agency for relief on any issue addressed in the order.

Added by Acts 1995, 74th Leg., ch. 20, § 1, eff. April 20, 1995. Amended by Acts 1995, 74th Leg., ch. 341, § 2.04, eff. Sept. 1, 1995. Redesignated from V.T.C.A., Family Code § 231.419 and amended by Acts 1997 75th Leg., ch. 911, § 80, eff. Sept. 1, 1997. Amended by Acts 1999, 76th Leg., ch. 556, § 66, eff. Sept. 1, 1999; Acts 2007, 80th Leg., ch. 972, § 57, eff. Sept. 1, 2007; Acts 2013, 83rd Leg., ch. 742 (S.B. 355), § 13, eff. Sept. 1, 2013.

### § 233.020. Contents of Petition for Confirmation of Nonagreed Order

(a) A petition for confirmation of a child support review order not agreed to by the parties:

(1) must include the final review order as an attachment to the petition; and

(2) may include a waiver of service executed under Section 233.018(b) and an agreement to appear in court for a hearing.

(b) Documentary evidence relied on by the Title IV–D agency, including, if applicable, an acknowledgment of paternity or a written report of a parentage testing expert, shall be filed with the clerk as exhibits to the petition, but are not required to be served on the parties. The petition must identify the exhibits that are filed with the clerk.

Added by Acts 1995, 74th Leg., ch. 20, § 1, eff. April 20, 1995. Amended by Acts 1995, 74th Leg., ch. 341, § 2.04, eff. Sept. 1, 1995. Redesignated from V.T.C.A., Family Code § 231.420 and amended by Acts 1997 75th Leg., ch. 911, § 80, eff. Sept. 1, 1997. Amended by Acts 1999, 76th Leg., ch. 556, § 67, eff. Sept. 1, 1999.

### § 233.021. Duties of Clerk of Court

(a) On the filing of an agreed child support review order or of a petition for confirmation of a nonagreed order issued by the Title IV-D agency, the clerk of court shall endorse on the order or petition the date and time the order or petition is filed.

(b) In an original action, the clerk shall endorse the appropriate court and cause number on the agreed review order or on the petition for confirmation of a nonagreed order.

(c) The clerk shall deliver by personal service or, if court-ordered, a method of substituted service, a copy of the petition for confirmation of a nonagreed review order and a copy of the order, to each party entitled to service who has not waived service.

(d) A clerk of a district court is entitled to collect in a child support review case the fees authorized in a Title IV-D case by Chapter 231.

Added by Acts 1995, 74th Leg., ch. 20, § 1, eff. April 20, 1995. Amended by Acts 1995, 74th Leg., ch. 341, § 2.04, eff. Sept. 1, 1995. Redesignated from V.T.C.A., Family Code § 231.421 and amended by Acts 1997 75th Leg., ch. 911, § 80, eff. Sept. 1, 1997. Amended by Acts 2021, 87th Leg., ch. 175 (S.B. 285), § 6, eff. Sept. 1, 2021.

Section 9 of Acts 2021, 87th Leg., ch. 175 (S.B. 285) provides:

"The change in law made by this Act to Section 233.021(c), Family Code, applies only to a petition for confirmation of a nonagreed order filed on or after the effective date [Sept. 1, 2021] of this Act. A petition filed before the effective date of this Act is governed by the law in effect on the date the petition was filed, and the former law is continued in effect for that purpose."

### § 233.022. Form to Request a Court Hearing on Nonagreed Order

(a) A court shall consider any responsive pleading that is intended as an objection to confirmation of a child support review order not agreed to by the parties, including a general denial, as a request for a court hearing.

(b) The Title IV-D agency shall:

(1) make available to each clerk of court copies of the form to request a court hearing on a nonagreed review order; and

(2) provide the form to request a court hearing to a party to the child support review proceeding on request of the party.

(c) The clerk shall furnish the form to a party to the child support review proceeding on the request of the party.

Added by Acts 1995, 74th Leg., ch. 20, § 1, eff. April 20, 1995. Amended by Acts 1995, 74th Leg., ch. 341, § 2.04, eff. Sept. 1, 1995. Redesignated from V.T.C.A., Family Code § 231.422 and amended by Acts 1997 75th Leg., ch. 911, § 80, eff. Sept. 1, 1997.

### § 233.023. Time to Request a Court Hearing

A party may file a request for a court hearing not later than the 20th day after the date the petition for confirmation of a nonagreed child support review order is delivered to the party.

Added by Acts 1995, 74th Leg., ch. 20, § 1, eff. April 20, 1995. Amended by Acts 1995, 74th Leg., ch. 341, § 2.04, eff. Sept. 1, 1995. Redesignated from V.T.C.A., Family Code § 231.423 and amended by Acts 1997 75th Leg., ch. 911, § 80, eff. Sept. 1, 1997.

### § 233.024. Confirmation of Agreed Order

(a) On the filing of an agreed child support review order signed by all parties, together with waiver of service, the court shall sign the order not later than the seventh day after the filing of the order. On expiration of the seventh day after the filing of the order, the order is considered confirmed by the court by operation of law, regardless of whether the court has signed the order. The court may sign the order before filing the order, but the signed order shall immediately be filed.

(b) On confirmation by the court, the Title IV-D agency shall immediately deliver to each party a copy of the signed agreed review order.

Added by Acts 1995, 74th Leg., ch. 20, § 1, eff. April 20, 1995. Amended by Acts 1995, 74th Leg., ch. 341, § 2.04, eff. Sept. 1, 1995. Redesignated from V.T.C.A., Family Code § 231.424 and amended by Acts 1997 75th Leg., ch. 911, § 80, eff. Sept. 1, 1997; Acts 2001, 77th Leg., ch. 1023, § 68, eff. Sept. 1, 2001; Acts 2003, 78th Leg., ch. 610, § 18, eff. Sept. 1, 2003. Amended by Acts 2017, 85th Leg., ch. 699 (H.B. 2048), § 3, eff. Sept. 1, 2017; Acts 2021, 87th Leg., ch. 175 (S.B. 285), § 7, eff. Sept. 1, 2021.

Section 10 of Acts 2021, 87th Leg., ch. 175 (S.B. 285) provides:

"The change in law made by this Act to Section 233.024(a), Family Code, applies only to an agreed child support review order filed on or after the effective date [Sept. 1, 2021] of this Act. An order filed before the effective date of this Act is governed by the law in effect on the date the order was filed, and the former law is continued in effect for that purpose."

### § 233.025. Effect of Request for Hearing on Nonagreed Order; Pleading

(a) A request for hearing or an order setting a hearing on confirmation of a nonagreed child support review order stays confirmation of the order pending the hearing.

(b) At a hearing on confirmation, any issues in dispute shall be heard in a trial de novo.

(c) The petition for confirmation and the child support review order constitute a sufficient pleading by the Title IV-D agency for relief on any issue addressed in the petition and order.

(d) The request for hearing may limit the scope of the de novo hearing by specifying the issues that are in dispute.

Added by Acts 1995, 74th Leg., ch. 20, § 1, eff. April 20, 1995. Amended by Acts 1995, 74th Leg., ch. 341, § 2.04, eff. Sept. 1, 1995. Redesignated from V.T.C.A., Family Code § 231.425 and amended by Acts 1997 75th Leg., ch. 911, § 80, eff. Sept. 1, 1997.

### § 233.026. Time for Court Hearing

(a) When a timely request for a court hearing has been filed as provided by Section 233.023, the court shall hold a hearing on the confirmation of a child support review order that has not been agreed to by the parties not later than the 30th day after the date the request was filed.

(b) A court may not hold a hearing on the confirmation of a nonagreed child support review order if a party does not timely request a hearing as provided by Section 233.023.

(c) If the court resets the time of the hearing, the reset hearing shall be held not later than the 30th day after the date set for the initial hearing.

Added by Acts 1995, 74th Leg., ch. 20, § 1, eff. April 20, 1995. Amended by Acts 1995, 74th Leg., ch. 341, § 2.04, eff. Sept. 1, 1995. Redesignated from V.T.C.A., Family Code § 231.426 and amended by Acts 1997 75th Leg., ch. 911, § 80, eff. Sept. 1, 1997; Acts 2003, 78th Leg., ch. 610, § 19, eff. Sept. 1, 2003.

### § 233.027. Nonagreed Order After Hearing

(a) After the hearing on the confirmation of a nonagreed child support review order, the court shall:

(1) if the court finds that the nonagreed order should be confirmed, immediately sign the nonagreed order and enter the order as a final order of the court;

(2) if the court finds that the relief granted in the nonagreed child support review order is inappropriate, sign an appropriate order at the conclusion of the hearing or as soon after the conclusion of the hearing as is practical and enter the order as an order of the court; or

(3) if the court finds that all relief should be denied, enter an order that denies relief and includes specific findings explaining the reasons that relief is denied.

(b) Repealed by Acts 2013, 83rd Leg., ch. 742 (S.B. 355), § 18.

(c) If the party who requested the hearing fails to appear at the hearing, the court shall sign the nonagreed order and enter the order as an order of the court.

Added by Acts 1995, 74th Leg., ch. 20, § 1, eff. April 20, 1995. Amended by Acts 1995, 74th Leg., ch. 341, § 2.04, eff. Sept. 1, 1995. Redesignated from V.T.C.A., Family Code § 231.427 and amended by Acts 1997 75th Leg., ch. 911, § 80, eff. Sept. 1, 1997; Acts 2003, 78th Leg., ch. 610, § 20, eff. Sept. 1, 2003. Amended by Acts 2013, 83rd Leg., ch. 742 (S.B. 355), §§ 14, 15, 18, eff. Sept. 1, 2013.

### § 233.0271. Confirmation of Nonagreed Order Without Hearing

(a) If a request for hearing has not been timely received, the court shall confirm and sign a nonagreed child support review order not later than the 30th day after the date the petition for confirmation was delivered to the last party entitled to service.

(b) The Title IV-D agency shall immediately deliver a copy of the confirmed nonagreed review order to each party, together with notice of right to file a motion for a new trial not later than the 30th day after the date the order was confirmed by the court.

Added by Acts 1997, 75th Leg., ch. 911, § 80, eff. Sept. 1, 1997.

### § 233.028. Special Child Support Review Procedures Relating to Establishment of Parentage

(a) If the parentage of a child has not been established, the notice of child support review delivered to the parties must include an allegation that the recipient is a biological parent of the child. The notice shall inform the parties that:

(1) not later than the 15th day after the date of delivery of the notice, the alleged parent of the child shall either sign a statement of paternity or an acknowledgment of paternity or deny in writing that the alleged parent is the biological parent of the child;

(2) either party may request that scientifically accepted parentage testing be conducted to assist in determining the identities of the child's parents;

(3) if the alleged parent timely denies parentage of the child, the Title IV-D agency shall order parentage testing; and

(4) if the alleged parent does not deny parentage of the child, the Title IV-D agency may conduct a negotiation conference.

(b) If all parties agree to the child's parentage, the agency may file an agreed child support review order as provided by this chapter.

(c) If a party denies parentage of a child whose parentage has not previously been acknowledged or adjudicated, the Title IV–D agency shall order parentage testing and give each party notice of the time and place of testing. If either party fails or refuses to participate in administrative parentage testing, the Title IV–D agency may file a child support review order resolving the question of parentage against that party. The court shall confirm the child support review order as a temporary or final order of the court only after an opportunity for parentage testing has been provided.

(d) If genetic testing identifies the alleged parent as the parent of the child and the results of a verified written report of a genetic testing expert meet the requirements of Chapter 160 for issuing a temporary order, the Title IV-D agency may conduct a negotiation conference to resolve any issues of support and file with the court a child support review order.

(e) If the results of parentage testing exclude an alleged parent from being the biological parent of the child, the Title IV-D agency shall issue and provide to each party a child support review order that declares that the excluded person is not a parent of the child.

(f) Any party may file a petition for confirmation of a child support review order issued under this section.

Added by Acts 1995, 74th Leg., ch. 20, § 1, eff. April 20, 1995. Amended by Acts 1995, 74th Leg., ch. 341, § 2.04, eff. Sept. 1, 1995. Redesignated from V.T.C.A., Family Code § 231.428 and amended by Acts 1997 75th Leg., ch. 911, § 80, eff. Sept. 1, 1997; Acts 2001, 77th Leg., ch. 821, § 2.17, eff. June 14, 2001. Amended by Acts 2015, 84th Leg., ch. 963 (S.B. 1727), § 6, eff. Sept. 1, 2015.

### § 233.029. Administrative Procedure Law Not Applicable

The child support review process under this chapter is not governed by Chapter 2001, Government Code.

Added by Acts 1995, 74th Leg., ch. 20, § 1, eff. April 20, 1995. Amended by Acts 1995, 74th Leg., ch. 341, § 2.04, eff. Sept. 1, 1995. Redesignated from V.T.C.A., Family Code § 231.429 and amended by Acts 1997 75th Leg., ch. 911, § 80, eff. Sept. 1, 1997.

## CHAPTER 234. STATE CASE REGISTRY, DISBURSEMENT UNIT, AND DIRECTORY OF NEW HIRES

### SUBCHAPTER A. UNIFIED STATE CASE REGISTRY AND DISBURSEMENT UNIT

Section



### SUBCHAPTER B. STATE DIRECTORY OF NEW HIRES



*Chapter 234, State Case Registry, Disbursement Unit, and Directory of New Hires, consisting of §§ 234.001 to 234.104, was added by Acts 1997, 75th Leg., ch. 911, § 94.*

*Another Chapter 234, Competitive Bidding for Child Support Collection Services, consisting of §§ 234.001 to 234.003, was added by Acts 1997, 75th Leg., ch. 420, § 27, and redesignated as V.T.C.A., Family Code Chapter 236 by Acts 1999, 76th Leg., ch. 62, § 19.01(25).*

### SUBCHAPTER A. UNIFIED STATE CASE REGISTRY AND DISBURSEMENT UNIT

### § 234.001. Establishment and Operation of State Case Registry and State Disbursement Unit

(a) The Title IV-D agency shall establish and operate a state case registry and state disbursement unit meeting the requirements of 42 U.S.C. Sections 654a(e) and 654b and this subchapter.

(b) The state case registry shall maintain records of child support orders in Title IV–D cases and in other cases in which a child support order has been established or modified in this state on or after October 1, 1998.

(c) The state disbursement unit shall:

(1) receive, maintain, and furnish records of child support payments in Title IV–D cases and other cases as authorized by law;

(2) forward child support payments as authorized by law;

(3) maintain records of child support payments made through the state disbursement unit; and

(4) make available to a local registry each day in a manner determined by the Title IV–D agency the following information:

(A) the cause number of the suit under which withholding is required;

(B) the payor's name and social security number;

(C) the payee's name and, if available, social security number;

(D) the date the disbursement unit received the payment;

(E) the amount of the payment; and

(F) the instrument identification information.

(d) A certified child support payment record produced by the state disbursement unit is admissible as evidence of the truth of the information contained in the record and does not require further authentication or verification.

Added by Acts 1997, 75th Leg., ch. 911, § 94, eff. Sept. 1, 1997. Amended by Acts 1999, 76th Leg., ch. 556, § 68, eff. Sept. 1, 1999; Acts 2001, 77th Leg., ch. 1023, § 69, eff. Sept. 1, 2001; Acts 2007, 80th Leg., ch. 972, § 58, eff. Sept. 1, 2007.

**§ 234.002. Integrated System for Child Support, Medical Support, and Dental Support Enforcement**

The statewide integrated system for child support, medical support, and dental support enforcement under Chapter 231 shall be part of the state case registry and state disbursement unit authorized by this subchapter.

Added by Acts 1997, 75th Leg., ch. 911, § 94, eff. Sept. 1, 1997. Amended by Acts 1999, 76th Leg., ch. 556, § 68, eff. Sept. 1, 1999; Acts 2015, 84th Leg., ch. 1150 (S.B. 550), § 53, eff. Sept. 1, 2018.

**§ 234.003. Expired**

**§ 234.004. Contracts and Cooperative Agreements**

(a) The Title IV-D agency may enter into contracts and cooperative agreements as necessary to establish and operate the state case registry and state disbursement unit authorized under this subchapter.

(b) To the extent funds are available for this purpose, the Title IV-D agency may enter into contracts or cooperative agreements to process through the state disbursement unit child support collections in cases not otherwise eligible under 42 U.S.C. Section 654b.

Added by Acts 1997, 75th Leg., ch. 911, § 94, eff. Sept. 1, 1997. Amended by Acts 2001, 77th Leg., ch. 1023, § 70, eff. Sept. 1, 2001.

**§ 234.005. Expired**

**§ 234.006. Rulemaking**

The Title IV–D agency may adopt rules in compliance with federal law for the operation of the state case registry and the state disbursement unit.

Added by Acts 1999, 76th Leg., ch. 556, § 68, eff. Sept. 1, 1999. Amended by Acts 2001, 77th Leg., ch. 1023, § 71, eff. Sept. 1, 2001; Acts 2007, 80th Leg., ch. 972, § 59, eff. Sept. 1, 2007.

**§ 234.007. Notice of Place of Payment**

(a) A court that orders a party to pay child support under a temporary or final order shall order that all child support payments be paid through the state disbursement unit, including any child support that the court orders an employer to withhold from the income of the obligor.

(b) In order to redirect payments to the state disbursement unit, the Title IV–D agency shall issue a notice of place of payment informing the obligor, obligee, and employer that income withheld for child support is to be paid to the state disbursement unit and may not be remitted to a local registry, the obligee, or any other person or agency. If withheld support has been paid to a local registry, the Title IV–D agency shall send the notice to the registry to redirect any payments to the state disbursement unit.

(c) A copy of the notice under Subsection (b) shall be filed with the court of continuing jurisdiction.

(d) The notice under Subsection (b) must include:

(1) the name of the child for whom support is ordered and of the person to whom support is ordered by the court to be paid;

(2) the style and cause number of the case in which support is ordered; and

(3) instructions for the payment of ordered support to the state disbursement unit.

(e) On receipt of a copy of the notice under Subsection (b), the clerk of the court shall file the notice in the appropriate case file.

(f) The notice under Subsection (b) may be used by the Title IV–D agency to redirect child support payments from the state disbursement unit of this state to the state disbursement unit of another state.

Added by Acts 1999, 76th Leg., ch. 556, § 68, eff. Sept. 1, 1999. Amended by Acts 2003, 78th Leg., ch. 1247, § 45, eff. Sept. 1, 2003; Acts 2013, 83rd Leg., ch. 742 (S.B. 355), § 16, eff. Sept. 1, 2013; Acts 2021, 87th Leg., ch. 552 (S.B. 286), § 10, eff. Sept. 1, 2021.

Section 12 of Acts 2021, 87th Leg., ch. 552 (S.B. 286) provides:

"The enactment of this Act does not constitute a material and substantial change of circumstances sufficient to warrant modification of a court order or portion of a decree that provides for the support of a child rendered before the effective date [Sept. 1, 2021] of this Act."

**§ 234.008. Deposit, Distribution, and Issuance of Payments**

(a) Not later than the second business day after the date the state disbursement unit receives a child support payment, the state disbursement unit shall distribute the payment to the Title IV–D agency or the obligee.

(b) The state disbursement unit shall deposit daily all child support payments in a trust fund with the state comptroller. Subject to the agreement of the comptroller, the state disbursement unit may issue checks from the trust fund.

(c) to (e) Repealed by Acts 2007, 80th Leg., ch. 972, § 65(5).

Added by Acts 1999, 76th Leg., ch. 556, § 68, eff. Sept. 1, 1999. Amended by Acts 2003, 78th Leg., ch. 1262, § 4, eff. Sept. 1, 2003; Acts 2005, 79th Leg., ch. 1232, § 1, eff. Sept. 1, 2005; Acts 2007, 80th Leg., ch. 972, §§ 60, 65(5), eff. Sept. 1, 2007.

### § 234.009. Official Child Support Payment Record

(a) The record of child support payments maintained by a local registry is the official record of a payment received directly by the local registry.

(b) The record of child support payments maintained by the state disbursement unit is the official record of a payment received directly by the unit.

(c) After the date child support payments formerly received by a local registry are redirected to the state disbursement unit, a local registry may accept a record of payments furnished by the state disbursement unit and may add the payments to the record of payments maintained by the local registry so that a complete payment record is available for use by the court.

(d) If the local registry does not add payments received by the state disbursement unit to the record maintained by the registry as provided by Subsection (c), the official record of child support payments consists of the record maintained by the local registry for payments received directly by the registry and the record maintained by the state disbursement unit for payments received directly by the unit.

Added by Acts 1999, 76th Leg., ch. 556, § 68, eff. Sept. 1, 1999.

### § 234.0091. Administrative Review of Child Support Payment Record

(a) On request, the state disbursement unit shall provide to an obligor or obligee a copy of the record of child support payments maintained by the unit. The record must include the amounts and dates of all payments received from or on behalf of the obligor and disbursed to the obligee.

(b) An obligor or obligee may request that the Title IV–D agency investigate an alleged discrepancy between the child support payment record provided by the state disbursement unit under Subsection (a) and the payment records maintained by the obligor or obligee. The obligor or obligee making the request must provide to the Title IV–D agency documentation of the alleged discrepancy, including a canceled check or other evidence of a payment or disbursement at issue.

(c) The Title IV–D agency shall respond to a request under Subsection (b) not later than the 20th day after the date the agency receives the request. If, after an investigation, the agency determines that the child support payment record maintained by the state disbursement unit should be amended, the state disbursement unit shall immediately make the required amendment to the record and notify the obligor or obligee who made the request under Subsection (b) of that amendment.

Added by Acts 2003, 78th Leg., ch. 1085, § 1, eff. June 20, 2003.

### § 234.010. Direct Deposit and Electronic Benefits Transfer of Child Support Payments

(a) The state disbursement unit authorized under this chapter may make a direct deposit of a child support payment to an obligee by electronic funds transfer into an account with a financial institution maintained by the obligee. It is the responsibility of the obligee to notify the state disbursement unit of:

(1) the existence of an account;

(2) the appropriate routing information for direct deposit by electronic funds transfer into an account; and

(3) any modification to account information previously provided to the state disbursement unit, including information that an account has been closed.

(b) Except as provided by Subsection (d), the state disbursement unit shall deposit a child support payment by electronic funds transfer into a debit card account established for the obligee by the Title IV–D agency if the obligee:

(1) does not maintain an account with a financial institution;

(2) fails to notify the state disbursement unit of the existence of an account maintained with a financial institution; or

(3) closes an account maintained with a financial institution previously used to accept direct deposit of a child support payment without establishing a new account and notifying the state disbursement unit of the new account in accordance with Subsection (a).

(c) The Title IV–D agency shall:

(1) issue a debit card to each obligee for whom a debit card account is established under Subsection (b); and

(2) provide the obligee with instructions for activating and using the debit card.

(c–1) Chapter 604, Business & Commerce Code, does not apply to a debit card issued under Subsection (c).

(d) An obligee may decline in writing to receive child support payments by electronic funds transfer into an account with a financial institution or a debit card account and request that payments be provided by paper warrants if the obligee alleges that receiving payments by electronic funds transfer would impose a substantial hardship.

(e) A child support payment disbursed by the state disbursement unit by electronic funds transfer into an account with a financial institution maintained by the obligee or into a debit card account established for the obligee under Subsection (b) is solely the property of the obligee.

Added by Acts 1999, 76th Leg., ch. 1072, § 6, Sept. 1, 1999. Redesignated from V.T.C.A., Family Code § 234.006 by Acts 2001, 77th Leg., ch. 1420, § 21.001(33), eff. Sept. 1, 2001. Amended by Acts 2009, 81st Leg., ch. 551, § 1, eff. June 19, 2009; Acts 2009, 81st Leg., ch. 767, § 30, eff. June 19, 2009.

### § 234.011. Repealed by Acts 2009, 81st Leg., ch. 551, § 4, eff. June 19, 2009; Acts 2009, 81st Leg., ch. 767, § 37, eff. June 19, 2009

### § 234.012. Release of Information from State Case Registry

Unless prohibited by a court in accordance with Section 105.006(c), the state case registry shall, on request and to the extent permitted by federal law, provide the information required under Sections 105.006 and 105.008 in any case included in the registry under Section 234.001(b) to:

(1) any party to the proceeding;

(2) an amicus attorney;

(3) an attorney ad litem;

(4) a friend of the court;

(5) a guardian ad litem;

(6) a domestic relations office;

(7) a prosecuting attorney or juvenile court acting in a proceeding under Title 3;[1] or

(8) a governmental entity or court acting in a proceeding under Chapter 262.

Added by Acts 2007, 80th Leg., ch. 972, § 61, eff. Sept. 1, 2007.

[1] V.T.C.A., Family Code § 51.01 et seq.

## SUBCHAPTER B. STATE DIRECTORY OF NEW HIRES

### § 234.101. Definitions

In this subchapter:

(1) "Employee" means an individual who is an employee within the meaning of Chapter 24 of the Internal Revenue Code of 1986 (26 U.S.C. Section 3401(c)) or an independent contractor as defined by the Internal Revenue Service. The term includes a driver who logs in to the digital network of a transportation network company, as those terms are defined by Section 2402.001, Occupations Code, regardless of whether the driver is considered an independent contractor under Section 2402.114, Occupations Code, and an individual who logs in to or otherwise uses a technology platform to make deliveries for compensation. The term does not include an employee of a state agency performing intelligence or counterintelligence functions if the head of the agency has determined that reporting employee information under this subchapter could endanger the safety of the employee or compromise an ongoing investigation or intelligence activity.

(2) "Employer" has the meaning given that term by Section 3401(d) of the Internal Revenue Code of 1986 (26 U.S.C. Section 3401(d)) and includes a governmental entity and a labor organization, as that term is identified in Section 2(5) of the National Labor Relations Act (29 U.S.C. Section 152(5)), including an entity, also known as a "hiring hall," used by the labor organization and an employer to carry out requirements of an agreement between the organization and an employer described in Section 8(f)(3) of that Act (29 U.S.C. Section 158(f)(3)). The term includes a transportation network company, as defined by Section 2402.001, Occupations Code, and a person that operates a technology platform used to make deliveries to customers.

(3) "Newly hired employee" means an employee who:

(A) has not previously been employed by or received earnings from the employer; or

(B) was previously employed by the employer but has been separated from that employment or has not received earnings from the employer for at least 60 consecutive days.

Added by Acts 1997, 75th Leg., ch. 911, § 94, eff. Sept. 1, 1997. Amended by Acts 2013, 83rd Leg., ch. 742 (S.B. 355), § 17, eff. Sept. 1, 2013; Acts 2015, 84th Leg., ch. 963 (S.B. 1727), § 7, eff. Sept. 1, 2015; Acts 2021, 87th Leg., ch. 446 (H.B. 458), § 2, eff. Sept. 1, 2021.

### § 234.102. Operation of New Hire Directory

In cooperation with the Texas Workforce Commission, the Title IV-D agency shall develop and operate a state directory to which employers in the state shall report each newly hired or rehired employee in accordance with the requirements of 42 U.S.C. Section 653a.

Added by Acts 1997, 75th Leg., ch. 911, § 94, eff. Sept. 1, 1997. Amended by Acts 1999, 76th Leg., ch. 178, § 12, eff. Aug. 30, 1999.

### § 234.103. Contracts and Cooperative Agreements

The Title IV-D agency may enter into cooperative agreements and contracts as necessary to create and operate the directory authorized under this subchapter.

Added by Acts 1997, 75th Leg., ch. 911, § 94, eff. Sept. 1, 1997. Amended by Acts 1999, 76th Leg., ch. 178, § 13, eff. Aug. 30, 1999.

### § 234.104. Procedures

The Title IV-D agency by rule shall establish procedures for reporting employee information and for operating a state directory of new hires meeting the requirements of federal law.

Added by Acts 1997, 75th Leg., ch. 911, § 94, eff. Sept. 1, 1997. Amended by Acts 1999, 76th Leg., ch. 178, § 14, eff. Aug. 30, 1999.

### § 234.105. Civil Penalty

(a) In addition to any other remedy provided by law, an employer who knowingly violates a procedure adopted under Section 234.104 for reporting employee information may be liable for a civil penalty as permitted by Section 453A(d) of the federal Social Security Act (42 U.S.C. Section 653a).

(b) The amount of the civil penalty may not exceed:

(1) $25 for each occurrence in which an employer fails to report an employee; or

(2) $500 for each occurrence in which the conduct described by Subdivision (1) is the result of a conspiracy between the employer and an employee to not supply a required report or to submit a false or incomplete report.

(c) The attorney general may sue to collect the civil penalty. A penalty collected under this section shall be deposited in a special fund in the state treasury.

Added by Acts 2007, 80th Leg., ch. 972, § 62, eff. Sept. 1, 2007.

## CHAPTER 235. SHARING INFORMATION IN STATE CASE REGISTRY [REPEALED]

**§§ 235.001 to 235.004. Repealed by Acts 2007, 80th Leg., ch. 972, § 65(6), eff. Sept. 1, 2007.**

## CHAPTER 236. COMPETITIVE BIDDING FOR CHILD SUPPORT COLLECTION SERVICES [REPEALED]

**§§ 236.001 to 236.003. Repealed by Acts 2017, 85th Leg., ch. 24 (S.B. 706), § 7(2), eff. Sept. 1, 2017**

# SUBTITLE E. PROTECTION OF THE CHILD

## CHAPTER 261. INVESTIGATION OF REPORT OF CHILD ABUSE OR NEGLECT

## SUBCHAPTER A. GENERAL PROVISIONS

### § 261.001. Definitions

In this chapter:

(1) "Abuse" includes the following acts or omissions by a person:

(A) mental or emotional injury to a child that results in an observable and material impairment in the child's growth, development, or psychological functioning;

(B) causing or permitting the child to be in a situation in which the child sustains a mental or emotional injury that results in an observable and material impairment in the child's growth, development, or psychological functioning;

(C) physical injury that results in substantial harm to the child, or the genuine threat of substantial harm from physical injury to the child, including an injury that is at variance with the history or explanation given and excluding an accident or reasonable discipline by a parent, guardian, or managing or possessory conservator that does not expose the child to a substantial risk of harm;

(D) failure to make a reasonable effort to prevent an action by another person that results in physical injury that results in substantial harm to the child;

(E) sexual conduct harmful to a child's mental, emotional, or physical welfare, including conduct that constitutes the offense of continuous sexual abuse of young child or disabled individual under Section 21.02, Penal Code, indecency with a child under Section 21.11, Penal Code, sexual assault under Section 22.011, Penal Code, or aggravated sexual assault under Section 22.021, Penal Code;

(F) failure to make a reasonable effort to prevent sexual conduct harmful to a child;

(G) compelling or encouraging the child to engage in sexual conduct as defined by Section 43.01, Penal Code, including compelling or encouraging the child in a manner that constitutes an offense of trafficking of persons under Section 20A.02(a)(7) or (8), Penal Code, solicitation of prostitution under Section 43.021, Penal Code, or compelling prostitution under Section 43.05(a)(2), Penal Code;

(H) causing, permitting, encouraging, engaging in, or allowing the photographing, filming, or depicting of the child if the person knew or should have known that the resulting photograph, film, or depiction of the child is obscene as defined by Section 43.21, Penal Code, or pornographic;

(I) the current use by a person of a controlled substance as defined by Chapter 481, Health and Safety Code, in a manner or to the extent that the use results in physical, mental, or emotional injury to a child;

(J) causing, expressly permitting, or encouraging a child to use a controlled substance as defined by Chapter 481, Health and Safety Code;

(K) causing, permitting, encouraging, engaging in, or allowing a sexual performance by a child as defined by Section 43.25, Penal Code;

(L) knowingly causing, permitting, encouraging, engaging in, or allowing a child to be trafficked in a manner punishable as an offense under Section 20A.02(a)(5), (6), (7), or (8), Penal Code, or the failure to make a reasonable effort to prevent a child from being trafficked in a manner punishable as an offense under any of those sections; or

(M) forcing or coercing a child to enter into a marriage.

(2) "Department" means the Department of Family and Protective Services.

(3) "Exploitation" means the illegal or improper use of a child or of the resources of a child for monetary or personal benefit, profit, or gain by an employee, volunteer, or other individual working under the auspices of a facility or program as further described by rule or policy.

(4) "Neglect" means an act or failure to act by a person responsible for a child's care, custody, or welfare evidencing the person's blatant disregard for the consequences of the act or failure to act that results in harm to the child or that creates an immediate danger to the child's physical health or safety and:

(A) includes:

(i) the leaving of a child in a situation where the child would be exposed to an immediate danger of physical or mental harm, without arranging for necessary care for the child, and the demonstration of an intent not to return by a parent, guardian, or managing or possessory conservator of the child;

(ii) the following acts or omissions by a person:

(a) placing a child in or failing to remove a child from a situation that a reasonable person would realize requires judgment or actions beyond the child's level of maturity, physical condition, or mental abilities and that results in bodily injury or an immediate danger of harm to the child;

(b) failing to seek, obtain, or follow through with medical care for a child, with the failure resulting in or presenting an immediate danger of death, disfigurement, or bodily injury or with the failure resulting in an observable and material impairment to the growth, development, or functioning of the child;

(c) the failure to provide a child with food, clothing, or shelter necessary to sustain the life or health of the child, excluding failure caused primarily by financial inability unless relief services had been offered and refused;

(d) placing a child in or failing to remove the child from a situation in which the child would be exposed to an immediate danger of sexual conduct harmful to the child; or

(e) placing a child in or failing to remove the child from a situation in which the child would be exposed to acts or omissions that constitute abuse under Subdivision (1)(E), (F), (G), (H), or (K) committed against another child;

(iii) the failure by the person responsible for a child's care, custody, or welfare to permit the child to return to the child's home without arranging for the necessary care for the child after the child has been absent from the home for any reason, including having been in residential placement or having run away; or

(iv) a negligent act or omission by an employee, volunteer, or other individual working under the auspices of a facility or program, including failure to comply with an individual treatment plan, plan of care, or individualized service plan, that causes or may cause substantial emotional harm or physical injury to, or the death of, a child served by the facility or program as further described by rule or policy; and

(B) does not include:

(i) the refusal by a person responsible for a child's care, custody, or welfare to permit the child to remain in or return to the child's home resulting in the placement of the child in the conservatorship of the department if:

(a) the child has a severe emotional disturbance;

(b) the person's refusal is based solely on the person's inability to obtain mental health services necessary to protect the safety and well-being of the child; and

(c) the person has exhausted all reasonable means available to the person to obtain the mental health services described by Sub-subparagraph (b); or

*Text of (4)(B)(ii), as added by Acts 2021, 87th Leg., ch. 8 (H.B. 567), § 5*

(ii) allowing the child to engage in independent activities that are appropriate and typical for the child's level of maturity, physical condition, developmental abilities, or culture.

*Text of (4)(B)(ii), as added by Acts 2021, 87th Leg., ch. 29 (H.B. 2536), § 2*

(ii) a decision by a person responsible for a child's care, custody, or welfare to:

(a) obtain an opinion from more than one medical provider relating to the child's medical care;

(b) transfer the child's medical care to a new medical provider; or

(c) transfer the child to another health care facility.

(5) "Person responsible for a child's care, custody, or welfare" means a person who traditionally is responsible for a child's care, custody, or welfare, including:

(A) a parent, guardian, managing or possessory conservator, or foster parent of the child;

(B) a member of the child's family or household as defined by Chapter 71;

(C) a person with whom the child's parent cohabits;

(D) school personnel or a volunteer at the child's school;

(E) personnel or a volunteer at a public or private child-care facility that provides services for the child or at a public or private residential institution or facility where the child resides; or

(F) an employee, volunteer, or other person working under the supervision of a licensed or unlicensed child-care facility, including a family home, residential child-care facility, employer-based day-care facility, or shelter day-care facility, as those terms are defined in Chapter 42, Human Resources Code.

(6) "Report" means a report that alleged or suspected abuse or neglect of a child has occurred or may occur.

(7) Repealed by Acts 2017, 85th Leg., ch. 316 (H.B. 5), § 36(1).

(8) Repealed by Acts 2015, 84th Leg., ch. 1 (S.B. 219), § 1.203(4).

(9) "Severe emotional disturbance" means a mental, behavioral, or emotional disorder of sufficient duration to result in functional impairment that substantially interferes with or limits a person's role or ability to function in family, school, or community activities.

Added by Acts 1995, 74th Leg., ch. 20, § 1, eff. April 20, 1995. Amended by Acts 1995, 74th Leg., ch. 751, § 86, eff. Sept. 1, 1995; Acts 1997, 75th Leg., ch. 575, § 10, eff. Sept. 1, 1997; Acts 1997, 75th Leg., ch. 1022, § 63, eff. Sept. 1, 1997; Acts 1999, 76th Leg., ch. 62, § 19.01(26), eff. Sept. 1, 1999; Acts 2001, 77th Leg., ch. 59, § 1, eff. Sept. 1, 2001; Acts 2005, 79th Leg., ch. 268, § 1.11, eff. Sept. 1, 2005; Acts 2007, 80th Leg., ch. 593, § 3.32, eff. Sept. 1, 2007; Acts 2011, 82nd Leg., ch. 1 (S.B. 24), § 4.03, eff. Sept. 1, 2011; Acts 2013, 83rd Leg., ch. 1142 (S.B. 44), § 1, eff. Sept. 1, 2013; Acts 2015, 84th Leg., ch. 1 (S.B. 219), §§ 1.120, 1.203(4), eff. April 2, 2015; Acts 2015, 84th Leg., ch. 432 (S.B. 1889), § 1, eff. Sept. 1, 2015; Acts 2015, 84th Leg., ch. 1273 (S.B. 825), § 4, eff. Sept. 1, 2015; Acts 2017, 85th Leg., ch. 316 (H.B. 5), § 36(1), eff. Sept. 1, 2017; Acts 2017, 85th Leg., ch. 319 (S.B. 11), § 7, eff. Sept. 1, 2017; Acts 2017, 85th Leg., ch. 1136 (H.B. 249), § 2, eff. Sept. 1, 2017; Acts 2021, 87th Leg., ch. 8 (H.B. 567), § 5, eff. Sept. 1, 2021; Acts 2021, 87th Leg., ch. 29 (H.B. 2536), § 2, eff. May 15, 2021; Acts 2021, 87th Leg., ch. 221 (H.B. 375), § 2.18, eff. Sept. 1, 2021; Acts 2021, 87th Leg., ch. 807 (H.B. 1540), § 39, eff. Sept. 1, 2021.

Section 15 of Acts 2021, 87th Leg., ch. 8 (H.B. 567) provides:

"The changes in law made by this Act apply only to a suit filed by the Department of Family and Protective Services on or after the effective date [Sept. 1, 2021] of this Act. A suit filed by the department before that date is governed by the law in effect on the date the suit was filed, and the former law is continued in effect for that purpose."

Section 3.01 of Acts 2021, 87th Leg., ch. 221 (H.B. 375) provides:

"The change in law made by this Act applies only to an offense committed on or after the effective date [Sept. 1, 2021] of this Act. An offense committed before the effective date of this Act is governed by the law in effect on the date the offense was committed, and the former law is continued in effect for that purpose. For purposes of this section, an offense was committed before the effective date of this Act if any element of the offense occurred before that date."

Section 63(d) of Acts 2021, 87th Leg., ch. 807 (H.B. 1540) provides:

"Except as otherwise provided by this section, the changes in law made by this Act apply only to an offense committed on or after the effective date [Sept. 1, 2021] of this Act. An offense committed before the effective date of this Act is governed by the law in effect on the date the offense was committed, and the former law is continued in effect for that purpose. For purposes of this section, an offense was committed before the effective date of this Act if any element of the offense occurred before that date."

## § 261.002. Central Registry

(a) The department shall establish and maintain a central registry of the names of individuals found by the department to have abused or neglected a child.

(b) The executive commissioner shall adopt rules necessary to carry out this section. The rules shall:

(1) prohibit the department from making a finding of abuse or neglect against a person in a case in which the department is named managing conservator of a child who has a severe emotional disturbance only because the child's family is unable to obtain mental health services for the child;

(2) establish guidelines for reviewing the records in the registry and removing those records in which the department was named managing conservator of a child who has a severe emotional disturbance only because the child's family was unable to obtain mental health services for the child;

(3) require the department to remove a person's name from the central registry maintained under this section not later than the 10th business day after the date the department receives notice that a finding of abuse and neglect against the person is overturned in:

(A) an administrative review or an appeal of the review conducted under Section 261.309(c);

(B) a review or an appeal of the review conducted by the office of consumer affairs of the department; or

(C) a hearing or an appeal conducted by the State Office of Administrative Hearings; and

(4) require the department to update any relevant department files to reflect an overturned finding of abuse or neglect against a person not later than the 10th business day after the date the finding is overturned in a review, hearing, or appeal described by Subdivision (3).

(c) The department may enter into agreements with other states to allow for the exchange of reports of child abuse and neglect in other states' central registry systems. The department shall use information obtained under this subsection in performing the background checks required under Section 42.056, Human Resources Code. The department shall cooperate with federal agencies and shall provide information and reports of child abuse and neglect to the appropriate federal agency that maintains the national registry for child abuse and neglect, if a national registry exists.

Added by Acts 1995, 74th Leg., ch. 20, § 1, eff. April 20, 1995. Amended by Acts 2005, 79th Leg., ch. 268, § 1.12, eff. Sept. 1, 2005; Acts 2015, 84th Leg., ch. 1 (S.B. 219), § 1.121, eff. April 2, 2015; Acts 2015, 84th Leg., ch. 432 (S.B. 1889), § 2, eff. Sept. 1, 2015; Acts 2017, 85th Leg., ch. 360 (H.B. 2849), § 1, eff. Sept. 1, 2017.

### § 261.003. Application to Students in School for Deaf or School for Blind and Visually Impaired

This chapter applies to the investigation of a report of abuse or neglect of a student, without regard to the age of the student, in the Texas School for the Deaf or the Texas School for the Blind and Visually Impaired.

Added by Acts 1995, 74th Leg., ch. 20, § 1, eff. April 20, 1995.

### § 261.004. Tracking of Recurrence of Child Abuse or Neglect Reports

(a) The department shall collect and monitor data regarding repeated reports of abuse or neglect:

(1) involving the same child, including reports of abuse or neglect of the child made while the child resided in other households and reports of abuse or neglect of the child by different alleged perpetrators made while the child resided in the same household; or

(2) by the same alleged perpetrator.

(b) In monitoring reports of abuse or neglect under Subsection (a), the department shall group together separate reports involving different children residing in the same household.

(c) The department shall consider any report collected under Subsection (a) involving any child or adult who is a part of a child's household when making case priority determinations or when conducting service or safety planning for the child or the child's family.

Added by Acts 2017, 85th Leg., ch. 319 (S.B. 11), § 8, eff. Sept. 1, 2017.

### § 261.005. Reference to Executive Commissioner or Commission

In this chapter:

(1) a reference to the executive commissioner or the executive commissioner of the Health and Human Services Commission means the commissioner of the department; and

(2) a reference to the Health and Human Services Commission means the department.

Added by Acts 2017, 85th Leg., ch. 316 (H.B. 5), § 10, eff. Sept. 1, 2017. Redesignated from V.T.C.A., Family Code § 261.004 by Acts 2019, 86th Leg., ch. 467 (H.B. 4170), § 21.001(12), eff. Sept. 1, 2019.

## SUBCHAPTER B. REPORT OF ABUSE OR NEGLECT; IMMUNITIES

### § 261.101. Persons Required to Report; Time to Report

(a) A person having reasonable cause to believe that a child's physical or mental health or welfare has been adversely affected by abuse or neglect by any person shall immediately make a report as provided by this subchapter.

(b) If a professional has reasonable cause to believe that a child has been abused or neglected or may be abused or neglected, or that a child is a victim of an offense under Section 21.11, Penal Code, and the professional has reasonable cause to believe that the child has been abused as defined by Section 261.001, the professional shall make a report not later than the 48th hour after the hour the professional first has reasonable cause to believe that the child has been or may be abused or neglected or is a victim of an offense under Section 21.11, Penal Code. A professional may not delegate to or rely on another person to make the report. In this subsection, "professional" means an individual who is licensed or certified by the state or who is an employee of a facility licensed, certified, or operated by the state and who, in the normal course of official duties or duties for which a license or certification is required, has direct contact with children. The term includes teachers, nurses, doctors, day-care employees, employees of a clinic or health care facility that provides reproductive services, juvenile probation officers, and juvenile detention or correctional officers.

(b–1) In addition to the duty to make a report under Subsection (a) or (b), a person or professional shall make a report in the manner required by Subsection (a) or (b), as applicable, if the person or professional has reasonable cause to believe that an adult was a victim of abuse or neglect as a child and the person or professional determines in good faith that disclosure of the information is necessary to protect the health and safety of:

(1) another child; or

(2) an elderly person or person with a disability as defined by Section 48.002, Human Resources Code.

(c) The requirement to report under this section applies without exception to an individual whose personal communications may otherwise be privileged, including an attorney, a member of the clergy, a medical practitioner, a social worker, a mental health professional, an employee or member of a board that licenses or certifies a professional, and an employee of a clinic or health care facility that provides reproductive services.

(d) Unless waived in writing by the person making the report, the identity of an individual making a report under this chapter is confidential and may be disclosed only:

(1) as provided by Section 261.201; or

(2) to a law enforcement officer for the purposes of conducting a criminal investigation of the report.

Added by Acts 1995, 74th Leg., ch. 20, § 1, eff. April 20, 1995. Amended by Acts 1995, 74th Leg., ch. 751, § 87, eff. Sept. 1, 1995; Acts 1997, 75th Leg., ch. 162, § 1, eff. Sept. 1, 1997; Acts 1997, 75th Leg., ch. 575, § 11, eff. Sept. 1, 1997; Acts 1997, 75th Leg., ch. 1022, § 65, eff. Sept. 1, 1997; Acts 1999, 76th Leg., ch. 62, § 6.29, eff. Sept. 1, 1999; Acts 1999, 76th Leg., ch. 1150, § 2, eff. Sept. 1, 1999; Acts 1999, 76th Leg., ch. 1390, § 21, eff. Sept. 1, 1999; Acts 2001, 77th Leg., ch. 1420, § 5.003, eff. Sept. 1, 2001; Acts 2005, 79th Leg., ch. 949, § 27, eff. Sept. 1, 2005; Acts 2013, 83rd Leg., ch. 395 (S.B. 152), § 4, eff. June 14, 2013; Acts 2015, 84th Leg., ch. 1 (S.B. 219), § 1.122, eff. April 2, 2015; Acts 2017, 85th Leg., ch. 1136 (H.B. 249), § 3, eff. Sept. 1, 2017; Acts 2021, 87th Leg., ch. 902 (H.B. 3379), § 1, eff. Sept. 1, 2021.

Section 2 of Acts 2021, 87th Leg., ch. 902 (H.B. 3379) provides:

"The changes in law made by this Act apply only to a report of suspected abuse or neglect of a child that is made on or after the effective date [Sept. 1, 2021] of this Act. A report of suspected abuse or neglect that is made before that date is governed by the law in effect on the date the report was made, and that law is continued in effect for that purpose."

### § 261.102. Matters to Be Reported

A report should reflect the reporter's belief that a child has been or may be abused or neglected or has died of abuse or neglect.

Added by Acts 1995, 74th Leg., ch. 20, § 1, eff. April 20, 1995. Amended by Acts 1995, 74th Leg., ch. 751, § 88, eff. Sept. 1, 1995.

### § 261.103. Report Made to Appropriate Agency

(a) Except as provided by Subsections (b) and (c) and Section 261.405, a report shall be made to:

(1) any local or state law enforcement agency;

(2) the department; or

(3) the state agency that operates, licenses, certifies, or registers the facility in which the alleged abuse or neglect occurred.

(b) A report may be made to the Texas Juvenile Justice Department instead of the entities listed under Subsection (a) if the report is based on information provided by a child while under the supervision of the

Texas Juvenile Justice Department concerning the child's alleged abuse of another child.

(c) Notwithstanding Subsection (a), a report, other than a report under Subsection (a)(3) or Section 261.405, must be made to the department if the alleged or suspected abuse or neglect involves a person responsible for the care, custody, or welfare of the child.

Added by Acts 1995, 74th Leg., ch. 20, § 1, eff. April 20, 1995. Amended by Acts 1995, 74th Leg., ch. 751, § 89, eff. Sept. 1, 1995; Acts 1999, 76th Leg., ch. 1477, § 24, eff. Sept. 1, 1999; Acts 2001, 77th Leg., ch. 1297, § 46, eff. Sept. 1, 2001; Acts 2005, 79th Leg., ch. 213, § 1, eff. Sept. 1, 2005; Acts 2015, 84th Leg., ch. 1 (S.B. 219), § 1.123, eff. April 2, 2015; Acts 2015, 84th Leg., ch. 734 (H.B. 1549), § 80, eff. Sept. 1, 2015.

### § 261.104. Contents of Report

The person making a report shall identify, if known:

(1) the name and address of the child;

(2) the name and address of the person responsible for the care, custody, or welfare of the child; and

(3) any other pertinent information concerning the alleged or suspected abuse or neglect.

Added by Acts 1995, 74th Leg., ch. 20, § 1, eff. April 20, 1995. Amended by Acts 1995, 74th Leg., ch. 751, § 90, eff. Sept. 1, 1995.

### § 261.105. Referral of Report by Department or Law Enforcement

(a) All reports received by a local or state law enforcement agency that allege abuse or neglect by a person responsible for a child's care, custody, or welfare shall be referred immediately to the department.

(b) The department shall immediately notify the appropriate state or local law enforcement agency of any report it receives, other than a report from a law enforcement agency, that concerns the suspected abuse or neglect of a child or death of a child from abuse or neglect.

(c) In addition to notifying a law enforcement agency, if the report relates to a child in a facility operated, licensed, certified, or registered by a state agency, the department shall refer the report to the agency for investigation.

(c–1) Notwithstanding Subsections (b) and (c), if a report under this section relates to a child with an intellectual disability receiving services in a state supported living center as defined by Section 531.002, Health and Safety Code, or the ICF–IID component of the Rio Grande State Center, the department shall proceed with the investigation of the report as provided by Section 261.404.

(d) If the department initiates an investigation and determines that the abuse or neglect does not involve a person responsible for the child's care, custody, or welfare, the department shall refer the report to a law enforcement agency for further investigation. If the department determines that the abuse or neglect involves an employee of a public or private elementary or secondary school, and that the child is a student at the school, the department shall orally notify the superintendent of the school district, the director of the open-enrollment charter school, or the chief executive officer of the private school in which the employee is employed about the investigation.

(e) In cooperation with the department, the Texas Juvenile Justice Department by rule shall adopt guidelines for identifying a report made to the Texas Juvenile Justice Department under Section 261.103(b) that is appropriate to refer to the department or a law enforcement agency for investigation. Guidelines adopted under this subsection must require the Texas Juvenile Justice Department to consider the severity and immediacy of the alleged abuse or neglect of the child victim.

Added by Acts 1995, 74th Leg., ch. 20, § 1, eff. April 20, 1995. Amended by Acts 1997, 75th Leg., ch. 1022, § 66, eff. Sept. 1, 1997; Acts 1999, 76th Leg., ch. 1477, § 25, eff. Sept. 1, 1999; Acts 2003, 78th Leg., ch. 374, § 3, eff. June 18, 2003; Acts 2009, 81st Leg., ch. 284, § 4, eff. June 11, 2009; Acts 2015, 84th Leg., ch. 1 (S.B. 219), § 1.124, eff. April 2, 2015; Acts 2015, 84th Leg., ch. 734 (H.B. 1549), § 81, eff. Sept. 1, 2015; Acts 2015, 84th Leg., ch. 1167 (S.B. 821), § 4, eff. Sept. 1, 2015; Acts 2019, 86th Leg., ch. 987 (S.B. 1231), § 1, eff. Sept. 1, 2019.

### § 261.1055. Notification of District Attorneys

(a) A district attorney may inform the department that the district attorney wishes to receive notification of some or all reports of suspected abuse or neglect of children who were in the county at the time the report was made or who were in the county at the time of the alleged abuse or neglect.

(b) If the district attorney makes the notification under this section, the department shall, on receipt of a report of suspected abuse or neglect, immediately notify the district attorney as requested and the department shall forward a copy of the reports to the district attorney on request.

Added by Acts 1997, 75th Leg., ch. 1022, § 67, eff. Sept. 1, 1997. Amended by Acts 2015, 84th Leg., ch. 1 (S.B. 219), § 1.125, eff. April 2, 2015.

### § 261.106. Immunities

(a) A person acting in good faith who reports or assists in the investigation of a report of alleged child abuse or neglect or who testifies or otherwise participates in a judicial proceeding arising from a report, petition, or investigation of alleged child abuse or neglect is immune from civil or criminal liability that might otherwise be incurred or imposed.

(b) Immunity from civil and criminal liability extends to an authorized volunteer of the department or a law enforcement officer who participates at the request of the department in an investigation of alleged or suspected abuse or neglect or in an action arising from an investigation if the person was acting in good faith and in the scope of the person's responsibilities.

(c) A person who reports the person's own abuse or neglect of a child or who acts in bad faith or with malicious purpose in reporting alleged child abuse or neglect is not immune from civil or criminal liability.

Added by Acts 1995, 74th Leg., ch. 20, § 1, eff. April 20, 1995. Amended by Acts 1995, 74th Leg., ch. 751, § 91, eff. Sept. 1, 1995.

### § 261.107. False Report; Criminal Penalty; Civil Penalty

(a) A person commits an offense if, with the intent to deceive, the person knowingly makes a report as provided in this chapter that is false. An offense under this subsection is a state jail felony unless it is shown on the trial of the offense that the person has previously been convicted under this section, in which case the offense is a felony of the third degree.

(b) A finding by a court in a suit affecting the parent-child relationship that a report made under this chapter before or during the suit was false or lacking factual foundation may be grounds for the court to modify an order providing for possession of or access to the child who was the subject of the report by restricting further access to the child by the person who made the report.

(c) The appropriate county prosecuting attorney shall be responsible for the prosecution of an offense under this section.

(d) The court shall order a person who is convicted of an offense under Subsection (a) to pay any reasonable attorney's fees incurred by the person who was falsely accused of abuse or neglect in any proceeding relating to the false report.

(e) A person who engages in conduct described by Subsection (a) is liable to the state for a civil penalty of $1,000. The attorney general shall bring an action to recover a civil penalty authorized by this subsection.

Added by Acts 1995, 74th Leg., ch. 20, § 1, eff. April 20, 1995. Amended by Acts 1995, 74th Leg., ch. 751, § 92, eff. Sept. 1, 1995; Acts 1997, 75th Leg., ch. 575, § 2, eff. Sept. 1, 1997; Acts 1997, 75th Leg., ch. 1022, § 68; Acts 1999, 76th Leg., ch. 62, § 6.30, eff. Sept. 1, 1999; Acts 2005, 79th Leg., ch. 268, §§ 1.13, 1.14(a), eff. Sept. 1, 2005.

### § 261.108. Frivolous Claims Against Person Reporting

(a) In this section:

(1) "Claim" means an action or claim by a party, including a plaintiff, counterclaimant, cross-claimant, or third-party plaintiff, requesting recovery of damages.

(2) "Defendant" means a party against whom a claim is made.

(b) A court shall award a defendant reasonable attorney's fees and other expenses related to the defense of a claim filed against the defendant for damages or other relief arising from reporting or assisting in the investigation of a report under this chapter or participating in a judicial proceeding resulting from the report if:

(1) the court finds that the claim is frivolous, unreasonable, or without foundation because the defendant is immune from liability under Section 261.106; and

(2) the claim is dismissed or judgment is rendered for the defendant.

(c) To recover under this section, the defendant must, at any time after the filing of a claim, file a written motion stating that:

(1) the claim is frivolous, unreasonable, or without foundation because the defendant is immune from liability under Section 261.106; and

(2) the defendant requests the court to award reasonable attorney's fees and other expenses related to the defense of the claim.

Added by Acts 1995, 74th Leg., ch. 20, § 1, eff. April 20, 1995.

### § 261.109. Failure to Report; Penalty

(a) A person commits an offense if the person is required to make a report under Section 261.101(a) and knowingly fails to make a report as provided in this chapter.

(a–1) A person who is a professional as defined by Section 261.101(b) commits an offense if the person is required to make a report under Section 261.101(b) and knowingly fails to make a report as provided in this chapter.

(b) An offense under Subsection (a) is a Class A misdemeanor, except that the offense is a state jail felony if it is shown on the trial of the offense that the child was a person with an intellectual disability who resided in a state supported living center, the ICF–IID component of the Rio Grande State Center, or a facility licensed under Chapter 252, Health and Safety Code, and the actor knew that the child had suffered serious bodily injury as a result of the abuse or neglect.

(c) An offense under Subsection (a–1) is a Class A misdemeanor, except that the offense is a state jail felony if it is shown on the trial of the offense that the actor intended to conceal the abuse or neglect.

Added by Acts 1995, 74th Leg., ch. 20, § 1, eff. April 20, 1995. Amended by Acts 2009, 81st Leg., ch. 284, § 5, eff. June 11, 2009; Acts 2013, 83rd Leg., ch. 290 (H.B. 1205), § 1, eff. Sept. 1, 2013; Acts 2015, 84th Leg., ch. 1 (S.B. 219), § 1.126, eff. April 2, 2015.

### § 261.110. Employer Retaliation Prohibited

(a) In this section:

(1) "Adverse employment action" means an action that affects an employee's compensation, promotion, transfer, work assignment, or performance evaluation, or any other employment action that would dissuade a reasonable employee from making or supporting a report of abuse or neglect under Section 261.101.

(2) "Professional" has the meaning assigned by Section 261.101(b).

(b) An employer may not suspend or terminate the employment of, discriminate against, or take any other adverse employment action against a person who is a professional and who in good faith:

(1) reports child abuse or neglect to:

(A) the person's supervisor;

(B) an administrator of the facility where the person is employed;

(C) a state regulatory agency; or

(D) a law enforcement agency; or

(2) initiates or cooperates with an investigation or proceeding by a governmental entity relating to an allegation of child abuse or neglect.

(c) A person may sue for injunctive relief, damages, or both if, in violation of this section, the person:

(1) is suspended or terminated from the person's employment;

(2) is discriminated against; or

(3) suffers any other adverse employment action.

(d) A plaintiff who prevails in a suit under this section may recover:

(1) actual damages, including damages for mental anguish even if an injury other than mental anguish is not shown;

(2) exemplary damages under Chapter 41, Civil Practice and Remedies Code, if the employer is a private employer;

(3) court costs; and

(4) reasonable attorney's fees.

(e) In addition to amounts recovered under Subsection (d), a plaintiff who prevails in a suit under this section is entitled to:

(1) reinstatement to the person's former position or a position that is comparable in terms of compensation, benefits, and other conditions of employment;

(2) reinstatement of any fringe benefits and seniority rights lost because of the suspension, termination, or discrimination; and

(3) compensation for wages lost during the period of suspension or termination.

(f) A public employee who alleges a violation of this section may sue the employing state or local governmental entity for the relief provided for by this section. Sovereign immunity is waived and abolished to the extent of liability created by this section. A person having a claim under this section may sue a governmental unit for damages allowed by this section.

(g) In a suit under this section against an employing state or local governmental entity, a plaintiff may not recover compensatory damages for future pecuniary losses, emotional pain, suffering, inconvenience, mental anguish, loss of enjoyment of life, and other nonpecuniary losses in an amount that exceeds:

(1) $50,000, if the employing state or local governmental entity has fewer than 101 employees in each of 20 or more calendar weeks in the calendar year in which the suit is filed or in the preceding year;

(2) $100,000, if the employing state or local governmental entity has more than 100 and fewer than

201 employees in each of 20 or more calendar weeks in the calendar year in which the suit is filed or in the preceding year;

(3) $200,000, if the employing state or local governmental entity has more than 200 and fewer than 501 employees in each of 20 or more calendar weeks in the calendar year in which the suit is filed or in the preceding year; and

(4) $250,000, if the employing state or local governmental entity has more than 500 employees in each of 20 or more calendar weeks in the calendar year in which the suit is filed or in the preceding year.

(h) If more than one subdivision of Subsection (g) applies to an employing state or local governmental entity, the amount of monetary damages that may be recovered from the entity in a suit brought under this section is governed by the applicable provision that provides the highest damage award.

(i) A plaintiff suing under this section has the burden of proof, except that there is a rebuttable presumption that the plaintiff's employment was suspended or terminated or that the plaintiff was otherwise discriminated against for reporting abuse or neglect if the suspension, termination, or discrimination occurs before the 61st day after the date on which the person made a report in good faith.

(j) A suit under this section may be brought in a district or county court of the county in which:

(1) the plaintiff was employed by the defendant; or

(2) the defendant conducts business.

(k) It is an affirmative defense to a suit under Subsection (b) that an employer would have taken the action against the employee that forms the basis of the suit based solely on information, observation, or evidence that is not related to the fact that the employee reported child abuse or neglect or initiated or cooperated with an investigation or proceeding relating to an allegation of child abuse or neglect.

(*l*) A public employee who has a cause of action under Chapter 554, Government Code, based on conduct described by Subsection (b) may not bring an action based on that conduct under this section.

(m) This section does not apply to a person who reports the person's own abuse or neglect of a child or who initiates or cooperates with an investigation or proceeding by a governmental entity relating to an allegation of the person's own abuse or neglect of a child.

Added by Acts 2001, 77th Leg., ch. 896, § 1, eff. Sept. 1, 2001. Amended by Acts 2019, 86th Leg., ch. 218 (H.B. 621), § 1, eff. Sept. 1, 2019.

Section 2 of Acts 2019, 86th Leg., ch. 218 (H.B. 621) provides:

"This Act applies only to an adverse employment action taken by an employer against an employee that occurs on or after the effective date [Sept. 1, 2019] of this Act. An adverse employment action taken by an employer against an employee that occurs before that date is governed by the law in effect on the date the action occurred, and the former law is continued in effect for that purpose."

### § 261.111. Refusal of Psychiatric or Psychological Treatment of Child

(a) In this section, "psychotropic medication" has the meaning assigned by Section 266.001.

(b) The refusal of a parent, guardian, or managing or possessory conservator of a child to administer or consent to the administration of a psychotropic medication to the child, or to consent to any other psychiatric or psychological treatment of the child, does not by itself constitute neglect of the child unless the refusal to consent:

(1) presents a substantial risk of death, disfigurement, or bodily injury to the child; or

(2) has resulted in an observable and material impairment to the growth, development, or functioning of the child.

Added by Acts 2003, 78th Leg., ch. 1008, § 3, eff. June 20, 2003. Amended by Acts 2015, 84th Leg., ch. 1 (S.B. 219), § 1.127, eff. April 2, 2015.

## SUBCHAPTER C. CONFIDENTIALITY AND PRIVILEGED COMMUNICATION

### § 261.201. Confidentiality and Disclosure of Information

(a) Except as provided by Section 261.203, the following information is confidential, is not subject to public release under Chapter 552, Government Code, and may be disclosed only for purposes consistent with this code and applicable federal or state law or under rules adopted by an investigating agency:

(1) a report of alleged or suspected abuse or neglect made under this chapter and the identity of the person making the report; and

(2) except as otherwise provided in this section, the files, reports, records, communications, audiotapes, videotapes, and working papers used or developed in an investigation under this chapter or in providing services as a result of an investigation.

(b) A court may order the disclosure of information that is confidential under this section if:

(1) a motion has been filed with the court requesting the release of the information;

(2) a notice of hearing has been served on the investigating agency and all other interested parties; and

(3) after hearing and an in camera review of the requested information, the court determines that the disclosure of the requested information is:

(A) essential to the administration of justice; and

(B) not likely to endanger the life or safety of:

(i) a child who is the subject of the report of alleged or suspected abuse or neglect;

(ii) a person who makes a report of alleged or suspected abuse or neglect; or

(iii) any other person who participates in an investigation of reported abuse or neglect or who provides care for the child.

(b-1) On a motion of one of the parties in a contested case before an administrative law judge relating to the license or certification of a professional, as defined by Section 261.101(b), or an educator, as defined by Section 5.001, Education Code, the administrative law judge may order the disclosure of information that is confidential under this section that relates to the matter before the administrative law judge after a hearing for which notice is provided as required by Subsection (b)(2) and making the review and determination required by Subsection (b)(3). Before the department may release information under this subsection, the department must edit the information to protect the confidentiality of the identity of any person who makes a report of abuse or neglect.

(c) In addition to Subsection (b), a court, on its own motion, may order disclosure of information that is confidential under this section if:

(1) the order is rendered at a hearing for which all parties have been given notice;

(2) the court finds that disclosure of the information is:

(A) essential to the administration of justice; and

(B) not likely to endanger the life or safety of:

(i) a child who is the subject of the report of alleged or suspected abuse or neglect;

(ii) a person who makes a report of alleged or suspected abuse or neglect; or

(iii) any other person who participates in an investigation of reported abuse or neglect or who provides care for the child; and

(3) the order is reduced to writing or made on the record in open court.

(d) The adoptive parents of a child who was the subject of an investigation and an adult who was the subject of an investigation as a child are entitled to examine and make copies of any report, record, working paper, or other information in the possession, custody, or control of the state that pertains to the history of the child. The department may edit the documents to protect the identity of the biological parents and any other person whose identity is confidential, unless this information is already known to the adoptive parents or is readily available through other sources, including the court records of a suit to terminate the parent-child relationship under Chapter 161.

(e) Before placing a child who was the subject of an investigation, the department shall notify the prospective adoptive parents of their right to examine any report, record, working paper, or other information in the possession, custody, or control of the department that pertains to the history of the child.

(f) The department shall provide prospective adoptive parents an opportunity to examine information under this section as early as practicable before placing a child.

(f-1) The department shall provide to a relative or other individual with whom a child is placed any information the department considers necessary to ensure that the relative or other individual is prepared to meet the needs of the child. The information required by this subsection may include information related to any abuse or neglect suffered by the child.

(g) Notwithstanding Subsection (b), the department, on request and subject to department rule, shall provide to the parent, managing conservator, or other legal representative of a child who is the subject of reported abuse or neglect information concerning the reported abuse or neglect that would otherwise be confidential under this section if the department has edited the information to protect the confidentiality of the identity of the person who made the report and any other person whose life or safety may be endangered by the disclosure.

(h) This section does not apply to an investigation of child abuse or neglect in a home or facility regulated under Chapter 42, Human Resources Code.

(i) Notwithstanding Subsection (a), the Texas Juvenile Justice Department shall release a report of alleged or suspected abuse or neglect made under this chapter if:

(1) the report relates to a report of abuse or neglect involving a child committed to the Texas Juvenile Justice Department during the period that the child is committed to that department; and

(2) the Texas Juvenile Justice Department is not prohibited by Chapter 552, Government Code, or other law from disclosing the report.

(j) The Texas Juvenile Justice Department shall edit any report disclosed under Subsection (i) to protect the identity of:

(1) a child who is the subject of the report of alleged or suspected abuse or neglect;

(2) the person who made the report; and

(3) any other person whose life or safety may be endangered by the disclosure.

(k) Notwithstanding Subsection (a), an investigating agency, other than the department or the Texas Juvenile Justice Department, on request, shall provide to the parent, managing conservator, or other legal representative of a child who is the subject of reported abuse or neglect, or to the child if the child is at least 18 years of age, information concerning the reported abuse or neglect that would otherwise be confidential under this section. The investigating agency shall withhold information under this subsection if the parent, managing conservator, or other legal representative of the child requesting the information is alleged to have committed the abuse or neglect.

(*l*) Before a child or a parent, managing conservator, or other legal representative of a child may inspect or copy a record or file concerning the child under Subsection (k), the custodian of the record or file must redact:

(1) any personally identifiable information about a victim or witness under 18 years of age unless that victim or witness is:

(A) the child who is the subject of the report; or

(B) another child of the parent, managing conservator, or other legal representative requesting the information;

(2) any information that is excepted from required disclosure under Chapter 552, Government Code, or other law; and

(3) the identity of the person who made the report.

Added by Acts 1995, 74th Leg., ch. 20, § 1, eff. April 20, 1995. Amended by Acts 1995, 74th Leg., ch. 751, § 93, eff. Sept. 1, 1995; Acts 1997, 75th Leg., ch. 575, § 12, eff. Sept. 1, 1997; Acts 1997, 75th Leg., ch. 1022, § 69, eff. Sept. 1, 1997; Acts 1999, 76th Leg., ch. 1150, § 3, eff. Sept. 1, 1999; Acts 1999, 76th Leg., ch. 1390, § 22, eff. Sept. 1, 1999; Acts 2003, 78th Leg., ch. 68, § 2, eff. Sept. 1, 2003; Acts 2005, 79th Leg., ch. 268, § 1.15, eff. Sept. 1, 2005; Acts 2007, 80th Leg., ch. 263, § 12, eff. June 8, 2007; Acts 2009, 81st Leg., ch. 713, § 1, eff. June 19, 2009; Acts 2009, 81st Leg., ch. 779, § 1, eff. Sept. 1, 2009; Acts 2009, 81st Leg., ch. 1377, § 13, eff. Sept. 1, 2009; Acts 2015, 84th Leg., ch. 1 (S.B. 219), § 1.128, eff. April 2, 2015; Acts 2015, 84th Leg., ch. 734 (H.B. 1549), § 82, eff. Sept. 1, 2015.

### § 261.202. Privileged Communication

In a proceeding regarding the abuse or neglect of a child, evidence may not be excluded on the ground of privileged communication except in the case of communications between an attorney and client.

Added by Acts 1995, 74th Leg., ch. 20, § 1, eff. April 20, 1995.

### § 261.203. Information Relating to Child Fatality

(a) Not later than the fifth day after the date the department receives a request for information about a child fatality with respect to which the department is conducting an investigation of alleged abuse or neglect, the department shall release:

(1) the age and sex of the child;

(2) the date of death;

(3) whether the state was the managing conservator of the child at the time of the child's death; and

(4) whether the child resided with the child's parent, managing conservator, guardian, or other person entitled to possession of the child at the time of the child's death.

(b) If, after a child abuse or neglect investigation described by Subsection (a) is completed, the department determines a child's death or a child's near fatality was caused by abuse or neglect, the department on request shall promptly release investigation information not prohibited from release under federal law, including the following information:

(1) the information described by Subsection (a), if not previously released to the person requesting the information;

(2) information on whether a child's death or near fatality:

(A) was determined by the department to be attributable to abuse or neglect; or

(B) resulted in a criminal investigation or the filing of criminal charges if known at the time the investigation is completed;

(3) for cases in which the child's death or near fatality occurred while the child was living with the child's parent, managing conservator, guardian, or other person entitled to possession of the child:

(A) a summary of any previous reports of abuse or neglect of the child or another child made while the child was living with that parent, managing conservator, guardian, or other person entitled to possession of the child;

(B) the disposition of any report under Paragraph (A);

(C) a description of any services, including family-based safety services, that were provided or offered by the department to the child or the child's family as a result of any report under Paragraph (A) and whether the services were accepted or declined; and

(D) the results of any risk or safety assessment completed by the department relating to the child; and

(4) for a case in which the child's death or near fatality occurred while the child was in substitute care with the department or with a residential child-care provider regulated under Chapter 42, Human Resources Code, the following information:

(A) the date the substitute care provider with whom the child was residing at the time of death or near fatality was licensed or verified;

(B) a summary of any previous reports of abuse or neglect investigated by the department relating to the substitute care provider, including the disposition of any investigation resulting from a report;

(C) any reported licensing violations, including notice of any action taken by the department regarding a violation; and

(D) records of any training completed by the substitute care provider while the child was placed with the provider.

(c) If the department is unable to release the information required by Subsection (b) before the 11th day after the date the department receives a request for the information or the date the investigation of the child fatality is completed, whichever is later, the department shall inform the person requesting the information of the date the department will release the information.

(d) Repealed by Acts 2015, 84th Leg., ch. 944 (S.B. 206), § 86(7).

(e) Before the department releases any information under Subsection (b), the department shall redact from the records any information the release of which would:

(1) identify:

(A) the individual who reported the abuse or neglect; or

(B) any other individual other than the deceased child or an alleged perpetrator of the abuse or neglect;

(2) jeopardize an ongoing criminal investigation or prosecution;

(3) endanger the life or safety of any individual; or

(4) violate other state or federal law.

(f) The executive commissioner of the Health and Human Services Commission shall adopt rules to implement this section.

Added by Acts 2009, 81st Leg., ch. 779, § 2, eff. Sept. 1, 2009. Amended by Acts 2015, 84th Leg., ch. 253 (S.B. 949), § 1, eff. Sept. 1, 2015; Acts 2015, 84th Leg., ch. 944 (S.B. 206), § 86(7), eff. Sept. 1, 2015.

### § 261.204. Annual Child Fatality Report

(a) Not later than March 1 of each year, the department shall publish an aggregated report using information compiled from each child fatality investigation for which the department made a finding regarding abuse or neglect, including cases in which the department determined the fatality was not the result of abuse or neglect. The report must protect the identity of individuals involved and contain the following information:

(1) the age and sex of the child and the county in which the fatality occurred;

(2) whether the state was the managing conservator of the child or whether the child resided with the child's parent, managing conservator, guardian, or other person entitled to the possession of the child at the time of the fatality;

(3) the relationship to the child of the individual alleged to have abused or neglected the child, if any;

(4) the number of any department abuse or neglect investigations involving the child or the individual alleged to have abused or neglected the child

during the two years preceding the date of the fatality and the results of the investigations;

(5) whether the department offered family-based safety services or conservatorship services to the child or family;

(6) the types of abuse and neglect alleged in the reported investigations, if any; and

(7) any trends identified in the investigations contained in the report.

(b) The report published under Subsection (a) must:

(1) accurately represent all abuse-related and neglect-related child fatalities in this state, including child fatalities investigated under Subchapter F, Chapter 264,[1] and other child fatalities investigated by the department; and

(2) aggregate the fatalities by investigative findings and case disposition, including the following dispositions:

(A) abuse and neglect ruled out;

(B) unable to determine cause of death;

(C) reason to believe abuse or neglect occurred;

(D) reason to believe abuse or neglect contributed to child's death;

(E) unable to complete review; and

(F) administrative closure.

(c) The department may release additional information in the annual report if the release of the information is not prohibited by state or federal law.

(d) The department shall post the annual report on the department's Internet website and otherwise make the report available to the public.

(e) The executive commissioner of the Health and Human Services Commission may adopt rules to implement this section.

(f) At least once every 10 years, the department shall use the information reported under this section to provide guidance for possible department policy changes.

Added by Acts 2015, 84th Leg., ch. 253 (S.B. 949), § 2, eff. Sept. 1, 2015. Amended by Acts 2017, 85th Leg., ch. 822 (H.B. 1549), § 1, eff. Sept. 1, 2017.

[1] V.T.C.A., Family Code §§ 264.501 et seq.

## SUBCHAPTER D. INVESTIGATIONS

### § 261.301. Investigation of Report

(a) With assistance from the appropriate state or local law enforcement agency as provided by this section, the department shall make a prompt and thorough investigation of a report of child abuse or neglect allegedly committed by a person responsible for a child's care, custody, or welfare. The investigation shall be conducted without regard to any pending suit affecting the parent-child relationship.

(b) A state agency shall investigate a report that alleges abuse, neglect, or exploitation occurred in a facility operated, licensed, certified, or registered by that agency as provided by Subchapter E.[1] In conducting an investigation for a facility operated, licensed, certified, registered, or listed by the department, the department shall perform the investigation as provided by:

(1) Subchapter E; and

(2) the Human Resources Code.

(c) The department is not required to investigate a report that alleges child abuse, neglect, or exploitation by a person other than a person responsible for a child's care, custody, or welfare. The appropriate state or local law enforcement agency shall investigate that report if the agency determines an investigation should be conducted.

(d) The executive commissioner shall by rule assign priorities and prescribe investigative procedures for investigations based on the severity and immediacy of the alleged harm to the child. The primary purpose of the investigation shall be the protection of the child. The rules must require the department, subject to the availability of funds, to:

(1) immediately respond to a report of abuse and neglect that involves circumstances in which the death of the child or substantial bodily harm to the child would result unless the department immediately intervenes;

(2) respond within 24 hours to a report of abuse and neglect that is assigned the highest priority, other than a report described by Subdivision (1); and

(3) respond within 72 hours to a report of abuse and neglect that is assigned the second highest priority.

(e) As necessary to provide for the protection of the child, the department shall determine:

(1) the nature, extent, and cause of the abuse or neglect;

(2) the identity of the person responsible for the abuse or neglect;

(3) the names and conditions of the other children in the home;

(4) an evaluation of the parents or persons responsible for the care of the child;

(5) the adequacy of the home environment;

(6) the relationship of the child to the persons responsible for the care, custody, or welfare of the child; and

(7) all other pertinent data.

(f) An investigation of a report to the department that alleges that a child has been or may be the victim of conduct that constitutes a criminal offense that poses an immediate risk of physical or sexual abuse of a child that could result in the death of or serious harm to the child shall be conducted jointly by a peace officer, as defined by Article 2.12, Code of Criminal Procedure, from the appropriate local law enforcement agency and the department or the agency responsible for conducting an investigation under Subchapter E.

(g) The inability or unwillingness of a local law enforcement agency to conduct a joint investigation under this section does not constitute grounds to prevent or prohibit the department from performing its duties under this subtitle. The department shall document any instance in which a law enforcement agency is unable or unwilling to conduct a joint investigation under this section.

(h) The department and the appropriate local law enforcement agency shall conduct an investigation, other than an investigation under Subchapter E, as provided by this section and Article 2.27, Code of Criminal Procedure, if the investigation is of a report that alleges that a child has been or may be the victim of conduct that constitutes a criminal offense that poses an immediate risk of physical or sexual abuse of a child that could result in the death of or serious harm to the child. Immediately on receipt of a report described by this subsection, the department shall notify the appropriate local law enforcement agency of the report.

(i) If at any time during an investigation of a report of child abuse or neglect to which the department has assigned the highest priority the department is unable to locate the child who is the subject of the report of abuse or neglect or the child's family, the department shall notify the Department of Public Safety that the location of the child and the child's family is unknown. If the Department of Public Safety locates the child and the child's family, the Department of Public Safety shall notify the department of the location of the child and the child's family.

(j) In geographic areas with demonstrated need, the department shall designate employees to serve specifically as investigators and responders for after-hours reports of child abuse or neglect.

(k) In an investigation of a report of abuse or neglect allegedly committed by a person responsible for a child's care, custody, or welfare, the department shall determine whether the person is an active duty member of the United States armed forces or the spouse of a member on active duty. If the department determines the person is an active duty member of the United States armed forces or the spouse of a member on active duty, the department shall notify the United States Department of Defense Family Advocacy Program at the closest active duty military installation of the investigation.

Added by Acts 1995, 74th Leg., ch. 20, § 1, eff. April 20, 1995. Amended by Acts 1995, 74th Leg., ch. 751, § 94, eff. Sept. 1, 1995; Acts 1995, 74th Leg., ch. 943, § 2, eff. Sept. 1, 1995; Acts 1997, 75th Leg., ch. 1022, § 70, eff. Sept. 1, 1997; Acts 1997, 75th Leg., ch. 1137, § 1, eff. Sept. 1, 1997; Acts 1999, 76th Leg., ch. 1150, § 4, eff. Sept. 1, 1999; Acts 1999, 76th Leg., ch. 1390, § 23, eff. Sept. 1, 1999; Acts 2003, 78th Leg., ch. 867, § 1, eff. Sept. 1, 2003; Acts 2005, 79th Leg., ch. 268, § 1.16(a), eff. Sept. 1, 2005; Acts 2015, 84th Leg., ch. 1 (S.B. 219), § 1.129, eff. April 2, 2015; Acts 2015, 84th Leg., ch. 1056 (H.B. 2053), § 1, eff. Sept. 1, 2015; Acts 2017, 85th Leg., ch. 319 (S.B. 11), § 9, eff. Sept. 1, 2017; Acts 2017, 85th Leg., ch. 356 (H.B. 2124), § 1, eff. Sept. 1, 2017; Acts 2017, 85th Leg., ch. 822 (H.B. 1549), § 2, eff. Sept. 1, 2017; Acts 2017, 85th Leg., ch. 1136 (H.B. 249), § 4, eff. Sept. 1, 2017; Acts 2019, 86th Leg., ch. 467 (H.B. 4170), § 21.001(13), eff. Sept. 1, 2019.

[1] V.T.C.A., Family Code § 261.401 et seq.

### § 261.3011. Joint Investigation Guidelines and Training

(a) The department shall, in consultation with the appropriate law enforcement agencies, develop guidelines and protocols for joint investigations by the department and the law enforcement agency under Section 261.301. The guidelines and protocols must:

(1) clarify the respective roles of the department and law enforcement agency in conducting the investigation;

(2) require that mutual child protective services and law enforcement training and agreements be implemented by both entities to ensure the integrity and best outcomes of joint investigations; and

(3) incorporate the use of forensic methods in determining the occurrence of child abuse and neglect.

(b) The department shall collaborate with law enforcement agencies to provide to department investigators and law enforcement officers responsible for investigating reports of abuse and neglect joint training relating to methods to effectively conduct joint investigations under Section 261.301. The training must include information on interviewing techniques, evidence gathering, and testifying in court for criminal investigations, as well as instruction on rights provided by the Fourth Amendment to the United States Constitution.

Added by Acts 2005, 79th Leg., ch. 268, § 1.17, eff. Sept. 1, 2005.

### § 261.3012. Repealed by Acts 2015, 84th Leg., ch. 944 (S.B. 206), § 86(8), eff. Sept. 1, 2015

### § 261.3013. Case Closure Agreements Prohibited

(a) Except as provided by Subsection (b), on closing a case, the department may not enter into a written agreement with a child's parent or another adult with whom the child resides that requires the parent or other adult to take certain actions after the case is closed to ensure the child's safety.

(b) This section does not apply to an agreement that is entered into by a parent or other adult:

(1) following the removal of a child and that is subject to the approval of a court with continuing jurisdiction over the child;

(2) as a result of the person's participation in family group conferencing; or

(3) as part of a formal case closure plan agreed to by the person who will continue to care for a child as a result of a parental child safety placement.

(c) The department shall develop policies to guide caseworkers in the development of case closure agreements authorized under Subsections (b)(2) and (3).

Added by Acts 2011, 82nd Leg., ch. 598 (S.B. 218), § 1, eff. Sept. 1, 2011.

### § 261.3015. Alternative Response System

(a) In assigning priorities and prescribing investigative procedures based on the severity and immediacy of the alleged harm to a child under Section 261.301(d), the department shall establish an alternative response system to allow the department to make the most effective use of resources to investigate and respond to reported cases of abuse and neglect.

(b) Notwithstanding Section 261.301, the department may, in accordance with this section and department rules, conduct an alternative response to a report of abuse or neglect if the report does not:

(1) allege sexual abuse of a child;

(2) allege abuse or neglect that caused the death of a child; or

(3) indicate a risk of serious physical injury or immediate serious harm to a child.

(c) The department may administratively close a reported case of abuse or neglect without completing the investigation or alternative response and without providing services or making a referral to another entity for assistance if the department determines, after contacting a professional or other credible source, that the child's safety can be assured without further investigation, response, services, or assistance.

(d) In determining how to classify a reported case of abuse or neglect under the alternative response system, the child's safety is the primary concern. The classification of a case may be changed as warranted by the circumstances.

(e) An alternative response to a report of abuse or neglect must include:

(1) a safety assessment of the child who is the subject of the report;

(2) an assessment of the child's family; and

(3) in collaboration with the child's family, identification of any necessary and appropriate service or support to reduce the risk of future harm to the child.

(f) An alternative response to a report of abuse or neglect may not include a formal determination of whether the alleged abuse or neglect occurred.

(g) The department may implement the alternative response in one or more of the department's administrative regions before implementing the system statewide. The department shall study the results of the system in the regions where the system has been implemented in determining the method by which to implement the system statewide.

Added by Acts 1997, 75th Leg., ch. 1022, § 71, eff. Sept. 1, 1997. Amended by Acts 2005, 79th Leg., ch. 268, § 1.19(a), eff. Sept. 1, 2005; Acts 2013, 83rd Leg., ch. 420 (S.B. 423), § 1, eff. Sept. 1, 2013; Acts 2015, 84th Leg., ch. 1 (S.B. 219), §§ 1.130, 1.131, eff. April 2, 2015.

### § 261.3016. Training of Personnel Receiving Reports of Abuse and Neglect

The department shall develop, in cooperation with local law enforcement officials and the Commission on State Emergency Communications, a training program for department personnel who receive reports of abuse and neglect. The training program must include information on:

(1) the proper methods of screening reports of abuse and neglect; and

(2) ways to determine the seriousness of a report, including determining whether a report alleges circumstances that could result in the death of or serious harm to a child or whether the report is less serious in nature.

Added by Acts 2005, 79th Leg., ch. 54, § 1, eff. Sept. 1, 2005; Acts 2005, 79th Leg., ch. 268, § 1.20, eff. Sept. 1, 2005.

### § 261.3017. Consultation with Physician Networks and Systems Regarding Certain Medical Conditions

(a) In this section:

(1) "Network" means the Forensic Assessment Center Network.

(2) "System" means the entities that receive grants under the Texas Medical Child Abuse Resources and Education System (MEDCARES) authorized by Chapter 1001, Health and Safety Code.

(b) Any agreement between the department and the network or between the Department of State Health Services and the system to provide assistance in connection with abuse and neglect investigations conducted by the department must require the network and the system to have the ability to obtain consultations with physicians licensed to practice medicine in this state and board certified in the relevant field or specialty, including radiologists, geneticists, orthopedists, and endocrinologists, to diagnose and treat certain unique health conditions, including:

(1) rickets;

(2) Ehlers–Danlos Syndrome;

(3) osteogenesis imperfecta;

(4) vitamin D deficiency; and

(5) other medical conditions that mimic child maltreatment or increase the risk of misdiagnosis of child maltreatment.

(c) During an abuse or neglect investigation authorized by this subchapter or an assessment provided under Subsection (b), the department shall refer the child's case for a specialty consultation if:

(1) the department determines the child requires a specialty consultation with a physician;

(2) the child's primary care physician or other primary health care provider who provided health care or treatment or otherwise evaluated the child recommends a specialty consultation; or

(3) the child's parent or legal guardian or, if represented by an attorney, the attorney of the parent or legal guardian requests a specialty consultation.

(c–1) For a case in which a specialty consultation is required by Subsection (c), the department shall refer the case to a physician who:

(1) is licensed to practice medicine in this state under Subtitle B, Title 3, Occupations Code;

(2) is board certified in a field or specialty relevant to diagnosing and treating the conditions described by Subsection (b); and

(3) was not involved with the report of suspected abuse or neglect.

(c–2) Before referring a child's case under Subsection (c), the department shall provide to the child's parent or legal guardian or, if represented by an attorney, the attorney of the parent or legal guardian written notice of the name, contact information, and credentials of the specialist. The parent, legal guardian, or attorney, as applicable, may object to the proposed referral and request referral to another specialist. The department and the parent, legal guardian, or attorney, as applicable, shall collaborate in good faith to select an acceptable specialist from the proposed specialists; however the department may refer the child's case to a specialist over the objection of the parent, legal guardian, or attorney.

(d) In providing assessments to the department as provided by Subsection (b), the network and the system must use a blind peer review process to resolve cases where physicians in the network or system disagree in the assessment of the causes of a child's injuries or in the presence of a condition listed under Subsection (b).

(e) This section may not be construed to prohibit a child's parent or legal guardian or, if represented by an attorney, the attorney of the parent or legal guardian from otherwise obtaining an alternative opinion at the parent's, legal guardian's, or attorney's, as applicable, own initiative and expense. The department shall accept and consider an alternative opinion obtained and provided under this section and shall document its analysis and determinations regarding the opinion.

Added by Acts 2017, 85th Leg., ch. 502 (H.B. 2848), § 1, eff. Sept. 1, 2017. Amended by Acts 2021, 87th Leg., ch. 1047 (S.B. 1578), § 1, eff. Sept. 1, 2021.

Section 8 of Acts 2021, 87th Leg., ch. 665 (S.B. 1578) provides:

"The changes in law made by this Act apply only to a suit affecting the parent-child relationship filed on or after the effective date [Sept. 1, 2021] of this Act. A suit affecting the parent-child relationship filed before the effective date of this Act is governed by the law in effect on the date the suit was filed, and the former law is continued in effect for that purpose."

## § 261.30171. Forensic Assessment Center Network Evaluation

*This section expires pursuant to (d)*

(a) In this section, "network" means the Forensic Assessment Center Network.

(b) The department, with the assistance of the Supreme Court of Texas Children's Commission, shall:

(1) evaluate the department's use of the network; and

(2) develop joint recommendations to improve:

(A) the evaluation of agreements between the department and the network; and

(B) the best practices for using assessments provided by the network in connection with abuse and neglect investigations conducted by the department.

(c) Not later than September 1, 2022, the department shall prepare and submit to the legislature a written report containing the department's findings and recommendations under Subsection (b) and any recommendations for legislative or other action.

(d) This section expires September 1, 2023.

Added by Acts 2021, 87th Leg., ch. 1047 (S.B. 1578), § 2, eff. Sept. 1, 2021.

Section 8 of Acts 2021, 87th Leg., ch. 665 (S.B. 1578) provides:

"The changes in law made by this Act apply only to a suit affecting the parent-child relationship filed on or after the effective date [Sept. 1, 2021] of this Act. A suit affecting the parent-child relationship filed before the effective date [Sept. 1, 2021] of this Act is governed by the law in effect on the date the suit was filed, and the former law is continued in effect for that purpose."

## § 261.30175. Mitigation of Provider Conflicts in Abuse or Neglect Investigation Consultations

(a) In this section:

(1) "Forensic assessment" means a medical examination, psychosocial evaluation, medical case review, specialty evaluation, or other forensic evaluation service conducted by a physician under Section 261.3017 in connection with any investigation of a suspected case of abuse or neglect for the primary purpose of providing the department, law enforcement, or the court with expert advice, recommendations, or testimony on the case.

(2) "Health care practitioner" means an individual licensed, certified, or otherwise authorized to administer health care services in the ordinary course of business or professional practice. The term includes a physician, medical student, resident physician, child abuse fellow, advanced practice registered nurse, nurse, and physician assistant.

(3) "Network" has the meaning assigned by Section 261.3017.

(4) "System" has the meaning assigned by Section 261.3017.

(b) A health care practitioner who reports suspected abuse or neglect of a child may not provide forensic assessment services in connection with an investigation resulting from the report. This subsection applies regardless of whether the practitioner is a member of the network or system.

(c) When referring a case for forensic assessment, the department shall refer the case to a physician authorized to practice medicine in this state under Subtitle B, Title 3, Occupations Code, who was not involved with the report of suspected abuse or neglect.

(d) This section may not be construed to:

(1) prohibit the department from interviewing the health care practitioner in the practitioner's capacity as a principal or collateral source; or

(2) otherwise restrict the department's ability to conduct an investigation as provided by this subchapter.

Added by Acts 2021, 87th Leg., ch. 1047 (S.B. 1578), § 3, eff. Sept. 1, 2021.

Section 8 of Acts 2021, 87th Leg., ch. 665 (S.B. 1578) provides:

"The changes in law made by this Act apply only to a suit affecting the parent-child relationship filed on or after the effective date [Sept. 1, 2021] of this Act. A suit affecting the parent-child relationship filed before the effective date [Sept. 1, 2021] of this Act is governed by the law in effect on the date the suit was filed, and the former law is continued in effect for that purpose."

## § 261.3018. Abbreviated Investigation and Administrative Closure of Certain Cases

(a) A department caseworker may refer a reported case of child abuse or neglect to a department supervisor for abbreviated investigation or administrative closure at any time before the 60th day after the date the report is received if:

(1) there is no prior report of abuse or neglect of the child who is the subject of the report;

(2) the department has not received an additional report of abuse or neglect of the child following the initial report;

(3) after contacting a professional or other credible source, the caseworker determines that the child's safety can be assured without further investigation, response, services, or assistance; and

(4) the caseworker determines that no abuse or neglect occurred.

(b) A department supervisor shall review each reported case of child abuse or neglect that has remained open for more than 60 days and administratively close the case if:

(1) the supervisor determines that:

(A) the circumstances described by Subsections (a)(1)–(4) exist; and

(B) closing the case would not expose the child to an undue risk of harm; and

(2) the department director grants approval for the administrative closure of the case.

(c) A department supervisor may reassign a reported case of child abuse or neglect that does not qualify for abbreviated investigation or administrative closure under Subsection (a) or (b) to a different department caseworker if the supervisor determines that reassignment would allow the department to make the most effective use of resources to investigate and respond to reported cases of abuse or neglect.

(d) The executive commissioner shall adopt rules necessary to implement this section.

(e) In this section, "professional" means an individual who is licensed or certified by the state or who is an employee of a facility licensed, certified, or operated by the state and who, in the normal course of official duties or duties for which a license or certification is required, has direct contact with children. The term includes teachers, nurses, doctors, day-care employees, employees of a clinic or health care facility that provides reproductive services, juvenile probation officers, and juvenile detention or correctional officers.

Added by Acts 2017, 85th Leg., ch. 523 (S.B. 190), § 1, eff. June 9, 2017. Redesignated from V.T.C.A., Family Code § 261.3017 by Acts 2019, 86th Leg., ch. 467 (H.B. 4170), § 21.001(14), eff. Sept. 1, 2019.

## § 261.3019. Expired

## § 261.302. Conduct of Investigation

(a) The investigation may include:

(1) a visit to the child's home, unless the alleged abuse or neglect can be confirmed or clearly ruled out without a home visit; and

(2) an interview with and examination of the subject child, which may include a medical, psychological, or psychiatric examination.

(b) The interview with and examination of the child may:

(1) be conducted at any reasonable time and place, including the child's home or the child's school;

(2) include the presence of persons the department determines are necessary; and

(3) include transporting the child for purposes relating to the interview or investigation.

(b–1) Before the department may transport a child as provided by Subsection (b)(3), the department shall attempt to notify the parent or other person having custody of the child of the transport.

(c) The investigation may include an interview with the child's parents and an interview with and medical, psychological, or psychiatric examination of any child in the home.

(d) If, before an investigation is completed, the investigating agency believes that the immediate removal of a child from the child's home is necessary to protect the child from further abuse or neglect, the investigating agency shall file a petition or take other action under Chapter 262 to provide for the temporary care and protection of the child.

(e) An interview with a child in which the allegations of the current investigation are discussed and that is conducted by the department during the investigation stage shall be audiotaped or videotaped unless:

(1) the recording equipment malfunctions and the malfunction is not the result of a failure to maintain the equipment or bring adequate supplies for the equipment;

(2) the child is unwilling to allow the interview to be recorded after the department makes a reasonable effort consistent with the child's age and development and the circumstances of the case to convince the child to allow the recording; or

(3) due to circumstances that could not have been reasonably foreseen or prevented by the department, the department does not have the necessary recording equipment because the department employee conducting the interview does not ordinarily conduct interviews.

(e–1) An interview with a child alleged to be a victim of physical abuse or sexual abuse conducted by an investigating agency other than the department shall be audiotaped or videotaped unless the investigating agency determines that good cause exists for not audiotaping or videotaping the interview in accordance with rules of the agency. Good cause may include, but is not limited to, such considerations as the age of the child and the nature and seriousness of the allegations under investigation. Nothing in this subsection shall be construed as prohibiting the investigating agency from audiotaping or videotaping an interview of a child on any case for which such audiotaping or videotaping is not required under this subsection. The fact that the investigating agency failed to audiotape or videotape an interview is admissible at the trial of the offense that is the subject of the interview.

(f) A person commits an offense if the person is notified of the time of the transport of a child by the department and the location from which the transport is initiated and the person is present at the location when the transport is initiated and attempts to interfere with the department's investigation. An offense under this subsection is a Class B misdemeanor. It is an exception to the application of this subsection that the department requested the person to be present at the site of the transport.

Added by Acts 1995, 74th Leg., ch. 20, § 1, eff. April 20, 1995. Amended by Acts 1995, 74th Leg., ch. 751, § 95, eff. Sept. 1, 1995; Acts 1997, 75th Leg., ch. 575, §§ 13, 14, eff. Sept. 1, 1997; Acts 1997, 75th Leg., ch. 1022, § 73, eff. Sept. 1, 1997; Acts 2005, 79th Leg., ch. 268, § 1.21, eff. Sept. 1, 2005; Acts 2015, 84th Leg., ch. 1 (S.B. 219), § 1.132, eff. April 2, 2015; Acts 2015, 84th Leg., ch. 944 (S.B. 206), § 19, eff. Sept. 1, 2015.

### § 261.3021. Casework Documentation and Management

Subject to the appropriation of money, the department shall identify critical investigation actions that impact child safety and require department caseworkers to document those actions in a child's case file not later than the day after the action occurs.

Added by Acts 2005, 79th Leg., ch. 268, § 1.22, eff. Sept. 1, 2005. Amended by Acts 2015, 84th Leg., ch. 944 (S.B. 206), § 20, eff. Sept. 1, 2015.

### § 261.3022. Child Safety Check Alert List

(a) The Department of Public Safety of the State of Texas shall maintain a child safety check alert list as part of the Texas Crime Information Center to help locate a child or the child's family for purposes of:

(1) investigating a report of child abuse or neglect;

(2) providing protective services to a family receiving family-based support services; or

(3) providing protective services to the family of a child in the managing conservatorship of the department.

(b) If the department is unable to locate a child or the child's family for a purpose described by Subsection (a) after the department has attempted to locate the child for not more than 20 days, the department shall notify the Texas Department of Public Safety that the department is unable to locate the child or the child's family. The notice must include the information required by Subsections (c)(1)–(10).

(c) On receipt of the notice from the department, the Texas Department of Public Safety shall notify the Texas Crime Information Center to place the child and the child's family on a child safety check alert list. The alert list must include the following information if known or readily available:

(1) the name, sex, race, date of birth, any known identifying numbers, including social security number and driver's license number, and personal descriptions of the family member alleged to have abused or neglected a child according to the report the department is attempting to investigate;

(2) the name, sex, race, date of birth, any known identifying numbers, including social security number and driver's license number, and personal descriptions of any parent, managing conservator, or guardian of the child who cannot be located for the purposes described by Subsection (a);

(3) the name, sex, race, date of birth, any known identifying numbers, including social security number and driver's license number, and personal descriptions of the child who is the subject of the report or is receiving services described by Subsection (a)(2) or (3);

(4) if applicable, a code identifying the type of child abuse or neglect alleged or determined to have been committed against the child;

(5) the family's last known address;

(6) any known description of the motor vehicle, including the vehicle's make, color, style of body, model year, and vehicle identification number, in which the child is suspected to be transported;

(7) the case number assigned by the department;

(8) the department's dedicated law-enforcement telephone number for statewide intake;

(9) the date and time when and the location where the child was last seen; and

(10) any other information required for an entry as established by the center.

Added by Acts 2005, 79th Leg., ch. 268, § 1.22, eff. Sept. 1, 2005. Amended by Acts 2015, 84th Leg., ch. 1056 (H.B. 2053), § 2, eff. Sept. 1, 2015; Acts 2015, 84th Leg., ch. 1202 (S.B. 1406), § 1, eff. Sept. 1, 2015.

## § 261.3023. Law Enforcement Response to Child Safety Check Alert

If a law enforcement officer encounters a child or other person listed on the Texas Crime Information Center's child safety check alert list, the law enforcement officer shall follow the procedures described by Article 2.272, Code of Criminal Procedure.

Added by Acts 2005, 79th Leg., ch. 268, § 1.22, eff. Sept. 1, 2005. Amended by Acts 2015, 84th Leg., ch. 1056 (H.B. 2053), § 3, eff. Sept. 1, 2015; Acts 2015, 84th Leg., ch. 1202 (S.B. 1406), § 2, eff. Sept. 1, 2015; Acts 2017, 85th Leg., ch. 324 (S.B. 1488), § 7.006, eff. Sept. 1, 2017.

## § 261.3024. Removal from Child Safety Check Alert List

(a) A law enforcement officer who locates a child listed on the Texas Crime Information Center's child safety check alert list shall report that the child has been located in the manner prescribed by Article 2.272, Code of Criminal Procedure.

(b) If the department locates a child who has been placed on the child safety check alert list established under Section 261.3022 through a means other than information reported to the department by a law enforcement officer under Article 2.272, Code of Criminal Procedure, the department shall report to the Texas Crime Information Center that the child has been located.

(c) On receipt of notice that a child has been located, the Texas Crime Information Center shall remove the child and the child's family from the child safety check alert list.

Added by Acts 2005, 79th Leg., ch. 268, § 1.22, eff. Sept. 1, 2005. Amended by Acts 2015, 84th Leg., ch. 1056 (H.B. 2053), § 4, eff. Sept. 1, 2015; Acts 2015, 84th Leg., ch. 1202 (S.B. 1406), § 3, eff. Sept. 1, 2015; Acts 2017, 85th Leg., ch. 324 (S.B. 1488), § 7.007, eff. Sept. 1, 2017.

## § 261.3025. Expired

## § 261.3027. Notice of Right to Record Interview

(a) Before conducting an interview with an alleged perpetrator, the department shall inform the person orally and in writing that:

(1) the person may create an audio or video recording of the interview but may not record the interview in any other manner;

(2) any audio or video recording made by the person may be subject to subpoena under a court order; and

(3) the person may request and receive a copy of the department's current recording policy.

(b) The department shall document in the case file that the department provided the notice required by Subsection (a).

(c) The department shall provide two copies of the written notice to be signed by the person. The department shall provide one signed notice to the person and retain the other signed notice in the case file.

(d) An audio or video recording of the department's interview with an alleged perpetrator may not be posted on an Internet website in a manner that could identify a party involved in the interview.

Added by Acts 2021, 87th Leg., ch. 789 (H.B. 135), § 1, eff. Sept. 1, 2021.

## § 261.303. Interference with Investigation; Court Order

(a) A person may not interfere with an investigation of a report of child abuse or neglect conducted by the department.

(b) If admission to the home, school, or any place where the child may be cannot be obtained, then for good cause shown the court having family law jurisdiction shall order the parent, the person responsible for the care of the children, or the person in charge of any place where the child may be to allow entrance for the interview, examination, and investigation.

(c) If a parent or person responsible for the child's care does not consent to release of the child's prior medical, psychological, or psychiatric records or to a medical, psychological, or psychiatric examination of the child that is requested by the department, the court having family law jurisdiction shall, for good cause shown, order the records to be released or the examination to be made at the times and places designated by the court.

(d) A person, including a medical facility, that makes a report under Subchapter B[1] shall release to the department, as part of the required report under Section 261.103, records that directly relate to the suspected abuse or neglect without requiring parental consent or a court order. If a child is transferred from a reporting medical facility to another medical facility to treat the injury or condition that formed the basis for the original report, the transferee medical facility shall, at the department's request, release to the department records relating to the injury or condition without requiring parental consent or a court order.

(e) A person, including a utility company, that has confidential locating or identifying information regarding a family that is the subject of an investigation under this chapter shall release that information to the department on request. The release of information to the department as required by this subsection by a person, including a utility company, is not subject to Section 552.352, Government Code, or any other law providing liability for the release of confidential information.

Added by Acts 1995, 74th Leg., ch. 20, § 1, eff. April 20, 1995. Amended by Acts 1995, 74th Leg., ch. 751, § 96, eff. Sept. 1, 1995; Acts 1999, 76th Leg., ch. 1150, § 5, eff. Sept. 1, 1999; Acts 1999, 76th Leg., ch. 1390, § 24, eff. Sept. 1, 1999; Acts 2007, 80th Leg., ch. 1406, § 6, eff. Sept. 1, 2007; Acts 2015, 84th Leg., ch. 1 (S.B. 219), § 1.133, eff. April 2, 2015.

[1] V.T.C.A., Family Code § 261.101 et seq.

## § 261.3031. Failure to Cooperate with Investigation; Department Response

(a) If a parent or other person refuses to cooperate with the department's investigation of the alleged abuse or neglect of a child and the refusal poses a risk to the child's safety, the department shall seek assistance from the appropriate attorney with responsibility for representing the department as provided by Section 264.009 to obtain a court order as described by Section 261.303.

(b) A person's failure to report to an agency authorized to investigate abuse or neglect of a child within a reasonable time after receiving proper notice constitutes a refusal by the person to cooperate with the department's investigation. A summons may be issued to locate the person.

Added by Acts 2005, 79th Leg., ch. 268, § 1.23, eff. Sept. 1, 2005. Amended by Acts 2007, 80th Leg., ch. 1406, § 7, eff. Sept. 1, 2007; Acts 2015, 84th Leg., ch. 1 (S.B. 219), § 1.134, eff. April 2, 2015.

## § 261.3032. Interference with Investigation; Criminal Penalty

(a) A person commits an offense if, with the intent to interfere with the department's investigation of a report of abuse or neglect of a child, the person relocates the person's residence, either temporarily or permanently, without notifying the department of the address of the person's new residence or conceals the child and the person's relocation or concealment interferes with the department's investigation.

(b) An offense under this section is a Class B misdemeanor.

(c) If conduct that constitutes an offense under this section also constitutes an offense under any other law, the actor may be prosecuted under this section or the other law.

Added by Acts 2005, 79th Leg., ch. 268, § 1.24, eff. Sept. 1, 2005.

## § 261.304. Investigation of Anonymous Report

(a) If the department receives an anonymous report of child abuse or neglect by a person responsible for a child's care, custody, or welfare, the department shall conduct a preliminary investigation to determine whether there is any evidence to corroborate the report.

(b) An investigation under this section may include a visit to the child's home, unless the alleged abuse or neglect can be confirmed or clearly ruled out without a home visit, an interview with and examination of the child, and an interview with the child's parents. In addition, the department may interview any other person the department believes may have relevant information.

(c) Unless the department determines that there is some evidence to corroborate the report of abuse, the department may not conduct the thorough investigation required by this chapter or take any action against the person accused of abuse.

Added by Acts 1995, 74th Leg., ch. 20, § 1, eff. April 20, 1995. Amended by Acts 2017, 85th Leg., ch. 416 (S.B. 1063), § 1, eff. Sept. 1, 2017.

## § 261.305. Access to Mental Health Records

(a) An investigation may include an inquiry into the possibility that a parent or a person responsible for the care of a child who is the subject of a report under Subchapter B[1] has a history of medical or mental illness.

(b) If the parent or person does not consent to an examination or allow the department to have access to medical or mental health records requested by the department, the court having family law jurisdiction, for good cause shown, shall order the examination to be made or that the department be permitted to have access to the records under terms and conditions prescribed by the court.

(c) If the court determines that the parent or person is indigent, the court shall appoint an attorney to represent the parent or person at the hearing. The fees for the appointed attorney shall be paid as provided by Chapter 107.

(d) A parent or person responsible for the child's care is entitled to notice and a hearing when the department seeks a court order to allow a medical, psychological, or psychiatric examination or access to medical or mental health records.

(e) This access does not constitute a waiver of confidentiality.

Added by Acts 1995, 74th Leg., ch. 20, § 1, eff. April 20, 1995. Amended by Acts 1997, 75th Leg., ch. 575, § 15, eff. Sept. 1, 1997; Acts 1999, 76th Leg., ch. 1150, § 6, eff. Sept. 1, 1999; Acts 1999, 76th Leg., ch. 1390, § 25, eff. Sept. 1, 1999; Acts 2015, 84th Leg., ch. 1 (S.B. 219), § 1.135, eff. April 2, 2015.

[1] V.T.C.A., Family Code § 261.101 et seq.

## § 261.306. Removal of Child from State

(a) If the department has reason to believe that a person responsible for the care, custody, or welfare of the child may remove the child from the state before the investigation is completed, the department may file an application for a temporary restraining order in a district court without regard to continuing jurisdiction of the child as provided in Chapter 155.

(b) The court may render a temporary restraining order prohibiting the person from removing the child from the state pending completion of the investigation if the court:

(1) finds that the department has probable cause to conduct the investigation; and

(2) has reason to believe that the person may remove the child from the state.

Added by Acts 1995, 74th Leg., ch. 20, § 1, eff. April 20, 1995. Amended by Acts 2015, 84th Leg., ch. 1 (S.B. 219), § 1.136, eff. April 2, 2015.

## § 261.307. Information Relating to Investigation Procedure and Child Placement Resources

(a) As soon as possible after initiating an investigation of a parent or other person having legal custody of a child, the department shall provide to the person:

(1) a summary that:

(A) is brief and easily understood;

(B) is written in a language that the person understands, or if the person is illiterate, is read to the person in a language that the person understands; and

(C) contains the following information:

(i) the department's procedures for conducting an investigation of alleged child abuse or neglect, including:

(a) a description of the circumstances under which the department would request to remove the child from the home through the judicial system; and

(b) an explanation that the law requires the department to refer all reports of alleged child abuse or neglect to a law enforcement agency for a separate determination of whether a criminal violation occurred;

(ii) the person's right to file a complaint with the department or to request a review of the findings made by the department in the investigation;

(iii) the person's right to review all records of the investigation unless the review would jeopardize an ongoing criminal investigation or the child's safety;

(iv) the person's right to seek legal counsel;

(v) references to the statutory and regulatory provisions governing child abuse and neglect and how the person may obtain copies of those provisions; and

(vi) the process the person may use to acquire access to the child if the child is removed from the home;

(2) if the department determines that removal of the child may be warranted, a proposed child placement resources form that:

(A) instructs the parent or other person having legal custody of the child to:

(i) complete and return the form to the department or agency;

(ii) identify in the form at least three individuals who could be relative caregivers or designated caregivers, as those terms are defined by Section 264.751;

(iii) ask the child in a developmentally appropriate manner to identify any adult, particularly an adult residing in the child's community, who could be a relative caregiver or designated caregiver for the child; and

(iv) list on the form the name of each individual identified by the child as a potential relative caregiver or designated caregiver; and

(B) informs the parent or other person of a location that is available to the parent or other person to submit the information in the form 24 hours a day either in person or by facsimile machine or e-mail; and

(3) an informational manual required by Section 261.3071.

(b) The child placement resources form described by Subsection (a)(2) must include information on the periods of time by which the department must complete a background check.

Added by Acts 1995, 74th Leg., ch. 20, § 1, eff. April 20, 1995. Amended by Acts 2005, 79th Leg., ch. 268, § 1.25(a), eff. Sept. 1, 2005; Acts 2019, 86th Leg., ch. 1294 (H.B. 3390), §§ 3, 4, eff. June 14, 2019.

### § 261.3071. Informational Manuals

(a) In this section:

(1) "Designated caregiver" and "relative caregiver" have the meanings assigned those terms by Section 264.751.

(2) "Voluntary caregiver" means a person who voluntarily agrees to provide temporary care for a child:

(A) who is the subject of an investigation by the department or whose parent, managing conservator, possessory conservator, guardian, caretaker, or custodian is receiving family-based safety services from the department;

(B) who is not in the conservatorship of the department; and

(C) who is placed in the care of the person by the parent or other person having legal custody of the child.

(b) The department shall develop and publish informational manuals that provide information for:

(1) a parent or other person having custody of a child who is the subject of an investigation under this chapter;

(2) a person who is selected by the department to be the child's relative or designated caregiver; and

(3) a voluntary caregiver.

(c) Information provided in the manuals must be in both English and Spanish and must include, as appropriate:

(1) useful indexes of information such as telephone numbers;

(2) the information required to be provided under Section 261.307(a)(1);

(3) information describing the rights and duties of a relative or designated caregiver;

(4) information regarding:

(A) the relative and other designated caregiver program under Subchapter I, Chapter 264[1], and the option for the relative or other designated caregiver to become verified by a licensed child-placing agency to operate an agency foster home, if applicable; and

(B) the permanency care assistance program under Subchapter K,[2] Chapter 264; and

(5) information regarding the role of a voluntary caregiver, including information on how to obtain any documentation necessary to provide for a child's needs.

Added by Acts 2005, 79th Leg., ch. 268, § 1.26, eff. Sept. 1, 2005. Amended by Acts 2009, 81st Leg., ch. 825, § 1, eff. June 19, 2009; Acts 2019, 86th Leg., ch. 375 (H.B. 1884), § 1, eff. Sept. 1, 2019.

[1] V.T.C.A., Family Code § 264.751 et seq.

[2] V.T.C.A., Family Code § 264.851 et seq.

### § 261.308. Submission of Investigation Report

(a) The department shall make a complete written report of the investigation.

(b) Repealed by Acts 2015, 84th Leg., ch. 944 (S.B. 206), § 86(9).

(c) Repealed by Acts 2015, 84th Leg., ch. 944 (S.B. 206), § 86(9).

(d) The department shall release information regarding a person alleged to have committed abuse or neglect to persons who have control over the person's access to children, including, as appropriate, the Texas Education Agency, the State Board for Educator Certification, the local school board or the school's governing body, the superintendent of the school district, the public school principal or director, the director of the open-enrollment charter school, or the chief executive officer of the private school if the department determines that:

(1) the person alleged to have committed abuse or neglect poses a substantial and immediate risk of harm to one or more children outside the family of a child who is the subject of the investigation; and

(2) the release of the information is necessary to assist in protecting one or more children from the person alleged to have committed abuse or neglect.

(e) On request, the department shall release information about a person alleged to have committed abuse or neglect to the State Board for Educator Certification if the board has a reasonable basis for believing that the information is necessary to assist the board in protecting children from the person alleged to have committed abuse or neglect.

Added by Acts 1995, 74th Leg., ch. 20, § 1, eff. April 20, 1995. Amended by Acts 1995, 74th Leg., ch. 751, § 97, eff. Sept. 1, 1995; Acts 2007, 80th Leg., ch. 1372, § 13, eff. June 15, 2007; Acts 2015, 84th Leg., ch. 1 (S.B. 219), § 1.137, eff. April 2, 2015; Acts 2015, 84th Leg., ch. 944 (S.B. 206), § 86(9), eff. Sept. 1, 2015; Acts 2019, 86th Leg., ch. 987 (S.B. 1231), § 2, eff. Sept. 1, 2019.

### § 261.309. Review of Department Investigations

(a) The executive commissioner shall by rule establish policies and procedures to resolve complaints relating to and conduct reviews of child abuse or neglect investigations conducted by the department.

(b) If a person under investigation for allegedly abusing or neglecting a child requests clarification of the status of the person's case or files a complaint relating to the conduct of the department's staff or to department policy, the department shall conduct an informal review to clarify the person's status or resolve the complaint. The division of the department responsible for investigating complaints shall conduct the informal review as soon as possible but not later than the 14th day after the date the request or complaint is received.

(c) If, after the department's investigation, the person who is alleged to have abused or neglected a child disputes the department's determination of whether child abuse or neglect occurred, the person may request an administrative review of the findings. A department employee in administration who was not involved in or did not directly supervise the investigation shall conduct the review. The review must sustain, alter, or reverse the department's original findings in the investigation.

(d) The department employee shall conduct the review prescribed by Subsection (c) as soon as possible but not later than the 45th day after the date the department receives the request, unless the department has good cause for extending the deadline. If a civil or criminal court proceeding or an ongoing criminal investigation relating to the alleged abuse or neglect investigated by the department is pending, the department may postpone the review until the court proceeding is completed.

(e) A person is not required to exhaust the remedies provided by this section before pursuing a judicial remedy provided by law.

(f) This section does not provide for a review of an order rendered by a court.

Added by Acts 1995, 74th Leg., ch. 20, § 1, eff. April 20, 1995. Amended by Acts 2015, 84th Leg., ch. 1 (S.B. 219), § 1.138, eff. April 2, 2015; Acts 2015, 84th Leg., ch. 944 (S.B. 206), § 21, eff. Sept. 1, 2015.

### § 261.3091. Notice of Right to Request Administrative Review

(a) Before conducting an interview with an alleged perpetrator, the department shall notify the person in writing that the person may request an administrative review of the department's findings under Section 261.309. The person shall sign the written notice to acknowledge receipt of the notice.

(b) The department shall document in the case file that the department provided the notice required by Subsection (a).

Added by Acts 2021, 87th Leg., ch. 789 (H.B. 135), § 2, eff. Sept. 1, 2021.

### § 261.310. Investigation Standards

(a) The executive commissioner shall by rule develop and adopt standards for persons who investigate suspected child abuse or neglect at the state or local level. The standards shall encourage professionalism and consistency in the investigation of suspected child abuse or neglect.

(b) The standards must provide for a minimum number of hours of annual professional training for interviewers and investigators of suspected child abuse or neglect.

(c) Repealed by Acts 2015, 84th Leg., ch. 944 (S.B. 206), § 86(10).

(d) The standards shall:

(1) recommend that videotaped and audiotaped interviews be uninterrupted;

(2) recommend a maximum number of interviews with and examinations of a suspected victim;

(3) provide procedures to preserve evidence, including the original recordings of the intake telephone calls, original notes, videotapes, and audiotapes, for one year; and

(4) provide that an investigator of suspected child abuse or neglect make a reasonable effort to locate and inform each parent of a child of any report of abuse or neglect relating to the child.

(e) The department, in conjunction with the Department of Public Safety, shall provide to the department's residential child-care facility licensing investigators advanced training in investigative protocols and techniques.

Added by Acts 1995, 74th Leg., ch. 20, § 1, eff. April 20, 1995. Amended by Acts 2005, 79th Leg., ch. 268, § 1.27, eff. Sept. 1, 2005; Acts 2015, 84th Leg., ch. 1 (S.B. 219), § 1.139, eff. April 2, 2015; Acts 2015, 84th Leg., ch. 944 (S.B. 206), § 86(10), eff. Sept. 1, 2015.

### § 261.3101. Repealed by Acts 2015, 84th Leg., ch. 944 (S.B. 206), § 86(11), eff. Sept. 1, 2015

### § 261.311. Notice of Report

(a) When during an investigation of a report of suspected child abuse or neglect a representative of the department conducts an interview with or an examination of a child, the department shall make a reasonable effort before 24 hours after the time of the interview or examination to notify each parent of the child and the child's legal guardian, if one has been appointed, of the nature of the allegation and of the fact that the interview or examination was conducted.

(b) If a report of suspected child abuse or neglect is administratively closed by the department as a result of a preliminary investigation that did not include an interview or examination of the child, the department shall make a reasonable effort before the expiration of 24 hours after the time the investigation is closed to notify each parent and legal guardian of the child of the disposition of the investigation.

(c) The notice required by Subsection (a) or (b) is not required if the department or agency determines that the notice is likely to endanger the safety of the child who is the subject of the report, the person who made the report, or any other person who participates in the investigation of the report.

(d) The notice required by Subsection (a) or (b) may be delayed at the request of a law enforcement agency if notification during the required time would interfere with an ongoing criminal investigation.

Added by Acts 1995, 74th Leg., ch. 20, § 1, eff. April 20, 1995. Amended by Acts 1997, 75th Leg., ch. 1022, § 74, eff. Sept. 1, 1997; Acts 2015, 84th Leg., ch. 1 (S.B. 219), § 1.140, eff. April 2, 2015.

### § 261.312. Review Teams; Offense

(a) The department shall establish review teams to evaluate department casework and decision-making related to investigations by the department of child abuse or neglect. The department may create one or more review teams for each region of the department for child protective services. A review team is a citizen review panel or a similar entity for the purposes of federal law relating to a state's child protection standards.

(b) A review team consists of at least five members who serve staggered two-year terms. Review team members are appointed by the commissioner of the department and consist of volunteers who live in and are broadly representative of the region in which the review team is established and have expertise in the prevention and treatment of child abuse and neglect. At least two members of a review team must be parents who have not been convicted of or indicted for an offense involving child abuse or neglect, have not been determined by the department to have engaged in child abuse or neglect, and are not under investigation by the department for child abuse or neglect. A member of a review team is a department volunteer for the purposes of Section 411.114, Government Code.

(c) A review team conducting a review of an investigation may conduct the review by examining the facts of the case as outlined by the department caseworker and law enforcement personnel. A review team member acting in the member's official capacity may receive information made confidential under Section 40.005, Human Resources Code, or Section 261.201.

(d) A review team shall report to the department the results of the team's review of an investigation. The review team's report may not include confidential information. The findings contained in a review team's report are subject to disclosure under Chapter 552, Government Code. This section does not require a law enforcement agency to divulge information to a review team that the agency believes would compromise an ongoing criminal case, investigation, or proceeding.

(e) A member of a review team commits an offense if the member discloses confidential information. An offense under this subsection is a Class C misdemeanor.

Added by Acts 1995, 74th Leg., ch. 943, § 3, eff. Sept. 1, 1995. Amended by Acts 1997, 75th Leg., ch. 575, § 16, eff. Sept. 1, 1997; Acts 2009, 81st Leg., ch. 1372, § 3, eff. June 19, 2009; Acts 2015, 84th Leg., ch. 1 (S.B. 219), § 1.141, eff. April 2, 2015.

### § 261.3125. Child Safety Specialists

(a) The department shall employ in each of the department's administrative regions at least one child safety specialist. The job responsibilities of the child safety specialist must focus on child abuse and neglect investigation issues, including reports of child abuse required by Section 261.101, to achieve a greater compliance with that section, and on assessing and improving the effectiveness of the department in providing for the protection of children in the region.

(b) The duties of a child safety specialist must include the duty to:

(1) conduct staff reviews and evaluations of cases determined to involve a high risk to the health or safety of a child, including cases of abuse reported under Section 261.101, to ensure that risk assessment tools are fully and correctly used;

(2) review and evaluate cases in which there have been multiple referrals to the department of child abuse or neglect involving the same family, child, or person alleged to have committed the abuse or neglect; and

(3) approve decisions and assessments related to investigations of cases of child abuse or neglect that involve a high risk to the health or safety of a child.

Added by Acts 1999, 76th Leg., ch. 1490, § 1, eff. Sept. 1, 1999. Amended by Acts 2005, 79th Leg., ch. 268, § 1.29, eff. Sept. 1, 2005.

## § 261.3126. Colocation of Investigators

(a) In each county, to the extent possible, the department and the local law enforcement agencies that investigate child abuse in the county shall colocate in the same offices investigators from the department and the law enforcement agencies to improve the efficiency of child abuse investigations. With approval of the local children's advocacy center and its partner agencies, in each county in which a children's advocacy center established under Section 264.402 is located, the department shall attempt to locate investigators from the department and county and municipal law enforcement agencies at the center.

(b) A law enforcement agency is not required to comply with the colocation requirements of this section if the law enforcement agency does not have a full-time peace officer solely assigned to investigate reports of child abuse and neglect.

(c) If a county does not have a children's advocacy center, the department shall work with the local community to encourage one as provided by Section 264.402.

Added by Acts 2005, 79th Leg., ch. 268, § 1.30, eff. Sept. 1, 2005.

## § 261.313. [Blank]

## § 261.314. Testing

(a) The department shall provide testing as necessary for the welfare of a child who the department believes, after an investigation under this chapter, has been sexually abused, including human immunodeficiency virus (HIV) testing of a child who was abused in a manner by which HIV may be transmitted.

(b) Except as provided by Subsection (c), the results of a test under this section are confidential.

(c) If requested, the department shall report the results of a test under this section to:

(1) a court having jurisdiction of a proceeding involving the child or a proceeding involving a person suspected of abusing the child;

(2) a person responsible for the care and custody of the child as a foster parent; and

(3) a person seeking to adopt the child.

Added by Acts 1995, 74th Leg., ch. 943, § 7, eff. Sept. 1, 1995.

## § 261.315. Removal of Certain Investigation Information from Records

(a) At the conclusion of an investigation in which the department determines that the person alleged to have abused or neglected a child did not commit abuse or neglect, the department shall notify the person of the person's right to request the department to remove information about the person's alleged role in the abuse or neglect report from the department's records.

(b) On request under Subsection (a) by a person whom the department has determined did not commit abuse or neglect, the department shall remove information from the department's records concerning the person's alleged role in the abuse or neglect report.

(c) The executive commissioner shall adopt rules necessary to administer this section.

Added by Acts 1997, 75th Leg., ch. 1022, § 75, eff. Sept. 1, 1997. Amended by Acts 2015, 84th Leg., ch. 1 (S.B. 219), § 1.142, eff. April 2, 2015.

## § 261.316. Exemption from Fees for Medical Records

The department is exempt from the payment of a fee otherwise required or authorized by law to obtain a medical record from a hospital or health care provider if the request for a record is made in the course of an investigation by the department.

Added by Acts 1997, 75th Leg., ch. 575, § 17, eff. Sept. 1, 1997. Redesignated from V.T.C.A., Family Code § 261.315 by Acts 1999, 76th Leg., ch. 62, § 19.01(27), eff. Sept. 1, 1999.

## SUBCHAPTER E. INVESTIGATIONS OF ABUSE, NEGLECT, OR EXPLOITATION IN CERTAIN FACILITIES

### § 261.401. Agency Investigation

(a) Repealed by Acts 2017, 85th Leg., ch. 319 (S.B. 11), § 32 and Acts 2017, 85th Leg., ch. 1136 (H.B. 249), § 14.

(b) Except as provided by Section 261.404 of this code and Section 531.02013(1)(D), Government Code, a state agency that operates, licenses, certifies, registers, or lists a facility in which children are located or provides oversight of a program that serves children shall make a prompt, thorough investigation of a report that a child has been or may be abused, neglected, or exploited in the facility or program. The primary purpose of the investigation shall be the protection of the child.

(c) A state agency shall adopt rules relating to the investigation and resolution of reports received as provided by this subchapter. The executive commissioner shall review and approve the rules of agencies other than the Texas Department of Criminal Justice or the Texas Juvenile Justice Department to ensure that those agencies implement appropriate standards for the conduct of investigations and that uniformity exists among agencies in the investigation and resolution of reports.

(d) The Texas School for the Blind and Visually Impaired and the Texas School for the Deaf shall adopt policies relating to the investigation and resolution of reports received as provided by this subchapter. The executive commissioner shall review and approve the policies to ensure that the Texas School for the Blind and Visually Impaired and the Texas School for the Deaf adopt those policies in a manner consistent with the minimum standards adopted by the executive commissioner under Section 261.407.

Added by Acts 1995, 74th Leg., ch. 20, § 1, eff. April 20, 1995. Amended by Acts 1995, 74th Leg., ch. 751, § 98, eff. Sept. 1, 1995; Acts 2001, 77th Leg., ch. 355, § 2, eff. Sept. 1, 2001; Acts 2007, 80th Leg., ch. 908, § 29, eff. Sept. 1, 2007; Acts 2009, 81st Leg., ch. 284, § 6, eff. June 11, 2009; Acts 2009, 81st Leg., ch. 720, § 18, eff. Sept. 1, 2009; Acts 2015, 84th Leg., ch. 1 (S.B. 219), § 1.143, eff. April 2, 2015; Acts 2017, 85th Leg., ch. 319 (S.B. 11), §§ 10, 32, eff. Sept. 1, 2017; Acts 2017, 85th Leg., ch. 1136 (H.B. 249), §§ 5, 14, eff. Sept. 1, 2017.

### § 261.402. Investigative Reports

(a) A state agency shall prepare and keep on file a complete written report of each investigation conducted by the agency under this subchapter.

(b) A state agency shall immediately notify the appropriate state or local law enforcement agency of any report the agency receives, other than a report from a law enforcement agency, that concerns the suspected abuse, neglect, or exploitation of a child or the death of a child from abuse or neglect. If the state agency finds evidence indicating that a child may have been abused, neglected, or exploited, the agency shall report the evidence to the appropriate law enforcement agency.

(c) A state agency that licenses, certifies, or registers a facility in which children are located shall compile, maintain, and make available statistics on the incidence in the facility of child abuse, neglect, and exploitation that is investigated by the agency.

(d) A state agency shall compile, maintain, and make available statistics on the incidence of child abuse, neglect, and exploitation in a facility operated by the state agency.

Added by Acts 1995, 74th Leg., ch. 20, § 1, eff. April 20, 1995. Amended by Acts 1995, 74th Leg., ch. 751, § 99, eff. Sept. 1, 1995; Acts 2001, 77th Leg., ch. 355, § 3, eff. Sept. 1, 2001; Acts 2015, 84th Leg., ch. 1 (S.B. 219), § 1.144, eff. April 2, 2015.

### § 261.403. Complaints

(a) If a state agency receives a complaint relating to an investigation conducted by the agency concerning a facility operated by that agency in which children are located, the agency shall refer the complaint to the agency's governing body.

(b) The governing body of a state agency that operates a facility in which children are located shall ensure that the procedure for investigating abuse, neglect, and exploitation allegations and inquiries in the agency's facility is periodically reviewed under the agency's internal audit program required by Chapter 2102, Government Code.

Added by Acts 1995, 74th Leg., ch. 20, § 1, eff. April 20, 1995. Amended by Acts 2001, 77th Leg., ch. 355, § 4, eff. Sept. 1, 2001; Acts 2015, 84th Leg., ch. 1 (S.B. 219), § 1.145, eff. April 2, 2015.

### § 261.404. Investigations Regarding Certain Children Receiving Services from Certain Providers

(a) The department shall investigate a report of abuse, neglect, or exploitation of a child receiving services from a provider, as those terms are defined by Section 48.251, Human Resources Code, or as otherwise defined by rule. The department shall also investigate, under Subchapter F, Chapter 48, Human Resources Code,[1] a report of abuse, neglect, or exploitation of a child receiving services from an officer, employee, agent, contractor, or subcontractor of a home and community support services agency licensed under Chapter 142, Health and Safety Code, if the officer, employee, agent, contractor, or subcontractor is or may be the person alleged to have committed the abuse, neglect, or exploitation.

(a–1) For an investigation of a child living in a residence owned, operated, or controlled by a provider of services under the home and community-based services waiver program described by Section 534.001(11)(B), Government Code, the department, in accordance with Subchapter E, Chapter 48, Human Resources Code,[2] may provide emergency protective services necessary to immediately protect the child from serious physical harm or death and, if necessary, obtain an emergency order for protective services under Section 48.208, Human Resources Code.

(a–2) For an investigation of a child living in a residence owned, operated, or controlled by a provider of services under the home and community-based services waiver program described by Section 534.001(11)(B), Government Code, regardless of whether the child is receiving services under that waiver program from the provider, the department shall provide protective services to the child in accordance with Subchapter E, Chapter 48, Human Resources Code.

(a–3) For purposes of this section, Subchapters E and F, Chapter 48, Human Resources Code, apply to an investigation of a child and to the provision of protective services to that child in the same manner those subchapters apply to an investigation of an elderly person or person with a disability and the provision of protective services to that person.

(b) The department shall investigate the report under rules developed by the executive commissioner.

(c) If a report under this section relates to a child with an intellectual disability receiving services in a state supported living center or the ICF–IID component of the Rio Grande State Center, the department shall, within one hour of receiving the report, notify the facility in which the child is receiving services of the allegations in the report.

(d) If during the course of the department's investigation of reported abuse, neglect, or exploitation a caseworker of the department or the caseworker's supervisor has cause to believe that a child with an intellectual disability described by Subsection (c) has been abused, neglected, or exploited by another person in a manner that constitutes a criminal offense under any law, including Section 22.04, Penal Code, the caseworker shall immediately notify the Health and Human Services Commission's office of inspector general and promptly provide the commission's office of inspector general with a copy of the department's investigation report.

(e) The definitions of "abuse" and "neglect" prescribed by Section 261.001 do not apply to an investigation under this section.

(f) Repealed by Acts 2015, 84th Leg., ch. 860 (S.B. 1880), § 15(1); Acts 2015, 84th Leg., ch. 1272 (S.B. 760), § 19(1).

Added by Acts 1995, 74th Leg., ch. 751, § 100, eff. Sept. 1, 1995. Amended by Acts 1999, 76th Leg., ch. 907, § 39, eff. Sept. 1, 1999; Acts 2009, 81st Leg., ch. 284, § 7, eff. June 11, 2009; Acts 2015, 84th Leg., ch. 1 (S.B. 219), § 1.146, eff. April 2, 2015; Acts 2015, 84th Leg., ch. 860 (S.B. 1880), §§ 11, 12, 15(1), eff. Sept. 1, 2015; Acts 2015, 84th Leg., ch. 1272 (S.B. 760), §§ 1, 2, 19(1), eff. Sept. 1, 2015.

1 V.T.C.A., Human Resources Code § 48.251 et seq.
2 V.T.C.A., Human Resources Code § 48.201 et seq.

## § 261.405. Investigations in Juvenile Justice Programs and Facilities

(a) Notwithstanding Section 261.001, in this section:

(1) "Abuse" means an intentional, knowing, or reckless act or omission by an employee, volunteer, or other individual working under the auspices of a facility or program that causes or may cause emotional harm or physical injury to, or the death of, a child served by the facility or program as further described by rule or policy.

(2) "Exploitation" means the illegal or improper use of a child or of the resources of a child for monetary or personal benefit, profit, or gain by an employee, volunteer, or other individual working under the auspices of a facility or program as further described by rule or policy.

(3) "Juvenile justice facility" means a facility operated wholly or partly by the juvenile board, by another governmental unit, or by a private vendor under a contract with the juvenile board, county, or other governmental unit that serves juveniles under juvenile court jurisdiction. The term includes:

(A) a public or private juvenile pre-adjudication secure detention facility, including a holdover facility;

(B) a public or private juvenile post-adjudication secure correctional facility except for a facility operated solely for children committed to the Texas Juvenile Justice Department; and

(C) a public or private non-secure juvenile post-adjudication residential treatment facility that is not licensed by the Department of Family and Protective Services or the Department of State Health Services.

(4) "Juvenile justice program" means a program or department operated wholly or partly by the juvenile board or by a private vendor under a contract with a juvenile board that serves juveniles under juvenile court jurisdiction. The term includes:

(A) a juvenile justice alternative education program;

(B) a non-residential program that serves juvenile offenders under the jurisdiction of the juvenile court; and

(C) a juvenile probation department.

(5) "Neglect" means a negligent act or omission by an employee, volunteer, or other individual working under the auspices of a facility or program, including failure to comply with an individual treatment plan, plan of care, or individualized service plan, that causes or may cause substantial emotional harm or physical injury to, or the death of, a child served by the facility or program as further described by rule or policy.

(b) A report of alleged abuse, neglect, or exploitation in any juvenile justice program or facility shall be made to the Texas Juvenile Justice Department and a local law enforcement agency for investigation.

(c) The Texas Juvenile Justice Department shall make a prompt, thorough investigation as provided by this chapter if that department receives a report of alleged abuse, neglect, or exploitation in any juvenile justice program or facility. The primary purpose of the investigation shall be the protection of the child.

(d) In an investigation required under this section, the investigating agency shall have access to medical and mental health records as provided by Subchapter D.[1]

(e) As soon as practicable after a child is taken into custody or placed in a juvenile justice facility or juvenile justice program, the facility or program shall provide the child's parents with:

(1) information regarding the reporting of suspected abuse, neglect, or exploitation of a child in a juvenile justice facility or juvenile justice program to the Texas Juvenile Justice Department; and

(2) the Texas Juvenile Justice Department's toll-free number for this reporting.

Added by Acts 1995, 74th Leg., ch. 751, § 100, eff. Sept. 1, 1995. Amended by Acts 1997, 75th Leg., ch. 162, § 2; Acts 1997, 75th Leg., ch. 1374, § 8, eff. Sept. 1, 1997; Acts 1999, 76th Leg., ch. 1150, § 7, eff. Sept. 1, 1999; Acts 1999, 76th Leg., ch. 1390, § 26, eff. Sept. 1, 1999; Acts 1999, 76th Leg., ch. 1477, § 26, eff. Sept. 1, 1999; Acts 2001, 77th Leg., ch. 1297, § 47, eff. Sept. 1, 2001; Acts 2003, 78th Leg., ch. 283, § 29, eff. Sept. 1, 2003; Acts 2005, 79th Leg., ch. 949, § 28, eff. Sept. 1, 2005; Acts 2007, 80th Leg., ch. 908, § 30, eff. Sept. 1, 2007; Acts 2015, 84th Leg., ch. 1 (S.B. 219), § 1.147, eff. April 2, 2015; Acts 2015, 84th Leg., ch. 734 (H.B. 1549), § 83, eff. Sept. 1, 2015; Acts 2017, 85th Leg., ch. 319 (S.B. 11), § 11, eff. Sept. 1, 2017; Acts 2017, 85th Leg., ch. 1136 (H.B. 249), § 6, eff. Sept. 1, 2017.

[1] V.T.C.A., Family Code § 261.301 et seq.

### § 261.406. Investigations in Schools

(a) On receipt of a report of alleged or suspected abuse or neglect of a child in a public or private school, the department shall perform an investigation as provided by this chapter.

(b) The department shall send a copy of the completed report of the department's investigation to the Texas Education Agency or, in the case of a private school, the school's chief executive officer. On request, the department shall provide a copy of the completed report of the department's investigation to the State Board for Educator Certification, the local school board or the school's governing body, the superintendent of the school district, the public school principal or director, or the chief executive officer of the private school, unless the principal, director, or chief executive officer is alleged to have committed the abuse or neglect, for appropriate action. On request, the department shall provide a copy of the report of investigation to the parent, managing conservator, or legal guardian of a child who is the subject of the investigation and to the person alleged to have committed the abuse or neglect. The report of investigation shall be edited to protect the identity of the persons who made the report of abuse or neglect. Except as otherwise provided by this subsection, Section 261.201(b) applies to the release of the report relating to the investigation of abuse or neglect under this section and to the identity of the person who made the report of abuse or neglect.

(c) Nothing in this section may prevent a law enforcement agency from conducting an investigation of a report made under this section.

(d) The executive commissioner shall adopt rules necessary to implement this section.

Added by Acts 1995, 74th Leg., ch. 751, § 100, eff. Sept. 1, 1995. Amended by Acts 1997, 75th Leg., ch. 575, § 18, eff. Sept. 1, 1997; Acts 1999, 76th Leg., ch. 1150, § 8, eff. Sept. 1, 1999; Acts 1999, 76th Leg., ch. 1390, § 27, eff. Sept. 1, 1999; Acts 2005, 79th Leg., ch. 213, § 2, eff. Sept. 1, 2005; Acts 2007, 80th Leg., ch. 1372, § 14, eff. June 15, 2007; Acts 2015, 84th Leg., ch. 1 (S.B. 219), § 1.148, eff. April 2, 2015; Acts 2015, 84th Leg., ch. 944 (S.B. 206), § 22, eff. Sept. 1, 2015; Acts 2019, 86th Leg., ch. 987 (S.B. 1231), § 3, eff. Sept. 1, 2019.

### § 261.407. Minimum Standards

(a) The executive commissioner by rule shall adopt minimum standards for the investigation under Section 261.401 of suspected child abuse, neglect, or exploitation in a facility.

(b) A rule or policy adopted by a state agency or institution under Section 261.401 must be consistent with the minimum standards adopted by the executive commissioner.

(c) This section does not apply to a facility under the jurisdiction of the Texas Department of Criminal Justice or the Texas Juvenile Justice Department.

Added by Acts 2001, 77th Leg., ch. 355, § 5, eff. Sept. 1, 2001. Amended by Acts 2015, 84th Leg., ch. 1 (S.B. 219), § 1.149, eff. April 2, 2015.

### § 261.408. Information Collection

(a) The executive commissioner by rule shall adopt uniform procedures for collecting information under Section 261.401, including procedures for collecting information on deaths that occur in facilities.

(b) The department shall receive and compile information on investigations in facilities. An agency submitting information to the department is responsible for ensuring the timeliness, accuracy, completeness, and retention of the agency's reports.

(c) This section does not apply to a facility under the jurisdiction of the Texas Department of Criminal Justice or the Texas Juvenile Justice Department.

Added by Acts 2001, 77th Leg., ch. 355, § 5, eff. Sept. 1, 2001. Amended by Acts 2015, 84th Leg., ch. 1 (S.B. 219), § 1.150, eff. April 2, 2015.

### § 261.409. Investigations in Facilities Under Texas Juvenile Justice Department Jurisdiction

The board of the Texas Juvenile Justice Department by rule shall adopt standards for:

(1) the investigation under Section 261.401 of suspected child abuse, neglect, or exploitation in a facility under the jurisdiction of the Texas Juvenile Justice Department; and

(2) compiling information on those investigations.

Added by Acts 2001, 77th Leg., ch. 355, § 6, eff. Sept. 1, 2001. Amended by Acts 2015, 84th Leg., ch. 734 (H.B. 1549), § 84, eff. Sept. 1, 2015.

### § 261.410. Report of Abuse by other Children

(a) In this section:

(1) "Physical abuse" means:

(A) physical injury that results in substantial harm to the child requiring emergency medical treatment and excluding an accident or reasonable discipline by a parent, guardian, or managing or possessory conservator that does not expose the child to a substantial risk of harm; or

(B) failure to make a reasonable effort to prevent an action by another person that results in physical injury that results in substantial harm to the child.

(2) "Sexual abuse" means:

(A) sexual conduct harmful to a child's mental, emotional, or physical welfare; or

(B) failure to make a reasonable effort to prevent sexual conduct harmful to a child.

(b) An agency that operates, licenses, certifies, or registers a facility shall require a residential child-care facility to report each incident of physical or sexual abuse committed by a child against another child.

(c) Using information received under Subsection (b), the agency that operates, licenses, certifies, or registers a facility shall, subject to the availability of funds, compile a report that includes information:

(1) regarding the number of cases of physical and sexual abuse committed by a child against another child;

(2) identifying the residential child-care facility;

(3) regarding the date each allegation of abuse was made;

(4) regarding the date each investigation was started and concluded;

(5) regarding the findings and results of each investigation; and

(6) regarding the number of children involved in each incident investigated.

Added by Acts 2005, 79th Leg., ch. 268, § 1.31, eff. Sept. 1, 2005.

## SUBCHAPTER F. PROTECTIVE ORDER IN CERTAIN CASES OF ABUSE OR NEGLECT

### § 261.501. Filing Application for Protective Order in Certain Cases of Abuse or Neglect

The department may file an application for a protective order for a child's protection under this subchapter on the department's own initiative or jointly with a parent, relative, or caregiver of the child who requests the filing of the application if the department:

(1) has temporary managing conservatorship of the child;

(2) determines that:

(A) the child:

(i) is a victim of abuse or neglect; or

(ii) has a history of being abused or neglected; and

(B) there is a threat of:

(i) immediate or continued abuse or neglect to the child;

(ii) someone illegally taking the child from the home in which the child is placed;

(iii) behavior that poses a threat to the caregiver with whom the child is placed; or

(iv) someone committing an act of violence against the child or the child's caregiver; and

(3) is not otherwise authorized to apply for a protective order for the child's protection under Chapter 82.

Added by Acts 2017, 85th Leg., ch. 317 (H.B. 7), § 14, eff. Sept. 1, 2017.

### § 261.502. Certification of Findings

(a) In making the application under this subchapter, the department must certify that:

(1) the department has diligently searched for and:

(A) was unable to locate the child's parent, legal guardian, or custodian, other than the respondent to the application; or

(B) located and provided notice of the proposed application to the child's parent, legal guardian, or custodian, other than the respondent to the application; and

(2) if applicable, the relative or caregiver who is jointly filing the petition, or with whom the child would reside following an entry of the protective order, has not abused or neglected the child and does not have a history of abuse or neglect.

(b) An application for a temporary ex parte order under Section 261.503 may be filed without making the findings required by Subsection (a) if the department certifies that the department believes there is an immediate danger of abuse or neglect to the child.

Added by Acts 2017, 85th Leg., ch. 317 (H.B. 7), § 14, eff. Sept. 1, 2017.

### § 261.503. Temporary Ex Parte Order

If the court finds from the information contained in an application for a protective order that there is an immediate danger of abuse or neglect to the child, the court, without further notice to the respondent and without a hearing, may enter a temporary ex parte order for the protection of the child.

Added by Acts 2017, 85th Leg., ch. 317 (H.B. 7), § 14, eff. Sept. 1, 2017.

### § 261.504. Required Findings; Issuance of Protective Order

(a) At the close of a hearing on an application for a protective order under this subchapter, the court shall find whether there are reasonable grounds to believe that:

(1) the child:

(A) is a victim of abuse or neglect; or

(B) has a history of being abused or neglected; and

(2) there is a threat of:

(A) immediate or continued abuse or neglect to the child;

(B) someone illegally taking the child from the home in which the child is placed;

(C) behavior that poses a threat to the caregiver with whom the child is placed; or

(D) someone committing an act of violence against the child or the child's caregiver.

(a–1) In making a determination whether the child is or has been a victim of abuse or neglect, the court shall consider the opinion of a medical professional obtained by an individual against whom a protective order is sought.

(b) If the court makes an affirmative finding under Subsection (a), the court shall issue a protective order that includes a statement of that finding.

Added by Acts 2017, 85th Leg., ch. 317 (H.B. 7), § 14, eff. Sept. 1, 2017. Amended by Acts 2021, 87th Leg., ch. 1047 (S.B. 1578), § 4, eff. Sept. 1, 2021.

Section 8 of Acts 2021, 87th Leg., ch. 665 (S.B. 1578) provides:

"The changes in law made by this Act apply only to a suit affecting the parent-child relationship filed on or after the effective date [Sept. 1, 2021] of this Act. A suit affecting the parent-child relationship filed before the effective date [Sept. 1, 2021] of this Act is governed by the law in effect on the date the suit was filed, and the former law is continued in effect for that purpose."

### § 261.505. Application of Other Law

To the extent applicable, except as otherwise provided by this subchapter, Title 4 applies to a protective order issued under this subchapter.

Added by Acts 2017, 85th Leg., ch. 317 (H.B. 7), § 14, eff. Sept. 1, 2017.

## CHAPTER 262. PROCEDURES IN SUIT BY GOVERNMENTAL ENTITY TO PROTECT HEALTH AND SAFETY OF CHILD

SUBCHAPTER A. GENERAL PROVISIONS



SUBCHAPTER B. TAKING POSSESSION OF CHILD



SUBCHAPTER C. ADVERSARY HEARING



SUBCHAPTER D. EMERGENCY POSSESSION OF CERTAIN ABANDONED CHILDREN



SUBCHAPTER E. RELINQUISHING CHILD TO OBTAIN CERTAIN SERVICES



SUBCHAPTER F. FAMILY PRESERVATION SERVICES PILOT PROGRAM

## SUBCHAPTER A. GENERAL PROVISIONS

### § 262.001. Authorized Actions by Governmental Entity

(a) A governmental entity with an interest in the child may file a suit affecting the parent-child relationship requesting an order or take possession of a child without a court order as provided by this chapter.

(b) In determining the reasonable efforts that are required to be made with respect to preventing or eliminating the need to remove a child from the child's home or to make it possible to return a child to the child's home, the child's health and safety is the paramount concern.

Added by Acts 1995, 74th Leg., ch. 20, § 1, eff. April 20, 1995. Amended by Acts 1999, 76th Leg., ch. 1150, § 10, eff. Sept. 1, 1999; Acts 1999, 76th Leg., ch. 1390, § 29, eff. Sept. 1, 1999.

### § 262.002. Jurisdiction

A suit brought by a governmental entity requesting an order under this chapter may be filed in a court with jurisdiction to hear the suit in the county in which the child is found.

Added by Acts 1995, 74th Leg., ch. 20, § 1, eff. April 20, 1995. Amended by Acts 1999, 76th Leg., ch. 1150, § 11, eff. Sept. 1, 1999; Acts 1999, 76th Leg., ch. 1390, § 30, eff. Sept. 1, 1999.

### § 262.0022. Review of Placement; Findings

At each hearing under this chapter, the court shall review the placement of each child in the temporary or permanent managing conservatorship of the Department of Family and Protective Services who is not placed with a relative caregiver or designated caregiver as defined by Section 264.751. The court shall include in its findings a statement on whether the department:

(1) asked the child in a developmentally appropriate manner to identify any adult, particularly an adult residing in the child's community, who could be a relative caregiver or designated caregiver for the child; and

(2) has the option of placing the child with a relative caregiver or designated caregiver.

Added by Acts 2017, 85th Leg., ch. 317 (H.B. 7), § 15, eff. Sept. 1, 2017. Amended by Acts 2019, 86th Leg., ch. 1294 (H.B. 3390), § 5, eff. June 14, 2019.

"(c) Except as otherwise provided by this section, the changes in law made by this Act apply only to a suit affecting the parent-child relationship filed on or after the effective date [Sept. 1, 2017] of this Act. A suit affecting the parent-child relationship filed before the effective date of this Act is subject to the law in effect at the time the suit was filed, and the former law is continued in effect for that purpose."

### § 262.003. Civil Liability

A person who takes possession of a child without a court order is immune from civil liability if, at the time possession is taken, there is reasonable cause to believe there is an immediate danger to the physical health or safety of the child.

Added by Acts 1995, 74th Leg., ch. 20, § 1, eff. April 20, 1995.

### § 262.004. Accepting Voluntary Delivery of Possession of Child

A law enforcement officer or a juvenile probation officer may take possession of a child without a court order on the voluntary delivery of the child by the parent, managing conservator, possessory conservator, guardian, caretaker, or custodian who is presently entitled to possession of the child.

Added by Acts 1995, 74th Leg., ch. 20, § 1, eff. April 20, 1995. Amended by Acts 1995, 74th Leg., ch. 751, § 101, eff. Sept. 1, 1995.

### § 262.005. Filing Petition After Accepting Voluntary Delivery of Possession of Child

When possession of the child has been acquired through voluntary delivery of the child to a law enforcement officer or juvenile probation officer, the law enforcement officer or juvenile probation officer taking the child into possession shall cause a suit to be filed not later than the 60th day after the date the child is taken into possession.

Added by Acts 1995, 74th Leg., ch. 20, § 1, eff. April 20, 1995. Amended by Acts 1995, 74th Leg., ch. 751, § 102, eff. Sept. 1, 1995.

### § 262.006. Living Child After Abortion

(a) An authorized representative of the Department of Family and Protective Services may assume the care, control, and custody of a child born alive as the result of an abortion as defined by Chapter 161.

(b) The department shall file a suit and request an emergency order under this chapter.

(c) A child for whom possession is assumed under this section need not be delivered to the court except on the order of the court.

Added by Acts 1995, 74th Leg., ch. 20, § 1, eff. April 20, 1995. Amended by Acts 2015, 84th Leg., ch. 1 (S.B. 219), § 1.151, eff. April 2, 2015.

### § 262.007. Possession and Delivery of Missing Child

(a) A law enforcement officer who, during a criminal investigation relating to a child's custody, discovers that a child is a missing child and believes that a person may flee with or conceal the child shall take possession of the child and provide for the delivery of the child as provided by Subsection (b).

(b) An officer who takes possession of a child under Subsection (a) shall deliver or arrange for the delivery of the child to a person entitled to possession of the child.

(c) If a person entitled to possession of the child is not immediately available to take possession of the child, the law enforcement officer shall deliver the child to the Department of Family and Protective Services. Until a person entitled to possession of the child takes possession of the child, the department may, without a court order, retain possession of the child not longer than five days after the date the child is delivered to the department. While the department retains possession of a child under this subsection, the department may place the child in foster care. If a parent or other person entitled to possession of the child does not take possession of the child before the sixth day after the date the child is delivered to the department, the department shall proceed under this chapter as if the law enforcement officer took possession of the child under Section 262.104.

Added by Acts 1995, 74th Leg., ch. 776, § 1, eff. Sept. 1, 1995. Amended by Acts 1999, 76th Leg., ch. 685, § 6, eff. Sept. 1, 1999; Acts 1999, 76th Leg., ch. 1150, § 12, eff. Sept. 1, 1999; Acts 1999, 76th Leg., ch. 1390, § 31, eff. Sept. 1, 1999; Acts 2015, 84th Leg., ch. 1 (S.B. 219), § 1.152, eff. April 2, 2015.

### § 262.008. Abandoned Children

(a) An authorized representative of the Department of Family and Protective Services may assume the care, control, and custody of a child:

(1) who is abandoned without identification or a means for identifying the child; and

(2) whose identity cannot be ascertained by the exercise of reasonable diligence.

(b) The department shall immediately file a suit to terminate the parent-child relationship of a child under Subsection (a).

(c) Repealed by Acts 2015, 84th Leg., ch. 1 (S.B. 219), § 1.203(5).

Added by Acts 1997, 75th Leg., ch. 600, § 4, eff. Jan. 1, 1998. Amended by Acts 2015, 84th Leg., ch. 1 (S.B. 219), §§ 1.153, 1.203(5), eff. April 2, 2015.

### § 262.009. Temporary Care of Child Taken Into Possession

An employee of or volunteer with a law enforcement agency who successfully completes a background and criminal history check approved by the law enforcement agency may assist a law enforcement officer or juvenile probation officer with the temporary care of a child who is taken into possession by a governmental entity without a court order under this chapter until further arrangements regarding the custody of the child can be made.

Added by Acts 2003, 78th Leg., ch. 970, § 1, eff. June 20, 2003.

### § 262.010. Child With Sexually Transmitted Disease

(a) If during an investigation by the Department of Family and Protective Services the department discovers that a child younger than 11 years of age has a sexually transmitted disease, the department shall:

(1) appoint a special investigator to assist in the investigation of the case; and

(2) file an original suit requesting an emergency order under this chapter for possession of the child unless the department determines, after taking the following actions, that emergency removal is not necessary for the protection of the child:

(A) reviewing the medical evidence to determine whether the medical evidence supports a finding that abuse likely occurred;

(B) interviewing the child and other persons residing in the child's home;

(C) conferring with law enforcement;

(D) determining whether any other child in the home has a sexually transmitted disease and, if so, referring the child for a sexual abuse examination;

(E) if the department determines a forensic interview is appropriate based on the child's age and development, ensuring that each child alleged to have been abused undergoes a forensic interview by a children's advocacy center established under Section 264.402 or another professional with specialized training in conducting forensic interviews if a children's advocacy center is not available in the county in which the child resides;

(F) consulting with a department staff nurse or other medical expert to obtain additional information regarding the nature of the sexually transmitted disease and the ways the disease is transmitted and an opinion as to whether abuse occurred based on the facts of the case;

(G) contacting any additional witness who may have information relevant to the investigation, including other individuals who had access to the child; and

(H) if the department determines after taking the actions described by Paragraphs (A)–(G) that a finding of sexual abuse is not supported, obtaining an opinion from the Forensic Assessment Center Network as to whether the evidence in the case supports a finding that abuse likely occurred.

(b) If the department determines that abuse likely occurred, the department shall work with law enforcement to obtain a search warrant to require an individual the department reasonably believes may have sexually abused the child to undergo medically appropriate diagnostic testing for sexually transmitted diseases.

Added by Acts 2011, 82nd Leg., ch. 598 (S.B. 218), § 2, eff. Sept. 1, 2011.

### § 262.011. Placement in Secure Agency Foster Home

A court in an emergency, initial, or full adversary hearing conducted under this chapter may order that the child who is the subject of the hearing be placed in a secure agency foster home verified in accordance with Section 42.0531, Human Resources Code, if the court finds that:

(1) the placement is in the best interest of the child; and

(2) the child's physical health or safety is in danger because the child has been recruited, harbored, transported, provided, or obtained for forced labor or commercial sexual activity, including any child subjected to an act specified in Section 20A.02 or 20A.03, Penal Code.

Added by Acts 2015, 84th Leg., ch. 338 (H.B. 418), § 1, eff. Sept. 1, 2015. Amended by Acts 2017, 85th Leg., ch. 317 (H.B. 7), § 16, eff. Sept. 1, 2017.

### § 262.012. Sealing of Court Records Filed Electronically

For purposes of determining whether to seal documents in accordance with Rule 76a, Texas Rules of Civil Procedure, in a suit under this subtitle, the court shall consider documents filed through an electronic filing system in the same manner as any other document filed with the court.

Added by Acts 2015, 84th Leg., ch. 455 (H.B. 331), § 1, eff. June 15, 2015. Redesignated from V.T.C.A., Family Code § 262.011 by Acts 2017, 85th Leg., ch. 324 (S.B. 1488), § 24.001(8), eff. Sept. 1, 2017.

### § 262.013. Voluntary Temporary Managing Conservatorship

In a suit affecting the parent-child relationship filed by the Department of Family and Protective Services, the existence of a parent's voluntary agreement to temporarily place the parent's child in the managing conservatorship of the department is not an admission by the parent that the parent engaged in conduct that endangered the child.

Added by Acts 2017, 85th Leg., ch. 317 (H.B. 7), § 17, eff. Sept. 1, 2017.

### § 262.014. Disclosure of Certain Evidence

On the request of the attorney for a parent who is a party in a suit affecting the parent-child relationship filed under this chapter, or the attorney ad litem for the parent's child, the Department of Family and Protective Services shall, before the full adversary hearing, provide:

(1) the name of any person, excluding a department employee, whom the department will call as a witness to any of the allegations contained in the petition filed by the department;

(2) a copy of any offense report relating to the allegations contained in the petition filed by the department that will be used in court to refresh a witness's memory; and

(3) a copy of any photograph, video, or recording that will be presented as evidence.

Added by Acts 2017, 85th Leg., ch. 317 (H.B. 7), § 17, eff. Sept. 1, 2017.

## § 262.015. Filing Requirement for Petition Regarding More Than One Child

Each suit under this chapter based on allegations of abuse or neglect arising from the same incident or occurrence and involving children that live in the same home must be filed in the same court.

Added by Acts 2017, 85th Leg., ch. 910 (S.B. 999), § 3, eff. Sept. 1, 2017. Redesignated from V.T.C.A., Family Code § 262.013 by Acts 2019, 86th Leg., ch. 467 (H.B. 4170), § 21.001(15), eff. Sept. 1, 2019.

## SUBCHAPTER B. TAKING POSSESSION OF CHILD

## § 262.101. Filing Petition Before Taking Possession of Child

An original suit filed by a governmental entity that requests permission to take possession of a child without prior notice and a hearing must be supported by an affidavit sworn to by a person with personal knowledge and stating facts sufficient to satisfy a person of ordinary prudence and caution that:

(1) there is an immediate danger to the physical health or safety of the child or the child has been a victim of neglect or sexual abuse;

(2) continuation in the home would be contrary to the child's welfare;

(3) there is no time, consistent with the physical health or safety of the child, for a full adversary hearing under Subchapter C;[1] and

(4) reasonable efforts, consistent with the circumstances and providing for the safety of the child, were made to prevent or eliminate the need for the removal of the child.

Added by Acts 1995, 74th Leg., ch. 20, § 1, eff. April 20, 1995. Amended by Acts 1995, 74th Leg., ch. 751, § 103, eff. Sept. 1, 1995; Acts 1997, 75th Leg., ch. 752, § 1, eff. June 17, 1997; Acts 1999, 76th Leg., ch. 1150, § 14, eff. Sept. 1, 1999; Acts 1999, 76th Leg., ch. 1390, § 33, eff. Sept. 1, 1999; Acts 2001, 77th Leg., ch. 849, § 1, eff. Sept. 1, 2001; Acts 2017, 85th Leg., ch. 910 (S.B. 999), § 4, eff. Sept. 1, 2017.

[1] V.T.C.A., Family Code § 262.201 et seq.

## § 262.1015. Removal of Alleged Perpetrator; Offense

(a) If the Department of Family and Protective Services determines after an investigation that child abuse has occurred and that the child would be protected in the child's home by the removal of the alleged perpetrator of the abuse, the department shall file a petition for the removal of the alleged perpetrator from the residence of the child rather than attempt to remove the child from the residence.

(a–1) Notwithstanding Subsection (a), if the Department of Family and Protective Services determines that a protective order issued under Title 4 [1] provides a reasonable alternative to obtaining an order under that subsection, the department may:

(1) file an application for a protective order on behalf of the child instead of or in addition to obtaining a temporary restraining order under this section; or

(2) assist a parent or other adult with whom a child resides in obtaining a protective order.

(b) A court may issue a temporary restraining order in a suit by the department for the removal of an alleged perpetrator under Subsection (a) if the department's petition states facts sufficient to satisfy the court that:

(1) there is an immediate danger to the physical health or safety of the child or the child has been a victim of sexual abuse;

(2) there is no time, consistent with the physical health or safety of the child, for an adversary hearing;

(3) the child is not in danger of abuse from a parent or other adult with whom the child will continue to reside in the residence of the child;

(4) the parent or other adult with whom the child will continue to reside in the child's home is likely to:

(A) make a reasonable effort to monitor the residence; and

(B) report to the department and the appropriate law enforcement agency any attempt by the alleged perpetrator to return to the residence; and

(5) the issuance of the order is in the best interest of the child.

(c) The order shall be served on the alleged perpetrator and on the parent or other adult with whom the child will continue to reside.

(d) A temporary restraining order under this section expires not later than the 14th day after the date the order was rendered, unless the court grants an extension under Section 262.201(e).

(e) A temporary restraining order under this section and any other order requiring the removal of an alleged perpetrator from the residence of a child shall require that the parent or other adult with whom the child will continue to reside in the child's home make a reasonable effort to monitor the residence and report to the department and the appropriate law enforcement agency any attempt by the alleged perpetrator to return to the residence.

(f) The court shall order the removal of an alleged perpetrator if the court finds that the child is not in danger of abuse from a parent or other adult with whom the child will continue to reside in the child's residence and that:

(1) the presence of the alleged perpetrator in the child's residence constitutes a continuing danger to the physical health or safety of the child; or

(2) the child has been the victim of sexual abuse and there is a substantial risk that the child will be the victim of sexual abuse in the future if the alleged perpetrator remains in the residence.

(g) A person commits an offense if the person is a parent or other person with whom a child resides, the person is served with an order containing the requirement specified by Subsection (e), and the person fails to make a reasonable effort to monitor the residence of the child or to report to the department and the appropriate law enforcement agency an attempt by the alleged perpetrator to return to the residence. An offense under this section is a Class A misdemeanor.

(h) A person commits an offense if, in violation of a court order under this section, the person returns to the residence of the child the person is alleged to have abused. An offense under this subsection is a Class A misdemeanor, except that the offense is a felony of the third degree if the person has previously been convicted under this subsection.

Added by Acts 1995, 74th Leg., ch. 943, § 4, eff. Sept. 1, 1995. Amended by Acts 1997, 75th Leg., ch. 575, § 19, eff. Sept. 1, 1997; Acts 2011, 82nd Leg., ch. 222 (H.B. 253), § 2, eff. Sept. 1, 2011; Acts 2011, 82nd Leg., ch. 598 (S.B. 218), § 3, eff. Sept. 1, 2011; Acts 2013, 83rd Leg., ch. 810 (S.B. 1759), § 6, eff. Sept. 1, 2013; Acts 2015, 84th Leg., ch. 1 (S.B. 219), § 1.154, eff. April 2, 2015; Acts 2017, 85th Leg., ch. 910 (S.B. 999), § 5, eff. Sept. 1, 2017.

[1] V.T.C.A., Family Code § 71.001 et seq.

## § 262.102. Emergency Order Authorizing Possession of Child

(a) Before a court may, without prior notice and a hearing, issue a temporary order for the conservatorship of a child under Section 105.001(a)(1) or a temporary restraining order or attachment of a child authorizing a governmental entity to take possession of a child in a suit brought by a governmental entity, the court must find that:

(1) there is an immediate danger to the physical health or safety of the child or the child has been a victim of neglect or sexual abuse;

(2) continuation in the home would be contrary to the child's welfare;

(3) there is no time, consistent with the physical health or safety of the child and the nature of the emergency, for a full adversary hearing under Subchapter C;[1] and

(4) reasonable efforts, consistent with the circumstances and providing for the safety of the child, were made to prevent or eliminate the need for removal of the child.

(b) In determining whether there is an immediate danger to the physical health or safety of a child, the court may consider whether the child's household includes a person who has:

(1) abused or neglected another child in a manner that caused serious injury to or the death of the other child; or

(2) sexually abused another child.

(b–1) A determination under this section that there is an immediate danger to the physical health or safety of a child or that the child has been a victim of neglect or sexual abuse may not be based solely on the opinion of a medical professional under contract with the Department of Family and Protective Services who did not conduct a physical examination of the child.

(c) If, based on the recommendation of or a request by the Department of Family and Protective Services, the court finds that child abuse or neglect has occurred and that the child requires protection from family violence by a member of the child's family or household, the court shall render a temporary order under Title 4[2] for the protection of the child. In this subsection, "family violence" has the meaning assigned by Section 71.004.

(d) The temporary order, temporary restraining order, or attachment of a child rendered by the court under Subsection (a) must contain the following statement prominently displayed in boldface type, capital letters, or underlined:

"YOU HAVE THE RIGHT TO BE REPRESENTED BY AN ATTORNEY. IF YOU ARE INDIGENT AND UNABLE TO AFFORD AN ATTORNEY, YOU HAVE THE RIGHT TO REQUEST THE APPOINTMENT OF AN ATTORNEY BY CONTACTING THE COURT AT [ADDRESS], [TELEPHONE NUMBER]. IF YOU

APPEAR IN OPPOSITION TO THE SUIT, CLAIM INDIGENCE, AND REQUEST THE APPOINTMENT OF AN ATTORNEY, THE COURT WILL REQUIRE YOU TO SIGN AN AFFIDAVIT OF INDIGENCE AND THE COURT MAY HEAR EVIDENCE TO DETERMINE IF YOU ARE INDIGENT. IF THE COURT DETERMINES YOU ARE INDIGENT AND ELIGIBLE FOR APPOINTMENT OF AN ATTORNEY, THE COURT WILL APPOINT AN ATTORNEY TO REPRESENT YOU."

Added by Acts 1995, 74th Leg., ch. 20, § 1, eff. April 20, 1995. Amended by Acts 1995, 74th Leg., ch. 751, § 104, eff. Sept. 1, 1995; Acts 1997, 75th Leg., ch. 752, § 2, eff. June 17, 1997; Acts 1999, 76th Leg., ch. 1150, § 15, eff. Sept. 1, 1999; Acts 1999, 76th Leg., ch. 1390, § 34, eff. Sept. 1, 1999; Acts 2001, 77th Leg., ch. 849, § 2, eff. Sept. 1, 2001; Acts 2003, 78th Leg., ch. 1276, § 7.002(m), eff. Sept. 1, 2003; Acts 2013, 83rd Leg., ch. 810 (S.B. 1759), § 7, eff. Sept. 1, 2013; Acts 2015, 84th Leg., ch. 1 (S.B. 219), § 1.155, eff. April 2, 2015; Acts 2017, 85th Leg., ch. 910 (S.B. 999), § 6, eff. Sept. 1, 2017; Acts 2021, 87th Leg., ch. 1047 (S.B. 1578), § 5, eff. Sept. 1, 2021.

[1] V.T.C.A., Family Code § 262.201 et seq.

[2] V.T.C.A., Family Code § 71.001 et seq.

Section 8 of Acts 2021, 87th Leg., ch. 1047 (S.B. 1578) provides:

"The changes in law made by this Act apply only to a suit affecting the parent-child relationship filed on or after the effective date [Sept. 1, 2021] of this Act. A suit affecting the parent-child relationship filed before the effective date [Sept. 1, 2021] of this Act is governed by the law in effect on the date the suit was filed, and the former law is continued in effect for that purpose."

### § 262.103. Duration of Temporary Order, Temporary Restraining Order, and Attachment

A temporary order, temporary restraining order, or attachment of the child issued under Section 262.102(a) expires not later than 14 days after the date it is issued unless it is extended as provided by the Texas Rules of Civil Procedure or Section 262.201(e).

Added by Acts 1995, 74th Leg., ch. 20, § 1, eff. April 20, 1995. Amended by Acts 2013, 83rd Leg., ch. 810 (S.B. 1759), § 8, eff. Sept. 1, 2013; Acts 2015, 84th Leg., ch. 1 (S.B. 219), § 1.156, eff. April 2, 2015; Acts 2017, 85th Leg., ch. 910 (S.B. 999), § 7, eff. Sept. 1, 2017.

### § 262.104. Taking Possession of a Child in Emergency Without a Court Order

(a) If there is no time to obtain a temporary order, temporary restraining order, or attachment under Section 262.102(a) before taking possession of a child consistent with the health and safety of that child, an authorized representative of the Department of Family and Protective Services, a law enforcement officer, or a juvenile probation officer may take possession of a child without a court order under the following conditions, only:

(1) on personal knowledge of facts that would lead a person of ordinary prudence and caution to believe that there is an immediate danger to the physical health or safety of the child;

(2) on information furnished by another that has been corroborated by personal knowledge of facts and all of which taken together would lead a person of ordinary prudence and caution to believe that there is an immediate danger to the physical health or safety of the child;

(3) on personal knowledge of facts that would lead a person of ordinary prudence and caution to believe that the child has been the victim of sexual abuse or of trafficking under Section 20A.02 or 20A.03, Penal Code;

(4) on information furnished by another that has been corroborated by personal knowledge of facts and all of which taken together would lead a person of ordinary prudence and caution to believe that the child has been the victim of sexual abuse or of trafficking under Section 20A.02 or 20A.03, Penal Code; or

(5) on information furnished by another that has been corroborated by personal knowledge of facts and all of which taken together would lead a person of ordinary prudence and caution to believe that the parent or person who has possession of the child is currently using a controlled substance as defined by Chapter 481, Health and Safety Code, and the use constitutes an immediate danger to the physical health or safety of the child.

(b) An authorized representative of the Department of Family and Protective Services, a law enforcement officer, or a juvenile probation officer may take possession of a child under Subsection (a) on personal knowledge or information furnished by another, that has been corroborated by personal knowledge, that would lead a person of ordinary prudence and caution to believe that the parent or person who has possession of the child has permitted the child to remain on premises used for the manufacture of methamphetamine.

(c) An authorized representative of the Department of Family and Protective Services, a law enforcement officer, or a juvenile probation officer may not take possession of a child under Subsection (a) based solely on the opinion of a medical professional under contract with the Department of Family and Protective

Services who did not conduct a physical examination of the child.

Added by Acts 1995, 74th Leg., ch. 20, § 1, eff. April 20, 1995. Amended by Acts 1997, 75th Leg., ch. 575, § 20, eff. Sept. 1, 1997; Acts 2005, 79th Leg., ch. 282, § 2, eff. Aug. 1, 2005; Acts 2015, 84th Leg., ch. 1 (S.B. 219), § 1.157, eff. April 2, 2015; Acts 2015, 84th Leg., ch. 338 (H.B. 418), § 2, eff. Sept. 1, 2015; Acts 2021, 87th Leg., ch. 1047 (S.B. 1578), § 6, eff. Sept. 1, 2021.

Section 8 of Acts 2021, 87th Leg., ch. 1047 (S.B. 1578) provides:

"The changes in law made by this Act apply only to a suit affecting the parent-child relationship filed on or after the effective date [Sept. 1, 2021] of this Act. A suit affecting the parent-child relationship filed before the effective date [Sept. 1, 2021] of this Act is governed by the law in effect on the date the suit was filed, and the former law is continued in effect for that purpose."

### § 262.1041. Repealed by Acts 2015, 84th Leg., ch. 944 (S.B. 206), § 86(12), eff. Sept. 1, 2015

### § 262.105. Filing Petition After Taking Possession of Child in Emergency

(a) When a child is taken into possession without a court order, the person taking the child into possession, without unnecessary delay, shall:

(1) file a suit affecting the parent-child relationship;

(2) request the court to appoint an attorney ad litem for the child; and

(3) request an initial hearing to be held by no later than the first business day after the date the child is taken into possession.

(b) An original suit filed by a governmental entity after taking possession of a child under Section 262.104 must be supported by an affidavit stating facts sufficient to satisfy a person of ordinary prudence and caution that:

(1) based on the affiant's personal knowledge or on information furnished by another person corroborated by the affiant's personal knowledge, one of the following circumstances existed at the time the child was taken into possession:

(A) there was an immediate danger to the physical health or safety of the child;

(B) the child was the victim of sexual abuse or of trafficking under Section 20A.02 or 20A.03, Penal Code;

(C) the parent or person who had possession of the child was using a controlled substance as defined by Chapter 481, Health and Safety Code, and the use constituted an immediate danger to the physical health or safety of the child; or

(D) the parent or person who had possession of the child permitted the child to remain on premises used for the manufacture of methamphetamine; and

(2) based on the affiant's personal knowledge:

(A) continuation of the child in the home would have been contrary to the child's welfare;

(B) there was no time, consistent with the physical health or safety of the child, for a full adversary hearing under Subchapter C;[1] and

(C) reasonable efforts, consistent with the circumstances and providing for the safety of the child, were made to prevent or eliminate the need for the removal of the child.

Added by Acts 1995, 74th Leg., ch. 20, § 1, eff. April 20, 1995. Amended by Acts 2001, 77th Leg., ch. 809, § 2, eff. Sept. 1, 2001; Acts 2015, 84th Leg., ch. 1 (S.B. 219), § 1.158, eff. April 2, 2015; Acts 2015, 84th Leg., ch. 944 (S.B. 206), § 86(13), eff. Sept. 1, 2015; Acts 2017, 85th Leg., ch. 910 (S.B. 999), § 8, eff. Sept. 1, 2017.

[1] V.T.C.A., Family Code § 262.201 et seq.

### § 262.106. Initial Hearing After Taking Possession of Child in Emergency Without Court Order

(a) The court in which a suit has been filed after a child has been taken into possession without a court order by a governmental entity shall hold an initial hearing on or before the first business day after the date the child is taken into possession. The court shall render orders that are necessary to protect the physical health and safety of the child. If the court is unavailable for a hearing on the first business day, then, and only in that event, the hearing shall be held no later than the first business day after the court becomes available, provided that the hearing is held no later than the third business day after the child is taken into possession.

(b) The initial hearing may be ex parte and proof may be by sworn petition or affidavit if a full adversary hearing is not practicable.

(c) If the initial hearing is not held within the time required, the child shall be returned to the parent, managing conservator, possessory conservator, guardian, caretaker, or custodian who is presently entitled to possession of the child.

(d) For the purpose of determining under Subsection (a) the first business day after the date the child is taken into possession, the child is considered to have been taken into possession by the Department of Family and Protective Services on the expiration of the five-day period permitted under Section 262.007(c) or 262.110(b), as appropriate.

Added by Acts 1995, 74th Leg., ch. 20, § 1, eff. April 20, 1995. Amended by Acts 1999, 76th Leg., ch. 1150, § 16, eff. Sept. 1, 1999; Acts 1999, 76th Leg., ch. 1390, § 35, eff. Sept. 1, 1999; Acts 2015, 84th Leg., ch. 1 (S.B. 219), § 1.159, eff. April 2, 2015; Acts 2017, 85th Leg., ch. 910 (S.B. 999), § 9, eff. Sept. 1, 2017.

### § 262.107. Standard for Decision at Initial Hearing After Taking Possession of Child Without a Court Order in Emergency

(a) The court shall order the return of the child at the initial hearing regarding a child taken in possession without a court order by a governmental entity unless the court is satisfied that:

(1) the evidence shows that one of the following circumstances exists:

(A) there is a continuing danger to the physical health or safety of the child if the child is returned to the parent, managing conservator, possessory conservator, guardian, caretaker, or custodian who is presently entitled to possession of the child;

(B) the child has been the victim of sexual abuse or of trafficking under Section 20A.02 or 20A.03, Penal Code, on one or more occasions and that there is a substantial risk that the child will be the victim of sexual abuse or of trafficking in the future;

(C) the parent or person who has possession of the child is currently using a controlled substance as defined by Chapter 481, Health and Safety Code, and the use constitutes an immediate danger to the physical health or safety of the child; or

(D) the parent or person who has possession of the child has permitted the child to remain on premises used for the manufacture of methamphetamine;

(2) continuation of the child in the home would be contrary to the child's welfare; and

(3) reasonable efforts, consistent with the circumstances and providing for the safety of the child, were made to prevent or eliminate the need for removal of the child.

(b) In determining whether there is a continuing danger to the physical health or safety of a child, the court may consider whether the household to which the child would be returned includes a person who has:

(1) abused or neglected another child in a manner that caused serious injury to or the death of the other child; or

(2) sexually abused another child.

Added by Acts 1995, 74th Leg., ch. 20, § 1, eff. April 20, 1995. Amended by Acts 1995, 74th Leg., ch. 751, § 105, eff. Sept. 1, 1995; Acts 2001, 77th Leg., ch. 849, § 3, eff. Sept. 1, 2001; Acts 2015, 84th Leg., ch. 338 (H.B. 418), § 3, eff. Sept. 1, 2015; Acts 2017, 85th Leg., ch. 910 (S.B. 999), § 10, eff. Sept. 1, 2017.

### § 262.108. Unacceptable Facilities for Housing Child

When a child is taken into possession under this chapter, that child may not be held in isolation or in a jail, juvenile detention facility, or other secure detention facility.

Added by Acts 1995, 74th Leg., ch. 20, § 1, eff. April 20, 1995. Amended by Acts 1997, 75th Leg., ch. 1374, § 9, eff. Sept. 1, 1997.

### § 262.109. Notice to Parent, Conservator, or Guardian

(a) The Department of Family and Protective Services or other agency must give written notice as prescribed by this section to each parent of the child or to the child's conservator or legal guardian when a representative of the department or other agency takes possession of a child under this chapter.

(b) The written notice must be given as soon as practicable, but in any event not later than the first business day after the date the child is taken into possession.

(c) The written notice must include:

(1) the reasons why the department or agency is taking possession of the child and the facts that led the department to believe that the child should be taken into custody;

(2) the name of the person at the department or agency that the parent, conservator, or other custodian may contact for information relating to the child or a legal proceeding relating to the child;

(3) a summary of legal rights of a parent, conservator, guardian, or other custodian under this chapter and an explanation of the probable legal procedures relating to the child; and

(4) a statement that the parent, conservator, or other custodian has the right to hire an attorney.

(d) The written notice may be waived by the court at the initial hearing:

(1) on a showing that:

(A) the parents, conservators, or other custodians of the child could not be located; or

(B) the department took possession of the child under Subchapter D;[1] or

(2) for other good cause.

Added by Acts 1995, 74th Leg., ch. 20, § 1, eff. April 20, 1995. Amended by Acts 1997, 75th Leg., ch. 1022, § 76, eff. Jan. 1, 1998; Acts 1999, 76th Leg., ch. 1150, § 17, eff. Sept. 1, 1999; Acts 1999, 76th Leg., ch. 1390, § 36, eff. Sept. 1, 1999; Acts 2001, 77th Leg., ch. 809, § 3, eff. Sept. 1, 2001; Acts 2015, 84th Leg., ch. 1 (S.B. 219), § 1.160, eff. April 2, 2015; Acts 2017, 85th Leg., ch. 910 (S.B. 999), § 11, eff. Sept. 1, 2017.

[1] V.T.C.A., Family Code § 262.301 et seq.

### § 262.1095. Information Provided to Relatives and Certain Individuals; Investigation

(a) When the Department of Family and Protective Services or another agency takes possession of a child under this chapter, the department:

(1) shall provide information as prescribed by this section in writing to each adult the department is able to identify and locate who is:

(A) related to the child within the fourth degree by consanguinity as determined under Chapter 573, Government Code;

(B) an adult relative of the alleged father of the child if the department has a reasonable basis to believe the alleged father is the child's biological father; or

(C) identified as a potential relative or designated caregiver, as defined by Section 264.751, on the proposed child placement resources form provided under Section 261.307; and

(2) may provide information as prescribed by this section to each adult the department is able to identify and locate who has a long-standing and significant relationship with the child.

(b) The information provided under Subsection (a) must:

(1) state that the child has been removed from the child's home and is in the temporary managing conservatorship of the department;

(2) explain the options available to the individual to participate in the care and placement of the child and the support of the child's family, the methods by which the individual may exercise those options, and any requirements the individual must satisfy to exercise those options, including:

(A) the requirement that the individual be evaluated by the Department of Family and Protective Services under Section 262.114 before the individual may serve as a substitute caregiver; and

(B) the deadlines before which the individual must respond to exercise those options;

(3) identify the options available to the individual that may be lost if the individual fails to respond in a timely manner;

(4) include, if applicable, the date, time, and location of the hearing under Subchapter C, Chapter 263[1]; and

(5) include information regarding the procedures and timeline for a suit affecting the parent-child relationship under this chapter.

(c) The department is not required to provide information to an individual if the individual has received service of citation under Section 102.009 or if the department determines providing information is inappropriate because the individual has a criminal history or a history of family violence.

(d) The department shall use due diligence to identify and locate all individuals described by Subsection (a) not later than the 30th day after the date the department files a suit affecting the parent-child relationship. In order to identify and locate the individuals described by Subsection (a), the department shall seek information from:

(1) each parent, relative, and alleged father of the child; and

(2) the child in an age-appropriate manner.

(d–1) Immediately after the Department of Family and Protective Services identifies and locates an individual described by Subsection (a)(1), the department shall provide the information required by this section.

(e) The failure of a parent or alleged father of the child to complete the proposed child placement resources form does not relieve the department of its duty to seek information about the person under Subsection (d).

Added by Acts 2011, 82nd Leg., ch. 1071 (S.B. 993), § 2, eff. Sept. 1, 2011. Amended by Acts 2015, 84th Leg., ch. 944 (S.B. 206), § 23, eff. Sept. 1, 2015; Acts 2021, 87th Leg., ch. 269 (H.B. 3041), § 1, eff. Sept. 1, 2021; Acts 2021, 87th Leg., ch. 710 (H.B. 2926), § 3, eff. Sept. 1, 2021.

[1] V.T.C.A., Family Code § 263.201 et seq.

Section 5 of Acts 2021, 87th Leg., ch. 269 (H.B. 3041) provides:

"The changes in law made by this Act to Section 262.1095, Family Code, apply only to a suit affecting the parent-child relationship filed on or after the effective date of this Act [Sept. 1, 2021]. A suit affecting the parent-child relationship filed before the effective date of this Act is governed by the law in effect immediately before the effective date of this Act, and the former law is continued in effect for that purpose."

### § 262.110. Taking Possession of Child in Emergency with Intent to Return Home

(a) An authorized representative of the Department of Family and Protective Services, a law enforcement officer, or a juvenile probation officer may take temporary possession of a child without a court order on discovery of a child in a situation of danger to the child's physical health or safety when the sole purpose is to deliver the child without unnecessary delay to the parent, managing conservator, possessory conservator, guardian, caretaker, or custodian who is presently entitled to possession of the child.

(b) Until a parent or other person entitled to possession of the child takes possession of the child, the department may retain possession of the child without a court order for not more than five days. On the expiration of the fifth day, if a parent or other person entitled to possession does not take possession of the child, the department shall take action under this chapter as if the department took possession of the child under Section 262.104.

Added by Acts 1995, 74th Leg., ch. 20, § 1, eff. April 20, 1995. Amended by Acts 1999, 76th Leg., ch. 1150, § 18, eff. Sept. 1, 1999; Acts 1999, 76th Leg., ch. 1390, § 37, eff. Sept. 1, 1999; Acts 2015, 84th Leg., ch. 1 (S.B. 219), § 1.161, eff. April 2, 2015.

### § 262.111. Repealed by Acts 2001, 77th Leg., ch. 849, § 10, eff. Sept. 1, 2001.

### § 262.112. Expedited Hearing and Appeal

(a) The Department of Family and Protective Services is entitled to an expedited hearing under this chapter in any proceeding in which a hearing is required if the department determines that a child should be removed from the child's home because of an immediate danger to the physical health or safety of the child.

(b) In any proceeding in which an expedited hearing is held under Subsection (a), the department, parent, guardian, or other party to the proceeding is entitled to an expedited appeal on a ruling by a court that the child may not be removed from the child's home.

(c) If a child is returned to the child's home after a removal in which the department was entitled to an expedited hearing under this section and the child is the subject of a subsequent allegation of abuse or neglect, the department or any other interested party is entitled to an expedited hearing on the removal of the child from the child's home in the manner provided by Subsection (a) and to an expedited appeal in the manner provided by Subsection (b).

Added by Acts 1995, 74th Leg., ch. 943, § 1, eff. Sept. 1, 1995. Redesignated from V.T.C.A., Family Code § 262.111 by Acts 1997, 75th Leg., ch. 165, § 31.01(29), eff. Sept. 1, 1997. Amended by Acts 2015, 84th Leg., ch. 1 (S.B. 219), § 1.162, eff. April 2, 2015.

### § 262.113. Repealed by Acts 2021, 87th Leg., ch. 8 (H.B. 567), § 13(1), eff. Sept. 1, 2021

Section 15 of Acts 2021, 87th Leg., ch. 8 (H.B. 567) provides:

"The changes in law made by this Act apply only to a suit filed by the Department of Family and Protective Services on or after the effective date [Sept. 1, 2021] of this Act. A suit filed by the department before that date is governed by the law in effect on the date the suit was filed, and the former law is continued in effect for that purpose."

### § 262.1131. Repealed by Acts 2021, 87th Leg., ch. 8 (H.B. 567), § 13(2), eff. Sept. 1, 2021

Section 15 of Acts 2021, 87th Leg., ch. 8 (H.B. 567) provides:

"The changes in law made by this Act apply only to a suit filed by the Department of Family and Protective Services on or after the effective date [Sept. 1, 2021] of this Act. A suit filed by the department before that date is governed by the law in effect on the date the suit was filed, and the former law is continued in effect for that purpose."

### § 262.114. Evaluation of Identified Relatives and other Designated Individuals; Placement

(a) Before a full adversary hearing under Subchapter C, [1] the Department of Family and Protective Services must perform a background and criminal history check of the relatives or other designated individuals identified as a potential relative or designated caregiver, as defined by Section 264.751, on the proposed child placement resources form provided under Section 261.307, including any adult identified by the child. The department shall evaluate each person listed on the form to determine the relative or other designated individual who would be the most appropriate substitute caregiver for the child and must complete a home study of the most appropriate substitute caregiver, if any, before the full adversary hearing. Until the department identifies a relative or other designated individual qualified to be a substitute caregiver, the department must continue to explore substitute caregiver options, including asking the child in a developmentally appropriate manner to identify any adult, particularly an adult residing in the child's community, who could be a relative or designated caregiver for the child. The time frames in this subsection do not apply to a relative or other designated individual located in another state.

(a–1) At the full adversary hearing under Section 262.201, the department shall, after redacting any social security numbers, file with the court:

(1) a copy of each proposed child placement resources form completed by the parent or other person having legal custody of the child;

(2) a copy of any completed home study performed under Subsection (a); and

(3) the name of the relative or other designated caregiver, if any, with whom the child has been placed.

(a–2) If the child has not been placed with a relative or other designated caregiver by the time of the full adversary hearing under Section 262.201, the department shall file with the court a statement that explains:

(1) the reasons why the department has not placed the child with a relative or other designated caregiver listed on the proposed child placement resources form, including any adult identified by the child; and

(2) the actions the department is taking, if any, to place the child with a relative or other designated caregiver.

(b) The department may place a child with a relative or other designated caregiver identified on the proposed child placement resources form, including any adult identified by the child, if the department determines that the placement is in the best interest of the child. The department must complete the background and criminal history check and conduct a preliminary evaluation of the relative or other designated caregiver's home before the child is placed with the relative or other designated caregiver. The department may place the child with the relative or designated caregiver before conducting the home study required under Subsection (a). Not later than 48 hours after the time that the child is placed with the relative or other designated caregiver, the department shall begin the home study of the relative or other designated caregiver. The department shall complete the home study as soon as possible unless otherwise ordered by a court. The department shall provide a copy of an informational manual required under Section 261.3071 to the relative or other designated caregiver at the time of the child's placement.

(c) The department shall consider placing a child who has previously been in the managing conservatorship of the department with a foster parent with whom the child previously resided if:

(1) the department determines that placement of the child with a relative or designated caregiver is not in the child's best interest; and

(2) the placement is available and in the child's best interest.

(d) In making a placement decision for a child, the department shall give preference to persons in the following order:

(1) a person related to the child by blood, marriage, or adoption;

(2) a person with whom the child has a longstanding and significant relationship;

(3) a foster home; and

(4) a general residential operation.

Added by Acts 2005, 79th Leg., ch. 268, § 1.33, eff. Sept. 1, 2005. Amended by Acts 2009, 81st Leg., ch. 527, § 1, eff. Sept. 1, 2009; Acts 2009, 81st Leg., ch. 856, § 1, eff. Sept. 1, 2009; Acts 2015, 84th Leg., ch. 944 (S.B. 206), § 24, eff. Sept. 1, 2015; Acts 2019, 86th Leg., ch. 1294 (H.B. 3390), § 6, eff. June 14, 2019; Acts 2021, 87th Leg., ch. 710 (H.B. 2926), § 4, eff. Sept. 1, 2021.

[1] V.T.C.A., Family Code § 262.201 et seq.

## § 262.115. Visitation with Certain Children; Temporary Visitation Schedule

(a) In this section, "department" means the Department of Family and Protective Services.

(b) This section applies only to a child:

(1) who is in the temporary managing conservatorship of the department; and

(2) for whom the department's goal is reunification of the child with the child's parent.

(c) The department shall ensure that a parent who is otherwise entitled to possession of the child has an opportunity to visit the child not later than the fifth day after the date the department is named temporary managing conservator of the child unless:

(1) the department determines that visitation is not in the child's best interest; or

(2) visitation with the parent would conflict with a court order relating to possession of or access to the child.

(d) Before a hearing conducted under Subchapter C,[1] the department in collaboration with each parent of the child must develop a temporary visitation schedule for the child's visits with each parent. The visitation schedule may conform to the department's minimum visitation policies. The department shall consider the factors listed in Section 263.107(c) in developing the temporary visitation schedule. Unless modified by court order, the schedule remains in effect until a visitation plan is developed under Section 263.107.

(e) The department may include the temporary visitation schedule in any report the department submits to the court before or during a hearing under Subchapter C. The court may render any necessary order regarding the temporary visitation schedule.

Added by Acts 2013, 83rd Leg., ch. 191 (S.B. 352), § 1, eff. Sept. 1, 2013. Amended by Acts 2015, 84th Leg., ch. 944 (S.B. 206), § 25, eff. Sept. 1, 2015.

[1] V.T.C.A., Family Code § 262.201 et seq.

### § 262.116. Limits on Removal

(a) The Department of Family and Protective Services may not take possession of a child under this subchapter based on evidence that the parent:

(1) homeschooled the child;

(2) is economically disadvantaged;

(3) has been charged with a nonviolent misdemeanor offense other than:

(A) an offense under Title 5, Penal Code;

(B) an offense under Title 6, Penal Code; or

(C) an offense that involves family violence, as defined by Section 71.004 of this code;

(4) provided or administered low-THC cannabis to a child for whom the low-THC cannabis was prescribed under Chapter 169, Occupations Code;

(5) declined immunization for the child for reasons of conscience, including a religious belief;

*Text of (a)(6), as added by Acts 2021, 87th Leg., ch. 8 (H.B. 567), § 6*

(6) allowed the child to engage in independent activities that are appropriate and typical for the child's level of maturity, physical condition, developmental abilities, or culture; or

*Text of (a)(6), as added by Acts 2021, 87th Leg., ch. 29 (H.B. 2536), § 3*

(6) sought an opinion from more than one medical provider relating to the child's medical care, transferred the child's medical care to a new medical provider, or transferred the child to another health care facility.

(7) tested positive for marihuana, unless the department has evidence that the parent's use of marihuana has caused significant impairment to the child's physical or mental health or emotional development.

(b) The department shall train child protective services caseworkers regarding the prohibitions on removal provided under Subsection (a).

(c) The executive commissioner of the Health and Human Services Commission may adopt rules to implement this section.

(d) This section does not prohibit the department from gathering or offering evidence described by Subsection (a) as part of an action to take possession of a child under this subchapter.

Added by Acts 2017, 85th Leg., ch. 317 (H.B. 7), § 19, eff. Sept. 1, 2017. Amended by Acts 2021, 87th Leg., ch. 8 (H.B. 567), § 6, eff. Sept. 1, 2021; Acts 2021, 87th Leg., ch. 29 (H.B. 2536), § 3, eff. May 15, 2021.

Section 15 of Acts 2021, 87th Leg., ch. 8 (H.B. 567) provides:

"The changes in law made by this Act apply only to a suit filed by the Department of Family and Protective Services on or after the effective date [Sept. 1, 2021] of this Act. A suit filed by the department before that date is governed by the law in effect on the date the suit was filed, and the former law is continued in effect for that purpose."

## SUBCHAPTER C. ADVERSARY HEARING

### § 262.201. Full Adversary Hearing; Findings of the Court

(a) In a suit filed under Section 262.101 or 262.105, unless the child has already been returned to the parent, managing conservator, possessory conservator, guardian, caretaker, or custodian entitled to possession and the temporary order, if any, has been dissolved, a full adversary hearing shall be held not later than the 14th day after the date the child was taken into possession by the governmental entity, unless the court grants an extension under Subsection (e) or (e–1).

(a–1) to (a–4) Expired.

(a–5) Repealed by Acts 2019, 86th Leg, ch. 467 (H.B. 4170), § 7.004(c).

(b) Repealed by Acts 2021, 87th Leg., ch. 8 (H.B. 567), § 13(3).

(c) Before commencement of the full adversary hearing, the court must inform each parent not represented by an attorney of:

(1) the right to be represented by an attorney; and

(2) if a parent is indigent and appears in opposition to the suit, the right to a court-appointed attorney.

(d) If a parent claims indigence and requests the appointment of an attorney before the full adversary hearing, the court shall require the parent to complete and file with the court an affidavit of indigence. The court may consider additional evidence to determine whether the parent is indigent, including evidence relating to the parent's income, source of income, assets, property ownership, benefits paid in accordance with a federal, state, or local public assistance program, outstanding obligations, and necessary expenses and the number and ages of the parent's dependents. If the appointment of an attorney for the parent is requested, the court shall make a determination of indigence before commencement of the full adversary hearing. If the court determines the parent is indigent, the court shall appoint an attorney to represent the parent.

(e) The court may, for good cause shown, postpone the full adversary hearing for not more than seven days from the date of the attorney's appointment to provide the attorney time to respond to the petition and prepare for the hearing. The court may shorten or lengthen the extension granted under this subsection if the parent and the appointed attorney agree in writing. If the court postpones the full adversary hearing, the court shall extend a temporary order, temporary restraining order, or attachment issued by the court under Section 262.102(a) for the protection of the child until the date of the rescheduled full adversary hearing.

(e–1) If a parent who is not indigent appears in opposition to the suit, the court may, for good cause shown, postpone the full adversary hearing for not more than seven days from the date of the parent's appearance to allow the parent to hire an attorney or to provide the parent's attorney time to respond to the petition and prepare for the hearing. A postponement under this subsection is subject to the limits and requirements prescribed by Subsection (e) and Section 155.207.

(f) The court shall ask all parties present at the full adversary hearing whether the child or the child's family has a Native American heritage and identify any Native American tribe with which the child may be associated.

(g) In a suit filed under Section 262.101 or 262.105, at the conclusion of the full adversary hearing, the court shall order the return of the child to the parent, managing conservator, possessory conservator, guardian, caretaker, or custodian entitled to possession from whom the child is removed unless the court finds sufficient evidence to satisfy a person of ordinary prudence and caution that:

(1) there was a danger to the physical health or safety of the child, including a danger that the child would be a victim of trafficking under Section 20A.02 or 20A.03, Penal Code, which was caused by an act or failure to act of the person entitled to possession and for the child to remain in the home is contrary to the welfare of the child;

(2) the urgent need for protection required the immediate removal of the child and reasonable efforts, consistent with the circumstances and providing for the safety of the child, were made to eliminate or prevent the child's removal; and

(3) reasonable efforts have been made to enable the child to return home, but there is a substantial risk of a continuing danger if the child is returned home.

(g–1) In a suit filed under Section 262.101 or 262.105, if the court does not order the return of the child under Subsection (g) and finds that another parent, managing conservator, possessory conservator, guardian, caretaker, or custodian entitled to possession did not cause the immediate danger to the physical health or safety of the child or was not the perpetrator of the neglect or abuse alleged in the suit, the court shall order possession of the child by that person unless the court finds sufficient evidence to satisfy a person of ordinary prudence and caution that, specific to each person entitled to possession:

(1) the person cannot be located after the exercise of due diligence by the Department of Family and Protective Services, or the person is unable or unwilling to take possession of the child; or

(2) reasonable efforts have been made to enable the person's possession of the child, but possession by that person presents a continuing danger to the physical health or safety of the child caused by an act or failure to act of the person, including a danger that the child would be a victim of trafficking under Section 20A.02 or 20A.03, Penal Code.

(h) In a suit filed under Section 262.101 or 262.105, if the court finds sufficient evidence to make the applicable finding under Subsection (g) or (g–1), the court shall issue an appropriate temporary order under Chapter 105.

(i) In determining whether there is a continuing danger to the physical health or safety of the child under Subsection (g), the court may consider whether the household to which the child would be returned includes a person who:

(1) has abused or neglected another child in a manner that caused serious injury to or the death of the other child; or

(2) has sexually abused another child.

(i–1) In making a determination whether there is an immediate danger to the physical health or safety of a child, the court shall consider the opinion of a medical professional obtained by the child's parent, managing conservator, possessory conservator, guardian, caretaker, or custodian.

(j) Repealed by Acts 2021, 87th Leg., ch. 8 (H.B. 567), § 13(3).

(k) If the court finds that the child requires protection from family violence, as that term is defined by Section 71.004, by a member of the child's family or household, the court shall render a protective order for the child under Title 4.[1]

(*l*) The court shall require each parent, alleged father, or relative of the child before the court to complete the proposed child placement resources form provided under Section 261.307 and file the form with the court, if the form has not been previously filed with the court, and provide the Department of Family and Protective Services with information necessary to locate any other absent parent, alleged father, or relative of the child. The court shall inform each parent, alleged father, or relative of the child before the court that the person's failure to submit the proposed child placement resources form will not delay any court proceedings relating to the child.

(l–1) The court shall ask all parties present at the full adversary hearing whether:

(1) the child has had the opportunity, in a developmentally appropriate manner, to identify any adult, particularly an adult residing in the child's community, who could be a relative or designated caregiver for the child; and

(2) each individual identified by the child as a potential relative or designated caregiver is listed on the proposed child placement resources form.

(m) The court shall inform each parent in open court that parental and custodial rights and duties may be subject to restriction or to termination unless the parent or parents are willing and able to provide the child with a safe environment.

(n) If the court does not order possession of a child by a parent, managing conservator, possessory conservator, guardian, caretaker, or custodian entitled to possession under Subsection (g) or (g–1), the court shall place the child with a relative of the child unless the court finds that the placement with a relative is not in the best interest of the child.

(n–1) For a child placed with a relative of the child, the court shall inform the relative of:

(1) the option to become verified by a licensed child-placing agency to operate an agency foster home, if applicable; and

(2) the permanency care assistance program under Subchapter K, Chapter 264.[2]

(*o*) When citation by publication is needed for a parent or alleged or probable father in an action brought under this chapter because the location of the parent, alleged father, or probable father is unknown, the court may render a temporary order without delay at any time after the filing of the action without regard to whether notice of the citation by publication has been published.

(p) For the purpose of determining under Subsection (a) the 14th day after the date the child is taken into possession, a child is considered to have been taken into possession by the Department of Family and Protective Services on the expiration of the five-day period permitted under Section 262.007(c) or 262.110(b), as appropriate.

(q) On receipt of a written request for possession of the child from a parent, managing conservator, possessory conservator, guardian, caretaker, or custodian entitled to possession of the child who was not located before the adversary hearing, the Department of Family and Protective Services shall notify the court and request a hearing to determine whether the parent, managing conservator, possessory conservator, guardian, caretaker, or custodian is entitled to possession of the child under Subsection (g–1).

Added by Acts 1995, 74th Leg., ch. 20, § 1, eff. April 20, 1995. Amended by Acts 1995, 74th Leg., ch. 751, § 107, eff. Sept. 1, 1995; Acts 1997, 75th Leg., ch. 575, § 21, eff. Sept. 1, 1997; Acts 1997, 75th Leg., ch. 600, § 5, eff. Jan, 1, 1998; Acts 1997, 75th Leg., ch. 603, § 1, eff. Jan. 1, 1998; Acts 1997, 75th Leg., ch; 752, § 3, eff. June 17, 1997; Acts 1997, 75th Leg., ch. 1022, § 77, eff; Jan. 1, 1998; Acts 1997, 75th Leg., ch. 1022, § 78, eff. Sept. 1, 1997; Acts 1999, 76th Leg., ch. 62, § 6.31, eff; Sept. 1, 1999; Acts 1999, 76th Leg., ch. 1150, § 20, eff. Sept. 1, 1999; Acts 1999, 76th Leg., ch; 1390, § 39, eff. Sept. 1, 1999; Acts 2001, 77th Leg., ch. 306, § 1, eff. Sept. 1, 2001; Acts 2001, 77th Leg., ch. 849, § 4, eff. Sept. 1, 2001; Acts 2005, 79th Leg., ch. 268, § 1.34(a), eff. Sept. 1, 2005; Acts 2009, 81st Leg., ch. 856, § 2, eff. Sept. 1, 2009; Acts 2013, 83rd Leg., ch. 810 (S.B. 1759), § 9, eff. Sept. 1, 2013; Acts 2015, 84th Leg., ch. 1 (S.B. 219), § 1.163, eff. April 2, 2015; Acts 2015, 84th Leg., ch. 128 (S.B. 1931), § 3, eff. Sept. 1, 2015; Acts 2015, 84th Leg., ch. 338 (H.B. 418), § 4, eff. Sept. 1, 2015; Acts 2015, 84th Leg., ch. 697 (H.B. 825), § 1, eff. Sept. 1, 2015; Acts 2017, 85th Leg., ch. 317 (H.B. 7), § 20, eff. Sept. 1, 2017; Acts 2017, 85th Leg., ch. 910 (S.B. 999), § 13, eff. Sept. 1, 2017; Acts 2019, 86th Leg., ch. 375 (H.B. 1884), § 2, eff. Sept. 1, 2019; Acts 2019, 86th Leg., ch. 467 (H.B. 4170), § 7.004, eff. Sept. 1, 2019; Acts 2019, 86th Leg., ch. 1294 (H.B. 3390), § 7, eff. June 14, 2019; Acts 2021, 87th Leg., ch. 8 (H.B. 567), §§ 7, 13(3), eff. Sept. 1, 2021; Acts 2021, 87th Leg., ch. 1047 (S.B. 1578), § 7, eff. Sept. 1, 2021.

[1] V.T.C.A., Family Code § 71.001 et seq.

[2] V.T.C.A., Family Code § 264.851 et seq.

Section 15 of Acts 2021, 87th Leg., ch. 8 (H.B. 567) provides:

"The changes in law made by this Act apply only to a suit filed by the Department of Family and Protective Services on or after the effective date [Sept. 1, 2021] of this Act. A suit filed by the department before that date is governed by the law in effect on the date the suit was filed, and the former law is continued in effect for that purpose."

Section 8 of Acts 2021, 87th Leg., ch. 1047 (S.B. 1578) provides:

"The changes in law made by this Act apply only to a suit affecting the parent-child relationship filed on or after the effective date [Sept. 1, 2021] of this Act. A suit affecting the parent-child relationship filed before the effective date [Sept. 1, 2021] of this Act is governed by the law in effect on the date the suit was filed, and the former law is continued in effect for that purpose."

## § 262.2015. Aggravated Circumstances

(a) The court may waive the requirement of a service plan and the requirement to make reasonable efforts to return the child to a parent and may accelerate the trial schedule to result in a final order for a child under the care of the Department of Family and Protective Services at an earlier date than provided by Subchapter D, Chapter 263,[1] if the court finds that the parent has subjected the child to aggravated circumstances.

(b) The court may find under Subsection (a) that a parent has subjected the child to aggravated circumstances if:

(1) the parent abandoned the child without identification or a means for identifying the child;

(2) the child or another child of the parent is a victim of serious bodily injury or sexual abuse inflicted by the parent or by another person with the parent's consent;

(3) the parent has engaged in conduct against the child or another child of the parent that would constitute an offense under the following provisions of the Penal Code:

(A) Section 19.02 (murder);

(B) Section 19.03 (capital murder);

(C) Section 19.04 (manslaughter);

(D) Section 21.11 (indecency with a child);

(E) Section 22.011 (sexual assault);

(F) Section 22.02 (aggravated assault);

(G) Section 22.021 (aggravated sexual assault);

(H) Section 22.04 (injury to a child, elderly individual, or disabled individual);

(I) Section 22.041 (abandoning or endangering child);

(J) Section 25.02 (prohibited sexual conduct);

(K) Section 43.25 (sexual performance by a child);

(L) Section 43.26 (possession or promotion of child pornography);

(M) Section 21.02 (continuous sexual abuse of young child or disabled individual );

(N) Section 43.05(a)(2) (compelling prostitution); or

(O) Section 20A.02(a)(7) or (8) (trafficking of persons);

(4) the parent voluntarily left the child alone or in the possession of another person not the parent of the child for at least six months without expressing an intent to return and without providing adequate support for the child;

(5) the parent has been convicted for:

(A) the murder of another child of the parent and the offense would have been an offense under 18 U.S.C. Section 1111(a) if the offense had occurred in the special maritime or territorial jurisdiction of the United States;

(B) the voluntary manslaughter of another child of the parent and the offense would have been an offense under 18 U.S.C. Section 1112(a) if the offense had occurred in the special maritime or territorial jurisdiction of the United States;

(C) aiding or abetting, attempting, conspiring, or soliciting an offense under Paragraph (A) or (B); or

(D) the felony assault of the child or another child of the parent that resulted in serious bodily injury to the child or another child of the parent; or

(6) the parent is required under any state or federal law to register with a sex offender registry.

(c) On finding that reasonable efforts to make it possible for the child to safely return to the child's home are not required, the court shall at any time before the 30th day after the date of the finding, conduct an initial permanency hearing under Subchapter D, Chapter 263. Separate notice of the permanency plan is not required but may be given with a notice of a hearing under this section.

(d) The Department of Family and Protective Services shall make reasonable efforts to finalize the permanent placement of a child for whom the court has made the finding described by Subsection (c). The court shall set the suit for trial on the merits as required by Subchapter D, Chapter 263, in order to facilitate final placement of the child.

Added by Acts 1997, 75th Leg., ch. 1022, § 79, eff. Sept. 1, 1997. Amended by Acts 1999, 76th Leg., ch. 1150, § 21, eff. Sept. 1, 1999; Acts 1999, 76th Leg., ch. 1390, § 40, eff. Sept. 1, 1999; Acts 2001, 77th Leg., ch. 849, § 5, eff. Sept. 1, 2001; Acts 2005, 79th Leg., ch. 268, § 1.35, eff. Sept. 1, 2005; Acts 2007, 80th Leg., ch. 593, § 3.33, eff. Sept. 1, 2007; Acts 2011, 82nd Leg., ch. 1 (S.B. 24), § 4.04, eff. Sept. 1, 2011; Acts 2015, 84th Leg., ch. 1 (S.B. 219), § 1.164, eff. April 2, 2015; Acts 2015, 84th Leg., ch. 944 (S.B. 206), § 26, eff. Sept. 1, 2015; Acts 2021, 87th Leg., ch. 221 (H.B. 375), § 2.19, eff. Sept. 1, 2021; Acts 2021, 87th Leg., ch. 831 (H.B. 2924), § 2, eff. Sept. 1, 2021.

[1] V.T.C.A., Family Code § 263.301 et seq.

Section 3.01 of Acts 2021, 87th Leg., ch. 221 (H.B. 375) provides:

"The change in law made by this Act applies only to an offense committed on or after the effective date [Sept. 1, 2021] of this Act. An offense committed before the effective date of this Act is governed by the law in effect on the date the offense was committed, and the former law is continued in effect for that purpose. For purposes of this section, an offense was committed before the effective date of this Act if any element of the offense occurred before that date."

Section 3 of Acts 2021, 87th Leg., ch. 831 (H.B. 2924) provides:

"The change in law made by this Act applies only to a court order for the involuntary termination of the parent-child relationship rendered on or after the effective date of this Act [Sept. 1, 2021]. A court order rendered before the effective date of this Act is governed by the law in effect on the date the order was rendered, and the former law is continued in effect for that purpose."

## § 262.202. Identification of Court of Continuing, Exclusive Jurisdiction

If at the conclusion of the full adversary hearing the court renders a temporary order, the governmental entity shall request identification of a court of continuing, exclusive jurisdiction as provided by Chapter 155.

Added by Acts 1995, 74th Leg., ch. 20, § 1, eff. April 20, 1995.

## § 262.203. Transfer of Suit

(a) On the motion of a party or the court's own motion, if applicable, the court that rendered the temporary order shall in accordance with procedures provided by Chapter 155:

(1) transfer the suit to the court of continuing, exclusive jurisdiction, if any, within the time required by Section 155.207(a), if the court finds that the transfer is:

(A) necessary for the convenience of the parties; and

(B) in the best interest of the child;

(2) order transfer of the suit from the court of continuing, exclusive jurisdiction; or

(3) if grounds exist for transfer based on improper venue, order transfer of the suit to the court having venue of the suit under Chapter 103.

(b) Notwithstanding Section 155.204, a motion to transfer relating to a suit filed under this chapter may be filed separately from the petition and is timely if filed while the case is pending.

(c) Notwithstanding Sections 6.407 and 103.002, a court exercising jurisdiction under this chapter is not required to transfer the suit to a court in which a parent has filed a suit for dissolution of marriage before a final order for the protection of the child has been rendered under Subchapter E, Chapter 263.[1]

(d) An order of transfer must include:

(1) the date of any future hearings in the case that have been scheduled by the transferring court;

(2) any date scheduled by the transferring court for the dismissal of the suit under Section 263.401; and

(3) the name and contact information of each attorney ad litem or guardian ad litem appointed in the suit.

(e) The court to which a suit is transferred may retain an attorney ad litem or guardian ad litem appointed by the transferring court. If the court finds that the appointment of a new attorney ad litem or guardian ad litem is appropriate, the court shall appoint that attorney ad litem or guardian ad litem before the earlier of:

(1) the 10th day after the date of receiving the order of transfer; or

(2) the date of the first scheduled hearing after the transfer.

Added by Acts 1995, 74th Leg., ch. 20, § 1, eff. April 20, 1995. Amended by Acts 1997, 75th Leg., ch. 575, § 22, eff. Sept. 1, 1997; Acts 1999, 76th Leg., ch. 1150, § 22, eff. Sept. 1, 1999; Acts 1999, 76th Leg., ch. 1390, § 41, eff. Sept. 1, 1999; Acts 2015, 84th Leg., ch. 211 (S.B. 1929), § 2, eff. Sept. 1, 2015; Acts 2017, 85th Leg., ch. 317 (H.B. 7), § 21, eff. Sept. 1, 2017; Acts 2017, 85th Leg., ch. 572 (S.B. 738), § 3; Acts 2017, 85th Leg., ch. 910 (S.B. 999), § 14, eff. Sept. 1, 2017.

[1] V.T.C.A., Family Code § 263.401 et seq.

"Sec. 4. The changes in law made by this Act apply to a suit affecting the parent-child relationship filed on or after the effective date [Sept. 1, 2017] of this Act. A suit affecting the parent-child relationship filed before the effective date of this Act is governed by the law in effect on the date the suit was filed, and the former law is continued in effect for that purpose.

## § 262.204. Temporary Order in Effect Until Superseded

(a) A temporary order rendered under this chapter is valid and enforceable until properly superseded by a court with jurisdiction to do so.

(b) A court to which the suit has been transferred may enforce by contempt or otherwise a temporary order properly issued under this chapter.

Added by Acts 1995, 74th Leg., ch. 20, § 1, eff. April 20, 1995.

## § 262.205. Repealed by Acts 2017, 85th Leg., ch. 910 (S.B. 999), § 15, eff. Sept. 1, 2017

## § 262.206. Ex Parte Hearings Prohibited

*Text of section effective only if specific appropriation is made as provided in Acts 2017, 85th Leg., ch. 317 (H.B. 7), § 74*

Unless otherwise authorized by this chapter or other law, a hearing held by a court in a suit under this chapter may not be ex parte.

Added by Acts 2017, 85th Leg., ch. 317 (H.B. 7), § 22.

## SUBCHAPTER D. EMERGENCY POSSESSION OF CERTAIN ABANDONED CHILDREN

### DISPOSITION TABLE

Showing where the subject matter of provisions contained in former Chapter 262, Subchapter D, Emergency Possession of Certain Abandoned Children, may be found in Chapter 262, Subchapter D, Emergency Possession of Certain Abandoned Children, as amended by Acts 2001, 77th Leg., ch. 809, § 4.

| Former Section | Amended Section |
|---|---|
| 262.301 | 262.302 |
| 262.302 | 262.303 |
| 262.303 | 262.304 |

### § 262.301. Definitions

In this chapter:

(1) "Designated emergency infant care provider" means:

(A) an emergency medical services provider;

(B) a hospital;

(C) a freestanding emergency medical care facility licensed under Chapter 254, Health and Safety Code; or

(D) a child-placing agency licensed by the Department of Family and Protective Services under Chapter 42, Human Resources Code, that:

(i) agrees to act as a designated emergency infant care provider under this subchapter; and

(ii) has on staff a person who is licensed as a registered nurse under Chapter 301, Occupations Code, or who provides emergency medical services under Chapter 773, Health and Safety Code, and who will examine and provide emergency medical services to a child taken into possession by the agency under this subchapter.

(2) "Emergency medical services provider" has the meaning assigned that term by Section 773.003, Health and Safety Code.

Amended by Acts 2001, 77th Leg., ch. 809, § 4, eff. Sept. 1, 2001; Acts 2015, 84th Leg., ch. 1 (S.B. 219), § 1.165, eff. April 2, 2015; Acts 2015, 84th Leg., ch. 260 (S.B. 1279), § 1, eff. Sept. 1, 2015.

### § 262.302. Accepting Possession of Certain Abandoned Children

(a) A designated emergency infant care provider shall, without a court order, take possession of a child who appears to be 60 days old or younger if the child is voluntarily delivered to the provider by the child's parent and the parent did not express an intent to return for the child.

(b) A designated emergency infant care provider who takes possession of a child under this section has no legal duty to detain or pursue the parent and may not do so unless the child appears to have been abused or neglected. The designated emergency infant care provider has no legal duty to ascertain the parent's identity and the parent may remain anonymous. However, the parent may be given a form for voluntary disclosure of the child's medical facts and history.

(c) A designated emergency infant care provider who takes possession of a child under this section shall perform any act necessary to protect the physical health or safety of the child. The designated emergency infant care provider is not liable for damages related to the provider's taking possession of, examining, or treating the child, except for damages related to the provider's negligence.

Amended by Acts 2001, 77th Leg., ch. 809, § 4, eff. Sept. 1, 2001.

### § 262.303. Notification of Possession of Abandoned Child

(a) Not later than the close of the first business day after the date on which a designated emergency infant care provider takes possession of a child under Section 262.302, the provider shall notify the Department of Family and Protective Services that the provider has taken possession of the child.

(b) The department shall assume the care, control, and custody of the child immediately on receipt of notice under Subsection (a).

Amended by Acts 2001, 77th Leg., ch. 809, § 4, eff. Sept. 1, 2001; Acts 2015, 84th Leg., ch. 1 (S.B. 219), § 1.166, eff. April 2, 2015.

### § 262.304. Filing Petition After Accepting Possession of Abandoned Child

A child for whom the Department of Family and Protective Services assumes care, control, and custody under Section 262.303 shall be treated as a child taken into possession without a court order, and the department shall take action as required by Section 262.105 with regard to the child.

Added by Acts 2001, 77th Leg., ch. 809, § 4, eff. Sept. 1, 2001. Amended by Acts 2015, 84th Leg., ch. 1 (S.B. 219), § 1.167, eff. April 2, 2015.

### § 262.305. Report to Law Enforcement Agency; Investigation

(a) Immediately after assuming care, control, and custody of a child under Section 262.303, the Department of Family and Protective Services shall report the child to appropriate state and local law enforcement agencies as a potential missing child.

(b) A law enforcement agency that receives a report under Subsection (a) shall investigate whether the child is reported as missing.

Added by Acts 2001, 77th Leg., ch. 809, § 4, eff. Sept. 1, 2001. Amended by Acts 2015, 84th Leg., ch. 1 (S.B. 219), § 1.168, eff. April 2, 2015.

### § 262.306. Notice

Each designated emergency infant care provider shall post in a conspicuous location a notice stating that the provider is a designated emergency infant care provider location and will accept possession of a child in accordance with this subchapter.

Added by Acts 2001, 77th Leg., ch. 809, § 4, eff. Sept. 1, 2001.

### § 262.307. Reimbursement for Care of Abandoned Child

The Department of Family and Protective Services shall reimburse a designated emergency infant care provider that takes possession of a child under Section 262.302 for the cost to the provider of assuming the care, control, and custody of the child.

Added by Acts 2001, 77th Leg., ch. 809, § 4, eff. Sept. 1, 2001. Amended by Acts 2015, 84th Leg., ch. 1 (S.B. 219), § 1.169, eff. April 2, 2015.

### § 262.308. Confidentiality

(a) All identifying information, documentation, or other records regarding a person who voluntarily delivers a child to a designated emergency infant care provider under this subchapter is confidential and not subject to release to any individual or entity except as provided by Subsection (b).

(b) Any pleading or other document filed with a court under this subchapter is confidential, is not public information for purposes of Chapter 552, Government Code, and may not be released to a person other than to a party in a suit regarding the child, the party's attorney, or an attorney ad litem or guardian ad litem appointed in the suit.

(c) In a suit concerning a child for whom the Department of Family and Protective Services assumes care, control, and custody under this subchapter, the court shall close the hearing to the public unless the court finds that the interests of the child or the public would be better served by opening the hearing to the public.

(d) Unless the disclosure, receipt, or use is permitted by this section, a person commits an offense if the person knowingly discloses, receives, uses, or permits the use of information derived from records or files described by this section or knowingly discloses identifying information concerning a person who voluntarily delivers a child to a designated emergency infant care provider. An offense under this subsection is a Class B misdemeanor.

Added by Acts 2005, 79th Leg., ch. 620, § 1, eff. Sept. 1, 2005.

### § 262.309. Search for Relatives Not Required

The Department of Family and Protective Services is not required to conduct a search for the relatives of a child for whom the department assumes care, control, and custody under this subchapter.

Added by Acts 2005, 79th Leg., ch. 620, § 1, eff. Sept. 1, 2005.

## SUBCHAPTER E. RELINQUISHING CHILD TO OBTAIN CERTAIN SERVICES

### § 262.351. Definitions

In this subchapter:

(1) "Commission" means the Health and Human Services Commission.

(1–a) "Department" means the Department of Family and Protective Services.

(1–b) "Relinquishment avoidance program" means the Health and Human Services Commission's program that provides mental health services to a child with a severe emotional disturbance without the child entering the managing conservatorship of the department.

(2) "Severe emotional disturbance" has the meaning assigned by Section 261.001.

Added by Acts 2013, 83rd Leg., ch. 1142 (S.B. 44), § 3, eff. Sept. 1, 2013. Amended by Acts 2021, 87th Leg., ch. 579 (S.B. 642), § 1, eff. June 14, 2021.

### § 262.352. Joint Managing Conservatorship of Child

(a) Before the department files a suit affecting the parent-child relationship requesting managing conservatorship of a child who suffers from a severe emotional disturbance in order to obtain mental health services for the child, the department must, unless it is not in the best interest of the child, discuss with the child's parent or legal guardian the option of seeking a court order for joint managing conservatorship of the child with the department.

(b) Expired.

(c) Expired.

Added by Acts 2013, 83rd Leg., ch. 1142 (S.B. 44), § 3, eff. Sept. 1, 2013. Amended by Acts 2015, 84th Leg., ch. 432 (S.B. 1889), § 3, eff. Sept. 1, 2015.

### § 262.353. Procedure for Relinquishing Child to Obtain Services

(a) The commission may not require the department to conduct a child abuse or neglect investigation before allowing a child to participate in the relinquishment avoidance program unless there is an allegation of abuse or neglect of the child.

(b) A local mental or behavioral health authority may refer a child directly to the relinquishment avoidance program without first contacting the department.

(c) The department and the commission shall:

(1) jointly adopt comprehensive guidance for providers and families that describes:

(A) how to access services under the relinquishment avoidance program; and

(B) the child's and family's rights when the child's parent or legal guardian:

(i) relinquishes the child in order to obtain mental health services for the child; or

(ii) accesses services under the relinquishment avoidance program;

(2) publish the information described by Subdivision (1) on the agency's Internet website; and

(3) make the information described by Subdivision (1) available to caseworkers and families with a child who has a severe emotional disturbance.

(d) The department and the commission shall jointly adopt clear and concise protocols for families at risk of relinquishing a child for the sole purpose of accessing mental health services for the child. The protocols must:

(1) include procedures for determining eligibility for the relinquishment avoidance program, including emergency eligibility procedures for children who are at immediate risk of relinquishment;

(2) include procedures for applying for the relinquishment avoidance program;

(3) identify who will manage the case of a family eligible for the relinquishment avoidance program;

(4) identify the funding and resources for the relinquishment avoidance program; and

(5) identify the role of each party involved in the relinquishment avoidance program, including the department, the commission, contracted residential treatment centers, and local mental and behavioral health authorities.

(e) The department and local mental and behavioral health authorities shall follow the protocols adopted under Subsection (d).

Added by Acts 2021, 87th Leg., ch. 579 (S.B. 642), § 2, eff. June 14, 2021.

## SUBCHAPTER F. FAMILY PRESERVATION SERVICES PILOT PROGRAM

### § 262.401. Definitions

In this subchapter:

(1) "Child who is a candidate for foster care" means a child who is at imminent risk of being removed from the child's home and placed into the conservatorship of the department because of a continuing danger to the child's physical health or safety caused by an act or failure to act of a person entitled to possession of the child but for whom a court of competent jurisdiction has issued an order allowing the child to remain safely in the child's home or in a kinship placement with the provision of family preservation services.

(2) "Department" means the Department of Family and Protective Services.

(3) "Family preservation service" means a time-limited, family-focused service, including a service subject to the Family First Prevention Services Act (Title VII, Div. E, Pub. L. No. 115–123), provided to the family of a child who is:

(A) a candidate for foster care to prevent or eliminate the need to remove the child and to allow the child to remain safely with the child's family; or

(B) a pregnant or parenting foster youth.

(4) "Family preservation services plan" means a written plan, based on a professional assessment,

listing the family preservation services, including services subject to the Family First Prevention Services Act (Title VII, Div. E, Pub. L. No. 115–123), to be provided to the family of a child who is:

(A) a candidate for foster care; or

(B) a pregnant or parenting foster youth.

(5) "Foster care" means substitute care as defined by Section 263.001.

Added by Acts 2021, 87th Leg., ch. 269 (H.B. 3041), § 2, eff. Sept. 1, 2021.

### § 262.402. Pilot Program for Family Preservation Services

(a) The department shall establish a pilot program that allows the department to dispose of an investigation by referring the family of a child who is a candidate for foster care for family preservation services and allowing the child to return home instead of entering foster care or by providing services to a pregnant or parenting foster youth. The department shall implement the pilot program in two child protective services regions in this state, one urban and one rural.

(b) The pilot program must be implemented in at least one child protective services region in this state in which community-based care has been implemented under Subchapter B–1, Chapter 264.

(c) In authorizing family preservation services for a child who is a candidate for foster care, the child's safety is the primary concern. The services may be modified as necessary to accommodate the child's circumstances.

(d) In implementing the pilot program, the department shall use:

(1) Title IV–E funds to:

(A) pay for legal representation for parents in the manner provided by Section 107.015; or

(B) provide to counties a matching reimbursement for the cost of the legal representation; and

(2) funds received under the Temporary Assistance for Needy Families (TANF) program or other department funds to provide enhanced in-home support services to families qualifying for prevention services under this subchapter to achieve the objectives in the family preservation services plan.

Added by Acts 2021, 87th Leg., ch. 269 (H.B. 3041), § 2, eff. Sept. 1, 2021.

### § 262.403. Court Order Required

(a) Subject to Subsection (b), the department must obtain a court order from a court of competent jurisdiction to compel the family of a child who is a candidate for foster care to obtain family preservation services and complete the family preservation services plan.

(b) The department is not required to obtain a court order to provide family preservation services to a pregnant or parenting foster youth.

Added by Acts 2021, 87th Leg., ch. 269 (H.B. 3041), § 2, eff. Sept. 1, 2021.

### § 262.404. Filing Suit; Petition Requirements

(a) The department may file a suit requesting the court to render an order requiring the parent, managing conservator, guardian, or other member of the child's household to:

(1) participate in the family preservation services for which the department makes a referral or services the department provides or purchases to:

(A) alleviate the effects of the abuse or neglect that has occurred;

(B) reduce a continuing danger to the physical health or safety of the child caused by an act or failure to act of the parent, managing conservator, guardian, or other member of the child's household; or

(C) reduce a substantial risk of abuse or neglect caused by an act or failure to act of the parent, managing conservator, guardian, or other member of the child's household;

(2) permit the child and any siblings of the child to receive the services; and

(3) complete all actions and services required under the family preservation services plan.

(b) A suit requesting an order under this section may be filed in a court with jurisdiction to hear the suit in the county in which the child is located.

(c) Except as otherwise provided by this subchapter, the suit is governed by the Texas Rules of Civil Procedure applicable to the filing of an original lawsuit.

(d) The petition for suit must be supported by:

(1) a sworn affidavit based on personal knowledge and stating facts sufficient to support a finding that:

(A) the child has been a victim of abuse or neglect or is at substantial risk of abuse or neglect; and

(B) there is a continuing danger to the child's physical health or safety caused by an act or failure to act of the parent, managing conservator, guardian, or other member of the child's household unless that person participates in family preservation services requested by the department; and

(2) a safety risk assessment for the child that documents:

(A) the process for the child to remain at home with appropriate family preservation services instead of foster care;

(B) the specific reasons the department should provide family preservation services to the family; and

(C) the manner in which family preservation services will mitigate the risk of the child entering foster care.

(e) In a suit filed under this section, the court may render a temporary restraining order as provided by Section 105.001.

(f) The court shall hold a hearing on the petition not later than the 14th day after the date the petition is filed unless the court finds good cause for extending that date for not more than 14 days.

Added by Acts 2021, 87th Leg., ch. 269 (H.B. 3041), § 2, eff. Sept. 1, 2021.

### § 262.405. Ad Litem Appointments

(a) The court shall appoint an attorney ad litem to represent the interests of the child immediately after a suit is filed under Section 262.404 but before the hearing to ensure adequate representation of the child. The attorney ad litem for the child has the powers and duties of an attorney ad litem for a child under Chapter 107.

(b) The court shall appoint an attorney ad litem to represent the interests of a parent for whom participation in family preservation services is being requested immediately after the suit is filed but before the hearing to ensure adequate representation of the parent. The attorney ad litem for the parent has the powers and duties of an attorney ad litem for a parent under Section 107.0131.

(c) Before the hearing commences, the court shall inform each parent of:

(1) the parent's right to be represented by an attorney; and

(2) for a parent who is indigent and appears in opposition to the motion, the parent's right to a court-appointed attorney.

(d) If a parent claims indigence, the court shall require the parent to complete and file with the court an affidavit of indigence. The court may consider additional evidence to determine whether the parent is indigent, including evidence relating to the parent's income, source of income, assets, property ownership, benefits paid in accordance with a federal, state, or local public assistance program, outstanding obligations, and necessary expenses and the number and ages of the parent's dependents. If the court finds the parent is indigent, the attorney ad litem appointed to represent the interests of the parent may continue the representation. If the court finds the parent is not indigent, the court shall discharge the attorney ad litem from the appointment after the hearing and order the parent to pay the cost of the attorney ad litem's representation.

(e) The court may, for good cause shown, postpone any subsequent proceedings for not more than seven days after the date of the attorney ad litem's discharge to allow the parent to hire an attorney or to provide the parent's attorney time to prepare for the subsequent proceeding.

Added by Acts 2021, 87th Leg., ch. 269 (H.B. 3041), § 2, eff. Sept. 1, 2021.

### § 262.406. Court Order

(a) Except as provided by Subsection (d), at the conclusion of the hearing in a suit filed under Section 262.404, the court shall order the department to provide family preservation services and to execute a family preservation services plan developed in collaboration with the family of the child who is a candidate for foster care if the court finds sufficient evidence to satisfy a person of ordinary prudence and caution that:

(1) abuse or neglect occurred or there is a substantial risk of abuse or neglect or continuing danger to the child's physical health or safety caused by an act or failure to act of the parent, managing conservator, guardian, or other member of the child's household;

(2) family preservation services are necessary to ensure the child's physical health or safety; and

(3) family preservation services are appropriate based on the child's safety risk assessment and the child's family assessment.

(b) The court's order for family preservation services must:

(1) identify and require specific services narrowly tailored to address the factors that make the child a candidate for foster care; and

(2) include a statement on whether the services to be provided to the family are appropriate to address the factors that place the child at risk of removal.

(c) The court may, in its discretion, order family preservation services for a parent whose parental rights to another child were previously terminated.

(d) If the court finds, by clear and convincing evidence, that the parent has subjected the child to aggravated circumstances described by Section 262.2015, the court may order that family preservation services not be provided.

Added by Acts 2021, 87th Leg., ch. 269 (H.B. 3041), § 2, eff. Sept. 1, 2021.

### § 262.407. Family Preservation Services Plan; Contents

(a) On order of the court under Section 262.406, the department in consultation with the child's family shall develop a family preservation services plan. The department and the family shall discuss each term and condition of the plan.

(b) The family preservation services plan must be written in a manner that is clear and understandable to the parent, managing conservator, guardian, or other member of the child's household and in a language the person understands.

(c) The family preservation services plan must:

(1) include a safety risk assessment of the child who is the subject of the investigation and an assessment of the child's family;

(2) state the reasons the department is involved with the family;

(3) be narrowly tailored to address the specific reasons the department is involved with the family and the factors that make the child a candidate for foster care;

(4) list the specific family preservation services the family will receive under the plan and identify the manner in which those services will mitigate the child's specific risk factors and allow the child to remain safely at home;

(5) specify the tasks the family must complete during the effective period of the plan and include a schedule with appropriate completion dates for those tasks; and

(6) include the name of the department or single source continuum contractor representative who will serve as a contact for the family in obtaining information related to the plan.

(d) The family preservation services plan must include the following statement:

"TO THE PARENT OF THE CHILD SERVED BY THIS PLAN: THIS DOCUMENT IS VERY IMPORTANT. ITS PURPOSE IS TO HELP YOU PROVIDE YOUR CHILD WITH A SAFE ENVIRONMENT WITHIN THE REASONABLE PERIOD SPECIFIED IN THIS PLAN. IF YOU ARE UNWILLING OR UNABLE TO PROVIDE YOUR CHILD WITH A SAFE ENVIRONMENT, YOUR CHILD MAY BE REMOVED FROM YOU, AND YOUR PARENTAL AND CUSTODIAL DUTIES AND RIGHTS MAY BE RESTRICTED OR TERMINATED. A COURT HEARING WILL BE HELD AT WHICH A JUDGE WILL REVIEW THIS FAMILY PRESERVATION SERVICES PLAN."

Added by Acts 2021, 87th Leg., ch. 269 (H.B. 3041), § 2, eff. Sept. 1, 2021.

### § 262.408. Family Preservation Services Plan: Signing and Effect

(a) The family of a child who is a candidate for foster care and the department shall sign the family preservation services plan, and the department shall submit a copy of the signed plan to the court for review.

(b) If the family is unwilling to participate in the development of the family preservation services plan, the department may submit the plan to the court without the parents' signatures.

(c) The family preservation services plan takes effect on the date the court certifies that the plan complies with the court's order for family preservation services and is narrowly tailored to address the factors that make the child a candidate for foster care. The court may hold a hearing to review the plan for compliance.

(d) The family preservation services plan remains in effect until:

(1) the 180th day after the date the court's order for family preservation services is signed, unless renewed by an order of the court; or

(2) the date the plan is amended or revoked by the court.

(e) A person subject to the family preservation services plan may file a motion with the court at any time to request a modification or revocation of the original or any amended plan.

Added by Acts 2021, 87th Leg., ch. 269 (H.B. 3041), § 2, eff. Sept. 1, 2021.

### § 262.409. Amended Family Preservation Services Plan

(a) A family preservation services plan may be amended at any time. The department or single source continuum contractor and the parents of a child who is a candidate for foster care shall jointly develop any amendment to the plan. The department or contractor must inform the parents of their rights related to the amended family preservation services plan process.

(b) The parents and the person preparing the amended family preservation services plan shall sign the amended plan, and the department or single source continuum contractor shall submit the amended plan to the court for review.

(c) If the parents are unwilling to participate in the development of the amended family preservation services plan, the department or single source continuum contractor may submit the amended plan to the court without the parents' signatures.

(d) The amended family preservation services plan takes effect on the date the court certifies that the amended plan complies with the court's order for family preservation services and is narrowly tailored to address the factors that make the child a candidate for foster care. The court may hold a hearing to review the amended plan for compliance.

(e) The amended family preservation services plan is in effect until:

(1) the 180th day after the date the court's order for family preservation services is signed, unless renewed by an order of the court; or

(2) the date the amended plan is modified or revoked by the court.

Added by Acts 2021, 87th Leg., ch. 269 (H.B. 3041), § 2, eff. Sept. 1, 2021.

### § 262.410. Court Implementation of Family Preservation Services Plan

(a) After reviewing and certifying an original or any amended family preservation services plan, the court shall incorporate the original and any amended plan into the court's order and may render additional appropriate orders to implement or require compliance with an original or amended plan.

(b) In rendering an order, a court may omit any service prescribed under the family preservation services plan that the court finds is not appropriate or is not narrowly tailored to address the factors that make the child a candidate for foster care and place the child at risk of removal.

Added by Acts 2021, 87th Leg., ch. 269 (H.B. 3041), § 2, eff. Sept. 1, 2021.

### § 262.411. Selection of Service Provider

(a) A parent, managing conservator, guardian, or other member of a household ordered to participate in family preservation services under this subchapter may obtain those services from a qualified or licensed provider selected by the person.

(b) Services provided by a provider selected under Subsection (a) must be similar in scope and duration to services described by the family preservation services plan adopted under Section 262.407 and achieve the stated goals of the service plan. The service provider must certify in writing that the parent, managing conservator, guardian, or other member of a household completed the services.

(c) A parent, managing conservator, guardian, or other member of a household who obtains family preservation services from a provider selected by the person is responsible for the cost of those services.

(d) A parent, managing conservator, guardian, or other member of a household who successfully completes the required family preservation services must obtain verification from the service provider of that completion. The department shall accept the service provider's verification provided under this subsection as proof that the person successfully completed the court-ordered family preservation services.

Added by Acts 2021, 87th Leg., ch. 269 (H.B. 3041), § 2, eff. Sept. 1, 2021.

### § 262.412. Status Hearing

Not later than the 90th day after the date the court renders an order for family preservation services under this subchapter, the court shall hold a hearing to review the status of each person required to participate in the services and of the child and to review the services provided, purchased, or referred. The court shall set subsequent review hearings every 90 days to review the continued need for the order.

Added by Acts 2021, 87th Leg., ch. 269 (H.B. 3041), § 2, eff. Sept. 1, 2021.

### § 262.413. Extension of Order

(a) The court may extend an order for family preservation services rendered under this subchapter on a showing by the department of a continuing need for the order, after notice and hearing. Except as provided by Subsection (b), the court may extend the order only one time for not more than 180 days.

(b) The court may extend an order rendered under this subchapter for not more than an additional 180 days only if:

(1) the court finds that:

(A) the extension is necessary to allow the person required to participate in family preservation services under the family preservation services plan time to complete those services;

(B) the department made a good faith effort to timely provide the services to the person;

(C) the person made a good faith effort to complete the services; and

(D) the completion of the services is necessary to ensure the physical health and safety of the child; and

(2) the extension is requested by the person required to participate in family preservation services under the family preservation services plan or the person's attorney.

Added by Acts 2021, 87th Leg., ch. 269 (H.B. 3041), § 2, eff. Sept. 1, 2021.

### § 262.414. Expiration of Order

On expiration of a court order for family preservation services under this subchapter, the court shall dismiss the case.

Added by Acts 2021, 87th Leg., ch. 269 (H.B. 3041), § 2, eff. Sept. 1, 2021.

### § 262.415. Contract for Services

(a) The department may contract with one or more persons to provide family preservation services under the pilot program. In a child protective services region in this state in which community-based care under Subchapter B–1, Chapter 264, has been implemented and in which the pilot program is implemented, the department may contract with the single source continuum contractor to provide family preservation services under the pilot program.

(b) The contract with the person selected to provide family preservation services must include performance-based measures that require the person to show that as a result of the services:

(1) fewer children enter foster care in the pilot program region in comparison to other regions of this state;

(2) fewer children are removed from their families after receiving the services in the pilot program region in comparison to other regions of this state; and

(3) fewer children enter foster care in the five years following completion of the services in the pilot program region in comparison to other regions of this state.

(c) The department shall collaborate with a person selected to provide family preservation services to identify children who are candidates for foster care or who are pregnant or parenting foster youth and to ensure that the services are appropriate for children referred by the department.

Added by Acts 2021, 87th Leg., ch. 269 (H.B. 3041), § 2, eff. Sept. 1, 2021.

### § 262.416. Limit on Finance of Services

If a court order for services under this subchapter includes services that are not subject to the Family First Prevention Services Act (Title VII, Div. E., Pub. L. No. 115–123), the order must identify a method of financing for the services and the local jurisdiction that will pay for the services.

Added by Acts 2021, 87th Leg., ch. 269 (H.B. 3041), § 2, eff. Sept. 1, 2021.

### § 262.417. Report to Legislature

(a) Not later than the first anniversary of the date the department commences a pilot program under this subchapter and every two years after that date, the department shall contract with an entity based in this state that is independent of the department and has demonstrated expertise in statistical, financial, logistical, and operational analysis to evaluate the implementation of the pilot program under this subchapter, assess its progress, and report its findings to the appropriate standing committees of the legislature having jurisdiction over child protective services and foster care matters. The report must include:

(1) a detailed description of the actions taken by the department to ensure the successful implementation of the pilot program;

(2) a detailed analysis of the role each of the following entities has in the pilot program:

(A) the courts;

(B) legal representatives;

(C) the investigations division of the department; and

(D) the department or other entity implementing the pilot program;

(3) an analysis of any barrier to the successful implementation of the pilot program and recommendations for overcoming those barriers;

(4) data on the performance-based outcomes described by Subsection (b) and achieved in the child protective services region in which the pilot program is implemented;

(5) a detailed comparison of outcomes achieved in the child protective services region in which the pilot program is implemented with outcomes achieved in other child protective services regions;

(6) a detailed description of the costs of the pilot program and services provided; and

(7) recommendations on whether to expand services described in this subchapter to other child protective services regions in this state based on the outcomes and performance of the pilot program.

(b) Performance-based outcomes for evaluating the pilot program must include:

(1) the number of children served;

(2) the number of families served;

(3) the percentage of children who do not have a reported finding of abuse, neglect, or exploitation;

(4) the percentage of children served who did not enter foster care at case closure;

(5) the percentage of children served who did not enter foster care within six months and one year of the date the case was closed;

(6) the number of families who received family preservation services under the pilot program for whom the department opens an investigation of abuse or neglect involving the family before the second anniversary of the date the case was closed; and

(7) the average length of time services are provided from the entry of an order for family preservation services to case dismissal.

Added by Acts 2021, 87th Leg., ch. 269 (H.B. 3041), § 2, eff. Sept. 1, 2021.

## CHAPTER 263. REVIEW OF PLACEMENT OF CHILDREN UNDER CARE OF DEPARTMENT OF FAMILY AND PROTECTIVE SERVICES

### SUBCHAPTER A. GENERAL PROVISIONS

**Section**



### SUBCHAPTER B. SERVICE PLAN AND VISITATION PLAN



### SUBCHAPTER C. STATUS HEARING



### SUBCHAPTER D. PERMANENCY HEARINGS

## SUBCHAPTER A. GENERAL PROVISIONS

### § 263.001. Definitions

(a) In this chapter:

(1) "Advanced practice nurse" has the meaning assigned by Section 157.051, Occupations Code.

(1–a) "Age-appropriate normalcy activity" has the meaning assigned by Section 264.001.

(1–b) "Department" means the Department of Family and Protective Services.

(2) "Child's home" means the place of residence of at least one of the child's parents.

(3) "Household" means a unit composed of persons living together in the same dwelling, without regard to whether they are related to each other.

(3–a) "Least restrictive setting" means a placement for a child that, in comparison to all other available placements, is the most family-like setting.

(3–b) "Physician assistant" has the meaning assigned by Section 157.051, Occupations Code.

(4) "Substitute care" means the placement of a child who is in the conservatorship of the department in care outside the child's home. The term includes foster care, institutional care, adoption, placement with a relative of the child, or commitment to the Texas Juvenile Justice Department.

(b) In the preparation and review of a service plan under this chapter, a reference to the parents of the child includes both parents of the child unless the child has only one parent or unless, after due diligence by the department in attempting to locate a parent, only one parent is located, in which case the reference is to the remaining parent.

(c) With respect to a child who is older than six years of age and who is removed from the child's home, if a suitable relative or other designated caregiver is not available as a placement for the child, placing the child in a foster home or a general residential operation operating as a cottage home is considered the least restrictive setting.

(d) With respect to a child who is six years of age or younger and who is removed from the child's home, if a suitable relative or other designated caregiver is not available as a placement for the child, the least restrictive setting for the child is placement in:

(1) a foster home; or

(2) a general residential operation operating as a cottage home, only if the department determines it is in the best interest of the child.

Added by Acts 1995, 74th Leg., ch. 20, § 1, eff. April 20, 1995. Amended by Acts 1995, 74th Leg., ch. 751, § 108, eff. Sept. 1, 1995; Acts 2005, 79th Leg., ch. 268, § 1.36, eff. Sept. 1, 2005; Acts 2009, 81st Leg., ch. 108, § 4, eff. May 23, 2009; Acts 2013, 83rd Leg., ch. 204 (H.B. 915), § 3, eff. Sept. 1, 2013; Acts 2015, 84th Leg., ch. 1 (S.B. 219), § 1.170, eff. April 2, 2015; Acts 2015, 84th Leg., ch. 262 (S.B. 1407), § 1, eff. Sept. 1, 2015; Acts 2017, 85th Leg., ch. 1022 (H.B. 1542), §§ 1, 2, eff. Sept. 1, 2017.

### § 263.002. Review of Placements by Court; Findings

(a) In a suit affecting the parent-child relationship in which the department has been appointed by the court or designated in an affidavit of relinquishment of parental rights as the temporary or permanent managing conservator of a child, the court shall hold a hearing to review:

(1) the conservatorship appointment and substitute care; and

(2) for a child committed to the Texas Juvenile Justice Department, the child's commitment in the Texas Juvenile Justice Department or release under supervision by the Texas Juvenile Justice Department.

(b) At each permanency hearing under this chapter, the court shall review the placement of each child in the temporary managing conservatorship of the department who is not placed with a relative caregiver or designated caregiver as defined by Section 264.751. The court shall include in its findings a statement whether the department:

(1) asked the child in a developmentally appropriate manner to identify any adult, particularly an adult residing in the child's community, who could be a relative or designated caregiver for the child; and

(2) placed the child with a relative or designated caregiver.

(c) At each permanency hearing before the final order, the court shall review the placement of each child in the temporary managing conservatorship of the department who has not been returned to the child's home. At the end of the hearing, the court shall order the department to return the child to the child's parent or parents unless the court finds, with respect to each parent, that:

(1) there is a continuing danger to the physical health or safety of the child; and

(2) returning the child to the child's parent or parents is contrary to the welfare of the child.

(d) This section does not prohibit the court from rendering an order under Section 263.403.

Added by Acts 1995, 74th Leg., ch. 20, § 1, eff. April 20, 1995. Amended by Acts 1995, 74th Leg., ch. 751, § 109, eff. Sept. 1, 1995; Acts 2009, 81st Leg., ch. 108, § 5, eff. May 23, 2009; Acts 2015, 84th Leg., ch. 1 (S.B. 219), § 1.171, eff. April 2, 2015; Acts 2017, 85th Leg., ch. 317 (H.B. 7), § 23, eff. Sept. 1, 2017; Acts 2019, 86th Leg., ch. 1294 (H.B. 3390), § 8, eff. June 14, 2019; Acts 2021, 87th Leg., ch. 8 (H.B. 567), § 8, eff. Sept. 1, 2021.

Section 15 of Acts 2021, 87th Leg., ch. 8 (H.B. 567) provides:

"The changes in law made by this Act apply only to a suit filed by the Department of Family and Protective Services on or after the effective date [Sept. 1, 2021] of this Act. A suit filed by the department before that date is governed by the law in effect on the date the suit was filed, and the former law is continued in effect for that purpose."

### § 263.00201. Review of Placement in Qualified Residential Treatment Program

(a) In this section, "qualified residential treatment program" has the meaning assigned by 42 U.S.C. Section 672(k)(4).

(b) Not later than the 60th day after the date the department places a child in a qualified residential treatment program, a court shall:

(1) consider any assessment, determination, and documentation made by a qualified individual in accordance with 42 U.S.C. Section 675a(c) regarding the child's placement;

(2) determine whether the child's needs can be met through placement in a foster home and, if not, whether:

(A) placing the child in a qualified residential treatment program provides the most effective and appropriate level of care for the child in the least restrictive environment; and

(B) placement in a qualified residential treatment program is consistent with the short-term and long-term goals for the child, as specified in the child's permanency plan; and

(3) approve or disapprove the placement.

(c) Any written documentation prepared for the review of the child's placement under this section and any documentation regarding the determination and approval or disapproval of the placement in a qualified residential treatment program by the court under Subsection (b) shall be included in and made part of the child's permanency plan.

(d) As long as a child remains in a qualified residential treatment program, the department shall at the status review hearing and each permanency hearing held with respect to the child provide the court with information:

(1) demonstrating that:

(A) ongoing assessment of the strengths and needs of the child continues to support the determination that the needs of the child cannot be met through placement in a foster home;

(B) placement in a qualified residential treatment program provides the most effective and appropriate level of care for the child in the least restrictive environment; and

(C) the placement is consistent with the short-term and long-term goals for the child, as specified in the child's permanency plan;

(2) documenting the specific treatment or service needs that will be met for the child in the placement and the length of time the child is expected to need the treatment or services; and

(3) documenting the efforts made by the department to prepare the child to return home or to be placed in a foster home or with a fit and willing relative, legal guardian, or adoptive parent.

(e) The department may include the information required by Subsection (d) in any report the department is required to provide to the court before the hearing.

(f) The review of a child's placement in a qualified residential treatment program may be conducted through a remote proceeding. For purposes of this subsection, "remote proceeding" means a proceeding before a court in which one or more of the participants, including a judge, party, attorney, witness, court reporter, child, or other individual, attends the proceeding remotely through the use of technology and the Internet.

Added by Acts 2021, 87th Leg., ch. 616 (S.B. 1575), § 1, eff. Sept. 1, 2021.

### § 263.0021. Notice of Hearing; Presentation of Evidence

(a) Notice of a hearing under this chapter shall be given to all persons entitled to notice of the hearing.

(b) The following persons are entitled to at least 10 days' notice of a hearing under this chapter and are entitled to present evidence and be heard at the hearing:

(1) the department;

(2) the foster parent, preadoptive parent, relative of the child providing care, or director or director's designee of the group home or general residential operation where the child is residing;

(3) each parent of the child;

(4) the managing conservator or guardian of the child;

(5) an attorney ad litem appointed for the child under Chapter 107, if the appointment was not dismissed in the final order;

(6) a guardian ad litem appointed for the child under Chapter 107, if the appointment was not dismissed in the final order;

(7) a volunteer advocate appointed for the child under Chapter 107, if the appointment was not dismissed in the final order;

(8) the child if:

(A) the child is 10 years of age or older; or

(B) the court determines it is appropriate for the child to receive notice; and

(9) any other person or agency named by the court to have an interest in the child's welfare.

(c) Notice of a hearing under this chapter may be given:

(1) as provided by Rule 21a, Texas Rules of Civil Procedure;

(2) in a temporary order following a full adversary hearing;

(3) in an order following a hearing under this chapter;

(4) in open court; or

(5) in any manner that would provide actual notice to a person entitled to notice.

(d) The licensed administrator of the child-placing agency responsible for placing the child or the licensed administrator's designee is entitled to at least 10 days' notice of a permanency hearing after final order.

(e) Notice of a hearing under this chapter provided to an individual listed under Subsection (b)(2) must state that the individual may, but is not required to, attend the hearing and may request to be heard at the hearing.

(f) In a hearing under this chapter, the court shall determine whether the child's caregiver is present at the hearing and allow the caregiver to testify if the caregiver wishes to provide information about the child.

Added by Acts 1995, 74th Leg., ch. 20, § 1, eff. April 20, 1995. Amended by Acts 1997, 75th Leg., ch. 600, § 10, eff. Jan. 1, 1998; Acts 1997, 75th Leg., ch. 603, § 5, eff. Jan. 1, 1998; Acts 1997, 75th Leg., ch. 1022, § 83, eff. Jan. 1, 1998; Acts 2001, 77th Leg., ch. 849, § 6, eff. Sept. 1, 2001; Acts 2013, 83rd Leg., ch. 885 (H.B. 843), § 1, eff. Sept. 1, 2013; Acts 2015, 84th Leg., ch. 1 (S.B. 219), § 1.178, eff. April 2, 2015. Redesignated from V.T.C.A., Family Code § 263.301 and amended by Acts 2015, 84th Leg., ch. 944 (S.B. 206), § 28, eff. Sept. 1, 2015. Amended by Acts 2017, 85th Leg., ch. 317 (H.B. 7), § 24, eff. Sept. 1, 2017.

## § 263.0025. Special Education Decision-Making for Children in Foster Care

(a) In this section, "child" means a child in the temporary or permanent managing conservatorship of the department who is eligible under Section 29.003, Education Code, to participate in a school district's special education program.

(a-1) A foster parent for a child may act as a parent for the child, as authorized under 20 U.S.C. Section 1415(b), if:

(1) the rights and duties of the department to make decisions regarding the child's education under Section 153.371 have not been limited by court order; and

(2) the foster parent agrees to the requirements of Sections 29.015(a)(3) and (b), Education Code.

(a-2) Sections 29.015(b-1), (c), and (d), Education Code, apply to a foster parent who acts or desires to act as a parent for a child for the purpose of making special education decisions.

(b) To ensure the educational rights of a child are protected in the special education process, the court may appoint a surrogate parent for the child if:

(1) the child's school district is unable to identify or locate a parent for the child; or

(2) the foster parent of the child is unwilling or unable to serve as a parent for the purposes of this subchapter.

(c) Except as provided by Subsection (d), the court may appoint a person to serve as a child's surrogate parent if the person:

(1) is willing to serve in that capacity; and

(2) meets the requirements of 20 U.S.C. Section 1415(b).

(d) The following persons may not be appointed as a surrogate parent for the child:

(1) an employee of the department;

(2) an employee of the Texas Education Agency;

(3) an employee of a school or school district; or

(4) an employee of any other agency that is involved in the education or care of the child.

(e) The court may appoint a child's guardian ad litem or court-certified volunteer advocate, as provided by Section 107.031(c), as the child's surrogate parent.

(f) In appointing a person to serve as the surrogate parent for a child, the court may consider the person's ability to meet the qualifications listed under Sections 29.0151(d)(2)-(8), Education Code.

(g) If the court prescribes training for a person who is appointed as the surrogate parent for a child, the training program must comply with the minimum standards for training established by rule by the Texas Education Agency.

Added by Acts 2013, 83rd Leg., ch. 688 (H.B. 2619), § 3, eff. Sept. 1, 2013. Amended by Acts 2017, 85th Leg., ch. 1025 (H.B. 1556), § 4, eff. Sept. 1, 2017.

## § 263.003. Information Relating to Placement of Child

(a) Except as provided by Subsection (b), not later than the 10th day before the date set for a hearing under this chapter, the department shall file with the court any document described by Sections 262.114(a-1) and (a-2) that has not been filed with the court.

(b) The department is not required to file the documents required by Subsection (a) if the child is in an adoptive placement or another placement that is intended to be permanent.

Added by Acts 2009, 81st Leg., ch. 856, § 3, eff. Sept. 1, 2009.

## § 263.004. Notice to Court Regarding Education Decision-Making

(a) Unless the rights and duties of the department under Section 153.371(10) to make decisions regarding the child's education have been limited by court order, the department shall file with the court the name and contact information for each person who has been:

(1) designated by the department to make educational decisions on behalf of the child; and

(2) assigned to serve as the child's surrogate parent in accordance with 20 U.S.C. Section 1415(b) and Section 29.001(10), Education Code, for purposes of decision-making regarding special education services, if applicable.

(b) Not later than the fifth day after the date an adversary hearing under Section 262.201 or 262.205 is concluded, the information required by Subsection (a) shall be filed with the court and a copy shall be provided to the school the child attends.

(c) If a person other than a person identified under Subsection (a) is designated to make educational decisions or assigned to serve as a surrogate parent, the department shall include the updated information in a permanency progress report filed under Section 263.303 or 263.502. The updated information must be provided to the school the child attends not later than the fifth day after the date of designation or assignment.

Added by Acts 2013, 83rd Leg., ch. 688 (H.B. 2619), § 4, eff. Sept. 1, 2013. Amended by Acts 2015, 84th Leg., ch. 944 (S.B. 206), § 29, eff. Sept. 1, 2015.

### § 263.0045. Education in Home Setting for Foster Children

On request of a person providing substitute care for a child who is in the managing conservatorship of the department, the department shall allow the person to provide the child with an education in a home setting unless:

(1) the right of the department to allow the education of the child in a home setting has been specifically limited by court order;

(2) a court at a hearing conducted under this chapter finds, on good cause shown through evidence presented by the department in accordance with the applicable provisions in the department's child protective services handbook (CPS August 2013), that education in the home setting is not in the best interest of the child; or

(3) the department determines that federal law requires another school setting.

Added by Acts 2015, 84th Leg., ch. 944 (S.B. 206), § 27, eff. Sept. 1, 2015.

### § 263.005. Enforcement of Family Service Plan

The department shall designate existing department personnel to ensure that the parties to a family service plan comply with the plan.

Added by Acts 1995, 74th Leg., ch. 943, § 5, eff. Sept. 1, 1995.

### § 263.006. Warning to Parents

At the status hearing under Subchapter C [1] and at each permanency hearing under Subchapter D [2] held after the court has rendered a temporary order appointing the department as temporary managing conservator, the court shall inform each parent in open court that parental and custodial rights and duties may be subject to restriction or to termination unless the parent or parents are willing and able to provide the child with a safe environment.

Added by Acts 1997, 75th Leg., ch. 600, § 6, eff. Jan. 1, 1998; Acts 1997, 75th Leg., ch. 603, § 2, eff. Jan. 1, 1998; Acts 1997, 75th Leg., ch. 1022, § 80, eff. Jan. 1, 1998.

[1] V.T.C.A., Family Code § 263.201 et seq.

[2] V.T.C.A., Family Code § 263.301 et seq.

### § 263.0061. Notice to Parents of Right to Counsel

(a) At the status hearing under Subchapter C [1] and at each permanency hearing under Subchapter D [2] held after the date the court renders a temporary order appointing the department as temporary managing conservator of a child, the court shall inform each parent not represented by an attorney of:

(1) the right to be represented by an attorney; and

(2) if a parent is indigent and appears in opposition to the suit, the right to a court-appointed attorney.

(b) If a parent claims indigence and requests the appointment of an attorney in a proceeding described by Subsection (a), the court shall require the parent to complete and file with the court an affidavit of indigence. The court may hear evidence to determine whether the parent is indigent. If the court determines the parent is indigent, the court shall appoint an attorney to represent the parent.

Added by Acts 2013, 83rd Leg., ch. 810 (S.B. 1759), § 10, eff. Sept. 1, 2013.

[1] V.T.C.A., Family Code § 263.201 et seq.

[2] V.T.C.A., Family Code § 263.301 et seq.

### § 263.007. Report Regarding Notification of Relatives

Not later than the 10th day before the date set for a hearing under Subchapter C,[1] the department shall file with the court a report regarding:

(1) the efforts the department made to identify, locate, and provide information to the individuals described by Section 262.1095;

(2) the name of each individual the department identified, located, or provided with information; and

(3) if applicable, an explanation of why the department was unable to identify, locate, or provide information to an individual described by Section 262.1095.

Added by Acts 2011, 82nd Leg., ch. 1071 (S.B. 993), § 3, eff. Sept. 1, 2011.

[1] V.T.C.A., Family Code § 263.201 et seq.

### § 263.008. Foster Children's Bill of Rights

(a) In this section:

(1) "Agency foster home" and "facility" have the meanings assigned by Section 42.002, Human Resources Code.

(2) Repealed by Acts 2015, 84th Leg., ch. 944 (S.B. 206), § 86(14).

(3) "Foster children's bill of rights" means the rights described by Subsection (b).

(b) It is the policy of this state that each child in foster care be informed of the child's rights provided by state or federal law or policy that relate to:

(1) abuse, neglect, exploitation, discrimination, and harassment;

(2) food, clothing, shelter, and education;

(3) medical, dental, vision, and mental health services, including the right of the child to consent to treatment;

(4) emergency behavioral intervention, including what methods are permitted, the conditions under which it may be used, and the precautions that must be taken when administering it;

(5) placement with the child's siblings and contact with members of the child's family;

(6) privacy and searches, including the use of storage space, mail, and the telephone;

(7) participation in school-related extracurricular or community activities;

(8) interaction with persons outside the foster care system, including teachers, church members, mentors, and friends;

(9) contact and communication with caseworkers, attorneys ad litem, guardians ad litem, and court-appointed special advocates;

(10) religious services and activities;

(11) confidentiality of the child's records;

(12) job skills, personal finances, and preparation for adulthood;

(13) participation in a court hearing that involves the child;

(14) participation in the development of service and treatment plans;

(15) if the child has a disability, the advocacy and protection of the rights of a person with that disability; and

(16) any other matter affecting the child's ability to receive care and treatment in the least restrictive environment that is most like a family setting, consistent with the best interests and needs of the child.

(c) The department shall provide a written copy of the foster children's bill of rights to each child placed in foster care in the child's primary language, if possible, and shall inform the child of the rights described by the foster children's bill of rights:

(1) orally in the child's primary language, if possible, and in simple, nontechnical terms; or

(2) for a child who has a disability, including an impairment of vision or hearing, through any means that can reasonably be expected to result in successful communication with the child.

(d) A child placed in foster care may, at the child's option, sign a document acknowledging the child's understanding of the foster children's bill of rights after the department provides a written copy of the foster children's bill of rights to the child and informs the child of the rights described by the foster children's bill of rights in accordance with Subsection (c). If a child signs a document acknowledging the child's understanding of the foster children's bill of rights, the document must be placed in the child's case file.

(e) An agency foster home or other residential child-care facility in which a child is placed in foster care shall provide a copy of the foster children's bill of rights to a child on the child's request. The foster children's bill of rights must be printed in English and in a second language.

(f) The department shall promote the participation of foster children and former foster children in educating other foster children about the foster children's bill of rights.

(g) The department shall develop and implement a policy for receiving and handling reports that the rights of a child in foster care are not being observed. The department shall inform a child in foster care and, if appropriate, the child's parent, managing conservator, or guardian of the method for filing a report with the department under this subsection.

(h) This section does not create a cause of action.

Added by Acts 2011, 82nd Leg., ch. 791 (H.B. 2170), § 1, eff. Sept. 1, 2011. Redesignated from V.T.C.A., Family Code § 263.007 by Acts 2013, 83rd Leg., ch. 161 (S.B. 1093), § 22.001(17), eff. Sept. 1, 2013. Amended by Acts 2015, 84th Leg., ch. 1 (S.B. 219), § 1.172, eff. April 2, 2015; Acts 2015, 84th Leg., ch. 944 (S.B. 206), § 86(14), eff. Sept. 1, 2015; Acts 2017, 85th Leg., ch. 317 (H.B. 7), §§ 25, 26, eff. Sept. 1, 2017.

### § 263.009. Permanency Planning Meetings

(a) The department shall hold a permanency planning meeting for each child for whom the department is appointed temporary managing conservator in accordance with a schedule adopted by the commissioner of the department by rule that is designed to allow the child to exit the managing conservatorship of the department safely and as soon as possible and be placed with an appropriate adult caregiver who will permanently assume legal responsibility for the child.

(b) At each permanency planning meeting, the department shall:

(1) identify any barriers to achieving a timely permanent placement for the child;

(2) develop strategies and determine actions that will increase the probability of achieving a timely permanent placement for the child; and

(3) use the family group decision-making model whenever possible.

(c) Repealed by Acts 2015, 84th Leg., ch. 944 (S.B. 206), § 86(15).

(d) Repealed by Acts 2015, 84th Leg., ch. 944 (S.B. 206), § 86(15).

(e) Repealed by Acts 2015, 84th Leg., ch. 944 (S.B. 206), § 86(15).

(f) Repealed by Acts 2015, 84th Leg., ch. 944 (S.B. 206), § 86(15).

Added by Acts 2013, 83rd Leg., ch. 1324 (S.B. 534), § 2, eff. Sept. 1, 2013. Amended by Acts 2015, 84th Leg., ch. 944 (S.B. 206), §§ 30, 86(15), eff. Sept. 1, 2015; Acts 2017, 85th Leg., ch. 316 (H.B. 5), § 11, eff. Sept. 1, 2017.

## SUBCHAPTER B. SERVICE PLAN AND VISITATION PLAN

### § 263.101. Department to File Service Plan

Except as provided by Section 262.2015, not later than the 45th day after the date the court renders a temporary order appointing the department as temporary managing conservator of a child under Chapter 262, the department shall file a service plan.

Added by Acts 1995, 74th Leg., ch. 20, § 1, eff. April 20, 1995. Amended by Acts 1999, 76th Leg., ch. 1150, § 24, eff. Sept. 1, 1999; Acts 1999, 76th Leg., ch. 1390, § 43, eff. Sept. 1, 1999; Acts 2015, 84th Leg., ch. 1 (S.B. 219), § 1.173, eff. April 2, 2015; Acts 2015, 84th Leg., ch. 944 (S.B. 206), § 31, eff. Sept. 1, 2015.

### § 263.1015. Repealed by Acts 2015, 84th Leg., ch. 1 (S.B. 219), § 1.203(6), eff. April 2, 2015

### § 263.102. Service Plan; Contents

(a) The service plan must:

(1) be specific;

(2) be in writing in a language that the parents understand, or made otherwise available;

(3) be prepared by the department in conference with the child's parents;

(4) state appropriate deadlines;

(5) specify the primary permanency goal and at least one alternative permanency goal;

(6) state steps that are necessary to:

(A) return the child to the child's home if the placement is in foster care;

(B) enable the child to remain in the child's home with the assistance of a service plan if the placement is in the home under the department's supervision; or

(C) otherwise provide a permanent safe placement for the child;

(7) state the actions and responsibilities that are necessary for the child's parents to take to achieve the plan goal during the period of the service plan and the assistance to be provided to the parents by the department or other agency toward meeting that goal;

(8) state any specific skills or knowledge that the child's parents must acquire or learn, as well as any behavioral changes the parents must exhibit, to achieve the plan goal;

(9) state the actions and responsibilities that are necessary for the child's parents to take to ensure that the child attends school and maintains or improves the child's academic compliance;

(10) state the name of the person with the department whom the child's parents may contact for information relating to the child if other than the person preparing the plan; and

(11) prescribe any other term or condition that the department determines to be necessary to the service plan's success.

(b) The service plan shall include the following statement:

TO THE PARENT: THIS IS A VERY IMPORTANT DOCUMENT. ITS PURPOSE IS TO HELP YOU PROVIDE YOUR CHILD WITH A SAFE ENVIRONMENT WITHIN THE REASONABLE PERIOD SPECIFIED IN THE PLAN. IF YOU ARE UNWILLING OR UNABLE TO PROVIDE YOUR CHILD WITH A SAFE ENVIRONMENT, YOUR PARENTAL AND CUSTODIAL DUTIES AND RIGHTS MAY BE RESTRICTED OR TERMINATED OR YOUR CHILD MAY NOT BE RETURNED TO YOU. THERE WILL BE A COURT HEARING AT WHICH A JUDGE WILL REVIEW THIS SERVICE PLAN.

(c) Repealed by Acts 2015, 84th Leg., ch. 944 (S.B. 206), § 86(16).

(d) The department or other authorized entity must write the service plan in a manner that is clear and understandable to the parent in order to facilitate the parent's ability to follow the requirements of the service plan.

(e) Regardless of whether the goal stated in a child's service plan as required under Subsection (a)(5) is to return the child to the child's parents or to terminate parental rights and place the child for adoption, the department shall concurrently provide to the child and the child's family, as applicable:

(1) time-limited family reunification services as defined by 42 U.S.C. Section 629a for a period not to exceed the period within which the court must render a final order in or dismiss the suit affecting the parent-child relationship with respect to the child as provided by Subchapter E;[1] and

(2) adoption promotion and support services as defined by 42 U.S.C. Section 629a.

(f) The department shall consult with relevant professionals to determine the skills or knowledge that the parents of a child under two years of age should learn or acquire to provide a safe placement for the child. The department shall incorporate those skills and abilities into the department's service plans, as appropriate.

(g) Repealed by Acts 2015, 84th Leg., ch. 944 (S.B. 206), § 86(16).

Added by Acts 1995, 74th Leg., ch. 20, § 1, eff. April 20, 1995. Amended by Acts 2005, 79th Leg., ch. 268, § 1.38(a), eff. Sept. 1, 2005; Acts 2007, 80th Leg., ch. 1406, § 8, eff. Sept. 1, 2007; Acts 2015, 84th Leg., ch. 1 (S.B. 219), § 1.174, eff. April 2, 2015; Acts 2015, 84th Leg., ch. 944 (S.B. 206), §§ 32, 86(16), eff. Sept. 1, 2015.

[1] V.T.C.A., Family Code § 263.401 et seq.

### § 263.103. Original Service Plan: Signing and Taking Effect

(a) The original service plan shall be developed jointly by the child's parents and a representative of the department, including informing the parents of their rights in connection with the service plan process. If a parent is not able or willing to participate in the development of the service plan, it should be so noted in the plan.

(a–1) Before the original service plan is signed, the child's parents and the representative of the department shall discuss each term and condition of the plan.

(b) The child's parents and the person preparing the original service plan shall sign the plan, and the department shall give each parent a copy of the service plan.

(c) If the department determines that the child's parents are unable or unwilling to participate in the development of the original service plan or sign the plan, the department may file the plan without the parents' signatures.

(d) The original service plan takes effect when:

(1) the child's parents and the appropriate representative of the department sign the plan; or

(2) the court issues an order giving effect to the plan without the parents' signatures.

(e) The original service plan is in effect until amended by the court or as provided under Section 263.104.

Added by Acts 1995, 74th Leg., ch. 20, § 1, eff. April 20, 1995. Amended by Acts 2011, 82nd Leg., ch. 598 (S.B. 218), § 4, eff. Sept. 1, 2011; Acts 2015, 84th Leg., ch. 1 (S.B. 219), § 1.175, eff. April 2, 2015.

### § 263.104. Amended Service Plan

(a) The service plan may be amended at any time. The department shall work with the parents to jointly develop any amendment to the service plan, including informing the parents of their rights in connection with the amended service plan process.

(b) The amended service plan supersedes the previously filed service plan and takes effect when:

(1) the child's parents and the appropriate representative of the department sign the plan; or

(2) the department determines that the child's parents are unable or unwilling to sign the amended plan and files it without the parents' signatures.

(c) A parent may file a motion with the court at any time to request a review and modification of the amended service plan.

(d) An amended service plan remains in effect until:

(1) superseded by a later-amended service plan that goes into effect as provided by Subsection (b); or

(2) modified by the court.

Added by Acts 1995, 74th Leg., ch. 20, § 1, eff. April 20, 1995. Amended by Acts 2011, 82nd Leg., ch. 598 (S.B. 218), § 5, eff. Sept. 1, 2011; Acts 2015, 84th Leg., ch. 1 (S.B. 219), § 1.176, eff. April 2, 2015.

### § 263.105. Review of Service Plan; Modification

(a) The service plan currently in effect shall be filed with the court.

(b) The court shall review the plan at the next required hearing under this chapter after the plan is filed.

(c) The court may modify an original or amended service plan at any time.

Added by Acts 1995, 74th Leg., ch. 20, § 1, eff. April 20, 1995. Amended by Acts 1999, 76th Leg., ch. 1150, § 25, eff. Sept. 1, 1999; Acts 1999, 76th Leg., ch. 1390, § 44, eff. Sept. 1, 1999; Acts 2011, 82nd Leg., ch. 1071 (S.B. 993), §§ 4, 5, eff. Sept. 1, 2011.

### § 263.106. Court Implementation of Service Plan

After reviewing the original or any amended service plan and making any changes or modifications it deems necessary, the court shall incorporate the original and any amended service plan into the orders of the court and may render additional appropriate orders to implement or require compliance with an original or amended service plan.

Added by Acts 1995, 74th Leg., ch. 20, § 1, eff. April 20, 1995. Amended by Acts 2011, 82nd Leg., ch. 598 (S.B. 218), § 6, eff. Sept. 1, 2011.

### § 263.107. Visitation Plan

(a) This section applies only to a child in the temporary managing conservatorship of the department for whom the department's goal is reunification of the child with the child's parent.

(b) Not later than the 30th day after the date the department is named temporary managing conservator of a child, the department in collaboration with each parent of the child shall develop a visitation plan.

(c) In determining the frequency and circumstances of visitation under this section, the department must consider:

(1) the safety and best interest of the child;

(2) the age of the child;

(3) the desires of each parent regarding visitation with the child;

(4) the location of each parent and the child; and

(5) the resources available to the department, including the resources to:

(A) ensure that visitation is properly supervised by a department employee or an available and willing volunteer the department determines suitable after conducting a background and criminal history check; and

(B) provide transportation to and from visits.

(d) Not later than the 10th day before the date of a status hearing under Section 263.201, the department shall file with the court a copy of the visitation plan developed under this section.

(e) The department may amend the visitation plan on mutual agreement of the child's parents and the department or as the department considers necessary to ensure the safety of the child. An amendment to the visitation plan must be in the child's best interest. The department shall file a copy of any amended visitation plan with the court.

(f) A visitation plan developed under this section may not conflict with a court order relating to possession of or access to the child.

Added by Acts 2013, 83rd Leg., ch. 191 (S.B. 352), § 4, eff. Sept. 1, 2013.

### § 263.108. Review of Visitation Plan; Modification

(a) At the first hearing held under this chapter after the date an original or amended visitation plan is filed with the court under Section 263.107, the court shall review the visitation plan, taking into consideration the factors specified in Section 263.107(c).

(b) The court may modify, or order the department to modify, an original or amended visitation plan at any time.

(c) A parent who is entitled to visitation under a visitation plan may at any time file a motion with the court to request review and modification of an original or amended visitation plan.

Added by Acts 2013, 83rd Leg., ch. 191 (S.B. 352), § 4, eff. Sept. 1, 2013.

### § 263.109. Court Implementation of Visitation Plan

(a) After reviewing an original or amended visitation plan, the court shall render an order regarding a parent's visitation with a child that the court determines appropriate.

(b) If the court finds that visitation between a child and a parent is not in the child's best interest, the court shall render an order that:

(1) states the reasons for finding that visitation is not in the child's best interest; and

(2) outlines specific steps the parent must take to be allowed to have visitation with the child.

(c) If the order regarding visitation between a child and a parent requires supervised visitation to protect the health and safety of the child, the order must outline specific steps the parent must take to have the level of supervision reduced.

Added by Acts 2013, 83rd Leg., ch. 191 (S.B. 352), § 4, eff. Sept. 1, 2013.

## SUBCHAPTER C. STATUS HEARING

### § 263.201. Status Hearing; Time

(a) Not later than the 60th day after the date the court renders a temporary order appointing the department as temporary managing conservator of a child, the court shall hold a status hearing to review the child's status and the service plan developed for the child.

(b) A status hearing is not required if the court holds an initial permanency hearing under Section 262.2015 and makes findings required by Section 263.202 before the date a status hearing is required by this section.

(c) The court shall require each parent, alleged father, or relative of the child before the court to submit the proposed child placement resources form provided under Section 261.307 at the status hearing, if the form has not previously been submitted.

Added by Acts 1995, 74th Leg., ch. 20, § 1, eff. April 20, 1995. Amended by Acts 1997, 75th Leg., ch. 600, § 8, eff. Jan. 1, 1998; Acts 1997, 75th Leg., ch. 603, § 3, eff. Jan. 1, 1998; Acts 1997, 75th Leg., ch. 1022, § 81, eff. Jan. 1, 1998; Acts 1999, 76th Leg., ch. 1150, § 26, eff. Sept. 1, 1999; Acts 1999, 76th Leg., ch. 1390, § 45, eff. Sept. 1, 1999; Acts 2005, 79th Leg., ch. 268, § 1.37(a), eff. Sept. 1, 2005; Acts 2011, 82nd Leg., ch. 1071 (S.B. 993), § 6, eff. Sept. 1, 2011.

### § 263.202. Status Hearing; Findings

(a) If all persons entitled to citation and notice of a status hearing under this chapter were not served, the court shall make findings as to whether:

(1) the department has exercised due diligence to locate all necessary persons, including an alleged father of the child, regardless of whether the alleged father is registered with the registry of paternity under Section 160.402; and

(2) the child and each parent, alleged father, or relative of the child before the court have furnished to the department all available information necessary to locate an absent parent, alleged father, or relative of the child through exercise of due diligence.

(b) Except as otherwise provided by this subchapter, a status hearing shall be limited to matters related to the contents and execution of the service plan filed with the court. The court shall review the service plan that the department filed under this chapter for reasonableness, accuracy, and compliance with requirements of court orders and make findings as to whether:

(1) a plan that has the goal of returning the child to the child's parents adequately ensures that reasonable efforts are made to enable the child's parents to provide a safe environment for the child;

(2) the child's parents have reviewed and understand the plan and have been advised that unless the parents are willing and able to provide the child with a safe environment, even with the assistance of a service plan, within the reasonable period of time specified in the plan, the parents' parental and custodial duties and rights may be subject to restriction or to termination under this code or the child may not be returned to the parents;

(3) the plan is narrowly tailored to address any specific issues identified by the department; and

(4) the child's parents and the representative of the department have signed the plan.

(b–1) After reviewing the service plan and making any necessary modifications, the court shall incorporate the service plan into the orders of the court and may render additional appropriate orders to implement or require compliance with the plan.

(c) Repealed by Acts 2011, 82nd Leg., ch. 1071 (S.B. 993), § 9.

(d) Repealed by Acts 2011, 82nd Leg., ch. 1071 (S.B. 993), § 9.

(e) At the status hearing, the court shall make a finding as to whether the court has identified the individual who has the right to consent for the child under Section 266.003.

(f) The court shall review the report filed by the department under Section 263.007 and inquire into the sufficiency of the department's efforts to identify, locate, and provide information to each adult described by Section 262.1095(a). The court shall order the department to make further efforts to identify, locate, and provide information to each adult described by Section 262.1095(a) if the court determines that the department's efforts have not been sufficient.

(f–1) The court shall ask all parties present at the status hearing whether the child or the child's family has a Native American heritage and identify any

Native American tribe with which the child may be associated.

(g) The court shall give the child's parents an opportunity to comment on the service plan.

(h) If a proposed child placement resources form as described by Section 261.307 has not been submitted, the court shall require each parent, alleged father, or other person to whom the department is required to provide a form to submit a completed form. The court shall ask all parties present at the status hearing whether:

(1) the child has had the opportunity, in a developmentally appropriate manner, to identify any adult, particularly an adult residing in the child's community, who could be a relative or designated caregiver for the child; and

(2) each individual identified by the child as a potential relative or designated caregiver is listed on the proposed child placement resources form.

(i) For a child placed with a relative of the child, the court shall inform the relative of:

(1) the option to become verified by a licensed child-placing agency to operate an agency foster home, if applicable; and

(2) the permanency care assistance program under Subchapter K, Chapter 264.[1]

Added by Acts 1995, 74th Leg., ch. 20, § 1, eff. April 20, 1995. Amended by Acts 1995, 74th Leg., ch. 751, § 111, eff. Sept. 1, 1995; Acts 1999, 76th Leg., ch. 1150, § 27, eff. Sept. 1, 1999; Acts 1999, 76th Leg., ch. 1390, § 46, eff. Sept. 1, 1999; Acts 2001, 77th Leg., ch. 306, § 2, eff. Sept. 1, 2001; Acts 2005, 79th Leg., ch. 268, §§ 1.38(b), 1.39, eff. Sept. 1, 2005; Acts 2011, 82nd Leg., ch. 1071 (S.B. 993), §§ 7, 9, eff. Sept. 1, 2011; Acts 2015, 84th Leg., ch. 1 (S.B. 219), § 1.177, eff. April 2, 2015; Acts 2015, 84th Leg., ch. 697 (H.B. 825), § 2, eff. Sept. 1, 2015; Acts 2019, 86th Leg., ch. 375 (H.B. 1884), § 3, eff. Sept. 1, 2019; Acts 2019, 86th Leg., ch. 1294 (H.B. 3390), § 9, eff. June 14, 2019; Acts 2021, 87th Leg., ch. 269 (H.B. 3041), § 3, eff. Sept. 1, 2021.

[1] V.T.C.A., Family Code § 264.851 et seq.

### § 263.203. Appointment of Attorney Ad Litem; Admonishments

(a) The court shall advise the parties of the provisions regarding the mandatory appointment of an attorney ad litem under Subchapter A, Chapter 107,[1] and shall appoint an attorney ad litem to represent the interests of any person eligible if the appointment is required by that subchapter.

(b) The court shall advise the parties that progress under the service plan will be reviewed at all subsequent hearings, including a review of whether the parties have acquired or learned any specific skills or knowledge stated in the plan.

Added by Acts 2011, 82nd Leg., ch. 1071 (S.B. 993), § 8, eff. Sept. 1, 2011.

[1] V.T.C.A., Family Code § 107.001 et seq.

## SUBCHAPTER D. PERMANENCY HEARINGS

### § 263.301. Redesignated as V.T.C.A., Family Code § 263.0021 and amended by Acts 2015, 84th Leg., ch. 944 (S.B. 206), § 28, eff. Sept. 1, 2015

### § 263.302. Child's Attendance at Hearing

The child shall attend each permanency hearing unless the court specifically excuses the child's attendance. A child committed to the Texas Juvenile Justice Department may attend a permanency hearing in person, by telephone, or by videoconference. The court shall consult with the child in a developmentally appropriate manner regarding the child's permanency plan, if the child is four years of age or older and if the court determines it is in the best interest of the child. Failure by the child to attend a hearing does not affect the validity of an order rendered at the hearing.

Added by Acts 1995, 74th Leg., ch. 20, § 1, eff. April 20, 1995. Amended by Acts 1997, 75th Leg., ch. 600, § 11, eff. Jan. 1, 1998; Acts 1997, 75th Leg., ch. 603, § 6, eff. Jan. 1, 1998; Acts 1997, 75th Leg., ch. 1022, § 84, eff. Jan. 1, 1998; Acts 2007, 80th Leg., ch. 1304, § 1, eff. June 15, 2007; Acts 2009, 81st Leg., ch. 108, § 6, eff. May 23, 2009; Acts 2015, 84th Leg., ch. 734 (H.B. 1549), § 85, eff. Sept. 1, 2015.

### § 263.3025. Permanency Plan

(a) The department shall prepare a permanency plan for a child for whom the department has been appointed temporary managing conservator. The department shall give a copy of the plan to each person entitled to notice under Section 263.0021(b) not later than the 10th day before the date of the child's first permanency hearing.

(b) In addition to the requirements of the department rules governing permanency planning, the permanency plan must contain the information required to be included in a permanency progress report under Section 263.303.

(c) The department shall modify the permanency plan for a child as required by the circumstances and needs of the child.

(d) In accordance with department rules, a child's permanency plan must include concurrent permanency goals consisting of a primary permanency goal and at least one alternate permanency goal.

Added by Acts 1997, 75th Leg., ch. 600, § 12, eff. Jan. 1, 1998; Acts 1997, 75th Leg., ch. 603, § 7, eff. Jan. 1, 1998; Acts 1997, 75th Leg., ch. 1022, § 85, eff. Jan. 1, 1998. Amended by Acts 2001, 77th Leg., ch. 809, § 5, eff. Sept. 1, 2001; Acts 2005, 79th Leg., ch. 620, § 3, eff. Sept. 1, 2005; Acts 2009, 81st Leg., ch. 1372, § 4, eff. June 19, 2009; Acts 2015, 84th Leg., ch. 944 (S.B. 206), § 33, eff. Sept. 1, 2015.

### § 263.3026. Permanency Goals; Limitation

(a) The department's permanency plan for a child may include as a goal:

(1) the reunification of the child with a parent or other individual from whom the child was removed;

(2) the termination of parental rights and adoption of the child by a relative or other suitable individual;

(3) the award of permanent managing conservatorship of the child to a relative or other suitable individual; or

(4) another planned, permanent living arrangement for the child.

(b) If the goal of the department's permanency plan for a child is to find another planned, permanent living arrangement for the child, the department shall document that there is a compelling reason why the other permanency goals identified in Subsection (a) are not in the child's best interest.

Added by Acts 2009, 81st Leg., ch. 1372, § 5, eff. June 19, 2009.

### § 263.303. Permanency Progress Report Before Final Order

(a) Not later than the 10th day before the date set for each permanency hearing before a final order is rendered, the department shall file with the court and provide to each party, the child's attorney ad litem, the child's guardian ad litem, and the child's volunteer advocate a permanency progress report unless the court orders a different period for providing the report.

(b) The permanency progress report must contain:

(1) information necessary for the court to conduct the permanency hearing and make its findings and determinations under Section 263.306;

(2) information on significant events, as defined by Section 264.018; and

(3) any additional information the department determines is appropriate or that is requested by the court and relevant to the court's findings and determinations under Section 263.306.

(c) A parent whose parental rights are the subject of a suit affecting the parent-child relationship, the attorney for that parent, or the child's attorney ad litem or guardian ad litem may file a response to the department's report filed under this section. A response must be filed not later than the third day before the date of the hearing.

Added by Acts 1995, 74th Leg., ch. 20, § 1, eff. April 20, 1995. Amended by Acts 1995, 74th Leg., ch. 751, § 112, eff. Sept. 1, 1995; Acts 1997, 75th Leg., ch. 600, § 13, eff. Jan. 1, 1998; Acts 1997, 75th Leg., ch. 603, § 8, eff. Jan. 1, 1998; Acts 1997, 75th Leg., ch. 1022, § 86, eff. Jan. 1, 1998; Acts 2005, 79th Leg., ch. 172, § 24, eff. Sept. 1, 2005; Acts 2009, 81st Leg., ch. 108, § 7, eff. May 23, 2009; Acts 2009, 81st Leg., ch. 1372, § 6, eff. June 19, 2009; Acts 2015, 84th Leg., ch. 1 (S.B. 219), § 1.179, eff. April 2, 2015; Acts 2015, 84th Leg., ch. 944 (S.B. 206), § 34, eff. Sept. 1, 2015.

### § 263.304. Initial Permanency Hearing; Time

(a) Not later than the 180th day after the date the court renders a temporary order appointing the department as temporary managing conservator of a child, the court shall hold a permanency hearing to review the status of, and permanency plan for, the child to ensure that a final order consistent with that permanency plan is rendered before the date for dismissal of the suit under this chapter.

(b) The court shall set a final hearing under this chapter on a date that allows the court to render a final order before the date for dismissal of the suit under this chapter. Any party to the suit or an attorney ad litem for the child may seek a writ of mandamus to compel the court to comply with the duties imposed by this subsection.

Added by Acts 1995, 74th Leg., ch. 20, § 1, eff. April 20, 1995. Amended by Acts 1995, 74th Leg., ch. 751, § 113, eff. Sept. 1, 1995; Acts 1997, 75th Leg., ch. 600, § 14, eff. Jan. 1, 1998; Acts 1997, 75th Leg., ch. 603, § 9, eff. Jan. 1, 1998; Acts 1997, 75th Leg., ch. 1022, § 87, eff. Jan. 1, 1998; Acts 2001, 77th Leg., ch. 1090, § 7, eff. Sept. 1, 2001.

### § 263.305. Subsequent Permanency Hearings

A subsequent permanency hearing before entry of a final order shall be held not later than the 120th day after the date of the last permanency hearing in the suit. For good cause shown or on the court's own motion, the court may order more frequent hearings.

Added by Acts 1995, 74th Leg., ch. 20, § 1, eff. April 20, 1995. Amended by Acts 1997, 75th Leg., ch. 600, § 15, eff. Jan. 1, 1998; Acts 1997, 75th Leg., ch. 603, § 10, eff. Jan. 1, 1998; Acts 1997, 75th Leg., ch. 1022, § 88, eff. Jan. 1, 1998.

**§ 263.306. Permanency Hearings Before Final Order**

(a) Repealed by Acts 2017, 85th Leg., ch. 324 (S.B. 1488), § 7.009.

(a–1) At each permanency hearing before a final order is rendered, the court shall:

(1) identify all persons and parties present at the hearing;

(2) review the efforts of the department or other agency in:

(A) locating and requesting service of citation on all persons entitled to service of citation under Section 102.009; and

(B) obtaining the assistance of a parent in providing information necessary to locate an absent parent, alleged father, relative of the child, or other adult identified by the child as a potential relative or designated caregiver;

(3) ask all parties present whether the child or the child's family has a Native American heritage and identify any Native American tribe with which the child may be associated;

(4) review the extent of the parties' compliance with temporary orders and the service plan and the extent to which progress has been made toward alleviating or mitigating the causes necessitating the placement of the child in foster care;

(5) review the permanency progress report to determine:

(A) the safety and well-being of the child and whether the child's needs, including any medical or special needs, are being adequately addressed;

(B) the continuing necessity and appropriateness of the placement of the child, including with respect to a child who has been placed outside of this state, whether the placement continues to be in the best interest of the child;

(C) the appropriateness of the primary and alternative permanency goals for the child developed in accordance with department rule and whether the department has made reasonable efforts to finalize the permanency plan, including the concurrent permanency goals, in effect for the child;

(D) whether the child has been provided the opportunity, in a developmentally appropriate manner, to express the child's opinion on any medical care provided;

(E) whether the child has been provided the opportunity, in a developmentally appropriate manner, to identify any adults, particularly an adult residing in the child's community, who could be a relative or designated caregiver for the child;

(F) for a child receiving psychotropic medication, whether the child:

(i) has been provided appropriate nonpharmacological interventions, therapies, or strategies to meet the child's needs; or

(ii) has been seen by the prescribing physician, physician assistant, or advanced practice nurse at least once every 90 days;

(G) whether an education decision-maker for the child has been identified, the child's education needs and goals have been identified and addressed, and there have been major changes in the child's school performance or there have been serious disciplinary events;

(H) for a child 14 years of age or older, whether services that are needed to assist the child in transitioning from substitute care to independent living are available in the child's community; and

(I) for a child whose permanency goal is another planned permanent living arrangement:

(i) the desired permanency outcome for the child, by asking the child;

(ii) whether, as of the date of the hearing, another planned permanent living arrangement is the best permanency plan for the child and, if so, provide compelling reasons why it continues to not be in the best interest of the child to:

(a) return home;

(b) be placed for adoption;

(c) be placed with a legal guardian; or

(d) be placed with a fit and willing relative;

(iii) whether the department has conducted an independent living skills assessment under Section 264.121(a–3);

(iv) whether the department has addressed the goals identified in the child's permanency plan, including the child's housing plan, and the results of the independent living skills assessment;

(v) if the youth is 16 years of age or older, whether there is evidence that the department has provided the youth with the documents and information listed in Section 264.121(e); and

(vi) if the youth is 18 years of age or older or has had the disabilities of minority removed, whether there is evidence that the department has provided the youth with the documents and information listed in Section 264.121(e–1);

(6) determine whether to return the child to the child's parents if the child's parents are willing and able to provide the child with a safe environment and the return of the child is in the child's best interest;

(7) estimate a likely date by which the child may be returned to and safely maintained in the child's home, placed for adoption, or placed in permanent managing conservatorship; and

(8) announce in open court the dismissal date and the date of any upcoming hearings.

(b) Repealed by Acts 2015, 84th Leg., ch. 944 (S.B. 206), § 86(18).

(c) In addition to the requirements of Subsection (a–1), at each permanency hearing before a final order is rendered the court shall review the department's efforts to:

(1) ensure that the child has regular, ongoing opportunities to engage in age-appropriate normalcy activities, including activities not listed in the child's service plan; and

(2) for a child placed with a relative of the child or other designated caregiver, inform the caregiver of:

(A) the option to become verified by a licensed child-placing agency to operate an agency foster home, if applicable; and

(B) the permanency care assistance program under Subchapter K, Chapter 264.

Added by Acts 1995, 74th Leg., ch. 20, § 1, eff. April 20, 1995. Amended by Acts 1995, 74th Leg., ch. 751, § 114, eff. Sept. 1, 1995; Acts 1997, 75th Leg., ch. 600, § 16, eff. Jan. 1, 1998; Acts 1997, 75th Leg., ch. 603, § 11, eff. Jan. 1, 1998; Acts 1997, 75th Leg., ch. 1022, § 89, eff. Jan. 1, 1998; Acts 1999, 76th Leg., ch. 1390, § 47, eff. Sept. 1, 1999; Acts 2001, 77th Leg., ch. 306, § 3, eff. Sept. 1, 2001; Acts 2001, 77th Leg., ch. 849, § 7, eff. Sept. 1, 2001; Acts 2009, 81st Leg., ch. 108, § 8, eff. May 23, 2009; Acts 2009, 81st Leg., ch. 1372, § 7, eff. June 19, 2009; Acts 2013, 83rd Leg., ch. 191 (S.B. 352), § 5, eff. Sept. 1, 2013; Acts 2013, 83rd Leg., ch. 204 (H.B. 915), § 4, eff. Sept. 1, 2013; Acts 2013, 83rd Leg., ch. 688 (H.B. 2619), § 5, eff. Sept. 1, 2013; Acts 2015, 84th Leg., ch. 1 (S.B. 219), § 1.180, eff. April 2, 2015; Acts 2015, 84th Leg., ch. 262 (S.B. 1407), § 2, eff. Sept. 1, 2015; Acts 2015, 84th Leg., ch. 697 (H.B. 825), § 3, eff. Sept. 1, 2015; Acts 2015, 84th Leg., ch. 944 (S.B. 206), §§ 35, 36, 86(17), 86(18), eff. Sept. 1, 2015; Acts 2017, 85th Leg., ch. 324 (S.B. 1488), § 7.009, eff. Sept. 1, 2017; Acts 2017, 85th Leg., ch. 937 (S.B. 1758), § 3, eff. Sept. 1, 2017; Acts 2019, 86th Leg., ch. 375 (H.B. 1884), § 4, eff. Sept. 1, 2019; Acts 2019, 86th Leg., ch. 1294 (H.B. 3390), § 10, eff. June 14, 2019.

### § 263.307. Factors in Determining Best Interest of Child

(a) In considering the factors established by this section, the prompt and permanent placement of the child in a safe environment is presumed to be in the child's best interest.

(b) The following factors should be considered by the court and the department in determining whether the child's parents are willing and able to provide the child with a safe environment:

(1) the child's age and physical and mental vulnerabilities;

(2) the frequency and nature of out-of-home placements;

(3) the magnitude, frequency, and circumstances of the harm to the child;

(4) whether the child has been the victim of repeated harm after the initial report and intervention by the department;

(5) whether the child is fearful of living in or returning to the child's home;

(6) the results of psychiatric, psychological, or developmental evaluations of the child, the child's parents, other family members, or others who have access to the child's home;

(7) whether there is a history of abusive or assaultive conduct by the child's family or others who have access to the child's home;

(8) whether there is a history of substance abuse by the child's family or others who have access to the child's home;

(9) whether the perpetrator of the harm to the child is identified;

(10) the willingness and ability of the child's family to seek out, accept, and complete counseling services and to cooperate with and facilitate an appropriate agency's close supervision;

(11) the willingness and ability of the child's family to effect positive environmental and personal changes within a reasonable period of time;

(12) whether the child's family demonstrates adequate parenting skills, including providing the child and other children under the family's care with:

(A) minimally adequate health and nutritional care;

(B) care, nurturance, and appropriate discipline consistent with the child's physical and psychological development;

(C) guidance and supervision consistent with the child's safety;

(D) a safe physical home environment;

(E) protection from repeated exposure to violence even though the violence may not be directed at the child; and

(F) an understanding of the child's needs and capabilities; and

(13) whether an adequate social support system consisting of an extended family and friends is available to the child.

(c) In the case of a child 16 years of age or older, the following guidelines should be considered by the court in determining whether to adopt the permanency plan submitted by the department:

(1) whether the permanency plan submitted to the court includes the services planned for the child to make the transition from foster care to independent living; and

(2) whether this transition is in the best interest of the child.

Added by Acts 1995, 74th Leg., ch. 20, § 1, eff. April 20, 1995. Amended by Acts 2015, 84th Leg., ch. 1 (S.B. 219), § 1.181, eff. April 2, 2015.

**§§ 263.308, 263.309. Repealed by Acts 1997, 75th Leg., ch. 603, § 13, eff. Jan. 1, 1998; Acts 1997, 75th Leg., ch. 1022, § 104(a), eff. Sept. 1, 1997.**

## SUBCHAPTER E. FINAL ORDER FOR CHILD UNDER DEPARTMENT CARE

### § 263.401. Dismissal After One Year; New Trials; Extension

(a) Unless the court has commenced the trial on the merits or granted an extension under Subsection (b) or (b–1), on the first Monday after the first anniversary of the date the court rendered a temporary order appointing the department as temporary managing conservator, the court's jurisdiction over the suit affecting the parent-child relationship filed by the department that requests termination of the parent-child relationship or requests that the department be named conservator of the child is terminated and the suit is automatically dismissed without a court order. Not later than the 60th day before the day the suit is automatically dismissed, the court shall notify all parties to the suit of the automatic dismissal date.

(b) Unless the court has commenced the trial on the merits, the court may not retain the suit on the court's docket after the time described by Subsection (a) unless the court finds that extraordinary circumstances necessitate the child remaining in the temporary managing conservatorship of the department and that continuing the appointment of the department as temporary managing conservator is in the best interest of the child. If the court makes those findings, the court may retain the suit on the court's docket for a period not to exceed 180 days after the time described by Subsection (a). If the court retains the suit on the court's docket, the court shall render an order in which the court:

(1) schedules the new date on which the suit will be automatically dismissed if the trial on the merits has not commenced, which date must be not later than the 180th day after the time described by Subsection (a);

(2) makes further temporary orders for the safety and welfare of the child as necessary to avoid further delay in resolving the suit; and

(3) sets the trial on the merits on a date not later than the date specified under Subdivision (1).

(b–1) If, after commencement of the initial trial on the merits within the time required by Subsection (a) or (b), the court grants a motion for a new trial or mistrial, or the case is remanded to the court by an appellate court following an appeal of the court's final order, the court shall retain the suit on the court's docket and render an order in which the court:

(1) schedules a new date on which the suit will be automatically dismissed if the new trial has not commenced, which must be a date not later than the 180th day after the date on which:

(A) the motion for a new trial or mistrial is granted; or

(B) the appellate court remanded the case;

(2) makes further temporary orders for the safety and welfare of the child as necessary to avoid further delay in resolving the suit; and

(3) sets the new trial on the merits for a date not later than the date specified under Subdivision (1).

(b–2) When considering under Subsection (b) whether to find that extraordinary circumstances necessitate the child remaining in the temporary managing conservatorship of the department for a case in which the court orders a parent to complete a substance abuse treatment program, the court shall consider whether the parent made a good faith effort to successfully complete the program.

(b–3) A court shall find under Subsection (b) that extraordinary circumstances necessitate the child remaining in the temporary managing conservatorship of the department if:

(1) a parent of a child has made a good faith effort to successfully complete the service plan but needs additional time; and

(2) on completion of the service plan the court intends to order the child returned to the parent.

(c) If the court grants an extension under Subsection (b) or (b–1) but does not commence the trial on the merits before the dismissal date, the court's jurisdiction over the suit is terminated and the suit is automatically dismissed without a court order. The court may not grant an additional extension that extends the suit beyond the required date for dismissal under Subsection (b) or (b–1), as applicable.

Added by Acts 1997, 75th Leg., ch. 600, § 17, eff. Sept. 1, 1997; Acts 1997, 75th Leg., ch. 603, § 12, eff. Jan. 1, 1998; Acts 1997, 75th Leg., ch. 1022, § 90, eff. Jan. 1, 1998. Amended by Acts 2001, 77th Leg., ch. 1090, § 8, eff. Sept. 1, 2001; Acts 2005, 79th Leg., ch. 268, § 1.40, eff. Sept. 1, 2005; Acts 2007, 80th Leg., ch. 866, §§ 2, 5, eff. June 15, 2007; Acts 2015, 84th Leg., ch. 944 (S.B. 206), §§ 37, 38, eff. Sept. 1, 2015; Acts 2017, 85th Leg., ch. 317 (H.B. 7), § 27, eff. Sept. 1, 2017; Acts 2017, 85th Leg., ch. 319 (S.B. 11), § 12, eff. Sept. 1, 2017; Acts 2019, 86th Leg., ch. 783 (H.B. 1780), § 1, eff. Sept. 1, 2019; Acts 2021, 87th Leg., ch. 8 (H.B. 567), § 9, eff. Sept. 1, 2021.

Section 2 of Acts 2019, 86th Leg., ch. 783 (H.B. 1780) provides:

"The changes in law made by this Act apply only to a suit affecting the parent-child relationship filed on or after the effective date [Sept. 1, 2019] of this Act. A suit affecting the parent-child relationship filed before that date is governed by the law in effect on the date the suit was filed, and that law is continued in effect for that purpose."

Section 15 of Acts 2021, 87th Leg., ch. 8 (H.B. 567) provides:

"The changes in law made by this Act apply only to a suit filed by the Department of Family and Protective Services on or after the effective date [Sept. 1, 2021] of this Act. A suit filed by the department before that date is governed by the law in effect on the date the suit was filed, and the former law is continued in effect for that purpose."

### § 263.4011. Rendering Final Order; Extension

(a) On timely commencement of the trial on the merits under Section 263.401, the court shall render a final order not later than the 90th day after the date the trial commences.

(b) The 90–day period for rendering a final order under Subsection (a) is not tolled for any recess during the trial.

(c) The court may extend the 90–day period under Subsection (a) for the period the court determines necessary if, after a hearing, the court finds good cause for the extension. If the court grants a good cause extension under this subsection, the court shall render a written order specifying:

(1) the grounds on which the extension is granted; and

(2) the length of the extension.

(d) A party may file a mandamus proceeding if the court fails to render a final order within the time required by this section.

Added by Acts 2021, 87th Leg., ch. 8 (H.B. 567), § 10, eff. Sept. 1, 2021.

Section 15 of Acts 2021, 87th Leg., ch. 8 (H.B. 567) provides:

"The changes in law made by this Act apply only to a suit filed by the Department of Family and Protective Services on or after the effective date [Sept. 1, 2021] of this Act. A suit filed by the department before that date is governed by the law in effect on the date the suit was filed, and the former law is continued in effect for that purpose."

### § 263.402. Limit on Extension

The parties to a suit under this chapter may not extend the deadlines set by the court under this subchapter by agreement or otherwise.

Added by Acts 1997, 75th Leg., ch. 600, § 17, eff. Sept. 1, 1997; Acts 1997, 75th Leg., ch. 603, § 12, eff. Jan. 1, 1997; Acts 1997, 75th Leg., ch. 1022, § 90, eff. Jan. 1, 1997. Amended by Acts 1999, 76th Leg., ch. 1390, § 48, eff. Sept. 1, 1999; Acts 2001, 77th Leg., ch. 1090, § 9, eff. Sept. 1, 2001; Acts 2007, 80th Leg., ch. 866, § 3, eff. June 15, 2007; Acts 2017, 85th Leg., ch. 317 (H.B. 7), § 28, eff. Sept. 1, 2017; Acts 2017, 85th Leg., ch. 319 (S.B. 11), § 13, eff. Sept. 1, 2017.

### § 263.403. Monitored Return of Child to Parent

(a) Notwithstanding Section 263.401, the court may retain jurisdiction and not dismiss the suit or render a final order as required by that section if the court renders a temporary order that:

(1) finds that retaining jurisdiction under this section is in the best interest of the child;

(2) orders the department to:

(A) return the child to the child's parent; or

(B) transition the child, according to a schedule determined by the department or court, from substitute care to the parent while the parent completes the remaining requirements imposed under a service plan and specified in the temporary order that are necessary for the child's return;

(3) orders the department to continue to serve as temporary managing conservator of the child; and

(4) orders the department to monitor the child's placement to ensure that the child is in a safe environment.

(a–1) Unless the court has granted an extension under Section 263.401(b), the department or the parent may request the court to retain jurisdiction for an additional six months as necessary for a parent to complete the remaining requirements under a service plan in a transition monitored return under Subsection (a)(2)(B).

(b) If the court renders an order under this section, the court shall:

(1) include in the order specific findings regarding the grounds for the order; and

(2) schedule a new date, not later than the 180th day after the date the temporary order is rendered, for dismissal of the suit unless a trial on the merits has commenced.

(c) If before the dismissal of the suit or the commencement of the trial on the merits a child placed with a parent under this section must be moved from that home by the department or the court renders a temporary order terminating the transition order issued under Subsection (a)(2)(B), the court shall, at the time of the move or order, schedule a new date for dismissal of the suit. The new dismissal date may not be later than the original dismissal date established under Section 263.401 or the 180th day after the date the child is moved or the order is rendered under this subsection, whichever date is later.

(d) If the court renders an order under this section, the court must include in the order specific findings regarding the grounds for the order.

Added by Acts 1997, 75th Leg., ch. 600, § 17, eff. Sept. 1, 1997; Acts 1997, 75th Leg., ch. 603, § 12, eff. Jan. 1, 1998; Acts 1997, 75th Leg., ch. 1022, § 90, eff. Jan. 1, 1998. Redesignated from V.T.C.A., Family Code § 263.402 by Acts 2001, 77th Leg., ch. 1090, § 9, eff. Sept. 1, 2001. Amended by Acts 2007, 80th Leg., ch. 866, § 4, eff. June 15, 2007; Acts 2017, 85th Leg., ch. 317 (H.B. 7), § 29, eff. Sept. 1, 2017; Acts 2021, 87th Leg., ch. 8 (H.B. 567), § 11, eff. Sept. 1, 2021.

Section 15 of Acts 2021, 87th Leg., ch. 8 (H.B. 567) provides:

"The changes in law made by this Act apply only to a suit filed by the Department of Family and Protective Services on or after the effective date [Sept. 1, 2021] of this Act. A suit filed by the department before that date is governed by the law in effect on the date the suit was filed, and the former law is continued in effect for that purpose."

### § 263.404. Final Order Appointing Department as Managing Conservator Without Terminating Parental Rights

(a) The court may render a final order appointing the department as managing conservator of the child without terminating the rights of the parent of the child if the court finds that:

(1) appointment of a parent as managing conservator would not be in the best interest of the child because the appointment would significantly impair the child's physical health or emotional development; and

(2) it would not be in the best interest of the child to appoint a relative of the child or another person as managing conservator.

(b) In determining whether the department should be appointed as managing conservator of the child without terminating the rights of a parent of the child, the court shall take the following factors into consideration:

(1) that the child will reach 18 years of age in not less than three years;

(2) that the child is 12 years of age or older and has expressed a strong desire against termination or has continuously expressed a strong desire against being adopted; and

(3) the needs and desires of the child.

Added by Acts 1997, 75th Leg., ch. 600, § 17, eff. Sept. 1, 1997. Redesignated from V.T.C.A., Family Code § 263.403 by Acts 2001, 77th Leg., ch. 1090, § 9, eff. Sept. 1, 2001. Amended by Acts 2015, 84th Leg., ch. 944 (S.B. 206), § 39, eff. Sept. 1, 2015.

### § 263.4041. Verification of Transition Plan

Notwithstanding Section 263.401, for a suit involving a child who is 14 years of age or older and whose permanency goal is another planned permanent living arrangement, the court shall verify that:

(1) the department has conducted an independent living skills assessment for the child as provided under Section 264.121(a–3);

(2) the department has addressed the goals identified in the child's permanency plan, including the child's housing plan, and the results of the independent living skills assessment;

(3) if the youth is 16 years of age or older, there is evidence that the department has provided the youth with the documents and information listed in Section 264.121(e); and

(4) if the youth is 18 years of age or older or has had the disabilities of minority removed, there is evidence that the department has provided the youth with the documents and information listed in Section 264.121(e–1).

Added by Acts 2017, 85th Leg., ch. 937 (S.B. 1758), § 4, eff. Sept. 1, 2017.

### § 263.405. Appeal of Final Order

(a) An appeal of a final order rendered under this subchapter is governed by the procedures for accelerated appeals in civil cases under the Texas Rules of Appellate Procedure. The appellate court shall render its final order or judgment with the least possible delay.

(b) A final order rendered under this subchapter must contain the following prominently displayed statement in boldfaced type, in capital letters, or underlined: "A PARTY AFFECTED BY THIS ORDER HAS THE RIGHT TO APPEAL. AN APPEAL IN A SUIT IN WHICH TERMINATION OF THE PARENT–CHILD RELATIONSHIP IS SOUGHT IS GOVERNED BY THE PROCEDURES FOR ACCELERATED APPEALS IN CIVIL CASES UNDER THE TEXAS RULES OF APPELLATE PROCEDURE. FAILURE TO FOLLOW THE TEXAS RULES OF APPELLATE PROCEDURE FOR ACCELERATED APPEALS MAY RESULT IN THE DISMISSAL OF THE APPEAL."

(b–1) Repealed by Acts 2011, 82nd Leg., ch. 75, § 5.

(c) The supreme court shall adopt rules accelerating the disposition by the appellate court and the supreme court of an appeal of a final order granting termination of the parent-child relationship rendered under this subchapter.

(d) to (i) Repealed by Acts 2011, 82nd Leg., ch. 75, § 5.

Added by Acts 2001, 77th Leg., ch. 1090, § 9, eff. Sept. 1, 2001. Amended by Acts 2005, 79th Leg., ch. 176, § 1, eff. Sept. 1, 2005; Acts 2007, 80th Leg., ch. 526, § 2, eff. June 16, 2007; Acts 2011, 82nd Leg., ch. 75 (H.B. 906), §§ 4, 5, eff. Sept. 1, 2011.

### § 263.4055. Supreme Court Rules

The supreme court by rule shall establish civil and appellate procedures to address:

(1) conflicts between the filing of a motion for new trial and the filing of an appeal of a final order rendered under this chapter; and

(2) the period, including an extension of at least 20 days, for a court reporter to submit the reporter's record of a trial to an appellate court following a final order rendered under this chapter.

Added by Acts 2017, 85th Leg., ch. 317 (H.B. 7), § 30, eff. Sept. 1, 2017.

### § 263.406. Court Information System

The Office of Court Administration of the Texas Judicial System shall consult with the courts presiding over cases brought by the department for the protection of children to develop an information system to track compliance with the requirements of this subchapter for the timely disposition of those cases.

Added by Acts 1997, 75th Leg., ch. 600, § 17, eff. Sept. 1, 1997. Redesignated from V.T.C.A., Family Code § 263.404 by Acts 2001, 77th Leg., ch. 1090, § 9, eff. Sept. 1, 2001.

### § 263.407. Final Order Appointing Department as Managing Conservator of Certain Abandoned Children; Termination of Parental Rights

(a) There is a rebuttable presumption that a parent who delivers a child to a designated emergency infant care provider in accordance with Subchapter D,[1] Chapter 262:

(1) is the child's biological parent;

(2) intends to relinquish parental rights and consents to the termination of parental rights with regard to the child; and

(3) intends to waive the right to notice of the suit terminating the parent-child relationship.

(a–1) A party that seeks to rebut a presumption in Subsection (a) may do so at any time before the parent-child relationship is terminated with regard to the child.

(b) If a person claims to be the parent of a child taken into possession under Subchapter D, Chapter 262, before the court renders a final order terminating the parental rights of the child's parents, the court shall order genetic testing for parentage determination unless parentage has previously been established. The court shall hold the petition for termination of the parent-child relationship in abeyance for a period not to exceed 60 days pending the results of the genetic testing.

(c) Before the court may render an order terminating parental rights with regard to a child taken into the department's custody under Section 262.303, the department must:

(1) verify with the National Crime Information Center and state and local law enforcement agencies that the child is not a missing child; and

(2) obtain a certificate of the search of the paternity registry under Subchapter E,[2] Chapter 160, not

earlier than the date the department estimates to be the 30th day after the child's date of birth.

Added by Acts 2001 77th Leg., ch. 809, § 6, eff. Sept. 1, 2001. Redesignated from V.T.C.A., Family Code § 263.405 by Acts 2003, 78th Leg., ch. 1275, § 2(54), eff. Sept. 1, 2003. Amended by Acts 2005, 79th Leg., ch. 620, § 2, eff. Sept. 1, 2005; Acts 2007, 80th Leg., ch. 1035, § 1, eff. June 15, 2007; Acts 2007, 80th Leg., ch. 1283, § 12, eff. Sept. 1, 2007.

[1] V.T.C.A., Family Code § 262.301 et seq.

[2] V.T.C.A., Family Code § 160.401 et seq.

### § 263.408. Requirements for Appointment of Nonparent as Managing Conservator

(a) In a suit in which the court appoints a nonparent as managing conservator of a child:

(1) the department must provide the nonparent with an explanation of the differences between appointment as a managing conservator of a child and adoption of a child, including specific statements informing the nonparent that:

(A) the nonparent's appointment conveys only the rights specified by the court order or applicable laws instead of the complete rights of a parent conveyed by adoption;

(B) a parent may be entitled to request visitation with the child or petition the court to appoint the parent as the child's managing conservator, notwithstanding the nonparent's appointment as managing conservator; and

(C) the nonparent's appointment as the child's managing conservator will not result in the eligibility of the nonparent and child for postadoption benefits; and

(2) in addition to the rights and duties provided under Section 153.371, the court order appointing the nonparent as managing conservator must include provisions that address the authority of the nonparent to:

(A) authorize immunization of the child or any other medical treatment that requires parental consent;

(B) obtain and maintain health insurance coverage for the child and automobile insurance coverage for the child, if appropriate;

(C) enroll the child in a day-care program or school, including prekindergarten;

(D) authorize the child to participate in school-related or extracurricular or social activities, including athletic activities;

(E) authorize the child to obtain a learner's permit, driver's license, or state-issued identification card;

(F) authorize employment of the child;

(G) apply for and receive public benefits for or on behalf of the child; and

(H) obtain legal services for the child and execute contracts or other legal documents for the child.

(b) The court must require evidence that the nonparent was informed of the rights and duties of a nonparent appointed as managing conservator of a child before the court renders an order appointing the nonparent as managing conservator of a child.

Added by Acts 2015, 84th Leg., ch. 182 (S.B. 314), § 1, eff. Sept. 1, 2015.

### § 263.409. Final Notification of Benefits Related to Kinship Verification

Before a court enters a final order naming a relative or another adult with a longstanding and significant relationship with a foster child as the permanent managing conservator for the child, the court shall verify that:

(1) the individual was offered the opportunity to become verified by a licensed child-placing agency to qualify for permanency care assistance benefits under Subchapter K, Chapter 264, and the individual declined the verification process and the permanency care assistance benefits; and

(2) the child-placing agency conducting the verification for the individual's permanency care assistance benefits has been notified of the individual's decision to decline the permanency care assistance benefits.

Added by Acts 2021, 87th Leg., ch. 621 (S.B. 1896), § 1, eff. June 14, 2021.

Section 35 of Acts 2021, 87th Leg., ch. 621 (S.B. 1896) provides:

"The Office of Community-Based Care Transition, the Department of Family and Protective Services, and the Health and Human Services Commission are required to implement this Act only if the legislature appropriates money specifically for that purpose. If the legislature does not appropriate money specifically for that purpose, the Office of Community-Based Care Transition, the Department of Family and Protective Services, and the Health and Human Services Commission may, but are not required to, implement this Act using other appropriations available for the purpose."

## SUBCHAPTER F. PERMANENCY HEARINGS AFTER FINAL ORDER

### § 263.501. Permanency Hearing After Final Order

(a) If the department has been named as a child's managing conservator in a final order that does not include termination of parental rights, the court shall conduct a permanency hearing after the final order is rendered at least once every six months until the department is no longer the child's managing conservator.

(b) If the department has been named as a child's managing conservator in a final order that terminates a parent's parental rights, the court shall conduct a permanency hearing not later than the 90th day after the date the court renders the final order. The court shall conduct additional permanency hearings at least once every six months until the department is no longer the child's managing conservator.

(c) Notice of each permanency hearing shall be given as provided by Section 263.0021 to each person entitled to notice of the hearing.

(d) Repealed by Acts 2015, 84th Leg., ch. 944 (S.B. 206), § 86(19).

(e) Repealed by Acts 2015, 84th Leg., ch. 944 (S.B. 206), § 86(19).

(f) The child shall attend each permanency hearing in accordance with Section 263.302.

(g) A court required to conduct permanency hearings for a child for whom the department has been appointed permanent managing conservator may not dismiss a suit affecting the parent-child relationship filed by the department regarding the child while the child is committed to the Texas Juvenile Justice Department or released under the supervision of the Texas Juvenile Justice Department, unless the child is adopted or permanent managing conservatorship of the child is awarded to an individual other than the department.

Added by Acts 1997, 75th Leg., ch. 600, § 17, eff. Sept. 1, 1997; Acts 1997, 75th Leg., ch. 603, § 12, eff. Jan. 1, 1998; Acts 1997, 75th Leg., ch. 1022, § 90, eff. Jan. 1, 1997. Amended by Acts 2001, 77th Leg., ch. 849, § 8, eff. Sept. 1, 2001; Acts 2007, 80th Leg., ch. 1304, § 2, eff. June 15, 2007; Acts 2009, 81st Leg., ch. 108, § 9, eff. May 23, 2009; Acts 2009, 81st Leg., ch. 1372, § 8, eff. June 19, 2009; Acts 2013, 83rd Leg., ch. 885 (H.B. 843), § 2, eff. Sept. 1, 2013; Acts 2015, 84th Leg., ch. 734 (H.B. 1549), § 86, eff. Sept. 1, 2015; Acts 2015, 84th Leg., ch. 944 (S.B. 206), §§ 41, 42, 86(19), eff. Sept. 1, 2015.

### § 263.502. Permanency Progress Report After Final Order

(a) Not later than the 10th day before the date set for a permanency hearing after a final order is rendered, the department shall file a permanency progress report with the court and provide a copy to each person entitled to notice under Section 263.0021.

(a–1) The permanency progress report must contain:

(1) information necessary for the court to conduct the permanency hearing and make its findings and determinations under Section 263.5031;

(2) information on significant events, as defined by Section 264.018; and

(3) any additional information the department determines is appropriate or that is requested by the court and relevant to the court's findings and determinations under Section 263.5031.

(a–2) For good cause shown, the court may:

(1) order a different deadline for filing the permanency progress report; or

(2) waive the reporting requirement for a specific hearing.

(b) Repealed by Acts 2015, 84th Leg., ch. 944 (S.B. 206), § 86(20).

(c) Repealed by Acts 2015, 84th Leg., ch. 944 (S.B. 206), § 86(20).

(d) Repealed by Acts 2015, 84th Leg., ch. 944 (S.B. 206), § 86(20).

Added by Acts 1997, 75th Leg., ch. 600, § 17, eff. Sept. 1, 1997; Acts 1997, 75th Leg., ch. 603, § 12, eff. Jan. 1, 1998; Acts 1997, 75th Leg., ch. 1022, § 90, eff. Jan. 1, 1998. Amended by Acts 2005, 79th Leg., ch. 268, § 1.41(a), eff. Sept. 1, 2005; Acts 2009, 81st Leg., ch. 108, § 10, eff. May 23, 2009; Acts 2009, 81st Leg., ch. 1372, § 9, eff. June 19, 2009; Acts 2011, 82nd Leg., ch. 91 (S.B. 1303), § 9.002, eff. Sept. 1, 2011; Acts 2013, 83rd Leg., ch. 1324 (S.B. 534), § 3, eff. Sept. 1, 2013; Acts 2015, 84th Leg., ch. 1 (S.B. 219), § 1.182, eff. April 2, 2015; Acts 2015, 84th Leg., ch. 944 (S.B. 206), §§ 43, 44, 86(20), eff. Sept. 1, 2015.

### § 263.503. Repealed by Acts 2021, 87th Leg., ch. 683 (S.B. 2058), § 2, eff. Sept. 1, 2021

Section 3 of Acts 2021, 87th Leg., ch. 683 (H.B. 2058) provides:

"The changes in law made by this Act apply only to a permanency hearing conducted under Chapter 263, Family Code, on or after the effective date [Sept. 1, 2021] of this Act. A permanency hearing conducted before the effective date of this Act is governed by the law in effect on the date the hearing was conducted, and the former law is continued in effect for that purpose."

### § 263.5031. Permanency Hearings Following Final Order

(a) At each permanency hearing after the court renders a final order, the court shall:

(1) identify all persons and parties present at the hearing;

(2) review the efforts of the department or other agency in notifying persons entitled to notice under Section 263.0021;

(3) for a child placed with a relative of the child or other designated caregiver, review the efforts of the department to inform the caregiver of:

(A) the option to become verified by a licensed child-placing agency to operate an agency foster home, if applicable; and

(B) the permanency care assistance program under Subchapter K, Chapter 264;[1] and

(4) review the permanency progress report to determine:

(A) the safety and well-being of the child and whether the child's needs, including any medical or special needs, are being adequately addressed;

(B) whether the child has been provided the opportunity, in a developmentally appropriate manner, to identify any adult, particularly an adult residing in the child's community, who could be a relative or designated caregiver for the child;

(C) whether the department placed the child with a relative or designated caregiver and the continuing necessity and appropriateness of the placement of the child, including with respect to a child who has been placed outside of this state, whether the placement continues to be in the best interest of the child;

(D) if the child is placed in institutional care, whether efforts have been made to ensure that the child is placed in the least restrictive environment consistent with the child's best interest and special needs;

(E) the appropriateness of the primary and alternative permanency goals for the child, whether the department has made reasonable efforts to finalize the permanency plan, including the concurrent permanency goals, in effect for the child, and whether:

(i) the department has exercised due diligence in attempting to place the child for adoption if parental rights to the child have been terminated and the child is eligible for adoption; or

(ii) another permanent placement, including appointing a relative as permanent managing conservator or returning the child to a parent, is appropriate for the child;

(F) for a child whose permanency goal is another planned permanent living arrangement:

(i) the desired permanency outcome for the child, by asking the child;

(ii) whether, as of the date of the hearing, another planned permanent living arrangement is the best permanency plan for the child and, if so, provide compelling reasons why it continues to not be in the best interest of the child to:

(a) return home;

(b) be placed for adoption;

(c) be placed with a legal guardian; or

(d) be placed with a fit and willing relative;

(iii) whether the department has conducted an independent living skills assessment under Section 264.121(a–3);

(iv) whether the department has addressed the goals identified in the child's permanency plan, including the child's housing plan, and the results of the independent living skills assessment;

(v) if the youth is 16 years of age or older, whether there is evidence that the department has provided the youth with the documents and information listed in Section 264.121(e); and

(vi) if the youth is 18 years of age or older or has had the disabilities of minority removed, whether there is evidence that the department has provided the youth with the documents and information listed in Section 264.121(e–1);

(G) if the child is 14 years of age or older, whether services that are needed to assist the child in transitioning from substitute care to independent living are available in the child's community;

(H) whether the child is receiving appropriate medical care and has been provided the opportunity, in a developmentally appropriate manner, to express the child's opinion on any medical care provided;

(I) for a child receiving psychotropic medication, whether the child:

(i) has been provided appropriate nonpharmacological interventions, therapies, or strategies to meet the child's needs; or

(ii) has been seen by the prescribing physician, physician assistant, or advanced practice nurse at least once every 90 days;

(J) whether an education decision-maker for the child has been identified, the child's education needs and goals have been identified and addressed, and there are major changes in the child's school performance or there have been serious disciplinary events;

(K) for a child for whom the department has been named managing conservator in a final order that does not include termination of parental rights, whether to order the department to provide services to a parent for not more than six months after the date of the permanency hearing if:

(i) the child has not been placed with a relative or other individual, including a foster parent, who is seeking permanent managing conservatorship of the child; and

(ii) the court determines that further efforts at reunification with a parent are:

(a) in the best interest of the child; and

(b) likely to result in the child's safe return to the child's parent; and

(L) whether the department has identified a family or other caring adult who has made a permanent commitment to the child.

(b) In addition to the requirements of Subsection (a), at each permanency hearing after the court renders a final order, the court shall review the department's efforts to ensure the child has regular, ongoing opportunities to engage in age-appropriate normalcy activities, including activities not listed in the child's service plan.

Added by Acts 2015, 84th Leg., ch. 944 (S.B. 206), § 45, eff. Sept. 1, 2015. Amended by Acts 2017, 85th Leg., ch. 317 (H.B. 7), § 31, eff. Sept. 1, 2017; Acts 2017, 85th Leg., ch. 937 (S.B. 1758), § 5, eff. Sept. 1, 2017; Acts 2019, 86th Leg., ch. 375 (H.B. 1884), § 5, eff. Sept. 1, 2019; Acts 2019, 86th Leg., ch. 1294 (H.B. 3390), § 11, eff. June 14, 2019; Acts 2021, 87th Leg., ch. 683 (H.B. 2058), § 1, eff. Sept. 1, 2021.

1 V.T.C.A., Family Code § 264.851 et seq.

Section 3 of Acts 2021, 87th Leg., ch. 683 (H.B. 2058) provides:

"The changes in law made by this Act apply only to a permanency hearing conducted under Chapter 263, Family Code, on or after the effective date [Sept. 1, 2021] of this Act. A permanency hearing conducted before the effective date of this Act is governed by the law in effect on the date the hearing was conducted, and the former law is continued in effect for that purpose."

## SUBCHAPTER G. EXTENDED JURISDICTION AFTER CHILD'S 18TH BIRTHDAY

### § 263.601. Definitions

In this subchapter:

(1) "Extended foster care" means a residential living arrangement in which a young adult voluntarily delegates to the department responsibility for the young adult's placement and care and in which the young adult resides with a foster parent or other residential services provider that is:

(A) licensed or approved by the department or verified by a licensed or certified child-placing agency; and

(B) paid under a contract with the department.

(2) "Guardianship services" means the services provided by the Department of Aging and Disability Services under Subchapter E, Chapter 161, Human Resources Code.

(3) "Institution" means a residential facility that is operated, licensed, registered, certified, or verified by a state agency other than the department. The term includes a residential service provider under a Medicaid waiver program authorized under Section 1915(c) of the federal Social Security Act that provides services at a residence other than the young adult's own home.

(3–a) "Trial independence" means the status assigned to a young adult under Section 263.6015.

(4) "Young adult" means a person who was in the conservatorship of the department on the day before the person's 18th birthday.

Added by Acts 2009, 81st Leg., ch. 96, § 1, eff. May 23, 2009. Amended by Acts 2011, 82nd Leg., 1st C.S., ch. 3 (H.B. 79), § 11.01, eff. Sept. 28, 2011; Acts 2011, 82nd Leg., 1st C.S., ch. 4 (S.B. 1), § 63.01, eff. Sept. 28, 2011; Acts 2013, 83rd Leg., ch. 456 (S.B. 886), § 1, eff. Sept. 1, 2013.

### § 263.6015. Trial Independence

(a) A young adult is assigned trial independence status when the young adult:

(1) does not enter extended foster care at the time of the young adult's 18th birthday; or

(2) exits extended foster care before the young adult's 21st birthday.

(b) Except as provided by Subsection (c), a court order is not required for a young adult to be assigned trial independence status. Trial independence is mandatory for a period of at least six months beginning on:

(1) the date of the young adult's 18th birthday for a young adult described by Subsection (a)(1); or

(2) the date the young adult exits extended foster care.

(c) A court may order trial independence status extended for a period that exceeds the mandatory period under Subsection (b) but does not exceed one year from the date the period under Subsection (b) commences.

(d) Except as provided by Subsection (e), a young adult who enters or reenters extended foster care after a period of trial independence must complete a new period of trial independence as provided by Subsection (b)(2).

(e) The trial independence status of a young adult ends on the young adult's 21st birthday.

Added by Acts 2013, 83rd Leg., ch. 456 (S.B. 886), § 2, eff. Sept. 1, 2013.

### § 263.602. Extended Jurisdiction

(a) Except as provided by Subsection (f), a court that had jurisdiction over a young adult on the day before the young adult's 18th birthday continues to have extended jurisdiction over the young adult and shall retain the case on the court's docket while the young adult is in extended foster care and during trial independence as described by Section 263.6015.

(b) A court with extended jurisdiction over a young adult in extended foster care shall conduct extended foster care review hearings every six months for the purpose of reviewing and making findings regarding:

(1) whether the young adult's living arrangement is safe and appropriate and whether the department has made reasonable efforts to place the young adult in the least restrictive environment necessary to meet the young adult's needs;

(2) whether the department is making reasonable efforts to finalize the permanency plan that is in effect for the young adult, including a permanency plan for independent living;

(3) whether, for a young adult whose permanency plan is independent living:

(A) the young adult participated in the development of the plan of service;

(B) the young adult's plan of service reflects the independent living skills and appropriate services needed to achieve independence by the projected date; and

(C) the young adult continues to make reasonable progress in developing the skills needed to achieve independence by the projected date; and

(4) whether additional services that the department is authorized to provide are needed to meet the needs of the young adult.

(c) Not later than the 10th day before the date set for a hearing under this section, the department shall file with the court a copy of the young adult's plan of service and a report that addresses the issues described by Subsection (b).

(d) Notice of an extended foster care review hearing shall be given as provided by Rule 21a, Texas Rules of Civil Procedure, to the following persons, each of whom has a right to present evidence and be heard at the hearing:

(1) the young adult who is the subject of the suit;

(2) the department;

(3) the foster parent with whom the young adult is placed and the administrator of a child-placing agency responsible for placing the young adult, if applicable;

(4) the director of the residential child-care facility or other approved provider with whom the young adult is placed, if applicable;

(5) each parent of the young adult whose parental rights have not been terminated and who is still actively involved in the life of the young adult;

(6) a legal guardian of the young adult, if applicable; and

(7) the young adult's attorney ad litem, guardian ad litem, and volunteer advocate, the appointment of which has not been previously dismissed by the court.

(e) If, after reviewing the young adult's plan of service and the report filed under Subsection (c), and any additional testimony and evidence presented at the review hearing, the court determines that the young adult is entitled to additional services, the court may order the department to take appropriate action to ensure that the young adult receives those services.

(f) Unless the court extends its jurisdiction over a young adult beyond the end of trial independence as provided by Section 263.6021(a) or 263.603(a), the court's extended jurisdiction over a young adult as described in Subsection (a) terminates on the earlier of:

(1) the last day of the month in which trial independence ends; or

(2) the young adult's 21st birthday.

(g) A court with extended jurisdiction described by this section is not required to conduct periodic hearings described in this section for a young adult during trial independence and may not compel a young adult who has elected to not enter or has exited extended foster care to attend a court hearing. A court with extended jurisdiction during trial independence may, at the request of a young adult, conduct a hearing described by Subsection (b) or by Section 263.6021 to review any transitional living services the young adult is receiving during trial independence.

Added by Acts 2009, 81st Leg., ch. 96, § 1, eff. May 23, 2009. Amended by Acts 2011, 82nd Leg., 1st C.S., ch. 3 (H.B. 79), § 11.02, eff. Sept. 28, 2011; Acts 2011, 82nd Leg., 1st C.S., ch. 4 (S.B. 1), § 63.02, eff. Sept. 28, 2011; Acts 2013, 83rd Leg., ch. 456 (S.B. 886), § 3, eff. Sept. 1, 2013.

### § 263.6021. Voluntary Extended Jurisdiction for Young Adult Receiving Transitional Living Services

(a) Notwithstanding Section 263.602, a court that had jurisdiction over a young adult on the day before the young adult's 18th birthday may, at the young adult's request, render an order that extends the court's jurisdiction beyond the end of trial independence if the young adult receives transitional living services from the department.

(b) Unless the young adult reenters extended foster care before the end of the court's extended jurisdiction described by Subsection (a), the extended jurisdiction of the court under this section terminates on the earlier of:

(1) the young adult's 21st birthday; or

(2) the date the young adult withdraws consent to the extension of the court's jurisdiction in writing or in court.

(c) At the request of a young adult who is receiving transitional living services from the department and who consents to voluntary extension of the court's jurisdiction under this section, the court may hold a hearing to review the services the young adult is receiving.

(d) Before a review hearing scheduled under this section, the department must file with the court a report summarizing the young adult's transitional living services plan, services being provided to the young adult under that plan, and the young adult's progress in achieving independence.

(e) If, after reviewing the report and any additional testimony and evidence presented at the hearing, the court determines that the young adult is entitled to additional services, the court may order the department to take appropriate action to ensure that the young adult receives those services.

Added by Acts 2011, 82nd Leg., 1st C.S., ch. 3 (H.B. 79), § 11.03, eff. Sept. 28, 2011; Acts 2011, 82nd Leg., 1st C.S., ch. 4 (S.B. 1), § 63.03, eff. Sept. 28, 2011. Amended by Acts 2013, 83rd Leg., ch. 456 (S.B. 886), § 4, eff. Sept. 1, 2013.

### § 263.603. Extended Jurisdiction to Determine Guardianship

(a) Notwithstanding Section 263.6021, if the court believes that a young adult may be incapacitated as defined by Section 1002.017(2), Estates Code, the court may extend its jurisdiction on its own motion without the young adult's consent to allow the department to refer the young adult to the Department of Aging and Disability Services for guardianship services as required by Section 48.209, Human Resources Code.

(b) The extended jurisdiction of the court under this section terminates on the earliest of the date:

(1) the Department of Aging and Disability Services determines a guardianship is not appropriate under Chapter 161, Human Resources Code;

(2) a court with probate jurisdiction denies the application to appoint a guardian; or

(3) a guardian is appointed and qualifies under the Estates Code.

(c) If the Department of Aging and Disability Services determines a guardianship is not appropriate, or the court with probate jurisdiction denies the application to appoint a guardian, the court under Subsection (a) may continue to extend its jurisdiction over the young adult only as provided by Section 263.602 or 263.6021.

(d) Notwithstanding any other provision of this subchapter, a young adult for whom a guardian is appointed and qualifies is not considered to be in extended foster care or trial independence and the court's jurisdiction ends on the date the guardian for the young adult is appointed and qualifies unless the guardian requests the extended jurisdiction of the court under Section 263.604.

Added by Acts 2009, 81st Leg., ch. 96, § 1, eff. May 23, 2009. Amended by Acts 2011, 82nd Leg., 1st C.S., ch. 3 (H.B. 79), § 11.04, eff. Sept. 28, 2011; Acts 2011, 82nd Leg., 1st C.S., ch. 4 (S.B. 1), § 63.04, eff. Sept. 28, 2011; Acts 2013, 83rd Leg., ch. 456 (S.B. 886), § 5, eff. Sept. 1, 2013; Acts 2017, 85th Leg., ch. 324 (S.B. 1488), § 22.020, eff. Sept. 1, 2017.

### § 263.604. Guardian's Consent to Extended Jurisdiction

(a) A guardian appointed for a young adult may request that the court extend the court's jurisdiction over the young adult.

(b) A court that extends its jurisdiction over a young adult for whom a guardian is appointed may not issue an order that conflicts with an order entered by the probate court that has jurisdiction over the guardianship proceeding.

Added by Acts 2009, 81st Leg., ch. 96, § 1, eff. May 23, 2009.

### § 263.605. Continued or Renewed Appointment of Attorney ad Litem, Guardian ad Litem, or Volunteer Advocate

A court with extended jurisdiction under this subchapter may continue or renew the appointment of an attorney ad litem, guardian ad litem, or volunteer advocate for the young adult to assist the young adult in accessing services the young adult is entitled to receive from the department or any other public or private service provider.

Added by Acts 2009, 81st Leg., ch. 96, § 1, eff. May 23, 2009.

### § 263.606. Duties of Attorney or Guardian ad Litem

An attorney ad litem or guardian ad litem appointed for a young adult who receives services in the young adult's own home from a service provider or resides in an institution that is licensed, certified, or verified by a state agency other than the department shall assist the young adult as necessary to ensure that the young adult receives appropriate services from the service provider or institution, or the state agency that regulates the service provider or institution.

Added by Acts 2009, 81st Leg., ch. 96, § 1, eff. May 23, 2009.

### § 263.607. Prohibited Appointments and Orders

(a) The court may not appoint the department or the Department of Aging and Disability Services as the managing conservator or guardian of a young adult.

(b) A court may not order the department to provide a service to a young adult unless the department:

(1) is authorized to provide the service under state law; and

(2) is appropriated money to provide the service in an amount sufficient to comply with the court order and the department's obligations to other young adults for whom the department is required to provide similar services.

Added by Acts 2009, 81st Leg., ch. 96, § 1, eff. May 23, 2009.

### § 263.608. Rights of Young Adult

A young adult who consents to the continued jurisdiction of the court has the same rights as any other adult of the same age.

Added by Acts 2009, 81st Leg., ch. 96, § 1, eff. May 23, 2009.

### § 263.609. Repealed by Acts 2011, 82nd Leg., 1st C.S., ch. 3 (H.B. 79), § 11.05, eff. Sept. 28, 2011; Acts 2011, 82nd Leg., 1st C.S., ch. 4 (S.B. 1), § 63.05, eff. Sept. 28, 2011

## CHAPTER 264. CHILD WELFARE SERVICES

### SUBCHAPTER A. GENERAL PROVISIONS



### SUBCHAPTER B. FOSTER CARE

SUBCHAPTER B–1. COMMUNITY–BASED CARE



SUBCHAPTER C. CHILD AND FAMILY SERVICES



SUBCHAPTER D. SERVICES TO AT–RISK YOUTH



SUBCHAPTER E. CHILDREN'S ADVOCACY CENTERS



SUBCHAPTER F. CHILD FATALITY REVIEW AND INVESTIGATION

## SUBCHAPTER A. GENERAL PROVISIONS

### § 264.001. Definitions

In this chapter:

(1) "Age-appropriate normalcy activity" means an activity or experience:

(A) that is generally accepted as suitable for a child's age or level of maturity or that is determined to be developmentally appropriate for a child based on the development of cognitive, emotional, physical, and behavioral capacities that are typical for the age or age group; and

(B) in which a child who is not in the conservatorship of the state is generally allowed to participate, including extracurricular activities, in-school and out-of-school social activities, cultural and enrichment activities, and employment opportunities.

(1–a) "Department" means the Department of Family and Protective Services.

(2) Repealed by Acts 2017, 85th Leg., ch. 316 (H.B. 5), § 36(1).

(3) Repealed by Acts 2017, 85th Leg., ch. 316 (H.B. 5), § 36(1).

(3–a) "Least restrictive setting" means a placement for a child that, in comparison to all other available placements, is the most family-like setting.

(4) "Residential child-care facility" has the meaning assigned by Section 42.002, Human Resources Code.

(5) "Standard of care of a reasonable and prudent parent" means the standard of care that a parent of reasonable judgment, skill, and caution would exer-

cise in addressing the health, safety, and welfare of a child while encouraging the emotional and developmental growth of the child, taking into consideration:

(A) the overall health and safety of the child;

(B) the child's age, maturity, and development level;

(C) the best interest of the child based on the caregiver's knowledge of the child;

(D) the appropriateness of a proposed activity and any potential risk factors;

(E) the behavioral history of the child and the child's ability to safely participate in a proposed activity;

(F) the importance of encouraging the child's social, emotional, and developmental growth; and

(G) the importance of providing the child with the most family-like living experience possible.

Added by Acts 1995, 74th Leg., ch. 20, § 1, eff. April 20, 1995. Amended by Acts 2005, 79th Leg., ch. 268, § 1.42, eff. Sept. 1, 2005; Acts 2015, 84th Leg., ch. 262 (S.B. 1407), § 4, eff. Sept. 1, 2015; Acts 2017, 85th Leg., ch. 316 (H.B. 5), § 36(1), eff. Sept. 1, 2017; Acts 2017, 85th Leg., ch. 1022 (H.B. 1542), § 3, eff. Sept. 1, 2017.

### § 264.0011. Reference to Executive Commissioner or Commission

In this chapter:

(1) a reference to the executive commissioner or the executive commissioner of the Health and Human Services Commission means the commissioner of the department; and

(2) a reference to the commission or the Health and Human Services Commission means the department.

Added by Acts 2017, 85th Leg., ch. 316 (H.B. 5), § 12, eff. Sept. 1, 2017.

### § 264.002. Specific Appropriation Required

(a) Repealed by Acts 2015, 84th Leg., ch. 944 (S.B. 206), § 86(22).

(b) Repealed by Acts 2015, 84th Leg., ch. 944 (S.B. 206), § 86(22).

(c) Repealed by Acts 2015, 84th Leg., ch. 944 (S.B. 206), § 86(22).

(d) Repealed by Acts 2015, 84th Leg., ch. 944 (S.B. 206), § 86(22).

(e) The department may not spend state funds to accomplish the purposes of this subtitle unless the funds have been specifically appropriated for those purposes.

Added by Acts 1995, 74th Leg., ch. 20, § 1, eff. April 20, 1995. Amended by Acts 2015, 84th Leg., ch. 944 (S.B. 206), §§ 46, 47, 86(22), eff. Sept. 1, 2015.

### § 264.003. Repealed by Acts 2001, 77th Leg., ch. 114, § 3, eff. Sept. 1, 2001

### § 264.004. Allocation of State Funds

(a) The department shall establish a method of allocating state funds for children's protective services programs that encourages and rewards the contribution of funds or services from all persons, including local governmental entities.

(b) Except as provided by this subsection, if a contribution of funds or services is made to support a children's protective services program in a particular county, the department shall use the contribution to benefit that program. The department may use the contribution for another purpose only if the commissioners court of the county gives the department written permission.

(c) The department may use state and federal funds to provide benefits or services to children and families who are otherwise eligible for the benefits or services, including foster care, adoption assistance, medical assistance, family reunification services, and other child protective services and related benefits without regard to the immigration status of the child or the child's family.

(d) The Health and Human Services Commission may use money appropriated from the trafficked persons program account established under Section 50.0153, Health and Safety Code, to establish, maintain, and operate facilities to provide care and recovery and to ensure the general well-being of children and youth who are victims of an offense of trafficking of persons as defined by Article 56B.003, Code of Criminal Procedure.

Added by Acts 1995, 74th Leg., ch. 20, § 1, eff. April 20, 1995. Amended by Acts 1997, 75th Leg., ch. 575, § 23, eff. Sept. 1, 1997; Acts 2021, 87th Leg., ch. 704 (H.B. 2633), § 3, eff. Sept. 1, 2021.

### § 264.005. County Child Welfare Boards

(a) The commissioners court of a county may appoint a child welfare board for the county. The commissioners court and the department shall determine the size of the board and the qualifications of its members. However, a board must have not less than seven and not more than 15 members, and the members must be residents of the county. The members shall serve at the pleasure of the commissioners court and may be removed by the court for just cause. The members serve without compensation.

(b) With the approval of the department, two or more counties may establish a joint child welfare board if that action is found to be more practical in accomplishing the purposes of this chapter. A board representing more than one county has the same powers as a board representing a single county and is subject to the same conditions and liabilities.

(c) The members of a county child welfare board shall select a presiding officer and shall perform the duties required by the commissioners court and the department to accomplish the purposes of this chapter.

(d) A county child welfare board is an entity of the department for purposes of providing coordinated state and local public welfare services for children and their families and for the coordinated use of federal, state, and local funds for these services. The child welfare board shall work with the commissioners court.

(e) A county child welfare board is a governmental unit for the purposes of Chapter 101, Civil Practice and Remedies Code.

(f) A county child protective services board member may receive information that is confidential under Section 40.005, Human Resources Code, or Section 261.201 when the board member is acting in the member's official capacity.

(g) A child welfare board may conduct a closed meeting under Section 551.101, Government Code, to discuss, consider, or act on a matter that is confidential under Section 40.005, Human Resources Code, or Section 261.201.

Added by Acts 1995, 74th Leg., ch. 20, § 1, eff. April 20, 1995. Amended by Acts 1997, 75th Leg., ch. 575, § 24, eff. Sept. 1, 1997.

### § 264.006. County Funds

The commissioners court of a county may appropriate funds from its general fund or any other fund for the administration of its county child welfare board. The court may provide for services to and support of children in need of protection and care without regard to the immigration status of the child or the child's family.

Added by Acts 1995, 74th Leg., ch. 20, § 1, eff. April 20, 1995. Amended by Acts 1997, 75th Leg., ch. 575, § 25, eff. Sept. 1, 1997.

### § 264.007. Repealed by Acts 2015, 84th Leg., ch. 1 (S.B. 219) § 1.203(7), eff. April 2, 2015

### § 264.008. Child Welfare Service Fund

The child welfare service fund is a special fund in the state treasury. The fund shall be used to administer the child welfare services provided by the department.

Added by Acts 1995, 74th Leg., ch. 20, § 1, eff. April 20, 1995.

### § 264.009. Legal Representation of Department

(a) Except as provided by Subsection (b), (c), or (f), in any action under this code, the department shall be represented in court by the county attorney of the county where the action is brought, unless the district attorney or criminal district attorney of the county elects to provide representation.

(b) If the county attorney, district attorney, or criminal district attorney is unable to represent the department in an action under this code because of a conflict of interest or because special circumstances exist, the attorney general shall represent the department in the action.

(c) If the attorney general is unable to represent the department in an action under this code, the attorney general shall deputize an attorney who has contracted with the department under Subsection (d) or an attorney employed by the department under Subsection (e) to represent the department in the action.

(d) Subject to the approval of the attorney general, the department may contract with a private attorney to represent the department in an action under this code.

(e) The department may employ attorneys to represent the department in an action under this code.

(f) In a county with a population of 2.8 million or more, in an action under this code, the department shall be represented in court by the attorney who represents the state in civil cases in the district or county court of the county where the action is brought. If such attorney is unable to represent the department in an action under this code because of a conflict of interest or because special circumstances exist, the attorney general shall represent the department in the action.

Added by Acts 1995, 74th Leg., ch. 20, § 1, eff. April 20, 1995. Amended by Acts 1995, 74th Leg., ch. 751, § 116, eff. Sept. 1, 1995; Acts 1997, 75th Leg., ch. 1022, § 91, eff. Sept. 1, 1997.

### § 264.0091. Use of Teleconferencing and Videoconferencing Technology

Subject to the availability of funds, the department, in cooperation with district and county courts, shall expand the use of teleconferencing and videoconferencing to facilitate participation by medical experts, children, and other individuals in court proceedings, including children for whom the department or a licensed child-placing agency has been appointed managing conservator and who are committed to the Texas Juvenile Justice Department.

Added by Acts 2005, 79th Leg., ch. 268, § 1.43, eff. Sept. 1, 2005. Amended by Acts 2009, 81st Leg., ch. 108, § 12, eff. May 23, 2009; Acts 2015, 84th Leg., ch. 1 (S.B. 219), § 1.184, eff. April 2, 2015.

### § 264.010. Child Abuse Plan; Limitation on Expenditure of Funds

(a) Funds appropriated for protective services, child and family services, and the purchased service system for the department may only be spent on or after March 1, 1996, in a county that provides the department with a child abuse prevention and protection plan. If a plan is not submitted to the department under this section, the department shall document the county's failure to submit a plan and may spend appropriated funds in the county to carry out the department's duties under this subtitle.

(b) A child abuse prevention and protection plan may be submitted by the governing body of a county or of a regional council of governments in which the county is an active participant.

(c) The department may not require a child abuse prevention and protection plan to exceed five double-spaced letter-size pages. The county or council of governments may voluntarily provide a longer plan.

(d) A child abuse prevention and protection plan must:

(1) specify the manner of communication between entities who are parties to the plan, including the department, the commission, local law enforcement agencies, the county and district attorneys, members of the medical and social service community, foster parents, and child advocacy groups; and

(2) provide other information concerning the prevention and investigation of child abuse in the area for which the plan is adopted.

Added by Acts 1995, 74th Leg., ch. 943, § 6, eff. Sept. 1, 1995. Amended by Acts 2015, 84th Leg., ch. 1 (S.B. 219), § 1.185, eff. April 2, 2015.

### § 264.011. Local Accounts

(a) The department may establish and maintain local bank or savings accounts for a child who is under the managing conservatorship of the department as necessary to administer funds received in trust for or on behalf of the child.

(b) Funds maintained in an account under this section may be used by the department to support the child, including for the payment of foster care expenses, or may be paid to a person providing care for the child.

Added by Acts 1997, 75th Leg., ch. 575, § 26, eff. Sept. 1, 1997.

### § 264.0111. Money Earned by Child

(a) A child for whom the department has been appointed managing conservator and who has been placed by the department in a residential child-care facility as defined by Chapter 42, Human Resources Code, is entitled to keep any money earned by the child during the time of the child's placement.

(b) The child may deposit the money earned by the child in a bank or savings account subject to the sole management and control of the child as provided by Section 34.305, Finance Code. The child is the sole and absolute owner of the deposit account.

(c) If a child earns money as described by this section and is returned to the child's parent or guardian, the child's parent or guardian may not interfere with the child's authority to control, transfer, draft on, or make a withdrawal from the account.

(d) In this section, a reference to money earned by a child includes any interest that accrues on the money.

(e) The executive commissioner may adopt rules to implement this section.

Added by Acts 2001, 77th Leg., ch. 964, § 3, eff. Sept. 1, 2001. Amended by Acts 2015, 84th Leg., ch. 1 (S.B. 219), § 1.186, eff. April 2, 2015; Acts 2017, 85th Leg., ch. 317 (H.B. 7), § 32, eff. Sept. 1, 2017.

### § 264.012. Repealed by Acts 2015, 84th Leg., ch. 944 (S.B. 206), § 86(23), eff. Sept. 1, 2015

### § 264.0121. Notice to Legislators of Foster Child's Death

Not later than the fifth day after the date the department is notified of the death of a child for whom the department has been appointed managing conservator, the department shall provide the information described by Section 261.203(a) for the child to the state senators and state representatives who represent:

(1) the county in which the child's placement at the time of the child's death was located; and

(2) the county in which a suit affecting the parent-child relationship involving the child is pending.

Added by Acts 2015, 84th Leg., ch. 722 (H.B. 1309), § 2, eff. June 17, 2015.

### § 264.013. Exchange of Information with other States

Subject to the availability of funds, the department shall enter into agreements with other states to allow for the exchange of information relating to a child for whom the department is or was the managing conservator. The information may include the child's health passport and education passport.

Added by Acts 2005, 79th Leg., ch. 268, § 1.44, eff. Sept. 1, 2005.

### § 264.014. Redesignated as V.T.C.A, Family Code § 264.121(e–1) and amended by Acts 2015, 84th Leg., ch. 944 (S.B. 206), § 56, eff. Sept. 1, 2015

### § 264.0145. Release of Case Record

(a) In this section, "case record" means those files, reports, records, communications, audio recordings, video recordings, or working papers under the custody and control of the department that are collected, developed, or used:

(1) in a child abuse or neglect investigation; or

(2) in providing services as a result of an investigation, including substitute care services for a child.

(b) The executive commissioner by rule shall establish guidelines that prioritize requests to release case records, including those made by an adult previously in the department's managing conservatorship.

(c) The department is not required to release a copy of the case record except as provided by law and department rule.

Added by Acts 2011, 82nd Leg., ch. 568 (H.B. 3234), § 1, eff. Sept. 1, 2011. Amended by Acts 2013, 83rd Leg., ch. 1069 (H.B. 3259), § 2, eff. Sept. 1, 2013; Acts 2015, 84th Leg., ch. 1 (S.B. 219), § 1.187, eff. April 2, 2015.

### § 264.015. Training

(a) The department shall include training in trauma-informed programs and services in any training the department provides to foster parents, adoptive parents, kinship caregivers, department caseworkers, and department supervisors. The department shall pay for the training provided under this subsection with gifts, donations, and grants and any federal money available through the Fostering Connections to Success and Increasing Adoptions Act of 2008 (Pub. L. No. 110–351). The department shall annually evaluate the effectiveness of the training provided under this subsection to ensure progress toward a trauma-informed system of care.

(b) The department shall require department caseworkers and department supervisors to complete an annual refresher training course in trauma-informed programs and services.

(c) To the extent that resources are available, the department shall assist the following entities in developing training in trauma-informed programs and services and in locating money and other resources to assist the entities in providing trauma-informed programs and services:

(1) court-appointed special advocate programs;

(2) children's advocacy centers;

(3) local community mental health centers created under Section 534.001, Health and Safety Code; and

(4) domestic violence shelters.

Added by Acts 2009, 81st Leg., ch. 1118, § 5, eff. Sept. 1, 2009. Amended by Acts 2011, 82nd Leg., ch. 371 (S.B. 219), § 1, eff. Sept. 1, 2011.

### § 264.016. Repealed by Acts 2015, 84th Leg., ch. 944 (S.B. 206), § 86(24), eff. Sept. 1, 2015

### § 264.017. Required Reporting

(a) The department shall prepare and disseminate a report of statistics by county relating to key performance measures and data elements for child protection.

(b) The department shall provide the report required by Subsection (a) to the legislature and shall publish the report and make the report available electronically to the public not later than February 1 of each year. The report must include, with respect to the preceding year:

(1) information on the number and disposition of reports of child abuse and neglect received by the department;

(2) information on the number of clients for whom the department took protective action, including investigations, alternative responses, and court-ordered removals;

(3) information on the number of clients for whom the department provided services in each program administered by the child protective services division, including investigations, alternative responses, family-based safety services, conservatorship, post-adoption services, and transitional living services;

(4) the number of children in this state who died as a result of child abuse or neglect;

(5) the number of children described by Subdivision (4) for whom the department was the children's managing conservator at the time of death;

(6) information on the timeliness of the department's initial contact in an investigation or alternative response;

(7) information on the response time by the department in commencing services to families and children for whom an allegation of child abuse or neglect has been made;

(8) information regarding child protection staffing and caseloads by program area;

(9) information on the permanency goals in place and achieved for children in the managing conservatorship of the department, including information on the timeliness of achieving the goals, the stability of the children's placement in foster care, and the proximity of placements to the children's home counties;

(10) the number of children who suffer from a severe emotional disturbance and for whom the department is appointed managing conservator, including statistics on appointments as joint managing conservator, due to an individual voluntarily relinquishing custody of a child solely to obtain mental health services for the child;

(11) the number of children who are pregnant or a parent while in the managing conservatorship of the department and the number of the children born to a parent in the managing conservatorship of the department who are placed in the managing conservatorship of the department;

(12) the number of children who are missing from the children's substitute care provider while in the managing conservatorship of the department; and

(13) the number of children who were victims of trafficking under Chapter 20A, Penal Code, while in the managing conservatorship of the department.

(c) To the extent feasible, the report must also include, for each county, the amount of funding for child abuse and neglect prevention services and the rate of child abuse and neglect per 1,000 children in the county for the preceding year and for each of the preceding five years.

(d) Not later than September 1 of each year, the department shall seek public input regarding the usefulness of, and any proposed modifications to, existing reporting requirements and proposed additional reporting requirements. The department shall evaluate the public input provided under this subsection and seek to facilitate reporting to the maximum extent feasible within existing resources and in a manner that is most likely to assist public understanding of department functions.

(e) In addition to the information required under Subsections (a) and (b), the department shall annually publish information on the number of children who died during the preceding year whom the department determined had been abused or neglected but whose death was not the result of the abuse or neglect. The department may publish the information described by this subsection in the same report required by Subsection (a) or in another annual report published by the department.

Added by Acts 2015, 84th Leg., ch. 944 (S.B. 206), § 48, eff. Sept. 1, 2015.

### § 264.018. Required Notifications

(a) In this section:

(1) "Child-placing agency" has the meaning assigned by Section 42.002, Human Resources Code.

(2) "Psychotropic medication" has the meaning assigned by Section 266.001.

(3) "Residential child-care facility" has the meaning assigned by Section 42.002, Human Resources Code.

(4) "Significant change in medical condition" means the occurrence of an injury or the onset of an illness that is life-threatening or may have serious long-term health consequences. The term includes the occurrence or onset of an injury or illness that requires hospitalization for surgery or another procedure that is not minor emergency care.

(5) "Significant event" means:

(A) a placement change, including failure by the department to locate an appropriate placement for at least one night;

(B) a significant change in medical condition;

(C) an initial prescription of a psychotropic medication or a change in dosage of a psychotropic medication;

(D) a major change in school performance or a serious disciplinary event at school;

(E) a placement in a qualified residential treatment program as that term is defined by 42 U.S.C. Section 672(k)(4); or

(F) any event determined to be significant under department rule.

(b) The notification requirements of this section are in addition to other notice requirements provided by law, including Sections 263.0021, 264.107(g), and 264.123.

(c) The department must provide notice under this section in a manner that would provide actual notice to a person entitled to the notice, including the use of electronic notice whenever possible.

(d) Not later than 24 hours after an event described by this subsection, the department shall make a reasonable effort to notify a parent of a child in the managing conservatorship of the department of:

(1) a significant change in medical condition of the child;

(2) the enrollment or participation of the child in a drug research program under Section 266.0041; and

(3) an initial prescription of a psychotropic medication.

(d–1) Except as provided by Subsection (d–2), as soon as possible but not later than 24 hours after a change in placement of a child in the conservatorship of the department, the department shall give notice of the placement change to the managed care organization that contracts with the commission to provide health care services to the child under the STAR Health program. The managed care organization shall give notice of the placement change to the primary care physician listed in the child's health passport before the end of the second business day after the day the organization receives the notification from the department.

(d–2) In this subsection, "catchment area" has the meaning assigned by Section 264.152. In a catchment area in which community-based care has been implemented, the single source continuum contractor that has contracted with the commission to provide foster care services in that catchment area shall, as soon as possible but not later than 24 hours after a change in placement of a child in the conservatorship of the department, give notice of the placement change to the managed care organization that contracts with the commission to provide health care services to the child under the STAR Health program. The managed care organization shall give notice of the placement change to the child's primary care physician in accordance with Subsection (d–1).

(e) Not later than 48 hours before the department changes the residential child-care facility of a child in the managing conservatorship of the department, the department shall provide notice of the change to:

(1) the child's parent;

(2) an attorney ad litem appointed for the child under Chapter 107;

(3) a guardian ad litem appointed for the child under Chapter 107;

(4) a volunteer advocate appointed for the child under Chapter 107; and

(5) the licensed administrator of the child-placing agency responsible for placing the child or the licensed administrator's designee.

(f) Except as provided by Subsection (d–1), as soon as possible but not later than the 10th day after the date the department becomes aware of a significant event affecting a child in the conservatorship of the department, the department shall provide notice of the significant event to:

(1) the child's parent;

(2) an attorney ad litem appointed for the child under Chapter 107;

(3) a guardian ad litem appointed for the child under Chapter 107;

(4) a volunteer advocate appointed for the child under Chapter 107;

(5) the licensed administrator of the child-placing agency responsible for placing the child or the licensed administrator's designee;

(6) a foster parent, prospective adoptive parent, relative of the child providing care to the child, or director of the group home or general residential operation where the child is residing; and

(7) any other person determined by a court to have an interest in the child's welfare.

(g) For purposes of Subsection (f), if a hearing for the child is conducted during the 10–day notice period described by that subsection, the department shall provide notice of the significant event at the hearing.

(h) The department is not required to provide notice under this section to a parent of a child in the managing conservatorship of the department if:

(1) the department cannot locate the parent;

(2) a court has restricted the parent's access to the information;

(3) the child is in the permanent managing conservatorship of the department and the parent has not participated in the child's case for at least six months despite the department's efforts to involve the parent;

(4) the parent's rights have been terminated; or

(5) the department has documented in the child's case file that it is not in the best interest of the child to involve the parent in case planning.

(i) The department is not required to provide notice of a significant event under this section to the child-placing agency responsible for the placement of a child in the managing conservatorship of the department, a foster parent, a prospective adoptive parent, a relative of the child providing care to the child, or the director of the group home or general residential operation where the child resides if that agency or individual is required under a contract or other agreement to provide notice of the significant event to the department.

(j) A person entitled to notice from the department under this section shall provide the department with current contact information, including the person's e-mail address and the telephone number at which the person may most easily be reached. The person shall update the person's contact information as soon as possible after a change to the information. The department is not required to provide notice under this section to a person who fails to provide contact information to the department. The department may rely on the most recently provided contact information in providing notice under this section.

(k) To facilitate timely notification under this section, a residential child-care facility contracting with the department for 24–hour care shall notify the department, in the time provided by the facility's contract, of a significant event for a child who is in the conservatorship of the department and residing in the facility.

(*l*) The executive commissioner of the Health and Human Services Commission shall adopt rules necessary to implement this section using a negotiated rulemaking process under Chapter 2008, Government Code.

Added by Acts 2015, 84th Leg., ch. 722 (H.B. 1309), § 1, eff. June 17, 2015; Acts 2015, 84th Leg., ch. 944 (S.B. 206), § 48, eff. Sept. 1, 2015. Amended by Acts 2017, 85th Leg., ch. 317 (H.B. 7), § 33, eff. Sept. 1, 2017; Acts 2017, 85th Leg., ch. 319 (S.B. 11), § 14, eff. Sept. 1, 2017; Acts 2019, 86th Leg., ch. 467 (H.B. 4170), § 7.005, eff. Sept. 1, 2019; Acts 2021, 87th Leg., ch. 616 (S.B. 1575), § 2, eff. Sept. 1, 2021.

### § 264.019. Collection and Reporting of Alcohol and Controlled Substance Statistics

(a) The department shall collect the following information and update the department's automated case tracking and information management system to allow caseworkers to record:

(1) the number of children reported to the department who at birth tested positive for the presence of alcohol or a controlled substance;

(2) the controlled substances for which the children described by Subdivision (1) tested positive;

(3) the number of children described by Subdivision (1) who were removed from their homes and have been diagnosed as having a disability or chronic medical condition resulting from the presence of alcohol or controlled substances; and

(4) the number of parents who test positive for the presence of a controlled substance during a department investigation of a report of abuse or neglect of the parent's child.

(b) Not later than November 1 of each year, the department shall:

(1) prepare for the preceding year a report containing:

(A) the information collected under Subsection (a); and

(B) the data collected under Section 531.02143, Government Code;

(2) post a copy of the report prepared under Subdivision (1) on the department's Internet website; and

(3) electronically submit to the legislature a copy of the report.

(c) The commissioner of the department shall adopt rules necessary to implement this section.

(d) The department is required to implement this section in a state fiscal biennium only if the commissioner of the department determines that the legislature has specifically appropriated an amount sufficient to update the department's automated case tracking and information management system. If the commissioner of the department does not make that determination, the department shall implement this section not later than the date of the department's next update of the automated case tracking and information management system.

Added by Acts 2019, 86th Leg., ch. 417 (S.B. 195), § 2, eff. Jan. 1, 2020.

## SUBCHAPTER B. FOSTER CARE

### § 264.101. Foster Care Payments

(a) The department may pay the cost of foster care for a child only if:

(1) the child has been placed by the department in a foster home or other residential child-care facility, as defined by Chapter 42, Human Resources Code, or in a comparable residential facility in another state; and

(2) the department:

(A) has initiated suit and been named conservator of the child; or

(B) has the duty of care, control, and custody after taking possession of the child in an emergency without a prior court order as authorized by this subtitle.

(a–1) The department shall continue to pay the cost of foster care for a child for whom the department provides care, including medical care, until the last day of the month in which the child attains the age of 18. The department shall continue to pay the cost of foster care for a child after the month in which the child attains the age of 18 as long as the child is:

(1) regularly attending high school or enrolled in a program leading toward a high school diploma or high school equivalency certificate;

(2) regularly attending an institution of higher education or a postsecondary vocational or technical program;

(3) participating in a program or activity that promotes, or removes barriers to, employment;

(4) employed for at least 80 hours a month; or

(5) incapable of performing the activities described by Subdivisions (1)–(4) due to a documented medical condition.

(a–2) The department shall continue to pay the cost of foster care under:

(1) Subsection (a–1)(1) until the last day of the month in which the child attains the age of 22; and

(2) Subsections (a–1)(2)–(5) until the last day of the month the child attains the age of 21.

(b) The department may not pay the cost of protective foster care for a child for whom the department has been named managing conservator under an order rendered solely under Section 161.001(b)(1)(J).

(c) The payment of foster care, including medical care, for a child as authorized under this subchapter shall be made without regard to the child's eligibility for federally funded care.

(d) The executive commissioner may adopt rules that establish criteria and guidelines for the payment of foster care, including medical care, for a child and for providing care for a child after the child becomes 18 years of age if the child meets the requirements for continued foster care under Subsection (a–1).

(d–1) The executive commissioner may adopt rules that prescribe the maximum amount of state money that a residential child-care facility may spend on nondirect residential services, including administrative services. The commission shall recover the money that exceeds the maximum amount established under this subsection.

(e) The department may accept and spend funds available from any source to pay for foster care, including medical care, for a child in the department's care.

(f) In this section, "child" means a person who:

(1) is under 22 years of age and for whom the department has been appointed managing conservator of the child before the date the child became 18 years of age; or

(2) is the responsibility of an agency with which the department has entered into an agreement to provide care and supervision of the child.

Added by Acts 1995, 74th Leg., ch. 20, § 1, eff. April 20, 1995. Amended by Acts 1997, 75th Leg., ch. 575, § 27, eff. Sept. 1, 1997; Acts 2005, 79th Leg., ch. 183, § 1, eff. May 27, 2005; Acts 2005, 79th Leg., ch. 268, § 1.45, eff. Sept. 1, 2005; Acts 2009, 81st Leg., ch. 1118, § 6, eff. Sept. 1, 2009; Acts 2009, 81st Leg., ch. 1238, § 6(b), eff. Oct. 1, 2010; Acts 2015, 84th Leg., ch. 1 (S.B. 219), § 1.188, eff. April 2, 2015; Acts 2015, 84th Leg., ch. 944 (S.B. 206), § 49, eff. Sept. 1, 2015.

### § 264.1015. Liability of Child's Estate for Foster Care

(a) The cost of foster care provided for a child, including medical care, is an obligation of the estate of the child and the estate is liable to the department for the cost of the care.

(b) The department may take action to recover from the estate of the child the cost of foster care for the child.

Added by Acts 1997, 75th Leg., ch. 575, § 28, eff. Sept. 1, 1997.

### § 264.102. County Contracts

(a) The department may contract with a county commissioners court to administer the funds authorized by this subchapter for eligible children in the county and may require county participation.

(b) The payments provided by this subchapter do not abrogate the responsibility of a county to provide child welfare services.

Added by Acts 1995, 74th Leg., ch. 20, § 1, eff. April 20, 1995.

### § 264.103. Direct Payments

The department may make direct payments for foster care to a foster parent residing in a county with which the department does not have a contract authorized by Section 264.102.

Added by Acts 1995, 74th Leg., ch. 20, § 1, eff. April 20, 1995.

### § 264.104. Parent or Guardian Liability

(a) The parent or guardian of a child is liable to the state or to the county for a payment made by the state or county for foster care of a child under this subchapter.

(b) The cost of foster care for a child, including medical care, is a legal obligation of the child's parents, and the estate of a parent of the child is liable to the department for payment of the costs.

(c) The funds collected by the state under this section shall be used by the department for child welfare services.

Added by Acts 1995, 74th Leg., ch. 20, § 1, eff. April 20, 1995. Amended by Acts 1997, 75th Leg., ch. 575, § 29, eff. Sept. 1, 1997.

### § 264.105. Repealed by Acts 2015, 84th Leg., ch. 1 (S.B. 219) § 1.203(8), eff. April 2, 2015

### § 264.106. Repealed by Acts 2015, 84th Leg., ch. 1 (S.B. 219) § 1.203(9), eff. April 2, 2015

### § 264.1061. Foster Parent Performance

The department shall monitor the performance of a foster parent who has been verified by the department in the department's capacity as a child-placing agency. The method under which performance is monitored must include the use of objective criteria by which the foster parent's performance may be assessed. The department shall include references to the criteria in a written agreement between the department and the foster parent concerning the foster parent's services.

Added by Acts 1997, 75th Leg., ch. 1022, § 92, eff. Sept. 1, 1997.

### § 264.1062. Repealed by Acts 2007, 80th Leg., ch. 1406, § 54(2), eff. Sept. 1, 2007

### § 264.1063. Repealed by Acts 2015, 84th Leg., ch. 1 (S.B. 219), § 1.203(10), eff. April 2, 2015

### § 264.107. Placement of Children

(a) Repealed by Acts 2015, 84th Leg., ch. 944 (S.B. 206), § 86(25).

(b) The department shall use an application or assessment developed by the department in coordination with interested parties for the placement of children in contract residential care.

(b–1) Expired.

(c) In selecting a placement for a child, the department shall consider whether the placement is in the child's best interest. In determining whether a placement is in a child's best interest, the department shall consider whether the placement:

(1) is the least restrictive setting for the child;

(2) is the closest in geographic proximity to the child's home;

(3) is the most able to meet the identified needs of the child; and

(4) satisfies any expressed interests of the child relating to placement, when developmentally appropriate.

(d) Repealed by Acts 2015, 84th Leg., ch. 944 (S.B. 206), § 86(25).

(e) In making placement decisions, the department shall:

(1) except when making an emergency placement that does not allow time for the required consultations, consult with the child's caseworker, attorney ad litem, and guardian ad litem and with any court-appointed volunteer advocate for the child; and

(2) use clinical protocols to match a child to the most appropriate placement resource.

(f) Repealed by Acts 2015, 84th Leg., ch. 1 (S.B. 219), § 1.203(11).

(g) If the department or single source continuum contractor is unable to find an appropriate placement for a child, an employee of the department or contractor who has on file with the department or contractor, as applicable, a background and criminal history check may provide temporary emergency care for the child. The employee may not provide emergency care under this subsection in the employee's residence. The department or contractor shall provide notice to the court for a child placed in temporary care under this subsection not later than the next business day after the date the child is placed in temporary care.

Added by Acts 1995, 74th Leg., ch. 20, § 1, eff. April 20, 1995. Amended by Acts 2005, 79th Leg., ch. 268, § 1.48, eff. Sept. 1, 2005; Acts 2007, 80th Leg., ch. 1406, § 14, eff. Sept. 1, 2007; Acts 2013, 83rd Leg., ch. 193 (S.B. 425), § 1, eff. Sept. 1, 2013; Acts 2015, 84th Leg., ch. 1 (S.B. 219), §§ 1.189, 1.203(11), eff. April 2, 2015; Acts 2015, 84th Leg., ch. 944 (S.B. 206), §§ 50, 86(25), eff. Sept. 1, 2015; Acts 2017, 85th Leg., ch. 1022 (H.B. 1542), § 4, eff. Sept. 1, 2017; Acts 2021, 87th Leg., ch. 621 (S.B. 1896), § 2, eff. June 14, 2021.

Section 35 of Acts 2021, 87th Leg., ch. 621 (S.B. 1896) provides:

"The Office of Community–Based Care Transition, the Department of Family and Protective Services, and the Health and Human Services Commission are required to implement this Act only if the legislature appropriates money specifically for that purpose. If the legislature does not appropriate money specifically for that purpose, the Office of Community–Based Care Transition, the Department of Family and Protective Services, and the Health and Human Services Commission may, but are not required to, implement this Act using other appropriations available for the purpose."

### § 264.1071. Office Stays Prohibited

The department may not allow a child to stay overnight in a department office.

Added by Acts 2021, 87th Leg., ch. 621 (S.B. 1896), § 3, eff. June 14, 2021.

Section 35 of Acts 2021, 87th Leg., ch. 621 (S.B. 1896) provides:

"The Office of Community–Based Care Transition, the Department of Family and Protective Services, and the Health and Human Services Commission are required to implement this Act only if the legislature appropriates money specifically for that purpose. If the legislature does not appropriate money specifically for that purpose, the Office of Community–Based Care Transition, the Department of Family and Protective Services, and the Health and Human Services Commission may, but are not required to, implement this Act using other appropriations available for the purpose."

### § 264.1072. Educational Stability

The department shall develop, in accordance with 42 U.S.C. Section 675, a plan to ensure the educational stability of a foster child.

Added by Acts 2013, 83rd Leg., ch. 688 (H.B. 2619), § 7, eff. Sept. 1, 2013.

### § 264.1073. Treatment Foster Care

The department and single source continuum contractors shall:

(1) lessen employment restrictions to allow single parents to participate in treatment foster care, when quality care is assured;

(2) expand the eligible age for treatment foster care to include children 10 years of age or older;

(3) prepare and plan for the subsequent placement not later than the 30th day after a child is placed in treatment foster care to assist in the transition to the least restrictive placement; and

(4) extend the length of time for a treatment foster care placement.

Added by Acts 2021, 87th Leg., ch. 621 (S.B. 1896), § 3, eff. June 14, 2021.

Section 35 of Acts 2021, 87th Leg., ch. 621 (S.B. 1896) provides:

"The Office of Community–Based Care Transition, the Department of Family and Protective Services, and the Health and Human Services Commission are required to implement this Act only if the legislature appropriates money specifically for that purpose. If the legislature does not appropriate money specifically for that purpose, the Office of Community–Based Care Transition, the Department of Family and Protective Services, and the Health and Human Services Commission may, but are not required to, implement this Act using other appropriations available for the purpose."

### § 264.1075. Assessing Needs of Child

(a) On removing a child from the child's home, the department shall use assessment services provided by a child-care facility, a child-placing agency, or the child's medical home during the initial substitute care placement. The assessment may be used to determine the most appropriate substitute care placement for the child, if needed.

(b) As soon as possible after a child is placed in the managing conservatorship of the department, the department shall assess whether the child has a developmental or intellectual disability.

(c) If the assessment required by Subsection (b) indicates that the child might have an intellectual disability, the department shall ensure that a referral for a determination of intellectual disability is made as soon as possible and that the determination is conducted by an authorized provider before the date of the child's 16th birthday, if practicable. If the child is placed in the managing conservatorship of the department after the child's 16th birthday, the determination of intellectual disability must be conducted as soon as possible after the assessment required by Subsection (b). In this subsection, "authorized provider" has the meaning assigned by Section 593.004, Health and Safety Code.

Added by Acts 1997, 75th Leg., ch. 1022, § 93, eff. Sept. 1, 1997. Amended by Acts 2005, 79th Leg., ch. 268, § 1.49, eff. Sept. 1, 2005; Acts 2015, 84th Leg., ch. 1 (S.B. 219), § 1.190, eff. April 2, 2015; Acts 2015, 84th Leg., ch. 944 (S.B. 206), § 51, eff. Sept. 1, 2015; Acts 2017, 85th Leg., ch. 822 (H.B. 1549), § 3, eff. Sept. 1, 2017.

### § 264.1076. Medical Examination Required

(a) This section applies only to a child who has been taken into the conservatorship of the department and remains in the conservatorship of the department for more than three business days.

(b) The department shall ensure that each child described by Subsection (a) receives an initial medical examination from a physician or other health care provider authorized under state law to conduct medical examinations not later than the end of the third business day after the date the child is removed from the child's home, if the child:

(1) is removed as the result of sexual abuse, physical abuse, or an obvious physical injury to the child; or

(2) has a chronic medical condition, a medically complex condition, or a diagnosed mental illness.

(c) Notwithstanding Subsection (b), the department shall ensure that any child who enters the conservatorship of the department receives any necessary emergency medical care as soon as possible.

(d) A physician or other health care provider conducting an examination under Subsection (b) may not administer a vaccination as part of the examination without parental consent, except that a physician or other health care provider may administer a tetanus vaccination to a child in a commercially available preparation if the physician or other health care provider determines that an emergency circumstance requires the administration of the vaccination. The prohibition on the administration of a vaccination under this subsection does not apply after the department has been named managing conservator of the child after a hearing conducted under Subchapter C, Chapter 262.[1]

(e) Whenever possible, the department shall schedule the medical examination for a child before the last business day of the appropriate time frame provided under Subsection (b).

(f) The department shall collaborate with the commission and selected physicians and other health care providers authorized under state law to conduct medical examinations to develop guidelines for the medical examination conducted under this section, including guidelines on the components to be included in the examination. The guidelines developed under this subsection must provide assistance and guidance regarding:

(1) assessing a child for:

(A) signs and symptoms of child abuse and neglect;

(B) the presence of acute or chronic illness; and

(C) signs of acute or severe mental health conditions;

(2) monitoring a child's adjustment to being in the conservatorship of the department;

(3) ensuring a child has necessary medical equipment and any medication prescribed to the child or needed by the child; and

(4) providing appropriate support and education to a child's caregivers.

(g) Notwithstanding any other law, the guidelines developed under Subsection (f) do not create a standard of care for a physician or other health care provider authorized under state law to conduct medical examinations, and a physician or other health care provider may not be subject to criminal, civil, or administrative penalty or civil liability for failure to adhere to the guidelines.

(h) The department shall make a good faith effort to contact a child's primary care physician to ensure continuity of care for the child regarding medication prescribed to the child and the treatment of any chronic medical condition.

(i) Not later than December 31, 2019, the department shall submit a report to the standing committees of the house of representatives and the senate with primary jurisdiction over child protective services and foster care evaluating the statewide implementation of the medical examination required by this section. The report must include the level of compliance with the requirements of this section in each region of the state.

Added by Acts 2017, 85th Leg., ch. 319 (S.B. 11), § 15(a), eff. Sept. 1, 2017.

[1] V.T.C.A., Family Code § 262.201 et seq.

## § 264.1077. Study Regarding Residential Treatment Center Placement

*Section expires pursuant to (c)*

(a) The Supreme Court of Texas Children's Commission, in collaboration with the department, shall establish and oversee a work group to examine the oversight of and best practices related to residential treatment center placements, including placements in qualified residential treatment programs as that term is defined by 42 U.S.C. Section 672(k)(4). The work group shall consider topics and changes to current practices the work group determines necessary to ensure the appropriate use of and to improve the transition into and out of residential treatment center placements, including:

(1) statutorily required judicial review of residential treatment center placements;

(2) fiscal implications of additional judicial review for residential treatment center placements;

(3) methods for improving the state's practices regarding the duration of residential treatment center placements, including best practices for transition planning and involving family and other relevant participants in preparing the child for a subsequent placement;

(4) proposed statutory changes regarding appropriate judicial findings, evidence required to be submitted by the department, and recommendations for information to be gathered from the child's attorney or guardian ad litem; and

(5) model court orders determined to be appropriate for the legal requirements for a particular placement.

(b) Not later than October 1, 2022, the Supreme Court of Texas Children's Commission shall submit a report to the legislature regarding the findings and recommendations from the work group established by Subsection (a).

(c) This section expires September 1, 2023.

Added by Acts 2021, 87th Leg., ch. 616 (S.B. 1575), § 3, eff. Sept. 1, 2021.

### § 264.108. Repealed by Acts 2015, 84th Leg., ch. 944 (S.B. 206), § 86(27), eff. Sept. 1, 2015

### § 264.1085. Foster Care Placement in Compliance with Federal Law Required

The department or a licensed child-placing agency making a foster care placement shall comply with the Multiethnic Placement Act of 1994 (42 U.S.C. Section 1996b).

Added by Acts 2015, 84th Leg., ch. 944 (S.B. 206), § 52, eff. Sept. 1, 2015.

### § 264.109. Assignment of Support Rights in Substitute Care Cases

(a) The placement of a child in substitute care by the department constitutes an assignment to the state of any support rights attributable to the child as of the date the child is placed in substitute care.

(b) If a child placed by the department in substitute care is entitled under federal law to Title IV-D child support enforcement services without the requirement of an application for services, the department shall immediately refer the case to the Title IV-D agency. If an application for Title IV-D services is required and the department has been named managing conservator of the child, then an authorized representative of the department shall be the designated individual entitled to apply for services on behalf of the child and shall promptly apply for the services.

(c) The department and the Title IV-D agency shall execute a memorandum of understanding for the implementation of the provisions of this section and for the allocation between the department and the agency, consistent with federal laws and regulations, of any child support funds recovered by the Title IV-D agency in substitute care cases. All child support funds recovered under this section and retained by the department or the Title IV-D agency and any federal matching or incentive funds resulting from child support collection efforts in substitute care cases shall be in excess of amounts otherwise appropriated to either the department or the Title IV-D agency by the legislature.

Added by Acts 1995, 74th Leg., ch. 751, § 117, eff. Sept. 1, 1995.

### § 264.110. Prospective Foster or Adoptive Parent Statement

(a) Repealed by Acts 2015, 84th Leg., ch. 944 (S.B. 206), § 86(28).

(b) Repealed by Acts 2015, 84th Leg., ch. 944 (S.B. 206), § 86(28).

(c) Repealed by Acts 2015, 84th Leg., ch. 944 (S.B. 206), § 86(28).

(d) Before a child may be placed with a foster or adoptive parent, the prospective foster or adoptive parent must sign a written statement in which the prospective foster or adoptive parent agrees to the immediate removal of the child by the department under circumstances determined by the department.

(e) Repealed by Acts 2015, 84th Leg., ch. 944 (S.B. 206), § 86(28).

(f) Repealed by Acts 2015, 84th Leg., ch. 944 (S.B. 206), § 86(28).

(g) Repealed by Acts 2015, 84th Leg., ch. 944 (S.B. 206), § 86(28).

(h) Repealed by Acts 2015, 84th Leg., ch. 944 (S.B. 206), § 86(28).

Added by Acts 1995, 74th Leg., ch. 943, § 8, eff. Sept. 1, 1995. Redesignated from V.T.C.A., Family Code § 264.109 by Acts 1997, 75th Leg., ch. 165, § 31.01(30), eff. Sept. 1, 1997. Amended by Acts 2015, 84th Leg., ch. 1 (S.B. 219), § 1.192, eff. April 2, 2015; Acts 2015, 84th Leg., ch. 944 (S.B. 206), §§ 53, 54, 86(28), eff. Sept. 1, 2015.

**§ 264.111. Repealed by Acts 2015, 84th Leg., ch. 713 (H.B. 1217), § 4, eff. Sept. 1, 2015; Acts 2015, 84th Leg., ch. 944 (S.B. 206), § 86(29), eff. Sept. 1, 2015**

**§ 264.112. Report on Children in Substitute Care**

(a) The department shall report the status for children in substitute care to the executive commissioner at least once every 12 months.

(b) The report shall analyze the length of time each child has been in substitute care and the barriers to placing the child for adoption or returning the child to the child's parent or parents.

Added by Acts 1997, 75th Leg., ch. 600, § 18, eff. Sept. 1, 1997. Amended by Acts 2015, 84th Leg., ch. 1 (S.B. 219), § 1.193, eff. April 2, 2015.

**§ 264.113. Foster Parent Recruitment**

(a) In this section, "faith-based organization" means a religious or denominational institution or organization, including an organization operated for religious, educational, or charitable purposes and operated, supervised, or controlled, in whole or in part, by or in connection with a religious organization.

(b) The department shall develop a program to recruit and retain foster parents from faith-based organizations. As part of the program, the department shall:

(1) collaborate with faith-based organizations to inform prospective foster parents about the department's need for foster parents, the requirements for becoming a foster parent, and any other aspect of the foster care program that is necessary to recruit foster parents;

(2) provide training for prospective foster parents recruited under this section; and

(3) identify and recommend ways in which faith-based organizations may support persons as they are recruited, are trained, and serve as foster parents.

(c) The department shall work with OneStar Foundation to expand the program described by Subsection (b) to increase the number of foster families available for the department and its private providers. In cooperation with the department, OneStar Foundation may provide training and technical assistance to establish networks and services in faith-based organizations based on best practices for supporting prospective and current foster families.

(d) The department shall work with the Department of Assistive and Rehabilitative Services to recruit foster parents and adoptive parents who have skills, training, or experience suitable to care for children with hearing impairments.

Added by Acts 2003, 78th Leg., ch. 957, § 1, eff. June 20, 2003. Amended by Acts 2007, 80th Leg., ch. 1406, § 16, eff. Sept. 1, 2007.

**§ 264.114. Immunity From Liability; Adverse Departmental Action Prohibited**

(a) A faith-based organization, including the organization's employees and volunteers, that participates in a program under this chapter is subject to civil liability as provided by Chapter 84, Civil Practice and Remedies Code.

(b) A faith-based organization that provides financial or other assistance to a foster parent or to a member of the foster parent's household is not liable for damages arising out of the conduct of the foster parent or a member of the foster parent's household.

(c) A foster parent, other substitute caregiver, family relative or other designated caregiver, or licensed child placing agency caring for a child in the managing conservatorship of the department is not liable for harm caused to the child resulting from the child's participation in an age-appropriate normalcy activity approved by the caregiver if, in approving the child's participation in the activity, the caregiver exercised the standard of care of a reasonable and prudent parent.

(d) A licensed child placing agency is not subject to adverse action by the department, including contractual action or licensing or other regulatory action, arising out of the conduct of a foster parent who has exercised the standard of care of a reasonable and prudent parent.

Added by Acts 2003, 78th Leg., ch. 957, § 1, eff. June 20, 2003. Amended by Acts 2015, 84th Leg., ch. 262 (S.B. 1407), §§ 5, 6, eff. Sept. 1, 2015.

**§ 264.115. Returning Child to School**

(a) If the department takes possession of a child under Chapter 262 during the school year, the department shall ensure that the child returns to school not later than the third school day after the date an order is rendered providing for possession of the child by the department, unless the child has a physical or mental condition of a temporary and remediable nature that makes the child's attendance infeasible.

(b) If a child has a physical or mental condition of a temporary and remediable nature that makes the child's attendance in school infeasible, the department shall notify the school in writing that the child is unable to attend school. If the child's physical or mental condition improves so that the child's attendance in school is feasible, the department shall ensure that the child immediately returns to school.

Added by Acts 2003, 78th Leg., ch. 234, § 1, eff. Sept. 1, 2003. Redesignated from V.T.C.A., Family Code § 264.113 by Acts 2005, 79th Leg., ch. 728, § 23.001(25), eff. Sept. 1, 2005.

## § 264.116. Texas Foster Grandparent Mentors

(a) The department shall make the active recruitment and inclusion of senior citizens a priority in ongoing mentoring initiatives.

(b) An individual who volunteers as a mentor is subject to state and national criminal background checks in accordance with Sections 411.087 and 411.114, Government Code.

(c) The department shall require foster parents or employees of residential child-care facilities to provide appropriate supervision over individuals who serve as mentors during their participation in the mentoring initiative.

(d) Chapter 2109, Government Code, applies to the mentoring initiative described by this section.

Added by Acts 2005, 79th Leg., ch. 268, § 1.50(a), eff. Sept. 1, 2005.

## § 264.1165. Expired

## § 264.117. Mentors for Foster Children

(a) The department and each single source continuum contractor in this state, in collaboration with local governmental entities and faith- and community-based organizations, shall examine the feasibility of designing a volunteer mentor program for children in congregate care settings.

(b) Not later than December 31, 2022, the department shall report its findings and recommendations for establishing a mentor program to the legislature.

(c) This section expires September 1, 2023.

Added by Acts 2021, 87th Leg., ch. 621 (S.B. 1896), § 4, eff. June 14, 2021.

Section 35 of Acts 2021, 87th Leg., ch. 621 (S.B. 1896) provides:

"The Office of Community-Based Care Transition, the Department of Family and Protective Services, and the Health and Human Services Commission are required to implement this Act only if the legislature appropriates money specifically for that purpose. If the legislature does not appropriate money specifically for that purpose, the Office of Community-Based Care Transition, the Department of Family and Protective Services, and the Health and Human Services Commission may, but are not required to, implement this Act using other appropriations available for the purpose."

## § 264.118. Annual Survey

(a) The department shall collect and report service and outcome information for certain current and former foster care youth for use in the National Youth in Transition Database as required by 42 U.S.C. Section 677(f) and 45 C.F.R. Section 1356.80 et seq.

(b) The identity of each child participating in a department survey is confidential and not subject to public disclosure under Chapter 552, Government Code. The department shall adopt procedures to ensure that the identity of each child participating in a department survey remains confidential.

Added by Acts 2005, 79th Leg., ch. 268, § 1.50(a), eff. Sept. 1, 2005. Amended by Acts 2011, 82nd Leg., ch. 598 (S.B. 218), § 7, eff. Sept. 1, 2011.

## § 264.119. Repealed by Acts 2015, 84th Leg., ch. 722 (H.B. 1309), § 5, eff. June 17, 2015; Acts 2015, 84th Leg., ch. 944 (S.B. 206), § 86(31), eff. Sept. 1, 2015

## § 264.120. Discharge Notice

(a) Except as provided by Subsection (b), a substitute care provider with whom the department contracts to provide substitute care services for a child shall include in a discharge notice the following information:

(1) the reason for the child's discharge; and

(2) the provider's recommendation regarding a future placement for the child that would increase the child's opportunity to attain a stable placement.

(b) In an emergency situation in which the department is required under the terms of the contract with the substitute care provider to remove a child within 24 hours after receiving the discharge notice, the provider must provide the information required by Subsection (a) to the department not later than 48 hours after the provider sends the discharge notice.

Added by Acts 2013, 83rd Leg., ch. 1324 (S.B. 534), § 4, eff. Sept. 1, 2013.

## § 264.121. Transitional Living Services Program

(a) The department shall address the unique challenges facing foster children in the conservatorship of the department who must transition to independent living by:

(1) expanding efforts to improve transition planning and increasing the availability of transitional family group decision-making to all youth age 14 or older in the department's permanent managing conservatorship, including enrolling the youth in the Preparation for Adult Living Program before the age of 16;

(2) coordinating with the commission to obtain authority, to the extent allowed by federal law, the state Medicaid plan, the Title IV–E state plan, and any waiver or amendment to either plan, necessary to:

(A) extend foster care eligibility and transition services for youth up to age 21 and develop policy to permit eligible youth to return to foster care as necessary to achieve the goals of the Transitional Living Services Program; and

(B) extend Medicaid coverage for foster care youth and former foster care youth up to age 21 with a single application at the time the youth leaves foster care;

(3) entering into cooperative agreements with the Texas Workforce Commission and local workforce development boards to further the objectives of the Preparation for Adult Living Program. The department, the Texas Workforce Commission, and the local workforce development boards shall ensure that services are prioritized and targeted to meet the needs of foster care and former foster care children and that such services will include, where feasible, referrals for short-term stays for youth needing housing;

(4) addressing barriers to participation in the Preparation for Adult Living Program for a youth who has a disability by making appropriate accommodations that allow the youth to meaningfully participate in the program; and

(5) documenting in the youth's case file any accommodations made under Subdivision (4).

(a–1) The department shall require a foster care provider to provide or assist youth who are age 14 or older in obtaining experiential life-skills training to improve their transition to independent living. Experiential life-skills training must be tailored to a youth's skills and abilities and must include training in practical activities that include grocery shopping, meal preparation and cooking, performing basic household tasks, and, when appropriate, using public transportation.

(a–2) The experiential life-skills training under Subsection (a–1) must include:

(1) a financial literacy education program developed in collaboration with the Office of Consumer Credit Commissioner and the State Securities Board that:

(A) includes instruction on:

(i) obtaining and interpreting a credit score;

(ii) protecting, repairing, and improving a credit score;

(iii) avoiding predatory lending practices;

(iv) saving money and accomplishing financial goals through prudent financial management practices;

(v) using basic banking and accounting skills, including balancing a checkbook;

(vi) using debit and credit cards responsibly;

(vii) understanding a paycheck and items withheld from a paycheck;

(viii) understanding the time requirements and process for filing federal taxes;

(ix) protecting financial, credit, and personally identifying information in personal and professional relationships and online;

(x) forms of identity and credit theft; and

(xi) using insurance to protect against the risk of financial loss; and

(B) assists a youth who has a source of income to:

(i) establish a savings plan and, if available, a savings account that the youth can independently manage; and

(ii) prepare a monthly budget that includes the following expenses:

(a) rent based on the monthly rent for an apartment advertised for lease during the preceding month;

(b) utilities based on a reasonable utility bill in the area in which the youth resides;

(c) telephone service based on a reasonable bill for telephone service in the area in which the youth resides;

(d) Internet service based on a reasonable bill for Internet service in the area in which the youth resides; and

(e) other reasonable monthly expenses; and

(2) for youth who are 17 years of age or older, lessons related to:

(A) insurance, including applying for and obtaining automobile insurance and residential property insurance, including tenants insurance;

(B) civic engagement, including the process for registering to vote, the places to vote, and resources for information regarding upcoming elections; and

(C) the documents the youth is required to receive under Subsection (e–1) prior to being discharged from foster care and how those documents may be used.

(a–3) The department shall conduct an independent living skills assessment for all youth in the department's conservatorship who are 16 years of age or older.

(a–4) The department shall conduct an independent living skills assessment for all youth in the department's permanent managing conservatorship who are at least 14 years of age but younger than 16 years of age.

(a–5) The department shall annually update the assessment for each youth assessed under Subsections (a–3) and (a–4) to determine the independent living skills the youth learned during the preceding year to ensure that the department's obligation to prepare the youth for independent living has been met. The department shall conduct the annual update through the youth's plan of service in coordination with the youth, the youth's caseworker, the staff of the Preparation for Adult Living Program, and the youth's caregiver.

(a–6) The department, in coordination with the Texas Higher Education Coordinating Board, shall establish a work group to develop a plan to ensure that foster youth who complete the standardized curriculum for the Preparation for Adult Living Program are eligible to receive college credit for completing the program. The work group must include representatives from urban and rural institutions of higher education, as defined by Section 61.003, Education Code. In developing its evidence-based recommendations, the work group shall consider the feasibility of implementing each recommendation, a foster youth's access to the Preparation for Adult Living Program, and the average length of time a foster youth will remain in a placement. The department shall report the plan to the legislature not later than November 1, 2022. This subsection expires September 1, 2023.

(a–7) The department shall ensure that before a youth leaves foster care, each youth who is 14 years of age or older has an e-mail address through which the youth may receive encrypted copies of personal documents and records.

(b) In this section:

(1) "Local workforce development board" means a local workforce development board created under Chapter 2308, Government Code.

(2) "Preparation for Adult Living Program" means a program administered by the department as a component of the Transitional Living Services Program and includes independent living skills assessment, short-term financial assistance, basic self-help skills, and life-skills development and training regarding money management, health and wellness, job skills, planning for the future, housing and transportation, and interpersonal skills.

(3) "Transitional Living Services Program" means a program, administered by the department in accordance with department rules and state and federal law, for youth who are age 14 or older but not more than 21 years of age and are currently or were formerly in foster care, that assists youth in transitioning from foster care to independent living. The program provides transitional living services, Preparation for Adult Living Program services, and Education and Training Voucher Program services.

(c) At the time a child enters the Preparation for Adult Living Program, the department shall provide an information booklet to the child and the foster parent describing the program and the benefits available to the child, including extended Medicaid coverage until age 21, priority status with the Texas Workforce Commission, and the exemption from the payment of tuition and fees at institutions of higher education as defined by Section 61.003, Education Code. The information booklet provided to the child and the foster parent shall be provided in the primary language spoken by that individual.

(d) The department shall allow a youth who is at least 18 years of age to receive transitional living services, other than foster care benefits, while residing with a person who was previously designated as a perpetrator of abuse or neglect if the department determines that despite the person's prior history the person does not pose a threat to the health and safety of the youth.

(e) The department shall ensure that each youth acquires a copy and a certified copy of the youth's birth certificate, a social security card or replacement social security card, as appropriate, and a personal identification certificate under Chapter 521, Transportation Code, on or before the date on which the youth turns 16 years of age. The department shall designate one or more employees in the Preparation for Adult Living Program as the contact person to assist a youth who has not been able to obtain the documents described by this subsection in a timely manner from the youth's primary caseworker. The department shall ensure that:

(1) all youth who are age 16 or older are provided with the contact information for the designated employees; and

(2) a youth who misplaces a document provided under this subsection receives assistance in obtaining a replacement document or information on how to obtain a duplicate copy, as appropriate.

(e–1) If, at the time a youth is discharged from foster care, the youth is at least 18 years of age or has had the disabilities of minority removed, the department shall provide to the youth, not later than the 30th day before the date the youth is discharged from foster care, the following information and documents unless the youth already has the information or document:

(1) the youth's birth certificate;

(2) the youth's immunization records;

(3) the information contained in the youth's health passport;

(4) a personal identification certificate under Chapter 521, Transportation Code;

(5) a social security card or a replacement social security card, if appropriate; and

(6) a Medicaid card or other proof of the youth's enrollment in Medicaid or an insurance card from a health plan that provides health coverage to foster youth.

(e–2) When providing a youth with a document required by Subsection (e–1), the department shall provide the youth with a copy and a certified copy of the document or with the original document, as applicable.

(e–3) When obtaining a copy of a birth certificate to provide to a foster youth or assisting a foster youth in obtaining a copy of a birth certificate, the department shall obtain the birth certificate from the state registrar. If the department is unable to obtain the birth certificate from the state registrar, the department may obtain the birth certificate from a local registrar or county clerk.

(e–4) The youth's caseworker shall:

(1) assist the youth with developing a plan for keeping the documents described by Subsection (e) in a safe place; and

(2) inform the youth about the documents the youth is required to receive before the date the youth is discharged from foster care.

(f) The department shall require a person with whom the department contracts for transitional living services for foster youth to provide or assist youth in obtaining:

(1) housing services;

(2) job training and employment services;

(3) college preparation services;

(4) services that will assist youth in obtaining a general education development certificate;

(5) services that will assist youth in developing skills in food preparation;

(6) nutrition education that promotes healthy food choices;

(7) a savings or checking account if the youth is at least 18 years of age and has a source of income;

(8) mental health services;

(9) financial literacy education and civic engagement lessons required under Subsection (a–2); and

(10) any other appropriate transitional living service identified by the department.

(g) For a youth taking prescription medication, the department shall ensure that the youth's transition plan includes provisions to assist the youth in managing the use of the medication and in managing the child's long-term physical and mental health needs after leaving foster care, including:

(1) provisions that inform the youth about:

(A) the use of the medication;

(B) the resources that are available to assist the youth in managing the use of the medication; and

(C) informed consent and the provision of medical care in accordance with Section 266.010(*l*); and

(2) for each youth who is 17 years of age or older and preparing to leave foster care, a program supervised by a health care professional to assist the youth with independently managing the youth's medication.

(h) An entity with which the department contracts for transitional living services for foster youth shall, when appropriate, partner with a community-based organization to assist the entity in providing the transitional living services.

(i) The department shall ensure that the transition plan for each youth 16 years of age or older includes provisions to assist the youth in managing the youth's housing needs after the youth leaves foster care, including provisions that:

(1) identify the cost of housing in relation to the youth's sources of income, including any benefits or rental assistance available to the youth;

(2) if the youth's housing goals include residing with family or friends, state that the department has addressed the following with the youth:

(A) the length of time the youth expects to stay in the housing arrangement;

(B) expectations for the youth regarding paying rent and meeting other household obligations;

(C) the youth's psychological and emotional needs, as applicable; and

(D) any potential conflicts with other household members, or any difficulties connected to the type of housing the youth is seeking, that may arise based on the youth's psychological and emotional needs;

(3) inform the youth about emergency shelters and housing resources, including supervised independent living and housing at colleges and universities, such as dormitories;

(4) require the department to review a common rental application with the youth and ensure that the youth possesses all of the documentation required to obtain rental housing; and

(5) identify any individuals who are able to serve as cosigners or references on the youth's applications for housing.

Added by Acts 2005, 79th Leg., ch. 268, § 1.51, eff. Sept. 1, 2005. Amended by Acts 2007, 80th Leg., ch. 1406, § 17, eff. Sept. 1, 2007; Acts 2009, 81st Leg., ch. 407, §§ 1, 2, eff. Sept. 1, 2009; Acts 2013, 83rd Leg., ch. 168 (S.B. 1589), § 1, eff. Sept. 1, 2013; Acts 2013, 83rd Leg., ch. 204 (H.B. 915), § 6, eff. Sept. 1, 2013; Acts 2013, 83rd Leg., ch. 342 (H.B. 2111), § 1, eff. June 14, 2013; Acts 2015, 84th Leg., ch. 1 (S.B. 219), § 1.194, eff. April 2, 2015; Acts 2015, 84th Leg., ch. 81 (S.B. 1117), § 1, eff. Sept. 1, 2015; Acts 2015, 84th Leg., ch. 944 (S.B. 206), §§ 55, 56, eff. Sept. 1, 2015; Acts 2015, 84th Leg., ch. 1236 (S.B. 1296), §§ 7.004, 7.005, 21.001(18), eff. Sept. 1, 2015; Acts 2017, 85th Leg., ch. 937 (S.B. 1758), § 6, eff. Sept. 1, 2017; Acts 2019, 86th Leg., ch. 707 (H.B. 53), § 1, eff. Sept. 1, 2019; Acts 2019, 86th Leg., ch. 1024 (H.B. 123), § 1, eff. Sept. 1, 2019; Acts 2021, 87th Leg., ch. 793 (H.B. 700), § 1, eff. Sept. 1, 2021.

Section 2 of Acts 2019, 86th Leg., ch. 707 (H.B. 53) provides:

"The changes in law made by this Act apply only to a person who enters into a contract with the Department of Family and Protective Services to provide transitional living services for foster youth on or after the effective date [Sept. 1, 2019] of this Act."

Section 8 of Acts 2019, 86th Leg., ch. 1024 (H.B. 123), provides:

"The changes in law made by this Act apply to an application for a driver's license, personal identification certificate, or birth record submitted on or after the effective date [Sept. 1, 2019] of this Act. An application for a driver's license, personal identification certificate, or birth record submitted before the effective date of this Act is governed by the law in effect on the date the application was submitted, and the former law is continued in effect for that purpose."

## § 264.1211. Career Development and Education Program

(a) The department shall collaborate with local workforce development boards, foster care transition centers, community and technical colleges, schools, and any other appropriate workforce industry resources to create a program that:

(1) assists foster care youth and former foster care youth in obtaining:

(A) a high school diploma or a high school equivalency certificate; and

(B) industry certifications that are necessary for occupations that are in high demand;

(2) provides career guidance to foster care youth and former foster care youth; and

(3) informs foster care youth and former foster care youth about the tuition and fee waivers for institutions of higher education that are available under Section 54.366, Education Code.

(b) Expired.

Added by Acts 2017, 85th Leg., ch. 419 (S.B. 1220), § 3, eff. June 1, 2017.

## § 264.1212. Facilitation of Transition to Institution of Higher Education

(a) In this section, "community resource coordination group" means a coordination group established under a memorandum of understanding under Section 531.055, Government Code.

(b) A department employee who is a member of a community resource coordination group shall inform the group about the tuition and fee waivers for institutions of higher education that are available to eligible children in foster care under Section 54.366, Education Code.

(c) Each school district, in coordination with the department, shall facilitate the transition of each child enrolled in the district who is eligible for a tuition and fee waiver under Section 54.366, Education Code, and who is likely to be in the conservatorship of the department on the day preceding the child's 18th birthday to an institution of higher education by:

(1) assisting the child with the completion of any applications for admission or for financial aid;

(2) arranging and accompanying the child on campus visits;

(3) assisting the child in researching and applying for private or institution-sponsored scholarships;

(4) identifying whether the child is a candidate for appointment to a military academy;

(5) assisting the child in registering and preparing for college entrance examinations, including, subject to the availability of funds, arranging for the payment of any examination fees by the department; and

(6) coordinating contact between the child and a liaison officer designated under Section 61.0908, Education Code, for students who were formerly in the department's conservatorship.

Added by Acts 2017, 85th Leg., ch. 333 (H.B. 928), § 1, eff. June 1, 2017. Redesignated from V.T.C.A., Family Code § 264.1211 by Acts 2019, 86th Leg., ch. 467 (H.B. 4170), § 21.001(16), eff. Sept. 1, 2019.

### § 264.1213. Records and Documents for Children Aging Out of Foster Care

The department in cooperation with volunteer advocates from a charitable organization described by Subchapter C, Chapter 107,[1] and the Department of Public Safety shall develop procedures to ensure that a foster child obtains a driver's license or personal identification card before the child leaves the conservatorship of the department.

Added by Acts 2017, 85th Leg., ch. 1076 (H.B. 3338), § 1, eff. June 15, 2017. Redesignated from V.T.C.A., Family Code § 264.1211 by Acts 2019, 86th Leg., ch. 467 (H.B. 4170), § 21.001(17), eff. Sept. 1, 2019.

[1] V.T.C.A., Family Code § 107.031.

### § 264.1214. Housing for Homeless Youth Aging Out of Foster Care

(a) For a youth who will voluntarily enter extended foster care on the youth's 18th birthday, the youth's caseworker shall, not later than six months before the youth's 18th birthday, complete any necessary transitional living or supervised independent living paperwork to ensure the youth has housing on the date the youth enters extended foster care. Not later than the 90th day before the youth's 18th birthday, the caseworker shall review the qualifications and requirements for the youth's housing.

(b) If a youth intends to continue living with the youth's substitute care provider after the youth's 18th birthday, the department shall waive any background check otherwise required for the youth to remain living with the substitute care provider.

(c) For a youth who continues living with the youth's substitute care provider after the youth's 18th birthday, the youth may share a bedroom with another youth who is 16 years of age or older provided the age difference between the youths does not exceed two years.

(d) A substitute care provider who prohibits a youth from living in the facility after the youth's 18th birthday shall notify the youth's caseworker of that fact:

(1) not later than:

(A) the 90th day before the youth's 18th birthday if the facility is a foster home; or

(B) six months before the youth's 18th birthday if the facility is a cottage family home or general residential operation; or

(2) as soon as possible if the youth is placed in a foster home, cottage family home, or general residential operation less than six months before the youth's 18th birthday.

(e) After receiving notice under Subsection (d), the youth's caseworker shall verbally communicate with the youth about the youth's living arrangements and document the substance of the communication in the youth's case file.

(f) The department shall assist a youth living in a supervised independent living program arrangement to develop a rental history by allowing the youth to cosign the lease for the youth's housing provided the property owner does not object.

(g) The department by rule shall establish a protocol that may be implemented for a youth to prevent the youth from aging out of a residential treatment center. The protocol, if implemented, must be implemented not later than the youth's 17th birthday or at the time the youth is placed in a residential treatment center after the youth's 17th birthday.

Added by Acts 2021, 87th Leg., ch. 793 (H.B. 700), § 2, eff. Sept. 1, 2021.

### § 264.122. Court Approval Required for Travel Outside United States by Child in Foster Care

(a) A child for whom the department has been appointed managing conservator and who has been placed in foster care may travel outside of the United States only if the person with whom the child has been placed has petitioned the court for, and the court has rendered an order granting, approval for the child to travel outside of the United States.

(b) The court shall provide notice to the department and to any other person entitled to notice in the suit if the court renders an order granting approval for the child to travel outside of the United States under this section.

Added by Acts 2007, 80th Leg., ch. 1406, § 18, eff. Sept. 1, 2007.

### § 264.123. Reports Concerning Children Who Are Missing or Victims of Sex Trafficking

(a) If a child in the department's managing conservatorship is missing from the child's substitute care provider, including a child who is abducted or is a runaway, the department shall notify the following persons that the child is missing:

(1) the appropriate law enforcement agencies;

(2) the court with jurisdiction over the department's managing conservatorship of the child;

(3) the child's attorney ad litem;

(4) the child's guardian ad litem; and

(5) the child's parent unless the parent:

(A) cannot be located or contacted;

(B) has had the parent's parental rights terminated; or

(C) has executed an affidavit of relinquishment of parental rights.

(b) The department shall provide the notice required by Subsection (a) not later than 24 hours after the time the department learns that the child is missing or as soon as possible if a person entitled to notice under that subsection cannot be notified within 24 hours.

(c) If a child has been reported as a missing child under Subsection (a), the department shall notify the persons described by Subsection (a) when the child returns to the child's substitute care provider not later than 24 hours after the time the department learns that the child has returned or as soon as possible if a person entitled to notice cannot be notified within 24 hours.

(d) The department shall make continuing efforts to determine the location of a missing child until the child returns to substitute care, including:

(1) contacting on a monthly basis:

(A) the appropriate law enforcement agencies;

(B) the child's relatives;

(C) the child's former caregivers; and

(D) any state or local social service agency that may be providing services to the child; and

(2) conducting a supervisory-level review of the case on a quarterly basis if the child is 15 years of age or younger to determine whether sufficient efforts have been made to locate the child and whether other action is needed.

(e) The department shall document in the missing child's case record:

(1) the actions taken by the department to:

(A) determine the location of the child; and

(B) persuade the child to return to substitute care;

(2) any discussion during, and determination resulting from, the supervisory-level review under Subsection (d)(2);

(3) any discussion with law enforcement officials following the return of the child regarding the child's absence; and

(4) any discussion with the child described by Subsection (f).

(f) After a missing child returns to the child's substitute care provider, the department shall interview the child to determine the reasons why the child was missing, where the child stayed during the time the child was missing, and whether, while missing, the child was a victim of conduct that constitutes an offense under Section 20A.02(a)(7), Penal Code. The department shall report to an appropriate law enforcement agency any disclosure made by a child that indicates that the child was the victim of a crime during the time the child was missing. The department shall make a report under this subsection not later than 24 hours after the time the disclosure is made. The department is not required to interview a missing child under this subsection if, at the time the child returns, the department knows that the child was abducted and another agency is investigating the abduction.

(g) The department shall collect information on each child in the department's managing conservatorship who is missing from the child's substitute care provider and on each child who, while in the department's managing conservatorship, is a victim of conduct that constitutes an offense under Section 20A.02(a)(7), Penal Code. The collected information must include information on:

(1) whether the managing conservatorship of the department is temporary or permanent;

(2) the type of substitute care in which the child is placed; and

(3) the child's sex, age, race, and ethnicity and the department region in which the child resides.

(h) The department shall prepare an annual report on the information collected under Subsection (g) and make the report available on the department's Internet website. The report may not include any individually identifiable information regarding a child who is the subject of information in the report.

Added by Acts 2011, 82nd Leg., ch. 1130 (H.B. 943), § 1, eff. Sept. 1, 2011. Amended by Acts 2015, 84th Leg., ch. 713 (H.B. 1217), §§ 2, 3, eff. Sept. 1, 2015.

### § 264.124. Day Care for Foster Child

(a) In this section, "day care" means the assessment, care, training, education, custody, treatment, or supervision of a foster child by a person other than the child's foster parent for less than 24 hours a day, but at least two hours a day, three or more days a week.

(b) The department, in accordance with department rules, shall implement a process to verify that each foster parent who is seeking monetary assistance from the department for day care for a foster child has attempted to find appropriate day-care services for the foster child through community services, including Head Start programs, prekindergarten classes, and early education programs offered in public schools. The department shall specify the documentation the foster parent must provide to the department to demonstrate compliance with the requirements established under this subsection.

(c) Except as provided by Subsection (d), the department may not provide monetary assistance to a foster parent for day care for a foster child unless the department receives the verification required under Subsection (b).

(d) The department may provide monetary assistance to a foster parent for a foster child without the verification required under Subsection (b) if the department determines the verification would prevent an emergency placement that is in the child's best interest.

Added by Acts 2013, 83rd Leg., ch. 423 (S.B. 430), § 1, eff. Sept. 1, 2013. Amended by Acts 2015, 84th Leg., ch. 1 (S.B. 219), § 1.195, eff. April 2, 2015.

### § 264.125. Age–Appropriate Normalcy Activities; Standard of Care

(a) The department shall use its best efforts to normalize the lives of children in the managing conservatorship of the department by allowing substitute caregivers, without the department's prior approval, to make decisions similar to those a parent would be entitled to make regarding a child's participation in age-appropriate normalcy activities.

(b) In determining whether to allow a child in the managing conservatorship of the department to participate in an activity, a substitute caregiver must exercise the standard of care of a reasonable and prudent parent.

(c) The department shall adopt and implement policies consistent with this section promoting a substitute caregiver's ability to make decisions described by Subsection (a). The department shall identify and review any departmental policy or procedure that may impede a substitute caregiver's ability to make such decisions.

(d) The department shall require licensed child placing agency personnel, residential child care licensing staff, conservatorship caseworkers, and other persons as may be determined by the department to complete a course of training regarding:

(1) the importance of a child's participation in age-appropriate normalcy activities and the benefits of such activities to a child's well-being, mental health, and social, emotional, and developmental growth; and

(2) substitute caregiver decision-making under the standard of care of a reasonable and prudent parent.

Added by Acts 2015, 84th Leg., ch. 262 (S.B. 1407), § 7, eff. Sept. 1, 2015.

### § 264.1251. Expired

### § 264.1252. Expired

### § 264.126. Redesignated as V.T.C.A., Family Code § 264.153 and amended by Acts 2017, 85th Leg., ch. 319 (S.B. 11), § 18(b), eff. Sept. 1, 2017

### § 264.1261. Foster Care Capacity Needs Plan

(a) In this section, "community-based care" has the meaning assigned by Section 264.152.

(b) Appropriate department management personnel from a child protective services region in which community-based care has not been implemented, in collaboration with foster care providers, faith-based entities, and child advocates in that region, shall use data collected by the department on foster care capacity needs and availability of each type of foster care and kinship placement in the region to create a plan to address the substitute care capacity needs in the region. The plan must identify both short-term and long-term goals and strategies for addressing those capacity needs.

(b–1) Notwithstanding Section 264.0011, the Health and Human Services Commission, in collaboration with the department and each single source continuum contractor in this state, shall develop a plan to increase the placement capacity in each catchment area of the state with the goal of eliminating the need to place a child outside of the child's community. In developing the plan, the commission shall:

(1) evaluate whether contracting for additional capacity at residential treatment centers, facilities that provide mental inpatient or outpatient beds for crisis intervention and stabilization purposes only for children with severe behavioral health or mental health needs, and other potential temporary placement options provides the best methods for meeting capacity shortages; and

(2) make a recommendation to the department regarding contracting for additional capacity.

(b–2) A plan developed under Subsection (b–1) that includes the use of an inpatient or outpatient mental health facility must require the facility to discharge a child placed in the facility not later than 72 hours after the treating health care provider determines it is not medically necessary for the child to remain in the facility.

(b–3) The plan developed under Subsection (b–1) must include information and contingency plans to ensure adequate capacity in other facilities to meet placement needs when a facility is placed on probation.

(b–4) The department and each single source continuum contractor shall contract with facilities for reserve beds to ensure the department may place each child in a facility if capacity is otherwise unavailable.

(c) A foster care capacity needs plan developed under Subsection (b) must be:

(1) submitted to and approved by the commissioner; and

(2) updated annually.

(d) The department shall publish each initial foster care capacity needs plan and each annual update to a plan on the department's Internet website.

Added by Acts 2017, 85th Leg., ch. 319 (S.B. 11), § 17(a), eff. Sept. 1, 2017; Acts 2017, 85th Leg., ch. 822 (H.B. 1549), § 4, eff. Sept. 1, 2017. Amended by Acts 2021, 87th Leg., ch. 621 (S.B. 1896), § 5, eff. June 14, 2021.

Section 35 of Acts 2021, 87th Leg., ch. 621 (S.B. 1896) provides:

"The Office of Community-Based Care Transition, the Department of Family and Protective Services, and the Health and Human Services Commission are required to implement this Act only if the legislature appropriates money specifically for that purpose. If the legislature does not appropriate money specifically for that purpose, the Office of Community-Based Care Transition, the Department of Family and Protective Services, and the Health and Human Services Commission may, but are not required to, implement this Act using other appropriations available for the purpose."

### § 264.128. Single Child Plan of Service Initiative

(a) In this section, "community-based care" has the meaning assigned by Section 264.152.

(b) In regions of the state where community-based care has not been implemented, the department shall:

(1) collaborate with child-placing agencies to implement the single child plan of service model developed under the single child plan of service initiative; and

(2) ensure that a single child plan of service is developed for each child in foster care in those regions.

Added by Acts 2017, 85th Leg., ch. 319 (S.B. 11), § 17(a), eff. Sept. 1, 2017.

### § 264.130. Pregnancy and Parenting Information

The department at developmentally appropriate stages shall ensure that children in the managing conservatorship of the department who are pregnant or who are minor parents receive information on and support in providing safe environments for children, including information and support regarding:

(1) safe sleeping arrangements;

(2) suggestions for childproofing potentially dangerous settings in a home;

(3) child development and methods to cope with challenging behaviors;

(4) selection of appropriate substitute caregivers;

(5) a child's early brain development, including the importance of meeting an infant's developmental needs by providing positive experiences and avoiding adverse experiences;

(6) the importance of paternal involvement in a child's life and methods for coparenting;

(7) the benefits of reading, singing, and talking to young children;

(8) the importance of prenatal and postpartum care for both the mother and infant, including the impact of and signs for perinatal mood disorders;

(9) infant nutrition and the importance of breastfeeding; and

(10) healthy relationships, including the prevention of intimate partner violence.

Added by Acts 2019, 86th Leg., ch. 1033 (H.B. 475), § 1, eff. Sept. 1, 2019.

## SUBCHAPTER B–1. COMMUNITY–BASED CARE

### § 264.151. Legislative Intent

(a) It is the intent of the legislature that the department contract with community-based nonprofit and local governmental entities that have the ability to provide child welfare services. The services provided by the entities must include direct case management to ensure child safety, permanency, and well-being, in accordance with state and federal child welfare goals.

(b) It is the intent of the legislature that the provision of community-based care for children be implemented with measurable goals relating to:

(1) the safety of children in placements;

(2) the placement of children in each child's home community;

(3) the provision of services to children in the least restrictive environment possible and, if possible, in a family home environment;

(4) minimal placement changes for children;

(5) the maintenance of contact between children and their families and other important persons;

(6) the placement of children with siblings;

(7) the provision of services that respect each child's culture;

(8) the preparation of children and youth in foster care for adulthood;

(9) the provision of opportunities, experiences, and activities for children and youth in foster care that are available to children and youth who are not in foster care;

(10) the participation by children and youth in making decisions relating to their own lives;

(11) the reunification of children with the biological parents of the children when possible; and

(12) the promotion of the placement of children with relative or kinship caregivers if reunification is not possible.

Added by Acts 2017, 85th Leg., ch. 319 (S.B. 11), § 18(a), eff. Sept. 1, 2017.

### § 264.152. Definitions

Except as otherwise provided, in this subchapter:

(1) "Alternative caregiver" means a person who is not the foster parent of the child and who provides temporary care for the child for more than 12 hours but less than 60 days.

(2) "Case management" means the provision of case management services to a child for whom the department has been appointed temporary or permanent managing conservator or to the child's family, a young adult in extended foster care, a relative or kinship caregiver, or a child who has been placed in the catchment area through the Interstate Compact on the Placement of Children, and includes:

(A) caseworker visits with the child;

(B) family and caregiver visits;

(C) convening and conducting permanency planning meetings;

(D) the development and revision of child and family plans of service, including a permanency plan and goals for a child or young adult in care;

(E) the coordination and monitoring of services required by the child and the child's family;

(F) the assumption of court-related duties regarding the child, including:

(i) providing any required notifications or consultations;

(ii) preparing court reports;

(iii) attending judicial and permanency hearings, trials, and mediations;

(iv) complying with applicable court orders; and

(v) ensuring the child is progressing toward the goal of permanency within state and federally mandated guidelines; and

(G) any other function or service that the department determines necessary to allow a single source continuum contractor to assume responsibility for case management.

(3) "Catchment area" means a geographic service area for providing child protective services that is identified as part of community-based care.

(4) "Community-based care" means the provision of child welfare services in accordance with state and federal child welfare goals by a community-based nonprofit or a local governmental entity under a contract that includes direct case management to:

(A) prevent entry into foster care;

(B) reunify and preserve families;

(C) ensure child safety, permanency, and well-being; and

(D) reduce future referrals of children or parents to the department.

Added by Acts 2017, 85th Leg., ch. 319 (S.B. 11), § 18(a), eff. Sept. 1, 2017. Amended by Acts 2021, 87th Leg., ch. 621 (S.B. 1896), § 6, eff. June 14, 2021.

Section 35 of Acts 2021, 87th Leg., ch. 621 (S.B. 1896) provides:

"The Office of Community-Based Care Transition, the Department of Family and Protective Services, and the Health and Human Services Commission are required to implement this Act only if the legislature appropriates money specifically for that purpose. If the legislature does not appropriate money specifically for that purpose, the Office of Community-Based Care Transition, the Department of Family and Protective Services, and the Health and Human Services Commission may, but are not required to, implement this Act using other appropriations available for the purpose."

## § 264.153. Community-Based Care Implementation Plan

(a) The department shall develop and maintain a plan for implementing community-based care. The plan must:

(1) describe the department's expectations, goals, and approach to implementing community-based care;

(2) include a timeline for implementing community-based care throughout this state, any limitations related to the implementation, and a progressive intervention plan and a contingency plan to provide continuity of the delivery of foster care services and services for relative and kinship caregivers if a contract with a single source continuum contractor ends prematurely;

(3) delineate and define the case management roles and responsibilities of the department and the department's contractors and the duties, employees, and related funding that will be transferred to the contractor by the department;

(4) identify any training needs and include long-range and continuous plans for training and cross-training staff, including plans to train caseworkers using the standardized curriculum created by the human trafficking prevention task force under Section 402.035(d)(6), Government Code, as that section existed on August 31, 2017;

(5) include a plan for evaluating the costs and tasks associated with each contract procurement, including the initial and ongoing contract costs for the department and contractor;

(6) include the department's contract monitoring approach and a plan for evaluating the performance of each contractor and the community-based care system as a whole that includes an independent evaluation of each contractor's processes and fiscal and qualitative outcomes; and

(7) include a report on transition issues resulting from implementation of community-based care.

(b) The department shall annually:

(1) update the implementation plan developed under this section and post the updated plan on the department's Internet website; and

(2) post on the department's Internet website the progress the department has made toward its goals for implementing community-based care.

Added by Acts 2015, 84th Leg., ch. 944 (S.B. 206), § 57, eff. Sept. 1, 2015. Redesignated from V.T.C.A., Family Code § 264.126 and amended by Acts 2017, 85th Leg., ch. 319 (S.B. 11), § 18(b), eff. Sept. 1, 2017.

## § 264.154. Qualifications of Single Source Continuum Contractor; Selection

(a) To enter into a contract with the commission or department to serve as a single source continuum contractor to provide services under this subchapter, an entity must be:

(1) a nonprofit entity that has:

(A) an organizational mission focused on child welfare; and

(B) a majority of the entity's board members residing in this state; or

(2) a governmental entity.

(b) In selecting a single source continuum contractor, the department shall consider whether a prospective contractor for a catchment area has demonstrated experience in providing services to children and families in the catchment area.

(c) The department shall request local stakeholders in a catchment area, including those listed in Section 264.155(a)(8), to provide any necessary information about the catchment area that will assist the department in:

(1) preparing the department's request for bids, proposals, or other applicable expressions of interest to provide community-based care in the catchment area; and

(2) selecting a single source continuum contractor to provide community-based care in the catchment area.

Added by Acts 2017, 85th Leg., ch. 319 (S.B. 11), § 18(a), eff. Sept. 1, 2017. Amended by Acts 2021, 87th Leg., ch. 621 (S.B. 1896), § 7, eff. June 14, 2021.

Section 35 of Acts 2021, 87th Leg., ch. 621 (S.B. 1896) provides:

"The Office of Community-Based Care Transition, the Department of Family and Protective Services, and the Health and Human Services Commission are required to implement this Act only if the legislature appropriates money specifically for that purpose. If the legislature does not appropriate money specifically for that purpose, the Office of Community-Based Care Transition, the Department of Family and Protective Services, and the Health and Human Services Commission may, but are not required to, implement this Act using other appropriations available for the purpose."

## § 264.155. Required Contract Provisions

(a) A contract with a single source continuum contractor to provide community-based care services in a catchment area must include provisions that:

(1) establish a timeline for the implementation of community-based care in the catchment area, including a timeline for implementing:

(A) case management services for children, families, and relative and kinship caregivers receiving services in the catchment area; and

(B) family reunification support services to be provided after a child receiving services from the contractor is returned to the child's family;

(2) establish conditions for the single source continuum contractor's access to relevant department data and require the participation of the contractor in the data access and standards governance council created under Section 264.159;

(3) require the single source continuum contractor to create a single process for the training and use of alternative caregivers for all child-placing agencies in the catchment area to facilitate reciprocity of licenses for alternative caregivers between agencies, including respite and overnight care providers, as those terms are defined by department rule;

(4) require the single source continuum contractor to maintain a diverse network of service providers that offer a range of foster capacity options and that can accommodate children from diverse cultural backgrounds;

(5) allow the department to conduct a performance review of the contractor beginning 18 months after the contractor has begun providing case management and family reunification support services to all children and families in the catchment area and determine if the contractor has achieved any performance outcomes specified in the contract;

(6) following the review under Subdivision (5), allow the department to:

(A) impose financial penalties on the contractor for failing to meet any specified performance outcomes; or

(B) award financial incentives to the contractor for exceeding any specified performance outcomes;

(7) require the contractor to give preference for employment to employees of the department:

(A) whose position at the department is impacted by the implementation of community-based care; and

(B) who are considered by the department to be employees in good standing;

(8) require the contractor to provide preliminary and ongoing community engagement plans to ensure communication and collaboration with local stakeholders in the catchment area, including any of the following:

(A) community faith-based entities;

(B) the judiciary;

(C) court-appointed special advocates;

(D) child advocacy centers;

(E) service providers;

(F) foster families;

(G) biological parents;

(H) foster youth and former foster youth;

(I) relative or kinship caregivers;

(J) child welfare boards, if applicable;

(K) attorneys ad litem;

(L) attorneys that represent parents involved in suits filed by the department; and

(M) any other stakeholders, as determined by the contractor; and

(9) require that the contractor comply with any applicable court order issued by a court of competent jurisdiction in the case of a child for whom the contractor has assumed case management responsibilities or an order imposing a requirement on the department that relates to functions assumed by the contractor.

(b) A contract with a single source continuum contractor under this subchapter must be consistent with the requirements of applicable law and may only include terms authorized by the laws or rules of this state.

(c) In regions identified for implementing community-based care and in regions where community-based care has been implemented, a contractor may apply to the department for a waiver from any statutory and regulatory requirement to increase innovation and flexibility for achieving contractual performance outcomes.

Added by Acts 2017, 85th Leg., ch. 319 (S.B. 11), § 18(a), eff. Sept. 1, 2017. Amended by Acts 2021, 87th Leg., ch. 621 (S.B. 1896), § 8, eff. June 14, 2021.

Section 35 of Acts 2021, 87th Leg., ch. 621 (S.B. 1896) provides:

"The Office of Community–Based Care Transition, the Department of Family and Protective Services, and the Health and Human Services Commission are required to implement this Act only if the legislature appropriates money specifically for that purpose. If the legislature does not appropriate money specifically for that purpose, the Office of Community–Based Care Transition, the Department of Family and Protective Services, and the Health and Human Services Commission may, but are not required to, implement this Act using other appropriations available for the purpose."

## § 264.156. Readiness Review Process for Community–Based Care Contractor

(a) The department shall develop a formal review process to assess the ability of a single source continuum contractor to satisfy the responsibilities and administrative requirements of delivering foster care services and services for relative and kinship caregivers, including the contractor's ability to provide:

(1) case management services for children and families;

(2) evidence-based, promising practice, or evidence-informed supports for children and families; and

(3) sufficient available capacity for inpatient and outpatient services and supports for children at all service levels who have previously been placed in the catchment area.

(b) As part of the readiness review process, the single source continuum contractor must prepare a plan detailing the methods by which the contractor will avoid or eliminate conflicts of interest. The department may not transfer services to the contractor until the department has determined the plan is adequate.

(c) Repealed by Acts 2021, 87th Leg., ch. 621 (S.B. 1896), § 26(1).

(d) If after conducting the review process developed under Subsection (a) the department determines that a single source continuum contractor is able to adequately deliver foster care services and services for relative and kinship caregivers in advance of the projected dates stated in the timeline included in the contract with the contractor, the department may adjust the timeline to allow for an earlier transition of service delivery to the contractor.

Added by Acts 2017, 85th Leg., ch. 319 (S.B. 11), § 18(a), eff. Sept. 1, 2017. Amended by Acts 2021, 87th Leg., ch. 621 (S.B. 1896), § 26(1), eff. June 14, 2021.

Section 35 of Acts 2021, 87th Leg., ch. 621 (S.B. 1896) provides:

"The Office of Community–Based Care Transition, the Department of Family and Protective Services, and the Health and Human Services Commission are required to implement this Act only if the legislature appropriates money specifically for that purpose. If the legislature does not appropriate money specifically for that purpose, the Office of Community–Based Care Transition, the Department of Family and Protective Services, and the Health and Human Services Commission may, but are not required to, implement this Act using other appropriations available for the purpose."

## § 264.157. Expansion of Community–Based Care

(a) Not later than the last day of the state fiscal biennium, the department shall:

(1) identify the catchment areas in the state where the department will implement community-based care; and

(2) following the implementation of community-based care services in those catchment areas, retain an entity based in this state that is independent of the department to conduct an evaluation of the implementation process and the single source continuum contractor performance in each catchment area.

(b) Notwithstanding the process for the expansion of community-based care described in Subsection (a), the department shall accept and evaluate unsolicited proposals from entities based in this state to provide community-based care services in a geographic service area where the department has not implemented community-based care. An entity that submits a proposal to provide community-based care services must ensure that it meets all criteria outlined by this subchapter and must demonstrate established connections to the area the entity proposes to serve. The Health and Human Services Commission in conjunction with the department shall adopt rules to ensure that proposals submitted under this subsection comply with state procurement laws and rules.

(c) In expanding community-based care, the department may change the geographic boundaries of catchment areas as necessary to align with specific communities or to enable satisfactory unsolicited proposals for community-based care services to be accepted and implemented.

(d) The department shall ensure the continuity of services for children and families during the transition period to community-based care in a catchment area.

Added by Acts 2017, 85th Leg., ch. 319 (S.B. 11), § 18(a), eff. Sept. 1, 2017. Amended by Acts 2021, 87th Leg., ch. 621 (S.B. 1896), § 9, eff. June 14, 2021.

Section 35 of Acts 2021, 87th Leg., ch. 621 (S.B. 1896) provides:

"The Office of Community–Based Care Transition, the Department of Family and Protective Services, and the Health and Human Services Commission are required to implement this Act only if the legislature appropriates money specifically for that purpose. If the legislature does not appropriate money specifically for that purpose, the Office of Community–Based Care Transition, the Department of Family and Protective Services, and the Health and Human Services

Commission may, but are not required to, implement this Act using other appropriations available for the purpose."

## § 264.158. Transfer of Case Management Services to Single Source Continuum Contractor

(a) In each initial catchment area where community-based care has been implemented or a contract with a single source continuum contractor has been executed before September 1, 2017, the department shall transfer to the single source continuum contractor providing foster care services in that area:

(1) the case management of children, relative and kinship caregivers, and families receiving services from that contractor; and

(2) family reunification support services to be provided after a child receiving services from the contractor is returned to the child's family for the period of time ordered by the court.

(b) The commission shall include a provision in a contract with a single source continuum contractor to provide foster care services and services for relative and kinship caregivers in a catchment area to which community-based care is expanded after September 1, 2017, that requires the transfer to the contractor of the provision of:

(1) the case management services for children, relative and kinship caregivers, and families in the catchment area where the contractor will be operating; and

(2) family reunification support services to be provided after a child receiving services from the contractor is returned to the child's family.

(c) The department shall collaborate with a single source continuum contractor to establish an initial case transfer planning team to:

(1) address any necessary data transfer;

(2) establish file transfer procedures; and

(3) notify relevant persons regarding the transfer of services to the contractor.

(d) A single source continuum contractor may implement its own procedures to execute the department's statutory duties the contractor assumes and is not required to follow the department's procedures to execute the assumed department duties.

Added by Acts 2017, 85th Leg., ch. 319 (S.B. 11), § 18(a), eff. Sept. 1, 2017. Amended by Acts 2021, 87th Leg., ch. 621 (S.B. 1896), § 10, eff. June 14, 2021.

Section 35 of Acts 2021, 87th Leg., ch. 621 (S.B. 1896) provides:

"The Office of Community-Based Care Transition, the Department of Family and Protective Services, and the Health and Human Services Commission are required to implement this Act only if the legislature appropriates money specifically for that purpose. If the legislature does not appropriate money specifically for that purpose, the Office of Community-Based Care Transition, the Department of Family and Protective Services, and the Health and Human Services Commission may, but are not required to, implement this Act using other appropriations available for the purpose."

## § 264.159. Data Access and Standards Governance Council

(a) The department shall create a data access and standards governance council to develop protocols for the interoperable electronic transfer of data from single source continuum contractors to the department to allow the contractors to perform case management functions and additional contracted services by the department.

(b) The council shall develop protocols for the access, management, and security of case data that is electronically shared between a single source continuum contractor and the department.

(c) The council shall develop protocols for the access, management, and security of data shared with an independent entity retained to conduct the independent evaluations required under this subchapter. The protocols shall ensure the entity has full, unrestricted access to all relevant data necessary to perform an evaluation.

(d) The council consists of single source continuum contractors with active contracts and department employees who provide data, legal, information technology, and child protective services. The council shall meet at least quarterly during each calendar year.

Added by Acts 2017, 85th Leg., ch. 319 (S.B. 11), § 18(a), eff. Sept. 1, 2017. Amended by Acts 2021, 87th Leg., ch. 621 (S.B. 1896), § 11, eff. June 14, 2021.

Section 35 of Acts 2021, 87th Leg., ch. 621 (S.B. 1896) provides:

"The Office of Community-Based Care Transition, the Department of Family and Protective Services, and the Health and Human Services Commission are required to implement this Act only if the legislature appropriates money specifically for that purpose. If the legislature does not appropriate money specifically for that purpose, the Office of Community-Based Care Transition, the Department of Family and Protective Services, and the Health and Human Services Commission may, but are not required to, implement this Act using other appropriations available for the purpose."

## § 264.160. Liability Insurance Requirements

A single source continuum contractor and any subcontractor of the single source continuum contractor providing community-based care services shall maintain minimum insurance coverage, as required in the contract with the department, to minimize the risk of insolvency and protect against damages. The executive commissioner may adopt rules to implement this section.

Added by Acts 2017, 85th Leg., ch. 319 (S.B. 11), § 18(a), eff. Sept. 1, 2017.

### § 264.161. Statutory Duties Assumed by Contractor

Except as provided by Section 264.163, a single source continuum contractor providing foster care services and services for relative and kinship caregivers in a catchment area must, either directly or through subcontractors, assume the statutory duties of the department in connection with the delivery of foster care services and services for relative and kinship caregivers in that catchment area.

Added by Acts 2017, 85th Leg., ch. 319 (S.B. 11), § 18(a), eff. Sept. 1, 2017.

### § 264.162. Review of Contractor Performance

The department shall develop a formal review process to evaluate a single source continuum contractor's implementation of placement services and case management services in a catchment area.

Added by Acts 2017, 85th Leg., ch. 319 (S.B. 11), § 18(a), eff. Sept. 1, 2017.

### § 264.163. Continuing Duties of Department

In a catchment area in which a single source continuum contractor is providing family-based safety services or community-based care services, legal representation of the department in an action under this code shall be provided in accordance with Section 264.009.

Added by Acts 2017, 85th Leg., ch. 319 (S.B. 11), § 18(a), eff. Sept. 1, 2017.

### § 264.164. Confidentiality

(a) The records of a single source continuum contractor relating to the provision of community-based care services in a catchment area are subject to Chapter 552, Government Code, in the same manner as the records of the department are subject to that chapter.

(b) Subchapter C, Chapter 261,[1] regarding the confidentiality of certain case information, applies to the records of a single source continuum contractor in relation to the provision of services by the contractor.

Added by Acts 2017, 85th Leg., ch. 319 (S.B. 11), § 18(a), eff. Sept. 1, 2017.

[1] V.T.C.A., Family Code § 261.201 et seq.

### § 264.165. Notice Required for Early Termination of Contract

(a) A single source continuum contractor may terminate a contract entered into under this subchapter by providing notice to the department and the commission of the contractor's intent to terminate the contract not later than the 60th day before the date of the termination.

(b) The department may terminate a contract entered into with a single source continuum contractor under this subchapter by providing notice to the contractor of the department's intent to terminate the contract not later than the 30th day before the date of termination.

Added by Acts 2017, 85th Leg., ch. 319 (S.B. 11), § 18(a), eff. Sept. 1, 2017.

### § 264.166. Contingency Plan in Event of Early Contract Termination

(a) In each catchment area in which community-based care is implemented, the department shall create a contingency plan to ensure the continuity of services for children and families in the catchment area in the event of an early termination of the contract with the single source continuum contractor providing foster care services in that catchment area.

(b) To support each contingency plan, the single source continuum contractor providing foster care services in that catchment area, subject to approval by the department, shall develop a transfer plan to ensure the continuity of services for children and families in the catchment area in the event of an early termination of the contract with the department. The contractor shall submit an updated transfer plan each year and six months before the end of the contract period, including any extension. The department is not limited or restricted in requiring additional information from the contractor or requiring the contractor to modify the transfer plan as necessary.

(c) If a single source continuum contractor gives notice to the department of an early contract termination, the department may enter into a contract with a different contractor for the sole purpose of assuming the contract that is being terminated.

Added by Acts 2017, 85th Leg., ch. 319 (S.B. 11), § 18(a), eff. Sept. 1, 2017.

### § 264.167. Attorney–Client Privilege

An employee, agent, or representative of a single source continuum contractor is considered to be a client's representative of the department for purposes of the privilege under Rule 503, Texas Rules of Evidence, as that privilege applies to communications with a prosecuting attorney or other attorney representing the department, or the attorney's representatives, in a proceeding under this subtitle.

Added by Acts 2017, 85th Leg., ch. 319 (S.B. 11), § 18(a), eff. Sept. 1, 2017.

### § 264.168. Review of Contractor Recommendations by Department

(a) Notwithstanding any other provision of this subchapter governing the transfer of case management authority to a single source continuum contractor, the department may review, approve, or disapprove a contractor's recommendation with respect to a child's permanency goal.

(b) Subsection (a) may not be construed to limit or restrict the authority of the department to include necessary oversight measures and review processes to maintain compliance with federal and state requirements in a contract with a single source continuum contractor.

(c) The department shall develop an internal dispute resolution process to decide disagreements between a single source continuum contractor and the department.

Added by Acts 2017, 85th Leg., ch. 319 (S.B. 11), § 18(a), eff. Sept. 1, 2017.

### § 264.169. Repealed by Acts 2021, 87th Leg., ch. 621 (S.B. 1896), § 26(2), eff. June 14, 2021; Acts 2021, 87th Leg., ch. 858 (S.B. 910), § 2(1), eff. June 16, 2021

Section 35 of Acts 2021, 87th Leg., ch. 621 (S.B. 1896) provides:

"The Office of Community-Based Care Transition, the Department of Family and Protective Services, and the Health and Human Services Commission are required to implement this Act only if the legislature appropriates money specifically for that purpose. If the legislature does not appropriate money specifically for that purpose, the Office of Community-Based Care Transition, the Department of Family and Protective Services, and the Health and Human Services Commission may, but are not required to, implement this Act using other appropriations available for the purpose."

Section 4 of Acts 2021, 87th Leg., ch. 858 (S.B. 910) provides:

"The Department of Family and Protective Services is required to implement a provision of this Act only if the legislature appropriates money specifically for that purpose. If the legislature does not appropriate money specifically for that purpose, the department may, but is not required to, implement a provision of this Act using other appropriations that are available for that purpose."

### § 264.1691. Study of Options for Implementing Family Preservation Services

*This section expires pursuant to (f)*

(a) In this section, "family preservation service" means a time-limited, family-focused service, including:

(1) a service subject to the Family First Prevention Services Act (Title VII, Div. E, Pub. L. No. 115–123), provided to the family of a child who is:

(A) a candidate for foster care to prevent or eliminate the need to remove the child and to allow the child to remain safely with the child's family; or

(B) a pregnant or parenting foster youth;

(2) enhanced in-home support services and nonrecurring financial support to promote safe and stable families; and

(3) services to promote self-sufficiency and prevent further need for interaction in the child welfare system.

(b) The department shall study and develop a comprehensive list of options for implementing family preservation services in existing catchment areas, including:

(1) contracting with single source continuum contractors to provide services; and

(2) procuring service providers through a competitive bidding process.

(c) In developing the options under Subsection (b), the department shall:

(1) examine existing department functions related to the stage of service the department describes as family-based safety services, including assessments of child safety and child removals, and make recommendations for incorporating the functions into a contracted model;

(2) consider the results from community needs assessments and capacity development plans conducted during the preceding 10 years; and

(3) consider:

(A) contingent on appropriation, including Title IV–E prevention services in the delivery of community-based family preservation services and the appropriate use of those services;

(B) the financial modeling used to determine implementation costs, including:

(i) start-up funding costs;

(ii) the cost of purchased client services;

(iii) strategies for shared financial risk; and

(iv) rate methodology;

(C) procedures for transitioning between case stages, including transitions from:

(i) investigation to family preservation; and

(ii) family preservation to foster care;

(D) ways to maximize evidence-based services and to increase the evidence base for family preservation programs in this state;

(E) requirements for complying with federal law to receive matching funds for certain prevention services;

(F) appropriate performance measures for contracted services, including associated financial remedies and incentives;

(G) ways to incorporate and to maximize existing funding methods for and programs related to behavioral health and substance use provided by the Health and Human Services Commission;

(H) appropriate contract provisions to ensure a clear distinction of money, personnel, and processes for family preservation services and foster care services;

(I) conflict resolution procedures between the department and contractors concerning:

(i) service plans;

(ii) services; and

(iii) case action for children or families served by a contractor;

(J) appropriate oversight structures to manage contract compliance, contractor performance, and child and family safety;

(K) appropriate contract provisions to ensure community engagement, including appropriate partnerships with faith-based organizations;

(L) recommendations for statutory changes necessary to support the department's implementation options; and

(M) any other information the department determines necessary for legislative direction of the department's implementation of community-based family preservation services.

(d) In developing implementation options under this section, the department shall:

(1) incorporate relevant information obtained from previous efforts and similar service models implemented in other states;

(2) collaborate with the Health and Human Services Commission as needed, including on:

(A) recommendations for the provision of behavioral health and substance use services; and

(B) appropriate rate methodology; and

(3) allow interested persons to comment on the provision of behavioral health and substance use services.

(e) The department may enter into any contracts the department determines necessary to comply with this section.

(f) This section expires August 31, 2023.

Added by Acts 2021, 87th Leg., ch. 858 (S.B. 910), § 1, eff. June 16, 2021.

Sections 3 and 4 of Acts 2021, 87th Leg., ch. 858 (S.B. 910) provide:

"Sec. 3. Not later than October 1, 2022, the Department of Family and Protective Services shall submit copies of the options described by Section 264.1691, Family Code, as added by this Act, along with any associated recommendations, to the:

"(1) governor;

"(2) lieutenant governor;

"(3) speaker of the house of representatives;

"(4) House Committee on Appropriations;

"(5) Senate Committee on Finance;

"(6) House Committee on Human Services; and

"(7) Senate Committee on Health and Human Services.

"Sec. 4. The Department of Family and Protective Services is required to implement a provision of this Act only if the legislature appropriates money specifically for that purpose. If the legislature does not appropriate money specifically for that purpose, the department may, but is not required to, implement a provision of this Act using other appropriations that are available for that purpose."

## § 264.170. Limited Liability for Single Source Continuum Contractor and Related Personnel

(a) A nonprofit entity that contracts with the department to provide services as a single source continuum contractor under this subchapter is considered to be a charitable organization for the purposes of Chapter 84, Civil Practice and Remedies Code, with respect to the provision of those services, and that chapter applies to the entity and any person who is an employee or volunteer of the entity.

(b) The limitations on liability provided by this section apply:

(1) only to an act or omission by the entity or person, as applicable, that occurs while the entity or person is acting within the course and scope of the entity's contract with the department and the person's duties for the entity; and

(2) only if insurance coverage in the minimum amounts required by Chapter 84, Civil Practice and Remedies Code, is in force and effect at the time a cause of action for personal injury, death, or property damage accrues.

Added by Acts 2019, 86th Leg., ch. 467 (H.B. 4170), § 7.006(a), eff. Sept. 1, 2019.

### § 264.171. Joint Legislative Oversight Committee on Community–Based Care Transition

(a) Notwithstanding Section 264.0011, in this section:

(1) "Commission" means the Health and Human Services Commission.

(2) "Committee" means the Joint Legislative Oversight Committee on Community–Based Care Transition.

(3) "Department" means the Department of Family and Protective Services.

(b) The Joint Legislative Oversight Committee on Community–Based Care Transition is composed of six voting members as follows:

(1) three members of the senate, appointed by the lieutenant governor; and

(2) three members of the house of representatives, appointed by the speaker of the house of representatives.

(c) The lieutenant governor and speaker of the house of representatives shall each appoint a member described by Subsection (b)(1) or (2), respectively, to serve as joint chairs of the committee.

(d) The committee shall meet at the call of the joint chairs and may consider public testimony.

(e) The committee may employ persons necessary to carry out this section through funds made available by the legislature.

(f) The committee shall monitor and report to the legislature on the following related to the implementation of community-based care:

(1) the funding of community-based care;

(2) the performance and outcomes of community-based care statewide and by region;

(3) statutory or regulatory barriers to the successful implementation of community-based care; and

(4) other challenges to the successful implementation of community-based care.

(g) The committee may request any relevant information from the commission, the department, or another relevant state agency, and the commission, department, or agency shall comply with the request, unless the provision of the information is prohibited by state or federal law.

(h) Not later than January 1 of each odd-numbered year, the committee shall submit a written report of the committee's findings and recommendations to the governor, the lieutenant governor, the speaker of the house of representatives, and each member of the standing committees of the senate and house of representatives having primary jurisdiction over child welfare issues.

(i) The committee shall monitor the continued implementation of community-based care and hold public hearings to receive comments from the public on the implementation of community-based care.

Added by Acts 2021, 87th Leg., ch. 621 (S.B. 1896), § 12, eff. June 14, 2021.

Section 35 of Acts 2021, 87th Leg., ch. 621 (S.B. 1896) provides:

"The Office of Community–Based Care Transition, the Department of Family and Protective Services, and the Health and Human Services Commission are required to implement this Act only if the legislature appropriates money specifically for that purpose. If the legislature does not appropriate money specifically for that purpose, the Office of Community–Based Care Transition, the Department of Family and Protective Services, and the Health and Human Services Commission may, but are not required to, implement this Act using other appropriations available for the purpose."

### § 264.172. Office of Community–Based Care Transition

(a) In this section:

(1) "Department" means the Department of Family and Protective Services.

(2) "Office" means the Office of Community–Based Care Transition created under this section.

(b) The Office of Community–Based Care Transition is a state agency independent of but administratively attached to the department.

(c) The office shall:

(1) assess catchment areas in this state where community-based care services may be implemented;

(2) develop a plan for implementing community-based care in each catchment area in this state, including the order in which community-based care will be implemented in each catchment area and a timeline for implementation;

(3) evaluate community-based care providers;

(4) contract, on behalf of the department, with community-based care providers to provide services in each catchment area in this state;

(5) measure contract performance of community-based care providers;

(6) provide contract oversight of community-based care providers;

(7) report outcomes of community-based care providers;

(8) identify the employees and other resources to be transferred to the community-based care provider to provide the necessary implementation, case management, operational, and administrative functions and outline the methodology for determining the employees and resources to be transferred;

(9) create a risk-sharing funding model that strategically and explicitly balances financial risk between this state and the community-based care provider and mitigates the financial effects of significant unforeseen changes in the community-based care provider's duties or the population of the region it serves; and

(10) require the annual review and adjustment of the funding based on updated cost and finance methodologies, including changes in policy, foster care rates, and regional service usage.

(d) The department shall provide any administrative support the office needs, and the department and the Health and Human Services Commission shall provide access to any information and legal counsel the office requires to implement community-based care.

(e) The governor shall appoint the director of the office to serve in that capacity at the pleasure of the governor. The director reports directly to the governor.

(f) The office shall report to the legislature at least once each calendar quarter regarding the implementation of community-based care in the state.

(g) A provision of this subchapter applicable to the department with respect to any duty assigned by this section to the office applies to the office in the same manner as the provision would apply to the department.

(h) Except as otherwise provided by this section, the department retains the powers and duties provided by this subchapter to the department.

(i) The office is abolished and this section expires on the date that community-based care is implemented in the last department region in this state.

Added by Acts 2021, 87th Leg., ch. 621 (S.B. 1896), § 12, eff. June 14, 2021.

Section 35 of Acts 2021, 87th Leg., ch. 621 (S.B. 1896) provides:

"The Office of Community–Based Care Transition, the Department of Family and Protective Services, and the Health and Human Services Commission are required to implement this Act only if the legislature appropriates money specifically for that purpose. If the legislature does not appropriate money specifically for that purpose, the Office of Community–Based Care Transition, the Department of Family and Protective Services, and the Health and Human Services Commission may, but are not required to, implement this Act using other appropriations available for the purpose."

## SUBCHAPTER C. CHILD AND FAMILY SERVICES

### § 264.201. Services by Department

(a) When the department provides services directly or by contract to an abused or neglected child and the child's family, the services shall be designed to:

(1) prevent further abuse;

(2) alleviate the effects of the abuse suffered;

(3) prevent removal of the child from the home; and

(4) provide reunification services when appropriate for the return of the child to the home.

(b) The department shall emphasize ameliorative services for sexually abused children.

(c) The department shall provide or contract for necessary services to an abused or neglected child and the child's family without regard to whether the child remains in or is removed from the family home. If parental rights have been terminated, services may be provided only to the child.

(d) The services may include in-home programs, parenting skills training, youth coping skills, and individual and family counseling. If the department requires or a court orders parenting skills training services through a parenting education program or practice, the program or practice must be an evidence-based program or practice or promising program or practice that is provided in the community in which the family resides, if available.

(e) The department may not provide and a court may not order the department to provide supervision for visitation in a child custody matter unless the department is a petitioner or intervener in the underlying suit.

Added by Acts 1995, 74th Leg., ch. 20, § 1, eff. April 20, 1995. Amended by Acts 1999, 76th Leg., ch. 1150, § 28, eff. Sept. 1, 1999; Acts 1999, 76th Leg., ch. 1390, § 49, eff. Sept. 1, 1999; Acts 2015, 84th Leg., ch. 1257 (H.B. 2630), § 1, eff. Sept. 1, 2015; Acts 2017, 85th Leg., ch. 324 (S.B. 1488), § 24.002(6), eff. Sept. 1, 2017; Acts 2021, 87th Leg., ch. 515 (S.B. 452), § 1, eff. Sept. 1, 2021.

### § 264.2011. Enhanced In–Home Support Program

(a) To the extent that funding is available, the department shall develop a program to strengthen families through enhanced in-home support. The program shall assist certain low-income families and children in child neglect cases in which poverty is believed to be a significant underlying cause of the neglect and in which the enhancement of in-home support appears likely to prevent removal of the child from the home or to speed reunification of the child with the family.

(b) A family that meets eligibility criteria for inclusion in the program is eligible to receive limited funding from a flexible fund account to cover nonrecurring expenses that are designed to help the family accomplish the objectives included in the family's service plan.

(c) The executive commissioner shall adopt rules establishing:

(1) specific eligibility criteria for the program described in this section;

(2) the maximum amount of money that may be made available to a family through the flexible fund account; and

(3) the purposes for which money made available under the program may be spent.

(d) The department shall evaluate the results of the program to determine whether the program is successful in safely keeping families together. If the department determines that the program is successful, the department shall continue the program to the extent that funding is available.

Added by Acts 2007, 80th Leg., ch. 1406, § 19, eff. Sept. 1, 2007.

### § 264.2015. Family Group Conferencing

The department may collaborate with the courts and other appropriate local entities to develop and implement family group conferencing as a strategy for promoting family preservation and permanency for children.

Added by Acts 2005, 79th Leg., ch. 268, § 1.52, eff. Sept. 1, 2005.

### § 264.202. Standards and Effectiveness

(a) The department, with assistance from national organizations with expertise in child protective services, shall define a minimal baseline of in-home and foster care services for abused or neglected children that meets the professionally recognized standards for those services. The department shall attempt to provide services at a standard not lower than the minimal baseline standard.

(b) The department, with assistance from national organizations with expertise in child protective services, shall develop outcome measures to track and monitor the effectiveness of in-home and foster care services.

Added by Acts 1995, 74th Leg., ch. 20, § 1, eff. April 20, 1995.

### § 264.203. Required Participation

(a) The department may file a suit requesting the court to render a temporary order requiring the parent, managing conservator, guardian, or other member of the child's household to:

(1) participate in the services for which the department makes a referral or services the department provides or purchases for:

(A) alleviating the effects of the abuse or neglect that has occurred;

(B) reducing a continuing danger to the physical health or safety of the child caused by an act or failure to act of the parent, managing conservator, guardian, or other member of the child's household; or

(C) reducing a substantial risk of abuse or neglect caused by an act or failure to act of the parent, managing conservator, guardian, or member of the child's household; and

(2) permit the child and any siblings of the child to receive the services.

(b) A suit requesting an order under this section may be filed in a court with jurisdiction to hear the suit in the county in which the child is located.

(c) Except as otherwise provided by this subchapter, the suit is governed by the Texas Rules of Civil Procedure applicable to the filing of an original lawsuit.

(d) The petition shall be supported by a sworn affidavit by a person based on personal knowledge and stating facts sufficient to support a finding that:

(1) the child has been a victim of abuse or neglect or is at substantial risk of abuse or neglect; and

(2) there is a continuing danger to the physical health or safety of the child caused by an act or failure to act of the parent, managing conservator, guardian, or other member of the child's household unless that person participates in services requested by the department.

(e) In a suit filed under this section, the court may render a temporary restraining order as provided by Section 105.001.

(f) The court shall hold a hearing on the petition not later than the 14th day after the date the petition is filed unless the court finds good cause for extending that date for not more than 14 days.

(g) The court shall appoint an attorney ad litem to represent the interests of the child immediately after the filing but before the hearing to ensure adequate representation of the child. The attorney ad litem for the child shall have the powers and duties of an attorney ad litem for a child under Chapter 107.

(h) The court shall appoint an attorney ad litem to represent the interests of a parent for whom participation in services is being requested immediately after the filing but before the hearing to ensure adequate representation of the parent. The attorney ad litem for the parent shall have the powers and duties of an attorney ad litem for a parent under Section 107.0131.

(i) Before commencement of the hearing, the court shall inform each parent of:

(1) the parent's right to be represented by an attorney; and

(2) for a parent who is indigent and appears in opposition to the motion, the parent's right to a court-appointed attorney.

(j) If a parent claims indigence, the court shall require the parent to complete and file with the court an affidavit of indigence. The court may consider additional evidence to determine whether the parent is indigent, including evidence relating to the parent's income, source of income, assets, property ownership, benefits paid in accordance with a federal, state, or local public assistance program, outstanding obligations, and necessary expenses and the number and ages of the parent's dependents. If the court determines the parent is indigent, the attorney ad litem appointed to represent the interests of the parent may continue the representation. If the court determines the parent is not indigent, the court shall discharge the attorney ad litem from the appointment after the hearing and shall order the parent to pay the cost of the attorney ad litem's representation.

(k) The court may, for good cause shown, postpone any subsequent proceedings for not more than seven days after the date of the attorney ad litem's discharge to allow the parent to hire an attorney or to provide the parent's attorney time to prepare for the subsequent proceeding.

(*l*) An order may be rendered under this section only after notice and hearing.

(m) At the conclusion of the hearing, the court shall deny the petition unless the court finds sufficient evidence to satisfy a person of ordinary prudence and caution that:

(1) abuse or neglect has occurred or there is a substantial risk of abuse or neglect or continuing danger to the physical health or safety of the child caused by an act or failure to act of the parent, managing conservator, guardian, or other member of the child's household; and

(2) services are necessary to ensure the physical health or safety of the child.

(n) If the court renders an order granting the petition, the court shall:

(1) state its findings in the order;

(2) make appropriate temporary orders under Chapter 105 necessary to ensure the safety of the child; and

(3) order the participation in specific services narrowly tailored to address the findings made by the court under Subsection (m).

(*o*) If the court finds that a parent, managing conservator, guardian, or other member of the child's household did not cause the continuing danger to the physical health or safety of the child or the substantial risk of abuse or neglect, or was not the perpetrator of the abuse or neglect alleged, the court may not require that person to participate in services ordered under Subsection (n).

(p) Not later than the 90th day after the date the court renders an order under this section, the court shall hold a hearing to review the status of each person required to participate in the services and the child and the services provided, purchased, or referred. The court shall set subsequent review hearings every 90 days to review the continued need for the order.

(q) An order rendered under this section expires on the 180th day after the date the order is signed unless the court extends the order as provided by Subsection (r) or (s).

(r) The court may extend an order rendered under this section on a showing by the department of a continuing need for the order, after notice and hearing. Except as provided by Subsection (s), the court may extend the order only one time for not more than 180 days.

(s) The court may extend an order rendered under this section for not more than an additional 180 days only if:

(1) the court finds that:

(A) the extension is necessary to allow the person required to participate in services under the plan of service time to complete those services;

(B) the department made a good faith effort to timely provide the services to the person;

(C) the person made a good faith effort to complete the services; and

(D) the completion of the services is necessary to ensure the physical health and safety of the child; and

(2) the extension is requested by the person or the person's attorney.

(t) At any time, a person affected by the order may request the court to terminate the order. The court shall terminate the order on finding the order is no longer needed.

Added by Acts 1995, 74th Leg., ch. 20, § 1, eff. April 20, 1995. Amended by Acts 2005, 79th Leg., ch. 268, § 1.55, eff. Sept. 1, 2005; Acts 2007, 80th Leg., ch. 1406, § 20, eff. Sept. 1, 2007; Acts 2021, 87th Leg., ch. 8 (H.B. 567), § 12, eff. Sept. 1, 2021.

Section 15 of Acts 2021, 87th Leg., ch. 8 (H.B. 567) provides:

"The changes in law made by this Act apply only to a suit filed by the Department of Family and Protective Services on or after the effective date [Sept. 1, 2021] of this Act. A suit filed by the department before that date is governed by the law in effect on the date the suit was filed, and the former law is continued in effect for that purpose."

### § 264.2031. Selection of Service Provider

(a) A parent, managing conservator, guardian, or other member of a household ordered to participate in services under Section 264.203(a) may obtain those services from a qualified provider selected by the person.

(b) A parent, managing conservator, guardian, or other member of a household who obtains services from a provider selected by the person is responsible for the cost of those services.

(c) A parent, managing conservator, guardian, or other member of a household who successfully completes the services ordered under Section 264.203(a) must obtain verification from the service provider of that completion. The department shall accept the service provider's verification provided under this subsection as proof that the person successfully completed the court-ordered services.

Added by Acts 2021, 87th Leg., ch. 269 (H.B. 3041), § 4, eff. Sept. 1, 2021.

### § 264.204. Community-Based Family Services

(a) The department shall administer a grant program to provide funding to community organizations, including faith-based or county organizations, to respond to:

(1) low-priority, less serious cases of abuse and neglect; and

(2) cases in which an allegation of abuse or neglect of a child was unsubstantiated but involved a family that has been previously investigated for abuse or neglect of a child.

(b) The executive commissioner shall adopt rules to implement the grant program, including rules governing the submission and approval of grant requests and the cancellation of grants.

(c) To receive a grant, a community organization whose grant request is approved must execute an interagency agreement or a contract with the department. The contract must require the organization receiving the grant to perform the services as stated in the approved grant request. The contract must contain appropriate provisions for program and fiscal monitoring.

(d) In areas of the state in which community organizations receive grants under the program, the department shall refer low-priority, less serious cases of abuse and neglect to a community organization receiving a grant under the program.

(e) A community organization receiving a referral under Subsection (d) shall make a home visit and offer family social services to enhance the parents' ability to provide a safe and stable home environment for the child. If the family chooses to use the family services, a case manager from the organization shall monitor the case and ensure that the services are delivered.

(f) If after the home visit the community organization determines that the case is more serious than the department indicated, the community organization shall refer the case to the department for a full investigation.

(g) The department may not award a grant to a community organization in an area of the state in which a similar program is already providing effective family services in the community.

(h) For purposes of this section, a case is considered to be a less serious case of abuse or neglect if:

(1) the circumstances of the case do not appear to involve a reasonable likelihood that the child will be abused or neglected in the foreseeable future; or

(2) the allegations in the report of child abuse or neglect:

(A) are general in nature or vague and do not support a determination that the child who is the subject of the report has been abused or neglected or will likely be abused or neglected; or

(B) if substantiated, would not be considered abuse or neglect under this chapter.

Added by Acts 2005, 79th Leg., ch. 268, § 1.53, eff. Sept. 1, 2005.

### § 264.2041. Cultural Awareness

The department shall:

(1) develop and deliver cultural competency training to all service delivery staff;

(2) increase targeted recruitment efforts for foster and adoptive families who can meet the needs of children and youth who are waiting for permanent homes;

(3) target recruitment efforts to ensure diversity among department staff; and

(4) develop collaborative partnerships with community groups, agencies, faith-based organizations, and other community organizations to provide culturally competent services to children and families of every race and ethnicity.

Added by Acts 2005, 79th Leg., ch. 268, § 1.54(a), eff. Sept. 1, 2005.

### § 264.2042. Nonprofit Organizations Providing Child and Family Services

(a) The department shall cooperate with nonprofit organizations, including faith-based organizations, in providing information to families in crisis regarding child and family services, including respite care, voluntary guardianship, and other support services, available in the child's community.

(b) The department does not incur any obligation as a result of providing information as required by Subsection (a).

(c) The department is not liable for damages arising out of the provision of information as required by Subsection (a).

Added by Acts 2017, 85th Leg., ch. 244 (H.B. 871), § 11, eff. Sept. 1, 2017.

### § 264.2043. Prohibition on Abuse or Neglect Investigation Based Solely on Request for Information

The department may not initiate an investigation of child abuse or neglect based solely on a request submitted to the department by a child's parent for information relating to child and family services available to families in crisis.

Added by Acts 2017, 85th Leg., ch. 244 (H.B. 871), § 11, eff. Sept. 1, 2017.

### § 264.2044. Grants for Faith-Based Community Collaborative Programs

(a) Using available funds or private donations, the governor shall establish and administer an innovation grant program to award grants to support faith-based community programs that collaborate with the department and the commission to improve foster care and the placement of children in foster care.

(b) A faith-based community program is eligible for a grant under this section if:

(1) the effectiveness of the program is supported by empirical evidence; and

(2) the program has demonstrated the ability to build connections between faith-based, secular, and government stakeholders.

(c) The regional director for the department in the region where a grant recipient program is located, or the regional director's designee, shall serve as the liaison between the department and the program for collaborative purposes. For a program that operates in a larger region, the department may designate a liaison in each county where the program is operating. The department or the commission may not direct or manage the operation of the program.

(d) The initial duration of a grant under this section is two years. The governor may renew a grant awarded to a program under this section if funds are available and the governor determines that the program is successful.

(e) The governor may not award to a program grants under this section totaling more than $300,000.

(f) The governor shall adopt rules to implement the grant program created under this section.

Added by Acts 2017, 85th Leg., ch. 319 (S.B. 11), § 19(a), eff. Sept. 1, 2017. Redesignated from V.T.C.A., Family Code § 264.2042 by Acts 2019, 86th Leg., ch. 467 (H.B. 4170), § 21.001(18), eff. Sept. 1, 2019.

### § 264.205. Swift Adoption Teams

(a) The department shall develop swift adoption teams to expedite the process of placing a child under the jurisdiction of the department for adoption. Swift adoption teams developed under this section shall, in performing their duties, attempt to place a child for adoption with an appropriate relative of the child.

(b) A swift adoption team shall consist of department personnel who shall operate under policies adopted by rule by the executive commissioner. The department shall set priorities for the allocation of department resources to enable a swift adoption team to operate successfully under the policies adopted under this subsection.

(c) Repealed by Acts 2011, 82nd Leg., ch. 1050 (S.B. 71), § 20; Acts 2011, 82nd Leg., ch. 1083 (S.B. 1179), § 25(27).

Added by Acts 1995, 74th Leg., ch. 943, § 9, eff. Sept. 1, 1995. Amended by Acts 2001, 77th Leg., ch. 306, § 4, eff. Sept. 1, 2001; Acts 2011, 82nd Leg., ch. 1050 (S.B. 71), § 20, eff. Sept. 1, 2011; Acts 2011, 82nd Leg., ch. 1083 (S.B. 1179), § 25(27), eff. June 17, 2011; Acts 2015, 84th Leg., ch. 1 (S.B. 219), § 1.196, eff. April 2, 2015.

### § 264.206. Repealed by Acts 2015, 84th Leg., ch. 1 (S.B. 219), § 1.203(12), eff. April 2, 2015

### § 264.207. Home Study Required Before Adoption

(a) The department must complete a home study before the date an applicant is approved for an adoption.

(b) Repealed by Acts 2015, 84th Leg., ch. 944 (S.B. 206), § 86(32).

Added by Acts 1997, 75th Leg., ch. 600, § 19, eff. Sept. 1, 1997; Acts 1997, 75th Leg., ch. 1022, § 94, eff. Sept. 1, 1997. Amended by Acts 2015, 84th Leg., ch. 944 (S.B. 206), §§ 58, 59, 86(32), eff. Sept. 1, 2015.

### § 264.208. Repealed by Acts 2015, 84th Leg., ch. 944 (S.B. 206), § 86(33), eff. Sept. 1, 2015

## SUBCHAPTER D. SERVICES TO AT-RISK YOUTH

### § 264.301. Services for At-Risk Youth

(a) The department shall operate a program to provide services for children in at-risk situations and for the families of those children.

(b) The services under this section may include:

(1) crisis family intervention;

(2) emergency short-term residential care;

(3) family counseling;

(4) parenting skills training;

(5) youth coping skills training;

(6) mentoring; and

(7) advocacy training.

Added by Acts 1995, 74th Leg., ch. 20, § 1, eff. April 20, 1995. Amended by Acts 1995, 74th Leg., ch. 262, § 58, eff. Jan. 1, 1996.

### § 264.302. Early Youth Intervention Services

(a) This section applies to a child who:

(1) is seven years of age or older and under 17 years of age; and

(2) has not had the disabilities of minority for general purposes removed under Chapter 31.

(b) The department shall operate a program under this section to provide services for children in at-risk situations and for the families of those children.

(c) The department may not provide services under this section to a child who has:

(1) at any time been referred to juvenile court for engaging in conduct that violates a penal law of this state of the grade of felony other than a state jail felony; or

(2) been found to have engaged in delinquent conduct under Title 3.[1]

(d) The department may provide services under this section to a child who engages in conduct for which the child may be found by a court to be an at-risk child, without regard to whether the conduct violates a penal law of this state of the grade of felony other than a state jail felony, if the child was younger than 10 years of age at the time the child engaged in the conduct.

(e) The department shall provide services for a child and the child's family if a contract to provide services under this section is available in the county and the child is referred to the department as an at-risk child by:

(1) a juvenile court or probation department as part of a progressive sanctions program under Chapter 59;

(2) a law enforcement officer or agency under Section 52.03; or

(3) a justice or municipal court under Article 45.057, Code of Criminal Procedure.

(f) The services under this section may include:

(1) crisis family intervention;

(2) emergency short-term residential care for children 10 years of age or older;

(3) family counseling;

(4) parenting skills training;

(5) youth coping skills training;

(6) advocacy training; and

(7) mentoring.

Added by Acts 1995, 74th Leg., ch. 262, § 58, eff. Jan. 1, 1996. Amended by Acts 1997, 75th Leg., ch. 1086, § 30, eff. Sept. 1, 1997; Acts 1997, 75th Leg., ch. 575, § 31, eff. Sept. 1, 1997; Acts 2001, 77th Leg., ch. 1514, § 16, eff. Sept. 1, 2001; Acts 2015, 84th Leg., ch. 944 (S.B. 206), § 60, eff. Sept. 1, 2015.

[1] V.T.C.A., Family Code § 51.01 et seq.

### § 264.303. Repealed by Acts 2015, 84th Leg., ch. 944 (S.B. 206), § 86(34), eff. Sept. 1, 2015

### § 264.304. Repealed by Acts 2015, 84th Leg., ch. 944 (S.B. 206), § 86(35), eff. Sept. 1, 2015; Acts 2017, 85th Leg., ch. 324 (S.B. 1488), § 7.011, eff. Sept. 1, 2017

### § 264.305. Repealed by Acts 2015, 84th Leg., ch. 944 (S.B. 206), § 86(36), eff. Sept. 1, 2015

### § 264.306. Repealed by Acts 2015, 84th Leg., ch. 944 (S.B. 206), § 86(37), eff. Sept. 1, 2015

## SUBCHAPTER E. CHILDREN'S ADVOCACY CENTERS

### § 264.401. Definition

In this subchapter, "center" means a children's advocacy center.

Added by Acts 1995, 74th Leg., ch. 255, § 1, eff. Sept. 1, 1995.

### § 264.402. Establishment of Children's Advocacy Center

On the execution of a memorandum of understanding under Section 264.403, a children's advocacy center may be established by community members and the participating agencies described by Section 264.403(a) to serve a county or two or more contiguous counties in which a center has not been established.

Added by Acts 1995, 74th Leg., ch. 255, § 1, eff. Sept. 1, 1995. Amended by Acts 2003, 78th Leg., ch. 185, § 1, eff. Sept. 1, 2003; Acts 2019, 86th Leg., ch. 396 (S.B. 821), § 1, eff. Sept. 1, 2019.

### § 264.403. Interagency Memorandum of Understanding

(a) A center shall enter into a memorandum of understanding regarding participation in the multidisciplinary team response under Section 264.406. The center and each of the following agencies must execute the memorandum of understanding:

(1) the department responsible for child abuse and neglect investigations;

(2) each county and municipal law enforcement agency with jurisdiction to investigate child abuse and neglect in the area to be served by the center; and

(3) each county or district attorney with jurisdiction to prosecute child abuse and neglect cases in the area to be served by the center.

(b) A memorandum of understanding executed under this section shall include the agreement of each participating agency to cooperate in:

(1) minimizing the revictimization of alleged abuse and neglect victims and nonoffending family members through the investigation, assessment, intervention, and prosecution processes; and

(2) maintaining a cooperative team approach to facilitate successful outcomes in the criminal justice and child protection systems through shared fact-finding and strong, collaborative case development.

(c) The memorandum of understanding must be reexecuted:

(1) at least every three years;

(2) on a significant change to the memorandum of understanding; or

(3) on a change of a signatory of a participating agency.

Added by Acts 1995, 74th Leg., ch. 255, § 1, eff. Sept. 1, 1995. Amended by Acts 2019, 86th Leg., ch. 396 (S.B. 821), § 2, eff. Sept. 1, 2019.

### § 264.4031. Multidisciplinary Team Working Protocol

(a) A center shall adopt a multidisciplinary team working protocol. The working protocol must include:

(1) the center's mission statement;

(2) the role of each participating agency on the multidisciplinary team and the agency's commitment to the center;

(3) specific criteria for referral of cases for a multidisciplinary team response and specific criteria for the referral and provision of each service provided by the center;

(4) processes and general procedures for:

(A) the intake of cases, including direct referrals from participating agencies described by Section

264.403(a) and reports from the department that involve the suspected abuse or neglect of a child or the death of a child from abuse or neglect;

(B) the availability outside scheduled business hours of a multidisciplinary team response to cases and provision of necessary center services;

(C) information sharing to ensure the timely exchange of relevant information;

(D) forensic interviews;

(E) family and victim advocacy;

(F) medical evaluations and medical treatment;

(G) mental health evaluations and mental health treatment;

(H) multidisciplinary team case review; and

(I) case tracking; and

(5) provisions for addressing conflicts within the multidisciplinary team and for maintaining the confidentiality of information shared among members of the multidisciplinary team.

(b) The working protocol must be executed by the participating agencies required to enter into the memorandum of understanding under Section 264.403.

(c) The working protocol must be reexecuted:

(1) at least every three years;

(2) on a significant change to the working protocol; or

(3) on a change of a signatory of a participating agency.

Added by Acts 2019, 86th Leg., ch. 396 (S.B. 821), § 3, eff. Sept. 1, 2019.

### § 264.404. Board Representation

(a) In addition to any other persons appointed or elected to serve on the governing board of a center, the governing board must include an executive officer of, or an employee with decision-making authority selected by an executive officer of:

(1) the department responsible for child abuse and neglect investigations;

(2) a law enforcement agency with jurisdiction to investigate child abuse and neglect in the area served by the center; and

(3) the county or district attorney's office with jurisdiction to prosecute child abuse and neglect cases in the area served by the center.

(b) Service on a center's board by an executive officer or employee under Subsection (a) is an additional duty of the person's office or employment.

(c) The governing board members required under Subsection (a) may not constitute a majority of the membership of a center's governing board.

Added by Acts 1995, 74th Leg., ch. 255, § 1, eff. Sept. 1, 1995. Amended by Acts 2003, 78th Leg., ch. 185, § 1, eff. Sept. 1, 2003; Acts 2019, 86th Leg., ch. 396 (S.B. 821), § 4, eff. Sept. 1, 2019.

### § 264.405. Center Duties

(a) A center shall:

(1) receive, review, and track department reports relating to the suspected abuse or neglect of a child or the death of a child from abuse or neglect to ensure a consistent, comprehensive approach to all cases that meet the criteria outlined in the multidisciplinary team working protocol adopted under Section 264.4031;

(2) coordinate the activities of participating agencies relating to abuse and neglect investigations and delivery of services to alleged abuse and neglect victims and their families;

(3) facilitate assessment of alleged abuse or neglect victims and their families to determine their need for services relating to the investigation of abuse or neglect and provide needed services; and

(4) comply with the standards adopted under Section 264.409(c).

(b) A center shall provide:

(1) facilitation of a multidisciplinary team response to abuse or neglect allegations;

(2) a formal process that requires the multidisciplinary team to routinely discuss and share information regarding investigations, case status, and services needed by children and families;

(3) a system to monitor the progress and track the outcome of each case;

(4) a child-focused setting that is comfortable, private, and physically and psychologically safe for diverse populations at which a multidisciplinary team can meet to facilitate the efficient and appropriate disposition of abuse and neglect cases through the civil and criminal justice systems;

(5) culturally competent services for children and families throughout the duration of a case;

(6) victim support and advocacy services for children and families;

(7) forensic interviews that are conducted in a neutral, fact-finding manner and coordinated to avoid duplicative interviewing;

(8) access to specialized medical evaluations and treatment services for victims of alleged abuse or neglect;

(9) evidence-based, trauma-focused mental health services for children and nonoffending members of the child's family; and

(10) opportunities for community involvement through a formalized volunteer program dedicated to supporting the center.

(c) The duties prescribed to a center under Subsection (a)(1) do not relieve the department or a law enforcement agency of its duty to investigate a report of abuse or neglect as required by other law.

Added by Acts 1995, 74th Leg., ch. 255, § 1, eff. Sept. 1, 1995. Amended by Acts 2019, 86th Leg., ch. 396 (S.B. 821), § 5, eff. Sept. 1, 2019.

### § 264.406. Multidisciplinary Team

(a) A center's multidisciplinary team must include employees of the participating agencies described by Section 264.403(a).

(b) A representative of any other entity may participate in the multidisciplinary team response as provided by the multidisciplinary team working protocol adopted under Section 264.4031 if:

(1) the entity participates in or provides the following:

(A) child abuse or neglect investigations;

(B) abuse or neglect investigations involving persons with a disability;

(C) services to alleged child abuse or neglect victims; or

(D) services to alleged victims who are persons with a disability;

(2) the center and the participating agencies agree in writing to the entity's participation; and

(3) the entity signs the memorandum of understanding executed under Section 264.403 and the working protocol adopted under Section 264.4031.

(c) A multidisciplinary team shall be actively involved in the following multidisciplinary team response:

(1) coordinating the actions of the participating agencies involved in the investigation and prosecution of cases and the delivery of services to alleged abuse or neglect victims and the victims' families; and

(2) conducting at regularly scheduled intervals multidisciplinary review of appropriate abuse or neglect cases as provided by the working protocol adopted under Section 264.4031.

(d) A multidisciplinary team may review an abuse or neglect case in which the alleged perpetrator is not a person responsible for a child's care, custody, or welfare.

(e) A multidisciplinary team member is authorized to share with and receive from other multidisciplinary team members information made confidential by Chapter 552, Government Code, Section 40.005 or 48.101, Human Resources Code, or Section 261.201 or 264.408 of this code when acting in the member's official capacity as an employee of a participating agency described by Section 264.403(a) or of another entity described by Subsection (b).

Added by Acts 1995, 74th Leg., ch. 255, § 1, eff. Sept. 1, 1995. Amended by Acts 1997, 75th Leg., ch. 575, § 32, eff. Sept. 1, 1997; Acts 2003, 78th Leg., ch. 185, § 1, eff. Sept. 1, 2003; Acts 2019, 86th Leg., ch. 396 (S.B. 821), § 6, eff. Sept. 1, 2019.

### § 264.4061. Multidisciplinary Team Response Required

(a) The department shall refer a case to a center and the center shall initiate a response by a center's multidisciplinary team appointed under Section 264.406 when conducting an investigation of:

(1) a report of abuse or neglect that is made by a professional as defined by Section 261.101 and that:

(A) alleges sexual abuse of a child; or

(B) is a type of case handled by the center in accordance with the working protocol adopted for the center under Section 264.4031; or

(2) a child fatality in which there are surviving children in the deceased child's household or under the supervision of the caregiver involved in the child fatality.

(b) Any interview of a child conducted as part of the investigation under Subsection (a) must be a forensic interview conducted in accordance with the center's working protocol adopted under Section 264.4031 unless a forensic interview is not appropriate based on the child's age and development or the center's working protocol adopted under Section 264.4031.

(c) Subsection (a) applies only to an investigation of abuse or neglect in a county served by a center that has executed an interagency memorandum of understanding under Section 264.403. If a county is not served by a center that has executed an interagency memorandum of understanding, the department may, if appropriate, directly refer a case to a center in an adjacent county to initiate a response by that center's multidisciplinary team.

Added by Acts 2017, 85th Leg., ch. 945 (S.B. 1806), § 1, eff. Sept. 1, 2017. Amended by Acts 2019, 86th Leg., ch. 396 (S.B. 821), § 7, eff. Sept. 1, 2019.

### § 264.407. Liability

(a) A person is not liable for civil damages for a recommendation made or an opinion rendered in good faith while acting in the official scope of the person's duties as a member of a multidisciplinary team or as a board member, staff member, or volunteer of a center.

(b) The limitation on civil liability of Subsection (a) does not apply if a person's actions constitute gross negligence.

Added by Acts 1995, 74th Leg., ch. 255, § 1, eff. Sept. 1, 1995.

### § 264.408. Use of Information and Records; Confidentiality and Ownership

(a) The files, reports, records, communications, and working papers used or developed in providing services under this chapter are confidential and not subject to public release under Chapter 552, Government Code, and may only be disclosed for purposes consistent with this chapter. Disclosure may be made to:

(1) the department, department employees, law enforcement agencies, prosecuting attorneys, medical professionals, and other state or local agencies that provide services to children and families; and

(2) the attorney for the alleged victim who is the subject of the records and a court-appointed volunteer advocate appointed for the alleged victim under Section 107.031.

(b) Information related to the investigation of a report of abuse or neglect under Chapter 261 and to the services provided as a result of the investigation is confidential as provided by Section 261.201.

(c) The department, a law enforcement agency, and a prosecuting attorney may share with a center information that is confidential under Section 261.201 as needed to provide services under this chapter. Confidential information shared with or provided to a center remains the property of the agency that shared or provided the information to the center. A request for confidential information provided to the center under this section must be made to the agency that shared or provided the information.

(d) An electronic recording of an interview with a child or person with a disability that is made by a center is the property of the prosecuting attorney involved in the criminal prosecution of the case involving the child or person. If no criminal prosecution occurs, the electronic recording is the property of the attorney involved in representing the department in a civil action alleging abuse, neglect, or exploitation. If the matter involving the child or person is not prosecuted, the electronic recording is the property of the department if the matter is an investigation by the department of abuse, neglect, or exploitation. If the department is not investigating or has not investigated the matter, the electronic recording is the property of the agency that referred the matter to the center.

(d–1) An electronic recording of an interview described by Subsection (d) is subject to production under Article 39.14, Code of Criminal Procedure, and Rule 615, Texas Rules of Evidence. A court shall deny any request by a defendant to copy, photograph, duplicate, or otherwise reproduce an electronic recording of an interview described by Subsection (d), provided that the prosecuting attorney makes the electronic recording reasonably available to the defendant in the same manner as property or material may be made available to defendants, attorneys, and expert witnesses under Article 39.15(d), Code of Criminal Procedure.

(e) The department shall be allowed access to electronic recordings of interviews of children or persons with a disability.

Added by Acts 1997, 75th Leg., ch. 575, § 33, eff. Sept. 1, 1997. Amended by Acts 2011, 82nd Leg., ch. 653 (S.B. 1106), § 4, eff. June 17, 2011; Acts 2013, 83rd Leg., ch. 1069 (H.B. 3259), § 3, eff. Sept. 1, 2013; Acts 2015, 84th Leg., ch. 299 (S.B. 60), § 1, eff. Sept. 1, 2015; Acts 2019, 86th Leg., ch. 396 (S.B. 821), § 8, eff. Sept. 1, 2019.

### § 264.409. Administrative Contracts

(a) The commission shall contract with one statewide organization that is exempt from federal income taxation under Section 501(a), Internal Revenue Code of 1986,[1] as an organization described by Section 501(c)(3) of that code and that is composed of individuals who have expertise in the establishment and operation of children's advocacy center programs. The statewide organization shall provide training, technical assistance, evaluation services, and funds administration to support contractual requirements under Section 264.411 for local children's advocacy center programs.

(b) The contract under this section must provide that the statewide organization may not spend annually in the performance of duties under Subsection (a) more than 12 percent of the annual amount appropriated to the commission for purposes of this section.

(c) The statewide organization with which the commission contracts shall develop and adopt standards for children's advocacy centers.

Added by Acts 1997, 75th Leg., ch. 575, § 33, eff. Sept. 1, 1997. Amended by Acts 1999, 76th Leg., ch. 347, § 1, eff. Sept. 1, 1999; Acts 2015, 84th Leg., ch. 597 (S.B. 354), § 1, eff. Sept. 1, 2015; Acts 2019, 86th Leg., ch. 396 (S.B. 821), § 9, eff. Sept. 1, 2019.

[1] 26 U.S.C.A. § 501(a).

### § 264.410. Contracts With Children's Advocacy Centers

(a) The statewide organization with which the commission contracts under Section 264.409 shall contract with eligible centers to establish, maintain, and enhance the services provided by the centers.

(b) The contract under this section may not result in reducing the financial support a center receives from another source.

(c) Repealed by Acts 2019, 86th Leg., ch. 396 (S.B. 821), § 12.

Added by Acts 1997, 75th Leg., ch. 575, § 33, eff. Sept. 1, 1997. Amended by Acts 1999, 76th Leg., ch. 347, § 2, eff. Sept. 1, 1999; Acts 2015, 84th Leg., ch. 597 (S.B. 354), § 2, eff. Sept. 1, 2015; Acts 2019, 86th Leg., ch. 396 (S.B. 821), §§ 10, 12, eff. Sept. 1, 2019.

### § 264.411. Eligibility for Contracts

(a) A public entity that operated as a center under this subchapter before November 1, 1995, or a nonprofit entity is eligible for a contract under Section 264.410 if the entity:

(1) has a signed memorandum of understanding as provided by Section 264.403;

(2) has a signed working protocol as provided by Section 264.4031;

(3) has a governing board as provided by Section 264.404;

(4) has a multidisciplinary team as provided by Section 264.406;

(5) regularly convenes the multidisciplinary team as provided by Section 264.406;

(6) employs an executive director who is accountable to the board of directors of the entity and who is not the exclusive salaried employee of any governmental agency; and

(7) fulfills the duties required by Section 264.405.

(b) The statewide organization described by Section 264.409 may waive the requirements specified in Subsection (a) if it determines that the waiver will not adversely affect a center's ability to carry out its duties under Section 264.405.

Added by Acts 1997, 75th Leg., ch. 575, § 33, eff. Sept. 1, 1997. Amended by Acts 1999, 76th Leg., ch. 347, § 3, eff. Sept. 1, 1999; Acts 2003, 78th Leg., ch. 185, § 2, eff. Sept. 1, 2003; Acts 2013, 83rd Leg., ch. 136 (S.B. 245), § 1, eff. Sept. 1, 2013; Acts 2015, 84th Leg., ch. 597 (S.B. 354), § 3, eff. Sept. 1, 2015; Acts 2019, 86th Leg., ch. 396 (S.B. 821), § 11, eff. Sept. 1, 2019.

## SUBCHAPTER F. CHILD FATALITY REVIEW AND INVESTIGATION

### § 264.501. Definitions

In this subchapter:

(1) "Autopsy" and "inquest" have the meanings assigned by Article 49.01, Code of Criminal Procedure.

(2) Repealed by Acts 2015, 84th Leg., ch. 1 (S.B. 219), § 1.203(13).

(3) "Child" means a person younger than 18 years of age.

(4) "Committee" means the child fatality review team committee.

(5) Repealed by Acts 2015, 84th Leg., ch. 1 (S.B. 219), § 1.203(13).

(6) "Health care provider" means any health care practitioner or facility that provides medical evaluation or treatment, including dental and mental health evaluation or treatment.

(7) "Meeting" means an in-person meeting or a meeting held by telephone or other electronic medium.

(8) "Preventable death" means a death that may have been prevented by reasonable medical, social, legal, psychological, or educational intervention. The term includes the death of a child from:

(A) intentional or unintentional injuries;

(B) medical neglect;

(C) lack of access to medical care;

(D) neglect and reckless conduct, including failure to supervise and failure to seek medical care; and

(E) premature birth associated with any factor described by Paragraphs (A) through (D).

(9) "Review" means a reexamination of information regarding a deceased child from relevant agencies, professionals, and health care providers.

(10) "Review team" means a child fatality review team established under this subchapter.

(11) "Unexpected death" includes a death of a child that, before investigation:

(A) appears to have occurred without anticipation or forewarning; and

(B) was caused by trauma, suspicious or obscure circumstances, sudden infant death syndrome, abuse or neglect, or an unknown cause.

Added by Acts 1995, 74th Leg., ch. 255, § 2, eff. Sept. 1, 1995; Acts 1995, 74th Leg., ch. 878, § 1, eff. Sept. 1, 1995. Amended by Acts 2001, 77th Leg., ch. 957, § 2, eff. Sept. 1, 2001; Acts 2015, 84th Leg., ch. 1 (S.B. 219), § 1.203(13), eff. April 2, 2015.

### § 264.502. Committee

(a) The child fatality review team committee is composed of:

(1) a person appointed by and representing the state registrar of vital statistics;

(2) a person appointed by and representing the commissioner of the department;

(3) a person appointed by and representing the Title V director of the Department of State Health Services;

(4) a person appointed by and representing the speaker of the house of representatives;

(5) a person appointed by and representing the lieutenant governor;

(6) a person appointed by and representing the governor; and

(7) individuals selected under Subsection (b).

(b) The members of the committee who serve under Subsections (a)(1) through (6) shall select the following additional committee members:

(1) a criminal prosecutor involved in prosecuting crimes against children;

(2) a sheriff;

(3) a justice of the peace;

(4) a medical examiner;

(5) a police chief;

(6) a pediatrician experienced in diagnosing and treating child abuse and neglect;

(7) a child educator;

(8) a child mental health provider;

(9) a public health professional;

(10) a child protective services specialist;

(11) a sudden infant death syndrome family service provider;

(12) a neonatologist;

(13) a child advocate;

(14) a chief juvenile probation officer;

(15) a child abuse prevention specialist;

(16) a representative of the Department of Public Safety;

(17) a representative of the Texas Department of Transportation;

(18) an emergency medical services provider; and

(19) a provider of services to, or an advocate for, victims of family violence.

(c) Members of the committee selected under Subsection (b) serve three-year terms with the terms of six or seven members, as appropriate, expiring February 1 each year.

(d) Members selected under Subsection (b) must reflect the geographical, cultural, racial, and ethnic diversity of the state.

(e) An appointment to a vacancy on the committee shall be made in the same manner as the original appointment. A member is eligible for reappointment.

(f) Members of the committee shall select a presiding officer from the members of the committee.

(g) The presiding officer of the committee shall call the meetings of the committee, which shall be held at least quarterly.

(h) A member of the committee is not entitled to compensation for serving on the committee but is entitled to reimbursement for the member's travel expenses as provided in the General Appropriations Act. Reimbursement under this subsection for a person serving on the committee under Subsection (a)(2) shall be paid from funds appropriated to the department. Reimbursement for other persons serving on the committee shall be paid from funds appropriated to the Department of State Health Services.

Added by Acts 1995, 74th Leg., ch. 255, § 2, eff. Sept. 1, 1995; Acts 1995, 74th Leg., ch. 878, § 1, eff. Sept. 1, 1995. Amended by Acts 2001, 77th Leg., ch. 957, § 3, eff. Sept. 1, 2001; Acts 2005, 79th Leg., ch. 268, § 1.56, eff. Sept. 1, 2005; Acts 2007, 80th Leg., ch. 396, § 1, eff. Sept. 1, 2007; Acts 2009, 81st Leg., ch. 933, § 3C.04, eff. Sept. 1, 2009; Acts 2011, 82nd Leg., ch. 1290 (H.B. 2017), § 42, eff. Sept. 1, 2011; Acts 2013, 83rd Leg., ch. 1145 (S.B. 66), § 1, eff. Sept. 1, 2013; Acts 2017, 85th Leg., ch. 822 (H.B. 1549), § 5, eff. Sept. 1, 2017.

### § 264.503. Purpose and Duties of Committee and Specified State Agencies

(a) The purpose of the committee is to:

(1) develop an understanding of the causes and incidence of child deaths in this state;

(2) identify procedures within the agencies represented on the committee to reduce the number of preventable child deaths; and

(3) promote public awareness and make recommendations to the governor and the legislature for changes in law, policy, and practice to reduce the number of preventable child deaths.

(b) To ensure that the committee achieves its purpose, the department and the Department of State Health Services shall perform the duties specified by this section.

(c) The department shall work cooperatively with:

(1) the Department of State Health Services;

(2) the committee; and

(3) individual child fatality review teams.

(d) The Department of State Health Services shall:

(1) recognize the creation and participation of review teams;

(2) promote and coordinate training to assist the review teams in carrying out their duties;

(3) assist the committee in developing model protocols for:

(A) the reporting and investigating of child fatalities for law enforcement agencies, child protective services, justices of the peace and medical examiners, and other professionals involved in the investigations of child deaths;

(B) the collection of data regarding child deaths; and

(C) the operation of the review teams;

(4) develop and implement procedures necessary for the operation of the committee;

(5) develop and make available training for justices of the peace and medical examiners regarding inquests in child death cases; and

(6) promote education of the public regarding the incidence and causes of child deaths, the public role in preventing child deaths, and specific steps the public can undertake to prevent child deaths.

(d–1) The committee shall enlist the support and assistance of civic, philanthropic, and public service organizations in the performance of the duties imposed under Subsection (d).

(e) In addition to the duties under Subsection (d), the Department of State Health Services shall:

(1) collect data under this subchapter and coordinate the collection of data under this subchapter with other data collection activities;

(2) perform annual statistical studies of the incidence and causes of child fatalities using the data collected under this subchapter; and

(3) evaluate the available child fatality data and use the data to create public health strategies for the prevention of child fatalities.

(f) Not later than April 1 of each even-numbered year, the committee shall publish a report that contains aggregate child fatality data collected by local child fatality review teams, recommendations to prevent child fatalities and injuries, and recommendations to the department on child protective services operations based on input from the child safety review subcommittee. The committee shall submit a copy of the report to the governor, lieutenant governor, speaker of the house of representatives, Department of State Health Services, and department and make the report available to the public. Not later than October 1 of each even-numbered year, the department shall submit a written response to the committee's recommendations to the committee, governor, lieutenant governor, speaker of the house of representatives, and Department of State Health Services describing which of the committee's recommendations regarding the operation of the child protective services system the department will implement and the methods of implementation.

(g) The committee shall perform the functions and duties required of a citizen review panel under 42 U.S.C. Section 5106a(c)(4)(A).

(h) Each member of the committee must be a member of the child fatality review team in the county where the committee member resides unless the committee member is an appointed representative of a state agency.

Added by Acts 1995, 74th Leg., ch. 255, § 2, eff. Sept. 1, 1995; Acts 1995, 74th Leg., ch. 878, § 1, eff. Sept. 1, 1995. Amended by Acts 2001, 77th Leg., ch. 957, § 4, eff. Sept. 1, 2001; Acts 2005, 79th Leg., ch. 268, § 1.57, eff. Sept. 1, 2005; Acts 2007, 80th Leg., ch. 396, § 2, eff. Sept. 1, 2007; Acts 2013, 83rd Leg., ch. 1145 (S.B. 66), § 2, eff. Sept. 1, 2013; Acts 2017, 85th Leg., ch. 822 (H.B. 1549), § 6, eff. Sept. 1, 2017.

### § 264.5031. Collection of near Fatality Data

(a) In this section, "near fatality" means a case where a physician has certified that a child is in critical or serious condition, and a caseworker determines that the child's condition was caused by the abuse or neglect of the child.

(b) The department shall include near fatality child abuse or neglect cases in the child fatality case database, for cases in which child abuse or neglect is determined to have been the cause of the near fatality. The department must also develop a data collection strategy for near fatality child abuse or neglect cases.

Added by Acts 2017, 85th Leg., ch. 822 (H.B. 1549), § 7, eff. Sept. 1, 2017.

### § 264.5032. Report on Child Fatality and near Fatality Data

(a) The department shall produce an aggregated report relating to child fatality and near fatality cases resulting from child abuse or neglect containing the following information:

(1) any prior contact the department had with the child's family and the manner in which the case was disposed, including cases in which the department made the following dispositions:

(A) priority none or administrative closure;

(B) call screened out;

(C) alternative or differential response provided;

(D) unable to complete the investigation;

(E) unable to determine whether abuse or neglect occurred;

(F) reason to believe abuse or neglect occurred; or

(G) child removed and placed into substitute care;

(2) for any case investigated by the department involving the child or the child's family:

(A) the number of caseworkers assigned to the case before the fatality or near fatality occurred; and

(B) the caseworker's caseload at the time the case was opened and at the time the case was closed;

(3) for any case in which the department investigation concluded that there was reason to believe that abuse or neglect occurred, and the family was referred to family-based safety services:

(A) the safety plan provided to the family;

(B) the services offered to the family; and

(C) the level of compliance with the safety plan or completion of the services by the family;

(4) the number of contacts the department made with children and families in family-based safety services cases; and

(5) the initial and attempted contacts the department made with child abuse and neglect victims.

(b) In preparing the part of the report required by Subsection (a)(1), the department shall include information contained in department records retained in accordance with the department's records retention schedule.

(c) The report produced under this section must protect the identity of individuals involved in a case that is included in the report.

(d) The department may combine the report required under this section with the annual child fatality report required to be produced under Section 261.204.

Added by Acts 2017, 85th Leg., ch. 822 (H.B. 1549), § 7, eff. Sept. 1, 2017.

### § 264.504. Meetings of Committee

(a) Except as provided by Subsections (b), (c), and (d), meetings of the committee are subject to the open meetings law, Chapter 551, Government Code, as if the committee were a governmental body under that chapter.

(b) Any portion of a meeting of the committee during which the committee discusses an individual child's death is closed to the public and is not subject to the open meetings law, Chapter 551, Government Code.

(c) Information identifying a deceased child, a member of the child's family, a guardian or caretaker of the child, or an alleged or suspected perpetrator of abuse or neglect of the child may not be disclosed during a public meeting. On a majority vote of the committee members, the members shall remove from the committee any member who discloses information described by this subsection in a public meeting.

(d) Information regarding the involvement of a state or local agency with the deceased child or another person described by Subsection (c) may not be disclosed during a public meeting.

(e) The committee may conduct an open or closed meeting by telephone conference call or other electronic medium. A meeting held under this subsection is subject to the notice requirements applicable to other meetings. The notice of the meeting must specify as the location of the meeting the location where meetings of the committee are usually held. Each part of the meeting by telephone conference call that is required to be open to the public shall be audible to the public at the location specified in the notice of the meeting as the location of the meeting and shall be tape-recorded. The tape recording shall be made available to the public.

(f) This section does not prohibit the committee from requesting the attendance at a closed meeting of a person who is not a member of the committee and who has information regarding a deceased child.

Added by Acts 1995, 74th Leg., ch. 255, § 2, eff. Sept. 1, 1995; Acts 1995, 74th Leg., ch. 878, § 1, eff. Sept. 1, 1995. Amended by Acts 2005, 79th Leg., ch. 268, § 1.58, eff. Sept. 1, 2005.

### § 264.505. Establishment of Review Team

(a) A multidisciplinary and multiagency child fatality review team may be established for a county to review child deaths in that county. A county may join with an adjacent county or counties to establish a combined review team.

(b) Any person who may be a member of a review team under Subsection (c) may initiate the establishment of a review team and call the first organizational meeting of the team.

(c) A review team must reflect the diversity of the county's population and may include:

(1) a criminal prosecutor involved in prosecuting crimes against children;

(2) a sheriff;

(3) a justice of the peace or medical examiner;

(4) a police chief;

(5) a pediatrician experienced in diagnosing and treating child abuse and neglect;

(6) a child educator;

(7) a child mental health provider;

(8) a public health professional;

(9) a child protective services specialist;

(10) a sudden infant death syndrome family service provider;

(11) a neonatologist;

(12) a child advocate;

(13) a chief juvenile probation officer; and

(14) a child abuse prevention specialist.

(d) Members of a review team may select additional team members according to community resources and needs.

(e) A review team shall select a presiding officer from its members.

Added by Acts 1995, 74th Leg., ch. 255, § 2, eff. Sept. 1, 1995; Acts 1995, 74th Leg., ch. 878, § 1, eff. Sept. 1, 1995. Amended by Acts 2005, 79th Leg., ch. 268, § 1.59, eff. Sept. 1, 2005; Acts 2017, 85th Leg., ch. 822 (H.B. 1549), § 8, eff. Sept. 1, 2017.

### § 264.506. Purpose and Duties of Review Team

(a) The purpose of a review team is to decrease the incidence of preventable child deaths by:

(1) providing assistance, direction, and coordination to investigations of child deaths;

(2) promoting cooperation, communication, and coordination among agencies involved in responding to child fatalities;

(3) developing an understanding of the causes and incidence of child deaths in the county or counties in which the review team is located;

(4) recommending changes to agencies, through the agency's representative member, that will reduce the number of preventable child deaths; and

(5) advising the committee on changes to law, policy, or practice that will assist the team and the agencies represented on the team in fulfilling their duties.

(b) To achieve its purpose, a review team shall:

(1) adapt and implement, according to local needs and resources, the model protocols developed by the department and the committee;

(2) meet on a regular basis to review child fatality cases and recommend methods to improve coordination of services and investigations between agencies that are represented on the team;

(3) collect and maintain data as required by the committee;

(4) review and analyze the collected data to identify any demographic trends in child fatality cases, including whether there is a disproportionate number of child fatalities in a particular population group or geographic area; and

(5) submit to the vital statistics unit data reports on deaths reviewed as specified by the committee.

(c) A review team shall initiate prevention measures as indicated by the review team's findings.

Added by Acts 1995, 74th Leg., ch. 255, § 2, eff. Sept. 1, 1995; Acts 1995, 74th Leg., ch. 878, § 1, eff. Sept. 1, 1995. Amended by Acts 2015, 84th Leg., ch. 1 (S.B. 219), § 1.197, eff. April 2, 2015; Acts 2017, 85th Leg., ch. 822 (H.B. 1549), § 9, eff. Sept. 1, 2017.

### § 264.507. Duties of Presiding Officer

The presiding officer of a review team shall:

(1) send notices to the review team members of a meeting to review a child fatality;

(2) provide a list to the review team members of each child fatality to be reviewed at the meeting;

(3) submit data reports to the vital statistics unit not later than the 30th day after the date on which the review took place; and

(4) ensure that the review team operates according to the protocols developed by the department and the committee, as adapted by the review team.

Added by Acts 1995, 74th Leg., ch. 255, § 2, eff. Sept. 1, 1995; Acts 1995, 74th Leg., ch. 878, § 1, eff. Sept. 1, 1995. Amended by Acts 2015, 84th Leg., ch. 1 (S.B. 219), § 1.198, eff. April 2, 2015.

### § 264.508. Review Procedure

(a) The review team of the county in which the injury, illness, or event that was the cause of the death of the child occurred, as stated on the child's death certificate, shall review the death.

(b) On receipt of the list of child fatalities under Section 264.507, each review team member shall review the member's records and the records of the member's agency for information regarding each listed child.

Added by Acts 1995, 74th Leg., ch. 255, § 2, eff. Sept. 1, 1995; Acts 1995, 74th Leg., ch. 878, § 1, eff. Sept. 1, 1995.

### § 264.509. Access to Information

(a) A review team may request information and records regarding a deceased child as necessary to carry out the review team's purpose and duties. Records and information that may be requested under this section include:

(1) medical, dental, and mental health care information; and

(2) information and records maintained by any state or local government agency, including:

(A) a birth certificate;

(B) law enforcement investigative data;

(C) medical examiner investigative data;

(D) juvenile court records;

(E) parole and probation information and records; and

(F) child protective services information and records.

(b) On request of the presiding officer of a review team, the custodian of the relevant information and records relating to a deceased child shall provide those records to the review team at no cost to the review team.

(b–1) The Department of State Health Services shall provide a review team with electronic access to the preliminary death certificate for a deceased child.

(c) This subsection does not authorize the release of the original or copies of the mental health or medical records of any member of the child's family or the guardian or caretaker of the child or an alleged or suspected perpetrator of abuse or neglect of the child which are in the possession of any state or local government agency as provided in Subsection (a)(2). Information relating to the mental health or medical condition of a member of of[1] the child's family or the guardian or caretaker of the child or the alleged or suspected perpetrator of abuse or neglect of the child acquired as part of an investigation by a state or local government agency as provided in Subsection (a)(2) may be provided to the review team.

Added by Acts 1995, 74th Leg., ch. 255, § 2, eff. Sept. 1, 1995; Acts 1995, 74th Leg., ch. 878, § 1, eff. Sept. 1, 1995. Amended by Acts 2005, 79th Leg., ch. 268, § 1.60, eff. Sept. 1, 2005; Acts 2017, 85th Leg., ch. 822 (H.B. 1549), § 10, eff. Sept. 1, 2017.

[1] So in enrolled bill.

### § 264.510. Meeting of Review Team

(a) A meeting of a review team is closed to the public and not subject to the open meetings law, Chapter 551, Government Code.

(b) This section does not prohibit a review team from requesting the attendance at a closed meeting of a person who is not a member of the review team and who has information regarding a deceased child.

(c) Except as necessary to carry out a review team's purpose and duties, members of a review team and persons attending a review team meeting may not disclose what occurred at the meeting.

(d) A member of a review team participating in the review of a child death is immune from civil or criminal liability arising from information presented in or opinions formed as a result of a meeting.

Added by Acts 1995, 74th Leg., ch. 255, § 2, eff. Sept. 1, 1995; Acts 1995, 74th Leg., ch. 878, § 1, eff. Sept. 1, 1995.

### § 264.511. Use of Information and Records; Confidentiality

(a) Information and records acquired by the committee or by a review team in the exercise of its purpose and duties under this subchapter are confidential and exempt from disclosure under the open records law, Chapter 552, Government Code, and may only be disclosed as necessary to carry out the committee's or review team's purpose and duties.

(b) A report of the committee or of a review team or a statistical compilation of data reports is a public record subject to the open records law, Chapter 552, Government Code, as if the committee or review team were a governmental body under that chapter, if the report or statistical compilation does not contain any information that would permit the identification of an individual.

(c) A member of a review team may not disclose any information that is confidential under this section.

(d) Information, documents, and records of the committee or of a review team that are confidential under this section are not subject to subpoena or discovery and may not be introduced into evidence in any civil or criminal proceeding, except that information, documents, and records otherwise available from other sources are not immune from subpoena, discovery, or introduction into evidence solely because they were presented during proceedings of the committee or a review team or are maintained by the committee or a review team.

Added by Acts 1995, 74th Leg., ch. 255, § 2, eff. Sept. 1, 1995; Acts 1995, 74th Leg., ch. 878, § 1, eff. Sept. 1, 1995.

### § 264.512. Governmental Units

The committee and a review team are governmental units for purposes of Chapter 101, Civil Practice and Remedies Code. A review team is a unit of local government under that chapter.

Added by Acts 1995, 74th Leg., ch. 255, § 2, eff. Sept. 1, 1995; Acts 1995, 74th Leg., ch. 878, § 1, eff. Sept. 1, 1995.

### § 264.513. Report of Death of Child

(a) A person who knows of the death of a child younger than six years of age shall immediately report the death to the medical examiner of the county in which the death occurs or, if the death occurs in a county that does not have a medical examiner's office or that is not part of a medical examiner's district, to a justice of the peace in that county.

(b) The requirement of this section is in addition to any other reporting requirement imposed by law, including any requirement that a person report child abuse or neglect under this code.

(c) A person is not required to report a death under this section that is the result of a motor vehicle accident. This subsection does not affect a duty imposed by another law to report a death that is the result of a motor vehicle accident.

Added by Acts 1995, 74th Leg., ch. 255, § 2, eff. Sept. 1, 1995; Acts 1995, 74th Leg., ch. 878, § 1, eff. Sept. 1, 1995.

### § 264.514. Procedure in the Event of Reportable Death

(a) A medical examiner or justice of the peace notified of a death of a child under Section 264.513 shall hold an inquest under Chapter 49, Code of Criminal Procedure, to determine whether the death is unexpected or the result of abuse or neglect. An inquest is not required under this subchapter if the child's death is expected and is due to a congenital or neoplastic disease. A death caused by an infectious disease may be considered an expected death if:

(1) the disease was not acquired as a result of trauma or poisoning;

(2) the infectious organism is identified using standard medical procedures; and

(3) the death is not reportable to the Department of State Health Services under Chapter 81, Health and Safety Code.

(a-1) The commissioners court of a county shall adopt regulations relating to the timeliness for conducting an inquest into the death of a child. The regulations adopted under this subsection must be as stringent as the standards issued by the National Association of Medical Examiners unless the commissioners court determines that it would be cost prohibitive for the county to comply with those standards.

(b) The medical examiner or justice of the peace shall immediately notify an appropriate local law enforcement agency if the medical examiner or justice of the peace determines that the death is unexpected or the result of abuse or neglect, and that agency shall investigate the child's death. The medical examiner or justice of the peace shall notify the appropriate county child fatality review team of the child's death not later than the 120th day after the date the death is reported.

(c) In this section, the terms "abuse" and "neglect" have the meaning assigned those terms by Section 261.001.

Added by Acts 1995, 74th Leg., ch. 255, § 2, eff. Sept. 1, 1995; Acts 1995, 74th Leg., ch. 878, § 1, eff. Sept. 1, 1995. Amended by Acts 1997, 75th Leg., ch. 1022, § 95, eff. Sept. 1, 1997; Acts 1997, 75th Leg., ch. 1301, § 2, eff. Sept. 1, 1997; Acts 1999, 76th Leg., ch. 785, § 3, eff. Sept. 1, 1999; Acts 2015, 84th Leg., ch. 1 (S.B. 219), § 1.199, eff. April 2, 2015; Acts 2017, 85th Leg., ch. 822 (H.B. 1549), § 11(a), eff. Sept. 1, 2017.

### § 264.515. Investigation

(a) The investigation required by Section 264.514 must include:

(1) an autopsy, unless an autopsy was conducted as part of the inquest;

(2) an inquiry into the circumstances of the death, including an investigation of the scene of the death and interviews with the parents of the child, any guardian or caretaker of the child, and the person who reported the child's death; and

(3) a review of relevant information regarding the child from an agency, professional, or health care provider.

(b) The review required by Subsection (a)(3) must include a review of any applicable medical record, child protective services record, record maintained by an emergency medical services provider, and law enforcement report.

(c) The committee shall develop a protocol relating to investigation of an unexpected death of a child under this section. In developing the protocol, the committee shall consult with individuals and organizations that have knowledge and experience in the issues of child abuse and child deaths.

Added by Acts 1995, 74th Leg., ch. 255, § 2, eff. Sept. 1, 1995; Acts 1995, 74th Leg., ch. 878, § 1, eff. Sept. 1, 1995.

## SUBCHAPTER G. COURT–APPOINTED VOLUNTEER ADVOCATE PROGRAMS

### § 264.601. Definitions

In this subchapter:

(1) "Abused or neglected child" means a child who is:

(A) the subject of a suit affecting the parent-child relationship filed by a governmental entity; and

(B) under the control or supervision of the department.

(2) "Volunteer advocate program" means a volunteer-based, nonprofit program that:

(A) provides advocacy services to abused or neglected children with the goal of obtaining a permanent placement for a child that is in the child's best interest; and

(B) complies with recognized standards for volunteer advocate programs.

Added by Acts 1995, 74th Leg., ch. 20, § 1, eff. April 20, 1995. Amended by Acts 2009, 81st Leg., ch. 1224, § 3, eff. Sept. 1, 2009.

### § 264.602. Contracts with Advocate Programs

(a) The statewide organization with which the commission contracts under Section 264.603 shall contract for services with eligible volunteer advocate programs to provide advocacy services to abused or neglected children.

(b) The contract under this section may not result in reducing the financial support a volunteer advocate program receives from another source.

(c) The commission shall develop a scale of state financial support for volunteer advocate programs that declines over a six-year period beginning on the date each individual contract takes effect. After the end of the six-year period, the commission may not provide more than 50 percent of the volunteer advocate program's funding.

(d) The executive commissioner by rule shall adopt standards for a local volunteer advocate program. The statewide organization shall assist the executive commissioner in developing the standards.

(e) The department, in cooperation with the statewide organization with which the commission contracts under Section 264.603 and other interested agencies, shall support the expansion of court-appointed volunteer advocate programs into counties in which there is a need for the programs. In expanding into a county, a program shall work to ensure the independence of the program, to the extent possible, by establishing community support and accessing private funding from the community for the program.

(f) Expenses incurred by a volunteer advocate program to promote public awareness of the need for volunteer advocates or to explain the work performed by volunteer advocates that are paid with money from the commission volunteer advocate program account under Section 504.611, Transportation Code, are not considered administrative expenses for the purpose of Section 264.603(b).

Added by Acts 1995, 74th Leg., ch. 20, § 1, eff. April 20, 1995. Amended by Acts 1995, 74th Leg., ch. 751, § 118, eff. Sept. 1, 1995; Acts 1997, 75th Leg., ch. 1294, § 7, eff. Sept. 1, 1997; Acts 2005, 79th Leg., ch. 268, § 1.61, eff. Sept. 1, 2005; Acts 2009, 81st Leg., ch. 1224, § 4, eff. Sept. 1, 2009; Acts 2015, 84th Leg., ch. 597 (S.B. 354), § 4, eff. Sept. 1, 2015.

### § 264.603. Administrative Contracts

(a) The commission shall contract with one statewide organization that is exempt from federal income taxation under Section 501(a), Internal Revenue Code of 1986,[1] as an organization described by Section 501(c)(3) of that code and that is composed of individuals or groups of individuals who have expertise in the dynamics of child abuse and neglect and experience in operating volunteer advocate programs to provide training, technical assistance, and evaluation services for the benefit of local volunteer advocate programs. The contract shall:

(1) include measurable goals and objectives relating to the number of:

(A) volunteer advocates in the program; and

(B) children receiving services from the program; and

(2) follow practices designed to ensure compliance with standards referenced in the contract.

(b) The contract under this section shall provide that not more than 12 percent of the annual legislative appropriation to implement this subchapter may be spent for administrative purposes by the statewide organization with which the commission contracts under this section.

Added by Acts 1995, 74th Leg., ch. 20, § 1, eff. April 20, 1995. Amended by Acts 1995, 74th Leg., ch. 751, § 119, eff. Sept. 1, 1995; Acts 1997, 75th Leg., ch. 600, § 20, eff. Sept. 1, 1997; Acts 2009, 81st Leg., ch. 1224, § 5, eff. Sept. 1, 2009; Acts 2015, 84th Leg., ch. 597 (S.B. 354), § 5, eff. Sept. 1, 2015; Acts 2021, 87th Leg., ch. 98 (S.B. 1156), § 1, eff. May 24, 2021; Acts 2021, 87th Leg., ch. 855 (S.B. 799), § 17, eff. Sept. 1, 2021.

1 26 U.S.C.A. § 501(a).

Sections 19 and 21 of Acts 2021, 87th Leg., ch. 855 (S.B. 799) provide:

"Sec. 19. The changes in law made by this Act apply only to a contract for which a state agency first advertises or otherwise solicits offers, bids, proposals, qualifications, or other applicable expressions of interest on or after the effective date [Sept. 1, 2021] of this Act. A contract for which a state agency first advertises or otherwise solicits offers, bids, proposals, qualifications, or other applicable expressions of interest before the effective date of this Act is governed by the law as it existed immediately before the effective date of this Act, and that law is continued in effect for that purpose."

"Sec. 21. If before implementing any provision of this Act a state agency determines that a waiver or authorization from a federal agency is necessary for implementation of that provision, the agency affected by the provision shall request the waiver or authorization and may delay implementing that provision until the waiver or authorization is granted."

### § 264.604. Eligibility for Contracts

(a) A person is eligible for a contract under Section 264.602 only if the person is a public or private nonprofit entity that operates a volunteer advocate program that:

(1) uses individuals appointed as volunteer advocates or guardians ad litem by the court to provide for the needs of abused or neglected children;

(2) has provided court-appointed advocacy services for at least six months;

(3) provides court-appointed advocacy services for at least 10 children each month; and

(4) has demonstrated that the program has local judicial support.

(b) The statewide organization with which the commission contracts under Section 264.603 may not contract with a person that is not eligible under this section. However, the statewide organization may waive the requirement in Subsection (a)(3) for an established program in a rural area or under other special circumstances.

Added by Acts 1995, 74th Leg., ch. 20, § 1, eff. April 20, 1995. Amended by Acts 1995, 74th Leg., ch. 751, § 120, eff. Sept. 1, 1995; Acts 1997, 75th Leg., ch. 1294, § 8, eff. Sept. 1, 1997; Acts 2009, 81st Leg., ch. 1224, § 6, eff. Sept. 1, 2009; Acts 2015, 84th Leg., ch. 597 (S.B. 354), § 6, eff. Sept. 1, 2015.

### § 264.605. Contract Form

A person shall apply for a contract under Section 264.602 on a form provided by the commission.

Added by Acts 1995, 74th Leg., ch. 20, § 1, eff. April 20, 1995. Amended by Acts 2015, 84th Leg., ch. 597 (S.B. 354), § 7, eff. Sept. 1, 2015.

### § 264.606. Criteria for Award of Contracts

The statewide organization with which the commission contracts under Section 264.603 shall consider the following in awarding a contract under Section 264.602:

(1) the volunteer advocate program's eligibility for and use of funds from local, state, or federal governmental sources, philanthropic organizations, and other sources;

(2) community support for the volunteer advocate program as indicated by financial contributions

from civic organizations, individuals, and other community resources;

(3) whether the volunteer advocate program provides services that encourage the permanent placement of children through reunification with their families or timely placement with an adoptive family; and

(4) whether the volunteer advocate program has the endorsement and cooperation of the local juvenile court system.

Added by Acts 1995, 74th Leg., ch. 20, § 1, eff. April 20, 1995. Amended by Acts 1995, 74th Leg., ch. 751, § 121, eff. Sept. 1, 1995; Acts 2015, 84th Leg., ch. 597 (S.B. 354), § 8, eff. Sept. 1, 2015.

### § 264.607. Contract Requirements

The commission shall require that a contract under Section 264.602 require the volunteer advocate program to:

(1) make quarterly and annual financial reports on a form provided by the commission;

(2) cooperate with inspections and audits that the commission makes to ensure service standards and fiscal responsibility; and

(3) provide as a minimum:

(A) independent and factual information in writing to the court and to counsel for the parties involved regarding the child;

(B) advocacy through the courts for permanent home placement and rehabilitation services for the child;

(C) monitoring of the child to ensure the safety of the child and to prevent unnecessary movement of the child to multiple temporary placements;

(D) reports in writing to the presiding judge and to counsel for the parties involved;

(E) community education relating to child abuse and neglect;

(F) referral services to existing community services;

(G) a volunteer recruitment and training program, including adequate screening procedures for volunteers;

(H) procedures to assure the confidentiality of records or information relating to the child; and

(I) compliance with the standards adopted under Section 264.602.

Added by Acts 1995, 74th Leg., ch. 20, § 1, eff. April 20, 1995. Amended by Acts 1995, 74th Leg., ch. 751, § 122, eff. Sept. 1, 1995; Acts 1997, 75th Leg., ch. 1294, § 9, eff. Sept. 1, 1997; Acts 2009, 81st Leg., ch. 1224, § 7, eff. Sept. 1, 2009; Acts 2015, 84th Leg., ch. 597 (S.B. 354), § 9, eff. Sept. 1, 2015.

### § 264.608. Report to the Legislature

(a) Not later than December 1 of each year, the commission shall publish a report that:

(1) summarizes reports from volunteer advocate programs under contract with the commission;

(2) analyzes the effectiveness of the contracts made by the commission under this chapter; and

(3) provides information on:

(A) the expenditure of funds under this chapter;

(B) services provided and the number of children for whom the services were provided; and

(C) any other information relating to the services provided by the volunteer advocate programs under this chapter.

(b) The commission shall submit copies of the report to the governor, lieutenant governor, speaker of the house of representatives, Legislative Budget Board, and members of the legislature.

Added by Acts 1995, 74th Leg., ch. 20, § 1, eff. April 20, 1995. Amended by Acts 2013, 83rd Leg., ch. 1312 (S.B. 59), § 21, eff. Sept. 1, 2013; Acts 2015, 84th Leg., ch. 597 (S.B. 354), § 10, eff. Sept. 1, 2015.

### § 264.609. Rule–Making Authority

The executive commissioner may adopt rules necessary to implement this subchapter.

Added by Acts 1995, 74th Leg., ch. 20, § 1, eff. April 20, 1995. Amended by Acts 2015, 84th Leg., ch. 597 (S.B. 354), § 11, eff. Sept. 1, 2015.

### § 264.610. Confidentiality

The commission may not disclose information gained through reports, collected case data, or inspections that would identify a person working at or receiving services from a volunteer advocate program.

Added by Acts 1995, 74th Leg., ch. 20, § 1, eff. April 20, 1995. Amended by Acts 2015, 84th Leg., ch. 597 (S.B. 354), § 12, eff. Sept. 1, 2015.

### § 264.611. Consultations

In implementing this chapter, the commission shall consult with individuals or groups of individuals who have expertise in the dynamics of child abuse and neglect and experience in operating volunteer advocate programs.

Added by Acts 1995, 74th Leg., ch. 20, § 1, eff. April 20, 1995. Amended by Acts 2015, 84th Leg., ch. 597 (S.B. 354), § 13, eff. Sept. 1, 2015.

### § 264.612. Funding

(a) The commission may solicit and receive grants or money from either private or public sources, including by appropriation by the legislature from the general revenue fund, to implement this chapter.

(b) The need for and importance of the implementation of this chapter by the commission requires priority and preferential consideration for appropriation.

Added by Acts 1995, 74th Leg., ch. 20, § 1, eff. April 20, 1995. Amended by Acts 1995, 74th Leg., ch. 751, § 128, eff. Sept. 1, 1995; Acts 2015, 84th Leg., ch. 597 (S.B. 354), § 14, eff. Sept. 1, 2015.

### § 264.613. Use of Information and Records; Confidentiality

(a) The files, reports, records, communications, and working papers used or developed in providing services under this subchapter are confidential and not subject to disclosure under Chapter 552, Government Code, and may only be disclosed for purposes consistent with this subchapter.

(b) Information described by Subsection (a) may be disclosed to:

(1) the department, department employees, law enforcement agencies, prosecuting attorneys, medical professionals, and other state agencies that provide services to children and families;

(2) the attorney for the child who is the subject of the information; and

(3) eligible children's advocacy centers.

(c) Information related to the investigation of a report of abuse or neglect of a child under Chapter 261 and services provided as a result of the investigation are confidential as provided by Section 261.201.

Added by Acts 2001, 77th Leg., ch. 142, § 1, eff. May 16, 2001.

### § 264.614. Internet Application for Case Tracking and Information Management System

(a) Subject to the availability of money as described by Subsection (c), the department shall develop an Internet application that allows a court-appointed volunteer advocate representing a child in the managing conservatorship of the department to access the child's case file through the department's automated case tracking and information management system and to add the volunteer advocate's findings and reports to the child's case file.

(b) The court-appointed volunteer advocate shall maintain the confidentiality required by this chapter and department rule for the information accessed by the advocate through the system described by Subsection (a).

(c) The department may use money appropriated to the department and money received as a gift, grant, or donation to pay for the costs of developing and maintaining the Internet application required by Subsection (a). The department may solicit and accept gifts, grants, and donations of any kind and from any source for purposes of this section.

(d) The executive commissioner shall adopt rules necessary to implement this section.

Added by Acts 2013, 83rd Leg., ch. 205 (H.B. 1227), § 1, eff. Sept. 1, 2013. Amended by Acts 2015, 84th Leg., ch. 1 (S.B. 219), § 1.200, eff. April 2, 2015.

## SUBCHAPTER H. CHILD ABUSE PROGRAM EVALUATION [REPEALED]

### § 264.701. Repealed by Acts 2015, 84th Leg., ch. 1 (S.B. 219) § 1.203(14), eff. April 2, 2015

## SUBCHAPTER H–1. TASK FORCE TO REDUCE CHILD ABUSE AND NEGLECT AND IMPROVE CHILD WELFARE [EXPIRED]

### §§ 264.721 to 264.728. Expired

## SUBCHAPTER I. RELATIVE AND OTHER DESIGNATED CAREGIVER PLACEMENT PROGRAM

*A former Subchapter I, Communities in Schools Program, consisting of §§ 264.751 to 264.758 was redesignated Subchapter E in Chapter 33 of the Education Code, consisting of V.T.C.A., Education Code §§ 33.151 to 33.158, by Acts 2003, 78th Leg., ch. 198, § 2.118(a) and Acts 2003, 78th Leg., ch. 1205, § 1.*

### § 264.751. Definitions

In this subchapter:

(1) "Designated caregiver" means an individual who has a longstanding and significant relationship with a child or the family of a child for whom the

department has been appointed managing conservator and who:

(A) is appointed to provide substitute care for the child, but is not verified by a licensed child-placing agency to operate an agency foster home under Chapter 42, Human Resources Code; or

(B) is subsequently appointed permanent managing conservator of the child after providing the care described by Paragraph (A).

(2) "Relative" means a person related to a child by consanguinity as determined under Section 573.022, Government Code.

(3) "Relative caregiver" means a relative who:

(A) provides substitute care for a child for whom the department has been appointed managing conservator, but who is not verified by a licensed child-placing agency to operate an agency foster home under Chapter 42, Human Resources Code; or

(B) is subsequently appointed permanent managing conservator of the child after providing the care described by Paragraph (A).

Added by Acts 2005, 79th Leg., ch. 268, § 1.62(a), eff. Sept. 1, 2005. Amended by Acts 2009, 81st Leg., ch. 1118, § 7, eff. Sept. 1, 2009; Acts 2009, 81st Leg., ch. 1238, § 6(c), eff. Sept. 1, 2009; Acts 2017, 85th Leg., ch. 317 (H.B. 7), § 34, eff. Sept. 1, 2017; Acts 2019, 86th Leg., ch. 1294 (H.B. 3390), § 12, eff. June 14, 2019.

### § 264.752. Relative and other Designated Caregiver Placement Program

(a) The department shall develop and procure a program to:

(1) promote continuity and stability for children for whom the department is appointed managing conservator by placing those children with relative or other designated caregivers; and

(2) facilitate relative or other designated caregiver placements by providing assistance and services to those caregivers in accordance with this subchapter and rules adopted by the executive commissioner.

(b) Repealed by Acts 2015, 84th Leg., ch. 944 (S.B. 206), § 86(38).

(c) The executive commissioner shall adopt rules necessary to implement this subchapter. The rules must include eligibility criteria for receiving assistance and services under this subchapter.

Added by Acts 2005, 79th Leg., ch. 268, § 1.62(a), eff. Sept. 1, 2005. Amended by Acts 2015, 84th Leg., ch. 944 (S.B. 206), § 86(38), eff. Sept. 1, 2015.

### § 264.753. Expedited Placement

The department shall expedite the completion of the background and criminal history check, the home study, and any other administrative procedure to ensure that the child is placed with a qualified relative or caregiver as soon as possible after the date the caregiver is identified.

Added by Acts 2005, 79th Leg., ch. 268, § 1.62(a), eff. Sept. 1, 2005. Amended by Acts 2015, 84th Leg., ch. 1 (S.B. 219), § 1.201, eff. April 2, 2015.

### § 264.754. Assessment of Proposed Placement

(a) In this section, "low-risk criminal offense" means a nonviolent criminal offense, including a fraud-based offense, the department determines has a low risk of impacting:

(1) a child's safety or well-being; or

(2) the stability of a child's placement with a relative or other designated caregiver.

(b) Before placing a child with a proposed relative or other designated caregiver, the department must conduct an assessment to determine whether the proposed placement is in the child's best interest.

(c) If the department disqualifies a person from serving as a relative or other designated caregiver for a child on the basis that the person has been convicted of a low-risk criminal offense, the person may appeal the disqualification in accordance with the procedure developed under Subsection (d).

(d) The department shall develop:

(1) a list of criminal offenses the department determines are low-risk criminal offenses; and

(2) a procedure for appropriate regional administration of the department to review a decision to disqualify a person from serving as a relative or other designated caregiver that includes the consideration of:

(A) when the person's conviction occurred;

(B) whether the person has multiple convictions for low-risk criminal offenses; and

(C) the likelihood that the person will commit fraudulent activity in the future.

(e) The department shall:

(1) publish the list of low-risk criminal offenses and information regarding the review procedure developed under Subsection (d) on the department's Internet website; and

(2) provide prospective relative and other designated caregivers information regarding the review procedure developed under Subsection (d).

Added by Acts 2005, 79th Leg., ch. 268, § 1.62(a), eff. Sept. 1, 2005. Amended by Acts 2017, 85th Leg., ch. 587 (S.B. 879), § 1, eff. Sept. 1, 2017.

### § 264.7541. Caregiver Visit with Child; Information

(a) Except as provided by Subsection (b), before placing a child with a proposed relative or other designated caregiver, the department must:

(1) arrange a visit between the child and the proposed caregiver; and

(2) provide the proposed caregiver with a form, which may be the same form the department provides to nonrelative caregivers, containing information, to the extent it is available, about the child that would enhance continuity of care for the child, including:

(A) the child's school information and educational needs;

(B) the child's medical, dental, and mental health care information;

(C) the child's social and family information; and

(D) any other information about the child the department determines will assist the proposed caregiver in meeting the child's needs.

(b) The department may waive the requirements of Subsection (a) if the proposed relative or other designated caregiver has a long-standing or significant relationship with the child and has provided care for the child at any time during the 12 months preceding the date of the proposed placement.

(c) Once a child is placed with a relative or other designated caregiver, the department shall inform the caregiver of:

(1) the option to become verified by a licensed child-placing agency to operate an agency foster home, if applicable; and

(2) the permanency care assistance program under Subchapter K.

Added by Acts 2013, 83rd Leg., ch. 426 (S.B. 502), § 1, eff. Sept. 1, 2013. Amended by Acts 2019, 86th Leg., ch. 375 (H.B. 1884), § 6, eff. Sept. 1, 2019.

### § 264.755. Caregiver Assistance Agreement

(a) The department shall, subject to the availability of funds, enter into a caregiver assistance agreement with each relative or other designated caregiver to provide monetary assistance and additional support services to the caregiver. The monetary assistance and support services shall be based on a family's need, as determined by Subsection (b) and rules adopted by the executive commissioner.

(a–1) When a relative or other designated caregiver enters into a caregiver assistance agreement under Subsection (a), the department shall inform the caregiver of:

(1) the option to become verified by a licensed child-placing agency to operate an agency foster home, if applicable; and

(2) the permanency care assistance program under Subchapter K.[1]

(b) The department shall provide monetary assistance under this section to a caregiver who has a family income that is less than or equal to 300 percent of the federal poverty level. Monetary assistance provided to a caregiver under this section may not exceed 50 percent of the department's daily basic foster care rate for the child. A caregiver who has a family income greater than 300 percent of the federal poverty level is not eligible for monetary assistance under this section.

(b–1) The department shall disburse monetary assistance provided to a caregiver under Subsection (b) in the same manner as the department disburses payments to a foster parent. The department may not provide monetary assistance to an eligible caregiver under Subsection (b) after the first anniversary of the date the caregiver receives the first monetary assistance payment from the department under this section. The department, at its discretion and for good cause, may extend the monetary assistance payments for an additional six months.

(b–2) The department shall implement a process to verify the family income of a relative or other designated caregiver for the purpose of determining eligibility to receive monetary assistance under Subsection (b).

(c) Monetary assistance and additional support services provided under this section may include:

(1) case management services and training and information about the child's needs until the caregiver is appointed permanent managing conservator;

(2) referrals to appropriate state agencies administering public benefits or assistance programs for which the child, the caregiver, or the caregiver's family may qualify;

(3) family counseling not provided under the Medicaid program for the caregiver's family for a period not to exceed two years from the date of initial placement;

(4) if the caregiver meets the eligibility criteria determined by rules adopted by the executive commissioner, reimbursement of all child-care expenses incurred while the child is under 13 years of age, or under 18 years of age if the child has a developmental disability, and while the department is the child's managing conservator; and

(5) if the caregiver meets the eligibility criteria determined by rules adopted by the executive commissioner, reimbursement of 50 percent of child-care expenses incurred after the caregiver is appointed permanent managing conservator of the child while the child is under 13 years of age, or under 18 years of age if the child has a developmental disability.

(d) The department, in accordance with department rules, shall implement a process to verify that each relative and designated caregiver who is seeking monetary assistance or additional support services from the department for day care as defined by Section 264.124 for a child under this section has attempted to find appropriate day-care services for the child through community services, including Head Start programs, prekindergarten classes, and early education programs offered in public schools. The department shall specify the documentation the relative or designated caregiver must provide to the department to demonstrate compliance with the requirements established under this subsection. The department may not provide monetary assistance or additional support services to the relative or designated caregiver for the day care unless the department receives the required verification.

(e) The department may provide monetary assistance or additional support services to a relative or designated caregiver for day care without the verification required under Subsection (d) if the department determines the verification would prevent an emergency placement that is in the child's best interest.

(f) If a person who has a family income that is less than or equal to 300 percent of the federal poverty level enters into a caregiver assistance agreement with the department, obtains permanent managing conservatorship of a child, and meets all other eligibility requirements, the person may receive an annual reimbursement of other expenses for the child, as determined by rules adopted by the executive commissioner, not to exceed $500 per year until the earlier of:

(1) the third anniversary of the date the person was awarded permanent managing conservatorship of the child; or

(2) the child's 18th birthday.

Added by Acts 2005, 79th Leg., ch. 268, § 1.62(a), eff. Sept. 1, 2005. Amended by Acts 2013, 83rd Leg., ch. 423 (S.B. 430), § 2, eff. Sept. 1, 2013; Acts 2013, 83rd Leg., ch. 426 (S.B. 502), § 2, eff. Sept. 1, 2013; Acts 2015, 84th Leg., ch. 1 (S.B. 219), § 1.202, eff. April 2, 2015; Acts 2017, 85th Leg., ch. 315 (H.B. 4), § 1; Acts 2019, 86th Leg., ch. 375 (H.B. 1884), § 7, eff. Sept. 1, 2019.

[1] V.T.C.A., Family Code § 264.851 et seq.

## § 264.7551. Fraudulent Agreement; Criminal Offense; Civil Penalty

*Text of section effective only if specific appropriation is made as provided in Acts 2017, 85th Leg., ch. 315 (H.B. 4), § 6*

(a) A person commits an offense if, with intent to defraud or deceive the department, the person knowingly makes or causes to be made a false statement or misrepresentation of a material fact that allows a person to enter into a caregiver assistance agreement.

(b) An offense under this section is:

(1) a Class C misdemeanor if the person entered into a fraudulent caregiver assistance agreement and received no monetary assistance under the agreement or received monetary assistance under the agreement for less than 7 days;

(2) a Class B misdemeanor if the person entered into a fraudulent caregiver assistance agreement and received monetary assistance under the agreement for 7 days or more but less than 31 days;

(3) a Class A misdemeanor if the person entered into a fraudulent caregiver assistance agreement and received monetary assistance under the agreement for 31 days or more but less than 91 days; or

(4) a state jail felony if the person entered into a fraudulent caregiver assistance agreement and received monetary assistance under the agreement for 91 days or more.

(c) If conduct that constitutes an offense under this section also constitutes an offense under any other law, the actor may be prosecuted under this section, the other law, or both.

(d) The appropriate county prosecuting attorney shall be responsible for the prosecution of an offense under this section.

(e) A person who engaged in conduct described by Subsection (a) is liable to the state for a civil penalty of $1,000. The attorney general shall bring an action to recover a civil penalty as authorized by this subsection.

(f) The commissioner of the department may adopt rules necessary to determine whether fraudulent activity that violates Subsection (a) has occurred.

Added by Acts 2017, 85th Leg., ch. 315 (H.B. 4), § 2.

### § 264.756. Assistance with Permanent Placement

The department shall collaborate with the State Bar of Texas and local community partners to identify legal resources to assist relatives and other designated caregivers in obtaining conservatorship, adoption, or other permanent legal status for the child.

Added by Acts 2005, 79th Leg., ch. 268, § 1.62(a), eff. Sept. 1, 2005.

### § 264.757. Coordination with other Agencies

The department shall coordinate with other health and human services agencies, as defined by Section 531.001, Government Code, to provide assistance and services under this subchapter.

Added by Acts 2005, 79th Leg., ch. 268, § 1.62(a), eff. Sept. 1, 2005.

### § 264.758. Funds

The department and other state agencies shall actively seek and use federal funds available for the purposes of this subchapter.

Added by Acts 2005, 79th Leg., ch. 268, § 1.62(a), eff. Sept. 1, 2005.

### § 264.759. Repealed by Acts 2013, 83rd Leg., ch. 1312 (S.B. 59), § 99(10), eff. Sept. 1, 2013

### § 264.760. Eligibility for Foster Care Payments and Permanency Care Assistance

Notwithstanding any other provision of this subchapter, a relative or other designated caregiver who becomes verified by a licensed child-placing agency to operate an agency foster home under Chapter 42, Human Resources Code, may receive foster care payments in lieu of the benefits provided by this subchapter, beginning with the first month in which the relative or other designated caregiver becomes licensed or is verified.

Added by Acts 2009, 81st Leg., ch. 1118, § 8, eff. Sept. 1, 2009; Acts 2009, 81st Leg., ch. 1238, § 6(d), eff. Sept. 1, 2009. Amended by Acts 2017, 85th Leg., ch. 317 (H.B. 7), § 35, eff. Sept. 1, 2017.

### § 264.761. Expired

### § 264.762. Annual Report

*Text of section effective only if specific appropriation is made as provided in Acts 2017, 85th Leg., ch. 315 (H.B. 4), § 6*

Not later than September 1 of each year, the department shall publish a report on the relative and other designated caregiver placement program created under this subchapter. The report must include data on permanency outcomes for children placed with relative or other designated caregivers, including:

(1) the number of disruptions in a relative or other designated caregiver placement;

(2) the reasons for any disruption in a relative or other designated caregiver placement; and

(3) the length of time before a relative or other designated caregiver who receives monetary assistance from the department under this subchapter obtains permanent managing conservatorship of a child.

Added by Acts 2017, 85th Leg., ch. 315 (H.B. 4), § 3.

## SUBCHAPTER J. FAMILY DRUG COURT PROGRAM

### § 264.801. Redesignated as V.T.C.A., Government Code § 122.001 and amended by Acts 2013, 83rd Leg., ch. 747 (S.B. 462), § 1.02, eff. Sept. 1, 2013

### § 264.802. Redesignated as V.T.C.A., Government Code § 122.002 and amended by Acts 2013, 83rd Leg., ch. 747 (S.B. 462), § 1.02, eff. Sept. 1, 2013

### § 264.803. Deleted

### § 264.804. Redesignated as V.T.C.A., Government Code § 122.003 by Acts 2013, 83rd Leg., ch. 747 (S.B. 462), § 1.02, eff. Sept. 1, 2013

### § 264.805. Redesignated as V.T.C.A., Government Code § 122.004 by Acts 2013, 83rd

Leg., ch. 747 (S.B. 462), § 1.02, eff. Sept. 1, 2013

## SUBCHAPTER K. PERMANENCY CARE ASSISTANCE PROGRAM

### § 264.851. Definitions

In this subchapter:

(1) Repealed by Acts 2015, 84th Leg., ch. 944 (S.B. 206), § 86(39).

(2) "Kinship provider" means a relative of a foster child, or another adult with a longstanding and significant relationship with a foster child before the child was placed with the person by the department, with whom the child resides for at least six consecutive months after the person becomes licensed by the department or verified by a licensed child-placing agency or the department to provide foster care.

(3) "Permanency care assistance agreement" means a written agreement between the department and a kinship provider for the payment of permanency care assistance benefits as provided by this subchapter.

(4) "Permanency care assistance benefits" means monthly payments paid by the department to a kinship provider under a permanency care assistance agreement.

(5) "Relative" means a person related to a foster child by consanguinity or affinity.

Added by Acts 2009, 81st Leg., ch. 1118, § 9, eff. Sept. 1, 2009; Acts 2009, 81st Leg., ch. 1238, § 6(e), eff. Sept. 1, 2009. Amended by Acts 2015, 84th Leg., ch. 944 (S.B. 206), § 86(39), eff. Sept. 1, 2015.

### § 264.852. Permanency Care Assistance Agreements

(a) The department shall enter into a permanency care assistance agreement with a kinship provider who is eligible to receive permanency care assistance benefits.

(b) The department may enter into a permanency care assistance agreement with a kinship provider who is the prospective managing conservator of a foster child only if the kinship provider meets the eligibility criteria under federal and state law and department rule.

(c) A court may not order the department to enter into a permanency care assistance agreement with a kinship provider unless the kinship provider meets the eligibility criteria under federal and state law and department rule, including requirements relating to the criminal history background check of a kinship provider.

(d) A permanency care assistance agreement may provide for reimbursement of the nonrecurring expenses a kinship provider incurs in obtaining permanent managing conservatorship of a foster child, including attorney's fees and court costs. The reimbursement of the nonrecurring expenses under this subsection may not exceed $2,000.

Added by Acts 2009, 81st Leg., ch. 1118, § 9, eff. Sept. 1, 2009; Acts 2009, 81st Leg., ch. 1238, § 6(e), eff. Sept. 1, 2009.

### § 264.8521. Notice to Applicants

At the time a person applies to become verified by a licensed child-placing agency to provide foster care in order to qualify for the permanency care assistance program, the department or the child-placing agency shall:

(1) notify the applicant that a background check, including a criminal history record check, will be conducted on the individual; and

(2) inform the applicant about criminal convictions that:

(A) preclude an individual from becoming a verified agency foster home; and

(B) may also be considered in evaluating the individual's application.

Added by Acts 2011, 82nd Leg., ch. 318 (H.B. 2370), § 1, eff. Sept. 1, 2011. Amended by Acts 2017, 85th Leg., ch. 317 (H.B. 7), § 36, eff. Sept. 1, 2017.

### § 264.853. Rules

The executive commissioner shall adopt rules necessary to implement the permanency care assistance program. The rules must:

(1) establish eligibility requirements to receive permanency care assistance benefits under the program; and

(2) ensure that the program conforms to the requirements for federal assistance as required by the Fostering Connections to Success and Increasing Adoptions Act of 2008 (Pub. L. No. 110–351).

Added by Acts 2009, 81st Leg., ch. 1118, § 9, eff. Sept. 1, 2009; Acts 2009, 81st Leg., ch. 1238, § 6(e), eff. Sept. 1, 2009.

### § 264.854. Maximum Payment Amount

The executive commissioner shall set the maximum monthly amount of assistance payments under a permanency care assistance agreement in an amount that does not exceed the amount of the monthly foster care maintenance payment the department would pay to a foster care provider caring for the child for whom the kinship provider is caring.

Added by Acts 2009, 81st Leg., ch. 1118, § 9, eff. Sept. 1, 2009; Acts 2009, 81st Leg., ch. 1238, § 6(e), eff. Sept. 1, 2009.

### § 264.855. Continued Eligibility for Permanency Care Assistance Benefits after Age 18

If the department first entered into a permanency care assistance agreement with a foster child's kinship provider after the child's 16th birthday, the department may continue to provide permanency care assistance payments until the last day of the month of the child's 21st birthday, provided the child is:

(1) regularly attending high school or enrolled in a program leading toward a high school diploma or high school equivalency certificate;

(2) regularly attending an institution of higher education or a postsecondary vocational or technical program;

(3) participating in a program or activity that promotes, or removes barriers to, employment;

(4) employed for at least 80 hours a month; or

(5) incapable of any of the activities described by Subdivisions (1)–(4) due to a documented medical condition.

Added by Acts 2009, 81st Leg., ch. 1118, § 9, eff. Sept. 1, 2009; Acts 2009, 81st Leg., ch. 1238, § 6(e), eff. Oct. 1, 2010.

### § 264.856. Appropriation Required

The department is not required to provide permanency care assistance benefits under this subchapter unless the department is specifically appropriated money for purposes of this subchapter.

Added by Acts 2009, 81st Leg., ch. 1118, § 9, eff. Sept. 1, 2009; Acts 2009, 81st Leg., ch. 1238, § 6(e), eff. Sept. 1, 2009.

### § 264.857. Repealed by Acts 2017, 85th Leg., ch. 290 (S.B. 203), § 1, eff. May 29, 2017

## SUBCHAPTER L. PARENTAL CHILD SAFETY PLACEMENTS

### § 264.901. Definitions

In this subchapter:

(1) "Caregiver" means an individual, other than a child's parent, conservator, or legal guardian, who is related to the child or has a long-standing and significant relationship with the child or the child's family.

(2) "Parental child safety placement" means a temporary out-of-home placement of a child with a caregiver that is made by a parent or other person with whom the child resides in accordance with a written agreement approved by the department that ensures the safety of the child:

(A) during an investigation by the department of alleged abuse or neglect of the child; or

(B) while the parent or other person is receiving services from the department.

(3) "Parental child safety placement agreement" means an agreement between a parent or other person making a parental child safety placement and the caregiver that contains the terms of the placement and is approved by the department.

Added by Acts 2011, 82nd Leg., ch. 1071 (S.B. 993), § 1, eff. Sept. 1, 2011.

### § 264.902. Parental Child Safety Placement Agreement

(a) A parental child safety placement agreement must include terms that clearly state:

(1) the respective duties of the person making the placement and the caregiver, including a plan for how the caregiver will access necessary medical treatment for the child and the caregiver's duty to ensure that a school-age child is enrolled in and attending school;

(2) conditions under which the person placing the child may have access to the child, including how often the person may visit and the circumstances under which the person's visit may occur;

(3) the duties of the department;

(4) the date on which the agreement will terminate unless terminated sooner or extended to a subsequent date as provided under department policy; and

(5) any other term the department determines necessary for the safety and welfare of the child.

(b) A parental child safety placement agreement must contain the following statement in boldface type and capital letters: "YOUR AGREEMENT TO THE PARENTAL CHILD SAFETY PLACEMENT IS NOT AN ADMISSION OF CHILD ABUSE OR NEGLECT ON YOUR PART AND CANNOT BE USED AGAINST YOU AS AN ADMISSION OF CHILD ABUSE OR NEGLECT."

(c) A parental child safety placement agreement must be in writing and signed by the person making the placement and the caregiver.

(d) The department must provide a written copy of the parental child safety placement agreement to the person making the placement and the caregiver.

Added by Acts 2011, 82nd Leg., ch. 1071 (S.B. 993), § 1, eff. Sept. 1, 2011.

### § 264.903. Caregiver Evaluation

(a) The department shall develop policies and procedures for evaluating a potential caregiver's qualifications to care for a child under this subchapter, including policies and procedures for evaluating:

(1) the criminal history of a caregiver;

(2) allegations of abuse or neglect against a caregiver; and

(3) a caregiver's home environment and ability to care for the child.

(a-1) The department shall expedite the evaluation of a potential caregiver under this section to ensure that the child is placed with a caregiver who has the ability to protect the child from the alleged perpetrator of abuse or neglect against the child.

(b) A department caseworker who performs an evaluation of a caregiver under this section shall document the results of the evaluation in the department's case records.

(c) If, after performing an evaluation of a potential caregiver, the department determines that it is not in the child's best interest to be placed with the caregiver, the department shall notify the person who proposed the caregiver and the proposed caregiver of the reasons for the department's decision, but may not disclose the specifics of any criminal history or allegations of abuse or neglect unless the caregiver agrees to the disclosure.

Added by Acts 2011, 82nd Leg., ch. 1071 (S.B. 993), § 1, eff. Sept. 1, 2011. Amended by Acts 2017, 85th Leg., ch. 822 (H.B. 1549), § 12, eff. Sept. 1, 2017.

### § 264.904. Department Procedures for Closing Case

(a) Before closing a case in which the department has approved a parental child safety placement, the department must develop a plan with the person who made the placement and the caregiver for the safe return of the child to the person who placed the child with the caregiver or to another person legally entitled to possession of the child, as appropriate.

(b) The department may close a case with a child still living with the caregiver in a parental child safety placement if the department has determined that the child could safely return to the parent or person who made the parental child safety placement but the parent or other person agrees in writing for the child to continue to reside with the caregiver.

(c) If the department determines that the child is unable to safely return to the parent or person who made the parental child safety placement, the department shall determine whether the child can remain safely in the home of the caregiver or whether the department must seek legal conservatorship of the child in order to ensure the child's safety.

(d) Before the department may close a case with a child still living in a parental child safety placement, the department must:

(1) determine and document in the case file that the child can safely remain in the placement without the department's supervision;

(2) obtain the written agreement of the parent or person who made the parental child safety placement, if possible;

(3) obtain the caregiver's agreement in writing that the child can continue living in the placement after the department closes the case; and

(4) develop a written plan for the child's care after the department closes the case.

(e) The department is not required to comply with Subsection (d) if the department has filed suit seeking to be named conservator of the child under Chapter 262 and been denied conservatorship of the child.

Added by Acts 2011, 82nd Leg., ch. 1071 (S.B. 993), § 1, eff. Sept. 1, 2011.

### § 264.905. Removal of Child by Department

This subchapter does not prevent the department from removing a child at any time from a person who makes a parental child safety placement or from a caregiver if removal is determined to be necessary by the department for the safety and welfare of the child as provided by Chapter 262.

Added by Acts 2011, 82nd Leg., ch. 1071 (S.B. 993), § 1, eff. Sept. 1, 2011.

### § 264.906. Placement Preference During Conservatorship

If, while a parental child safety placement agreement is in effect, the department files suit under Chapter 262 seeking to be named managing conservator of the child, the department shall give priority to placing the child with the parental child safety placement caregiver as long as the placement is safe and available.

Added by Acts 2011, 82nd Leg., ch. 1071 (S.B. 993), § 1, eff. Sept. 1, 2011.

## CHAPTER 265. PREVENTION AND EARLY INTERVENTION SERVICES

### SUBCHAPTER A. PREVENTION AND EARLY INTERVENTION SERVICES



### SUBCHAPTER A. PREVENTION AND EARLY INTERVENTION SERVICES

#### § 265.001. Definitions

In this chapter:

(1) "Department" means the Department of Family and Protective Services.

(2) "Division" means the prevention and early intervention services division within the department.

(3) "Prevention and early intervention services" means programs intended to provide early intervention or prevent at-risk behaviors that lead to child abuse, delinquency, running away, truancy, and dropping out of school.

Added by Acts 1999, 76th Leg., ch. 489, § 2, eff. Sept. 1, 1999. Amended by Acts 2007, 80th Leg., ch. 632, § 1, eff. June 15, 2007.

#### § 265.002. Prevention and Early Intervention Services Division

(a) The department shall operate a division to provide services for children in at-risk situations and for the families of those children and to achieve the consolidation of prevention and early intervention services within the jurisdiction of a single agency in order to avoid fragmentation and duplication of services and to increase the accountability for the delivery and administration of these services. The division shall be called the prevention and early intervention services division and shall have the following duties:

(1) to plan, develop, and administer a comprehensive and unified delivery system of prevention and early intervention services to children and their families in at-risk situations;

(2) to improve the responsiveness of services for at-risk children and their families by facilitating greater coordination and flexibility in the use of funds by state and local service providers;

(3) to provide greater accountability for prevention and early intervention services in order to demonstrate the impact or public benefit of a program by adopting outcome measures; and

(4) to assist local communities in the coordination and development of prevention and early interven-

tion services in order to maximize federal, state, and local resources.

(b) The department's prevention and early intervention services division must be organizationally separate from the department's divisions performing child protective services and adult protective services functions.

Added by Acts 1999, 76th Leg., ch. 489, § 2, eff. Sept. 1, 1999. Amended by Acts 2015, 84th Leg., ch. 837 (S.B. 200), § 1.13, eff. Sept. 1, 2015.

### § 265.003. Consolidation of Programs

(a) In order to implement the duties provided in Section 265.002, the department shall consolidate into the division programs with the goal of providing early intervention or prevention of at-risk behavior that leads to child abuse, delinquency, running away, truancy, and dropping out of school.

(b) The division may provide additional prevention and early intervention services in accordance with Section 265.002.

Added by Acts 1999, 76th Leg., ch. 489, § 2, eff. Sept. 1, 1999.

### § 265.004. Use of Evidence–Based Programs for At–Risk Families

(a) To the extent that money is appropriated for the purpose, the department shall fund evidence-based programs, including parenting education, home visitation, family support services, mentoring, positive youth development programs, and crisis counseling, offered by community-based organizations that are designed to prevent or ameliorate child abuse and neglect. The programs funded under this subsection may be offered by a child welfare board established under Section 264.005, a local governmental board granted the powers and duties of a child welfare board under state law, a children's advocacy center established under Section 264.402, or other persons determined appropriate by the department.

(a–1) The department shall ensure that not less than 75 percent of the money appropriated for parenting education programs under Subsection (a) funds evidence-based programs or practices described by Section 265.151(b) and that the remainder of that money funds promising programs or practices described by Section 265.151(c) or evidence-informed programs or practices described by Section 265.151(d).

(a–2) The department shall actively seek and apply for any available federal funds to support parenting education programs provided under this section.

(b) The department shall place priority on programs that target children whose race or ethnicity is disproportionately represented in the child protective services system.

(c) The department shall periodically evaluate the evidence-based abuse and neglect prevention programs to determine the continued effectiveness of the programs.

Added by Acts 2005, 79th Leg., ch. 268, § 1.64, eff. Sept. 1, 2005. Amended by Acts 2007, 80th Leg., ch. 526, § 4, eff. June 16, 2007; Acts 2015, 84th Leg., ch. 1257 (H.B. 2630), § 3, eff. Sept. 1, 2015; Acts 2017, 85th Leg., ch. 324 (S.B. 1488), § 24.002(7), eff. Sept. 1, 2017; Acts 2021, 87th Leg., ch. 515 (S.B. 452), § 2, eff. Sept. 1, 2021.

### § 265.0041. Collaboration with Institutions of Higher Education

(a) Subject to the availability of funds, the Health and Human Services Commission, on behalf of the department, shall enter into agreements with institutions of higher education to conduct efficacy reviews of any prevention and early intervention programs that have not previously been evaluated for effectiveness through a scientific research evaluation process.

(b) Subject to the availability of funds, the department shall collaborate with an institution of higher education to create and track indicators of child well-being to determine the effectiveness of prevention and early intervention services.

Added by Acts 2017, 85th Leg., ch. 319 (S.B. 11), § 20, eff. Sept. 1, 2017.

### § 265.005. Strategic Plan

(a) The department shall develop and implement a five-year strategic plan for prevention and early intervention services. Not later than September 1 of the last fiscal year in each five-year period, the department shall issue a new strategic plan for the next five fiscal years beginning with the following fiscal year.

(b) A strategic plan required under this section must:

(1) identify methods to leverage other sources of funding or provide support for existing community-based prevention efforts;

(2) include a needs assessment that identifies programs to best target the needs of the highest risk populations and geographic areas;

(3) identify the goals and priorities for the department's overall prevention efforts;

(4) report the results of previous prevention efforts using available information in the plan;

(5) identify additional methods of measuring program effectiveness and results or outcomes;

(6) identify methods to collaborate with other state agencies on prevention efforts;

(7) identify specific strategies to implement the plan and to develop measures for reporting on the overall progress toward the plan's goals;

(8) identify strategies and goals for increasing the number of families receiving prevention and early intervention services each year, subject to the availability of funds, to reach targets set by the department for providing services to families that are eligible to receive services through parental education, family support, and community-based programs financed with federal, state, local, or private resources; and

(9) identify specific strategies to increase local capacity for the delivery of prevention and early intervention services through collaboration with communities and stakeholders.

(c) The department shall coordinate with interested parties and communities in developing the strategic plan under this section.

(d) The department shall annually update the strategic plan developed under this section.

(e) The department shall post the strategic plan developed under this section and any update to the plan on its Internet website.

Added by Acts 2015, 84th Leg., ch. 944 (S.B. 206), § 62, eff. Sept. 1, 2015; Acts 2015, 84th Leg., ch. 1257 (H.B. 2630), § 4, eff. Sept. 1, 2015. Amended by Acts 2017, 85th Leg., ch. 319 (S.B. 11), § 21, eff. Sept. 1, 2017; Acts 2017, 85th Leg., ch. 822 (H.B. 1549), § 13, eff. Sept. 1, 2017; Acts 2019, 86th Leg., ch. 467 (H.B. 4170), § 7.007, eff. Sept. 1, 2019.

### § 265.006. Prohibition on Use of Agency Name or Logo

The department may not allow the use of the department's name or identifying logo or insignia on forms or other materials related to the department's prevention and early intervention services that are:

(1) provided by the department's contractors; or

(2) distributed by the department's contractors to the department's clients.

Added by Acts 2015, 84th Leg., ch. 837 (S.B. 200), § 1.14, eff. Sept. 1, 2015.

### § 265.007. Improving Provision of Prevention and Early Intervention Services

(a) To improve the effectiveness and delivery of prevention and early intervention services, the department shall:

(1) identify geographic areas that have a high need for prevention and early intervention services but do not have prevention and early intervention services available in the area or have only unevaluated prevention and early intervention services available in the area; and

(2) develop strategies for community partners to:

(A) improve the early recognition of child abuse or neglect;

(B) improve the reporting of child abuse and neglect; and

(C) reduce child fatalities.

(b) The department may not use data gathered under this section to identify a specific family or individual.

Added by Acts 2017, 85th Leg., ch. 822 (H.B. 1549), § 14, eff. Sept. 1, 2017.

### § 265.008. Evaluation of Prevention and Early Intervention Services

(a) The department may enter into agreements with institutions of higher education to conduct efficacy reviews of any prevention and early intervention services provided under this chapter that have not previously been evaluated for effectiveness in a research evaluation. The efficacy review shall include, when possible, a cost-benefit analysis of the program to the state and, when applicable, the return on investment of the program to the state.

(b) The department may not enter into an agreement to conduct a program efficacy evaluation under this section unless:

(1) the agreement with the institution of higher education is cost neutral; and

(2) the department and institution of higher education conducting the evaluation under this section protect the identity of individuals who are receiving services from the department that are being evaluated.

Added by Acts 2017, 85th Leg., ch. 822 (H.B. 1549), § 14, eff. Sept. 1, 2017.

## SUBCHAPTER B. CHILD ABUSE AND NEGLECT PRIMARY PREVENTION PROGRAMS

### § 265.051. Definitions

In this subchapter:

(1) "Children's trust fund" means a child abuse and neglect primary prevention program.

(2) "Primary prevention" means services and activities available to the community at large or to families to prevent child abuse and neglect before it occurs. The term includes infant mortality prevention education programs.

(3) "Operating fund" means the Department of Family and Protective Services child abuse and neglect prevention operating fund account.

(4) "State agency" means a board, commission, department, office, or other state agency that:

(A) is in the executive branch of the state government;

(B) was created by the constitution or a statute of this state; and

(C) has statewide jurisdiction.

(5) "Trust fund" means the child abuse and neglect prevention trust fund account.

Added by Acts 2001, 77th Leg., ch. 957, § 1, eff. Sept. 1, 2001. Amended by Acts 2015, 84th Leg., ch. 1 (S.B. 219), § 4.208, eff. April 2, 2015. Redesignated from V.T.C.A., Human Resources Code § 40.101 by Acts 2015, 84th Leg., ch. 944 (S.B. 206), § 63, eff. Sept. 1, 2015; Acts 2015, 84th Leg., ch. 1257 (H.B. 2630), § 5, eff. Sept. 1, 2015.

### § 265.052. Child Abuse and Neglect Primary Prevention Programs

(a) The department shall operate the children's trust fund to:

(1) set policy, offer resources for community primary prevention programs, and provide information and education on prevention of child abuse and neglect;

(2) develop a state plan for expending funds for child abuse and neglect primary prevention programs that includes an annual schedule of transfers of trust fund money to the operating fund;

(3) develop eligibility criteria for applicants requesting funding for child abuse and neglect primary prevention programs; and

(4) establish funding priorities for child abuse and neglect primary prevention programs.

(b) The children's trust fund shall accommodate the department's existing rules and policies in procuring, awarding, and monitoring contracts and grants.

(c) The department may:

(1) apply for and receive funds made available by the federal government or another public or private source for administering programs under this subchapter and for funding for child abuse and neglect primary prevention programs; and

(2) solicit donations for child abuse and neglect primary prevention programs.

Added by Acts 2001, 77th Leg., ch. 957, § 1, eff. Sept. 1, 2001. Redesignated from V.T.C.A., Human Resources Code § 40.102 by Acts 2015, 84th Leg., ch. 944 (S.B. 206), § 63, eff. Sept. 1, 2015; Acts 2015, 84th Leg., ch. 1257 (H.B. 2630), § 5, eff. Sept. 1, 2015.

### § 265.053. Administrative and Other Costs

(a) Administrative costs under this subchapter during any fiscal year may not exceed an amount equal to 50 percent of the interest credited to the trust fund during the preceding fiscal year.

(b) Funds expended under a special project grant from a governmental source or a nongovernmental source for public education or public awareness may not be counted as administrative costs for the purposes of this section.

Added by Acts 2001, 77th Leg., ch. 957, § 1, eff. Sept. 1, 2001. Redesignated from V.T.C.A., Human Resources Code § 40.104 by Acts 2015, 84th Leg., ch. 944 (S.B. 206), § 63, eff. Sept. 1, 2015; Acts 2015, 84th Leg., ch. 1257 (H.B. 2630), § 5, eff. Sept. 1, 2015.

### § 265.054. Child Abuse and Neglect Prevention Trust Fund Account

(a) The child abuse and neglect prevention trust fund account is an account in the general revenue fund. Money in the trust fund is dedicated to child abuse and neglect primary prevention programs.

(b) The department may transfer money contained in the trust fund to the operating fund at any time. However, during a fiscal year the department may not transfer more than the amount appropriated for the operating fund for that fiscal year. Money transferred to the operating fund that was originally deposited to the credit of the trust fund under Section 118.022, Local Government Code, may be used only for child abuse and neglect primary prevention programs.

(c) Interest earned on the trust fund shall be credited to the trust fund.

(d) The trust fund is exempt from the application of Section 403.095, Government Code.

(e) All marriage license fees and other fees collected for and deposited in the trust fund and interest earned on the trust fund balance shall be appropriated each biennium only to the operating fund for child abuse and neglect primary prevention programs.

Added by Acts 2001, 77th Leg., ch. 957, § 1, eff. Sept. 1, 2001. Amended by Acts 2007, 80th Leg., ch. 632, § 4; Acts 2015, 84th Leg., ch. 1 (S.B. 219), § 4.209, eff. April 2, 2015. Redesignated from V.T.C.A., Human Resources Code § 40.105 and amended by Acts 2015, 84th Leg., ch. 944 (S.B. 206), § 63, eff. Sept. 1, 2015; Acts 2015, 84th Leg., ch. 1257 (H.B. 2630), § 5, eff. Sept. 1, 2015.

### § 265.055. Department Operating Fund Account

(a) The operating fund is an account in the general revenue fund.

(b) Administrative and other costs allowed in Section 265.053 shall be taken from the operating fund. The department may transfer funds contained in the operating fund to the trust fund at any time.

(c) The legislature may appropriate the money in the operating fund to carry out the provisions of this subchapter.

(d) The operating fund is exempt from the application of Section 403.095, Government Code.

Added by Acts 2001, 77th Leg., ch. 957, § 1, eff. Sept. 1, 2001. Amended by Acts 2015, 84th Leg., ch. 1 (S.B. 219), § 4.210, eff. April 2, 2015. Redesignated from V.T.C.A., Human Resources Code § 40.106 and amended by Acts 2015, 84th Leg., ch. 944 (S.B. 206), § 63, eff. Sept. 1, 2015; Acts 2015, 84th Leg., ch. 1257 (H.B. 2630), § 5, eff. Sept. 1, 2015.

### § 265.056. Contributions

(a) The department may solicit contributions from any appropriate source.

(b) Any other contributions for child abuse and neglect primary prevention or other prevention and early intervention programs shall be deposited into a separate designated fund in the state treasury and shall be used for that designated purpose.

(c) A person may contribute funds to either the trust fund, the operating fund, or a fund designated by the department for a specific child abuse and neglect primary prevention or other prevention or early intervention purpose.

(d) If a person designates that a contribution is intended as a donation to a specific fund, the contribution shall be deposited in the designated fund.

Added by Acts 2001, 77th Leg., ch. 957, § 1, eff. Sept. 1, 2001. Redesignated from V.T.C.A., Human Resources Code § 40.107 by Acts 2015, 84th Leg., ch. 944 (S.B. 206), § 63, eff. Sept. 1, 2015; Acts 2015, 84th Leg., ch. 1257 (H.B. 2630), § 5, eff. Sept. 1, 2015.

### § 265.057. Community Youth Development Grants

(a) Subject to available funding, the department shall award community youth development grants to communities identified by incidence of crime. The department shall give priority in awarding grants under this section to areas of the state in which there is a high incidence of juvenile crime.

(b) The purpose of a grant under this section is to assist a community in alleviating conditions in the family and community that lead to juvenile crime.

Added by Acts 1997, 75th Leg., ch. 165, § 21.03(a), eff. Sept. 1, 1997. Redesignated from V.T.C.A., Human Resources Code § 40.0561 by Acts 2015, 84th Leg., ch. 944 (S.B. 206), § 64, eff. Sept. 1, 2015; Acts 2015, 84th Leg., ch. 1257 (H.B. 2630), § 6, eff. Sept. 1, 2015.

## SUBCHAPTER C. NURSE-FAMILY PARTNERSHIP COMPETITIVE GRANT PROGRAM

*Acts 2015, 84th Leg., ch. 837 (S.B. 200), § 1.15 redesignated V.T.C.A., Government Code Chapter 531, Subchapter Q as V.T.C.A., Family Code Chapter 265, Subchapter C, consisting of §§ 265.101 to 265.110.*

*Another Subchapter C, Parenting Education, consisting of §§ 265.101 to 265.105, was redesignated as Subchapter D, consisting of §§ 265.151 to 265.155, by Acts 2017, 85th Leg., ch. 324 (S.B. 1488), § 24.001(9).*

### § 265.101. Definitions

In this subchapter:

(1) "Competitive grant program" means the nurse-family partnership competitive grant program established under this subchapter.

(2) "Partnership program" means a nurse-family partnership program.

Added by Acts 2007, 80th Leg., ch. 348, § 1, eff. Sept. 1, 2007. Redesignated from V.T.C.A., Government Code § 531.451 by Acts 2009, 81st Leg., ch. 87, § 27.001(37), eff. Sept. 1, 2009. Redesignated from V.T.C.A., Government Code § 531.651 by Acts 2015, 84th Leg., ch. 837 (S.B. 200), § 1.15(a), eff. Sept. 1, 2015.

### § 265.102. Operation of Nurse–Family Partnership Competitive Grant Program

(a) The department shall operate a nurse-family partnership competitive grant program through which the department will award grants for the implementation of nurse-family partnership programs, or the expansion of existing programs, and for the operation of those programs for a period of not less than two years.

(b) The department shall award grants under the program to applicants, including applicants operating existing programs, in a manner that ensures that the partnership programs collectively:

(1) operate in multiple communities that are geographically distributed throughout this state; and

(2) provide program services to approximately 2,000 families.

Added by Acts 2007, 80th Leg., ch. 348, § 1, eff. Sept. 1, 2007. Redesignated from V.T.C.A., Government Code § 531.452 by Acts 2009, 81st Leg., ch. 87, § 27.001(37), eff. Sept. 1, 2009. Amended by Acts 2015, 84th Leg., ch. 1 (S.B. 219), §§ 2.188, 2.189, eff. April 2, 2015. Redesignated from V.T.C.A., Government Code § 531.652 and amended by Acts 2015, 84th Leg., ch. 837 (S.B. 200), § 1.15(a), eff. Sept. 1, 2015.

### § 265.103. Partnership Program Requirements

A partnership program funded through a grant awarded under this subchapter must:

(1) strictly adhere to the program model developed by the Nurse–Family Partnership National Service Office, including any clinical, programmatic, and data collection requirements of that model;

(2) require that registered nurses regularly visit the homes of low-income, first-time mothers participating in the program to provide services designed to:

(A) improve pregnancy outcomes;

(B) improve child health and development;

(C) improve family economic self-sufficiency and stability; and

(D) reduce the incidence of child abuse and neglect;

(3) require that nurses who provide services through the program:

(A) receive training from the office of the attorney general at least once each year on procedures by which a person may voluntarily acknowledge the paternity of a child and on the availability of child support services from the office;

(B) provide a mother with information about the rights, responsibilities, and benefits of establishing the paternity of her child, if appropriate;

(C) provide assistance to a mother and the alleged father of her child if the mother and alleged father seek to voluntarily acknowledge paternity of the child, if appropriate; and

(D) provide information to a mother about the availability of child support services from the office of the attorney general; and

(4) require that the regular nurse visits described by Subdivision (2) begin not later than a mother's 28th week of gestation and end when her child reaches two years of age.

Added by Acts 2007, 80th Leg., ch. 348, § 1, eff. Sept. 1, 2007. Redesignated from V.T.C.A., Government Code § 531.453 by Acts 2009, 81st Leg., ch. 87, § 27.001(37), eff. Sept. 1, 2009. Redesignated from V.T.C.A., Government Code § 531.653 by Acts 2015, 84th Leg., ch. 837 (S.B. 200), § 1.15(a), eff. Sept. 1, 2015.

### § 265.1035. Expired

### § 265.104. Application

(a) A public or private entity, including a county, municipality, or other political subdivision of this state, may apply for a grant under this subchapter.

(b) To apply for a grant, an applicant must submit a written application to the department on a form prescribed by the department in consultation with the Nurse–Family Partnership National Service Office.

(c) The application prescribed by the department must:

(1) require the applicant to provide data on the number of low-income, first-time mothers residing in the community in which the applicant proposes to operate or expand a partnership program and provide a description of existing services available to those mothers;

(2) describe the ongoing monitoring and evaluation process to which a grant recipient is subject under Section 265.109, including the recipient's obligation to collect and provide information requested by the department under Section 265.109(c); and

(3) require the applicant to provide other relevant information as determined by the department.

Added by Acts 2007, 80th Leg., ch. 348, § 1, eff. Sept. 1, 2007. Redesignated from V.T.C.A., Government Code § 531.454 and amended by Acts 2009, 81st Leg., ch. 87, §§ 27.001(37), 27.002(7), eff. Sept. 1, 2009. Redesignated from V.T.C.A., Government Code § 531.654 and amended by Acts 2015, 84th Leg., ch. 837 (S.B. 200), § 1.15(a), eff. Sept. 1, 2015.

### § 265.105. Additional Considerations in Awarding Grants

In addition to the factors described by Sections 265.102(b) and 265.103, in determining whether to award a grant to an applicant under this subchapter, the department shall consider:

(1) the demonstrated need for a partnership program in the community in which the applicant proposes to operate or expand the program, which may be determined by considering:

(A) the poverty rate, the crime rate, the number of births to Medicaid recipients, the rate of poor birth outcomes, and the incidence of child abuse and neglect during a prescribed period in the community; and

(B) the need to enhance school readiness in the community;

(2) the applicant's ability to participate in ongoing monitoring and performance evaluations under Section 265.109, including the applicant's ability to collect and provide information requested by the department under Section 265.109(c);

(3) the applicant's ability to adhere to the partnership program standards adopted under Section 265.106;

(4) the applicant's ability to develop broad-based community support for implementing or expanding a partnership program, as applicable; and

(5) the applicant's history of developing and sustaining innovative, high-quality programs that meet the needs of families and communities.

Added by Acts 2007, 80th Leg., ch. 348, § 1, eff. Sept. 1, 2007. Redesignated from V.T.C.A., Government Code § 531.455 and amended by Acts 2009, 81st Leg., ch. 87, §§ 27.001(37), 27.002(8), eff. Sept. 1, 2009. Redesignated from V.T.C.A., Government Code § 531.655 and amended by Acts 2015, 84th Leg., ch. 837 (S.B. 200), § 1.15(a), eff. Sept. 1, 2015.

### § 265.106. Partnership Program Standards

The commissioner, with the assistance of the Nurse–Family Partnership National Service Office, shall adopt standards for the partnership programs funded under this subchapter. The standards must adhere to the Nurse–Family Partnership National Service Office program model standards and guidelines that were developed in multiple, randomized clinical trials and have been tested and replicated in multiple communities.

Added by Acts 2007, 80th Leg., ch. 348, § 1, eff. Sept. 1, 2007. Redesignated from V.T.C.A., Government Code § 531.456 by Acts 2009, 81st Leg., ch. 87, § 27.001(37), eff. Sept. 1, 2009. Redesignated from V.T.C.A., Government Code § 531.656 by Acts 2015, 84th Leg., ch. 837 (S.B. 200), § 1.15(a), eff. Sept. 1, 2015. Amended by Acts 2017, 85th Leg., ch. 316 (H.B. 5), § 15, eff. Sept. 1, 2017.

### § 265.107. Use of Awarded Grant Funds

The grant funds awarded under this subchapter may be used only to cover costs related to implementing or expanding and operating a partnership program, including costs related to:

(1) administering the program;

(2) training and managing registered nurses who participate in the program;

(3) paying the salaries and expenses of registered nurses who participate in the program;

(4) paying for facilities and equipment for the program; and

(5) paying for services provided by the Nurse–Family Partnership National Service Office to ensure a grant recipient adheres to the organization's program model.

Added by Acts 2007, 80th Leg., ch. 348, § 1, eff. Sept. 1, 2007. Redesignated from V.T.C.A., Government Code § 531.457 by Acts 2009, 81st Leg., ch. 87, § 27.001(37), eff. Sept. 1, 2009. Redesignated from V.T.C.A., Government Code § 531.657 by Acts 2015, 84th Leg., ch. 837 (S.B. 200), § 1.15(a), eff. Sept. 1, 2015.

### § 265.108. State Nurse Consultant

Using money appropriated for the competitive grant program, the department shall hire or contract with a state nurse consultant to assist grant recipients with implementing or expanding and operating the partnership programs in the applicable communities.

Added by Acts 2007, 80th Leg., ch. 348, § 1, eff. Sept. 1, 2007. Redesignated from V.T.C.A., Government Code § 531.458 by Acts 2009, 81st Leg., ch. 87, § 27.001(37), eff. Sept. 1, 2009. Redesignated from V.T.C.A., Government Code § 531.658 and amended by Acts 2015, 84th Leg., ch. 837 (S.B. 200), § 1.15(a), eff. Sept. 1, 2015.

### § 265.109. Program Monitoring and Evaluation; Annual Committee Reports

(a) The department, with the assistance of the Nurse–Family Partnership National Service Office, shall:

(1) adopt performance indicators that are designed to measure a grant recipient's performance

with respect to the partnership program standards adopted by the commissioner under Section 265.106;

(2) use the performance indicators to continuously monitor and formally evaluate on an annual basis the performance of each grant recipient; and

(3) prepare and submit an annual report, not later than December 1 of each year, to the Senate Health and Human Services Committee, or its successor, and the House Human Services Committee, or its successor, regarding the performance of each grant recipient during the preceding state fiscal year with respect to providing partnership program services.

(b) The report required under Subsection (a)(3) must include:

(1) the number of low-income, first-time mothers to whom each grant recipient provided partnership program services and, of that number, the number of mothers who established the paternity of an alleged father as a result of services provided under the program;

(2) the extent to which each grant recipient made regular visits to mothers during the period described by Section 265.103(4); and

(3) the extent to which each grant recipient adhered to the Nurse–Family Partnership National Service Office's program model, including the extent to which registered nurses:

(A) conducted home visitations comparable in frequency, duration, and content to those delivered in Nurse–Family Partnership National Service Office clinical trials; and

(B) assessed the health and well-being of mothers and children participating in the partnership programs in accordance with indicators of maternal, child, and family health defined by the department in consultation with the Nurse–Family Partnership National Service Office.

(c) On request, each grant recipient shall timely collect and provide data and any other information required by the department to monitor and evaluate the recipient or to prepare the report required by this section.

Added by Acts 2007, 80th Leg., ch. 348, § 1, eff. Sept. 1, 2007. Redesignated from V.T.C.A., Government Code § 531.459 and amended by Acts 2009, 81st Leg., ch. 87, §§ 27.001(37), 27.002(9), eff. Sept. 1, 2009. Amended by Acts 2015, 84th Leg., ch. 1 (S.B. 219), § 2.190, eff. April 2, 2015. Redesignated from V.T.C.A., Government Code § 531.659 and amended by Acts 2015, 84th Leg., ch. 837 (S.B. 200), § 1.15(a), eff. Sept. 1, 2015. Amended by Acts 2017, 85th Leg., ch. 316 (H.B. 5), § 16, eff. Sept. 1, 2017.

### § 265.110. Competitive Grant Program Funding

(a) The department shall actively seek and apply for any available federal funds, including federal Medicaid and Temporary Assistance for Needy Families (TANF) funds, to assist in financing the competitive grant program established under this subchapter.

(b) The department may use appropriated funds from the state government and may accept gifts, donations, and grants of money from the federal government, local governments, private corporations, or other persons to assist in financing the competitive grant program.

Added by Acts 2007, 80th Leg., ch. 348, § 1, eff. Sept. 1, 2007. Redesignated from V.T.C.A., Government Code § 531.460 by Acts 2009, 81st Leg., ch. 87, § 27.001(37), eff. Sept. 1, 2009. Redesignated from V.T.C.A., Government Code § 531.660 and amended by Acts 2015, 84th Leg., ch. 837 (S.B. 200), § 1.15(a), eff. Sept. 1, 2015.

## SUBCHAPTER D. EVIDENCE-BASED PROGRAMS AND PRACTICES

*This Subchapter was added as Subchapter C, Parenting Education, consisting of §§ 265.101 to 265.105, by Acts 2015, 84th Leg., ch. 1257 (H.B. 2630), § 7. Acts 2017, 85th Leg., ch. 324 (S.B. 1488), § 24.001(9) redesignated it as Subchapter D and redesignated the sections as §§ 265.151 to 265.155.*

### § 265.151. Requirements for Programs and Practices on Evidence–Based Spectrum

(a) Repealed by Acts 2021, 87th Leg., ch. 515 (S.B. 452), § 9.

(b) An evidence-based program or practice is a program or practice that:

(1) is research-based and grounded in relevant, empirical knowledge and program-determined outcomes;

(2) has comprehensive standards ensuring the highest quality service delivery with continuous improvement in the quality of service delivery;

(3) has demonstrated significant positive outcomes;

(4) has been evaluated by at least one rigorous, random, controlled research trial across heterogeneous populations or communities with research results that have been published in a peer-reviewed journal;

(5) substantially complies with a program or practice manual or design that specifies the pur-

pose, outcomes, duration, and frequency of the program or practice services;

(6) employs well-trained and competent staff and provides continual relevant professional development opportunities to the staff; and

(7) is associated with an organization in this state, a national organization, an institution of higher education, or a national or state public health institute.

(c) A promising program or practice is a program or practice that:

(1) has an active impact evaluation of the program or practice or demonstrates a schedule for implementing an active impact evaluation of the program or practice;

(2) has been evaluated by at least one outcome-based study demonstrating effectiveness or random, controlled trial in a homogeneous sample;

(3) substantially complies with a program or practice manual or design that specifies the purpose, outcomes, duration, and frequency of the program or practice services;

(4) employs well-trained and competent staff and provides continual relevant professional development opportunities to the staff; and

(5) is research-based and grounded in relevant, empirical knowledge and program- or practice-determined outcomes.

(d) An evidence-informed program or practice is a program or practice that:

(1) combines well-researched interventions with clinical experience and ethics, and client preferences and culture, to guide and inform the delivery of treatments and services;

(2) has an active impact evaluation of the program or practice or demonstrates a schedule for implementing an active impact evaluation of the program or practice;

(3) substantially complies with a program or practice manual or design that specifies the purpose, outcome, duration, and frequency of the program or practice services; and

(4) employs well-trained and competent staff and provides continual relevant professional development opportunities to the staff.

Added by Acts 2015, 84th Leg., ch. 1257 (H.B. 2630), § 7, eff. Sept. 1, 2015. Redesignated from V.T.C.A., Family Code § 265.101 by Acts 2017, 85th Leg., ch. 324 (S.B. 1488), § 24.001(9), eff. Sept. 1, 2017. Amended by Acts 2021, 87th Leg., ch. 515 (S.B. 452), §§ 4, 5, 9, eff. Sept. 1, 2021.

### § 265.152. Outcomes of Evidence-Based Prevention and Early Intervention Programs and Practices

The department shall ensure that a prevention and early intervention program or practice provided under this subchapter achieves favorable behavioral outcomes in at least two of the following areas:

(1) improved cognitive development of children;

(2) increased readiness for and participation and performance in school;

(3) reduced child abuse, neglect, and injury;

(4) improved child safety;

(5) improved social-emotional development of children and youth;

(6) increased protective factors, including nurturing, bonding, and other parenting skills;

(7) improved family economic self-sufficiency;

(8) reduced parental or youth involvement with the criminal justice system; and

(9) increased paternal involvement and support.

Added by Acts 2015, 84th Leg., ch. 1257 (H.B. 2630), § 7, eff. Sept. 1, 2015. Redesignated from V.T.C.A., Family Code § 265.102 by Acts 2017, 85th Leg., ch. 324 (S.B. 1488), § 24.001(9), eff. Sept. 1, 2017. Amended by Acts 2021, 87th Leg., ch. 515 (S.B. 452), § 6, eff. Sept. 1, 2021.

### § 265.153. Evaluation of Prevention and Early Intervention Programs and Practices

(a) The department shall adopt outcome indicators to measure the effectiveness of prevention and early intervention programs and practices provided under this subchapter in achieving desired outcomes.

(b) The department may work directly with the model developer of a prevention and early intervention program or practice to identify appropriate outcome indicators for the program or practice and to ensure that the program or practice substantially complies with the model.

(c) The department shall develop internal processes to share information with prevention and early intervention service providers to assist the department in analyzing the performance of the programs or practices.

(d) The department shall use information obtained under this section to:

(1) monitor prevention and early intervention programs and practices;

(2) continually improve the quality of the programs and practices; and

(3) evaluate the effectiveness of the programs and practices.

Added by Acts 2015, 84th Leg., ch. 1257 (H.B. 2630), § 7, eff. Sept. 1, 2015. Redesignated from V.T.C.A., Family Code § 265.103 by Acts 2017, 85th Leg., ch. 324 (S.B. 1488), § 24.001(9), eff. Sept. 1, 2017. Amended by Acts 2021, 87th Leg., ch. 515 (S.B. 452), § 7, eff. Sept. 1, 2021.

### § 265.154. Reports to Legislature

(a) Not later than December 1 of each even-numbered year, the department shall prepare and submit a report on state-funded prevention and early intervention programs and practices to the standing committees of the senate and house of representatives with jurisdiction over child protective services.

(b) A report submitted under this section must include:

(1) a description of the prevention and early intervention programs and practices implemented and of the models associated with the programs and practices;

(2) information on the families served by the programs and practices, including the number of families served and their demographic information;

(3) the goals and achieved outcomes of the implemented programs and practices;

(4) information on the cost for each family served, including any available third-party return-on-investment analysis; and

(5) information explaining the percentage of money spent on evidence-based programs and practices, on promising programs and practices, and on evidence-informed programs and practices.

Added by Acts 2015, 84th Leg., ch. 1257 (H.B. 2630), § 7, eff. Sept. 1, 2015. Redesignated from V.T.C.A., Family Code § 265.104 by Acts 2017, 85th Leg., ch. 324 (S.B. 1488), § 24.001(9), eff. Sept. 1, 2017. Amended by Acts 2021, 87th Leg., ch. 515 (S.B. 452), § 8, eff. Sept. 1, 2021.

### § 265.155. Rules

The commissioner of the department may adopt rules as necessary to implement this subchapter.

Added by Acts 2015, 84th Leg., ch. 1257 (H.B. 2630), § 7, eff. Sept. 1, 2015. Amended by Acts 2017, 85th Leg., ch. 316 (H.B. 5), § 14, eff. Sept. 1, 2017. Redesignated from V.T.C.A., Family Code § 265.105 by Acts 2017, 85th Leg., ch. 324 (S.B. 1488), § 24.001(9), eff. Sept. 1, 2017.

## CHAPTER 266. MEDICAL CARE AND EDUCATIONAL SERVICES FOR CHILDREN IN CONSERVATORSHIP OF DEPARTMENT OF FAMILY AND PROTECTIVE SERVICES



*Chapter 266, Medical Care and Educational Services for Children in Foster Care, consisting of V.T.C.A., Family Code §§ 266.001 to 266.011, was added by Acts 2005, 79th Leg., ch. 268, § 1.65(a). Another Chapter 266, Interagency Coordinating Council for Building Healthy Families, was added by Acts 2005, 79th Leg., ch. 587, § 1, and was redesignated as V.T.C.A., Family Code Chapter 267 by Acts 2007, 80th Leg., ch. 632, § 3.*

### § 266.001. Definitions

In this chapter:

(1) "Advanced practice nurse" has the meaning assigned by Section 157.051, Occupations Code.

(1–a) "Commission" means the Health and Human Services Commission.

(1–b) "Commissioner" means the commissioner of the Department of Family and Protective Services.

(2) "Department" means the Department of Family and Protective Services.

(2–a) "Drug research program" means any clinical trial, clinical investigation, drug study, or active medical or clinical research that has been approved by an institutional review board in accordance with the standards provided in the Code of Federal Regulations, 45 C.F.R. Sections 46.404 through 46.407, regarding:

(A) an investigational new drug; or

(B) the efficacy of an approved drug.

(3) "Executive commissioner" means the executive commissioner of the Health and Human Services Commission.

(4) Repealed by Acts 2015, 84th Leg., ch. 944 (S.B. 206), § 86(40).

(4–a) "Investigational new drug" has the meaning assigned by 21 C.F.R. Section 312.3(b).

(5) "Medical care" means all health care and related services provided under the medical assistance program under Chapter 32, Human Resources Code, and described by Section 32.003(4), Human Resources Code.

(6) "Physician assistant" has the meaning assigned by Section 157.051, Occupations Code.

(7) "Psychotropic medication" means a medication that is prescribed for the treatment of symptoms of psychosis or another mental, emotional, or behavioral disorder and that is used to exercise an effect on the central nervous system to influence and modify behavior, cognition, or affective state. The term includes the following categories when used as described by this subdivision:

(A) psychomotor stimulants;

(B) antidepressants;

(C) antipsychotics or neuroleptics;

(D) agents for control of mania or depression;

(E) antianxiety agents; and

(F) sedatives, hypnotics, or other sleep-promoting medications.

Added by Acts 2005, 79th Leg., ch. 268, § 1.65(a), eff. Sept. 1, 2005. Amended by Acts 2007, 80th Leg., ch. 506, § 1, eff. Sept. 1, 2007; Acts 2013, 83rd Leg., ch. 204 (H.B. 915), § 7, eff. Sept. 1, 2013; Acts 2015, 84th Leg., ch. 944 (S.B. 206), § 86(40), eff. Sept. 1, 2015; Acts 2017, 85th Leg., ch. 316 (H.B. 5), § 17, eff. Sept. 1, 2017.

### § 266.002. Construction with Other Law

This chapter does not limit the right to consent to medical, dental, psychological, and surgical treatment under Chapter 32.

Added by Acts 2005, 79th Leg., ch. 268, § 1.65(a), eff. Sept. 1, 2005.

### § 266.003. Medical Services for Child Abuse and Neglect Victims

(a) The department shall collaborate with the commission and health care and child welfare professionals to design a comprehensive, cost-effective medical services delivery model, either directly or by contract, to meet the needs of children served by the department. The medical services delivery model must include:

(1) the designation of health care facilities with expertise in the forensic assessment, diagnosis, and treatment of child abuse and neglect as pediatric centers of excellence;

(2) a statewide telemedicine system to link department investigators and caseworkers with pediatric centers of excellence or other medical experts for consultation;

(3) identification of a medical home for each foster child on entering foster care at which the child will receive an initial comprehensive assessment as well as preventive treatments, acute medical services, and therapeutic and rehabilitative care to meet the child's ongoing physical and mental health needs throughout the duration of the child's stay in foster care;

(4) the development and implementation of health passports as described in Section 266.006;

(5) establishment and use of a management information system that allows monitoring of medical care that is provided to all children in foster care;

(6) the use of medical advisory committees and medical review teams, as appropriate, to establish treatment guidelines and criteria by which individual cases of medical care provided to children in foster care will be identified for further, in-depth review;

(7) development of the training program described by Section 266.004(h);

(8) provision for the summary of medical care described by Section 266.007; and

(9) provision for the participation of the person authorized to consent to medical care for a child in foster care in each appointment of the child with the provider of medical care.

(b) The department shall collaborate with health and human services agencies, community partners, the health care community, and federal health and social services programs to maximize services and benefits available under this section.

(c) The commissioner shall adopt rules necessary to implement this chapter.

(d) The commission is responsible for administering contracts with managed care providers for the provision of medical care to children in foster care. The department shall collaborate with the commission to ensure that medical care services provided by managed care providers match the needs of children in foster care.

Added by Acts 2005, 79th Leg., ch. 268, § 1.65(a), eff. Sept. 1, 2005. Amended by Acts 2017, 85th Leg., ch. 316 (H.B. 5), § 18, eff. Sept. 1, 2017.

### § 266.0031. Expired

### § 266.004. Consent for Medical Care

(a) Medical care may not be provided to a child in foster care unless the person authorized by this section has provided consent.

(b) Except as provided by Section 266.010, the court may authorize the following persons to consent to medical care for a foster child:

(1) an individual designated by name in an order of the court, including the child's foster parent or the child's parent, if the parent's rights have not been terminated and the court determines that it is in the best interest of the parent's child to allow the parent to make medical decisions on behalf of the child; or

(2) the department or an agent of the department.

(c) If the person authorized by the court to consent to medical care is the department or an agent of the department, the department shall, not later than the fifth business day after the date the court provides authorization, file with the court and each party the name of the individual who will exercise the duty and responsibility of providing consent on behalf of the department. The department may designate the child's foster parent or the child's parent, if the parent's rights have not been terminated, to exercise the duty and responsibility of providing consent on behalf of the department under this subsection. If the individual designated under this subsection changes, the department shall file notice of the change with the court and each party not later than the fifth business day after the date of the change.

(d) A physician or other provider of medical care acting in good faith may rely on the representation by a person that the person has the authority to consent to the provision of medical care to a foster child as provided by Subsection (b).

(e) The department, a person authorized to consent to medical care under Subsection (b), the child's parent if the parent's rights have not been terminated, a guardian ad litem or attorney ad litem if one has been appointed, or the person providing foster care to the child may petition the court for any order related to medical care for a foster child that the department or other person believes is in the best interest of the child. Notice of the petition must be given to each person entitled to notice under Section 263.0021(b).

(f) If a physician who has examined or treated the foster child has concerns regarding the medical care provided to the foster child, the physician may file a letter with the court stating the reasons for the physician's concerns. The court shall provide a copy of the letter to each person entitled to notice under Section 263.0021(b).

(g) On its own motion or in response to a petition under Subsection (e) or Section 266.010, the court may issue any order related to the medical care of a foster child that the court determines is in the best interest of the child.

(h) Notwithstanding Subsection (b), a person may not be authorized to consent to medical care provided to a foster child unless the person has completed a department-approved training program related to informed consent and the provision of all areas of medical care as defined by Section 266.001. This subsection does not apply to a parent whose rights have not been terminated unless the court orders the parent to complete the training.

(h–1) The training required by Subsection (h) must include training related to informed consent for the administration of psychotropic medication and the appropriate use of psychosocial therapies, behavior strategies, and other non-pharmacological interventions that should be considered before or concurrently with the administration of psychotropic medications.

(h–2) Each person required to complete a training program under Subsection (h) must acknowledge in writing that the person:

(1) has received the training described by Subsection (h–1);

(2) understands the principles of informed consent for the administration of psychotropic medication; and

(3) understands that non-pharmacological interventions should be considered and discussed with the prescribing physician, physician assistant, or advanced practice nurse before consenting to the use of a psychotropic medication.

(i) The person authorized under Subsection (b) to consent to medical care of a foster child shall participate in each appointment of the child with the provider of the medical care.

(j) Nothing in this section requires the identity of a foster parent to be publicly disclosed.

(k) The department may consent to health care services ordered or prescribed by a health care provider authorized to order or prescribe health care services regardless of whether the services are provided under the medical assistance program under Chapter 32, Human Resources Code, if the department otherwise has the authority under this section to consent to health care services.

Added by Acts 2005, 79th Leg., ch. 268, § 1.65(a), eff. Sept. 1, 2005. Amended by Acts 2007, 80th Leg., ch. 727, § 1, eff. June 15, 2007; Acts 2013, 83rd Leg., ch. 204 (H.B. 915), § 8, eff. Sept. 1, 2013; Acts 2015, 84th Leg., ch. 944 (S.B. 206), § 65, eff. Sept. 1, 2015.

## § 266.0041. Enrollment and Participation in Certain Research Programs

(a) Notwithstanding Section 266.004, a person may not authorize the enrollment of a foster child or consent to the participation of a foster child in a drug research program without a court order as provided by this section, unless the person is the foster child's parent and the person has been authorized by the court to make medical decisions for the foster child in accordance with Section 266.004.

(b) Before issuing an order authorizing the enrollment or participation of a foster child in a drug research program, the court must:

(1) appoint an independent medical advocate;

(2) review the report filed by the independent medical advocate regarding the advocate's opinion and recommendations concerning the foster child's enrollment and participation in the drug research program;

(3) consider whether the person conducting the drug research program:

(A) informed the foster child in a developmentally appropriate manner of the expected benefits of the drug research program, any potential side effects, and any available alternative treatments and received the foster child's assent to enroll the child to participate in the drug research program as required by the Code of Federal Regulations, 45 C.F.R. Section 46.408; or

(B) received informed consent in accordance with Subsection (h); and

(4) determine whether enrollment and participation in the drug research program is in the foster child's best interest and determine that the enrollment and participation in the drug research program will not interfere with the appropriate medical care of the foster child.

(c) An independent medical advocate appointed under Subsection (b) is not a party to the suit but may:

(1) conduct an investigation regarding the foster child's participation in a drug research program to the extent that the advocate considers necessary to determine:

(A) whether the foster child assented to or provided informed consent to the child's enrollment and participation in the drug research program; and

(B) the best interest of the child for whom the advocate is appointed; and

(2) obtain and review copies of the foster child's relevant medical and psychological records and information describing the risks and benefits of the child's enrollment and participation in the drug research program.

(d) An independent medical advocate shall, within a reasonable time after the appointment, interview:

(1) the foster child in a developmentally appropriate manner, if the child is four years of age or older;

(2) the foster child's parent, if the parent is entitled to notification under Section 264.018;

(3) an advocate appointed by an institutional review board in accordance with the Code of Federal Regulations, 45 C.F.R. Section 46.409(b), if an advocate has been appointed;

(4) the medical team treating the foster child as well as the medical team conducting the drug research program; and

(5) each individual who has significant knowledge of the foster child's medical history and condition, including any foster parent of the child.

(e) After reviewing the information collected under Subsections (c) and (d), the independent medical advocate shall:

(1) submit a report to the court presenting the advocate's opinion and recommendation regarding whether:

(A) the foster child assented to or provided informed consent to the child's enrollment and participation in the drug research program; and

(B) the foster child's best interest is served by enrollment and participation in the drug research program; and

(2) at the request of the court, testify regarding the basis for the advocate's opinion and recommendation concerning the foster child's enrollment and participation in a drug research program.

(f) The court may appoint any person eligible to serve as the foster child's guardian ad litem, as defined by Section 107.001, as the independent medical advocate, including a physician or nurse or an attorney who has experience in medical and health care, except that a foster parent, employee of a substitute care provider or child placing agency providing care for the foster child, representative of the department, medical professional affiliated with the drug research program, independent medical advocate appointed by an institutional review board, or any person the court determines has a conflict of interest may not serve as the foster child's independent medical advocate.

(g) A person otherwise authorized to consent to medical care for a foster child may petition the court for an order permitting the enrollment and participation of a foster child in a drug research program under this section.

(h) Before a foster child, who is at least 16 years of age and has been determined to have the capacity to consent to medical care in accordance with Section 266.010, may be enrolled to participate in a drug research program, the person conducting the drug research program must:

(1) inform the foster child in a developmentally appropriate manner of the expected benefits of participation in the drug research program, any potential side effects, and any available alternative treatments; and

(2) receive written informed consent to enroll the foster child for participation in the drug research program.

(i) A court may render an order approving the enrollment or participation of a foster child in a drug research program involving an investigational new drug before appointing an independent medical advocate if:

(1) a physician recommends the foster child's enrollment or participation in the drug research program to provide the foster child with treatment that will prevent the death or serious injury of the child; and

(2) the court determines that the foster child needs the treatment before an independent medical advocate could complete an investigation in accordance with this section.

(j) As soon as practicable after issuing an order under Subsection (i), the court shall appoint an independent medical advocate to complete a full investigation of the foster child's enrollment and participation in the drug research program in accordance with this section.

(k) This section does not apply to:

(1) a drug research study regarding the efficacy of an approved drug that is based only on medical records, claims data, or outcome data, including outcome data gathered through interviews with a child, caregiver of a child, or a child's treating professional;

(2) a retrospective drug research study based only on medical records, claims data, or outcome data; or

(3) the treatment of a foster child with an investigational new drug that does not require the child's enrollment or participation in a drug research program.

(*l*) The department shall annually submit to the governor, lieutenant governor, speaker of the house of representatives, and the relevant committees in both houses of the legislature, a report regarding:

(1) the number of foster children who enrolled or participated in a drug research program during the previous year;

(2) the purpose of each drug research program in which a foster child was enrolled or participated; and

(3) the number of foster children for whom an order was issued under Subsection (i).

(m) A foster parent or any other person may not receive a financial incentive or any other benefit for recommending or consenting to the enrollment and participation of a foster child in a drug research program.

Added by Acts 2007, 80th Leg., ch. 506, § 2, eff. Sept. 1, 2007. Amended by Acts 2015, 84th Leg., ch. 722 (H.B. 1309), § 3, eff. June 17, 2015; Acts 2015, 84th Leg., ch. 944 (S.B. 206), § 66, eff. Sept. 1, 2015.

### § 266.0042. Consent for Psychotropic Medication

Consent to the administration of a psychotropic medication is valid only if:

(1) the consent is given voluntarily and without undue influence; and

(2) the person authorized by law to consent for the foster child receives verbally or in writing information that describes:

(A) the specific condition to be treated;

(B) the beneficial effects on that condition expected from the medication;

(C) the probable health and mental health consequences of not consenting to the medication;

(D) the probable clinically significant side effects and risks associated with the medication; and

(E) the generally accepted alternative medications and non-pharmacological interventions to the medication, if any, and the reasons for the proposed course of treatment.

Added by Acts 2013, 83rd Leg., ch. 204 (H.B. 915), § 9, eff. Sept. 1, 2013.

### § 266.005. Finding on Health Care Consultation

If a court finds that a health care professional has been consulted regarding a health care service, procedure, or treatment for a child in the conservatorship of the department and the court declines to follow the recommendation of the health care professional, the court shall make findings in the record supporting the court's order.

Added by Acts 2017, 85th Leg., ch. 317 (H.B. 7), § 38, eff. Sept. 1, 2017.

### § 266.006. Health Passport

(a) The commission, in conjunction with the department, and with the assistance of physicians and other health care providers experienced in the care of foster children and children with disabilities and with the use of electronic health records, shall develop and provide a health passport for each foster child. The passport must be maintained in an electronic format and use the department's existing computer resources to the greatest extent possible.

(b) The executive commissioner, in collaboration with the commissioner, shall adopt rules specifying the information required to be included in the passport. The required information may include:

(1) the name and address of each of the child's physicians and health care providers;

(2) a record of each visit to a physician or other health care provider, including routine checkups conducted in accordance with the Texas Health Steps program;

(3) an immunization record that may be exchanged with ImmTrac;

(4) a list of the child's known health problems and allergies;

(5) information on all medications prescribed to the child in adequate detail to permit refill of prescriptions, including the disease or condition that the medication treats; and

(6) any other available health history that physicians and other health care providers who provide care for the child determine is important.

(c) The system used to access the health passport must be secure and maintain the confidentiality of the child's health records.

(d) Health passport information shall be part of the department's record for the child as long as the child remains in foster care.

(e) The commission, in collaboration with the department, shall provide training or instructional materials to foster parents, physicians, and other health care providers regarding use of the health passport.

(f) The department shall make health passport information available in printed and electronic formats to the following individuals when a child is discharged from foster care:

(1) the child's legal guardian, managing conservator, or parent; or

(2) the child, if the child is at least 18 years of age or has had the disabilities of minority removed.

Added by Acts 2005, 79th Leg., ch. 268, § 1.65(a), eff. Sept. 1, 2005. Amended by Acts 2017, 85th Leg., ch. 316 (H.B. 5), § 19, eff. Sept. 1, 2017.

### § 266.007. Judicial Review of Medical Care

(a) At each hearing under Chapter 263, or more frequently if ordered by the court, the court shall review a summary of the medical care provided to the foster child since the last hearing. The summary must include information regarding:

(1) the nature of any emergency medical care provided to the child and the circumstances necessitating emergency medical care, including any injury or acute illness suffered by the child;

(2) all medical and mental health treatment that the child is receiving and the child's progress with the treatment;

(3) any medication prescribed for the child, the condition, diagnosis, and symptoms for which the medication was prescribed, and the child's progress with the medication;

(4) for a child receiving a psychotropic medication:

(A) any psychosocial therapies, behavior strategies, or other non-pharmacological interventions that have been provided to the child; and

(B) the dates since the previous hearing of any office visits the child had with the prescribing physician, physician assistant, or advanced practice nurse as required by Section 266.011;

(5) the degree to which the child or foster care provider has complied or failed to comply with any plan of medical treatment for the child;

(6) any adverse reaction to or side effects of any medical treatment provided to the child;

(7) any specific medical condition of the child that has been diagnosed or for which tests are being conducted to make a diagnosis;

(8) any activity that the child should avoid or should engage in that might affect the effectiveness of the treatment, including physical activities, other medications, and diet; and

(9) other information required by department rule or by the court.

(b) At or before each hearing under Chapter 263, the department shall provide the summary of medical care described by Subsection (a) to:

(1) the court;

(2) the person authorized to consent to medical treatment for the child;

(3) the guardian ad litem or attorney ad litem, if one has been appointed by the court;

(4) the child's parent, if the parent's rights have not been terminated; and

(5) any other person determined by the department or the court to be necessary or appropriate for review of the provision of medical care to foster children.

(c) At each hearing under Chapter 263, the foster child shall be provided the opportunity to express to the court the child's views on the medical care being provided to the child.

Added by Acts 2005, 79th Leg., ch. 268, § 1.65(a), eff. Sept. 1, 2005. Amended by Acts 2013, 83rd Leg., ch. 204 (H.B. 915), § 12, eff. Sept. 1, 2013.

### § 266.008. Education Passport

(a) The department shall develop an education passport for each foster child. The department shall determine the format of the passport. The passport may be maintained in an electronic format. The passport must contain educational records of the child, including the names and addresses of educational providers, the child's grade-level performance, and any other educational information the department determines is important.

(b) The department shall maintain the passport as part of the department's records for the child as long as the child remains in foster care.

(c) The department shall make the passport available to:

(1) any person authorized by law to make educational decisions for the foster child;

(2) the person authorized to consent to medical care for the foster child; and

(3) a provider of medical care to the foster child if access to the foster child's educational information is necessary to the provision of medical care and is not prohibited by law.

(d) The department shall collaborate with the Texas Education Agency to develop policies and procedures to ensure that the needs of foster children are met in every school district.

Added by Acts 2005, 79th Leg., ch. 268, § 1.65(a), eff. Sept. 1, 2005. Amended by Acts 2013, 83rd Leg., ch. 688 (H.B. 2619), § 8, eff. Sept. 1, 2013; Acts 2017, 85th Leg., ch. 316 (H.B. 5), § 20, eff. Sept. 1, 2017.

### § 266.009. Provision of Medical Care in Emergency

(a) Consent or court authorization for the medical care of a foster child otherwise required by this chapter is not required in an emergency during which it is immediately necessary to provide medical care to the foster child to prevent the imminent probability of death or substantial bodily harm to the child or others, including circumstances in which:

(1) the child is overtly or continually threatening or attempting to commit suicide or cause serious bodily harm to the child or others; or

(2) the child is exhibiting the sudden onset of a medical condition manifesting itself by acute symptoms of sufficient severity, including severe pain, such that the absence of immediate medical attention could reasonably be expected to result in placing the child's health in serious jeopardy, serious impairment of bodily functions, or serious dysfunction of any bodily organ or part.

(b) The physician providing the medical care or designee shall notify the person authorized to consent to medical care for a foster child about the decision to provide medical care without consent or court authorization in an emergency not later than the second business day after the date of the provision of medical care under this section. This notification must be documented in the foster child's health passport.

(c) This section does not apply to the administration of medication under Subchapter G, Chapter 574, Health and Safety Code, [1] to a foster child who is at least 16 years of age and who is placed in an inpatient mental health facility.

Added by Acts 2005, 79th Leg., ch. 268, § 1.65(a), eff. Sept. 1, 2005.

[1] V.T.C.A., Health & Safety Code § 574.101 et seq.

### § 266.010. Consent to Medical Care by Foster Child at Least 16 Years of Age

(a) A foster child who is at least 16 years of age may consent to the provision of medical care, except as provided by Chapter 33, if the court with continuing jurisdiction determines that the child has the capacity to consent to medical care. If the child provides consent by signing a consent form, the form must be written in language the child can understand.

(b) A court with continuing jurisdiction may make the determination regarding the foster child's capacity to consent to medical care during a hearing under Chapter 263 or may hold a hearing to make the determination on its own motion. The court may issue an order authorizing the child to consent to all or some of the medical care as defined by Section 266.001. In addition, a foster child who is at least 16 years of age, or the foster child's attorney ad litem, may file a petition with the court for a hearing. If the court determines that the foster child lacks the capacity to consent to medical care, the court may consider whether the foster child has acquired the capacity to consent to medical care at subsequent hearings under Section 263.5031.

(c) If the court determines that a foster child lacks the capacity to consent to medical care, the person authorized by the court under Section 266.004 shall continue to provide consent for the medical care of the foster child.

(d) If a foster child who is at least 16 years of age and who has been determined to have the capacity to consent to medical care refuses to consent to medical care and the department or private agency providing substitute care or case management services to the child believes that the medical care is appropriate, the department or the private agency may file a motion with the court requesting an order authorizing the provision of the medical care.

(e) The motion under Subsection (d) must include:

(1) the child's stated reasons for refusing the medical care; and

(2) a statement prepared and signed by the treating physician that the medical care is the proper course of treatment for the foster child.

(f) If a motion is filed under Subsection (d), the court shall appoint an attorney ad litem for the foster child if one has not already been appointed. The foster child's attorney ad litem shall:

(1) discuss the situation with the child;

(2) discuss the suitability of the medical care with the treating physician;

(3) review the child's medical and mental health records; and

(4) advocate to the court on behalf of the child's expressed preferences regarding the medical care.

(g) The court shall issue an order authorizing the provision of the medical care in accordance with a motion under Subsection (d) to the foster child only if the court finds, by clear and convincing evidence, after the hearing that the medical care is in the best interest of the foster child and:

(1) the foster child lacks the capacity to make a decision regarding the medical care;

(2) the failure to provide the medical care will result in an observable and material impairment to the growth, development, or functioning of the foster child; or

(3) the foster child is at risk of suffering substantial bodily harm or of inflicting substantial bodily harm to others.

(h) In making a decision under this section regarding whether a foster child has the capacity to consent to medical care, the court shall consider:

(1) the maturity of the child;

(2) whether the child is sufficiently well informed to make a decision regarding the medical care; and

(3) the child's intellectual functioning.

(i) In determining whether the medical care is in the best interest of the foster child, the court shall consider:

(1) the foster child's expressed preference regarding the medical care, including perceived risks and benefits of the medical care;

(2) likely consequences to the foster child if the child does not receive the medical care;

(3) the foster child's prognosis, if the child does receive the medical care; and

(4) whether there are alternative, less intrusive treatments that are likely to reach the same result as provision of the medical care.

(j) This section does not apply to emergency medical care. An emergency relating to a foster child who is at least 16 years of age, other than a child in an inpatient mental health facility, is governed by Section 266.009.

(k) This section does not apply to the administration of medication under Subchapter G, Chapter 574, Health and Safety Code, [1] to a foster child who is at least 16 years of age and who is placed in an inpatient mental health facility.

(*l*) Before a foster child reaches the age of 16, the department or the private agency providing substitute care or case management services to the foster child shall advise the foster child of the right to a hearing under this section to determine whether the foster child may consent to medical care. The department or the private agency providing substitute care or case management services shall provide the foster child with training on informed consent and the provision of medical care as part of the Preparation for Adult Living Program.

Added by Acts 2005, 79th Leg., ch. 268, § 1.65(a), eff. Sept. 1, 2005. Amended by Acts 2015, 84th Leg., ch. 944 (S.B. 206), § 67, eff. Sept. 1, 2015.

[1] V.T.C.A., Health & Safety Code § 574.101 et seq.

### § 266.011. Monitoring Use of Psychotropic Drug

The person authorized to consent to medical treatment for a foster child prescribed a psychotropic medication shall ensure that the child has been seen by the prescribing physician, physician assistant, or advanced practice nurse at least once every 90 days to allow the physician, physician assistant, or advanced practice nurse to:

(1) appropriately monitor the side effects of the medication; and

(2) determine whether:

(A) the medication is helping the child achieve the treatment goals; and

(B) continued use of the medication is appropriate.

Added by Acts 2013, 83rd Leg., ch. 204 (H.B. 915), § 13, eff. Sept. 1, 2013.

### § 266.012. Comprehensive Assessments

(a) Not later than the 45th day after the date a child enters the conservatorship of the department, the child shall receive a developmentally appropriate comprehensive assessment. The assessment must include:

(1) a screening for trauma; and

(2) interviews with individuals who have knowledge of the child's needs.

(b) The department shall develop guidelines regarding the contents of an assessment report.

(c) A single source continuum contractor under Subchapter B–1, Chapter 264,[1] providing therapeutic foster care services to a child shall ensure that the child receives a comprehensive assessment under this section at least once every 90 days.

Added by Acts 2015, 84th Leg., ch. 11 (S.B. 125), § 1, eff. Sept. 1, 2015. Amended by Acts 2017, 85th Leg., ch. 319 (S.B. 11), § 22, eff. Sept. 1, 2017.

[1] V.T.C.A., Family Code § 264.151 et seq.

### § 266.013. Continuity of Services Provided by Commission

(a) In addition to the requirements of Section 266.003(d), the commission shall continue to provide any services to children in the conservatorship of the department that the commission provided to those children before September 1, 2017.

(b) Subsection (a) does not apply to any services provided by the commission in relation to a child's education passport created under Section 266.008.

Added by Acts 2017, 85th Leg., ch. 316 (H.B. 5), § 21, eff. Sept. 1, 2017.

## CHAPTER 267. INTERAGENCY COORDINATING COUNCIL FOR BUILDING HEALTHY FAMILIES [EXPIRED]

*This Chapter, added as Chapter 266, Interagency Coordinating Council for Building Healthy Families, by Acts 2005, 79th Leg., ch. 587, § 1, was redesignated as Chapter 267 by Acts 2007, 80th Leg., ch. 632, § 3.*

### §§ 267.001, 267.002. Expired

# PENAL CODE

## TITLE 6. OFFENSES AGAINST THE FAMILY

### CHAPTER 25. OFFENSES AGAINST THE FAMILY



**§ 25.03. Interference with Child Custody**

(a) A person commits an offense if the person takes or retains a child younger than 18 years of age:

(1) when the person knows that the person's taking or retention violates the express terms of a judgment or order, including a temporary order, of a court disposing of the child's custody;

(2) when the person has not been awarded custody of the child by a court of competent jurisdiction, knows that a suit for divorce or a civil suit or application for habeas corpus to dispose of the child's custody has been filed, and takes the child out of the geographic area of the counties composing the judicial district if the court is a district court or the county if the court is a statutory county court, without the permission of the court and with the intent to deprive the court of authority over the child; or

(3) outside of the United States with the intent to deprive a person entitled to possession of or access to the child of that possession or access and without the permission of that person.

(b) A noncustodial parent commits an offense if, with the intent to interfere with the lawful custody of a child younger than 18 years, the noncustodial parent knowingly entices or persuades the child to leave the custody of the custodial parent, guardian, or person standing in the stead of the custodial parent or guardian of the child.

(c) It is a defense to prosecution under Subsection (a)(2) that the actor returned the child to the geographic area of the counties composing the judicial district if the court is a district court or the county if the court is a statutory county court, within three days after the date of the commission of the offense.

(c–1) It is an affirmative defense to prosecution under Subsection (a)(3) that:

(1) the taking or retention of the child was pursuant to a valid order providing for possession of or access to the child; or

(2) notwithstanding any violation of a valid order providing for possession of or access to the child, the actor's retention of the child was due only to circumstances beyond the actor's control and the actor promptly provided notice or made reasonable attempts to provide notice of those circumstances to the other person entitled to possession of or access to the child.

(c–2) Subsection (a)(3) does not apply if, at the time of the offense, the person taking or retaining the child:

(1) was entitled to possession of or access to the child; and

(2) was fleeing the commission or attempted commission of family violence, as defined by Section 71.004, Family Code, against the child or the person.

(d) An offense under this section is a state jail felony.

Acts 1973, 63rd Leg., p. 883, ch. 399, § 1, eff. Jan. 1, 1974. Amended by Acts 1979, 66th Leg., p. 1111, ch. 527, § 1, eff. Aug. 27, 1979; Acts 1987, 70th Leg., ch. 444, § 1, eff. Sept. 1, 1987; Acts 1989, 71st Leg., ch. 830, § 1, eff. Sept. 1, 1989; Acts 1993, 73rd Leg., ch. 900, § 1.01, eff. Sept. 1, 1994; Acts 2001, 77th Leg., ch. 332, § 1, eff. May 24, 2001; Acts 2007, 80th Leg., ch. 272, § 1, eff. Sept. 1, 2007; Acts 2011, 82nd Leg., ch. 840 (H.B. 3439), § 2, eff. Sept. 1, 2011; Acts 2011, 82nd Leg., ch. 1100 (S.B. 1551), § 3, eff. Sept. 1, 2011.

**§ 25.031. Agreement to Abduct From Custody**

(a) A person commits an offense if the person agrees, for remuneration or the promise of remuneration, to abduct a child younger than 18 years of age by force, threat of force, misrepresentation, stealth, or unlawful entry, knowing that the child is under the care and control of a person having custody or physical possession of the child under a court order, including a temporary order, or under the care and control of another person who is exercising care and control with the consent of a person having custody or physical possession under a court order, including a temporary order.

(b) An offense under this section is a state jail felony.

Added by Acts 1987, 70th Leg., ch. 444, § 3, eff. Sept. 1, 1987. Amended by Acts 1993, 73rd Leg., ch. 900, § 1.01, eff. Sept. 1, 1994; Acts 2007, 80th Leg., ch. 272, § 2, eff. Sept. 1, 2007.

### § 25.05. Criminal Nonsupport

(a) An individual commits an offense if the individual intentionally or knowingly fails to provide support for the individual's child younger than 18 years of age, or for the individual's child who is the subject of a court order requiring the individual to support the child.

(b) For purposes of this section, "child" includes a child born out of wedlock whose paternity has either been acknowledged by the actor or has been established in a civil suit under the Family Code or the law of another state.

(c) Under this section, a conviction may be had on the uncorroborated testimony of a party to the offense.

(d) It is an affirmative defense to prosecution under this section that the actor could not provide support for the actor's child.

(e) The pendency of a prosecution under this section does not affect the power of a court to enter an order for child support under the Family Code.

(f) An offense under this section is a state jail felony.

Acts 1973, 63rd Leg., p. 883, ch. 399, § 1, eff. Jan. 1, 1974. Amended by Acts 1987, 70th Leg., 2nd C.S., ch. 73, § 13, eff. Nov. 1, 1987; Acts 1993, 73rd Leg., ch. 900, § 1.01, eff. Sept. 1, 1994; Acts 2001, 77th Leg., ch. 375, § 1, eff. May 25, 2001.

*Subsection (d) [formerly subsec. (f)] of this section was declared unconstitutional by Lowry v. State, 671 S.W.2d 601 (1984).*

### § 25.07. Violation of Certain Court Orders or Conditions of Bond in a Family Violence, Child Abuse or Neglect, Sexual Assault or Abuse, Indecent Assault, Stalking, or Trafficking Case

(a) A person commits an offense if, in violation of a condition of bond set in a family violence, sexual assault or abuse, indecent assault, stalking, or trafficking case and related to the safety of a victim or the safety of the community, an order issued under Subchapter A, Chapter 7B, Code of Criminal Procedure, an order issued under Article 17.292, Code of Criminal Procedure, an order issued under Section 6.504, Family Code, Chapter 83, Family Code, if the temporary ex parte order has been served on the person, Chapter 85, Family Code, or Subchapter F, Chapter 261, Family Code, or an order issued by another jurisdiction as provided by Chapter 88, Family Code, the person knowingly or intentionally:

(1) commits family violence or an act in furtherance of an offense under Section 20A.02, 22.011, 22.012, 22.021, or 42.072;

(2) communicates:

(A) directly with a protected individual or a member of the family or household in a threatening or harassing manner;

(B) a threat through any person to a protected individual or a member of the family or household; or

(C) in any manner with the protected individual or a member of the family or household except through the person's attorney or a person appointed by the court, if the violation is of an order described by this subsection and the order prohibits any communication with a protected individual or a member of the family or household;

(3) goes to or near any of the following places as specifically described in the order or condition of bond:

(A) the residence or place of employment or business of a protected individual or a member of the family or household; or

(B) any child care facility, residence, or school where a child protected by the order or condition of bond normally resides or attends;

(4) possesses a firearm;

(5) harms, threatens, or interferes with the care, custody, or control of a pet, companion animal, or assistance animal that is possessed by a person protected by the order or condition of bond; or

(6) removes, attempts to remove, or otherwise tampers with the normal functioning of a global positioning monitoring system.

(a–1) For purposes of Subsection (a)(5), possession of a pet, companion animal, or assistance animal by a person means:

(1) actual care, custody, control, or management of a pet, companion animal, or assistance animal by the person; or

(2) constructive possession of a pet, companion animal, or assistance animal owned by the person or for which the person has been the primary caregiver.

(b) For the purposes of this section:

(1) "Family violence," "family," "household," and "member of a household" have the meanings assigned by Chapter 71, Family Code.

(2) "Firearm" has the meaning assigned by Chapter 46.

(2–a) "Global positioning monitoring system" has the meaning assigned by Article 17.49, Code of Criminal Procedure.

(3) "Assistance animal" has the meaning assigned by Section 121.002, Human Resources Code.

(4) "Sexual abuse" means any act as described by Section 21.02 or 21.11.

(5) "Sexual assault" means any act as described by Section 22.011 or 22.021.

(6) "Stalking" means any conduct that constitutes an offense under Section 42.072.

(7) "Trafficking" means any conduct that constitutes an offense under Section 20A.02.

(8) "Indecent assault" means any conduct that constitutes an offense under Section 22.012.

(c) If conduct constituting an offense under this section also constitutes an offense under another section of this code, the actor may be prosecuted under either section or under both sections.

(d) Reconciliatory actions or agreements made by persons affected by an order do not affect the validity of the order or the duty of a peace officer to enforce this section.

(e) A peace officer investigating conduct that may constitute an offense under this section for a violation of an order may not arrest a person protected by that order for a violation of that order.

(f) It is not a defense to prosecution under this section that certain information has been excluded, as provided by Section 85.007, Family Code, or Article 17.292, Code of Criminal Procedure, from an order to which this section applies.

(g) An offense under this section is a Class A misdemeanor, except the offense is:

(1) subject to Subdivision (2), a state jail felony if it is shown at the trial of the offense that the defendant violated an order issued under Subchapter A, Chapter 7B , Code of Criminal Procedure,[1] following the defendant's conviction of or placement on deferred adjudication community supervision for an offense, if the order was issued with respect to a victim of that offense; or

(2) a felony of the third degree if it is shown on the trial of the offense that the defendant:

(A) has previously been convicted two or more times of an offense under this section or two or more times of an offense under Section 25.072, or has previously been convicted of an offense under this section and an offense under Section 25.072; or

(B) has violated the order or condition of bond by committing an assault or the offense of stalking.

(h) For purposes of Subsection (g), a conviction under the laws of another state for an offense containing elements that are substantially similar to the elements of an offense under this section or Section 25.072 is considered to be a conviction under this section or Section 25.072, as applicable.

Added by Acts 1983, 68th Leg., p. 4049, ch. 631, § 3, eff. Sept. 1, 1983. Amended by Acts 1985, 69th Leg., ch. 583, § 3, eff. Sept. 1, 1985; Acts 1987, 70th Leg., ch. 170, § 1, eff. Sept. 1, 1987; Acts 1987, 70th Leg., ch. 677, § 8, eff. Sept. 1, 1987; Acts 1989, 71st Leg., ch. 614, §§ 23 to 26, eff. Sept. 1, 1989; Acts 1989, 71st Leg., ch. 739, §§ 4 to 7, eff. Sept. 1, 1989; Acts 1991, 72nd Leg., ch. 366, § 2, eff. Sept. 1, 1991. Redesignated from V.T.C.A., Penal Code § 25.08 and amended by Acts 1993, 73rd Leg., ch. 900, § 1.01, eff. Sept. 1, 1994. Amended by Acts 1995, 74th Leg., ch. 658, §§ 2, 3, eff. June 14, 1995; Acts 1995, 74th Leg., ch. 660, §§ 1, 2, eff. Sept. 1, 1995; Acts 1995, 74th Leg., ch. 1024, § 23, eff. Sept. 1, 1995; Acts 1997, 75th Leg., ch. 1, § 2, eff. Jan. 28, 1997; Acts 1997, 75th Leg., ch. 1193, § 21, eff. Sept. 1, 1997; Acts 1999, 76th Leg., ch. 62, § 15.02(c), eff. Sept. 1, 1999; Acts 2001, 77th Leg., ch. 23, § 1, eff. Sept. 1, 2001; Acts 2003, 78th Leg., ch. 134, § 1, eff. Sept. 1, 2003; Acts 2007, 80th Leg., ch. 66, § 2, eff. May 11, 2007; Acts 2007, 80th Leg., ch. 1113, §§ 1, 2, eff. Jan. 1, 2008; Acts 2009, 81st Leg., ch. 87, § 19.001, eff. Sept. 1, 2009; Acts 2011, 82nd Leg., ch. 136 (S.B. 279), §§ 3, 4, eff. Sept. 1, 2011; Acts 2013, 83rd Leg., ch. 96 (S.B. 743), § 2, eff. Sept. 1, 2013; Acts 2013, 83rd Leg., ch. 543 (S.B. 555), § 3, eff. Sept. 1, 2013; Acts 2013, 83rd Leg., ch. 760 (S.B. 893), §§ 4 to 6, eff. Sept. 1, 2013; Acts 2015, 84th Leg., ch. 1086 (H.B. 2645), §§ 2, 3, eff. Sept. 1, 2015; Acts 2015, 84th Leg., ch. 1133 (S.B. 147), §§ 1 to 3, eff. Sept. 1, 2015; Acts 2017, 85th Leg., ch. 317 (H.B. 7), § 68, eff. Sept. 1, 2017; Acts 2017, 85th Leg., ch. 317 (H.B. 7), § 69; Acts 2019, 86th Leg., ch. 469 (H.B. 4173), § 2.58, eff. Jan. 1, 2021; Acts 2019, 86th Leg., ch. 955 (S.B. 194), § 11(b), (c), 13, eff. Sept. 1, 2019; Acts 2019, 86th Leg., ch. 1066 (H.B. 1343), § 4, eff. Sept. 1, 2019; Acts 2021, 87th Leg., ch. 787 (H.B. 39), § 11, eff. Sept. 1, 2021.

[1] Vernon's Ann. Texas C.C.P. art. 7B.001 et seq.

Section 11(a), (e) of Acts 2019, 86th Leg., ch. 955 (S.B. 194) provides:

"(a) This section takes effect only if the comptroller determines that Sections 14 and 69, H.B. 7, Acts of the 85th Legislature, Regular Session, 2017, took effect as provided by H.B. 7."

"(e) Sections 25.07 and 25.072, Penal Code, as amended by this section, apply only to an offense committed on or after the effective date [Sept. 1, 2019] of this Act. An offense committed before the effective date of this Act is governed by the law in effect when the offense was committed, and the former law is continued in effect for that purpose. For purposes of this subsection, an offense was committed before the effective date of this Act if any element of the offense occurred before that date."

# CONSTITUTION OF THE STATE OF TEXAS 1876

## ARTICLE XVI

## GENERAL PROVISIONS



### § 15. Separate and community property of husband and wife

Sec. 15. All property, both real and personal, of a spouse owned or claimed before marriage, and that acquired afterward by gift, devise or descent, shall be the separate property of that spouse; and laws shall be passed more clearly defining the rights of the spouses, in relation to separate and community property; provided that persons about to marry and spouses, without the intention to defraud pre-existing creditors, may by written instrument from time to time partition between themselves all or part of their property, then existing or to be acquired, or exchange between themselves the community interest of one spouse or future spouse in any property for the community interest of the other spouse or future spouse in other community property then existing or to be acquired, whereupon the portion or interest set aside to each spouse shall be and constitute a part of the separate property and estate of such spouse or future spouse; spouses also may from time to time, by written instrument, agree between themselves that the income or property from all or part of the separate property then owned or which thereafter might be acquired by only one of them, shall be the separate property of that spouse; if one spouse makes a gift of property to the other that gift is presumed to include all the income or property which might arise from that gift of property; spouses may agree in writing that all or part of their community property becomes the property of the surviving spouse on the death of a spouse; and spouses may agree in writing that all or part of the separate property owned by either or both of them shall be the spouses' community property.

Amended Nov. 2, 1948; Nov. 4, 1980; Nov. 3, 1987; Nov. 2, 1999.

# INDEX

## Abbreviations

| | |
|---|---|
| **Const. Art.** | **Constitution of Texas** |
| **Fam** | **Family Code** |
| **Pen** | **Penal Code** |

# INDEX

# INDEX

# INDEX

# INDEX